D0085865

THEODORE OF MOPSUESTIA:

THE COMMENTARIES ON THE MINOR EPISTLES OF PAUL

Society of Biblical Literature

Writings from the Greco-Roman World

John T. Fitzgerald, General Editor

Editorial Board

David Armstrong
Elizabeth Asmis
Brian E. Daley, S.J.
David Konstan
Wendy Mayer
Margaret M. Mitchell
Ilaria Ramelli
Michael J. Roberts
Johan C. Thom
James C. VanderKam

Number 26

THEODORE OF MOPSUESTIA:
THE COMMENTARIES ON THE MINOR EPISTLES OF PAUL

Volume Editors
John C. Cavadini and John T. Fitzgerald

Theodore of Mopsuestia:
The Commentaries on the Minor Epistles of Paul

Translated with an Introduction by

Rowan A. Greer

Society of Biblical Literature
Atlanta

THEODORE OF MOPSUESTIA: *THE COMMENTARIES ON THE MINOR EPISTLES OF PAUL*

Copyright © 2010 by the Society of Biblical Literature.

All rights reserved.

No part of this work may be reproduced or transmitted in any form or by any means, electronic or mechanical, including photocopying and recording, or by means of any information storage or retrieval system, except as may be expressly permitted by the 1976 Copyright Act or in writing from the publisher. Requests for permission should be addressed in writing to the Rights and Permissions Department, Society of Biblical Literature, 825 Houston Mill Road, Suite 350, Atlanta, GA 30329, USA.

Library of Congress Cataloging-in-Publication Data

Theodore, Bishop of Mopsuestia, ca. 350–428 or 9.
[Commentaries on the minor epistles of Paul. English]
The commentaries on the minor epistles of Paul / Theodore of Mopsuestia ; translated with an introduction by Rowan A. Greer.
        p. cm. — (Society of Biblical Literature writings from the Greco-Roman world ; no. 26)
Includes bibliographical references and index.
ISBN 978-1-58983-279-4 (paper binding : alk. paper)
   1. Bible. N.T. Epistles of Paul—Commentaries. I. Greer, Rowan A. II. Title.

BS2650.53.T4413 2010
227′.07–dc22   2010021021

---

18 17 16 15 14 13 12 11 10 — 5 4 3 2 1

Printed on acid-free, recycled paper conforming to ANSI/NISO Z39.48-1992 (R1997) and ISO 9706:1994 standards for paper permanence.

∞

Table of Contents

Abbreviations

BZNW	Beiheft zur Zeitschrift für die neutestamentliche Wissenschaft
CSCO	Corpus scriptorum christianorum orientalium
FC	Fathers of the Church
JTS	*Journal of Theological Studies*
PO	*Patrologia orientalis*
RBén	*Revue bénédictine*
SacEr	*Sacris erudiri: Jaarboek voor Godsdienstwetenschappen*
SBLWGRW	Society of Biblical Literature Writings from the Greco-Roman World
ST	Studi e testi

Introduction

The writings of Theodore of Mopsuestia are available to us only in a sadly fragmentary way. His commentaries on the twelve lesser prophets alone remain in a complete Greek text. Two other works have survived in their entirety in Syriac translations, namely, the commentary on John and the catechetical homilies. Robert Devreesse, however, assembled the surviving Greek and Latin fragments of Theodore's commentary on the Psalms and so has given us reasonably complete evidence for Theodore's interpretation of the first eighty psalms.[1] Robert Hill has translated Devreesse's edition into English, and what we can know of Theodore's commentary on the Psalms is now available to the English reader.[2] Considerable fragments of Theodore's exegetical work have been preserved by the catenists. Moreover, a body of dogmatic fragments remain largely because of their citation in the Nestorian controversy of the fifth century and the dispute over the "Three Chapters" in the sixth. Most of these fragments appear as an appendix in Swete's edition of Theodore's commentaries on the minor epistles of Paul.[3] Theodore's writings, of course, suffered condemnation at the fifth general council in 553, and the vicissitudes of Nestorian Christianity explain why so little remains of the Syriac translations of Theodore's works.

One other complete work of Theodore has managed to survive in a Latin translation. His commentaries on the minor epistles of Paul have been edited by Henry B. Swete, and the translation that follows is of his edition. That Theodore wrote

---

[1] Robert Devreesse, ed., *Le commentaire de Théodore de Mopsueste sur les Psaumes (I-LXXX)* (ST 93; Vatican City: Biblioteca Apostolica Vaticana, 1939).

[2] Robert C. Hill, trans., *Theodore of Mopsuestia: Commentary on Psalms 1–81* (SBLWGRW 5; Atlanta: Society of Biblical Literature, 2006).

[3] Henry B. Swete, ed., *Theodori episcopi Mopsuesteni In epistolas b. Pauli commentarii* (2 vols.; Cambridge: Cambridge University Press, 1880–1882). Hereafter cited in the notes as "Swete," followed by volume and page number(s). References to Swete within the main text list only the volume and page number(s). The discussion that follows in this section of the introduction depends entirely upon Swete's introduction and is no more that an attempt to summarize his conclusions. Full study requires the reader to consult Swete.

commentaries on all fourteen Pauline letters is certain and is wit-
nessed by Cyril of Alexandria, Facundus, Vigilius, and Leontius
of Byzantium. Moreover, these commentaries must have been
known to the Greek catenists, who assembled patristic comments
on scripture as early as the sixth century, continuing to the work
of Nicetas of Heraclea in the eleventh century and beyond. It is
the excerpts from Theodore's comments on the minor epistles of
Paul found in the catenae, primarily in the eleventh-century Paris
manuscript *Coislin 204*, that demonstrate our Latin text to be, in
fact, Theodore's work. In *Coislin 204* there are 130 excerpts assigned to Theodore, largely in marginal notes but in thirty cases
in the text itself.

Turning to the Latin evidence, as early as the seventeenth
century the Benedictine editors of Ambrose called attention to a
manuscript that had belonged to the monastery of Corbie that preserved commentaries on Romans and the Corinthian letters the
same as those attributed to Ambrosiaster, but commentaries on
the other letters save for Hebrews that were obviously not to be
assigned to Ambrosiaster. In 1852 J. B. Pitra argued that these
commentaries should be attributed to Hilary of Poitiers, but two
years later J. L. Jacobi disproved this conclusion and suggested
that the original was the Greek text of Theodore's commentaries.
In 1859 F. J. A. Hort reached the same conclusion independently.
Despite Jacobi's attempt to provide an edition and so to confirm
the attribution of the Corbie commentaries on the minor epistles to Theodore, the task devolved upon H. B. Swete. He based
his edition upon the Corbie manuscript, which is to be dated in
the ninth or tenth century and is now at Amiens: *Codex Ambianensis, olim Corbeiensis* (C). Hort had also discovered a second
Latin manuscript in the Harley collection at the British Museum:
a ninth-century manuscript, *Codex Harleianus 3063, olim Cusanus* (H). Swete argues that C, though later, is the more reliable
manuscript, that C and H are independent, and that they do not
reflect the same original. Swete's edition, then, largely follows
C and places the corresponding Greek fragments from the catenae in relation to the Latin text, thus confirming its attribution to
Theodore.

When the Greek parallels enable us to form a judgment,
the Latin translation is more often than not faithful, and Swete
argues for the "substantial integrity of the Latin trans-

lation."[4] At the same time, there are some obvious mistakes.
Indeed, the very attempt of the translator to supply a literal translation often results in great obscurity. This affects the translation
of the scriptural text itself, since the translator tends to render the
Greek text word for word in the same order and at the same time is
influenced by the Old Latin and Vulgate translations. Moreover,
the Latin itself is not only difficult but has "a limited vocabulary
drawn in great part from the vulgar idiom rather than from classi-
cal Latinity."[5] As well, Swete suggests that the translator employs
an African dialect and frequently "in his choice of words . . . continually treads in the steps of the law-books and jurists."[6]

Theodore almost certainly wrote his commentaries on the
Pauline epistles late in his career. From his birth circa 350 until
392, when he became bishop of Mopsuestia, he lived in Antioch,
where he was a pupil of the pagan rhetor Libanius and a disciple of Diodore of Tarsus. His earliest work was the commentary
on Psalms and may well have been the product of his studies under the guidance of Diodore. Several considerations lead Swete
to date Theodore's Pauline commentaries during his episcopate
(392–428).[7] The reference at 1 Thess 5:1 to another "heading"
(*capitulum*) corresponds with the sixth chapter of Euthalius's division of the epistles, divisions that may be derived from Theodore's
own work and can take us back to 396. Next, Theodore's references in our text to his commentaries on the Gospels (Col 1:17;
1 Tim 1:4; 3:16), as well as his citations of the Old Testament,
suggest that the Pauline commentaries are later than his other exegetical work. His comments on the dispute between Peter and
Paul at Antioch (Gal 2:11–14) may reflect his knowledge of the
correspondence on the problem between Chrysostom and Jerome
in 404. Finally, it is not impossible that Theodore knew Pelagius's
commentary on the Pauline letters, probably to be dated about
412.

It is impossible to know when and by whom Theodore's
commentaries were translated into Latin and brought West.
Swete points out that the translator must have been a friend rather
than a foe of Theodore and suggests four possible settings for his

---

[4] Swete, 1:xxxv.
[5] Swete, 1:xxxvii.
[6] Swete, 1:xli.
[7] See Swete's discussion (1:lxi-lxiii).

work. The first two of these presuppose the connection of the Pelagians with the Antiochenes, and we may think either of Pelagius's own supporters in the West or of the so-called semi-Pelagians in Gaul. Either view would date the translation sometime in the fifth century. A third possibility is that the translator was a defender of the Three Chapters, and that would take us to the sixth century. Finally, Theodore's Christology may have been congenial to the Spanish adoptionists in the seventh century. In Swete's judgment, it is the third of these possibilities that seems most likely. The Latinity of the translation seems too late for the first two possibilities, and its North African character could easily explain its circulation in Spain and Italy. Moreover, in the latter part of the sixth century many in North Africa suffered persecution for their defense of the Three Chapters.

I have already noted the difficulty and obscurity of the Latin translation, but similar judgments may be made about Theodore's own Greek style. Photius in the ninth century found fault, among other things, with his obscurity, diffuseness, harshness, and want of grace.[8] Part of Swete's conclusion is worth citing:

> All these imperfections are distinctly visible in the present work, even through the veil of the translation. The translator has idiosyncrasies of his own ... but on the whole he is faithful to his author and makes no attempt to hide his blemishes. Indeed he may be said to exaggerate them, for, where comparison is possible, the Latin proves to be more obscure, more diffuse and harsh than the Greek, and at least as full of verbal repetition. It may in part, though certainly not altogether, be owing to the clumsiness of the Latin medium that one rises from a perusal of these commentaries with a feeling in which weariness and interest are strangely mingled. Seldom is so much originality of thought to be found in connexion with so dull a manner; or such great acuteness with such needless and ambiguous iteration.

In what follows let me turn to some reflections and observations concerning the interest these commentaries can afford us in describing Theodore's exegesis and his theology.

---

[8] Swete, 1:lxiii.

THEODORE'S EXEGESIS

Up to a point Theodore reveals a concern for the correct reading of the scriptural text. Of course, it is not always easy to be sure of his own reading. The translator often seems to be following one of the existing Latin texts, and there are even places where the Latin translation in the commentary reflects a text that differs from the one the translator gives. In appendix B of his second volume, Swete supplies an indispensable tool for examining the question of Theodore's text of the Pauline letters. I have tried to call attention in the notes on the translation to the more interesting places where textual problems appear. Sometimes the issue is no more than a question of punctuation. For example, at Eph 1:4–5 Theodore attaches "in love" to verse 5 rather than to verse 4; Eph 1:7–9 and Phil 3:9–10 supply other examples of the same thing, and even noting the way the text is broken up demonstrates the importance of punctuation for interpretation. Next, let me give several examples of places where Theodore's text does have manuscript support but is not always the one we should choose. At Eph 5:9 Theodore reads "fruit of the Spirit" instead of "light of the Spirit." He adopts the reading "Christ will shine on you," rejecting "Christ will touch you," at Eph 5:14. "We are reproached" is favored over "we struggle" at 1 Tim 4:10, and 2 Tim 4:22 reads "with us" rather than "with you." In a few cases Theodore appears to have an idiosyncratic reading, and the interested reader may consult as examples Eph 2:21; 3:15; 4:6; Phil 1:1; 1 Thess 4:3; and 2 Tim 3:16.

Far more interesting and important, however, is Theodore's lengthy discussion of Gal 4:21–31, including the problematic statement of verse 24: "now this is an allegory." Since Theodore's treatise against the allegorists is lost, this discussion is the best surviving evidence for the Antiochene antipathy to allegorism.[9]

---

[9] Let me call attention to four English translations of part or all of Theodore's discussion. Maurice Wiles and Mark Santer in *Documents in Early Christian Thought* (Cambridge: Cambridge University Press, 1975), 151–54, have translated Swete, 1:73–79. Karlfried Froehlich in *Biblical Interpretation in the Early Church* (Sources of Early Christian Thought; Philadelphia: Fortress, 1984), 95–103, has translated Swete, 1:72–87. Joseph W. Trigg in *Biblical Interpretation* (Message of the Fathers of the Church 9; Wilmington, Del.: Glazier,

He articulates his complaint against the allegorists as follows (1:73): "There are people who have great zeal for overturning the meaning of the divine scriptures, and by breaking up [*intercipere*] everything placed there they fabricate [*confingere*] from themselves certain foolish fictions [*fabulas quasdam ineptas*] and give their folly the name of allegory." The most difficult word is the one I have translated "breaking up." *Intercipio* can mean "separate off, take away" or "break the continuity of, interrupt." And I should suggest that the Latin word translates διαλαμβάνω, which can mean "take or receive severally" or "divide" or "mark off." As well, κατὰ διάληψιν can mean "separately." The same Latin verb occurs once more a little later in Theodore's discussion: "by breaking up the narrative [*historiam intercipientes*] they no longer have a narrative [*historiam*]."[10] Though it is with some hesitation, what I want to suggest is that Theodore's first problem with the allegorists is purely exegetical. Their mistake is to break up the narrative and to interpret its component parts without reference to the narrative as a whole. This suggestion depends in part upon arguing that "history" is a highly misleading translation of *historia*. For example, in Gregory of Nyssa's *Life of Moses*, the *historia* supplies the basis for his spiritual interpretation, the *theoria*, and it is obviously what Gregory supposes to be the plain narrative of scripture about Moses' life, by no means excluding midrashic elaborations of the text. It has seemed to me better to speak of "the narrative meaning" than to speak of the historical or literal sense of the text for the simple reason that "historical" and "literal" are terms that run the risk of importing anachronistic ideas into our understanding of patristic exegesis.

Theodore does, however, insist that the "narrative" is a true one, and I should cite two passages from his discussion. First, "the apostle does not do away with the narrative [*historiam*], nor

---

1988), 172–77, has translated Swete, 1:72–81. Frederick G. McLeod in *Theodore of Mopsuestia* (The Early Church Fathers; London: Routledge, 2009), 120–21, has translated Swete 1:73–75 and four lines of 1:79.

[10] Swete, 1:75. See the English translations noted. Wiles and Santer translate *intercipere* "thwart" in the first passage and "start removing" in the second. Froehlich translates both instances as "serve their own ends." Trigg has "rob it of any meaning" for the first and "play tricks" for the second. McLeod translates the first instance as "misappropriating" and the second as "entangling." In the second passage the first three translators render *historia* as "history," while McLeod has "historical narrative."

does he get rid of what happened long ago [*res dudum factas*]"
(1:73–74). Second, "if their view is true and what is written does
not preserve an account [*narrationem*] of what really happened [*rerum gestarum*] but points to something else profound. . ."[11] The
first passage seems to me to imply a distinction between med-
dling with the narrative and denying that what it recounts really
happened, while the second passage might show that the word
Theodore associates with the relation of true events is *narratio*
rather than *historia*. In any case, while Theodore does insist that
the narrative about Abraham's two children is a true one, he also is
clear that the factual account does not preclude a spiritual or theological use. Paul "put [what happened long ago] down as what
had actually taken place at that time, but in such a way that he
also used the narrative of what had actually happened for his own
interpretation" (1:74). Theodore does not speak of the Old Testament story as a type; indeed, in these commentaries "type" tends
to refer to baptism as an anticipation of "the good things" of the
age to come. In explaining Paul's reference to "allegory" (Gal
4:24) he says that Paul "calls an allegory that comparison [*comparationem*/ἐκ παραθέσεως πρὸς σύγκρισιν] which can be made between
events that happened long ago and present circumstances" (1:79).
Nevertheless, this definition so closely approximates his definition
elsewhere of "type" that it is reasonable to conclude that he wishes
to insist upon what we have come to call a typological understanding of Gal 4. At the same time, Paul's "use" of the Old Testament
need not be confined to typology. He cites Isa 54:1 in Gal 4:27 not
because the verse was "spoken prophetically of the resurrection"
but because it included the word "barren" (1:84). Similarly, in
Eph 4:8 Paul changes "received gifts" to "gave gifts" in Ps 67:19,
using the verse "not as it was spoken prophetically, but as we are
often accustomed to use scriptural testimonies when we speak in
church" (1:166).

Despite his recognition of the spiritual meaning of scripture and of uses that go beyond the narrative meaning, Theodore's

---

[11] Swete, 1:75. The English translators treat *narrationem* in the second
passage somewhat differently. Wiles and Santer have "a record of things that
happened"; Froehlich, "the narrative of actual events"; Trigg, "one account of
actual events." McLeod conflates *retinent* and *narrationem*, and he translates
"the text does not relate what has actually happened."

commentaries primarily deal with the narrative. As I have suggested, he wants to respect the *historia* and so is concerned with its order (ἀκολουθία). In a sense, Paul's letters are narratives, and one of Theodore's preoccupations is the attempt to discern the logical order that lies beneath the text and represents the argument Paul is making. For example, he notes in his comment on Col 1:21–22 that Paul in this letter observes the same "logical order" (*sequentiam*) he follows in Ephesians, since he moves from Christ and his work to the church and then to the people he is addressing (1:277). Discovering Paul's "order," however, is no easy task, and there are serious obstacles that derive from Paul's style. When he is "upset" and "perplexed" (Gal 4:20b), he is not merely an orator "acting a part" but is genuinely a father weeping for his lost children (1:71). His letter to the Galatians is "terse and embellished with various emotions," including anger, and angry people "touch many emotions and say everything often and succinctly, nowhere drawing out at length their emotion" (1:93). This observation helps explain why Paul is so often obscure. His succinctness can lead him to omit words and to express himself incompletely, thereby giving his interpreter no small task.[12] A second kind of obstacle stems from the fact that Paul "usually pays no attention to grammar. . . . For he had not studied the discipline of rhetoric, nor did he think it suitable to devote himself to this study" (2:70). He does not place conjunctions in their proper order (1:16), and he usually understands "so that" as a reference to result rather than purpose.[13] One particular instance of Theodore's attempts to overcome these obstacles is his explanation of 1 Tim 5:24–25. The verses bear no obvious relation to their context, but Theodore ties them to the preceding verse, where Paul urges Timothy to take a little wine. Generally speaking, Theodore tries to unearth the logical order of the letters by isolating "insertions." He clearly has no wish to rewrite Paul's letters, but identifying the insertions depends upon

---

[12] See, e.g., Eph 3:2–4: "All his discussions in this letter . . . have a good deal of obscurity because of the concise way he expresses himself" (Swete, 1:155). See also Phlm 16c: "What has been said is indeed obscure on account of too much succinctness, because the apostle in his wish to expound some things succinctly often wrapped his words in obscurity" (2:282). Examples of omissions include Titus 2:2 and 2:9 (2:246, 249), where "teach" must be supplied.

[13] See the comments on Gal 5:17; Col 1:18; 1 Tim 1:20; 2 Tim 1:4; Phlm 13.

an extremely close reading of the text and often results in interesting, often persuasive, comments.[14]

If one concern that can be identified in Theodore's polemic
against the allegorists revolves around respecting the narrative
meaning and discovering its logical order, the other one has to do
with his insistence that we must take seriously what actually happened. Each of the commentaries has an introduction that the
Latin translator has labeled *argumentum* and that I have translated
"the setting." My reason for doing so is that in the commentary
on Psalms, in places where both the Greek and Latin survive, *argumentum* translates the Greek ὑπόθεσις.[15] The word, of course,
could mean "theme" or "subject matter,"[16] but Theodore, somewhat surprisingly, states that Ps 36 is "without a setting" (ἐκτὸς
ὑποθέσεως).[17] That is, this psalm cannot be associated with any
particular scriptural event. For this reason, it has seemed to me
that the "setting" is more than the theme or subject matter of the
text and has to do with the actual circumstances presupposed by
the text.[18] Indeed, it is easy to form the impression that Theodore
is concerned with the actual circumstances that explain Paul's

---

[14] The insertions can be identified as Gal 2:3–6, 8; 3:1b, 19b; Eph 2:2–4,
5b; 3:2–13; 4:17–24; 1 Tim 3:16–5:2, 5:4–8; 2 Tim 1:3b; Titus 1:1b-3.

[15] See Devreesse, *Le commentaire de Théodore*, 90 (Ps 15) and 477 (Ps 72);
see also Hill, *Theodore of Mopsuestia*, 180, 954.

[16] See Frances Young, "The Rhetorical Schools and Their Influence on
Patristic Exegesis," in *The Making of Orthodoxy: Essays in Honour of Henry
Chadwick* (ed. Rowan Williams; Cambridge: Cambridge University Press,
1989), 190–91: "Summary and paraphrase is a persistent Antiochene technique
for bringing out the gist of the argument, and the *hupothesis* usually includes
this, together with historical or circumstantial introductory material." See also
Frances Young, *The Art of Performance: Towards a Theology of Holy Scripture*
(London: Darton, Longman & Todd, 1990), 98; and idem, *Biblical Exegesis and
the Formation of Christian Culture* (Cambridge: Cambridge University Press,
1997; repr., Peabody, Mass: Hendrickson, 2002), 173–75

[17] Devreesse, *Le commentaire de Théodore*, 206; Hill, *Theodore of Mopsuestia*, 412.

[18] See Christoph Schäublin, *Untersuchungen zu Methode und Herkunft
der antiochenischen Exegese* (Theophaneia: Beiträge zur Religions- und Kirchengeschichte des Altertums 23; Köln: Hanstein, 1974), 94: "Damit ist schon
gesagt, dass Theodors Hypotheseis höher zu bewerten sind denn als 'blosse In-
haltsangaben', fassen sie doch bereits die Ergebnisse eigener sprachlicher und
besonders historischer Forschung."

letters. In the "setting" that introduces the commentary on Ephesians, he argues that John the apostle came to Ephesus long after Paul had sent Timothy there. It was only at the beginning of the revolt of the Jews against Rome that the apostles left Judea and that John came to Ephesus. Theodore concludes this "historical" discussion by saying he has said all this "for the sake of accuracy so that no one might suppose the meaning of the divine scriptures should be accepted without reference to the occasion and historical connection" (1:117). The last phrase in this translation, though it follows Swete's suggestion, may go too far, since a more literal translation would be that we should not interpret the meaning of scripture "simply and accidentally" (*absolute, fortuitu*). It is the context of the statement that suggests the bolder translation. There are many other reasons for supposing that Theodore is concerned with what we should call the historical background of the letters. He speaks of the persecution of the Judean Christians by the Jews in his comment on 1 Thess 2:14 (2:14) and has a good deal to say about the Judaizing Christians not only in commenting on Galatians but also in identifying them as the opponents in 2 Corinthians, Philippians, and Colossians. The setting of 1 Thessalonians reflects Luke's account in Acts 16–17 and makes a specific reference to Acts. Paul writes Philippians during his first imprisonment in Rome, while his second letter to Timothy has its setting in his second imprisonment, immediately before his martyrdom. It would be possible to elaborate these considerations and tempting to suppose that Theodore has correlated the letters with the Acts of the Apostles, giving us a full reconstruction of Paul's career and where to locate his letters in it.[19]

What at first seems puzzling is that such a supposition finds very little warrant in the commentaries. A closer examination of Theodore's account of the setting of 1 Thessalonians in its relation to Acts 16–18 illustrates the point. Theodore's emphasis is

---

[19] It is true that Theodore assumes the framework of Acts. See Gal 2:7–9 (Swete, 1:20), which refers to Paul's persuasion of the ruler of the synagogue in Corinth (Acts 18:8); Phil 1:1–2 (1:199), which refers to Paul's sending of Timothy and Erastus to Macedonia (Acts 19:22); 1 Thess 5:19–21 (2:38), which refers to the Jewish exorcists of Acts 19:13; 1 Tim 3:1 (2:107), which refers to Simon Magus (Acts 8:14–24); 1 Tim 3:8a (2:120–21), which refers to Paul and the elders of Ephesus (Acts 20:17, 28); 1 Tim 5:17 (2:168), which refers to the widows' tables (Acts 6:2).

upon Paul's sending Timothy back to Thessalonica from Athens (3:1–2) and Timothy's report upon his return (3:6). But in Acts Paul leaves Thessalonica for Beroea with Silas (17:10), then is sent to the coast, leaving Silas and Timothy behind, apparently in Beroea (17:14). Paul's escorts take him to Athens, where they leave him with instructions to have Silas and Timothy join him (17:15). They do so once Paul has moved on to Corinth (18:5). Theodore pays no attention to any of this. The same sort of puzzle occurs in the "prison" letters. In the commentary on Philemon, Theodore notes that it is only in the salutation of this letter that Paul refers to himself as a prisoner and not as an apostle or servant and that he does so even though he wrote a good many other letters from prison, "as one can see from his letters and especially from the one he is seen to have written to the Ephesians" (2:267). But in the commentary on Ephesians, despite the clear references at 3:1 and 4:1, Theodore makes almost nothing of Paul as a prisoner. The same judgment can be made regarding his interpretation of Colossians, where the specific reference to Paul as a prisoner in 4:18 ("Be mindful of my chains") merely provokes Theodore to paraphrase the statement as though it meant "do not be displeased even at suffering for the truth by imitating me." It seems obvious that both Ephesians and Colossians are supposed to be prison letters, yet Theodore comes close to ignoring the fact. Perhaps this is because he argues that both of these letters, like that to the Romans, are written to churches that Paul has not yet seen and so belong early in his career, certainly before he was arrested and sent to Rome. If Theodore supposes that the only imprisonments of Paul are the two in Rome, then he cannot account for an earlier imprisonment, nor does he show any sign of perceiving the problem. Even in his comments on Philemon, which make much of the fact that Paul is a prisoner, he gives no indication of when or where Paul is in prison.[20]

---

[20] It would be easy to multiply problems of this sort. Why does Theodore fail to deal with Paul's circumcision of Timothy (Acts 16:3) when he is discussing Paul's refusal to circumcise Titus (Gal 2:3)? Since Silvanus is associated with Paul and Timothy in sending both letters to the Thessalonians, why does Theodore fail to say anything about Silvanus/Silas, even though he is more prominent than Timothy in the account of the so-called third missionary journey in Acts? Why does Theodore's commentary on Philemon fail to note that Onesimus is mentioned in Col 4:7–9?

It becomes obvious that the "setting" cannot be identified with any comprehensive understanding of Paul's career or with any attempt to bring the information in the letters into any full or persuasive relationship with the framework supplied by Acts. At the same time, the settings do include what Theodore regards as the particular circumstances of both Paul and those to whom he is writing. One possible way of explaining this peculiarity is to argue that the "setting" is not an end in itself but a point of departure for fuller interpretation. Our modern sensibilities would suggest that specifying the "historical" setting of each letter on the basis of deductions made from the text itself would supply a basis for the larger task of reconstructing the historical picture more broadly and of reconciling the evidence of the letters with what we find in Acts. But Theodore sees his task a different way. In at least two places in the commentary on Psalms Theodore points out that the "settings" are a basis for more general exhortation, instruction, and praise. Psalm 32 is a kind of hymn of victory to celebrate the miraculous destruction of the Assyrians in the time of Hezekiah (2 Kgs 19:35–37), but it is also to be understood as a general hymn. We need to know the setting to understand the psalm, but in the psalms David turns from the setting to "instructive exhortation" (καταχητικὴν παραίνεσιν). The setting of Ps 72 is the Babylonian captivity, but it looks toward the common benefit of all.[21] What I am suggesting is that, while Theodore takes the actual circumstances that supply the setting for the scriptural texts quite seriously, he regards the task of interpretation as one that moves toward an articulation of the religious and theological meaning of scripture. Philemon belongs in the canon because it supplies a lesson for "our own times" (2:261). All bishops in the present day should study 1 Timothy carefully (2:68). Indeed, from a historical perspective Theodore's commentaries inadvertently give us more interesting evidence for his own times than anything that would enable us to come to historical conclusions about Paul's letters.[22]

---

[21] See Devreesse, *Le commentaire de Théodore*, 142 and 477; Hill, *Theodore of Mopsuestia*, 284 and 954.

[22] See especially his lengthy discussions regarding bishops and the meaning of "the husband of one wife" (2:99–108, 117–26), as well as his argument for the value of the letter to Philemon (2:258–66).

THEODORE'S THEOLOGY AND HIS RELIGIOUS MESSAGE

I have already argued that Theodore is preoccupied with scripture as a narrative and with its logical order, and this would be one way of trying to show that it is more than a contemporary emphasis upon "story" that enables us to conclude that Theodore's theology is fundamentally a story. The idea of creation as God's dispensation of two successive world orders, two "ages," seems to me central to Theodore's thought. Paul's reference to "the present wicked age" in Gal 1:4 triggers an extensive and more general comment from Theodore that provides an excellent example of how he thinks of the Christian story. He begins with Adam, who "was created in such a way that if he had remained immortal, the present life would certainly not have come to be" (1:6). From this perspective it looks as though the first and mortal age is the unfortunate consequence of the fall of Adam. On the other hand, God made us "mortals in this present life" without in any way "contravening his own judgment, moved to wrath because of Adam's one sin" (1:25–26). The second of these statements fits Theodore's larger picture better than the first.[23] Far from being no more than a punishment, the present mortal age exists "for the training of virtues and the teaching of what is right for us to do" (1:26). The age to come is the goal of this training, and it is largely identified with the resurrection and immortality. Thus, the two successive ages represent a transition from mortality to immortality, and the second age is an increment on the first, completing and perfecting it. This general perspective, of course, is common to most of the church fathers. Even Augustine sees the transition from paradise to the perfected city of God as one from "the possibility of sinning" to "the impossibility of sinning." But the Greek fathers tend to think of the fundamental human problem as mortality rather than sinfulness; what we inherit from Adam is mortality but not spiritual or eternal death.

[23] For the problem of Adam's original condition, see the discussion in Richard A. Norris, *Manhood and Christ: A Study in the Christology of Theodore of Mopsuestia* (Oxford: Clarendon, 1963), 173–78.

Theodore tends to explain sin as the consequence of our mortality.[24] Sin is "strong among us by custom. . . . Nor was there anything that could make us free of sin; rather, the very weakness of our nature kept on drawing us to sin" (1:8). "Flesh" in Paul's letters usually means mortality, but it can also refer to the sin that is its product (1:37, 94). Although the passions belong, at least in part, to the soul, they are "carried out in mortal nature" (1:99). Mortality, then, means not only that humans must die but also that there is an unstable relationship between the governing mind or soul and the body together with the passions that are the product of the soul's union with the body. It is important to add that this understanding is far from an Augustinian view of original sin. Granted that our mortal nature explains the many wrong choices we make; nevertheless, we retain the power to choose better things. "For the Lord makes us rational and wishes to promote that very rationality in us and make it efficacious, because it could be manifested in no other way save by distinguishing contraries by which the choice of what is better can be acquired— for this is the highest knowledge for all rational beings" (1:27). Theodore continues by appealing to Rom 7 and argues that the "opposition within us" is what distinguishes us from irrational creatures because it obliges us to choose the good freely. In this way our progress toward the virtues is really a question of learning from our mistakes, and true freedom is the steadfast election of the good. Education in virtue, however, requires a teacher, and like the other Greek fathers Theodore accepts in a general way the view taken by Origen of the relationship between human free choice and divine providence. Theodore paraphrases the juxtaposition between our working and God's in Phil 2:12–13 by saying, "let your enthusiasm find God's grace working with it, since it necessarily works with you, so that you may think and do those things that are pleasing to God" (1:225). The "fruits of the Spirit" in Gal 5:22–23 contrast with the "works of the flesh," because "it is by grace through the cooperation of the Spirit that we can attain, as it were, these fruits. For we can never ourselves perfect

---

[24] See the discussion in Norris, *Manhood and Christ*, 182–84, where he argues for a tension in Theodore's thought with respect to the relationship of sin and mortality. Without denying the tension, it might be possible to resolve it by arguing that Adam's sin is the ultimate problem, while for us it is mortality. Christ, of course, is thought to abolish both sin and mortality.

the work of virtue, just as we cannot reap the fruits of the earth, even if we should toil to a great extent, if God had not seen fit to give them" (1:101).

What lies behind this understanding seems to me an identification of grace or providence with God's love, as well as the conviction that love can never compel. Human life is placed within the context of grace, and when human beings sin, they are really misusing God's love. That love not only dispensed the two ages in such a way as to give humans freedom, but it is also constantly at work to bestow gifts that will assist humans to move toward the perfection of their freedom. But we must distinguish the gift from its effect; only when it is rightly used in freedom will it have its intended effect. Timothy's election and the prophecy that attended it demonstrate "grace in a preeminent way, but it will be your task to confirm that very election." The election of Judas by Christ brought him no help because he misused it (2:82–83). The same point attaches to baptism, a gift that was misused by Simon Magus and so did him no good. "It is not the nature of water, but the faith of those receiving it, that is fitted to draw the perfect generosity of God into baptism" (2:107–8). Baptism is God's generous gift, but its perfection depends upon the baptized life. In this way Theodore underlines the central importance of grace without denying human freedom. Dependence upon God's grace is what enables moral autonomy. The law is a gift of grace meant to assist humans in their knowledge of the good, thereby curbing sin. Yet Theodore argues that the law has to do only with this age, and he sometimes seems to mean not only the Jewish law but also the natural law. Perhaps for this reason he can say that the law remains necessary in this present life (1:49, 85), but he can also say that the law does no more than demonstrate our weakness because we inevitably violate it (1:28, 51). While this mortal life is a training ground and an education, it can never be the completion of that training and education.

It is impossible to read Theodore's commentaries without noting his emphasis upon the age to come and the good things that will be found there. The general resurrection with the immortality that follows it is central to his religious convictions and his theology. "All of us who share with him [Christ] both in the resurrection and in that immortality that follows the resurrection will be made as one with him" (1:57). The abolition of mortality will

be the abolition of sin (1:8, 31, 98–99). For this reason the law will be useless, since there will no longer be any need to condemn sin. As well, all human divisions will end when we are all made Christ's body (1:139–43, 170–71, 263–64). Moreover, the salvation perfected in the age to come will be a new creation. Christ will be "the bond for the harmony of the whole creation" (1:128–31, 267–69). And by "Christ" Theodore here means the human Christ, the assumed Man. In Adam we find human nature constituted as a "pledge" for the harmony finally effected by Christ, since the soul allies humanity to the invisible creation and the body to the visible creation. Theodore's comments on Eph 1:10, Phil 2:5–11, and Col 1:15–20 provide good evidence for the main lines of his Christology. He insists upon a clear distinction between the two natures, the Man and God the Word. But he has no wish to make that distinction a division and is equally insistent that Paul speaks of "a single person" and that "the union of person" is "undivided" (1:219–20). It would be necessary to consult the dogmatic fragments in order to assess how Theodore tries to solve the major problem of his Christology, that is, how to explain the union of the two natures. But in these commentaries his concern is to describe the saving work of Christ. The Man is the proximate agent of salvation, but to say this depends upon recognizing that he is indwelt by the Word of God. Thus, the Man is not merely the first instance of the general resurrection but its firstfruits and first principle. Theodore imagines the age to come in a Christocentric fashion.

The present life for Christians represents an anticipation of the age to come. "All of us who believe in Christ in this present life are, as it were, between both the present and the future life" (1:30). It seems to me arguable that Theodore correctly sees the Pauline tension between the "already" and the "not yet." And like Paul he thinks of our present anticipation of the future as one made possible by faith. "By faith we see ourselves as though already translated to the life to come, especially when we have received baptism (because baptism has the type of Christ's death and resurrection), since at that time we also receive the Holy Spirit given in baptism" (1:30). The type of baptism, then, gives Christians the firstfruits of what is to come in the future age (1:173–74, 287–89), and the gift of the Spirit is a pledge and down payment that points toward the perfection yet to come (1:43, 132–34; 2:200). All this is

by way of a promise that comes to Christians from the future but
is based upon Christ's death and resurrection. But the promise is
also a demand. "For the blessing that takes place by God is completed in us by what we do" (1:121), and what we do is the fulfilling
of the law (Gal 5:14), for the law prohibits sin "by threats and terrors, nor is it easily able to correct those who submit themselves
to it. But love accomplishes this with complete delight and ease
and with full urgency" (1:95). The demand, then, is the demand
of love, and it asks Christians to imitate the life to come so far as
that is possible (1:299; 2:24, 77). It is in this way that the law becomes "useless for those who in a special way possess the guidance
of the law" (2:76).

It will be obvious that much more could be said regarding Theodore's exegesis and theology. My remarks have been no
more than an attempt to indicate ways in which the evidence of
these commentaries can assist us in understanding Theodore's approach not only to scripture but to the use made of it in the church.
It is certainly true that he sees his aim as designed to explain
the scriptural text. Indeed, his commentaries seem primarily designed to elucidate the difficult passages in scripture even if that
means passing over texts that would prove central to the preacher.
Nevertheless, it has seemed to me that in the long run his exegesis is both religious and theological. To be sure, he employs the
rhetorical conventions of his day and has not escaped the influence
of Greek philosophy on theology. But he assumes that the message
of Paul is one that can inform his own time with the promise and
demand of the gospel. It is even tempting to suggest that his theology is really quite Pauline, however much it differs from the sort
of interpretation of Paul provided by Augustine and many modern
interpreters. Coming to terms with these commentaries may be a
twofold task. On the one hand, to understand the details of what
Theodore is doing requires careful reading and constant consulta-
tion of the scriptural text. It is not always easy to follow him. On
the other hand, less patience is required in examining the longer
discursive parts of the commentaries. They have the appearance
of notes or appendices, and they repay study.

THE TRANSLATION

It would have been impossible to translate the text in any way without the assistance of Swete's notes, and there is no way this translation can be a substitute for Swete's edition. I have frequently called attention to his notes, particularly where he makes suggestions that are really conjectural emendations of the text. His notes also supply details regarding Latin translations of the Pauline letters and frequently make comparisons between Theodore's interpretation and that of others, particularly John Chrysostom and Theodoret. I have retained the page numbers from Swete's edition, placing them in brackets; these numbers do not correspond to the pagination in the text printed in this work. When the translation has two columns, the first represents the Latin with marks indicating the beginning (†) and ending (*) of what correlates with the catenist's Greek; the second column represents the Greek fragment. I have also retained the Septuagint's numbering of the psalms. Rightly or wrongly, I have decided to be as literal as possible in the translation. This will be particularly obvious in the translation of the scriptural text, but there it is designed to show that the Pauline text poses very real problems of meaning, problems to some degree obscured by our modern translations. It is easy to forget that a translation is also an interpretation. Let me note, as well, that I have decided to translate *pietas* as "true religion." This is obviously unsatisfactory, but I have been unable to think of anything that would be fully adequate. Unfortunately, *pius* becomes "godly," and *impius*, "ungodly."

THE TEXT AND ITS APPARATUS

It is important to point out to readers that the text that follows, while it does print Swete's Latin and Greek texts, does not observe his pagination. Moreover, Swete printed the Greek parallels as footnotes. The present edition, by using parallel columns, should make it easier for readers to compare the Greek fragments with the Latin text. As well, the apparatus printed in this volume is

also Swete's, but it has been adapted to the present text by replacing Swete's line notations with those found in the new pagination.

As well, Swete himself supplies "addenda et corrigenda" for his printed text both in volume 1 (312) and in volume 2 (286). Many of these notes correct mistakes, particularly in the Greek accents; they also correct punctuation. All these changes have been followed in the present text. Although most of Swete's conjectural emendations, however persuasive, seem designed to improve the Latin of the translation without any clear manuscript support, a few of them are compelling and persuasive; they have been adopted. Moreover, Ulrich Wickert in his *Studien zu den Pauluskommentaren Theodors von Mopsuestia* (BZNW 27; Berlin: Töpelmann, 1962) appended to his study a list of "Korrekturen" that included a number of notes relating to Swete's edition (206–12 nn. 51–79). Wickert's emendations are generally conjectural, but two them have been accepted in this text (see his nn. 58 and 60). Though I have been cautious in accepting emendations without clear manuscript support, the real value of the suggestions made by Swete and Wickert is to alert students of Theodore to obscure passages in the text of the commentaries.[25]

As noted at the beginning of this introduction, Swete depends primarily on three manuscripts, two Latin and one Greek. It will be useful to say a little more about them and to indicate some of the other manuscripts Swete consulted. In this way it will be possible to supply readers with what is lacking in Swete's edition, namely, a list of *sigla* that will enable them to use the apparatus. In his preface to volume 1, Swete explains in some detail the manuscripts he has used in preparing his edition. The better of the two Latin manuscripts he primarily uses is *Codex Ambianensis 88*, olim *Corbiensis* (*C*). Dating from the ninth or tenth century, the second volume includes all the commentaries from Galatians to Philemon. Originally at Corbie, this manuscript was moved to Amiens in the late eighteenth century. Swete also consults *Codex Harleianus 3063*, olim *Cusanus* (*H*), a manuscript that once belonged to the Hospital of St. Nicholas near Cusa, a foundation of Nicholas of Cusa (d. 1464). By Swete's time, this ninth-century manuscript was part of the Harley Collection in the British Museum. The opening eight quires of the manuscript have been lost,

[25] See the "Appended Note" that begins after the listing of *sigla* on p. xxix.

and what remains begins with the early part of Ambrosiaster's commentary on 2 Corinthians. With the prologue to Galatians the Latin translation of Theodore's commentaries replaces Ambrosiaster's work. These two Latin manuscripts appear unrelated to one another and do not seem derived directly from a single original.

Swete has taken the Greek fragments he prints largely from the eleventh-century catena in the Bibliothèque Nationale, *Coislin 204*. This manuscript was printed by J. A. Cramer in volumes 6 and 7 of his *Catenæ Græcorum Patrum in Novum Testamentum* (8 vols.; Oxford: E Typographeo Academico, 1838–44), and Otto Fridolin Fritzsche extracted from Cramer and edited most of the fragments attributed to Theodore in his *Theodori episcopi Mopsuesteni In novum testamentum commentariorum quae reperiri potuerunt* (Turici: Meyer et Zeller, 1847). Occasionally Swete cites in his apparatus other catenae found in Paris.

As I have mentioned, unfortunately, Swete does not supply *sigla* for his apparatus. Nevertheless, he includes in it a number of references to other Latin texts that have a bearing upon the readings of *C* and *H*. Rabanus Maurus, who was abbot of Fulda (825–847) and who died in 856 as Archbishop of Mainz, completed his *Enarrationes* on Paul about 842. The manuscript from Fulda that he apparently used seems to have attributed the commentaries it included to Ambrose. But beginning with the commentary on Philippians Rabanus's texts depend upon a (lost) Latin manuscript translating Theodore's commentaries that Swete suggests is "near of kin to the archetype of *C* and *H*" (1:xxxiii). For Rabanus's work Swete uses the *editio princeps*, printed in Cologne, 1626. Lanfranc (ca. 1010–1089) entered the abbey of Bec in 1042 and was prior from 1045 until 1063. In his commentary on Paul, Lanfranc preserved extracts from what may have been the manuscript used by *C*, and Swete has used Abbé Migne's reprint of J. L. D'Achery's edition of the Lanfranc manuscript then belonging to the Benedictine monastery of St. Melanius at Redon in Brittany, published in Paris, 1646. Depending upon Lanfrance, Robert of Bridlington (fl. 1180) wrote his *Compilationes in epistolas Pauli apostoli*, preserved in two manuscripts now found at Cambridge. Finally, Cardinal J. B. Pitra published in 1852 the Latin translation of Theodore's commentaries on Galatians, Ephesians, and Philemon, with selections from the intervening commentaries (published in J. B. Pitra, ed.,

Spicilegium solesmense complectens sanctorum patrum scriptorumque ecclesiasticorum anecdota hactenus opera, selecta e graecis oriental- ibusque et latinis codicibus [4 vols.; Paris: Didot, 1852–58]).

With all this in mind it is possible to supply an abbreviated list of *sigla* as follows:

C = *Codex Ambianensis 88*
H = *Codex Harleianus 3063*
Coisl. 204 = *Coislin 204*
Cr. = Cramer (see above)
Fr. = Fritzsche (see above)
r = Rabanus Maurus
l = Lanfranc
Pitra = Cardinal Pitra, 1852
g = Greek

APPENDED NOTE

The purpose of this note is to supply readers who wish to examine problems with Swete's text with a preliminary guide for doing so.[26] First, I shall list the changes recommended by Swete himself and by Wickert that have been accepted in the text published in this book. References will be to the emended text by page and line, followed by the volume, page, and line in Swete's original edition, and by any comments that seem necessary. Second, I shall make some observations about the proposals made by Swete and Wickert that have not been accepted. Finally, Professor John Fitzgerald has called my attention to four secondary articles, three of which report newly found manuscript evidence for the Latin translation of Theodore's commentaries.

Corrections and Emendations of Swete's Text Accepted in This Volume

A number of Swete's suggestions in his two "Addenda et Corrigenda" are quite simply corrections of his text. The most obvious example is the substitution of diuinarum for the typographical

---

[26] Both volumes of Swete's edition are available online for free viewing or download, so readers can consult on their own Swete's text, apparatus, notes, and addenda and corrigenda (1:312; 2:286). For volume 1, see: http://www.archive.org/details/theodoriepiscopo1theogoog; for volume 2, see: http://www.archive.org/details/theodoriepiscopooswetgoog.

error diuianrum (178.5, Swete 1:117.14). Another typographical error occurs at 314.21 (Swete 1:216.3), where quoniam should
not have been italicized. In several places Swete corrects the
spelling and accentuation of the Greek parallels (86.30, Swete
1:57.21; 96.29, Swete 1:63.19; 210.28, Swete 1:141.10; 294.6,
Swete 1:200.18; 298.32, Swete 1:204.26; 400.29, Swete 1:284.21;
568.4–5, Swete 2:102.12).

Other corrections involve the apparatus:

46 formam *H* refers to line 23 (Swete corrects the line number on 1:30 from 13 to 17)

60 for line 2 read nobis instead of uobis (Swete 1:39: 6 *corr.*
nobis)

100 for line 6 read uideretur *C** instead of uideretur *C* (Swete
1:65: 5 *C**)

114 add to line 30 cum haec *H* (Swete 1:75.16 adds this
manuscript reading)

118 Swete's correction of 1:77, *read* 12 for 11, has been made
by the adaptation of his apparatus to the present pagination and lines.

210 for lines 31–32 incircumscriptione instead of incircum-
scriptionem (Swete 1:141.3 corrects to incircumscriptione *C** *H*)

294 (at line 32 in apparatus) and 314 (at line 11 in apparatus)
delete l̄ēc̄. (Swete 1:202 and 1:215 *dele* l̄ēc̄.)

In addition to the obvious corrections just listed, Swete
changes his punctuation in a number of places. Sometimes it is
merely a question of changing a misprinted comma to a period
(190.11, Swete 1:125.14; 258.4, Swete 1:174.16; 316.18; Swete
1:218.3). Several other changes in the punctuation have also been
accepted:

112.32 (Swete 1:73.26: *punctuate* nit. et ipsi,). The change
makes ipsi the subject of nituntur, rather than understanding it with the participle intelligentes. This
improves the Latin but does not alter the sense of the
passage.

124.2 (Swete 1:82.25: *add comma after* πληροῦται) The addition of the comma clarifies the passage by preventing the following prepositional phrase from being understood in reference to the fulfilling of the law in the present Jerusalem.

208.24 (Swete 1:139.12: *punctuate* regenerationem, illam) This changes "we participating by that regeneration, gain the participation that is with him" to "we participating by regeneration, gain that participation that is with him." This makes for a smoother reading.

304.23 (Swete 1:208.12: *dele comma after* quidem) Here the comma seems superfluous and even confusing.

308.19 (Swete 1:211.4: *add comma after* eo) The comma prevents the clause beginning with licet from intruding upon the main clause of the sentence.

368.18 (Swete 1:258.18: *dele comma after* eo) The comma is superfluous and interrupts the flow of the Latin.

394.25 (Swete 1:279.9: *dele comma after* ostendens) Again the comma is superfluous.

752.1–2 (Swete 2:242.19–20: *read* 'eorum' poetam 'prophetam') This is an important change: from "their own poet" to "their own prophet." The correction conforms Theodore's comment to the scriptural text: *proprius eorum propheta.*

At three places Swete has added a bracketed word to the scriptural text:

476.28 (Swete 2:30.2: *read* in obu. [Domini]) The addition reflects Theodore's comment: rapti ducantur in aërem obuiam Domini.

556.7 (Swete 2:92.2: *add* [aut] *after* crinibus) This not only makes better sense of the scriptural passage but also reflects Theodore's comment: ex auro aut margaritas aut flexu crinium aut pretiosa ueste.

758.30 (Swete 2:249.8: *after* in omnibus *add* [placentas]) In his note 78 Wickert appears to misunderstand Swete's note to line 17, attributing it to line 8, where Swete has added [placentas] because of the Greek text and in light of Theodore's comment: si hoc dominis libitum fuerit.

In two places Swete restores the reading of *C* and *H*. At 456.24 (Swete 2:15.15: *dele* [ad]) Swete upon reflection abandons his use of Rabanus in favor of the omission of ad by *C* and *H*. The word is scarcely necessary for the meaning of the passage. At 706.4 (Swete 2:208.3) Swete follows *C* and *H* by omitting [nisi], a qualification of quia mendacia confirmare cupiunt that lacks manuscript support.

Three other of Swete's emendations have been accepted and may be noted as follows:

> 36.10–11 (Swete 1:23.18: *after* quemadmodum *add* [non]). The addition of "not" is necessary to make sense of the passage. Theodore argues that the conflict between Paul and Peter might well have led to division and asserts that this did not happen because of their later agreement. How would division *not* have been brought about, had not agreement intervened? The emendation is a *construction ad sensum*, but it surely seems necessary despite the lack of manuscript support.

> 372.25 (Swete 1:263.2: *read* uideri *and dele note*). Here Swete follows Jacobi's emendation of uidere to read uideri. Theodore is discussing an image that is seen in contrast to the unseen original. Swete's original text would have meant "[people make images] so that there may be a recollection of those not seen for those who are nevertheless able to see." The emended text would mean: "a recollection of those not seen by the images that can nevertheless be seen." The improvement is obvious.

> 484.14 (Swete 2:35.2: *read* et illi.). The reading of *C* (*corr*) is ut et illi tunc uiuent. Swete has opted for et rather than ut: *both* those alive at Christ's coming *and* those already dead. The emendation supplies a better Latin reading and has some manuscript support.

Of Wickert's twenty-eight notes on Swete's text, not all of which suggest emendations, only two have been accepted, both on the basis of their support by the manuscript evidence:

> 426.21 (Swete 1:304.9). In note 58 Wickert points out that Swete's text (consequentem ei doctrinae) fails to follow the reading eis found in *C*, *H̄*, and Rabanus. Presumably, Swete construed ei as an adjectival dative agreeing

with doctrinae: "following that doctrine." Swete's note *ad loc.* argues that to accept eis as the reading would require rejecting doctrinae as a gloss. Wickert's proposed emendation requires reading eis as ei<u>s: "his doctrine" rather than "that doctrine." The emendation is more securely based in the manuscript evidence than Swete's, and it conforms to two parallel expressions on the same page: Christi doctrina on Swete's line 5 (426.18) and eius doctrina on line 10 (426.21).

458.25 (Swete 2:17.4). In note 60 Wickert observes that Swete has followed Jacobi's conjecture, substituting uenire for the reading finire found in *C, H,* and Rabanus. He suggests reading finiri as a presumed translation of a Greek ὁρίζεσθαι. Thus, instead of "we expect the reward to *come to us,*" we should translate "we expect the reward to be *determined for us.*" The emendation is persuasive because it is more securely based upon the manuscripts.

Emendations Not Accepted in This Edition

Many of the proposals made by Swete and Wickert, however persuasive, seem purely conjectural, and it is primarily for this reason that they have been rejected. As well, few of the changes recommended affect the fundamental sense of the text first established by Swete. It would go beyond the purpose of this note to examine in detail all the suggestions that have been made, and in what follows I shall try to limit my discussion. The volume, page, and line numbers refer to Swete's printed edition.

Several of Swete's "additions" are just that: proposing a possible Greek original for the Latin (1:37.16, 1:198.17), determining the meaning of a Latin word (1:20.8), or referring to other sources that could be consulted (1:162.14, 1:222.18sq.). Some of his corrections involve no more than a change in the spelling of the Latin word (1:7.5, 1:130.12, 1:235.10, 1:248.10sq., 1:271.13, 1:272.6). Sometimes it is a question of changing the Latin word itself without seriously affecting the sense (1:3.1, 1:33.9, 1:41.20, 1:49.15, 1:95.1, 1:165.16, 1:219.16, 1. :247.18, 1:269.16). At one point Swete revises his punctuation but in a way that makes only a minor difference in the sense (1:155.15). In two places he has made slight changes to the scriptural text (1:60.10, 1:63.7). None of these changes affects the sense, and they often have no manuscript

support and are sometimes qualified by a "perhaps." The aim appears to be finding a clearer Latin text. For these reasons, none of them has been accepted.

There are six places where Swete has accepted Jacobi's conjectures. Three of them are clearly designed to improve the Latin but have no warrant in the manuscript tradition, judging by Swete's apparatus (1:21.3, 1:201.9, 1:219.14). At 1:251.4–5 Swete "perhaps" follows Jacobi's judgment that communionem ... accepit should "be expunged as a marginal gloss on the preceding sentence." Jacobi's two other conjectures followed by Swete are more interesting because they are attempts to improve the sense of the text:

> 1:32.12 (50.9 in this edition) *for* arrogantiam *read perh.* angustiam [so Jacobi, *l.c.*]. Here Theodore is speaking of the apostle's obscurity, and Jacobi's emendation rests soley on his understanding that the problem rests in Paul's lapidary style. "Arrogantia" does, indeed, seem a strange word in the context, since its usual meaning would be "haughtiness" or "arrogance." But the Oxford Latin Dictionary gives a meaning of the verb arrogo (2b): "to import or introduce (additional matter)." I have attempted to make sense of the passage by translating arrogantia as "exaggeration." This is because the scriptural text (Gal 2:17) includes Paul's (false) conclusion that "Christ is a servant of sin." Thus, we could understand Theodore's comment as a reference not only to Paul's lapidary style but also to his rhetorical use of arguments that are so exaggerated as to carry with them their own refutation. In any case, while the difficulty certainly remains, Jacobi's emendation is purely conjectural.

> 1:130.11 (196.18) *dele* nos [Jacobi, *l.c.*]. Here Theodore speaks of the "recapitulation" of all things in Christ as "the bond for the harmony of the whole creation." He goes on to say that the whole creation was looking to *us* for this, because God the Word indwelt him (the assumed Man): omni creatura ad illud <u>nos</u> inspiciente, propter inhabitantem Deum Uerbum. *C* in fact omits nos, but both *C* and *H* employ the accusative rather than the ablative, thereby rendering the Latin unintelligible.

Granted the difficulty, it does not seem to me impossible to understand "us." The clearer reference would be to the human Christ, but Theodore's strong insistence upon the identity of humans with the assumed Man could well be the point. God's purpose was to employ humanity as the bond linking the invisible and visible creations. Adam was a pledge of this harmony, and the new humanity in Christ ("us") fulfills that pledge. Again, the difficulty remains, but removing the nos does not necessarily clarify the passage.

Many of Swete's own emendations appear to be attempts to clarify or to improve the Latin of the text (1:2.28, 1:10.11, 1:13.1, 1:31.30, 1:38.18, 1:97.15, 1:116.7, 1:132.9, 1:242.14, 1:255.17, 1:294.6, 2:11.14). At two places he slightly modifies the Greek text (1:61.26, 2:8.23). He changes the tense of the verb to the future (ostendet) at 1:240.5 in order to conform Theodore's paraphrase to the future tense employed by the scriptural verse. In the commentary on Colossians at 1:276.1 he suggests the future (adimpletur) for the citation of Eph 1:22, on the grounds that in the commentary on Ephesians the verse is rendered this way. None of these changes significantly alters the meaning of the text. Again, few of them have firm manuscript support, while most of them are qualified by "perhaps." As with Jacobi's emendations, so with Swete's, the more interesting proposals have to do with attempts to expose the meaning of the passages in question. The following examples may be cited:

> 1:47.10 (72.13) *read* [mortales] const. Swete rightly sees that constituti dangles: literally, "since all of us constituted necessarily commit many transgressions." Adding mortales would not only clarify the Latin but also would reflect Theodore's idea that our mortality is the cause of our sinfulness. The English translation solves the problem by using the phrase "so constituted that" we transgress. Swete's solution is attractive, but it has no basis in the manuscripts and has seemed unnecessary to me.

> 1:49.14 (74.20) *om*. non [?]. Theodore argues that the law was imposed for the sake of transgressions, quasi quod iam ultra lex in nobis <u>non</u> habeat locum, post Christi aduentum.

In note 53 Wickert rejects this emendation. He supposes that Swete was "disturbed" by the following sentence, where Theodore recognizes that "in the present life and after Christ's coming we are plainly still subject to committing transgressions." In other words, Swete sees an apparent contradiction between the implied absence of transgressions in lines 12–14 and their recognition in lines 15–17. But the contradiction has to do with the tension between the "already" and the "not yet." Wickert correctly argues: "Es handelt sich aber um die Doppeldeutigkeit des Interim.... 'Der Apostel sagt also, das Gesetz sei um der Übertretungen willen gegeben, in der Meinung (quasi quod = ὡς ἄν), daß nunmehr weiterhin das Gesetz eine Stätte habe bei uns, nach Christi Erscheinung': das klingt, angesichts des die Epoche bezeichnenden iam = ἤδη, sehr unwahrscheinlich und erweist sich im Blick auf Gal 3 19 als sachlich unmöglich. Der folgende Satz (quoniam autem etc.) führt übrigens deutlich einen Gegensatz zum Vorigen ein."

1:168.10 (248.23) *read* percipiant. The first clause in the sentence beginning on line 10 reads: et quoniam in hoc sermonem adtraxit. Swete apparently wishes to replace adtraxit with percipiant. "When they understood his discourse on this point" substitutes for "When Paul drew his discourse to this point." I fail to understand the point of the emendation. There is no manuscript support, and the revised meaning makes no more sense than the one it replaces.

2:7.3 (446.7) *for* placitis doctrinis *read perh.* pl. [uel] d. Swete takes placitis as a noun meaning tenets, opinions, or doctrines. This would yield a translation "how by our tenets or doctrines you left idol worship." But the text as it stands could be understood as an ablative absolute: "our teachings having been pleasing." In note 59 Wickert deals with the same passage. He refers not only to Swete's suggestion but also Jacobi's conjecture (enim for quidem, and plac<e>tis for placitis). Wickert's own suggestion is to read: nostris placiti doctrinis. This emendation would scarcely differ from construing the text as it stands as an ablative absolute.

Wickert's notes (51–79) are not always "Korrekturen," nor is it easy to categorize them. The comments that follow will be in the order of his notes, followed by an indication of the volume, page, and line numbers of Swete's edition and this edition.

51. (1:28.14 = 44.4) A difficult passage. Wickert wants to read: "If God had made us ... establishing *us* (no<s> rather than non) as a nature (natura rather than naturam) concurring with this (sc. the legitimo animo, instinctively obedient to the natural law)." But there is no manuscript evidence for changing non to nos. I prefer my translation (45.3–5), which depends upon the adversative meaning of concurrere: "If God had employed some kind of single character for our complete existence so as to prepare us for choosing the best by a soul ruled by the law, and had *not* also made us by establishing in us a nature that *runs counter* to this, we should necessarily differ in no way from irrational beasts." These alternatives really make little difference, since Theodore's main point is clear for both of them: humans possess free choice.

52. (1:29.17 = 46.1) Wickert is concerned with Swete's note on cum uita ista diuidens saecula. Swete suggests replacing ista with ipsa, reflecting a hypothetical Greek: ἅμα αὐτῇ τῇ ζωῇ. Wickert questions this retroversion and suggests that the Greek may have been μετὰ τοῦτον τὸν βίον διαιρῶν τοὺς αἰῶνας, which the Latin translator misunderstood as μετὰ τούτου τοῦ βίου. He does not suggest emending the Latin text.

53. (1:49.12 = 74.18) See the discussion of Swete's correction at 1:49.14 above. Wickert also rejects Swete's change of ultro in line 14 to ultra.

54. (1:61.24 = 94.1) Here Wickert emends the Greek, rendering three datives as accusatives on the basis of the Latin. This may improve the Greek, but it does not change the sense. Should we seek to correct the Greek by the Latin?

55. (1:106.2 = 160.30) Wickert's emendation (nos for non) would yield "it is unbecoming for *us* in the present to undergo toil" instead of "it is *not* unbecoming in

the present to undergo toil." I think Wickert misses Theodore's point, based on the cryptic ending of the scriptural verse: "when we are not tired." Theodore takes the reference to be to the rest of the age to come, when toil will disappear. In the present, however, toil is appropriate and necessary.

56. (1:132.22 = 200.4) Here the Latin attaches "bound" to the miracles, while the Greek attributes the binding to the Spirit. Wickert wants to conform the Greek to the Latin by substituting ἐπισφιγγόν<των> for ἐπισφιγγόν (200.4). It is hard to see any fundamental difference in meaning, and it is more reasonable to suppose the Latin has misunderstood the Greek than the other way round.

57. (1:147.14 = 220.10) Wickert's emendation takes perfectam with directionem and changes uirtutem to uirtutum: "make progress toward the perfect achievement of virtues" instead of "make progress in the straight path leading to perfect virtue." The emendation is purely speculative and scarcely changes the basic meaning of the passage.

58. (1:304.9 = 426.21) Wickert's emendation has been accepted. See above.

59. (2:7.1= 446.5) This note has been discussed in reference to Swete 2:7.3 above.

60. (2:17.4 = 458.25) Wickert's emendation has been accepted. See above.

61. (2:22.15 = 466.12) The problem is ut adultera in line 17. We should expect the husband rather than the wife as the adulterer. The Greek parallel, which exists for this passage, has ὅταν μὴ πρὸς ἑτέραν ῥυπαίνηται: "when he is not defiled with another woman." The Latin would mean "he means the time when [the wife?] is not defiled as an adulteress." Wickert suggests that the original Latin translation may have been: quando non ad <a>ltera<m> sordidatur, later corrupted to the present text, ut adultera. This conjecture is both ingenious and persuasive, and the only reason it has not been accepted is its lack of manuscript support.

62. (2:24.14 = 468.30) Wickert's note concerns the expression sanctificationem possessionis in line 15, where Theodore explains the text of 1 Thess 4:7 and its mention of sanctificationem alone. Wickert does not propose changing the text, but rejects Swete's note *ad loc.* associating the expression with Acts 7:5, 45. He rightly links the expression to 1 Thess 4:4: τὸ ἑαυτοῦ σκεῦος κτᾶσθαι ἐν ἁγιασμῷ. Theodore's reference is primarily to the age to come. "Es geht um jene Heiligkeit, die wir einst ganz besitzen werden, um die wir uns aber hier schon κατὰ μίμησιν bemühen—auch in den geschlechtlichen Beziehungen."

63. (2:58.2 = 512.23) Wickert accepts Jacobi's change of in ueritate caritatis to in caritate ueritatis, thereby conforming Theodore's paraphrase to the expression in 2 Thess 2:10. The emendation is attractive but has not been accepted partly because there is no manuscript warrant and partly because it is not possible to be sure that the Latin translator has followed Theodore's Greek text of the scriptural verse.

64. (2:58.7 = 512.28) Here there is a Greek parallel. On this basis Wickert approves of Swete's correction of concessione in *C H r* to concessionem, an emendation Swete's apparatus explains as based on the Greek text. But Wickert argues that Swete might have gone further by changing Dei to Deo. He suggests that the reading concessione may have explained the Dei: "by the permission of God." This would then allow the following words (opus eius) to be a reference to the devil's or antichrist's work, leaving quasi and esse without any clear meaning. The argument is ingenious and may help explain why the Latin text is muddled, but Wickert apparently does not propose an emendation.

65. (2:63.11 = 520.13) Theodore comments on 2 Thess 3:12: "He [Paul] does not say that they should work without qualification, but he added *with modesty*, quod erant adimentes, so that they might not be inquisitive...." Wickert remains unconvinced by the attempts of Swete and Jacobi to conjecture the original Greek, and he suspects the phrase underlined above is a gloss. On the

other hand, if we accept "ut de uita aliena," the reading of *C(corr.)*, rather than "ut ne," that of *H* for line 12, the text could be read: adiecit 'cum modestia,' quod erant ad<nit>entes (= σπουδάζοντες?) ut de uita aliena curiose agerent. Wickert does not press his solution and ends with a *non liquet*.

66. (2:77.4 = 538.17) Wickert notes the tautology in the text: 'euangelium' uero 'gloriae' uocat illam praedicationem quae de euangelio est. He also points out that illa in line 7 "hangs in the air" and that line 11 reads: haec ergo praedicatio est de futuris. Thus, in the first phrase we should read quae de futuris est rather than quae de euangelio est. This certainly makes good sense, and Wickert rightly alludes to the Antiochene tendency to identify glory with the age to come. But the emendation has no clear manuscript support.

67. (2:83.6 = 546.12) Here Theodore paraphrases Paul's advice to Timothy, urging him to persevere in his life and teaching, hoc enim magnum tibi prouidebit iuuamen et consequenter eligenti istae gratiae. Wickert notes that all the manuscripts have eligent. He rejects Jacobi's conjecture: consequenter <uivere> eligent, which would mean: "and consequently they (sc. those to whom Timothy preaches) will choose to live by that grace." He approves of Swete's simpler conjecture (eligenti for eligent).

68. (2:86.5 = 550.5) The problem is aliter in line 7. Wickert refers to Swete's note *ad loc.*, suggesting a possible reading altera. But he does not emend the text and asks: "Warum sollte der bersetzer nicht 'ἄλλως' gelesen haben?"

69. (2:98.22 = 564.11) The difficulty is that here the episcopate is *not* to be desired, whereas in 1 Tim 3:16 and Theodore's following comments it is to be desired as a good work. Wickert approves of Swete's note on line 23, noting the difficulty. But he rejects the reading Swete suggests in his note: ut intellegerent non [absolute quidem] esse concupiscendum. Wickert proposes reading: hoc enim erat suadere ut intelligerent non esse <non> concupiscendum, debere uero scire, etc., arguing that

the second non has dropped out by haplography. Thus, we could translate: "to persuade them that it was not the case that the episcopate was not to be desired, but that they ought to know how to desire it." This is an attractive proposal and, in fact, honors the spirit of Swete's note. The English translation makes a similar qualification, but it has seemed to me preferable to leave the difficulty in the text untouched and simply to call attention to it in a note.

70. (2:104.4 = 570.30) Wickert suggests changing utrisque in line 5 to utrosque, thereby following the Greek, which has the accusative. But utriusque in line 3 is equally troubling. The emendation clarifies the Latin but is purely conjectural.

71. (2:142.16 = 618.14) Wickert emends arbitrio eorum prauitatem to arbitrii eorum prauitatem, following the reading of C (corr.) and Rabanus. He also appeals to 2:111.5, where we find arbitrii sui prauitate. The emendation has manuscript support, but it is hard to see that it changes the sense of the passage.

72 (2:142.21 = 618.18) Wickert refers to Swete's note on 2:142.22, where he suggests the possibility of reading talia instead of alia and understands de illis in line 23 to refer to the faithful. Wickert admits the possibility of reading talia, but his concern is to reject Swete's interpretation of de illis, arguing that the reference is not to the faithful but to the foods. Thus, he proposes no emendation.

73. (2:146.7 = 622.26) quae alios ita instruere deproperat ita ut sit.... Wickert suggests the possibility of striking the second ita. This would improve the Latin, but ita ut could well be an example of the barbarous Latin of the translation.

74. (2:157.18 = 638.26) Wickert approves of Swete's note on line 19, which points out that "the alternative clause seems to be wanting." Wickert suggests that the problem may be the result of a homoteleuton and that we could supply a phrase parallel to that following the first and existing siue. He does not appear to emend the text.

75. (2:177.16 = 664.29) Wickert makes a slight change in order to improve the Greek text in the parallel (τῷ instead
of τό).

76. (2:193.23 = 686.30) Wickert suggests using the Latin to
correct the Greek parallel, by changing ἡνίκα to ἅτινα.
This is a reasonable proposal, but one that makes no
significant change in the meaning and argues (problem-
atically, I think) from the Latin to the Greek.

77. (2:218.5 = 718.17) Wickert proposes inserting accipere
qui instead of Swete's simple insertion of qui. Thus, we
should translate "it would be ridiculous to accept Moses,
who..." instead of "it would be ridiculous that Moses,
who...." I find it hard to see that the change makes any
real difference.

78. (2:249.8 = 758.30) See Swete's addition of [placentes] in
this place. Wickert's note has been discussed in commenting on accepting Swete's amendment (758.30 in
this edition).

79. (2:254.18 = 766.25) Wickert's emendation changes necessitate addictus to necessitate add<u>ctus, that is,
"led by necessity." But since the present reading means
"bound by necessity," the emendation scarcely seem
necessary.

Articles Dealing with Swete's Text

In two articles Donatien de Bruyne called attention to newly
found manuscript evidence for the Latin translation of Theodore's
commentaries on the Pauline epistles. In *Revue bénédictine* 33
(1921): 53–54 he reported his discovery of a manuscript in the
Bibliothèque Nationale of Paris that includes Theodore's commentaries on the two letters to Timothy and the letters to Titus
and Philemon. Leaves 5–12 of MS 17.177 are in an Anglo-Saxon
script of the tenth century, though leaves 9–12 are mutilated. The
leaves are to be arranged in the order 11, 10, 5, 6, 7, 8. DeBruyne
also correlated the content of these leaves with Swete's printed
text. He then chose three passages that call Swete's text into question, arguing that P supplies a better text at these points (Swete
2:189.1, 2:250.3, 2:255.16). Several years later (in *Revue bénédictine* 47 [1935]: 305) DeBruyne pointed out that the manuscript he

had discovered (now labeled Paris B.N. 17177) was missing two
leaves between 5 and 6. These two leaves turned out to have been
preserved in a mutilated condition in the Vatican Library (Vatic.
lat. 340). They are described as in an Anglo-Saxon script of the
eighth or ninth century, though DeBruyne failed to note that in
his earlier article he gave the date as tenth century.

Dom Eligius Dekkers almost twenty years later published
an article entitled "Un nouveau manuscrit du commentaire de
Théodore de Mopsueste aux Épîtres de S. Paul" (*Sacris erudiri*
6 [1954]: 429–33). Swete dated *C* in the ninth or tenth century, *H* in the ninth. But Dekker claims that both are from the
eighth or ninth century and that their provenance is northeast
France and probably from Corbie. He also notes the Paris-Vatican
manuscript DeBruyne had found. His own discovery is of a
manuscript in the Bibliothèque Universitaire of Gaud (Ganda-
vensis 455). This manuscript, a quarto consisting of two hundred
leaves, is dated to the ninth century, "provenant, comme tant
d'autres manuscripts gantois, de S. Maximin de Trèves." Apart
from the apparently later addition of a diploma of Otto I, dated
10 March 956, and a poem on creation, the manuscript includes
commentaries on all the Pauline epistles save for Romans and
Hebrews. Only the commentaries on the Corinthian letters give
Ambrosiaster's text, while the rest of them preserve the Latin
translation of Theodore's commentaries. Since a number of Car-
olingian and medieval writers have preserved this combination
of Ambrosiaster and Theodore, attributing both to Ambrose,
there remains the possibility of discovering other witnesses to
Theodore's commentaries in the many manuscripts attributed to
Ambrosiaster. Dekkers points out that *G* reproduces the "particu-
larités" of *C* and *H*. Therefore, it belongs to the same family but is
closer to *H*. Dekkers's reconstruction of the manuscript tree proposes a common archetype for *C* and a hypothical *y*, which is then
to be regarded as the archetype of *H* and *G*.

The last of the four articles Prof. Fitzgerald sent me does not
include any new manuscript evidence but is simply a note on a passage in Theodore's commentary on 1 Timothy. W. L. Lorimer, in
Journal of Theological Studies 44 (1943): 58–59, corrects Swete's
note on 2:123. The Greek fragment reads: "But when there came
to be a great increase of true religion, not only the *largest* [μέγισται]
cities, but also the country places belonged to believers." The

Latin translation reads: "But when true religion appears to have gained increase, then not only cities but country regions were *filled* [repletae] with believers." Swete's note observes that the Greek has lost the word corresponding with repletae, while μέγισται finds no place in the Latin. Lorimer's conclusion is that "Theodore wrote, and the translator read, μεσταὶ not μέγισται."

Conclusion

In considering the various ways in which Swete himself and others have attempted to improve his edition, I have been struck by the fact that none of these attempts and, so far as one can tell, none of the new manuscript evidence seriously calls into question Swete's achievement. Indeed, not only are the various proposals concerned with small details in Swete's text, but they also fail to make any significant change in that text. To be sure, the work of emendation may well polish and sharpen the text Swete has established, but they can scarcely replace it. The real value of the observations and emendations discussed in this note may well be to call attention to the difficulties in the text and to help readers discern Theodore's meaning, which so often lies concealed beneath the obscurity not only of the Latin translation but, as well, of his Greek.

THEODORUS MOPSUESTENUS IN EPISTOLAM B. PAULI AD GALATAS

ARGUMENTUM*

BEATUS apostolus Paulus fidem quae in Christo est euangeli-
zans uenit ad gentem Galatarum; quos et per gratiam sancti Spiritus ita sua inluminauit doctrina, ut etiam credentes non modo
baptizarentur, sed etiam sancti Spiritus gratiam ad instar cetero-
5   rum fidelium adsequerentur. quidam uero ex Iudaeis qui Christo crediderant, praua ducti aemulatione, multam sollicitudinem
expendebant ad hoc ut suaderent illis qui ex gentibus crediderant
etiam legis seruare mandata. est autem argumentum huius epistolae plurima in parte concordans in illis quae in secunda ad Corin-
10 thios epistola expressa esse uidentur, si quis tamen eius argumentum ueraciter cum istius epistolae argumento comparare uoluerit.
uenerunt ergo hi et ad gentem Galatarum, plurimum derogantes
apostolum Paulum, cupientes modis omnibus legis firmare decreta; dicentes quoniam 'nullum iuuamen ex ea fide quae in Christo
15 est poterint credentes adsequi, si non etiam et legis Moysaicae impleuerint decreta.' dicebant enim quia et primum lex a Deo data sit ea ratione ut custodientes eam bonorum ab ea percipiamus
fruitionem, utpote iusti et qui opere ipso legis impleuerimus decreta. si uero neglegendam existimauerimus esse legis custodiam,
20 indubie diuinae subiciemur sententiae. dicebant autem et apostolos omnes qui fuerant cum Christo uehementer legis custodiam

---

‖ INCIPIT . ARGUM̄TVM . IN EPISTOLA BEATI PAVLI APOSTOLI AD GALATHAS
EXPOSITUM A BEATO AMBROSIO EPISCOPO C   3   modo *om* H   9   conc. illis
C (*corr.*) [cf. p. 51, l. 1]   11   argumentum C* H   12   et hi H   15   poterant
C (*corr.*) H [cf. Rönsch, 294: Bensly, 72 n, 88]   ‖   leges C*   17   ab eo H   20
ad apost. H

THEODORE OF MOPSUESTIA ON BLESSED PAUL'S LETTER TO THE GALATIANS

THE SETTING

[1] The blessed apostle Paul came to the Galatians preaching the good news of faith in Christ. By the grace of the Holy Spirit he so illuminated them by his teaching that, as soon as they believed, they were not only baptized but also acquired the grace of the Holy Spirit in just the same way as the rest of the faithful. But certain of the Jews who had believed in Christ, prompted by perverse rivalry, spent great and anxious care to persuade the believing Gentiles that they should keep the requirements of the law. Indeed, the setting of this letter agrees in large part with what appears to be described in 2 Corinthians, at least if someone is willing accurately to compare its setting with that of this letter. Thus, these Jewish Christians came to the Galatians, slandering the apostle Paul as much as possible and wishing [2] to establish the commandments of the law in all ways. And so they said that "believers could gain no benefit from faith in Christ unless they also fulfilled the commandments of the Mosaic law." For they said that the law was given by God at first on the principle that if we keep it we should receive from it the enjoyment of good things, since, of course, those of us who fulfill the commandments of the law by doing them are righteous. But if we think that keeping the law must be disregarded, we shall doubtless be liable to divine judgment. Moreover, they also said that all the apostles who had been with Christ

cum omni seruare diligentia. haec autem dicebant ut legis quidem auctoritatem omni uirtute augerent, gloriam uero Pauli modis omnibus abolerent; derogantes eius doctrinae ac dicentes quoniam 'non uere similis hic ceteris apostolis. nec enim est fas ut tan-
5   tos relinquentes, isti uni et soli uelitis intendere.' adicientes etiam
dicebant quia 'illi quidem discipuli fuerunt Christi, et cum eo per
omne tempus conuersati sunt, et ab eo omni dogmatum scrupulositate sunt edocti; hic uero idem Paulus Christum nec uidere nec
ab eo discere quicquam potuit, sed horum ipsorum fuit discipulus.
10 a quo enim altero potuit discere ueritatem, postquam Christus in
caelum ascendit? itaque modis omnibus conuenit non huic intendere talia docenti, sed ceteris apostolis, apud quos multa sollicitudo erga legis obseruantiam esse inuenitur.' his sermonibus suaserunt Galatis qui ex gentibus Christo crediderant, docentes eos
15 qui a beato Paulo baptisma perceperant et diuersas gratias spiritales fuerant adsecuti ut legitimae obseruationi succumberent, in
tantum ut et quidam eorum circumcisionem carnis accipere ad-
quieuissent. quo facto apostolus de tali gestu probat ut conuenerat feruens aemulatione, scribens ad eos hanc epistolam; ad omnia
20 quae ab aduersariis de eo dicta fuerant prudenter respondens, et
comprobans quod enim illa quae de se fuerant dicta uana essent.
cum debita uero modestia instruxit eos ac docuit quoniam post
Christi aduentum minime conueniat legis inseruire custodiae. do-
cebit autem nos cautissime de singulis his illa interpretatio quae
25 Deo auctore suo ordine explanabitur in subsequentibus.

I

Paulus apostolus, non ab hominibus neque per hominem, sed per Ie-
sum Christum, et Deum Patrem, qui suscitauit eum ex mortuis.

Diximus iam et in superioribus argumentum explicantes, quoniam aduersarii ad destructionem Pauli plurimam abusi fuissent
30 derogationem, dummodo eius euacuarent gloriam, sicque doctri-

---

2   auctoritate in o. u. *H*   4   hic similis *H*   ‖   cet. est ap. *C* (*corr.*)   7   omne
d. scrupolisitate *C**   omnes d. scrupulositate *C* (*corr.*)   11   asc. in c. *H*   12
alia doc. *H*   ‖   et (*for* sed) *H*   14   docentes eos beato P. qui et bapt. perc. *C**
detrahentes b. P. qui et bapt. ab eo perc. *C* (*corr.*)   16   obseruatione *C**   17-18
adquiuissent *C H*   18   probata *C*   19   scribit *C*   21   enimuero (*for* enim) *C*
(*corr.*)   28   etiam (*for* iam) *H*

firmly observed keeping the law with all diligence. They said this, then, in order to magnify the authority of the law as much as possible, but also to destroy Paul's reputation in all respects by setting aside his teaching and saying that "he is not truly like the other apostles. Nor is it right for you to desert such great men and be willing to pay attention to that one and him alone." They said in addition that "those men who were indeed Christ's disciples were his companions during the whole time of his ministry and learned from him his teaching with all exactness. But this Paul was unable either to see Christ or to learn anything from him. Instead, he was the disciple of those very others. Indeed, from what other source could he have learned the truth after Christ had ascended into heaven? And so in every way it is right to pay no attention to him when he teaches such things, but to attend to the other apostles among whom there is found great care for observing the law." By these words they persuaded the Galatians who had believed in Christ when they were Gentiles. They taught those who had received baptism from blessed Paul and had acquired various spiritual graces that they should submit to observing the law to such a degree as to accept the circumcision of their flesh. When this happened, the apostle demonstrates that he had been right regarding this matter. He is roused to opposition, and he writes this letter to them. He wisely answers everything that his opponents had said about him [3] and demonstrates that it was groundless. Moreover, with due modesty he instructed them and taught that after Christ's coming it was not at all right to be slaves by keeping the law. And so, the interpretation expounded in what follows, in order and with God's inspiration, will give us the soundest teaching concerning each of these points.

BOOK I

1:1 *Paul, an apostle, not from humans nor through a human being, but through Jesus Christ and God the Father, who raised him from the dead—*

We have already said above in explaining the setting that Paul's opponents had falsely employed the greatest possible slander to

nam eius repudiare facerent. necessarium enim erat, eius opinione imminuta, simul etiam et doctrinae eius titulum aboleri. propter hoc et ipse cogitur de illis quae erga se sunt satisfacere, arguens aduersarios uniuersa fuisse mentitos. in quibus et demiratione di-
5 gna est apostolica prudentia, quemadmodum sua firmans nullo in loco grauis aliquibus uisus est extitisse; sed quasi qui pro se satisfacere sit coactus, ita sub specie referentis uniuersa simpliciter et absolute dixit. quod et protinus ab ipsa praefatione custodisse repperitur. dicebant enim aduersarii discipulum eum fuisse beati
10 Petri et ceterorum, ut praecellente illorum doctrina per omnia ab istius doctrina abscedentes, legis confirmarent obseruantiam utpote necessariam; quam etiam et ceteri apostoli ut in Iudaea commorantes ob aliorum utilitatem seruare necessario cogebantur.

    non dixit secundum suam consuetudinem: *Paulus apostolus*
15 *Christi*, aut *Dei;* sed interiecit: *non ab hominibus, neque per homi-nem*, hoc est, 'sicut aduersarii dicunt.' unde illud et diuisit, dicens: *non ab hominibus, neque per hominem;* id ipsum quidem dicens, quoniam non homines apostolatus illi causa extiterat. diuidit autem illud, ut ostendat ipsa multitudine narrationis nullo mo-
20 do illos uerum dixisse. denique adicit: *sed per Iesum Christum et Deum Patrem*, in commune ponens illud quod dixit *per*, id est, et in 'Patre' et in 'Iesu Christo.' non enim dixit *et a Deo Patre;* sed simpliciter: *et Deum Patrem, per Iesum Christum* pariter illud complectens. optime autem usus est et delectionem qua adicit dicens:
25 *qui suscitauit eum ex mortuis.* nouitatem enim designare cupit futurae uitae, cuius primitiae dominica extitit resurrectio; in qua locum nullum habere potest legis obseruantia. nec enim circumcisio nec sacrificium nec temporum custodia locum ullum habere poterint tunc quando inmortalem illam uitam perceperimus per resur-
30 rectionem.

    deinde quia et multitudine uolebant differentiam eius ostende-

---

6 qui *om C** 10 P. et ut cet. *C** ‖ praecellentem, doctrinam *C H* ‖ eorum (*for* ill.) *H* 11 discedentes *H* 13 cogebant *H* 16 et illud *H* 18 hominis *C H* 20 dicere *l* 21 ponens ponens *H* ‖ idem (*for* id est) *C H* 22 Patre *om C* 24 dilectionem *C H* 27 obseruantiae *C H* 28-29 poterunt tum *C* 31 quae (*for* quia) *C* ‖ multitudinem *C* multitudini *H*

destroy him. By taking away his reputation they sought to bring about the repudiation of his teaching. For if he lost esteem, it would necessarily follow that the claim of his teaching would be destroyed at the same time. For this reason Paul is compelled to give satisfactory answers to the charges made against him by proving that his opponents had lied about everything. Here, too, the apostle's wisdom is worth admiring for the way he builds up his case without the least heavy-handedness against anyone. But inasmuch as he was compelled to give a satisfactory account of himself, in presenting his reply to all the charges he spoke simply and completely. Right from the start in his very salutation he is found to have observed this approach. For his opponents were saying that he was a disciple of blessed Peter and the others, and so those who abandoned Peter's teaching were abandoning a teaching far superior in all things to their own. They said this in order to establish the observance of the law as necessary. As well, they said that the rest of the apostles, inasmuch as they remained in Judea, were also necessarily obliged to preserve the law's observance because of its advantage for others.[1]

[4] He did not say in his usual way *Paul, an apostle of Christ* or *of God*, but he inserted *not from humans nor through a human being*, that is, "as my opponents say." This is why he divides his statement in two, saying *not from humans nor through a human being*. He means the same thing, since human beings had not been the source of his apostolic office; but he divided his statement to demonstrate by his very lengthening of it that they had in no way spoken the truth. Then he adds *but through Jesus Christ and God the Father*, using the word *through* for both, that is, both the Father and Jesus Christ. For he did not say *and from God the Father*, but simply *and God the Father*, including these words equally with *through Jesus Christ*. He also quite effectively employs charm by adding to his words *who raised him from the dead*. For he wants to indicate the novelty of the life to come, the firstfruits of which are the Lord's resurrection, where observing the law can have no place. For neither circumcision nor sacrifice nor the observances of special times can have any place at that time when we take possession of immortal life through the resurrection.

Then because they wanted to demonstrate his difference from

---

[1] Perhaps the "others" are potential converts from Judaism.

re, ex comparatione scilicet ceterorum apostolorum, quasi quia et
unus idem et solus sit, non debere ceteris hunc uel praehonorari
vel exaequari, ait:

   et qui mecum sunt omnes fratres, ecclesiis Galatiae.

5   ostendens quoniam multi sunt etiam cum ipso apostolo, communicantes ei in hac doctrina.

   gratia uobis et pax a Deo patre nostro et domino Iesu Christo.

   hoc quidem posuit consuete; connectit uero alia praeter consuetudinem, illa quae sibi conuenire ad praesens argumentum exi-

10   stimabat:

   qui dedit semetipsum pro peccatis nostris, ut eriperet nos ex prae-
   senti saeculo maligno secundum uoluntatem Dei et patris nostri, cui
   gloria in saecula saeculorum. amen.

   ad eos qui opinantur ex his dictis posse ostendere quoniam na-

15   tura est aliqua uel mala uel maligna, quod non est praesentis temporis longam de istis facere prosecutionem, alio sermonis extanti
proposito; tantum sufficit dicere, quod

†saeculum non est natura, quae   αἰὼν δέ ἐστιν οὐ φύσις ἐν ὑποστάσει
in sua possit agnosci substantia.   γνωριζομένη, ἀλλὰ διάστημα ὅπως

20   saeculum autem dicitur omnis   ποτὲ ἐπινοούμενον χρόνου εἴτε μι-
temporum prolixitas uel distan-   κρὸν εἴτε μέγα· μικρὸν μὲν ὡς ὅταν
tia, qualitercumque fuerit exco-   τὴν ἡμετέραν ζωὴν οὕτως καλῇ· ὁ
gitata, siue in modicum, siue in   αἰὼν ἡμῶν εἰς φωτισμὸν τοῦ προσ-
maius. in modicum quidem, si-   ώπου σου.

25   cut est nostra uita, quam ita uocat: *saeculum nostrum in inlumi-*
natione uultus tui.

in magnum uero, sicut quando   μέγα δὲ ὡς ὅτε τὸ πᾶν διάστημα
omnem dicit distantiam illam,   οὕτως λέγει τὸ ἀπὸ τῆς τοῦ κόσ-

30   quae est ab euangelii constitu-   μου καταβολῆς ἄχρι τῆς δευτέρας
tione usque ad secundum Chri-   τοῦ Χριστοῦ παρουσίας ἐπὶ συντε-
sti aduentum; quod erit in con-   λείᾳ τοῦ παρόντος βίου γινομένης
summationem praesentis uitae,   νοούμενον. περὶ οὗ ἐν τοῖς εὐαγγε-
de qua in euangeliis Dominus   λίοις ὁ κύριος φησίν· ἰδοὺ ἐγὼ μεθ'

35   ait: *ecce ego uobiscum sum omni-*   ὑμῶν εἰμὶ πάσας τὰς ἡμέρας ἕως

---

1   quae (*for* quia) C   2   hunc cet. H   8   aliam C H   9   illam H   ‖   pr. ad
arg. H   18   sq. Coisl. 204 f. 5 b, [Cr. vi. 12, Fr. 121]. θεοδώρου (marg.).   22   ὁ
Cr.   25   uita nostra H   30   [a mundi const. g]   32   αὐτοῦ παρόντος Cr. αὐτοῦ
τοῦ παρ. conj. Fr.   34   euangelio H   35   sum *om.* C*

the many, that is, by comparison with the other apostles, as though he were one and alone and ought not be honored before or equaled with the rest, he says:

1:2 *and all the brothers who are with me, to the churches of Galatia.*

[5] He shows that there are many also with him, the apostle, sharing with him in this teaching.

1:3 *Grace to you and peace from God our Father and the Lord Jesus Christ,*

He placed this here as usual, but contrary to his custom he intertwines other statements that he thought suited the present setting:

1:4–5 *who gave himself for our sins to rescue us from the present wicked age, according to the will of our God and Father, to whom be the glory to the ages of ages. Amen.*

Because there is no time now to supply an extended refutation of those who think they can demonstrate from these words that there is another nature that is either evil or wicked,[2] and since there is another discussion existing in published form, it is enough to say that

†an age is not a nature that can be recognized in an existing substance. But an age is said to be the entire extension or interval of times, however it may be conceived, whether moderate or [6] greater. In moderate form, such as our life, scripture names it thus (Ps 89:8): *our age is in the light of your face.*[3]	an age is not a nature recognized in an existing substance but is an interval of time however conceived, whether small or great. It is small as when scripture names our life this way (Ps 89:8): *our age is in the light of your face.*
But it is in great form such as when scripture speaks of that entire interval that exists from the establishment of the gospel to the second coming of Christ, which will take place at the consummation of the present life.	It is great as when scripture means us to understand the entire interval from the foundation of the world until the second coming of Christ at the end of the present life. Concerning this the Lord says in the

---

[2] The Manichaeans.

[3] Cf. Ps 90:10 (LXX 89:10), where human life is limited to seventy or eighty years.

bus diebus usque ad consummatio-
nem saeculi.

quod enim et *instans saeculum*
alibi apostolus dixit; sic uocans
illud, quasi quia in eo etiam
praesentem hanc uitam uiuamus.

quemadmodum ergo uidebimus
distantiam, quae nec in substantia sua esse uidetur, nec bona esse, nec mala secundum suam
potest esse naturam?

sed illud quod uult apostolus ad
praesens dicere, ob propositam
nobis interpretationem explicare iustum censemus.

    primus homo adubi factus
est, si inmortalis mansisset,
praesens utique non esset uita;
eo quod nec finem idem haberet
uitae, inmortalis manendo.

uerum quia mortalis factus est
per peccatum, praesens uocatur
uita *instans* uita, in comparatione futurae illius uitae quam in
ultimo fieri expectamus. in hac
igitur uita, quia peccare possumus, lex nobis est necessaria,*

qua prohibeamur ab illis actibus qui nobis non conueniunt. nam
et ante legem Moysaicam erant legitima quaedam apud homines,
quae secundum Dei sapientiam datam inerant nobis. non enim
nobis licebat homicidium facere neque adulterium, neque furtum
neque aliud inconueniens.

†in futuro uero saeculo neque
lex nobis erit necessaria, neque
obseruantia alicuius praecepti;

τῆς συντελείας τοῦ αἰῶνος.

ὃν δὴ καὶ ἐνεστῶτα αἰῶνα ὁ ἀπόστολος λέγει· οὕτως καλῶν αὐτὸν ὡς
ἂν ἐν αὐτῷ τὴν παροῦσαν ταυτηνὶ
ζωὴν ζώντων ἡμῶν.

πῶς οὖν ἂν γένοιτο διάστημα, ὃ
μηδὲ ἐν ὑποστάσει θεωρεῖται, ἢ
καλὸν ἢ κακὸν κατὰ φύσιν;

ἀλλ᾽ ὅπερ βούλεται εἰπεῖν ὁ ἀπόστολος τοῦτό ἐστιν.

ὁ πρῶτος ἄνθρωπος ὡς ἐγένετο,
εἰ μὲν ἀθάνατος ἔμεινεν, ἐνεστὼς
βίος οὐκ ἂν ἦν, ἅτε δὴ τέλος οὐκ
ἔχων·

ἐπειδὴ δὲ θνητὸς ἐγένετο διὰ τὴν
ἁμαρτίαν, ἐνεστὼς καλεῖται βίος
ὡς εἰκὸς ἡ παροῦσα ζωὴ πρὸς τὴν
μέλλουσαν ὕστερον. ἐν ταύτῃ μὲν
οὖν καὶ ἁμαρτάνειν ἐπιδεχόμεθα,
ὅθεν καὶ νομίμων ἡμῖν χρεία·

ἐπὶ δέ γε τοῦ μέλλοντος αἰῶνος
οὐδὲ διατάξεως χρεία ἡμῖν τινός,
ἐπείπερ ἔξω πάσης ἁμαρτίας τῇ τοῦ

3 instantem *C H* 4 alibi *om g* 14 positam *H* 17 at ubi *C* 24 idem *C*
id est *H* (*ins before* instans) 27 peccare *om C** 29 quae *C H* 32 n. liceat
*C** licebat n. *H* 35 διὰ τάξεως Cr. 36 obseruantiae *C H*

In the Gospels the Lord speaks of this (Matt 28:20): *Behold, I am with you all the days until the consummation of the age.*

Elsewhere the apostle spoke of it as the *age at hand* (Rom 8:38; Heb 9:9), giving it this name on the grounds that we live this present life in it.

Therefore, how shall we see an interval that neither [7] appears in its own substantial existence nor can be good or evil by its own nature?

But we think it right to explain for the present what the apostle means in view of the interpretation we propose.

The first human was created in such a way that if he had remained immortal, the present life would certainly not have come to be because he would not have had an end of life by remaining immortal.

But because he was made mortal by sin, the present life is called *at hand* by comparison with the future life that we expect to come about at the last day. Thus, in this life, because we can sin, the law is necessary for us.*

By it we are kept apart from those actions unfitting for us. For even before the Mosaic law there were certain legal prescriptions among humans that were implanted in us according to the wisdom given by God. For we were not permitted to commit murder, adultery, theft, or any other wrong act.

†But in the age to come neither will the law be necessary for us

Gospels (Matt 28:20): *Behold, I am with you all the days until the consummation of the age.*

Indeed, the apostle speaks of it as the *age at hand*, giving it this name since we live this life in it.

Therefore, how would an interval that is not seen in substantial existence be either good or evil by nature?

Rather, what the apostle means is this:

When the first human came into existence, if he had remained immortal, the present life would not have existed, since he would have had no end of life.

But when he became mortal because of his sin, life is called *at hand*, since the present life is compared to the one that will come to be later. Thus, in this life we expect to sin, which is why we need laws.

But in the age to come we need no commandment at all, since

eo quod ab omni peccato liberi
per gratiam sancti Spiritus custodiemur.*

ostendens itaque apostolus quanta sit differentia de illis qui secun-
5 dum Christum sunt et de illis qui secundum legem sunt, haec posuit,

†uolens docere quoniam 'data
quidem erat lex; peccatum uero
non erat ablatum, sed et ualde
10 uersabatur in nobis; eo quod et
per singula praeuaricamus momenta, quando quidem ista,
quando uero illa contra legis decreta agentes. nec erat quic-
15 quam quod nos posset a peccato liberari; sed ipsa naturae in-
becillitas adtrahebat nos ad peccatum. Christus uero ueniens
et morti succumbens pro nobis
20 et exsurgens, in commune omnibus beneficium praestitit, donans nobis per se etiam resurrectionis communionem. liberauit enim nos a praesentis sae-
25 culi uita, in qua multa de illis quae non conueniebant agere
uidebamur; constituitque nos in
spe futurae uitae, quam adsequi
ultra expectamus, in inmortali-
30 tatem persistentes, et in inpassi-
bilitatem extra omne consistentes peccatum; quod nullo modo
praestare nobis lex ualuit. ultra
ergo nec legis indigemus custo-
35 diam nec praeceptorum, sed nec
constitutiones ullas.'

πνεύματος χάριτι φυλαττόμεθα.

βούλεται τοίνυν εἰπεῖν ὅτι δέδοται
μὲν ὁ νόμος, ἁμαρτία δὲ οὐκ ἀνή-
ρητο, ἀλλὰ γὰρ καὶ σφόδρα ἡμῖν
ἐπολιτεύετο· ἐπειδὴ γὰρ ἑκάστοτε
παραβαίνομεν, ποτὲ μὲν ταῦτα ποτὲ δὲ ἐκεῖνα παρὰ τὴν τοῦ νόμου
διαπραττόμενοι διάταξιν, καὶ ἦν οὐδὲν τὸ τοῦ ἁμαρτάνειν ἡμᾶς ῥυόμε-
νον, ἀλλ' αὐτὴ ἡ τῆς φύσεως ἀσ-
θένεια καθεῖλκεν ἐπὶ τὸ πταίειν· ὁ
δέ γε Χριστὸς ἀποθανὼν ὑπὲρ ἡμῶν
καὶ ἀναστάς, παρασχόμενος δι' αὐτοῦ καὶ ἡμῖν τὴν τῆς ἀναστάσεως
μετουσίαν, ἀπήλλαξεν ἡμᾶς τῆς τοῦ
παρόντος βίου ζωῆς, ἐν ᾗ πολλὰ
τῶν οὐ προσηκόντων διαπραττόμε-
θα· καὶ κατέστησεν ἐπὶ ἐλπίδι τῆς
μελλούσης ζωῆς, λοιπὸν ἀθάνατοί
τε καὶ ἀπαθεῖς διαμένοντες καὶ ἔξω
πάσης ἁμαρτίας· ὃ μηδαμῶς πα-
ρασχεῖν ἡμῖν ὁ νόμος ἐξίσχυσεν.

---

14 "v. τὸ fortasse delenda" Fr.   15   non (for nos) C   18-19   αὐτοῦ edd.   28
quia C   ‖   et serui (for ads.) C H   29-30   inmortalitate, inpassibilitate C
(corr.)

nor the observance of any command, since we shall be kept free from all sin by the grace of Holy Spirit.*

we are kept from all sin by the grace of the Spirit.

And so the apostle in demonstrating how great a difference there is between Christ's dispensation and that of the law put these words down in his

†wish to teach that "the law had been given, [8] but sin had not been taken away. Rather, it was strong among us by custom, since we transgress moment by moment, sometimes doing one thing, sometimes another against the law's commandments. Nor was there anything that could make us free of sin; rather, the very weakness of our nature kept on drawing us to sin. But when Christ came, yielded to death for us, and rose again, he bestowed his benefit on all of us in common, giving us also through himself participation in the resurrection. For he freed us from the life of the present age in which we plainly commit many acts that are not right. And he established us in the hope of the future life that we await to obtain hereafter, when we shall continue in immortality and be placed in impassibility apart from all sin. In no way was the law strong enough to supply us with this. Therefore, we shall no longer need to keep the law and its precepts or any decrees."

Therefore, he wants to say that the law was given but that sin was not taken away. Rather, it was strong among us by custom, since we transgress all the time, sometimes doing one thing, sometimes another against the law's commandment. Nor was there anything to rescue us from sinning; rather, the very weakness of our nature drew us on to falling into sin. But when Christ died for us and rose again, giving us also through himself participation in the resurrection, he delivered us from the life of the present world in which we commit many acts that are not right. And he established us in the hope of the life to come, when we shall continue thereafter immortal and impassible and free from sin. In no way was the law strong enough to supply us with this.

quod et bene constringens at- | ὃ καὶ καλῶς ἐπισφίγγων προσέθη-
que confirmans, adicit dicens: | κεν· κατὰ τὸ θέλημα τοῦ θεοῦ καὶ
secundum uoluntatem Dei et pa- | πατρὸς ἡμῶν.
*tris nostri;**

5 ut non solum magnitudine rerum sed et adiectione uolens *Dei uo-*
luntatem suadere illis qui haec incessanter proponere adtempta-
bant, dicentes quoniam 'Dei est lex.' ostendebat enim sufficienter quoniam necessarium est in his perseuerare, quae sub differentia multum superiora esse legi ostendebantur; Deus enim sic
10 illa uoluit fieri, eo quod et melius quidem nobis fieri comprobauit.
haec, ut dixi, coniunxit illi dictioni qua dixit: *gratia nobis et pax a*
Deo patre nostro et domino Iesu Christo. quod etiam et competenter praecedentibus iunxit. incipit uero in subsequentibus uerba ad
eos depromere:

15 *miror quod sic cito transferimini ab eo qui uocauit uos in gratiam*
Christi, in aliud euangelium.

conueniens principium nouitati factorum; sic enim posuit *mi-*
ror, quasi quia et res accidit, quae numquam fieri credebatur. alienos enim mores et consuetudines habemus demirari. sed et

20 †per singula verba auxit illi- | διὰ πάντων ηὔξησεν τὴν ἀτοπίαν
ci[tum transductionis, *sic* dicens, | τῆς μεταβολῆς· τὸ οὕτως εἰπών,
quod multam habet ostensio- | πολλὴν ἔχον τὴν ἔνδειξιν· καὶ τὸ τα-
nem; coniungens et illi *ci*]*to*. et | χέως ἐπισυνάψας. καὶ τὸ μετατί-
quia adiecit *transferimini*, non | θεσθε προστεθεικώς, οὐ μετάγεσ-
25 dixit *transducimini*, sed *transfe-* | θε· ὡς ἐπὶ ἀψύχων θησὶν μετατί-
rimini; quasi [in] exanimes ali- | θεσθε.
quos,*

et qui animi motum non habeant. et quod dixit: *ab eo qui uocauit*
uos in gratiam Christi, ut ne uiderentur a Christo tantum discedere,
30 sed et a Deo. adiecit illis omnibus:

†*in aliud euangelium;* ut uidea- | εἰς ἕτερον εὐαγγέλιον· ἵνα δοκῇ
tur plenaria pietatis esse trans- | παντελὴς εἶναι εὐσεβείας μετάθεσις·
latio. et ne uideretur concedere | καὶ ἵνα μὴ δόξῃ συγχωρεῖν ἕτερον

5 magnitudinem, adiectionem *C H* ‖ uolentes *C H* 6 suaderet *H* 7
ostendebant *H* 11 illi dict. q. d. *om H* 12 patre et dom. nostro *C* 13
iunxit *om C* 18-19 alienas *C H* [Rönsch, 434; Bensly, 18] 20 illic cito *C H*
(*corr.*) (*H** illi) ‖ sq. Coisl. 204 f. 7 b [Cr. vi. 16, Fr. 123]. Θεόδωρος. ἄλλος
δὲ πάλιν οὕτως ἑρμηνεύει τὰ εἰρημένα· διὰ πάντων, κ.τ.λ.] 22 εἶχον Cr. 23
at quae *C* (*corr.*) 25 dicit *b l* 26 quia *C* *H* 29 gratia *C*

To make his point fully cohe-
rent and solid, he adds the phrase *according to the will of our
God and Father,**

Rightly bringing this all together, he added: *according to the
will of our God and Father.*

so that not only by the greatness of the facts but also by his
addition of *the will of God*, [9] he wishes to persuade those who
were constantly attacking his claims by saying that "the law is
God's." For he was demonstrating sufficiently that it is necessary
to persevere in these claims because by contrast they are proved
far superior to the law. For God willed the facts on which they
rest to take place because he gave his sanction that something
better should be dispensed for us. As I have said, he joined these
facts to the phrase in which he said *grace to you and peace from
God our Father and the Lord Jesus Christ.* He also suitably joined
this phrase to what preceded it. But in what follows he begins to
address his words to them:

1:6 *I am astonished that you have been so quickly changed from the
one who called you in the grace of Christ to a different gospel.*

The beginning suits the unexpected character of what had
happened. For he put *I am astonished* first as though to indicate
that what took place was something he believed never would
happen. For we hold in utter astonishment strange customs and
habits.

†Moreover, by individual
words he heightened the wickedness of the change, saying *so*
because it was quite openly displayed, and joining to it *quickly*. And because he adds *you
have been changed*—he did not
say *you have been led astray* but
you have been changed—[10] it
is as though they were changed
into lifeless things,*

In every way he heightened
the wickedness of the change,
saying *so* because it was quite
openly displayed, and joining
to it *quickly*. And he added *you
are changed* rather than *you are
led astray*, as though he said *you
are changed* to lifeless things.

and people who have no activity in their rational soul. And he said
from the one who called you in the grace of Christ to indicate that they
had plainly departed not only from Christ but also from God. He
adds to all this:

†*to a different gospel,* so that the
change might appear a total de-

to a different gospel, so that the
change might appear a total de-

esse aliud euangelium, adiecit:
 quod non est aliud.
 quomodo dixit ergo aliud?
 nisi sunt quidam qui contur-
5 *bant uos, et uolunt conuertere*
euangelium Christi.
 transductionem uero euangelii aliud euangelium esse dixit. deinde aduersus eos qui
10 personas apostolorum illi oppo-
nendas esse existimabant:
 sed et si nos.
 ut ostendat quoniam non illis praeponit [se], sed uerita-
15 tem uindicat, excepta qua nec se
ipsum esse aliquid existimabat.
unde illud et auget:
 aut angelus de caelo.
 de caelo adiecit, ut neque lo-
20 ci dignitas, neque personae co-
niunctio exaequari umquam ueritati posse existimetur.*
 euangelizauerit uobis praeter quod euangelizamus uobis, anathema
sit.
25 et ut ne uideretur futurae quodammodo tantum pondus sententiae expressisse, qua neque angelis parceret:
 sicut praediximus, et nunc iterum dico: siquis uobis euangelizauerit
praeter quod suscepistis, anathema sit.
 'si omnes siue nos (inquit), siue inuisibiles uirtutes, quae prae-

εὐαγγέλιον εἶναι·
ὃ οὐκ ἔστιν ἄλλο.
πῶς οὖν εἶπας ἕτερον;
εἰ μή τινές εἰσιν οἱ ταράσσοντες
ὑμᾶς, καὶ θέλοντες μεταστρέψαι τὸ
εὐαγγέλιον τοῦ χριστοῦ.
τὴν ἀπὸ τοῦ ὄντος εὐαγγελίου
μεταβολὴν ἕτερον εἰπὼν εὐαγγέλιον. εἶτα ἐπειδὴ τὰ τῶν ἀποστόλων πρόσωπα προεβάλλοντο·

[ἀλλὰ καὶ ἐὰν ἡμεῖς]·
ὥστε δεῖξαι ὅτι οὐχ ἑαυτὸν ἐκείνων προτιμᾷ ἀλλὰ τὴν ἀλήθειαν, ἧς
ἐκτὸς οὐδὲ ἑαυτὸν εἶναί τι νενόμι-
κεν. ὅθεν αὐτὸ καὶ ἐπαύξων ἔλεγεν·

ἢ ἄγγελος ἐξ οὐρανοῦ·
ἵνα μηδὲ ἡ τοῦ τόπου ἀξιοπισ-
τία μετὰ τοῦ προσώπου συναφθεῖσα
ἀντίρροπος τῆς ἀληθείας εἶναι νομί-
ζηται.

3 ergo dixit *H* 4 quidem *C* * *H* 11 addidit *add C* (*corr.*) 13 ostendant *H*
‖ non illis praeponit sed &c. *C* * *H* non i. se pr. sed &c. *C* (*corr.*) non se illis
&c. *l* 17 et illud aug. *C* (*corr.*) 19 et ut ne *H*

sertion from true religion. And lest he seem to grant that there was another gospel, he added:

1:7a *which is not another,*

Therefore, what did he mean by *another*?

1:7b *unless there are some who are confusing you and want to alter the gospel of Christ.*

What he really meant was that *a different gospel* was changing the gospel. Then he addresses those who thought that the roles of the apostles ought to be placed above him:

1:8a *But even if we*

He says this to demonstrate that he is not putting himself before them but is laying claim to the truth, apart from which he thought himself to be of no account. Then he heightens his point:

1:8b *or an angel from heaven*

[11] He added *from heaven* so that neither the dignity of the place nor of the role associated with it would ever be thought capable of being deemed equal in value with the truth.*

sertion from true religion. And lest he seem to grant that there was another gospel, he says *which is not another.*

Therefore, what did he mean by *another*?

Unless there are some who are confusing you and want to alter the gospel of Christ.

He calls the change from the real gospel *a different gospel.* Then, since the roles of the apostles were being placed above him,

[he says *but even if we*] to demonstrate that he is honoring not himself but the truth above them; apart from the truth he thought himself to be of no account.

Then, heightening his point, he said,

or an angel from heaven,

so that the trustworthy dignity of the place joined with the role might not be thought to have the same value as truth.

1:8c *should proclaim to you a gospel contrary to what we proclaimed to you, let that one be accursed!*

And so that he would not appear to have spoken some great and weighty utterance of a future judgment by which he would not even spare the angels:

1:9 *As we have said before, and now I say again, if anyone proclaims to you a gospel contrary to what you received, let that one be accursed!*

"Whether it is all of them or we (he says) or the invisible powers, they are worthless in importance compared with the truth that

dictae ueritati nullius digna sunt momenti.' dein transiturus ad
sui defensionem, ut ostenderet se quia pro ueritate huiusmodi uerba deprompsit, nullius momenti illos qui sibi derogauerant existimans, ait:

5   *modo enim hominibus suadeo, an Deo? aut quaero hominibus pla-*
cere?

et ostendens ex rebus ipsis quoniam nulla huiusmodi cura est
illi, adiecit:

si enim adhuc hominibus placerem, Christi seruus non essem.

10   'igitur tunc hominibus placebam, quando pro lege uniuersa
agebam; quae nullius momenti feci, eo quod Christo ulterius seruire me probaui.'

notum autem uobis facio, fratres, euangelium quod euangelizatum
est a me, quoniam non est secundum hominem.

15   'illa igitur quae erga me sunt nota uobis facio, ut non humana
me quadam adinuentione doctrinam quam abutor praesumpsisse
existimetis.' sed unde ergo habes illam acceptam?

nec enim ego ab homine suscepi illud, neque didici illud, sed per
reuelationem Iesu Christi.

20   deinde et probationem rebus ipsis implet, referens ea quae secundum se sunt, et qualis erat dudum pro lege desudans, et quoniam nemo hominum uolens eum corrigere; hocque ex comparatione ueterum uult ostendere, quoniam non legem spreuit, sed
quod melius est et recognouit et elegit. et aperte uult conprobare
25 quoniam a Christo didicit solo illa quae ad praesens tenere uidetur, per illam reuelationem quae de caelo facta est ad eum; quando
se ei manifestans eundem uisus est correxisse, quando et legis erat
uehemens aemulator:

audistis enim conuersationem meam aliquando in iudaismo, quo-
30 *niam supra modum persequebar ecclesiam Dei, et uastabam eam. et*
proficiebam in iudaismo supra multos coaetaneos meos in genere meo,
abundantius aemulator existens paternarum mearum traditionum.

bene et *coaetaneos* dixit; hoc enim erat maius, si et iuuenibus
uehementior esse uidebatur in illis laboribus quos pro lege subire
35 nitebatur. 'talia igitur erant illa quae erga me erant, et talis eram

---

1 transsi tu rus (*sic*) *H*   2 qui (*for* quia) *l*   3-4 aestimans *b*   11 qui (*for*
quae) *C* H* quod *C* (*corr.*)   17 existimetur *C**   ‖ sed *om C* (*corr.*) *H*   19
relationem *C**   23 ueteri *H*   25-26 uidentur *H*   27 erit *C**   29 etiam
(*for* enim) *H*   34 quod (*for* quos) *C* H*

was preached." Then, as he is about to turn to his own defense, to demonstrate that he uttered words like this on behalf of the truth and reckoning that those who had disparaged him were of no importance, he says:

1:10a *Am I now persuading humans or God? Or am I seeking to please people?*

And to show from the facts themselves that he had no concern of this kind, he added:

[12] 1:10b *If I were still pleasing people, I would not be a servant of Christ.*

"Therefore, I was pleasing people at the time when I was acting in all ways on behalf of the law. I made this of no importance because later on I consented to serve Christ."

1:11 *For I make known to you, brothers, the gospel that was proclaimed by me that it is not according to a human being;*

"Therefore, I make known to you those matters that concern me so that you will not think that I assumed the teaching I employed by any human contrivance." But from what source then did you receive it?

1:12 *for I did not receive it from a human source, nor was I taught it, but I received it through a revelation of Jesus Christ.*

Then he completes his proof by the facts themselves, referring to his own career, both how for a long time he exerted himself in defending the law and that no human being was willing to set him right. By this he wants to show on the basis of a comparison with his former life that he did not scorn the law but that he both recognized and chose what is better. And he wants frankly to prove that it was from Christ alone and through that revelation made to him from heaven that he learned the views he plainly holds now. By manifesting himself to him, Christ appeared to set him right at the very time he was a forceful zealot for the law:

1:13–14 *For you have heard of my life once in Judaism, that above measure I was persecuting the church of God and was trying to destroy it, and I advanced in Judaism beyond many among my people of the same age, being far more zealous for the traditions of my ancestors.*

He rightly said *of the same age*, for it was a stronger argument if he was plainly more forceful even than youths in those efforts he struggled to undergo on behalf of the law. "Therefore, such were my concerns, and such was I for a long time in the law. Now it

dudum in lege. uestrum iam ultra est probare utrum spernentis legem est doctrina ista quam nunc doceo sequendam, pro quibus et tanta faciens perseueraui; aut, sicut conuenit, illud quod melius est praehonoraui.'

5   quemadmodum ergo es conuersus?

cum uero complacuit ei qui me segregauit ex utero matris meae et uocauit per gratiam suam, reuelare filium suum in me, ut euangelizem eum in gentibus.

†bene illud ad praescientiam | καλῶς αὐτὸ ἐπὶ τὴν πρόγνωσιν
10 retulit Dei, ut et antequam ipse | ἀνήνεγκεν τοῦ θεοῦ, ὥστε καὶ πρὸ
esset, uideretur de eo hoc fuisse | τῆς αὐτοῦ ὑπάρξεως φαίνεσθαι τῷ
placitum Deo; tantumque abes- | θεῷ τοῦτο δεδογμένον· τοσοῦτον
set ut leuiter nouitas ulla aut ho- | ἀποδέον τοῦ καινότητα εἶναί τινα
minum adinuentio ipsa existi- | καὶ εὕρεσιν ἀνθρώπων τὸ κήρυγμα.
15 maretur esse praedicatio.*

miraculo dignum et multa praeditum humilitate, eo quod suam uocationem simpliciter retulit. et quidem poterat magnifice eam explicare, concurrentibus sibi ad hoc negotiis; eo quod de caelo sibi cum tanta claritate Christus fuerat ostensus.

20   uocatus ergo, quid egisti?

statim non adquieui carni et sanguini; neque abii in Hierosolimam ad praecessores meos apostolos; sed abii in Arabiam, et iterum reuersus sum Damascum.

'implebam statim rem mihi commissam, circuiens et docens ea
25 quae de Christo sunt. nec enim referre illis super doctrinam meam ullam curam habui; quia et in tantum me cohibui ut aliquid discerem ab illis qui ante me fuerunt apostoli, ita ut nec irem protinus ad eos, sed nec uiderem eos, nec consilium caperem eorum de his quae mihi fuerant ostensa; superfluum esse iudicans post
30 reuelationem Christi hominum expectare doctrinam.' bene autem

---

1 spernente lege C* H spernendo legem C (corr.) 2 sequenda C H 9 sq. Coisl. 204 f. 11 a [Cr. vi. 23, Fr. 124]. θεόδωρος. καὶ ἄλλος δὲ εἰς τό· ὅτε δὲ εὐδόκησεν ὁ θεὸς ὁ ἀφ. με ἐκ κοιλ. μητρ. μου, φησίν· καλῶς, κ.τ.λ. 11 esse C H 12-13 adesse ut nec C H [abesse ut g] 13 illa C 15 multo C H 26 qui (for quia) C (corr.) 28 nec uid. eos sed nec H

is up to you next to examine [13] whether the doctrine that I now teach must be followed involves scorning the law—you for whom I also persisted in such great endeavors—or, as is right, that what is better should be held in greater honor."

How, then, were you converted?

1:15–16a *But when he who had set me apart from my mother's womb and called me through his grace was pleased to reveal his Son in me, so that I might proclaim him among the Gentiles,*

†He rightly assigned this to God's foreknowledge, so that even before he existed it might appear that this had been resolved by God concerning him. So far removed was his preaching from being lightly thought some novelty or contrivance of humans.*

He rightly assigned this to God's foreknowledge, so that even before his existence it might appear that this had been resolved by God. So far removed was his preaching from being something new and a contrivance of humans.

The fact that he records his calling with simplicity is worth admiring and is endowed with great humility. Indeed, he could have given a longer account of it boastfully. The commission that came suddenly upon him might have led to this, because Christ appeared to him from heaven with such great brightness.

Then, when you were called, what did you do?

1:16b–17 *At once I did not obey flesh and blood, nor did I go away to Jerusalem to those who were already apostles before me, but I went away into Arabia, and again I returned to Damascus.*4

"At once I began to fulfill my commission, going about and teaching [14] the dispensation of Christ.5 For I had no concern to confer with them about my teaching. For this reason I restrained myself from learning anything from those who had been apostles before me to such an extent that I neither went to them right away nor saw them nor took their advice about what had been revealed to me, judging it needless after Christ's revelation to wait

---

4 "Obey" (*adquieui*) is the reading of the Old Latin and the Vulgate, but, as we shall see, it does not seem to have been Theodore's reading. "Go away to Jerusalem" implies ἀπῆλθον rather than ἀνῆλθον, possibly a mistake of the scribe or the translator.

5 Literally, "those things that are about Christ" (*ea quae de Christo sunt*). The translation here and hereafter is meant to avoid the awkwardness of a literal translation.

et rem ipsam quasi non necessariam detraxit, non dicens *aposto-*
lis, sed neque *hominibus*; sed *carni et sanguini;* ualde cum debita id
obseruantia dicens et scrupulositate. et quia dixit: *statim non expo-*
sui; exposuit enim postea illis, ascendens secundum reuelationem
5   hoc ipsud, sicut ipse post pauca dicit. et ut ne uideatur per omnia
contempsisse apostolos:
   deinde post annos tres ascendi Hierosolimis uidere Petrum.
   et ita affectum quem erga Petrum uidendum habebat explicans,
et quod sollicitudinem expenderet, ut redderet ei quod debebat.
10   *et mansi apud eum dies quindecim.*
   de aliis uero quid?
   alium apostolorum autem non uidi, nisi Iacobum fratrem Domini.
   euidens est ergo quoniam neque tunc ut aliquid disceret ascendit, siquidem post tres annos haec fecit; quando apostolatus sui
15   opus iam in multis ante expedierat. sic igitur ea quae secundum se
erant referens destruxit ipsis rebus illa quae ab aduersariis fuerant
contra se dicta; nullo in loco grauem se illis exhibens, commendans uero fideliter ea quae a se dicta fuerant; eo quod conueniebat
et hoc ita fieri.
20   *quae autem scribo uobis, ecce in conspectu Dei quoniam non men-*
tior. deinde ueni in partibus Syriae et Ciliciae.
   illud perficiens quod conueniens sibi erat.
   eram autem ignotus facie ecclesiis Iudaeae quae erant in Christo.
   uult dicere quoniam 'illis qui in Iudaea crediderant in Chri-
25   sto per omnia eram ignotus secundum personae uisum; eo quod
et tunc, quando ascendi Hierosolimam, Petrum uidi solum et fratrem Domini Iacobum, alium autem neminem; eo quod et omnes
dies quindecim Hierosolimis fecerim tantum.'
   tantum autem audientes erant: 'qui persequebatur nos aliquando,
30   *nunc euangelizat fidem, quam aliquando expugnabat.' et glorifica-*
bant in me Deum.

1   necessarium *H*   1-2   ap. neque h. (*om* sed) *H* apostolus sed, &c. *l* (*ed*)   5
ipsum *C* (*corr.*)   12   autem apost. *C* (*corr.*) *H*   13-14   et (*after* disceret) *add*
C   14   hoc *C*   15   si (*for* sic) *H*   18   fuerant dicta *H*   21   ciliae (*sic*) *H*   24
crediderunt *C*   27   Iac. fr. Dom. *H*

for human teaching." Moreover, he also rightly excluded this course of action as unnecessary by saying *flesh and blood* rather than "apostles" or "humans." He uses this expression powerfully with due precaution and exactness. And for this reason he said *I did not confer*, for later on he did confer with them when he went up by revelation for this very purpose, as he says himself soon after.[6] And lest he seem to have despised the apostles altogether:

1:18a *Then after three years I did go up to Jerusalem to visit Cephas,*

And so he makes clear the affection he had for Peter when he saw him and that he spent great care to give him his due.

1:18b *And I stayed with him fifteen days;*

But what about the others?

1:19 *but I did not see any other of the apostles except James the Lord's brother.*

Therefore, it is evident that not even then did he go up to learn anything, inasmuch as he did this after three years, when [15] his work as an apostle had already prospered in many ways. Thus, by recounting his circumstances he refuted by the facts themselves what had been said against him by his opponents. Nowhere does he show himself overbearing to them, but he faithfully commends what he had said because it was right to do so this way.

1:20–21 *In what I am writing to you, before God, I do not lie! Then I went into the regions of Syria and Cilicia*

Accomplishing what was right for him.

1:22 *And I was unknown by sight to the churches of Judea that were in Christ,*

He means that "to those in Judea who had believed in Christ I was entirely unknown by personal appearance, because even when I went up to Jerusalem I saw only Peter and James the Lord's brother, but no one else. That is the only thing I did in Jerusalem the entire fifteen days."

1:23–24 *and they only were hearing, "The one who once was persecuting us is now proclaiming the faith he once tried to destroy." And they glorified God because of me.*

---

[6] Here the text of 1:16b is cited as "confer" (*exposui*). Swete's note (1:14) reads in part: "*Adquieui*, though retained in the text from the O.L. and Vulg., has been abandoned by the translator in the commentary, where the meaning attached to προσανεθ. by Th. comes clearly into view."

'audita didicerant illa quae de me erant; quam ob causam et mi-
rabantur, quasi noua et gloria digna illa esse existimantes.' 'quemadmodum (inquit ille) qui tanta pro lege contra eos gesserat,
nunc conuersus uniuersis illam quae in Christo est fidem praedi-
5   cat; maxime cum nemo hominum perspiciatur qui conuersionis
eius auctor esse uideatur?'

deinde post quattuordecim annos iterum ascendi Hierosolimam
cum Barnaba, adsumens mecum et Titum.

cum iam longum tempus apostolatus sui expedisset, ipsis rebus
10   ac operibus sibi adtestantibus. dicitur deinde et quomodo ascen-
derit:

ascendi autem secundum reuelationem.

qua de causa ascenderet, euoluit reuelatio.

et exposui illis euangelium quod praedico in gentibus, secreto his qui
15   *uidebantur aliquid esse; ne quoquo modo in uacuum currerem aut cu-*
currissem.

nam quod dicitur: *ne quoquo modo*, non dubitationis causa dicitur; sed quia 'suscepi reuelationem ita ut ascendens referrem et ex-
ponerem egregiis apostolorum de doctrina hac quam gentibus tra-
20   didi, ut credant Christo sine ulla legis obseruantia; ita ut non uidear uane et putatiue circuire, et tantos subire labores eorum causa
qui Christo credunt; ne quando existimer proprium quoddam iter
exequi et ceteris apostolis inconueniens. unde et hoc placuit, ut et
illorum consensus in his quae a me fiebant haberetur.' deinde in-
25   teriecit in ipsa factorum sequentia illud quod maius est:

sed nec Titus, qui mecum ex gentibus erat, conpulsus est circumcidi
propter subintroductos autem falsos fratres, qui subintroierant explora-
re libertatem nostram, quam habemus in Christo Iesu, ut nos in serui-
tutem redigerent; quibus nec ad horam cessimus subiectioni, ut ueritas
30   *euangelii permaneat apud uos.*

nam quantum est ad sequentiam dictum, superflue hoc in lo-

2   esse *om H*   10   dicit et (*for* dicitur) *H*   13   quae *H*   ‖   reuoluit *H*   18
suscipi *C*   20   ullam l. obseruantiam *C* H*   22   existimarer *b l*   23   et *om*
C (corr.)   29   redirent *C**   31   sequentia dicti *C (corr.)*

"They had become acquainted with what they heard about me. For this reason they marveled, since they thought it strange and worth praising." "How is it (he says) that he who had played so great a part for the law against them is now converted and preaches to the whole world faith in Christ, especially when no human being may be discerned as appearing to be the agent of his conversion?"

2:1 *Then after fourteen years I went up again to Jerusalem with Barnabas, taking Titus along with me.*

It was when he had already flourished as an apostle for a long time, as the facts and his deeds bore witness for him. It is said then how he went up.

2:2a *I went up in response to a revelation,*

The revelation explains why he went up.

[16] 2:2b *and I conferred to them the gospel that I proclaim among the Gentiles, privately to those who seemed to be of importance, lest I should in any way be running or had run in vain.*

To be sure, the expression *lest in any way* is not used because of uncertainty but because "I received a revelation that I should go up to report to those of the apostles who were distinguished and to explain to them the teaching I have handed over to the Gentiles, that they should believe in Christ without any observance of the law. This was so that I might not appear in vain or in my own fancy[7] to travel about and to undergo such great trials for the sake of those who believe in Christ, and lest I be thought at any time to follow some path of my own and be out of harmony with the other apostles. This is why it seemed good to me that their agreement should also be gained for what I was myself doing." Then he introduced into his account of what had happened something more important:

2:3–5 *Yet not even Titus, who was with me from the Gentiles, was compelled to be circumcised. But because of false brothers secretly brought in, who slipped in to spy on our freedom that we have in Christ Jesus, so that they might return us to slavery—we did not submit to them even for a moment, so that the truth of the gospel might always remain with you.*

Certainly, so far as the logical order of words goes, *but* appears

---

[7] Swete (1:16) suggests the possibility of understanding *putative* "as a mere conceit or fancy of my own."

co *autem* positum esse uidetur (multis enim in locis coniunctiones
a beato Paulo non cum debita sequentia positas esse ostendimus);
est enim *propter subintroductos falsos fratres.* quod quidam non adtendentes, nouitatem intellectus somniati sunt. uult autem dicere
5 quoniam 'ascendens Hierosolimam, habebam mecum Titum qui
ex gentibus erat, et hunc habebam incircumcisum; et non circumcidi eum, istis satisfaciens qui simulabant quidem se esse fratres.
subintroduxerunt autem se nobis non bene. non enim sapiunt illa
quae conueniunt, neque illa quae pietatis sunt continua, sed insi-
10 diantes libertatem nostram, quam ob rem illam quam in Christo
habemus necessario abutimur, eo quod a seruitute legis liberi sumus effecti, solummodo incusare sciunt illa quae a nobis fiunt, legem ubique proferentes, et contendentes sub eius nos seruitutem
redigere.' hoc est dici: *ut nos in seruitutem redigant.* 'qui et liber-
15 tatem nostram qua liberati sumus a necessitate et legis obseruantia non cessimus, neque passi sumus aliquid illorum causa facere, praeterquam quod fieri a nobis decebat; sed custodiuimus Titum incircumcisum, ut uobis omnibus qui ex gentibus credidistis
sit euidens probatio euangelium nostrum ueritate esse praeditum.
20 quod cum omni fiducia sumus abusi, nullum aduersariorum, neque tunc quando apud illos eramus, pertimescentes.' et quoniam
apostolos ubique proferebant aduersarii, utpote legem custodientes, adicit:

    ab his autem qui uidentur esse aliquid, quales aliquando fuerunt
25 *nihil mihi interest.*

    et ut ne uideatur uane contra maiores se extollere:

    personam (inquit) *hominis Deus non accipit.*

    ueritas enim erat qui iudicabat, non persona. haec quidem in-
teriaciens, ut dixi, ab illo loco quo dixit: *sed neque Titus qui mecum*
30 *erat, gentilis cum esset;* sequitur deinceps suam sequentiam, illa do-

---

1 ut *C H* [autem *g*]   6   nunc (*for* non) *C* H*   11   a *om C**   12   incusari *H*
13   praeferentes *H* [cf. Hildebrand, *Ap.* i., 1021].   19   ueritatem *C H: om l*
|| praedictum *H* praedicatum *l*   22   praef. *H*   28   quidam *C H*   28-29
interiacens *C H*   29   quod dixi *C H*

to be placed here superfluously.[8] (For we can show that in many passages blessed Paul does not place the conjunctions in their proper order.) [17] For the text should read simply *because of false brothers secretly brought in.* Some people who have not paid attention have dreamed up a novel way of interpreting the verse. Surely what he means is that "when I went up to Jerusalem, I had with me Titus, who was a Gentile, and I kept him uncircumcised. And I did not circumcise him to satisfy those who pretended to be brothers. But they slipped themselves into our midst secretly and wrongly. For they did not understand what was right or what was bound up with true religion. Rather, they treacherously attacked our freedom that we necessarily employ because of that advantage we have in Christ because we have been freed from the slavery of the law. They only knew how to blame what we were doing, promoting the law in all circumstances and striving to drive us back to its slavery." This is the meaning of *so that they might return us to slavery.* "But we did not yield our freedom by which we have been delivered from the necessity and observance of the law, nor did we submit to doing anything because of them save for what was proper for us to do. Indeed, we kept Titus uncircumcised so that there might be clear proof to all of you who are Gentile believers that our gospel had been proclaimed in truth. We have managed it with complete confidence, frightened by not one of our opponents, not even at the time we were with them." And since his opponents everywhere held up the apostles as people who kept the law, he adds:

2:6a *But from those who appeared to be of importance, whatever they were makes no difference to me,*

And lest he should seem to extol himself vainly against his elders:

2:6b *God* (he says) *does not accept the person of a human.*   προσωπον

For it was truth that rendered judgment, not a person. [18] Indeed, he inserts these verses [3–6], as I have said, beginning with the passage where he said *Yet not even Titus who was with me, since he was a Gentile.*[9] Afterwards he resumes his own order,

---

[8] Theodore appears to be reading "not even Titus was compelled to be circumcised because of false brothers..." The "but" before "false brothers" might imply that Titus *was* circumcised, a view held by Pelagius and one that Theodore is concerned to refute. See Swete's note (1:17).

[9] What he means is that 2:3–6 interrupt the logic that would see verse 2

cere properans, quae illi fuerat cum apostolis habita disceptatio,
quando ascendit *secundum reuelationem*, ut illis exponeret euangelium. conueniebat enim eum coniungere cum sensu suo etiam illorum sententiam, ut in aperto consisteret qualiter sibi erga nego-
5   tium consensum praebuerant apostoli.

    mihi enim qui uidentur esse aliquid nihil contulerunt.

    'conferre' dicitur communicare consilium super aliquod nego-
tium; sic enim et nos in consuetudinem dicimus. similiter autem
et apostolus manifestus est hac uoce fuisse abusus. in superioribus
10   enim dixit: *statim non adquieui carni et sanguini*, hoc est: 'nullius
participatus sum consilio.' et post hoc: *contuli cum illis evangelium*,
hoc est: 'participatus sum consilio, et manifestum feci illis qui est
modus meae praedicationis.' sic ergo et hoc in loco: *nihil contule-*
runt, hoc est, 'ipsi quidem mihi nihil adiecerunt, neque participati
15   sunt mihi consilium de aliquo.' quod autem additum est:

    sed e contrario uidentes quoniam creditum est mihi euangelium
praeputii, sicut et Petro circumcisionis (qui enim operatus est Petro in
apostolatum circumcisionis, operatus est et mihi inter gentes); et co-
gnoscentes gratiam quae data est mihi, Iacobus et Cephas et Iohan-
20   *nes, qui uidebantur columnae esse, dextras dederunt mihi et Barnabae*
communionis, ut nos quidem in gentibus, ipsi uero in circumcisione.

    quidam sic legerunt, *sed e contrario;*—perfectum sensum con-
cludentes. ad plenum uero intendere ordini uerborum noluerunt.
est enim sensus hic: *sed e contrario uidentes quoniam creditum est*
25   *mihi euangelium praeputii, sicut et Petro circumcisionis, et cognoscen-*
tes gratiam quae data est mihi, et cetera. post interiectionem quae

---

3   assensu *H* [*C**?] 15   de aliquid *C H* [Rönsch, 410, 523; Tisch. *Cod. Amiat.*
prol. p. xxxi.] 19-20   Ioh. et Cephas *C* 22   legerant *H*

hurrying on to tell of the debate that took place between him and the apostles when he went up *in response to a revelation* to explain his gospel to them. For it was right for him to join even their judgment with his understanding so that it might be openly established how the apostles had given him their consent in the matter.

2:6c *those who appeared to be of importance conferred nothing to me*

"To confer" means to give advice about a matter of some kind, for so we customarily speak. And similarly the apostle also made it clear he had employed this meaning. For above he said *At once I did not confer*[10] *with flesh and blood* (1:16), that is, "I shared in no one's advice." But later on *I conferred with them about the gospel* (2:2),[11] that is, "I shared in counsel and made clear to them the manner of my preaching." The meaning is the same in this passage: *they conferred nothing*, that is, "in fact they made no additional requirements of me, nor did they take part in advising me about anything." Moreover, he added:

2:7–9 *On the contrary, when they saw that I had been entrusted with the gospel of the uncircumcision, just as Peter had been entrusted with the gospel of the circumcision (for he who worked through Peter for the apostolate of the circumcision also worked through me among the Gentiles), and James and Cephas and John, who were seen to be pillars, recognizing the grace that had been given to me, gave to me and Barnabas* [19] *the right hand of fellowship, so that we should go to the Gentiles and they to the circumcision.*

Some commentators have read *on the contrary* so as to complete the full meaning of the preceding verse. But they have not been willing to pay strict attention to the order of the words. For the sense is as follows: *On the contrary, when they saw that I had been entrusted with the gospel of the uncircumcision, just as Peter had been entrusted with the gospel of the circumcision, and when they*

---

followed by verse 7: "I explained to them the gospel... when they saw that I had been entrusted with the gospel..."

[10] The text actually has "obey" (*adquieui*), but the sense requires "confer" (*exposui, contulerunt*). See n. 5.

[11] Here the text of 2:2 is *contuli cum illis evangelium*. Above the text is cited *et exposui illis evangelium*. The confusion is partly to be explained by the translator's use of the Old Latin and partly by the difficulty of translating προσανατίθημι (1:16; 2:6) and ἀνατίθημι (2:2).

est ab illo loco: *sed neque Titus*, consequenter praecedentibus iunctum est, ut sit: *qui enim operatus est Petro in apostolatum circumcisionis, operatus est et mihi inter gentes.* quod in mediis sermonibus secundum interiectiones positum esse uidetur, ad comprobandum quod in nullam partem minorationem sustineat euangelium; eo quod idem sit Deus qui et hoc Petro iniunxit, et illud sibi. uult autem dicere quoniam 'illi quidem *nihil contulerunt mihi; e contrario uero* ipsi audientes a me euangelii modum quem praedicabam, et edocti huiusmodi gratiam, ad hoc adsequi promerui, ut probatissimi apostolorum, Iacobus et Johannes et Cephas, non solum non reprobauerint mea, sed et doctrinae assensum praebuerint, ita ut dextras communionis mihi quoque darent et Barnabae, ut uideremur (licet nos gentibus praedicaremus, ipsi uero illis qui in circumcisione sunt) [quod] tunc unius essemus sententiae; [et] unam intentionem habentes, uniuersos per fidem Christo offeramus.' nam et discretio haec non alia ex causa diuina gratia est dispensata, nisi ut Iudaei, qui ex uetere legis consuetudine non patiebantur gentibus permisceri, eo quod lege dudum fuerant segregati, ideo et per beatum Petrum ad fidem quae in Christo est inducerentur; illi uero qui ex gentibus erant itidem per beatum Paulum ad fidem perducerentur. congregauit autem eos postea in unum fidei similitudo; unum quidem omnes operati, sicut et factum esse ex ipsis rebus euidenter ostenditur. denique et Paulus quantos poterat Iudaeorum ad fidem deuocabat, sicuti et Corintho fecit, ipsum principem synagogae Christo credere suadens; et multis in locis euidens est in synagogis disputasse Iudaeis. Petrus quoque gentibus, quotiescumque potuit, hoc ipsud facere non piguit; quod et inprimis secundum diuinam reuelationem erga Cornelium uisus est perfecisse. et quoniam diuisos eos dixit, pandit horum quoque et illorum doctrinae diligentiam. uidebatur autem

---

2 apostolatu *C* (*corr.*) 5 in *om H** ‖ sustinet *H** 9 edoctus *C* 11 reprobauerunt *C** *H* 11-12 praebuerunt *C** *H* 12 Barnebae *C** 13 praedicaremur *C** *H* 14 quod, et, *om C** *H* 20 inducebantur, perducebantur *C H* 23 est *C** 24 sicut *H* 26 eum disp. cum I. *C* (*corr.*) ‖ Petro *C* 27 ipsum *C* (*corr.*)

recognized the grace that had been given to me, and the rest. After the insertion that begins where it says *Yet not even Titus* (2:3), there follows another insertion joined to what precedes, that is, *for he who worked through Peter for the apostolate of the circumcision also worked through me among the Gentiles* (2:8).[12] What seems to be placed in the midst of the text by way of insertion is designed to demonstrate that the gospel should admit no narrowing in any part, because it is the same God who committed one group to Peter and the other to him. And so he means that "they in fact *conferred nothing to me, but on the contrary,* when they heard from me the manner of the gospel I was preaching and learned about the grace to which I had promised to cleave, James and John and Cephas, as the most highly regarded of the apostles, not only did not condemn my convictions but even gave their assent to my teaching so that they gave the right hand of fellowship to me and Barnabas. This was so that we might be at that time of one opinion and by having a single aim might offer up all people through faith in Christ—even though we were to preach to the Gentiles, but they to those who were circumcised." For even this distinction makes no difference, since it was a dispensation of divine grace, [20] except that the Jews, who by the ancient custom of the law were not allowed to associate with Gentiles because they had for long been separated from them by the law, were to be admitted to faith in Christ through blessed Peter, while the Gentiles would similarly be conducted to faith through blessed Paul. But afterwards the shared character of the faith brought them together as one. Indeed, they all worked as one, as is clearly shown to be the case by the facts themselves. In fact, even Paul called as many of the Jews as he could to faith, as he did in Corinth, when he persuaded the ruler of the synagogue himself to believe in Christ (Acts 18:8). And it is clear in many places that he disputed with the Jews in the synagogues. Peter also went to the Gentiles as often as he could and did not disdain to do so. He plainly did this fully at first with Cornelius by divine revelation. And since

---

[12] As Swete points out, the translator may be having difficulty with the original. What Theodore appears to mean is that, just as 2:3–6 can be regarded as an insertion interrupting the connection of verse 2 to verse 7, so in verse 8 what the NRSV has placed in parentheses is an insertion that interrupts the flow of the words. The confusion is compounded by the idea that *on the contrary* belongs to verse 7, not to verse 6.

multis in locis sollicitudinem expendere de illis sanctis qui in Iudaea erant, et paupertate tenebantur; eo quod illos qui Christo credebant tunc Iudaei, ante expugnationem sui, propriis rebus nudare more tyrannorum properabant. pro quibus etiam Galatis super
hoc disputasse signauit apostolus. denique et Corinthiis scribens,
dicit: *sicut ordinaui ecclesiis Galatiae, sic et uos facite.* ostendens
quoniam, neque hoc excepto, quod disposuerant inter se facere faciebant:

tantum pauperum ut memores essemus; quod et festinans hoc ipsud
facere.

'hoc erat solum placitum nobis, ut et nos illis pauperibus qui
apud eos erant diligentiam adhiberemus, ob communem utilitatem et consensus nostri probationem; quod etiam et sollicitus fui
facere.' et ostendens quoniam adquieuerunt etiam illi in eius doctrinam sic dicit:

cum autem uenisset Petrus Antiochiae, in faciem illi restiti, quo-
niam erat reprehensus.

quidam quia incusabant illa quae ab eo fiebant. quae autem
erant ilia?

priusquam uenirent quidam ab Iacobo, cum gentibus manducabat;
postquam uero uenerunt, subtrahebat et segregabat seipsum, timens eos
qui erant ex circumcisione; et ducti sunt in illam simulationem etiam
ceteri Iudaei, ita ut et Barnabas duceretur in eorum simulationem.
sed quando uidi quia non recte incedunt ad ueritatem euangelii, di-
xi Petro coram omnibus: si tu Iudaeus cum sis, gentiliter uiuis et non
iudaice, quid gentes cogis iudaizare?

uult quidem ostendere, quoniam non scriptis tantum abutitur
uerbi fiduciam, sed et in faciem restitit Petro. quando Iudaei ab
Iacobo fratre Domini, qui Hierosolimorum ecclesiam regere fuerat constitutus, Antiochiam uenerunt, cessans edere cum illis qui
ex gentibus crediderant, quod primum indiscrete facere uideba-

1 in *om H* 10 facere *om C* 11 hoc erat *om H* 14-15 doctrina erat reprehensus sic dicit et erant *C* doctrinam sic dicit erat repr. *C (corr.)* doctrinam erat
repr. sicut dicit et erant *H* 17 erat *om CH* reprehensibilis erat quia quidam
C (corr.) reprehensus quidem quia *H* 20 manducabant *C* 22 et *om H* 24
incederent *H* 26 quomodo (*for* quid) *H* 27 abutimur *C*H* 28 fidutia *H*
‖ facie *C H** 31 facere indiscrete *H*

he called the Gentiles excluded, God opened him to a concern for teaching both parties.[13] And Paul in many passages plainly spent great care for those saints who were in Judea and were bound fast by poverty. This was because at that time the Jews, before the destruction of their land, were eager in a tyrannical way to strip those who believed in Christ of their possessions. The apostle indicated even to the Galatians that he had taken up their cause because of this. Later, when he wrote to the Corinthians, he says (1 Cor 16:1): *you should follow the directions I gave to the churches of Galatia*. He shows that with no exception they were doing what they had arranged among themselves to do:

2:10 *only that we remember the poor, which was actually what I was eager to do.*

"Only this was decided for us, that we should diligently assist those poor who were among them because of its common usefulness and its proof of our agreement. I was also anxious to do this." And to show that they agreed with him in his teaching, he says as follows:

[21] 2:11 *But when Peter came to Antioch, I opposed him to his face, because he had been rebuked.*[14]

Because certain people were condemning what he was doing. What in fact was this?

2:12–14 *Before certain people came from James, he used to eat with the Gentiles. But after they came, he drew back and kept himself separate, fearing those who were from the circumcision. And the other Jews were also led into this hypocrisy, so that even Barnabas was led astray by their hypocrisy. But when I saw that they were not acting rightly toward the truth of the gospel, I said to Peter before them all, "If you, though you are a Jew, live like a Gentile and not like a Jew, why do you compel the Gentiles to live like Jews?"*

He surely wants to prove that he did not so much employ writing as confident speech, and he even opposed Peter to his face. When Jews came to Antioch from James the Lord's brother, who had been appointed to rule the church in Jerusalem, Peter by

---

[13] Taking *diuisos eos* as the Gentiles divided from the Jews and God as the subject of *pandit*, I suggest understanding this cryptic sentence in the light of Acts 10.

[14] "Peter" instead of "Cephas" is the Old Latin reading. The translation of the verse reflects Theodore's understanding. Chrysostom agrees with Theodore in taking κατεγνωσμένος as passive rather than middle.

tur, seipsum ab eorum coepit custodire communione. 'in qua hoc factum: non solum Iudaeis communicantibus illi, sed et Barnaba meo socio, propter illos qui a Iudaea uenerant ad eos, solus ego ex omnibus illis, praehonorans ueritatem, praecellenti et omnium maiori Petro stans in faciem dixi quoniam "non est iustum te, Iudaeum secundum naturam extantem, frequenter sine legitima obseruatione cibum sumere cum illis qui crediderunt ex gentibus; illos uero qui ex gentibus sunt ad legis obseruantiam deuertere." '

bene autem et secundum ordinem ea quae erga se fuerant probare uidetur—primum quidem dicens qualis erat erga legem; deinde quia ad fidem transiit, non per hominem; post illud, quoniam et apostoli complacuerunt in eius doctrinam; post omnia uero, quoniam necessitate cogente nec resistere dubitauit pro hoc ipso Petro. per omnia enim haec et illa quae sua erant confirmabat, et falsa aduersariorum esse uerba ostendebat. quoniam ergo beatus Paulus illis nunc abusus est, ut ostenderet quoniam publice pro illis qui ex gentibus sunt et iustitiam uindicare et arguere eligantissimum apostolorum non piguit. et quoniam suscepit ille quae ab hoc dicebantur euidens est. si enim aliqua controuersia de hoc fuisset oborta aut contentio adnata, alterum isto stabiliente, alterum illo firmante, necessario utique et differentia aliqua huiusmodi fuisset facta inter Christianos, aliis Paulo aliis Petro intendentibus; et aliis quidem illa quae istius erant, aliis illa quae illius suscipientibus. et multo magis hoc fiebat, eo quod Iudaei pro lege omni nitebantur intentione; illi uero qui ex gentibus erant plurima ex parte non patiebantur subici legitima obseruatione. illud autem dico, quoniam siue consensu ipsam controuersiam inter se simulauerunt pro aliorum utilitate, sunt uere quidem mirandi, eo quod omnia ad aliorum utilitatem facere adquieuerunt; siue quia Petrus illorum curam habens qui ex Iudaeis crediderant, uisus est se cohibere a communione illorum qui ex gentibus erant—Paulus uero horum qui ex gentibus crediderant curam habens, resultare et arguere eum in faciem non piguit, utrique sunt demirandi de

---

1   in quo facto *C* (*corr.*)   2   Barnabae *H*   6   existente *H** exstante *H* (*corr.*)
9   sua erant (*for* fuerant) *C*   19   euid. ratio est *H*   20   stabiliante *C**   23
quidam *C**   26   legitimi obseruatione *C** legitimae obseruationi *C* (*corr.*)   28
mirandi quidem *H*

ceasing to eat with the believing Gentiles—something he plainly did at first without making any distinction—began to keep himself back from communion with them. "When this was done not only by the Jews who were in communion with him but even by my companion Barnabas, because of those who had come to them from Judea, [22] I was the only one of them all to honor truth more highly. Standing face to face with Peter, who was more distinguished and greater than all of them, I said to him, 'It is not right for you, who are a Jew by birth, without observing the law, to eat frequently with Gentile believers, and then to turn the Gentiles aside to the observance of the law.'"

Indeed, Paul appears to prove the case concerning his circumstances rightly and in proper order. First of all, he speaks of his manner of life under the law, then that he changed his allegiance to the faith, but not by human agency. Next he says that the apostles endorsed his teaching. But after all this he describes how he did not even hesitate to oppose Peter himself on this account, though he was compelled by necessity. For by all these explanations he both established his own claims and proved that his opponents' words were false. Therefore, blessed Paul now employed these arguments to show that it was not irksome for him publicly both to claim justice for the Gentile Christians and to accuse the most distinguished of the apostles. And it is clear from this that he took up the case that was being discussed. For if some controversy had arisen concerning this matter or a conflict had come about with different people supporting different views, it necessarily followed that a division of this kind had taken place among Christians, some attending to Paul and others to Peter, some upholding the one's opinion and some the other's. And this happened all the more because the Jews exerted themselves for the law with all their might, but the Gentile Christians were for the most part intolerant of being subjected to the observance of the law. Moreover, I am putting it this way to leave open two interpretations. If Peter and Paul agreed with one another to feign the controversy [23] for the benefit of others, they must truly be admired because they trusted they were doing everything for the benefit of others. But if Peter appeared to keep himself separate from the Gentile Christians because he was concerned for the Jewish Christians, while Paul did not hesitate to retaliate and accuse him to his face because he was concerned for the Gentile Christians, both of them must be ad-

suis sententiis et arbitriis. hic quidem qui praehonorandam omnibus credidit ueritatem, et propter hanc non piguit nec praecellenti insigni apostolorum in faciem resistere; ille uero, licet uideretur argui, tamen qui adquieuit, totum ferens silentio; et quidem ex
5 multis negotiis primatum sibi sufficiens uindicare, illa quae erga se
fuerant nullius momenti faciens ueritatem hominibus praehonorandam esse existimauit. quoniam autem contentio illorum nullam fecerit separationem, consensus eorum in consequente tempore demonstrauit. si enim uilissimorum hominum differentia et
10 de friuolis rebus facta saepe uniuersas separauit ecclesias; quemadmodum [non] talium contentio et de talibus negotiis effecta, si
non consensus interfuisset? utique magnam omnium fecisset separationem, nullo ultra sufficiente coniungere scissam multitudinem, quae ex illorum controuersia semel fuerat separata. utrique
15 enim dignitate contendentes, proponentes pro partibus suis, stultum esse censerent, alii post Petrum, alii post Paulum; alium quidem recipere ueritatis magistrum.

usque in hunc locum bene de se Paulus satisfacere sub specie
referentis properauit. omnia quidem quae sua fuerant compro-
20 bans, omnia uero quae ab aduersariis dicta de se fuerant falsa esse
ostendens; ita autem modeste cuncta explicauit, ut per omnia fu-
gere uideretur pondus eorum uerborum quae ad sui faciebat excusationem. incipit uero hinc ipsa dogmata examinare et ostendere quia nulla ratione iustum est eos post fidem quam in Christo
25 acceperant ultra legi inseruire. bene ex illis sermonibus quos ad
beatum Petrum fecisse uidetur principium dogmatum et exami-
nis sumpsit, ita dicens:

---

1 quidam *H*   4   qui *om C (corr.)* tamenque *H*   8   consequenti *C (corr.)*   9
demonstrabit *H*   10   saepe *om H**   13   ultro *C H*   14   qui *H*   16-17   quidam
C* H   23   dogmate *C* H* (ipso dogmate *H (corr.)*)   25   b. autem ex i. *H (corr.)*

mired for their opinions and decisions. Paul must be admired because he believed that truth must be honored before everything,
and for it he did not hesitate to oppose the most excellent and distinguished of the apostles to his face. But Peter must be admired because, granted that he appeared to be convicted, nevertheless he remained quiet, bearing it all with silence. Though he was
capable of asserting his primacy on the basis of many considerations, he treated his own affairs as of no importance and thought
that people should honor truth above all. But their agreement in
the time that followed has demonstrated that their dispute did not
cause any division.[15] For if the differences between the most con-
temptible people, occurring even because of trifling matters, have
often divided the churches throughout the world, how would the
conflict of such people, a conflict brought about over important
matters, not have done so had not agreement intervened? Doubtless there would have followed a great division of all of them, and
nothing would have sufficed thereafter to unite the multitude cut
in two once they had been divided by their controversy. [24] For
both parties, striving honorably and making the case for their respective sides, some following Peter and others Paul, would have
deemed it foolish to accept the other as a teacher of truth.

Up to this point Paul has rightly been eager to give a satisfactory assurance about himself in the form of a report. Indeed, he
confirmed everything that concerned himself, while he showed
that everything his opponents had said about him was false. But
he developed his entire account with such modesty so that in everything he might plainly avoid weighty words that would have justified him. From this point, however, he begins to examine his
teachings themselves and to show that it is for no reason right that
those who have once accepted faith in Christ should any longer be
enslaved to the law. On the basis of the words he appears to have
addressed to blessed Peter,[16] he rightly takes up the beginning of
his teachings and their examination, saying:

---

[15] See especially the correspondence of Jerome and Augustine on this passage.
Jerome argues that the dominant interpretation is the first one, that Paul and
Peter conspired in a medicinal lie. As Swete points out, Theodore seems
inclined to Augustine's opinion that Peter was honest but deserved his rebuke.
But Theodore's idea that the dispute did not cause division goes beyond what
Jerome and Augustine argue.

[16] Theodore regards verse 14 as the end of Paul's speech to Peter.

nos autem natura Iudaei et non ex gentibus peccatores, scientes quo-
niam non iustificatur homo ex operibus legis, nisi per fidem Iesu Chri-
sti, et nos [in] Iesum Christum credimus, ut iustificemur ex fide Chri-
sti et non ex operibus legis; eo quod non iustificabitur ex operibus legis
5 *omnis caro.*

'nos quidem non ex gentibus ad legem accessimus; sed ab origi-
ne ex Iudaeorum stirpe descendimus. uerumtamen scientes quoniam non est possibile ex operibus legis iustificari quemquam,
Christo credimus, simul per illam fidem quae est in Christo expec-
10 tantes et ipsi iustificari; eo quod ex operibus legis iustificari non
possumus.' hunc quidem sensum et in epistola posuit quam ad
Romanos scripsit, quoniam non est possibile ex operibus legis iustificari. simul et illam quae ex fide est iustitiam comparauit illi iustitiae quae ex lege est; cuius etiam dignitatem multis modis publi-
15 care deproperauit. hoc autem idem et hoc in loco facit, necessitate
maxima se conpellente. ad ostendendum uero euidentem intellectum, uolo latius pandere quid uoluit dicere illam iustitiam quae ex
fide est; quid uero illam quae ex operibus legis est, quam neque
adquirere alicui possibile est. etenim modum quendam non modi-
20 ca secundum intellectum pluribus hinc dubietas adnasci uidetur,
maxime illis qui cautius considerare talia consueuerunt, quia nos
extra legem non sumus; licet Moysaicam legem non eandem cum
Iudaeis custodiamus, tamen sunt et apud nos aliqua quae et festi-
namus non praeuaricare. etenim homicidium cauemus facere, et
25 adulterium; et ex integro illa quae cauere nos diuina monet scriptura sub lege nos esse ostendunt. omnis enim constitutio aliud agi
praecipit, aliud iubet caueri; haec autem et lex est et dicitur.

Dominus Deus mortales quidem nos secundum praesentem uitam instituit. resuscitans uero, iterum inmortales nos facere pro-
30 misit et faciet. nec enim illud contra suam ueniens sententiam, ob

8 iustificare *C* H* 9 illum *C* H* 12-13 iustificare *C* H* 14 etiam et
dign. *H* 19 quondam *C* H**: *corr.*. quodam 22 eam quam *C H*

2:15–16 And we ourselves are Jews by birth and not sinners from the Gentiles, knowing that a person is justified not by the works of the law unless through faith in Jesus Christ. And we have believed in Jesus Christ, so that we might be justified by faith in Christ, and not by the works of the law, because no flesh will be justified by the works of the law.

"Indeed, we did not assent to the law as a Gentile. Rather, we were descended from the race of the Jews to begin with. Nevertheless, because we came to know that it is impossible for anyone to be justified by the works of the law, we believed in Christ, at the same time expecting that by that faith in Christ we should also be justified ourselves, because we could not be justified by the works of the law." He put this same opinion in the letter he wrote to the Romans (Rom 3:20), namely, that it is impossible [25] to be justified by the works of the law. At the same time, he also contrasted the righteousness based on faith with the righteousness based on the law and also hastened to explain its worth publicly in many ways. He does the same thing also in this passage, where the greatest necessity urges him on. But in order to demonstrate his meaning clearly, I wish to expand more broadly my discussion of what he meant by that righteousness that is based on faith, as well as by that righteousness based on the works of the law, which is impossible for anyone to acquire. The fact is that in some measure no small uncertainty in understanding appears to have arisen for many concerning this, especially for those accustomed to examine such matters quite carefully, because we are not outside law. Granted that we do not keep the same Mosaic law as the Jews, nevertheless there are even among us some rules we are not anxious to violate. So we avoid committing murder and adultery and on the whole those deeds that the divine scripture warns us to avoid. This shows that we are under a law. For this entire system advises one thing to be done and orders another to be avoided. And this both is and is said to be a law.

The Lord God assuredly established us as mortals in this present [26] life. But by raising us up he promised to make us immortal again, and he will do it.[17] Nor, indeed, does he seem

---

[17] The future tense, "he will do it" (*faciet*) appears to contradict the perfect tense in the next sentence, "to have done it" (*fecisse*). It would be possible to resolve the difficulty by understanding "he will do it" as a reference to the

solum Adae peccatum ira commotus, fecisse uidetur— indecens
enim id erga Deum existimare; neque secundum quod nos facit inmortales, poenitentia ductus id facit, aut quia de his melius postea
uoluit cogitare. sed inenarrabili sapientia a primordio illa quae de
5   nobis sunt omnia instituit, sicut et fas est nos sentire de illo, qui
bonitate sola nos faciebat et factos tuebatur. dedit autem nobis
praesentem hanc uitam mortalem, ut dixi, ad exercitationem uirtutum et doctrinam illorum quae nos conueniunt facere. multas in
ea patimur uertibilitates, quasi qui et in natura mortali; nunc qui-
10 dem hoc, nunc eligentes illud et facientes; in quibus non modica
de illis quae non conueniunt et lege sunt interdicta facimus. omni autem ex parte rationabilitas in nos et eligendi potestas exerce-
tur. et quod data lege possit meliorum electio adesse nobis, exinde autem et correctionem suscipimus et tristes efficimur quidem
15 utpote in tali constituti natura. multa enim per singula momenta
accidentia nobis prudentes nos exhibent, et tolerantiam nostram
in accidentibus ostendunt casibus; exercemur enim in istis ipsis,
et ad uirtutes prouocamur. sic autem uitam mortalem et multis
passionibus subditam, ad discendam uirtutem opportunam fecis-
20 se uisus est; legesque nobis uarias ad adiutorium dedit et mores
illos qui sunt secundum animae electionem; ita ut non deteriora
eligamus, bonum autem inde discentes, ad huius magis curramus
electionem. nam sine scriptura ad primos homines locutus esse uidetur; per scripturam uero, sicut est lex quae per Moysen data est.
25 talem etiam et naturam nostram fecit, ut opportuna esse uideatur
ad ediscenda ista in quibus neque multum expendere nec cessemus
laborare, ut scire possimus quid conueniens sit. sed sufficit nobis
sola commonitio, ut firmam possimus habere apud nos si uoluerimus bonitatis cognitionem. rationabiles nos enim faciens Domi-
30 nus, ipsamque rationabilitatem in nobis efficacem expedire uolens,
quia nec aliter uideri possit, nisi discretione contrariorum, ex qui-

1   ita (*for* ira) *H*   8   eas (*for* in ea) *C* H** in eis *H* (*corr.*)   11-12   omnia *C* H*
13   vobis *H*   14   accipimus *H*   ‖   quidem (*before* eff.) *add C*   26   cessemur
C*   29   rat. enim nos *C*

to have done it by contravening his own judgment when moved to wrath because of Adam's one sin—for it is not fitting to think such a thing of God. Neither is it the case that because he makes us immortal that he is led to do so by our repentance, or because he willed to have better thoughts about this later on. Rather, by his ineffable wisdom from the first beginning he established everything that concerns us, just as it is also right for us to be aware that he made us by his goodness alone and that he preserved us once we were made. Indeed, he gave us this present mortal life, as I have said, for the training of virtues and the teaching of what is right for us to do. In it we suffer many vicissitudes, as one might expect of those living in a mortal nature. We choose and do now one thing, now another. In these choices we commit a great many acts that are wrong and prohibited by law. But in all respects our rational nature and its power of choosing is exercised. And because the choice of better things can be available to us once the law is given, for that reason we both accept reproof and are made sorrowful by the fact that we are established in such a nature. For many chance events that happen to us from time to time bring to light our wisdom and demonstrate our endurance in the misfortunes that happen. For we are trained by these very circumstances and are summoned to the virtues. So in this way he appears to have made the life that is mortal and subject to many passions an opportunity for learning virtue. And he gave us various laws for a help, as well as that character that accords with the soul's choice, so that we might not choose what is worse but by learning what is good in this way might be eager all the more to choose it. Moreover, he seems to have spoken to the first humans without scripture, but he also speaks through scripture just as in the law given through Moses. And he also made our nature capable of discerning occasions for learning [27] what we should not cease either spending great effort upon or working for, so that we might be able to know what is right. This reminder alone suffices us to be able to have within us a firm knowledge

---

resurrection and immortality and "to have done it" as a reference to God's promise. But Theodore goes on to say "he *makes* us immortal." Presumably, God does so in baptism. Consequently, despite the awkward use of tense and the absence of an object for "do," we can understand what Theodore means by appealing to his idea of baptism as a pledge and type of what will be in the age to come.

bus et meliorum electio adquiri potest—haec enim summa est cognitio rationabilium omnium; sic quodam modo illa quae secundum nos sunt composuit, ut et aliqua uideatur inesse contrarietas
apud nos, exercitationem rationabilitatis expedire sufficiens. na-
5 turalis equidem mortalitas multam nos fecit praesentium habere
cupiditatem. hinc nobis cupiditatis pecuniariae inest passio, hinc
gloriae appetitio, hinc uoluptatum; ex quibus dum unum quodcumque horum facimus, sub peccato cadimus. temporalis enim
ista uita horum nobis, ut moris est, causam praestare uidetur; ob
10 quam et pecunias concupiscimus, et gloriam appetimus, et uoluptatis causas sumimus. inmortales uero effecti neque alicuius horum indigemus, neque perficimus aliquid horum. etenim mortalitate naturae ad illa quae in praesenti sunt concurrentibus nobis,
legis nos decreto magis fecit cautos uidere, bonitatis cognitionem
15 firmam in nos collocans, nec ab isto subduci animae suadens proposito, cupere uero illa quae sunt uirtutum; licet summo cum labore illa nos adquirere conueniat. hinc licet ab illa quae in natura
est infirmitate ad delictum deferamur, semper cauentes et homicidium facere et adulterium et furtum, et omnia illa quae ad al-
20 terius pertinent nocibilitatem—quae quoniam mala sunt, omnes
uno consensu confitemur; sed non per hoc ualemus extra omne delictum nos plenius conseruare. e contrario uero, et praeter id quod
nobis ex legis placet doctrina, multa propter naturae facimus infirmitatem, utpote mortales. haec et beatus Paulus Romanis scri-
25 bens latius uidetur explicasse, dicens: *non enim quod uolo hoc facio bonum, sed quod nolo malum hoc ago.* et, *inuenio legem uolenti
mihi facere quod bonum est; quoniam mihi malum adiacet.* et, *con-
delector legi Dei secundum interiorem hominem; uideo autem aliam
legem in membris meis, repugnantem legi mentis meae.* et illa quae in
30 illa parte epistolae memoratus est, docens nos quam multa et per
naturae infirmitatem contra propositum nostrum delinquimus, et
quidem lege quod bonum est edocti. quae etiam cautius cognosce-

2-3   sec. non s. *H**   6   pecuniae rei *C** *H* (pecuniariae rei *C* (*corr.*))   7   hinc
nos delectatio uolupt. *H*.   12-13   mortalitatem *CH*   13   praesente *H**   18
deferimur *H* (*corr.*)   20   nobilitatem *C* (*corr.*)   ‖   malae *C**   22   pl. nos *C*
24-25   scribere *C** *H*   31   deliquimus *C**

of the good, if we are willing. For the Lord makes us rational and wishes to promote that very rationality in us and make it efficacious, because it could be manifested in no other way save by distinguishing contraries by which the choice of what is better can be acquired—for this is the highest knowledge for all rational beings. So the Lord composed the elements that make us up in such a way that there would plainly be a kind of opposition within us, sufficient for the training of our rationality. Indeed, our natural mortality has caused us to have a great desire for present goods. This explains our innate passion for desiring wealth; from it comes the pursuit of fame, from it, the desire for sensual pleasure. As long as we act on the basis of one or another of these passions, we fall into sin. For that temporal life of ours customarily seems to supply the cause of this. This is why we desire wealth, seek fame, and seize what causes sensual pleasure. But once we are made immortal, we need none of these things, nor do we accomplish any of them. Moreover, by the law's decree the Lord made us look more carefully at what pertains to our present circumstances, which attach to the mortal aspect of our nature, thereby settling in us a secure knowledge of the good and persuading the soul not to be subject to what is proposed to it but to desire what belongs to the virtues—though it is right we should acquire them with the greatest toil. In this way—by always avoiding committing murder, adultery, and theft, and everything that tends to injure someone else, since we are all agreed in recognizing these deeds as evil— we are allowed to be carried away from the weakness in our nature that inclines us to offend. Nevertheless, we are not strong enough in this way to keep ourselves completely free from all offense. On the contrary, even aside from what is decreed for us on the basis of the law's teaching, we do many things because of the [28] weakness of our nature, since we are mortal. Blessed Paul plainly explained this at greater length in writing to the Romans, when he says (Rom 7:19, 21–23): *For I do not do the good I want, but the evil I do not want is what I do* and *I find it to be a law that, when I want to do what is good, evil lies close at hand* and *I delight in the law of God in my inmost self, but I see in my members another law at war with the law of my mind.* By what he recorded in that part of the letter he teaches us how many offenses we commit against what we intend because of the weakness of our nature and even though we have been taught by the law what is good. Anyone can

re quis poterit, si discutere uoluerit interpretationem illam epistolae quam ipsi exposuisse uidemur. qui si una quadam specie erga
nos ad plenum usus fuisset, qua nos legitimo animo praeparasset
praeeligere, ad hoc etiam non naturam instituens concurrere fecis-
5   set, nihil differre iumentis inrationalibus uideremur, inuiti magis
ad bonitatis actum inpulsi. illa uero quae existimatur contrarietas
inesse nobis, sicut nuper diximus, rationabilitatem ipsam in opere uideri perficit. euidenter autem nos nostrae uoluptatis dominos
instituit, ut quod uolumus eligamus, natura quidem propter illam
10 quae inest ei mortalitatem ad hoc nos adtrahente, legibus uero nos
e contrario docentibus; et animae auctoritate discretionem eorum
ad id quod sibi libitum fuerit secundum ut conueniens est facien-
te, sed nec deuiante umquam a suo proposito, a meliorum gloria,
licet naturali infirmitate in contrarios deducatur actus. iustificari
15 tamen in praesenti uita scrupulose, secundum legis conuersationem et maxime Moysaicae quae multa habet praecepta, et multa
indiget cautela, inpossibile est. uerumtamen non sine nostra utilitate res ipsa efficitur; ut autem firmam accipiamus instructionem
bonitatis, discamus etiam odire peccatum, non modicum auxilii
20 ad hoc lex conferre nobis uidetur. et quidem ad exercitationem
uirtutum fert nobis auxilium desiderantibus illa facere, quae bona
de legis doctrina esse existimamus. in futuro uero saeculo perfectam multam iustificationem per gratiam Dei percipiemus. illa est
quam in praesenti uita a diuersis didicimus exercitationibus, ad-
25 hortante nos ad hoc legitimo decreto quae et conueniunt, nobis,
sicut diximus, in contrarium perspicere uolentibus, ut maiori disciplina bonitatis concupiscentiam ex comparatione tali suscipere possimus. haec tunc in nobis opere implebuntur, gratia sancti Spiritus inuertibilitate per omnia custodiente nos in bonis illis,
30 quorum desiderium cum et odio peccati in praesenti uita suscipimus, eo quod et hoc primitus nobis necessarie adesse conueniebat.
siue enim illud secundum se erat existens, inrationabilitate quadam uidebamur magis in bonis mansisse; siue hoc quidem fiebat,
quod secundum praesentem hanc uitam fieri in nobis exercitatio

1   discurre *C** discurrere *C* (*corr.*) 2   ipse *C* ‖ uidetur *C* (*corr.*) 7   diximus
om H   11   auctoritatem *C H*   12   fuerat *H**   16   multam ind. cautelam *H*
17   nostram *H**   20   quidam *C**   22-23   perfecta multa *C** perfecte multam
C (*corr.*)   23   percipimus *C*   24   quae *C* H*   25   de leg. decr. *H**   26
maioribus *C**   34   uobis *H**

also more carefully understand the point if he is willing to consult the interpretation of that letter that we have seen fit to publish ourselves. If God had employed some kind of single character for our complete existence so as to prepare us for choosing the best by a soul ruled by the law and had not also made us by establishing in us a nature that runs counter to this, we should necessarily differ in no way from irrational beasts, since we should have been driven for the most part to do the good involuntarily. But it is that opposition thought to be innate in us, as we have already said, that causes our very rationality to appear. But God clearly established us as masters of our own desire, so that we should choose what we wish. Indeed, because of that mortality innate in it, our nature draws us to this, while the laws teach us the contrary. And although the soul's authority distinguishes what is pleasing to it according to what is right and never deviates from its intention and from the boast of what is better, it is permitted to be led to contrary acts because of natural weakness. Yet it is impossible to be justified with exactness in the present life by acquaintance with the law, especially that of Moses, which has many commandments and requires great carefulness. Nevertheless, this very impossibility does not take place without benefiting us. The law plainly gives us no small help in accepting instruction about the good [29] and also in learning to hate sin. Indeed, it brings help to us for training in the virtues, when we desire to do what we think to be good because of the law's teaching. But in the age to come we shall receive far more perfect justification by the grace of God. The justification we learn by various exercises in this life, with the law's decree urging us to what is right for this purpose, examines us, as we have said, so that we can gain a desire for the good by greater discipline on the basis of such a contrast. This will be fulfilled in us in actuality at that time when the grace of the Holy Spirit will keep us unchangeable in all ways in those good things, the desire for which we accept in our present life together with hatred of sin, because it was right that this firstfruits should necessarily be present to us. For if that desire for good and hatred of sin had existed by itself in us, we should plainly have remained in those goods more by some irrational inclination than by reason. But if the desire for good was to come about gradually, then what happens to us in this life

bonitatis erat futura. unde bene cum uita ista diuidens saecula, hoc quidem saeculum nobis fecit aptum, ut et exercitari in eo, et cum conuenienti discretione discere quod bonum est possimus; et animo firmo accipere uirtutis desiderium et peccati odium. futu-
5 rum uero saeculum uel uita quae post horum [finem] est, praebebit nobis et quod ipsi nobis adquirere minime sufficiebamus, eo quod nullo modo excepto peccato custodiri poteramus. quia ergo Christus uenit, dirigens per suam resurrectionem illa quae futura sunt, praestitit uero et nobis illorum promissionem. omnes qui
10 in praesenti hac uita credimus Christo, quasi medii quidam sumus praesentis quoque uitae et futurae, secundum illud quidem quod mortales sumus natura, et superuenientes nobis suscipimus uertibilitates. utpote in tali consistentes natura, legem et doctrinam, ut moris est, indigemus; quae nos docet illa facere quae conue-
15 niunt, et a quibus caueri. nec enim sine labore et sudore ad uirtutes possumus dirigi, licet plurimum eius animo uideamur habere desiderium. fide autem quasi iam translatos nos in futura uita uidemus, et maxime adubi baptisma perceperimus (quod baptisma formam habet mortis et resurrectionis Christi), simul accipientes
20 et Spiritum sanctum qui in baptismate datur. qui quasi primitiae quaedam sunt futurorum, eo quod ad perfectam inmortalitatem dandus est nobis Spiritus sanctus. ideo et regenerationis dicimus Spiritum, secundum quod et forma suae inoperationis quasi in secunda uita uidetur nos regenerare. et propter hoc a corporalibus
25 praeceptis et illis quae propria sunt legis securi consistimus; circumcisionem adsero, et sacrificia, et dierum obseruantiam, et illorum quae eiusmodi sunt, quorum nulla in futuro saeculo lucra habemus. custodimus autem illa, ne homicidium faciamus aut adulterium aut furtum, et uniuersa illa quae ad propinqui nociuitatem
30 a nobis fieri possunt; a quibus etiam et in futura nos continebimus uita, cum multo, ut fas est, studio perfectam caritatem et erga proximos et erga Deum nos habere ipso opere ostendentes. con-

2 hunc C H ǁ quidam H 5 finem om C* H 7 custodire C H 10 praesentem C* ǁ qui si (for quasi) H* ǁ medii quidem C* H medium quiddam C (corr.) 13 lege et doctrina C (corr.) 14 doceat C (corr.) 15 oportet add (after caueri) H 16 uideamus H 18 ubi (for adubi) C (corr.) passim 23 formam H ǁ operationis C (corr.) 29 nocitatem H nocibilitatem C (corr.)

was to be a training for the good in the age to come.[18] Therefore,
God rightly distinguished two ages for our life. Surely he made
this age for us as one suitable for our being trained in it and for
the possibility of our learning by rightly distinguishing what is
good and by accepting with a steadfast mind the desire for virtue
and the hatred of sin. But the age to come or the life that will be
when this has been accomplished is what he will provide for us—
something we were by no means sufficient to acquire for ourselves
because we were in no way [30] capable of being kept free from
sin. Therefore, since Christ came to arrange what was to come
in the future age by his own resurrection, he truly bestowed upon
us its promise. All of us who believe in Christ in this present life
are, as it were, between both the present and the future life. It
is by the first that we are mortal by nature and are subject to the
vicissitudes that come upon us, with the result that since we exist
in such a nature, we customarily need the law and the teaching that
instruct us in what we should do and what we should avoid. Nor
can we be directed to the virtues without toil and sweat, however
much we appear to have a desire for them in our mind. But by faith
we see ourselves as though already translated to the life to come,
especially when we have received baptism (because baptism has
the type of Christ's death and resurrection), since at that time we
also receive the Holy Spirit given in baptism. In this way there
are, as it were, a kind of firstfruits of the things to come, because
the Holy Spirit must be given to us for perfect immortality. We
call him the Spirit of rebirth, because the type of his working
plainly gives us new birth as in a second life. For this reason we
stand free from bodily precepts and those commands proper to the
law—I mean circumcision, sacrifices, the observance of days, and
things like them, from which we shall have no profit in the age to
come. But we keep those laws that are against murder, adultery, or
theft, and against all we might do to harm our neighbor. [31] In
them we shall even maintain ourselves in the life to come, showing
with much zeal by what we do, as is right, that we have perfect
love toward our neighbors and toward God. And we shall no

---

[18] Cf. Swete's paraphrase (1:29): "If we had been impeccable by nature, our
perseverance would have been due to an unreasoning compliance; as it is, the
good within us is of gradual growth, and this life is our practice-ground for the
world to come."

cupiscentiam autem turpem neque in sensu nostro ultra accipere poterimus, non lege quadam aut denuntiatione prohibiti, sed cooperatione solius gratiae perficientis in nos omnia quae cum labore et sudore multo uix in praesenti legis doctrinam sequentes dirige-
5 re possumus. et nec sic ad plenum a delicto possumus esse securi, propter naturae infirmitatem. quoniam ergo necdum in fruitionem futurorum bonorum quae per Christum nobis extiterunt ad perfectionem sumus constituti, per fidem autem illam quae illorum est eorum spem et promissionem suscepimus, utpote per
10 formam in hisdem effecti; iusta ratione illa quae Christi sunt illis quae in lege sunt comparans, fidem legi e contrario sistit, eo quod necdum rerum potiti fide sola adsequi ea interim uidemur. hoc ergo uult et eo loco dicere, quoniam inpossibile est iustificari ex operibus legis, eo quod sumus natura mortales; licet ualde ad uir-
15 tutem inspiciamus. sed ut plerumque non peccemus, nullo modo fieri potest. interimere enim scit iustitiam obortum peccatum, lege condempnante illos qui delinquunt et non considerante utrum multa recte agentes erga exigua deliquerint; sed illos qui quoquo modo deliquerunt scit sub poena concludere. haec est legis natura,
20 ut peccantem sine aliqua excusatione poenae subiciat. necessarie inquit illa quae a Christo praestita sunt nobis; qui et consummauit illa quae deerant nobis propter naturae infirmitatem, quae etiam ex fide percepimus, et tamquam in illis iam esse uidemur. non ergo iustum est denuo nos ad legem recurrere ex qua nihil lucri ad-
25 quirere possumus. sed haec dicta sunt latius, ut magis apostolicum sensum intelligere possimus, et maxime eadem causa qua in multis causis illa exequi id uideretur. sed recurrendum est ad sequentiam narrationis.

in praecedentibus enim apostolus ex utriusque qualitate secun-
30 dum comparationem ostendit eorum esse differentiam. multum supereminere uidentur illis ea quae secundum Christum sunt, si quidem illis qui sub lege uiuunt labor et sudor frequens sit necessarius; adiecto illo quod non possint plenariam peccati habere libertatem, propter naturae infirmitatem. apud Christum uero

---

2 nam (*for* non) *H*   4 uita *add* (*after* in praes.) *H*   12 uidentur *H*   13 quo (*for* quoniam) *C*   16 ob ortum (*appy*) *H*   18 delinquerunt *C** (*bis*) *H* delinquerint, delinquerunt *C* (*corr.*) (cf. Rönsch, 287; Bensly, 15)   27 uidetur *C* (*corr.*)   ‖   sequentia *C H*

longer be able to receive shameful concupiscence in our senses, not because we are prohibited by any law or admonition but because of the assistance of grace that alone will perfect us in everything in which we were scarcely able to direct our path in this life with toil and much sweat by following the law's teaching. Not even this way were we able to be completely free of offense because of the weakness of our nature. Therefore, since we have not yet been established in the enjoyment of the good things to come that Christ called into existence for our perfection, we receive their hope and promise by our very faith in them, since we have been fashioned in them by type. A comparison by right reasoning of what pertains to Christ with what is found in the law establishes faith and the law as contraries, because, though we have not yet gained those good things, we plainly do acquire them for the time being by faith alone. Therefore, this is what Paul means in this passage: that it is impossible to be justified by the works of the law because we are mortal by nature, however much we set our sight on virtue. Indeed, it is impossible in any way that we should for the most part refrain from sin. For Paul knows that sin, when it springs to life, destroys righteousness, since the law condemns those who transgress and does not consider whether they have transgressed in small ways, though acting rightly in many ways. Rather, he knows that those who have transgressed in any way are consigned to punishment. This is the nature of law, that it subjects the sinner to punishment without any excuse. Of necessity he speaks about what Christ established for us. He completed what we lacked because of the weakness of our nature, and we receive this by faith and appear to be as though we were already in this condition. Therefore, it is not right from now on for us to rush back to the law from which we can gain nothing to benefit us. We have spoken at some length so that we can better understand the apostle's meaning, and especially because for many reasons the subject seems worth pursuing. But we must return to the order of the narrative.

In what he has just said Paul shows the difference between faith and the law by comparing them on the basis of their character. Convictions based on Christ are plainly far superior, [32] even if toil and constant sweat are necessary for those who live under the law, since Christ gives in addition the fuller freedom from sin that they cannot have because of the weakness of their nature.

optima quaedam est futurorum promissio, indubiam et confessam habens bonorum fruitionem. aliud adicit multo fortius praeceden-ti, cuius maxime fortitudo amplior esse ab illis quae praedicta sunt ostendi poterit euidenter:

5 *si autem quaerentes iustificari in Christo inuenti sumus et ipsi pec-catores, ergo Christus peccati minister est. absit.*

est quidem obscuritate inuolutus intellectus apostolicus, a mul-ta atque compendiosa prosecutione; structuram enim uerbi sui in multam produxit arrogantiam. uult enim dicere, quoniam 'se-
10 cundum legem iustificari minime poterimus. accessimus ad Chri-stum, quasi per eum adsecuti iustitiam. si autem hac spe credentes in eum inuenimur peccantes, quia legem non custodimus, uidetur aduentu suo idem peccatorum nobis extitisse prouisor. euidens est enim quoniam conuenit ad fidem nos se illam quae in se est euo-
15 care, non ut legis nos custodiam doceat diligenter seruare; qua de causa et ante eius aduentum lex erat posita. si autem illa quae in eum est fides peccare facit illos qui legem non custodiunt, peccati nobis extitit prouisor.' et propter inconuenientiam dictorum, ut consuetudo illi est in talibus negotiis, adiecit, *absit!*
20 *si enim quae destruxi, haec iterum aedifico, praeuaricatorem meip-sum conuinco.*

'praeuaricator legis dicor (hoc est, non iusta constituor ratio-ne), cum ab ea recessisse uidebor. et aliter indecens est me haec docere alios, a quorum cura uel diligentia ipse recessi. hoc enim
25 est me ipsum conuincere praeuaricatorem, inconuenienter a pri-mordio discessisse a lege, si nunc quasi me ipsum reprehendens denuo ad illorum concurrere uoluero confirmationem.' et quia hoc sententialiter magis dictum esse uidebatur, quam probationem ali-quam habere (necdum enim erat manifestum ne quando et ipse

---

1 optime *C H*: txt *coniec. Pitra* ‖ confersam *H* 7 apostolici *C** apostoli *C* (*corr.*) 8 structorum *C H* 9 autem (*for* enim) *l b* 10 poteramus *C* ‖ per (*for* ad) *H** 12 peccatores (*for* peccantes) *l b* 13 peccati (*for* peccatorum) *l* 14 nosse illam *C H* 22 dicitur *H* ‖ constituo *C H*: txt *coniec. Pitra* 26 non (*for* nunc) *C* H* 28 sentialiter *C* H** essentialiter *H* (*corr.*)

With Christ there is truly a certain best promise of what is to come, a promise that holds the undoubted and acknowledged enjoyment of good things. Paul adds another consideration much more convincing than the preceding one, the strength of which can quite clearly be shown to be fuller than what he has already said:

2:17 *But if seeking to be justified in Christ, we ourselves have been found to be sinners, Christ is a servant of sin. Certainly not!*

To be sure, the apostle's meaning is wrapped in obscurity because of the highly succinct character of its order; for he draws out the arrangement of his words with great exaggeration. What he means is that "by the law we could by no means be justified. We have drawn near to Christ because we gain righteousness through him. But if when we believe in him with this hope we are found to be sinners because we have not observed the law, he will appear at his coming to take his stand for us as the one who provides against sins. For it is clear that what accords with faith is that we should call upon what it contains and that it does not teach us to be slaves in keeping the law [33] with diligence because the law was imposed before Christ's coming. But if faith in him makes sinners of those who do not keep the law, he has taken his stand as the one who provides against sin." And because what he has said is inappropriate, as is his custom in such matters, he added *Certainly not!*

2:18 *For if I build up again the very things that I have torn down, then I demonstrate that I am a transgressor.*

"I am called a transgressor of the law (that is, I am found such by incorrect reasoning), since I shall be seen to have departed from it. If I had not done so, it would be inappropriate for me to instruct others in teachings from the careful observance of which I have myself departed.[19] If I were now to turn round and agree all over again to the establishment of legal requirements by, as it were, rebuking myself, that is what would be to convict myself as a transgressor and to have been wrong by deserting the law in the first place." And because this seems to have been said more by way of an opinion than as something having the force of proof (for it was not yet clear when and by what right reasoning he

---

[19] See Swete's paraphrase (1:33): "I am charged with having committed a sin in abandoning the standpoint of the law. To teach compliance with legal ordinances now, would be to admit my guilt."

non iusta ratione ab illa discessisset), ostendit non esse praeuaricatum ab illa discedere:

ego enim per legem legi mortuus sum, ut Deo uiuam.

'in ipsa lege praedicatum inueniens Christum, cui et per legem
5   oblatus, et credens, mortuus sum legi, exter factus a praesenti hac
uita; illam uero quae Dei est in promissione per baptisma iam adsecutus sum.' et idipsum latius explicans:

*Christo confixus sum cruci. uiuo autem iam non ego; uiuit uero in
me Christus.*

10 †eo quod in baptismate mor-   ἐπειδὴ ἐν τῷ βαπτίσματι τοῦ τε
tis quoque et resurrectionis for-   θανάτου καὶ τῆς ἀναστάσεως τύπον
mam implebant, concrucifigi   ἐπλήρουν, συσταυροῦσθαι ἐλέγοντο
dicebantur Christo qui baptiza-   τῷ χριστῷ, ὡς ἂν αὐτοῦ μὲν διὰ
bantur; eo quod idem per cru-   σταυροῦ τὸν θάνατον δεξαμένου καὶ
15 cem mortem suscipiens et a   ἀναστάντος· αὐτοὶ δὲ κατὰ τύπον
praesenti hac uita exter factus,   τοῦ βαπτίσματος ἐν τοῖς ὁμοίοις
postquam resurrexit, inmorta-   γιγνόμενοι ἐπ' ἐλπίδι τοῦ καὶ πάντη
lem uitam sumpsit. ipsi uero se-   ποτὲ μετασχεῖν τῶν ὁμοίων, ὅταν
cundum formam baptismatis in   τῆς κοινῆς πάντων ἀναστάσεως ἐν
20 similitudinem sumus facti, spe   τῇ τοῦ αἰῶνος συντελείᾳ τὸν καιρὸν
illa quod ut et aliquando assi-   παρεῖναι συμβαίνῃ.
milemur [et] horum necessario
participemur, quando communis omnium resurrectio in con-
25 summatione saeculi perficietur
tempore concurrenti,*

sicut et in epistola quam ad Romanos scripsit dixisse uidetur: *hoc
cognoscentes quoniam uetus homo noster crucifixus est, ut destruatur
corpus peccati; ut ultra non seruiamus peccato.*

30 †hoc ergo dicit quoniam 'con-   τοῦτο οὖν λέγει, ὅτι συνεσταύρωμαι
crucifixus sum Christo*, nullam   (φησὶν) τῷ χριστῷ, οὐδεμίαν πρὸς
ad praesentem hanc uitam ha-   τὴν παροῦσαν ταύτην ζωὴν κοινω-
bens communionem, in qua se-   νίαν ἔχων, ἐν ᾗ κατὰ νόμον πολι-
cundum legem nos necesse sit   τεύεσθαι ἡμᾶς ἀνάγκη.

4   praeuaricatum (*for* praed.) *C H*   6   illa *C* H*   10   sq. Coisl. 204 f. 20 b
[Cr. vi. 42. Fr. 124]. θεόδωρος. ἄλλος πάλιν ὧδε φησίν· ἐπ., κ.τ.λ.   12   cum
crucifigi *C**   13-14   cum bapt. *H* (*corr.*)   18-19   sec. f. in b. s. *C H** sec. hanc
f., &c., *H* (*corr.*): txt *g*   23   participamur *C* (*corr.*)   30-31   cumcrucifixus sum
C* cumcrucifixi sumus *C* (*corr.*)   31-32   n. ergo ad pr. *H* (*corr.*)

had deserted the law), he shows that he had not transgressed by deserting it:

2:19a *For through the law I died to the law, so that I might live to God.*

"I found Christ predicted in the law itself, and I gave myself up to his keeping through the law. Believing in him I died to the law because I became a stranger to the present life. In truth I have already approached that life that is God's by promise through baptism." He explains this very thing more fully:

2:19b–20a *I have been crucified with Christ, and it is no longer I who live, but it is Christ who lives in me.*

[34] †Since in baptism people fulfilled the type of both death and resurrection, those who were baptized were said to be crucified with Christ, because Christ received death through the cross and became a stranger to the present life. After he rose again he embraced immortal life. In truth we have been made like him according to the type of baptism in the hope that we shall some day assume this likeness and necessarily share in these goods when the general resurrection of all happens at the same time as the consummation of this age.*

Since in baptism people fulfilled the type of both death and resurrection, they were said to be crucified with Christ, since he received death through the cross and rose again. And they have come to be in similar things according to the type of baptism in the hope of someday sharing in all ways in the like, when the time of the general resurrection of all happens to take place at the consummation of this age.

He seems to have spoken the same way in the letter he wrote to the Romans (Rom 6:6): *We know that our old self was crucified with him so that the body of sin might be destroyed, and we might no longer be enslaved to sin.*

†Therefore, he says "*I have been crucified with Christ,* since I have no share in this present life in which we must conduct ourselves according to the law.*

Therefore, he says *I have been crucified with Christ,* since he has no share in this present life in which we must conduct ourselves according to the law.

conuersari.*

transiens uero a praesenti uita, quasi iam in illam uitam me aestimo uiuere, secundum quam etiam Christus in me uiuit. cui per
resurrectionem adiunctus, membrum eius (id est Christi) effectus
5   sum, dignus corpori eius copulatus esse'—caput, ut moris est, ipsum sibi adscribens. sic enim et alibi dicit: *etenim nos omnes in uno*
Spiritu in unum corpus baptizati sumus.

nam illud quod dixit: *uiuo autem iam non ego*, hoc est, praesentem uitam; utpote post mortem alter, et non ipse existens. nam
10 quod dixit, *uiuit in me Christus*, quoniam illius uitam uiuit illi inmortalem. ea enim quae tunc erunt ipsis rebus, haec quasi iam facta dicit, secundum quod in formam illorum per baptisma transisse
uidetur; et de futuris, quia erunt, firmam habet fidem.

deinde, quoniam adhuc mortalem hanc uitam uidetur uiuere,
15 necdum in illa existens:

quod autem nunc uiuo in carne, in fide uiuo Fili Dei qui me dilexit,
et tradidit semetipsum pro me.

'carnem' consuete pro mortalitate dicit, hoc dicens quoniam 'si
adhuc aestimor mortalem hanc uitam et temporalem uiuere, sed
20 fide iam uitam illam uiuere existimor, indubiam ultra per Filium
Dei futurorum spem habens, eo quod et *dilexit me, et dedit seipsum*
pro me. hac de causa dubitare ultra de futuris non possum.' quod
autem dixit, quod 'nunc uiuo in carne, sed in fide uiuo,' et cetera.
et quasi iam sufficienter memorans illa quae a Filio Dei data sunt
25 nobis futura, confirmans cum fiducia adicit:

non sperno gratiam Dei.

et iterum probationem dictorum complectens:

si enim per legem iustitia, ergo Christus gratis mortuus est.

iure id dixit; si enim pro nostra iustificatione omnia fiunt, hoc
30 est, si autem nobis ex lege adquiri poterat, superflua utique fuit
mors Christi, nihil amplius perficiens. deinde uertitur ad fidei
confirmationem. et quia probationem erat adiecturus, nullam ambiguitatem sustinere sufficientem, eo quod non uerbis autem opere eius erat futura probatio; ad increpationem incipit, confidens

---

2   in illa uita *H* (*corr.*)   4   eff. esse *C* H*   16   filii *C* (*corr.*)   23   non (*for* nunc)
C H   27   complector *C H** [*for. leg.* complectitur]   30   omnia (*for* autem) *C*
(*corr.*) aut *H*   ‖   poterant *C* (*corr.*)   33   aut *C H*   34   eius f. e. approbatio *H*

In truth, by moving on from the present life, I consider that I am already as though I were living in that life by which Christ also lives in me. Joined to him through his resurrection, I have been made a member of him (that is, of Christ) worthy of being associated with his body"—regarding him as its head, as is his custom. For he makes this point elsewhere by saying (1 Cor 12:13): *For in the one Spirit we were all baptized into one body.*

[35] For the fact that he said *it is no longer I who live* refers to the present life, since as we might expect he exists as someone different and not himself after death. And he said *Christ lives in me*, since he lives his immortal life in him. For what will come to pass in fact at that future time, he speaks of as though it had already taken place, because he has plainly moved on to its type through baptism. And he has a steadfast faith that what is to come will be.

Then, since he is plainly still living this mortal life and does not yet exist in the one to come:

2:20b *And what I now live in the flesh I live in faith in the Son of God, who loved me and gave himself for me.*

He customarily uses "flesh" to mean mortality. What he means is: "If I am still deemed to be living this mortal and temporal life, yet by faith I consider I am living that other life, since I have an unwavering faith in what is to come through the Son of God, because *he loved me and gave himself for me.* For this reason I can have no further doubt concerning what is to come." And this is what he meant by saying *I now live in the flesh*, but *I live in faith*, and the rest. And as though he now were sufficiently calling to mind those good things to come given us by the Son of God, he confidently supports what he is saying by adding:

2:21a *I do not scorn the grace of God,*

And again including proof of what he has said:

2:21b *for if righteousness comes through the law, then Christ died for nothing.*

[36] He said this with good reason. If, indeed, all this happened for our justification, that is, if, indeed, it could have been secured for us by the law, doubtless Christ's death would have been useless, since it would have accomplished nothing more. He then turns his attention to confirming the faith. And because he was about to add a proof sufficient to admit no doubt and because the proof was to be not in words but in deed, he begins his reproach, confident that

nullam posse sustinere controuersiam illa quae a se dicenda erant:

> *o insensati Galatae, quis uos fascinauit? quibus ante oculos Iesus Christus proscriptus est, et in uobis crucifixus est.*

uult quidem dicere quoniam 'cum multo affectu uerba crucis audistis. propter quod et credidistis illis bonis quae nobis per eum adquisita sunt, ita ut et ante oculos uestros paulo minus depingeretis ipsam crucem et illa quae eo tempore facta sunt. qua ergo fascinatione tantum abiecistis affectum, quem erga Christum habere uidebamini?' interiectum est autem totum ab illo loco, quo dixit, *quis uos fascinauit;* poterat enim ipsam increpationem curuare. nam ad illud quod dixit: *o insensati Galatae,* consequenter postea adiecit:

> *hoc solum uolo discere a uobis; ex operibus legis Spiritum accepistis, an ex auditu fidei?*

'manifestum est; miraculorum etenim magnitudo testimonium perhibet dati uobis Spiritus. dicite ergo mihi: quemadmodum accepistis Spiritum? unde tantae donationis participationem sumpsistis? utrum ex custodia legis hoc uobis conlatum est? quando enim cura uobis fuit de lege? gentes enim antea eratis, et a nobis nihil tale docti, sed credentes solummodo in Christo, tantam accepistis gratiam. deinde (tanta quaedam uos contigit insipientia) quasi qui per fidem, excepta lege, Spiritum accepistis, denuo uoluistis recurrere ad legis obseruantiam, ut quid exinde maius accipiatis? nam cum nihil sit bonum quod exaequari possit donationi Spiritus sancti, adhuc et bonorum omnem participationem uobis non aliunde expectetis tribui; hinc et resurrectionem adsecuturi, et inmortales autem mansuri, et inuertibilitatem expectatam potituri.' et post probationem iterum adicit cum increpatione:

> *sic insensati estis? inchoantes Spiritu, nunc ut in carne consummamini?*

euidenter ostendens quoniam ideo eos insensatos uocauit, quoniam non perspexerunt quod illis qui in Christo crediderunt su-

---

3　praescriptus *C* [cf. p. 17, I. 11, vv. II.]　‖　et *om H*　6　adquaesita *C H*　7　quia (*for* qua) *H*　8　abiectis *H**　9　quod dixit *C* H*　13　Christum (*for* Spiritum) *C H*　15　enim (*for* etenim) *H*　17　donationi *C* dominationi *H*　18　collatum est uobis *H*　19　etiam (*for* enim) *H*　20　tantum *C*　21　quaenam (*for* quaedam) *C*　‖　uobis (*for* uos) *C* (*corr.*) *H* (*corr.*)　24　posset *C* H*　27　et inmortali autem m. *C** et in inmortalitate a. m. *C* (*corr.*) et inmortali m. *H** et inmortales m. *H* (*corr.*)　28　increpationem *C*

what he had to say could admit no dispute:

3:1 *You foolish Galatians! Who has bewitched you? It was before your eyes that Jesus Christ was publicly exhibited and was crucified in your*[20] *midst.*

What he means is that "you heard the words about the cross with great affection. Because of this you also so believed those good things we have gained through him that you all but painted before your eyes that very cross and what happened at that time. By what witchery, then, have you thrown away that great affection we saw you had for Christ?" Moreover, he inserted everything following the words *who has bewitched you?* For he could have brought his reproach full circle [by continuing immediately with 3:2]. In that case he would have added next in logical sequence the following verse to his statement *You foolish Galatians.*

3:2 *The only thing I want to learn from you is this: Did you receive the Spirit by the works of the law or from the hearing of faith?*

[37] "It is obvious, for the fact is that the greatness of the miracles bears witness to the Spirit that was given to you. So tell me: How did you receive the Spirit? From what source did you take up your share in so great a gift? Was it granted to you because you kept the law? For when did you have any concern for the law? Indeed, you were previously Gentiles and were taught no such thing by us. Instead, you received so great a grace only by believing in Christ. Then (such a great folly befell you), since you actually received the Spirit through faith apart from the law, have you all at once turned around, running to observe the law so as to receive something more from it? For since there is nothing good that can be equal to the gift of the Holy Spirit, up until now you would have expected the entire share in good things to be bestowed upon you from no other source. From that gift you will draw near to the resurrection, and you will also remain immortal and will possess what you have hoped for unchangeably." After his proof he adds a repetition of his reproach:

3:3 *Are you so senseless? Having started with the Spirit, are you now ending with the flesh?*

He clearly shows that he has called them senseless because they have failed to recognize that observing the law is useless for those who have believed in Christ, inasmuch as the Spirit has

---

[20] Theodore, like Chrysostom and Theodoret, reads ὑμῖν rather than ἡμῖν.

perflua iam sit legis custodia, si quidem et Spiritus hinc illis datus sit, quia et ob magnas tribuendus est promissiones. sicut enim
'carnem' causa mortalitatis accepit, eo quod nihil inmortale dicitur caro; sic et 'Spiritum' causa accepit inmortalitatis, eo quod per
5 eum expectamus exsurgentes in inmortalem illam uiuere uitam.
unde et 'primitias' uocat illum Spiritum qui nunc nobis sed in spe
tribuitur futurorum. quae futura etiam et percipiemus, perfectam
Spiritus sancti suscipientes inoperationem, sicut et ipse apostolus
dicit: *non solum autem, sed et ipsi primitias Spiritus habentes, et nos*
10 *ipsi in nobis ipsis ingemiscimus, filiorum adoptionem expectantes, re-*
demptionem corporis nostri. hoc ergo dicit: 'sic insensati estis, ut
neque scire possitis in quorum exemplo Spiritus sanctus sit uobis
datus, sed recurritis iterum a melioribus ad deteriora; et

†suscipientes Spiritum sanctum   δεξάμενοι τὸ πνεῦμα ἐπ' ἐλπίδι
15 in spe inmortalitatis, quando et   τῆς ἀναστάσεως καὶ τῆς ἀθανασίας,
per gratiam ab omni erimus ex-   ὅτε χάριτι πάσης ἐκτὸς ἁμαρτίας
tranei peccato, iterum quasi mor-   ἐσόμεθα, αὖθις ὡς θνητοί τινες ὑπὸ
tales quidam et usque ad prae-   τὴν τοῦ νόμου φυλακὴν ἑαυτοὺς
sentem uitam totum definien-   ποιεῖτε;
20 tes, sub legis custodiam uos ipsos facere uultis?'*

deinde interponit inter medias probationes illud quod maxime
eos poterat ad uerecundiam perducere:
tanta passi estis sine causa?
25 'ut autem omnia praetermittam, quae passi estis pro Christo
non erubescitis? illa etenim omnia praesentia hac uertibilitate uana nunc esse monstrastis.'
et, ut ne uideatur ad plenum desperasse de eis:
si nunc et sine causa;
30 id dicens ostendit se bonam de illis adhuc spem haberc, expectans simul quia et se cohibebunt ab illicita aduersariorum doctrina. et post interiectionem uerborum, iterum anteriorem intellec-

---

2   ob magnis promissionibus *C H* [Rönsch, 408]   5   in (*bef.* inmort.) *om C*
(*corr.*)   6   quae *C H**   7   tribuetur *C* H** tribuentem *C* (*corr.*)   ‖   etiam
perc. *C* (*corr.*)   8   operationem *C* (*corr.*)   12   sit uobis (*om* datus) *C** s. d. u *C*
(*corr.*)   14   sq. Coisl. 204, f. 22 a [Cr. vi. 46]. ἄλλος δέ φησιν· δεξάμενοι, κ.τ.λ.
18   quidem *C* (*corr.*)   26   praesenti *C* (*corr.*)   28   adiecit (*aft.* de eis, *in marg*)
add H (*corr.*)   29   non (*for* nunc) *C H*   31   simulq. etsi c. se ab &c. *C H*

been given them from now on and that he has been bestowed on account of great promises. For just as he understands "flesh" by its reference to mortality, since flesh is said in no way to be immortal, so he understands "Spirit" by its reference to immortality, since we hope through him to ascend to live [38] in that immortal life. This is why he calls the Spirit—now bestowed upon us, but in the hope of what is to come—the "firstfruits." Those things to come that we shall acquire when we receive the perfect working of the Holy Spirit will be just as the apostle himself says (Rom 8:23): *and not only the creation, but we ourselves, who have the firstfruits of the Spirit, groan inwardly while we wait for the adoption of sons, the redemption of our bodies.* Therefore, he says: "Are you so senseless that you cannot even know what the Holy Spirit has been given to us to typify, but are running back again to worse from better?

†Though you received the Holy Spirit in the hope of immortality when we shall be by grace outside all sin, do you wish again to put yourselves under the guardianship of the law like mere mortals and people restricting everything to the present life?"*

Though you received the Spirit in the hope of the resurrection and of immortality when we shall be by grace outside all sin, are you again putting yourselves under the guardianship of the law like mere mortals?

Then he introduces in the midst of his proofs what could have led them to be greatly ashamed of themselves:

3:4a *Did you experience so much for nothing?*

"Are you not ashamed that I should fail to mention all that you experienced for Christ? Indeed, you have shown that all your experiences are now in vain because of your present changeableness."

And lest he seem to have totally despaired of them:

3:4b *if it really was for nothing.*

[39] By saying this he shows that he still has good hope for them, expecting at the same time that they will also keep themselves apart from the forbidden teaching of his opponents.

tum resumit:

qui ergo ministrat uobis Spiritum, et inoperatur uirtutes in uobis,
ex operibus legis aut ex auditu fidei?

et statuens fidem de Spiritus sancti datam fuisse largitate,
5 ostendit eius dignitatem, simul et personae magnitudinem:

sicut 'Abraham (inquit) *credidit Deo, et reputatum est illi ad iusti-*
tiam.'

'omnium (inquit) dixi Abraham apud uos eligantiorem; a quo
et omne uestrum habetur principium. hic igitur, sicut diuina
10 scriptura de eo dicit, per fidem iustitiam adsecutus est.' et, quoniam Iudaei naturae adfinitatem proponentes plus sibi aliquid
uindicare uidebantur, quod nullo modo illis qui ex gentibus erant
adesse poterat, ait:

scitote ergo quoniam [qui] ex fide sunt, [hi sunt filii Abrahae].

15 itaque non delinquit quicumque hos dixerit esse filios Abrahae
et maxime eius familiares secundum iustificationem, qui per fidem
expectant adsequi iustificationem, sicut et ille est adsecutus. et,
ut ne uideretur ipse uiolenter adsecutus, illud confirmare poterat,
dicens:

20 *praeuidens autem scriptura, quoniam ex fide iustificat Deus gentes,*
ante euangelizauit Abrahae, quoniam 'benedicentur in te omnes gentes.'

dictum est in diuina scriptura Abrahae a Deo quoniam uniuersae gentes illi communicabunt in benedictione. nam quod dixit: *benedicentur in te;* hoc est, 'tecum benedicentur, et communi-
25 cabunt tibi benedictionem; principatorem te huius benedictionis
existiment.' diuina igitur scriptura in omnes gentes benedictionem uenire promittit; hoc autem quemadmodum fieri poterit super illos qui extra legem sunt, et cognationi Abrahae minime pertinere uidentur? sed non sola natura propinquitas est, quae hoc il-
30 lis praestare possit; aut illa ratio, qua sub lege minime habeantur.
euidens est enim quoniam non aliter participare eius benedictione
possibile est eos qui extra legem sunt, et secundum progeniem nihil pertinentes ad Abraham, sed si similitudine eius uniuersitatis

---

2 operator *C (corr.) H* ‖ nobis *H** 4 largitatem *C* H* 8 quae (*bef.*
dixi) *add C (corr.)* ‖ eligantior est *C (corr.)* 9 habet *H* ‖ hoc *H* 11
affinitate *H* 12 de illis *H* 14 quia *add C (corr.)* ‖ hi s. f. *A om C H*
17 iustificationem *om C (corr.)* 21 qui (*bef.* ante) *add C H* 25 ut (*bef.*
princip.) *add C (corr.)* 30 posset *C* 31 participari *C (corr.)* 33 si *om H*
‖ similitudinem *C H*

After introducing these words, he resumes his earlier argument:

3:5 *Therefore, the one who supplies you with the Spirit and works miracles among you, was it by the works of the law or by the hearing of faith?*

And declaring that faith had been given and distributed by the Holy Spirit, he shows its worth and at the same time the greatness of the person [who gives it]:

3:6 *Just as "Abraham* (he says) *believed God, and it was reckoned to him as righteousness."*

"I have told you (he says) that Abraham was more distinguished than anyone else, and in him is held your entire first principle. This is because, as divine scripture says of him, he acquired righteousness through faith." And since the Jews were plainly setting forth as some greater claim for themselves natural affinity, because it could by no means be present in those who were Gentiles, he says:

3:7 *Know, therefore, that those who are from faith, these are the sons of Abraham.*

And so whoever would say that those hoping to attain justification through faith, just as Abraham attained it, are Abraham's sons and in a special sense members of his household by justification would not be mistaken. And lest he should seem to have reached this conclusion violently by himself, he was able to establish it by saying:

3:8 *And the scripture, foreseeing that God would justify the Gentiles by faith, declared the gospel beforehand to Abraham, saying, "All the Gentiles shall be blessed in you."*

In divine scripture God told Abraham that all the Gentiles would share with him in his blessing. For he said *they shall be blessed in you*, meaning "they shall be blessed with you [40] and will share the blessing with you. They will regard you as the principal cause of this blessing." Thus, divine scripture promised that the blessing would come to all the Gentiles. But how could this come to pass additionally to those who are outside the law and seem by no means to have any blood relationship with Abraham? But nature is not the only relationship that can make this kinship available to them, nor is that reasoning by which they are held to be by no means under the law of any force. For it is clear that it is impossible for those who are outside the law and have no relation to Abraham by blood descent to share in his blessing in

Deo credunt; et sic per fidem cum eo a Deo potiuntur benedictionem. unde et probationis considerans firmitatem uehementius
instruxit:

> *itaque qui ex fide sunt, benedicentur cum fideli Abraham.*

5   non est possibile aliter extraneos illos constitutos suscipere
communionem ad eum, praeterquam si crediderint eius Deo. et
quia omni ex parte fidem firmam ostendit tam a dato, id est, Spiritu, quam etiam de Abrahae eligantia, et ex illo promisso, quod
a Deo ad illum fuerat factum; ostendit secundum conparationem
10 etiam legis differentiam:

> *quotquot enim ex operibus legis sunt, sub maledicto sunt; sicut*
> *scriptum est: 'maledictus omnis qui non permanet in omnibus quae*
> *scripta sunt in libro legis, ut faciat ea'*

tantum autem abest ut omnes gentes communicare illi in be-
15 nedictionem per opera legis possint, ut et ipsi qui sub lege sunt,
[sub maledicto sint. et] a maledictione liberum esse dicit illum qui
in omnibus permanet, et omnia semper cum omni implet cautela;
hoc autem inpossibile est humanae naturae. non peccare enim nos
nullo modo possibile est. itaque etiamsi aliquis in lege benedica-
20 tur, contra legis id fit decretum, diuina gratia legis definitionem
uincente. deinde ex scriptura iterum firmat illa quae secundum
fidem sunt, intercipiens illa quae in lege sunt:

> *quoniam autem in lege nemo iustificatur apud Deum, manifestum*
> *est; quoniam 'iustus ex fide uiuit.'*

25   euidens est sententia: 'non aliunde iustum quemquam posse
uiuere, et ut aeternorum mercedem promissionum adquirere posset, nisi solum si per fidem potiatur ista.' et confidens firmitate
probationum, ostendit quoniam intercipitur illud quod ex lege est
ab illo quod ex fide est:

30   *lex autem non est ex fide; sed qui fecerit ea, uiuet in eis.*

multa autem est contrarietas. lex enim recta opera exquirit,
et illum qui impleuerit eius, id est, legis decretum, hunc adsequi
promittit illas mercedes; quae exinde promittit, quia nihil accep-

---

3 instruit *H*   4 fide A. *H**   6 propter q. *H**   ‖ et qui *C H*   8 promissio *H*   11 sicut scr. e. m. *om H**   14 habet (*for* abest) *C H*   14-15
benedictione *H* (*corr.*)   15 et ipsi quoque qui (*om* ut) *H* (*corr.*)   16 sub mal.
sint et *om C* H*   ‖ dicat *C* (*corr.*)   18 nobis *C* (*corr.*)   21 uincere *H*   26-27
non (*bef.* posset) *add H* (*corr.*)   28 probationem *C H**   ‖ legem *C*   29 illud
C H   32 eiusdem (*for* eius i. e.) *H*   33 quae (*for* quia) *H**

any way other than by believing in the God of the universe like Abraham. Thus, it is through faith that they gain God's blessing with him. From this argument, taking the firmness of the proof into consideration, he gave his instruction more energetically:

3:9 *And so those who are from faith will be blessed with faithful Abraham.*

It is impossible for those placed outside Abraham's household to take up fellowship with him in any other way than by believing in his God. And he demonstrates that faith is firm in every way as much as by what is given, that is, the Spirit, as also from Abraham's election and on the basis of the promise God made to him. He also demonstrates by comparison the different character of the law:

3:10 *For as many as are from the works of the law are under a curse, for it is written, "Cursed is everyone who does not remain in all the things written in the book of the law to do them."*

[41] And it is so far from the case that all the Gentiles could share with Abraham in the blessing by the works of the law that even those subject to the law are under a curse. And scripture says that the person who remains in all [the commandments] and fulfills all of them with all carefulness is freed from the curse. But this is impossible for human nature, for it is in no way possible for us not to sin. And so even if someone is blessed in the law, this takes place against the law's decree, since divine grace prevails over the law's ruling. Then he again confirms from scripture what has to do with faith as distinct from what is in the law:

3:11 *Now it is evident that no one is justified before God by the law; since "the one who is righteous through faith will live."*

The meaning is clear: "No righteous person whatsoever can be able to live and to gain the reward of eternal promises from any other source unless he obtains them only by faith." Trusting in the validity of his proofs, he demonstrates that what is based on the law is quite distinct from what is based on faith:

3:12 *But the law is not from faith; but whoever does them will live in them.*

There is, then, a great contrast. For the law exacts right deeds, and it promises that the person who fulfills its decrees, that is,

turum dicit, si non primitus illa recte expedierit. qui autem ex fide
potiturus est uitam, manifestum est non de sua directione posse
adquiri eam; sed de diuina gratia debere eum expectare salutem.
erant enim omnia firmitate eius probationis munita, eo quod omni
5 ex parte ualidissimum fidei struxit sermonem; equidem et secundum comparationem excludens illa quae legis erant, et quod inpossibile sit exinde percipere iustificationem. ex abundanti autem
ultra ostendere temptat superfluum illis esse ut secundum legem
uiuant; eo quod locum [nullum] habere uidebatur, postquam illis
10 ea quae praedicta sunt sine ulla struxisse uidebatur controuersia.

†nam et ultra superflua nobis le-   ἄλλως τε καὶ περιττὴ λοιπὸν ἡμῖν
gis est custodia. debitum enim   ἡ τοῦ νόμου τήρησις, φησίν. ὁ γὰρ
quod debebatur legi super cu-   ὠφείλετο τῷ νόμῳ χρέος τῆς φυλα-
stodienda ab omnibus, hoc Chri-   κῆς παρὰ τῶν ἀνθρώπων, τοῦτο ὁ
15 stus persoluit nobis; utpote ho-   Χριστὸς κατέβαλεν ὑπὲρ ἡμῶν.
mo existens secundum quod ui-
debatur, et quod pro nobis suscepit.

cum omni etenim cautela legem   μετὰ γὰρ πάσης αὐτὸν τῆς ἀκρι-
20 impleuit, et quasi quaedam pro   βείας πληρώσας, καὶ ὥσπερ τινὰ
nostra redemptione adpendens,   λύτρα καταβαλὼν ὑπὲρ ἡμῶν, ἐξ-
redemit nos ab eius seruitute, et   ηγόρασέν τε ἡμᾶς τῆς ἐκεῖθεν δου-
a maledicto legis securos esse   λείας, καὶ τῆς ἀπὸ τοῦ νόμου κατ-
per omnia fecit. qualiter, uel   άρας ἀπήλλαξεν. πῶς καὶ τίνι τρό-
25 quomodo?   πῳ;

  factus pro nobis maledictum*   γενόμενος ὑπὲρ ἡμῶν κατάρα.
(scriptum est enim: 'maledictus omnis qui pendet in ligno'); ut in gentibus benedictio Abrahae fieret in Christo Iesu; ut promissionem Spiritus accipiamus per fidem.

30   latius conuenit dicere illum, qui manifestum legentibus cupit
apostoli facere sensum. 'lex (inquit) omnem qui super lignum
pendet maledictum esse existimat; eo quod huiusmodi poena illis statuta est, qui ultimi sceleris rei esse inueniuntur. sed Chri-

---

4 munitae C* H   6 eo (for et) H (corr.)   7 ex in habundanti C ex in habun-
dantia H ex hab. H (corr.)   9 illi (aft. locum) add C* illis C (corr.) ‖ illi H
10 ullam, controversiam C* H*   11 sq. Coisl. 204 f. 24b [Cr. vi. 52]. ἄλλος
δέ φησιν· ἄλλως, κ.τ.λ.   13 legis C* H legi super custodiendae C (corr.)   28-29
spiritus om H*   32 pendit C* H

the law's, will gain those rewards that it promises on the condition that not one of them will be received if he does not first accomplish these deeds rightly. But it is obvious that the one who will gain life on the basis of faith cannot attain it by his own right activity. Rather, he must hope for salvation from divine grace. Now all these points were drawn up to defend the strength of his proof, because he constructed his discussion in every part as the strongest possible defense of faith, cutting out indeed what concerned the law both by comparison and because it is impossible by it to acquire justification. Moreover, over and above what was necessary he tries to show further that it is useless for them [42] to live according to the law, because it plainly had no place after its predictions for them were established beyond question.

†Moreover, keeping the law is from now on useless for us. For *Christ* discharged us from the obligation that was owed under the law concerning what must be kept by all, inasmuch as he existed as a human being according to what was seen, and he undertook this for our sake.

Moreover, keeping the law is from now on useless for us, he says. For *Christ* abolished for us the obligation owed by humans to the law for keeping it.

For he fulfilled the law with all carefulness, and paying the price for our redemption *he redeemed us* (3:13a) from slavery to the law and made us free from its curse in all respects. In what way or how?

For when he had fulfilled the law with all exactitude and had established, as it were, a ransom for us, *he redeemed us* (3:13a) from slavery to the law and delivered us from its curse. How and in what way?

3:13b–14 *by becoming a curse for us**—

3:13b *by becoming a curse for us*

for it is written, "Cursed is everyone who hangs on a tree"—that in Christ Jesus the blessing of Abraham might come to the Gentiles, so that we might receive the promise of the Spirit through faith.

It is right for anyone who wants to make the apostle's meaning clear to the readers to explain this at greater length. [43] "The law (he says) considers everyone who hangs on a tree to be cursed (Deut 21:23), because a punishment of this kind was appointed for those found guilty of the most extreme crime. But Christ, even

stus nihil delinquens—e contrario uero secundum omnem conuersatus cautelam, et neque sententiae mortis reus existens, eo quod
nec aliquid peccauit—patiebatur eos qui se crucifigere et occidere uolebant. et quoniam non iusta ratione puniebatur, omni autem
ex parte iustitia sibi opitulante, liberari a morte iustissime poterat;
exsurrexit quidem ipse a morte, eo quod nec iuste ab ea tenebatur;
in communi uero omnibus spem resurrectionis praestitit. tribuit
etiam nobis et Spiritum sanctum, quem credentes in eum quasi
arram quandam percipimus in spe futurorum; credentes quod et
ipsi aequam resurrectionem simus adsecuti. sicque extra necessitatem legis uicturi sumus, eo quod post illam fidem quae in eo est,
et Spiritus sancti participationem, nihil cum praesenti uita commune habebimus. sed in futuram illam uitam commigrantes, illam
quae a Christo est benedictionem cuncti suscepimus; cuius promissum etiam dudum ad Abraham factum esse uidetur.' nam illud
quod dixit, *ut in gentibus*, et iterum, *ut promissionem*, non quasi ex
causa descendens dixit, sed illud quod sequitur consuete adiecit.
sicque ultra et superflua nobis inuenietur legis custodia; et nullum
locum ex ipsis rebus poterit habere. superfluum et quidem ultra
est; redditum est ei debitum a Christo, quod a nobis debebatur.
locum autem non habens, quoniam res non admittit eos qui semel
transmigrauerunt in futuram uitam praesentis uitae succumbere
negotiis.

   et iterum ad probationem uertitur, ex ipso tempore illorum
ostendens quae ex lege fuerant ista quae fidei sunt honorabiliora
esse:

   fratres, secundum hominem dico; tamen hominis confirmatum te-
stamentum nemo spernit aut superordinat. Abrahae autem dictae sunt
promissiones, et semini eius. non dicit: 'et seminibus,' quasi in multis,
sed quasi in uno: 'et semini tuo,' qui est Christus. hoc autem dico: te-
stamentum, ante confirmatum a Deo in Christum, illa quae post qua-
dringentos et triginta annos facta est lex, non euacuat ad destruendam
promissionem.

7   commune *C* (*corr.*) communione *H*   8   et *om H*   ‖   sanctum *om C*   10
ipse *C**   12-13   communi *C H*   16   ut (*aft.* dixit) *om H*   27   tunc *C* H*
tamen *C* (*corr.*)   30   semine *C** (*bis*)

though he transgressed in nothing at all—but, on the contrary, conducted himself with entire carefulness and was not guilty so as to be sentenced to death, since he sinned in absolutely no way—submitted to those who wanted to crucify and kill him. And since he was punished for no just cause, while instead justice was serving him in every way, he would have been able most justly to be freed from death. Indeed, he rose from death himself because he was not held by it justly. In truth, he supplied all in common with the hope of the resurrection. He also bestowed on us the Holy Spirit. By believing in him we gain in him, as it were, a kind of deposit in the hope of the things to come. And we believe that we have gained a resurrection equal to his. And thus we shall be victors beyond the law's requirements, because after that faith in Christ and our participation in the Holy Spirit we shall have nothing in common with the present life. Instead, passing over to that future life, we have received [44] that universal blessing that comes from Christ and the promise of which had plainly been given to Abraham long ago." For he said that [in Christ Jesus the blessing of Abraham might come] to the Gentiles and that [we might receive] the promise not as though these statements depended upon a cause but because he added what customarily results.[21] And so from now on keeping the law will be found useless for us and can have no place because of these very facts. Indeed, something more is useless. The obligation we owed the law has been paid back to it by Christ. And the law has no place, since this fact does not permit those who have once passed over to the future life to submit to the preoccupations of this life.

Again he turns to his proof, demonstrating from their time of occurrence that what belongs to faith confers greater honor than what had been from the law:

3:15–17 *Brothers, I speak in a human way. Nevertheless, once a person's testament has been ratified, no one scorns it or adds to it. Now the promises were made to Abraham and to his seed; it does not say "and to his seeds," as of many, but it says as of one "and to your seed," who is Christ. And I mean this: the law, which came 430 years later, does not annul a testament previously ratified by God in Christ[22] so as to destroy the promise.*

---

[21] The two instances of "that" (*ut*) in 3:14 indicate result rather than purpose.
[22] The reading reflects the Old Latin version.

ualida probatio, et omnis controuersiae superior: 'hominis (inquit) testamentum neque euoluit quisquam, neque emendat. Deo
autem promittente omnes gentes in Abraham debere benedici et
semine eius (quod et in Christum impletum esse ipsis rebus inuenimus, in quem et omnes credimus, eo quod ex Abraham originem trahit), patrem quoque nobis Abraham adscribimus; et illam
benedictionem, quae a Deo est, expectamus. hancne euoluit lex,
quae post tanto tempore facta est?' et ostendens quoniam secundum legem uiuere contrarium est illi promissioni, quae ad Abraham facta est, adiecit:

*si enim ex lege est hereditas, iam non est ex promissione. Abrahae
uero per repromissionem donauit Deus.*

†'uox illa quae facta est ad   ἡ πρὸς τὸν Ἀβραὰμ φωνὴ ἐπ-
Abraham promissionis est (in-   αγγελίας ἐστίν, φησίν. ὁ δὲ νόμος
quit), quae quasi magnum ali-   κατορθῶσαι ἀπαιτεῖ, καὶ τότε δί-
quid donare ei promittit. lex   δωσιν τὸν μισθόν· ὥστε εἰ μὲν ἀπὸ
autem integritatem uitae exigit,   τοῦ νόμου ταῦτα περιμένομεν, πε-
et tunc dat mercedem. itaque si   ριττὴ ἡ ἐπαγγελία· ὁ γὰρ ἡμέτε-
ex lege haec dari nobis expec-   ρος κάματος καὶ οὐχ ἡ τοῦ Θεοῦ
tamus, superflua est promissio.   ἐπαγγελία τὸν μισθὸν ἡμῖν ἀποδί-
noster enim labor, et non Dei   δωσιν· εἰ δὲ ἡ ἐπαγγελία γεγένηται
promissio mercedem nobis re-   τὴν τοῦ ὑποσχομένου χάριν ἐμφαί-
stituet. si autem promissio fac-   νουσα, οὐκ ἄρα ἡ τοῦ νόμου κατόρ-
ta est quae promittentis gratiam   θωσίς ἐστιν, ἀλλ' ἡ τοῦ θεοῦ ὑπόσ-
demonstraret, non utique legis   χεσις ἡ τὴν κοινωνίαν ἡμῖν τῆς εὐ-
directio est necessaria; sed Dei   λογίας χαριζομένη.
promissio, quae nobis commu-
nionem donat benedictionis.'*

illud autem notare in apostolicis dictis dignum est, quoniam
dixit: *non dicit: 'et seminibus,' quasi in multis; sed, quasi in uno:
'et semini tuo,' qui est Christus.* non quod non possit dictum esse quod dixerit: *et semini tuo,* in commune et de omnibus intellegi, in contentione posuit; sed quoniam facta fuerat ad Abraham
promissio et ad semen eius, ut uniuersae gentes, tam ipsius quam
etiam seminis eius, communicarent benedictionem. praeueniens

---

4 semini *H* ‖ Christo *C (corr.)* 13 sq. Coisl. 204 f. 26 b [Cr. vi. 54,
Fr. 124]. θεόδωρος. ἄλλος πάλιν φησίν· ἡ πρὸς τὸν Ἀβ., κ.τ.λ. 31 quae (*for*
quod) *C** quia *C (corr.)* 33 aut (*bef.* in cont.) add *C H: for. leg.* hoc.

A strong proof and one beyond dispute: "no one (he says) overturns or emends a person's testament. Thus, because of God's promise that all the Gentiles must be blessed in Abraham and his seed (something we find fulfilled by the facts themselves in Christ, in whom we all believe because he takes his origin from Abraham), we also assign Abraham as our father, [45] and we await that blessing that is from God. Did not the law reveal the blessing that became a fact after so great a time?" And to show that living according to the law is contrary to the promise made to Abraham, he added:

3:18 *For if the inheritance is from the law, it no longer is from the promise; but God granted it to Abraham through the promise.*

†That word of promise that came to Abraham, he says, is one that promises to give him something indeed great. But the law requires an upright life and then gives the reward. And so if we expect this to be given us from the law, the promise is useless. For our own toil and not God's promise would restore the reward to us. But if the promise was made to demonstrate the grace of the one who promised, then the guidance of the law is by no means necessary. Rather, God's promise is what gives us our share in the blessing.*

The word addressed to Abraham is one of promise, he says. But the law requires uprightness and then gives the reward, with the result that, if we expect it from the law, the promise is useless, for our own toil and not God's promise would give us the reward. But if the promise took place to demonstrate the grace of the one who promised, then the guidance of the law is nothing. Rather, God's promise is what gives us our share in the blessing.

Moreover, it is worth calling attention to the apostle's words, when he says: *it does not say "and to his seeds," as of many, but it says as of one "and to your seed," who is Christ.* He was not disputing the possibility that the text that reads *to your seed* could be understood in a general sense and of all. But he reads the expression this way because the promise had been made to Abraham that all the Gentiles should share so in his blessing as in his seed's. Anticipating his argument he demonstrates that it

ostendit quoniam inpossibile sit in omnibus gentibus impleri promissionem, nisi per fidem solam. ex rebus ipse iterum probauit,
quoniam per Christum hoc nobis adquisitum est, in quem credentes accepimus Spiritum. et illam familiaritatem quae ad Abraham
5 est per fidem accepimus, promissionis benedictionem adsequentes. uidit scripturarum uoce illud quod rebus ipsis probari poterat, tale aliquid dicens, quoniam

'†et *semini eius* absolute dictum,   τὸ δὲ τῷ σπέρματι αὐτοῦ εἰρημένον
in Christo uerissime inuenimus   οὕτως ἁπλῶς εὑρίσκομεν ἐπὶ τοῦ
10 impletum. hic enim semen qui-   χριστοῦ ἀκριβῶς πληρούμενον· οὗ-
dem est eius secundum natu-   τος γὰρ σπέρμα μὲν αὐτοῦ κατὰ φύ-
ram, sicuti et ceteri qui origi-   σιν, ὡς οὖν καὶ οὐ λοιποὶ οἱ τὸ γέ-
nem exinde trahunt. credimus   νος ἐκεῖθεν κατάγοντες. πιστεύομεν
autem in eum, deinde et Abra-   δὲ ἐπ' αὐτὸν, εἶτα καὶ τὸν Ἀβρα-
15 ham patrem nobis adscribimus;   ὰμ πατέρα ἐπιγραφόμεθα καὶ οὕτως
et sic benedictionis communio-   τῆς εὐλογίας τὴν κοινωνίαν δεχόμε-
nem adsequimur. itaque quod   θα. ὥστε τὸ εἰρημένον ὡς ἐφ' ἑν-
dictum est *quasi in unum*, potest   ός, δυνάμενον δὲ κατὰ κοινοῦ ὡς ἐπὶ
uero et in communi *quasi in mul-*   πολλῶν νοεῖσθαι, τῷ σπέρμα αὐτοῦ
20 *tis* intellegi, eo quod semen eius   εἶναι πάντας τοὺς ἐκεῖθεν τὸ γένος
sunt omnes gentes, qui exinde   κατάγοντας, ἐπὶ τοῦ χριστοῦ κυ-
originem trahunt, in Christum   ρίως ἐπ' αὐτῶν πληρούμενον τῶν
uerissime ex ipsis rebus imple-   πραγμάτων εὑρίσκομεν.
tum esse inuenimus.'*

25   hoc et quidem nos pro maiori cautela notauimus. apostolus uero, eo quod per omnia haec fidem confirmauit, lege eiecta, et euidentem sententiam protulit; quoniam et inpossibile est illud promissum Dei, quod ad Abraham factum est, a lege illa solui, quae
post tanto delata est tempore. illam autem (id est, fidem, uel pro-
30 missum) tenere et erga nos iustum est; siquidem non est lex domi-
na soluere illa, eo quod et multo posterior ab illis esse inuenitur.
   itaque ut ne lex superflua fuisse existimaretur, aut inepte et uane fuisse subintroducta, bene obiecit sibi, quod ab aliis sibi obici
poterat; et soluit illud, quod maxime ambiguitatem facere uideba-
35 tur:

4 illa familiaritate *C H* 5 accipimus *C** 14 dein et *H* 19 σπέρματι, Cr.
Fr. 20 et (*for* eo) *C H* 21 quae *C* (*corr.*) 25 hoc q. et nos *H* 27 et (*bef.*
inposs.) *om C* 29 deleta *C** || idem (*for* id est) *H* || uelut (*for* uel) *C H*

is impossible for the promise to be fulfilled save by faith alone. Once more he proved from the facts that [46] we have acquired this through Christ, since it is by believing in him that we receive the Spirit. And we receive that close relationship with Abraham by attaining the blessing of the promise. He sees in the words of the scriptures what was capable of being proved by the facts themselves and so speaks of something definite, since

†we find the expression *and to his seed* understood singly to have been most truly fulfilled in Christ. For this seed is his by nature, just like the others who also trace their origin from this source. But we believe in him and then appoint Abraham as our father and in this way gain our share in the blessing. And so the expression *as of one* can truly be understood *as of many* because we find that the fact that all the Gentiles who trace their origin from Abraham are his seed is most truly fulfilled in Christ on the basis of the facts themselves.*

We find the expression *to his seed* understood singly to have been fulfilled exactly in Christ. For this seed is his by nature, just like the others who also trace their origin from this source. But we believe in him and then appoint Abraham as father and in this way receive our share in the blessing. As a result, the expression *as of one* can be understood in the general sense *as of many*. We find this properly fulfilled in Christ by the facts themselves because his seed is all those who trace their origin from him.

We have ourselves mentioned this for the sake of greater accuracy. But the apostle also expressed a clear meaning because he confirmed faith by all these considerations, leaving the law to one side. This was because it is impossible that God's promise given to Abraham could be annulled by the law that was handed down after such a long time. But it is right for us to hold fast to that faith or promise inasmuch as the law has no power to annul them, because it originated much later than they did.

And so lest the law be thought to have been useless or to have been slipped in foolishly or in vain, he rightly raised an objection that could have been made by others to his argument. And he resolves the point that seems to make for the greatest possible ambiguity:

quid ergo lex?

†secundum hypocrisin; in 'lege' debet manere. 'sed interrogas (inquit) quae sit legis necessitas, si nunc promissionem et gratiam tenere conueniebat?'

*praeuaricationum causa adiecta est,**

καθ' ὑπόκρισιν ἀναγνωστέον. ἀλλὰ τοῦτο ἐρωτᾶς· τίς ἡ τοῦ νόμου χρεία, εἴπερ δὴ τὴν ἐπαγγελίαν καὶ τὴν χάριν ἔδει κρατεῖν;

τῶν παραβάσεων χάριν προσετέθη.

donec ueniat semen cui promissum est; disposita per angelos in manu mediatoris.

promissio quidem Dei de omnibus gentibus ad Abraham fecta est, sicut de diuina scriptura id discere possibile. quod iam in Christo exitum sumpsisse uidetur. quoniam omnes constituti multa praeuaricamus necessario, nobis lex data est cohibens nos a peccato suis decretis, usque ad tempus illud, quo promissio finem conuenientem adsequatur, uiso eo per quem futurorum bonorum accepturi sumus promissum.

†quod autem dixit: *usquedum ueniat semen cui promissum est;* interiectio est. nam sequentia erat: *quid ergo lex? praeuaricationum causa posita est, disposita per angelos in manu mediatoris;* ut illud quod dixit *disposita* de lege dictum fuisse intellegatur.**

ἄχρις οὗ ἔλθῃ τὸ σπέρμα ᾧ ἐπήγγελται. τοῦτο δὲ παρέγκειται· ἡ γὰρ ἀκολουθία· τί οὖν ὁ νόμος; τῶν παραβάσεων χάριν προσετέθη, διαταγεὶς δι' ἀγγέλων ἐν χειρὶ μεσίτου· ἵνα ᾖ διαταγεὶς ἐπὶ τοῦ νόμου νοούμενον.

sic et illud quod dixit ad Hebraeos, de ipsa dicit lege: *si enim quod per angelos narratum est uerbum, fuit firmum, et omnis praeuaricatio et inoboedientia iustam accepit mercedum retributionem.* dicit autem *per angelos* legem fuisse dispositam, quasi angelis tum ministrantibus, quando lex dabatur. nam et in morte primitiuorum angelum esse dixit Moyses, qui primitiuos Aegyptiorum interfecit. et

1   propter transgressionem posita est *add C H* (v. note)   2   sq. Coisl. 204 f. 26 b [Cr. vi. 55]. καθ' ὑπόκρ. ἀναγν., φησίν· κ.τ.λ. In margin, τοῦ χρυσοστόμου. 3-4   interrogans *C H*   4-5   necesse *C** H*   5   non (*for* nunc) *C H* txt *g*   12 est (*aft.* disc.) *C* (*corr.*)   13   iam (*aft.* exitum) *add C** H*   15   discretis usque ad t. ad i. *C**   21   erit *C*   22   ἀγγέλου Coisl. 204, ἀγγέλων Coisl. 26.

[47] 3:19a *Why then the law?*

†He is acting a part; "law" should remain before the break in the sense.[23] "But you ask (he says) why the law is necessary if it has now become right to hold fast to the promise and grace."

It must be read as though he is acting a part. "But you ask this question: What need is there for the law if it has become necessary to hold fast to the promise and grace?"

3:19b *It was added because of transgressions,* *

3:19b *It was added because of transgressions.*

until the seed would come to whom the promise had been made, and it was ordained through angels by the hand of a mediator.

Indeed, God's promise about all the Gentiles was made to Abraham, just as it is possible to learn this from divine scripture. It already has plainly found its fulfillment in Christ. Since all of us are so constituted that we necessarily commit many transgressions, the law was given us to restrain us from sin by its decrees until that time when the promise should attain its proper end, through which, once it appeared, we were to receive the promise of the good things to come.

†But his statement *until the seed would come to whom the promise had been made* is an insertion. For the logical order was: *Why then the law? It was added because of transgressions, ordained through angels by the hand of a mediator,* so that [48] the word *ordained* is understood to have been spoken of the law.*

Until the seed would come to whom the promise had been made. This is inserted. For the logical order is: *Why then the law? It was added because of transgressions, ordained through angels by the hand of a mediator,* so that *ordained* may be understood of the law.

Thus, what he said in the letter to the Hebrews also refers to the law (Heb 2:2): *For if the word declared through angels was valid, and every transgression and disobedience received a just retribution.* And he says that the law was dispensed *through angels* inasmuch as the angels were ministering at the time when the law was given. For even in the death of the firstborn Moses said it was an angel who

---

[23] "Acting a part" (*secundum hypocrisin,* καθ᾽ ὑπόκρισιν) apparently refers to the imaginary objector. The Latin (*in 'lege' debet manere*) adds the idea that we should not read verse 19 as though it said: "What, then? The law was added because of transgressions…"

de manna beatus Dauid dixit: *panem angelorum manducauit homo,* quasi qui per illos fuerat datus. omnia autem haec ad legis concurrunt datum, nam quod dixit: *in manu mediatoris,* Moysi dicit. et bene adicit:

5   *mediator autem unius non est. Deus autem unus est.*

hoc dicens, quoniam 'Moyses quidem Dei et hominum illorum, qui legem accipiebant, mediator erat. *Deus autem unus est,* idem qui et legem tunc dedit; et nunc illa, quae secundum Christum sunt, excellentiora demonstrauit.' conuenit autem non
10 rerum intendere differentiae, sed operantis dignitatem, sincera mente perspicientes rerum differentiam; et competentem de illis et consentaneam diuino iudicio depromere sententiam, ita ut meliora haec esse reputentur, quae apud uniuersitatis Deum talia esse uidentur. considerandum est hinc etiam illud quod dicebamus,
15 quoniam illa quae secundum Christum sunt, in futuro saeculo ueram adsequentur plenitudinem; quando neque peccare possumus, neque legitimorum indigemus aliquorum. etenim si etiam et fides iam in illis esse uideatur; sed et praeuaricamus, et lege prohibemur peccare. apostolus ergo praeuaricationum gratia legem adpo-
20 sitam esse dixit, quasi quod iam ultra lex in nobis non habeat locum, post Christi aduentum; eo quod neque inpossibile sit nos ultro praeuaricare. quoniam autem secundum praesentem uitam, et post aduentum Christi, subditi adhuc esse uidemur ut delinquamus, et hac de causa legem indigemus; cui et intendentes a delicto,
25 secundum ut possumus, nos extrahere properamus. nemo istis potest contradicere, eo quod interim medii quidam sumus, sicut et in superioribus dixi. secundum fidem quidem in illis iam sumus constituti; commoramur uero in istis adhuc, fratres, naturae mortalitate. unde et apostolus, rerum dignitate considerata, iusta ratione
30 de futuris comprobare properat; eo quod per fidem illa percipimus interim. ideo et fidei rationem modis omnibus comprobare festinat. dicens autem apostolus sufficienter in praecedentibus legis necessitatem, adiecit:

---

7 erant *C**   ‖   unius *H*   9   nos *(for* non) *C (corr.)*   10   differentias et *C (corr.)*   12   ne *(aft.* ut) *add C H*   13   reputantur *C*H*   ‖   apud *om H*   17   sic *(for* etenim si) *H*   19   gratiam *C*H*   24   lege *C (corr.)*   28-29   mortalitatem *C**

slew the firstborn of the Egyptians. And blessed David said of the manna (Ps 77:25) *humans ate the bread of angels*, since it had been given through them. And all these references harmonize with the giving of the law. For when he said *by the hand of a mediator*, he means Moses. And he rightly adds:

3:20 *Now a mediator is not of one, but God is one.*

He says this because "Moses indeed was a mediator between God and those people who received the law. *But God is one,* [49] the same one who both gave the law at that time and now has revealed a more excellent dispensation, that of Christ." And it is right that we should not pay attention to the difference between the two but should discern with a clear mind the importance of the one who effected the different dispensations. And we should set forth a view that recognizes that they are in harmony and consistent with God's judgment so that the dispensation reckoned to be better is seen to be such before the God of the universe. In this connection there must also be considered the point we made, namely, that the dispensation of Christ will attain true fullness in the age to come when we are both unable to sin and without the need of any legal ordinances. The fact is that, even if faith plainly already participates in this fulfillment, yet we both continue to transgress and are kept from sinning by the law. Therefore, the apostle said that the law was imposed for the sake of transgressions inasmuch as the law should now have no further place among us after Christ's coming, but not because it is impossible for us to transgress any more. And because in the present life and after Christ's coming we are plainly still subject to committing transgressions, for this reason we need the law and by attending to it are eager to draw ourselves away from transgression as much as we can. No one can contradict these conclusions because we are indeed for the time being between two ages, as I have said in my earlier comments. By faith we are indeed already established in the age to come, but we still tarry in this age, my brothers, because of the mortality of our nature. This is why the apostle, having taken account of the importance of these matters, hastens by right reasoning to prove the truth of the things to come, because we perceive them by faith for the time being. For this reason he is also eager to prove the truth of the principle of faith [50] in every way. The apostle, then, saying enough about the necessity of the law in the preceding verses, added:

lex ergo aduersus promissa Dei? absit.

haec ergo eius est necessitas, non ut euoluat Dei promissa. ex ipsis rebus ostendens illum esse uerum:

si (inquit) *data fuisset lex quae poterat uiuificare, uere utique ex* 5 *lege esset iustitia. sed conclusit scriptura omnia sub peccato, ut promissio ex fide Iesu Christi detur credentibus.*

†'si quidem talis aliqua uirtus aderat legi, ut illis qui sub se conuersabantur fructum et 10 iustificationis et aeternae uitae conferre posset; intercipere utique promissionem poterat lex, ipsa pro illa praestans nobis iustificationem. nunc uero ex 15 contrario execratur quidem peccatum; liberare uero a peccato non praeualet eos, qui propter naturae infirmitatem corruunt in peccato. per quae hanc ma 20 gis arguit infirmitatem nostram, quam ad iustificationem habemus, immo, ut plenius dicam, inpossibilitatem; ostendens nos necessario indigere Christi gra 25 tiam.*

εἰ γὰρ τοιαύτη τις δύναμις τῷ νόμῳ προσῆν, ὥστε τοὺς ὑπ᾽ αὐτῷ πολιτευομένους καὶ δικαιοῦσθαι καὶ τῆς αἰωνίου δύνασθαι τυγχάνειν ζωῆς, ἀναιρετικὸς ἦν τῆς ἐπαγγελίας ὁ νόμος, αὐτὸς ἀντ᾽ ἐκείνης τὴν δικαίωσιν παρέχων· νυνὶ δὲ τὸ ἐναντίον, ἀπαγορεύων μὲν τὴν ἁμαρτίαν, ἀπαλλάττειν δὲ αὐτῆς οὐκ ἰσχύων τοὺς διὰ τὴν τῆς φύσεως ἀσθένειαν καταπίπτοντας εἰς αὐτήν, καὶ διὰ τούτου μειζόνως ἐλέγχων ἡμῶν τὸ πρὸς δικαίωσιν ἄτονον, μᾶλλον δὲ πάντη ἀδύνατον, ἀναγκαίως τῆς τοῦ Χριστοῦ χάριτος δεομένους δείκνυσιν ἡμᾶς.

cuius maxime fruitionem percepimus, secundum uerum Dei promissum, per fidem illam quae in Christo est; quae sub lege nobis conuersantibus adquiri a nobis minime potuit. haec per illam fidem quam in Christo habemus percipiemus.' ualde concordat hoc 30 in loco dictum *conclusit*, cum illo dicto quod et ad Romanos di-

3 uenturum (*for* uerum) H 7 sq. Coisl. 204 f. 26 b [Cr. vi. 55, Fr. 125]. Θεόδωρος δέ φησω· εἰ γάρ, κ.τ.λ. 9 δικοῦσθαι (*sic*) cod. 10 iustificationes C ǁ et (*aft.* iustif.) *om* C (*corr.*) H 11 possit C* H 12 ὁ ν. αὐτός (*sic*) edd. 19 quem (*for* quae) C H 24-25 gratia C (*corr.*) 27 est (*aft.* lege) *add* C* 28 per f. i. H 30 ad *om* H*

3:21a *Is the law then opposed to the promises of God? Certainly not!*

Therefore, the necessity of the law does not result in overturning God's promises. He shows this to be true on the basis of the facts themselves:

3:21b–22 *For if a law had been given that could make alive, then righteousness would indeed come through the law. But the scripture has imprisoned all things under the power of sin, so that what was promised through faith in Jesus Christ might be given to those who believe.*

†"If indeed there had been such power in the law that those who led their lives under it could reap the fruit both of justification and of eternal life, the law could certainly have taken away the promise, since it instead of the promise would have furnished us with justification. But on the contrary, as it is, the law detests sin but is not strong enough to deliver from sin those who fall into sin because of the weakness of their nature. By these considerations he all the more proves the weakness, indeed to speak more fully, the impossibility we have of attaining justification, demonstrating that we necessarily need Christ's grace.*

For if there had been such power in the law that those who led their lives under it could have gained both justification and eternal life, the law would have taken away the promise by furnishing justification instead of the promise. But on the contrary, as it is, the law condemns sin but is not strong enough to deliver from it those who fall into it because of the weakness of their nature. In this way by all the more proving our incapacity for justification, and still more its total impossibility, he demonstrates that we necessarily need Christ's grace.

We have most fully acquired his benefits according to God's true promise through that faith that is in Christ. What we could in no way have acquired when we led our lives under the law, we shall acquire by the faith we have in Christ."[24] [51] The word *imprisoned* that he uses here fully agrees with what he said to the

---

[24] Following Prof. Cavadini's suggestion, the translation alters Swete's punctuation, starting a new sentence with *quae sub lege* and placing a comma rather than a period after *a nobis minime potuit.*

xit: *conclusit enim Deus omnes in incredulitate.* simile enim est et
uoce et negotio. illic enim secundum hoc dicit nos esse conclu-
sos, secundum quod in praesenti saeculo infirmitas nostra arguitur; tunc uero Dei potiemur misericordiam. quod maxime cogno-
5 scere quis poterit, cautius si nostram decurrere uoluerit interpretationem, in qua latius id explicasse uidemur. et hoc in loco hoc
dicit quoniam 'infirmitas nostra ostensa est illa lege quae dudum
data est, eo quod dirigere illud quod nobis conueniens est non possumus. in quantum enim lex peccata cauere decernit, tanto magis
10 scientes eius prauitatem cogimur propriam sentire infirmitatem,
eo quod non possumus agere illud quod nobis bonum esse uidetur;
ita ut ex ipsa comparatione Dei in nos maior adpareat gratia, qui
nobis fecit inesse cum omni facilitate, quod ipsi nobis nec cum labore maximo adquirere potuimus securi, et quidem scientes quo-
15 niam malum est peccare. quod et cauere ualde uolumus, eo quod
ipsa lex nobis ostendit; sed non possumus id expedire, fratres, naturae infirmitate.'

ad suam iterum sequentiam recurrit apostolus. ostendit quidem legis utilitatem, ex cuius comparatione magnitudinem eorum
20 publicat quae sunt secundum Christum.

priusquam ueniret (inquit) *fides, sub lege custodiebamur conclusi in*
eam fidem, quae incipiebat reuelari.

†notandum est in his illud   ἐπισημαντέον ἐκεῖνο, ὅτι τῶν
maxime, quod multis utile esse   κατὰ Χριστὸν ποιεῖται μὲν ἀπὸ τῶν
25 uidetur (illis tamen qui sciunt),   μελλόντων ὡς εἰκὸς τὴν ἀπόδειξιν,
quoniam illorum quae secun-   ἐπειδὴ πᾶσα τῶν παρ' αὐτοῦ κατορ-
dum Christum sunt de illis quae   θωμάτων ἡμῖν ἡ φανέρωσις ἐπὶ τῶν
futura sunt facit probationem;   πραγμάτων γίνεται τότε.
eo quod et uniuersa illa quae ab
30 eo directa sunt, tunc nobis rebus ipsis erunt manifesta.*

complectitur uero cum illis fidei simul et promissionis uocabulum,
nec non et gratiam, sic illa nominans. et in his omnibus examinat
illa.

35 †uocat autem ista 'fidem' qui-   καλεῖ δὲ πίστιν μέν, ἐπειδὴ μηδέ-

---

9 peccati *C*   12   magis (*for* maior) *C* (*corr.*)   13   facultate *H*   17   infirmitatem *C**   23   inquit (*aft.* est) *add C H* ‖ sq. Coisl. 204 f. 28 b [Cr. vi. 57,
Fr. 125]. θεοδώρου. ἐπισημαντέον, κ.τ.λ.   27   qui (*for* quae) *H*   33   illam (*for*
illa) 1°, *C* (*corr.*) 2°, *C*   35   istam *C H*

Romans (Rom 11:32): *For God has imprisoned all in disbelief.* The two passages are alike both in their words and in their subjects. For there he says that we are imprisoned because our weakness in the present age is to blame, but then we shall obtain God's mercy. Anyone can understand this most fully if he is willing quite carefully to consult our commentary in which we plainly explained this at greater length. In this passage he means that "our weakness is demonstrated by that law given long ago, because we are unable to direct ourselves to what is right for us. For to the degree that the law decrees the avoidance of sins, by so much the more are we compelled to have a sense of our weakness by knowing its wickedness, because we cannot do what seems good to us. And so the law's purpose is that God's grace may seem greater in our eyes by contrast, since he implanted in us with great ease a sense that of ourselves we are unable to be confident of acquiring the ability to do the good even with the greatest toil because we indeed know that it is evil to sin. We strongly want to avoid sin because the law itself shows us what it is, but we are unable to accomplish this, brothers, because of the weakness of our nature."

Now the apostle turns back to the logical order of his argument. He does demonstrate the law's usefulness. But by contrast with it he makes known the greatness of Christ's dispensation.

3:23 *Now before faith came* (he says) *we were guarded under the law, imprisoned for that faith which was beginning to be revealed.*

†What must be especially noted in these words is what seems to many to be useful (at least to those who know), namely, that [52] he is giving a proof of Christ's dispensation from what is to come, since all that has been accomplished by him will at that time be clear to us by the facts themselves.*

It must be noted that he is, as it seems, giving a proof of Christ's dispensation from what is to come, since the entire manifestation of what he accomplished for us will take place in fact at that time.

In fact, he includes in this simultaneously with faith also the idea of the promise and indeed grace, indicating them in this way. And he considers Christ's dispensation under all these terms.

dem eo quod necdum rebus ipsis in illis sumus, sed interim
credimus de illis; 'promissionem' uero, eo quod iam de il-
5 lis promissionem adsecuti fuerimus; et 'gratiam' iure illa nominat, eo quod donum quoddam euidens est Dei quod nobis tribuitur, non de nostro me-
10 rito, sed de illius liberalitate habens principium. discutit uero
cum illis omnibus iusta ratione
legem conferens.*

πω γεγονότες ἐπὶ τῶν πραγμάτων,
πιστεύομεν τέως περὶ αὐτῶν, ἐπαγγελίαν δέ, ὡς ἂν τὴν περὶ αὐτῶν ὑπόσχεσιν ἤδη κεκομισμένων
ἡμῶν, καὶ χάριν δὲ εἰκότως αὐτὰ ὀνομάζει μάλιστα, ἐπειδὴ δω-
ρεὰ σαφής τις τοῦ θεοῦ ἐστιν τὰ
διδόμενα, οὐκ ἀπὸ τῆς ἡμετέρας
ἀξίας, ἀλλ᾽ ἀπὸ τῆς αὐτοῦ φιλοτιμίας ἔχοντα τὴν ἀρχήν· ἀντιπαρεξε-
τάζει δὲ τὸν νόμον πᾶσιν εἰκότως.

siue enim futura quis examinare uoluerit, quando ipsa rerum fit
15 demonstratio, superflua est lex; eo quod nullum tunc indigemus
praeceptum, quando per diuinam gratiam excepto omni seruamur
peccato. siue quis fidem examinans aut promissionem aut gratiam,
comparare illis uoluerit legem, superflua lex inuenietur, istis uim
suam uindicantibus; eo quod, lege extante, nihil adsequi boni pos-
20 sibile est, si non primitus uitam suam quis direxerit secundum legis decretum. et superflua erit fides, si haec ita se habent. superflua autem erit et promissio; eo quod nihil eos adiuuare poterit,
si non legitima custodierint. et gratia quoque nullum habebit locum, si legitima conuersatio a nobis scrupulose est exquirenda. si
25 autem et credentes iustificamur, et promissae ad nos promissiones
confessam bonorum accipiunt consummationem, uacat omnis legis dirigendae sollicitudo; Domino Deo iustificationem nobis sua
misericordia per fidem donante, secundum suum promissum. unde et apostolus frequenter fidem gratiam nominans manifestus est.
30 et sicut dixi, sicuti et in praesenti epistola inperfectioribus dicit:
*miror quod sic cito transferimini ab eo qui uocauit uos in gratiam Chri-
sti;* similiter itaque et in praesenti sermone nominat 'fidem,' hoc
dicens quoniam 'ante Christi aduentum, et priusquam nobis ista
adessent quae nunc adquisita sunt per eum, eramus sub legis doc-
35 trina custoditi, ita ut possemus ista tempore adsequi competenti.

1-4   necdum—uero *om (per homoeotel.)* H*   6   illam C illi H   7   bonum (*for*
donum) H   16   seruamus H   24   legitime C H   26   omnes leges C*   29
suam (*for* fidem) C H   30   inperfectionibus C*   33   dominum [dn̄m] (*for*
quoniam [qn̄m]) C H   34-35   doctrinam H   35   possimus C*

†And he calls it "faith" because we do not yet exist in it by the facts themselves, but for the time being we believe in it. And he calls it "promise" because we have already received the promise of it. And he rightly names it "grace" because it is clear that it is given us as some kind of gift of God, not for our merit, but because of his generosity. In fact, by all these, making his comparison by right reason, he overturns the law.*

And he calls it "faith" since we have not yet come to be in the facts, but for the time being we have faith in them. And he calls it "promise" since we have already received the guarantee of them. And he rightly names them especially "grace" since what has been given is a clear gift of God, not based on our worth, but one that has its principle in his generosity. And he rightly contrasts the law with all of them.

For if anyone should be willing to consider what is to come, when the demonstration of the facts will itself take place, the law is useless because we shall need no commandment at that time when we are saved by divine grace with all sin excluded. Or if anyone in considering faith or the promise or grace should be willing to compare the law to them, the law will be found useless, since these assert their own power. This is because while the law exists it is possible to attain nothing of the good unless someone has guided his life from start to finish according to the law's decrees. And faith would be useless if this were the case. The promise, too, would be useless because nothing could help them if they did not keep the law's ordinances. Grace also would have no place if we are required to live our lives scrupulously in a legal fashion. But if by believing we are justified and the promises made to us receive the acknowledged consummation of good things, all care for the law's direction goes away, [53] since the Lord God gives us justification by his mercy through faith according to his promise. This is why the apostle frequently indicates faith by mentioning grace. And as I have said [elsewhere], so in this letter he says in a rather incomplete way (1:6) *I am astonished that you are so quickly changed from the one who called you in the grace of Christ.* And so similarly in his present discussion he mentions "faith" (3:23), meaning that, "before Christ's coming and before those things were present to

uirtutum enim doctrina et diuinae cognitionis communicatio secundum [legem] diuinam nobis aderant; et prophetarum prophetiae a longo tempore nos praemonebant expectare Christum, aptos
nos ad eorum susceptionem esse facientes, ita ut illorum instructi
5 doctrina, nullam inesse nouitatem in his quae postea manifesta-
bantur aestimaremus, nihilque esse extraneum aut nouum de illis
reputaremus, quae praeter omnem accidebant spem. ex nobis etenim qui sub lege eramus, adparuit Christus, et nos primos habuit
in se credentes; sicque ex nobis in omnes homines suam defundere
10 fecit cognitionem. quae tamquam uia quidem extitit omnibus qui
eum susceperunt, illa quae in lege et prophetis scripta erant de eo;
unum quidem, quia segregati eramus nos a ceterorum permixtione per legis doctrinam; ita ut pii seruati opportuni esse uideremur
illa quae secundum Christum sunt suscipere. nam prophetis ante
15 multorum temporum spatia id praedicantibus, cognoscentes ante
exitum negotii illa quae secundum Christum sunt iam uidemus,
sicque illa recipimus postquam facta sunt.' in euangeliis et quidem
uidetur ad Petrum Andreas frater eius dixisse: *quem scripsit Moy-*
ses in lege, et prophetae, inuenimus Messiam, qui est Christus. magis
20 quoque aduenientibus, dum Herodes legisperitos interrogaret, re-
sponderunt ei quoniam in Bethleem eundem uenturum expectant
secundum propheticam uocem. et multa huiusmodi inueniet quis
in euangeliis inserta. quibus unusquisque a primordio denuntiatione praecedentium prophetarum de Christo instructus, praedi-
25 cationem euangeliorum uisus est suscepisse; eo quod et dudum et
ex longo tempore ab illis id fieri sperabatur, fratres. quod bene dicit apostolus:

    itaque lex paedagogus noster fuit in Christo, ut ex fide iustificemur.

    'iustificatio igitur ista et bonorum omnium caput Christi exti-
30 tit aduentus. ex quo et resurrectionem percepimus, et inmortalem
uitam potiti sumus. in qua existentes, ultra non peccabimus; sed
in multa constituti delectatione custodiemur, affectum erga Deum
inlibatum seruantes, et nullum occursum tristitiae sustinentes. lex

1 uirtutem *C** ‖ diuini *C H* 2 legem *om C H* 4 eius (*for* eorum) *C*
(*corr.*) 6 aestimaret nos *C H* 7 accedebant *C* [cf. Hild. *Apul.* i. 316] 9
difundere *C* (*corr.*) *H* (*corr.*) 13 pii s. oportune *C* H* pie s. oportuni *C* (*corr.*)
[oport. (*passim*) *C H*] 15 id spatia *H* (*corr.*) 26 fratres *om C* (*corr.*) 29
ergo (*for* igitur) *H* 32 delectione *C** 33 tristitia *C** tristitiam *H*

us that we have now acquired through him, we were guarded under the law's teaching so that we could acquire them at the suitable time. For the teaching of virtues and the impartation of knowledge of God were present to us by God's gift.[25] And the prophets' prophecies from time long gone admonished us ahead of time to await Christ by making ourselves fit to receive him. This happened so that, instructed by their teaching, we might not suppose there to be any novelty in what was afterwards manifested and might consider that nothing in what took place above all hope was foreign or novel. Indeed, Christ appeared for those of us who were under the law and had us as the first to believe in him. And so it was from us that he made knowledge [of the gospel] spread to all people. What was written in the Law and the Prophets about him concerned the way that has come to exist for all who have received him. Indeed, the only reason that we were separated [54] from association with the others by the law's teaching was so that we might plainly be kept godly and available to receive Christ's dispensation. For since the prophets long ago predicted this, we were already aware of Christ's dispensation and knew about it before its fulfillment, and so we accepted it after it took place." Indeed, in the Gospel, Andrew, Peter's brother, plainly said to him (John 1:41, 45): *The one about whom Moses wrote in the Law and also the Prophets, we have found him, the Messiah who is Christ.*[26] Also when the wise men came and Herod questioned the experts in the law, they answered him that they expected Christ to come in Bethlehem according to the prophetic word (Matt 2:4). Anyone will find many examples of this kind included in the Gospels. Each one of the Evangelists, instructed from the earliest proclamation of Christ by the prophets who came before them, clearly took up their predictions, since of old and for a long time they kept on hoping this would take place, brothers. This is what the apostle rightly says:

3:24 *And so the law was our pedagogue to Christ, so that we might be justified by faith.*

"Therefore, that justification and Christ's coming as the head of all good things came into existence. By it we have also gained

---

[25] I have supplied "gift," following Swete's suggestion (1:53).

[26] The citation conflates what Andrew says in 1:41 with what Philip says in 1:45.

autem bona est, quae paedagogi locum implens ad ista nos perdu-
xit, et sua doctrina horum nobis manifestauit aduentum. itaque et
utilis est nobis, eo quod ad magnitudinem istorum nos perducere
ualuit. et ut nec esset ultra, iustum est, eo quod intentio eius fine
5 conclusa est; aduentu rerum perfectarum finem est consecuta.'

ualde huc mirifice legem laudauit, et magnitudinem gratiae supereminentem publicauit. quod et magis ostendit, paedagogum
uocans legem. nam paedagogi utiles quidem sunt puerulis paruu-
lis propter paruulitatem eorum. non sunt autem necessarii, quan-
10 do puer in usu effectus ad perfectam profecerit doctrinam. quoniam autem sufficienter legis utilitatem ostendit, temptat ultra ex
comparatione etiam gratiae publicare magnitudinem, simul comprobans ex his, quoniam ultra locum non habent illa tenere:
ueniente autem fide, iam non sumus sub paedagogo.
15 quare?
omnes enim filii Dei estis per fidem, quae est in Christo Iesu.

†hoc est ut dicat, 'perfec- ἀντὶ τοῦ εἰπεῖν τέλειοι· τοῦτο
ti estis.' hoc enim erat conse- γὰρ ἀκόλουθον πρὸς τὸ ὑπὸ παιδα-
quens, ut post paedagogi me- γωγόν, τὸ υἱοὶ θεοῦ εἰπεῖν. τῷ γὰρ
20 moriam, filios Dei diceret. filio υἱῷ τοῦ θεοῦ οὐδὲν λείπει πρὸς τε-
enim Dei nihil minus est, quo λειότητα.
non sit perfectus.*

sed quoniam probationem filiorum adoptionis inmortalitatem
diuina scit esse scriptura, et quod non decet filios Dei mori, si-
25 cut et Dauid in psalmis dicit: *ego dixi: dii estis, et filii Excelsi omnes; uos autem sicut homines moriemini,* quasi quia non deceat mori
illos qui filii Dei nuncupati sunt; quod nullo modo illis accidere
fas erat, si uirtutibus donatam sibi adoptionem filiorum custodire uoluissent; ideo filiorum adoptionem apostolus resurrectionem
30 esse dicit, eo quod inmortales erimus tunc—secundum hoc enim

3 nobis *om* C (*corr.*) H 4 ne cesset H (*corr.*) 6 ualde hoc C (*corr.*) 10
perfecerit H 17 sq. Coisl. 204 f. 28 b [Cr. vi. 58, Fr. 125]. θεόδωρος (marg)

the resurrection and acquired immortal life. By existing in it we shall no longer sin but shall be kept steadfast in great joy, keeping our affection for God undiminished and giving way to no assault of misfortune. But the law is good because by filling the office of a pedagogue it has guided us to these things, and its teaching about them has manifested to us their coming. And so it is useful to us because it [55] had the power to lead us to the greatness of those things. And it is right that it should no longer be, because its purpose has been completed by its end; it achieved its end by the coming of perfect things."

To this degree he strongly and remarkably praised the law and also proclaimed the surpassing excellence and greatness of grace. He demonstrated this all the more by calling the law a pedagogue, for pedagogues are indeed useful to small children because of their immaturity. But they are not necessary when a boy brought up by practice progresses to perfect teaching. And since he has sufficiently demonstrated the usefulness of the law, he makes a further attempt to proclaim by comparison the greatness of grace, at the same time proving on this basis that the law's ordinances have no further place to hold:

3:25 *But now that faith has come, we are no longer subject to a pedagogue.*

Why?

3:26 *For you are all sons of God through faith that is in Christ Jesus.*

†This means "you are perfect." For it was in logical order, after mentioning the pedagogue, for him to say *sons of God*. For there is nothing missing for a son of God by which he may not be perfect.*

Instead of saying "perfect." For it was in logical order to say *sons of God* after *subject to a pedagogue*. For there is nothing lacking in perfection for a son of God.

But divine scripture knows that immortality is the proof of the adoption of sons and that it is not fitting for the sons of God to die, as David says in the psalm (Ps 81:6–7): *I said, "You are gods and all of you sons of the Most High, but you shall die like human beings."* He says this inasmuch as it is not fitting that those [56] who are called sons of God should die, because it was in no way right for this to happen to them if they had been willing by their virtues to keep the adoption of sons given them. For this reason the apostle says

et in baptismate filiorum adoptionem adsequi dicimur, secundum quod in baptismi primitias suscepimus, formam in eodem baptismate mortis quoque et resurrectionis implentes. sic enim et ad Romanos scribens dicit: *non solum autem, sed et ipsi primitias Spiritus habentes nos ipsi in nobis ipsis ingemiscimus, filiorum adoptionem expectantes, redemptionem corporis nostri;* filiorum adoptionem uerum uocans, eo quod tunc post resurrectionem inmortales effecti permanebimus. sic et in hoc loco dicit quoniam 'credentes in Christum filii Dei facti estis;' hoc est, 'a morte extitistis securi, et ab omni passione liberi.' qui autem huiusmodi sunt, perfecti (ut fas est) effecti, ultra non poterunt peccare, inmortalitatem semel potiti. lex autem quae paedagogi locum implebat, in his qui huiusmodi sunt locum habere non poterat. quid enim est quod minus illis possit esse, quod et a paedagogo adsequi possint? 'itaque neque inmortalibus uobis iam factis locum legitima obseruatio in uobis poterit habere; illa enim corporalia sunt mandata, quae et ad praesentem hanc et temporalem uitam competere uidentur.' et quoniam ista in futuro erunt saeculo, nunc autem illa necdum potiti sumus, nisi solummodo in forma; ideo ad baptismatis transit rationem, in quo illorum forma suscepta est, et quasi iam de confessis apud eosdem rebus baptismi referat uirtutem:

> *quotquot* (inquit) *in Christo baptizati estis, Christum induistis; non est Iudaeus neque gentilis; non est seruus neque liber, non est masculus neque femina; omnes enim uos unum estis in Christo Iesu.*

quod dicit tale est:

†'praesentis uitae principium omnium Adam extitit. residui uero homines, omnes quicumque in praesenti uita nati esse noscuntur, communem ab illo habuerunt essentiam. ratione autem naturae, unus homo omnes sumus; ad communem enim

τῆς παρούσης ζωῆς ἀρχὴ μὲν τοῖς πᾶσιν ὁ Ἀδάμ. εἷς δὲ ἄνθρωπος οἱ πάντες ἐσμὲν τῷ λόγῳ τῆς φύσεως, πρὸς γὰρ δὴ τὸ κοινὸν ὡσπερεὶ μέλους τάξιν ὁ καθεῖς ἡμῶν ἐπέχει·

---

1 adoptionem *om H* * ins* (*bef.* fil.) *H* (*corr.*) 2 in (*bef.* bapt.) *om C* (*corr.*) 3 quique *C** 6-7 ueram *C om H* 7 nunc (*for* tunc) *C* 11 inmortalitate *C* (*corr.*) 12-14 locum—paedagogo *om H.* 16 illa (*bef.* habere) *add H* 18 quo (*for* quoniam) *C* ‖ nunciauit (*aft.* saeculo) *add H* (*corr.*) 21 hisdem (*for* eosd.) *C H* 26 sq. Coisl. 204, f. 29 a, b [Cr. vi. 59, 60, Fr. 125, 126]. Θεόδωρος. ἄλλος τις τὸ αὐτὸ ῥητὸν οὕτως λέγει· τῆς παρ., κ.τ.λ. 31 rationem *H*

that the adoption of sons is the resurrection, because it is at that time that we shall be immortal. It is according to this that we are also said to acquire the adoption of sons in baptism, because we receive its firstfruits in baptism when we fulfill the type of both death and resurrection in that same baptism. For he also says this when writing to the Romans (8:23): *and not only the creation, but we ourselves, who have the firstfruits of the Spirit, groan inwardly while we wait for the adoption of sons, the redemption of our bodies.* He calls this the true adoption of sons because at that time after the resurrection we shall remain fashioned immortal. So also in this passage he says that "by believing in Christ you have been made sons of God"; that is, "you have taken an existence immune from death and free from all passion." Those who are like this have been made perfect (as is right); they can no longer sin once they have acquired immortality. But the law that used to fill the office of a pedagogue could not have had a place in things of this kind. Why is it, then, that it is not at all possible for them to be able to attain this by a pedagogue? "And so the observation of the law's ordinances cannot have any place in you once you have been made immortal, for they are bodily commands that appear suitable for this present temporal life." And since those things will come to pass in the age to come, we have not yet now gained possession of them save only in type. For this reason he goes on to the meaning of baptism in which the type of those things is received, as if he had not already referred to the power of baptism in speaking of the things confessed by them:

3:27–28 *As many of you as were baptized into Christ have clothed yourselves with Christ. There is neither Jew nor Gentile, there is neither slave nor free, there is neither male nor female; for all of you are one in Christ Jesus.*

[57] What he means is this:

†"Adam stands as the beginning of the present life for everyone. In fact, other humans, all those whatsoever who are known to be born in this present life, have taken their common essence from him. And by the principle of nature we are all one human being, for each one of us plainly

Adam is the beginning of the present life for everyone. All of us are one human being by the principle of nature, for each one of us holds his rank as a member in what is common.

humanitatem, tamquam mem-
bri alicuius ordinem unusquisque nostrum implere uidetur.
sic itaque et in futura uita il-
5 la inmortali, quae post resurrectionem erit, principium quidem
uitae illius est in Christo. omnes
autem qui communicamus ei et
in resurrectione et in inmorta-
10 litate illa quae post resurrectionem est, tamquam unus efficimur ad eum, dum similitudine rerum membri ordinem unusquisque nostrum obtinere ui-
15 detur ad illum quod commune
est.

οὕτως δὴ καὶ ἐπὶ τῆς μελλούσης
ζωῆς ἀρχὴ μὲν ὁ Χριστός, πάντες
δὲ οἱ κοινωνοῦντες αὐτῷ τῆς ἀναστάσεως καὶ τῆς μετὰ τὴν ἀνάστασιν
ἀθανασίας ὥσπερ εἷς γινόμεθα πρὸς
αὐτόν, τῇ ὁμοιότητι τοῦ πράγματος μέλους τάξιν πρὸς τὸ κοινὸν τοῦ
καθ' ἕνα ἡμῶν ἐπέχοντες.

tunc igitur *neque masculus, ne-*
que femina uidebitur: non enim
est nubere aut nuptu tradi. *ne-*
20 *que Iudaeus, neque gentilis:* non
enim locum habet circumcisio
in inmortali natura; neque discernere quisquam poterit cir-
cumcisum ab eo qui praepu-
25 tium habet. *neque seruus, neque*
liber: omnis enim rerum uarie-
tas erit tunc interempta.'

τότε τοίνυν οὔτε ἄρσεν οὔτε θῆ-
λυ θεωρεῖται, οὐ γάρ ἐστιν γαμῆ-
σαι ἢ γαμηθῆναι· οὔτε Ἰουδαῖος οὔτε Ἕλλην, οὐδὲ γὰρ περιτομὴ ἐν
ἀθανάτῳ φύσει χώραν ἔχει, ὥστε
διακριθῆναι περιτετμημένου ἀκρό-
βυστον· οὔτε δοῦλος οὔτε ἐλεύθε-
ρος, πᾶσα γὰρ ἀνωμαλία πραγμάτων ἀνήρηται.

quia ergo secundum formam
per baptisma in illis efficimur,
30 hoc dicit*

ἐπειδὴ τοίνυν κατὰ τύπον διὰ
τοῦ βαπτίσματος ἐν ἐκείνοις γινόμεθα, τοῦτο λέγει.

quoniam *in Christo baptizati, induti estis Christum:* hoc est, 'participes estis effecti inmortalis eius naturae; ut hoc uideamini existentes quod ille est post resurrectionem, ita ut Christus in omnibus uobis uideatur, nulla in uobis uisa discretione.' si igitur et
35 unus omnes homines sumus, caput nobis adscribentes Christum,

9 in resurrectionem et inmortalitatem illa *H* 12-13 similitudinem *C* H* 19
esse (*for* est) *C* H* 22 περιτετμημένον Cr. 26 omnes *C** 31 estis induti *H*
31-32 participati *H* 32 inmortali *H* 34 uid. uobis *H* ‖ discretionem
C* discretus *H*

fulfills his rank in the common humanity as members of one another.

So it will also be in that future immortal life that will come to pass after the resurrection, and the beginning of that life is indeed in Christ. And all of us who share with him both in the resurrection and in that immortality that follows the resurrection will be made as one with him, while by the actual likeness each one of us will be seen to obtain our rank as a member in relation to what is common to all. Therefore, at that time there will be seen *neither male nor female*, for there will be neither marrying nor giving in marriage; *neither Jew nor Gentile*, for circumcision has no place in immortal nature, nor could anyone distinguish a circumcised man from an uncircumcised; *neither slave nor free*, for all diversity of circumstance will then be done away."

So, too, Christ is the beginning for the life to come, and all of us who share with him in the resurrection and the immortality following the resurrection shall be one with him, having by actual likeness the rank of individual members in relation to what is common to all.

Therefore, at that time there will be seen *neither male nor female*, for there is neither marrying nor giving in marriage; *neither Jew nor Greek*, for circumcision has no place in immortal nature so that uncircumcision could be distinguished from circumcision; *neither slave nor free*, for all diversity of circumstance will be done away.

[58] Therefore, because according to the type through baptism we are brought into these things,*

Therefore, he says this since we come to be in that state according to the type through baptism.

he says that since you *were baptized into Christ, you have clothed yourselves with Christ*: that is, "you have been made partakers of his immortal nature, so that by this you may appear as what he is after his resurrection in such a way that Christ may be seen in all of you with no division appearing among you." If, therefore, all of us humans are one, ascribing Christ as our head, we are also held to be brought to perfection in a certain single body (as is

et in uno quodam (ut fas est) corpore consummati habemur; sicuti
et alibi dicit: *uos estis corpus Christi et membra de membro.* et alibi euidentius similitudinem quam habebimus ad eum significans,
dicit: *quoniam quos praesciuit, praeordinauit conformes fieri imagi-*
5 *nis Filii sui.* etenim si multum omnibus nobis praecellit, et differt
honore et dignitate (eo quod ab omnibus adorabitur); sed secundum rationem resurrectionis et inmortalitatis, per gratiam et nos
ad eum suscipimus similitudinem.

et optime dixit quoniam unus sumus omnes, per eam copula-
10 tionem quam habemus in Christo, unde et adiecit:

si autem uos Christi, utique Abrahae semen estis; et secundum pro-
missionem heredes.

admirabilis uirtus sermonis! paulo etenim minus comprobauit
quoniam et naturaliter filii Abraham facti essent.

15 †'si enim uos corpus Christi   εἰ γὰρ ὑμεῖς τοῦ Χριστοῦ σῶμα διὰ
propter regenerationem illam   τὴν ἐπὶ τοῦ βαπτίσματος ἀναγέννη-
quam in baptismate estis con-   σιν τύπον ἔχουσαν τῆς τότε παρεσο-
secuti, quae formam habet il-   μένης ὑμῖν πρὸς αὐτὸν ὁμοιότητος,
lius similitudinis quae tunc uo-   ὁ δὲ Χριστὸς τοῦ Ἀβραὰμ σπέρμα·
20 bis erit ad eum; Christus au-   ἀνάγκη καὶ ὑμᾶς, τὸ ἐκείνου σῶμα,
tem est Abrahae semen; neces-   τούτου εἶναι σπέρμα οὗπερ δὴ κά-
sarium est et uos quoque, eius   κεῖνος·
corpus, huius esse semen, cuius
est et ille.*

25 alioquin inpossibile est unum esse corpore, et existimare caput
quidem alterius esse, residuum uero corpus alterius.

†unde iusta ratione et promis-   ὅθεν εἰκότως καὶ τῆς ἐπαγγελίας
sionis heredes facti estis.*   κληρονόμοι.

sicut enim ad illum qui ex eo est copulationem accepistis, in id ip-
30 sum ei reputamini necessario, et horum eritis heredes; quoniam et
illi participati estis promissionibus illis quae ad illum factae sunt a
Deo, patrem quidem eundem adscribentes uobis, benedictionem
uero a Deo consequenter illis promissionibus quae ad eum factae
sunt iure et ipsi accipientes.'

35 horum quidem dictorum fortitudinem, et quod sine ulla con-

---

1 habemus *H*   6 se (*for* sed) *H*   10 adicit *C*   22 que (*for* quoque) *C** qui
C (*corr.*): *adding* estis *aft.* corp.   25 corpus *C* (*corr.*)   26 quidem *om H**   27
iusta rationem *C** iuxta r. *H*   30 ei *om H**   32 patre *C*   34 ipse *C**

right). He says the same thing elsewhere (1 Cor 12:27): *You are the body of Christ and individually members of it*. And in another passage to indicate more clearly the likeness we have to him, he says (Rom 8:29): *For those whom he foreknew he also predestined to be conformed to the image of his Son*. For even if he greatly excels all of us and differs from us in honor and worth (because he will be worshiped by all), yet according to the principle of resurrection and immortality we have ourselves received likeness to him through grace.

[59] And he said most effectively that we are all one by that union we have in Christ. For this reason he added:

3:29 *And if you belong to Christ, then you are Abraham's seed and heirs according to the promise.*

What an admirably powerful statement! He has all but proved that they have been made Abraham's sons by nature.

†"For if you have attained the body of Christ because of that regeneration in baptism, which holds the type of that likeness that will be yours with him at that future time, and if Christ is Abraham's seed, it necessarily follows that you, his body, are also the seed of him whose seed he is.*

For if you are the body of Christ because of the regeneration of baptism, which has the type of the likeness to him that will then be yours, and if Christ is Abraham's seed, it necessarily follows that you as his body are also the seed of him whose seed he is.

Otherwise, it would be impossible for them to be one in body, and one might suppose the head to be of one and the rest of the body of another.

†Thus, with good reason you have also been made heirs of the promise.*

Thus, you are rightly also heirs of the promise.

For just as you have received union with that which is from him, you are necessarily reckoned to be in a condition the same as his and will come to be heirs of it. This is because you are those who have shared in those promises God made to him, ascribing to yourselves the same Father and receiving yourselves in truth God's blessing that follows those promises made to him by oath."

No one could ever marvel enough at the boldness of these

trouersia dictum habeatur, nemo digne umquam poterit demira-
re. praestabat enim eis et ad illorum sensum, qui aestimabantur
per uim fuisse ab eo adtracti, abundantem probationem simul et
confirmationem baptismatis ab inoperatione illa Spiritus sancti,
5 quae tunc in opere miraculorum ostendebatur. quoniam autem
sufficienter in his ostendit perfecta esse illa quae secundum Christum sunt, ab ipsis ultra quae dicta sunt secundum comparationem ostendit quoniam et primitus justa ratione sub lege conuersabantur, et nunc sub lege conuersari nullo modo illis sit aptum:
10 *dico autem quanto tempore heres paruulus est, nihil differt a seruo,*
dominus cum sit omnium; sed sub tutoribus et dispensatoribus est usque
ad [prae] finitum tempus a patre. sic et nos cum essemus paruuli, sub
elementis mundi eramus seruientes.

elementa quidem mundi solem nominat et lunam, ex quibus
15 quoque et menses perficiuntur et anni. haec enim uarie obserua-
bant illi qui erant in lege, secundum data sibi praecepta. uult autem dicere quoniam 'si quis moriens heredem instituerit suum filium, paruulum adhuc aetate constitutum, habere quidem eum
statim integram relictorum potestatem non patitur; tempus uero
20 quoddam statuet ei, post quod perfectam habens aetatem, ultra
possit illa quae secundum se sunt gubernare, dispensatores et tu-
tores rerum in medio constituens tempore. necessarium est filium
eum et heredem, usque *ad praefinitum tempus a patre*, nihil differre a seruo, nullam habentem potestatem suorum, sub aliorum ue-
25 ro degentem potestate; eo quod et ipse et substantia autem relicta,
sub potestate habetur illorum qui a patre sunt dispensatores constituti, nihil illi ad praesens conferente dominatione quam habere
uidetur, fracta aetatis imbecillitate. sic et nos quando eramus in-
perfecti, necdum inmortalitatis suscipientes fruitionem, sicut sub
30 tutoribus et dispensatoribus eramus sub istius mundi elementis,
dies obseruantes et tempora et menses, ut non secundum omnem
potestatem quod nobis uidebatur absolute ageremus. horum uero custodia faciebat nos paternas persentire leges, quibus nos cum
pudicitia et multa scrupulositate uiuere uolebat.'

---

2 ad *om H*   3   per *om H*   12   sicut (*for* sic et) *H**   21   posset *C* H*   24   a
om H   ‖   potestate *H*   25   degente *H*   ‖   ei (*for* autem) *C* (*corr.*) haut *H* [cf.
p. 37, 1. 13, n]   27   nihili *H*   ‖   qua *C**   28   imbecillitatem *C**   ‖   erramus
*C**   33   sentire *C*

words and at their restraint from disputation. For he was presenting to them also abundant proof for the meaning of those teachings that were thought to have been violently dragged in by him, [60] and at the same time he was presenting a confirmation of baptism by the activity of the Holy Spirit that was then being demonstrated by the working of miracles. And since he sufficiently showed by this that Christ's dispensation is perfect, he shows by what he goes on to say by way of comparison that with good reason they had at first led their lives under the law and that now it would be in no way suitable for them to do so:

4:1–3 *And I say that as long as the heir is a minor, he differs in no way from a slave, though he is master of all; but he is under guardians and trustees until the date set by the father. So with us; while we were minors we were enslaved to the elements of the world.*

He calls the sun and the moon, from which both months and years are brought about, the elements of the world. For those who were in the law used to observe them in various ways according to the commandments given them. What he means is that "if someone who dies has appointed his son heir, if the son is still a minor, he is not allowed to have entire power over what has been left him. In fact, the father will establish a certain time after which, when he attains his majority, he can then take charge of what belongs to him, though in the meantime the father appoints trustees and guardians for his legacy. It is necessary that the son and heir should differ in no way from a slave until *the date set by the father*, since he has no power over his possessions but continues under the power of others. This is because both he and the property left him are held under the power of those whom the father appointed as trustees, since the authority that plainly obtains conveys nothing to him for the present because the immaturity of his age prevents it. So we, too, when we were imperfect and had not yet received the fruit of immortality, were as though under guardians and trustees [61] by being under the elements of this world, observing days and seasons and months, so that we spent our lives not according to all the power that was perfectly provided for us. Indeed, observing these things was making us conscious of our Father's laws by which he wanted us to live with purity and great carefulness."

†substantiam quidem apostolus posuit esse uirtutes, et illam caritatem quam erga Deum
et erga proximos exercere debe
5 mus; usum uero eius, non ut conueniebat, nos fuisse abusos, eo
quod contraria facientibus nobis, exterminabatur ipsa substantia.*

οὐσίᾳ μὲν ὑπέθετο τὴν ἀρετὴν ὁ
ἀπόστολος, τῇ περὶ τὸν θεὸν ἀγάπῃ
καὶ τῇ περὶ τὸν πλησίον γνωριζο
μένῃ, χρῆσιν δὲ αὐτῆς οὐκ εἰς δέον,
τῷ τἀναντία διαπραττομένους ἀφα
νίζειν αὐτῆς τὴν ὑπόστασιν.

10 horum autem possessio tunc nobis firma aderit, quando illam quae
per inmortalitatem est acceperimus perfectionem; eo quod nec
possibile erit tunc peccare, aut aliquid contrarium uirtutibus facere. nunc uero quia et delinquere nos adhuc res patitur, ne ad
plenum traditam nobis exterminemus substantiam, tamquam
15 †sub tutoribus facti sumus, sub
huius mundi elementis; dies obseruantes et tempora et menses, ut assidua horum custodia
et quod in iisdem cotidie co
20 nuersamur, ad memoriam semper adducamur Dei, qui nobis leges huiusmodi dedit; ut
sic pudice uiuentes traditam nobis substantiam non extermine
25 mus, usque tunc dum futura institerit perfectio, firmam et integram nobis substantiae praestans fruitionem; utpote sufficientibus nobis tunc integram
30 hereditatem custodire paternam.'*
unde et adicit:

ὑπὸ ἐπιτρόπους τοίνυν καὶ οἰκο
νόμους γεγόναμεν, ἵνα ἡ συνεχὴς
τούτων παρατήρησις εἰς ὑπόμνησιν
ἄγῃ πάντοτε ἡμᾶς τοῦ δεδωκότος
θεοῦ τοὺς νόμους, καὶ οὕτως σω
φρονέστερον βιοῦντες μὴ τὴν παρα
δοθεῖσαν ἡμῖν παραφανίζωμεν οὐ
σίαν, ἄχρις ἂν ἡ τότε ἐπιστᾶσα τε
λειότης βεβαίαν καὶ ὁλοτελῆ τῆς
οὐσίας παράσχῃ τὴν ἀπόλαυσιν, ἅτε
δὴ καὶ φυλάττειν τότε ἀκέραιον τὴν
πατρῴαν δυναμένοις κληρονομίαν.

1 sq. Coisl. 204, f. 29 b-30 a. [Cr. vi. 60, 61, Fr. 126]. Θεόδωρος. ἄλλος φησίν·
οὐσίᾳ, κ.τ.λ.   12 contr. aliquit H   19 isdem H   25 tunc om C (corr.)   27
sq. substantiae ... nobis om (per homoeot.) H

†Indeed, the apostle assumed possessions to be the virtues and that love we ought to practice toward God and our neighbors, and he assumed that we had misused this "substance" by employing it for what was not right because that very substance was being wasted since we were engaged in harmful deeds.*²⁷

The apostle was comparing virtue to property, recognized in the love of God and neighbor, and meant that by doing the opposite we were using it for what was not right and wasting its substance.

And the possession of these virtues will be assured for us at that time when we shall receive that perfection that will be ours through immortality because it will then be impossible to sin or to do anything contrary to the virtues. But now, because our condition allows us to transgress, lest we should totally waste the substance given us,

†We have been placed under guardians, under the elements of this world. And we observed days and seasons and months so that by keeping them regularly and because we lived our lives daily in these observations we might always be led to remember God who gave us laws of this kind. This was so that by living purely we might not waste the substance given us until that time when the future perfection should be established, presenting us with the steadfast and complete enjoyment of our substance, seeing that we would in fact be sufficient at that time to take charge of our full paternal inheritance.*

This is why he adds:

Therefore, we were under guardians and trustees so that the continual keeping of these observances might always lead us to the recollection of God who gave the laws and so by living quite continently might not waste the substance given us, until the perfection established at that time should furnish us with the steadfast and complete enjoyment of our substance, seeing that we would then be able to take charge of our full paternal inheritance.

---

²⁷ See the parable of the prodigal son in Luke 15:11–32.

cum ergo uenit plenitudo temporis, misit Deus Filium suum factum
ex muliere, factum sub lege, ut illos qui sub lege erant redimeret; ut
filiorum adoptionem recipiamus.

'quoniam autem tempus uenit secundum quod ad perfectum
5 occurrere digni habeamur, liberi effecti a morte et a corruptione
et omni passione, uenit Dei Filius, factus ex muliere, hoc est, habens naturam quam et nos; qui et sub lege factus est, utpote homo constitutus secundum naturam, et quidem legi debitum resti-
tuens quod a nobis debebatur. sicque ipse exsurgens inmortalem
10 illam uitam adsumpsit, consistens in illam integritatem quam olim
speramus; et simillimorum nobis prouisor extitit bonorum, omnes nos a seruitute liberans legis.' quoniam autem filiorum adoptionem et inmortalitatem adquiremus post resurrectionem, et superius euidenter ostendimus. considerandum est autem et ex his
15 quae hoc in loco dicta sunt, quoniam perfectio illorum quae secundum Christum sunt in futuro saeculo nobis aderit, quando et illa
quae ab apostolo dicta sunt ipsis rebus uera esse monstrabuntur;
interim illa ipsa in promissa accipientibus nobis in praesenti uita.

nam quod dixit: *misit Deus Filium suum factum ex muliere;* eui-
20 dens quidem est, quoniam de homine dicit, qui et ex muliere factus est et sub lege conuersatus est. filium autem eum iure uocat, utpote praeter omnes homines participatum filii adoptionem,
propter copulationem illam qua Deus Verbum qui ex Patre est genitus eum sibi copulare dignatus est. et quoniam dixit nos filiorum
25 accipere adoptionem, hoc est, illam inmortalitatem quae ex resurrectione est, rebus ipsis illud confirmat:

quoniam autem estis filii Dei, misit Deus Spiritum Filii sui in cor-
dibus uestris clamantem: Abba, Pater.

†sequebantur enim tunc da-   ἠκολούθει τότε τῇ δόσει τοῦ
30 tum Spiritum miracula illa quae   πνεύματος τὰ γινόμενα θαύματα,
fiebant, sicut saepius dixi. quae   ὅπερ ἀναμφίβολον αὐτοῖς τὴν δόσιν
ipsi accipiebant, faciebant, in-   ὡς εἰκὸς ἐποίει τοῦ πνεύματος·
dubie sibi datum Spiritum os-   ἐντεῦθεν δὲ καὶ τὸ τῆς υἱοθεσίας
tendentes.   hinc autem et fi-   μετειληφέναι ἐπίστευον. ὅθεν καὶ

---

5 a *om H*   ‖ correptione *C** 7 sicut (*for* quam) *H*   9 sic quia *H*   11
spirabamus *C* (*corr.*)   ‖ simillorum *H**   13   et (*bef.* inmort.) *om H*   14 et
(*bef.* ex his) *om H*   15   in hoc 1. *H*   ‖   quo (*for* quoniam) *C*   18 ipsa *om H*.
20 munere (*for* muliere) *C** 23 quia (*for* qua) *H*   28 nostris (*for* uestris) *H*
[ὑμῶν Chr. Thdt.]   29 sq. Coisl. 204, f. 30 b. [Cr. vi. 61, Fr. 127]. θεόδωρος
(marg.)

[62] 4:4–5 *Therefore, when the fullness of time had come, God sent his Son, born of a woman, born under the law, in order to redeem those who were under the law, so that we might receive the adoption of sons.*

"And when the time came at which we should be held worthy of arriving at perfection, made free from death and from corruption and all passion, the Son of God came, born of a woman, that is, having a nature just as ours. He also was born under the law so that constituted as a human by nature he might pay back the debt we owed to the law. And so rising again himself he gained that immortal life, taking his stand in that wholeness that we hope someday will be ours. And he has been found the provider of similar good things for us, freeing all of us from slavery to the law." And we have clearly demonstrated earlier[28] that we shall attain the adoption of sons and immortality after the resurrection. But we must also bear in mind on the basis of what is said in this passage that the perfection of Christ's dispensation will be present to us in the age to come when what the apostle says will be shown to be true by the facts themselves. For the time being in the present life, those future goods are ours because we receive them by promises.

Now because he said *God sent his Son, born of a woman,* it is quite clear that he is speaking of the man who was both born of a woman and led his life under the law. And he [63] rightly calls him Son as one who partook of adoption as a son beyond all humans because of that union by which God the Word, begotten of the Father, saw fit to unite him to himself. And since he said that we receive the adoption of sons, that is, the immortality that comes from the resurrection, he confirms the point by the facts themselves:

4:6 *And because you are God's sons, God has sent the Spirit of his Son into your hearts, crying, "Abba! Father!"*

†For at that time those miracles that took place followed the gift of the Spirit, as I have quite often said. They were receiving them and doing them, demonstrating that the Spirit had without doubt been given to them. On this basis they also believed	At that time the miracles that took place followed the gift of the Spirit and in all likelihood made the gift of the Spirit something they could not doubt. On this basis they also believed that they had partaken of the adoption of sons. For this rea-

---

[28] See his discussion of 3:26.

liorum adoptionem se adsecu-
tos esse credebant. unde et
ipse confidens firmitati probationum, utpote ex ipsis rebus
5 sumptae, quae et apud illos erant
indubia, adicit:

   itaque iam non es seruus, sed
filius; si autem filius, et heres Dei
per Christum.
10 'sic nulla tibi (inquit) communio ultra est ad eos qui sub
lege uiuunt.*

αὐτὸς θαρρήσας τῷ ἰσχυρῷ τῆς
ἀποδείξεως, ὡς ἅτε δὴ ἀπὸ τῶν
πραγμάτων εἰλημμένῳ τῶν καὶ
παρ' αὐτοῖς ἀναμφιβόλων ἐπάγει·

   ὥστε οὐκέτι εἶ δοῦλος, ἀλλὰ
υἱός· εἰ δὲ υἱός, καὶ κληρονόμος
θεοῦ διὰ χριστοῦ.

οὕτως οὐδεμία σοι (φησὶν) πρὸς
τοὺς ὑπὸ νόμον ζῶντας κοινωνία
λοιπόν.

quoniam autem Spiritum adsecuti estis, euidens est. hunc uero
participantes, nec quod filii sitis negare poteritis. facti autem filii,
15 necessario estis et heredes, cum multa libertate degentes et omni
metu liberi et omni necessitate et, ut fas est, securi. tantum ergo abest ut sitis serui, quod obprobrium est illorum qui sub lege
sunt.' nam quod dixit *per Christum*, iure id dixit, eo quod omnium
horum idem sit auctor. deinde post probationem adicit quod ualde
20 erat graue:

   sed tunc quidem nescientes Deum, seruistis his qui non sunt natura
dii. nunc autem cognoscentes Deum, magis autem cogniti a Deo, quo-
modo conuertimini iterum ad infirma et egena elementa, quibus iterum
denuo seruire uultis?

25   elementa et superius et in hoc loco solem dicit et lunam et stel-
las; ex quibus dies quoque et menses fiunt et anni et tempora. seruire ergo elementis dicit, eo quod illa, id est, dies et menses ob-
seruarent, quasi ab illis facta. et quod dixit: *seruistis autem his qui*
non sunt natura dii; de ipsis dicit sole et luna et stellis; eo quod ado-
30 rabant illa cum essent gentes ut deos, secundum legem gentium.

   et haec diximus ut nihil obscurum inquirenti esse uideatur.
sensus uero apostolicus multam habet profunditatem. etenim
paulo minus ostendit eos non iudaismum tenentes, sed ad gentili-
tatis iterum recurrisse obseruationem. dicit enim quoniam 'primi-

---

3-4 probationem *H*   3 εἰλημμένων cod. edd. cf. lat.   7 est (*for* es) *H*   8
heredes *H* ‖ εἰ δὲ υἱός om. edd.   19 probatione *C* H*   22 cognoti *C**
[cf. Rönsch, 295]   26 mensens *C**   28 seruis *H* (*corr.*)   29 soli *H* ‖ et
(*for* eo) *H*   32 apostolus *H* ‖ multum *C** ‖ produntatem (*sic*) *H*   33
iudaismo *C* H*

that they had attained the adoption of sons. For this reason he was also confident in the validity of the proofs as certainly drawn from the very facts that were undoubted also by them. So he adds:

4:7 *So you are no longer a slave but a son, and if a son, then also an heir of God through Christ.*

"Thus, he says, you no longer have any fellowship with those who live under the law.*

son he was also confident in the validity of the proof as certainly drawn from the facts that were also undoubted by them. He continues:

4:7 *So you are no longer a slave but a son, and if a son, then also an heir of God through Christ.*

Thus, he says, you no longer have any fellowship with those who live under the law.

And that you have acquired the Spirit is clear. [64] Indeed, since you participate in him, you could not deny that you are sons. And made sons you are necessarily also heirs, living with great freedom, delivered from all fear and all neediness and, as is right, untroubled. Therefore, it is quite far from the case that you are slaves, which is the shame of those who are under the law." Indeed, he said *through Christ* with good reason, since he is in fact the originator of all these goods. Then after the proof he adds an extremely serious point:

4:8–9 *But then, when you did not know God, you were enslaved to beings that by nature are not gods. Now, however, that you have come to know God, or rather to be known by God, how can you turn back again to the weak and beggarly elements? How can you want to be enslaved to them again?*

Both earlier and in this passage he means the sun, moon, and stars by which both days and months and years and seasons take place. Thus, he says they were enslaved to the elements because they observed them, that is, days and months, inasmuch as those things were effected by them. And his statement *you were enslaved to beings that are not by nature gods* refers to them, to the sun, moon, and stars, because they used to worship them since they are for the Gentiles as gods by the law of the Gentiles.

We have said this so that nothing may seem obscure to the inquirer, In fact, the apostle's meaning has great profundity. Indeed, he all but proves that they were not cleaving to Judaism but had again returned to keeping the Gentile religion. For he

tus quidem nescientes uerum Deum, seruistis autem istis, (tamquam diceretur) qui non erant dii. quoniam enim cognouistis aliquando uerum Deum. magis autem cogniti estis a Deo (non enim
scientibus aut uidentibus diuina uobis quodammodo inluxit scien-
5 tia); iterum ergo illis ipsis elementis seruire deproperatis sub alia
specie?' id ipsum iterum ut uideret peragere festinantes, probauit
propemodo quoniam hac ratione ad praesens eos inculpat, eo quod
alio quodam modo ad antiquos ritus rursum recurrere nitantur,
per illud quod dixit: *quomodo conuertimini iterum?* conuertere ete-
10 nim quis uera ratione dicitur, quando ad illa ipsa iterum regredi-
tur. ostendens quemadmodum illis seruiunt:

dies obseruatis et menses et tempora et annos.

'haec (inquit) ex illis, id est, elementis perficiuntur. itaque si
horum obseruantiam magnam quandam esse existimatis, cum ti-
15 more illa implentes, rursus illis seruire uidemini.' et sciens dictorum suorum firmitatem, adicit:

estote sicut ego, quoniam et ego sicut uos.

'eram (inquit) et ego sub lege; sed praeelegi extra legem uiuere,
sicut et uos per eam quae in Christo est fidem uiuebatis. imitamini
20 ergo et uos me, cum illa quae in Christo est fide a conuersatione
legitima uosmetipsos extraneos facientes.'

II

Frequentibus ualde probationibus et quae omnem excludunt
controuersiam omnifarie apostolus abusus, suam prosecutionem
ueram esse sufficienter comprobauit; ex rerum qualitate ostendens
25 eorum differentiam, et quod multo meliora sint illa quae secundum Christum sunt ab illis quae erant in lege, eo quod hic quidem facile est iustificari, illic uero durum ualde et propemodum
inpossibile. fidem uero firmans ratione, et dignitatem eius per omnia ostendens, tam de tributo credentibus Spiritu, [quam de] il-

---

1 autem istis *om C*   4   uobis *add (aft.* scient.) *H*   6   uideretur *C** uidetur
C (*corr.*) uidere *H*   7   propemodum *H*   15   scientes *C* H*   17   uos *om H*
18   sub in lege *H*   ‖   praelegi *H* post elegi *l*   20   mecum, illam *C* (*corr.*)   21
uosmetipsis *H*   ‖   EXPLICIT LIBER PRIMUS GALATHARUM, INCIPIT LIBER SE-
CUNDUS EORUNDEM add (*aft* facientes) *C H*   27   iustificare *C* H*   28   fide *H*
‖   rationem *C* H*   29   tributum *C* H*   ‖   Spiritum *C H*   29   illic *C H*

says "formerly when you did not know the true God, you served instead [65] those (as should be said) who were not gods. Some time later you came to know the true God, or rather were known by God (for a certain divine knowledge began to shine upon you in your ignorance and blindness). Are you, then, ending up rushing to serve those same elements under another form?" Inasmuch as it seemed they were in a hurry to accomplish the same slavery once more, he next proved that he was at present blaming them for this reason, because they were struggling to go back again in another way to their old religious observances. This is why he said *how can you turn back again?* In fact, someone is said with good reason to "turn back" when he reverts again to those same things. He shows how they served them:

4:10 *You are observing days and months and seasons and years.*

"These (he says) are accomplished from those, that is, the elements. And so if you suppose that observing them is of great importance, fulfilling those observances with fear, you are plainly enslaved to them again." And knowing the validity of his words he adds:[29]

4:12 *Be as I am, for I also have been as you are.*

"For (he says) I was also myself under the law, but I decided it was better to live outside the law, just as you also were living through that faith that is in Christ. Therefore, imitate me, you also, by making yourselves through faith in Christ strangers to life under the law's ordinances."

BOOK 2

[66] By vigorously employing in all sorts of ways a great many proofs that shut out all dispute, the apostle has sufficiently proved the truth of his case. He demonstrated the difference between the two ways of life by their character and that Christ's dispensation is far better than that of the law because by it justification is easily obtained, whereas by the law it is in fact quite difficult and well nigh impossible. In truth, confirming faith by reasoning and demonstrating its importance in every way, he made his proclamation as much on the basis of the Spirit's bestowal

---

[29] Note that the comment on verse 11 is omitted here and placed at the beginning of book 2.

lis quae secundum Abraham facta fuerant, et scripturalibus testimoniis, quibus locum non posse habere legem, istis tenentibus,
pronuntiauit. sed ex comparatione utilitatem dicens legis, eminentiam illorum quae secundum Christum sunt insinuauit. haec
5 quidem uniuersa euidenter cognoscere poterit quis ex illis quae in
anterioribus diximus; in quibus et cum competenti scrupulositate
per omnia, ut potens erat, dicebat. ueneranda uerba apostoli sunt
intellectus facientis. interpretationi autem quoniam in praeeun-
tibus probationibus competentem suis sermonibus adhibuisse ui-
10 sus est uirtutem; in medio uero etiam duris usus sermonibus, eos
fuerat adgressus, neque stultos eos uocare dubitans, ubi res ipsa
locum ei praebebat increpationis necessarium; iure ergo ait:

　　timeo uos, ne forte sine causa laborauerim in uobis.

　　quare? 'quoniam aliter uenerari adceleratis, quibus antea se-
15 ruiebatis.'

　　et post increpationem ad uerecundiam eos inuitans adicit, in-
pensa sollicitudine curans sanare eos, sciens quoniam grauis est
increpatio homini, etiamsi et iuste ei inferri uideatur:

　　fratres, obsecro uos, nihil me nocuistis.

20 　　satisfacit illis pro pondere uerborum grauissimorum. 'nihil nocitus sum (inquit) a uobis; itaque ne quis me existimet ira et recor-
datione malitiae ad hos uenisse sermones.'

　　scitis autem quoniam per infirmitatem carnis euangelizaui uobis in
　　primis, et temptationem meam quae est in carne mea non sprevistis,
25 　　*neque respuistis; sed sicut angelum Dei suscepistis me, sicut Christum*
　　Iesum.

　　'e contrario uero cum essem in persecutionibus et miseriis et
tribulationibus multis, ad uos ueni; et tunc propter illa mala quae
mihi imminebant, non respuistis me. sed *sicut angelum Dei susce-*
30 *pistis me*, immo uero ut ipsum Christum.' *infirmitatem* enim *carnis*
et temptationem, eam quae in corpore est tribulationem dicit.

　　quae ergo erat beatitudo uestra?

　　†in hoc loco dicens: 'quae　　　τὸ οὖν τίς ἐνταῦθα ἀντὶ τοῦ ποῦ
erat beatitudo?' hoc est, 'ubi est　ὁ μακαρισμός; οἴχεται, ἀπώλετο.
35 beatitudo illa, qua beatos dice-　καλῶς οὐκ ἀποφηνάμενος, ἀλλὰ δι'

3-4 imminentiam *C* H* 8 facientes *C H* ‖ interpretationem *C H* 10
duris etiam *H* 12 increpationes necessariorum *C* H* 17 curauit *C* H* 21
ita ut (*for* itaque) *H* 28 tamen (*for* tunc) *H* (*corr.*) 33 Coisl. 204, f. 32 b [Cr.
vi. 66, Fr. 127]. θεόδωρος marg.

on believers as on the basis of what had taken place regarding Abraham and the scriptural testimonies that for those who grasp them prove that the law has no place. Though he spoke of the comparative usefulness of the law, he introduced the superiority of Christ's dispensation. Indeed, anyone can know all this quite clearly on the basis of what we have said in commenting on the previous arguments in which he spoke with suitable carefulness in all respects so far as he was able. The words of the apostle must be revered when he is engaged in rational argumentation. And in his explanation in the preceding proofs he plainly applied suitable strength to his words. But even in their midst he used harsh words and attacked them, not even hesitating to call them foolish where the situation itself gave him a necessary occasion for rebuke. Therefore, he says with good reason:

4:11 *I am afraid that my work for you may have been wasted.*

Why? "Since you have rushed to worship in a different way those you were accustomed to serve formerly."

And after the rebuke he adds an inducement to shame them, taking care to heal them with extreme solicitude, well aware that people find rebuke hard to bear even when it seems to be given them with just cause:

4:12 *Brothers, I beg you ... you have done me no wrong.*

He makes amends to them for the severity of his extremely harsh words. [67] "I have not been wronged by you (he says) in any way. And so let no one suppose that I have resorted to these words in anger and malice aforethought."

4:13–14 *You know that it was because of infirmity of the flesh that I first announced the gospel to you, and you did not scorn my testing in the flesh or despise me but welcomed me as an angel of God, as Christ Jesus.*[30]

"On the contrary, in truth I came to you when I was in persecutions, afflictions, and many tribulations, and at that time you did not despise me because of those evils that pressed closely upon me. Instead, *you welcomed me as an angel of God*, indeed even as Christ himself." For by *infirmity of the flesh* and *testing* he means bodily tribulation.

4:15a *What was your blessing?*

†In this passage he says: Therefore, *what* is used here in-

---

[30] Theodore reads "*my* testing" rather than "*your* testing."

bant uos omnes pro tali affec- ἐρωτήσεως ἐνδειξάμενος.
tu quem erga praedicationem
ostendistis, per illum honorem
qui tunc mihi a uobis est prae-
5 bitus? ubi ergo est ille honor?'
id est, fuit, periit. beneque non
dixit id sententialiter, sed inter-
rogatiue id ostendit.*
et adhuc conlaudans ipsam beatitudinem adicit:
10   *testimonium enim perhibeo uobis, quoniam si possibile esset, oculos*
uestros eruentes utique dedissetis mihi.

et quia honorem illum qui sibi ab illis fuerat praestitutus dixit, ostendens simul qui et qualis fuerit, quamue magnus, et quam
sufficiens, ut etiam secundum hoc et reuerentiam illorum haberet,
15 sed nunc omnibus negotiis ueritatem praehonorandam esse existimaret, adicit:

itaque inimicus uobis factus sum uerum dicens uobis?

'sed ecce talia a uobis adsecutus inimici ordinem nunc uideor
implere, ueritatem praehonorans.' optime autem adiecit, *uerum*
20 *dicens uobis*, ita ut non solum ueritatis sollicitudinem habere existimaretur, sed cum eorum prouidentia id se fecisse doceret. ostendit enim quoniam propter illos et hoc ita fuerit gestum, et ut ne a
ueritate extorres fierent; ita ut species quidem uideretur esse ini-
micitiae, opus uero ipsud amicitiae, et inimicos ex comparatione
25 incusans, adicit:

aemulantur uos non bene.

bona adiectio illa quae adiecit dicens: *non bene.* est enim et bene
aemulari, quando quis bonum demirans uult eum imitari.

sed excludere uos uolunt, ut illos aemulemini.

30 'uolunt enim uos propellere ab illo intellectu perfecto, in quo
nunc estis; ita ut sub legis constituti conuersatione, inueniamini
apud illos ordinem implere discipulorum, quasi qui et aliquid melius illis facientibus imitari eos uelitis.'

bonum autem aemulari in bono semper.

5 ubi est ergo *C* (*corr.*) *H* 7 sentialiter *C* H* 12 praestitus *H* 15 non
(*for* nunc) *C H* (*corr.*) ‖ ut (*bef.* non) *add C* (*corr.*) 18 a *om C** 24 opus u.
i. amicitiae *om H* ipsum *C* (*corr.*) 27 qua *C** : *corr.* quam 28 aemulare *C* H*
‖ enim (*for* eum) *C* H* ‖ imitare *C** 30 praecellere (*for* propellere) *H*
33 uellitis *C** 34 bono (*for* bonum) *H* ‖ aemulare *C*

"What was the blessing?" that is, "where is that blessing by which everyone was calling you blessed for the kind of affection you demonstrated for the preaching by that honor you showed me at that time?[31] Where, then, is that honor?" That is, it is no more; it has perished. And he rightly did not say this as a declarative opinion [68] but made it known as a question.*

stead of where *was the blessing?* It is gone; it has perished. He rightly made this known not by a declarative opinion but by a question.

And still praising that blessedness he adds:

4:15b *For I bear testimony to you that, had it been possible, you would have torn out your eyes and given them to me.*

And he demonstrates at the same time what that honor was he said they rendered him and of what sort it was—how great and how sufficient for his possession by it of their respect. But now so that truth may be honored before all else he adds:

4:16 *Have I now become your enemy by telling you the truth?*

"But, look, you have engaged in such pursuits that now I seem to be ranked as an enemy because I honor truth above all." And he most effectively added *telling you the truth* so that he might be thought not only to have a care for truth but to be teaching them that he had done this with consideration for them. For he demonstrated that he had done even this for them so that they would not be banished from truth. So, in order that the appearance of enmity might be seen in truth the very work of friendship, he blames the enemies by comparison and adds:

4:17a *They are jealous for you, but not rightly.*

The addition he makes by saying *not rightly* is a good one. For there is also a good jealousy when someone who admires a good person wants to imitate him.

4:17b *But they want to exclude you, so that you may be jealous of them.*

[69] "For they want to drive you away from that perfect understanding in which you now are, so that established in a way

---

[31] Theodore has the reading τίς rather than ποῦ, and this explains his puzzle over the text. He also takes ὑμῶν as an objective genitive in "your blessing."

'melius est ergo talia uos facere, ita ut ab omnibus aemulemini; ut et alii uos, sicut conuenit, aemulentur, et imitari uos festinent; residui uero inuidentes uobis, nihil uos possint nocere.' et quasi qui talia primitus facerent, adicit:

5 *et non solum in aduentu meo ad uos.*

potentissime eos in hisce uerbis curauit, ita ut et aduersariorum ex comparatione argueret sententiam. ex commemoratione uero praeteritorum subito animo accensus, et propter hoc a praecedentibus abstractus sermonibus, ad uerba flectitur fletus, dicens:

10 *filioli mei quos iterum parturio usquedum formetur Christus in uobis.*

demirabilis admodum sermo, et multam habens affectionis ostensionem. primum quidem quasi in fletu subito exclamantis locum implet, dicens: *filioli mei*, et ut quis ita dicat, cum dulcissi-

15 mus pater filios amissos fletu euocet. deinde, quod non dixit *filii*, sed *filioli;* quod maiorem egerentis ostendere poterat dolorem. et quod adiecit: *parturio;* quia multum graue illis qui in partu sunt esse uidetur.

†et quod dixit: *iterum;* ita ut τὸ δὲ πάλιν, ὥστε τῶν παλαιῶν
20 et antiquos dolores partus ad- ὠδίνων ἀγαγεῖν εἰς μνήμην· τὸ δὲ
duceret in memoriam. nam et ἄχρις οὗ μορφωθῇ χριστὸς ἐν ὑμῖν,
quod dixit: *usquedum formetur* ἐπίτασιν ἔχει τοῦ πάθους, οὐδὲ γὰρ
Christus in uobis; pondus indi- εἰδότος ἐστὶν ποῦ ποτε στήσεται
cat passionis esse inmensum, et αὐτῷ τὰ τῶν ὠδινῶν.
25 nec scientis quo statu quoque fine
partus ipsius concludantur dolores.*

bene autem dixit: *donec formetur Christus;* ex proprietate partus id accipiens dictum, post quem et solui solent dolores. et hoc

---

3 uobis (*for* uos) H ‖ possent C* 8 praeteritarum C 13 osfensionem (*sic*) C* offensionem (*for* ostens.) H 19 sq. Coisl. 204, f. 33 b [Cr. vi. 67, Fr. 127]. Θεόδωρος (marg.). 21 et (*aft.* nam) om H 25 scientes C H

of life regulated by the law you may be ranked as their disciples insofar as you are willing to imitate them as though they were doing something better."

4:18a *It is good to be jealous for a good purpose at all times,*

"Therefore, it is better for you to do such things as will make everyone jealous of you, so that some others may be jealous of you, as is right, and may be eager to imitate you. But the rest, though they envy you, can do you no harm." And inasmuch as they had at first acted in an exemplary fashion, he adds:

4:18b *and not only when I am present with you.*

Most powerfully has he taken care of them by these words in such a way that by comparison be might prove the opponents' opinion wrong. He is suddenly stirred to deep emotion by bringing to mind what has passed, and for this reason he is drawn away from his preceding words and is turned to words of lamentation, saying:

4:19 *My little children, for whom I am again in the pain of childbirth until Christ is formed in you.*

An absolutely marvelous statement and one with a great show of affection. He carries out the first part of what he says as though he were suddenly exclaiming in lamentation, saying *my little children*, just as someone might say when as the most affectionate of fathers he calls upon his lost children with weeping. Moreover, the reason he did not say *children* but *little children* is because he was able to show a grief greater than he could put into words. And the reason he adds *I am in the pain of childbirth* is that it is obviously the case that those in childbirth have much that is hard to bear.

†And the reason he says *again* is so that he could bring to mind the former pains of childbirth. Again, [70] by saying *until Christ is formed in you* he indicates the immense burden of suffering, for he does not know in what condition or to what conclusion his pains will be brought to an end.* *Again* so as to bring to mind the former pains of childbirth. And *until Christ is formed* in you intensifies the suffering, for he does not know where or when the pains of childbirth will stop for him.

He also rightly said *until Christ is formed*, taking the word from what is proper to childbirth after which the pains are customarily loosed. And in this passage, inasmuch as it concerns

in loco quasi de illis qui nati sunt in Christum per fidem et baptisma, deinde abolere temptauerunt ipsam effigiem ueritatis, aliam
formationem expectat in illis fieri, quae impleri poterit ab affectu
illo qui erga Christum erit perfectus; ita ut et ad plenum ultra a le-
5 gitimis discedant custodiis. uerumtamen et post talem tantamque
fletus exclamationem, et uerba illa quae multum ei inesse affectum
ostendebant; quasi qui uictus fuerit passione ita ut nec proloqui
aliquid ulterius posset, in tantum in quantum et uult; et quod nec
deceat scribentem summam miserabilitatem suis exprimere litte-
10 ris:

> *uolebam autem uenire ad uos nunc et mutare uocem meam.*

'uolebam uenire magis et mutare sermones meos, et alia quidem dicere, sicut lex lugentem ac deflentem dicere postulat; dicere
autem pariter qualia et quanta uolebam.' summa autem adiectione
15 suorum dictorum abusus esse uidetur:

> *quoniam aporior (confundor) in uobis;*

eo quod in tantum passione sit uictus, ut et quasi quadam aporia teneatur, neque quid conueniat sibi loqui scire possit.

quanti oratores, in unum uenientes, aut matrem deflentem filios
20 suos aut patrem imitare uolentes, tantam compassionis molem aliquando suis poterunt explicare sermonibus, quantum in praesenti ostendit beatus Paulus; simulans quidem nihil, sed secundum
insitum sibi affectum quem erga eos habebat uniuersa enarrans.
quod in his ostendisse uidetur sermonibus; quasi qui et ingemi-
25 scens et cum lamento deflens, et passione uictus, simulque et pro-
tractus ab illis solis quae sibi deceant retineri uidetur. et propter
hoc optans ad illos uenire, ut omnia illa impleret quae sibi passio
fieri suggerebat; quoniam abunde defleuit transductionem eorum
in deterius factam, et illos sermones quos in primordio duriores
30 uisus fuerat dixisse, curauit sufficienter, uertitur iterum ad uerba

1 qua (*for* qui) *H*   3   implere *C H*   4   effectu *H*   17   tanta *H* (*corr.*)   20
imitari *C* (*corr.*)   ‖   compassione *C**   23   insitum *om H*   26   solo *C* (*corr.*)
‖   retinere *C H*   30   fuerit *H*

those who had been born in Christ by faith and baptism and
had then tried to efface that image of truth, he hopes that
there will take place in them another formation capable of being
fulfilled by that affection for Christ that will be perfected, so that
from now on they may completely leave the observance of the
law's ordinances. Nevertheless, even after such and so great an
exclamation of lamentation and after those words that showed the
great affection he had for them, as though he had become someone
so overwhelmed by emotion that he could no longer say anything
as much as he wanted, and because it was not fitting for him in
writing to express his excessive distress in the letter:

4:20a *And I wanted to come to you now and to change my voice,*

"I wanted to come all the more both to change my words and
to say such additional ones inasmuch as [the question of] the law
requires me to speak with grief and tears. But I wanted to speak
such and so great words face to face." And he plainly used this
addition to sum up his words:

4:20b *since I am perplexed, upset about you.*[32]

[71] Because he has been so greatly overwhelmed by emotion
that he is held fast as by a measure of perplexity and is unable to
know what he should say.

How many orators coming together in their wish to portray
either a mother or a father weeping for their sons could ever
have displayed such a vast amount of compassion by their words
as blessed Paul shows in his present argument?[33] Indeed, he is
in no way just acting a part but is describing everything fully
according to the deep-seated affection he had for them. He plainly
demonstrated this in these words, inasmuch as he groans and
weeps in lamentation and is overwhelmed by emotion, and at the
same time has also deferred only what is fitting for him to hold
back. This is why he wants to come to them so as to satisfy
everything that his emotion was suggesting he should do. Since
he has amply lamented their change for the worse and has taken
sufficient trouble over those harsh words that he plainly used at
the beginning of the letter, he turns once more to words that he
could treat as relevant to what had happened:

---

[32] The Latin text reads *aporior* (*confundor*). Swete suggests (1:70 and 1:5) that
the translator sometimes uses two words when he is uncertain how to translate
the Greek.

[33] *Pace* Swete, who does not take the sentence as a question.

quae ei cum re poterant coaequare:

dicite mihi: qui sub lege uultis esse, legem non audistis?

†bona ad illos facta est co-   καλὴ δὲ καὶ ἡ πρὸς ἐκείνους
nuersio uerborum, et qualem   ἀποστροφὴ τῶν λόγων· διὰ γὰρ
5 fieri conueniebat ab eo qui rebus   πάντων φαίνεται ὁ ἀπόστολος ὑπὸ
ipsis fuerat incitatus; per omnia   τῆς τῶν γεγονότων ὀργῆς συνεχεῖς
etenim haec uidetur apostolus   τὰς μεταβολὰς δεχόμενος, καὶ τὰ
ob usurpatorum iram frequen-   μὲν πρὸς τούτους ἀγανακτῶν, τὰ δὲ
tes dictorum sustinere mutabi-   πρὸς ἐκείνους, τὸ δὲ καὶ ἀλγῶν ὡς
10 litates. et modo quidem indi-   ἐπὶ τέκνοις ἀπολωλόσιν. καὶ ὅλως
gnatur aduersus hos, modo ue-   ἀκριβῶς τις σκοπούμενος, πολλὴν
ro aduersus illos; pro aliis uero   ἴδοι ἂν ἐν τοῖς γεγραμμένοις τῶν
et dolet, quasi de filiis amissis.   παθῶν τὴν ἐναλλαγήν.
et ad plenum si quis caute consi-
15 derare uoluerit, multam passionum inueniet mutabilitatem in
his quae scripta sunt,*
et qualem res ipsa a Paulo fieri exigebat; tanto ardore praedica-
to, ut omnes Christo properaret offerre, eo quod et omnes uole-
20 bat iungere Christo ob enormem affectum quem erga eum habere
uidebatur. dicit autem quoniam 'uos qui legi oboedire promittitis
non intenditis illa quae lex dicit.' quibus ista in subsequentibus
adicit:

scriptum est quoniam 'Abraham duos filios habuit, unum de ancil-
25 *la et unum de libera.' sed ille quidem qui de ancilla fuerat secundum*
carnem natus est; ille uero qui de libera per promissionem.

superius nullam posse habere communionem legem cum promissionibus ostendit, eo quod lex quidem exigit hoc ut impleatur,
promissio uero donantis comprobat liberalitatem. per omnia ue-
30 ro gratiae confirmare properauit rationem, ideoque et fidei et promissionum facit memoriam cum et illis quae nobis adesse speramus. omnibus autem illis e contrario posuit legem, quae quasi aliqua sequentia praebere uidetur iustitiam, siquidem eis qui primitus legem impleuerint, ea praebere promittit; fraudat uero mul-

---

2 legistis (*for* aud.) *H*   3 sq. Coisl. 204, f. 34 a [Cr. vi. 68, Fr. 127]. Θεόδωρος
(marg.).   9 dictorum *om H*   14 et ad plenum *bis C**   16 mutab. inuen. *H*
20 inormem *C* H*   22 istis *C* H*   26 repromissionem *H*   31 cum illis
et *C* (*corr.*)

4:21 Tell me, you who desire to be subject to the law, do you not hear the law?

†Changing his words to them was appropriate and something right for him to do, since he had been provoked by what had actually happened. For in all these respects the apostle seems to put up with frequent changes of his subject because of his anger at what was carried out. And he is indignant now at these, now at those, but for others he grieves [72] as for lost sons. And altogether if someone were willing to make a careful examination, he would find a great alternation of emotions in his writings,*

Changing his words to them was appropriate, for in all respects the apostle seems to admit frequent changes because of his anger at what had happened. And he is indignant now at these, now at those, and he grieves as for lost children. And altogether if someone were to examine carefully, he would see a great alternation of emotions in his writings.

the kind of alternation that the situation itself compelled Paul to make. He preached with such great enthusiasm so that he might be eager to offer all people to Christ, because he wanted all to join Christ because of the immense affection he plainly had for him. And what he means is: "You who have promised to obey the law are paying no attention to what the law says." He adds what this is in what follows:

4:22–23 For it is written that Abraham had two sons, one by a slave woman and the other by a free woman. One, the child of the slave, was born according to the flesh; the other, the child of the free woman, was born through the promise.

Above he demonstrated that the law could have nothing in common with the promises because the law required that its ordinances be fulfilled, while the promise ratified the generosity of the one who gave it. In all respects, however, he was eager to establish the principle of grace, and so he mentioned faith and the promise together with what we hope to be ours. And he placed the law in contrast to all of these, because it plainly offered righteousness in a certain order. It promises to offer these goods at any rate to those who have first fulfilled the law. But it deceives many—or to speak more truly—probably all, because those who

tos, et, ut uerius dicam, propemodum omnes, propter inpossibilitatem illorum qui legem implere adnituntur. ideo maxime illam quae ex gratia est iustitiam meliorem esse ab illa quae ex lege est, dixit; quoniam hanc sua liberalitate praestat Deus, nemine ob naturalem excluso infirmitatem. id ipsud autem et in praecedentibus ostendens ex illa parabola quae secundum Abraham est, memoratus et quoniam fuerunt ei duo filii, quorum alter naturae sequentia natus est, alter uero per gratiam. propter quod lex dicit quoniam *Abraham duos filios habuit, unum de ancilla, et unum de libera. sed ille quidem qui de ancilla, secundum carnem natus est.* hoc est, naturali sequentia natus est; sic nominans, *secundum carnem*, quoniam et carni adest secundum naturam partus. et Ismahel naturali sequentia carnis natus est, siue secundum Abraham, siue secundum Agar. nam *ille qui de libera natus est secundum promissionem natus est*, hoc est, secundum gratiam. omnis enim promissio per gratiam solet fieri. ordine enim naturae Isaac nequaquam fuisse natus dicitur, eo quod Sarra duplici ratione edere partum non poterat. erat enim una passio sterilitatis, et alia quae illam ob longaeuitatem prohibebat parere. et ipse Abraham aetate senectutis fuerat prouectior effectus. sed natus est praeter omnem spem et naturae sequentiam, propter solam promittentis uirtutem pariter et liberalitatem. sic et illa quae secundum Abraham sunt referens, secundum ut et in diuinis scripturis scriptum esse uidetur, ostendere uero cupiens qua de causa illis sit abusus, adicit:

quae sunt per allegoriam dicta.

qui studium multum habent interuertere sensus diuinarum scripturarum et omnia quae illuc posita sunt intercipere, fabulas uero quasdam ineptas ex se confingere, et allegoriae nomen suae ponere desipientiae; hanc uocem apostoli abutentes, quasi qui hinc uideantur sumpsisse potestatem ut et omnes intellectus diuinae exterminent scripturae, eo quod secundum apostolum *per allegoriam* dicere nituntur et ipsi, non intellegentes quantum differt quod ab illis et ab apostolo hoc in loco dictum sit. apostolus enim non interimit historiam, neque euoluit res dudum factas; sed sic posuit illa ut tune fuerant facta, et historiam illorum quae fue-

---

4 suam liberalitatem *C* H* ‖ neminem *C** ‖ ob naturali excl infirmitate *H* 5 ipsum *C (corr.) H* 7 ei *om H* 8 lex *om C* 12 id est (*for* adest) *H* 19 par. proh. *C* 22 et (*aft.* sic) *om C* 30 uideatur *C H* uid. sumps. uid. *H*

strive to fulfill the law are unable to do so. For this reason he said that the righteousness that comes from grace is to the greatest extent better than that which comes from the law, since God bestows it by his own generosity with no one excluded because of natural weakness. And demonstrating the same conclusions as in what preceded on the basis of the illustration about Abraham, he reminded them that Abraham had two sons, one born according to the order of nature but the other through grace. About this the law [73] says that *Abraham had two sons, one by a slave woman and the other by a free woman. One, the child of the slave, was born according to the flesh*; that is, he was born by the natural order. He calls this *according to the flesh*, since childbirth by nature belongs to the flesh. And Ishmael was born by the natural order of the flesh both by Abraham and by Hagar. But *the child of the free woman was born through the promise*, that is, according to grace. For every promise customarily takes place through grace. Now Isaac is said by no means to have been born in the order of nature, because Sarah was unable to give birth for two reasons. For one thing, she was barren, and for another, she was prevented from giving birth by her great age. And Abraham himself was far advanced in old age. Yet Isaac was born beyond all hope and beyond the order of nature only because of the power, as well as the generosity, of the one who promised. So he refers to the story of Abraham as it appears written in the divine scriptures. But since he wishes to show why he employed it, he adds:

4:24a *Now this is by an allegory.*

There are people who have great zeal for overturning the meaning of the divine scriptures, and by breaking up[34] everything placed there they fabricate from themselves certain foolish fictions and give their folly the name of allegory. They use this term of the apostle's so as to take from it the right to dismiss the entire meaning of divine scripture by depending on the apostle's expression *by an allegory*. But they fail to understand how great the difference is between their view and what the apostle says in this passage. For the apostle does not do away with the narrative, nor [74] does he get rid of what happened long ago. Instead, he put it down as what had actually taken place at that time, but in such a way that he also used the narrative of what had

---

[34] Latin *intercipere*. See the introduction for the explanation of my translation.

runt facta ad suum usus est intellectum, quando quidem dicens:
confinis est eius quae nunc est Hierusalem; quando uero quoniam *si-*
cut tunc is qui secundum carnem natus erat, persequebatur illum qui
secundum Spiritum. sic pro omnibus negotiis historiam confessus
est. nec enim confinia esse dixisset illa quae secundum Agar fuerunt *illius quae nunc est Hierusalem*, quam nunc esse confitebatur.
neque *sicut* posuisset, quem non esse existimabat. nam quod dixit,
sicut, similitudinem utique ostendit; similitudo autem fieri non
poterit, rebus non stantibus. addito et quod dixerat *tunc*, incertum
existimans quantum tempus designans dicit. superflua autem erit
et temporum diuisio, si tamen non fuerit factum. sed apostolus
quidem ita dicit; isti uero omnia e contrario faciunt, omnem de
diuina scriptura historiam somniorum nocturnorum nihil differre uolentes; nec enim Adam, Adam esse dicunt, quando maxime
eos de diuina scriptura 'spiritaliter' enarrare acciderit—spiritalem
etiam interpretationem suam uolunt uocari desipientiam—neque
paradisum, paradisum, neque colubrum, colubrum esse dicentes.
ad quos uolebam illud dicere, ut historiam intercipientes, ultra
non habuerint historiam. hoc autem facto, dicant unde habent adserere, quisnam primus homo factus est? aut quomodo inoboe-
diens existit? aut quomodo introducta est mortis sententia? et siquidem de scripturis ista didicerunt, necessario illa quae ab illis
dicitur allegoria est manifesta desipientia, quia et superflua esse
per omnia arguitur. si autem hoc uerum est, et illa quae scripta
sunt non rerum gestarum retinent narrationem, aliud uero quid
profundum indicant et quod intellegi debeat, siue et spiritale, sicut ipsi uolunt dicere, quod et deprehenderunt, utpote spiritales
quidam ipsi existentes; unde eorum ergo acceptam habent cognitionem? quemadmodum autem illa et dicunt, quasi de diuina ideo
docti locuntur scriptura? et sileo interim illud, quoniam haec cum
ita se habeant, neque illa quae secundum Christum sunt uidebuntur qua ratione facta sint. reuocauit enim, sicut apostolus dicit,

5   confinis *C* H*   7   quam *C H*   15   de, scriptura *om C*   ‖   accederit *C**
18   historia *C (corr.)*   19   abuterentur *C* habuterint (*sic*) *H (corr.)*   21   extitit
H (corr.)   26   indicat *H*   ‖   et (*bef.* spir.) *om. C (corr.)*   27   ipse *C**   28
quidem *C (corr.)*   ‖   unde ergo eor. *C*   30   dum (*for* docti) *H*   ‖   haec cum *C*
cum haec *H*   32   sunt (*for* sint) *C*

actually happened for his own interpretation, as when he says *she corresponds to the present Jerusalem* (4:23), or when he says *just as at that time the child who was born according to the flesh persecuted the child who was born according to the Spirit* (4:29). In this way he acknowledged the narrative in all these matters. Otherwise he would not have said that what concerned Hagar corresponds *to the present Jerusalem,* which he acknowledges exists at the present time. Nor would he have put down *just as* to refer to someone he did not think existed. For when he said *just as*, he was doubtless making a comparison, and no comparison can be made unless the terms of the comparison continue to exist. Furthermore, when he said *at that time*, though he supposes it to be unspecified, he meant to indicate a definite time. And the distinction of times would be meaningless if what happened had nevertheless not taken place. This is, indeed, what the apostle means; but those people invert the meaning of everything since they wish the whole narrative of divine scripture to differ in no way from dreams of the night. For they say that not even Adam actually existed as Adam, since it strikes them they should interpret scripture as much as possible "spiritually"—they want their folly to be called spiritual interpretation. [75] So they say that paradise did not exist as paradise nor the serpent as the serpent. I should like to say to them that by breaking up the narrative they no longer have a narrative. And if they do this, let them say where they get the basis for answering these questions: Who, pray tell, was the first man created? Or how was he found disobedient? Or how was the sentence of death introduced? And if they have learned answers to these questions from the scriptures, it necessarily follows that what they call allegory is obvious folly because it is proved to be in all respects useless. And if their view is true and what is written does not preserve an account of what really happened but points to something else profound and that must be understood intellectually—something spiritual, as they want to say, which they can discern since they are themselves spiritual people—where have they acquired this knowledge? And how can they make these assertions as if they are placed in office because they have been taught by divine scripture? For the present I pass over the fact that, if what they claim were the case, then neither will it appear for what reason Christ's dispensation has taken place. For, as the apostle says, he revoked Adam's disobedience and removed the

inoboedientiam Adae, et mortis sententiam soluit. quae sunt illa
quae olim facta esse dicuntur, et ubi sunt facta? siquidem historia
quae de his est, non ista, sed altera aliqua secundum eos significat.
quem autem locum obtinebit apostolica dictio: *timeo autem ne si-*
5 *cut coluber Euam seduxit;* si neque coluber fuit, neque Eua, neque
seductio alias erga illum extitit? et multis in locis euidens est apostolus historiam antiquorum ut ueritatem per omnia fuisse abusus. et hoc loco quasi de gestis negotiis et illis quae apud Iudaeos
in confessione erant deducta, adsertionem suam comprobare ad-
10 nititur; quod ei et ab initio fuerat propositum. quid autem illud
est? ut maiora illa quae secundum Christum sunt ostenderentur
ab illis quae sunt in lege, et multum praehonorabilior perspice-
retur illa quae apud nos est iustitia ab illa quae in lege est. ideo
duo testamenta esse dixit; unum quod per Moysen, aliud quod
15 per Christum. uocat autem testamentum in Christum, resurrectionem quam promisit omnibus nobis, primus ipse ex mortuis exsurgens. et hoc in epistola illa quae ad Hebraeos est interpretantes
ostendimus euidentius.

†sicut enim illa quae per Moy-   [ὥσπερ γὰρ τὰ διὰ Μωϋσέως δο-
20 sen fuerant data hanc habebant   θέντα ὑπὸ τὸν νόμον] ἐβούλετο πο-
intentionem, ut sub lege hi qui   λιτεύεσθαι [τοὺς αὐτὸν παρειληφό-
eam acceperant conuersarentur,   τας], καὶ τὴν ἐκεῖθεν δικαίωσιν δέ-
et illam iustitiam quae inde erat   χεσθαι·
susciperent (propter quod et de
25 Aegypto exierunt, et remoto in
loco fuerunt constituti; ut ab
omni gentium permixtione segregati, cum competenti cautela
custodire possent legem sibi da-
30 tam);

4-5 siue (*for* sicut) *C*   5   sine (*for* si neque) *H*   6   ergo *C**   7   antiq. ut
uer. antiquorum (*sic*) *H**   ‖   fuisset *H**   8   digestis *H*   14   testamento *H*
15   in Christo *C* (*corr.*)   19   sq. Coisl. 204 f. 34 b, [Cr. vi. 70, Fr. 127] ὥσπερ
γὰρ (φησὶν) ὁ Ἰσμαὴλ κατὰ σάρκα γεγέννηται, οὕτως καὶ ἐνταῦθα ὁ νόμος τοὺς
ὑπ' αὐτὸν ἐβούλετο πολιτεύεσθαι καὶ τὴν ἐκ. δικ. δέχεσθαι· καὶ ὥσπερ ὁ Ἰσαὰκ
κατὰ χάριν γεγέννηται [p. 84, l. 15 sq.] (τοῦτο γὰρ ἡ ἐπαγγελία, τῆς ἀκολουθίας
τοῦτο μὴ βουλομένης), οὕτως καὶ τῶν κ. Χ., κ.τ.λ.   20   fuerant *om H**   29
sidatam (*for* sibi d.) *H**

sentence of death. What are the events said to have happened once upon a time, and where did they take place, if we assume that the narrative about them does not refer to them but to some other meaning they have? And what room will be left for the apostle's words (2 Cor 11:3): *But I am afraid that as the serpent deceived Eve*, if there was neither a serpent nor Eve nor her subsequent seduction by him? And it is clear in many passages that the apostle employed the narrative of things of old as true in all respects. [76] And in this passage it is on the basis of events that actually took place and of those traditions acknowledged by the Jews as true that he strives to prove his own claim, which he sets forth from the outset. But what is that claim? He wants to demonstrate that Christ's dispensation is greater than that of the law and that our righteousness should be perceived as far more excellent than that found in the law. Thus, he said that there were two testaments, one through Moses and the other through Christ. And he calls the testament in Christ the resurrection that he promised to all of us, since he rose himself the first of the dead. In our commentary on his letter to the Hebrews we have demonstrated this more clearly.

†For the dispensation given through Moses intended that those who received it [77] should live their lives under the law and should receive that righteousness that came from it. For this reason they left Egypt and were established in a distant place, so that by being separated from all association with the Gentiles they might keep the law given them with suitable care.

For the dispensation given by Moses willed that those who received it should live their lives under the law and receive the righteousness that came from it.

sic et illa quae secundum Christum sunt hanc habent intentionem et finem, ut soluatur quidem mors, resurgant uero omnes homines qui quolibet tempore fuerunt, et in inmortali ultra degant natura, nec peccare ulterius ullo modo possint
propter illam gratiam Spiritus
quae inest illis;*

οὕτως καὶ τῶν κατὰ Χριστὸν ὁ
σκοπὸς οὗτος ἦν καὶ τὸ τέλος, λυ-
θῆναι μὲν τὸν θάνατον, ἀναστάντας
δὲ ἅπαντας τοὺς πώποτε γεγονότας
ἀνθρώπους ἐν ἀθανάτῳ διάγειν τῇ
φύσει, μηδαμῶς ἁμαρτεῖν ἐπιδεχο-
μένους ἔτι διὰ τὴν ἐνοῦσαν αὐτοῖς
ἔτι τότε χάριν τοῦ πνεύματος.

per quam et ab omni peccato securi habebimur. haec enim iustificatio et uera est et perfecta. iusta ergo ratione et *testamenta* similiter utraque uocauit, eo quod illa ipsa quae lex docebat, haec
et gratia per opera dirigebat; scilicet ut et Deus diligatur et pro-
ximus. haec autem ipsa etiam lex seruare praecipiebat, discernens
atque docens nullo modo debere peccare. gratia autem id operibus
implet per resurrectionem et illam inmortalitatem quae tunc nobis
aderit per Spiritum; a quo et gubernati tunc peccare nequaquam
poterimus.

iustificatio equidem est et in lege [et] apud Christum. sed in
lege quidem adquiritur ab illo qui labore multo et sudore eam adquirere poterit; quod erat durissimum, immo (ut uerius dicam) inpossibile, si tamen pro legum scrupulositate id quis uellet iudicare; nam non peccare ex integro hominem existentem inpossibile
est. hic uero per solam gratiam adquiritur; nec enim peccare ultra
poterimus tunc quando et excepto omni labore, illam quae a Christo est obtinebimus iustificationem. ideo memoratus est Agar et
Sarram (ex quibus altera quidem secundum sequentiam naturae
peperit, altera uero cum parere non posset, et per gratiam peperit
Isaac; in quibus multum nimis ille qui secundum gratiam fuit natus praehonorabilior est inuentus), ut ex comparatione tali ostendat, quoniam et nunc illa quae secundum Christum est iustificatio
multo melior est ab illa, eo quia per gratiam adquiritur; bene pro
illa quidem quae in lege est iustificatio illam quae ordine naturae

7 degeant *C H* 10 est in illis *H* 11 habebantur *H* 13 ultraque *C **
H 15 ipsa lex etiam *H* 16 posse peccare debere *H*: corr.*, pecc. deb. 26
omne *C** 28 Saram (*so nearly always*) *H* 29 possit et *C*: corr.*, posset (*om
et*) 34 iustificatione *C (corr.)* ‖ illam quae ordinem *C** illa quae ordinem *H*

So, too, Christ's dispensation has this intention and purpose, that death should be destroyed and that all people who had lived at whatever time should rise again and thereafter live in an immortal nature no longer capable of sinning in any way because of the grace of the Spirit that is within them,* So, too, the aim and purpose of Christ's dispensation was that death should be destroyed and that all people who had ever been, by rising again should live in an immortal nature, no longer admitting sinning in any way because of the grace of the Spirit within them at that time. a grace by which we shall be kept safe from all sin. For this justification is both true and perfect. Therefore, with good reason he called both dispensations alike *testaments*, because grace by its guidance was putting into effect those very teachings of the law, namely, the love of God and the neighbor. For the law kept on commanding the keeping of these same commandments, emphasizing them and teaching the duty of not sinning in any way. But grace brings this to fulfillment by the resurrection and that immortality that will then be ours through the Spirit, since when we shall then be guided by him, we shall by no means sin.

Justification, then, is both in the law and with Christ. But in the law it would in fact be acquired only by the person able to acquire it by much toil and sweat. This would prove extremely difficult, indeed, to speak more truly, impossible, if at any rate one wanted to judge according to a scrupulous keeping of the laws. For it is impossible that any human existing would be completely sinless. Indeed, this is acquired only by grace, for we shall be incapable of sinning any longer at that time when apart from all toil we shall obtain the justification that comes from Christ. [78] Thus, Paul mentioned Hagar and Sarah, the first of whom gave birth according to the order of nature, but the other, since she could not give birth, bore Isaac according to grace. Of the two sons the one born according to grace was found far and away much the more distinguished. Paul mentioned them so that by such a comparison he might demonstrate that now, as well, justification according to Christ is far better than that other justification because it is acquired by grace. He rightly took the woman who gave birth by the order of nature as standing for the justification that is in the law, and he set down the woman seen to have given birth beyond hope as standing for justification that is by grace. He does this

peperit accipiens; pro illa uero iustificatione quae in gratia est, illam posuit quae praeter spem peperisse uidetur; eo quod illis qui
in praesentia sunt legitima competit conuersatio; illis uero qui semel resurrexerunt, et facti sunt incorrupti, et circumcisio superflua est et oblatio et sacrificiorum nec non et dierum obseruantia.

†sunt autem quaedam quae   ἔστιν δὲ ἀκολουθία μὲν γινομένη
secundum naturae fiunt sequen-   φύσεως, ἡ εἰς τόνδε τὸν βίον
tiam, id est, nascentium in hac   τῶν τικτομένων πάροδος· ἐφ' οὗ
uita transitus, in quibus etiam   τὴν κατὰ νόμον πολιτείαν χώραν
legitima conuersatio locum ha-   ἔχειν συμβέβηκεν. χάριτος δὲ ἡ
bere uidetur. gratiae uero il-   γέννησις ἐκείνη καθ' ἣν ἀνιστάμενοι
la est natiuitas secundum quam   πάντες εἰς τὴν μέλλουσαν ζωὴν
resurgentes omnes in futuram   ἀποτίκτονται.
uitam nascuntur;*

in qua Christi maxime impletur iustificatio. sic ergo pro illa quae
secundum legem est iustificatione, illam accepit quae naturae sequentia peperit, utpote lege locum habente tenere illos qui in hac
uita nascuntur, qui et secundum naturae nascuntur sequentiam;
pro illa uero iustificatione, quae secundum Christum est, illam
quae per gratiam peperit; eo quod et uerissime impletur in illis qui
semel resurrexisse uidentur, qui per gratiam praeter omnem spem
secundam illam expectant natiuitatem. ob hanc igitur edixit: *quae
sunt per allegoriam dicta:*

†allegoriam uocans illam com-   ἀλληγορίαν ἐκάλεσεν τὴν ἐκ παρα-
parationem quae ex dudum fac-   θέσεως τῶν ἤδη γεγονότων πρὸς τὰ
tis negotiis comparari poterat il-   παρόντα σύγκρισιν.
lis quae ad praesens sunt*
unde et adicit

  *haec autem sunt duo testamenta; unum quidem a monte Sina, in
seruitutem generans, quae est Agar.*

  tales etenim sunt. ad illud autem redit quod dixit: *quae sunt
per allegoriam dicta;* ut sit: 'haec enim sunt duo testamenta, quae
sunt per allegoriam dicta.' uult autem dicere quoniam per allego-

2 periisse *H** 3 quae *H** 5 necnon et sanctarum siue dierum obs. *C** so-
lempnitatum (*after* sanct.) *add C* (*corr.*) necnon dier. obs. *H* 6 sq. Coisl. 204,
f. 34 b, [Cr. vi. 70, Fr. 127]. 7-8 sequentia *C* sapientia *H* 16 iustificationem
*C*H* ‖ quam *C* 17 legem *C H* ‖ habentem *C H* 18 sequentia *C H*
(*corr.*) 22 se dixit *C* *H* esse d. *C* (*corr.*) 24 Coisl. 204 *l.c.* θεόδωρος (marg.)
καὶ ἄλλος δέ· ἀλλ. (φησὶν) ἐκάλεσεν κ.τ.λ. 31 enim (*for* etenim) *H*

because living according to the law is relevant for those who are in the present, but for those who have once risen again and been made incorruptible, circumcision is useless as well as the offering of sacrifices, to say nothing of the observance of days.

†There are certain events that take place according to the order of nature, that is, the passage to this life of those who are born. Among them living a life according to the law also appears to have a place. But the birth of grace is one by which all are born to the life to come by rising again.*

There is an order that takes place in nature, the passage to this life of those who are born. In this passage it came to pass that living a life according to the law has a place. But the birth of grace is one by which all are born to the life to come by rising again.

This life is the one in which the justification of Christ is perfectly fulfilled. Therefore, he took the woman who gave birth by the order of nature to stand for that justification that is according to the law, inasmuch as the law holds the place of binding those who are born into this life, born according to the order of nature. But the woman who gave birth by grace stands for that justification that [79] is according to Christ, because it is most truly fulfilled in those who plainly have once and for all been raised and in those who by grace hope beyond all hope for that birth. Therefore, this is why he said *Now this is by an allegory.*

†He calls an allegory that comparison that can be made between events that happened long ago and present circumstances.*

He called allegory the comparison made by relating events that had already taken place to present circumstances.

Then he adds:

4:24b *And they are two testaments, one in fact from Mount Sinai, giving birth for slavery, which is Hagar.*

"They" refers to the two women. He alludes to what he said, *this is by an allegory*, as though the verse read: "For these women are the two testaments spoken of by an allegory." And what he means is that by allegory one can compare the two testaments.

riam similare poterit quis illis duobus, id est, Agar et Sarrae, duo
testamenta; ita ut sit Agar quidem in ordine legitimorum praeceptorum, quia etiam lex data est in monte Sina. generat autem in seruitutem. illi enim qui sub lege conuersantur in ordine seruorum
et praecepta accipiunt et legem; puniuntur uero sine aliqua excusatione, si peccasse fuerint inuenti; laudantur uero, si secundum
omnem scrupulositatem legem observare uoluerint. quod ualde
arduum est, et cum multo expeditur labore. seruorum autem est
proprium et non liberorum, hoc modo sub lege teneri. et ostendens quoniam ipsa comparatio quae de Agar facta est non est extranea veteri testamento, adicit:

Agar enim Sina mons est in Arabia; coniungitur uero ei qui nunc
est Hierusalem, seruit autem cum filiis suis.

†Arabia antiquis temporibus 'Αραβία τὸ παλαιὸν οὐχ ἡ νῦν
non illa quae nunc nominatur οὕτως ὀνομαζομένη μόνον ἐλέγετο,
sola erat; sed et solitudo omnis, ἀλλὰ γὰρ ἥ τε ἔρημος πᾶσα καὶ
et illae partes quae circa solitu- τὰ περὶ αὐτὴν οἰκούμενα μέρη, καὶ
dinem habitabantur; nec non et μὴν καὶ τῆς Αἰγύπτου μέρος οὐκ
Aegypti pars non modica,* ἐλάχιστον.

in qua et locus erat ille in quo habitabant Israhelitae eo in tempore quo commorabantur in Aegypto. sic enim dicebatur locus ille,
sicut de divina id discimus Scriptura, quoniam *in terram Gessen*
Arabiae habitant. quia ergo indc erat Agar et Sina mons ad Ara-
bios uoluit ostendere. quoniam apta est similitudo Agar ad uetus
testamentum, eo quod in illo sit data loco, qui locus ad gentem pertinet illam unde erat et Agar.

†nam quod dixit: *adfinis est* [ὃ γὰρ εἶπεν· συνστοιχεῖ τῇ νῦν
eius quae nunc est Hierusalem, de ἱερουσαλήμ,] περὶ τῆς Ἄγαρ [λέ-
Agar dicit; ut dicat quoniam 'il- γει· ἵνα εἴπῃ] ὅτι τῇ παρ' ἡμῖν Ἱε-
la quae apud nos est Hierusa- ρουσαλήμ, τουτέστιν τῇ κατὰ τὸν
lem, hoc est, quae in saeculum βίον τοῦτον θεωρουμένη, ἰσοδυνα-
hoc esse uidetur, aequam uirtu- μεῖ ἡ Ἄγαρ, ταύτην ἡμῖν τὴν τά-
tem habet ad Agar; hunc no- ξιν ἐπεχούσης τῆς νῦν Ἱερουσαλήμ,

2 in ordinem *H* 8 autem *om H* 10 non extr. (*om* est) *H* 12 enim *om H*
14 sq. Coisl. 204, f. 35 b [Cr. vi. 71, Fr. 128]. Θεόδωρος (marg.) καὶ ἄλλος δέ
φησιν· 'Αραβία, κ.τ.λ. 16 ἀλλᾱγαρ (*sic*) cod. ἀλλ' Ἄγαρ edd. 20 eo temp. *H*
22 gesen *C* (*corr.*) 23 Arabii *H* 25 sita (*for* data) *H* 27 Coisl. 204 *l.c.*
τοῦτο οὖν θέλει εἰπεῖν περὶ τῆς Ἄγαρ, ὅτι τῇ παρ' ἡμῖν, κ.τ.λ. 31 seculo *C*
(*corr.*) 33 hoc n. ordine retinente illam *C** (ordinem *C* (*corr.*) *H*: retinentem
H): txt *g*

to those two, that is, to Hagar and Sarah, so that Hagar may be ranked in the law's commands, because the law was given on Mount Sinai and gives birth to slavery. For those who live their lives under the law are so ranked as slaves, and they accept both the commands and the law. [80] But they are punished without any excuse if they are found to have sinned, while they are praised if with all scrupulous care they are willing to observe the law. This is extremely difficult and is accomplished with great toil. And it is appropriate for slaves and not for free people to be held under the law in this way. Then, to demonstrate that the comparison made from Hagar is not foreign to the Old Testament, he adds:

4:25 *Now Hagar is Mount Sinai in Arabia and corresponds to the present Jerusalem and is in slavery with its sons.*

†In times of old Arabia was not only the region that now has that name but included the entire desert and the places that were inhabited round about the desert, not least of which was the part of Egypt*

Of old Arabia was not only said to be what now has that name but was also the entire desert and the inhabited parts round about it, not least of which was part of Egypt.

[81] in which there was also the place the Israelites inhabited during their stay in Egypt. For this was the way that place was spoken of, as we learn from divine scripture: *they dwell in the land of Goshen in Arabia*.[35] Therefore, he wanted to demonstrate from this that Hagar and Mount Sinai pertain to Arabia. Consequently, the comparison of Hagar to the Old Testament is suitable because it was given in the place belonging to the nation from which Hagar came.[36]

†Now by saying *corresponds to the present Jerusalem* he refers to Hagar, so that he means "that Jerusalem which is with us, [82] that is, which is seen to exist in this age, has the same worth as Hagar, since the present Jerusalem retains for us the system in which the legal ordinan-

For he said *corresponds to the present Jerusalem* of Hagar, in order to say that Hagar is the equivalent of our Jerusalem, that is, the one to be seen in this life, since the present Jerusalem includes for us the system in which the legal ordinances of that testament are fulfilled in

---

[35] See Gen 45:10 and 46:34 in the LXX.
[36] According to Gen 16:1 Hagar was an Egyptian.

bis ordinem retinente illa quae
nunc est Hierusalem, in qua testamenti illius legitima implen-
tur, ad comparationem illorum
5 quae expectantur, quae etiam
frui in futuro speramus saeculo.' quam et continere uidebatur Agar, Sarrae comparata.
nam quod dixit: *seruit autem*
10 *cum filiis suis,* non de Agar id
dicit, sed ad testamentum quod
datum est in Sina*

ἐφ' ἧς τὰ τῆς διαθήκης ἐκείνης νόμιμα πληροῦται, πρὸς τὰ προσδοκώμενα, ὧν δὴ καὶ τεύξεσθαι ἐπὶ
τοῦ μέλλοντος ἐλπίζομεν αἰῶνος, ἣν
ἐπεῖχεν ἡ Ἄγαρ πρὸς τὴν Σάρραν
κρινομένη. τὸ μέντοι δουλεύει μετὰ τῶν τέκνων αὐτῆς, οὐ περὶ τῆς
Ἄγαρ λέγει, ἀλλὰ περὶ τῆς ἐν τῷ
Σινᾶ δοθείσης διαθήκης.

reddidit illud, ut statuat illud quod dixit: *unum quidem ex monte*
Sina, in serutitutem generans. filios eius illos esse dixit qui sub illa
15 conuersantur. bene autem dixit quod et ipsa *cum filiis suis seruit.*
testamentum enim quale sit in illis utique cognoscitur qui illud susceperunt. nec enim secundum suam substantiam perspicitur; itaque seruit, quando illi, qui secundum illud sunt, seruire uidentur.

    conueniebat allegoriae sectatores ad illud respicere quod dixit:
20 *confinis est eius quae nunc est Hierusalem;* euidenter enim non in-
tercipientis est illa quae secundum Agar, sed aequam eas habere uirtutem ostendere uoluit, secundum quod significatione id ipsum sunt. beatus uero Paulus primum testamentum dicens, dicit
et aliud:

25   *quae autem sursum est Hierusalem, libera est; quae est mater om-*
nium nostrorum.

    sursum Hierusalem non somnia colligens dicit apostolus, ad si-
militudinem illorum qui uniuersa in allegoriam iactanda esse existimant; sed quoniam testamentum secundum scit nuncupare re-
30 surrectionem, quam expectabant illi qui adsecuti sunt, qui etiam
et in caelo morandi licentiam adsequi sperabant, liberi ab omni
existentes peccato. ad comparationem ergo huius illam nominauit
quae sursum est Hierusalem; conuersationem nostram illam quam
in caelis habemus hoc modo indicans, eo quod illo commorabimur
35 simul cum Christo degentes; in qua etiam secundum omnem co-

---

3 δεῖ cod., Cr.: δὲ Fr.   5 quia etiam *H*   13 redigit (*for* reddidit) *s*   17 secundum *om H**   21 eos *C H*   26 nostrum *C* (*corr.*) *H* (*corr.*)   28 uniuersam,
iactandam *C* H*   31 se sperant *C*   35 quo *C*

ces of that testament are fulfil-led in contrast to what was ex-pected, what we also hope to en-joy in the age to come." And what Hagar plainly included is contrasted with Sarah. For he said *and is in slavery with its sons* not of Hagar, but he harks back to the testament given on Sinai*

contrast to the expectations we hope to gain in the age to come. What Hagar includes is distin-guished from Sarah. He says *and is in slavery with its children* not of Hagar but of the covenant given on Sinai.

in order to establish what he had said (4:23): *one from Mount Sinai, bearing children for slavery*. He said that those who live their lives under that testament are its sons. And he rightly said that it *is in slavery with its sons*. For the character of the testament is certainly recognized in those who have received it. For it is not described by its own substance, and so it is in slavery when those who follow it are plainly in slavery.

It would be right for those devoted to allegory to pay attention to what he said: *she corresponds to the present Jerusalem*. For it is quite clearly not a question of breaking up the account of Hagar, but what he wanted to show is that Hagar and the present Jerusalem have a like worth because they have the same meaning. Blessed Paul speaks of the first testament and then makes another statement:

4:26 *But the Jerusalem above is free; she is the mother of us all*.

[83] The apostle does not say *Jerusalem above* by concocting dreams as those people do who suppose that everything must be tossed into allegory. Rather, he uses the expression since he knows how to designate the second testament as the resurrection that those who attained it were awaiting, those who were indeed also hoping to attain the privilege of dwelling in heaven freed from all sin. Therefore, he used the expression *which is the Jerusalem above* in relation to this, pointing out in this way that form of life of ours that we have in the heavens because we shall dwell and live there together with Christ and shall conduct ourselves with perfect diligence. At any rate, he used the expression *Jerusalem above* in this way to refer to the heavenly dwelling, since even

nuersabimur industriam. at *sursum Hierusalem* caeleste habitaculum sic nominans, quoniam et Judæi in locis Hierusalem commorantes cum Deo se commorare existimabant; ubi et debitum Deo
persoluere seruitium properabant, hunc locum competentem esse
sibi existimantes, eo quod neque sacrificium neque holocaustum
neque aliud aliquid secundum legem alibi perficere poterant. illa enim *quae sursum est Hierusalem, libera est; quae est mater om-*
nium nostrum. ut dicat quoniam 'resurrectionem adsecuti, et secundam illam et gloriosam percipientes natiuitatem, cuius propter
et in caelo commorabimur, illam Hierusalem nostram esse existimantes, in libertate plurima omnes simul erimus; legitima praecepta aut alia quae eiusmodi sunt implere non indigentes. cum
multa autem fiducia illo commorabimur, eo quod nec peccatis ultra subiacere poterimus.' et utitur scripturale testimonium:

scriptum est enim: *'lactare, sterilis quae non paris; erumpe et cla-*
ma, quae non parturis; quoniam multi filii desertae magis quam eius
quae habet uirum.'

hoc non tamquam prophetice de resurrectione dictum posuit;
sed testimonium abusus est propter nomen *sterilis,* eo quod, steri-
lem constitutam Sarram in ordinem secundi accipit testamenti; ut
dicat quoniam 'omnia illa erunt praeter spem. exsurgemus enim
qui mortui sumus; ita ut et numero multo ampliores ab illis inue-
niamur. multo enim ampliores erimus qui in hoc concurrimus testamento. illi enim qui sub lege sunt testamento, gens est una. nos
uero qui resurrectionis testamentum adsequi habemus, omnes sumus filii.' unde et adicit:

nos autem, fratres, secundum Isaac promissionis sumus filii.

quod dixit: *secundum Isaac,* hoc est, 'erimus secundum Isaac;
non secundum naturam, sed secundum gratiam. sicut enim Isaac
praeter omnem spem natus est; eo quod et gratiae est resurrectio,
non naturae.' et quouiam ab illis quae in diuina tenentur scriptura probauit testamentorum differentiam, ostendens quoniam illorum quae secundum naturam sunt, multo meliora sunt illa quae
secundum gratiam; ipsa ergo praeditus sequentia, etiam praesen-

---

1   Abraham *(for* at sursum) *C H*   ‖   caelestem *C H*   3   commorari *C (corr.)*
5   sibi ex. esse *H*   8-9   secundum *C H*   9   et *om* 2° *H*   ‖   gloriam *(after*
propret) *add in marg. C (corr.)*   10   commorabuntur *H*   12   non *om H*   13
illuc *(for* illo) *H*   16   multae filiae *C H*   21   erant *H*   24   legis *C (corr.)*   25
recsurrectionis *C**   26   filii *om H*   34   praesentia *H*

the Jews who dwelt in the environs of Jerusalem used to think they were dwelling with God. Jerusalem was where they hastened to discharge the slavery they owed to God, since they thought this the right place for them, because they could nowhere else accomplish sacrifice or whole burnt offering or anything else according to the law. This is why that *Jerusalem which is above is free, which is the mother of us all.* What he means is that "by attaining the resurrection and by it also discerning the glorious new birth by which we shall also dwell in heaven, and by thinking that to be our Jerusalem, we shall be at the same time in the greatest freedom, since we shall no longer need to fulfill the law's ordinances or anything else of this kind. And we shall dwell there with great confidence because we shall no longer be capable of submitting to sin." And he employs a scriptural testimony (Isa 54:1):

[84] 4:27 *For it is written, "Rejoice, you barren one, you who bear no children, burst into song and shout, you who endure no birth pangs; for the sons of the desolate woman are more numerous than of the one who has a husband."*

He did not cite this verse as though it were spoken prophetically of the resurrection, but he employed the testimony because of the word *barren*, since he takes Sarah as the barren woman in the rank of the second testament. What he means is that "all that will be beyond hope. For we who have died will rise again so that we shall be found more numerous than those others. For we who come together in this testament shall be much more numerous. Those, however, who are in the testament under the law are a single nation. But we who hold fast to our attainment of the testament of the resurrection shall all be sons." This is why he adds:

4:28 *Now we, brothers, are sons of the promise, like Isaac.*

When he said *like Isaac*, he meant "we shall be like Isaac, not according to nature, but according to grace. For just as Isaac was born beyond all hope, [so it is for us] because the resurrection is by grace and not by nature." And since he has proved by what is found in divine scripture the difference between the two testaments, he shows that the dispensation of grace is much better than that of nature. Therefore, following this train of thought, he also makes full use of the present circumstances:

4:29 *But just as at that time he who was born according to the flesh persecuted the one born according to the Spirit, so it is now also.*

tibus abutitur negotiis:

sed sicut [tunc] is qui secundum carnem natus erat, persequebatur
eum qui secundum Spiritum, sic et nunc.

de illis qui secundum Christum sunt,

5 †non solum quae fidei sunt et
promissionis, ponit nomen (sicuti et in superioribus iam ostendimus), sed et Spiritus; et
multis in locis hac uel maxime
10 abutitur uoce, sicuti et ad Romanos quis euidenter perspicere poterit; eo quod expectamus
participatione Spiritus fruitionem accipere futurorum bono-
15 rum.

sic igitur et de illis qui secundum legem sunt, illud quod corporis est dicit; eo quod secundum praesentem hanc uitam lex
20 utilis esse potest. nam quia 'carnem' temporale dicit, et quod
facile soluitur, cum nostram
[non] nominauerit naturam,*

οὐ τὸ τῆς πίστεως καὶ τῆς ἐπαγγελίας μόνον ἐντίθησιν ὄνομα, ἀλλὰ γὰρ καὶ τὸ τοῦ πνεύματος· ἅτε
δὴ προσδοκώντων ἡμῶν τῇ μετουσίᾳ τοῦ πνεύματος τὴν ἀπόλαυσιν
δέξασθαι τῶν μελλόντων·

οὑτωσὶ δὲ καὶ ἐπὶ τῶν κατὰ νόμον
τὸ τῆς σαρκός, ἅτε δὴ κατὰ τὸν
παρόντα τουτονὶ βίον χρησιμεύειν
τοῦ νόμου δυναμένου· σάρκα γὰρ τὸ
πρόσκαιρον καὶ εὐδιάλυτον λέγει,
ὅταν μὴ τὴν ἡμετέραν ὀνομάζῃ
φύσιν.

multis in locis id ostendimus in interpretatione apostolica; et ple-
25 naria nostra expositio id euidenter ostendit, illis tamen qui cautissime uolunt dictis intendere. et quoniam Agar eicitur quae sequentia naturali peperisse uidebatur, quae formam acceperat ue-
teris testamenti, eo quod et tenere [ordinem] poterat, secundum
praesentem uitam, illorum qui naturali ordine nascuntur; quod et
30 nuper ediximus. *sicuti ergo tunc ille qui* ex naturae ordine *fuerat na-*
tus illum persequebatur qui per promissionem *fuerat natus,*
†*sic et* hic illi qui *nunc* legis exi-
stunt uindices illa quae gratiae

[οὕτως καὶ νῦν] οἱ τοῦ νόμου
προεστάναι δῆθεν βουλόμενοι, τὰ

---

2 tunc *om C H*   5   sq. Coisl. 204, f. 36 b [Cr. vi. 73, Fr. 128] ἄλλος δέ θησιν·
οὐ τὸ τῆς π., κ.τ.λ.   6   ponet *C**   8   et multis et multis *H**   13   participationem *H*   18   υἱὸν (for βίον) Cr. (per incuriam).   21   temporalem *C H* txt *g*
22   soluit *C H*   23   non *om C H* txt *g*   26   qui (*for* quae 1°) *H*   28   ordinem
om C H   30   nuber ediximus *C* nubere diximus *H*   32   οἱ τοίνυν τοῦ νόμου
κ.τ.λ. cod. and edd. See lat.

[85] Of those who are according to Christ

†he uses not only the words *faith* and *promise* (as we have already demonstrated above) but also the word *Spirit*. In many passages he makes special use of this word, as one can clearly see in Romans,[37] because we await our reception of the good things to come by participation in the Spirit.

He uses not only the words *faith* and *promise* but also the word *Spirit*, since we expect to receive the enjoyment of the good things to come by participating in the Spirit.

Therefore, in this way he also speaks of those who are according to the law in reference to what belongs to the body, because it is in this present life that the law can be useful. Moreover, that fact that he speaks of flesh as temporal and something easily destroyed when he speaks of our nature*

So, too, he uses the word *flesh* of those who live by the law, since the law can be useful in this present life. For he speaks of flesh as temporal and easily destroyed, whenever he speaks of our nature.

is something we have demonstrated in many passages in interpreting the apostle's writings. Our fuller discussion has clearly demonstrated this, at least to those willing to examine his words with the greatest care. And since Hagar, who plainly gave birth by natural order, is driven out, she held the type of the Old Testament because it was capable of keeping a system in the present life for those born in the order of nature, as we have just said. Therefore, *just as at that time he who was born* by the order of nature *persecuted the one born* by promise,

---

[37] E.g., Rom 8:2.

sunt indagare adnituntur.*   τῆς χάριτος ἀπελαύνουσιν.
bene autem *secundum Spiritum* dixit, hoc est, ut dicat eum qui
secundum promissionem est; eo quod nostram personam ad similitudinem illius erat e contrario positurus. in quibus *Spiritus*
5 nomen ueraciter ponebatur propter illa quae ab illis creduntur.
optimos uero allegoristas uolebam hoc in loco illud interrogare,
utrum diuina scriptura retulit nobis quoniam Ismahel persequebatur Isaac, hoc significans quoniam quidam erant illorum qui
ex circumcisione sunt, qui in nouissimis temporibus aliquando il-
10 los, qui ex Galatis Christo crediderant, transducturi erant ad legem? et quis poterit condigne aliquando id deridere? itaque si nihil aliud, saltem hoc eos perspicere conueniebat, quoniam historiam apostolus quasi uere factorum negotiorum, et in confessione
deductorum existentem, in sua posuit narratione ut confirmaret il-
15 la quae dixerat. secundum comparationem uero uoluit ostendere
historiam ad illam similitudinem. unde et illa quae facta fuerant
illis ab extraneis abusus esse uidetur. quibus inconsequenter simul
et magnifice adicit:
    sed quid dicit scriptura? 'eice ancillam et filium eius; non enim he-
20 res erit filius ancillae cum filio liberae.'
    ut dicat quoniam 'nihil prodest illis laborare, sicuti nec illi tunc
profuit.
†nec enim est aliqua commu-   οὐδὲ γάρ ἐστίν τις κοινωνία τῶν
nio praesentibus ad futura, sed   παρόντων καὶ τῶν μελλόντων· οὐδ'
25 nec habere possunt locum le-   ἔχει χώραν τὰ νόμιμα ἐπὶ τῆς
gitima in nostram conuersatio-   καθ' ἡμᾶς διαίτης, ἣν κατὰ τύπον
nem, quam secundum formam   πληροῦμεν τῆς ἀναστάσεως. καὶ
implemus resurrectionis. quid   λοιπὸν ὡς ἐπὶ τῶν προκειμένων
ergo festinant illi eos qui in Chri- ἐπισυλλογίζεται.
30 sto crediderunt etiam ad legis
custodiam trahere?' deinde quasi qui ex praecedentibus colligere poterat negotium dicens:*

---

2 Spiritum Spiritum *H**   3   nostra persona *C H*   4   positura *C H*   ‖   Spiritum *H* [*for. leg.* Spiritum nomen … ponebat]   8   erant quidem *C* quidem
erant *H*   10   transducti erant *C** transducti sunt *H*   12   saltim *C** [cf. Wagner
orth. Verg. v. 470, cited by Hild. *Ap.* ii. 633]   14   delictorum (*for* deduct.) *H*
19   enim *om C*   23   nec enim talia *H*   26   in legitima *H** in legitimum *H*
(*corr.*)   32-33   collidere *H*

†*so also* those who *now* present so it is now also. Those, then,
themselves as champions of the who wish to be champions of
law strive to hunt out what be- the law, drive away what belongs to grace.* longs to grace.

[86] And he rightly said *according to the Spirit*, so as to mean
that Isaac was according to the promise, because he was about to
describe our position by comparing it to the likeness of Isaac's.
The word *Spirit* was truthfully used of both because of what was
believed because of them. I should like to ask those most excellent
allegorists whether in this passage divine scripture records for us
that Ishmael persecuted Isaac because it really means that there
would be certain people from the circumcision who in the most
recent times would try to hand over those Galatian Christians
to the law. Who would ever be able to make enough fun of
such an idea? And so if nothing else, it would at least be right
for them to recognize that the apostle put the narrative in his
discussion as one of events that really happened and one handed
down acknowledged as such, and that he did so to establish what
he had said. He did indeed want to display the narrative by
comparison with its likeness. This is why he plainly employed
what had actually happened in reference to circumstances foreign
to those events. He adds inconsistently but at the same time
splendidly:

4:30 *But what does the scripture say? "Drive out the slave and her
son, for the son of the slave will not be the heir with the son of the free
woman."*

He means that "toiling profits them nothing, just as it did not
profit him at that time.

†For neither is there anything For neither is there anything
in common between the present in common between the present
and the future, nor can the or- and the future, nor can the ordinances of the law have a place dinances of the law have a place
in our way of life, which we ac- in our way of life, which we accomplish according to the type complish according to the type
of the resurrection. Why, there- of the resurrection.
fore, are those people eager also
to drag those who have believed
in Christ to the observance of
the law?"

Then, as though he had been Then he draws a subsequent

itaque, fratres, non sumus ancillae filii, sed liberae.

cui dicto etiam exhortationem connectit:

libertate qua nos Christus liberauit state, et nolite iterum iugo se-
ruitutis obduci.

5 ab illis quae ostensa sunt ab eo exhortationem faciens, 'ne (inquit) *a libertate qua* uos *Christus liberauit* discedentes; iterum uos
sub *iugo seruitutis* legitimae constituatis.'

et ultra confidens et multitudini [et] magnitudini probationum
quae nullam controuersiam admittebant (alia quidem ex rebus
10 perspicuis, alia uero de diuinis sumpta scripturis, alia uero aliunde, omnia autem summe expressa habebantur); dicit in subsequentibus, quasi de rebus indubiis contestationem faciens:

ecce ego Paulus dico uobis quoniam si circumcidamini, in Christo
uobis nihil proderit.

15 bene posuit: *ecce ego Paulus*, quasi confidens super contestatio-
nis factae iustitiam, et quod numquam negari possit ob rerum ueritatem. 'circumcisi enim, a Christo nihil expectetis percipere, eo
quod nec est uobis ad eum ultra communio.' deinde quod fecit in
praecedenti negotio, ponit illud et uoce:

20 *testificor autem iterum omni homini circumcidenti se, quoniam de-*
bitor est totam legem implere.

nam quod dixit: *testificor*, euidenter id posuit. et quod dixit *ite-*
rum, contestatio enim et haec erat, et illud quod superius fuerat
dictum: 'ecce (inquit) et aliud contestor, quoniam qui circumci-
25 dit se obnoxius est implere legem omnem. quare? quoniam circumcisio confessio est legis seruandae. debet autem is qui confitetur, pactus sui implere conditionem. si autem hoc possibile sit
uobis, uos uideritis.' quoniam inpossibile est, eo quod et multa ni-

3 liberauit. state *H*   8   et 3° *om C* H* ac *C* (*corr.*)   10   prospicuis *H*   11
habebuntur. *H*   ‖   adicit (*for* dicit) *C*   13   ecce *om H**   ‖   Christus *H* (*corr.*)
16   negare *C* H*   19   ponet *C**   25   omnem legem *C*

able to deduce his case from what preceded, he says:* inference from what precedes.

[87] 4:31 *And so, brothers, we are not sons of the slave but of the free woman.*

He also joins an exhortation to this statement:

5:1 *Stand firm in the freedom by which Christ has freed us, and do not submit again to a yoke of slavery.*

He makes his exhortation from what has been demonstrated. "Do not (he says) desert *the freedom by which Christ has freed* you and again put yourselves under the *yoke of slavery* to the law's ordinances.

Furthermore, he confidently trusts in many and great proofs that allow no dispute, some of which are taken from the obvious facts and others from the divine scriptures and still others from other considerations—but all of them compelling in the highest degree. He then speaks in what follows as though he were making a solemn declaration about facts that could not be doubted:

5:2 *Listen! I, Paul, am telling you that if you are circumcised, in Christ[38] nothing will profit you.*

He rightly put down *Listen! I, Paul,* inasmuch as he trusted in the validity of the solemn declaration he was making and that it could never be denied because of the truth of the facts. "For if you are circumcised, you can expect to receive nothing from Christ, because you will no longer have fellowship with him." Then he puts into words what he had drawn up in his previous argument:

5:3 *Once again I testify to every man who circumcises himself that he is a debtor to fulfill the entire law.*

Now when he said *I testify,* he made the point quite clearly. And he said *once again,* for this solemn declaration was the same one he had spoken earlier. "Listen! (he says) I am making another attestation that whoever circumcises himself is liable to fulfill the entire law. Why? [88] Since circumcision is an acknowledgement that the law must be kept, whoever makes that acknowledgement must fulfill the conditions of his agreement. And you will see whether this is possible for you." The fact

---

[38] Swete finds some manuscript support in the witnesses to Theodore's commentary but points out the peculiarity of the reading "in Christ" and says: "It is difficult to account for this reading, unless we suppose that the scribe or translator had his eye upon v. 6 *infra*" (1:87).

mis praeuaricabant, et ipsi perspicere poterant facile et statim ante
omnia, eo quod praeceptum fuerat nihil illorum quae ad honorem
pertinent diuinitatis alibi debere implere praeter in locum Hierusalem. aut enim non implebant illud quod constitutum erat, aut
5   implentes praeuaricabant. posuit autem illud, ualde perspicuum
existens in his maxime quae praeuenerant, si tamen circumcisi ab
illis donationibus quae erant a Christo extranei constituebantur; et
a lege nullum iuuamen adsequi poterant, eo quod nec custodirent
illam sicut conueniebat. deinde et aliud adicit:
10   *destructi estis a Christo, qui in lege iustificamini.*
'nulla uobis est cum Christo ultra communio, qui ex lege iustificamini. itaque et ipsa simulatio qua uos credere in eum confin-
gitis superflua esse inuenitur, et nullum habet iuuamen.' et ostendens hoc ex ipsis rebus ita se habere:
15   *a gratia excidistis.*
'illa quae a Christo sunt, gratiae sunt. lex autem non est gratia.
quae ergo nobis erit cum aduersariis communio?'
mirabilis uero per omnia uidetur apostolus, et frequentia sensuum est talis qualis habet fieri a uiro in mediis constricto necessi-
20   tatibus et ui legum impulso et contestanti super his quae sibi fiunt,
ita ut in tempore suas possit exequi iustitias ante iudicem ipsum,
cum uindicare ueritatem tempus inuenerit; et quia nihil eorum
quae secundum se erant reliquit in tempore uiolentiae, neque adquieuit illis quae non bene fiebant; e contrario uero et contradixit
25   et contestatus est, litigans pro uirtutis suae possibilitate. talium
enim proprium est ut omnia illa dicant quae competere suis partibus existimant, et frequenter dicere illa et compendiose, sicut et

---

8   nullum *om H*   12-13   confiditis *H*   19   et (*for* est) *C H*   ‖   at uero (*for*
a uiro) *C H*   20   contestantem *C H*   21   ipsi *C: om H*

that this is impossible is because they transgressed too much in many ways and could themselves easily and at once discern what was plain to all, that it had been commanded that it was necessary to fulfill what pertained to the honor of divinity in no other place than in Jerusalem. For either they would not fulfill what had been appointed, or, if they did fulfill it, they would still transgress.[39] And he made this point, since it was especially obvious, particularly because of what had already happened, that if they were circumcised, they would have been placed outside those gifts that come from Christ and would have been able to gain no benefit from the law, because they would not keep the law as was right. Then he adds another point:

5:4a *You who want to be justified by the law have cut yourselves off from Christ.*

"You no longer have any fellowship with Christ if you are justified by the law. And so that very pretense by which you imagine you believe in him is found to be useless and to have no benefit." And on the basis of the facts themselves he demonstrates that this is the situation:

5:4b *You have fallen away from grace.*

"What Christ gives belongs to grace, but the law is not grace. Therefore, what fellowship can exist between us and our opponents?"

Indeed, the apostle is plainly admirable in all respects, and his frequent bursts of emotion are such as take place in a man held fast by difficulties, constrained by the force of the laws, and making his appeal concerning what has happened to him so that in due time he might be able to pursue his rights before [89] the judge himself, when he might find the occasion to claim the truth. He would have abandoned none of his concerns in a time of violence, nor would he have been satisfied with the evils that were taking place. On the contrary, he would have both objected and made his appeal, arguing as forcefully as possible. For it is characteristic of such people to tell their children everything they suppose suitable and to do so often and succinctly. This is what Paul has plainly

---

[39] This comment is obscure. Perhaps Theodore means that, even if the Galatians succeeded in observing the law, they would still transgress because it would be unlikely they would travel to Jerusalem to discharge the law's commands there.

hoc in loco Paulus fecisse uidetur. denique postquam arguit malitiam actus eorum, e contrario etiam sua posuit—quod et hoc ipsud
proprium est illorum qui contestantur:

nos enim Spiritu ex fide spem iustitiae expectamus.

5   solummodo quia non clamat et dicit quoniam 'nihil horum nostrum est; nullam cum istis habemus communionem. nos iustificari speramus per fidem, Spiritus expectantes gratiam per quam
et perfectam bonorum participationem adquirimus.' et adhuc his
sua connectens:

10   *in Christo* (inquit) *Iesu neque circumcisio quid ualet, neque praeputium; sed fides [quae] per caritatem inoperatur.*

'talia sunt illa quae secundum Christum sunt ita ut non in circumcisione, non in praeputio ueritas sit definita. fides enim est
apud nos quae omnia implet; quam etiam et erga illa quae ex-
15 pectantur consequentem illius promissis conuenit demonstrari, in
caritate perfectam fidem exhibentes. caritatem autem dicit illam
quae erga Deum est et erga proximum. qui enim credidit non
absoluta quadam intentione, sed cum animae suae firmitate, sicut et est credere conueniens, euidens est quoniam et diligere eum
20 adceleret utpote omnium bonorum nobis conlatorum auctorem;
nec non et proximum diligat. nam illa caritas quae erga Deum
est, etiam proximum diligere ut fas est praecipit, et maxime illum
qui eiusdem fidei esse uidetur. hunc enim diuina scriptura 'proximum' uocat. diligens uero proximum, opere utique suae animae
25 demonstrat affectum. nec enim possibile est illum qui Deum diligit non opus facere aliquod, unde et dilectionis euidentem poterit ostendere probationem. ille enim qui proximum diligit, necessario in opere suam ostendit amicitiam. hoc ergo dixit *fidem quae
per caritatem inoperatur,* quod cum uera fide erga Deum ostendit
30 caritatem, pariter etiam et erga proximum itidem subsequentem
ostendit caritatem. caritas uero necessario in opere debet cognosci, eo quod uerae sit fidei, quam conuenit habere illos qui Christo crediderunt; quia per caritatem in operibus debet demonstrari

---

1   hoc *om H**   2   ipsum *C (corr.) H*   4   Spiritum *C H*   5   conclamat (*for
non clamat*) *C (corr.)* ‖ dicat *H*   10   aliquid *H (corr.)*   11   quae *om C* H*
15   in caritatem perfectam *C** in caritate perfecta *C (corr.)*   17   proximos (*for
erga proximum*) *H*   19   et (*aft.* conuen.) *add C* ‖ dignum (*bef.* est cred.)
add C (corr.)   21   diligit *C*   22   praecepit *C* H*   26-27   poteris *C* H*   28
hanc *H (corr.)*   30   ut idem (*for* itidem) *C*   32   uere *C H*

done in this passage. Then, after he has condemned their wicked behavior, he turned, as well, to points about himself—something also characteristic of those making appeals:

5:5 *For through the Spirit, by faith, we await the hope of righteousness.*

Almost shouting aloud he says that "none of them are on our side; we have no fellowship with those people. We hope to be justified by faith, since we wait for the grace of the Spirit by which we also gain our perfect share in good things." And he further joins his own claims to this:

5:6 *In Christ Jesus* (he says) *neither circumcision counts for anything nor uncircumcision, but faith that works through love.*

"The dispensation of Christ is such that the truth is determined neither by circumcision nor uncircumcision. For it is faith that completes everything for us. And it is right for it to be a sign consistent with the promises we await, when we display perfect faith in love. And he means that love that is of God and the neighbor. For whoever has believed not only with a perfect intent but also with steadfastness of soul, as it is right to believe, will clearly be eager to love God, since he is the source of all the good things bestowed on us, and he will surely also love his neighbor. [90] For that love that is directed to God, as is right, also commands the love of neighbor and especially of the one who is plainly of the same faith. For it is this one that divine scripture calls 'neighbor.' Indeed, loving the neighbor surely displays in deed the affection of a person's soul. For it is impossible that someone who loves God should fail to practice that love in some way, since practice can give clear proof of love. Whoever loves his neighbor necessarily shows his friendship by what he does. Therefore, he said *faith that works through love* to demonstrate that love of God accompanies true faith and that equally the love of neighbor likewise follows. Indeed, love must necessarily be recognized in deed because it belongs to true faith that it is right for those who have believed in Christ to love, since who and of what character a person is must be given clear proof by love in

qui qualisue sit. 'haec quidem apud nos cum sollicitudine debita
aguntur; circumcisionis uero et praeputii nullam curam habemus.'
et quasi qui sufficienter fuerit contestatus, iterum ad exhortationem suum uertit sermonem:

5   *currebatis bene: qui uos impediuit ueritati non suaderi?*

ad summam eos uerecundiam adducit, dum illa quae primitus
ab eis fide integra gesta fuerant cum illis comparat quae ad praesens faciebant, reprehendens simul factum eorum. uidetur enim
per omnia perspici eos, et demiratione dignos eos ostendere, ex il-
10 lis quae dudum gesserant.

     persuasio non est ex uocante [*uos*].

     haec uult dicere: quoniam
†'gratia erat Dei ut uocaret uos,   τῆς χάριτος θεοῦ ἦν τὸ καλέσαι,
quod et fecit, dans Spiritus   τὸ δοῦναι τοῦ πνεύματος τὴν χάριν,
15 sancti gratiam, promittens fu-   ὑποσχέσθαι τὰ μέλλοντα· τὸ μέντοι
tura. nam permanere firmos   μένειν βεβαίους ἐπὶ τῆς πίστεως
in fide, non erat illius, sed ue-   οὐκ ἦν ἐκείνου, ἀλλ' ὑμέτερον.
strum.*

hoc enim solum conferre uos conueniebat; residua uero omnia ex
20 illius accedebant gratia. et ecce et hoc facere distulistis.' deinde
malitiam admissam detegens, adicit:

     modicum fermentum totam massam fermentat.

     'non solum illa quae fiunt defleo, sed illa quae hinc oriuntur
pertimesco. doctrina enim non bona, semel principium mali ac-
25 cipiens, augmentum in tempore scit adquirere.'

     et ut ne aestimaretur non bonam de illis habere spem, simul et
sanans eos adicit:

     ego confido in uobis in Domino quoniam nihil aliud sapietis.

     sufficiens erat Galatas desperantes confirmare et reducere ad fi-
30 dei integritatem, eo quod et Paulus bona de illis sperabat. ad haec
curans Galatas, aduersariis sese inuehit dicens:

     qui autem conturbat uos, portabit iudicium, quicumque est ille.

     demiratione dignum est quod dixit: *quicumque est ille;* osten-
dens quoniam non ueretur personam, quando ueritatis discutitur

---

1   quis (*for* qui) *H* (*corr.*)   3   quasi quia *C*   8   faciebat *H*   ‖   eorum *om H*
11   persuasione euocante *C* p. ex uocante *H*   13   sq. Coisl. 204, f. 38 a [Cr.
vi. 77, Fr. 129] θεόδωρος. ἄλλος δέ φησιν· τῆς χάριτος, κ.τ.λ.   14   facit *H*   25
in tempores scit *H*   30   sperat *C*   ‖   adhuc *C*   31   esse (*for* sese) *C**: *corr.*
se   34   persona *H*

works. This, then, is what we ought to do with due care. But we have no concern for circumcision or uncircumcision." And as though he had sufficiently made his appeal, he turns again to exhortation:

5:7 *You were running well; who prevented you from being persuaded by the truth?*

He brings them to the greatest shame, since he compares what they had formerly done with pure faith to what they were presently doing, and at the same time he rebukes them for what they have done. For he plainly demonstrates that he has examined them in all respects and that they are worthy of admiration because of what they had done in the past.

5:8 *Such persuasion does not come from the one who calls you.*

[91] He means that

†"It was God's grace that called you. He accomplished this by giving the grace of the Holy Spirit and promising the things to come. But to remain steadfast in the faith was not his task but yours.*

Calling, giving the grace of the Spirit, and promising the things to come belonged to God's grace. But remaining steadfast in the faith was not his task but yours.

It was right to bestow this alone upon you, but everything else followed upon his grace. And, look, you have put off doing your part." Then, exposing the wickedness that had found its way in, he added:

5:9 *A little yeast leavens the whole batch of dough.*

"Not only do I lament what has happened, but I am quite fearful of what will result from it. For a teaching that is not good, once it receives the beginning of evil, knows how to gain increase over time."

And lest he be thought not to have good hope for them, and at the same time healing them, he adds:

5:10a *I am confident about you in the Lord that you will not think otherwise.*

It was sufficient to encourage the Galatians in their despair and to bring them back to the soundness of faith that even Paul was hoping for good things from them. Healing the Galatians in this way, he attacks the opponents, saying:

5:10b *But whoever it is that is confusing you will pay the penalty.*

That he said *whoever it is* is worth admiring. He showed that he

ratio. et quoniam interposuit consilium quod illis dabat, sua euidenter comprobauit. iterum ad circumcisionis recurrit uerba, et in
sua persona id examinans, probationem eorum facit; eo quod illa
quae de eo dicebantur, etiam ceteris apostolis similiter competere
poterant, eo quod et illi propter illam quam in Christo habebant
fidem, eius implentes doctrinam, ad similitudinem eius similiter
persecutionem patiebantur. et maxime a Judaeis id pati uidebam-
tur.

*ego autem, fratres, si circumcisionem adhuc praedico, quid adhuc
persecutionem patior? ergo destructum est scandalum crucis.*

'si per legem (inquit) est iustificatio, et praedicari conuenit circumcisionem ad legis custodiam, sicut illi dicunt, utpote minime
nobis iuuatis de sola illa quae in Christo est fide, si non et legem
custodierimus; uana quidem sunt omnia illa quae secundum crucem sunt, et quod hinc infirmi scandalum patiuntur. uane autem
et nos persecutionem patimur, siue ego siue ceteri qui et praedicant illam quae in Christo est fidem. et propter hoc quoniam ipsi persecutionem patiuntur similiter sicut et ego, cum liceat nobis
illa quae legis sunt docere et omnem carere molestiam, simul lu-
crantes cotidianos angores. sed non ita se res habet; nec enim possibile est per legem iustificari. sed gratia in nobis Christi ista implere uidetur, qui propter hoc et crucifixus est et mortuus, ut exsurgens communem nobis bonorum illorum quae inde sunt praebeat fruitionem. ideo praedicamus, quia non erubescentes ignobilitatem illam quae ex ea esse existimatur, gloriamur uero in illis bonis quae per illam facta sunt. ideoque etiam si persecutionem pati
conueniat, non abhorremus; maiores enim fructus exinde per passionem sumere expectamus, in tantum communicare ei sperantes
in gloriam, in quantum ignobilitati et passionibus communicare
uoluerimus.' et quoniam euidenter ostendit superfluam esse circumcisionem, siquidem illa quae secundum Christum sunt interceptionem faciunt legis, cuius uim obtinere uidetur circumcisio;
exaestuauit ira motus contra illos homines qui pro nihilo solicitudinem expendere properant:

3   ei (*aft*. facit) *H*   5   illis *H*   6   ad similitudinem eius similitudinem perse-
cutionum *H*   11   eius (*for* est) *H*   15   patiantur *C**   19   dicere *H*   20-21
impossibile *H*   23   commune *C*H*   ‖   quae desunt *C*   23-24   praebeant *H*
26   patimur (*for* pati conu.) *H*   30   superfluum *H*   32   faciunt *om H*   33
iram *H*

feared no one when the discussion concerned a principle of truth. And since he inserted the advice he was giving them, he clearly proved his own claims. Again he returns to talk of circumcision, [92] and by examining the question from his own perspective he gives evidence for his claims. What was being said about him could similarly apply, as well, to the other apostles, since they, too, were suffering persecution just as he was because of their faith in Christ and their fulfillment of his teaching. And they were plainly suffering this especially from the Jews.

5:11 *But, brothers, if I am still preaching circumcision, why am I still suffering persecution? Therefore, the offense of the cross has been done away.*

"If justification (he says) is by the law and it is right to preach circumcision for the keeping of the law, as those people say, certainly that faith that is only in Christ will not benefit us at all, if we do not also keep the law. If so, everything that depends on the cross is vain, as well as that offense the weak experience from it. And it is in vain that we suffer persecution, whether it is I myself or the others who also preach faith in Christ. And it is for this that they suffer persecution just as I do, even though we might be permitted to teach what the law requires and be free of all trouble and at the same time spared of all our daily anxieties. But this is not the case, for it is impossible to be justified by the law. Rather, the grace of Christ plainly accomplishes this for us. This is why he was crucified and died, so that by rising again he might bestow on us our common enjoyment of those good things that come from this source. And so we preach because we are not ashamed of the humility thought to belong to the cross, but we boast in those good things accomplished by it. And so, even if it is right to suffer persecution, we do not shrink back, for we look forward to gaining greater fruit from it by suffering, hoping to share with him in glory as much as we have been willing to share with him in humility and sufferings." He has clearly demonstrated that circumcision is useless, since [93] Christ's dispensation takes away the law, the validity of which rests in circumcision. This is why he seethed with rage against those who were eager to spend much care for nothing:

utinam et abscidantur qui conturbant uos.

'ad plenum (inquit) si salutem nobis et perfectionem per Christum adesse speramus, et corporis friuolam excisionem bonum quid esse iudicant, etiam integra membra genitalia sibi excidant,
5   ut maiores adquirant lucros, si tamen carnis excisione iuuari se existimant.'

et ad plenum quis considerans illa quae in hac sunt epistola, tam quae extra probationem sunt, siue ad Galatas dicta siue ad aduersarios, inueniet densam eam esse et sensus uarietate illustra-
10   tam; nunc quidem ista, nunc uero illa dicentem. quod proprium est illorum qui irascuntur, ita ut et multa contingant, et omnia frequenter et compendiose dicant, nullo in loco sensum dilatantes. beatus uero Paulus inuehens se aduersariis sufficienter, ad exhortationem Galatarum recurrit, perfectam super uirtutibus faciens
15   ad illos doctrinam, ita ut ostendat eis quod hoc multo aptius illis esse uidetur, qui non sub lege, sed sub gratia Christi conuersantur. disputans uero ad eos de his quae sibi maxime imminere uidebat, ita ut res ipsa exigebat, etiam et caritatis uerba permiscuit:

uos autem, fratres, in libertatem uocati estis.

20   optime ab illis quae ante a se fuerant ostensa exhortationis sumpsit principium. '*uocati* (inquit) *estis*, ut participes sitis libertatis.' et confirmans dictum suum:

tantum ne libertatem in occasione carnis detis.

'non enim est iustum libertatem uos abuti ad peccandum.' uti-
25   le autem esse uidetur, ut et illud dicatur quod dixit: *in occasione carnis*, qua ratione illud posuit pro 'peccare'; et maxime propter eos qui existimant 'carnem' multis in locis peccatum ab scriptura nominari, cum diuina scriptura, nominibus aliud quid significantibus, alia nullo in loco nominari patitur absolute; sed cum qua-
30   dam ratione abuti solet nominum mutabilitate, sicut et hoc in loco fecit. 'carnem' enim apostolus, sicut in multis locis ostendimus, illud quod temporale est et mortale et solubile scit uocare, eo quod et omnis caro talis est. quoniam ergo disputat et de praesenti statu et de futuro qui per Christum praestitus est nobis. est autem

1   abscidentur *C**   10   dicente *C*H*   15   ad illos *om H*   24   libertate *C*

5:12 *I wish those who unsettle you would castrate themselves!*

"If we hope (he says) that salvation to the utmost and perfection are ours through Christ and claim that the cutting off of the flesh they judge to be good is worthless, let them also cut off all their genitals so as to gain greater profit—if, at any rate, they think they are benefited by cutting off the flesh."

If someone considers as fully as possible the contents of this letter insofar as they are outside his proof, whether it is what he says to the Galatians or what he says to the opponents, he will find the letter terse and embellished with various emotions. Indeed, he now says one thing, now another. This is characteristic of people who are angry, so that they touch many emotions and say everything often and succinctly, nowhere drawing out at length their emotion. Indeed, blessed Paul, sufficiently attacking his opponents, returns to exhorting the Galatians. He completes his teaching for them by treating the virtues, so that he may show them that this is plainly far more in keeping with those who live their lives not under the law but under the grace of Christ. Arguing with them about what seemed to him the greatest threat, as the circumstances required, he also mingled in words of love:

5:13a *For you were called to freedom, brothers,*

He most effectively took the beginning of his exhortation from what he had previously demonstrated. "*You were called* (he says) so that you might participate in freedom." And confirming his words:

[94] 5:13b *only do not use your freedom as an opportunity for the flesh,*

"For it is not right for you to use your freedom for sinning." And it is plainly useful that he said *as an opportunity for the flesh*. With good reason he used the word "flesh" instead of "to sin," especially because of those who think that scripture calls sin "flesh" in many passages. Since names in divine scripture mean different things, scripture does not allow the different names to be taken absolutely in any passage. But since with good reason scripture customarily employs names in changeable senses, that is what it has done in this passage. For the apostle, as we have demonstrated in many passages, is aware of calling "flesh" what is temporal, mortal, and capable of dissolution, because this is what all flesh is like. Thus, he argues for a distinction between the present age and the future one that Christ has bestowed upon us. And the latter

inmortalis quidem ille status, et omni peccato liber; mortalis uero iste, et peccato succumbens. pro ergo 'peccare,' *in occasionibus
carnis* posuit, ut dicat quoniam 'non conuenit propter libertatem
qua praediti estis ista agere quae mortales sequuntur. diligentiam
5 uero illorum debetis habere, quae etiam decere uobis existimatis,
eo quod et in spe uocati estis inmortalitatis, in qua et uerae libertatis participationem habetis.' et quoniam modo quodam contrarium esse uidebatur, quod et liberos eos esse dicebat, et ab actu
certo eos excludebat, hoc [autem] erat iterum alia ratione sub le-
10 ge eos quidem constituere, quod opus seruorum esse euidenter in
superioribus ipse pronunciauit:

    sed per caritatem seruite inuicem.

est et aliter non peccare, quando quis caritatem saluam custodit; ille enim qui talis est non solum a nocibilitate aliorum sese co-
15 hibet, sed et compellitur bonum facere. neque seruire piget aliquando dilecto sibi, si non hoc usus exegerit; eo quod nec necessitate legum adactus id facit. unde de stabilitate confidens caritatis
quae omnem excludit controuersiam, neque 'seruire in inuicem'
ponere distulit, et quidem contrarium id esse libertati ualde sciens.
20 omnis enim libertas hanc seruitutem libenter subit, eo quod nec
mos est obsequium illorum qui se diligunt grauiter ferre, siquando sibi in inuicem seruierint; pusillanimes uero tunc efficiuntur,
quando seruitii opus non secundum suum propositum implere uidentur. deinde et latius caritatis opus explicans, dicit:

25   *omnis enim lex in uno uerbo impletur: 'diliges proximum tuum sicut
teipsum.'*

'compendiose (inquit) in hoc omnis legis impletur intentio.
nam non occidere, neque adulterium facere nec furtum et quodcumque istis est simile quae ad nociuitatem aliorum fieri solent,
30 haec lex quidem minis et terroribus prohibet fieri, et nec sic facile potest illos qui subiacent sibi corrigere. caritas uero cum omni
illa delectatione et facilitate et omni implet instantia. etenim quisnam modo patietur nocere illum, quem maxime uidetur dilige-

---

4 quam *C H* [cf. p. 17, l. 18, vv. ll.] ‖ secuntur *H*   5 dicere *C H*   7
quidam *H*   9 autem *om C H*   11 praenuntiauit *H*   16 si non hoc si *C** si
non *H*   17 stabilite *H*   18 in (*bef.* inuicem) *om H**   19 liberati *C**   20
subdit *H*   21 more (*for* mos est) *C** norit *C* (*corr.*) morem *H*   22 in (*bef.*
inuicem) *om C* (*corr.*)   29 nocibilitatem *C* (*corr.*)   32-33 q. non solummodo
patietur non nocere *C* (*corr.*)

condition is indeed immortal and free from all sin, but the former condition is mortal and subject to sin. Therefore, he put down *as opportunities for the flesh* instead of "to sin" in order to mean that "it is not right because of the freedom with which you have been endowed to engage in those acts that mortals pursue. Instead, you ought to be diligent in what you also think becomes you because you have been called in the hope of immortality by which you have participation in true freedom." In some way he seemed to contradict himself because he said they were free and yet shut them out from a particular kind of conduct that would again put them under the law for a different reason, a conduct that he had clearly pronounced to be the work of slaves earlier in the letter. For this reason:

5:13c *but through love become slaves to one another.*

[95] In another way someone does not sin when he keeps love unimpaired. For whoever is like this not only prevents himself from harming others but is also compelled to do good. Nor is he ever displeased to be the slave of someone he loves if custom does not exact this, because he acts without being compelled by the law's necessity. Thus, trusting in the steadfastness of love that excludes all dispute, Paul did not hesitate to put down "being slaves to one another," even though he knew it was quite contrary to freedom. For all freedom submits to this slavery freely, because it is not the custom for people to bear under pressure the subservience of those who love them whenever they are slaves of one another. But they are then made small-minded when they plainly accomplish the work of slavery against their own inclination. Then, to explain the work of love more fully, he says:

5:14 *For the whole law is summed up in a single commandment, "You shall love your neighbor as yourself."*

"The purpose of the entire law (he says) is succinctly fulfilled in this, for the commandments not to murder and not to commit adultery or theft and whatever is like them are ones that customarily prohibit harm from being done to others. The law, however, prohibits these deeds by threats and terrors, nor is it easily able to correct those who submit themselves to it. But love accomplishes this with complete delight and ease and with full urgency. For who would ever allow himself to harm someone he plainly loved to the greatest degree? Rather, he would bestow upon him goods as much as he was capable of giving in his eagerness to pursue the law

re? sed et bona illi praestare pro uirium suarum possibilitate, pro quo amicitiae legem adcelerat. sic et illos qui non sunt sub lege, possibile est illa quae legis sunt implere. caritas enim non ex lege impleri solet, sed solo animi arbitrio. hanc autem sequitur neces-
5 sarie, ut legis impleat uoluntatem. maxime autem uos caritatis decet implere legem, qui futuram illam et inmortalem uitam expectatis, quando inuiolata in uobis caritatis custodita fuerit lex, nihil existente in rebus humanis quod eam ultra soluere possit.' multis in locis manifestus est apostolus et propemodum in omnibus
10 locis multam exhortationem faciens super caritatem, eo quod scit omnia bona continere; et quod excepta hac nihil ex illis quae conueniunt umquam fieri posse. hac uero permanente inlibata, facile est et illa ferre quae dura esse uidentur. et hoc in loco non solum propter exhortationis utilitatem, sed et propter praesentium,
15 euidenter ad ista exisse uidetur; eo quod apud Galatas, quibus ita fuerat persuasum ab illis qui ex circumcisione erant ad legis accedere custodiam, ut et carnis susciperent circumcisionem, schismata uero inter hos et non leues hinc adnascebantur contentiones, ab illis uel maxime qui nullam transductionem fidei fuerant perpes-
20 si. qui non ratione quadam aut exhortatione illos qui auersi fuerant cum debita modestia corrigere properabant, sed uehementer in illos insurgebant, insultantes illis eo quod et a ueritate fuerant extorres effecti. necessarie ergo et propter hanc causam etiam caritatis explicare poterat rationem; eo quod ad omnem correctionem
25 uirtutum necessaria sit caritas, et maxime in praesenti negotio illis conueniens. unde adicit:

si autem in inuicem uos mordetis et consumitis, uidete ne ab inuicem consumamini.

nociuitatem ualde et aperte in his contentionibus ostendit. ap-
30 tissime etiam uerborum est abusus ordinem, ne ista talia insuadibilia esse uiderentur, quae ab ordine dictorum nullo modo fieri possunt. nam deuorare in inuicem et consumi inpossibile est, quantum ad homines uidetur. quod apte composuit, dicens in praecedentibus, *mordetis.* nam morderi interea res patitur. et quia

of friendship. In this way it is possible for those who are not under the law to fulfill the law's requirements. For love is customarily fulfilled not by the law but only by the judgment of the soul. But fulfilling what the law wills is the necessary consequence of love. And it is especially fitting for you to fulfill the law of love because you [96] await that future and immortal life when you will keep the law of love inviolate, since there will be nothing in human affairs capable any longer of breaking it." In many passages the apostle explained love, and in almost all of them he gives abundant exhortation about it, because he knows that it includes all good things and that without it nothing that is right can be done. And when love remains unimpaired, it is plainly easy to bear what is hard to endure. In this passage he plainly digressed not only because of the usefulness of the exhortation but also because of the present circumstances. Among the Galatians divisions and no small disputes were arising between those whom the people from the circumcision had so persuaded to agree to keep the law that they accepted the circumcision of the flesh and those who as much as possible had tolerated no betrayal of the faith. Some were eager to reform those who had turned away, but not with any good argument or exhortation and without due restraint. Instead, they were rising up against them violently, insulting them because they had been banished from the truth. Therefore, Paul was necessarily able to explain the purpose of love also for this reason, because love is necessary for full guidance toward the virtues and was especially suitable for them in the present situation. Thus, he adds:

5:15 *But if you bite and consume one another, take care that you are not consumed by one another.*

He vigorously and openly demonstrated the harm in these disputes. And quite appropriately he employed an ordering of his words lest such statements should appear unpersuasive because they could in no way be derived from the order of the words. For to devour one another and be consumed [97] is impossible so far as human beings are concerned. He appropriately composed

morsum solet sequi esca et consumi (illud autem quod manducatur, necessario et consumitur et expenditur), non [autem] de homine id fieri solet; ergo primum illud posuit, quod fieri poterat.
deinde coniunxit illa quae de ordine quodam naturaliter fieri poterant, ut ex dictorum ordine etiam illa quae dixerat necessario confirmaret, et quod uidebatur in illis esse insuadibile dictorum sub-
terfugere uideretur iactantiam. uult autem dicere quoniam

†si uolueritis aduersus alteru-	εἰ μέλλετε πρὸς ἀλλήλους οὕτως φι-
trum sic pertinaciter contende-	λονεικεῖν ἀνενδότως, οὐ μόνον οὐδὲν
re, non solum nihil adiuuabi-	ὠφελεῖτε τοὺς ἁμαρτάνοντας, ἀλλὰ
tis illos qui peccauerunt, sed e	γὰρ τοὐνατίον ἔξω παντελῶς γενέσ-
contrario alienos eos a pietate	θαι αὐτοὺς τῆς εὐσεβείας παρασ-
perficietis, praeeligentibus inte-	κευάζετε. ὃ καὶ καλῶς 'ἀναλίσκεσ-
rea illis hoc sustinere, propter	θαι' ἐκάλεσεν, ἅτε δὴ μείωσιν ἐρ-
contentionis uestrae enormita-	γαζομένων τῷ κοινῷ τῶν τῆς εὐ-
tem.' quod et bene 'consumi'	σεβείας ἀποχωρούντων.

posuit, eo quod scit huiusmodi
res peractam minorationem in
communi inferre, cum quidam a
pietate discedunt.*

et hoc dicens ad integram primum progreditur doctrinam. deinde
recurrit iterum ad illa quae proposita sibi erant:

dico autem: Spiritu ambulate, et desiderium carnis non perficietis.

his euidenter ostendit illud quod a nobis fuerat dictum; e contrario enim 'carni' statuit 'Spiritum.' nam et 'Spiritum' pro resurrectione accepit et futura inmortalitate; eo quod et per Spiritum
ista nobis adquiri sperantur. sicut et 'carnem' sumpsit ad mortalitatem, eo quod carnem sequitur ut peccet; inmortalitatem uero,
quod nequaquam possit peccare. 'compendiose (inquit) illud di-

---

1-3 consumi non de homine id fieri solet (soleat H) illud (id H) autem quod
manducatur necessario (nec. om H) et cons. et exp., ergo, &c. C H   4   de om
C   8   sq. Coisl. 204, f. 40 a [Cr. vi. 81, Fr. 129] Θεόδωρος. ἄλλος δέ φησιν· εἰ
μέλλετε, κ.τ.λ.   10   solumque C   15   contentiones uestras C*   18   in oratione
C minoratione H

his words by saying first *you bite*. For something allows itself to be bitten little by little. And because a piece bitten off goes with food and is consumed (and what is chewed is necessarily both consumed and parceled out), this does not ordinarily happen with respect to a human being. Thus, he put first what could have happened first. Then he joined what could have happened in some order naturally, so that by the order of his words he might necessarily establish what he had said and might appear by subterfuge to put to one side what was unpersuasive in his words.[40] What he means is that

†"If you want to contend with one another so stubbornly, not only will you give nothing by way of help to those who have sinned, but on the contrary you will complete their alienation from true religion, since they will prefer to resist because of the enormity of your contentiousness." And he rightly put down "be consumed," because he knew that something of this kind brought loss to the community since some had deserted the true religion.*

If you are going to contend with one another so stubbornly, not only are you giving nothing by way of help to those who have sinned, but on the contrary you are causing them to be entirely removed from true religion. And he rightly used the words "be consumed," since those who were deserting the true religion were bringing loss to the community.

Saying this, he goes on first to sound teaching. Then he goes back again to what he had set forth:

5:16 *And I say, walk by the Spirit, and do not complete the desire of the flesh.*

[98] By these words he clearly demonstrated what we have said, for he defined "Spirit" as the opposite of "flesh." And he took "Spirit" to mean the resurrection and the immortality yet to come, because it is by the Spirit that we hope to acquire them. Similarly, he took "flesh" in reference to mortality, because it accords with the flesh to sin, whereas immortality is something that can by no means sin. "I say this (he says) succinctly: you have received

---

[40] The argument is obscure. Theodore apparently means that "bite" can also mean to hurt or to criticize, while "consume" must refer to eating. He seems disturbed by the metaphor.

co: in spe inmortalitatis accepistis Spiritum. illa ergo agite quae
consentanea uestrae existunt promissioni; in inmortalitatem ergo
uiuere, secundum ut nobis est possibile. illa uero quae sequuntur
mortalitatem nolite facere.'

5   *caro enim concupiscit aduersus Spiritum, Spiritus uero aduersus*
carnem; haec autem contraria sibi sunt in inuicem, ut non illa quae
uultis faciatis.

nam quod dixit, *concupiscit aduersus Spiritum*, hoc est, 'interimit illa quae illius sunt;' ut dicat:

10 '†interimit quidem mortalitas	ἀναιρετικὸν μὲν θνητότητος ἀθανα-
inmortalitatem, et inmortalitas	σία, ἀθανασία δὲ θνητότητος, οὐδὲ
excludit mortalitatem. nec enim	γὰρ συμφωνεῖ ταῦτα ἀλλήλοις· ὅθεν
consentiunt sibi ista in inuicem.	οὐδὲ ἡμῖν ἔξεστιν ποιεῖν ἅπερ βου-
unde nec nobis licet facere illa	λόμεθα, ἐπεὶ μηδὲ δυνατὸν ἐν ἐκεί-
15 quae uolumus. nec enim possu-	νοις ὄντας τὰ τῆς θνητότητος πράτ-
mus in illa per fidem existentes,	τειν. τὸ γὰρ ἵνα οὐκ ἐπὶ αἰτίας εἶ-
illa quae mortalitatis sunt face-	πεν, ἀλλ' ὡς ἀκόλουθον, κατὰ τὸ
re.' nam quod dixit, non *ut* in	οἰκεῖον ἰδίωμα.
causando illud dixit, sed qua-	
20 si consequens, secundum suam	
proprietatem.*	

admirabiliter uero in his ostendit magis illis uirtutem debere competere (eo quod et in forma futurae uitae consistunt), quam imitari
eos secundum uirium qualitatem in praesenti conuenit uita. dein-
25   de ex illis ipsis etiam omnis sermonis comprobat propositum:

si autem Spiritu ducimini, non estis sub lege.

'ad plenum (inquit) secundum illa uiuitis, nec sub lege ultra uos
uiuere est possibile.' optime in id ipsud utraque colligit ex illis
quae ab illis credebantur, quod non conueniat eos peccare, neque
30   sub lege esse. nam mortales et peccare possunt, et legem habent
necessariam quae illos a peccato possit prohibere; superflua uero
utraque uidebantur erga illos qui et a morte sunt securi, et peccare
ulterius non possunt. deinde et euidenter utrumque ab alterutro
separat, dicens:

35   *manifesta, autem sunt opera carnis; quae sunt adulterium, forni-*

---

2 in inmortalitate ergo uiuite *C* (*corr.*)   3 secuntur *H*   5 uero *om H*   6 in
om H   10 sq. Coisl. 204, f. 40 b, [Cr. vi 82, Fr. 129] θεόδωρος. ἄλλος δέ φησιν·
ἀναιρετικόν, κ.τ.λ..   13 in *om H*   18 ut *om H*   ‖ in *om C*   28 in *om H*

the Spirit in the hope of immortality. Therefore, do what is appropriate to your promise, to live in immortality as far as that is possible for us. But do not do what accords with mortality."

5:17 *For the flesh desires against the Spirit, and the Spirit desires against the flesh; for these are opposed to each other, so that you may not do what you want.*

For when he said *it desires against the Spirit*, that is, "it destroys what belongs to him," what he means is:

†"mortality destroys immortality, and immortality excludes mortality, for they do not agree with one another. This is why it is not permitted for us to do what we wish. For if we exist in immortality by faith, we are incapable of doing what belongs to mortality." For he said *so that* not to mean purpose but to indicate result, as is characteristic of him.*

Immortality destroys mortality, and immortality is destroyed by mortality, for they do not agree with one another. This is why it is not permitted for us to do what we wish, since it is impossible for those who are in that state [of immortality] to do what belongs to mortality. For he said *so that* not to mean purpose but to indicate result, according to his own peculiar style.

Indeed, he marvelously demonstrates by these words that it is necessary for them to seek virtue in what is future and immortal (because they stand fast in the type [99] of the life to come) rather than to imitate what suits the present life according to its characteristic powers. Then on the basis of these very considerations he also proves what he has set forth in his entire argument:

5:18 *But if you are led by the Spirit, you are not subject to the law.*

"To the utmost extent (he says) you live by those things, nor is it possible you should live any longer under the law." Most effectively he combines both points in the same statement on the basis of what they believed—that it was not right for them to sin nor to be under the law. For mortals are both able to sin and have the law as necessary because it can keep them from sin. But both were clearly useless for those securely freed from death and no longer able to sin. Then he clearly distinguishes the one way of life from the other, saying:

5:19–21a *Now the works of the flesh are obvious; they are adul-*

catio, immunditia, impudicitia, idolorum seruitus, ueneficia, inimici-
tiae, contentiones, aemulationes, prouocationes, dissensiones, haereses,
inuidiae, homicidia, ebrietates, comessationes, et his similia.

quoniam non sicut quidam haereticorum existimauerunt, car-
5 nem naturam nostram uult dicere, euidens est. nam et inimicitiam
et idolorum culturam et inuidiam et iram et alia quae huiusmodi
sunt, carnis esse dixit; quae passiones solius animae perspicue esse
uidentur. dicit autem quoniam manifestata sunt illa quae in natura
mortali peragi possunt. 'quae illa? illa quae praedixi:'
10 *quae et ante dico uobis, sicut et praedixi; quoniam qui talia agunt*
regnum Dei non possidebunt.

bene posuit illud quod dixit, *ante praedixi*, ut ne nunc in primis
necessitate adactus illud dicere uideretur: 'tantum abest ut aptari
uobis possint huiusmodi actus ita ut nec possibile sit illos qui in his
15 sunt regnum adquirere. illa enim quae regnum Dei fieri non admittit, nec status ille qui tunc erit patitur, illi qui talia agunt participare illorum nequaquam poterunt; eo quod et contraria illorum
quae tunc erunt ad praesens agere pertemptant.' deinde transit ad
aliam partem:
20 *fructus* (inquit) *Spiritus est caritas, gaudium, pax, patientia, bo-*
nitas, benignitas, fides, mansuetudo, continentia.

bene indicans [fructum] Spiritus caritatem omnibus anteposuisse uidetur, reliqua uero adiecit. haec enim quae secundum
praesentem sunt uitam necessaria sunt illis qui custodiunt illam
25 quae in futuro uel maxime implebitur. 'fructum' ergo 'Spiritus'
dicit, hoc est, illa quae per mortalitatem a nobis adquiri uidentur.
et iustum est nos qui in illis iam sumus, secundum illa conuersari.
quaedam autem sunt ex illis quae dicta sunt, quae neque tempus
habere poterunt ut in futuro impleantur saeculo; quale est illud
30 quod dixit: 'patientiam' et 'continentiam.' tunc enim superflua
erit patientia, quando nemo inuenitur qui tristare aliquem possit.
superflua autem erit continentia, dum non sunt illa quae mouere

---

4 non, naturam *om H*   7   animae *om H*   8   quod (*for* quon.) *H*   ‖   non
(*bef.* manif.) *add C**   ‖   quae illam *C**   9   mortales *H*   13   illud dicere ...
actus *om* (*per homoeotel.*) *H*   15-16   admittunt *C H*   17-18   poterant, erant *C**
H: *C* (*corr.*) *remodels the sentence thus:* nec status ille qui tunc erit patitur illos
qui talia ag. part. illorum, eo quod et contr. illorum quae tunc erunt, &c.   22
fructum *om C* H*   24   nec (*bef.* necess) *add C**   ‖   illa *H*   26   uidetur *H**
31   tristari al. possint *C* (*corr.*)

tery, fornication, impurity, licentiousness, idolatry, sorcery, enmities, strifes, jealousies, quarrels, dissensions, factions, envies, murders, drunkennesses, carousings, and things like these.[41]

It is clear that he does not want "flesh" to mean our nature, as some of the heretics have supposed. For he said that enmity, the worship of idols, envy, wrath, and other things of this kind belong to the flesh. These passions unmistakably appear to belong to the soul alone. And he says that they are obvious because they can be carried out in mortal nature. "What are they? The ones I told you about before":

[100] 5:21b *I am telling you what also was before, just as I also previously said, that those who do such things will not inherit the kingdom of God.*

He rightly made his point by saying *before ... I previously said*, so that it might be plain that he was not saying this for the first time because he had been compelled by necessity: "It is so far from the case that acts of this kind could be suitable for you that it is impossible for those who do them to gain the kingdom. For the kingdom of God does not allow these acts to be done, nor will that condition that will come to be at that time permit them. Those who commit such deeds will by no means be able to share in those things [bestowed in the kingdom] because they constantly try to attain in this present life what is contradictory of what will then be the case." Then he moved on to the other way of life:

5:22–23a *The fruits of the Spirit* (he says) *are love, joy, peace, endurance, kindness, generosity, faith, gentleness, continence.*[42]

Rightly pointing out the fruit of the Spirit, he plainly put love before all and then added the others. For in the present life they are necessary for those who keep love, which will be fulfilled to the greatest extent in the future. Therefore, by "the fruit of the Spirit" he means the virtues we plainly gain through mortal life. And it is right that we should already participate in them and live our lives by them. And some of the ones that are mentioned can have no occasion for fulfillment in the age to come, such as endurance and continence. For at that future time endurance would be useless, since no one will be found capable of causing anyone misfortune. And continence would be useless, since [101]

---

[41] Theodore's list differs slightly from our text.
[42] Again, this list differs slightly from the usual one.

quemquam possint. necessarie ergo caritatem anteposuit. secundum praesentem enim uitam si quis sub hanc esse uoluerit, etiam cetera facillime poterit expedire. in futuro saeculo caritas omnia secum habet, cessantibus tunc omnibus nobis; laborem ad uirtutum inoperationem inicere ad praesens uidetur. bene ergo carni 'opera' aptauit, eo quod et a nobis illa aguntur; Spiritum uero dicens, 'fructum' posuit, eo quod gratia tamquam fructus aliquos per Spiritus cooperationem illa adsequi possumus. nec enim ipsi aliquando secundum nos ipsos uirtutis opera perficere possumus; sicuti nec fructus terrae adsequi possimus, etiam si multum laboremus, si non Deus dare illos fuerit dignatus. deinde dicens illa quae sunt Spiritus, quod et multa demiratione [dignum est] adicit:

aduersus huiusmodi non est lex.

quae enim erit lex aduersus bona, excludens ea? alioquin iusta ratione non *lex*, sed potius iniquitas eiusmodi uocabitur, quando uel maxime bonos prohibet actus. sic per omnia ostendit et uirtutem magis competere nostrae promissioni, et quod sub lege ultra esse non possumus; eo quod nec possimus in futuro saeculo peccare, in cuius superna iam nunc consistere uidemur, eo quod et possibile sit et in praesenti uita nos ab omni legitima obseruatione esse securos, consequenter intentioni nostrae illa agentes quae per caritatem impleri conueniunt. unde et adicit:

illi autem qui sunt Christi, carnem crucifixerunt cum passionibus et concupiscentiis.

'nos (inquit) qui Christo credidimus euidens est, etsi non re, forma tamen baptismatis concrucifixi sumus Christo, mortui existentes praesenti uitae, ita ut neque passio neque concupiscentia locum in nobis ullum possit habere. migrauimus enim in futuram illam uitam per regenerationem Spiritus.' et sicuti recapitulans illa quae dixerat, adicit:

uiuimus ergo Spiritu, et Spiritu constamus.

'conuenit ergo nos in uita illa constitutos in qua per Spiritum sumus regenerati, illa quae consentanea sunt illius uitae agere.' haec quidem apostolus de futuris adfirmauit. quoniam autem la-

---

2 hac *C** 5 uidentur *C H (corr.)* 8 possimus *C* 11 dignatos *C** 12 dign. est *om C H* 16 iniq. *om H* ‖ uocabit *C** 17 actos *C** 18 prouisione *C* 22 quia (*for* quae) *H* 26 reformata tamen *H* 29 migrabimus *H*

there would be nothing able to disturb anyone. Therefore, he necessarily put love first. For in the present life, if anyone is willing to be subject to love, he can quite easily accomplish the rest. In the age to come, love holds everything with itself, since at that time we shall rest from all activity. In the present, toil is plainly introduced for the task of gaining the virtues. Therefore, he rightly joined "works" to flesh, because they are done by us. But when he spoke of the Spirit, he put down "fruit," because it is by grace through the cooperation of the Spirit that we can attain, as it were, those fruits. For we can never by ourselves perfect the works of virtue, just as we cannot reap the fruits of the earth, even if we should toil as much as possible, if God had not seen fit to give them. Then, in speaking of what belongs to the Spirit, because it is worthy of great admiration, he adds:

5:23b *There is no law against such things.*

For what would be a law against good things, excluding them? Otherwise, it would with good reason be called not *law* but rather wickedness of some kind, since it would prohibit good deeds as much as possible. Thus, in all respects he shows both that virtue all the more accords with our promise and that we can no longer be under the law. Because we are unable to sin in the age to come, on whose heights we plainly stand even now, and because it is possible even in the present life for us to be freed from all observation of the law's ordinances, we do what it is right to accomplish by love in accordance with our intent. And so he adds:

5:24 *And those who belong to Christ have crucified the flesh with its passions and desires.*

[102] "It is clear (he says) that we who have believed in Christ have been crucified with Christ, even though not in actual fact, yet in the type of baptism. We are dead to the present life so that neither passion nor desire can have any place in us. For we have crossed over to the life to come by the rebirth of the Spirit." And as though he were summing up what he had said, he adds:

5:25 *Therefore, we live by the Spirit; we also continue in the Spirit.*[43]

"Therefore, it is right for us, even though we are placed in this life, to do what is appropriate to that other life because we have

---

[43] As Swete points out, there is some manuscript evidence for this reading, even though Theodore's comments may suggest the more usual reading.

bor nobis est necessarius secundum praesentem uitam, et quasi
medii quidam praesentis interim uitae sumus et futurae, latius nobis dictum est in superioribus, et illa ipsa frequenter dicere inconueniens esse existimamus.

5 sic de integra conuersatione exhortatus ad proposita recurrit,
dans illis consilium non ultra litigare aduersus alterutrum, competenti uero sermone corrigere debere illos magis qui peccauerunt:

non efficiamur (inquit) *uanae gloriae appetitores, alterutrum
prouocantes, alterutrum inuidentes.*

10 et inueniebat enim aliquos apud eos, de illis qui non fuerant
transducti, magna sapere super firmitatem arbitrii sui, et saepe illud ad ostentationem sui proferre. unde fiebat ut illi qui persua-
si fuerant, prouocati uenirent ad contentiones; necessarium enim
erat illos utpote homines dictis illorum permoueri, et maxime cum
15 propria pulsarentur conscientia; unde et facile ad contentionem
prorumpebant. bene ergo *uanae gloriae* illos uocauit, eo quod
ostendere se ipsos uolentes et gloriam ab hominibus inquirentes,
pro quibus non fuerant seducti sua sententia. 'prouocare' autem
dixit, eo quod magna de se iactantes, ad contentionem commoue-
20 bant illos qui negauerant. et quod adiecit *inuidentes*, grauiter admodum id et opportune adiecit. 'sicut enim inuidentes illorum saluti, ita hisce sermonibus uidemini eos ad contentionem prouocare, ut omni ex parte a uestra discedant communione; cum conueniat uos, (sed non salutem eorum uera ratione desideratis), exhor-
25 tatione potius eos ad id quod melius est reuocare.' unde inpro-
perans eos pro quibus non bene egerant, adicit, simul docens eos
quemadmodum facere deberent:

*fratres, etsi praeoccupatus fuerit homo in aliquo delicto, uos qui spi-
ritales estis, instruite eum qui eiusmodi est, in spiritu mansuetudinis;
30 considerans teipsum, ne et tu tempteris.*

'sic magis conuenit facere uos qui estis perfecti, uerbis lenissi-
mis eos qui peccauerunt reuocantes, simulque reputantes quoniam

5 exortator *C* 10 inquit (*for* enim) *C* 12 quae (*for* qui) *H* 14 permouere
C* H 18 namque f. s. &c. *C** non f. s. ab sua sent *C* (*corr.*) iamque f. s. sua
sent *H* 19-20 commonebant *H* 20-22 grauiter … saluti *om H* 23 coin
(*for* omni) *H* 24 si (*for* sed non) *C* (*corr.*) ‖ desideratis *om H* 28 etiam
etsi *H*

been born anew by the Spirit." The apostle affirmed this about the things to come. And we have spoken earlier at greater length about the fact that we have unavoidable toil in the present life and are for the time being, as it were, in between the present life and the one to come. For this reason we think it inappropriate to say the same things over and over again.

So, once he has made his exhortation about a pure way of life, he returns to his argument and advises them not to quarrel with one another any longer but that they ought all the more to admonish those who had sinned with suitable words:

5:26 *Let us not become people who seek vainglory, challenging one another, envying one another.*

For he found among them some of those who had not been carried off, who thought highly of the validity of their judgment and who often made an open display of it. Thus, it came about that those who had been persuaded [by the opponents], when challenged, would enter into disputes with them, For it was unavoidable for the backsliders, since they were only human, not to be disturbed by their words and to be assailed in their own conscience to the greatest extent. This is why they easily forced disputes to break forth. Therefore, he rightly called them [*people who seek*] *vainglory*, [103] because they wanted to make a display of themselves and were searching for glory from human beings by taking the side of those who had not been led astray in their opinion. And he said that they were *challenging* because by boasting great things about themselves they were stirring up those who repudiated them to disputation. And by adding *envying* he makes an addition that is extremely serious and opportune. "For it is insofar as you envy them their salvation that you plainly challenge them to disputation by these words so that in every way they may depart from your fellowship, since it is this that suits you rather than an exhortation calling them back to what is better. Indeed, you do not desire their salvation for the true reason." Thus, blaming them for their ill behavior and at the same time teaching them how they ought to behave, he adds:

6:1 *Brothers, even if a person is detected in some transgression, you who are spiritual restore him in a spirit of gentleness, considering yourself lest you should be tempted.*

"Thus, it is all the more right for you who are perfect, in calling back those who have sinned, to use the gentlest words, bearing in

homines et uos estis, sicut et illi, qui multam perpeti mutabilitatem ob naturae potestis inbecillitatem. et illa ipsa struens:

    inuicem onera uestra portate, et sic adimplebitis legem Christi.

    †ut dicat 'caritatem.' hanc   [ἵνα εἴπῃ τὴν ἀγάπην· ταύτην
5 enim uocat *legem Christi.* 'sed   γὰρ λέγει] νόμον Χριστοῦ. ἀλ-
communicare eis secundum uir-   λὰ καὶ κοινωνῆσαι [αὐτοῖς κατὰ τὸ
tutem unusquisque uestrum de-   δυνατὸν ἕκαστος ὑμῶν ὀφείλει, τὸ
bet, sarcinam eorum subleuans.   φορτίον αὐτῶν βαστάζων. καὶ πῶς
quomodo autem hoc fieri pote-   ἂν γένοιτο τοῦτο ;] ὅταν διὰ παραι-
10 rit? si per exhortationem et le-   νέσεως καὶ χρηστότητος ἐπικουφί-
nitatem uerborum animam eius   ζῃς αὐτῷ τὴν ψυχὴν ὑπὸ τῆς τοῦ
recreare acceleraueris, quae pec-   ἁμαρτήματος συνειδήσεως βεβαρη-
cati conscientia grauata admo-   μένην.
dum esse uidetur;*

15 si sanis consiliis animum eius erigere, si exhortatione eundem recreare uolueris; si animaequiorem feceris, inuitans eum ad promissionem meliorum.' et modum illis ostendens quod facere eos
conueniens erat, iterum inuehit se illis qui ob fidem seruatam magna de se sapiebant:

20   *si enim uidetur quis esse aliquid, cum nihil sit, seipsum seducit.*

    bene posuit: *cum nihil sit;* qualiscumque enim quisquis ille fue-
rit, scrupulositati iudicis comparatus, nihil esse uidebitur, utpote
homo existens. et quoniam uidebatur firma propositio eos extollere:

25   *opus autem suum probet unusquisque, et tunc in seipsum solum ha-*
bebit gloriam, et non in alterum. unusquisque enim suum pondus por-
tabit.

    'igitur si te hoc faciat magna sapere eo quod permanseris inuer-
tibilis in fidem, secundum teipsum gloriare, si tamen tibi hoc utile
30 esse uidetur. noli autem te extollere aduersus proximum, eo quod
nec aliquid ei prodesse potes per tuam stabilitatem. unusquisque
enim pro se rationem est redditurus.' optime autem ostendit non
debere illum qui stat extollere se aduersus illum qui peccauit, siquidem nihil illum de sua iuuabit stabilitate. primum quod non

---

2 astruens *C* (*corr.*)   4 sq. Coisl. 204 f. 42 b [Cr. vi. 86, Fr. 129] Θεόδωρος.
ἄλλος δέ φησιν· νόμον Χριστοῦ τὴν ἀγάπην φησίν. ἀλλὰ καὶ κοινωνῆσαι αὐτῷ
τὸ φορτίον ὀφείλεις· τοῦτο δὲ γίνεται ὅταν, κ.τ.λ.   6 eos *C* H*   22 scrupulositate *H*   ‖   uidebatur *C**   25 seipso, altero *C* (*corr.*)   29 fide *C* (*corr.*)
31 potest *C*   32 is (*for* non) *H*

mind at the same time that you are human beings just as they are and that you are capable of undergoing great inconstancy because of the weakness of your nature." And he puts the same idea in these words:

6:2 *Bear one another's burdens, and in this way you will fulfill the law of Christ.*

†He means "love," for he calls this *the law of Christ*. "But [104] each one of you ought to share with them so far as you can, by supporting their load. How can this be done? If by exhortation and gentleness of words you are eager to restore the soul that is plainly greatly weighed down by consciousness of sin,*

He means "love," for he calls this *the law of Christ*. But each one of you ought to share with them as much as possible, by supporting their load. How can this be? When by exhortation and kindness you lighten the soul weighed down by the consciousness of sin.

if by sound advice you are willing to raise up his mind, if by exhortation you are willing to restore him, if you make him more calm-minded, inviting him to the promise of better things." Showing them how it was right for them to behave, he attacks them again because they thought highly of themselves because they had kept the faith:

6:3 *For if anyone thinks he is something when he is nothing, he deceives himself.*

He rightly put down *when he is nothing*, for whatever character anyone has, if he is evaluated by the meticulous care of the judge, he will plainly be nothing, since he is human. And because the statement of his case was plainly well-founded for raising them up:

6:4–5 *And let each one test his own work, and then he will have pride in himself alone and not in another, for each one will carry his own load.*

"Therefore, if the fact that you remained steadfast in the faith causes you to think highly, take pride in yourself, at any rate if that seems to you useful. But do not exalt yourself against your neighbor, because you can do nothing to profit him by your steadfastness. For each individual is to give an account for himself." And quite effectively he demonstrates that the person who stands fast ought not to exalt himself against one who has sinned, since he will give him no help from his own steadfastness. He first declared that it was not right for them

conueniat de his magna sapere pronunciauit, instruens ut suam respicientes naturam, solliciti magis sint per singula momenta de illis incertis quae accidere solent naturae mortali. et quoniam eueniebat aliquos esse inter illos, nam tales plurimam diligentiam
5 properabant implere ut illos qui deliquerant reducerent ad fidei antiquitatem:

communicet (inquit) *is qui catechizatur uerbum ei qui se catechizat in omnibus bonis.*

'si est quidam qui docet illa quae doceri conueniunt, conue-
10 nit illum qui docetur ualde intendere dictis illius, et in bonis suis participem illum recipere; ita ut de quibus habet, usibus eius ministret; eo quod non est demiratione dignum, si in spiritalibus adiuuatus, corporalia ei ad inuicem fuerit uisus ministrare.' hoc autem utile utrisque poterat esse; et illis qui docebant, ut animae-
15 quiores existentes docerent, et illis similiter qui discebant. nam conligare cupiebat eos in affectu doctorum, a quibus et eruditi quasi debitores eorum seipsos deberent existimare. hoc faciebat etiam, ut et dictorum iuuamen cum multa susciperent reuerentia. deinde iterum ad integram exhortationem proficit:

20 *nolite errare. Deus non irridetur. quod enim quis seminauerit, hoc et metet; quoniam qui seminat in carne sua, de carne metet corruptionem; qui autem seminat in Spiritu, de Spiritu metet uitam aeternam.*

compendiose inquit: 'siue illa quis quae carnis sunt agit, talia recipiet; siue meliora, mercedem accipiet aequam suo labori.' et
25 quia laborem habebat uirtutum directio, adicit:

bonum autem facientes non deficiamus. tempore enim suo metemus non fatigati.

bene ad semen redit, messem dicens mercedum esse retributionem. optime autem adiecit: *non fatigati*, quia sufficiens est ad
30 uerecundiam inuitare; eo quod inconueniens est non in praesente sustinere seminis laborem (siquidem et cum multo labore etiam

---

3 accedere *C** 5 delinquerant *C** 7 catecizatur, catecizat, *C* catezizatur, catezizat *H* ‖ uerbis *H* 9 quidem *C* (*corr.*.) ‖ docere *C** *H* 13 adiutus *C* (*corr.*) ‖ ad uicem *C* 20 qui *C** 21 de (*for* in) *H* 26 suum metemur *C** 29 autem *om H** ‖ his (*aft.* adiecit) *add H* (*corr.*) 30-31 praesenti *C* (*corr.*)

to think highly about this, drawing up his argument so that by examining their own nature they might be more apprehensive about those uncertainties that moment by moment customarily happen [105] to mortal nature. And since it happened that some of them were the sort of people eager to apply the greatest diligence in bringing those who had transgressed back to their former faith:

6:6 *Let him* (he says) *who is taught the word share with the one who teaches him in all good things.*

"If there is someone who teaches correct doctrine, it is right that the student should pay close attention to his words and should accept him as a participant in his own goods, so that he may minister to his needs from what he has. This is because there would be nothing worth admiring if, when the student had been helped in spiritual matters, he would not be seen to respond by ministering to his teacher in bodily matters." And this had the possibility of being useful to both of them, to the teachers so that they might teach with a more tranquil mind, and likewise to the students. For he wanted to bind them to their teachers in affection, since the students ought to regard themselves as debtors to those by whom they had been trained. He was also trying to bring it about that they would accept the help of their teaching with great respect. Then he goes on again to pure exhortation:

6:7–8 *Do not err. God is not mocked; for whatever someone sows, that he will also reap. Because whoever sows in his own flesh will reap corruption from the flesh, but whoever sows in the Spirit will reap eternal life from the Spirit.*

He says succinctly: "If anyone does what belongs to the flesh, he will receive like things. But if he does what is better, he will receive a reward equal to his toil." And because making the path of the virtues straight required toil, he adds:

6:9 *So let us not grow weary in doing what is right, for we will reap in its own time, when we are not tired.*[44]

He rightly goes back to sowing, saying that the harvest is the recompense of rewards. [106] And he most effectively adds *when we are not tired* because it was capable of inducing shame in them. This is because it is not unbecoming in the present to undergo toil in sowing (and we can assume that we are also compelled to

---

[44] The last phrase reflects Theodore's interpretation, one he shares with Chrysostom and Theodoret.

messem colligere compellimur), pro uirtutibus uero nolle laborare
quarum retributio nullum uidetur habere laborem. in requie enim
constituti mercedem earum recipiemus. deinde quasi iam de confessis bonis adicit:

5   *itaque dum tempus habemus, operemur quod bonum est ad omnes,*
maxime ad domesticos fidei.

'in hoc saeculo operandi tempus est. non praetermittamus illud; laborantibus enim indubia est mercedum retributio.' bene
autem dixit: *operemur quod bonum est;* in communionis intellectu
10   id posuit siue eorum qui docere debent, siue eorum qui opus habent discere; quod et ad plenum de omni actu uirtutum significari
potest. optimum enim omne est quod uirtutibus est praeditum;
quod et erga omnes debet esse, eo quod et nobis optimum esse uidetur. nam quod dixit, *ad domesticos fidei;* ostendit et quod aliis
15   uideatur. ego autem cupiebam his intendere illos qui aestimant indiscrete nocendos esse eos qui sunt nobis alieni a fide. quos conueniebat illud excogitare, quoniam non omne quod quis pati dignus
sit, hoc et nobis deceat facere. quapropter plurimam nos adhibere
conuenit diligentiam.

20   quoniam uero et exhortationem consummauit, siue illam quae
ex integro est siue de illis de quibus cogebatur consummare epistolam, incipiens iterum ad negotii propositum recurrit:

uidete qualibus litteris uobis scripsi mea manu.

†inuehere se cupiens aduer-   μέλλων καθάπτεσθαι τῶν ἐναν-
25   sariis ualde maioribus litteris   τίων ἄγαν μείζοσιν ἐχρήσατο γράμ-
usus est, designans quoniam ne-   μασιν, ἐμφαίνων ὅτι οὔτε αὐτὸς
que ueretur eos, neque negat illa   ἐρυθριᾷ οὔτε ἀρνεῖται τὰ λεγόμενα.
sua esse quae dicit,*

sed et ualde arguere eos, si usus exegerit, sufficiens sit. propter hoc
30   primum ostendens litterarum magnitudinem adicit:

---

1   nollo C* nollum [i. e. nullum (?)] C (*corr.*)   ‖   conuenit (*for* laborare) C
(*corr.*)   2   idem (C: id est H) noli considerare laborem (*aft.* laborare) *add* C H
11   discernere H   12   est *om* H   13   aptum (*for* opt.) C   14   quod et H   15
existimant H   17   illos (*aft..* conu.) *add* C* H   18   nos C (*corr.*)   20   uero
om C (*corr.*)   24   Coisl. 204, f. 44 b [Cr. vi. 90, Fr. 129] θεοδώρου. ἄλλος δέ
φησίν· μέλλων, κ.τ.λ.   27   negant C*

reap the harvest with great toil) and yet be unwilling to toil for the virtues, the recompense of which plainly requires no toil. For it is when we are placed in rest from toil that we shall receive virtue's reward. Then, as if he is speaking about obvious goods, he adds:

6:10 *So then, while we have time, let us work what is good for all, and especially for those of the family of faith.*

"In this age there is a time for working. Let us not fail to take advantage of it, for the recompense of rewards for those who toil cannot be doubted." And he rightly said *let us work what is good.* He made the statement to mean all in common, referring either to those who ought to teach or to those who have the task of learning. The statement can also be given the fullest possible meaning by understanding it of every virtuous act. For everything bestowed by the virtues is best, and we ought to have all the virtues because this is plainly best for us. For when he said *for those of the family of faith,* he also showed what should plainly be the case also for others. But I wanted to bring this to the attention [107] of those who suppose that people who are foreign to us by faith may be harmed with impunity. It would be right for them to reflect upon this, since not everything someone deserves to suffer is right for us to cause. We ought to employ the greatest diligence about this matter.

Since, then, he has completed his exhortation, whether his latest one or the one concerning the situation that compelled him to write the letter, he returns to what he has set forth about the situation, beginning once more:

6:11 *See with what letters I am writing to you in my own hand.*

†In his desire to attack his opponents he used extremely large letters, pointing out that he was neither afraid of them nor denying that what he said was his own*

Since he was going to attack his opponents, he used extremely large letters, pointing out that he was neither blushing nor denying what he had said.

but that it was enough to prove them quite wrong that he was obliged to use them.[45] For this reason he first shows the great size of the letters and then adds:

---

[45] Swete points out that Chrysostom disagrees with this interpretation and understands the large letters to be a reference to his "formless" style. Theodoret mentions both interpretations.

quicumque uolunt placere in carne, hi cogunt uos circumcidi, tan-
tum ne crucis Christi persecutionem patiantur.

'qui uolunt (inquit) secundum praesentem hanc uitam placere aduersariis pietatis, (ut dicat Iudaeis) ita ut persecutionem non
patiantur propter Christum, ista facere adnituntur.' et quia ualde
erat graue ut infidelium gratia talia facerent, ipsi simulantes se fidem tenere, ut ne uideatur a se id confinxisse, properat confirmare
illud quod dixit:

nec enim hi qui circumcisi sunt ipsi legem custodiunt; sed uolunt uos
circumcidi, ut in uestra carne glorientur.

'quoniam multa legis praecepta praeuaricant manifestum est.
nec enim sacrificia implent, quae definitis in lege tribus temporibus annue in Hierosolimis adscendere adcelerant, secundum legis praeceptum. alia etiam plurima quis eos praeuaricantes inueniet, modo si diligenter considerare uoluerit. itaque si affectu legis circumcisionem simulant tenere, id erga legis ostendant custodiam. si autem legem praeuaricare indiscrete adcelerant, quemadmodum uos circumcisionem suscipere suadent? euidens est quoniam in ablatione carnis uestrae gloriam sibi apud homines con-
locare deproperant, ut ab aduersariis, quasi familiares quidam legis existentes, nullam persecutionem patiantur.' sufficienter uero
ostendens illos non affectu legis ista agere, e contrario sua illis contrasistit cum ualida et nimis compendiosa probatione:

mihi autem absit gloriari, nisi in cruce domini nostri Iesu Christi;
per quem mihi mundus crucifixus est, et ego mundo.

bene posuit, *absit;* quia qui deuotat se, ne aliquando in aliud
aliquid magnum sapiat cupit. 'sed haec (inquit) mihi semper dignum gloriae reputari, id est, crucem Christi, per quem mihi praesens mundus uidetur esse mortuus, dum animo iam illa quae futura sunt considero. nam et ego praesenti uitae sum emortuus, in
illis iam me conuersare existimans.' et quidem hoc ad praesens;
nunc uero ad illa quae inquiruntur:

1   eos (*for* uos) C*   7   id a se H   ‖   confix. C [confinx. *coniec. Pitra*]   13
annua C   26   in *om* C (*corr.*)   29   iam *om* H   30   mundo (*for* uitae) H   31
illius C* H illa C (*corr.*)   ‖   conuersari C (*corr.*)

6:12 *Those who want to be pleasing in the flesh, these are compelling you to be circumcised—only that they may not be persecuted for
the cross of Christ.*

"Those who want (he says) in this present life to please the
opponents of true religion (he means the Jews) strive to do this so
that they may not suffer persecution on account of Christ." And
because it was an extremely serious matter that they were doing
such things for the sake of the unbelievers, pretending that they
were keeping faith with them, Paul is eager to confirm what he has
said, so that he may not seem to have fabricated it by himself:

[108] 6:13 *Even those who have been circumcised do not themselves
keep the law, but they want you to be circumcised so that they may
boast about your flesh.*

"It is obvious that they transgress many of the law's commandments. For they do not even accomplish the sacrifices that require
the ascent to Jerusalem at the three times in the year fixed by the
law according to the law's commandment. Anyone will find them
transgressing in a great many other ways, if he is only willing to
make a careful examination. And so if they pretend to keep circumcision because of their affection for the law, they do demonstrate the keeping of the law in this respect. But if they promote
the transgression of the law in other respects, how is it that they
are persuading you to accept circumcision? It is clear that by cutting off your flesh they are eager to gain praise from human beings
so that they may suffer no persecution from their opponents, as
though they belong to the family of the law." Indeed, by sufficiently demonstrating that what they did was not motivated by
their affection for the law, he opposed and contrasted his position
to theirs with a proof valid and quite succinct:

6:14 *And far be it from me to boast of anything except the cross of
our Lord Jesus Christ, through whom the world has been crucified to
me, and I to the world.*

He rightly put down *far be it*, because he is devoted to his desire
never to think highly of anything else. "But this (he says) I always
think worthy of my boast, that is, the cross of Christ by whom the
present world seems dead to me, while with my mind I already
contemplate what is yet to be. For I have died to the present
life, supposing myself already living my life in those good things
to come." So much for the moment, but now he speaks of the
questions being raised:

*nec enim circumcisio aliquid ualet neque praeputium, sed noua
creatura.*

'Christo enim omnia renouante per suum aduentum, omnis
status praesens iam uidetur esse solutus; ita ut nec aliquem locum
5 possit habere examen circumcisionis et praeputii. quae enim et
fieri poterit discretio in inmortali natura? ad illa igitur inspicio:
illam ego incorruptibilitatem et inmortalitatem quae tunc erit considero, quando et omnium illorum quae in lege sperantur erit renouatio. haec enim nobis Christus per suam prouidit crucem; in
10 qua etiam magna semper superopto, non illam ignobilitatem quae
uidetur erubesci, sed illa lucra quae exinde adnascuntur considerans.' et confidens magnitudini rerum, adicit:

*et quicumque regulam hanc sectantur, pax super illos et misericor-
dia, et super Israel Dei.*

15 †ut dicat quoniam 'omnes   ἵνα εἴπῃ ὅτι πάντες οἱ κατὰ ταῦ-
quotquot secundum ista propo-   τα προῃρημένοι τυγχάνουσιν τῶν
situm habent, illa bona fruantur παρ' αὐτοῦ καλῶν· τὴν μὲν εἰρήνην
quae ab eo sunt.' 'pacem' qui- εἰπών, ὡς ἂν τότε πάσης λυομέ-
dem dicens, eo quod tunc omnis νην διαστάσεως· τὸ δὲ ἔλεος, ἐπειδὴ
20 dissensio dissoluetur et omnis φιλανθρωπίᾳ ἅπαντα ἡμῖν τὰ πρὸς
tristitia tunc erit exclusa. 'mi- αὐτοῦ προσγίνεται ἀγαθά. ὅμοιον
sericordiam' autem dixit, quo- δέ ἐστιν τὸ χάρις ὑμῖν καὶ εἰρήνη,
niam tunc nobis omnia bona tri- ἐπεὶ μηδὲ διαφέρει τὸ ἔλεος τῆς χά-
buentur sola eius misericordia. ριτος.
25 simile autem est illi dictioni et
illud quod dixit: *gratia uobis et
pax*, quod et in omnibus ante-
ponit epistolis; eo quod nec aliquam habet differentiam secun-
30 dum significationem misericordia a gratia.*

optima autem omnibus est facta adiectio:

de cetero laborem mihi nemo adhibeat; ego enim stigmata domini

---

1 in Christo enim Iesu (*bef.* nec enim) *add C H* ‖ enim 2° *om C* (*corr.*) 5
etsi (*for* et) *H* 10 quia (*aft.* qua) *add H* 14 et super Israel *om H* 15 sq.
Coisl. 204, f. 46 a [Cr. vi. 93] Θεοδώρου (om. Cr.). ἄλλος δὲ ὧδε λέγει· καὶ ὅσοι
τῷ κανόνι τούτῳ στοιχήσουσιν· ἵνα εἴπῃ, κ.τ.λ. 16 istam *C* H* istum (*om*
secundum) *C* (*corr.*) 25 simili est autem *H* 28 nec (*aft.* quod) *om C* aliam
(*bef.* aliquam) *add H* 29-30 secunde *C**

[109] 6:15 *For neither circumcision nor uncircumcision is of any value, but a new creation.*

"For since Christ renewed everything by his coming, the entire present order is plainly already dissolved, so that distinguishing circumcision and uncircumcision can have no place. For what difference between them could be made in an immortal nature? Therefore, I look to these things: I contemplate the incorruptibility and immortality that will come to pass at that time when there will be a renewal of everything hoped for in the law. Christ made this available to us ahead of time by his cross, by which I also pray always and above all for those great benefits, not considering that humility which makes me blush, but those riches which arise from it." Trusting in the greatness of these matters, he adds:

6:16 *And those who follow this rule, peace upon them and mercy, and upon the Israel of God.*

†He means that "all, however many, who have chosen their way of life according to those things, enjoy the good things that come from him." He said *peace* because then all disagreement will be destroyed and all sorrow will then be excluded. And he said *mercy* since then all good things will be bestowed upon us only by his mercy. And this is similar to his expression *grace to you and peace*, which he uses as a preface in all his letters, since mercy has no difference in meaning [110] from grace.*

He means that all who have chosen their way of life according to these things gain good things from him. He said *peace* because then all disagreement will be destroyed, and *mercy* since all the good things that come from him will be ours by his beneficence. And this is similar to *grace to you and peace*, since mercy differs in no way from grace.

And most effectively he makes this addition to all this:

6:17 *From now on, let no one trouble me, for I carry the marks of the Lord Jesus Christ on my body.*

Iesu Christi in corpore meo fero.

†quasi qui in multis labori-   ὡς εἰς πολλοὺς καμάτους ἀπὸ
bus ob eorum inciderit mali-   τῆς ἐκείνων ἐμπεπτωκὼς κακίας.
tiam,*

5 et ideo modo pro se satisfacere cogitur, modo graui se ira inuehere,
plurima etiam contra suam uoluntatem et suos mores et sententiam peragere; Galatis increpare, et arguere illos qui uidebantur
esse praeclari propter praehonorationem ueritatis, ut nec angelis
pepercisse uideatur. et tandem aliquando, postquam omnia com-
10 pleuisse uidetur, laborem praesentiens adicit:

†'discedant (inquit) et non fiant   ἀπαλλασσέσθωσαν (φησίν) καὶ μὴ
mihi prouisores laborum. me   γινέσθωσαν πρόξενοι καμάτων· ἐμὲ
enim a Christi discedere confes-   γὰρ ἀποστῆναι τῆς τοῦ Χριστοῦ
sione per omnia est inpossibi-   ὁμολογίας τῶν ἀδυνάτων, ὑπὲρ ἧς
15 le: pro qua multa passus, paulo   πολλὰ παθὼν μικροῦ κατέστιγμαι
minus toto corpore sum confos-   τὸ σῶμα.
sus.'*

consueto uero fine epistolam credidit esse claudendam:

   gratia domini nostri Iesu Christi cum spiritu uestro, fratres. amen.

20   neque hoc in loco 'Spiritum' sine causa posuit, sed quasi proui-
sorem existentem expectatae resurrectionis, in qua nullum habet
locum legitimorum custodia. solum quia non est contestatus et
hoc in loco, quoniam 'inpossibile est eos gratiae Christi participare et illa bona frui quae inde sunt, si non illo modo quem gratia
25 flagitat, fuerint conuersati.'

---

2 ὡς γὰρ cod. edd.   7 Galatas *C*   8 agilis *C H*   16-17 confusus *C H*
txt *g*   19 fratres *om H*   22 quae (*for* quia) *H*   23-24 participari *C* (*corr.*)
24 sed non *C* H* si *C* (*corr.*) ‖ quam *C*H*   25 explicit (*aft* conuers.) *add*
C

†Inasmuch as he had fallen into many troubles because of their wickedness,* As he had fallen into many troubles because of their wickedness

and so is compelled now to make an apology for himself, now to mount an attack with harsh anger, and for the most part to conduct himself against his own wish, his own practices and opinion—to reproach the Galatians and to condemn those who seemed especially distinguished because he gave highest honor to the truth, so that he might seem to have spared not even the angels. And at length, after he seems to have completed everything, apprehending trouble yet to come, he adds:

†"Let them go away (he says) and not become sources of troubles for me. For it is entirely impossible for me to turn away from the confession of Christ; for it I have suffered much and have almost been pierced in my whole body."* Let them go away (he says) and not become sources of troubles. For it is an impossibility that I should desert the confession of Christ for which I have endured many sufferings and almost been branded on my body.

But he believed the letter should be concluded with his customary ending:

6:18 *The grace of our Lord Jesus Christ be with your Spirit, brothers. Amen.*

Not even in this verse did he put "Spirit" for no reason, but as the cause of the expected resurrection in which [111] keeping the law's observances has no place. This is because this is not the only place where he attested that "it is impossible for them to participate in Christ's grace and to enjoy those good things that come from it unless they have lived their lives the way grace demands."

THEODORUS
MOPSUESTENUS
IN EPISTOLAM B. PAULI
AD EPHESIOS

ARGUMENTUM*

SCRIBIT Ephesiis hanc epistolam beatus Paulus, eo modo quo
et Romanis dudum scripserat quos necdum ante uiderat. et hoc
euidenter ipse ostendit, in ipsa epistola sic scribens: *propter hoc et
ego audiens eam fidem quae in uobis est in domino Iesu, et caritatem*
quam in omnes sanctos habetis, non cesso gratias agere pro uobis. numquam profecto dixisset se auditu de illis cognoscentem gratiarum
pro illis facere actionem, si eos alicubi uel uidisset, uel ad notitiam
eius ulla ratione uenire potuissent.

    habet autem ipsa epistola aliqua ex parte similitudinem secun-
dum intellectum ad illam epistolam quam ad Romanos dudum
scripsisse uidetur. nam et in illa adnititur ostendere Christi aduentum hominibus multorum bonorum causam extitisse conlatorum;
quod et in hac epistola similiter fecisse uidetur. in hac ergo parte
similitudo saluatur epistolae. in schemate uero et ceteris illis quae
ad promissionem sui abusus est propositi plurimam inueniet quis
immutationem, modo si caute dictis intendere uoluerit. illic enim
disputationem cum multo agone et examine faciens docuisse uidetur. primo in loco, quod aduersariorum arguerit dogmata, gentium, inquio, et Iudaeorum. deinde comparatione ostendit Christi aduentus utilitatem; et hoc non simpliciter neque absolute, sed

|| INCIPIT ARGUMENTUM *C H*   6   cognoscente *C* H*   7   alicui *C* H* mali
(*bef.* alicui) *add H*   8   potuisset *C* H*   11   nam etiam illa ad notitiam (*for*
nam—adnititur) *H*   14   seruatur (*for* saluatur) *C* (*corr.*)   15   ad *om H*   19
inquit *H*   20   sed (*for* neque) *H*

THEODORE
OF MOPSUESTIA
ON BLESSED PAUL'S LETTER
TO THE EPHESIANS

THE SETTING

[112] Blessed Paul writes this letter to the Ephesians the way he had previously written to the Romans, that is, to those he had not already seen. He reveals this quite clearly himself by writing in this letter as follows (1:15–16): *Because of this I, too, hearing of the faith that is in you in the Lord Jesus and the love that you have for all the saints, do not cease to give thanks for you.*[1] He would certainly never have said that he [113] was giving thanks for them because of what he had heard, either if he had seen them at some time or if they had been able to make his acquaintance for some other reason.

Moreover, in another respect this letter resembles in its meaning the letter he seems to have written earlier to the Romans. For also in it he strives to show that Christ's coming has become the cause of the many good things to be bestowed upon humans. Similarly, in this letter that is what he has plainly done. Therefore, in this respect the similarity of the letter to the Romans is preserved. At the same time, in the plan and in other details that he used in setting forth his argument, anyone will find a good deal of difference, at least if he is willing to examine Paul's words carefully. For in Romans he plainly gave his teaching by constructing an argument with great anguish and critical scrutiny, first of all because he found fault with the doctrines of the opposing sides, I mean the Gentiles and the Jews. Then he shows the benefit of Christ's coming by comparing the two, and he plainly did

---

[1]The Latin translation of Eph 1:15–16 in the commentary (1:135) differs in detail from this citation. Swete suggests that the translator takes a somewhat free approach. See his notes on 1:112 and 1:135.

cum multo examine id egisse uidetur, ut nihil inexaminatum sub-
relinqueret ex illis quae aduersarii ad destructionem dogmatum
pietatis inuenire se posse existimabant. nam illa quae doctrinam
habere uidentur eorum quae a Christo nobis sunt praestita ualde quis et caute considerans, infirmiora inueniet illis quae aduersus aduersarios dicta sunt ab eo; et hoc optime quis recognoscet,
si epistolae a nobis interpretatae textum decurrens, librare secum
dicta uoluerit. in hac uero epistola, sub specie gratiarum actionis
illa explicat quae a Christo nobis sunt praestita, simul ostendens
quod aduentu suo multorum bonorum nobis omnibus causa extiterit; de quibus etiam et doctrinam absolutam fecisse uidetur.

  habet autem similitudinem ad illam epistolam et in hac parte,
eo quod dogmaticos primum consummans sermones— dogmatici
autem sunt sermones qui narrationem aduentus continent Christi,
simul indicantes et illa bona quae suo nobis praestitit aduentu—
quibus finitis, ad ethicam postea transit exhortationem, singulas
prosecutiones suas discernens. aequum etiam principium ethicorum fecisse uidetur uerborum. illic enim post dogmaticorum consummationem, ad ethicos transiens sermones, sic inchoauisse uidetur: *obsecro autem uos, fratres, per misericordiam Dei.* et in hac
epistola similiter: *obsecro,* inquit, *uos ego uinctus in Domino.* obsecrationem ethicorum uerborum in utrisque epistolis principium
suorum fecisse uidetur. quando uero dicimus dogmaticos aut ethicos sermones, discernentes a proposito, eos ita dicimus compro-
bantes. fieri enim potest ut et dogmatici sermones ethicis permi-
sceantur, non a sola sequentia, sed interdum et ad probationem
dictorum; apostolo maxime consueto et dogmaticis sermonibus

2 adstructionem *C* H* 8   noluerit *H* 13   consummat *C (corr.)* 20   ut (*for*
et) *C** ‖ hac (*bef.* ep.) *om C* H* 23   uerborum (*aft.* suorum) *add C H* 25
dogmaticis serm. ethici *C* 26   ad (*for* a) *H*

so not simply or unambiguously but with critical scrutiny, so that he might leave unexamined none of the opinions that the opposing groups thought they could discover for the destruction of the doctrines of true religion. For if anyone examines with great care the points of their teaching about what Christ bestowed on us, he will find them much weaker than what Paul said against the opposing sides. Anyone will quite clearly recognize this if he is willing to consult our commentary on the letter and weigh what we have said for himself. But in this letter it is in the form of a thanksgiving that he expounds what Christ bestowed on us, demonstrating at the same time that by his coming [114] he became for us the cause of many good things. And it is about them that he plainly gave his unambiguous teaching.

And Ephesians also resembles Romans in the following respect. First of all, he completes his doctrinal discussions, and the doctrinal discussions are those that include the account of Christ's coming and at the same time point out those good things bestowed on us by his coming. Then when these discussions are finished, he passes on to moral exhortation, distinguishing each of his points in their logical order.[2] And he plainly made a smooth beginning of his moral discourse. For in Romans when he passes on to moral discussions after he has finished his treatment of doctrine, he plainly began as follows (Rom 12:1): *And I entreat you, brothers, by the mercy of God.* Similarly, in this letter he says (Eph 4:1): *I, the prisoner in the Lord, entreat you.*[3] He plainly made "entreaty" the point of departure for moral statements in both letters. But when we speak of doctrinal or moral discussions, distinguishing the two by their purpose, we do so in such a way as to recognize their unity in the argument.[4] For it can happen that doctrinal discussions may be mixed into moral ones not by the logical order alone but sometimes to prove what is said. It is especially the apostle's custom to prove his moral points by

---

[2] Swete (1:114) points out that *prosecutio* renders ἀκολουθία.

[3] Theodore notes that "beseech" (παρακαλῶ) occurs in both passages.

[4] See Swete's paraphrase (1:114–15): "When we speak of one portion on an Ep. as doctrinal and of another as ethical, distinguishing the two portions by their respective purposes and intents..., we use these terms to point out their relation to the argument. It is S. Paul's habit to base his exhortations upon doctrine, and with this view ethics and dogma are sometimes interwoven, at other times, as in these two Epistles, kept distinct."

probationem facere ethicorum. epistolae igitur argumentum, ut compendiose dicamus, hoc est: doctrina illorum bonorum quae a Christi aduentu in nos conlata esse uidentur, quae et sub specie gratiarum actionis sunt explicata. hoc est autem dogmatis com-
5 probatio, cum et exhortationem illorum quae ad uirtutem pertinent explicat.

†illud autem ualde demira-   ἐπῆλθέν μοι σφόδρα θαυμάζειν
tione dignum mihi accidit de il-   ἐκεῖνα τῶν εἰρηκότων
lis qui dixerunt*

10 beatum Paulum propter hoc uel maxime laudare Ephesiorum fidem, ut ostendat quemadmodum recepit dogmatum illorum traditionem quae ab Iohanne euangelista ad eos dudum fuerat facta. uidentur enim illud dixisse absolute ex sola coniectura, eo quod et fuisse dicatur ad Ephesios beatissimus Iohannes, existimantes

15 †quod et idem illis inprimis fi-   τὸν μακάριον Ἰωάννην τὸν εὐαγγε-
dem eam quae in Christum est   λιστὴν πρῶτον τοῖς Ἐφεσίοις πα-
tradiderit, non considerantes   ραδεδωκέναι τὸν τῆς εὐσεβείας λό-
quoniam Iohannes in nouissi-   γον· οὐκ ἐνενόησαν γὰρ ὡς Ἰωάν-
mis temporibus Ephesi acces-   νης τοὺς ὑστέρους χρόνους παρ'
20 sit; uixit enim usque ad tem-   Ἐφεσίοις ἐγένετο, διαγενόμενος
pora Traiani imperatoris a tem-   ἄχρι τῶν Τραϊανοῦ τοῦ βασιλέως
poribus Neronis incipiens. a   καιρῶν, ἀπὸ τῶν Νέρωνος ἀρξάμε-
quo Nerone Paulus ob pietatis   νος, ἀφ' οὗ Παῦλος ἀπετμήθη τὴν
praedicationem capitalem uide-   κεφαλὴν καὶ ὁ Ἰουδαϊκὸς πόλεμος
25 tur subiisse sententiam, quan-   ἀρχὴν ἐδέξατο. ἐπὶ τούτου γὰρ δὴ
do contigit et Iudaïcum bellum   τοῦ πολέμου πάντας μὲν ἀναχωρῆ-
sumpsisse principium. hoc igi-   σαι τοὺς ἀποστόλους τῆς Ἰουδαίας
tur bello omnes apostoli a Iu-   ἐγένετο· τότε δὲ καὶ Ἰωάννης εἰς
daea discesserunt; quod bellum   τὴν Ἔφεσον γενόμενος διετέλεσεν
30 magnum existens multis malis   ἐπ' αὐτῆς, ἄχρι τῶν Τραϊανοῦ δια-
Iudaeos adfecisse uidetur. tunc   γεγονὼς ὡς ἔφην καιρῶν. Παῦλος
ergo Iohannes Ephesi accessit,   δὲ οὐδὲ τεθεαμένος αὐτοὺς ἐπιστέλ-
et commoratus est in ea; usque   λων φαίνεται· καταλιμπάνει δὲ Τι-
ad tempus etenim Traiani in   μόθεον μετὰ τοῦτο ἐπιστατήσοντα

---

1   tam (for ut) H   2-3   a Chr. aduentum C* H ad, &c. C (corr.)   4   hoc autem est C   7   sq. Coisl. 204, f. 47 b [Cr. vi 97, Fr. 130] θεόδωρος δέ φησιν· ἐπῆλθεν, κ.τ.λ.   13   uidetur H   23   ἐφ' οὗ is suggested by Fr.; cod., Cr., as in text.   24   praedicatione H   25   subisse H   31   id fecisse C* H afflixisse C (corr.)

doctrinal discussions. Therefore, the setting of the letter, if we may speak succinctly, is as follows: the teaching of those good things plainly bestowed on us by Christ's coming and expounded in the form of a thanksgiving is the proof of the doctrines, while it also unfolds the exhortation of what pertains to virtue.

[115] †But the greatest astonishment has come upon me from those who have said* The greatest astonishment has come upon me because of those who have said that blessed Paul gave special praise to the faith of the Ephesians for this reason, namely, to show how he accepted the tradition of those teachings that John the Evangelist had given them long ago. For they seem to have made this assertion only by conjecture, because that most blessed John is said to have been with the Ephesians. They supposed

†that he was the same one who first handed over to them the faith in Christ, though they did not take note of the fact that John came to Ephesus much later. For he lived to the time of the emperor Trajan, beginning with the time of Nero. It was by this Nero that Paul plainly suffered capital punishment because he preached the true religion, and this was at the same time that the Jewish war took its beginning. Thus, in this war all the apostles fled from Judea because once [116] this great war took place, it plainly afflicted the Jews with many evils. Therefore, it was at that time that John went to Ephesus and dwelt there, for he plainly dwelt in this city up to the time of Trajan, as we have just said. But Paul wrote them this letter at a time when he had not yet seen them. Afterwards, when

that blessed John the Evangelist first handed over to the Ephesians the account of true religion. For they did not understand that John was with the Ephesians at a later time, since he lived up to the time of the emperor Trajan, beginning from Nero, by whom Paul was beheaded and in whose time the Jewish war had its beginning. For at the time of this war it came about that all the apostles withdrew from Judea.

And it was at that time that John went to Ephesus and dwelt there up to the time of Trajan, as I have said. But Paul appears to have sent them the letter when he had not seen them.

Afterwards, once he had appa-

hac ciuitate uisus est commo-
rasse, sicut et superius diximus.
Paulus uero hanc epistolam
scripsit ad eos illo tempore quo
adhuc non uiderat eos. reliquit
autem Timotheum post hoc ut
curam ecclesiae eorum adhiberet; qui iam et fuerat apud illos.*

τῇ παρ' αὐτοῖς ἐκκλησίᾳ, γεγονὼς
ἤδη παρ' αὐτοῖς ὡς εἰκός.

cui et scribit, adsignans qui et qualis et quemadmodum in ecclesiasticum debeat creari ministerium; quemadmodum autem et erga uiduas dispensationem implere debeat. instruit eum simul et de
ceteris omnibus, sicut et ex ipsa est euidenter discernere epistola.
†quis autem sic fatuus qui exi-
stimet, praesente Iohanne, Timotheum relictum fuisse ad ecclesiarum dispensationem, uel
isdem fuisse praepositum? sed
et illud necessario reputari conueniens est, quoniam*

τίς δὲ οὕτως ἠλίθιος ὥστ' ἂν οἰη-
θῆναι ὅτι παρόντος Ἰωάννου Τιμόθεον ἐπὶ τῷ τὴν ἐκκλησίαν οἰκο-
νομεῖν κατελίμπανεν; ἔτι καὶ τοῦτο πρὸς τοῖς εἰρημένοις λογίζεσθαι
χρή,

beatus Paulus bis Romae accessit regnante Nerone. et primum
quidem adpellans Festum apud Iudaeam, dum ille in gratiam Iudaeorum eundem Hierosolimis mittere uellet, sicque Romae in
uinculis ductus, inde iudicio Neronis liberatus, securus abire iussus est. duobus uero annis commoratus Romae, exinde egressus,
multis pietatis doctrinam praedicasse uisus est. secunda uero uice
Romam accedens, dum illo adhuc moraretur; contigit ut sententia
Neronis ob praedicationem pietatis capite puniretur.
†Ephesios autem uidit multum
antequam Romae ab Iudaea duceretur (quod ex libro Actuum
apostolorum discere quis euidenter poterit), quando etiam et
ceteri apostoli adhuc in Iudaea
commorabantur. igitur adparet
eum omni ex parte multo ante

ὡς Ἐφεσίους ἐθεάσατο πολλῷ πρότερον ἢ ἐπὶ τὴν Ῥώμην ἀπὸ τῆς
Ἰουδαίας ἀναχθῆναι ὅλως, ὡς ἐν
ταῖς Πράξεσιν τῶν ἀποστόλων μά-
θοι ἄν τις σαφέστερον· ὥστε φαίνεσθαι αὐτὸν πανταχόθεν πολλῷ
πρότερον τῆς Ἰωάννου διατριβῆς
ταῦτα γράφοντα πρὸς αὐτούς.

1 uita (for civitate) H   15 praesentem Iohannem C*H   19 reputare C   22
gratia C*H   28 praedicatione H   31 quo C*

he had already been with them, he left Timothy to take charge of their church.*5 / rently been with them, he left Timothy to take charge of their church.

And Paul writes to Timothy, setting down what person and of what character a minister should be and how appointment should be made for the church's ministry, and as well how he ought to carry out the superintendence of widows. At the same time, he instructs him about everything else, as is obviously seen in that letter.

†And who would be so foolish as to suppose that if John had been present, Timothy would have been left to manage the affairs of the church or to have been put in charge of them? But it is necessarily right to take into consideration the fact that* / And who would be so foolish as to suppose that if John had been present, he would have left Timothy to manage the church? Moreover, it is necessary to take into consideration this fact in addition to what has been said,

blessed Paul went to Rome twice during the reign of Nero. Indeed, he first appealed to Festus in Judea [to send him to Rome], while [117] Festus wanted to send him to Jerusalem as a favor to the Jews.6 Thus, he was taken to Rome in chains and was there freed by Nero's judgment and ordered to depart in safety. For two years he dwelt at Rome and then seems to have left and preached the teaching of true religion to many. But he came to Rome a second time, and while he was still dwelling there, it came about that he received capital punishment by Nero's sentence because of his preaching of the true religion.

†And he saw the Ephesians long before he was taken to Rome from Judea (which anyone can clearly learn from the Acts of the Apostles), at the time when the other apostles were still dwelling in Judea. Therefore, it is evident from all sides that / namely, that he saw the Ephesians long before he was taken to Rome from Judea, as anyone can more clearly learn from the Acts of the Apostles. As a result, it is evident from all sides that he wrote this to them long before John's stay there.

---

5 For Paul's first visit to Ephesus see Acts 18:19. The reference to Timothy depends upon 1 Tim 1:3. See the introduction for the puzzles created by Theodore's view.

6 See Acts 25:1–12.

hanc epistolam Ephesiis scripsisse quam Iohannes illo commoratus.*

et haec contemplatione cautelae doctrinae dicta sunt a nobis, ut ne
5 quis absolute sensus diuinarum scripturarum fortuitu existimet
accipiendos. intendi autem ulterius debet interpretationi quae per
partes fit, ex quibus possibile est nos apostolici intellectus prudentiam perspicere, quod uel maxime plus omnibus necessarium esse
conuenit. his autem obsistit nihil neque ullam adiectionem facit
10 aut minorationem, utrum Iohannes beatus euangelista Ephesiis
uideatur ante eius litteras fidem tradidisse, utrum alter aliquis sit,
qui Ephesios ad Christi adduxit credulitatem. tantum uero adice-
re dictis uolo quoniam multam difficultatem ipsa epistola etiam in
uerbis habere uideatur, ita ut interpretare eam uolenti, non faci-
15 le sit manifestum eius facere sensum. hac de causa optimum esse
arbitratus sum non solum omnem interpretationem exponere uerborum, sed et ipsa obscura uerba interpretare, ubi id fieri res exigit. sic enim perspicuum erit omni uolenti discutere hanc scripturam, quo possit intellectus apostolici sensus perspicuus haberi;
20 quod et praehonorabilius omnibus esse existimo et opto id euenire, si tamen id contigerit nobis per diuinam gratiam posse proue-
niri, ut euidenter sensum apostolicum cunctis uolentibus legere
publicemus.

Paulus apostolus Iesu Christi per uoluntatem Det, sanctis omnibus
25 *qui sunt Ephesi et fidelibus in Christo Iesu: gratia uobis et pax a Deo*
patre nostro et domino Iesu Christo.

†in his et quidem secundum   ἐν τούτῳ κατὰ τὸ εἰωθὸς αὐτῷ
consuetudinem suam epistolae   τῆς ἐπιστολῆς τὴν προγραφὴν συν-
praefationem consummasse ui-   επέρανεν· παραπλήσιόν τι τῇ παρ’
30 detur, simile aliquid faciens il-   ἡμῖν συνηθείᾳ ποιῶν· ὡς ὅταν ἐπισ-
lius consuetudinis quae est apud   τέλλοντες λέγομεν, ‘ὁ δεῖνα τῷ δεῖνι
nos; cum enim nos scribere uo-   χαίρειν.’

---

1 Ephesis C* H   3   esset (aft commor.) add C (corr.)   4   contemplationem
C* H   5   esse (aft exist) add C   6   per om H*   12   ad Chr. om H   12-13
adiecere C*   13   ipsa epst C ipse post H (for ipsa epistola)   14   interpretari C
17   interpretari C (corr.)   19   habere C*   21   contingerit C*   ‖   per om
H   23   EXPLICIT ARGUMENTUM [+ EPHESIORUM EPISTOLAE C] INCIPIT EPI-
STOLA EORUNDEM EPHESIORUM (aft publicemus) add C H   27   sq. Coisl. 204,
f. 47 b-48 a [Cr. vi. 100].   28   hanc (for suam) C

he wrote this letter to the Ephesians long before John dwelt
there.*

We have said this for the sake of accuracy,[7] so that no one might
suppose the meaning of the divine scriptures should be accepted
without reference to the occasion and historical connection.[8] But
still more attention must be paid to a detailed interpretation by
which it is possible for us to discern the wisdom of the apostle's
meaning. It is right that this should be necessary to the greatest
possible extent in all cases. And nothing stands in the way of this,
nor [118] does it add or detract anything whether blessed John
the Evangelist may seem to have handed down the faith to the
Ephesians before Paul's letter or whether it was someone else who
brought the Ephesians to their belief in Christ. But I only want
to add to what I have said that this letter plainly also poses great
difficulty in its language, so that it is not easy for someone who
wishes to interpret it to make its meaning clear. For this reason
I have thought it best not only to supply a general interpretation
but also to explain the obscure words where the text requires
me to do this. For in this way it will be clear to everyone who
wants to analyze this scripture how the meaning of the apostle's
understanding can be kept clear. I think this is to be honored
before everything else, and I pray that it will result in our making
clearly and generally known the apostle's meaning to all who are
willing to read the commentary, provided at any rate that we may
have the good fortune to be prospered by divine grace.

1:1–2 *Paul, an apostle of Jesus Christ by the will of God, to all the*
saints who are in Ephesus and to the faithful in Christ Jesus: Grace
to you and peace from God our Father and the Lord Jesus Christ.

†By these words, as is his custom, he plainly completed the
salutation of the letter, doing something similar to our custom,
for when we want to write a letter, we say, "this person to that

By this, as is his custom, he
completed the salutation of the
letter, doing what is similar to
our custom, since when writing
a letter we say, "such a one to
such a one, greetings."

---

[7] Swete (1:117) suggests this translation of *contemplatione cautelae* and points
out that "the phrase appears to be almost confined to the writings of jurists and
legal documents."

[8] Again, Swete (1:117) suggests this translation of *absolute* (perhaps including
fortuitu). Literally, we could translate "accepted not simply and accidentally."

lumus, dicimus: 'ille illi salutem'.*

  Christi autem apostolum seipsum iure pronuntiat, utpote illam
bonitatem quae ex aduentu Christi accedit docere illos praesenti-
5 bus adproperans scriptis.

†adiecit autem, *per uoluntatem*	προσέθηκεν δὲ τὸ διὰ θελήματος
Dei, simul connectens utrum-	θεοῦ, ὅμου τε συνδέων αὐτὰ ὡς
que, ita ut nihil discretum ne-	μηδὲν διακεκρίσθαι μηδὲ ἀπεσπάσ-
que scissum esse uideatur ab il-	θαι δοκεῖν τοῦ θεοῦ τῶν διὰ τοῦ
10 lis quae Dei sunt illorum quae	Χριστοῦ γενομένων· ὅμου δὲ καὶ
per Christum effecta sunt; si-	τὸ τῆς ἀποστολῆς ἔργον ἀναγκαιό-
mul autem et apostolatus sui	τατον ἑαυτῷ πανταχόθεν δεικνύς·
opus necessarium sibi undique	πλήν γε δὴ ὅτι σύντομον τὴν προ-
ostendit. uerumtamen quoniam	γραφὴν ἐποιήσατο,
15 compendiosam praefationem lit-	
terarum fecisse uidetur*	

(et quidem cum in multis epistolis consequentia suorum scriptorum ipso argumento aliqua interiecisse uideatur cum praefatione
scripturae, ita ut ex hoc saepe prolongaret praefationem—hoc au-
20 tem uiderit quis in epistolis quas uel ad Romanos, uel ad Galatas
maxime scripsit—sed hoc in loco compendiose prosecutus est)

†consequenter et hoc proposi-	καταλλήλως καὶ τοῦτο τῇ προθέσει
tione suorum faciens uerborum.*	τοῦ λόγου ποιῶν.

memores enim sumus et in argumento ipso dixisse, quoniam

25 †propositum habet aduentus	πρόκειται γὰρ αὐτῷ τῆς τοῦ Χρισ-
Christi utilitatem sub specie	τοῦ παρουσίας τὸ ὠφέλιμον εἰπεῖν
gratiarum actionis compendio-	ἐν εὐχαριστίας εἴδει συντόμως, οὐχ
se dicere; non sicut in illa epi-	ὡς ἐπὶ τῆς πρὸς Ῥωμαίους ἐξερ-
stola quam ad Romanos scrip-	γαστικώτερον καὶ μετὰ τοῦ πρὸς
30 sit, quam et cum multa edi-	τοὺς ἐναντίους λόγου.
dit cautela, aduersariorum si-	
mul retundens obiectiones.*	

consummans uero praesentis epistolae praescriptionem, in his statim adicit, propositum suum explanare cupiens:
35   *benedictus Deus et Pater domini nostri Iesu Christi.*

---

4 accidit *H*   5 deproperans *H*   10 illa (*for* illorum) *C H*: txt *g*   12 apostolus *H*   13 πλὴν γε δεῖ cod.; so Cr., adding: "sic. νοεῖν aut simile uerbum
excidit."   17 consequentem *H*   25 aduentum *H*   33 haec (*for* in his) *C*
(*corr.*)

person, greetings."*

[119] And he rightfully proclaims himself an apostle of Christ, since he was eager in the present letter to teach them about the kindness that drew near because of Christ's coming.

†And he added *by the will,* of *God,* binding both expressions together at the same time so that there would seem to be no distinction or division between what belongs to God and what was brought about by Christ. And at the same time he also demonstrated in all respects that his work as an apostle was most necessary for him. Nevertheless, he plainly made the salutation of the letter succinct,*	And he added *by the will of God,* binding both expressions together at the same time so that there would seem to be no distinction or division between what belongs to God and what came to pass through Christ. And at the same time he also demonstrated in all respects that his work as an apostle was most necessary for him. Nevertheless, he made the salutation succinct,

(to be sure, in many of his letters he plainly inserted in his salutation some statements appropriate to the argument of his writings, so that because of this he would often lengthen the salutation—one may see this especially in the letters he wrote to the Romans or to the Galatians—yet in this passage he took a succinct approach),

†doing this in accordance with the argument he would make.*	doing this in accordance with the argument he would make.

For we are mindful of having said in our account of the setting that

†what he proposes is to speak succinctly of the benefit of Christ's coming in the form of a thanksgiving—not as in the letter he wrote to the Romans, which he composed with much care, at the same time blunting the charges of the opposing parties.*	For what he proposes is to speak succinctly of the benefit of Christ's coming in the form of a thanksgiving—not as in the letter to the Romans in greater detail and with an argument against the opposing parties.

But when he has completed [120] the salutation of the present letter, since he wishes to make what he proposes evident, he immediately adds:

1:3a *Blessed be the God and Father of our Lord Jesus Christ,*

quoniam gratiarum actionis—ita ut statim et a primordio uideatur illud expedire quod diximus—quoniam sub specie gratiarum actionis illorum bonorum quae nobis praestita sunt a Christo
faciat doctrinam. 'benedicere' enim dicitur laudare, extollere, bo-
5 na narrare.

†quod enim dixit: *benedictus,*   τὸ εὐλογητὸς ἀντὶ τοῦ 'ἐπαινεῖσθαι
hoc est, 'laudari et demirari di-   καὶ θαυμάζεσθαι ἄξιος·' τὸ μέντοι
gnus.' nam quod dixit: *Deus*   ὁ θεὸς καὶ πατὴρ τοῦ κυρίου
et Pater domini nostri Iesu Chri-   ἡμῶν Ἰησοῦ Χριστοῦ δύναται μὲν
10 *sti* poterat equidem et separatim   καὶ διῃρημένως λέγεσθαι, ἵν' ᾖ τὸ
dici, ut sit illud quod dixit *Deus*   μὲν θεὸς κατὰ διαίρεσιν ἀπολύτως
separatim. continuata uox eui-   νοούμενον, τὸ δὲ πατὴρ καθ' ἑαυτό.
dens est, et absolute praestat in-
tellectum,*

15 sicut et illud quod scriptum est: *et fecit Deus; et dixit Deus;* et si
qua huiusmodi sunt.

†nam *Pater* secundum se in   εἰ δέ τις αὐτὸ ἐπισυμπλέκειν φιλο-
Christo accipitur. si quis uero   νεικοίη ὡσὰν καὶ τοῦ θεὸς καὶ τοῦ
illud connectere fuerit adnisus,   πατὴρ ἐπὶ τοῦ προσώπου νοεῖσθαι
20 ita ut et Deus et Pater erga per-   ὀφείλοντος τοῦ Χριστοῦ, οὐδὲ πρὸς
sonam intellegi debeat Christi,   τοῦτο μαχόμεθα.
neque in hoc litigamus.*

alioquin et Deus pater adsumpti aptissime diceretur, utpote et homine illo existente per naturam. quoniam autem de hoc disputat
25 per omnes sermones dogmaticos illos qui in hac sunt epistola, id
poterit euidenter ostendi. deinde dicit et pro quibus sit benedictus:

---

1 actiones *C H* 3 praestita est *H* 6 Coisl. 204, f. 49 b [Cr. vi. 104. Fr. 131]
Θεόδωρος δέ φησιν τὸ εὐλογ. κ.τ.λ. 7 Deus (*aft.* bened.) add *H* ‖ laudare
C H 9 δύναται το μὲν (*sic*) cod., δύναται τὸ μὲν Cr.; Fr. as in text. 15 et
dixit D. et fecit D. *H* 23 consumpti *H* ‖ dicere *C H* 23-24 hominem
illum existentem *C H*

This is because he is giving thanks—so that immediately and from the beginning he may be seen to work out what we have said—since it is in the form of a thanksgiving that he gives his teaching about those good things Christ has bestowed on us. For by "bless" is meant praise, extol, tell of good things.

†When he said *blessed*, he meant "worthy of being praised and admired." Indeed, when he said *the God and Father of our Lord Jesus Christ*, it could even have been understood as separate statements, so that *God* might be taken by itself. It is clear that the expression can be a sentence and supplies a meaning by itself,*⁹

Blessed means "worthy of being praised and admired." The phrase *the God and Father of our Lord Jesus Christ* can also be read as separate statements, so that *God* would be understood separately and unconditionally, and *Father* by itself.

just as it is written: *and God made, and God said*, and other verses like this.

[121] †For *Father* by itself is to be referred to Christ. But if someone were to insist on a connection so that both *God* and *Father* should be understood to refer to Christ's person, we do not quarrel with this.*

But if someone were to contend that a connection is made, as though both *God* and *Father* should be understood to refer to Christ's person, we do not quarrel with this.

In any case, God would quite appropriately be called the Father of the assumed Man, even though he was a human by nature. And it could clearly be demonstrated that he argues about this in all the doctrinal discussions in this letter.¹⁰ Then he speaks of those things for which God is blessed:

---

⁹The idea, at least in the Latin translation, seems to be that "blessed be God" forms a complete sentence and that "God" can be understood apart from "Father." See Swete's note, 1:120. The issue is whether or not we should understand "God *and* Father" to mean simply God the Father, that is, the first person of the Trinity rather than the single essence of God.

¹⁰"God the Father," as a reference to the first person of the Trinity, would more clearly refer to the eternal generation of the Word. Here, however, Theodore understands "our Lord Jesus Christ" to refer to—or at least to include—the assumed Man. Presumably, God as Father is the Father of the assumed Man by grace and because of the union of the divine Son with the Man. Theodore more clearly expresses his understanding in commenting on 1:17a.

qui benedixit nos in omni benedictione spiritali in caelestibus in
Christo.

nostra benedictio quae fit in Deo, confessio sola est illorum bonorum quae nobis praestita sunt ab eo. nam illa benedictio quae
5 a Deo fit, in nobis opere impletur, pro quibus nos suis beneficiis
sublimans demirationi exhibet dignos. dignus ergo est ut et demiretur a nobis, et ut gratiarum illi referamus actiones; quoniam sic
nos gloriosos, sua in nos conferens bona, efficere est dignatus, omne nobis bonum spiritale donans per illam dispensationem quam
10 per Christum misisse uidetur. hoc enim dicit *in Christo.* nam quod
dixit: *in caelestibus;* hoc est, 'quae in caelo morantes participabimus.' dixit namque futura illa bona—resurrectionem, inquio, et
illam quae tunc erit inmortalitatem; et quod iam ultra peccare non
poterimus, sed inuertibiles permanebimus in bonis. in caelo enim
15 conuersantes, ista tunc expectamus adesse nobis per Spiritus gratiam. sicut enim in epistola illa quam scripsit ad Corinthios super resurrectionem disputans dixisse uidetur quoniam corpus nostrum 'seminatur quidem in corruptione et ignobilitate et infirmitate; surget autem in incorruptela et honore et uirtute;' adiecit: *se-*
20 *minatur corpus animale, surget corpus spiritale;* in illum cuncta coa-
dunans, id est, Spiritum ex quo omnia nobis ista aderunt. unde et
hoc in loco, *in omni benedictione* dicens, *spiritali* adiecit, ad ostensionem quia omnia nobis bona aderunt tunc per Spiritum.

et quoniam magna erunt tam illa quae promissa sunt quam
25 quae expectantur, uidebatur autem ipsa nouitas rerum mentem
turbare, quapropter non ante multum temporis tanta nobis donas-
set, sed neque dixisset aperte quae sunt illae spiritales benedictiones; simul etiam de nouitate satisfaciens et benedictiones ipsas manifestius explanans, adiecit:
30 *sicut elegit nos in ipso ante constitutionem mundi, esse nos sanctos*
et immaculatos coram eo.

'olim (inquit) et ante mundi totius fabricam hanc fecerat dispensationem, secundum suam praescientiam, segregans nos in

---

5 opere *om l* 6 exibit dignos *C* exibet d. *H* exbibet dignus *C (corr.)* 8 nos
(*bef.* glor.) *om H* 11 qui (*for* quae) *CH* quam *l* 11-12 participauimus *C* 12
inquo *C H* 19 autem *om H* 20-21 adunans *H** 27-28 bened. spir. *H*
33 praesentiam *H*

1:3b *who has blessed us in Christ with every spiritual blessing in the heavenly,*

Our blessing that takes place in God is only the acknowledgement of those good things he has bestowed on us. For the blessing that takes place by God is completed in us by what we do, in return for which he lifts us up by his favors and shows us worthy of admiration. Therefore, it is right that we should admire him and return thanks to him, since he has seen fit to make us glorious by conferring his own good things on us, giving us every spiritual good by the dispensation he plainly sent in Christ. For he speaks of this as *in Christ*. When he said *in the heavenly*, he meant "those things [122] we shall share when we dwell in heaven." For he meant those good things to come—I mean the resurrection and the immortality that will come to be at that time and that we shall no longer be able to sin but shall remain steadfast in good things. For by living our lives in heaven[11] by the grace of the Spirit, we await the time of their presence in us. It is just as he plainly said in the letter he wrote to the Corinthians in his argument about the resurrection (1 Cor 15:42–44): our body "is indeed sown in corruption and dishonor and weakness, but it will rise in incorruption and honor and power." And he added *it is sown a physical body, it is raised a spiritual body*, joining all this to him, that is, to the Spirit from whom all those things will be present to us. For this reason in this passage when he says *with every blessing*, he added *spiritual* to demonstrate that all good things will then be present to us through the Spirit.

And since what has been promised will be as great as what is looked forward to, the very novelty of these realities seemed to disturb his mind as to why God had not given us such great gifts long ago and had not said openly what those spiritual blessings were. Both giving an assurance about the novelty and at the same time explaining more clearly the blessings themselves, he added:

1:4a *just as he chose us in him before the foundation of the world to be holy and blameless before him.*[12]

"Long ago (he says) and before the fashioning of the entire world, he had made this dispensation by his foreknowledge,

---

[11] Perhaps an echo of Phil 3:20: "our citizenship is in heaven."

[12] Note that Theodore divides the text differently than the NRSV, taking "in love" with verse 5.

Christo; ut potiti eius bona in sanctitate permaneamus perfecta,
nullam maculam peccatorum ultra suscipientes; sed ut simus secundum eius probationem et decretum sine ulla culpa.' hoc enim
dicit *coram eo;* ut dicat, 'ualde ab omni culpa securos.' uere enim
5 ille est omni excusationi superior, quemcumque talem esse de-
creuerit Deus. nam quod dicit, *elegit;* id est, 'ad hoc segregauit.'
et quod dicit, *in ipso;* Christo dicit, eo quod per eundem occasionem accepimus tantorum bonorum potiri donationem. euidens
est quoniam *sancti et immaculati,* quales Paulus dicit, in futuro
10 saeculo per inoperationem Spiritus erimus. dixi namque et in epistola Galatarum,

†quoniam de futuris mos est il-	πρόδηλον ὡς ἀπὸ τῶν μελλόν-
li ea quae secundum Christum	των ἔθος αὐτῷ τῶν κατὰ Χριστὸν
sunt comprobare, eo quod et	ποιεῖσθαι τὴν ἀπόδειξιν, ἅτε δὴ τό-
15 tunc in ipsis rebus donationes	τε φαινομένων ἐπὶ τοῦ πράγματος.
perspicientur; nunc enim in pro-	νῦν γὰρ ἐν ἐπαγγελίᾳ μόνον αὐτῶν
missione eorum sumus tantum	ἐσμὲν διὰ πίστεως.
per fidem.*	

deinde et quod maius est aditur:
20 *in caritate praeordinans nos in filiorum adoptionem per Iesum*
Christum in ipsum.

nam quod dicit, *in caritate* praeordinatos nos *in filiorum adop-*
tionem,

†maiorem dictorum ostendit es-	τοῦτο ἐπίτασιν ἔχει τοῦ προκειμέ-
25 se affectum duabus ex parti-	νου διχόθεν, ἐπείπερ ἡμῖν ἀγάπη
bus. nam caritas praeelectione	τῆς ἐκλογῆς μείζων,
uel praeordinatione maior est.*	

electio potest etiam liberalitate quadam fieri; caritas uero insitum
affectum ostendit, ex quo et magnitudo uidetur liberalitatis.

30 †maius autem horum est et illud	καὶ τὸ τῆς υἱοθεσίας τοῦ ἁγίους καὶ
quod dixit: *filiorum adoptionem,*	ἀμώμους.
ab illo quod dixerat: *sanctos et*	
*immaculatos.**	

similiter enim et hoc superiori sensui connexum esse uidetur. nam

---

5 illum (*aft.* quemc.) add *C*H* 5-6 decreuit *H* 6 adhuc *H* 8 donatione
C (*corr.*) 9 dixit *CH* 12 sq. Coisl. 204, f. 50 a [Cr. vi. 105, Fr. 131] θεόδωρος
δέ φησιν· πρόδηλον, κ.τ.λ. 16-17 promissionem *H* 19 additur *C* (*corr.*) 24
sq. Coisl. 204, f. 50 b [Cr. vi. 106, Fr. 131] θεόδωρος δέ φησιν· τοῦτο, κ.τ.λ. 26
electione *C*H* 34 sensu *H*

separating us out in Christ so that by acquiring his good things we might remain in perfect holiness, receiving no longer any spot of sins, and so that we might be without any fault according to his determination and decree." For this is what he means by *before him*, that is "quite free from fault." For in truth whoever God should decree to be such is above all need for pardon. For when he said *he chose*, he meant "he separated out for this." And when he says *in him*, he means Christ, because [123] by him we have received the opportunity of acquiring the gift of such great things. It is clear that, by the working of the Spirit, in the age to come we shall be *holy and blameless*, as Paul says. Indeed, also in commenting on the letter to the Galatians I have said[13]

†that it is his custom to prove the dispensation of Christ by the things to come, because it is then that they will be discerned in the facts themselves, for we now have only the promise of them by faith.*	It is evident that it is his custom to prove the dispensation of Christ by the things to come, because it is then that they will appear in fact, for we now have only the promise of them by faith.

Then what is greater is added:

1:4b-5a *In love he predestined us for the adoption of sons through Jesus Christ in himself,*

For when he says that *in love* we are predestined *for the adoption of sons,*

†he shows that the affection expressed in his words is greater for two reasons. For love is greater than election or predestination. Election can come about by some kind of generosity, but love demonstrates a deep-seated affection by which it appears greater than generosity. And greater than having said *holy and blameless* is his reference to *the adoption of sons.**	He emphasizes what he sets forth in two ways, since love is greater than election

and *the adoption of sons* than *holy and blameless.* |

[124] For in a similar way the adoption of sons appears connected

---

[13] See Gal 3:23 and Theodore's comment (1:51).

alterum illorum, id est, *sanctos, et ut sint immaculati*, etiam sola
potest gratia tribuentis ostendi.

†nam filiorum adoptio propin-   οἰκειότητος γὰρ ἀπόδειξιν ἔχει ταῦ-
quitatis magnam uindicat osten-   τα μεγίστην.

5 sionem*,

quam et omnium bonorum sequitur copia. quo enim poterit frau-
dari bono ille qui semel in ordinem filii fuerit factus? hoc enim
uoluit dicere, quoniam *elegit nos* non absolute sed *in caritate;* et
ostendit *sanctos et immaculatos* faciens nos—tantam nobis ad illum
10 propinquitatem donauit. optime autem memorans *filiorum adop-*
tionem, coniunxisse illis uisus est *per Iesum Christum;* eo quod per
illum nobis regeneratio quoque et Spiritus adoptionis filiorum do-
natus esse uidetur. nam quod dixit *in ipsum*, de Deo dixit; hoc
est, 'ut eius dicatur filius.' quoniam ergo dixit: *praeordinans nos in*
15 *filiorum adoptionem*, incertum autem erat cuius diceret filios esse
adoptiuos; adiecit

†*in ipsum*, hoc est, 'in sui ipsius,'   τὸ δὲ εἰς αὐτόν· ἵνα αὐτοῦ υἱοὶ
ut illius filii et dicamur et nun-   λεγώμεθά τε καὶ χρηματίζωμεν.
cupemur.*

20 et iterum augens, illud dicit:

secundum bonum placitum uoluntatis eius.

†ut dicat quoniam 'ualde pla-   ἵνα εἴπῃ ὅτι σφόδρα ἤρεσεν αὐ-
cita fuerunt ei, ut ista erga nos   τῷ ταῦτα περὶ ἡμᾶς διαπράξασθαι·
ordinaret; et ualde uoluit in his   ὡς γὰρ ἐν εὐχαριστίας προσχήμα-
25 nos participes fieri.' sicut enim   τι λέγων αὐτά, πανταχόθεν αὔξει
sola specie gratiarum actionis il-   τῶν γεγονότων τὴν χάριν τῷ μεγέ-
la dicens, omni ex parte auxisse   θει τῶν πραγμάτων.
uidetur factorum gratiam ma-
gnitudine rerum.*

30 tale est et illud quod dixit: *benedixit nos in omni benedictione spiri-*
tali in caelestibus; et: *ut simus sancti et immaculati;* et quod dixit: *in*
filiorum adoptionem praeordinatos. antiquam fuisse Dei de his probationem ostendit, quale est illud quod dixit: *praeelegit nos.* adhuc autem etiam et affectum de rebus huiusmodi implens ostendit.

---

1 sanctitas *C* s̄citios (*sic*) *H*   6 enim *om C*   11 illi *H*   17 ipsa (*for in*
ipsum) *H* ‖ sq. Coisl. 204 f. 51 a [Cr. vi. 108, Fr. 131] Θεόδωρος δέ φησω· ἵνα
εἴπῃ, κ.τ.λ.   18 λεγοίμεθα cod. and edd.   21 uoluntatem *C**   28 gratia *H*
28-29 magnitudinem *C* H*   30 in *om H*   33-34 quale—ostendit *om* (*per*
homoeotel.) *H**   34 impletis *C*

to his reference to "holy and blameless" (1:4).[14] For the second of the phrases, that is, *holy* and that they may be *blameless*, can be displayed only by the grace of the one bestowing it.

†For the adoption of sons asserts a great proof of intimacy,*

For this has the greatest proof of intimacy.

which the abundance of all good things follows. For in what circumstances could he who had once taken his place as a son be defrauded of good? Indeed, this is what he meant, since *he chose us* not without qualification but *in love*. And he demonstrated this by making us *holy and blameless*—so great was the intimacy he gave us with himself. And quite effectively in mentioning *the adoption of sons* he plainly joined to these words *through Jesus Christ*, since it is through him that both rebirth and the Spirit of the adoption of sons are plainly given us. Now he said the words *in him* of God, that is, "so as to be called his son." Therefore, since when he said *predestining us for the adoption of sons*, it was uncertain whose adopted sons he meant, he added

†*in him*, that is, "in himself," so that we might both be said to be and be named his sons.*

And *in him*, so that we might both be said to be and be called his sons.

And again to amplify this, he says:

1:5b *according to the good pleasure of his will*

†To mean that "it greatly pleased him to arrange these things for us, and he greatly willed that we should share in them." For by saying this only in the form of a thanksgiving he plainly in all respects amplified the grace by the greatness of the favors done.*

He means that it greatly pleased him to arrange these things for us, for since he says this in the form of a thanksgiving, in all respects he amplifies the grace by the greatness of the favors done.

Like this is also [125] what he said (1:3b-4a): *he has blessed us with every spiritual blessing in the heavenly* and *that we might be holy and blameless* and *predestined for the adoption of sons*. He showed that God's approval of this was from of old, for example, when he said *he chose us before*.[15] Furthermore, he also showed the full measure

---

[14]Theodore means that, just as love is greater than election, so sonship is greater than a blameless life. That is, grace is greater than our own efforts.

[15]*Praeelegit* instead of *elegit*, as in the citation of 1:4a above.

nam quod dixit: *in caritate*, et, *secundum bonum placitum uoluntatis suae*, haec ostendit. omni autem ex parte augens donationum magnitudinem, consequenter adiecit:

in laude gloriae gratiae eius.

†'itaque dignus est pro his laudari a nobis, et omni demiratione dignus haberi, pro quibus sua gratia tantam nobis communicare dignatus est gloriam.'*

ὥστε (φησὶν) ὑπὲρ τούτων ἐπαινεῖσθαι καὶ θαυμάζεσθαι δίκαιον αὐτὸν παρ' ἡμῶν, ἀνθ' ὧν οἰκείᾳ χάριτι τοσαύτης ἡμῖν μετέδωκεν δόξης.

deinde dicit iterum gratiae ipsius gloriam:

in qua gratificauit nos in dilecto.

nam quod dixit: *gratificauit*, id signare uoluit quoniam 'omni nos repleuit gratia.' et quod dixit: *in dilecto*, 'in Christo' dixit. omni enim ex parte illa quae de nobis fiunt memorans adicit *per ipsum* et *in ipso*, utpote in ordine primitiarum eodem Christo adsumpto; et illa omnia quae erga illum pro communi salute sunt gesta. sic enim et participare ei resurrectionem et incorruptelam, et commorari cum eo in caelis sperans, et ostendens multitudinem donationum per illud quod dixit *gratificauit nos*; dicit et illud quod omnibus uidetur eminere, et ad quod omnes maxime congregare faciebat:

in quo habemus redemptionem per sanguinem eius, remissionem delictorum, secundum diuitias gratiae eius quam abundare fecit in nobis.

nam quod dicit: *in quo*, iterum 'in Christo' dicit. inde originem omnium et fruitionem habere ostendens, ita ut magis eos in caritate coniungeret Christi; 'in ipso (inquit) Christo, qui pro nobis suscipere mortem dignatus est, hoc est dici, per sanguinem eius peccatorum accepimus remissionem; quam nullo modo adsequi poteramus, si non multa quaedam Dei erga nos fuisset gratia.' *remissionem* enim hoc in loco, non confessionem, sed plenariam dicit

---

1 dicit C ‖ in car. *om* C 2 siue hoc (*for* suae haec) C ‖ agens H 5 sq. Coisl. 204, *l.c.* Θεόδωρος δὲ ὧδε λέγει· ὥστε, κ.τ.λ. 7 αὐτοῦ Cr. 14 sunt (*for* fiunt) C 15 in *om* C 17 incorruptibilem H 18 commorare C 29 quaedam *om* C (*corr.*) 30 non *om* H

of God's affection from gifts like these. Indeed, he showed this by saying *in love* and *according to the good pleasure of his will*. And because he was amplifying the greatness of the gifts in all respects, in logical order he added:

> 1:6a *to the praise of the glory of his grace*

†And so he is worthy to be praised by us for these gifts and to be held worthy of all admiration because he saw fit to share such great glory with us by his own grace.*

As a result (he says), it is right that he should be praised and admired by us for these gifts because he gave us a share in such great glory by his own grace.

Then he speaks again of the glory of his grace:

> 1:6b *in which he graced us in the Beloved,*

Now when he said *he graced*, he wanted to indicate that "he filled us with all grace." And when he said *in the Beloved*, he meant "in Christ." For every time he calls to mind what took place for us, he adds *through him* and *in him*, since, of course, Christ was taken into the order of the firstfruits for the same purpose. And everything that concerns him took place for the salvation of all. For it is because Paul hopes in this way to share with him in the resurrection and incorruption, and to dwell with him in the heavens, and because he is showing the greatness of the gifts, that he said *he graced us*. He speaks of gifts that excel everything and were bringing about as much as possible the gathering together of all people to them:

> [126] 1:7–8a *in whom we have redemption through his blood, the remission of our transgressions, according to the riches of his grace that he made to abound in us.*[16]

For when he says *in whom*, again he means "in Christ." He shows that the source and enjoyment of all things have their origin in him, so that he may all the more bind them together in the love of Christ. "In Christ himself (he says), who saw fit to undergo death for us, that is to say, through his blood, we have received the remission of sins, which we could in no way have gained had not some abundant grace of God been present to us." For by *remission* in this verse he speaks not of confession but instead of

---

[16]Comparison with the NRSV will show the ways Theodore divides the text differently.

peccatorum abolitionem. simile est autem et hoc dictum illi dicto, *ut simus sancti et immaculati;* quod et in superioribus iam dixisse uidetur. quoniam ergo sub sententia eramus mortis; mortales uero cum essemus, sequebatur et ut delinqueremus, eo quod
5　nec fieri potest mortalem aliquando posse uideri sine culpa; moriens ergo pro nobis et exsurgens pro nobis donauit nobis cum participatione Spiritus inmortalem illam uitam, in qua possibile est
commorantes nos liberos esse a peccato. unde bene *redemptionem
dixit,* eo quod per mortalitatem tenebamur sub arcta necessitate
10　*peccatorum*; uerum quia quasi quaedam redemptio pro nobis datus
est Christus, qui et eripuit nos a mortis potentia, praebuit autem
nobis resurrectionis spem, cum qua et expectamus excepto omni
uiuere peccato. hoc in loco notandum est quod dicebamus, quoniam per omnia haec quae dicit de Christo, de suscepto homine
15　dicit, inde illa quae secundum nos sunt firmare cupiens; ex quibus hoc in loco euidenter adposuit *per sanguinem eius.*

　　deinde dicit et aliud multo praecellentius illis quae praedicta
sunt:

　　in omni sapientia et prudentia notum nobis faciens mysterium uo
20　*luntatis suae, secundum bonum placitum quod proposuit in ipso.*

†*mysterium uoluntatis* Dei dicit absconditam eius uoluntatem et omnibus incertam; *mysterium* illud uocans, utpote incertum interim omnibus ante Christi extans aduentum. quod ergo dicit, tale est: 'olim illi placitum et praeordinatum erat hoc, quod cum multa sapientia et prudentia notum fecit nobis.' ut dicat, 'ipsis ostendit rebus.'*	μυστήριον τοῦ θελήματος τοῦ θεοῦ λέγει τὸ ἀποκεκρυμμένον αὐτοῦ θέλημα καὶ ἄδηλον τοῖς πᾶσιν· μυστήριον αὐτὸ καλῶν. ὅπερ οὖν (φησὶν) πόρρωθεν αὐτῷ δοκοῦν καὶ προωρισμένον ἦν, τοῦτο μετὰ πολλῆς σοφίας καὶ φρονήσεως ἐγνώρισεν ἡμῖν· ἵνα εἴπῃ· ἐπ' αὐτῶν ἔδειξεν τῶν πραγμάτων.

　2　id (*for* iam) *H*　4　et *om C* (*corr.*)　6　uero (*for* ergo) *H*　‖　cum *om C*
(*corr.*)　8　peccatore *C** dixit red. *H*　11　de (*for* a) *H*　15　non (*for* nos) *H*
16　posuit *H*　21　sq. Coisl. 204, f. 54 b [Cr. vi. 114, Fr. 131–2] καὶ Θεόδωρος
δέ φησιν· μυστήριον, κ.τ.λ.

the complete abolition of sins.[17] Moreover, this is similar to what he had already plainly said in what precedes (1:4): *that we might be holy and blameless*. Thus, we were under the sentence of death, and since we were truly mortal, it followed that we should also commit transgressions because it cannot happen that a mortal could ever be found without fault. Because of this, therefore, by dying and rising again for us Christ gave us, together with participation in the Spirit, that immortal life in which it is possible for us to dwell free from sin. This is why he rightly said *redemption*, because we were held fast by mortality under the binding necessity of sins. But because Christ was given for us as some kind of ransom[18] to rescue us from the power of death, he bestowed on us the hope of the resurrection with which we await a life with all sin excluded. In this passage what we said must be pointed out, that in everything he says about Christ he speaks of the assumed Man, [127] since he wants to establish the fact that it is from him that all that concerns us derives. On the basis of this he clearly put down in this passage *through his blood*.

Then he says something else far more excellent than what he had said before:

1:8b-9 *with all wisdom and insight making known to us the mystery of his will, according to the good pleasure that he set forth in him*

†By *the mystery of the will* of God he means his will that is hidden and unclear to all. He calls it a *mystery*, since it was unclear to all during the time before the coming of Christ. Therefore, what he means is like this: "What long ago pleased him and was predestined, this he made known to us with great wisdom and insight."

By *the mystery of the will* of God he means his will that is hidden and unclear to all, calling it a *mystery*. Therefore, (he says) what long ago pleased him and was predestined, this he made known to us with great wisdom and insight, so as to say he demonstrated this by the facts themselves.

---

[17] Swete (1:126) suggests that *confessio* is here used as the equivalent of *absolutio*. He paraphrases Theodore's comment: "not simply the present process of penitence crowned by the formal absolution of the Church, but the final destruction of sin at the resurrection." See Heb 9:26, where removing sin (ἀθέτησιν) seems contrasted with forgiving sin (ἄφεσιν).

[18] *Quaedam redemptio.*

uult enim dicere quoniam illud quod dudum ei placebat, incertum interim erat; quod rebus ipsis nunc cum multa manifestauit sapientia per eam dispensationem quam secundum Christum fecisse uidetur.

†quare autem nunc?*

    in dispensatione plenitudinis temporum.

†eo quod secundum ordinem omnia dispensari conueniebant. quando ergo impleta sunt tempora ceterorum, tunc secundum ordinem qui dudum fuerat dispensatus in suis temporibus etiam illa quae secundum Christum sunt ostendi effecit.*

διὰ τί δὲ νῦν;

εἰς οἰκονομίαν τοῦ πληρώματος τῶν καιρῶν·

ἐπειδὴ κατὰ τάξιν πάντα οἰκονομεῖσθαι ἔδει. ὅτε οὖν ἐπληρώθησαν οἱ καιροὶ τῶν λοιπῶν, τότε κατὰ τὴν ἄνωθεν οἰκονομουμένην τάξιν ἐπὶ τῶν οἰκείων καιρῶν καὶ τὰ περὶ τὸν Χριστὸν ἐδείχθη.

quae sunt autem illa? quae olim quidem illi placuerunt, nunc autem illa in opus perduxisse uidetur secundum proprium tempus consequenter illis quae dudum dispensabantur, et

    instaurare (uel potius *recapitulare*) *omnia in Christo, quae in caelis sunt et quae in terra, in ipso.*

'recapitulatio' euidenter dicitur multorum sensuum uelox resumptio. quod autem uult dicere, tale est: 'uniuersitatis Deus fecerat quidem omnem creaturam quasi unum quoddam corpus, ex multis compositum membris, tam rationabilium ordinum quam sensibilium. fabricauit autem animal unum, id est, hominem, qui et ad inuisibiles naturas propinquitatem sibi anima uindicaret, et uisibilibus naturis corpore iungeretur. ex quattuor enim integris elementis, terra, inquio, et aere et aqua et igne, corpus composuit nostrum; et quasi quoddam amicitiae pignus totius creaturae fecit esse hominem, utpote omnibus in eum coadunatis. mouentur

12-13 (quae, fuerant, dispensata *CH: cf. g and p.* 81, *l.* 7, *note.* 15 ostendi efficit *C** ostendit effici *C* (*corr.*) 23 quoddam unum *H* 28 inquit *CH*

This is to say that "he demonstrated this by the facts themselves."*

For he means that what long ago pleased him was for the time
being unclear. But now by the facts themselves he has made this
clear with much wisdom through the dispensation he plainly made
by Christ.

†But why now?	But why now?
1:10a *for a dispensation of the fullness of times*	1:10a *for a dispensation of the fullness of times*
Because all things were rightly dispensed in order. Therefore, when the times of the others had been fulfilled, then in [128] the order that had long ago been dispensed he caused the things concerning Christ also to be shown in their own times.*	Since it was necessary that all things be dispensed in order. Therefore, when the times of the others were fulfilled, then according to the order long ago dispensed, the things concerning Christ were shown in their own times.

But what are they? What, indeed, pleased him of old, but what he
has plainly brought to actualization in its own time according to
what had been dispensed long ago, and

    1:10b *to renew* (or rather *to recapitulate*)[19] *all things in Christ,
things that are in the heavens and things on earth, in him,*

"Recapitulation" is evidently said of a simple summing up of
many meanings. But what he wants to say is something like this:
"The God of the universe in fact made the entire creation as a kind
of single body [129] composed of many members, both intelligible
and sensible orders. But he fashioned one living being, that is,
man, who would claim a relationship to the invisible natures by his
soul and would be joined to the visible natures by his body. For
God composed our body from the four prime elements, I mean
earth, air, water, and fire. And he made humanity to be, as it
were, a kind of pledge for the harmony of the entire creation with
everything being united together in humanity. And everything

---

[19]The translator occasionally uses two words to translate the Greek. Here
Swete suggests (1:128) that "Our translator appears to have been unwilling
to desert the Vulg., supported as it was by the majority of the Latin fathers;
but he sees clearly that Th.'s interpretation points to a deeper sense of
ἀνακεφαλαιώσασθαι than the Vulg. represents."

autem omnia quae sunt sensibilia propter hominis necessitatem.
rationabiles uero uirtutes insistunt pro nobis uisibilibus, ut commoueant ea secundum nostram necessitatem. ministrant uero et
illis rebus quae pro nostra sunt salute, si tamen uerum sit illud
5 quod a Paulo dictum est: *nonne omnes* (inquit) *sunt ministrationis*
spiritus, in ministerium missi propter eos qui capiunt hereditare salu-
tem? sed subintroducta est mors peccantibus nobis; fiebat autem
hinc separatio quaedam utrorumque. anima enim a corpore separabatur; et corpus separatum solutionem plenariam sustinebat.
10 dissoluebatur ergo secundum hoc creaturae copulatio. omnia ergo
tam illa quae in caelis sunt, quam quae super terram, 'instaurauit,'
(uel potius 'recapitulauit') *in Christo*, quasi quandam compendiosam renouationem et redintegrationem totius faciens creaturae per
eum. faciens enim incorruptum corpus et inpassibile per resur-
15 rectionem, et reddens illud ad inmortale suae animae, ita ut ultra
ad illud separari non possit corruptum, uniuersae creaturae uinculum amicitiae uisus est condonasse. quod et multo amplius in ipso
factum est, omni creatura ad illud nos inspiciente, propter inhabitantem Deum Verbum, dum diuina in illum natura ab omnibus
20 per hanc existimatur intueri. hanc ergo 'capitulationem omnium'
uocauit, eo quod omnia collecta sunt in unum, et ad unum quoddam inspiciunt, concordantes sibi; eo quod hanc intentionem olim
Opifex habuit et ad hoc omnia a principio construxit, quod nunc
impleuit cum multa facilitate, in illis quae erga Christum extitisse
25 uidentur. hoc autem in futuro saeculo erit, quando homines cuncti necnon et rationabiles uirtutes ad illum inspiciant, ut fas exigit,
et concordiam inter se pacemque firmam obtineant.'

et dicens duo illa quae a Christo sunt facta, unum quidem quod
proprium est nobis, alterum uero quod in commune bonum, adi-
30 cit:

in quo et sorte constituti sumus, praeordinati secundum propositum
eius, qui in omnia inoperatur secundum consilium uoluntatis suae; ut
simus in laudem gloriae eius nos qui et ante sperauimus in Christo.

praecedentibus illud reddidit, hoc dicens, quoniam 'in omni-
35 bus his bonis et nos uocati sumus, olim in hoc a Deo praeordi-

---

1   homines *C**   3   eam *CH*   16   sperari *C* H*   18   omnem creaturam ad
illud inspicientem *C* o. cr. ad illud nos inspicientem *H*   21   collata *H*   29   illis
(*bef.* nobis) *add H**   31   praepositum *H*   34   est (*bef.* dicens) *add C* H*

that is sensible is moved to serve the needs of humans. In fact, the intelligible powers attend to visible things on our behalf, so that they may move them according to our needs. And they also minister in those matters that exist for our salvation, if at any rate what Paul said is true (Heb 1:14): *Are they not all* (he says) *spirits of ministration sent to minister for the sake of those who are to inherit salvation?* But death slipped into us when we sinned, and from this a certain separation of the two orders took place. For the soul was separated from the body, and [130] the body once separated suffered a complete dissolution. Thus, because of this the linking together of creation was loosed. Therefore, God "renewed" (or rather "recapitulated") everything, both what is in the heavens and what is on earth, *in Christ*, making, as it were, a kind of concise renewal and restoration of the whole creation through him. For by making his body incorruptible and impassible by the resurrection and restoring it to the immortality of his soul so that it could no longer be separated and so corrupted, God plainly gave him as the bond for the harmony of the whole creation. This was done in him much more abundantly than in the whole creation that was looking to us for this, because God the Word indwelt him, while the divine nature may be thought discerned in him by all because of this. Therefore, he called this "the heading up of all things," because all things were gathered together in one and, when they are in harmony with one another, they appear as a kind of unity. Because the Creator had this intention and from the beginning fashioned everything for this purpose, he has now fulfilled that purpose with great ease by what has plainly come to be by Christ's dispensation. But its consummation will come to pass in the age to come, when [131] all people, to say nothing of the intelligible powers, will look to him, as right requires, and will gain harmony and steadfast peace with one another.

And speaking of those two accomplishments of Christ, one proper to us but the other for the common good [of the universe], he adds:

1:11–12 *in whom we have also been established in a heritage, having been predestined according to the purpose of him who accomplishes all things according to the counsel of his will, so that we who hoped beforehand in Christ might be for the praise of his glory,*

He referred this to what precedes it, meaning that "we have been called in all these good things, predestined of old for this

nati.' uolens enim omni ex parte illa extollere, quod multo digna
sunt gratiarum actionis, frequenter dicit *praeordinationem*, et *bo-*
num placitum, et *uoluntatem*, gratiam illam deliberatam docens et
liberalitatem; sicut et praeordinauit et uoluit illa quae secundum
5 nos sic facere, nihil nobis conferentibus de proprio nostro. bene
autem dixit: *qui et ante sperauimus in Christo;* ut dicat quoniam
'horum maxime bonorum adepti, causa illi demirationis erimus,
ob eam quam erga nos exhibuit liberalitatem, qui et ante exitum
rei credidimus Christo, et de his spem accepimus.' non enim, si-
10 cut quidam existimauerunt, eos qui et ante sperauerunt dicit, hoc
est, illos qui tunc crediderunt antequam ceteri in nouissimis crederent temporibus. stultum est enim aestimare erga illos solos fieri
illa bona quae expectantur, et ad laudem gloriae Dei solos illos pertinere; cum in commune omnibus qui usque ad consummationem
15 saeculi erunt Christi donatio proposita esse uideatur. nam quod
dixit *qui ante sperauimus*, in comparatione incredulorum dicit; ut
dicat illos qui ante exitum rei, per illam fidem quae in Christo est,
qui etiam et ista se adquirere sperant; optime de his dicens, qui
maxime adepti sunt illa bona quae expectantur, qui maiorem Deo
20 gloriam reportare uidebantur. nam quod dicit *nos* non de illis qui
tunc erant dicit, sed in communi de omnibus qui quolibet tempore
credunt. et quoniam usque ad praesens in communi omnia dixit
in persona credentium, adicit:

in quo et uos, audientes uerbum ueritatis, euangelium salutis
25 *uestrae—in quo credentes signati estis Spiritu promissionis sancto, ar-*
ra hereditatis nostrae in redemptionem adquisitionis, in laudem gloriae
eius.

'†ipso enim modo et uos uer-   'τῷ γὰρ αὐτῷ δὴ τρόπῳ (φησὶν)
ba euangelii audistis, et ad fi-   τῶν τοῦ εὐαγγελίου ῥημάτων ἀκού-
30 dem accessistis, et Spiritus par-   σαντες, τῇ τε πίστει προσεληλύθα-
ticipatione confirmationem ac-   τε καὶ τῇ τοῦ πνεύματος μετουσίᾳ
cepistis,' hoc enim dicit, *signati*   τὴν βεβαίωσιν ἐδέξασθε·' τοῦτο γὰρ
estis. adquirebatur autem eis fir-   λέγει τὸ ἐσφραγίσθητε. προσεγίνε-

2 actiones *C* H* actione *C* (*corr.*)   4   sic (*for* sicut) *H*   5   sic *om C* (*corr.*) ||
benedixit autem dixit *H**   9   Christum *H*   12   enim est *C*   14   cum *om H*   15
et (*for* erunt) *H*   21   erat *H*   22   in commune *H*   26   adquisitionem *C*   28
sq. Coisl. 204, f. 56 a [Cr. vi. 117, Fr. 132] θεόδωρός φησιν· τῷ αὐτῷ δὴ τρόπῳ,
κ.τ.λ.   30-31   participationem *C* H: see g.*   33   estis *om H* || adquerebatur
C* adquirebat *H*

by God." For since he wants in every respect to extol those goods because they quite deserve thanksgiving, he repeatedly says *predestination* and *good pleasure* and *will*. He is teaching about the grace God resolved to give and his generosity, inasmuch as he predestined and willed to do what concerns us this way, even though we contribute nothing of our own. And he rightly said *we who hoped beforehand in Christ*, meaning that "when we have obtained these good things as much as possible, we shall be a reason for admiring God because of the generosity he displayed toward us. We have believed in Christ before the consummation of his purpose and have received the hope of these good things." For he does not mean, as some have thought, those who had believed before, that is, those who had believed at a time before the rest believed in most recent times. For it would be foolish to judge that those good things that were awaited would have come to pass only for them and that they alone would be relevant for the praise of God's glory, since Christ's gift was plainly offered generally to all who will come to be until the consummation of this age. Indeed, when he said *we who hoped beforehand*, he means "we" in contrast to unbelievers, so that he is speaking of those who, before the consummation of his purpose, by faith in Christ [132] hope they will also obtain these things. He speaks quite effectively of them because they have as much as possible obtained those good things that are expected and have plainly brought greater glory to God. Indeed, by saying *we* he is not referring to those who existed at that time alone but in general to all who believe at whatever time. And since up until now he has said everything in the common person of believers, he adds:

1:13–14 *in whom you also, when you had heard the word of truth, the gospel of your salvation—believing in whom you were sealed with the Holy Spirit of promise, the pledge of our inheritance for the redemption of possession to the praise of his glory.*

†"For in the same way you heard the words of the gospel, you came forward to the faith, and you received its confirmation by participation in the Spirit." For this is what he means by *you were sealed*. And confirmation by the grace of the Spirit

"For in the same way (he says) by hearing the words of the gospel, you both came forward to the faith and received its confirmation by participation in the Spirit." For this is what he means by *you were sealed*. And the confirmation of the miracles

mitas per gratiam Spiritus, per
illa miracula quae tunc a credentibus fiebant, quae erga fidem maiori eos nexu stringe
5 bant. bene autem illud Spiritum *promissionis* uocauit, quoniam omnia bona quae expectantur in future saeculo adesse
credentibus Spiritus sancti par
10 ticipatione expectantur.*

το δὲ αὐτοῖς διὰ τῆς τοῦ πνεύματος
χάριτος ἡ βεβαίωσις τῶν ἀκολου
θούντων ὡς εἰκὸς θαυμάτων, μει
ζόνως εἰς τὴν πίστιν ἐπισφίγγον
αὐτούς. καλῶς δὲ αὐτὸ πνεῦμα τῆς
ἐπαγγελίας ἐκάλεσεν, ἐπειδὴ πάν
τα τὰ προσδοκώμενα αὐτοῖς ἐπὶ τοῦ
μέλλοντος αἰῶνος πρόσεσται ἀγαθὰ
τῇ τοῦ πνεύματος μετουσίᾳ.

sicut enim et in superioribus diximus, quoniam de his quae potituri sunt promissionem accipiebant, in qua ordine primitiarum
particulam quandam gratiae in praesenti uita ad confirmationem
futurorum percipiebant, sicut et apostolus Romanis scribit dicens:
15 *non solum autem, sed et ipsi primitias Spiritus habentes, et ipsi in no*
bis ipsis ingemiscimus filiorum adoptionem expectantes, redemptionem
corporis nostri. unde illud et manifestius explanans adiecit: *qui est*
arra hereditatis nostrae;

'†hereditatem' quidem illam
20 fruitionem quae tunc erit uocans, eo quod et firme illis dabitur; 'arram' uero hereditatis,
donum quod hic praebetur dicit Spiritus, eo quod de futu
25 ris promissiones accipientes, et
perfectam Spiritus expectantes
participationem, exiguas quasdam, sicut dixi, primitias in
praesenti accipere uidebantur,*

κληρονομίαν τῶν τότε καλεῖ τὴν
ἀπόλαυσιν ἅτε δὴ βεβαίως αὐ
τοῖς διδομένων· ἀρραβῶνα δὲ τῆς
κληρονομίας, τὴν ἐνταῦθα δόσιν
τοῦ πνεύματος, ἐπειδὴ τὰς περὶ
τῶν μελλόντων ἐπαγγελίας δεχόμε
νοι καὶ τὴν τελείαν τοῦ πνεύματος
προσδοκῶντες μετάδοσιν, βραχεῖάν
τινα, ὥσπερ οὖν εἶπον, ἀπαρχὴν τοῦ
παρόντος ἐλάμβανον.

30 quod et ordinem arrae obtinere uidebatur; necessarie per illud
quod dabatur eis iam hinc expectantibus et illud quod perfectum
est tempore sibi tribui competenti. 'audientes ergo uos et credentes, de futuris promissionem percepistis, et quasi quandam arram
futurorum Spiritus gratiam accepistis. tunc uero ab omnibus istis
35 liberabimini tristitiis, et familiariter ei eritis adiuncti, et eius glo-

---

3 quia *C (corr.)* 7-8 expectamus *H (bis)* creduntur (2°) *C (corr.)* 8 προσ
έσθαι Cr. 12 ordinem *C* H* 23 praebet Sp. d. *H* 25 promissionis *C**
promissionibus *C (corr.)* ‖ accipientis *C** ‖ ex *(for* et) *C* H* 32 et *(aft.*
ergo) *add C* 35 liberamini *H**

was acquired by them through those miracles that were done at that time by believers and that bound them with greater ties to the faith. And he rightly called the Spirit *of promise*, since [133] all the good things awaited in the age to come are awaited as present to believers by participation in the Holy Spirit.*

that in all likelihood followed came to them through the grace of the Spirit, who bound them all the more to the faith. And he rightly called the Spirit *of promise*, since all the good things they expected in the age to come will be present to them by participation in the Spirit.

For, as we have said above, since they received the promise of what they will possess, they acquired in the order of firstfruits a certain portion of grace in the present life for the confirmation of the things to come, just as the apostle writes to the Romans, saying (Rom 8:23): *and not only the creation, but we ourselves, who have the firstfruits of the Spirit, groan inwardly, while we wait for the adoption of sons, the redemption of our bodies.* Thus, to explain this more clearly he added *which is the pledge of our inheritance.*

†He calls the enjoyment that will then come to pass the "inheritance," because it will be given them in a steadfast way. But he says "the pledge" of the inheritance is the gift of the Spirit that is bestowed here because by receiving the promises of the things to come and by awaiting perfect participation in the Spirit, they plainly received in the present some small firstfruits, as I have said,*

He calls the enjoyment of the things that will then come to pass the "inheritance," since they will be given them in a steadfast way. And he calls the gift of the Spirit here "the pledge" of the inheritance, since by receiving the promises of the things to come and by awaiting perfect participation in the Spirit, they obtained in the present some small firstfruits, as I said.

because they plainly obtained the payment of the pledge. Necessarily, what was given by it was theirs because already from it they expect what is complete to be bestowed on them at the proper time. "Therefore, because you have heard and believed, you have acquired the promise of the things to come, [134] and you have received the grace of the Spirit as a kind of pledge of the things to come. But at that future time you will be freed from all those mis-

riae participabitis; ita ut et multa laus ei pro uobis hinc possit adnasci.' 'adquisitionem' enim dicit illam familiaritatem quae ad
Deum est;

†*redemptionem* autem, id est, *ad-*
5 *quisitionis*, quae per resurrectionem et inmortalitatem tunc
aderit illis, liberantem eos a peccato, et familiaritatem illam
quae apud eum est hisdem tri-
10 buentem; ex quibus eius gloriae participabunt.   qua ergo
ratione demiratione dignum illum ostendebamus, qui tantorum bonorum nobis causa exti-
15 tit. hoc enim dicit: *in laudem*
*gloriae eius.**

ἀπολύτρωσιν περιποιήσεως τὸ διὰ
τῆς ἀναστάσεως καὶ τῆς ἀθανασίας
τῶν ἐντεῦθεν ἀπαλλαττομένους κα-
κῶν τὴν πρὸς αὐτὸν οἰκείωσιν λαμ-
βάνειν· ἀφ' ὧν τῆς παρ' αὐτοῦ με-
τασχόντες δόξης εἰκότως θαυμαστὸν ἐκεῖνον ἐνδείκνυμεν τὸν τοσούτων αἴτιον ἡμῖν τῶν ἀγαθῶν γεγο-
νότα· τοῦτο γὰρ λέγει τὸ εἰς ἔπαι-
νον τῆς δόξης αὐτοῦ.

deinde et ampliores eos laudibus faciens, libera est enim humana
natura, et ad id quod expetit laudibus magis solet accendi:

propter hoc et ego audiens illam quae est secundum uos fidem in do-
20 *mino Iesu et caritatem quam habetis in omnibus sanctis, non cesso gra-*
tias agens pro uobis, memoriam uestri faciens in orationibus meis.

†hoc autem necessarie adiecit; non solum propter eos, sed
ut ne existimaretur quod in-
25 cusans illam quam acceperant
doctrinam, suam uellet abuti.
etiamsi non Iohannes illis, sed
alter aliquis praedicator pietatis fuisset, qui ueritatis dogmata
30 illis tradiderat, necessaria erat
adiectio.**

τοῦτο ἀναγκαίως προστέθεικεν
οὐκ αὐτῶν μόνον ἕνεκεν, ἀλλ' ὥστε
καὶ μὴ δοκεῖν, ἐπιμεμφόμενον οἷς
ἤδη παρέλαβον, κεχρῆσθαι τῇ πρὸς
αὐτοὺς διδασκαλίᾳ. εἰ γὰρ καὶ
μὴ Ἰωάννης ἀλλ' ἕτερός τις τῶν
εὐσέβειαν κηρυττόντων ἦν ὁ τὰ τῆς
ἀληθείας δόγματα αὐτοῖς παραδούς,
ἀναγκαία ἡ προσθήκη.

---

1 eius (*for* ei) H   ‖   pro uobis *om* H   4   sq. Coisl. 204, f. 58 b [Cr. vi. 122,
Fr. 132] Θεόδωρός φησιν· ἀπολύτρωσιν, κ.τ.λ.   7   aderunt, liberantes C H   ‖
αὐτὸν cod., Cr.   9   isdem C (*corr.*)   11   ea (*after* part.) *add* C H   13   ostendemus C (*corr.*) [ostendimus g]   17   enim est C   18   aliud (*for* ad id) C H   22
προτέθεικεν cod., Fr.   26   sua C (*corr.*)   29   dogma H

fortunes. You will be intimately joined to him, and you will share in his glory so that from this much praise can arise for him because of you." For he calls intimacy with God *possession*.

†And *the redemption*, that is, *of possession* is what will then be present to them through the resurrection and immortality, which frees them from sin and bestows on them intimacy with him. By this they will share in his glory. Therefore, we showed for what reason he is worthy of admiration, since he exists as the cause for us of such great good things. For this is what he means by saying *to the praise of his glory*.*

The *redemption of possession* refers to the fact that through the resurrection and immortality they are delivered henceforth from evils and receive intimacy with him. Because of this and by sharing in the glory that comes from him, we rightly show that he is admirable, since he has become the cause for us of such great things. For this is what he means by *to the praise of his glory*.

Then he magnifies them by his praises, for human nature is free and by praises is accustomed to be all the more roused to what it seeks to obtain:

[135] 1:15–16 *Because of this I, too, hearing of your faith in the Lord Jesus and the love you have for all the saints, do not cease giving thanks for you, making mention of you in my prayers,*

†And he necessarily added this, not only because of them, but so that it might not be thought that by finding fault with the teaching they had received he wished to employ his own. Even if it had not been John but some other preacher of true religion who had come to them to hand down to them the doctrines of truth, the addition was necessary.*

He necessarily added this, not only because of them, but so that it might not seem that by finding fault with what they had already received he was instructing them. For even if it had not been John but some other one of those preaching true religion who had handed down to them the doctrines of truth, the addition was necessary.

et quoniam dixit non solum gratias se agere, sed et orare pro eis,
adicit ipsam orationem quae continet doctrinam conuenientium
illis, quam et ipsius orationis explanans narrationem publicare uidetur:

5   *ut Deus domini nostri Iesu Christi, Pater gloriae.*

hic ostendit quoniam Christi Deum dicit, susceptum indicans
hominem. 'Deum' enim dicens 'Christi' 'Patrem' uero 'gloriae,'
eo quod et consuetudo est ei gloriae nomen erga diuinam ponere
naturam; et quod et gloriosa sit et demirabilis, sicut et ad Hebraeos
10   dicit, *qui est splendor gloriae;* pro quibus debuit dicere 'Dei' siue
'diuinae naturae.'

det uobis Spiritum sapientiae et reuelationis in cognitione ipsius,
inluminatos habere oculos cordis uestri.

†'hoc (inquit) postulo, ut
15   praestetur uobis a Deo Spiritus
sancti gratia; ut repleat uos sapientia et cognitione Dei, suscipientes inenarrabilium reuelationem; ita ut sensus uestri ad
20   instar luminis per cognitionem
Spiritus claritate emicantes habeantur.' quapropter?

ut sciatis quae est spes uocatio-
nis uestrae.

25   hoc est, 'in qua spe estis uocati ab eo.' uocati autem sumus
in spe utique futurorum; unde
adicit:

et quae sunt diuitiae gloriae
30   *hereditatis eius in sanctis.*

τοῦτο αἰτῶ (φησὶν) ὡς ἂν πα-
ρασχεθείη ὑμῖν παρὰ τοῦ θεοῦ πνεύματος χάρις εἰς τὸ σοφίας τε ὑμᾶς
πληρωθῆναι καὶ ἐπιγνώσεως τοῦ
θεοῦ, δεξαμένους τῶν ἀπορρήτων
τὴν ἀποκάλυψιν, ὥστε τὴν διάνοιαν ὑμῶν φωτὸς δίκην τῇ ἀπὸ τοῦ
πνεύματος καταλάμπεσθαι γνώσει.
τίνος ἕνεκεν;

εἰς τὸ εἰδέναι ὑμᾶς τίς ἐστιν ἡ
ἐλπὶς τῆς κλήσεως αὐτοῦ·

ἀντὶ τοῦ· ἐπὶ ποίαις ἐλπίσιν
κεκλήμεθα παρ' αὐτοῦ

καὶ τίς ὁ πλοῦτος τῆς δόξης τῆς
κληρονομίας αὐτοῦ ἐν τοῖς ἁγίοις·

6 Domini (*for* Deum) *C*   8 divina *C H*   11 diuina *C*   13 cordis *om H*
14 sq. Coisl. 204, f. 61 a, b [Cr. vi. 128, Fr. 132] θεόδωρος δέ φησιν εἰς τὸ δώῃ
ὑμῖν πνεῦμα σοφίας καὶ ἀποκαλύψεως καὶ τὰ ἑξῆς· τοῦτο αἰτῶ, κ.τ.λ.   16-17
sapientiae *C**   19 ad *om C* (*corr.*)   21 claritatem *C H*

And since he said that he not only gave thanks but also prayed for them, he adds the very prayer that includes the teaching of what was right for them, a teaching he plainly makes known by expounding the content of the prayer itself:

1:17a *that the God of our Lord Jesus Christ, the Father of glory*

Here he shows that he says " the God of Christ" to indicate the assumed Man. For he speaks of "the God of Christ" but of "the Father of glory," inasmuch as he customarily uses the word "glory" to refer to the divine [136] nature because it is both glorious and wonderful, as he says in Hebrews (1:3): *who is the brightness of glory*. He ought to have said "of God" or "of the divine nature."[20]

1:17b-18a *may give you the Spirit of wisdom and revelation by knowing him, to have the eyes of your heart enlightened,*

†"I ask this (he says) that the grace of the Holy Spirit may be bestowed on you by God, so that he may fill you with wisdom and the knowledge of God by receiving the revelation of ineffable things, so that your senses like light may be kept radiant with brilliance through knowledge of the Spirit. Why?	I ask this (he says) that the grace of the Spirit may be bestowed on you by God, so that you may be filled with wisdom and the knowledge of God by receiving the revelation of ineffable things, so that your understanding like light may be illuminated by knowledge from the Spirit. Why?
1:18b *so that you may know what is the hope of your calling*	1:18b *so that you may know what is the hope of your calling*
That is, "in what hope you have been called by him." And we have been called in the hope, of course, of the things to come. And so he adds:	Instead of "to what kind of hopes we have been called by him."
1:18c *and what are the riches of the glory of his inheritance in the saints*	1:18c *and what are the riches of the glory of his inheritance in the saints*

---

[20]What Theodore means is that "God" and "Father" are to be understood differently in relation to Christ. "God" implies the assumed Man, since we can understand the word to imply the distinction between the Creator and what is created. "Father," however, refers to the first person of the Trinity and implies the eternal generation of the Word, who indwells the assumed Man.

'et quanta aderit fruitio bonorum sanctis Dei in futuro saeculo.' bene autem *gloriam here-*
ditatis uocauit, eo quod et glo-
5 riosi efficiemur tunc per magnitudinem donationis. *diuitias*
autem *gloriae* dixit, ut dicat donationum eminentiam.*

καὶ ὅση τις περίεσται κτῆσις
ἀγαθῶν τοῖς τοῦ θεοῦ ἁγίοις ἐπὶ
τοῦ μέλλοντος αἰῶνος· καλῶς δὲ
δόξαν μὲν κληρονομίας ἐκάλεσεν ὡς
ἂν ἐπιδόξων τότε γινομένων ἡμῶν·
πλοῦτον δὲ δόξης, ἵνα εἴπῃ τῶν
δωρεῶν τὴν ὑπερβολήν.

etenim multa quaedam est erga nos Dei liberalitas, siquidem so-
10 luta morte in incorruptibilitate constituti, ultra peccare non poterimus; sed in multa quadam commorabimur claritate, perpetuam
erga Deum habentes coniunctionem.

   et quae sit supereminens magnitudo uirtutis eius in nos qui credidi-
mus.

15 'et qualia uel quam magna erga nos, qui in eum credidimus, ab
eo efficientur.'

   considera autem et hoc in loco quemadmodum modis omnibus
extollit uerbum sub gratiarum actione, prout conueniens erat; non
dicens *gloriam hereditatis* absolute, sed *diuitias gloriae;* neque *uir-*
20 *tutem eius quae in nobis est*, sed neque *magnitudinem uirtutis* solum,
sed uehementius secundum id quod esse uidetur, dixit: *superemi-*
nens magnitudo uirtutis.

   secundum operationem potentiae fortitudinis eius.

   et hoc in loco non dixit *fortitudinis* absolute, sed *secundum po-*
25 *tentiam fortitudinis;* ut dicat: illius magnae et potentis

   quam operatus est in Christo, suscitans eum ex mortuis.

   bene explanans magnitudinem illorum quae erga nos facta
sunt, illa memoratus est quae secundum Christum sunt; a quo omnis erga nos liberalitas principium sumpsisse uidetur. hoc ergo di-
30 cit, quoniam 'oro ut cognoscatis illa quae erga nos facta sunt; quam
magnam habent ostensionem uirtutis, et quemadmodum suscitauit Christum ex mortuis.' deinde adicit quod maius est:

   et sedere fecit in dexteram suam in caelestibus, super omnem princi-

[137] "And what great enjoyment of good things will be present to the saints in the age to come." And he rightly called it *the glory of inheritance* because we shall at that time be made glorious by the greatness of the gift. And he said *riches of glory* to mean the excellence of the gifts.*[21]

And what a great possession of good things will surround the saints of God in the age to come. And he rightly called it *the glory of inheritance* since we shall at that time be glorious, and *the riches of glory* to mean the excellence of the gifts.

And indeed God shows much generosity toward us, since once death is destroyed and we are established in incorruptibility we shall no longer be able to sin, but we shall also dwell in some kind of great brightness by having perpetual union with God.

1:19a *and what is the preeminent greatness of his power in us who have believed,*

"And of what sort or how great are the deeds accomplished by him for us who have believed in him."

Consider also in this passage how in all sorts of ways he lifts his speech up in thanksgiving, so far as was right. He did not simply say *the glory of inheritance*, but *the riches of the glory*; nor did he say *the power that is in us* or only *the greatness of the power*, but as is plainly more forceful he said *the preeminent greatness of power*.

1:19b *according to the working of the power of his might,*

And in this passage he did not say simply *of his might* but *according to the power of his might*, in order to mean that it is great and powerful.

1:20a *which he put to work in Christ, when he raised him from the dead*

[138] Rightly explaining the greatness of those things accomplished for us, he mentioned those according to Christ, from whom all [God's] generosity toward us plainly took its origin. Therefore, what he means is: "I pray that you may know those things that have been accomplished for us, what a great demonstration of power they have, and how God raised Christ from the dead." Then he adds what is greater:

1:20b *and seated him at his right hand in the heavenly places,*

---

[21] In other words, in the phrase "the riches of the glory of his inheritance" the glory attaches both to the inheritance and to the riches.

patum et potestatem et uirtutem et dominationem et omne nomen quod
nominatur non solum in saeculo hoc, sed et in futuro.

    nam quod dicit, *sedere fecit in dexteram suam,* hoc est, 'partici-
pem illum honoris accepit,' de suscepto homine id dicens; eo quod
5   propter inhabitantem in eum naturam Dei Verbi ab omnibus habet adorari. unde adicit: *super omnes.* quod etiam et maius ostendere uolens, adicit: *et omne nomen quod nominatur [non solum] in*
saeculo hoc sed et in futuro; hoc est, 'siue aliquid secundum praesentem uitam nominatur et cognoscitur esse magnum apud nos,
10 siue in futuro cognoscere poterimus quod nunc forsitan nescimus,
omnium illorum superiorem illum fecit.' unde illud et confirmans
adicit:

    et omnia subiecit sub pedibus eius.

    compendiose dicere uoluit, 'omnium illum dominum consti-
15 tuit.' et quidem apud nos

    ipsum dedit caput super omni ecclesia quae est corpus eius, pleni-
tudo eius qui omnia in omnibus adimpletur.

    'commune (inquit) est hoc bonum omnibus nobis, qui credi-
mus.' quare? 'quoniam corpus eius sumus omnes nos qui cre-
20 dimus, similitudine naturae participationem suscipientes gratiae
Spiritus illius qui in eo factus est. quod enim erga illum factum
est in chrismatis ordine susceptum—*Spiritus* (inquit) *Domini su-*
per me, propter quod unxit me—huic Spiritui et nos participantes
per regenerationem, illam participationem percepimus quae apud
25 eum est; ueram quidem copulationem in futuro saeculo percipientes, quando et resurrectionis eius participes efficiemur. nam primitias quasdam Spiritus ex eo accepimus in baptismate secundum
praesens saeculum, quod baptisma formam habere mortis et resurrectionis existimatur; in quorum et formam constitui iam amo-
30 do credimus, corpus quidem eius omnes esse eos qui credunt existimantes. 'ecclesiam' enim fidelium nuncupat congregationem;
'caput' autem nostrum, illum esse designat. sic et Corinthiis scri-

---

5 eo (*for* eum) *C* (*corr.*)   ‖ hominibus (*for* omnibus) *H* 7 non solum *om C*
H 8 sed *om H* 13 sub *om H* 17 quia *C H: see note* 22 susceptus *C* H*
suscepistis *C* (*corr.*) 25 uerum *H* 28 praesentem *C* H* 29 existimamur
C H

above all rule and authority and power and dominion, and above every name that is named, not only in this age but also in the one to come,

For when he says *seated him at his right hand*, he means "he received him as a partaker of his honor," saying this of the assumed Man, because he possesses the worship of all because of the nature of God the Word that indwelt him. So he adds *above all*, and since he wishes to demonstrate something still greater, he adds *and every name that is named*, [*not only*] *in this age but also in the one to come*. That is, "whether it is anything named in the present life and is known among us to be great or anything we shall be able to know in the age to come that we perhaps do not know now—God made him superior to all of them." Then, to confirm this he adds:

[139] 1:22a *and he has put all things under his feet*.

He wanted to say succinctly, "He established him as Lord of all." And so far as we are concerned:

1:22b-23 *He gave him to be the head above all the church,*[22] *which is his body, the fullness of him who is filled all in all*.

"This good (he says) is common to all of us who believe." Why? "Since all of us who believe are his body, through likeness of nature we receive participation in the grace of the Spirit of the one who was working in him [the assumed Man].[23] For what was at work in him was assumed by means of unction—*the Spirit of the Lord is upon me, because he has anointed me*.[24] We, too, by participating in the Spirit through rebirth, have gained that participation with him, even though in fact we shall gain true union in the age to come, when we shall also be made partakers of his resurrection. For in the present age we have received a kind of firstfruits of the Spirit from him in baptism, since baptism is considered to possess the type of death and resurrection. As soon as we believe we are already established in their type, since we consider that all who believe are his body. For he names the assembly of the faithful "the church," but [140] he designates him to be our "head." Thus, in writing to the Corinthians he says (1

---

[22] As Swete points out, the reading *super omni ecclesia* is replaced in Theodore's later citations of the verse (1:142 and 1:275, where he comments on Col 1:19) by *super omnem ecclesiam*, a reading found in Ambrosiaster and Augustine. Both readings contradict the Greek, which means "above all, for the church."

[23] That is, the Word who was working in the assumed Man.

[24] See Isa 61:1; Luke 4:18.

bens dicit: *etenim in uno Spiritu nos omnes in unum corpus bapti-*
zati sumus. et multis in locis in apostolica interpretatione hunc
sensum latius dixisse uidemur, non ex nobis absolute interiectionem eius facientes; sed beatus Paulus frequenter illud adorsus est,
5 quod et aliorum dictorum probatio in hoc consistere uidetur. sicut
ergo in uno corpore eligantiorem partem caput esse existimamus,
a quo omnis uirtus uiuacitatis ad ceterum deducitur corpus; sic secundum praesentem uitam *unum corpus omnes sumus* homines, eo
quod et unius sumus naturae; caput nobis adscribentes Adam, a
10 quo omnis causa ut essemus deriuasse uidetur in nobis. secundum
futurum uero factum, secundum quod exsurgentes erimus inmortales, corpus quidem unum erimus omnes; eo quod communem
suscepimus resurrectionem, et illam inmortalitatem quae per resurrectionem erit. in ordine uero caput nobis Christus erit, ex quo
15 omnis causa secundae regenerationis in nos deriuasse uidetur. unde et hoc in loco dicens: *supereminens magnitudo uirtutis eius in nos*
qui credidimus, illa quae secundum Christum sunt memoratus est
primum, a quo omnis aptata esse uidetur liberalitas. et dicens illa
quae erga eum sunt magnifice sicut se ueritas habebat, adicit illa
20 quae nostra esse uidentur; quoniam hoc commune nostrum est bonum. in corporis enim ordine ei consistimus; in ultimo quidem ipsis rebus, in forma uero et promissionibus secundum praesentem
uitam. caput illum nostrum esse existimamus; ergo communicamus ei in omni honore, et commune bonum omnium est nostrum
25 quodcumque fuerit erga illum. corpus est ecclesia *et plenitudo eius,*
qui omnia in omnibus adimpletur.

†non dixit 'omnia implet,' sed
quia ipse *in omnibus adimpletur;*
hoc est, 'in omnibus plenus est.'
30 totus enim in unumquemque
est propter naturae incircum-
scriptionem, non secundum
partes diuisus. necessaria autem est et illa adiectio qua di-
35 xit, *omnia in omnibus;* osten-

οὐκ εἶπεν ὅτι τὰ πάντα πληροῖ, ἀλλ'
ὅτι αὐτὸς ἐν πᾶσιν πληροῦται, τουτέστιν, ἐν πᾶσιν πλήρης ἐστιν· ὅλος
ὢν ἐν ἑκάστῳ διὰ τὸ τῆς φύσεως
ἀπερίγραφον, οὐ κατὰ μέρη διαι-
ρούμενος. ἀναγκαία δὲ καὶ ἡ τοῦ
'τὰ πάντα' προσθήκη, δεικνύντος
ὅτι ἐν πᾶσίν ἐστιν ὅλος ὢν ἐν ἑκάστῳ καθότι ἄν τις ἐννοήσειεν, εἴτε

2 interpretationem *H* 4 faciens *C H* 10 diriuasse *C H* ‖ in nobis *om*
H 11 uero futurum *H* 21 ordinem *H* ‖ ei *om H* 23 et (*bef.* caput) *add*
H 25 ecclesiae *C H* 26 quia *H* 27 sq. Coisl. 204, f. 61 b [Cr. vi. 129].
31-32 incircum scriptione *C* H*

Cor 12:13): *For in one Spirit we were all baptized into one body.* And in many passages in our commentaries on the apostle's writings we have plainly spoken at greater length about this meaning, though we have not made this observation simply on our own. Rather, blessed Paul introduced this idea repeatedly because the proof of other assertions plainly rests upon it. Therefore, just as we consider the more attractive part in a single body to be the head from which all the power of vitality is carried down to the rest of the body, so in the present life *all of us* humans *are one body* because we are of a single nature. And we assign Adam as our head, from whom the entire cause of our existence has plainly derived. But according to what will happen in the future when we shall be immortal by rising again, we shall all be one body because we shall have received the general resurrection and the immortality that will come to be through the resurrection. And in rank Christ will be our head because it is from him that that the entire cause of our second birth has plainly derived. Thus, in this passage by saying *the preeminent greatness of his power in us who have believed* (1:19), he first called to mind the dispensation of Christ by whom all God's generosity has plainly been made available (1:20–21). Then, speaking splendidly of those acts that concerned Christ, as their truth possessed him, Paul adds what is plainly ours (1:22–23), since this common good belongs to us.[25] For we are established in Christ by being ordered in his body— by the facts themselves in our final state, but in type and by promises in the present life. We consider him to be our head; therefore, we share with him in every honor. And the common good of all—whatever may come to pass because of him—is ours. The church is his body *and the fullness of him who is filled all in all.*[26]

[141] †He did not say "he fills all things" but that *he is* himself *filled in all*; that is, "he is full in all." For he is in each in-

He did not say that he fills all things but that *he* himself *is filled in all*; that is, he is full in all, since he is in each individual

---

[25] Theodore appears to be giving a summary of 1:19–23.

[26] Swete's note (1:141) reads in part: "Th. (1) takes the clause τοῦ ... πληρουμένου to refer either to God the Word or perhaps rather (cf. the comm. on Col. i.19) to the Father.... (2) He regards πληροῦσθαι as = πλήρης εἶναι, and τὰ πάντα as nearly equivalent to ὅλος, so that the clause will mean: 'who by virtue of His omnipresence is in all things with the fulness of His indivisible Deity.'"

dens quando in omnibus est,
totus existens in unumquemque prout quis cogitare uoluerit, siue essentia siue inoperatione siue uirtute siue potestate siue et alio quolibet modo,
eo quod per omnia sit incircumscriptus. et ideo in unumquemque totus per omnia esse uidetur, eo quod omnia in omnibus sic esse eum et posse, sicut possibile est eum esse, qui in
unumquemque totus est*

οὐσίᾳ εἴτε ἐνεργείᾳ εἴτε δυνάμει εἴτε ἐξουσίᾳ εἴτε ὅτῳ δήποτε ἑτέρῳ,
διὰ τὸ κατὰ πάντα εἶναι αὐτὸν ἀπε-
ρίγραφον· καὶ διὰ τοῦτο ἐν ἑκάστῳ ὅλον κατὰ πάντα θεωρεῖσθαι,
τῷ πάντα ἐν πᾶσιν εἶναί τε αὐτὸν
καὶ δύνασθαι, ὡς εἰκὸς τὸν ἑκάστῳ
ὅλον ὄντα.

sufficienter ergo illum honorem qui erga nos est ostendit, corpus
nos dicens esse Christi, et plenitudinem eius *qui omnia in omni-*
bus adimpletur. hoc dicens: 'quoniam nos fideles corpus quidem
sumus Christi. habemus autem prae ceteris in nobis illum qui est
incircumscriptus (ut totus sit omnia in omnibus), eligantem quandam ad eum accipientes familiaritatem; siquidem corpus sumus
nos Christi, maiorem prae ceteris copulationem ad eum habere digni existimati. caput autem nostrum ille est, in quo diuina natura
affectu inhabitat eliganti.' bene et ualde scrupulose quod non dixerit absolute de Christo qui secundum carnem est, de quo omnis
illi sermo hactenus fuit, quoniam dedit eum caput ecclesiae, quando *super omnem ecclesiam caput eum dedit.* caput quidem omnium
est secundum quod et omnes aliquam ad eum cognationem habere uidentur; unde et recapitulari omnia in Christo in superioribus
dixit. *super omnia* autem nostrum esse caput uidetur, quantum et

11-13   sic esse eum qui unumq. totus est *H*   14   quae *C** H*   20   ceteros *H*   ‖
haberi *CH*   21   est ille *H*   22-23   dixit *H*   26   cognitionem *H*   28   quanto
C: cf. *Bensly*, M. F., p. 87

dividual as a whole because his nature is uncircumscribed, not divided into parts. And Paul's additional statement *all in all* is necessary, since it demonstrates that it is by existing as a whole in each individual that he is in all, however one would wish to understand this, whether by essence or operation or power or authority or in any other way, because he is uncircumscribed in all respects. Because of this he is seen to be in each individual as a whole in all respects, [142] because he can also be in this way *all in all*, since he is in each individual as a whole.*

Therefore, he sufficiently demonstrates the honor that attaches to us by saying that we are the body of Christ and the fullness of him *who is filled all in all*. What he means is that "we, the faithful, are in fact the body of Christ, And we have beyond others in us the one who is uncircumscribed (so that he may be as a whole all in all), since we receive a certain special intimacy with him. If we are indeed the body of Christ, we have been considered worthy of having a greater union with him than others. And our head is the one in whom the divine nature dwells with special affection." Rightly and quite carefully he would not have said this simply of Christ according to the flesh, about whom his whole discussion has been up to this point, since God gave him as the head of the church when *he gave him to be the head above all the church*. Indeed, he is the head of all because of the fact that all people [143] appear to have some relationship with him. That is why Paul said above (1:10) that all things are recapitulated in Christ. But he is plainly our head *above all*,²⁷ insofar as a greater intimacy with him has

---

²⁷Here Theodore seems to understand the phrase in 1:22 to mean "most of all for the church," instead of "over all the church." This may suggest that the Latin in 1:22 contradicts Theodore's understanding, which reflects the Greek text of the verse, which does not treat "all" as modifying "church."

maior nobis ad eum ex similitudine consistere uidetur familiaritas. et quoniam ostendit magna quidem illa quae secundum Christum sunt usque ad nos uero exinde extendi, gratiam auget datam ex arbitrio suscipientium:

5   *et uos cum essetis mortui in delictis et peccatis uestris, in quibus aliquando ambulastis secundum saeculum mundi huius.*

ut dicat, 'in hac praesente uita'; adiciens enim hoc ostendit quoniam saeculum non creaturam dicit, sed temporalem huius saeculi conuersationem qua uiuimus nos in homines.

10   *secundum principem potestatis aeris spiritus, qui nunc operatur in filios diffidentiae.*

dicit quidem diabolum. uocat autem eum *principem potestatis aeris spiritus;* eo quod omnes inuisibiles uirtutes imminent uisibilibus ut commoueant ea, secundum communem omnium necessi-
15   tatem. sunt autem ex illis qui et aeris imminent motui, inter quos diabolus erat. unde illum et *principem potestatis aeris spiritus* uocauit. hoc est, acceperat mandatum ut principaretur aeri, et potestatem haberet commouere eum. hoc enim dicit *spiritus*, eo quod et motum aeris flatum nuncupare consueuimus. bene autem dixit:
20   *qui nunc inoperatur in filios diffidentiae;* eo quod et ab illa sit reiectus potestate, et hoc ultro operatur propter arbitrii sui mutabilitatem. 'haec igitur agebatis dudum, eo quod et diabolicum sequebamini intellectum, et cum praesenti hac uita omnia uestra definiri censebatis'. et quoniam dixit, *uos*, ut ne subtrahere se existimare-
25   tur ab illis qui necessariam habere uidebantur gratiam, adicit:

in quibus et nos omnes conuersati sumus aliquando in desideriis carnis nostrae, facientes uoluntatem carnis et cogitationum; et eramus natura filii irae, sicut et ceteri.

omni ex parte propositum habet diuinam augere gratiam, si-
30   cut et in illam narrationem quam de illis expediit quae a Deo facta sunt, nominibus abusus talibus quibus illa cum augmento commendaret. sic et ab arbitrio eorum qui susceperant, uolens augere Dei liberalitatem; quoniam cum ualde essent mali et indigni donationes frui illas quae a Deo sunt, tamen et multa et magna adepti

---

1   similitudinem *H*   9   quae *C*   ‖   in *om C H (corr.)*   14   eas *CH*   18 habere *H*   20   operatur *H*   21   ultra *C* H*   23   definire *H**   27   uestrae (*for* nostrae) *H*   ‖   uestrae (*aft.* carnis) *add H**   29   diuinum *H*   30   in *om H**   ‖   illa narratione *C (corr.)* expetiit *C* H*   31   in omnibus (*for* nom.) *H*   32   ab *om H*   34   illas frui *H*

come into existence for us by our likeness to him. And since Paul is demonstrating that those great acts relating to Christ are in truth extended to us from that source, he magnifies the grace that has been given on the basis of the judgment of those receiving it:

2:1–2a *And when you were dead in transgressions and your sins in which you once walked according to the age of this world,*

He means "in this present life." For by adding this he demonstrates that he does not mean that the age is a created being but is rather the temporal life of this age, the life we live as humans.

2:2b *according to the ruler of the authority of the wind of the air who is now at work in the sons of unfaith,*

Of course, he means the devil. And he calls him *the ruler of the authority of the wind of the air* because all the invisible powers oversee visible things to move them according to the common needs of all. And there are some of them who oversee the motion of the air, among whom was the devil. This is why he called him *the ruler of the authority of the wind of the air.* That is, he had received the commission of ruling over the air and having power to move it. [144] For he calls this *wind* because we customarily give this name to the blowing motion of the air.[28] And he rightly said *who is now at work in the sons of unfaith,* because he had been rejected from that authority and from that time on is at work by the inconstancy of his judgment. "Therefore, you were formerly acting this way because you were following the devil's understanding and since you imagined that all your deeds were determined by this present life." And since he said *you,* so that he might not be thought to make himself an exception from those who plainly considered grace necessary, he adds:

2:3 *among whom all of us once lived in the desires of our flesh, doing the wish of the flesh and the senses, and we were sons of wrath by nature, just as also the others.*

In every respect he has the purpose of magnifying divine grace, just as also in the account he supplied of what God has done he employed such words as would make it attractive by magnifying it. Thus, he wants to magnify God's generosity also by the judgment of those who had received it, since although they were quite wicked and unworthy of enjoying God's gifts, nevertheless

---

[28]Theodore's point, of course, is that the same word in Greek (and Latin) means both "wind" and "spirit."

sunt bona. quorum et cum maxima accusatione exaggerare nititur malitiam. ideo *uoluntates carnis et cogitationum* dicit; et, *era-*
mus natura filii irae et cetera; quibus uehementer antiquam eorum
incusat malitiam. cum ergo tales essemus, quid accidit?

5   *Deus autem diues cum esset in misericordia, propter multam ca-*
ritatem suam qua dilexit nos, et cum essemus mortui in delictis et in
peccatis.

nam *cum essemus* hoc in loco dicens, signat quod fuimus; retulit autem illud ad principium uerbi. sic enim coepit: *et uos cum*
10   *essetis mortui delictis et peccatis uestris.* unde et interiecit cetera,
quae malitiam eorum uehementem poterant ostendere. resump-
sit iterum illud in illa narratione donationis Dei, ultra non dicens
uos, sed *nos;* ut ostendat quoniam et malitiam aestimat esse communem et gratiam similiter. eos autem qui huiusmodi erant quid
15   fecit?

conuiuificauit Christo.

totum reddidit praecedentibus illis quae de Christo dixerat,
ostendens quoniam communionem ad eum habemus tam ex similitudine naturae quam ex copulatione resurrectionis.

20   deinde adicit resurrectionis lucrum:

gratia estis saluati.

uult dicere quoniam 'suscitat uos, ut ultra salutem per gratiam
adquiratis.' 'salutem' nominat hanc, id est, 'ut ne ultra pro delictis poenam aliquam expectetis;' eo quod et 'perditionem' diuina
25   scriptura poenam nominare consueuit. sicut Dominus in euangeliis dicit: *timete magis illum qui potest et animam et corpus perdere*
in gehennam. sed nunc illud euidentius dixit, eo quod et inperfec-
tum hoc in loco sensum reliquit; adicit illa quae sequuntur illud

2-4 ideo ... malitiam *om H*   9 cepit *C* H*   10 et (*bef.* cet.) *add H*   12
donationes *C H*   13 aestimant *C H*   18-19 similitudinem *H*   23 idem (*for*
id est) *C H*   27 gehenna *C* (*corr.*)   ‖ euidentius illud *H*

they had acquired many and great good things. And he strives to exaggerate their wickedness by rebuking them as much as possible. And so he speaks of *the wishes of the flesh and the senses*, and says *we were sons of wrath by nature*, and the rest. By these words he vigorously condemns their former wickedness. Therefore, since we were like this, what happened?

2:4–5a *But God, who is rich in mercy, because of the great love with which he loved us, and when we were dead in transgressions and in sins,*

For by saying *when we were* in this passage, he means that we have been,[29] [145] and he refers this to the beginning of the passage.[30] For he begins this way (2:1): *And when you were dead in transgressions and your sins.* Thus, he inserts the rest (2:2–4) because it was capable of demonstrating their excessive wickedness. He took this up again in his account of God's gift, no longer saying *you* (2:1), but *we* (2:5) in order to show that he reckoned wickedness common to both and likewise grace. But what did God do for those who were like this?

2:5b *he made us alive together with Christ—*

He turned the whole discussion back to what he had said about Christ in the preceding verses, demonstrating that we have fellowship with him as much by the likeness of nature as by union with the resurrection.

Then he adds what is gained by the resurrection:

2:5c *by grace you have been saved—*

He wants to say that "he raises you up so that from now on you may acquire salvation by grace." He uses the word *saved* for salvation to mean "that you may no longer expect any punishment for transgressions," because divine scripture customarily uses the word "lost" to mean punishment. For example, in the Gospels the Lord says (Matt 10:28): *rather fear him who can lose both soul and body in Gehenna.* Here he said this more clearly, because in this passage he left the meaning incomplete.[31] He adds what follows to

---

[29] The comment makes sense only by realizing that the Latin clause translates the Greek participle. Theodore probably said: "For by saying *us being*, he means that we were."

[30] See Swete's note (1:145): "v. 5 takes up the thread of v. 1, vv. 2–4 being parenthetic."

[31] The comment is somewhat unclear. Presumably Matt 10:28 makes the point more clearly, but since 2:5c is an insertion, the meaning is incomplete.

dictum quod dixit *conuiuificavit Christo.* quid dicens?

    et conresuscitauit et consedere fecit in caelestibus in Christo Iesu.

    uides quoniam illa quae dixit de Christo, illis nos ait communi-
casse per illam quae apud eum est coniunctionem; ostendens quo-
5 niam non incassum memoratus est illa, scilicet non solum ea quae
de Christo sunt manifestat; sed ut ex illis liberalitatem erga nos
Christi ostendat. deinde adicit:

    ut ostendat in saeculis superuenientibus superabundantes diuitias
gratiae suae in bonitate super nos in Christo Iesu.

10 bene *in saeculis superuenientibus* dixit, quando ipsa rerum demonstratio manifestam erga nos ostendit Dei bonitatem, et gratiam illam quam perficere dignatus est per illa quae secundum
Christum sunt. eo quod omni in loco illa magna quae per Christum praestita sunt nobis, de futuris probare est adnisus. neces-
15 sarie ergo et hoc adiecit, ita ut non in praesenti uita dictorum exi-
gerent documenta; perfectam uero de nobis et plenariam reddidit
rationem. resumit uero illud quod dixerat:

    gratia enim estis saluati [per fidem].

    regenerationis lucrum quod erit docens nos et dicit:

20 *et hoc non ex uobis, Dei donum; non ex operibus, ut ne quis glorie-*
tur. ipsius enim sumus factura, creati in Christo Iesu in operibus bonis,
quae praeparauit Deus ut in illis ambulemus.

    nam quod dixit: *ipsius enim sumus factura,*

†hoc in loco non secundum pri-	ἐνταῦθα οὐ κατὰ τὴν πρώτην λέγει
mam dicit opificationem, sed	δημιουργίαν, ἀλλὰ κατὰ τὴν δευτέ-
secundam; secundum quam et	ραν, καθ᾽ ἣν ἀνακτιζόμεθα διὰ τῆς
recreamur, per resurrectionem	ἀναστάσεως.
iterum effecti.*	

unde adiecit: *creati in Christo Iesu;* sicut et ad Corinthios dicit: *si*
30 *qua in Christo noua creatura.* quod autem dicere uult indiget latitudinem, ita ut legentibus manifestum fieri posset. mortales cum

1   inquid (*sc.* inquit) *C* (*corr.*) quod *H*   6   manifesta *C H*   18   per fidem *om C*
H   20   non ex. op. *om H*   24   sq. Coisl. 204, f. 68 a [Cr. vi. 142, Fr. 133] Θεόδωρος δέ φησιν εἰς τὸ ‘αὐτοῦ γάρ ἐσμεν ποίημα, κτισθέντες ἐπ᾽ ἔργοις ἀγαθοῖς᾽·
ἐνταῦθα, κ.τ.λ.   27-28   creamur per res. eff. iterum *H*   30-31   latitudine *C*
(*corr.*)

his statement: *he made us alive together with Christ.*[32] What does he say?

2:6 *and he raised us up with him and seated us with him in the heavenly places in Christ Jesus,*

You see that he says we share in those things he has said of Christ by our union with him. He shows [146] that it is not without a purpose that he has mentioned them; that is, he does so not only to make clear the things that concern Christ but also to show from them Christ's generosity toward us. Then he adds:

2:7 *so that in the ages to come he might show the immeasurable riches of his grace in kindness toward us in Christ Jesus,*

He rightly said *in the ages to come,* when the very revelation of the facts shows the obvious kindness of God toward us and the grace he saw fit to perfect through the dispensation of Christ. Because those great gifts bestowed on us through Christ are in every place, he strove to prove them by what was to come. Thus, he necessarily added this phrase so that the teachings of his words might not be restricted to the present life but would give a perfect and complete explanation with regard to us. And he takes up again what he had said (2:5c):

2:8a *for by grace you have been saved [through faith],*

Teaching us what the profit of rebirth will be he says:

2:8b-10 *and this is not from you; it is the gift of God—not from works, so that no one may boast. For we are what he has made us, created in Christ Jesus for good works, which God has prepared for us to walk in.*

For when he said *for we are what he has made us,*

†in this passage he is not speaking of the first fashioning but of the second by which we are created again, made again by the resurrection.*

Here he is not speaking of the first fashioning but of the second by which we are created anew by the resurrection.

[147] This is why he added *created in Christ Jesus,* just as he says to the Corinthians (2 Cor 5:17): *if there is a new creation in Christ.*[33] But what he means requires a longer discussion to make it clear to the reader. Since we are mortal in this present life, a tendency to

---

[32] That is, verse 5c is an insertion that interrupts the flow of the language.

[33] Swete (1:147) points out that this punctuation of the verse is common to "the great majority of the Latin authorities." Cf. 2 Cor 5:17 in NRSV: "so if anyone is in Christ, there is a new creation."

simus secundum praesentem uitam, sequitur quodammodo mortalitatem facilitas peccandi. est enim quando quidem a uolupta-
te, quando uero a cupiditate pecuniaria, frequenter et ob praesentem gloriam quam et adpetere properamus, in delictum incurri-
5   mus. hinc contingit in multitudinem nos peccatorum et profunditatem impietatis praecipites duci; nihil iuuati neque ex illis legibus
quae a Deo datae sunt nobis, nisi solum hoc, quoniam lex ostendebat illa nos agere quae non conueniebant. quid ergo fecit Dominus, cum nos minime possemus propter infirmitatem illam quae
10 nobis aderat per mortalitatem, et cum non sufficeremus ad perfectam uirtutem proficere directionem? iterum nos secundo creauit,
secundam illam uitam inmortalem donans nobis; in qua effecti, et
naturalem abicientes infirmitatem, utpote erepti a mortalitate et
ab omni passione liberi effecti, inmortali habebimur natura ut nec
15 peccare ultra possimus. quoniam ergo dixit quia eramus *mortui delictis, facientes uoluntates carnis et cogitationum, et eramus natura filii irae*, sed cum tales essemus, conresuscitauit nos Christo, ut ultra
per gratiam salutem adsequi possemus; haec adiecit, latius comprobare illam salutem uolens, quae nobis effecta est per gratiam.
20 quid enim? quando hoc nobis praestitit, id est, resurrectionem. eo
quod non ex nobis neque ex nostris operibus salutem adsequi poteramus, sicut et praeteritum ostendit tempus, sufficienter arguens
in his nostram infirmitatem. et ideo denuo creauit nos in Christo,
secundam illam uitam condonans nobis in qua effecti peccare qui-
25 dem nullomodo poterimus. omne uero quodcumque bonum est,
permanebimus facientes illud. hoc enim dicit: *creati in Christo Iesu in operibus bonis;*

†ut illa quae per nostrum propositum agere nullomodo ualui-
30 mus (eo quod naturalis infirmitas repugnabat nobis), haec sine labore aliquo cum multa facilitate per gratiam eius, qui nos
ad hoc iterum creauit, perficere

ἵν᾽ ἅπερ ἀπὸ τῆς οἰκείας προαι-
ρέσεως κατορθῶσαι οὐδαμῶς οἷοί
τε ἐγενόμεθα τῷ τὴν φυσικὴν ἀν-
τιπράττειν ἡμῖν ἀσθένειαν, ταῦτα
δίχα πόνου παντὸς σὺν εὐμαρείᾳ
πολλῇ χάριτι τοῦ πρὸς τοῦτο ἡμᾶς
ἀνακτίζοντος ἐπιτελέσαι ἡμῖν ἐγγέ-

6 iuuat *H*   7   sunt *om H*   8   non *om C*   9   possimus *C*   10   non *om H**
12   secundum (*for* secundam) *C* H*   15   possemus *C* H*   17   nos, salutem
om H   18   possumus *H** possimus *H* (*corr.*)   21-22   poterimus *C* H*   24
secundum *C* H*   28   sq. Coisl. 204 *l. c.*   32   multa *om H*

sin somehow follows upon mortality. For sometimes by sensual pleasure, sometimes by desire for money, and often because of present honor we are eager to claim, we rush into a transgression. From this it happens that we are led headlong into a multitude of sins and a depth of godlessness. Nor are we helped in any way by the laws God has given us, save only that the law showed us what it was not right to do. Therefore, what did God do when we by no means had any capacity for good because of the weakness present in us through mortality and when we were not strong enough to make progress on the straight path leading to perfect virtue? He created us a second time, giving us immortality according to that life. When we are fashioned in it and have put off our natural weakness, in fact rescued from mortality and made free of all passion, we shall be kept in an immortal nature so that we shall no longer be able to sin. He said that we were *dead in transgressions* (2:1), *doing the wishes of the flesh and the senses, and we were sons of wrath by nature* (2:3), yet even though we were like this, he raised us up together with Christ (2:6) so that thereafter we might be able to acquire salvation by grace. Therefore, since he has said all this, he added these verses (2:8–10) in his wish to confirm at greater length the salvation that has been brought about for us by grace. What is it, then? It is when he bestowed this upon us, that is, the resurrection. In these verses he sufficiently condemns our weakness, because we were unable to acquire salvation of ourselves or by our works, as time gone by demonstrates. And so he created us anew in Christ, giving us with him the gift of that life in which we are to be made [148] incapable of sinning in any way. Instead, we shall persevere in doing everything whatsoever that is good. This is what he means by saying *created in Christ Jesus for good works,*

†so that what we were not strong enough in any way to do by our own purpose (because our natural weakness resisted us), this we might be able to accomplish without any toil and with great ease by the grace of him who created us again for this.*	so that what we were in no way able to succeed in doing by our own free choice, because our natural weakness opposed us, this became possible for us to accomplish without any toil and with great ease by the grace of the one who created us anew for this.

In this part of the letter he speaks of the resurrection as a good

potuerimus.*　　　　　　　　νηται.

dicens uero in hisce resurrectionis bonum, quod commune erat omnibus, siue illis qui ex gentibus crediderunt, siue illis qui ex Iudaeis; in subsequentibus illud adicit quod lucrum illorum tantum
5　erat qui ex gentibus erant, eo quod Ephesii ex gentibus ad fidem Christi accesserunt. et uehementius Deo gratias agere deproperat, eo quod non solum pro communibus, sed pro suis propriis debitores erant id facere:

　　propter quod memores estote quoniam uos qui dudum eratis gentes,
10　*in carne qui dicebamini praeputium.*

　　quod dicit, *in carne*, adici illi debet *qui dicimini*, non in illo dicto quo *gentes* dixit; ut sensus hic esse uideatur: *qui in carne dicimini praeputium.* adicit enim:

　　ab illa quae dicitur circumcisio in carne manu facta.
15　　*in carne* praeputiatos debere dici adserens, eo quod et circumcisio erga carnem uideri potest.

　　quoniam eratis tempore illo sine Christo.

　　'necdum enim credideratis in eum.' non debet autem quisquam sermonum obscuritatem inhaerere; sed examinare debet
20　apostolicorum uerborum intellectum.

　　abalienati a conuersatione Israel, et peregrini testamentorum promissionis, spem non habentes, et sine Deo in hoc mundo.

　　'reputamini (inquit) uos qui ex gentibus credidistis, quia ab illis qui in circumcisione sunt *praeputium dicimini.* et quasi natura-
25　lem quandam discretionem ad Iudaeos in carne habere uidemini; quando secundum tempus illud, priusquam credidissetis Christo, nulla erat uobis ad Deum communio, neque habebatis bonas aliquas spes, alieni ab Israel extantes, et a promissionibus et testamentis quae ad illos fuerant factae, quorum summum bonum erat
30　is qui expectabatur Christus.' quid ergo?

　　nunc autem in Christo Iesu uos qui aliquando eratis longe, prope facti estis in sanguine Christi.

　　'sed

†nunc Christi mors resurrectio-　'νῦν ὁ τοῦ Χριστοῦ θάνατος τὴν

1　poterimus *C* poteramus *H*　2　erant (*for* erat) *C**　11　dicebamini *C* (*corr.*)
|| illi (*for* in illo) *C* (*corr.*)　13　abicit *C H*　18　crederatis *C**　19　obscuritati
C (*corr.*)　20　apostolicum *C*　21　Israhel *C*　26　quandam *H*　|| credissetis
*C**　27　erit *C**　28　Israhel *C*　34　sq. Coisl. 204, f. 69 a [Cr. vi 145, Fr. 133]
Θεόδωρος δέ φησιν· νῦν ὁ τοῦ Χριστοῦ θ., κ.τ.λ.

common to all, whether they are Gentile or Jewish Christians. In what follows he adds what those who had been Gentiles gained, since the Ephesians had come to faith in Christ from the Gentiles. And he was eager for them to give thanks to God all the more intensely because they were obliged to do this not only for the gifts given to all but also for those that were particularly theirs:

2:11a *Because of this remember that you who were formerly Gentiles in the flesh were called the uncircumcision*

His expression *you are called* must be connected to *in the flesh* rather than to *Gentiles*, so that the meaning here is plainly: "you are called in the flesh the uncircumcision."[34] For he adds:

2:11b *by what is called the circumcision made in the flesh by hand,*

[149] He maintains that they should be called the uncircumcision *in the flesh* because circumcision is obviously related to the flesh.

2:12a *since you were at that time without Christ,*

"For you had not yet believed in him." And no one ought to stick to the obscurity of what is said. Instead, he should pay attention to the meaning of the apostle's words.

2:12b *being aliens from the way of life of Israel, and strangers to the testaments of promise, having no hope and without God in this world.*

"You who believed as Gentiles (he says) are reckoned to be like this because *you are called the uncircumcision* by those who are circumcised. And inasmuch as you are seen to have in the flesh a certain natural difference from the Jews, at that time before you believed in Christ you had no fellowship with God, nor did you possess any good hopes, since you were aliens from Israel and from the promises and testaments given to them, of which the greatest good was that Christ who was expected." What then?

2:13 *But now in Christ Jesus you who once were far off have been brought near by the blood of Christ.*

"But

| †now Christ's death, by giving the resurrection and introducing a life other than the present one, has joined you who were | Now Christ's death, by giving the resurrection and introducing a life other than the present one, has joined you who were |

---

[34]That is, we should read "formerly Gentiles, in the flesh were called" rather than "formerly Gentiles in the flesh, were called." In his commentary Theodore uses the present tense instead of the imperfect of the Latin rendition of the text.

nem donans et alteram uitam
pro praesente inducens, coniunxit uos qui eratis multum separati.' qualiter aut quomodo?*

ἀνάστασιν χαρισάμενος καὶ ἕτερον
ἀντὶ τοῦ παρόντος ἐπεισαγαγὼν
βίον, συνῆψεν ὑμᾶς τοὺς ἀφεστῶτας
πολύ.' πῶς καὶ τίνα τρόπον;

5   *ipse est enim pax nostra, qui fecit utraque unum, et medium parie-
tem maceriae soluit inimicitiam in carne sua; legem mandatorum in
edictis destituens, ut duos condat in se in unum hominem nouum, faciens pacem; et reconciliet utrosque in uno corpore Deo per crucem,
interficiens inimicitiam in ipso.*

10   lex per circumcisionem suos ab alienis discreuit; unde nec aliqua communio gentibus cum Iudaeis poterat esse. circumcisione
et quidem habebant potestatem. sed dominus

†Christus per resurrectionem inmortalitatem nobis praestans,
15 destruxit hanc diuisionem; in
inmortali etenim natura circumcisio nequaquam poterit celebrari. circumcisione uero non
extante, nulla uidebitur praepu-
20 tii et circumcisionis esse discretio; sed et ipsorum praeceptorum legem hinc cessare fecit,
superflua enim tunc omnis est
definitio legis,*

ὁ Χριστὸς τὴν διὰ τῆς ἀναστάσεως
ἀθανασίαν ἡμῖν παρασχών, κατέλυ-
σεν τὴν διαίρεσιν ταύτην· ἐν γὰρ
ἀθανάτῳ φύσει περιτομὴ μὲν οὐκ ἂν
γένοιτο· τούτου δὲ οὐκ ὄντος, οὐδεμία φανήσεται ἀκροβύστου καὶ περιτετμημένου διάκρισις. ἀλλὰ μὴν
καὶ αὐτῶν τῶν ἐντολῶν τὸν νόμον
ἐντεῦθεν ἔπαυσεν· περιττὴ γὰρ τότε πᾶσα τοῦ νόμου διάταξις.

25 eo quod iam ultra nec peccare poterimus. hoc ergo uult dicere,
quoniam 'ipse pacis nobis extitit auctor, qui illam inimicitiam et
separationem quae inerat ex circumcisione carnis dissoluit per resurrectionis gratiam, inmortales nos ultra exhibens, apud quos circumcisio locum non habet ulterius; quid enim et conferre poterit
30 inmortalibus circumcisio, ubi praeputii discretio ultra non poterit
inueniri?

†hanc autem inimicitiam abstulit, non circumcisionem solum
auferens, sed et ipsam legem
35 cessare faciens per sua decreta.'

[ταύτην δὲ τὴν ἔχθραν ὀφεῖλεν, οὐ
μόνον ἀφελὼν τὴν περιτομὴν ἀλλὰ καὶ αὐτὸν τὸν νόμον παύσας]
διὰ τῶν ἰδίων δογμάτων· ἵνα εἴ-

---

11 circumcisionem C H   13 Coisl. 204 *l. c.*   15 iussionem (*for* divis.) C
H: txt g   ‖ in *om* H   16 enim H*   21 et *om* H*   23-24 edefinitio (*for*
est def.) C*   30 praeputio C*   32 Coisl. 204, f. 71 a [Cr. vi. 149, Fr. 133]
θεόδωρος δέ φησιν· ἵνα εἴπῃ διὰ τῶν ἰδίων δογμάτων, κ.τ.λ.   33 solam H

quite separated." How and in what way?*

[150] 2:14–16 *For he is our peace, who made both one and has broken down the middle partition of the wall, the hostility, in his flesh, destroying the law of commandments by decrees so that he might compose in himself one new human, making peace, and might reconcile both in one body to God through the cross, putting to death the hostility in him.*

By circumcision the law separated its own people from aliens, and so there was no possibility of any fellowship for Gentiles with Jews. It was by circumcision that they had such authority, but the Lord

†Christ, by bestowing on us immortality through his resurrection, destroyed this division, for circumcision could by no means be observed in an immortal nature. And once circumcision ceases to exist no distinction will appear between uncircumcision and circumcision. Rather, from then on he made *the law of* those *commandments* to cease its operation, for at that future time the entire ruling of the law is useless,*

because we shall no longer be able to sin. Therefore, he means that "he is the author of peace for us, because by the grace of the resurrection he destroyed the hostility and division present because of the circumcision of the flesh, displaying us from now on as immortal and as people among whom circumcision no longer has a place. For what benefit could circumcision give to those who are immortal, where there could no longer be found any difference made by uncircumcision?

†And he took away this hostility not only [151] by removing circumcision but also by stopping the law itself by his own [And he took away this hostility not only by removing circumcision but also by stopping the law itself]35 by his own decrees,

---

35 The brackets indicate Swete's conjectural rendering of the Greek text.

quae autem sunt decreta? resurrectio, incorruptela, inmortali-
tas. haec enim 'decreta' uocauit,
quasi quia et in re sint, ex qui-
5 bus efficitur, ut iam ultra peccare non possimus, opere id diuina
gratia in nobis expediente; ita
ut neque praecepta ulterius in-
digeamus, neque ulla mandata
10 quae alia quidem nos facere uolunt, alia prohibent.*

πη, τῆς ἀναστάσεως, τῆς ἀφθαρ-
σίας, τῆς ἀθανασίας· δόγματα καλέσας ταῦτα ὡς ἐν πράγμασιν ὄντα, τῆς θείας χάριτος ἐν ἡμῖν κατα-
πραττομένης, ὡς μηδὲ προσταγμά-
των ἡμᾶς δεῖσθαι καὶ ἐντολῆς τῆς
τόδε τι ποιεῖν ἢ μὴ ποιεῖν βουλομένης ἡμᾶς.

illam ergo inimicitiam et separationem quae ex circumcisione
fiebat cum omni lege fecit cessare; duos nos, id est, illum qui ex
gentibus erat et qui ex Iudaeis, unum quendam nouum hominem
15 per resurrectionem faciens inmortalem, apud quem nulla circumcisionis et praeputii habetur discretio. sic enim nos in unum corpus illud inmortale habere effecit, in pace nos constituens, familiaritatem utriusque nobis illam quae ad Deum est hinc donans. quae
cuncta efficit *per* propriam *crucem*, ut dicat 'per passionem et mor-
20 tem,' omnem inimicitiam quae inesse nobis uidebatur adimens,
utpote et ipsam mortem per resurrectionem destruens. optime autem illam separationem quae ex circumcisione fiebat *medium pa-
rietem maceriae* uocauit; ostendens nullomodo posse nos inuicem
propinquare, ad similitudinem eorum, qui, maceria quadam me-
25 diante, propinquare sibi prohibentur; eo quod nec erat possibile
secundum legis praeceptum eos qui in praeputio erant aliquam ad
circumcisos habere communionem, praeterquam si circumcisionem suscipere uoluissent, quod erat illius partis semel fieri. prudentia uero apostolica est demiranda, eo quod memorans resurrec-
30 tionem et illa quae exinde adquisita sunt gentibus, simul adtraxit
et Iudaeos, eo quod reconciliationem similiter et isti sicut et illi per

7 τι om edd. 17 efficit *C* 18 illa *C* H* 24 maceriae *C H* 26 praeputium *C** 27 propter quam *H* 29 est *om H* 30 ex (*for* et) *C* ea *H*   ‖
qui ita (*for* adquisita) *H*

decrees."[36]   What decrees are they? The resurrection, incorruption, immortality.   For he called these "decrees" because insofar as they exist in fact they have the effect that we can no longer sin, since the working of divine grace provides this for us, so that we no longer need ordinances or any commandment, some commanding us what to do, others giving us prohibitions.*

that is, the resurrection, incorruption, immortality. He called them *decrees* because when they exist in fact, with divine grace operating in us, we need no ordinances or a command willing us to do or not to do something.

Therefore, he stopped the hostility and division that resulted from circumcision together with the entire law. And he made the two of us, that is, the one from the Gentiles and the other from the Jews, a kind of single new human, immortal through the resurrection, a new humanity in which no distinction of circumcision and uncircumcision obtains. For in this way he brought about the keeping of us in that one immortal body, establishing us in peace, and from this giving both of us intimacy with God. He brought all this about *through* his own *cross*, that is, "through his suffering and death," removing all the hostility present to us, just as he also [152] destroys death itself through the resurrection. And quite effectively he called the division that came about because of circumcision *the middle partition of the wall*, demonstrating that we could in no way draw near to one another, in the same way that people are prevented from drawing near to one another when some wall stands in the middle. This was because it was impossible according to the ordinance of the law for the uncircumcised to have any fellowship with the circumcised, unless they were willing to receive circumcision, which was to be done once for all in their judgment. But the apostle's wisdom is to be admired, because by mentioning the resurrection and what the Gentiles had gained from it he at the same time brought in the Jews. This was because both groups alike had gained reconciliation through the resurrection, so that the Jews might not seem to think highly of themselves inasmuch as they had just the

---

[36] *Per sua decreta*, instead of *in edictis*, as in the text of 2:15.

illam potiti sunt; ut ne uideantur magna sapere Iudaei, quasi qui nil minus habuerint. unde iterum dicit:

et ueniens euangelizauit pacem uobis qui longe estis et qui prope.

prope dicens, Iudaeos designauit, propter legis disciplinam.
5 adicit illud quod praecedentibus consequenter iungi poterat:

quoniam [per eum] habemus accessum utrique in uno Spiritu ad Patrem.

'utrique (inquit) similiter eandem Spiritus participati gratiam potuimus accedere per eum ad Deum, ita ut et patrem illum ad-
10 scribamus proprium. quod numquam neque Iudaei ex lege huius-modi familiaritatem adquirere potuerant; e contrario uero et poe-nae eos lex subiciebat, minime ab illis scrupulose seruata.' et quo-niam ostendit quia et Iudaeis Christi aduentus maximum con-tulit lucrum, licet gentibus uideretur alienis extantibus eligan-
15 tem quandam illam praebuisse familiaritatem quae nullomodo illis pertinere poterat; resumit iterum illud, quasi ad illos proloquens qui ex gentibus crediderunt:

itaque iam ultra non estis peregrini et aduenae, sed conciues sanc-torum et domestici Dei, aedificati supra fundamentum apostolorum et
20 *prophetarum.*

id ipsud dicens quod et in superioribus dixerat, quoniam 'ul-tra *non estis alieni* a pietate; *domestici* enim *Dei* estis effecti, illam quae ad apostolos et prophetas est communionem suscipientes per illam fidem quae est in Christo.' et quoniam dixit *superaedificati,*
25 seruans exempli ipsius sequentiam adicit:

existente angulari lapide ipso Iesu Christo, in quo omne tactum

2 nihil *H* 10 neque *om H** 11 assequi (*for* adquirere) *H* 13 aduentum *C* H* 18 ciues *H* 21 id ipsum *C (corr.) H* 26 existente [existens *H*] angulare [- i *C (corr.)*] lapide ipsum Iesum Christum *C H* ‖ tactu *C*

same privileges as the Gentiles. Thus, he goes on to say:

2:17 *And he came and preached peace to you who are far off and who are near,*[37]

By *near* he indicated the Jews because of the study of the law. He adds what could have been joined in logical order to the preceding verse:

2:18 *for [through him] both of us have access in one Spirit to the Father.*

"Both of us (he says) by having alike participated in the same grace of the Spirit have been able through him to draw near to God, so that we assign him as our own Father. Not even the Jews by the law had ever been able to acquire an intimacy of this kind. On the contrary, the law [153] used to subject them to punishment if they kept it with less than scrupulous care." And since he shows that Christ's coming conferred the greatest gain also to the Jews, even though he plainly bestowed on the Gentiles who were alien that sort of excellent intimacy that had never in any way been possible for the Jews to have, he picks up his argument again, inasmuch as he is addressing Gentile believers:

2:19–20a *And so you are no longer strangers and aliens, but you are fellow citizens of the saints and members of the household of God, built upon the foundation of the apostles and prophets,*

He is saying the same thing he said above (2:12), that "*you are no longer aliens* from true religion.[38] For you have been made *members of the household of God*, since you have received fellowship with the apostles and prophets through faith in Christ." And since he said *built upon*, he keeps the logic of his illustration and adds:

2:20b-22 *with Jesus Christ himself as the cornerstone, in whom the whole touch[39] joined together grows into a holy temple in the Lord, in whom you also are built together into a dwelling place for God in the*

---

[37] See Swete's note (1:152): "The Vulg. supplies *fuistis*. The second εἰρήνην, which is represented in all the versions excepting the Syriac, appears to have been wanting in Th.'s text. It is omitted also by Chrys. and Thdt., followed by the later Greek expositors."

[38] In 2:12 the reading is *abalienati ... peregrini* (ἀπηλλοτριωμένοι ... ξένοι), while in 2:19 it is *peregrini ... advenae* (ξένοι ... πάροικοι).

[39] See Swete's note (1:154). Theodore is apparently reading ἀφή here instead of οἰκοδομή, understanding it to mean "touch" rather than ligament, as his following commentary shows. Swete says: "I can only account for this singular error by supposing that Th. wrote without reference to his codex, and that he has blended c. ii. 21 ... with iv. 16."

coaptatum crescit in templo sancto in Domino, in quo et uos coaedifi-camini in habitaculum Dei in Spiritu.

'angularis lapidis ordinem nobis Christus tenere uidetur, super quem et illi qui ex gentibus et nos qui ex Iudaeis credidimus utri-
5 que coniungimur, discretione nulla ultra in nobis intercedente;

†eo quod in templum Dei coap-
tamur similiter utrique eadem
uirtute Spiritus per regenerationem, ita ut adsequi merea-
10 mur in uno consistere aedificio.'
nam quod dixit: *in quo omne
tactum coaptatum*, ut dicat 'omnis lapis qui sub tactu cadit;' a
quadam proprietate ita dicens,
15 in ordine uidelicet hominis lapi-
dem dicens.*

ἐπειδὴ εἰς ναὸν τοῦ θεοῦ τελοῦ-
μεν ἀμφότεροι, τῇ αὐτῇ δυνάμει τοῦ
πνεύματος διὰ τῆς ἀναγεννήσεως τὸ
συντελεῖν εἰς μίαν οἰκοδομὴν δεξάμενοι. τὸ δὲ ἐν ᾧ πᾶσα ἁφὴ συν-
αρμολογουμένη, ἵνα εἴπῃ· πᾶς λίθος
ὑπὸ ἁφὴν πίπτων· ἀπό τινος ἰδιώ-
ματος οὕτως εἰπών, ἐν τάξει δηλονότι ἀνθρώπου τὸν λίθον λέγων.

et quoniam omni ex parte retulit Dei gratiam quae in nos est et resurrectionis lucrum et illorum quae expectamus magnitudinem, adicit:

20 *huius rei gratia ego Paulus, uinctus Christi Iesu pro uobis gentibus.*

et non dixit illa quae huius rei gratia dici uoluerat, sed relin-quens in ultimo eius supplementum ad illud cucurrit quod dixit; *uinctus pro uobis gentibus.* illa quae subsequebantur adicit, osten-dens quemadmodum illi pertinere uidetur gentium euangelium,
25 pro quo etiam uinctum se esse dicit:

si tamen audistis dispensationem gratiae Dei quae data est mihi in uobis, quoniam [secundum reuelationem notum] factum est mihi my-sterium, sicut praescripsi in paucibus, prout potestis legentes intelle-gere prudentiam meam in mysterium Christi.

30 multam habent obscuritatem ob sermonum compendiosam ex-

---

3 lapis, Christi *H*   6 sq. Coisl. 204, f. 73 a. [Cr. vi. 152, Fr. 133] Θεόδωρος δέ φησιν· ἐπειδή, κ.τ.λ.   7-8 eandem uirtutem *C H*   8-9 τοῦ συντελεῖν cod., edd.; txt conj. Fr.   9 adepti (*aft.* reg.) *add C* (*corr.*)   12 πίστεως (*for* πίπτων) edd.   14 ista (*for* ita) *C* (*corr.*)   17 gratia *C**   ‖ nobis *C* (*corr.*)   27 sec. reuel. notum *om C H*   28 scripsi *H*   ‖ paucis *C* (*corr.*)   30 multum *C H* ‖ ob *om H*

Spirit.

Christ plainly holds the rank of cornerstone for us. Upon him both those from the Gentiles and we from the Jews have believed we are both joined together with no distinction any longer placed between us,

†because both of us alike are joined together in the temple of God by the same power of the Spirit through rebirth, so that we are granted the right to attain [154] our position in a single building." For when he said *in whom the whole touch is joined together,* he means "every stone that falls beneath a touch." He says this in some peculiar way, apparently comparing a human being to a stone.*

since both of us find our goal in the temple of God, receiving by the same power of the Spirit through the resurrection our joint perfection in one building. The phrase *in whom the whole touch is joined together* means every stone that falls beneath a touch. He said this in some peculiar way, apparently comparing a human being to a stone.

And since everywhere he referred God's grace in us to the riches of the resurrection and to the greatness of those things we await, he adds:

3:1 *For this reason I, Paul, a prisoner of Christ Jesus for you Gentiles—*

He did not explain what he had wanted to say *for this reason,* but leaving until later what he wanted to add, he rushes on to his words *a prisoner for you Gentiles.*⁴⁰ He adds what follows to show how the gospel for the Gentiles plainly was his concern. And he says that it was for it that he is a prisoner:

3:2–4 *if, at any rate, you have heard of the dispensation of God's grace that was given me for you, that the mystery was made [known] to me [by revelation], as I wrote above in a few words, a reading of which will enable you to perceive my understanding of the mystery of Christ,*

[155] All his discussions in this letter, even the doctrinal ones, have a good deal of obscurity because of the concise way he expresses himself. And this is especially true of that part of the letter we now propose to interpret. Therefore, we must pay close

---

⁴⁰See Swete's comment (1:154): "Th. regards the thread of the argument as taken up again in verse 14."

pressionem uniuersa etenim illa quae dogmatica sunt in praesenti
epistola; maxime autem ista pars epistolae quae a nobis nunc interpretari est proposita. intendendum est ergo ad intellectum sermonum, cuius doctrinam praehonorabilem omnibus existimare de-
5 bemus.

     statim uero [*quae*] *data est*, pro *datam* dicit;

†uult enim dicere quoniam 'ne-   βούλεται εἰπεῖν ὅτι 'πάντως που
cessarie aliqua ex parte audistis   ἠκούσατε τὴν παρασχεθεῖσάν μοι
datam mihi in uobis gratiae di-   τῆς εἰς ὑμᾶς χάριτος οἰκονομίαν·
10 spensationem, et quoniam se-   καὶ ὅτι κατὰ ἀποκάλυψιν ἐδεξάμην
cundum reuelationem suscepi   τοῦ μυστηρίου τούτου τὴν γνῶσιν·
mysterii istius cognitionem. de   περὶ οὗ δὴ καὶ γεγράφηκα ὑμῖν
quibus et scripsi uobis ut fas ad-   ὡς ἐνῆν διὰ βραχέων, ἐπὶ τῷ
mittebat de paucis, ut cognosca-   γνῶναι καὶ ὑμᾶς τοῦ μυστηρίου τὴν
15 tis et uos illam quam suscepi   σύνεσιν.'
prudentiam de hoc mysterio.'*

sicuti ad Corinthios scribit; *sic nos existimet homo, sicut ministros
Christi et dispensatores mysteriorum Dei*; hoc est, 'ordinatos ut de
inenarrabilibus omnibus distribuamus uobis doctrinam.' et quod
20 sit ipsum mysterium, dicens *secundum reuelationem notum est.*

    *quod aliis generationibus non innotuit filiis hominum, sicut nunc
reuelatum est sanctis apostolis eius et prophetis, in Spiritu; esse gentes
coheredes et concorporales et conparticipes promissionis eius in Christo.*

25   hoc quod ab antiquis quidem ignorabatur, nunc autem manifestum est *et apostolis et prophetis;* 'prophetas' dicens illos qui eo
in tempore prophetiae gratia digni habiti esse ostendebantur. quoniam placuit Deo ut gentes communionem habeant omnis promissionis quae est in Christo, quae et expectatur ut suum exitum su-
30 mat. ideo optime dixit *sicut praescripsi.* dixerat enim in superioribus de hoc, quoniam magna sunt illa quae in nos sunt a Deo conlata; quorum participationem etiam gentes dignae habitae sunt.
deinde dicens mysterium, resumit dictum *si tamen audistis dispen-*

2-3 interpretare *C**   3 posita *H*   7 sq. Coisl. 204, *l. c.* [Cr. vi. 153]   9
κοινωνίαν (for οἰκ.) Cr.   13-14 ἐπὶ τὸ γνῶναι Cr.   16 misterium *C**   17
sicuti et *H* ‖ ut (*for* sicut) *H*   18 dispensatorum *H* ‖ ministeriorum
(*for* myst.) *C**   30 scripsi *H*   32 habiti *C* H*   33 resumet *C**

attention to understand the discussions of one whose teaching we ought to consider more distinguished than anyone else's.

And immediately he says *that was given* instead of *given*.[41]

†He means that "you have inevitably somehow heard of the gracious dispensation given me for you and that it was by revelation that I received knowledge of that mystery. I wrote you about this, as far as was permitted in a few words, so that you might also know the understanding I received about this mystery."*

He wants to say that "you have inevitably somehow heard of the gracious dispensation given me for you and that it was by revelation that I received knowledge of this mystery. I wrote you about this, as far as it was possible in a few words, so that you might also know the understanding of the mystery."

He writes this way to the Corinthians (1 Cor 4:1): *Let a person think of us this way, as servants of Christ and dispensers of God's mysteries*, that is, "appointed so that we may distribute to you teaching about all the ineffable doctrines." And he explains what this very mystery is by saying it *was made known by revelation*.

3:5–6a *what was not made known in other generations to the sons of men as* [156] *it has now been revealed to his holy apostles and prophets by the Spirit, that the Gentiles are fellow heirs and members of the same body and fellow sharers in his promise in Christ*

What was unknown to those of old has now been manifested to both *the apostles and prophets*. By "prophets" he means those who at that time were openly held worthy of the grace of prophecy. This was because it pleased God that the Gentiles should have a share in the whole promise in Christ that is expected to find its fulfillment. And so he quite effectively said *as I wrote above* (3:3).[42] For he had spoken above of this, saying that what God confers on us is great and that the Gentiles are held worthy of sharing it. Then, speaking of the mystery, he resumes what he said (3:2): *if at any rate you have heard of the dispensation of God's grace that was given me for you:*

3:6b-9 *through the gospel of which I have become a minister according to the gift of God's grace that was given me by the working*

---

[41]That is, "given" refers to the dispensation rather than to the grace.

[42]That is, in 2:13ff., or possibly in the whole of the letter following the salutation.

sationem gratiae Dei quae data est mihi in uobis:

per euangelium, cuius factus sum ego minister secundum dationem gratiae Dei quae data est mihi secundum inoperationem uirtutis ejus.
mihi minima omnium sanctorum data est gratia ista, in gentibus euan-
5 *gelizare inuestigabiles diuitias Christi, et inluminare omnes quae esset dispensatio mysterii quod absconditum fuit a saeculis in Deo qui omnia creauit.*

idipsum dicit et hoc in loco, quoniam 'datum est mihi mysterium euangelii, ita ut omnibus gentibus praedicem uoluntatem
10 Dei, illam quae erga illos extitit; et ut ostendam illis doctrinam
huius mysterii quod absconditum fuerat et omnibus erat occultum, soli uero Deo erat cognitum, ei qui omnia fecit.' et ostendens
quemadmodum omnibus erat occultum, adicit:

ut innotescat nunc principatibus et potestatibus in caelestibus per
15 *ecclesiam multiformis sapientia Dei, secundum propositum saeculo-*
rum quod fecit in Christo Iesu domino nostro; in quo habemus fidu-
ciam et accessum in confidentia per fidem eius.

sic enim omnibus hoc occultum erat quod erat dispensandum
per Christum, ita ut nec principatus nec potestates (ut dicat 'inui-
20 sibiles uirtutes') potuissent primitus scire illa quae erant futura;
quae uere recognouissent nouam et gloriosam Dei sapientiam de
his quae dudum illi et ante saecula fuerant placita, nunc uero manifestata per illa quae erga ecclesiam facta sunt—ut dicat 'erga fideles,' qui per fidem nouati, et futurorum spem suscipientes per-
25 fectam, offerimus cum multa confidentia Deo, utpote qui et magna
quadam fiducia constituemur. et qualis est illa? talis quae iam ultra peccare nos non patitur, neque ab illis quae nos decent excedere
nos ultra sinat.

haec omnia interiecit ad illud quod dixit: *Paulus uinctus pro uo-*
30 *bis gentibus.* et quasi confirmans illud adicit:

propter quod postulo non deficere in tribulationibus meis pro uobis,
quae est gloria uestra.

'pro his ergo non solum gauisus sum quoniam uinctus sum,

4   ista *om H*   8   mihi *om H*   12   et (*for* ei) *H*   ‖   facit *C*   14   ostendat (*for* innot.) *H*   ‖   principibus *H*   15   multiformi *H*   16   quam *C H*   18   hoc *om H*   21   cognouissent *H*   23   facta est [ἐγένετο ?] *C H*   24   renouati *C* (*corr.*)   24-25   perfectum *H*   26   fiducia quadam *H**.   28   sinant *C H*   32   mea (*for* uestra) *H*   33   gravis (*for* gauisus) *C**   ‖   sum (1°) *om C H* (*corr.*)

of his power. To me the very least of all the saints was that grace given to preach to the Gentiles the good news of the unsearchable riches of Christ and to illuminate all as to what is the dispensation of the mystery that was hidden for ages in God who created all things,

[157] In this passage he says the same thing [he said in 3:2], that "the mystery of the gospel has been given me so that I might preach to all the Gentiles God's will that stands firm for them and that I might show them the teaching of this mystery that had been hidden and concealed from all, but known to God alone, to him who made all things." And to show how it had been concealed from all, he adds:

3:10–12 *so that now to the rulers and authorities in the heavenly places the manifold wisdom of God might be made known through the church according to the purpose of the ages, which he accomplished in Christ Jesus our Lord, in whom we have boldness and access in confidence through faith in him.*

For this was concealed from all in this way because it was destined to be dispensed [158] through Christ, so that neither the rulers nor the authorities (he means "the invisible powers") could have at first known the things that were to come. But they recognized them as God's new and glorious wisdom concerning what had been his good pleasure long ago and before the ages came to be, but now manifested by what took place with respect to the church—he means "with respect to the faithful," we who renewed by faith and receiving the perfect hope of the things to come, make our offering to God with great confidence, since we have been established in a certain great boldness. And what is that like? It is such that we are no longer allowed to sin, nor are we any longer permitted to depart from what is suitable for us.

He inserts all this (3:2–12) after he said *Paul, a prisoner for you Gentiles* (3:1). And as though to confirm this, he adds:

3:13 *Because of this I pray not to lose heart in my afflictions for you, which is your glory.*

"Therefore, for these reasons I am not only glad that I am a

sed et oro ut non cedam illis quae pro uobis sunt tribulationibus;
sciens quoniam uestrum est lucrum, si ergo passiones sustinens
tolerauero, non discedens ab illis quae conueniunt.' et quoniam
omnia ista ad illud retulit quod dixerat, *Paulus uinctus pro uobis*
5　*gentibus*; resumit iterum quod dixerat, *huius rei gratia*. et quod ibi
dicere supra proposuerat, hoc in isto loco adicit:

huius rei gratia, flecto genua mea ad patrem domini nostri Iesu
Christi, ex quo omnis congregatio in caelis et super terram nominatur.

†quidam *paternitas* legerunt,　τινὲς πατριὰ ἀνέγνωσαν, οὐ συν-
10　non intellegentes quod positum　ιέντες τὸ κείμενον· ἔστιν δὲ φρα-
erat ab apostolo; est autem *con-*　τρία. πατριὰ μὲν γὰρ ἡ συγγένεια
gregatio. nam *patria* uel *pater-*　λέγεται, φρατρία δὲ τὸ σύστημα·
nitas, cognatio dicitur; *congre-*　ἐν δὲ τοῖς οὐρανοῖς συγγένεια μὲν
gatio autem collectio esse insi-　οὐδεμία, συστήματα δὲ καὶ πολλά.
15　nuatur. in caelis namque co-　τὸ τοίνυν τούτου χάριν ἄνωθεν μὲν
gnatio quidem est nulla; con-　ἀποδεδωκὼς πρὸς τὰ προκείμενα,
gregationes autem sunt pluri-　διήγησιν ἔχοντα τοῦ μεγέθους τῆς
mae. nam quod dixit: *huius*　περὶ ἡμᾶς χάριτος τοῦ θεοῦ, ἐνταῦ-
rei gratia, sursum quidem red-　θα δὲ αὐτὸ μετὰ τὰ παρεντεθέντα
20　didit ad illa quae praedicta fue-　ἀναλαβών, τοῦτο λέγει, ὅτι 'ὑπὲρ
rant ei, quae narrationem ex-　τούτων ἁπάντων ὧν ἡμῖν παρέσ-
plicabant magnitudinis gratiae　χεν, καὶ ὡς προεῖπον οὕτως ὄντων
Dei illius quae erga nos facta es-　μεγάλων καὶ θαυμαστῶν, ἑκάστοτε
se uidebatur. hoc uero in loco　προσπίπτω τῷ πατρὶ τοῦ Χριστοῦ,
25　illud post interiectionem resu-　ὃν ἅπαν σύστημα εἴτε ἐν οὐρανοῖς
mens, hoc dicit, quoniam 'pro　εἴτε ἐπὶ γῆς οἰκεῖον καλεῖ τε καὶ
his omnibus quae nobis praesti-　ἡγεῖται δεσπότην.'
tit, sicut praedixi, quia sic sunt
magna et demiratione digna et
30　nimium praeclara, per singula momenta genua flecto patri
Christi, quem omnis congrega-

1 ero (*for* oro) *H* 3 non discedetis ab illis quae uobis conu. *C* (*corr.*) 6
super (*for* supra) *C* H* 8 terra *H* 9 legunt *C* (*corr.*) ‖ sq. Coisl. 204,
f. 76 a [Cr. vi. 159, Fr. 134] θεόδωρος δέ φησιν· τινές, κ.τ.λ. ‖ πατριὰν cod.
10-11 φατρία cod. 13 μὲν om edd. 14 esse *om H g* 19 rursum (*for*
sursum) *C* ‖ αὐτῷ, Cr. 20 praedicata *C* 21 eisque (*for* ei quae) *C* 21-
22 explicabat *C H* ‖ παρεῖχε edd. 22 προειπὼν Cr. 26 καλεῖται cod.,
edd. 31 flecti *C H* 32 Christo *C* H*

prisoner, but I also pray that I may not yield to those afflictions that are for your sake.[43] I know that the profit is yours if, indeed, I persevere in bearing my sufferings and not deserting convictions that are right." And since he has referred all this to what he had said (3:1), *Paul, a prisoner for you* [159] *Gentiles*, he repeats the statement he had made (3:1), *for this reason*. He adds at this place what he had also set forth at that previous place:

3:14–15 *For this reason I bow my knees before the Father of our Lord Jesus Christ, from whom every association in the heavens and on earth takes its name,*

†There are some who have read *fatherhood* by failing to understand what the apostle put down, but the reading is *association*. For *fatherland* or *fatherhood* is spoken of blood relationship, but *association* has the connotation of an assembly. There is, of course, no blood relationship in the heavens, but there are a great many associations.[44] For when he said *For this reason*, he turned back to what he had previously said above, which [160] gave an account of the greatness of God's grace that plainly came about for us. But in this passage, when he resumes his argument after the insertion,[45] he says this because "for all these gifts he has bestowed on us, as I said before, since they are great and worthy of admiration and

Some people have read *fatherland*, failing to understand what is put down; the reading is *association*.

For *fatherland* is said of blood relationship, but an *association* is an assembly.

And in the heavens there is no blood relationship, but there are many assemblies. Therefore, the expression *for this reason*, which he used above, shows he has turned back to what precedes, since it contains an account of the greatness of God's grace concerning us. But here when he resumes his argument after what he had inserted, he says this because "for all these gifts he has bestowed on us, as I said before, since they are so great and marvelous, I constantly bend my knees to the Father

---

[43] That is, Paul risks losing heart, not the Ephesians.

[44] Theodore's reading of φρατρία instead of πατριά (*congregatio* instead of *paternitas* or *patria*) is idiosyncratic, unsupported by any manuscript or version. What seems to bother him is the implication of blood relationship in heaven and possibly the fact that the Gentiles have no blood relationship with Israel.

[45] The insertion is 3:2–13, and "for this reason," occurs in 3:1 and 3:14.

tio *siue ea quae in caelis est siue
ea quae super terram est*, proprium uocat et aestimat esse dominum.'*

5   quid depostulans ab eo?

*ut det uobis secundum diuitias gloriae suae uirtutem confortari per
Spiritum eius in interiorem hominem; habitare Christum per fidem in
cordibus uestris; in caritate radicati et fundati.*

'postulo (inquit) ab eo, ut secundum suam bonitatem praebeat
10   uobis Spiritus gratiam, ut confirmet uos in ea quae secundum
Christum est fide; ita ut aestimetur idem inhabitare in uestris ani-
mis, uobis erga eum habentibus caritatem, quasi quandam radi-
cem et fundamentum firmissimum.' et aliud adicit:

*ut possitis comprehendere cum omnibus sanctis, quae sit latitudo et
15   longitudo et profundum et altitudo; cognoscere etiam supereminentem
scientiae caritatem Christi.*

†nam quod dicit, *cognosce-*   τὸ γνῶναι ἀντὶ τοῦ ἀπολαῦσαι
re, frui dicit; ipsis rebus dicens   λέγει· ἐπὶ πραγμάτων εἰπὼν τὴν
cognitionem, sicut et in psal-   γνῶσιν, ὡς ἐν τῷ ψαλμῷ τὸ ἐγνώ-
20   mo: *notas mihi fecisti uias ui-*   ρισάς μοι ὁδοὺς ζωῆς· [πληρώσεις
tae; adimplebis me laetitia cum   με εὐφροσύνης μετὰ τοῦ προσώ-
uultu tuo, hoc est, 'in fruitione   που σου]· ἀντὶ τοῦ· 'ἐν ἀπολαύσει
uitae me constituisti.' similiter   με τῆς ζωῆς κατέστησας.' ὁμοίως
autem et quod dixit, *ut possitis*   δὲ καὶ τὸ ἐξισχύσητε καταλαβέσθαι
25   *comprehendere;* 'ut in fruitione   τὸ ἐν ἀπολαύσει καταστῆναι τοῦ
(inquit) rerum consistatis.' et   πράγματος λέγει. καὶ τοῦτο δεί-
hoc ostendit ex illo quod [ait],   κνυσιν διὰ τοῦ σὺν τοῖς ἁγίοις. τὸ
cum sanctis. nam 'latitudinem   δὲ πλάτος καὶ μῆκος καὶ βάθος καὶ
et longitudinem et profundum   ὕψος, ἵνα εἴπῃ τῆς χάριτος τὸ μέγε-
30   et altitudinem,' ut dicat gratiae   θος ἀπὸ τῶν παρ' ἡμῶν ὀνομάτων.
magnitudinem ex illis nomini-   'εὔχομαι τοίνυν ὥστε ὑμᾶς συναπο-
bus quae apud nos esse magna   λαῦσαι τοῖς ἁγίοις τῆς οὕτως με-
uidentur. 'oro (inquit) ut frua-   γάλης καὶ θαυμαστῆς δωρεᾶς τοῦ
mini cum sanctis illa tam magna   θεοῦ, ἣν πολλὴ τοῦ Χριστοῦ περὶ
35   et demiratione digna donatione   ἡμᾶς ἀγάπη παρέσχεν ἡμῖν.'
Dei quam praestitit nobis cari-

1 et *(for* ea 2°) *C*   6   confortare *CH*   7   fidem *H*   17   sq. Coisl. 204, f. 78 a
[Cr. vi. 163, Fr. 134] Θεόδωρός φησιν· τὸ γνῶναι, κ.τ.λ.   25   fruitionem *H*   27
ex illud quod cum s. *C* H* illud quod ait c. s. *C (corr.)*

exceedingly magnificent, I constantly bend my knees to the Father of Christ, whom every association, whether *in the heavens* or *on earth* calls its own Father and considers him to be Lord."*

What does he pray for from him?

3:16–17 *that, according to the riches of his glory, he may grant that you may be strengthened in your inner man with power through his Spirit, and that Christ may dwell in your hearts through faith, as you are being rooted and grounded in love,*

"I pray (he says) from him that according to his kindness he may bestow on you the grace of the Spirit to strengthen you in your faith in Christ, so that he may be thought to dwell in your souls when you have a love for him as solid as possible, like a root or a foundation." And he adds something else:

3:18–19a *that you may be able to comprehend, with all the saints, what is the breadth and length and depth and height,*[46] *and to know the love of Christ that surpasses knowledge,*

[161] For when he says *know*, he means "enjoy," since he is speaking of the knowledge of those realities, as in the psalm (15:11): *You have made known to me the paths of life; you will fill me with joy with your countenance*; that is, "you have established me in the enjoyment of life." And similarly he said *that you may be able to comprehend*, to mean "that you may stand fast in the enjoyment of the realities." And he shows this by saying *with the saints*, for *the breadth and length and depth and height* mean the great-

He says *know* instead of "enjoy," since he was speaking of the knowledge of realities, as in the psalm (15:11): *You have made known to me the paths of life; [you will fill me with joy with your countenance]*, that is, "you have established me in the enjoyment of life." And similarly he said *that you may have the power to comprehend* to mean standing fast in the enjoyment of the reality. And he shows this by saying *with the saints*, for *the breadth and length and depth and height* mean the greatness of the grace, indicated by our

---

[46]The reversal of "height" and "depth" also occurs in the commentary and in Chrysostom and Theodoret.

tas Christi, multa erga nos existens.'*
et quod lucrum ex hoc erit nobis?
   ut adimpleamini in omnem plenitudinem Dei.
5   'ita ut et ipsi in portione communis corporis uideamini, in quod
uel maxime inhabitat Deus.' et orat taliter pro illis. post propositam gratiae narrationem concludit dogmaticos sermones sub specie gratiarum actionis, eo quod et sub tali specie expositionem eorum fecisse uidetur. quibus adicit:
10   *ei autem qui potens est super omnia facere superabundanter quae*
petimus aut intellegimus, secundum uirtutem quam inoperatus est in
nobis; ipsi gloria in ecclesia in Christo Iesu, in omnes progenies saeculi
saeculorum. amen.
   'praestabit enim ista Deus qui potens est et ista et ampliora fa-
15   cere ab illis quae petimus et intellegimus, qui in illis quae per Christum erga ecclesiam facta sunt per singulas generationes et per
omne saeculum gloriosus esse et uidetur et uidebitur.' nam quod
dixit, *ei autem qui potens est super omnia facere*, dictum est *autem*
χατ᾽ ἔλλειψιν. quod enim uult dicere, iam in praecedentibus a no-
20   bis dictum est manifestius.
   obsecro ergo uos ego uinctus in Domino.
   dogmaticos sermones hucusque consummans, incipit hic ethicos. et primum quidem illis disputat de caritate et concordia quam
erga se debent in inuicem exercere; quam et maxime omnibus il-
25   lis plus esse necessariam existimat, omni in loco de illa dispu-

5   et ipsi et *C*   6   post *om H*   7   dogmatico sermone *H*   14   et ista *om C*
‖   et ampliora *om H*   17   omnem *C**   ‖   uideretur (*for* uidetur) *C**   18-19
dictum est autem catelipsin *C** (catalipsin *C* (*corr.*)) dictum est catelipsin *H*   19
tam (*for* iam) *H*   21   autem (*for* ergo) *H*   22   hic *om H*   24   in (*bef.* inuicem)
om H   25   illud *H*

ness of grace indicated by our usage of these words. "I pray (he says) that you may enjoy with the saints such great and marvelous things by God's gift, which Christ's love bestowed on us, since his love is abundant toward us."*

usage of these words. "Therefore, I pray that you may enjoy with the saints so great and marvelous a gift of God, a gift the great love of Christ for us has bestowed on us."

And what profit will we have from this?

3:19b *that you may be filled with all the fullness of God.*

"So that we ourselves may be seen in our share of the common body in [162] which God dwells to the greatest possible extent." This is how he prays for them. After setting forth his account of grace, he concludes his doctrinal discussions in the form of a thanksgiving, because he plainly constructed his exposition of these themes in such a form.[47] He adds to them:

3:20–21 *And to him who is able to accomplish more than abundantly above all we ask or understand, according to the power that has been at work[48] in us, to him be glory in the church in Christ Jesus to all generations of the ages of ages. Amen.*

"For God will bestow these things because he is able to accomplish them, and more than what we ask or understand; and he is both seen and will be seen to be glorious in what has been accomplished for the church through Christ generation after generation and through every age." For when he said *and to him who is able to accomplish above all,* he said *and* as an ellipsis.[49] For we have explained more clearly above what he wants to say.

[163] 4:1a *I, therefore, the prisoner in the Lord, entreat you*

At this point he completes his doctrinal discussions and begins his moral ones. First of all he reasons with them about love and the concord they ought to practice with one another. He thinks

---

[47]Swete's note (1:162) reads in part: "Theodore means to say: 'The *gratiae narratio* which formed the substance of the *dogmatici sermones* ends (iii.20) as it began (i.3) with a *gratiarum actio.*'"

[48]The translation, missing the force of the present participle in Greek, may use the past tense to conform to Theodore's interpretation, but, as Swete also suggests (1:162), there may be a "reminiscence" of 1:20.

[49]See Swete's note (1:162): "I.e. 'The δέ is elliptical; it glances back at the various reasons for thanksgiving upon which the Ap. has enlarged in the preceding chapters.'"

tans. optimum equidem principium ab exhortatione et obsecratione sumpsisse uidetur. scit enim magis ad reuerentiam inuitare
tali exhortatione, maxime quia et adiecit, *uinctus in Domino;* siquidem et ipsa uincula propter praedicationem habere uidetur. cum
5 quibus et obsecratur eos dicens:

    ut digne ambuletis uocatione qua uocati estis.

et hoc dicens ad uerecundiam eos inuitat; si tamen propriae uocationi digna illos agere deprecatur. quid autem est quod postulat?

    cum omni humilitate et mansuetudine, cum patientia, sustinentes
10 *in inuicem in caritate.*

quoniam hoc dicebat, quia Christus equidem diuinam habens
in se naturam, tamen multa humilitate abusus omnia uoluit pro
nostra pati salute. hoc ergo dicit conueniens esse uocatione, ita
ut Christi imitantes humilitatem sustineant se inuicem, etiam etsi
15 delinquere aliquem aliquando extiterit. bene autem in ultimo posuit *in caritate,* eo quod si hanc habeant inter se, et humilitatem
et mansuetudinem et patientiam et omnia in opere ostendere poterint.

    adcelerantes seruare unitatem Spiritus, in uinculo pacis.

20 omni ex parte illis necessariam esse ostendit concordiam et caritatem. 'ab Spiritu enim regenerati, unum quod facti estis. hanc
igitur unitatem inlibatam custodite; conligate uobis inuicem per
pacem et caritatem.' unde et multis modis ostendere nititur quoniam necessarius sit illis consensus:

25   *unum corpus, et unus Spiritus.*

    †'Spiritus, qui uos regene-   πνεῦμα, τὸ ἀναγεννῆσαν· σῶμα,
rauit; corpus uero, in quod per   εἰς ὅπερ διὰ τῆς ἀναγεννήσεως
regenerationem consistere uide-   κατέστητε.
mini.'*

30   *sicut et uocati estis in una spe uocationis uestrae.*

    †'una enim proposita est spes   μία [γὰρ] πρόκειται ἡ τῶν
nobis illorum quae expectamus.'* προσδοκωμένων ἐλπίς.

    unus Dominus, una fides, unum baptisma.

---

7 proprie uocatione *C*   10 in (*bef.* inuicem) *om H*   13 uocationi *C* (*corr.*)
uocationem *H*   19 uirtutem (*for* unit.) *C H*   21 quod *om H*   26 Coisl. 204,
f. 79 a [Cr. vi. 165, Fr. 134] Θεόδωρος δέ φησιν· πνεῦμα, κ.τ.λ. The edd. punctuate (but ag. cod.), πν. τὸ ἀναγεννῆσαν σῶμα, εἰς, κ.τ.λ.   27 inquit (*for* in
quod) *C H*   ‖ unum (*aft.* in quod) *add H: txt g*   32 illorumque *C**

concord is more necessary and especially for all of them, reasoning about it everywhere. He certainly has plainly taken the best point of departure from his exhortation and entreaty. For he knows how to induce people all the more to deference, especially because he added *the prisoner in the Lord*—and he certainly is seen to have those chains because of his preaching. With them he entreats them, saying:

4:1b *that you may walk worthily in the calling by which you have been called,*

By saying this he induces them to shame, at least if he is begging them to do what is worthy of their own calling. But what is he demanding?

4:2 *with all humility and gentleness, with patience, supporting one another in love,*

He said this because Christ, even though he had the divine nature in himself, nevertheless made use of everything with much humility and was willing to suffer for our salvation. Therefore, he says that this is what befits their calling, so that by imitating Christ's humility they may support one another even if someone at some time should be found to have transgressed. And he rightly put *in love* last, because if they were to have love among themselves, they would be able to show it at work in humility, gentleness, endurance, and everything.

4:3 *being eager to keep the unity of the Spirit in the bond of peace.*

[164] In every respect he shows that concord and love are necessary for them. "For you have been born anew by the Spirit, and you have been made one. Therefore, guard this unity unimpaired. Bind yourselves together through peace and love." Thus, he strives in many ways to show that agreement is necessary for them:

4:4a *There is one body and one Spirit,*

†"The Spirit because he has given you new birth, and the body in which you are seen established by the new birth.*

The Spirit that gave new birth, the body into which you have been established by the new birth.

4:4b *just as you were called in one hope of your calling,*

†"For there is one hope of what we await set forth for us.*

[For] one hope of what is awaited lies before.

4:5 *one Lord, one faith, one baptism,*

"Thus, you are in no part divided, but all things are common

'sic nulla ex parte estis diuisi, sed omnia uobis sunt communia.'
unus Deus et Pater omnium.

euidens est quoniam

†neque *unus Dominus* dicens, ad
5 interceptionem Patris dicit; neque *unus Deus* dicens, ad interceptionem Filii dicit. sed tamquam si ut dicat: 'non diuersos dominos, neque diuersos deos
10 esse existimamus. inseparabilis enim apud nos est et deitatis et dominationis confessio. nec enim essentias diuidimus secundum numerum personarum, sed similiter scimus ado-
15 rare.'*

μήτε τὸ εἷς κύριος ἐπ' ἀναιρέσει τοῦ πατρὸς νοητέον, μήτε τὸ εἷς θεὸς ἐπ' ἀναιρέσει τοῦ υἱοῦ. ἀλλ' ἵνα εἴπῃ· 'οὐ διαφόρους κυρίους οὐδὲ διαφόρους νομίζομεν θεούς· ἀδιάσπαστος γὰρ ἡμῖν τῆς θεότητος καὶ τῆς κυριότητος ἡ ὁμολογία, οὐ διαιρουμένων τῶν γνωμῶν ἡμῶν κατὰ τὸν τῶν προσώπων ἀριθμόν, ἀλλὰ τὴν ὁμοίαν ἀποδιδόντων προσκύνησιν.'

qui super omnes et per omnia et in omnibus nobis.

†qui omnibus supereminet:
hoc enim dicit *super omnes.* quia
20 *et per omnia* nobis suam ostendit
prouidentiam, *in omnibus* quoque *nobis* et esse et habitare creditur. et quoniam per omnia ista ostendit illis necessariam
25 esse concordiam, uidebatur autem quaedam eis inesse differentia ob gratiarum uarietatem:
unicuique autem nostrum data est gratia secundum mensuram
30 *donationis Christi.*

ὁ ἐπὶ πάντων δέ, ἵνα εἴπῃ 'ὁ πάντων ὑπερέχων καὶ διὰ πάντων ἡμῶν τὴν οἰκείαν ἐπιδεικνύμενος πρόνοιαν, ἐν πᾶσίν τε ἡμῖν εἶναι καὶ οἰκεῖν πιστευόμενος.' καὶ ἐπειδὴ διὰ πάντων ἔδειξεν αὐτοῖς τὴν ὁμόνοιαν, ἐδόκει δέ τις αὐτοῖς εἶναι διαφορὰ ἀπὸ τῆς τῶν χαρισμάτων ποικιλίας, ἐπιφέρει·

ἑνὶ δὲ ἑκάστῳ ἡμῶν ἐδόθη ἡ χάρις κατὰ τὸ μέτρον τῆς δωρεᾶς τοῦ χριστοῦ.

'si autem propriam quandam gratiam spiritalem unusquisque nostrum habet, differentia uero facta est, prout suum donum
35 unicuique nostrum dominus di-

εἰ δὲ ἴδιόν τι χάρισμα ἕκαστος ἡμῶν ἔχει, ἡ διαφορὰ γέγονεν καθὼς τὴν ἑαυτοῦ δωρεὰν ἑκάστῳ ἡμῶν ὁ δεσπότης ἐπεμέτρησεν Χριστός. ὅ τε γὰρ δεδωκὼς ἡμῖν,

4 Coisl. 204, f. 80 b [Cr. vi. 168, Fr. 134 –5] Θεόδωρος δέ φησιν· μήτε, κ.τ.λ. 5
dicit (1°) *om H* 7-8 sed uel quasi [+ ut *corr.*] dicat nec diu. *H* 13 uidemur
(*for* diuid.) *C** diuidemus *C* (*corr.*) *H* 23 super *H* 26 inesse eis *H*

among you."

4:6a *one God and Father of all,*

It is clear that

†when he says *one Lord*, he does not mean to exclude the Father, nor when he says *one God* does he mean [165] to exclude the Son. But it is as if he were saying: "We do not suppose there to be separate Lords or separate Gods. For the confession of divinity and lordship is undivided for us. For we do not divide essences according to the number of the persons, but we know how to worship them alike."*

4:6b *who is above all and through all and in all of us.*[50]

†Who excels all, for this is what *above all* means, and *through all* demonstrates his providence toward us; and he is also believed both to be and to dwell *in all* of us. And since he demonstrated that in all respects concord was necessary for them, but there seemed to be some difference among them because of the diversity of gifts:

4:7 *But to each one of us grace was given according to the measure of Christ's gift,*

"But if each one of us has some spiritual grace of his own, the difference is made insofar as the Lord Christ saw fit to distribute his gift to each one of

One Lord must not be understood to exclude the Father nor *one God* to exclude the Son. Rather, he means "we do not suppose these are different Lords or different Gods, for our confession of divinity and lordship is undivided, since our judgments are not divided according to the number of the persons, but we ascribe a like worship."

who is above all means the one who excels all, and *through all* demonstrates his characteristic providence toward us; and he is believed to be and to dwell *in all* of us. And since he demonstrated that in all respects concord was necessary for them, but there seemed to be some difference among them because of the diversity of gifts, he continues:

4:7 *But to each one of us grace was given according to the measure of Christ's gift,*

But if each one of us has some gift of his own, the difference has taken place just as the Lord Christ has measured out his own gift to each one of us.

---

[50] I am unaware of any manuscript evidence for the addition of *nobis* ("all of us"), but it reflects Theodore's comment here and on the verse that follows.

mittere dignatus est Christus.   εἰς· καὶ τὸ δοθὲν ἡμῖν πνεῦμα, ἕν.
nam is qui dedit nobis unus est;
et qui datus est nobis Spiritus
unus.'*

5   deinde profert uerbum, docens etiam qualiter dedit, aut si habuit dandi potestatem; de illo dicens qui secundum carnem est
Christus, sicuti et ipsa sequentia ostendit:
   propter quod dicit: 'ascendens in altum captiuam duxit captiuitatem, dedit dona hominibus.'

10   hoc quidem iacet in psalmo; utitur autem hoc testimonium non
quasi prophetice dictum, sed sicut nos in ecclesiastica allocutione
scripturalibus frequenter solemus uti testimoniis.

†denique et commutans illud   ὑπαλλάξας δὲ τὸ ἔλαβεν δόματα,
quod in psalmo positum fuerat: οὕτως ἐν τῷ ψαλμῷ κείμενον, ἔδω
15   *accepisti dona, dedisti dona* di   κεν δόματα εἶπεν, τῇ ὑπαλλαγῇ
xit, demutatione uerbi ob fir   πρὸς τὴν οἰκείαν χρησάμενος ἀκοmitatem suae est usus prosecu   λουθίαν· ἐκεῖ μὲν γὰρ πρὸς τὴν ὑπόtionis. illic enim ad explanan   θεσιν τὸ ἔλαβεν ἥρμοττεν, ἐνταῦdum negotium aptum erat *ac   θα δὲ τῷ προκειμένῳ τὸ ἔδωκεν
20   cepisti*. hic uero praecedentibus   ἀκόλουθον ἦν. βούλεται δὲ εἰπεῖν
consequens erat dicere *dedisti*.   ὅτι ἀγῶνα ὑπὲρ ἡμῶν ἐνστησάμενος
uult enim dicere quoniam 'cer   πρὸς τὸν διάβολον καὶ ὥσπερ ποtamen pro nobis aduersus dia   λέμου νόμῳ νικήσας αὐτόν, ἐπειδὴ
bolum arripiens, et tamquam   ἀφεῖλεν ἑαυτὸν τοῦ θανάτου πρό
25   lege belli uincens eum (eo quod   τερος ἀναστάς, κοινὴν ἐπὶ πάντων
et subtraxit se a morte, primus   ἡμῶν τοῦ θανάτου τὴν λύσιν ἐποιex mortuis resurgens), commu   ήσατο· ὥσπερ αἰχμαλώτους τινὰς
nem nobis omnibus mortis ex   τοὺς ἀνθρώπους καὶ ὑπὸ τὴν τοῦ
pediit solutionem; quasi cap   διαβόλου τυραννίδα κατεχομένους,
30   tiuos quosdam nos homines et   τῆς ἐκείνου καταδυναστείας αὐτοὺς
sub diaboli tyrannide retenta   ἀφελὼν ἀνῆλθεν εἰς τοὺς οὐρανούς.
tos, ab eius eripuit impressione. sicque pro hominibus omnibus aduersus diabolum de
35   certans, uictoriam obtinuit; et

1 Chr. dign. est *H*   7 Christum *C H*   10 ita et (*for* iacet) *H*   11 prophetiae *C*   12 solumus *C**   16 περὶ (*for* πρὸς) edd.   21 ἐνστησόμενος Cr. ὁ
Χριστὸς add. Fr.   23 uobis *C**   26 subtraxisse *C**   27 καὶ ὥσπερ Fr.   31
ἀνῆγεν Fr.

us. [166] For he who gave it to us is one, and the Spirit that is given to us is one.*

For he who gave to us is one, and the Spirit given to us is one.

Then he sets forth a scriptural verse, teaching as well how Christ gave or on what basis he had the power of giving. He is speaking of the one who is Christ according to the flesh, as he shows in the very words that follow:

4:8 *Therefore, it says* (Ps 67:19): *"When he ascended on high, he led captivity captive; he gave gifts to humans."*

To be sure, this verse is found in the psalm, but Paul uses this testimony not as it was spoken prophetically but as we are often accustomed to use scriptural testimonies when we speak in the church.

†Then, changing what had been put down in the psalm—*you have received gifts*—he said, *you have given gifts*; he used the change in the words to confirm the logical order of his discourse. For in the psalm *you have received* was suitable for explaining the subject matter, but here it was in accord with what comes before, to mean *you have given*. He means that "by taking control of the contest [167] against the devil on our behalf and by conquering him by, so to speak, the law of war—because he rescued himself from death, rising again as the first from the dead—he brought about the general destruction of death for all of us. When we humans were like captives and were held fast by the devil's tyranny, Christ delivered us from his oppression. And so by fighting for all humans against the devil, he gained the

He changed *he received gifts*, which is what is found in the psalm, and said *he gave gifts*, using the change for his own logical order. For in the psalm *he received* was suitable for the setting. But here *he gave* was in accord with his purpose.

He wants to say that by taking control of the contest against the devil on our behalf and by conquering him by, so to speak, the law of war—because he rescued himself from death, rising again as the first—he brought about the general destruction of death for all of us. When humans were like captives and were held fast by the devil's tyranny, Christ delivered them from his oppression and ascended into the heavens.

ascendens in caelum*

et accipiens Spiritus gratiam dedit omnibus nobis, unicuique
suam gratiam secundum quod sibi placitum fuit demetiens.' et
quia incredibile erat hoc de homine dictum:

5   *quod autem ascendit, quid est, nisi quia et descendit primum in in-*
feriores partes terrae?

    nam quod dicit, *in inferiores partes terrae*, non sub terram dicit.
nam illa quae sub terra sunt, iam ultra terram esse non poterunt.
in inferiores autem *partes*, ipsam terram nominat in comparatio-
10 ne caeli. uult autem dicere quoniam non ascenderat, nisi primum
in illum diuina aliqua extitisset natura, quae etiam et super caelos
erat; cui et complacuit in illum habitare, qui super terram erat, et
super terram morabatur. deinde adicit:

    qui descendit, ipse est et qui ascendit super omnes caelos, ut impleret
15 *omnia.*

    non qui descendit ipse est et qui ascendit; quemadmodum enim
fieri poterat, ut ille qui adsumptus est homo ipse sit et qui de caelo descendit? simile est autem hoc dictum illi dicto: *nemo ascendit*
in caelum, nisi qui de caelo descendit; uult enim dicere quoniam is
20 in quem diuina descendit natura super omnes effectus est caelos,
illo ascendens; ita ut et in omnibus idem esse uideatur, omnibus
ad eum intuentibus propter inhabitantem naturam. et quoniam in
hoc sermonem adtraxit, uolens dicere unde et quomodo illi qui secundum carnem est Christo id extitit ut ista adsequeretur ita ut et
25 aliis possit tribuere spiritales donationes, recurrit iterum ad suam
illam sequentiam, dicens quomodo demetita est gratia unicuique
a Christo:

    et ipse dedit quosdam quidem apostolos, quosdam uero prophetas,
quosdam euangelistas, quosdam uero pastores et doctores, ad consum-
30 *mationem sanctorum, in opus ministerii, in aedificium corporis Chri-*
sti.

    'haec donationum (inquit) est differentia, ita ut alii quidem ista,
alii uero illa percipient ad commune incrementum dominici corporis, expedientes et illis qui per singula credunt momenta.'

35   *donec occurramus omnes in unitatem fidei et cognitionem Filii Dei*

2   bonis (*for* nobis) *H*   3   demitiens *C* H*   5   quod est *C*   9-10   incom-
parabile *H*   21   in *om C**   ‖   hominibus (*for* omn.) *C* (*corr.*)   23   sermone
C* H   24   istam *C* H*   25   diuitias (*for* donat.) *H*   33   communem *C**   ‖
domini *C**   34   quae *H*

victory. And by ascending into
heaven*
and receiving the grace of the Spirit, he gave it to all of us,
measuring out his grace to each individual according to his
pleasure." And because it was incredible that this should be said
of a man:

4:9 *And that he ascended, what is it but that he also descended first
into the lower parts of the earth?*

Now when he says *into the lower parts of the earth*, he does not
mean beneath the earth. Indeed, those places beneath the earth
would no longer be "the earth." But he names the earth itself *the
lower parts* by comparison with heaven. And he means that he
would not have ascended unless first a divine nature that was even
above the heavens had taken its existence in him. He who was
above the earth and remained above the earth was well pleased to
dwell in him. Then he adds:

[168] 4:10 *He who descended is the one who ascended above all
heavens, so that he might fill all things.*

It is not the case that the one who descended is himself also
the one who ascended. For how could it have come to pass that
the Man who was assumed should also be the one who descended
from heaven? This verse is like the one that reads (John 3:13):
*No one has ascended into heaven except the one who descended from
heaven.* What in fact he means is that he to whom the divine nature
descended was made to be above all heavens by ascending with
him [the Word], so that he might appear to be the same in all
respects, since all fixed their gaze on him because of the indwelling
nature. And when Paul drew his discourse to this point, he wanted
to say from what source and how it came to be for Christ according
to the flesh that he accomplished this so that he could bestow
spiritual gifts on others. He returns to the logical order of his
discourse and says how grace is measured out to each individual
by Christ:

4:11–12 *And he gave some to be apostles, and some prophets, some
evangelists, and some pastors and teachers for the equipping of the
saints for the work of ministry, for building up the body of Christ,*

"This diversity of gifts (he says) exists so that different people
receive different ones for the common growth of the Lord's body,
since they make provision for those who believe through each
successive moment of time."

in uirum perfectum, in mensuram aetatis plenitudinis Christi.

factum praesentem paruulum se dicit esse, ad comparationem futurorum. sic et ad Galatas scribens dicit: *quando eramus paruuli, sub elementa mundi eramus seruientes.* hoc ergo dicit, quoniam 'ipsa gratiarum differentia propter aliorum fit necessitatem, ita ut ecclesia augmentum adsequatur, usquedum per fidem et cognitionem Filii Dei congregemur ad illud perfectum quod expectamus, quando nulla in parte minus aliquid apud nos esse reperietur; omnes uero corpus extiterimus Christi, in ipso repleti et ipsum habentes in nobis perspicuum.'

cum ergo tali ex causa differentia gratiarum fiat, quid nobis faciendum est?

ut ultra non simus paruuli fluctuantes, et circumferamur omni uento doctrinae in astutia hominum, in uersutia, ad remedium erroris.

'itaque illis quae expectamus aequa utique et sapere debemus, ita ut ultra non more paruulorum abstrahamur a qualibet uentosa doctrina illorum, qui nos huc atque illuc circumducere uolunt per suam astutiam, quam et utuntur uarie, illa quae erroris sunt perficientes.'

ueritatem autem facientes in caritate, crescere faciamus in ipsum omnia qui est caput, Christus.

'ueram autem erga Christum caritatem ostendentes contineamus nos in eius affectum, sicut conuenit capiti corpus esse coniunctum.' et quoniam caput illum uocauit, ostendit quod adsint ei illa quae sunt capitis; ita ut rebus ipsis ostendat necessariam nobis esse huiusmodi copulationem ad eum:

ex quo omne corpus coaptatum et productum per omne tactum subministrationis, secundum inoperationem in mensuram uniuscuiusque partis incrementum corporis facit ad aedificium sui in caritate.

quoniam sicut de nostro capite in residuum corpus omnis uiua-

---

3 ad *om H*   4 Christi (*for* mundi) *C H*   ‖   quando (*for* quoniam) *H*   7 fili *C**   8 reperitur *C** reperiatur *H*   14 in uersutia *om C* (*corr.*)   18 qua (*for* quam) *C* (*corr.*)   ‖   errore *C**   28 operationem *C** (?)   30 sicut *om H*

4:13 *until all of us come to the unity of the faith and to the knowledge of the Son of God, to the perfect man, to the measure of the age of the fullness of Christ,*

He means that what is presently the case is quite insignificant by comparison with [169] what is to come. So he also says when he writes to the Galatians (Gal 4:3): *when we were small children, we were enslaved to the elements of the world.* Here he means that "the very difference of graces takes place because of the needs of others, so that the church may gain increase until we are gathered together by faith and the knowledge of the Son of God into that perfect body we await, when nothing that falls short of perfection will be found in us in any respect. And we shall all exist as the body of Christ, fulfilled in him and having him clearly visible in us."

Therefore, since the diversity of graces takes place for such a reason, what must we do?

4:14 *so that we may no longer be small children tossed to and fro and may not be carried about by every wind of doctrine, by people's trickery, by craftiness, to the false medicine of error,*[51]

"And so we must practice and think about what matches the goods we await so that we may no longer be drawn aside like small children by any windy doctrine whatsoever taught by those who want to lead us hither and thither by their trickery, which they employ in various ways to accomplish what belongs to error."

4:15 *but doing the truth in love, let us make everything grow into him who is the head, Christ,*

"And by showing true love for Christ, let us persevere in our affection for him, just as the body must be joined to the head." And since he called him the head, he shows that what belongs to the head applies to him, so that by the facts themselves he may show that we need such a union with him:

[170] 4:16 *from whom the whole body, joined together and brought forth through every sinew*[52] *of its equipment, according to the working of each part in its measure, causes the growth of the body for the building up of himself in love.*

---

[51] *Ad remedium erroris.* Swete's note (1:169) points out that "*Remedium* is the O.L. rendering of μεθοδεία (in the sense of a *nostrum*, 'quack-medicine' ...)."

[52] See Theodore's comment on 2:20b-22 and note 39. Here he apparently understands ἀφή to mean "sinew" rather than "touch."

citatis fertur uirtus, ex quo unumquodque membrorum et uiuit et
mouetur et reliquo corpori est coaptatum; sic et spiritalis gratia
in nobis quasi de capite Christo aduenit, per quam gratiam regenerationis in uno corpore sic ad eum communionem suscepimus.
5 membrorum differentiam in gratiarum differentia ostendens. hoc
enim dicit, quia 'ex ipso Christo quasi de capite copulatur et continetur nouum ecclesiae corpus, secundum ut in unoquoque nostrum spiritalis efficitur inoperatio, quam unusquisque nostrum
inenarrabili quadam ratione suscipiens in communi suum prae-
10 stat ministerium.' nam quod dixit: *in aedificium sui in caritate*, de
Christo dicit; ut dicat quoniam 'ita facit Christus propter proprii
corporis aedificium ob illam caritatem quam erga nos habere uidetur;' ostendat uero per ista quoniam differentiam gratiarum, non
necessitatem diuisionis imponit; non solum quia unus est Chri-
15 stus, et unus nobis ista tribuit, sed et unum quoddam corpus suum
omnes spiritali effecti regeneratione.

et quoniam communis est omnium necessitas, unoquoque hoc
quod potest in communi conferente, ita ut nec ille qui infirmam uidetur habere gratiam, minus esse ad communem existimetur per-
20 fectionem, siquidem et in corpore membrorum unam constat esse naturam; insuper etiam et communem de omnibus membris
habemus sollicitudinem, omnia similiter ad stabilitatem communis corporis perficere existimantes; et propter hoc nullum nostrae
prouidentiae indignum esse arbitramur, utpote minimum ab illis.
25 et quoniam ob gratiarum differentiam quae uidebantur esse illa
quae conueniebant edixit, adicit:

hoc ergo dico et testificor in Domino.

necessarie posuit *testificor*, post praecedentium probationem,
in quibus omni ex parte ostendit necessarium illis esse consensum.
30 *ita ut ultra non ambuletis, sicut et ceterae gentes ambulant in ua-*
nitate mentis suae, excaecati intellectu, abalienati a uita Dei propter
ignorantiam quae est in illis, propter caecitatem cordis eorum.

†hoc dicit compendiose, quo-   τοῦτο λέγει συντόμως· 'οὐ δί-

5 differentiam (*for* differentia) C* 6-7 continet H 8-9 qua in uniuscuiusque n. inenarrabile [-i C (*corr.*)] quadam [quaedam H] rat. susc. C H 11 ista
(*for* ita) C (*corr.*) 13 quam (*for* quoniam) C 17 unumquemque C H 18 hi
firmam C* infirma H 19 gratia H ‖ minimus (*for* minus) C 20-21 una,
natura C 29 quo H 33 sq. Coisl. 204, f. 85 a [Cr. vi. 177, Fr. 135] Θεόδωρος
δέ φησιν· τοῦτο, κ.τ.λ.

This is because just as there is brought down from our head to the rest of the body the entire vital force by which each one of our members lives and is moved and is joined to the rest of the body, so, too, spiritual grace comes to us from Christ as our head. It is by this grace of rebirth that we so receive fellowship with him in one body. He shows the diversity of the members in the diversity of graces. For he means that "from Christ himself, as from the head, the new body of the church is joined and held together by the fact that in each one of us there is effected the spiritual working that each one of us receives by some ineffable principle, and by which he supplies his own ministry for the common good." For when he said *for the building up of himself in love,* he is speaking of Christ. He means that "Christ works this way to build up his own body because of the love he is seen to have for us." And Paul says this to demonstrate that the diversity of graces does not involve the necessity of division, not only because Christ is one and as one has bestowed these gifts on us, but also because we have all been made his one body by spiritual rebirth.

And what is needed is common to all, while each individual [171] contributes what he can to the common good, so that even the one who appears to have a weak grace may not be considered to fall short of the common perfection, assuming that it is agreed that there is a single nature of the members in the body. Furthermore, we have a common concern for all the members, since we think that all of them alike work to perfect the steadfastness of the common body. For this reason we judge that no one is unworthy of our oversight, not even the least of them.

And since he has declared what was plainly suitable because of the diversity of graces, he adds:

4:17a *Therefore, I say this and testify in the Lord,*

He necessarily put down *I testify* after the preceding proof, in which in every respect he demonstrated that it was necessary for them to agree.

4:17b-18 *so that you may no longer walk as the other Gentiles walk in the futility of their mind, blinded in their understanding, alienated from the life of God because of the ignorance that is in them, because of the blindness of their heart,*

| †He says this concisely: "It is not right for you to behave like the Gentiles, who know nothing | He says this concisely: "It is not right for you to do what accords with the Gentiles, who |

niam 'non est iustum uos ad similitudinem gentium agere, qui
nihil sciunt de illis quae sibi conueniunt, sed tamquam in te-
5 nebris ambulantes et a pietate
elongauerunt, et a Dei uita alieni sunt effecti;' ut dicat, 'a resurrectione illa quae fieri expectatur.'*

καιον ὑμᾶς ἀκόλουθα πράττειν τοῖς
ἔθνεσιν, οἳ μηδὲν ἐπιστάμενοι τῶν
δεόντων ὥσπερ ἐν σκότει διάγου-
σιν, τῆς εὐσεβείας μακρὰν τυγχά-
νοντες καὶ τῆς τοῦ θεοῦ ζωῆς ἀλ-
λότριοι καθεστῶτες·' ἵνα εἴπῃ, τῆς
προσδοκωμένης ἀναστάσεως.

10 quid uero illi?

  *qui desperantes semetipsos tradiderunt impudicitiae, in operatio-
nem omnis immunditiae et auaritiae.*

    bene
†dixit *desperantes*, ex illa ratio-
15 ne illud sumens qua solent saepe aliqua membra passione corporis mortificari; quibus exinde non solum dolor nullus adnascitur, sed neque membri ip-
20 sius excisio sensum aliquod illis
praestare uidetur.*

τὸ δὲ ἀπηλγηκότες ὥσπερ τῶν ἀπὸ
πάθους τινὸς μέρη πολλάκις τοῦ
σώματος νενεκρωμένων, οἷς οὐ μόνον ἄλγος οὐδὲν ἐκεῖθεν ἐγγίνεται,
ἀλλ' οὐδὲ ἡ τοῦ μέρους ἀφαίρεσις
αἴσθησιν ἐμποιεῖ.

'illi (inquit) neque malorum illorum quae agunt sensum suscipere
uolunt, in omnem actum prauum semel seipsos ingurgitantes.' et
cum multa expressione illa quae illorum fuerant edicens, contra-
25 sistit sua:

  *uos autem non ita didicistis Christum, si tamen illum audistis, et
in illo docti estis, sicut est ueritas in Iesu.*

    nam quod dixit *si tamen illum audistis*, hoc est, 'necessarie eum
audistis;' sicut et in superioribus, *si audistis dispensationem gratiae
30 Dei quae data est mihi in uobis.*

†hoc enim dicit, quoniam 'omni
ex parte *audistis et docti estis*
de Christo ista, quae et uera
consistunt et sic se habent.'*

τοῦτο λέγει, ὅτι 'πάντως ποῦ καὶ
ἠκούσατε καὶ ἐδιδάχθητε περὶ τοῦ
Χριστοῦ ταῦτα· ἅπερ δὴ καὶ ἀληθῆ
καθέστηκεν καὶ οὕτως ἔχει.'

35 *deponere uos secundum pristinam conuersationem ueterem homi-*

of what is right for them, but walking as though in darkness have both wandered far from true religion [172] and have been made alien from the life of God." He means "from the resurrection that is awaited to take place."*

because they know nothing of what they ought to do live as if in darkness, being far from true religion and made alien from the life of God." He means "from the resurrection that is awaited."

But what about the Gentiles?

4:19 *who by despairing*[53] *have handed themselves over to unchastity, to the working of every uncleanness and greed.*

Rightly †he said *by despairing*, taking the expression from that cause by which some members of the body are often wont to be deadened to feeling. Because of this not only does no pain arise in them, but not even the amputation of the member seems to give them any sensation.*

By having lost sensitivity, just as when people in parts of their body are often deadened to feeling, not only does no pain come to them from this member, but not even the amputation of the member causes sensation.

"These people (he says) are unwilling to accept any sense of those evil deeds they commit, once they have immersed themselves in every possible perverse deed." And declaring quite openly what their behavior was like, he contrasted it with his own:

4:20–21 *But you have not so learned Christ, if at any rate you have heard him and been taught in him, as truth is in Jesus,*

When he said *if at any rate you have heard him*, he means "you have necessarily heard him," as above he says (3:2): *if*[54] *you have heard of the dispensation of God's grace that was given me for you.*

†For he says this because [173] "in all respects *you have heard and been taught* those things that concern Christ, which both are established as true and are thus the case."*

He says this because "you have somehow inevitably both heard and been taught those things that concern Christ, which both are established as true and are the case."

---

[53] See Swete's comment (1:172): "It is strange that Th.'s exposition has not compelled the translator to abandon at least in the comm. this inadequate rendering of ἀπηλγηκότες." The verb can, of course, mean "be despondent," but Theodore clearly understands it to mean "cease to feel pain."

[54] *Si* rather than *si tamen*, as in the text of 3:2 above.

nem, qui corrumpitur secundum concupiscentiam erroris; renouamini
autem spiritu mentis uestrae, et induite uos nouum hominem, qui se-
cundum Deum creatus est in iustitia et sanctitate et ueritate.

†et quod mortales sequitur
5 ut peccent, inmortales uero effecti in futuro saeculo peccare
ultra non poterimus; forma autem illius est spiritalis regeneratio quam in baptismate implere
10 uidemur, quasi hinc iam recreati
et secundum formam regenerati
spe illorum quae et fieri expectamus; hoc dicit quoniam 'non
ignoratis solutum quidem esse
15 ueterem illum hominem mortalem. nouus uero quidam pro
illo indutus est incorruptus, in
cuius formam illam quae in baptismate est [renouationem] per-
20 cepistis, simul et primitias Spiritus accipientes. itaque iustum
est uos consentanee illis et sapere et conuersari,*

ἐπειδὴ τοῖς θνητοῖς ἕπεται τὸ
ἁμαρτάνειν, ἀθάνατοι δὲ γενόμενοι
ἐπὶ τοῦ μέλλοντος αἰῶνος ἁμαρτεῖν οὐκ ἐπιδεχόμεθα· σύμβολον δὲ
ἐκείνου ἡ τοῦ πνεύματος ἀναγέννη-
σις ἣν ἐν τῷ βαπτίσματι πληροῦμεν, ὥσπερ ἀνακτιζόμενοι ἐντεῦθεν
ἤδη καὶ ἀναγεννώμενοι κατὰ τύπον
ἐλπίδι τῶν προσδοκωμένων· τοῦτο
λέγει, ὅτι 'πάντως οὐκ ἀγνοεῖτε ὅτι
λέλυται μὲν ὁ παλαιὸς ἄνθρωπος ὁ
θνητὸς ἐκεῖνος, καινὸς δέ τις ἀντε-
πεισῆκται ἄφθαρτος, οὗπερ εἰς τύπον ἐπὶ τοῦ βαπτίσματος ἀνακαι-
νισμὸν ἐδέξασθε, τὴν τοῦ πνεύματος ἀπαρχὴν κομισάμενοι. ὥστε δίκαιον ὑμᾶς ἀκόλουθα τούτοις καὶ
φρονεῖν καὶ πολιτεύεσθαι.'

qui maxime cum Spiritus regeneratione etiam sensus renouatio-
25 nem estis adsecuti, et ueterem conuersationem deponentes cum
omni ueteri actu secundum omnem iustitiam conuersamini.' haec
enim omnia secundum interiectionem magis ab illo sunt dicta. de
consensu enim disputans illis interiecit, id est, illa quae [de] differentia erant gratiarum. iterum regressus est ad propositum suum
30 ut de caritate disputaret. unde et adicit:

propter quod deponentes mendacium, loquimini ueritatem unusqui-
sque cum proximo suo.

mendacium et *ueritatem* hoc in loco non uerborum dicit; sed

2 autem *om C** 14 solum tum (*for* solutum) *H* 18 illa *C H* 19 renouationem *om C H* 22 conuersare *C* 28 de *om C H* 30 disputet *H*

4:22–24 that you put away according to the former way of life the old man that is corrupted according to the lust of error and be renewed in the spirit of your mind and clothe yourselves with the new man, which is created according to God in righteousness and holiness and truth.

†And this is because it is a consequence for mortals that they should sin, but when we are made immortal in the age to come, we shall no longer be able to sin. And the spiritual rebirth that we are seen to fulfill in baptism is a type of this, since from it we are already created anew and born again in type by the hope of what we look forward to taking place. For this reason he says that "you are not unaware that the old mortal man has been destroyed, but the new man, put on instead of the old man, is uncorrupted, and it is in his type that you have received new birth in baptism [174], receiving at the same time the firstfruits of the Spirit. And so it is right for you to think and to live in accordance with these things,*

Since to sin is a consequence for mortals, but when we become immortal in the age to come, we shall not admit the possibility of sinning. And the rebirth of the Spirit that we fulfill in baptism is a token of this, since from it we are already created anew and born again in type by the hope of what we expect. For this reason he says that "you are certainly not unaware that the old man, that mortal one, has been destroyed, but that a new incorruptible one has been introduced in its place, in whose type you have received the renewal in baptism by acquiring the firstfruits of the Spirit. As a result, it is right for you to think and to live in accordance with these things.

since as much as possible you have also acquired the renewal of your mind together with the rebirth of the Spirit, and by putting away your old way of life with every old deed, you live according to all righteousness." Indeed, he said all this rather parenthetically, for he inserted it into his argument about concord, that is, about what had to do with the diversity of graces.[55] Again he returned to the argument he proposed about love. And so he adds:

4:25a Therefore, putting away falsehood, let each one of us speak the truth with his neighbor,

---

[55] The insertion appears to be 4:17–24.

ut dicat, 'omnem simulationem et hypocrisin deponite; perfecta mente uobis in inuicem narrate.' et magis magisque suadens eis, adiecit:

quoniam sumus alterutrum membra.

5   prudenter simul omnem contradictionem exclusit, et ex ipsa differentia dictorum suorum probationem fecisse uidetur. ideo non dixit: 'corpus sumus.' sed *membra;* eo quod et membrorum illorum quae ad nos pertinere uidentur multam sollicitudinem habemus, partes communes corporis similiter omnia illa esse existi-
10 mantes.

   deinde condescendens docet eos modeste; eo quod uidebat etiam tristitias inter eos commoueri, utpote inter homines:

irascimini (inquit) *et nolite peccare.*

'sed etsi ad iram commoueris, non tamen ad peccatum exire de-
15 bes et prorumpere, iniustum aliquid aduersus proximum tuum faciens.' et ut ne uideatur concedere iram sine iniustitia exerceri, terminum irae statuit, dicens:

sol non occidat super iracundiam uestram.

bene cum diei et operum termino etiam finem illorum quae ex
20 ira adnasci solent fecisse uidetur. et rei ipsius utilitatem ostendens adicit:

et nolite locum dare diabolo.

'si (inquit) in longum tetenderis iram, accipit locum diabolus, ut et ad iniustitiam te propellat.'

25   et quoniam perfectum de concordia et caritate sermonem reddit, profert iterum et de illis exhortationem, de plurimis et necessariis illis disceptans:

*qui furabatur iam non furetur; magis autem laboret operando quod bonum est manibus suis, ut habeat retribuere ei qui necessitatem susti-
30 net.*

bene a persona furis retulit dicens, *magis autem laboret operando quod bonum est manibus suis.* si enim non potest operari necessaria, nec furtum facere poterit; si autem potest, melius est laborare illum operantem, ut et aliis tribuere possit. non enim in commu-
35 ne posuit legem operandi aduersus omnes, uel maxime illos qui

3 adicit *C* 7 sum *C** 11 ueniebat *C** eueniebat *C* (*corr.*) 15 contra prox. (*om* tuum) *H* 16 sine iniustitiam *C** siue in. *C* (*corr.*) sine iustitia *H* 17 sterminum [*sic*] *H* 23 accepit *C** 24 ad iustitiam *H* 32 operare *C** 34 posset *C**

In this passage by *falsehood* and *truth* he is not referring to words, but he means "put away all pretense and hypocrisy; speak to one another with your mind perfected." More and more persuading them, he added:

4:25b *since we are members of one another.*

He wisely excluded all contradiction and at the same time plainly proved his point by the very diversity of his words. And so he did not say "we are a body," but we are *members*, because we have great concern for those members that are seen to belong to us, regarding them all alike as common parts of the body.

Then, stooping down, he teaches them mildly, because he saw that gloomy looks were being stirred up among them, as is natural among human beings:

4:26a *Be angry* (he says) *and do not sin;*

[175] "But even if you are stirred to anger, nevertheless, you ought not to go on and break forth into sin by committing some wrong against your neighbor." And lest he should seem to be granting that anger may be indulged without unrighteousness, he established a limit for anger, saying:

4:26b *do not let the sun go down on your anger,*

He is rightly seen to have made the end of what customarily arises from anger coincide with the end of the day and its works. And to show the benefit of the rule itself he adds:

4:27 *and do not make a place for the devil.*

"If (he says) you hold on to anger for a long time, the devil gains a place so that he may urge you on to unrighteousness."

And since he is returning to the discourse he had made about concord and love,[56] he again sets forth an exhortation about them, arguing about a good many and necessary points:

4:28 *Let the one who stole steal no longer, but let him rather toil by working what is good with his own hands so that he may have something to hand over to the one who suffers need.*

He rightly mentioned the person of a thief, saying *but let him rather toil by working what is good with his own hands.* For if he were unable to work for necessities, he would not have committed theft. But if he could, it would be better for him to toil by working

---

[56]That is, 4:1–16, which is resumed in 4:25ff. with 4:17–24 regarded as the insertion.

non possunt operari. ubi et de se propter imminentem sibi doctrinae necessitatem dicit: *numquid non habemus potestatem ut non
operemur?* et ut bonum opus erga sanctos fiat, frequenter uidetur
sollicitudinem impendere; quod utique superfluum erat facere, si
operandi lex omnibus incumbebat.

*omnis sermo nequam ex ore uestro non procedat; sed si quis bonus
ad aedificationem necessitatis, ut det gratiam audientibus.*

'inconueniens nihil nos proloqui uult, sed magis illa quae audientibus sunt utilia, quae et de necessariis sciunt iuuamen praestare; in quibus etiam et laetari conuenit eos qui audiunt.' et quod
per omnia eos possit ad reuerentiam inuitare, adiecit:

*et nolite contristare Spiritum sanctum Dei in quo signati estis in
die redemptionis.*

dein et aliam inducit exhortationem:

*omnis amaritudo et ira et indignatio et clamor et blasphemia tol-
latur a uobis cum omni malitia.*

compendiose per omnia ista cauere nos uult ab odio illo quod
in inuicem solet fieri; propter quod et adiecit:

estote in inuicem benigni, misericordes.

et quoniam illa quae adnascuntur saepe solent mentem hominis
conturbare:

donantes uobis ipsis.

deinde quia graue esse uidebatur, ut is qui nocitus est remitteret
nocenti se:

sicut et Deus (inquit) *in Christo donauit uobis.*

et confidens exemplo probato:

estote ergo imitatores Dei.

deinde et condecentem ostendens esse ipsam imitationem:
sicut filii dilecti.

1-2 necess. doctr. deo (*for* doctr. n. dicit) *H* 10 laetare *C* 11, 18 adicit *C*
14 deinde *C* (*corr.*) ‖ inducet *C*H* 17 ut (*aft.* uult) *add H* ‖ qui (*for*
quod) *C H* 19 in (*bef.* inu.) *om H* 25 nobis *H* 27 ergo *om C** 28
condecenter *H*

for what he could also hand over to others.[57] For Paul did not establish a law of working for all in common, especially for those who could not work. This is why, [176] because of the necessity of teaching that pressed upon him, he says of himself (1 Cor 9:6): *Do we not have the right not to work?* And it often appears that a concern that good work be done for the saints weighs upon him. It would, of course, be useless to do this if the law of working applied to everyone.

4:29 *Let no evil talk come out of your mouth, but only what is good for the building up of what is necessary, so that it may give grace to those who hear.*

"He wants us to speak nothing that is unsuitable, but rather words useful to those who hear them and words able to give help in their needs. And it is right that those who hear them should rejoice in these words." And because he was able in everything to induce them to a feeling of deference, he added:

4:30 *And do not grieve the Holy Spirit of God, in whom you were sealed for the day of redemption.*

Then he introduces another exhortation:

4:31 *Let all bitterness and wrath and anger and clamor and slander be taken away from you, together with all malice,*

Concisely by all these he wants us to beware of the hatred that is wont to take place with one another. Therefore, he added:

4:32a *be kind to one another, tenderhearted,*

And since those emotions that arise are often wont to disturb the human mind:

4:32b *excusing yourselves,*[58]

Then, because it seemed to be a serious matter that the one harmed should forgive the one who harmed him:

[177] 4:32c *as God also in Christ has excused you.*

And confident in the proof of the example:

5:1a *Therefore, be imitators of God,*

Then also demonstrating that the imitation itself is appropriate:

5:1b *as beloved sons;*

---

[57] Is the point that those unable to work, such as the apostles (and perhaps others who were unable by their circumstances), could depend upon the charity of the church and so need not steal?

[58] *Donantes vobis ipsis.* The Latin must represent χαριζόμενοι ἑαυτοῖς, "forgiving one another."

et imitationis factae documenta ostendit:
et ambulate in caritatem.
et iterum exemplo utitur, simul discutiens illud:
sicut et Christus dilexit nos, et seipsum tradidit pro nobis oblatio-
5 *nem et sacrificium Deo in odorem bonae suauitatis.*
sicut et Dominus dicit: *ut diligatis in inuicem, sicut et ego dilexi*
uos; maiorem hoc caritatem nemo habet ut quis animam suam ponat
pro amicis suis. et post caritatis uerba iterum ad alia transit dicens:
fornicatio autem et omnis immunditia aut auaritia nec nominetur
10 *in uobis.*
immunditiam dicit fornicationis nimiam pertinaciam. et quoniam dixit, *neque nominetur in uobis*, ad uerecundiam eos inuitans
adiecit:
sicut decet sanctos.
15 et non solum hoc, sed
et turpitudo et stultiloquium et scurrilitas, quae ad rem non perti-
net; sed magis gratiarum actio.
stultiloquium dicit, quando de rebus non necessariis loquimur;
scurrilitatem uero dicit derogationem illam quam in proximos fa-
20 cimus. deinde et timorem illis incutiens:
hoc enim scitote, cognoscentes quoniam omnis fornicarius aut in-
mundus aut auarus (quod est idolorum seruitus) non habet heredita-
tem in regno Christi et Dei.
auaritiae autem pondus ex similibus demonstrauit, 'idolorum
25 seruitutem' illam vocans; eo quod similiter a Deo potest auertere,
et quia haec apud gentes absolute tunc agebantur, eo quod nolebant credere aliquod esse examen illorum quae hic agimus.
nemo uos seducat inanibus uerbis; propter haec enim uenit ira Dei
super filios diffidentiae. nolite ergo fieri conparticipes eorum.
30 id ostendens quemadmodum illis non sit aptum ultra id facere.
eratis enim aliquando tenebrae, nunc uero lumen in Domino.
hoc est ut dicat: 'ignorabatis Deum; nunc autem cognouistis.'
bene ignorantiam quidem 'tenebras' uocauit, scientiam uero, 'lumen'; non solum propter rerum differentiam, sed et ut opportu-

2 caritate *H*   6 in (*bef.* inu.) *om H*   7 hanc *C* H*   11 fornicationes *C**
13 adicit *C*   19 scurrilitates *H*   27 hic *om H*

And he shows what proves the imitation has been accomplished:

5:2a *and walk in love,*

And again he uses the example, at the same time elaborating it:

5:2b *as also Christ loved us and gave himself up for us as an offering and sacrifice to God in an odor of good fragrance.*

As the Lord says (John 15:12–13): *that you love one another as I have loved you. No one has greater love than this, to lay down his life for his friends.* And after speaking about love, he turns his attention to other matters, saying:

5:3a *But fornication and all impurity or greed, let it not even be mentioned among you,*

By *impurity* he means excessive persistence in fornication; and when he said *let it not even be mentioned among you,* inducing them to shame, he added:

5:3b *as becomes saints,*

And not only this, but:

5:4 *also filthy conduct and foolish talk and jesting, which is out of place; but rather thanksgiving.*

By *foolish talk* he means when we speak of unnecessary things. And by *jesting* he means slandering our neighbors. Then, striking fear into them:

[178] 5:5 *For know this, understanding that no fornicator or impure person or one who is greedy (that is, slavery to idols) has an inheritance in the kingdom of Christ and of God.*

And he demonstrated the gravity of greed on the basis of its similarity to the other vices, calling it *slavery to idols* because it can similarly turn someone away from God and because these things were being practiced unreservedly at that time among the Gentiles, since they were unwilling to believe there was anything worth taking account of in what we are urging here.

5:6–7 *Let no one lead you astray with empty words, for because of these things the wrath of God comes on the sons of disobedience. Therefore, do not be associated with them.*

He shows how it is not suitable for them to behave this way any longer.

5:8a *For once you were darkness, but now light in the Lord.*

This means: "You did not know God, but now you do know him." He rightly called ignorance *darkness* and knowledge *light,* not only because of their difference, but also by using the most

nissimis abusus nominibus ad eruditionem eos inuitaret uirtutum.
unde et adiecit:

tamquam filii luminis ambulate.

'sicut decet illos qui in lumine consistunt.' et aliter illa osten-
5   dere cupiens quae illos deceant:

fructus enim Spiritus in omni bonitate et iustitia et ueritate.

'sed et illius Spiritus tales sunt donationes; itaque talia decet
agere uos qui accepistis eundem Spiritum.' et recurrens iterum
ad exemplum quod usus est:

10   *probantes quid sit beneplacitum Domino; et nolite communicare*
operibus infructuosis tenebrarum, magis autem et redarguite.

'curam igitur magis adhibere illorum quae placent Domino, nihil perficientes tale quale et illi qui Deum nesciunt. decet enim uos
sic a peccato modis omnibus auerti, ita ut et illa quae huiusmodi
15   ab aliis fiunt arguatis, ob utilitatem communem.' sic et ad Timotheum scribit, dicens *eos qui peccant coram omnibus arguere, ut et*
ceteri timorem habeant.

et ostendens qualia sunt quae ab illis fiebant:

quae enim in occulto fiunt ab illis, turpe est et dicere.

20   dein quod dixit, *magis autem et arguite,* ostendens ipsius rei utilitatem, adiecit:

omnia enim dum arguuntur, a lumine manifestantur.

nam dum illius actus qui arguitur fiunt manifesti, sciunt etiam
alterius corrigere. dictum est autem ab apostolo non integre, dixit
25   enim nihil amplius nisi quia *manifestantur;* illud uero quod sequebatur silentio tradidit, eo quod posset ipsa manifestatio adiuuare. omnis enim quicumque est, ille super suum delictum confu-
sionem patietur tunc quando eius delictum fuerit manifestatum.
deinde adiecit:

30   *omne quod manifestatur, lumen est.*

ad illud retulit quod dixit: *et nolite communicare operibus tene-*
brarum, hoc est: 'uos decet non illorum opera imitari, sed et talia agere quae si fuerint manifestata, tristes uos minime faciant.'

2   adicit *C*   7   et *om H*   9   quo (*for* quod) *C* (*corr.*)   10   probans *C H*   11
op. infruct. *om H*   12   adhibete *C* (*corr.*)   ‖   illorumque *C*   19   inquit (*aft.*
enim) *add C* (*corr.*)   21   adicit *C*   28   manifestum *C**   29   adicit *C*

advantageous words to attract them to instruction in the virtues. And so he added:

5:8b *Walk as sons of light,*

"As becomes those who are established in light." And he wants to show what becomes them in another way:

5:9 *for the fruit of the Spirit*[59] *is in all kindness and righteousness and truth,*

"Moreover, such are the gifts of the Spirit, and so such behavior becomes you who have received the same Spirit." And repeating the example he used:

[179] 5:10–11 *testing what is well-pleasing to the Lord, and take no part in the unfruitful works of darkness but rather rebuke them.*

"Therefore, take care all the more for what pleases the Lord, doing nothing such as those do who do not know God. For it becomes you in this way to avoid sin in all ways, so that for the benefit of all you may rebuke deeds of this kind done by others." So he writes to Timothy, saying (1 Tim 5:20): *as for those who sin, rebuke them in the presence of all, so that the rest also may have fear.*

And showing what their deeds were like:

5:12 *For it is shameful even to speak of what such people do secretly;*

Then, because he said *but rather rebuke them* to show the benefit of doing so, he added:

5:13 *for as long as all things are rebuked, they are made manifest by light;*

For when the deeds of one who is rebuked become manifest, they also are skillful in mending the ways of someone else. But the apostle's statement is incomplete, for he said no more than that *they are made manifest.* But he handed over to silence what would follow—that the manifestation itself could bring help. For everyone, whoever he is, suffers anxiety over his transgression whenever his transgression becomes manifest. Then he added:

5:14a *everything that is manifested is light,*

[180] He returned to what he had said (5:11): *and take no part in the works of darkness*; that is, "it becomes you not to imitate their works but to do such things that would by no means make you sorrowful if they were made manifest." For the works of light are

---

[59] A variant reading (instead of "light") that has support in the manuscripts but that may be a corruption introduced by the recollection of Gal 5:22.

luminis enim sunt opera illa quae in manifesto fiunt. talia autem
sunt opera uirtutum; tenebrarum uero opera illa sunt quae occul-
tantur. talia autem sunt opera malitiae.

deinde adiecit et testimonium:

5   *propter quod dicit: 'surge qui dormis, et exsurge ex mortuis, et in-*
luminabit tibi Christus'

alii *continget te Christus* legerunt; habet autem nullam sequentiam. de lumine enim disputans, abusus est hoc testimonium; dicit autem de peccato et impietate. atubi enim credentes in Christo
10   resipiscere uoluerimus, et quasi de somno et morte quadam exper-
gefacti fuerimus, suscipimus illam cognitionem et gratiam quae
exinde ad instar luminis in nos defertur; quibus decens est nos
consentanea agere.

quidam dixerunt quoniam multae erant illo in tempore gratiae
15   Spiritus quae dabantur illis; dabatur etiam cum ceteris gratia ut
et psalmos facerent, sicuti et beato David ante Christi aduentum
id tribui euenit. unum quidem hoc erat, quod tunc cantantes illi
qui gratiam talem acceperant dicebant. quod apostolus in testimonium ad praesens abusus fuisse uidetur. uerumtamen qualiter-
20   cumque se habet, nos sensum apostoli examinare debemus. ponens enim ipsud testimonium adiecit exhortationem dicens:

uidete etenim quomodo caute ambuletis, non sicut insipientes, [sed
ut sapientes]; redimentes tempus, quoniam dies mali sunt. propter hoc
nolite fieri insipientes, sed intellegentes quae sit uoluntas Domini.

25   bene posuit *redimentes;* eo quod is qui aliquid emit ad suam utilitatem, illud quod emit utitur. 'et tu (inquit) quia praesens uita
malitiae repleta est, accelera cum sapientia abuti illa conuenienter; quasi redimens teipsum per uirtutem, ut uoluntatem Dei in
uitam praesentem implens, adsequaris aeternas mercedes.' et ite-
30   rum connectit consilium:

2   sunt illa *H*   4   adicit (*for* adiecit) *C*   5   a (*for* ex) *H*   7   contempnentes
non Christum *C* contempn. Chr. (*om* non) *H* [*see note*]   7-8   consequentiam
C (*corr.*)   8   autem (*for* enim) *H*   9   adubi *C*   12   adstar (*for* ad instar) *H*
14   in. temp, illo *H*   17   que (quae?) *C** quod *H*   21   ipsum *C* (*corr.*) *H*   22
enim *H*   22-23   sed ut sap. *om C H*   28   in uita praesenti *C* (*corr.*)

those that take place in what is manifest, and such are the works of the virtues. But the works of darkness are those that are kept secret, and such are the works of wickedness.

Then he added a testimony:

5:14b *therefore it says: "Sleeper, awake and rise from the dead! And Christ will shine on you."*

Others have read *Christ will touch you.*[60]   But this does not keep the logical order. For Paul used this testimony while he was reasoning about light, and he is speaking of sin and godlessness. For whenever we are willing to come to our senses by believing in Christ and so have become like people wakened from sleep and some kind of death, we receive the knowledge and grace brought down to us from this source like light. And it is right for us to do what agrees with this.

[181] There are some who have said that in former times there were many graces of the Spirit given to those people. Among other things grace was also given for them to compose psalms, for example, as this came to be bestowed on blessed David before Christ's coming. Those who make this point, then, have said that this verse was one of the psalms that those who had received such a grace sang at that time. And they said that the apostle appears to have used it as a testimony in the present verse. Nevertheless, however this may be, we must examine the apostle's meaning. For in putting down this testimony he added an exhortation, saying:

5:15–17 *See, then, how you should walk carefully, not as unwise people [but as wise], purchasing the time, because the days are evil. Therefore, do not be foolish, but understanding what the will of the Lord is.*

He rightly put down *purchasing*, because someone who buys something for his own use, uses what he has bought. "And you (he says), because the present life is filled with wickedness, hurry to use those things rightly with wisdom, as though you were purchasing yourself by virtue so that by fulfilling God's will in the present life you may acquire eternal rewards." And again he links advice to what he says:

---

[60]The alternate reading is ἐπιψαύσει instead of ἐπιφαύσει, and it is reflected in the Old Latin versions. Chrysostom and Theodoret are aware of the reading but do not accept it.

et nolite inebriari uino, in quo est omnis luxuria, sed replemini in
Spiritu; loquentes uobis psalmis et hymnis et canticis spiritalibus, can-
tantes et psallentes in cordibus uestris Domino; gratias agentes semper
pro omnibus, in nomine domini nostri Iesu Christi, Deo et Patri.

5   'ab ebrietate quidem cavete ex qua luxuria impletur. adcelerate uero uos ipsos dignos exhibere ut Spiritu repleamini, uirtutibus
intendentes, psalmis quoque et spiritalibus canticis semper corda uestra inlustrantes; proque omnibus illis quae uobis per Christum conlata sunt gratiarum actionem reddere Deo properate, ita
10   ut numquam minus faciatis quin animo uestro laudetis Deum.
quam laudem conuenit pro illis quae uobis tributa sunt illi cum
gratiarum reddere actione.'

et iterum adiecit illa, unde coepit, de quibus et multa in medio
uerba fecisse uidetur:
15   *subiecti inuicem in timore Christi.*

'ante omnia (inquit) propter timorem Christi caritatem quae
inuicem est ostendentes; neque subici uobis in inuicem differatis,
propter illum lucrum quod hinc uobis adnasci uidetur.'

et quoniam communem ad omnes hanc fecisse uidetur exhorta-
20   tionem, incipit ultra de his propria quae unicuique sunt disputare,
et quae ultra non ad omnes similiter pertinere poterant. et alia quidem proprie scribit mulieribus ita ut erga maritos suos suum se-
ruent affectum; alia uero uiris scribit ita ut erga suas uxores integro
sint arbitrio. parentibus quoque scribit ut erga filios suos affectum
25   habeant inlibatum. filiis quoque scribit ut parentes suos omni honore dignos existiment. seruis quoque et dominis scribit, unicuique suadens ut quod iustum est alter alteri praebeat. tres uero hos
affectus memoratus est, ex quibus unum est quod debeant mariti et uxores in inuicem se diligere; alterum quod debeant parentes
30   cum suis habere filiis; aliud quemadmodum debeant esse serui et
domini. et primum quidem naturalem memoratus est affectum,
deinde subintroductum. talis enim est affectus inter seruos et do-

1   inebriare *C**   5   luxurias impetur (*sic*) *C**   5-6   ad celeritate *C**   10   qui
in (*for* quin) *H* 13 et (2°) *om C*   15   in (*bef.* inu.) *add C* (*corr.*) *H*   17   in (*bef.*
inu.) *add C* (*corr.*) *H*   18   illud *C* (*corr.*)   24   effectum *C*H*   28   affectos *C**

5:18–20 And do not get drunk with wine, in which is all⁶¹ profligacy, but be filled [182] with the Spirit, speaking with yourselves in psalms and hymns and spiritual songs, singing and playing the harp in your hearts to the Lord, giving thanks always for everything in the name of our Lord Jesus Christ to God the Father.

"Beware of drunkenness by which profligacy is filled up. But hasten to show yourselves worthy so that you may be filled with the Spirit, concentrating on the virtues and always enlightening your hearts with psalms and spiritual songs. Hasten to give God thanks for everything that has been granted you by Christ so that you may never fail to praise God sincerely. It is right to render this praise to him, together with thanksgiving, for what has been bestowed on you."

And again he added the idea with which he began and about which he is seen to have said a good deal in the intervening discussion:⁶²

5:21 Be subject to one another in the fear of Christ.

"Before all (he says), because of the fear of Christ, show love for one another, and do not delay being subject to one another because of the profit that will be seen to arise for you from this."

And since he plainly composed this exhortation as one common for all, he begins what follows with an argument appropriate for each one of them, and what follows could not similarly have applied to everyone. Indeed, he writes some things appropriate for wives so that they may keep their affection for their husbands, and he writes other things to the husbands so that they may be purely disposed toward their wives. He also writes to parents so that they may have unimpaired affection for their children; he also writes to children so that they may esteem their parents as worthy of all honor. [183] And he also writes to slaves and to masters, advising both to furnish what is just one to the other. He mentioned three forms of affection. One of them is the love husbands and wives ought to have for one another; the second is what parents ought to have with their children; the third, how slaves and masters should be. Indeed, he first mentioned natural affection and then affection introduced secondarily. For such is the

---

⁶¹ An addition to the text.

⁶² The reference may be to 4:1–16, the beginning of his "moral discussions," while 5:21 returns to the theme of concord in the community.

minos; nec enim in natura inest seruitus, sicut est in natura nuptialis cohabitatio et filiorum procreatio. et neque de illis dicens,
corrupit ordinem; primum enim de uiris et mulieribus, eorumque
explicauit affectum, eo quod nuptiae praecedere soleant, deinde
5 sequitur filiorum propagatio. tamen in unoquoque affectum ab in-
firmioribus inchoauit, primum mulieribus disputans, deinde uiris;
et antequam parentibus aliquid diceret, filiis illa quae conueniebant suasit. sed et de dominis disputans, illa quae conueniebant
ad seruos narrauit, ostendens quoniam ante omnia necesse est il-
10 los debitum implere obsequium, eo quod et hinc maxime illa quae
meliora sunt accipiunt in melius incrementum; quae etsi non impleantur, excusationem nullam habere poterunt peccatorum. incipit ergo a mulieribus. *subiecti* (inquit) *in inuicem in timore Christi;*
consequenter adiciens:
15   *mulieres propriis maritis sicut Domino subditae sint.*

hoc est, 'subiectae sint.' et quoniam dignum fidei esse uidebatur quod dixerat, *sicut Domino* non uidebatur autem ratione id suadere; adiecit:
     quoniam uir caput est mulieris; sicut et Christus caput ecclesiae, et
20 *ipse est saluator corporis*

†illum enim ordinem quem
Christus habet ad ecclesiam, eo
quod ex illo secundae uitae causam ecclesia habere uidetur, ex
quo et ecclesiastici corporis sta-
25 tus est effectus (hoc enim isto
in loco dicit: *ipse est saluator*
corporis, hoc est, causam praebens status ecclesiastici corporis); hunc ordinem etiam uir ha-
30 bet ad mulierem; eo quod et ut
sit et ut consistat, mulier ex uiro accepit.*

ἣν γὰρ ἐπέχει τάξιν ὁ Χριστὸς
τῇ ἐκκλησίᾳ, [ἅτε δὴ ἐκεῖθεν τὴν
αἰτίαν λαβούσῃ τῆς δευτέρας ὑπάρ-
ξεως, ἐξ οὗ καὶ τοῦ ἐκκλησιαστικοῦ
σώματος γίνεται ἡ σύστασις (τοῦτο
γὰρ λέγει] τὸ αὐτό[ς] ἐστιν ὁ σωτὴρ
[τοῦ σώματος], ἀντὶ τοῦ ʽὁ τὴν αἰτίαν παρασχόμενος τῇ συστάσει τοῦ
ἐκκλησιαστικοῦ σώματος')· ταύτην
ἐπέχει τὴν τάξιν ὁ ἀνὴρ τῇ γυναικί,
ἅτε δὴ τὸ εἶναί τε καὶ συνεστάναι
ἐκεῖθεν λαβούσῃ.

---

4 procedere *H* 16 subditae sint *H* 18 adicit *C* 21 sq. Coisl 304, f. 98
a [Cr. vi. 202, Fr. 135] θεόδωρος δέ φησιν· ἣν γὰρ ἐπέχει τάξιν ὁ Χριστὸς τῇ
ἐκκλησίᾳ, τὸ αὐτό ἐστιν ὁ σωτήρ· ἀντὶ τοῦ, κ.τ.λ.

affection between slaves and masters, for slavery is not natural as marital cohabitation and the procreation of children are natural. Nor in speaking of these three relations did he harm the proper order. For he explained the affection of husbands and wives first because marriage customarily comes first, and then there follows the procreation of children. Yet in each case he begins his account of affection with the weaker, arguing first about the wives and then about the husbands. And before he says anything to the parents, he advised the children what was right for them. Moreover, in arguing about masters, he gave an account of what was right for slaves, showing that before all it was necessary for them to fulfill the service they owed, because it is especially from this that they receive what is better for higher promotion, although if they should not fulfill their duties, they would have no excuse for their sins. Therefore, he begins with the wives. *Be subject* (he says) *to one another in the fear of Christ*, adding in logical order:

5:22 *Wives, be subject to your husbands as you are to the Lord,*

That is, "be subject."[63] And since what he said, *as to the Lord*, seemed worthy of belief but did not seem to give a persuasive reason, he added:

5:23 *for the husband is the head of the wife just as Christ is the head of the church, and he is the Savior of the body.*

†For that order which Christ has to the church, [184] because from him the church plainly has the cause of the second life, from whom also the organization of the church's body has come to be (for in this passage he says *he is the Savior of the body*; that is, he supplies the cause of the organization of the church's body), this order also the husband has to the wife, since the wife receives from the

The order that Christ has to the church, [because from him it takes the cause of the second existence, from whom also the organization of the church's body has come to be (for he says] *he is the Savior [of the body]*, meaning "he supplies the cause of the organization of the church's body"), this order the husband has to the wife, since she takes from him both her existence and her ordering.[64]

---

[63] Theodore's comment assumes that his text of verse 22 does not include "be subject," a reading with strong manuscript support.

[64] The brackets indicate where Swete has partly reconstructed the Greek conjecturally on the basis of the Latin.

sed ut ecclesia subdita est Christo, sic et mulieres suis maritis in om-
nibus,

et quidem sunt quidam in ecclesia qui non sunt subiecti. sed
eiusmodi homines iam non esse ecclesiae existimantur, eo quod
5   nec illa quae corporis sunt sapiant. subditam autem Christo esse
ecclesiam dixit; de illis dicit, qui subditi sunt, quos et corpus ecclesiae esse existimat. non est autem demiratione dignum, si adiecit *in omnibus*, quod absolute quasi ad pios disputans adiecit; de
quibus superfluum erat excogitare nequando in deterius suas uel-
10   lent adducere uxores.

uiri, diligite uxores uestras sicut et Christus dilexit ecclesiam, [et]
seipsum tradidit pro illa.

demirandum est eo quod uno eodemque exemplo, et ut subiectae sint mulieres, et ut uiri eas diligant et affectum ut conuenit erga
15   eas ostendant, instruxit. 'talem (inquit) et uos erga uestras uxores
iustum est ostendere caritatem, qualem et Christus erga ecclesiam
ostendit.' unde et caritatis indicia latius in Christo nititur publicare dicens:

ut illam sanctificet, mundans per lauacrum aquae in sermone; ut
20   *exhibeat eam sibi ipsi gloriosam ecclesiam, non habentem maculam aut*
rugam aut aliquid horum, sed ut sit sancta et immaculata.

hoc non solum caritatis Christi continebat demonstrationem,
sed et ad eruditionem illis proficiebat, ut custodirent uxoribus suis
nuptialis conscientiae foedus; eo quod sic eos conligatos esse er-
25   ga uxores caritatis ratio depostulabat, sicut Christus ecclesiam sibi
coniunxit ita ut numquam eos qui in ecclesia sunt relinquat, usque
dum affectum erga eum integrum uelint seruare.

unde adiecit:

sic debent uiri diligere suas uxores sicut sua corpora.

30   hoc est, 'sic Christus ecclesiam diligit, sicut corpus suum.'
deinde ex ipsa similitudine etiam ad rationem naturae decurrit,
ostendens quoniam ipsa ratio illis competere uideatur secundum
principalem opificationem:

1   et (*bef.* ut) *add* C (*corr.*)   9   interius *H**   11   et *om* C H   15   ostendit *C**
20   eam *om* H   22   ad (*bef.* car.) *add* C (*corr.*)   23   et *om* H   ‖   custodiret
C*   28   adicit C

husband both her existence and
her ordering.*

5:24 *But as the church is subject to Christ, so also wives to their husbands in all.*

Even though there are some in the church who are not subject, yet people of this kind are no longer considered to belong to the church, because they do not have a sense of what belongs to the body. But he said that the church is subject to Christ. He speaks of those who are subject, whom he also considers to be the body of the church. And it is not worth being astonished that he added *in all*, which he added simply because he was making his case with the godly, of whom it would be idle to think they would ever be willing to lead their wives to the worse.

5:25 *Husbands, love your wives, just as Christ loved the church [and] gave himself up for her*

This statement must be admired because by one and the same example he gave instruction both that wives should be subject and that husbands should love them and show proper affection [185] toward them. "It is right (he says) for you to show such love toward your wives as Christ shows toward the church." And so he strives to proclaim at greater length the tokens of love in Christ, saying:

5:26–27 *in order to sanctify her, cleansing her with the washing of water by the word, so as to present the church to himself in splendor, without a spot or wrinkle or anything of the kind—but so that she may be holy and without blemish.*

This not only included a description of Christ's love but also helped to instruct them to guard the marriage contract with their wives in good conscience, because the loving relationship required them to be bound together with their wives, just as Christ united the church to himself in such a way that he would never desert those in the church as long as they were willing to keep their affection for him unimpaired.

And so he added:

5:28a *In the same way husbands should love their wives as they do their own flesh.*

That is, "in the same way that Christ loves the church as his own body." Then he turns from this resemblance also to the relation of nature, demonstrating that this relation is seen to be relevant to them according to the first creation:

qui diligit suam uxorem, se ipsum diligit; nemo enim aliquando suam carnem odio habuit, sed nutrit et fouet eam.

ut dicat quoniam 'secundum primam opificationem una caro erat mulieris et uiri; eo quod et mulier portio mariti erat. itaque
5 qualem solicitudinem uel diligentiam erga proprium corpus exhibemus, talem iustitiae ratio postulat ut uiri erga suas exhibeant uxores.' et complectens exemplum illud quod secundum Christum est, adiecit:

sicut et Christus ecclesiam.

10 eo quod et corpus Christi est ecclesia, corpus uero mariti uxor; et complectitur utrumque, ostendens quoniam et a natura et a ratione pietatis aptum est illis, ut connexi suis uxoribus habeantur. etenim non absolute ampliorem ad uiros fecit sermonem, incitans eos ad illam caritatem quam debeant erga suas seruare uxores; eo
15 quod facilius hi nuptiales leges spernere consueuerunt, cum aliis se, praetermissis suis uxoribus, permiscentes. quoniam autem dixit, *sicut et Christus ecclesiam,* persistit docere quoniam illam rationem habet uxor ad maritum secundum primam opificationem, quam uindicat rationem ecclesia a Christo; ita ut non uideatur ua-
20 ne abusus fuisse exemplo illo quod secundum Christum et ecclesiam est. deinde adiecit:

quoniam membra sumus corporis eius, de carne eius et de ossibus eius.

'†sicut enim portio fuit Adae   ὥσπερ μέρος ἐγένετο τοῦ ᾿Αδὰμ
25 mulier ex ossibus eius et carne   ἡ γυνὴ ἐκ τῶν ὀστῶν αὐτοῦ καὶ ἐκ
eius sumpta; sic et nos dominici   τῆς σαρκὸς αὐτοῦ ληφθεῖσα· οὕτως
corporis sumus membra, sicuti   καὶ ἡμεῖς τοῦ δεσποτικοῦ σώματος
ex carne eius et ex ossibus eius   ἐσμὲν μέλη, ὥσπερ ἐκ τῆς σαρκὸς
facti*,   αὐτοῦ καὶ ἐκ τῶν ὀστέων αὐτοῦ
     γεγονότες.

30 eo quod gratiam ex illo Spiritu qui in eum est accepimus, ut ad similitudinem eius resurrectionem et inmortalitatem potiamur.' deinde permanens in ipso exemplo, ostendere cupiens eius similitudinem, scripturalem ponit uocem dicens:

propter hoc relinquet homo patrem suum et matrem suam, et adiun-

2 fouit *C H* 4 fortior marito (*for* portio mariti) *H* 8 adicit *C* 12 pietati *C* ‖ connexis *C* H* 16 se *om C* 21 adicit *C* 24 sq. Coisl. 204, f. 99 b [Cr. vi. 205, Fr. 136] Θεόδωρος δέ φησιν· ὥσπερ μέρος, κ.τ.λ. μέλος (*for* μέρος) Fr. 30 eo (*for* eum) *H* 31 resurrectione et immortalitate *H* 34 relinquit *C H*

5:28b-29a *He who loves his wife loves himself, for no one ever hates his own body, but he nourishes it and tenderly cares for it,*

What he means is that "according to the first creation there was one flesh of wife and husband, because the wife was a portion of the husband. And so the kind of tender and diligent care we show toward our own body is such as the relation righteousness demands husbands should show toward their wives." And including the example that has to do with Christ, he added:

[186] 5:29b *just as also Christ the church,*

Because the body of Christ is the church, and the body of the husband is the wife. And he includes both, demonstrating that both by nature and by the relation of true religion it is appropriate for them to be kept joined to their wives. Of course, it was not for nothing that he composed a longer address to the husbands, urging them to the love they ought to preserve for their wives. It was because they were accustomed quite easily to scorn the laws of marriage by having intercourse with other women and neglecting their wives. And since he said *just as also Christ the church,* he persists in teaching that the relation the wife has to the husband according to the first creation is the one that the church claims from Christ. This is so that he may not seem to have used the example of Christ and the church in an empty way. Then he added:

5:30 *because we are members of his body, of his flesh and bones.*[65]

†"For just as the woman was a portion of Adam, taken from his bones and his flesh, so we are members of the Lord's body, just as though we were made of his flesh and of his bones,*

For just as the woman was a portion of Adam, taken from his bones and his flesh, so we are members of the Lord's body, just as though we had come to be from his flesh and from his bones.

because we have received grace from that Spirit who is in him, so that we may gain the resurrection and immortality after his likeness." Then, keeping [187] to his example and wishing to show its likeness, he puts down a scriptural text (Gen 2:24) and says:

---

[65] The addition of "of his flesh and bones" has support in the manuscripts and in the Latin versions. The allusion is to Gen 2:23.

getur ad uxorem suam; et erunt duo in carne una.

quibus et adiecit:

mysterium hoc magnum est.

et ut ne uideatur de uirorum et mulierum copulatione dicere
5 quoniam 'magnum est mysterium' caute prospexit:

ego autem dico in Christo et in ecclesia.

†hoc uult dicere quoniam 'il- ὅπερ (φησὶν) εἴρηται ἐν ἀρχῇ
lud quod dictum in principium τῆς δημιουργίας περὶ τῶν γυναι-
opificationis de mulieribus et κῶν καὶ τῶν ἀνδρῶν, τοῦτο μυστι-
10 maritis, hoc mystice in Christo κώτερον ἐπὶ τοῦ Χριστοῦ καὶ τῆς
et in ecclesia impletum est. om- ἐκκλησίας πεπλήρωται· πάντες γὰρ
nes enim ab illa natiuitate quae τῆς ἐκ πατρὸς καὶ μητρὸς γεννή-
ex patre et matre erat segrega- σεως ἔξω γενόμενοι, ἅτε δὴ καὶ θα-
ti sunt, eo quod et morte ab il- νάτῳ χωρισθέντες τῆς ζωῆς ἐκεί-
15 la uita sunt separati. spirita- νης, πνευματικῇ τῇ ἀναγεννήσει
li uero regeneratione resurrec- τὴν ἀνάστασιν δεχόμεθα, ἀπορρή-
tionem percipimus, inenarrabi- τῳ λόγῳ τῷ Χριστῷ συναπτόμενοι,
li ratione Christo copulati, et si- καὶ τὴν πρὸς αὐτὸν ὁμοιότητα τῆς
militudinem inmortalitatis eius ἀθανασίας ἀκριβῆ λαμβάνοντες.
20 cautam percipimus.'*

et ostendens per omnia similitudinem illorum quae a Christo sunt,
et quoniam similiter illis et secundum rationem naturae et secundum rationem fidei aptus est consensus ille qui est cum uxoribus,
adiecit:

25 *uerumtamen et uos singuli, unusquisque suam uxorem sic diligat sicut seipsum.*

deinde et de mulieribus:

uxor uero, ut timeat maritum.

exinde uertitur ad alium affectum, deinde et ad parentes:

30 *filii, oboedite parentibus uestris in Domino; hoc enim iustum est.*

ostendere uero cupiens quoniam de his etiam antiqua lex id
praeceperat:

honora (inquit) *patrem tuum et matrem, quod est primum mandatum in promissione; ut bene tibi fiat, et sis longaeuus super terram. et*
35 *uos, patres, nolite exacerbare filios uestros; sed nutrite eos in disciplina*

---

2 adicit *C* 4 ut *om C* ‖ copulationem *C** 7 sq. Coisl. 204, f. 100 b [Cr.
vi. 207, Fr. 136] Θεόδωρος δέ φησιν· ὅπερ, φησίν, κ.τ.λ. 17-18 inenarrabile *H**
20 percepimus *C* 25 ut (*bef.* suam) add *C* 28 uero *om H* 29 alienum
(*for* alium) *H* 30 fili *C* 32 praeceperit *C*

5:31 *"For this reason a man will leave his father and his mother and will be joined to his wife, and the two will become one flesh."*

To which he added:

5:32a *This is a great mystery,*

And lest he seem to be saying that the union of husbands and wives "is a great mystery," he carefully anticipated the misunderstanding:

5:32 *and I am speaking of Christ and the church.*

†He means that "what was said in the beginning of creation concerning wives and husbands has been fulfilled mystically in Christ and the church. For all of us have been excluded from birth through a father and a mother, because we have been separated from that life by death. But we receive the resurrection by spiritual rebirth, joined to Christ by an ineffable relation, and we receive a secure likeness of his immortality.*

What was said in the beginning of creation (he says) concerning wives and husbands has been fulfilled more mystically in Christ and the church. For all of us, when we come to be outside birth from a father and a mother, since we have been separated from that life by death, receive the resurrection by spiritual rebirth, joined to Christ by an ineffable relation and receiving an exact likeness with him of immortality.

And showing throughout the similarity of those things that come from Christ, and because concord with wives is associated with them both by the relation of nature and by the relation of faith, he added:

5:33a *Nevertheless, each of you individually, each one of you should love his wife as himself;*

And then concerning the wives:

5:33b *and a wife should honor her husband.*

[188] From there he turns to other forms of affection, beginning with parents:

6:1 *Children, obey your parents in the Lord, for this is right.*

And wishing to demonstrate that the old law had given a precept about this (Exod 20:12; Deut 5:16):

6:2–4 *"Honor* (it says) *your father and mother"—this is the first*

et admonitione Domini.

nam quod dicit, *nolite exacerbare,* hoc est, 'nolite despicere neque respuere, sed fouete magis eos, et sustinete delinquentes.' et iterum ad alterum migrat affectum:

serui, oboedite dominis (inquit) *secundum carnem cum timore et tremore ; in simplicitate cordis uestri, tamquam Christo.*

et quoniam incertum erat illud quod dixerat *sicut Christo,* modum quo illud dixerat pandit:

non ad oculum serui, sicut hominibus placentes, sed sicut serui Christi, facientes uoluntatem Dei ex animo; cum bona uoluntate seruientes Domino et non hominibus.

'serui (inquit) estis Christi. conuenit ergo uos erga uestros dominos bonam exhibere uoluntatem, eo quod hoc uult Deus, ut perfecto animo adimpleatis ei uicem; ut serui Christi propter Christi faciatis legem, quasi Christo ipsi ista implentes; ita ut illa quae fiunt, Deo propter uestrum reputentur arbitrium.' et quod magis poterat eos ad reuerentiam adducere et placare, ut serui cum bona uoluntate suis seruiant dominis, quasi ipsi Christo seruientes:

scientes quoniam quodcumque fecerit unusquisque uestrum bonum, hoc et recipiet a Deo, siue seruus siue liber.

'licet seruus sis, accipies a Deo mercedem tuam, faciens illa et quae conueniunt. et liber quoque ab illo mercedem expectat. itaque nulla tibi differentia est apud Deum secundum mercedum receptionem. ergo sicut illi seruiens a quo et mercedem recipere expectas, sic omnia debes adimplere.'

et uos, domini, haec eadem facite ad eos, remittentes minas.

hoc est: 'benignissimos uos illis exhibete, tribuentes ueniam delictis eorum, cum illa examinatis.' bene autem quia non dixit 'auferentes,' sed et *remittentes.* non enim corrigere seruos, si pertinaciter permanent in peccatis, prohibet, aut ad plenum existimat auferendam esse disciplinam; sed ut humane et cum uenia illud agant praecepit. nam et adiectio est demiranda et sufficiens ad uerecundiam eos inuitare qui auctoritate abutuntur dominationis:

scientes quoniam et uester et eorum dominus est in caelist, et per-

1   admonitionem *C* H*   5-6   et tremore *om C**   8   quod *H*   9   non ad oc. seruientes *C* (*corr.*)   11   Deo (*for* Domino) *H*   17   placere *H*   18   dominos *C**   23   mercedem *C*   23-24   retributionem (*for* recept.) *H*   24   ille *C H*   24-25   expectans *C H*   26   uos *om H**   28   examine natis *C**   29   et *om H*   33   qua *C*

commandment with a promise—"so that it may be well with you and you may live long on the earth." And you, fathers, do not provoke your children, but bring them up in the discipline and instruction of the Lord.

When he says *do not provoke*, he means "do not despise and reject them but rather cherish them and bear with them when they do wrong." And again he passes on to another form of affection:

6:5 Slaves (he says), *obey your masters according to the flesh with fear and trembling, in the singleness of your heart, as you obey Christ,*

And since it was unclear what he meant by *just as*[66] *Christ*, he discloses the way he had meant it:

6:6–7 not slaves to the eye, as pleasing men, but as slaves of Christ, doing the will of God from the mind, with goodwill serving the Lord and not men,

"You are (he says) slaves of Christ. Therefore, it is right for you to display goodwill toward your masters, because God wishes you to carry out your function for him with enthusiasm, so that as slaves of Christ you may perform your contract as though you were performing your duties for Christ himself. This is so that what is done may be considered done for God because of your choice." And [189] because it could lead and dispose them all the more to deference, so as to serve their masters as slaves with goodwill, as if they were serving Christ himself:

6:8 knowing that whatever good each one of you does, he will get it back from God, whether he is slave or free.

"Granted you are a slave, you will receive your reward from God by doing what is right. The free person also awaits his reward from him. And so God makes no distinction about you with respect to receiving rewards. Therefore, you ought to perform all your duties as though you were serving him from whom you expect to receive a reward."

6:9a And you, masters, do the same to them, relaxing threats,

That is, "show yourselves to them as kind as possible, pardoning their faults when you examine them." And it is right that he did not say "taking away" but *relaxing*. For he does not forbid chastising slaves if they stubbornly persist in sins, nor does he think that discipline should be completely taken away. Rather, he advises them to do this humanely and with pardon. Indeed, what he

---

[66] *Sicut* instead of *tamquam*, as in the citation of the text.

sonarum acceptio non est apud eum.

hoc est: 'aestima tecum quoniam licet et in praesenti uidearis supereminere seruis, sed communis uester dominus est in caelis, qui nullum erubescens, omnium faciet examen; non relinquens
5 nec dominos impunitos, si praeterquam conuenit delinquant. igitur qualem uis illum esse erga te, talis ipse esto erga proprios seruos.' implens autem et specialem exhortationem, iterum in communi disputat de illis quae omnibus similiter aptari poterant:

de cetero, fratres mei, confortamini in Domino, et in potentia uir-
10 *tutis eius.*

'omnia cum sollicitudine et uirtute illa quae Deo placita sunt perficite.' et quoniam dixit: *confortamini*, adiecit:

induite uos omnia arma Dei.

sicut consuetudo est militibus dicere, quibus cum fortitudine
15 etiam arma sunt necessaria. deinde dicit et aduersus quos est bellum illis; conueniebat enim et hoc manifestum facere illum, quia omnia arma indui praecipiebat:

ita ut possitis stare aduersus uersutias diaboli.

'itaque nolite locum dare diabolicis machinationibus.' et haec
20 dicens quasi ad bellum illos adhortans, adiecit:

quoniam non est nobis conluctatio aduersus sanguinem et carnem,
sed aduersus principatus et aduersus potestates, aduersus mundi rec-
tores tenebrarum saeculi huius, aduersus spiritalia nequitiae in caele-
stibus.

25 inconsequens esse uidetur ut is qui de armis omnibus sumendis et bello disputauit conluctationem memoretur; sed nihil differre existimat, eo quod neque uera ratione de conluctatione aut de militia illi erat ratio, sed abusiue ueritatis, quoniam omnibus est abusus ad confirmationem certaminis illius, quod proprietatem aduer-
30 sus diabolum inire uidetur. quoniam autem *principatus* et *potesta-*
tes inuisibilium uirtutum scit ordines esse, euidens est ex quibus et Colossensibus scribens dicit *siue sedes siue dominationes siue prin*

---

1   Deum (*for* eum) *H*   2   aestimatio (*for* aest. tec.) *C H*   ‖   et *om H*   11 D. sunt pl. *H*   20   adicit *C*   21   uobis *H*   ‖   carnem et sang. *H*   25   de arma omnia sumenda et bellum *C H*

adds is to be admired and is sufficient to shame those who abuse their authority as masters:

6:9b *knowing that both your and their master is in the heavens, and there is no partiality with him.*

That is, "consider in yourself that even though at the present time you seem to be superior to your servants, yet your common master is in the heavens. With special respect for no one, he will examine everyone and will not leave even masters unpunished if they have transgressed beyond what is right. [190] Therefore, as you wish him to be toward you, so be yourself toward your own slaves." And completing his particular exhortation, he again reasons generally about what could apply to all alike:

6:10 *For the rest, my brothers, be brave in the Lord and in the strength of his power.*

"Accomplish everything pleasing to God with great care and power." And since he said *be brave*, he added:

6:11a *Put on the whole armor of God,*

Just as it is the custom to say to soldiers, who need arms as well as bravery. Then he also says against whom they have gone to war. For it was right for him to make this clear because he was advising them to put on the whole armor:

6:11b *so that you may be able to stand against the wiles of the devil.*

"And so, do not give place to the devil's contrivances." Saying this as if he were urging them on to war, he added:

6:12 *For our wrestling is not against blood and flesh but against the rulers and against the authorities, against the world rulers of the darkness of this age, against the spiritual powers of iniquity in the heavenly places.*

It seems to be out of order that he who has been arguing about taking up the whole armor and about war should mention wrestling. But he thinks this makes no difference because his argument was really not about wrestling or about military service. Rather, he is speaking figuratively,[67] since he used all his words [191] for encouragement in that contest that is seen to be joined against the devil as a special kind of war. And that he understands *rulers* and *authorities* to be orders of invisible powers is clear from what he says when writing to the Colossians (Col 1:16): *whether*

---

[67] See Swete's note (1:190): "*abusiue ueritatis*] 'using the words figuratively, καταχρηστικῶς' (sc. abutendo ueritatem, abusione ueritatis) [?]."

cipatus siue potestates. hoc ergo in loco principatus et potestates daemonum ordines uidetur dicere; eo quod et euidens est quoniam de illo ordine erant illi qui in deterius uersi sunt. unde et superius dixit: *secundum principem potestatis aeris spiritus*, de diabolo id dicens. hoc ergo dicit, quoniam 'non aduersus homines infirmos nobis est certamen (nam *sanguinem et carnem* hoc uult dicere) sed aduersus uirtutes inuisibiles, et qui multam habent potentiam in praesente uita, omne quodcumque est pessimum operantes.' hoc enim dicit *spiritalia nequitiae*. nam quod dicit, *in caelestibus;* ut dicat, 'pro caelestibus,' hoc est, pro regno caelorum aduersus illos nobis certamen. quidam uero pro multa fatuitate mutauerunt illud quod dixerat, *in caelestibus*, et ita legere uoluerunt dicentes: 'in his quae sub caelo sunt;' existimantes dicere apostolum, quoniam sub caelum nobis est certamen cum illis. nouam adiectionem et dignam illorum stultitiae! qui sic intellexerunt, ut ne existimaremus quoniam aduersus illos super caelum habemus pugnare. sed non sic se ratio habet; sed uoluit dicere quoniam 'pro illis quae adquirere properamus; cum caelesti enim commoratione etiam et illa bona quae in caelis sunt potiri uolumus; pro quibus aduersus inuisibiles uirtutes nobis est bellum. itaque sic nos conuenit esse paratos, quasi qui et pro talibus et aduersus tales bellum habere uideamur.' tamen adiciens dictum illum quia *non est nobis conluctatio*, hoc est, bellum, et abusus indifferenter conluctationis nomen, sequitur iterum suam sequentiam, quasi qui de bello disputet, et dicit:

propter hoc resumite omnia arma Dei, ut possitis resistere in die maligno, et omnia perficientes stare.

nam quod dicit *in die maligno*, ut dicat 'in tempore pessimo,' praesentem uitam sic nominans, eo quod mala in hoc saeculo in praesente uita aguntur. et quae sint *omnia arma* dicit:

---

4 huius (*for* spiritus) *H* 6 carnem et sang. *H* 8 praesenti *H* 18 caelestem, commorationem *C** ‖ et *om H** 19 potire *C* ‖ aduersis *H* 23 conluctationes *H** 28 maligna *C H* 30 praesenti *H*

thrones or dominions or rulers or authorities. Therefore, in this passage the rulers and authorities appear to refer to orders of demons, because it is clear that those who were turned to the worse were of that order.[68] That is why he said above (2:2) *according to the ruler of the authority of the spirit of the air*, speaking this of the devil. Therefore, he says this because "our contest is not against weak men (for this is what he means by *blood and flesh*) but against invisible powers who also have much strength in the present life, working whatever is the worst possible wickedness." This is what he means by *the spiritual powers of iniquity*. Now when he says *in the heavenly places*, he means "for the heavenly places"; that is, our contest is against them for the kingdom of the heavens. But some people with great foolishness have changed the reading *in the heavenly places*. They have wanted to read "in those places that are under heaven," because they think the apostle was saying that our contest with them is under heaven.[69] [192] A novel addition and one worthy of their stupidity! They adopted this reading so that we might not suppose that we are obliged to fight them above heaven. But this reasoning does not hold. Rather, Paul wanted to say that "[we fight] for what we are eager to acquire; that is, together with our heavenly dwelling we also want to gain possession of those good things that are in the heavens. Our war against the invisible powers is for them. And so it is right for us to be prepared, inasmuch as we are plainly at war for such things and against such beings." Nevertheless, when he adds the words *our wrestling is not*, that is, our war, and so used the word *wrestling* as making no difference, he again follows his own logical order, as though someone were arguing about a war, and says:

6:13 *Therefore, take up the whole armor of God, so that you may be able to withstand on the evil day, and having done everything to stand firm.*

When he says *on the evil day*, he means "at the worst possible time," naming the present life this way, because the evils in this age are done in the present life. And he says what the whole armor is:

---

[68] Theodore's point is that the orders mentioned in Colossians are created and good; here they are fallen spiritual powers.

[69] The alternate reading is ὑπουρανίοις instead of ἐπουρανίοις. Swete's note (1:191) reads in part: "No known MS. of S. Paul's Epp. presents the reading … in this place. Possibly Th. refers to the Peshito, which translates as if ὑπ had stood in the text."

state ergo circumcinctum habentes lumbum uestrum in ueritate;
et induite loricam iustitiae, et calciati pedes uestros in praeparatione
euangelii pacis.

circumcingere ueritatem, uestire iustitiam, calciare pacem, ut
5   dicat: 'de his uobis sit sollicitudo, id est, de ueritate et iustitia et
pace. haec uobis imponite; istis uos armis munite.' et quoniam
omnia illis erant tradenda, quae militibus adsunt, adiecit:

super omnibus autem adsumentes scutum fidei, in quo possitis om-
nia iacula inimici ignita exstinguere.

10   *scutum* clypeum esse dicit. 'nam pro scuto (inquit) sit uobis fides, per quam omnia diaboli machinamenta facile percutere poteritis.'

et galeam salutarem accipite.

'horum (inquit) diligentiam adhibentes, habebitis illam salu-
15   tem quae est a Deo, quae et pro galea communiet uos; ita ut uulnus
a diabolo in locis uiuacibus minime percipiatis.'

et gladium Spiritus, qui est sermo Dei.

'pro gladio Spiritus sumite gratiam, quam habentes uel maxime terribiles eritis daemonibus.'

20   †bene autem dixit: *quod est ser-*   καλῶς τὸ ὅ ἐστιν ῥῆμα θεοῦ, εἰς
mo Dei, ad ostensionem poten-   παράστασιν τοῦ δυνατοῦ τῆς ἐν-
tiae inoperationis Spiritus. nam   εργείας τοῦ πνεύματος· ῥῆμα γὰρ
quod dicit: *sermo Dei,* hoc est   θεοῦ λέγει ἀντὶ τοῦ 'θεοῦ ἐνέργεια,'
'Dei inoperatio;' sicut et alibi   ὡς τὸ τῷ λόγῳ κυρίου οἱ οὐρανοὶ
25   dictum est: *uerbo Domini cae-*   ἐστερεώθησαν, ἀντὶ τοῦ 'τῇ ἐνερ-
li firmati sunt, hoc est, 'inope-   γείᾳ καὶ τῇ δυνάμει τοῦ θεοῦ ταῦτα
ratione et uirtute Dei ista sunt   συνέστη.' οὕτως καὶ παρὰ τοῖς προ-
constituta.' sic etiam et apud   φήταις κεῖται συνεχῶς τὸ ῥῆμα τοῦ
prophetas positum est frequen-   θεοῦ ὃ ἐγένετο, καὶ λόγος κυρίου ὅς
30   ter: *sermo Domini qui factus est;*   ἐγένετο, ἀντὶ τοῦ 'ἡ ἀποκάλυψις ἡ
et: *uerbum Domini quod fac-*   κατ' ἐνέργειαν τοῦ θεοῦ ἐναποτεθεῖ-
tum est, hoc est, 'reuelatio illa   σα.' κἀνταῦθα τοίνυν θεοῦ ῥῆμα τὴν
quae secundum inoperationem   τοῦ πνεύματος ἐκάλεσεν ἐνέργειαν.
Dei est menti impressa.' et hoc
35   in loco Dei sermonem Spiritus

---

2 luricam *C H* ‖ calciate *H* 11 diaboli *om H* 13 salutaria *C* 15
muniet *H* 20 qui *C* ‖ sq. Coisl. 204 f. 107 a [Cr. vi. 221, Fr. 136]. θεοδώ-
ρος. καλῶς, κ.τ.λ. 23 dixit *C* 29-30 sequenter *C**(?) 31 Dei *C* 31-32
εὐαποτεθεῖσα Cr. 35 operationem (*for* serm.) *C H: txt g*

6:14–15 *Stand therefore, having your loins girded with truth, and put on the breastplate of righteousness, and with shoes on your feet for the preparation of the gospel of peace,*

To gird with truth, to clothe with righteousness, to put on the shoes of peace—these expressions mean "let your concern be about these, that is, about truth and righteousness and peace. Put these on you. Defend yourselves with these arms." And since everything handed over to them is what belongs to soldiers, he added:

6:16 *and above all of these taking the long shield of faith with which you may be able to quench all the flaming arrows of the enemy;*[70]

[193] He says that a shield is a *long shield*.[71] "Let faith (he says) be a long shield for you, by which you can easily strike down all the devil's contrivances."

6:17a *and take the helmet of salvation*

"By employing (he says) the diligent use of these arms you will have salvation from God, with which he will fortify you instead of with a helmet, so that you may by no means receive a wound from the devil in your vital parts."

6:17b *and the sword of the Spirit, which is the spoken word of God,*

"Take the grace of the Spirit for a sword, since when you have it you will certainly strike terror in the demons to the greatest possible extent."

†And he rightly said *which is the spoken word*[72] *of God* to set forth the strength of the Spirit's working. For by *spoken word of God* he means "the working of God," as was said elsewhere (Ps 32:6): *By the word of the Lord the heavens were established,* that is, "by the working and power of God they were established." So, too, in the prophets [194] there is of-

---

[70] For "enemy" (*inimici*), see Swete's note (1:192): "The Gk. text gives τοῦ πονηροῦ without variant, and the Latin versions correspond. Our translation suggests a gloss ... but possibly it is a mere oversight."

[71] The text reads "long shield" (*scutum*, θυρεόν). Shield is *clypeus*, ἀσπίς.

[72] "Spoken word" translates *sermo* and ῥῆμα; "word," *verbum* and λόγος. Theodore treats them as synonyms.

operationem esse uocauit,*
simul etiam et Spiritus dignitatem ostendens. nec enim Dei operatio erit Spiritus operatio, si non idem Spiritus primum sit Deus.
simul etiam quasi magnum aliquod bonum esse ostendens ipsius
5 Spiritus participationem. et post plenariam exhortationem adiecit:

per omnem orationem et obsecrationem orantes in omni tempore in
Spiritu; et in ipso uigilantes in omni assiduitate et oratione pro om-
nibus sanctis. et pro me, ut detur mihi sermo in apertione oris mei in
10 *fiducia notum facere mysterium euangelii, pro quo legationem fungor*
in catenis, ut in ipso fiducialiter agam prout oportet me loqui.

praecepit illis intentissime orare pro se, ita ut eueniat illi cum
fiducia praedicare pietatem. et adiecit:

ut autem sciatis et uos illa quae erga me sunt, quid ago, omnia uobis
15 *nota faciet Tychicus, carissimus frater et fidelis minister in Domino.*
quem misi uobis in hoc ipsum, ut sciatis quae de nobis sunt, et ut con-
solentur corda uestra in Domino.

'eo quod illa quae secundum me sunt omnia uobis Tychicus
nota faciet, qui est fidelis minister Christi, frater uero noster di-
20 lectus; quem propter hoc misi, ut nota uobis faciat illa quae circa
nos sunt et consoletur uos suis sermonibus.'

pax fratribus et caritas cum fide a Deo Patre et domino Iesu Chri-
sto.

exoptans pacem et caritatem fratribus cum fide a Deo Patre et
25 domino Iesu Christo. omni enim loco uidetur plurimis sermonibus fuisse abusus de caritate, eo quod et maxime necessaria sit ad
uirtutum incorruptionem. adiecit:

1 uocatur *C* H* 4 aliquid *C (corr.)* 5-6 adicit *C* 10 legatione *C (corr.)*
11 aeternis *(for* catenis) *C H* 13 adicit *C* 15 titicus *C (corr.)* [*C*?*] 16
misi ad uos *C* 18 tychius *H* 20 misit *(for* misi ut) *C** 24 exoptans—
Christo *om (per homoeotel.) C** 27 adicit *C*

ten put down *the spoken word of the Lord that came to pass* and *the word of the Lord that came to pass*, that is, "the revelation stamped on the mind according to God's working." And in this passage he called the working of the Spirit *the spoken word of God,**

down *the spoken word of the Lord that came to pass* and *the word of the Lord that came to pass* instead of "the revelation stamped according to God's working." And here, therefore, he called the working of the Spirit *the spoken word of God*.

at the same time also demonstrating the excellence of the Spirit. For the working of the Spirit would not be the working of God if the Spirit were not, indeed, first of all God. At the same time he also demonstrated that participation in the Spirit himself is something great. And to conclude his exhortation he added:

6:18–20 *praying in the Spirit at all times in every prayer and entreaty, and in him keeping awake in all constancy and prayer for all the saints, and for me, that a spoken word may be given to me in the opening of my mouth to make known in confidence the mystery of the gospel, for which I serve as an ambassador in chains, so that I may act confidently in it so far as it is necessary for me to speak.*

He advised them to pray as earnestly as possible for him so that it would come to pass that he would preach the true religion with confidence. And he added:

6:21–22 *So that you may also know how I am and what I am doing, Tychicus, my dearly beloved brother and a faithful minister in the Lord, will make everything known to you. I have sent him to you for this very purpose, that you may know how we are and that your hearts may be encouraged in the Lord.*

[195] "Because Tychicus will make known to you all my affairs. He is a faithful minister of Christ, indeed our beloved brother. I have sent him for this purpose, that he may make known to you what our situation is and may encourage you with his discourses."

6:23 *Peace to the brothers and love with faith from God the Father and the Lord Jesus Christ.*

He intercedes for the brothers and prays for peace and love with faith from God the Father and the Lord Jesus Christ. For everywhere he is seen to have employed a great many discourses about love, because it was to the greatest extent necessary for keeping the virtues unimpaired. He added:

gratia cum omnibus qui diligunt dominum nostrum Iesum Chri-
stum, et caste conuersantur.

hoc est,

† 'omnibus adsit Dei gratia, qui
5   diligunt Christum et caste conuersantur.' uidetur autem non
dixisse secundum suam consuetudinem *gratia uobiscum;* sed
absolute [*cum omnibus*] *qui dili-*
10 *gunt Dominum in incorruptione,*
ita ut doceat eos multam istius
rei facere diligentiam; quasi illi qui tales sunt gratiam a Deo
plurimam perfrui possent,*

'πᾶσιν δὲ προσείη τοῦ θεοῦ ἡ
χάρις τοῖς ἀγαπῶσιν τὸν Χριστὸν
καὶ ἐν ἀφθαρσίᾳ πολιτευομένοις.'
ἔοικεν δὲ μὴ εἰρηκέναι ἡ χάρις
μεθ' ὑμῶν συνηθῶς· ἀλλ' ἁπλῶς
[μετὰ πάντων] τῶν ἀγαπώντων
τόν κύριον ἐν ἀφθαρσίᾳ· ἐπὶ τῷ
παιδεῦσαι αὐτοὺς πολλὴν τούτου
ποιεῖσθαι τὴν ἐπιμέλειαν, ὡς ἂν
τῶν τοιούτων καὶ τῆς παρὰ τοῦ
θεοῦ χάριτος ἀπολαύειν δυναμένων.

15 talem qualem et erga Deum caritatem ostendere uoluerint. monet etiam eos castitatem diligenter custodire. nam in superioribus
plurima uidetur de his dixisse, suadens illis ut pudice uiuant, et
non luxuriose, secundum ritum gentium qui alieni sunt a pietate.
eo quod erant ex gentibus ipsi Ephesii, gentibus autem luxurio-
20 se uiuere moris erat; siquidem et ipsis illis quae sua mystica esse
existimabant plurima talia agere uidebantur. necessarie ergo plurimam ad eos exhortationem super his facere uidetur, ut ne antiqua consuetudine protracti neglegerent pudice uiuere. ideo et diligentiam eos istius rei habere suadet; eo quod illis qui pie uiuere
25 deproperant, condecens est et necessarium ut in sanctam perseue-
rent conuersationem.

---

4   assit *H*   ‖   sq. Coisl. 204 f. 108 b [Cr. vi. 225] θεόδωρός φησιν· πᾶσιν δέ,
κ.τ.λ. Cr., θεοῦ φησίν. 9   cum omn. *om C H*   15   et *om C (corr.) H*   19   eresi
(*for* Ephesii) *C*   23   neglegerint *H*   26   explicit *add C (corr.)*

6:24 *Grace be with all who love our Lord Jesus Christ and live purely.*[73]

That is,

†"May God's grace be with all who love Christ and live purely." But he apparently did not say, as was his custom, *grace be with you,* but simply [*with all*] *who love the Lord in integrity.* This was to teach them to take special care about this, inasmuch as such people are able to enjoy greater grace from God,*

"May God's grace be with all who love Christ and live with integrity." But he apparently did not say, as was his custom, *grace be with you,* but simply [*with all*] *who love the Lord in integrity.* This was to teach them to take special care about this, since such people are able to enjoy grace from God.

as much as the love they would be willing [196] to show toward God. And he advises them to guard continence carefully, for he is seen to have said a good deal about this earlier in the letter, urging them to live chastely and not licentiously after the practice of the Gentiles, who were alien to true religion. This was because the Ephesians were themselves Gentile Christians, and it was the custom of the Gentiles to live licentiously, even if they apparently thought that much of such behavior belonged to their sacred mysteries. Therefore, he necessarily is seen to address them with a rather long exhortation about these matters, lest attracted by their former custom they should neglect living chastely. And so he urges them to have great care about this matter, because it was fitting for those who were eager to live godly lives and necessary for them to persevere in a holy way of life.

---

[73] "Purely" (*caste*). The Greek is ἐν ἀφθαρσίᾳ. See Swete's note (1:195): "Probably substituted here by an error of the scribes for *in incorruptione,* which stands in the text as quoted in the comm. just below."

THEODORUS MOPSUESTENUS IN EPISTOLAM B. PAULI AD PHILIPPENSES

ARGUMENTUM*

PHILIPPENSES uiri erant eligantes et contemplatione uirtutum multis erant meliores, qui et ad usus necessarios beati Pauli multam semper expendebant sollicitudinem, debitores se eius esse existimantes utpote apostoli, et quia ob aliorum utilitatem mul-
5 tum sustinere uidebatur laborem. et hoc quis recognoscere poterit ex illis quae in fine epistolae ab eodem Paulo sunt scripta. sed euenit de primatu contentionem oboriri inter quosdam illorum, et hoc inter illos qui maxime uirtutibus ornati esse uidebantur. deducti uero sunt ad hanc contentionem sicut saepe solet inter ho-
10 mines fieri, maxime cum illis adfuerint illa quae possunt primatum illis praestare. uirtus enim hoc uel maxime conferre potest, licet si et aliqua alia sint quae id praestare possint; haec tamen, quantum aliis melior esse perspicitur, tanto uehementius id uindicat sibi, si non quis naturae perpendens infirmitatem ab animo
15 suo omnem repulerit elationem. his additur, quoniam illi qui ex circumcisione erant suadere properabant illis fidelibus qui ex gentibus crediderunt ut legem custodirent; de quibus apostolus in secunda ad Corinthios epistola et ad Galatas plurima uidetur scripsisse. ex quibus quidam uenerunt et ad Philippenses temptantes
20 subrepere eis; qui etiam et docebant eos, dicentes quod illos qui Christo crediderunt non conueniat legem neglegere. scribit ergo

‖ *Incipit argumentum in epistola ad Philippenses C (corr.) 7 aboriri C H:
txt r 10 dum (for cum) r ‖ illa (bef. quae) om C 12 licet et alia aliqua r
13 meliores se perspiciunt C* H r 13-14 uindicant r 18 Chorinthios H
20 subripere C H surripere r ‖ illis (for illos) r 21 in Chr. H

THEODORE
OF MOPSUESTIA
ON BLESSED PAUL'S LETTER
TO THE PHILIPPIANS

THE SETTING

[197] The Philippians were distinguished men, and in their attentive consideration of the virtues they were better than most. They always used to spend much care for the needs of blessed Paul, since they considered themselves indebted to him as their apostle and because he plainly endured great toil for the benefit of others. Anyone would be able to recognize this because of what the same Paul wrote at the end of the letter (4:10–18). But it happened that a dispute arose among some of them about who held first place, and this was among those who were seen to be especially adorned with virtues. Of course, they were drawn to this dispute just the way this usually happens with some frequency among people, especially when they have qualities capable of affording them first place. For virtue especially can have this effect, granted that there are also some other things that can produce it. Nevertheless, the more virtue is regarded better than other things, the more vigorously does it claim first place for itself, if a person [198] should fail to drive all arrogance from his soul by weighing the weakness of his nature. In addition, those who came from the circumcision were eagerly trying to persuade the Gentile Christians to keep the law. The apostle plainly has written about them at considerable length in his second letter to the Corinthians and in his letter to the Galatians. Some of them had come even to the Philippians, trying to creep into their midst. And they, too, were teaching them, saying that it was not right for those who have believed in Christ to neglect the law. Therefore, in the present

in praesenti epistola beatus Paulus de humilitate custodienda illa
quae scribi conueniebant, scribens eis simul et de illis qui custodire eos legem suadebant, ut non intenderent dictis eorum; complectens et aliqua, quae ad ineundum consilium idonea illis esse
5 existimabat. demonstrabuntur uero cautius omnia ista in illa interpretatione quae per partes futura est, cum et illis quae his dicit,
et residua omnia quae in epistola dixisse uidetur. tantum uero adi-
cere dictis dignum est ad manifestandum textum epistolae, quoniam scribit ista ad eos ab urbe Roma, cum esset in uinculis, quan-
10 do contigit eum Caesarem adpellare et propterea a Iudaea ductus
est Romae, Nerone illo in tempore regnante.

*Paulus et Timotheus, servi Iesu Christi, omnibus sanctis qui sunt
Philippis, coepiscopis et diaconibus. gratia vobis et pax a Deo patre
nostro et domino Iesu Christo.*

15 haec est praescriptio epistolae. sociauit uero Timotheum secum, eo quod et miserat eum aliquando in Macedoniam cum Era-
sto, et quod notus est et illis. notandum uero est et illud, quoniam
episcopos dixit illos qui nunc presbyteri dicuntur, sic illos nominans; nec enim ordinis erat, multos in una ciuitate esse illos, qui
20 nunc episcopi nuncupantur, siquidem nec per singulas ciuitates
erant antiquis temporibus qui functionem hanc adimplebant. sed
episcopis dicens statim memoratus est et diacones. non utique re-
lictis presbyteris diacones dixisset inferiores eorum. sed ista quis
melius recognoscet ex illis quae ad Titum scripta sunt, in quibus
25 dicit: *ut constituas per ciuitates presbyteros, sicut ego tibi praecepi;*
et adiciens quales, *oportet,* (inquit) *episcopum inreprehensibilem esse,* 'presbyteros' episcopos euidenter nominans.

hoc uero in loco
†intendendum est, quoniam di-   προσεκτέον ὅτι τὸ συνεπισκόποις
30 xit *coepiscopis;* non sicut qui-   λέγει οὐχ ὡς τινες ἐνόμισαν, ὥσπερ
dam intellexerunt, *coepiscopis*   ἡμεῖς 'συμπρεσβυτέροις' γράφειν
dixit, sicut et nos et 'conpre-   εἰώθαμεν· οὐ γὰρ πρὸς τὸ ἑαυτοῦ
sbyteris' scribere consueuimus.   πρόσωπον εἶπεν τὸ σύν, ἵνα ᾖ συν-

---

4 ad in eundem *C H: txt r*   5 existimabant *C H: txt r*   6 patres (*for* partes)
C*   11 Romam *r*   13 quo episcopis *H* cum ep. *C* (*corr.*)   16 Macedonia *H*
17 et (*bef.* illud) om *l* ‖ notum est et illis *C** notus esset illis *C* (*corr.*) *r*   22
episcopos *r* ‖ diaconos (*bis*) *r*   23 dixisse *H*   29 sq. Coisl. 204, f. 110
b–111 a [Cr. vi. 232, Fr. 137] θεόδωρος. ἄλλος φησίν· προσεκτέον, κ.τ.λ. ‖
συν ἐπισκοποις (*sic*) cod.   30 cum episcopis *r*   33-294.1 σὺν ἐπισκόποις cod.
[ἰσὴν ἐπισκόποις (*sic*) Cr.]

letter blessed Paul writes what was suitable about the necessity of preserving humility, at the same time writing to them about those who were trying to persuade them to keep the law, so that they would pay no attention to their words. He includes also other matters that he thought suitable for them in forming his advice. But all these points will be demonstrated more carefully in the detailed commentary that follows, including both what he says to them regarding the former points and everything else he is seen to have written in the letter. Only it is worth adding to what I have said, so as to make the composition of the letter clear, that he writes it to them from the city of Rome, when he was in chains. This happened after he had appealed to Caesar and for this reason was led from Judea to Rome during the reign of Nero.

1:1–2 *Paul and Timothy, servants of Jesus Christ, to all the saints who are at Philippi, to the fellow bishops*[1] *and the deacons. Grace to you and peace from God our Father and the Lord Jesus Christ.*

[199] This is the salutation of the letter. And he associated Timothy with himself because he had once sent him to Macedonia with Erastus (Acts 19:22) and because he was known to the Philippians. Moreover, it must be noted that he said that those now called presbyters were bishops, giving them that name. For it was not part of the church order that there should be in a single city many of those who now have the title of bishop, even if we grant that in early times there were people in particular cities who used to fulfill this function. And when he said *to the bishops,* he immediately mentioned the deacons as well. He would certainly not have called the deacons next in rank to them if the presbyters had been left out. But anyone may better recognize the point by what was written to Titus, where Paul says (Titus 1:5, 7): *that you may appoint throughout* [200] *the cities presbyters, as I have instructed you*; and adding of what sort they were, *a bishop* (he says) *ought to be above reproach*, clearly naming bishops "presbyters." Indeed, in this passage

it must be noted that when he	It must be noted that he says
said *fellow bishops,* he did not,	*fellow bishops* not, as some have
as some have understood it, say	supposed, the way we have been

---

[1] *Coepiscopis.* The Greek, of course, has "with the bishops." Swete (1:199) suggests that "Th. writes in view of the reading συνεπισκόποις, and rejects both that reading and the interpretation which had been put upon it."

non enim ad suam personam redigens dixit *coepiscopis*, ut intellegi possit 'coepiscopis nostris,'
sed ad illud quod dixit *omni-*
5 *bus sanctis in Christo Iesu;* ut
intellegi possit quoniam 'omnibus qui sunt Philippis sanctis
cum illis [qui illic] sunt coepiscopis et diaconibus;' non ab-
10 solute designans horum nomina, sed quia humilitatis exhortatio illis magis apta esse uidebatur, qui et ceteros instruere
poterant, et ante alios seipsos
15 formam ceteris praebere in his
quae conueniebant uel agi debebant.*

ἐπισκόποις ἡμῶν, ἀλλὰ πρὸς τὸ
πᾶσιν [τοῖς ἁγίοις ἐν Χριστῷ Ἰησοῦ, ἵνα ᾖ· πᾶσιν] τοῖς ἐν Φιλίπ-
ποις ἁγίοις σὺν τοῖς αὐτόθι ἐπισκόποις τε καὶ διακόνοις· οὐχ ἁπλῶς
ἐπισημηνάμενος τὰ τούτων ὀνόματα, ἀλλ' ὡς μάλιστα τῶν περὶ τῆς
μετριοφροσύνης λόγων τούτοις ἁρ-
μοττόντων οἳ τοὺς ἑτέρους ὤφειλον
διδάσκειν καὶ πρὸ τῶν λοιπῶν αὐτοὶ
μετιέναι τὸ δέον.

gratias ago Deo meo super omni memoria uestra semper in omni
oratione mea pro omnibus uobis, cum gaudio et orationem meam fa-
20 *ciens, in communionem uestram in euangelio a prima die usque nunc.*

frequenter quidem a gratiarum actione incipit scribere; hoc uero in loco uidetur etiam aliquam illis adtestare uirtutem, si tamen
non solum pro illis gratias se agere semper edicitur *super omni [me-*
moria illorum *in omni] oratione*, sed et *cum gaudio* pro illis facit ora-
25 tionem, *communionem* eorum *in euangelio ex prima die usque nunc*
demirans. nam quod gaudere se pro illis in orationibus edicit, indicium eorum uirtutis habere uidetur; et quod *a prima die usque*
nunc dixit, inmobilitatem eorum indicat probatissimam, eo quod
numquam mutabilitatem aliquam fuerunt perpessi. et quoniam
30 incautum esse uidebatur gaudere pro omnibus, quorum exitus erat
incertus, adiecit:

confidens hoc ipsum, quoniam qui inchoauit in uobis opus bonum,

---

1-2　rediens *C r*　3　τοῖς ἁγίοις—πᾶσιν om. cod. edd.: see note.　6　cum (*for*
quoniam) *r*　8　cum sanctis illis sunt *C H* ut in sanctis illic suis coep. et diaconis
r: txt *g*　10　αὐτούς cod. Cr.; txt Fr.　14　aliis *H* ‖ seipsis f. ceteros *C H*
r　18　omni *om H**　22　attestari *r*　23　se gratias *H* se *om r* ‖ edicitur
C H: txt r　23-24　mem. ill. in omni *om CHr*　24　iam (*for* cum) *r*　24-25
orat. communem *C r* communem orat. *H*　25　eorum *om r*　31　adicit *C r*　32
confidimus in domino Iesu (*marg*) *H*

"fellow bishops," as we have been accustomed to write "fellow presbyters." For he did not say *fellow bishops* in reference to his own person, so that it can be understood as "our fellow bishops." Rather, he tied it to what he had said, that is, *to all the saints in Christ Jesus*, so that it can be understood as "to all the saints who are at Philippi together with those who are there fellow bishops and deacons," not simply indicating their names, but because an exhortation to humility seemed more suitable for those who [201] were able to instruct others and were obliged before others to present themselves as a pattern of correct behavior.*

accustomed to write "fellow presbyters." For he did not say *fellow²* regarding his own person, so as to mean "to *our* fellow bishops." Rather, he said it as tied to *all the saints in Christ Jesus*, so as to mean "to all the saints in Philippi together with those there who are bishops and deacons," not simply indicating their names, but because his words concerning modesty were as much as possible suitable for those who were obliged to teach others and who ought themselves to pursue before the rest what is right.

1:3–5 *I thank my God for every remembrance of you, always in every prayer of mine for you all, with joy also making my prayer for your fellowship in the gospel from the first day until now,*

Indeed, he often begins writing with a thanksgiving, but in this passage he plainly also bears witness to their virtue, if indeed he not only declares that he always gives thanks for them *for every remembrance* of them *in every prayer*, but also makes his prayer for them with joy by marveling at their *fellowship in the gospel from the first day until now*. For the fact that he declares that he rejoices for them in his prayers plainly indicates their virtue, and the fact that he said *from the first day until now* points out their most tried and true steadfastness, because they had never undergone any inconstancy. And since it seemed incautious to rejoice for all of those whose fate was uncertain, he added:

[202] 1:6 *confident of this very thing, that he who has begun a good*

---

²Literally, "with" (σύν). That is, we should read σὺν ἐπισκόποις rather than συνεπισκόποις.

perficiet usque in diem Christi Iesu.

    bene autem et principium et finem Christi gratiae aptauisse
perspicitur, non solum quoniam confirmabatur illa quae in Christo est fides; quoniam et istos plus esse firmos erga bonum facie-
5 bat, dum discerent quia causam illorum quae fiunt Deo conuenit
aptari, ipsi etiam pro praeteritis debent gratiarum referre actiones.
nam ita in illis persistere confirmationem illis de futuris praestare
uidebatur.

    sicut est iustum mihi hoc sapere pro omnibus uobis, eo quod habeam
10 *uos in corde meo, et in uinculis meis et in omni defensione et confirma-*
tione euangelii comparticipes gratiae omnes uos esse.

    hoc ad illud quod in superioribus est dictum retulit, ubi dixit:
cum gaudio et orationem faciens super communionem uestram in euan-
gelium; uolens dicere quoniam 'mihi uel maxime decet talia de uo-
15 bis credere, qui semper uos in corde meo habeo, licet si in uinculis,
licet ob defensionem meam tenear pro opere meo. sic enim me ad-
fectari facit de uobis, ut sciam quoniam praedicationem et doctrinam meam confirmastis per uestram fidem, tributae mihi gratiae
in apostolatum comparticipes facti;' ut dicat quoniam 'habeo uos
20 in animo semper eo quod credidistis.'

†'confirmationem' enim 'in euangelio' illorum dicit creduli-tatem, eo quod credentes, quan-tum ad illos pertinet, confir-mant praedicationem, quod ue-ra habeatur; sicut et in euan-gelio scriptum est: *qui accipit eius testimonium, signauit quo-niam Deus uerax est;* hoc est: 'credens confirmauit quantum ad se est illa quae a Deo sunt, utpote uera.' nam et *compar-ticipes gratiae meae* quia dixit, idipsum dicit. eo quod ipse ac-	βεβαίωσιν τοῦ εὐαγγελίου τὸ πισ-τεῦσαι λέγει, ὡς ἂν τῶν πιστευόν-των τό γε ἐπ' αὐτοῖς βεβαιούντων τὸ κήρυγμα ὅτι ἀληθές· ὡς ἐν τοῖς εὐαγγελίοις τὸ ὁ λαβὼν αὐτοῦ τὴν μαρτυρίαν ἐσφράγισεν ὅτι ὁ θεὸς ἀληθής ἐστιν, ἀντὶ τοῦ 'τῷ πιστεῦ-σαι ἐβεβαίωσεν τά γε ἐπ' αὐτῷ τὰ παρὰ τοῦ θεοῦ γινόμενα ὡς ἀληθῆ.' καὶ συνκοινωνοὺς δέ μου τῆς χάρι-τος τὸ αὐτὸ λέγει· ἐπειδὴ γὰρ αὐτὸς εἰλήφει χάριν ἀποστολῆς εἰς τὸ πισ-τεύειν ἑτέρους, ὁ πιστεύων ὡς εἰκὸς ἐκοινώνει τῆς χάριτος.

4-5   faciebant *C H*: *txt r*   5   qui causam *C* quia causa *r*   6   actiones ref *H*   7
confirmatione *C*   14   me (*for* mihi) *r*   15   sim (*for* si) *C* (*corr.*) *r*   18   tribuit *H r*
‖   gratiam *H*   21   sq. Coisl. 204, f. 112 a [Cr. vi. 234, Fr. 137] Θεοδώρου. ἄλλος
φησίν· βεβαίωσιν, κ.τ.λ.   23   τότε cod., Cr.: txt conj. Fr.   28   testomonium *H*
‖   ἐκβεβαιώσει edd.: txt cod. (corr. ἐβεβαίωσε τό γε, κ.τ.λ.).

work in you will perfect it until the day of Christ Jesus,

Moreover, one can perceive that he has well joined both the beginning and the end of Christ's grace, not only since faith in Christ was established, but also since it was continuing to make them more steadfast in good—provided they would recognize that it is right to attribute the cause of what took place to God and to know that they were obliged to give him thanks for past favors. For persevering in those things this way was plainly furnishing them with a confirmation of the things to come.

1:7 *as it is right for me to have this mind for all of you, because I hold you in my heart to be, all of you, fellow sharers of grace both in my chains and in every defense and confirmation of the gospel.*

He referred this to what was said above, when he said: *with joy also making prayer for your fellowship in the gospel.* He wants to say that "it becomes me even to the greatest extent to have such beliefs about you, since I always hold you in my heart, even if I am in chains, even if I am held prisoner because of my defense on behalf of my work. For my being moved by affection for you in this way makes me know that you have confirmed my preaching and teaching by your faith and have been made fellow sharers in the grace given me for my apostleship." Thus, he means, "I have you in mind always because you have believed."

†For he calls their belief "confirmation in the gospel" because so far as they are concerned by believing they are [203] confirming the preaching because it is held to be true—just as it is also written in the Gospel (John 3:33): *whoever receives his testimony has sealed that God is true*; that is, "by believing he has confirmed that so far as he is concerned those things that are from God are indeed true. The fact that he said *fellow sharers of my³ grace* means the same thing. This is because he had himself

He calls having believed *confirmation of the gospel* since, so far as they were concerned, by believing they are confirming the truth of the preaching—as in the Gospels (John 3:33): *whoever receives his testimony has sealed that God is true*, instead of "by having believed he has confirmed so far as he is concerned the things that come to be from God as true."

And *fellow sharers of my grace* means the same thing. For since he had himself received

---

³Note that "my" does not appear in the text of verse 7.

ceperat gratiam apostolatus ut
crederent alii, sicut et Romanis
scribens dicit: *per quem acce-*
pimus gratiam et apostolatum in
5 *oboedientia fidei in omnibus gen-*
tibus; qui credebat communica-
bat utique gratiae.*
et copiose suum erga eos affectum ostendens dicit:

testis enim mihi est Deus, quemadmodum desidero omnes uos in
10 *uisceribus Christi Iesu; et hoc oro, ut caritas uestra magis magisque*
abundet in cognitione et omni sensu, ut probetis utiliora, ut sitis since-
res et sine offensione in die Christi, repleti fructum iustitiae illum qui
per Iesum Christum est in gloriam et laudem Dei.

nam quod dixit: *in uisceribus Christi,* dicere uoluit: 'in caritate
15 illa quae secundum Christum est.' et quod dixit: *caritas uestra,*
'illa utique quae et erga Deum est et erga alterutrum est.'

†uult ergo dicere quoniam 'testis est mihi Deus, qualiter erga uos affectum teneo, et oro
20 per singula momenta abundare magis in uobis illam caritatem, quae et erga Deum et erga
alterutrum est. scientiam uero
conuenientem habere uos cupio
25 de illis quae ad uirtutem pertinent, probantes quae sint utiliora; et erga illa magis sollicitudinem expendite, ita ut in
futura die sine ulla adpareatis
30 reprehensione, plurimam direc-
tionum copiam obtinentes, pro
quibus poterit et in praesenti uita glorificari in uobis Deus, omnibus super uestra uirtute illum
35 conlaudantibus, in cuius nomi-

βούλεται εἰπεῖν ὅτι 'μάρτυς μου ὁ
θεὸς ὅπως περὶ πάντας ὑμᾶς διά-
κειμαι, καὶ προσεύχομαι ἑκάστοτε πλεονάζειν μὲν ὑμῶν τὴν περὶ τὸν θεὸν καὶ τὴν περὶ ἀλλήλους
ἀγάπην, γνῶσιν δὲ ἔχειν ὑμᾶς τὴν
προσήκουσαν περὶ τῶν εἰς ἀρετὴν
συντεινόντων, δοκιμάζοντας τίνα τὰ
κρείττονα, καὶ περὶ ταῦτα μᾶλλον
ἐσπουδακότας, ὥστε ὑμᾶς ἐν τῇ
μελλούσῃ ἡμέρᾳ ἀμέμπτους κατὰ
πάντα φανῆναι, ὄγκον ἐπαγομένους
κατορθωμάτων, ἐφ' οἷς δυνατὸν καὶ
κατὰ τὸν παρόντα βίον θαυμάζεσθαι ἐφ' ὑμῖν τὸν θεόν, πάντων ὡς
εἰκὸς ἐπὶ τῇ ὑμετέρᾳ ἀρετῇ ἐκεῖνον
ἐκπληττομένων, οὕπερ ἐπ' ὀνόματι
ταῦτα ποιεῖτε.'

3-4 accipimus *C* 9 uos omnes *H* 12 fructu ... illum *H r* 15 est *om H*
16 et (I°) *om C* 17 sq. Coisl. 204, f. 112 b [Cr. vi. 236, Fr. 138] Θεοδώρου.
ἄλλος φησίν· βούλεται, κ.τ.λ. 18 ὑμῶν edd.: txt cod. 30 confusione (*for*
repreh.) *H* 30-31 directionis *H*

received the grace of apostleship in order that others might believe, as he says when writing to the Romans (Rom 1:5): *through whom we have received grace and apostleship for the obedience of faith in all the Gentiles*; the one who believed would undoubtedly share in the grace.*

the grace of apostleship so that others would believe, the believer would in all likelihood share in the grace.

And eloquently showing his own affection for them, he says:

1:8–11 *For God is my witness how I long for you all in the innermost parts of Christ Jesus. And this I pray, that your love may more and more abound in knowledge and in every sense, so that you may test the things that are more advantageous, so that you may be pure and without blame in the day of Christ, filled with that fruit of righteousness that is through Jesus Christ to the glory and praise of God.*

[204] For when he said *in the innermost parts of Christ*, he meant "in that love that is according to Christ." And when he said *your love*, he meant undoubtedly that love that is both toward God and toward one another.

†Therefore, he wants to say "God is my witness how I have affection for you, and I pray at all times that there may abound all the more in you that love that is toward God and toward one another. But I wish you to have a right knowledge of those things that pertain to virtue, testing what things are more advantageous. So all the more spend great care on those things, so that on the day that is to come you may appear found without any fault, gaining a very great supply of right deeds, in return for which even in the present life God may be able to be glorified in you, when

He wants to say "God is my witness how well-disposed I am to you all, and I pray at all times that your love for God and for one another may abound and that you may have knowledge proper to the things that contribute to virtue, testing what things are better and being all the more zealous for them, so that on the day that is to come you may appear blameless in all things, procuring for yourselves a great weight of virtuous deeds, by which it is possible even in the present life for God to be admired in you, when all people, as is likely, because of your virtue are struck with admira-

ne haec facitis.'*

ista quidem scripsit ad eos, affectum proprium quem erga eos habebat ostendens. et quidem uerissimis laudibus ad eorum est exhortationem abusus. incipit uero in subsequentibus ea quae de se
5 erant nota facere illis simul quidem quasi affectiosis et qui ualde
pro illo solliciti, siquidem sumptus misisse uidentur; conueniebat
enim talibus et illa quae secundum se erant nota facere, simulque
et ad doctrinam illis proficere poterant. nam quia sub arcta erat
necessitate apostolus pietatis contemplatione, sufficiens erat eru-
10 dire illos eius imitatione etiam grauiora tolerare pro uirtute. incipit uero sic:

scire autem uos uolo, fratres, quoniam ea quae erga me sunt magis
ad profectum euangelii peruenerunt, ita ut uincula mea manifesta, in
Christo fierent in toto praetorio et ceteris omnibus, et plures fratrum
15 *in Domino confidentes uinculis meis abundantius auderent sine timore*
uerbum loqui.

†beatus Paulus adpellans Festum eo quod uolebat eum Iudaeis tradere, et postulans se
20 mitti ad Caesarem, ductus est in
uinculis Romae. inductus uero
ante Neronem, et defensionem
sui faciens, biennio illo demora-
tus, plenariam adeptus est secu-
25 ritatem.*

ὁ μακάριος Παῦλος ἐφέσει κατὰ
τοῦ Φήστου χρησάμενος βουληθέν-
τος αὐτὸν Ἰουδαίοις ἐκδοῦναι, καὶ
διὰ τοῦτο Καίσαρα ἐπικαλεσάμε-
νος, ἀνήχθη δέσμιος εἰς τὴν Ῥώ-
μην· εἰσαχθεὶς δὲ τῷ Νέρωνι καὶ
ὑπὲρ τῶν καθ' ἑαυτὸν ἀπολογησά-
μενος διετῆ χρόνον αὐτόθι διέτρι-
ψεν, παντελοῦς τετυχηκὼς τῆς ἀφέσεως.

ideo et in secunda ad Timotheum epistola, quam a Roma ad eum
scripsit, non tunc quando et ad Philippenses scribebat—etenim
tunc cum ipso ad illos scripsit—sed secunda uice, quando illic ca-
30 pite est punitus, scribens dicit: *in prima mea defensione nemo mihi*
adfuit, sed omnes me reliquerunt; non illis imputetur. Dominus autem
adstitit mihi et confortauit me, ut per me praedicatio impleatur, omnes
gentes; et liberatus sum ex ore leonis (Neronem indicans).

---

2 quidam *C*   4 in (*bef.* uer.) add *C H r*   5 affectuosus *r*   6 erant (*bef.*
soll.) *add H*   8 erant *C* r*   9 contemplationem *C H r*   10 imitationem *C*
r   17 sq. Coisl. 204, f. 113 a [Cr. vi. 238, Fr. 138] θεοδώρου. ἄλλος φησίν· ὁ
μακ. Π., κ.τ.λ.   21 Romam *r*   25-26 ἐφέσεως edd.: txt cod.   28 ad (*bef.*
Philipp.) *om H* Philippensibus *r*   31 affuit *C* (*corr.*) *H*   ‖   relinquerunt *C**
dereliquerunt *H*

all people in concert because of your virtue praise him in whose name you accomplish these deeds."*

tion for him in whose name you accomplish these deeds."

Indeed, he wrote those words to them, showing his own affection that he had for them. And he surely employed the truest praises to encourage them. But in what follows he begins to make his affairs known to them, both because they were affectionate and because they were greatly concerned for him, [205] if at any rate they had indeed sent money. For it was right for him to make known to such people even his own affairs, and they had at the same time the ability to profit by them for instruction. For because the apostle was fast bound in straitened circumstances for the sake of true religion, it was enough to instruct them how to endure even graver things for virtue by following his example. So he begins this way:

1:12–14 *And I want you to know, brothers, that what has happened to me has come more for the advancement of the gospel, so that my chains have been made apparent in Christ in the whole praetorium and to all the rest; and most of the brothers, having been made confident in the Lord by my chains, dare to speak the word more abundantly without fear.*

†Blessed Paul, appealing to Festus because he wanted to hand him over to the Jews, and demanding to be sent to Caesar, was led to Rome in chains. And brought before Nero and making a defense for himself, he stayed there for a period of two years and gained complete safety.*

Blessed Paul, gaining permission from Festus, who wanted to hand him over to the Jews, and for this reason appealing to Caesar, was led to Rome as a prisoner. And brought before Nero and making his apology for the charges against him, spent two years there, having gained a complete release.

And so in the second letter to Timothy, which he wrote to him from Rome, not at the time he was writing to the Philippians—for then it was with Timothy that he wrote to them—but on a second occasion when he underwent capital punishment there, he wrote and said (2 Tim 4:16–17): [206] *at my first defense no one came to my support, but all deserted me. May it not be counted against them! But the Lord stood by me and strengthened me so that through me the preaching might be fulfilled and all the Gentiles might hear it. And I was freed from the lion's mouth* (indicating Nero).

†tunc quidem existimabant omnes beatum Paulum interfici a
Nerone, eo quod crudelissimus
erat; et maxime, quia noua quaedam illis in temporibus docere
uidebatur, multum extranea illorum quae apud Romanos tunc
ritu deorum colebantur. praeter omnem uero spem introductus est defendens causam suam;
non solum quia nihil passus est,
uerum etiam et plenam securitatem est adsecutus, ita ut et
a Roma postea discederet, et
consueto more doctrinae immi-
neret. omnes uero ad demirationem impellebat illud quod
fuerat factum, et plurimam fiduciam fidelibus tribuebat, ita
ut excepto omni terrore pacatus
dogmata doceret.*

τότε τοίνυν προσεδόκων μὲν ἅπαν-
τες τὸν μακάριον Παῦλον πάντως
ἀναιρεῖσθαι ὑπὸ τοῦ Νέρωνος, ὠμο-
τάτου τὸν τρόπον ὄντος, καὶ μάλιστα ἐπειδή πως καὶ καινὰ ἐδόκει διδάσκειν, πολὺ τῆς τότε παρὰ Ῥωμαίοις κρατούσης περὶ θεὸν
δόξης ἀλλότρια. ἔτυχεν οὖν παντελοῦς ἀφέσεως, ὡς καὶ ἀναχωρῆσαι
τῆς Ῥώμης καὶ τῷ συνήθει τρόπῳ χρήσασθαι τῆς διδασκαλίας· ἐξ-
έπληττέν τε ἅπαντας τὸ γενόμενον
καὶ παρρησίαν ἐνεποίει τοῖς πιστοῖς
τοῦ διδάσκειν.

nam quod dixit *in toto praetorio*, ut dicat: 'in regiis, et illis quae
circa eum sunt;' 'praetorium' illud nominans, quod nunc ex consuetudine 'palatium' nominamus.

†hoc ergo dixit: 'uolo uos (inquit) scire, eo quod illa quae
doctrinae meae sunt in singulis diebus incrementa accipiunt.
nam uinctus ad omnium notitiam perueni, inductus defensione mea adfui; et sic ab omni periculo liberatus, ut multi fideles docerent illa quae pietatis
sunt, ex illis quae erga me facta
sunt fiduciam accipientes.'*

τοῦτο οὖν λέγει, ὅτι 'βούλομαι ὑμᾶς
εἰδέναι, ὡς τὰ τῆς διδασκαλίας ὁσ-
ημέραι προκόπτει τῆς ἐμῆς· δῆ-
λος γὰρ ἐπὶ τοῖς δεσμοῖς μου ἅπασιν ἐγενόμην, καὶ εἰσαχθεὶς περὶ τῶν καθ' ἑαυτὸν ἀπελογησάμην,
καὶ οὕτως ἀπήλλαξα ἀκινδύνως ὥστε πολλοὺς τῶν ὁμοπίστων διδάσκειν τὰ τῆς εὐσεβείας ἀπὸ τῶν κατ'
ἐμὲ τὴν παρρησίαν εἰληφότας.'

5 in *om* r ‖ docebatur uidebatur *H* 18 et *om H* r 20 peccatus *C** 21
dogma *H* 23 nos (*for* nunc) *H* 28 incrementum *C* 30 peruenit *r* 31
affui *C* (*corr.*) *H* 33 cum fiducia (*aft.* fideles) *add C*

†Indeed, at that time everyone thought that blessed Paul would be killed by Nero, because Nero was extremely cruel and especially because at that time he was apparently teaching certain novel customs quite foreign to those that were then being cultivated among the Romans in worshiping the gods. So Paul was brought in beyond all hope to defend his own cause. Then not only did he suffer nothing, but he also even gained complete safety, so that he also left Rome afterwards and in his usual manner gave his attention to teaching. What had happened drove everyone to amazement and furnished the faithful with greater confidence, so that with all fear removed he could teach his doctrines in peace.*

Therefore, at that time everyone expected that blessed Paul would inevitably be killed by Nero, because Nero was extremely cruel in character and especially since somehow he was also apparently teaching novel customs quite foreign to the popular opinion about God that prevailed among the Romans at that time.

Then Paul gained a complete release, so that he left Rome and in his usual manner busied himself with teaching. What happened amazed everyone and produced in the faithful confidence for teaching.

For when he said *in the whole praetorium*, he means "in the royal residence and the places that are around it," giving the name "praetorium" to what [207] we are now accustomed to name "the palace."

†Therefore, he said this: "I want you to know (he says) that the results of my teaching are receiving increases day by day. For being bound I came to everyone's notice. Brought in, I was present at my defense, and so I have been freed from all danger, so that many of the faithful might teach what belongs to true religion, receiving confidence because of what happened to me."*

Therefore, he means this: "I want you to know that the results of my teaching advance day by day. For I became conspicuous to all in my bonds, and, brought in, I made my apology concerning the charges against me, and so I got off free without danger, so that many of my fellow believers are teaching what belongs to true religion, since they have received confidence from what happened to me."

*quidam quidem et propter inuidiam et contentionem, quidam uero
et propter bonum placitum Christum adnuntiant.*

et latius significans quid sit, quod dixerit: *propter inuidiam et
contentionem*, adicit:

5   *alii quidem ex contentione Christum adnuntiant, non sincere, existimantes tribulationem inferre uinculis meis.*

'quidam (inquit) inuidentes rebus bene erga me gestis, et quoniam nihil mali passus sum inductus ante Neronem, sed et illa
quae erga me fuerunt edicens solui ab eo promerui; contra me
10   suam contentionem exercentes discurrunt, non fiducia aliqua id
agentes, sed nequitia (ut ita dixerim) pietatis dogmata docere deproperant, ut illi qui in principatu et potestate sunt ex eorum fiducia permoti secum reputent, quoniam quia horum omnium causa
illa extitit, quod ego sine periculo negotium transierim; ut iterum
15   aduersus me conuertantur, et poena mea ceteros corrigant.' hoc
autem quis erga beatum Paulum effectum intellegens nequaquam
demirabitur, quasi qui ob inuidiam fuerit aliquid perpessus. deinde quia dixit: *et per bonum placitum Christum praedicant*, euidenter
illud significauit dicens:

20   *quidam quidem ex caritate, scientes quoniam in defensionem euangelii positus sum.*

hoc est: 'quidam caritate illa quam erga Christum habebant
praedicant, confidentes quidem meum esse opus ut praedicetur
pietas; abutuntur uero fiducia, eo quod ita erga me diuina donante
25   gratia sit dispensatum, ut fiduciam cuncti adsequerentur.' dicens
euidentius horum quoque et illorum arbitrium:

quid enim? dum omnimodo, siue occasione siue ueritate, Christus

---

11 impietatis *C H r* 11-12 properant *H* 12 principatum et potestatem *H*
13 quia *om r* 14 existit *r* ‖ ego *om H* 15 aduersum *r* ‖ corrigantur *r*
20 defensione *C (corr.) H* 22 caritatem illam *C H r*

1:15 *Some, indeed, even because of envy and rivalry, but others also because of good will, proclaim Christ.*[4]

And indicating at greater length what he meant when he said *because of envy and rivalry*, he adds:

1:17 *Some, indeed, proclaim Christ from rivalry, not sincerely, thinking to inflict tribulation on my chains,*

"Some (he says), envying me the good outcome—since I suffered nothing evil when I was brought before Nero but even deserved to be acquitted by him when I declared my circumstances—are running about in different ways, practicing their rivalry against me and doing so not with any confidence, but it is by wickedness, if I may say so, [208] that they are eager to teach the doctrines of true religion, so that those in leadership and authority, upset by their confidence, might reflect among themselves that the cause of all this had really come about because I had passed through the affair without danger and so that they might again turn against me and correct the rest by punishing me."[5] And anyone who understands what took place with respect to blessed Paul will by no means be astonished if it turns out that he will suffer something because of envy.[6] Then, because he said *also because of goodwill they preach Christ*,[7] he pointed this out more clearly by saying:

1:16 *some, indeed, from love, knowing that I have been placed for the defense of the gospel.*

That is, "some preach by the love they had for Christ, surely trusting that it is my work that true religion be preached, and they make full use of confidence because the dispensation of divine grace given to me is so that all may acquire confidence." Speaking more clearly of the judgment of both the former people and the latter:

1:18a *What then? Provided that in every way, whether by chance*

---

[4] In what follows verses 16 and 17 are transposed, as they are also by Chrysostom and Theodoret. The verbs in the Latin translation of verses 15, 17, and 18 do not correspond exactly to the Greek. In verse 15 *adnuntiant* corresponds to κηρύσσουσιν; in verse 17 *adnuntiant* to καταγγέλλουσιν; in verse 18 *praedicetur* to καταγγέλλεται.

[5] That is, the motive of their bold preaching was to provoke the Roman authorities to take further action against Paul and so to compromise the spread of the gospel rather than to further it.

[6] Swete (1:208) suggests that Theodore is thinking of his own experience.

[7] *Praedicant* instead of *adnuntiant*, as in the Latin rendering of the verse.

praedicetur.

multa demiratione dignum est id quod a Paulo dictum est, licet sit et aliquid aliud simile. 'non (inquit) discutio arbitrium illorum, licet ad nociuitatem meam per inuidiam fiat quod fit; tan-
5 tum cunctos doceant Christo credere.' nec enim, ut quidam existimauerunt, licentiam in his beatus Paulus praestat illis qui interuertere pietatis cupiunt dogma; qui tantum nos uult erga hae-
reticos odium habere, sicut ipse scribens dicit: *haereticum hominem post primam et secundam correptionem deuita.* sed de illis hoc
10 in loco loquitur, qui sanam quidem doctrinam docent dogmatum,
faciunt autem illud non ob ipsam pietatem, sed ut commoueant
contra eum insidias. et ostendens quoniam consequenti ratione ita
persistit de illis qui non integre illud faciunt, sed insidias ei cupiunt commouere:

15 *et hoc gaudeo, sed et gaudebo; scio enim quoniam hoc mihi proficiet*
in salutem, per uestram orationem et subministrationem Spiritus Iesu
Christi.

'his ita affectis gaudio cumulor, sciens quoniam in futuro saeculo plus gratulabor, quando pro his mercedem recipiam uobis oran-
20 tibus, et Christo gratiam Spiritus copiosam nobis pro istis prae-
bente;' eo quod et resurrectionem per Spiritum sanctum fieri expectabant, et fruitionem futurorum bonorum, eo quod ante adsequi sperabant. euidens autem est, quoniam et futurae gloriae
splendorem pro modo fidei uel laborum a Spiritu sibi itidem da-
25 ri expectabant. bene ergo *subministrationem Spiritus* dixit, ut lar-
gam mercedem significaret et retributionum magnitudinem illam,
quam decet Spiritum tribuere. et quoniam licet magna sint illa
quae expectantur, sed et tribulationes praesentes magnae erant,

---

2 a *om r*　5 non (*for* nec) *H*　7 pietatis *om H*　11 commouere cupiunt *r*
15 ego (*bef.* gaudebo) *add H**　16 in *om C * H r*　18 gaudeo comulor (*sic*)
*C**　24 laborem *C H r*　24-25 dare *C* H r*

or by truth Christ is preached.

What Paul has said would be worthy of much astonishment, granted that one thing is like the other. "I do not (he says) pull to pieces the judgment of those people, granted that what takes place does so by envy to harm me, if the only thing that matters is that they are teaching all to believe in Christ." Nor, indeed, as some people have thought, does blessed Paul by these words furnish license to those who [209] want to set aside the doctrine of true religion.[8] He wants us to have such a great hatred for heretics as, for example, he himself says when he writes (Titus 3:10): *A person who is a heretic, after a first correction and a second, avoid.* But as for those he speaks of in this passage, they are surely giving sound teaching of doctrines, but they are doing this not because of true religion itself but in order to stir up plots against him. And showing that it is for a consistent reason that he stands firm regarding them because they do this not honestly, but wish to stir up plots against him:

1:18b-19 *And in that I rejoice, but I also shall rejoice, for I know that this will turn out for me for salvation through your prayer and the provision of the Spirit of Jesus Christ,*

"Since advances have been made in this way, I am overwhelmed with joy, knowing that in the age to come I shall give thanks all the more, when I shall receive a reward for them while you offer your prayers and Christ bestows on us the abundant grace of the Spirit for these things." This is because they were looking forward to the resurrection's taking place through the Holy Spirit and to the enjoyment of the good things to come, because they were hoping beforehand to acquire them. And it is clear that [210] they were likewise looking forward to the splendor of the glory to come to be given them by the Spirit according to the measure of faith (see Rom 12:3) or of toils. Therefore, he rightly said *the provision of the Spirit* so that he might indicate the lavish reward and the greatness of the compensations that it becomes the Spirit to bestow. And since even though those things that are expected are great, yet

---

[8] See Swete's note (1:209): "from the united protest of Chrys., Th. and Thdt. it is clear that at the beginning of the fifth century the Apostle's words were used by many as an argument against the prevalent attacks upon heresy.... With this latitudinarian party ... Th. had no sympathy, notwithstanding his dislike of coercive measures."

siquidem et tales insidiae aduersus eum ab his qui eiusdem fidei erant praeparabantur:

secundum desperationem et spem meam quia in nullis confundar, sed in omni fiducia, sicut semper et nunc magnificabitur Christus in
5   *corpore meo, siue per uitam, siue per mortem.*

desperationem euidenter illud dicit, quod sperare non possit. uult enim dicere quoniam 'licet in tantis constringar malis, ut desperem de praesentibus, et nullam subrelictam mihi spem salutis esse existimem, sed tunc spero non confundi, ualde edoctus, quo-
10   niam magnus per illa quae erga me sunt uidebitur Christus, siue uiuam, siue moriar; neque mortem meam fieri Christo absolute concedente aut uane.' et quoniam dixit quia *magnificabitur Christus*, hoc autem necdum probationem habebat illorum quae erga eum erant, ostendens quoniam et hoc sufficiens sit sibi si Christus
15   magnificabitur, adiecit:

mihi autem uiuere Christus est et mori lucrum.

'nec enim si uiuam, inquam, alterius alicuius rei curam habeo, nisi solum illam, quae ad gloriam pertinet Christi; licet moriar pro eo, magna me lucrasse confido. uado enim, ut sim cum illo.' unde
20   et summa cum demiratione adicit:

si autem uiuere in carne, hic mihi fructus operis, et quid eligam, ignoro. coarctor enim ex duobus, desiderium habens ut resoluar et cum Christo sim, multo magis melius; permanere autem in carne necessarium est propter uos.

25   'itaque et in aporia uertor, ignorans quid me conueniat eligere. oblectat enim me huius uitae exitus, eo quod Christo me facit adesse; gratum autem mihi est et ut sim in uita, eo quod multos ex illis qui Christo extranei sunt ad eius pote sum perducere fidem. itaque etsi melius est mihi hinc discedere ut sim cum Chri-
30   sto, sed tamen plus praesentiam meam *propter uos* necessariam esse iudico'—ut dicat 'uos, qui ad fidem acceditis.' et quoniam ista dixit suum arbitrium publicans, ut ne uideatur uera ratione aporiatus nescire ea quae secundum se sunt, uel in quibus sit, adiecit:

---

3 dispensationem *C H r* 6 dispensationem *C** desparationem *H** desperationem *C (corr.) H (corr.)* 8 mihi *om r* 12 quia *om H* 19 lucratum esse *r* 20 cum *om H* 25 dubitationem (*for* aporia) *r* 26 fecit *H* 27 multis *C H r* 28 possum *C (corr.)* potes *H* potero *r* 28-29 finem (*for* fidem) *H* 29 melior *C H* 31 ut ducam (*for* ut dicat) *r* 32 dixit ista *H* 32-33 apparatus *r* 33 nec scire *C* H* nec ea scire *r* ‖ adicit *C r*

present tribulations were also great, if indeed such plots were also being planned against him by those who were of the same faith:

1:20 *according to despair[9] and my hope that I shall in nothing be put to confusion, but in all confidence that just as always, so now Christ will be magnified in my body whether by life or by death.*

He clearly says *despair* because he was unable to hope. For he wants to say, "granted that I am fast bound in such great evils that I despair of present things and think there is no hope of safety left to me, yet at the time to come I do hope not to be put to confusion, firmly taught that Christ will be seen to be great through what happens to me, whether I live or die—not even if Christ permits my death to take place simply and for nothing." And since he said *Christ will be magnified*, but this did not yet have a proof about those things that happened to him that would demonstrate that even this would be enough for him, if Christ would be magnified, he added:

[211] 1:21 *And for me to live is Christ, and to die is gain.*

"For not even if I should live, I say, do I have any concern about one thing or the other, except only that concern that pertains to the glory of Christ. Even should I die for him, I am confident that I should have gained great profit. For I am going forward so that I may be with him." For this reason quite marvelously he adds:

1:22–24 *And if to live in the flesh, this is for me the fruit of work; and what I should choose I do not know. For I am hard pressed from two things, having the desire that I be released and be with Christ, by far the better, but to remain in the flesh is necessary for you.*

"And so I am also turned about in perplexity, not knowing what is right for me to choose. For departure from this life delights me because it would make me present to Christ; but it is acceptable to me, as well, that I should be in life, because I am able to lead many of those who are alien to Christ to faith in him. And so, even though it is better for me to leave this life in order to be with Christ, nevertheless, I judge my presence to be more necessary *for you*"—meaning "you who have drawn near to faith." And since he said those things to make his judgment public, so that he might not seem perplexed with true reason in not knowing what his affairs were or in what circumstances he was, he added:

---

[9] *Desperationem*, a possible meaning of ἀποχαραδοχίαν.

et hoc confidens scio quoniam manebo et compermanebo omnibus
uobis ad uestrum profectum et gaudium fidei, ut gloriatio vestra abun-
det in Christo Iesu in me per meum aduentum iterum ad uos.

'sed haec quidem secundum meum affectum locutus sum; scio
5   autem quoniam ero in hac uita, ita ut et ad uos iterum ueniam,
et profectum suum in fide etiam illa quae secundum uos sunt habeant, adiuncta uobis multitudine copiosa quae per me ad fidem
deducetur, ita ut et ampliorem habeam occasionem gloriandi de
uobis secundum Christum.' nam *uestrum* dicens non ad plenum
10 de persona Philippensium dicit, sed ut dicat illos qui per eum sint
credituri ex gentibus; ex illorum persona illud dicens, quasi quia
et ipsi sic crediderunt.

tantum digne euangelio Christi conuersamini.

hinc incipit de concordia et humilitate illis disputare, docens
15 eos, non de primatu concertare. ualde autem illos ad uerecundiam
inuitat dicto illo quo dixit, *ita ut digne euangelio Christi conuerse-*
mini; si igitur hoc quaerit ab illis, ut promissione sua consentanea
agant. cui demiranda adiectio quam adiecit:

ut siue ueniens et uidens uos, siue absens audiero illa quae de uobis
20 *sunt.*

licet praesens sit, licet absens, similiter sollicitus est de illis, ut
illa quae meliora sunt recognoscant, et propter hoc semper aequo
studio diligentiam implere meliorem optent. quod est autem eius
consilium?

25 *quoniam statis in uno spiritu unianimes.*

hoc est, 'concordatis uobis.' et quae sit utilitas concordiae explicans:

concertantes in fide euangelii; et non terreamini in nullo ab aduer-
sariis, quae est illis causa perditionis, uobis autem salutis.

30 'poteritis (inquit) concordantes auxilium uobis inuicem praestare in fide, ita ut non concedatis illis quae ab aduersariis uobis
inferuntur; quae illorum quidem perditionis habent probationem,
qui iusta ratione poenas luent pro quibus in uobis talia agunt. uobis uero salus ex hoc erit, quam adquiretis pro quibus in praesenti

5   uitam (*for* uos) *C H r: see note*   10   sunt *H*   12   si (*for* sic) *C*   16-17
conuersamini *C H r*   17   sic (*for* si) *H*   ‖   promissione sine *C* r* prom. sibi
C (*corr.*) [promissioni suae *conj. Jacobi*]   18   cuius *C r*   19   et (*for* ut) *C* (*corr.*)
25   unanimes *C* (*corr.*) *H r*   28   in ullo *C* (*corr.*) *r*   29   illa (*for* illis) *C H*   31
cedatis *H*   34   exoceret (*sic: for* ex hoc erit) *C**

1:25–26 *And confident of this, I know that I shall remain and continue with [212] you all for your progress and joy in faith, so that your boast may abound in Christ Jesus for me by my coming again to you.*

"But I have spoken these words, of course, in accord with my affection, and I know that I shall be in this life so that I may come again to you and also that your situation affords its own progress in the faith, since an abundant multitude led by me to faith has been joined to you, so that I may have a fuller opportunity of boasting about you in Christ." For by saying *your [progress]* he does not mean to restrict "your" to the person of the Philippians, but refers to those from the Gentiles who were going to believe through him. He says this to refer to them inasmuch as the Philippians, too, came to belief in this way.

1:27a *Only live worthily in the gospel of Christ,*

From this point he begins to reason with them about concord and humility, teaching them not to contend with one another for first place. And he firmly induces them to shame by the expression he used: *so that[10] you may live worthily in the gospel of Christ*, if at least he is asking of them that they act in accordance with their promise. The addition he made to this is to be admired:

1:27b *so that whether coming and seeing you or absent I shall hear those things that concern you,*

No matter whether he were present or absent, he is equally concerned about them, [213] so that they may recognize what are better actions and because of this may always choose a better attentiveness with reasonable zeal. What, then, is his advice?

1:27c *that you stand in one spirit, sharing a single mind,*

That is, "when you are in concord." And to explain what the benefit of concord is:

1:27d–28a *contending together in the faith of the gospel, and may you not be terrified in anything by the opponents, which is for them a cause of destruction but for you of salvation,*

"You will be able (he says) by being in concord to furnish help to one another in faith, so that you may not yield to the things that are inflicted upon you by the opponents, which they have surely as a proof[11] of the destruction of those who with just reason pay the

---

[10] *Ita ut* instead of *tantum* in the citation of the verse.

[11] *Probationem*, apparently reflecting ἔνδειξις in the text of 1:28, which the

uita contemplatione pietatis passionibus obiectamini.' et prouo-
cans eos ad passionem ineundam:

et hoc a Deo; quoniam uobis datum est pro Christo non solum ut in
illum credatis, sed et pro illo patiamini.

sufficienter illis et hisce dictis alacritatem praestitit, siquidem
sic bonum est pati pro Christo, ita ut et dignum sit illi pro hoc
etiam gratias agere ob illos lucros qui illis hinc adnascuntur.

deinde exemplo sui magis eos adhortatur:

idem certamen habentes quod uidistis in me et nunc audistis de me.

deinde sumens exhortationem, dicens:

si qua ergo consolatio in Christo, si quod solatium caritatis, si
qua societas Spiritus, si qua et uiscera miserationis, implete gaudium
meum.

bene quia dixit *si qua ergo*, eo quod uidebantur curam eius habere propter imminentem ei necessitatem, ita ut mitterent et illa
quae usui eius sciebant esse necessaria; 'omnimodo (inquit) si uobis cura est de nostra consolatione, et diligentes nos condoletis nobis talia patientibus, illa facite quae perfectum nobis gaudium de
uobis reddere poterunt.'

ut idipsum sapiatis, eandem caritatem habentes, unanimes, unum
sapientes.

quae illa? uarie dixit, ut dicat 'concordantes et diligentes alterutrum.' deinde et abdicans illa quae ab illis fiebant, monuit:

nihil secundum concertationem aut uanam gloriam.

'nec enim cupiditate uanae gloriae super primatum debetis
contendere; sed quid magis conuenit uos facere?'

sed humilitate in inuicem existimantes supereminere uobis.

'melius est, inquam, per humilitatem etiam et illos, qui aequales uobis sunt, meliores existimare, et sic omnem illis honorem im-
pigre tribuere.' et quod maxime sciebat posse intercipere huius-

1   adiectamini *H* oblectamini *r*   7   illa lucra *r*   8   suo *H*   9   in me *om C**   16
usum *C* H* ad usum *C (corr.)*: *txt r*   ‖   omnino (*for* omnimodo) *r*   17   mea
(*for* nostra) *H*   20-21   ut idipsum—sapientes *om r*   23   faciebant (*for* fiebant) *r*
25   cupiditatem *H*   26   uobis *r*

penalties for doing such things among you. But from this you will have salvation, which you will gain in return for the sufferings you are subject to in the present life for the sake of true religion." And challenging them to undergo suffering:

1:28b-29 *and this from God, because it has been given to you for Christ not only that you should believe in him but also that you should suffer for him,*

He sufficiently set forth enthusiasm with his former words and with these, if at any rate it is good to suffer for Christ in this way, so that it may be appropriate even to thank him for this because of those profits that arise for them from this source.

Then he exhorts them all the more by his own example:

1:30 *having the same contest that you see in me and now hear about me.*

[214] Then, summing up the exhortation, saying:

2:1–2a *Therefore, if there is any encouragement in Christ, if there is the consolation of love, if there is any fellowship of the Spirit, if there are also any innermost parts of compassion, fill up my joy,*

The reason he rightly said *therefore, if any* is because they plainly had a concern for him because of the difficulty that threatened him, so that they would send him what they knew to be necessary for his needs. "If in all circumstances (he says) your concern is to console us, and if in your love for us you grieve with us when we suffer such things, do what can bring about my perfect joy about you."

2:2b *so that you may have the same mind, having the same love, sharing a single mind, minding one thing,*

What are those things? In various ways he said this to mean "being in concord with and loving one another." Then, disavowing what they were doing, he warned:

2:3a *nothing from rivalry or vainglory,*

"For you ought not compete for first place by a desire for vainglory. But what is it right for you to do instead?"

[215] 2:3b *but in humility reckoning of one another to be more excellent than you,*

"It is better, I say, by humility to reckon even those who are equal to you as better and so actively to attribute all honor to them." And he added what he especially knew could prevent

---

Latin translation of the text renders as *causa*.

modi contentionem, adiecit, consilium dans eis:

ut non solum sua unusquisque consideret, sed et quae alterius sunt singuli.

'noli (inquit) considerare, quemadmodum ipse primatum te-
5   neas, sed reputa, quoniam si tibi iucundum est ceteris praeesse, multo magis alteri intolerable est, ut secundum locum teneat. co-
gitans autem similia et de ceteris, diligentiam magis ex aequalitate adhibebis.'

deinde et exemplo admodum necessario utitur ad humilitatis
10   doctrinam illam, edicens quae secundum Christum sunt:

hoc enim (ait) *sapiatur* (uel *sentiatur*) *in uobis quod in Christo Ie-su.*

hoc est, 'talia sapite et qualia Christus uidetur sapuisse.' qualia illa?

15   *qui in forma Dei extans non rapinam arbitratus est esse se aequalem Deo.*

rapere hominibus est moris illa, ex quibus aliquid adquirere se-
se posse existimant. dicimus enim frequenter quoniam 'rem illam rapiendam esse existimauit,' hoc est, 'cum celeritate illud susce-
20   pit, quasi quia magnum illi lucrum possit conferre.' hoc ergo dicit de Christo, quoniam *non rapinam arbitratus est, ut sit aequalis Deo;* hoc est, 'non magnam reputauit illam quae ad Deum est aequalitatem, et elatus in sua permansit dignitate; sed magis pro alio-
rum utilitate praeelegit humiliora sustinere negotia quam secun-
25   dum se erant, et quidem cum in forma Dei extaret'—ut dicat: 'Dei existens;' hoc est, 'dominus et dominator et uniuersitatis auctor.' haec enim omnia quae dicta sunt nuncupationem Dei subsequi uidentur ueraciter. quid autem fecit?

sed se ipsum exinaniuit formam serui accipiens.

30   †'exinanitum' diuina scrip-   κένωσιν ἡ θεία γραφή φησιν τὸ
tura pro nihilo uocat, sicut ali-   μηδέν, ὡς τὸ κεκένωται ἡ πίστις,
bi scriptum est: *euacuata est fi-*   ἀντὶ τοῦ 'οὐδὲν ἀποπέφανται·' καὶ
des, hoc est, 'nulla esse ostensa   κενὸν ἄρα τὸ κήρυγμα ἡμῶν, ἀντὶ

---

7   ex qualitate *C*H*   9   et *om r*   10   illam *C*   11   hoc enim sentite (*marg*) *H*
‖   uel sent. sap. *C**   13-14   hoc est—illa *om r*   13   et *om C* (*corr.*)   15   se *om*
H*   21   rapina *H*   24   utilitatem *C*H*   30   sq. Coisl. 204, f. 124 a, b [Cr.
vi. 259, Fr. 138–9] Θεόδωρος. καὶ ἄλλος δέ φησιν· κένωσιν, κ.τ.λ.   31   nihilum.
C H   31-32   ab illis. (*for* alibi) *H*   32   ἀπέφανται cod., Cr.: πέφανται Fr.

competition of this kind, giving them advice:

2:4 *so that each one may consider not only his own things but also what belongs to each of the others.*

"Do not think about (he says) how you may yourself keep first place, but bear in mind that if it is pleasing for you to be superior to others, it is much more unbearable for someone else that he should be kept in second place. And by pondering similar thoughts as well about others, you will all the more behave with diligence because of equality."

Then he employs an example altogether necessary for his teaching about humility, declaring what has to do with Christ:

2:5 *For* (he says) *let this be the mind* (or *let this be the sense*) *in you that is in Christ Jesus,*

That is, "mind such things as Christ also is seen to have minded." What are those things?

2:6 *who, being found in the form of God, did not think it robbery that he was equal to God,*

It is usual for people to rob those things by which they think they can acquire some gain for themselves. For we often say [216], "He thought that thing something to be robbed"; that is, "he took that with haste, as though it were the case that it could bring him great profit." Therefore, this is what he says about Christ, that *he did not think it robbery that he should be*[12] *equal to God*; that is, "he did not consider that equality with God great, and he remained on high in his own high rank. But he chose as more profitable for the benefit of others to undergo difficulties more humble than were appropriate for him, even though he was found in the form of God—meaning "existing as God," that is, "as Lord and Ruler (see Jude 4) and Founder of the universe." For all these expressions are seen in truth to accord with the name of God. What, then, did he do?

2:7a *but he emptied himself, taking the form of a slave,*

†Divine scripture uses the word "emptying" to mean nothing, just as it is written elsewhere (Rom 4:14): *faith has been emptied,* that is, "has been shown to be nothing," [217] and

Divine scripture calls nothing "emptying," as in (Rom 4:14) *faith has been emptied* instead of "has been shown to be nothing," and (1 Cor 15:14) *therefore, our preaching is empty* in-

---

[12] *Ut sit* rather than *esse,* as in the Latin rendering of the verse.

est;' *euacuata est ergo praedica-*
tio nostra, hoc est, nulla est et
uana. nam quod dicit *seipsum*
[*exinaniuit,* hoc est, 'non osten-
5   dit seipsum], formam enim serui accipiens dignitatem illam
abscondit; hoc solum a uidentibus se esse existimabatur, quod
et uideri poterat.*

τοῦ 'οὐδὲν καὶ εἰκαῖον.' τὸ οὖν ἑαυτὸν ἐκένωσεν, ἀντὶ τοῦ 'οὐκ ἔδειξεν
ἑαυτόν· μορφὴν γὰρ δούλου λαβὼν
τὴν ἀξίαν ἐκείνην ἀπέκρυψεν, τοῦτο
τοῖς ὁρῶσιν εἶναι νομιζόμενος ἅπερ
ἐφαίνετο.'

10   diuina enim natura cunctis erat occulta.' *formam* autem *serui,* ut
dicat 'naturam serui,' humanam sic uocans naturam, seruilis enim
est humana natura; sicut et illud quod dixit *in forma Dei,* in diuina dicit natura, hoc est, 'diuinae naturae existens.' et quoniam
dixit *formam serui,* commune autem erat hoc et hominibus et iu-
15   mentis et angelis, formae enim seruorum sunt et illi siquidem facti
sunt, adiecit et illud quod proprietatem significaret, instruere uolens quoniam dixerit *formam serui:*
   in similitudinem hominis factus.
   factus quod dixit pro 'habitus' posuit. nam quod dixit *in simi-*
20   *litudinem hominis,* ut dicat 'in homine;' similitudo enim hominis
homo est. haec omnia coniunxit, de Dei Verbo dicens; unde et
adiecit:
   in schemate (uel *specie*) *inuentus est ut homo.*
   ad comparationem illius naturae, quae in nulla specie uel sche-
25   mate perspici potest, schema et speciem posuit, ut dicat quoniam
'inuisibilis et omni schemate liber existens, sicut fas est, uoluit in
homine uideri.'
   humiliauit se ipsum.
   usque in hunc locum illa quae diuinae naturae condecebant, ui-
30   sus est edixisse; in subsequentibus uero ad illa transit, quae humanae possunt aptari naturae:
   factus oboediens usque ad mortem, mortem autem crucis.
   de homine quidem condecent ut ista dicantur; diuinae autem

---

1   ut ipsum sapiatis eandem caritatem habentes unanimes unum sapientes (*bef.*
euac. est) *add C H r: see note*   4   exinaniuit—seipsum *om C H r (per homoeo-*
tel.): *txt g*   5   enim *om r*   9   uidere *C*   11   uocatus *C* uocas *H** [humana
sic uocatur natura *r*]   12   in d. n. dicit *r*   17   quam (*for* quoniam) *C* (*corr.*)
quod *r*   19   habitans *C* [*r*?] /   22   adicit *C*   23   est *om H*   29   concedebant
C *H r*   30   dixisse *r*

(1 Cor 15:14) *therefore our preaching is emptied*; that is, it is nothing and vain. For when he says *he emptied himself*, he means "he did not show himself, for by *taking the form of a slave* he hid that high rank; he was thought by those who saw him only that which could also be seen.*

stead of "nothing and purposeless." For *he emptied himself* is instead of "he did not show himself," for by *taking the form of a slave* he hid that high rank, thought by those who saw him to be what he appeared to be.

For the divine nature was hidden from all." And *form of a slave* means "the nature of a slave." This is what he calls human nature, for human nature is servile, just as when he said *in the form of God*, he is speaking in reference to the divine nature, that is, "existing in a divine nature." And since he said *the form of a slave* and yet this was, however, common both to humans and to beasts of burden and angels, for they are also forms of slaves if indeed they are created, he added also what [218] would indicate a specific meaning in his wish to instruct them as to what he had meant by *form of a slave*:

2:7b *made in the likeness of a man,*

The expression he used, *made*, he put down instead of "held to be." For he said *in the likeness of a man* to mean "in a man," for the likeness of a man is a man. He joined all these things together in speaking of the Word of God, and so he also added:

2:7c *he was found in shape* (or *appearance*) *as a man,*

He put down shape and appearance by contrast with that nature that cannot be discerned in any appearance or shape, so as to mean that "he who exists as invisible and free from every shape, as is right, has willed to be seen in a man,"

2:8a *he humbled himself,*

Up to this place it is those things that were appropriate to the divine nature [219] that he has plainly declared. But in what follows he goes on to those things that can be applied to human nature.

2:8b *made obedient up to death, even the death of the cross,*

Surely it is appropriate to say those things of a man, and by no means can they be applied to a divine nature. For that nature

naturae nequaquam aptari possunt ista. nec enim mortem pati natura illa potest, quae et mortuum suscitare promisit, euidenter Domino ipso dicente: *soluite templum hoc, et in tribus diebus suscitabo illud.* et solutionem quidem templo aptauit, resurrectionis
5 uero operationem sibi aptauit. statim in ipso principio dicens: *in Christo Iesu,* singulariter et ut moris erat de una persona dicens, duarum et rationum memoratus est et naturarum, dicens: *qui in forma Dei extans ... formam serui* accepit, euidenter aliud quod dicens Dei formam, aliud etiam serui; illud quidem sumptum di-
10 cens, hunc uero sumentem. ut autem diuisio haec dictorum non alterum aliquem ad plenum praeter Christum faciat intellegi, serui formam unicuique reddidit. secundum ut et in promptu perspici possit, illud quidem quod dixit: *qui in forma existens* et reliqua, omnia illa dixit quae in persona intelleguntur Christi; *for-*
15 *mam* uero *serui,* ne aliud quid praeter Christum esse existimetur reputasse, eo quod et ab eo sit accepta. dicens uero quaecunque oportebant de diuina dici natura, ad humilitatis augmentum coniunxit et illa quae humanitatis sunt propria in una eademque persona. dicens illum honorem, qui erga eum post passionem exi-
20 stit, adiecit: *quoniam dominus Iesus Christus,* euidenter ostendens, quoniam non alium aliquem praeter Christum existimat esse susceptum hominem; et uirtute illorum quae significantur naturarum differentiam ostendit. nam ex illo quod in una persona omnia dixit, copulationem sufficienter ostendit. omnia quidem in lo-
25 co ubi de Christo disputat, quasi de una persona uniuerse dicit; et illa, quae uirtute sunt differentia secundum naturarum diuisionem, in unum omnia collegit, ita ut indiuisam custodiat personae copulationem. hoc uero in loco et maxime hoc prudenter simul et necessarie egisse uidetur. non propter consuetudinem solam
30 quam abutitur ad scrupulosam doctrinam dogmatis, sed et quantum ad praesens argumentum, ualde haec species narrationis illi conueniebat. propositum illi erat enim ut doceret et Philippenses, quoniam bona est humilitas et ualde sufficiens agenti illud lucros conferre. et hoc ex illo exemplo, quod secundum Christum est,
35 confirmat; conueniebat enim ad maiorem doctrinam omni ex parte

---

7　et *(bis) om* C *(corr.)*　‖　rationem *C H r*　17　dicit *(for* dici) *r*　22　uirtutem *C H r*　23　quo diuina *(for* quod in una) *r*　25　uniuersa *C (corr.) r*　27 colligit *H*　‖　diuisam *C* H r*　29　nam *(for* non) *r*　33　lucra *r*　34　ex *om r*　35　enim *om r*

that has promised even to raise the dead is not able to suffer death, since the Lord himself clearly says (John 2:14): *destroy this temple, and in three days I will raise it*. And he applied the destruction to the temple, but he applied the working of the resurrection to himself. At once in the very beginning of this passage (Phil 2:5) he says *in Christ Jesus* by a single expression and by speaking, as was his custom, of a single person. But he mentioned two principles and natures by saying that *he who was found in the form of God* took *the form of a slave*, clearly meaning that the form of God is one thing and the form of a slave another, speaking of the one as assumed but of the other as in truth assuming. And he attributes the form of a slave to one of the two in such a way that this division of words would not lead to the understanding that there is someone completely other than Christ. Accordingly, so that this could readily be perceived, what he surely [220] said (*who existing in the form* and the rest), he said in its entirety so as to be understood in the person of Christ, lest, in truth, he should be thought to have considered *the form of a slave* anything other than Christ, because it was taken up by the Word. But saying whatever was required to be said of the divine nature, to enlarge the humility of the Word he joined also those things proper to humanity in one and the same person. Speaking of that honor that came to be for the Man after his passion, he added (Phil 2:11) *that Jesus Christ is Lord*, clearly demonstrating that he did not think that the assumed Man is someone other than Christ; and he demonstrated the difference of the natures by virtue of those properties that are mentioned. For because of the fact that he said everything in one person, he sufficiently demonstrated the union. Indeed, he says everything in the passage where he is reasoning about Christ in relation to one person with respect to the whole, and those properties that are different in power according to the distinction of natures—he gathered all of them together in one so that he might keep the union of person undivided. Indeed, in this place, and especially here, he is seen to have accomplished his work wisely and at the same time necessarily. It was not alone because of the practice he habitually employed for minute care in teaching doctrines, but as much for his present argument that this form of discourse perfectly suited him. For it was his purpose to teach the Philippians also that humility is good and quite sufficient to profit the one practicing [221] it. And he confirms this by the

augeri exemplum. quemadmodum? si enim deitatis solius fecisset mentionem, sufficienter ostendere poterat, quod ualde conueniat humilia sapere; etenim tantum diuinam naturam ostendebat
humilitate rem efficientem, quae multum a sua dignitate distare
uidebatur. nam quia erat res ipsa agenti lucratiua ostendere nullomodo poterat, eo quod nec poterat comprobare aliquid hinc illam naturam potuisse adquirere. si autem humanam naturam tantummodo fuisset memoratus, lucratiuam rem esse ab illis quae ei
adquisita fuerant ostendebat; quod uero conueniat humilia sapere cum simili dignitate hinc non poterit confirmare. nam et illud
quod dixit: *foctus oboediens usque ad mortem*, homini aptatum nihil poterat illorum quae ad humilitatem pertinent comprobare, si
non et diuina natura inesse ei fuisset ostensa, per quam licebat et
huic non subici morti. nam secundum se non oboeditionis opus
implebat morti subcumbens; sustinebat enim mortem et nolens,
secundum dudum positum terminum naturae. prudenter uero,
sicut dixi, quasi in una persona omnia retulit, colligens in unum
illa quae uirtute differre uidebantur, secundum naturarum diuisionem, ita ut ex utroque quod utile erat deduceret ad exhortationem. de illis quidem sermonibus qui erant deitatis, suadebat
nobis ut necessarie in nostris cogitationibus humilitatem ostende-
remus, siquidem Deus Verbum talia sponte fecisse uidebatur, ita
ut pro aliorum salute praehonorandam omnibus existimaret humilitatem. de illis uero quae secundum humanitatem facta sunt,
ostendebat lucratiuam esse rem agere uolenti, ex quibus ille post
passionem in tanta constitit gloria. unde dicens: *factus oboediens
usque ad mortem, mortem autem crucis;* quod quidem erat humanitatis proprium, quae humanitas etiam et passionem suscepisse
uidebatur, ostendebatur uero ex diuinitatis sermonibus ad exhortationem humilitatis, per quam licebat non pati, si uoluisset, adiecit:

> *propter quod et Deus illum superexaltauit.*

nescio si aliquis sic stultus inueniri possit, ita ut post passio-

3 diuinam tantum *H* 4 humilitatem rem efficiens *C H r* 5 namque *C H*
nam quae *r* 10 huic *C H r*: *txt conj. Jacobi* ‖ poterat *r* ‖ et *om H**
11 autem (*aft.* homini) *add r* 14 hinc *C H r*: *txt conj. Jacobi* 17 dixit *C*
H r: Jacobi, "fortasse dixi." 18-19 diuis. natur. *H* 21 necessario *r* 30-31
adicit *C r*

example found in Christ, for the example was suitable in every way for the elaboration of greater teaching. How? For if he had mentioned divinity alone, he could have sufficiently shown that it was quite right to be humble-minded, and, indeed, so great was the deed he was showing the divine nature accomplishing by humility that it seemed to be far distant from its high rank. For the fact is that the deed itself could in no way show how it could profit the one doing it, because it could not prove that that nature could have acquired anything from it. But if he had merely mentioned human nature, he would have shown that the deed was profitable because of what it gained, but he could not have confirmed on this basis with similar worth that it would be right to be humble-minded. For his statement (Phil 2:8) *made obedient up to death*, applied to the Man, could have proved none of those things that pertain to humility, if the divine nature had not also been shown to be present in him, the nature by which it was also permitted to him not to be subject to death. For of himself, by yielding to death he would not have completed his work of obedience, for he would have undergone death even unwillingly according to the limit of nature long ago put in place. But wisely, as I have said, he referred everything as though to one person, bringing together in one those things that plainly differed in power according to the distinction of natures, so that he might draw from both what was beneficial for [222] his exhortation. So from those discussions that were about the divinity he was persuading us that we should necessarily show humility in our thoughts, if indeed God the Word was seen to have done such things of his own accord so as to think humility should be honored above all things for the salvation of others. But from those discussions composed in reference to the humanity, he was showing that it was a profitable thing for the person willing to act this way, because the Man stood fast in such great glory after his passion. For this reason when he says *made obedient up to death, even the death of the cross*, it was because the statement was appropriate to humanity, since it was the humanity that plainly underwent even the passion. Yet because this was being demonstrated by his discussions exhorting to humility, based on the divinity by which it would have been permitted for him not to suffer if he so chose, he added:

2:9a *because of which God also has highly exalted him,*

I do not know if anyone can be found so foolish as to suppose

nem exaltatum fuisse Dei Verbum existimet. quae est autem ipsa exaltatio?

et donauit illi nomen quod est super omne nomen.

nomen; euidens est quoniam non uocabulum, sed rem quandam dicit adquisitam ei, sicut illud quod scriptum est: *et cogno-*
scant quoniam nomen tibi Dominus, hoc est, 'quoniam tu Dominus.'
interpretatur uero ipse quid sit illud nomen:

ut in nomine Iesu omne genu flectatur caelestium et terrestrium et
infernorum, et omnis lingua confiteatur quoniam dominus Iesus Chri-
stus in gloria est Dei Patris.

hoc enim illi donauit, ut omnes illum adorent, et ut omnes
Deum confiteantur Iesum Christum in gloria Dei patris effectum;
hoc est, talem potitum gloriam, qualem fas est illum qui sibi patrem adscribit Deum potiri, propter illam copulationem quam habet ad Unigenitum. quoniam autem haec post passionem adquisita sunt illi qui adsumptus est, nemo qui nesciat; Deo autem Verbo
aderant a principio, utpote omnium factori, quod neminem aestimo contradicere, nisi forte ualde cedat insaniae. *caelestium* quidem dicit 'inuisibilium uirtutum;' *terrestrium* uero 'uiuorum hominum;' *infernorum* etiam 'illorum qui mortui sunt,' qui et ipsi per
resurrectionem Dominum confitebuntur resurrectionis suae auctorem.

illud inter cetera est explicandum, quod quidam haereticorum
interuertere uolentes testimonium illud quod dictum est: *non ra-*
pinam arbitratus est, esse se aequalem Deo, sic intellexerunt, quoniam 'existimauit (inquit) Christus conuenire sibi, ut non raperet
illam aequalitatem, quam Deus habere uidebatur.' dictum ipsum
multae stultitiae habet probationem; hoc enim quando excogitare
potuit Christus, si tamen secundum illorum sententiam eius factura est ex nihilo factus, qui et auctorem suum scit illum esse fac-
torem suum et creatorem? nisi forte hoc dicant, quoniam secundum daemones exaequare se Deo non usurpauit. quod haereti-
cos quidem conuenit intellegere, qui et semper plena insaniae uer-

---

5 illi *r*   11   et *om H**   18   nisi si *H*   ‖   forti *C H r*   26   existimabit *C**
H r   ‖   Chr. inquit *H*   28   stultie (*sic*) *H*   30   auditorem (*for* auct.) *H*

that it was the Word of God who was exalted after the passion. But what is the exaltation itself?

2:9b *and he has given him a name that is above every name,*

Name; it is obvious that he is not speaking of a designation but of a fact acquired by the Man, as it is written (Ps 82:19): *let them know that your name is Lord,* that is "that you are Lord." And he himself explains what that name is:

2:10–11 *so that at the name of Jesus every knee should bow, of things in heaven and on earth and under the earth, and that every tongue should confess that Jesus Christ is Lord in the glory of God the Father.*

For he gave the Man the gift that all should worship him and that all [223] should confess that Jesus Christ has been made God in the glory of God the Father; that is, he has obtained such glory as is right to obtain for him who assigns God as his own Father because of that union he has with the Only Begotten. And there is no one ignorant of the fact that the assumed Man acquired these things after his passion, but they were present to God the Word from the beginning, since he is, of course, the maker of all things—a fact I think no one disputes, unless by chance he quite submits to insanity. Indeed, by *things in heaven* he means the invisible powers, but by *things on earth*, living human beings, and by *things under the earth*, those who have died and will themselves by the resurrection confess the Lord to be the author of their resurrection.

Among other points it must be explained how some of the heretics in their wish to overturn the testimony have taken *he did not think it robbery that he was equal to God* (Phil 2:6). They have understood the verse this way: "Christ thought it was right for him not to rob that equality that God is seen to have." The opinion [224] is of itself proof of much stupidity; for when could Christ have thought this out, if at any rate in their opinion his fashioning was made from nothing and he knows that the one who begets him is his maker and creator?[13] Unless by chance they say this because he did not usurp for himself equality with God as the demons did. This, indeed, would have suited the understanding of the heretics,

---

[13] A polemic against the Arians, who equated Christ's refusal to "rob" equality with God with their claim that the Word of God is a creature and who interpreted equality with God as *res rapta* rather than *res rapienda*.

ba loquuntur; Paulo uero non conueniebant haec uerba, quasi ut quid magnum diceret de Christo, licet talia esse quis dicat illa quae secundum Filium sunt, qualia illi dicunt. uidentur autem neque sensum apostoli perspexisse dicentis: *humilitate uos existimantes*
5 *alterutrum uobis supereminere.* euidens est enim quoniam in hisce uerbis non minores docet debitum honorem maioribus persolue- re, sed exaequatos honore admonet ut per humilitatem alterutrum se sibi supereminere existiment. unde et *alterutrum* posuit, ut et isti erga illos et illi erga istos paria sapiant. ad hoc etiam exem-
10 plum aptasse uisus est, siquidem Christus, ad Patrem secundum diuinam naturam aequalitatem uindicans, adquieuit in hominem habitare, et sic exiguam apud homines opinionem adquirere, ita ut nec aestimarent eum aliud quid tunc esse praeter hominem solum, quod et esse uidebatur; ultra uero non erat aptum, si nullam ha-
15 bens ad Patrem aequalitatem, praeceptum solummodo implebat natura ipsa, ut obtemperaret ei, necessitatem illi inponente. ita- que et ridiculum erat secundum apostoli intentionem ut diceret quoniam et Christus non insurrexit aduersus Patrem, neque co- natus est rapere illam aequalitatem quam cum Patre habebat; con-
20 silia illis dante, ut [quos] aequales sibi existimarent per bonorum actuum cooperationem, per humilitatem supereminere sibi existi- marent. itaque beatus Paulus sic per omnia exhortationem faciens

1 locuntur *C H*   3 illic *C* H r* illa *C* (*corr.*)   4 praespexisse *r*   ‖ humili- tatem *r*   5 quoniam *om H*   11 homine *r*   13 nec (*aft.* tunc) *add C H r*   ‖ propter (*for* praeter) *r*   14 ultro *C*   16 necessitate *C H*   ‖ imponentem *r* 19-20 consilio *C H r*   20 quos *om C H r*

who always speak words filled with insanity. But such words were not suitable for Paul, inasmuch as he was saying something great about Christ, granted that someone might say that there are such things concerning the Son as they say of him.[14] And they seem not to have discerned the meaning of the apostle when he says (Phil 2:3): *in humility reckoning of one another that they are more excellent than you.* For it is clear that by these words he is not teaching that inferiors should pay the honor due to superiors but is urging them to be equal in honor so that by humility they may think one another to be more excellent than themselves. This is why he put down *one another*, so that those to these and these to those might be equal-minded. He plainly applied his example to this point, if indeed Christ, though claiming equality with the Father in accordance with his divine nature, was satisfied to dwell in a man and thus to acquire a reputation of small importance among human beings, so that they thought him to be at that time nothing other than a mere man, which he also seemed to be. Furthermore, it would not have been fitting if, having no equality with the Father, the nature by itself had fulfilled the precept [of humility], so that he would comply with it because his nature assigned the obligation to him. And so it would have been absurd according to the apostle's aim for him to say that even Christ did not rebel against the Father, nor try to rob him of that equality that [225] he did have with the Father. This is because Paul is giving them advice to think of one another by humility to be the more excellent ones, since they were equal with one another by their working together for good actions.[15] And so blessed Paul, making

---

[14]The meaning of the last clause is unclear. Swete (1:224) suggests the paraphrase: "Granting that the Arian view of the Person of Christ were correct, S. Paul would have said nothing so little to the honour of his Master as that He barely abstained from seizing upon Divine prerogatives to which He had no just claim." Could it be also that Theodore recognizes that some of the things the Arians say about the Word would make sense were they applied to the assumed Man?

[15]Theodore's argument is rather obscure. He seems to be distinguishing two ideas: (1) that Christ's example of humility has to do with the divine Word's "emptying" and *not* with the Man; thus, the "robbery" of Phil 2:6 is *res rapienda* rather than *res rapta*; and (2) that humility must be located at the same natural level, so that when the divine example of humility is applied to the human level, it means treating one another as equals. See Theodore's discussion following Phil 2:8 (Swete, 1:221).

adiecit:

itaque carissimi mihi, sicut semper oboedistis non solum in prae-
sentia mea, sed et nunc multo magis in absentia mea, cum timore et
tremore uestram salutem operamini.

5 optime et memoria praeteritorum persuasit illis nihil indignum
sibi sapere, sed talia facere, qualia et primitus fiebant coram ipso.
et animiaequiores faciens eos super conuenienti illis studio adiecit:

Deus enim est, qui inoperetur in uobis et uelle et inoperari pro bono
placito.

10 'sic enim alacritas uestra cooperariam inuenerit sibi Dei gratiam, necessarie eo cooperante uobis, ut cogitetis et agatis illa quae
sunt Deo placita'—sic enim dicit *pro bono placito.* deinde ad exhortationem perducit uerbum:

omnia facite sine murmuratione et disceptationibus.

15 ut dicat: 'alacriter et sollicite.'

ut efficiamini inreprehensibiles et sinceres, filii Dei immaculati, in
media generatione praua et peruersa, in quibus adpareatis sicut lumi-
naria in mundo, uerbum uitae retinentes in gloria mihi in diem Christi.

† 'sic enim inter medios ho-
20 mines illos, qui deteriorum plurimam habent sollicitudinem,
adparebitis inreprehensibiles, et
quales decet adparere illos qui
in ordine sunt filiorum Dei ef-
25 fecti, ita ut uirtutibus inlustra-
ti, fulgentes inter illos ad similitudinem luminariorum, expectantes illam aeternam uitam in
futuro illo die; in quo et mi-
30 hi proueniet gloriari.' et ostendens quod illorum prouectus
multam et illi praestabit fiduciam, qui fiet in melius:*

ὅυτως ἐν μέσῳ τῶν ἀνθρώ-
πων, οἷς περὶ τὰ χείρονα κατά γε
τὸ πλεῖστον ἡ σπουδή, φανήσεσθε
ἄμεμπτοι καὶ οἵους πρέπει φαίνεσθαι τοὺς ἐν υἱῶν τάξει γεγονότας,
ὡς διαλάμπειν ὑμᾶς ἐν αὐτοῖς φωσ-
τήρων δίκην κατὰ τὴν ἀρετήν· ἀπ-
εκδεχομένους τὴν αἰώνιον ζωὴν ἐν
τῇ μελλούσῃ ἡμέρᾳ. ἀφ' οὗ δὴ καὶ
ἐμοὶ τὸ καυχᾶσθαι ὡς εἰκὸς προσ-
γενήσεται.' καὶ δεικνὺς ὡς πολλὴν
καὶ αὐτῷ παρέξει τὴν παρρησίαν ἡ
ἐν τοῖς βελτίοσιν ἐκείνων προκοπὴ
...

---

1 adicit *C r*   5 memoriam *C H r*   6 faciebat (*for* fiebant) *H*   7 animaequiores *C* (*corr.*) *r*   ‖ adicit *C r*   8 inoperatur *H r*   ‖ in uobis (*aft* inop.)
add H   10 sibi inu. gr. D. ut nec., &c. *H*   19 sq. Coisl. 204, f. 125 b [Cr. 262]
ἄλλος ·φησίν· οὕτως (φησίν), κ.τ.λ.   20 deteriorem *C H r*: txt *g*   23 apparare
*C**   25 in (*bef.* uirt.) *add H*   27-28 expectatis *C* (*corr.*)   31 profectus *r*   32
illa *r*

his exhortation this way by all these points, added:

2:12 *And so, my dearly beloved, as you have always obeyed not only in my presence, but also now much more in my absence, work your salvation with fear and trembling,*

And by reminding them of what had previously taken place he quite effectively persuaded them to mind nothing unworthy among themselves and to accomplish such deeds as at first took place when he was with them in person. And to make them equal-minded concerning the zeal appropriate for them, he added:

2:13 *for it is God who works in you both to will and to work for good pleasure.*

"For let your enthusiasm find God's grace working with it, since it necessarily works with you, so that you may think and do those things that are pleasing to God"—for this is what he means by *for good pleasure.* Then he brings his discourse over to exhortation:

2:14 *Do everything without murmuring and debates,*

To mean "enthusiastically and carefully."

2:15–16a *so that you may be made without fault and pure, spotless sons of God, [226] in the midst of a crooked and perverse generation, among whom you appear like lights in the world, holding fast to the word of life for my boast in the day of Christ,*

†"For thus in the midst of those people who have greater care for what is worse, you will appear without fault and such as it becomes those who have been placed in the rank of God's sons to appear, so that illumined by virtues, shining among one another like lights, awaiting eternal life in that day to come in which it will come to pass for me to boast."[16] And showing that their progress, which is taking place for the better, will furnish him with much confidence:*

"Thus, in the midst of people who have at least for the most part a zeal for what is worse, you will appear blameless and such as it becomes those who have been placed in the rank of God's sons to appear, since you shine among them like lights because of virtue, awaiting eternal life in the day to come. From this, then, it will in all likelihood come to pass for me to boast." And showing that their progress in better things will give him much confidence:

---

[16]See Swete's note (1:226): "The translator seems to have inadvertently left the sentence without a finite verb, forgetting that he had rendered ὡς by *ut*."

quoniam non in uacuum cucurri, nec in uacuum laboraui. sed etsi libor in sacrificio et functione fidei uestrae, gaudeo et congaudeo omnibus uobis; idipsum autem et uos gaudete et congaudete mihi.

†'uobis sollicitis de uirtute existentibus gratulor et ipse spe illa, qua et in futuro saeculo sum de uobis exultaturus; sciens quia non uane pro fide laboraui, sed iusta ratione omnia sustineo, licet pro uobis etiam mortem subire sim paratus, uobis quasi aliquod sacrificium fidem uestram Deo offerentibus, me autem ad instar libationis proprium sanguinem uobis infundente.' bene autem dixit: *hoc ipsum et uos facite;* 'hoc et iustum est, et uos, ex quibus agitis, ut socii adpareatis gaudii mei.'*

ὑμῶν ἐπιμελομένων ἀρετῆς καὶ αὐτὸς ἐλπίδι [χαίρω] τοῦ καὶ ἐπὶ τοῦ μέλλοντος αἰῶνος ἐφ' ὑμῖν εὐφρανθήσεσθαι, εἰδὼς ὅτι οὐ μάτην ὑπὲρ ὑμῶν ἐκοπίασα, ἀλλὰ καὶ εἰκότως ἅπαντα ὑπομένω κἂν εἰ τὸν ὑπὲρ ὑμῶν ἐλοίμην θάνατον· ὑμῶν μὲν ὥσπερ τινὰ θυσίαν τὴν πίστιν τῷ θεῷ προσκομιζόντων, ἐμοῦ δὲ δίκην σπονδῆς ἐπιχέοντος ὑμῖν τὸ οἰκεῖον αἷμα.' καλῶς δὲ τὸ δ' αὐτὸ καὶ ὑμεῖς ἀντὶ τοῦ· 'δίκαιον καὶ ὑμᾶς δι' ὧν πράττετε κοινωνοῦντάς μοι φαίνεσθαι τῆς χαρᾶς.'

deinde adiecit:

spero autem in domino Iesu Timotheum cito mittere uobis, ut ego bono animo sim, cognoscens quae circa uos sunt. neminem enim habeo aequanimem, qui sincera affectione de uobis sollicitus sit. omnes enim quae sua sunt quaerunt, non quae Iesu Christi.

'quoniam spero (inquit) cito mittere uobis Timotheum, ita ut magis bono animo sim, per illum cautissime uobis instructis; eo quod neque habeo alium sic unanimem et affectiose de uobis sollicitum, omnibus illa considerantibus quae sua sunt.' indicat enim de illis qui ex circumcisione sunt. et ostendere cupiens quoniam ista non in gratiam Timothei dicit, ipsorum utitur testimonium, utpote scientibus eum, et dicit:

experimentum autem eius cognoscitis, quoniam tamquam patri filius mecum seruiuit in euangelio.

1 et (*for* etsi) C   4 ὅτι οὐκ εἰς κενόν φησιν ἔδραμον· οὐδὲ εἰς κενὸν ἐκοπίασα· ὑμῶν γάρ φησιν, κ.τ.λ. cod.   6 seculorum (*for* saec. sum) C*   23 quae circa uos sunt neminem enim *om* C* H   24 tam (*bef.* aeq.) *add* C (*corr.*)   27 instructus H   28 unianimem H   31 Timotheum H   32 dixit H   33 cognoscetis C* H   34 metum C*

2:16b-18 that I have not run in vain nor toiled in vain. But even if I am poured out in sacrifice and service for your faith, I rejoice, and I rejoice together with all of you, and you, in the same way, both rejoice and rejoice together with me.

[227] †"Because you are people who take great care for virtue, I rejoice in you, and I myself rejoice in that hope by which also in the age to come I shall be exultant because of you, knowing that I have not toiled for the faith in vain, but with just reason I endure all things, granted that I am prepared to undergo even death for you, since you are offering your faith to God as some kind of sacrifice, while I pour out my own blood for you like a libation." And he rightly said, "You also, do the same thing. This also is right, that you also should appear as partners of my joy because of what you are doing."* Then he added:

"Since you care greatly about virtue, I myself also rejoice in the hope that also in the age to come I shall be exultant because of you, knowing that I have not toiled for you in vain;

but I also endure all things suitably even should I choose death for your sake, since you are offering your faith to God as a kind of sacrifice, while I am pouring out my own blood for you like a libation." And he rightly said *and you in the same way* instead of "it is right also for you to appear as people sharing with me in joy because of what you are doing."

2:19–21 And I hope in the Lord Jesus to send Timothy quickly to you, so that I may be of good cheer, knowing what concerns you. For I have no one of equal mind who is concerned about you with pure affection; for all are seeking the things that are their own, not the things that are Jesus Christ's.

"For I hope (he says) to send Timothy quickly to you, so that I may be of good cheer, since you have been instructed by him with the greatest care—and because I have no one else so of one mind and affectionately concerned about you, since everyone is looking to his own affairs." For he is pointing out [228] those from the circumcision. And wishing to show that he is not saying those things to please Timothy, he employs their own testimony, since, of course, they knew him, and says:

2:22 And you know his tried character, that as a son to a father he has served with me in the gospel.

et iterum adiecit:

hunc equidem spero mittere, atubi uidero ea quae erga me sunt, confestim.

'quoniam mittam illum uobis, atubi illa quae secundum me sunt uidero et sciero in quibus sunt, omni dilatione postposita.'

confido autem in Domino, quoniam et ipse cito ueniam ad uos.

adiecit autem quoniam et ipse ualde credidit Deo uenire ad eos. unde adiecit:

necessarium autem existimaui Epaphroditum fratrem et cooperarium et commilitonem meum, uestrum autem apostolum et ministrum necessitatum mearum mittere ad uos, eo quod desiderans erat omnes uos et aestuans animo, eo quod audistis quoniam infirmatus est. etenim infirmatus est prope mortem, sed Deus ei misertus est; non solum autem illi, sed et mei, ut ne tristitiam super tristitiam habeam.

'quoniam nunc interim necessarium existimaui Epaphroditum mittere ad uos, qui cooperarius meus est secundum euangelium, apostolus autem uester est et minister necessitatum mearum'—ut dicat: 'per quem transmisistis illa, quae in usus meos necesse habebantur.' deinde et commendans eum illis dicit: 'quoniam et ipse desiderabat uos et maxime, illa quae de uobis sunt per neminem cognoscens; quoniam audistis eundem infirmantem. tristabatur enim reputans tristitiam uestram illam, quam pro eo habere uidebamini. nam et uere infirmatus est, ita ut et propinquaret morti; misertus est autem ei Deus, magis autem et mihi et illi, liberans eum ab infirmitate, ut ne circumuallatus multa tristitia adiectionem alterius tristitiae ex eius sustinerem morte.' quibus et adiecit:

festinantius ergo misi eum, ut uidentes eum iterum gaudium habeatis [et ego sine tristitia sim].

'uelocitate, ut et uos uidentes eum gaudio repleamini, et ego ultra non sim tristis, sciens quoniam consolabitur uos illius aduentus.' his ergo adiecit:

suscipite ergo eum in Domino cum omni gaudio, et eos qui huiusmodi sunt in honore habete; quoniam propter opus Domini usque ad mortem adpropinquauit, in incertum tradens animam, ut suppleat uestram

---

1 adicit *C r* 2 adubi *C* H* ‖ quidam *H* 4 uobis illum *H* ‖ adubi *C* H* 7 adicit *C r* ‖ uos (*for* eos) *H* 8 adicit *C r* 14 tristitia (1°) *H* 20 enim (*aft.* neminem) *add C H r* 23 et *om r* 29 uelocius eum misi inquit (*for* uelocitate) *C* (*corr.*) de eius uelocitate *r* ‖ ut *om H* 34 propinquauit *H**

And he further added:

2:23 Indeed, I hope to send him, when I shall have seen to the things that are to me, without delay.

"I shall send him to you, when I shall have seen to my affairs and shall have known how they are, with all delay set aside."

2:24 And I am confident in the Lord that I shall also myself come quickly to you.

And he added that, as well, he himself in God strongly believed that he would come to them. Then he added:

2:25–27 And I have thought it necessary to send to you Epaphroditus, my brother and fellow worker and fellow soldier, and your apostle, and the minister to my needs, because he was longing for all of you and distressed in mind because you heard that he was sick. And indeed he was sick, close to death, but God had mercy on him, and not only on him, but also on me, so that I might not have sorrow upon sorrow.

[229] "Now for the time being I have thought it necessary to send to you Epaphroditus, who is my fellow worker in the gospel, and he is your apostle and the minister of my needs"—meaning "through whom you have sent those things that are indispensable for my requirements." Then, commending him to them, he says: "because he also was longing for you, especially not knowing from anyone how you were, since you had heard he was sick. For he was sorrowful in considering the sorrow you apparently had for him. Indeed, he was in fact sick, so that he was even close to death. But God had mercy on him, still more both on me and him, freeing him from his sickness, so that surrounded by many sorrows I might not undergo the addition of another sorrow by his death." To this he added:

2:28 Therefore, I have sent him more speedily so that seeing him again you may have joy, and I may be without sorrow.

"With swiftness, so that when you see him, you may be filled with joy, and I may no longer be sorrowful, knowing that his arrival will be a comfort to you." Therefore, he added to this:

2:29–30 Therefore, receive him in the Lord with all joy, and hold in honor those who are like this, because on account of the Lord's work he drew near to death, handing his soul over to uncertainty in order

minorationem ad meum ministerium.

obsecrans eos ut suscipiant eum libenter, et consilium illis dat,
ut ad plenum in honore habeant eos qui tales sunt. ostendit autem
quoniam uera ratione dignus sit honore apud eos, 'ex quibus (di-
5 cit) quod ministrauerit uestrae uoluntati, apportans illa quae mihi a uobis missa sunt, in tantum inciderit periculum.' *opus* quidem *Domini* ministerium ipsum uocans; supplementum uero eorum minorationis ad suum obsequium hoc idem uocans, ita ut cupientes mittere illa, quae ad usus erant necessaria, minime uale-
10 rent, eo quod unusquisque quaecunque illi dare uoluerant per se
perferre non poterant. hoc ergo dixit: 'ipse suppleuit et quae uobis deerant; ille ab omnibus accipiens et omnium supplens uota
apportauit.' et haec dicens de Timotheo quidem memoratus est,
quoniam missurus sit eum; de Epaphrodito uero, quoniam misit
15 eum cum suis scriptis. adiecit uero ad omnia:

de cetero, fratres mei, gaudete in Domino.

orans pro illis ista dicit, hoc est: 'contingat uobis ita omnia pati
per diuinam gratiam, ut semper gaudio sitis repleti in illis bonis
quae ab eo nobis sunt praestita.' bene autem posuit *in Domino*, eo
20 quod est gaudere et non bene, quando quis a bonis praesentibus
delectari uidetur erga possessiones et fruitionem earum, id sibi bonum esse existimans.

haec eadem scribere uobis mihi quidem impigrum, uobis autem cau-
tum.

25 †hinc incipit illos reprehen-   ἐντεῦθεν ἄρχεται τῶν ἐκ περιτο-
dere qui erant ex circumcisio-   μῆς καθάπτεσθαι, οἳ πείθειν αὐτοὺς
ne, qui suadere illis conaban-   ἐπειρῶντο κατὰ νόμον ζῆν. τὸ τὰ
tur, ut secundum legem uiue-   αὐτὰ γράφειν οὐχ ὡς καὶ ἤδη γρά-
rent. nam quod dixit *haec ea-*   ψας λέγει, οὐδαμοῦ γὰρ τῆς ἐπισ-
30 *dem scribere*, non quia iam scrip-   τολῆς φαίνεται περὶ αὐτῶν εἰπών,
serat dicit; nullo enim in lo-   ἑτέραν δὲ ὅτι γεγράφηκεν πρὸς αὐ-
co in epistola id uidetur dixis-   τοὺς ἐπιστολὴν οὐδαμόθεν ἐμάθο-
se, alteram autem quando scrip-   μεν· ἀλλ' ὡς διαλεχθεὶς αὐτοῖς πολ-
sit ad eos epistolam nullomo-   λὰ περὶ τούτων ὅτε παρῆν τοῦτο λέ-
35 do didicimus. sed quia docue-   γει, ὅτι 'ἐμοὶ περὶ ὧν ὑμῖν διελέχ-

---

1 inorationem (*for* minor.) *H*   6-7 enim (*for* quidem) *H*   7 misterium *C*
15 adicit *C*   20 in (*for* a) *r*   25 sq. Coisl. 204, f. 128 b [Cr. vi. 268, Fr. 139].
Θεόδωρος. ἄλλος δέ φησιν· ἐντεῦθεν, κ.τ.λ.   27 τῷ (*for* τὸ) cod. edd.

to fill up your deficiency for my ministry.

[230] Beseeching them to receive him gladly, he also advises them to hold in honor to the fullest extent those who are like him. And he shows that it is for a true reason that he may be held worthy of honor among them, "because (he says) he ministered to your wish by bringing me what you sent to me, he fell into such great danger." He calls the ministry itself *the Lord's work*; and he calls the same thing the filling up of their deficiency for his own service, so that even though they wanted to send those things necessary for his requirements, they were by no means strong enough because none of them could carry out by themselves whatever they had wanted to give him. Therefore, he said "Epaphroditus himself filled up even what was lacking from you; he was the one who, receiving from all and filling up the desires of all, brought it." What he mentioned in speaking of Timothy is that he was going to send him, but of Epaphroditus, that he sent him with his letter. And to all this he added:

3:1a *For the rest, my brothers, rejoice in the Lord.*

He says this praying for them, that is, "may it so happen to you to suffer everything by divine grace so that you may always be filled with joy in those good things that God has bestowed on you." And he rightly put down *in the Lord*, because rejoicing in the wrong way is when someone is seen to take delight from present goods in possessions and their enjoyment, thinking this to be good for himself.

3:1b *To write these same things to you is indeed not troublesome to me, but it is safe for you.*

[231] †From here he begins to rebuke those from the circumcision who were trying to persuade them to live according to the law. For he said *to write these same things* not because he is speaking of what he had already written, for there is no place in the letter where he appears to have said this, and we have in no way learned that he wrote them another letter. Rather, because he had taught

From here he begins to rebuke those from the circumcision who were trying to persuade them to live according to the law. He says *to write the same things* not because he had already written them, for nowhere in the letter does he appear to have spoken about them, and from no source have we learned that he wrote them another letter. Rather, since he had spoken much with them about

rat eos instantissime de his ipsis
negotiis quando illo fuerat, hoc
dicit quoniam 'mihi de quibus
frequenter uobis locutus sum,
5 de illis ipsis scribere impigrum
est, eo quod frequens commonitio cautelam uobis ampliorem
praebere uidetur.'*
quae sunt ergo ista?
10   *uidete canes, uidete malos operarios.*

†*canes* uocauit eos, eo quod
nullam habent uerecundiam,
sed et frequenter reprehensi pro
praua et uana doctrina in hi-
15 sdem persistere uideantur; *ma-*
los autem *operarios* dicit, eo quod
non illa docere festinent quae
pietati conveniunt.*

θην, περὶ τῶν αὐτῶν καὶ γράφειν
ὄκνος οὐδείς, ἐπειδήπερ ἀσφάλειαν
ὑμῖν ἡ συνέχεια παρέχει τῶν ῥημάτων.'

κύνας δὲ αὐτοὺς καλεῖ ὡς ἀναισ-
χύντους καὶ πολλάκις ἐλεγχθέντας
ἐφ' οἷς οὐ καλῶς διδάσκουσιν, ἐπι-
μένοντας δὲ ὅλως· κακοὺς δὲ ἐργά-
τας ὡς οὐ τὰ προσήκοντα διδάσκειν
ἐσπουδακότας.

'opus' autem uocat doctrinam, sicut et alibi dixit: *si cuius opus*
20 *manserit quod superaedificauit, mercedem accipiet; si cuius opus ar-*
serit, detrimentabitur. de doctrinis enim illa dixisse euidenter cognoscitur.
    uidete concisionem.
    bene *concisionem* dixit, eo quod quando id fieri Deo complace-
25 bat, circumcisio erat; quia uero nunc non secundum Dei fit uoluntatem, sed conciduntur tantum ad corporis nociuitatem. ideo
et suam illis comparat personam dicens:
    nos enim sumus circumcisio.
    hoc est, 'qui illa agimus quae placita sunt Deo, et custodes cau-
30 tissimi sumus illorum quae Deo placent; quod proprium est illorum, qui se habere promittunt circumcisionem.' ex ipsis rebus id
confirmans adiecit:
    qui spiritu Deo seruimus et gloriamur in Christo Iesu et non in car-
ne confidimus.

---

18 pietatis C r   19-20 si cuius—accipiet *om* C*   24 autem (*aft.* bene) *add*
r   26 nouitatem C*   27 ad (*for* et) C* H r   29-30 cautissime C H r   30-31
Deo—qui *om* H   32 adicit C r   34 confidemus H

them about these matters with the greatest urgency when he had been there, what he means is: "Since I have often spoken to you about them, it is not troublesome to me to write about the same things, because frequent warning plainly furnishes you with greater safety."*

these things when he was present there, what he means is: "It is no trouble to me also to write about the same things about which I have spoken with you, since the frequency of the words furnishes you with safety."

Therefore, what are those things?

3:2a *Watch out for the dogs, watch out for the evil workers,*

†He called them *dogs* because they have no shame, but [232] also are often rebuked for the crooked and vain teaching in which they are seen to persist. And he says that they are *evildoers* because they are not quick to teach what accords with true religion.*

And he calls them *dogs* because they are shameless and often convicted for teaching things that are not good and for entirely persisting in them. And he calls them *evildoers* because they are eager to teach things that are not proper.

And he calls the teaching "work," as he also said elsewhere (1 Cor 3:14–15): *if someone's work, which he built on the foundation, should remain, he will receive a reward; but if someone's work should be burned up, he will suffer loss.* For it is clearly recognized that he said this about teachings.

3:2b *Watch out for the concision,*

He rightly said *concision,* because when it was pleasing to God that this should be done, it was circumcision; but because now it takes place not in accordance with God's will, they are cut only for the harm of the body. And so, he also contrasts his own person to them, saying:

3:3a *for it is we who are the circumcision,*

That is, "we who do those things that are pleasing to God and are the most careful guardians of those things that please God, which is the property of those who profess that they have the circumcision." Confirming this from the facts themselves, he added:

3:3b *we who serve God in the Spirit*[17] *and boast in Christ Jesus and have no confidence in the flesh,*

---

[17]Presumably reflecting the reading πνεύματι Θεῷ instead of πνεύματι Θεοῦ.

†'qui non carnalem Deo functionem reddimus, sed sicut est conueniens; et gloriamur in Christo, qui horum nobis auctor extitit, non tamen in illis quae secundum carnem sunt pietatem esse definimus.'*

'οἱ ἀσώματον τῷ θεῷ τὴν λατρείαν ἀποδιδόντες, ὥσπερ οὖν προσῆκον ἐστίν, καὶ καυχώμενοι ἐπὶ τῷ Χριστῷ τῷ τούτων ἡμῖν αἰτίῳ γεγονότι, οὐ μὴν ἐν τοῖς περὶ τὴν σάρκα τὴν εὐσέβειαν ὁριζόμενοι.'

sic et Dominus in euangeliis dicit: *etenim Pater tales quaerit qui se adorent. spiritus est Deus, et qui adorant eum, in spiritu et ueritate debent adorare.* quae et ad Samaritanam dicebat, quae æstimabat in loco oportere adorare diuinitatem, docens quoniam incorporea est diuina natura et tali arbitrio conueniet eam adorari. et ut ne uideatur ex superfluo illos incusare ipse nihil tale habens ad sui probationem, illis habentibus, unde glorietur:

et quidem ego habens confidentiam et in carne; si quis uidetur alter in carne confidere, ego magis.

'si de his (inquit) bonum erat magna sapere, nulli eorum infirmior sum secundum hanc rationem.' deinde et per partes dicit omnia illa, quae uidebantur esse magna illis qui secundum legem conuersabantur:

circumcisione octauae diei.

bene posuit octauam diem, ut ostenderet non se fuisse aduenam, in quibus solet postea celebrari circumcisio; sed et ab initio et secundum legem.

ex genere Israel.

ex cuius genere descendere omnes uidentur qui in qualibet sunt tribu.

de tribu Beniamin.

necessaria fuit etiam tribus adiectio ad ostensionem quod non aduena fuerit, sed a primordio inde originem traxerit. unde et euidentius illud insinuans dicit:

Hebraeus ex Hebraeo.

non dixit, 'Iudaeus ex Iudaeis,' nouella enim erat haec nuncupatio; sed '*Hebraeus ex Hebraeis,*' de antiqua nuncupatione anti-

1 quoniam (*for* qui non) *C H r: txt g*   ‖ sq. Coisl. 204, *l. c.* [Cr. vi. 269, Fr. 139] Θεόδωρος. οἱ ἀσώματον, κ.τ.λ. 8 dicit in euan. *H* 10 qui (*for* quae) *r* 11 adorari *H* 13 illo *H** illa *r*   ‖ adicit (*for* ad) *C* (*corr.*) 16 confidere *om C H* 21 circumcisionem *C* (*corr.*) *H*   ‖ octaui *C* (*corr.*) 23 celebrare *C* H* 25 Israhel *C* 32 Ebraeus, &c. *C H*

[233] †"We who render no fleshly service to God, just as is right. And we boast in Christ, who has become for us the source of these things; only, we do not define true religion to be in those things that are according to the flesh."*

"Who render bodiless service to God, as indeed is right, and who boast in Christ, who became for us the source of these things, only not defining true religion in the things that concern the flesh."

Thus, the Lord also says in the Gospels (John 4:23–24): *for indeed the Father seeks such to worship him. God is Spirit, and those who worship him must worship in spirit and truth.* He said this even to the Samaritan woman, who thought it was right to worship the divinity in a place. He was teaching that the divine nature is bodiless and that it would be fitting to worship him with such a judgment. And so that he might not seem to be condemning his opponents uselessly, as though he had himself no proof of the basis of his boasting, as they did:

3:4 *even though I, having confidence in the flesh; if anyone else seems to have confidence in the flesh, all the more I,*

"Even if it were good (he says) to think highly of these things, I am second to none of them on this account." Then even in detail [234] he speaks of all those things that seemed great to those who lived by the law:

3:5a *in circumcision of the eighth day,*

He rightly put down the eighth day to show that he was not a convert for whom circumcision was customarily observed later on; rather, he was circumcised even from the beginning and according to the law.

3:5b *from the race of Israel,*

From whose race all apparently traced their descent, no matter what tribe they belonged to.

3:5c *of the tribe of Benjamin,*

The addition of the tribe, as well, was necessary to show that he was not a convert but traced his origin from that tribe to begin with. Thus, making this still more clearly known, he says:

3:5d *a Hebrew from the Hebrew,*[18]

He did not say "a Jew from the Jews," for this would have

---

[18]As Swete points out (1:234), the singular appears to be "a slip, possibly of Th.'s own pen."

quitatem suae originis confirmauit. deinde et illa quae sunt eius propositi:

  secundum legem (inquit) *Pharisaeus.*

  illi enim qui in hanc consistebant haeresin cauti interpretes le-
5 gis esse existimabantur, et illa docere properabant quae in lege habere uidebantur. hinc ostendi poterat:

  secundum aemulationem persequens ecclesiam.

  et quoniam [non] in persecutione habebat perfectam probationem—fieri enim poterat, ut hoc ferocitate sola faceret, simulatione
10 illa qua pro aemulatione pietatis id facere uidebatur—adiecit:

  secundum iustitiam quae in lege est, factus sine querela.

  bene autem dixit *quae in lege est,* eo quod non erat possibile sine
querela ad plenum posse aliquem inuenire. omnia uero decurrens
et ostendens, quod nihil deerat ei bonum ex illis quae secundum
15 legem erant:

  *sed quaecunque mihi erant lucra, haec existimo propter Christum
detrimenta.*

  lucra quidem dicens, ut ostendat quoniam [non] necessarie tunc
agebantur;

20 †adiciens uero 'illa quae erant,'   τὸ ἦν εἰς σύστασιν τοῦ ποτὲ κέρδος
ad confirmationem dicit quo-   ἔχειν τὴν περὶ ταῦτα σπουδήν.
niam lucra habebat illa sollicitu-
do quae erga illa erat,*

nunc uero magis sunt *detrimenta* in comparatione Christi reputata.
25 unde ad comparationem Christi:

  *sed et existimo omnia detrimenta esse propter supereminentem
scientiam Iesu Christi domini mei.*

  bene posuit *domini mei* quasi ex comparatione cognoscens ipsam differentiam. unde et motus amore dominum suum Deum
30 dixit, ut post maiorum bonorum illi causam existentem. deinde
adiecit:

  propter quem omnia detrimentatus sum et existimo stercora esse.

---

1 qui (*for* quae) *r* ‖ ei (*for* eius) *H* 5 existimantur *C* H r* ‖ illo *C* H*
6 ostendit (*for* ost. poterat) *r* 8 non *om C H r* 10 illa qua pro aemulatione
bis H ‖ adicit *C r* 13 inueniri *C* (*corr.*) 14 qui (*for* quae) *H* 18 non
om C H r ‖ necessario *r* 20 sq. Coisl. 204, f. 130 a [Cr. vi. 272, Fr. 139]
Θεόδωρος. καὶ ἄλλος δὲ ὁμοίως φησίν· τὸ ἦν, κ.τ.λ. 22 illos (*for* illa 2°) *C r*
23 erant *C* H r* 30 causa existente *C H r* 31 adicit *C r*

been a novel designation, but *a Hebrew from the Hebrews*. So he confirmed the antiquity of his origin from the ancient designation. Then, also those things belonging to his chosen way of life:

3:5e *according to the law* (he says) *a Pharisee,*

For those who took their place in this sect were considered to be careful interpreters of the law and were eager to teach the tenets seen to be in the law. From this he was able to show:

[235] 3:6a *according to zeal persecuting the church,*

And since he did not have complete proof in persecution—for it could have happened that he did this by savagery alone, pretending to do it by zeal for true religion, he added:

3:6b *according to the righteousness that is in the law, carried out without fault.*

And he rightly said *that is in the law*, because it was impossible to find anyone capable of being entirely without fault. Indeed, running through everything and demonstrating that he lacked no good of those things that are according to the law:

3:7 *But whatever gains were mine, these I think losses because of Christ.*

Indeed, he says *gains* to show that they were necessarily produced at that time.

†But by adding that they *were*, he means to confirm that the great care for those things used to have gains,*

Were, to establish that zeal for these things once had gain.

but now they are all the more losses when considered by comparison to Christ. Then, with respect to the comparison with Christ:

3:8a *Moreover, I think all things losses because of the surpassingly excellent knowledge of Jesus Christ, my Lord,*

He rightly put down *my Lord*, inasmuch as he knew the difference itself by the comparison. For this reason, and moved by love, he called God[19] his Lord, [236] as the one who had afterward come to be for him the source of greater goods. Then he added:

3:8b *because of whom I have suffered the loss of all things, and I think them to be dung,*

---

[19] "God" is clearly an error, and Swete suggests that the copyist may have misread an abbreviation. The text probably read: "he called Jesus his Lord."

†et quoniam contumeliosa uidebantur, ut stercora uocaret illa quae legis sunt, uelociter adiecit:

ἐπειδὴ ἐφύβριστον ἦν τὸ σκύβαλα καλέσαι τὰ τοῦ νόμου, μάλα ὀξέως ἐπήγαγεν

5 *ut Christum lucrifaciam;*

ἵνα Χριστὸν κερδήσω·

ostendens quoniam comparatio illorum quae secundum Christum sunt, ista talia facit uideri.*

δεικνὺς ὅτι ἡ παράθεσις ἐκείνων ταῦτα τοιαῦτα εἶναι ποιεῖ.

10 qualiter aut quomodo?

et inveniar in illum habens non meam iustitiam quae ex lege est, sed illam quae ex fide est Christi, quae ex Deo est iustitia ex fide.

'cupio (inquit) illam iustitiam adsequi, quae ex Deo est, quam adsequi possumus per illam fidem quae in Christo est; et ideo de-
15 spicio meam iustitiam quae ex lege est, sciens eam et laboriosam esse et inpossibilem ad directionem; facilius enim mihi ex lege peccare est quam dirigi.' et manifestius faciens, quae sit illa ex Deo iustitia, quae per illam fidem quae in Christo est adquiritur:

in fidem ut cognoscam eum et uirtutem resurrectionis eius.

20 non dixit 'resurrectionem' sed *uirtutem resurrectionis.* quae est autem resurrectionis eius uirtus? quoniam pro omnibus facta est ut et omnes similem adsequantur resurrectionem. 'credens enim Christo credo etiam et uirtutem resurrectionis eius cognoscere, hoc est, adsequi resurrectionem; in qua effectus in inmortali et
25 inpassibili natura ab omni peccato liber ero, ultra non indigens legem. nec enim erunt consentanea simul etiam et affectus eius quam erga legem cum labore et sudore uirtutem sum directurus, sed diuina gratia custodibor in bonis, eo quod tunc nec peccare ultra potero.'

30 *et communicationem passionum eius, conformis factus morti eius, si*

---

1 sq. Coisl. *l. c.* θεοδώρου. Cr.: "non Theodori sed Chrys. est schol." 2 uidebantur contumeliosa *r* ‖ uacare *C* uocare *H r* 4 adicit *C r* 7 qui (*for* quae) *r* 8 faciunt *C H r* 9 adicit (*aft.* uid.) *add C* (*corr.*) 12 effide (*for* ex f. *aft.* iustitia) *C** 19 resurr.—uirt. *om C* [*per homoeotel.*] 22 et ut omn. *H r* 24 immortalia *r* 26 lege *C* (*corr.*) *r* ‖ erant *C H* ‖ et (*bef.* aff.) *om H* 30 communicatione *C H: txt r*

†And since it seemed insulting to call what had to do with the law *dung*, he quickly added:

3:8c *so that I may gain Christ,*

Showing that it was the comparison with these things that had to do with Christ that makes those things seem like this.*
Of what kind or how?

Since it was insulting to call what had to do with law *dung*, quite quickly he continued:

3:8c *so that I may gain Christ,*

Showing that the comparison with those things makes these things to be like this.

3:9 *and may be found in him, having not my own righteousness that is from the law, but that which is from faith in Christ, which is the righteousness from God from faith,*

"I desire (he says) to gain that righteousness that is from God, which we are able to gain by faith in Christ. And so I despise my own righteousness that is from the law, knowing that it involves much toil and is impossible to achieve; for it is easier [237] for me to sin on the basis of the law than to be guided by it." And to make more evident what that righteousness is that is from God and is gained by faith in Christ:

3:9b-10a *in faith[20] that I may know him and the power of his resurrection,*

He did not say "resurrection" but *the power of resurrection.* What, then, is the power of his resurrection? That it took place for all, so that all might also gain a like resurrection. "For by believing in Christ I also believe in knowing his resurrection, that is, gaining the resurrection. When I have been brought to be in it, I shall be in an immortal and impassible nature, free from all sin with no further need of the law. For this condition will not accord with the law's disposition toward virtue, since I am to be guided by it to virtue with toil and sweat.[21] Instead, by divine grace I shall be kept in good things because at that time I shall no longer be able to sin.

[238] 3:10b-11 *and the sharing of his sufferings, made conformable*

---

[20] "From faith" and "in faith" both represent the Greek text at the end of verse 9. It seems likely that Theodore understands the phrase to belong to verse 10 and that the copyist has missed the point.

[21] The Latin here is virtually unintelligible. Swete (1:237) paraphrases: "our resurrection-state will not harmonize with the mode of attaining virtue prescribed by the law, which involves toil and labour—things unknown to immortal natures."

quomodo occurram in eam resurrectionem quae est ex mortuis.

'propter hoc (inquit) et communicare passionibus eius cupio,
consimilis factus morti eius, eo quod ad similitudinem eius contemplatione pietatis ab alienis ad mortem pertrahor; spe illa qua
5 confido particeps fieri eius resurrectionis, quae etiam multa et in-
mensa repleta est gloria.'

non quia iam acceperim, aut iam perfectus sim; persequor autem,
si et comprehendam in quo et comprehensus sum a Christo Iesu.

eo quod desursum illi adparuit et de caelo Christus suam illi
10 ostendit gloriam. hoc dicit: 'in illud quod perfectum est necdum
constitutio, expecto enim illud adhuc. omnia autem facio enite-
scens adsequi participationem eorum, in quibus ipse oculis meis
perspexi esse Christum, quando me persequentem per suam reuelationem praeueniens in suam me cognitionem conuerterat.' et in-
15 sistens illis ipsis:

fratres, ego memet ipsum non aestimo comprehendisse; unum tan-
tum, illa quae posteriora sunt obliuiscens, illis quae ante sunt coexten-
dor; ad destinatum persequor, ad brauium supernae uocationis Dei in
Christo Iesu.

20 †'effectum me ueraciter perfectum non praenuncio, necdum enim in fruitionem con-
sisto illorum quae expectantur;
tamen sciens illorum magnitu-
25 dinem, ueterum omnium nullam facio rationem, ad plenum
illa obliuioni tradens; ad futura
uero et quae expectantur meum
cogitatum extendo, unam ha-
30 bens intentionem, ad quam re-
spiciens omnia ago ita ut ad-
sequar proposita mihi praemia

'γεγενῆσθαι ἐμαυτὸν ἐν τῇ ἀλη-
θινῇ τελειότητι οὐκ ἀποφαίνομαι,
οὐδέπω γὰρ ἐν ἀπολαύσει τῶν
προσδοκωμένων κατέστημεν. ἀλλ'
ὅμως εἰδὼς ἐκείνων τὸ μέγεθος,
τῶν μὲν παλαιῶν ἁπάντων οὐδένα
ποιοῦμαι λόγον, πρὸς δὲ τὰ μέλλοντα ἐμαυτοῦ λογισμὸν ἐκτείνων, ἕνα
σκοπὸν ἔχω, πρὸς ὃν ἀφορῶν ἅπαντα πράττω, ὅπως ἅπως ἂν τύχοι-
μι τῶν προκειμένων ἡμῖν ἐπάθλων
εἰς τὴν ἄνω κλῆσιν· ἵνα εἴπῃ τὴν
ἐν τοῖς οὐρανοῖς δίαιταν, ἧς ἐπὶ τῷ

3 contemplationem *r* 7 ut (*for* aut) *C* 11 constitutus *C* (*corr.*) constituto *r*
14 conuenerat *C H* 16 met. ipsum *C** meipsum *H* 20 sq. Coisl. 204,
f. 132 b [Cr. vi. 276, Fr. 139] θεόδωρος. ταύτην δὲ τὴν ἐξήγησιν θεόδωρος οὐ
προσίεται. βούλεται γὰρ ἀπὸ τοῦ 'τὰ αὐτὰ γράφειν ὑμῖν ἐμοὶ μὲν οὐκ ὀκνηρόν,'
δι' ὅλου περὶ τοῦ μὴ δεῖν πείθεσθαι τοῖς κατὰ νόμον ζῆν αὐτοὺς [ἡμῖν αὐτοῖς Cr.
per incur.; cf. Fr.] βουλομένοις πείθεσθαι· τοῦτο γάρ ἐστιν ὅ φησιν γεγενῆσθαι·
ἐμαυτὸν (*sic*), κ.τ.λ. 24 tantum (*for* tamen) *H* 27 obliuione *C** *r* 31-32
adsequor *C* H* (ass.) *r* 32 ἐπὶ τὸ τ. edd.

to his death, if somehow I may attain that resurrection that is from the dead,

"For this reason (he says) I desire also to share in his sufferings, made like him in his death, because after his likeness I am being dragged to death by strangers for observing right religion, for that hope by which I am confident I shall become a sharer in his resurrection, which is filled also with much and immeasurable glory."

3:12 *not because I have already obtained or already have been made perfect, but I press on if I also may take hold of it, in which I am also taken hold of by Christ Jesus.*

Because he appeared to him from above, and Christ showed him his glory from heaven. This is what he means: "My condition is not yet in what is perfect, for I am still awaiting that. But I do everything striving to attain a share in those things in which I myself with my own eyes saw Christ existing, when by preventing me through his revelation while I was persecuting he had converted me to knowledge of him." And dwelling on the same things:

3:13–14 *Brothers, I do not think myself that I have taken hold of it, only one thing, forgetting the things that are behind, I am stretched out to those things that are before; I am pressing on to the goal, to the prize of the high calling of God in Christ Jesus.*

[239] †"I do not declare that I have truly been made perfect, for I am not yet established in the enjoyment of those things that are awaited. Nevertheless, since I know their greatness, I take no account of all the old things, handing them over completely to oblivion, but I stretch out my thinking to the things to come that are also awaited, having a single aim. Looking to it, I do everything so that I may attain the rewards held out to me in the high calling," meaning "dwelling in heaven," to which we are all called so as

"I do not declare that I myself have come to be in true perfection, for we have not yet been established in the enjoyment of the things awaited. Nevertheless, since I know their greatness, I take no account of all the old things, but stretching out my own thinking to the things to come, I have one aim.

Looking to it, I do everything so that I may gain the prizes held out to us for the high calling," meaning "dwelling in heaven, which all of us are called to gain."

in superna uocatione'—ut dicat   τυχεῖν κεκλήμεθα πάντες.
'caelestem commorationem,' ad
quam ut adsequamur omnes sumus uocati,*

5   unde et regnum dicitur caelorum; resurgentes enim incorrupti et
inmortales in caelesti commorare secundum datum nobis promissum speramus. ex comparatione uero uoluit ostendere, quantum
legi illa quae nostra sunt praecellere uidentur. et quoniam dixit
suum erga ista propositum, docere nititur qualem oporteat de his
10 habere sententiam; adiecit etenim exhortationem:

quicunque ergo sumus perfecti, hoc sapiamus.

'itaque qui illud frui quod perfectum est concupiscimus, haec
debemus sapere, porro abicientes illa omnia quae sunt corporalia,
et futuro statui consentanea sentire debemus.'

15 *et si quid aliud sapitis, et hoc uobis Deus reuelabit.*

†'etenim si nescimus futura   εἰ καὶ μὴ ἴσμεν ἀκριβῶς τὰ
qualia sint; sed ipsis rebus nobis   μέλλοντα ὁποῖα καθέστηκεν, ἀλλ᾽
illa ostendit Deus.'*   ἐπὶ τῶν πραγμάτων αὐτὰ ἡμῖν
                                        δείξει ὁ θεός.

uerumtamen ad quod occurrimus, eadem constare regula, idipsum
20 *sapere.*

†'interim (inquit) in quibus   ῾τέως (φησὶν) ἐν οἷς ἐσμὲν καὶ ἐν
sumus et in quibus uocati su-   οἷς ἐκλήθημεν ἐπιμένειν ὀφείλομεν,
mus, permanere debemus, con-   σύμφωνον τὴν περὶ αὐτὰ διάθεσιν
sentaneum erga illos affectum   ἐπιδεικνύμενοι καὶ μὴ ἐξιστάμενοι
25 ostendentes, et non discedentes   τῆς τῶν μελλόντων προσδοκίας
ab expectatione futurorum, sed   καὶ τοῦ κατ᾽ ἐκεῖνα τὸν ἑαυτοῦ
secundum illam uitam nostram   ῥυθμίζειν βίον.᾽
dirigere debemus.'*

hinc enim praecedentium uerborum est sensus. quidam uero non
30 intendentes sequentiae, quasi apostolo de uirtute disputante, sic
illa susceperunt; et quod dixit: *illa quae posteriora sunt obliuiscens,*
ad illa uero quae in ante sunt me extendens, et cetera omnia similiter susceperunt. habent enim se non sic. ab illo enim loco quo

2   commemorationem *C*H*   10   adicit enim hanc exh. *r*   13   temporalia (*for*
corp.) *r*   16   sq. Coisl. 204, f. 133 a [Cr. vi. 277] ἄλλος δέ φησιν· εἰ καὶ, κ.τ.λ.
17   quanta futura qualia sint *C H* et (*bef.* qualia) *add C (corr.) r: txt g*   19   in
eandem (*for* ead.) *C (corr.)* || regulam *C H*   24   illis *C H: txt r*   27   uitam
om H   29   enim *om r*

to attain it,*

hence it is also called the kingdom of the heavens. For by rising again incorruptible and immortal, we hope to dwell like this in the heavenly place according to the promise given us. And he wanted to show by contrast how much those things that are ours excel the law. And since he spoke of his own purpose in regard to those things, he strives to teach what sort of opinion it is fitting to have about them. And so he added an exhortation:

3:15a *Therefore, let those of us who are perfect be of this mind;*

"And so those of us who desire to enjoy what is perfect [240] ought to mind these things, throwing far away all that is bodily; and we ought to have a sense of what accords with our future condition."

3:15b *and if you mind anything else, God will reveal also this to you.*

†"Even if we do not know what the things to come are like, yet God shows them to us by the facts themselves."*	Even if we do not know accurately the things to come the way he has established them, yet God will show them to us in the facts.
3:16 *Nevertheless, to what we have attained, stand fast in the same rule, mind the same thing.*	
†"For the time being (he says) we ought to persevere in our present condition and calling, showing an affection in harmony with those things; and not abandoning our expectation of the things to come, we ought to guide our life by that expectation."*	"For the time being (he says) we ought to persevere in our present condition and calling, showing an affection in harmony with these things and not abandoning the expectation of the things to come and guiding one's own life by them.

For from this the preceding discussion takes its meaning. But some people, failing to understand the logical order, as though the apostle were reasoning about virtue, have taken his words this way, when he said *forgetting those things that are behind,* [241] *but stretching forward to those things that are before me.*[22] And

---

[22] "The things behind" represents *posteriora*. The interpretation Theodore rejects interprets this to mean what is worse, as opposed to virtue, which lies ahead.

dixit: *haec eadem scribere uobis mihi quidem impigrum*, per omnia docet eos eo quod non conueniat obtemperare illis qui secundum legem eos uiuere suadent, sicuti et interpretatione ostendimus. et ostenditur id etiam ex subsequentibus melius; adiecit enim:

5   *imitatores mei estote, fratres mei.*

†hoc est, 'nolite sub lege   ἀντὶ τοῦ 'μὴ ὑπὸ νόμον ζῶντες, uiuere, sicuti nec ego uiuo sub   ἀλλ' ὁμοίως ἐμοί.' lege.'*

et ostendens, quoniam non sui causa ista dicit, sed talem uitae co-
10 nuersationem eosdem habere cupit; unde et adiecit:

    considerate eos qui sic ambulant sicut habetis formam nostram.

†'ad plenum (inquit) ad illos   'καὶ καθόλου (φησὶν) πρὸς τοὺς respicite, qui sic uiuunt sicut et   οὕτως ζῶντας ἀφορᾶτε, κἀκείνους nos; illis obtemperate, et illos   μιμεῖσθε.'
15 imitari festinate.'*

deinde arguens aduersarios uehementer illis insistit:

    multi enim ambulant quos frequenter dixi uobis, nunc autem et flens dico, inimicos crucis Christi.

sufficiens erat inuitare Philippenses ad odium illorum, siqui-
20 dem illa quae contraria erant cruci docere temptabant. unde et adiecit:

    quorum finis perditio.

†quid enim aliud erit suspi-   τί γὰρ ἕτερον εἴη ἂν καὶ ὑπο-
cari de illis qui repugnant Chri-   λαβεῖν ἐπὶ τῶν ἐναντιουμένων τῷ
25 sto et minorare properant ilia   Χριστῷ καὶ ἐλαττούντων τὰ περὶ
quae erga Christum sunt, sol-   αὐτὸν τῇ περὶ τὰ νόμιμα σπουδῇ;
licitudinem erga legem impen-
dentes?*

    quorum deus uenter est.

30 †'hoc manduca, illud noli   'τόδε φάγε καὶ τόδε μὴ φάγῃς·'
manducare'; et circa studia sua   καὶ περὶ τοῦτο ἑαυτοὺς ἀσχολοῦντες
se uertunt, quasi deo cuidam   ὥσπερ θεῷ τῇ κοιλίᾳ προσέχοντες,
uentri suo intendentes, et idip-   καὶ τὸ εὐσεβεῖν ἐν τῷ τάδε αὐτῇ
sum pietatem esse existimant,   προσκομίζειν ἢ μὴ τάδε τιθέμενοι.

---

4 adicit *C* ‖ adicit enim *om r*   6 sq. Coisl. 204, f. 133 b [Cr. vi. 278, Fr. 140] θεόδωρος. ἄλλος φησίν· ἀντὶ τοῦ, κ.τ.λ.   9 causam *C*   10 unde et *om r* adicit *C*   13 et *om C r*   15 imitare *C*   18 cruce *C* ‖ ergo (*bef.* Chr.) *r*   21 adicit *C r*   23 sq. Coisl. 204, *l. c.* [Cr. vi 278] ἄλλος δέ φησιν· τί γάρ, κ.τ.λ.   26 αὐτῶν cod., Cr.   33 ad ipsum *C* (*corr.*)

all the rest they have taken in a similar way. But this is not so. For from the place where he said (Phil 3:1) *to write these same things to you is indeed not troublesome to me*, he is teaching them by everything that it is not right to submit to those trying to persuade them to live according to the law, as we have demonstrated in our interpretation. And this is demonstrated still better by what follows. For he added:

3:17a *Be imitators of me, my brothers;*

†That is, "do not live under the law, just as I do not live under the law."*

Instead of "not living under the law, but like me."

And to demonstrate that he said this not because of himself, but that he wanted them to have such a way of life, he added:

3:17b *observe those who walk this way just as you have our example.*

†"Look entirely (he says) to those who live this way, as we do; submit to them and be quick to imitate them."*

"And look entirely (he says) to those who live this way and imitate them."

Then, condemning the opponents, he vigorously attacked them:

3:18 *For many walk, about whom I have often spoken to you, and now speak of even weeping, as enemies of the cross of Christ,*

It was enough to urge the Philippians to a hatred of them, if indeed they were trying to teach what was contradictory to the cross. Then he added:

3:19a *whose end is destruction,*

†For what else will be suspected about those who oppose Christ [242] and are eager to belittle what has to do with Christ by spending great care on the law?*

For what else would there be to suppose of those who oppose Christ and belittle what has to do with him in their zeal for the law's ordinances?

3:19b *whose God is the belly,*

†"Eat this; do not eat that." They go round about in their own pursuits, concentrating on their belly as though it were some kind of god, and they think this very thing is true religion, because they are eager

"Eat this, and do not eat this." And they occupy themselves with this, concentrating on the belly as though it were God, regarding the practice of true religion to be in providing it with some things or not with other

quod alia quidem illi offerre,
alia minime offerre studeant.*
illud etenim quod ultra non secundum uoluntatem Dei fit, obseruantia est pura nihil continens bonitatis; iniquitatem uero perficit
5 euidentem. unde illud et ex abundantia extenuat dicens:
et gloria in confusione eorum.

†magnum aliquid esse exi- μέγα (φησὶν) νομίζουσιν τὸ μὴ
stimant, ut alia quidem man- τάδε φαγεῖν, ἀλλὰ τάδε· οὐκ ἐννο-
ducentur, alia non manducen- οῦντες ὅτι κόπρος γίνεται ὅπερ ἂν
10 tur, non considerantes quoniam φάγωσιν, ἣν καὶ ὁρᾶν αἰσχύνονται·
omnis esca, quaeque illa fue- ἰδοὺ τῆς σπουδῆς αὐτῶν τὸ τέλος.
rit insumpta, in stercore uerti-
tur, quod et inspicere confun-
dentur; ecce studiorum eorum
15 qui est finis.*
et ad plenum eos incusans adiecit:
qui terrena sapiunt.

'nam legitimae obseruationes ad praesentem uitam sunt neces-
sariae, siue circumcisio sit, siue sacrificium, siue escarum obse-
20 ruantiae, siue sabbatorum custodiae; omnia autem haec in futuro
saeculo otiosa erunt, in quo constituti expectantes iam secundum
formam in illis esse existimamur.'

nostra autem conuersatio in caelis habetur, unde saluatorem expec-
tamus dominum Iesum Christum, qui transfigurabit corpus humilitatis
25 *nostrae, ut fiat ipsum conforme corpori gloriae eius secundum bonum*
placitum, ut possit ipse et subicere sibi omnia.

'nostra autem conuersatio non est terrena, sed caelestis, ubi ire
expectamus, unde et nostras primitias expectamus, ipsum Christum, qui hoc corpus quod nunc humiliatum est sub morte ad in-
30 mortalitatem transferat, simile illud suo corpori faciens. quia non
solum hoc potest facere, sed omnia renouans sibi coniungit; ita ut
omnis corruptela soluatur et omnia ad illum inspiciant, quasi principatorem et auctorem incorruptionis sibi existentem.' nam quod

4 efficit uidentem *H* perficite uid. *r* 5 unde et illud *H* 6 eorum (*aft.* gloria)
add C 7 sq. Coisl. 204, f. 134 a [Cr. vi. 279, Fr. 140] Θεόδωρος. ἄλλος δέ· οὕτως
μέγα φ., κ.τ.λ. cod.: txt edd. 12 stercora *C* (*corr.*) 13-14 confunduntur *C*
(*corr.*) 16 adicit *C r* 21 erunt et *H* ‖ in quem constituit *C* H* in quem
constituti *r* ‖ expectando *C* (*corr.*) 24 transfigurauit *C H* 27 celestistis *H*
‖ quo (*for* ubi) *r* 30 transferet *r*

to provide it some things and   things.
by no means to provide it other
things.*

And indeed, because this takes place superfluously, not in accord with God's will, it is nothing but an observance, involving nothing to do with moral excellence. Then he belittles this also because of its excess, saying:

3:19c *and the glory is in their shame,*

| †They think it something great that some things are eaten, while others are not eaten, because they do not consider that every food, whatever may be consumed, is changed into excrement, which they are ashamed to look at. See what the end of their pursuits is!* | They think (he says) it great not to eat some things but to eat others, because they do not consider that whatever they eat becomes excrement, which they are ashamed to see. See the end of their pursuit! |

And completely condemning them, he added:

[243] 3:19d *who mind earthly things.*

"For the observances of the law are necessary for the present life, whether it be circumcision or sacrifice or observances about foods or the ways to keep the Sabbath. But all these will have no purpose in the age to come, in which we are established because we await it and are people existing already by type in those good things."

3:20–21 *But our way of life is held in the heavens, from which we await the Lord Jesus Christ, who will change the form of the body of our humiliation so that it may be conformed to the body of his glory according to good pleasure that he should be able himself also to subject all things to himself.*

"But our way of life is not on earth but in heaven, where we expect to go and from which we expect our firstfruits, Christ himself, who will change the form of this body, now humiliated beneath death, to immortality, making it like his own body. In fact, he is not only able to do this, but by renewing all things he also joins them to himself so that all corruption may be destroyed and all things may look to him as the one who became for them the cause and founder of incorruption." For when he said in this place

hoc in loco dixit *subicere*, non in seruitute illa quae ex necessitate est dicit—non enim hoc in loco propositum est—sed quoniam
coniungit sibi per illa beneficia quae illis praebet, ita ut omnia ad
illum inspiciant quasi principatorem et auctorem bonorum. tale
est et illud quod ad Corinthios scriptum est: *tunc ipse Filius sub-*
ditus erit; non quia seruiet, sed manet coniunctus illi per se omnia
offerens—de suscepto homine ista dicens. deinde firmat exhortationem consolatione:

   itaque fratres mei carissimi et desiderantissimi, gaudium meum et
corona mea, sic state in Domino, carissimi.

   hoc est, 'tali modo conuersamini.' ostendit in his, quoniam
multum eos diligebat et uenerabatur quasi industrios, 'carissimos
et desiderantissimos' fratres nuncupans eos, et 'gaudium suum et
coronam' eos esse pronuncians; et omnibus illis adiciens iterauit
carissimi.

   Euodiam rogo et Syntychen obsecro idipsum sapere in Domino.

   †euidens est, quoniam et ip-   δῆλον ὅτι καὶ αὗται πρὸς ἀλλή-
sae aduersus alterutram decer-   λας ἐστασίαζον περὶ πρωτείων ἐρί-
tabant, contendentes super pri-   ζουσαι, ἐνάρετοι οὖσαι καὶ ὡς εἰ-
matum, utpote uirtutibus ador-   κὸς εἰς τὴν περὶ τῶν τοιούτων ἔριδα
natae, et ut fieri solet, in huiu-   καταπίπτουσαι.
smodi contentione prouocaban-
tur.*

unde et nominatim earum memoratus est, secundum multam
reuerentiam, ita ut suaderet eis illa quae bona erant, simul ut et
quod decebat personis earum redderet. hoc in loco maxime illud
possibile est conspicere, quoniam nulla eo in tempore discretio uirorum erat et mulierum, quando similiter contemplatione pietatis
adcelerabatur, ubi et ad omnem plebem scribens nominatim memorare has non dubitaret, plurimam illis reuerentiam in suis sermonibus adtestans; nihil pertimescens, ne aliquam sibi reprehen-

---

1   in seruite *H* seruituti *r*   2   est *om H*   8   consolationem *H* [et consolationem
in sequenti capite *r*]   9   karissimi, karissimos *C H*   ‖   et (*bef.* gaud.) *add C*
(*corr.*)   ‖   meum (*aft.* gaud.) *om C*: *txt H r*   10   karissimi, karissimos *C H*
12   karissimi, karissimos *C H*   14   adicens *H*   15   karissimi, karissimos *C H*
16   Euchodiam, Sinticen *C* Synticen *H*   17   quo (*for* quoniam) *H* alterutrum
C alterum *H*: *txt r*   ‖   sq. Coisl. 204, f. 135 a [Cr. vi. 281, Fr. 140] ἄλλος δέ
φησιν· δῆλον, κ.τ.λ.   24   sed cum (*for* secundum) *C* (*corr.*) *r*   27   possibile *om*
H   28   ac (*for* et) *r*

to subject, he is not referring to a slavery tied to necessity—for in this place that [244] is not set forth—but rather to that fact that he joins all things to himself by the benefits he bestows on them, so that all things may look to him as the cause and founder of good things. What is written to the Corinthians is also like this (1 Cor 15:28): *then the Son himself will be subjected*, not because he will be a slave, but the Man remains joined to the Word by offering up all things through himself—speaking this of the assumed Man. Then he strengthens the exhortation with consolation:

4:1 *And so, my dearly beloved and most greatly missed brothers, my joy and my crown, stand fast this way, dearly beloved.*

That is, "live your lives in such a fashion." By these words he shows how much he loved them and revered them for their zeal, naming them *dearly beloved and most greatly missed brothers* and declaring them to be his *joy and crown*. And to add to all this he repeated *dearly beloved*.

4:2 *I ask Euodia and I beseech Syntyche to have the same mind in the Lord.*

†It is clear that these women were at enmity with one another, [245] competing for first place, since they were adorned with virtues and, as usually happens, were provoked to a competition of this kind.*

It is clear that these women were at enmity with one another, quarreling about the first place, since they were virtuous and, as is likely, fell into a rivalry about such things.

For this reason he mentioned them even by name with much respect, so that he might persuade them of what was good and at the same time might pay due respect to their persons. In this place especially it is possible to see that at that time no distinction was made between men and women when it was a question of urging both alike to the observance of true religion. And here, though he was writing to all the people, he did not hesitate to mention the women by name, testifying very much respect for them by his words and in no way afraid that this would be a cause for blaming him. And it is clear that he was not hesitant even about women for

sionem ob ipsam causam prouideret. euidens est autem quoniam
neque de mulieribus dubitabat, ne quando edoleant, eo quod coram omnibus sint reprehensae. tanta erat commonitio apud illos
qui tunc erant, et sic omnia apud illos in caritate fiebant, ut delec-
5 tarentur potius coram omnibus reprehensae, quae tamen opus habebant ut reprehenderentur; et nemo illa quae fiebant secundum
ullam incusabat rationem.

etiam rogo et te, coniugalis affectiose, adiuua eas.

quidam beatum Paulum existimauerunt hinc uxorem habuis-
10 se et ad illam scribere [et] rogasse, quasi Philippis commorantem;
neque ad illud inspicientes, quoniam

†dixit *affectiose* et non 'affec-   τὸ γνήσιε [εἶπεν], ὃ ἀνδρὶ μὲν ἁρ-
tiosa,' quod uiro quidem apta-   μόττει, γυναικὶ δὲ οὐκέτι. δέον αὐ-
ri potest, mulieri autem nequa-   τοὺς κἀκεῖνο ἐννοῆσαι, ὅτι σύζυγον
15 quam. quos conueniebat etiam   ἡ θεία γραφὴ οὐδαμοῦ τὸν γάμῳ
illud cogitare, quoniam 'coniu-   συνημμένον λέγει, ἀλλὰ τὸν ὑπὸ τὴν
galem' diuina scriptura nullo in   αὐτὴν πίστιν.
loco illum qui nuptiis sociatus
est dicit, sed illum qui sub ea-
20 dem fide est.*

nam et Dominus *iugum* uocat illam conuersationem quae sub lege
est; *tollite* (inquit) *iugum meum, quoniam suaue est.* uidetur ergo ad
aliquem scribere affectu et fide illis coniunctum, quem et hortatur ut ad concordiam eas suo reducat studio (de qua pace disputat
25 illis), et consilia illis tribuat bona et omnia agat summa cum diligentia, ita ut ad unanimitatem illas faciat recurrere. et ostendens
quoniam dignae sunt multae diligentiae:

quae in euangelio simul mecum decertauerunt.

euidens est quoniam alicubi iter eius secutae sunt, et mini-

---

1 etiam (*for* autem) *r*   2 ad (*for* de) *C**   ‖   dubitabit *C**   ‖   hae doleant *r*   4
tunt (*for* tunc) *C**   8 eos *C H*   10 scribere rogasse *C* scr. rogasset *H* scribens
rogasse *r*   18 nuptis *C H r*   23 affectum *C H* affectus *r*   25 tribuit, agit *C*
(*corr.*)   ‖   cum s. d. *r*   26 illa *C**

fear they would be aggrieved because they were rebuked publicly before all. So great was admonition among the people of that time and so in love did everything take place among them, that they gladly preferred to be rebuked publicly before all even when they did something for which they deserved rebuke, and no one found fault with what took place for any reason.

4:3a *Indeed, I ask also you, affectionate yokefellow, help them,*

Because of this some people have thought that blessed Paul had a wife, [246] and was writing his request to her as if she were dwelling in Philippi. But they have paid no attention to the fact that

†he said *affectionate* in the masculine and not the feminine gender, so that the word can be applied to a man but by no means to a woman. And it would have been suitable for them to recognize that divine scripture nowhere uses the word "yokefellow" to refer to someone joined in marriage but to the person who is under the same faith.*	He said *affectionate* in the masculine gender, which applies to a man but not at all to a woman. They ought to recognize also this, that divine scripture nowhere uses the word "yokefellow" as applied to marriage but to refer to someone under the same faith.

Moreover, the Lord calls that way of life that is under the law[23] a *yoke* (Matt 11:29–30): *take up* (he says) *my yoke, since it is pleasant.* Therefore, Paul seems to be writing to some man joined to those women by affection and faith, and he urges him to bring them back to concord by his own zeal in reasoning with them about peace, to give them good advice, and to do everything with the greatest diligence so that he may hasten their return to being of one mind. And showing that the women are worthy of much careful attention:

4:3b *these women who have contended in the gospel together with me,*

[247] It is clear that the women followed his path somewhere else, and they ministered to him by fulfilling the teaching of right religion. And so that he might not seem to be speaking of a mere

---

[23] *Sub lege*, which must either be a mistake or a reference to the law of the gospel. Cf. "the law of faith" in Rom 3:27.

strauerunt ei implenti doctrinam pietatis. et ut ne uideatur puram
quandam dicere decertationem:

cum Clemente et ceteris cooperariis meis, quorum nomina sunt in
libro uitae.

5　　hoc est, 'similiter sicut illi conlaborauerunt mihi ad doctrinam
pietatis.' euidens est enim hinc etiam illud quoniam quando dicit
ad Corinthios: *numquid non habemus potestatem sororem mulierem*
circumducere? non quia numquam circumduxerit dicit, sed quia
non semper; quod et cautius nobis notatum est et ostensum est in
10　expositione ipsius epistolae. et iterum orat pro illis:

gaudete in Domino semper; et iterum duo, gaudete.

hoc est, 'semper uobis talia adsint a Deo, pro quibus gaudio
possitis impleri.' deinde et ad exhortationem uertitur, quae inap-
tari poterat illi exhortationi quae humilitati fuerat facta:

15　　*modestia uestra nota fiat omnibus hominibus.*

'sicut et uos uolo esse modestos, ita ut omnes super uestram
modestiam de uobis gratulentur.' et quoniam modestia frequenter solet noceri adiecit:

Dominus prope est; nihil solliciti sitis.

20　　'licet nociuitatem sustinetis, nolite solliciti esse; prope est
Deus, qui uobis nocitis ferat auxilium, qui et potens est eos qui
nocent uos punire.' quid ergo conuenit facere eos nocitos?

sed in omni oratione et postulatione cum gratiarum actione postu-
lationes uestrae innotescant ad Deum.

25　　'tantum uos per omnia gratias agite Deo, postulantes ab eo tristitiae solutionem quae est huius rei merces.'

et pax Dei quae supereminet omnem intellectum custodiat corda
uestra et sensus uestros in Christo Iesu.

hoc est, 'ipse uobis praestet perfectam pacem qui ab omnibus
30　plus potest.' nam pacem Dei supereminere dixit omnia, ut dicat
'Deum.'

---

1 impletae *H* 7 numquam *H* ‖ sororem *om r* 12 assint *H* 13 quem
aptari *C** quae apt. *C (corr.)* 14 humilitate *r* 17 modestis (*for* modestia) *C*
(*corr.*) modesti, solent *r* 18 adicit *C r* 20 sustineatis *r* 21 indigentibus
(*for* nocitis) *r* 22 quibus nocetur (*for* nocitos] *r* 25-26 tantum—merces *om r*

contending:[24]

4:3c *with Clement and the rest of my fellow workers, whose names are in the book of life.*

That is, "in the same way, just as those who worked with me in teaching true religion." For it is clear from this also what he means when he writes to the Corinthians (1 Cor 9:5): *do we not have authority to lead around a sister wife?* He does not say that he had never led one around but that he had not always done so. We have also pointed this out more carefully in our commentary on that letter. And again he prays for them:

4:4 *Rejoice in the Lord always, and again I say, rejoice.*

That is, "may such things be always present to you from God for which you can be filled with joy." Then he turns to an exhortation that could have been applied to the exhortation to humility he had made (Phil 2:2–11):

4:5a *Let your gentleness be made known to all people.*

"As, indeed, I also want you to be gentle so that everyone may be glad because of you for your gentleness." And because gentleness usually often suffers harm, he added:

4:5b-6a *The Lord is near. Be anxious for nothing,*

"Granted that you suffer harm, do not be anxious. God is near and will bring you help when you are harmed, and he has power to punish those who harm you." Therefore, what should those who are harmed do?

[248] 4:6b *but in everything by prayer and supplication with thanksgiving make your supplications[25] known to God.*

"Only give God thanks by everything, supplicating him for a loosing of sorrow, which is the reward for doing this."

4:7 *And may[26] the peace of God that surpasses all understanding keep your hearts and your thoughts in Christ Jesus.*

That is, "may he himself bestow upon you perfect peace, which is more powerful than all things." For he said that the peace of God surpasses all things so as to mean "God."

4:8–9 *For the rest, brothers, whatever things are true, whatever are*

---

[24]That is, to show that the women "contended" not only by witnessing but also by teaching.

[25]*Postulatione ... postulationes,* an unusual translation of δεήσει ... αἰτήματα.

[26]*Custodiat.* See Swete's note (1:248): "The error *custodiat* runs through nearly all the Latin authorities, and strangely enough finds an apparent support in the comments of the Gk. expositors."

de cetero, fratres, quaecunque sunt uera, quaecunque pudica, quae-
cunque iusta, quaecunque casta, quaecunque dilectionis, quaecunque
bonae opinionis, si qua uirtus, et si qua laus, haec cogitate; quae et di-
dicistis et accepistis, et audistis et uidistis in me, haec agite, et Deus
5 *pacis erit uobiscum.*

'ueritatis (inquit) diligentiam adhibete, pudicitiae, iustitiae, castitatis;' ut dicat: 'abstinete uos a prauis negotiis (sicuti et alibi dixit: *in omnibus uos comprobastis castos esse in negotio*), ut ageretis illa
quae omnibus placent;' hoc est, illa quae ab omnibus cognoscun-
10 tur esse bona. 'nam et apud omnes similis est bonorum confessio,
ex quibus operibus bona uos opinio subsequi poterit. quaecunque sunt uirtutum opera, quaecunque laudem uobis ab omnibus
prouidere possunt, hoc uidentes in nobis, hoc docti a nobis, haec
agite, et habebitis semper Deum uobiscum profundam uobis suam
15 pacem praebentem.' consummans uero omnia illa quae exhortationis fuerunt, scribit ultra de his quae missa fuerant sibi ab illis:

gauisus sum autem in Domino magnifice, quoniam tandem aliquan-
do refloruistis, ut pro me saperetis; in quo et sapiebatis, tempus uero
non habuistis.

20 bene quia dixit *in Domino*, ut non uideretur ob pecuniam di-
rectam sibi laetari, sed ob propositum illorum qui miserunt. dicit enim quoniam 'laetatus sum pro quibus pertinuit uobis de me;
sciebam etenim quoniam et dudum uobis pertinebat, tempus uero
non habebatis, ut faceretis illud quod uolebatis.' nam

25 †quod dixit, *tempus non habui-*   τὸ ἠκαιρεῖσθε φησὶν ἀντὶ τοῦ
stis, hoc dicit: 'hoc prohibiti   ἐκωλύεσθε καὶ οὐκ εἴχετε τοῦτο
estis, tempus non habentes ut   ποιῆσαι ὅπερ ἐβούλεσθε.'
faceretis quod uolebatis.'*

et caute confirmans eos, ut ne existimarent eum propter datas pe-
30 cunias haec dicere:

non quia secundum minorationem dico, ego enim didici in quibus
sum sufficient esse; scio et humiliari, scio et abundare, omnia et in om-
nibus imbutus sum, et saturari, et esurire, et abundare, et minorari.

---

7 ibi *for* alibi *C H* 8 cogeretis (*for* ag.) *H* 13 prouideri *H* ‖ in uobis (*for* a
nobis) *C H: txt r* 18 per me *C* 21 ob *om C* H r* 23 et (*bef.* dudum) *om r* ‖
pert. uobis *H* 24–30 nam quod dixit—haec dicere *om r* 25 sq. Coisl. 204,
f. 136 b [Cr. vi. 285, Fr. 140] θεόδωρος. ἄλλος δέ· τὸ ἠκαιρεῖσθε φησὶν ἀντὶ τοῦ,
κ.τ.λ. 26 prohibuistis *H* 29 ut me *C** uti ne *C* (*corr.*) 33 abundari *C* H*

honorable, whatever are just, whatever are pure, whatever belongs to love, whatever to good reputation, if there is any virtue and if any praise, think about these things. The things you have both learned and received, both heard and seen in me, these things do, and the God of peace will be with you.

"Hold fast (he says) to the diligent care of truth, of what is honorable, of justice, of purity," meaning, "keep yourselves away from perverse matters—as he said elsewhere (2 Cor 7:11): *in all things you have proved yourselves pure in the matter*—so that you may do those things pleasing to all," that is, what all know to be good. "For among all people there is a like acknowledgement of the things that are good; by doing them a good reputation may be capable of following you. [249] Whatever are the deeds of virtues, whatever can bring you praise from all people when they see this in us—do these things, taught by us, and you will always have with you God, who bestows on you his own deep peace." Then, completing everything that had to do with his exhortation, he writes further about what they had sent him:

4:10 *And I rejoiced in the Lord greatly that at long last you have blossomed again, so that you mind about me, and you were minding, but you did not have the opportunity.*

He rightly said *in the Lord* so that he might not seem glad because of the money sent to him, but because of the intent of those who sent it. For he says "I was glad for the fact that you were concerned about me, for I know that this was from long ago your concern, but you did not have the opportunity to do what you wished."

†For by saying *you did not have the opportunity* he means, "you were prevented, since you did not have the opportunity to do what you wished.*

you did not have the opportunity instead of "you were prevented and were not able to do what you wished."

And carefully strengthening them so that they would not think that he was saying these things because of the money given:

4:11–12 *Not that I am speaking with respect to being in need, for I have learned to be self-sufficient in what conditions I am. I know also how to be humiliated; I know also how to abound. I have been introduced to all things and in all ways, both to be filled to repletion and to suffer hunger, both to abound and to be in need.*

[250] "I am saying this (he says) not because I am bearing a

'hoc dico (inquit) non quia inopiam fero grauiter; in consuetudinem enim me ipsum constitui, ut sufficiens sim illis quae inueniuntur in praesenti.' et quoniam nulla ex parte conturbatur ex illis quae sibi accidebant, suscipiebat uero et illa quae requiei erant
5 et illa quae tristitiae prudenti ac sobrio intellectu; et in duris quidem rebus consueuerat non illa ferre grauiter, in prosperis uero
non laxari deliciis, sed disponere illa quae erga se erant per omnia
conuenienter. et ut ne uideatur magna de se sapere haec dicens:
  omnia praeualeo in eo qui me confortat, Christo.
10 'ipse (inquit) est qui praestat mihi sic posse, ut et requiem conuenienti arbitrio abutar et tristitias forti animo feram.' et ut ne
aestimetur contempnere illa quae ab illis missa fuerant, tale habens institutum, adiecit:
  uerumtamen bene fecistis communicantes tribulationi meae.
15 'uos quidem omni laude estis digni, pro quibus communicastis
tribulationibus meis, mittentes sumptus subleuantes necessitatem
meam; ex quibus necesse est, ut et mercedis uobis adsit communio.'
  scitis et uos, Philippenses, quoniam in principio euangelii, quando
20 *exii a Macedonia, nulla mihi ecclesia communicauit in ratione dati et*
accepti, nisi uos soli; quoniam et Thessalonicae et semel et bis ad usus
meos misistis.
  deinde dicit quoniam 'et quando inprimis uobis praedicaui pietatem cum ceteris Macedonibus, et exinde sum egressus, neque
25 dedit mihi quis alter, neque suscepi ab altero, nisi a uobis solis; etenim et Thessalonicae commoranti mihi et semel et bis illa quae ad
usus necessabantur misistis.' nam quod dixit *communicastis in ra-*
tionem dati et accepti, hoc dicit, non quia aliqua quidem ipse dedit,
alia uero illi, sed quod illi quidem dederunt, ipse uero acceperit.
30 'communionem dati et accepti' hoc dixit, eo quod illi quidem dederunt, ipse uero accepit. et iterum ostendens, quoniam non pro
illis quae data sibi fuerunt ista dicit:

---

1   haec *C* haec inq. (*om* dico) *r*   5   in (*bef.* duris) *om H*   7   diuitiis *H*   ‖   his
ponere (*for* disp.) *C* H r*   10   est *om H*   12   talem *C H*   13   adicit *C r*   15
estis *om r*   17   mercedes *r*   ‖   assit *H*   21   nisi soli uos *H*   25   qui saltem
(*for* quis alter) *C** quis saltem *C* (*corr.*) *r*   27   necessaria habebantur *C* (*corr.*)
necesse habebantur *r*   ‖   missistis *C* (*corr.*)   ‖   numquid (*for* nam quod) *r*
29   acciperit *C** acciperet *r*

heavy load of poverty, for I have put myself in the habit of being self-sufficient in whatever circumstances are encountered in the present." And he was in no way disturbed by what happened to him, but he accepted what had to do with rest from toil and what had to do with misfortune with a wise and sober mind. Indeed, in harsh circumstances he had the habit of not bearing them heavily, but in favorable ones, the habit of not being slackened by luxuries. Rather, in everything his habit was to manage what happened to him in a proper way. And so that he would not seem to think highly of himself because of this, he says:

4:13 *I prevail over all things in the one who strengthens me, Christ.*

"He it is (he says) who bestows on me in this way the ability to employ rest from toil with a right judgment and to bear misfortunes with a strong mind." And so that he might not be thought to despise what they had sent him because he had this habit, he added:

4:14 *Nevertheless, you have done well by sharing in my affliction.*

"Indeed, you are worthy of all praise for what you have shared with me in my afflictions, by sending expenses to relieve my needs, because of which it is necessary that a share in the reward should also be yours."

4:15–16 *And you also know, Philippians, that in the beginning of the gospel, when I left Macedonia, there was no church that shared with me in the account of giving and receiving except you alone, since you sent also to Thessalonica both once and twice for my needs.*

Then he says, "and when I first preached true religion to you with the other Macedonians and left from there, neither did anyone else give anything to me, nor did I receive anything from anyone else, except from you alone. And indeed, when I was dwelling in Thessalonica, both once and twice [251] you sent me what was necessary for my needs." For when he said *you shared in the account of giving and receiving*, he means not that he himself gave some things and they gave others but that they gave while he received.[27] He said "sharing in giving and receiving" because they gave, but he received. And again, to show that he is not saying this because of what they have given:

---

[27] Apparently Theodore rejects the idea that what Paul gave was spiritual and what the Philippians gave was material support.

non quia requiro datum, sed requiro fructum, qui abundat in ratio-
nem uestram.

'hoc dico (inquit) non propter illa quae data sunt, sed institutum uestrum conlaudo, cuius euidentes sunt et fructus. dantes
enim multam uobis mercedum retributionem prouidistis.' deinde adiecit:

habeo autem omnia et abundo; repletus sum, suscipiens ab Epaph-
rodito quae a uobis missa sunt, odorem suavitatis, sacrificium accep-
tabile, bene placens Deo.

'quoniam omnia recepi quae a uobis missa sunt; magis autem et
ampliora suscepi, quae per Epaphroditum a uobis fuerant missa.'
ostendens quoniam et multas illis refert gratias pro quibus dederunt, propositum illorum plus praehonorans quam illa quae missa
sunt. orat autem pro illis, ut sacrificium boni odoris illa ipsa ante
Deum adpareant, quorum recepit quidem propositum, retribuit
uero eis illam quae a se erat gratiam:

Deus autem meus repleat omnem necessitatem uestram secundum
diuitias suas in gloria in Christo Iesu.

orat pro illis, ut et secundum praesentem uitam omnis illorum
necessitas a Deo impleatur, nullam minorationem hisdem susti-
nentibus.

Deo autem et patri nostro gloria in saecula saeculorum. amen.

quoniam pro omnibus Deo et Patri gloriam referre dignum est.

salutate omnem sanctum in Christo Iesu. salutant [uos qui mecum
sunt fratres. salutant] uos omnes sancti, maxime autem qui ex Caesa-
ris domo sunt.

salutat quidem omnem sanctum apud illos; salutat etiam eos et
ab illis fratribus qui secum sunt, et ab omnibus qui Romac sanctis,
ut dicat 'fidelibus;' et [ab illis qui] sunt de Caesaris domo; erant
enim qui exinde crediderant. et super omnibus adiecit sibi con-
suetum finem epistolis inponens:

gratia domini Iesu Christi cum omnibus uobis.

5   mercede *C** mercedis *C (corr.)* mercedem *H r*   ‖   et *(aft.* mercedem) *add r*
6   adicit *C*   11   ab Ephafroditum a uobis missa fuerant *H*   13   praehonoras
C*   15   recipit *r*   20   iisdem *r*   22   et *om r*   24   uos—salutant *om C H: txt r*
28   sunt *(aft.* Romae) *add r*   29   ab illis qui *om C H r*   30   adicit *C r*   30-31
cum sibi suetum *C* H*

4:17 *Not that I seek the gift, but I seek the fruit that abounds to your account.*

"I am saying this (he says) not because of the things that were given, but I praise your habit of which they are the evidence and the fruit. For by giving you have provided yourselves with much recompense in reward." Then he added:

4:18 *And I have everything, and I abound. I have been filled, accepting from Epaphroditus the things that have been sent by you, a smell of sweet savor, an acceptable sacrifice, well-pleasing to God.*

"Since I have received all that you sent, I have rather accepted as even more than enough what you sent by Epaphroditus." He is showing that he sends them much thanks for what they have given, while giving greater honor to their intention than to what was sent. And he prays for them that those very gifts may appear before God as a sacrifice of sweet odor. He has, indeed, received their intention, and he has paid his thanks to them:

4:19 *And may[28] God fill up every need of yours according to his riches in glory in Christ Jesus.*

He prays for them that even in the present life every need of theirs [252] will be fulfilled by God without their suffering any lack.

4:20 *And to God our Father be glory to the ages of ages. Amen.*

Since it is right to render glory to God the Father for all things.

4:21–22 *Greet every saint in Christ Jesus. The brothers who are with me greet you. All the saints greet you, and especially those who are of Caesar's household.*

He greets every saint among them, and he sends them greetings also from those brothers who are with him and from all the saints at Rome, meaning "the faithful," and from those who are of Caesar's household. For there were some there who had believed. And he added to everything what he was accustomed to put down as the conclusion of his letters:

4:23 *The grace of the Lord Jesus Christ be with all of you.*

---

[28] *Repleat*, the subjunctive replacing the future of the Greek.

THEODORUS MOPSUESTENUS IN EPISTOLAM B. PAULI AD COLOSSENSES

ARGUMENTUM*

SCRIBIT Colossensibus beatus Paulus sicut scripsit Ephesiis quos antequam scriberet non uiderat. ostendit autem hoc ipse in suis scriptis, quando quidem dicens: *audientes fidem uestram in Christo et caritatem quam habetis in omnes sanctos;* quando uero
5 scribit: *uolo autem uos scire, quale certamen habeam pro uobis et his qui in Laodicia sunt et quotquot non uiderunt faciem meam in carne.* est autem argumentum epistolae tale. consuetudo illi est, ubicunque uel ad quoscunque scribit quos ante non uiderat, illa quae secundum Christum sunt extollere, et ostendere illorum magnitu-
10 dinem quae per eum directa sunt; eo quod nec possibile erat aliter magnum quid et utile ostendi illis, qui illam sectantur fidem quae in eum est. hoc uero in loco non solum secundum hunc modum necessariam sibi hanc esse perspiciebat rationem, sed propter illos qui ex circumcisione erant, qui omni in loco peragrantes illos qui
15 ex gentibus crediderunt persuadere properabant ut cum illa fide quam in Christo habent etiam legis custodirent decreta; quia ergo et ad Colossenses uenerant et paulo minus aliquibus eorum suaserunt ut legitimis inseruirent decretis. nam dum ostendit illorum eminentiam quae a Christo directa sunt, infirmam utique osten-
20 debat esse legem, superfluam simul et uanam eius diligentiam et custodiam esse ostendens. utraque ergo ex causa ita scribit, una quod apta illi esse poterant talia inprimis scribenti, altera quod il-

4 quandoquidem uero *C (corr.)* 6 laetitia (*for* laodicia) *C H* 10 qui per e. directi sunt *C H r* 15 et (*for* ut) *C* r* 22 poterat *r*

THEODORE OF MOPSUESTIA ON BLESSED PAUL'S LETTER TO THE COLOSSIANS

THE SETTING

[253] Blessed Paul writes to the Colossians, just as he wrote to the Ephesians, as to people whom he had not seen before writing. And he shows this himself in the letter when he says (Col 1:4), *hearing of your faith in Christ and of the love you have for all the saints*, and when he writes (Col 2:1), *and I want you to know what kind of contest I have for you and for those who are in Laodicea and as many as have not seen my face in the flesh.*[1] Now such is the setting of the letter. It is his habit [254] whenever he writes to any people he had not previously seen to praise what has to do with Christ and to show the greatness of his dispensations, because it was not possible in any other way that what is great and beneficial could be shown to those who follow faith in Christ. But in this place he recognized that this reason was necessary for him not only in this way but also because of those from the circumcision who, wandering about everywhere, were eager to persuade Gentile believers also to keep the commandments of the law together with their faith in Christ. This, then, was because they had come also to the Colossians and all but persuaded some of them to become slaves of the law's commandments. For while he showed the superior excellence of Christ's dispensations, he was also certainly showing that the law was invalid, demonstrating that diligence in keeping it was at the same time useless and vain. Thus, he writes this way for two reasons: one because his words could be suitable for him when he was writing to them for

---

[1] The second citation differs somewhat from the translation of the verse in the commentary proper.

lorum causa qui erant ex circumcisione extollere illa properabat
quae sunt secundum Christum, sicut et conueniens erat, magnitudinem eorum quae sunt gesta explicans. deinde et post hoc euidenter exhortatur ut non suadeantur ab illis qui talia eos docere
5   pertemptant, omni ex parte pronuntians quod non sit illis ultra necessaria legis custodia; et post hoc ad exhortationem egressus super multis et necessariis rebus omnibus illis loquitur. inchoabimus
uero in subsequentibus eam facere narrationem, quae per partes
esse uidetur; eo quod illa quae ad argumentum epistolae pertine-
10 bant, in his sufficienter patefacta sunt.

Paulus apostolus Christi Iesu per uoluntatem Dei, et Timotheus
frater, his qui sunt Colossenses sanctis et fidelibus fratribus in Christo
Iesu; gratia uobis et pax a Deo patre nostro.

hanc consuetam epistolae praescriptionem faciens incipit hoc
15 modo:

gratias agimus Deo patri domini nostri Iesu Christi, semper pro uo-
bis orantes, audientes fidem uestram in Christo Iesu et caritatem quam
habetis in omnes sanctos.

sic et illam epistolam quam ad Romanos scripsit a gratiarum
20 actione inchoauit scribere eis. adicit autem in hac *pro uobis oran-*
tes, ostendens quoniam non pro quibus crediderunt tantum gratias
agit, sed et pro residuo tempore orat. quae est autem oratio eius?

propter spem quae reposita est uobis in caelis.

'ita ut adsequi possitis caelestia bona, quorum custoditur uo-
25 bis spes firma, si tamen illa quae a uobis sunt concurrerunt.' et
ostendens quoniam non aliud quid dicit praeterquam illam quam
cognouerunt:

quam ante audistis in uerbo ueritatis euangelii, quod uenit in uobis.

'dico autem ista quae cognouistis cum ueritate euangelii susci-
30 pientes doctrinam.' et ad maiorem exhortationem eorum ostendens quoniam non soli illi ista praeter ceteros cognouerunt homines; alioquin et magis eos continere in fide poterat, quod illa pietas
quae ab omnibus in commune tenetur etiam ab his teneatur:

sicut in omni mundo.

---

4   non *om r* ‖ suadantur *C*H* suadentur *r* 5   praeceptant (*for* pertempt.) *r*
9   uidentur *C*H r* ‖ quae *om H* 14   consuetae *r* ‖ ep. *om H* 19   in
illa epistola *C* (*corr.*) 21   non *om H* 27   agnouerunt *H* 28   qui (*for* quod)
C H 30   et *om r* 33   in communi *C* (*corr.*)

the first time, and the other because it was on account of those from the circumcision that he was eager to praise what had to do with Christ, expounding the greatness of his mighty deeds as was right. And after this he then quite clearly exhorts them not to be persuaded by those trying to teach them such things, proclaiming in every respect that it is no longer necessary for them to keep the law. And after this, leaving behind his exhortation, he speaks to them about many things and all of them necessary. Now in what follows we shall enter upon an orderly account of what appears in the different sections, because what would attach to the setting of the letter is sufficiently disclosed in them.

[255] 1:1–2 *Paul, an apostle of Christ Jesus by the will of God, and Timothy the brother, to those saints who are Colossians and to the faithful brothers in Christ Jesus; grace to you and peace from God our Father.*

Making this customary salutation of the letter, he begins this way:

1:3–4 *We give thanks to God the Father of our Lord Jesus Christ, always praying for you, hearing of your faith in Christ and of the love you have for all the saints,*

He began writing to them with a thanksgiving, the same way he wrote the letter to the Romans. And he adds to it *praying for you,* showing that he not only gives thanks because they have believed but also prays for the time that still lies ahead. What, then, is his prayer?

1:5a *for the hope that is laid up for you in the heavens,*

"So that you may be able to attain the heavenly goods by which your hope is kept steadfast, if indeed your contribution harmonizes with them." And to show that what he says is no different from what they have known:

1:5b-6a *which you have heard before in the word of the truth of the gospel, which came to you,*

[256] "And I am saying what you have known, because you received teaching with the truth of the gospel." And to strengthen the exhortation he shows that they are not the only ones, set apart from other people, who have known these things. And besides, the fact that the true religion held in common by all was also held by them was capable of holding them together all the more in faith:

1:6b *as in all the world,*

et rei magnitudinem ostendens:

et est fructificans et crescens.

'non solum (inquit) cognitum est illis qui in omni sunt orbe, sed et augmentum suscipit per singulos dies.' deinde ut ne uideatur
5 euangelii quidem cognitio communis illis esse cum omnibus, sicut dixit 'in omnibus'—ne ergo illi aestimarent, quod euangelium non et augmentum apud omnes consequitur, adicit:

sicuti et in uobis ex qua die audistis et cognouistis gratiam Dei in ueritate.

10 'cognouistis (inquit) uos pietatem, sicut et omnes; augmentum etiam suscipit omni in loco per singulos dies, sicut et apud uos. sic omni in loco euangelium uim suam obtinet, et augmentum per singulos accipit dies, et apud uos et apud omnes qui sunt in orbe terrarum.' hoc autem sufficiens erat hos et adhortari et suadere
15 ut in fide manerent, si tamen cum consensu omnes haec uera esse cognouissent. deinde indicat et a quo sint docti:

sicut didicistis ab Epaphra carissimo conseruo nostro, qui est fidelis pro uobis minister Christi; qui et nunciauit nobis uestram caritatem in Spiritu.

20 euidenter enim in hisce ostendit quoniam ab Epaphra euange-lium susceperunt, quem et iusta ratione laudauit, uenerabilem il-lis exhibens, quem etiam commendauit illis, eo quod nota sibi fe-cisset illa quae de illis erant; sciens quoniam necessarium quidem et utile est ad plenum, ut uenerabilis et desiderabilis sit discipulis
25 magister. maxime autem erga hunc aptissime illud fecisse uidetur, ita ut doceat eos cum multo affectu persistere in eius doctrina. in his et sequestrata lege tradiderat illis euangelium. itaque non lau-dasset eius doctrinam, si non hoc modo fuisset effecta; qui enim fieri poterat ut is qui docebat illa non deberet custodire? deinde

---

2 et *om* C* H quae (*bef.* est) *add* C (*corr.*): *txt* r 4 euangelium (*for* augm.) r ‖ suscepit C r 6 cum omn. (*for* in omn.) C H: *txt* r 7 ad (*for* et) r 11 suscepit C r 15 esse *om* H 18 uobis (*for* nobis) C* 24 uenerabis et diserabilis (*sic*) H 26 deceat r 27 eo quod (*for* et) C (*corr.*) 28 non (*bef.* fuisset) *add* H ‖ affecta r ‖ quibus (*for* qui enim) H quo r 29 debere C H r

And to show the greatness of the matter:

1:6c *and it is bearing fruit and growing,*

"Not only (he says) is it known to those in the whole round world, but it also receives increase day by day." Then, so that it might not seem that while the knowledge of the gospel is common to them with all—as he said "in all"—the gospel but not its increase is following for all.[2] Lest they should think that, he adds:

1:6d *just as also in you from the day you heard and knew the grace of God in truth,*

[257] "You have known (he says) true religion, just as all have. It also receives increase everywhere day by day, just as also among you. Thus, everywhere the gospel gains its power and receives increase day by day, both among you and among all who are in the inhabited round world." And this was enough both to exhort and to persuade them to persevere in faith, if indeed all with a common mind should know these things to be true. Then he points out also the one by whom they were taught:

1:7–8 *as you have learned from Epaphras, our dearly beloved fellow servant, who is a faithful minister of Christ on your behalf, who has also brought word to us of your love in the Spirit.*

For by these words he showed clearly that they received the gospel from Epaphras, whom he also praised with just reason, presenting him as worthy of their respect, and about whom he gave them a favorable report because he had made their circumstances known to him. He knew that it is necessary and entirely beneficial that a teacher should be respected and longed for by disciples. And he seems especially to have composed this with the greatest appropriateness regarding Epaphras, so that he might teach them to persevere in his teaching with much affection. In his teaching Epaphras had handed over to them the gospel, with the law excluded. And so Paul would not have praised his teaching if it had not been done in this way. For how could it have happened that the one who taught them the gospel should have been obliged to praise the keeping of the law? Then, picking up again what he

---

[2]Swete (1:256) interprets this difficult sentence as follows: "Th. says: 'The Apostle had stated that the Gospel (1) had reached the Colossians as it had reached the rest of the world; and (2) was continually yielding fruit and making increase. To the latter statement he immediately adds, καθὼς καὶ ἐν ὑμῖν, to prevent the inference that whilst the knowledge of the Gospel was shared by all nations alike, its fruitfulness was confined to the Colossians."

quod dixit *semper pro uobis orantes*, et cetera, resumens dicit:

pro quo nos ex qua die audiuimus non cessamus pro uobis orantes et
postulantes, ut impleamini cognitione uoluntatis eius in omni sapientia
et intellectu spiritali; ambulare uos digne Deo ad omne bonum placi-
tum, in omni opere bono fructificantes et crescentes in cognitione Dei,
in omni uirtute confortati secundum potentiam gloriae eius in omnem
patientiam et longanimitatem cum gaudio.

per omnia optasse illis bona uidetur, sub specie orationis edocens eos illa quae eis conueniebant. dicit autem quoniam 'ex quo
illa quae de uobis sunt audiuimus, sine dilatione oramus ita ut omni sensu spiritali repleti cognoscere possitis Dei uoluntatem, digne ei conuersantes et per omnia placere ei properantes; ita ut boni actus multiplicentur in uobis per singulos dies cum et Dei cognitione, qui poterit uos secundum suam potentiam respicientes
ad se sua replere patientia, ita ut possitis ferre patienter uniuersa
illa quae tristitiae sunt; ita ut gaudium habeatis in illis, propter illam mercedem quae uobis in futuro saeculo pro his est retribuen-
da.' hoc quidem, ut dixi, optasse se eis dixit; et in eo dum dicit illa
quae orationis sunt, docet eos diligentiam conuenientium adhibere. sumens uero et gratiarum actionem quam pro eis impleuerat,
initium sumit doctrinae, sicut in Ephesiorum fecit epistola, ubi
sub specie gratiarum actionis illa quae sunt dogmatum eos uisus
est instruxisse; propter quod dicit:

gratias agentes Patri, qui dignos uos habuit in partem sortis sanc-
torum in lumine.

'haec (inquit) postulamus ante omnia, gratias agentes Deo pro
uobis, quoniam dignos uos per suam cognitionem sanctorum collegio esse pronuntiauit, cum essetis alieni a pietate et idolorum
eratis sectatores.' nam quod dixit *in lumine*, ut dicat 'per suam cognitionem;' et quod dixit *qui dignos uos habuit*, hoc est, 'dignos esse
pronuntiauit.' et quod illud est lucrum? ut sanctorum iungantur
collegio.

qui eripuit nos de potestate tenebrarum et transtulit in regnum filii
caritatis suae.

3 agnitione *H* 7 pacientia *H* 10 orabamus *r* ‖ ita ut et *C* (*corr.*) ut *r* 13
et (*aft.* cum) *om C* (*corr.*) *r* 18 ei (*for* eis) *C* H r* 19-20 adhibere conu. *H*
21 epistolam *C** 26 agens *C H: txt r* 27 agnitionem *H* 33 uos *C* (*corr.*)
‖ trantulit (*sic*) *C**

had said (Col 1:3), *always praying for you* and the rest, he says:

[258] *1:9–11 Because of this we, from the day we heard it, do not cease praying for you and asking that you may be filled with the knowledge of his will in all wisdom and spiritual understanding, for you to walk worthily for God to all good pleasure, bearing fruit in every good work and growing in the knowledge of God, strengthened in every virtue according to the power of his glory for all endurance and long-suffering with joy,*

In everything he has plainly prayed that good things may be theirs, teaching them in the form of a prayer what was right for them. And he is saying that "beginning with the time we heard of your circumstances, we keep praying without delay that filled with every spiritual sense you may be able to know the will of God, living worthily for him and being eager to please him in all things, so that good deeds may be multiplied among you day by day together with the knowledge of God. May he be able by his own power to fill you with his own endurance when you fix your sight on him, so that you may be capable of bearing with endurance every single thing that belongs to misfortune, so that you may rejoice in this because of that reward to be bestowed on you for it in the age to come." Indeed, as I have said, he said that he had prayed this for them, and while he utters the words of his prayer, he is teaching them to hold fast to the diligent care of what is right. Indeed, by taking up the thanksgiving he had completed for them, he takes up the point of departure for teaching, just as he did in the letter to the Ephesians, where he plainly instructed them in the teaching of doctrine under the form of a thanksgiving. Because of this he says:

1:12 giving thanks to the Father, who has held you worthy for a share in the inheritance of the saints in light.

"We ask these things (he says) before all, thanking God [259] for you, since he has proclaimed you to be worthy of joining the society of the saints through your knowledge of him, even though you were strangers to true religion and were followers of idols." For he said *in light* to mean "through knowledge of him." And his statement *who held you worthy* is the equivalent of "he pronounced you to be worthy." And what is that gain? To be joined to the society of the saints.

1:13 He has rescued us from the power of darkness and has transferred us into the kingdom of the Son of his love,

'non solum (inquit) abstulit uos ab errore et daemonum potentia, sed et participes uos pronuntiauit regni esse Christi.' nam
quod dicit *transtulit in regnum filii caritatis suae*, hoc dicit sicut et
in alio loco: *si sustinemus, et conregnabimus.* unde bene quia

5 †non dixit *filii* tantum, sed filii
caritatis suae. nec enim participes regni Dei Verbi efficimur—
qui enim fieri potest, ut uniuersitatis Opifici iungamur?—sed
10 suscepto homini dicit, cui et
participabimus honoris propter
naturae similitudinem, quando
affectum erga eum ipsis operibus ostendere ualuerimus. unde
15 et 'filium caritatis' eum uocauit,
eo quod non secundum naturam Patris est filius, sed caritate filiorum adoptionem est adsecutus.*

οὐκ εἶπεν τοῦ υἱοῦ, ἀλλὰ τοῦ υἱοῦ
τῆς ἀγάπης αὐτοῦ· οὐ γὰρ κοινωνοὶ
τῆς βασιλείας τοῦ θεοῦ λόγου γινό
μεθα, ἀλλὰ τοῦ ἀναληφθέντος ἀν
θρώπου, ᾧ κοινωνοῦμεν τῆς τιμῆς
διὰ τὴν φυσικὴν ὁμοιότητα, ὅταν
πρὸς αὐτὸν διάθεσιν ἐπὶ τῶν ἔργων
ἐπιδειξώμεθα· ὅθεν καὶ υἱὸν ἀγάπης
αὐτὸν ἐκάλεσεν, ὡς οὐ φύσει τοῦ
πατρὸς ὄντα υἱὸν ἀλλ' ἀγάπῃ τῆς
υἱοθεσίας ἀξιωθέντα.

20 per omnia enim propositum habet illa quae secundum Christum
sunt ostendere magna, sicut et in argumentum praediximus, et
comprobare properat illorum magnitudinem quae ab eo correcta
sunt. unde et de suscepto homine disputat, quasi de primitiis nostris, et quia prouisor nobis bonorum extiterit multorum. unde et
25 adiecit:

   in quo habemus redemptionem, remissionem peccatorum.

'per ipsum enim omnem peccatorum securitatem sumus adsecuti.' dicit autem futurum statum, in quo per resurrectionem ef-

---

5 sq. Coisl. 204, f. 143 a [Cr. vi. 302, Fr. 141] ἀλλ' ὁ ἀνόσιος Θεόδωρος τούτοις
ἀντιφθεγγόμενος, ἕνα σκοπὸν ἔχων ἰουδαϊκῶς καὶ βλασφήμως τὰς θείας γραφὰς
ἑρμηνεύειν τὰς δεικνύσας τοῦ χριστοῦ τὴν θεότητα, καὶ τὴν προκειμένην χρῆσιν
οὕτως ἐξηγήσατο· οὐκ εἶπεν (φησίν), κ.τ.λ. ...... τούτων τί ἂν εἴη ἀσεβέστερον
τοῖς ἐντυγχάνουσιν καταλείψω σκοπεῖν. Cf. Coisl. 26, f. 279 a, ἀλλ' ὁ ἀνόσιος
Θεόδωρος ὁ μόψου ἑστίας βλασφήμως κενολογῶν· οὐκ εἶπεν (φησίν, κ.τ.λ. ......
ἀλλ' ὁ μὲν ἐρρέτω μετὰ τῆς ἀσεβείας αὐτοῦ· ἡ δὲ ἀλήθεια ἐχέτω τὸ βέβαιον.
8 quo (*for* qui) r   9 opificii C   10 cuius r   11 participauimus H   ‖
honori C H   13 effectum C H   14 uoluerimus H   15 ἀξιωθέντα τούτων
edd.: ἀξιωθέντα· τούτων, κ.τ.λ. cod.   17 patris *om* r   17-18 caritatem r   18
adoptionis r   21 argumento C (*corr.*) r   25 adicit C r

"Not only (he says) has he taken you out of error and the power of demons, but he has also pronounced you to be sharers in the kingdom of Christ." For he makes his statement *he has transferred into the kingdom of the Son of his love* just as he says in another place (2 Tim 2:12): *if we endure, we shall also reign with him.* And so it was right that

†he did not merely say *Son* but Son *of his love.* For we are not made sharers in the kingdom of God the Word—for how could it happen [260] that we should be joined to the Maker of the universe? Rather, he is speaking of the assumed Man, with whom we, too, shall share in honor because of the likeness of nature, when we are strong enough to show affection toward him by our very works. For this reason he also called him "Son of love," because he is not the Father's Son by nature but acquired the adoption of sons by love.*

He did not say *Son* but *Son of his love.* For we do not become sharers in the kingdom of God the Word but in that of the assumed Man, with whom we share in honor because of natural likeness, when we show affection for him in deeds. This is why he called him "Son of love," since he is not the Father's Son by nature but was made worthy of sonship by love.

For in everything his purpose is to show that what has to do with Christ is great, just as we have said above in connection with the setting, [261] and he is eager to establish the greatness of his accomplishments. That is why he reasons about the assumed Man as about our firstfruits and because he has become for us the provider of many good things. So he also added:

1:14 *in whom we have redemption, the forgiveness of sins.*

"For by him we have gained entire safety from sins." And he is speaking of the future condition in which we shall no longer be able to sin, once we have been made this way by the resurrection,

fecti, natura nostra inmortali extante, peccare ulterius non poterimus. tale est et illud quod ad Ephesios dictum est: *ita ut simus
sancti et immaculati.* deinde dicit et illam dignitatem quae erga
eum est:

5　　*qui est imago Dei inuisibilis.*

bene *inuisibilis* adiecit, non quod sit et uisibilis Deus, sed ad
ostensionem magnitudinis; si tamen in isto quasi in imagine inuisibilem illam naturam uidemus, eo quod copulatus est Deo Verbo et iudicabit omnem orbem terrarum, adparens ipse secundum
10　suam, ut fas est, naturam, in futuro saeculo cum multa gloria ueniens de caelo. imaginis ordinem nobis retinet, euidenter quoniam
omnes in eum quasi in imaginem quandam diuinam conicimus naturam, in qua refertur magnitudo illorum quae efficiuntur, non uisibili natura iudici auctoritatem reputantes. demiratus sum autem
15　illos, qui in diuinam naturam hoc susceperunt; qui primum quidem non uiderunt, quoniam et beatus Moyses de homine dicit,
quoniam *in imaginem Deus fecit eum;* et beatus Paulus: *uir quidem
non debet uelare caput, imago et gloria Dei extans*, quod numquam
de hominibus dictum fuisset, si diuinae naturae proprium erat.
20　deinde neque illud prospexerunt, quoniam omnis imago, dum ipsa uidetur, illud ostendit quod non uidetur. fieri ergo [non] potest ut talis fiat imago, quae non uidetur, cum sit euidens quoniam
imagines propter hoc fieri consuetae sunt apud illos qui aut honoris aut affectus gratia easdem faciunt, ita ut recordatio sit eorum
25　qui non uidentur, illis qui tamen uideri possunt. deinde adiecit:

primogenitus totius creaturae.

hinc maxime quidam ualde prudentium de diuina natura dici
illud quod dixit, *imago Dei inuisibilis*, adstruxerunt, quasi quia non
possit *primogenitus* erga humanitatem aut uideri aut recipi; cum
30　conueniens esset eos perspicere, quoniam non potest hoc uel maxime aptari diuinae naturae. si enim sicut creatura *primogenitus* es-

---

1　incorruptibiles (*aft.* effecti) *add C* (*corr.*)　6　adicit *C r*　7　imaginem *C**
H　8　Dei *H*　9　omnem *om H*　10　magna (*for* multa) *r*　11　in magnis *C**
H r: txt C (*corr.*) *l*　‖　ordinem *om H*　12　in eo quasi in imagine *C* (*corr.*)
‖　continemus *l*　13-14　uisibilis *C* (*corr.*)　14　naturae *r*　21　non *om C H r:*
txt conj. Jacobi.　24　affectu *C r*　‖　gratiae *r*　25　adicit *C r*　30　est (*for*
esset) *C*

when our nature will exist immortal. Such also is what is said to the Ephesians (Eph 1:4): *so that we might be holy and blameless*.[3] Then he speaks of the dignity that belongs to him [the assumed Man]:

1:15a *He is the image of the invisible God,*

He rightly added *invisible*, not because there is also a visible God but to demonstrate his greatness, if indeed we see that invisible nature in that one [the Man] as in an image, because he has been joined to God the Word and will judge the entire inhabited round world, appearing himself in his own nature, as is right, when in the future age he comes from heaven with great glory. He retains the rank of image for us, [262] since clearly in him as in some kind of image all of us form our conclusions about the divine nature to which the greatness of those deeds that took place is referred, bearing in mind that the authority of judgment does not belong to the visible nature. But I am astonished at those people who have taken this verse as a reference to the divine nature. First of all, they have not seen that blessed Moses is speaking of a human being when he says (see Gen 1:27): *God made him in the image*. Also blessed Paul says (1 Cor 11:7): *indeed, a man ought not to veil his head, since he is the image and glory of God*. This would never have been said of human beings if it were peculiarly appropriate to the divine nature. Next, neither have they taken the trouble to look at the fact that every image, while it is itself seen, shows what is not seen. Therefore, it is impossible that such a thing as is not seen should become an image, since it is obvious that images are customarily made for this purpose among those who [263] make them for the sake of honor or thanks, so that there may be a recollection of those not seen by the images that can nevertheless be seen. Then he added;

1:15b *the firstborn of the whole creation,*

It is especially from this phrase that some of those who are quite sagacious have built their argument that, when Paul said *the image of the invisible God*, he was speaking of the divine nature—on the grounds that *firstborn* can neither be seen nor accepted as a reference to humanity, though it would have been right for them to notice that this word cannot even especially be applied to the

---

[3] The text from Ephesians is rendered a different way by the Latin in the commentary on Ephesians.

set, 'primocreatus' debuerat utique dici; si autem genitum aiunt,
multa dicti ipsius diuersitas esse uidebitur, si tamen is, qui non
est creatus, creaturarum primogenitus esse dicatur. nam primogenitus qui dicitur, illorum utique dici poterit primogenitus, qui
5 similitudinem illam quae ad eum est necessario saluare uidentur;
et hoc ostendit apostolus euidenter, dicens ad Romanos: *quoniam
quos praesciuit, et praeordinauit conformes fieri imaginis filii sui, ut
sit ipse primogenitus in multis fratribus*, euidenter fratrem eum primogenitum esse dicens eorum; et qui conformes illi sunt propter
10 similitudinem illam quam a Deo habent, iusta ratione eum sibi ad-
scribunt primogenitum, utpote supereminentem secundum hanc
rationem. etenim illic non dixit *conformes filii*, sed *imaginis filii*,
imaginem filii uisibilem naturam euidenter dicens. sed interrogant, quemadmodum susceptus homo *primogenitus* potest uideri
15 *totius creaturae*, cum non sit ante omnem creaturam, sed ut esset
in nouissimis accepit temporibus; non intellegentes, quoniam

†primogenitus non tempore di-	τὸ πρωτότοκος οὐκ ἐπὶ χρόνου λέ-
citur solum sed et praehonora-	γεται μόνον, ἀλλὰ γὰρ καὶ ἐπὶ προ-
tione frequenter, eo quod pri-	τιμήσεως πολλάκις, ὡς τὸ· ἐπικα-
20 mogenitus dicitur ueraciter illo-	λέσεταί με, πατήρ μου εἶ σύ, καὶ
rum, qui post illum geniti fue-	ἐγὼ πρωτότοκον θήσομαι αὐτόν,
rint. ille tamen qui prior fuerit	οὐ τοῦτο εἰπόντος τοῦ θεοῦ, ὅτι
natus, hunc sequitur necessario	ἕκαστον αὐτῶν πρότερον ποιήσω
ut et praehonoretur, sicuti et na-	τῷ χρόνῳ τῶν λοιπῶν,’ ἀλλ’ ὅτι
25 turae ratio et lex diuinae egit	‘περὶ πολλοῦ ποιήσομαι·’ λέγει δὲ
scripturae. est quidem quan-	ταῦτο ὁ Δαβίδ, τῶν πρὸς αὐτὸν
do et in tempore utitur nominis	ἐπαγγελιῶν τοῦ θεοῦ μνημονεύων,
huius translatione, saepe autem	ὡς ἂν ὑποσχομένου τοὺς ἐξ αὐτοῦ
et honoris causa. etenim bea-	κατὰ διαδοχὴν οἰκειώσεσθαι. ὁ δὲ
30 tus Dauid promissa Dei quae ad	ἀπόστολός φησιν τό [ἀλλὰ προσε-
se facta fuerant commemorans,	ληλύθατε σιὼν ὄρει καὶ πόλει Θεοῦ
in quibus promisit illos qui ex	ζῶντος ἱερουσαλὴμ ἐπουρανίῳ καὶ
successione eius sunt ad fami-	μυριάσιν ἀγγέλων πανηγύρει καὶ]
liaritatem suam recipere, quasi	ἐκκλησίᾳ πρωτοτόκων ἀπογεγραμ-

---

1 aut (*aft.* autem) *add* C H: *txt* r   5 seruare *r*   7 praedestinauit (*for*
praeord.) *H*   8 eum fr. *H*   9 et *om* C (*corr.*)   10-11 adscribit C   12 illud (*for* illic) *H*   17 sq. Coisl. 204, f. 145 a [Cr. vi. 306, Fr. 142] θεόδωρος δέ
φησιν· τὸ πρωτότοκος, κ.τ.λ. [Coisl. 26, f. 280 a].   25 λέγει δὲ ταῦτα (φησὶν)
ὁ Δ. cod.; Cr.: om. φ. Fr.   30-33 ἀλλὰ...καὶ om. cod. edd.   32 ex *om* r

divine nature. For if *firstborn* were meant to mean created, he surely ought to have been called "first-created." But if they affirm the meaning "begotten," there will plainly be much ambiguity in the word itself, if at least he who was not created is said to be the firstborn of creatures. For the one who is called firstborn could surely be called the firstborn of those who are seen necessarily to preserve likeness to him. And this is what the apostle clearly demonstrates when he says to the Romans (Rom 8:29): *For those whom he foreknew he also predestined* [264] *to be conformed to the image of his Son, so that he might be himself the firstborn among many brothers*, obviously meaning that the one who is firstborn is their brother. And those conformed to him because of that likeness that they have from God, with good reason assign him to themselves as the firstborn, since he clearly is greatly superior for this reason. Moreover, because of the fact that he did not say *conformed to the Son* but *to the image of the Son*, he is clearly calling the visible nature the image of the Son. But they ask how the assumed Man can be seen as *the firstborn of the whole creation* when he is not in existence before the whole creation, but received his existence in very recent times. They do not understand that

†"firstborn" is not only said with respect to time but also often with respect to higher honor, because one is said to be firstborn of those to be born after him. Nevertheless, it is necessarily a consequence for the one who may have been born earlier that he should be given higher honor, as both the principle of nature and [265] the law of divine scripture have urged. Of course, sometimes scripture uses this word in reference to time, but it also often uses it to express honor. Indeed, blessed David, when relating the promises God had made to him, including his promise that he would admit David's successors

"Firstborn" is said not only of time but also often of higher honor,

as in (Ps 88:27–28) *he will call*

ipso Deo dicente, ita ait: *ipse inuocabit me, pater meus es tu ... et ego primogenitum ponam eum;* non hoc dicente Deo quoniam 'unumquemque eorum ceteris tempore priorem faciam,' sed quoniam 'plurimum illis feram auxilium.' apostolus uero ad Hebraeos manifeste hoc idem ostendit, sic dicens: *sed accessistis Sion monti et ciuitati Dei uiui, Hierusalem caelesti et denis millibus angelorum nundinae et ecclesiae primitiuorum adscriptorum in caelo;* ut dicat, 'illorum qui multo honore digni habiti sunt.' non enim uult dicere aliquos anteriores esse aliorum filiorum. et alibi: *filius meus primogenitus Israel,* hoc est 'honorabilis mihi.' nam et erant et alii ante Israel qui filiorum Dei nuncupatione digni fuerant habiti; de quibus Moyses dicit: *uidentes filii Dei filias hominum quoniam bonae sunt, acceperunt sibi ab omnibus quibus elegerunt.* sic et hoc in loco quod dixerat: *primogenitus totius creaturae;* hoc est, 'super omnem creaturam honorabilis.' si quidem dixisset absolute *primogenitus,* 'honorabilem' tantummodo dicebat. nam quia adiecit *omnis creaturae,* illum desi-

μένων ἐν οὐρανοῖς· ἵνα εἴπῃ, 'τῶν πολλῆς ἄγαν ἠξιωμένων τῆς τιμῆς.' καὶ τό· υἱὸς πρωτότοκός μου ἰσραήλ· ἀντὶ τοῦ 'τίμιος ἐμοί.' οὕτως φησὶν κἀνταῦθα· πρωτότοκος πάσης κτίσεως· ἀντὶ τοῦ 'παρὰ πᾶσαν τὴν κτίσιν τιμώμενος.'

1-2 τὸν... ἠξιωμένον cod. Cr.: txt conj. Fr.   2 inuocauit *C*   6-7 for. leg. πάσης τῆς κτίσεως. Cf. ll. 31-32, supra.   11 Syoni *H* ‖ ciuitatem *C H* (ad Syon montem et ad civ., &c. *r*)   13 nundinam *C H*   26 erant pulchrae (*for* bonae sunt) *r*   27 quas (*for* quibus) *r*

to familial intimacy with him, says, as though God himself were speaking (Ps 88:27–28): *he will call upon me, "You are my Father" ... and I will place him as firstborn.* God does not say "I will make some of them earlier in time than the others," but "I will give them the greatest help." And the apostle obviously shows the same thing to the Hebrews, when he says (Heb 12:22–23): *but you have come to Mount Sion and to the city of the living God, to the heavenly Jerusalem, and to the throng of ten thousand angels and to the church of the firstborn who have been enrolled in heaven,* [266] meaning, "of those who have been held worthy of much honor." For he did not want to say that some were older than other sons. And elsewhere (Exod 4:22): *my firstborn son, Israel,* that is, "held in honor by me." For there were also others before Israel who had been held worthy of the designation "sons of God." Moses says of them (Gen 6:2): *When the sons of God saw the daughters of men that they were good, they took to themselves [wives] from all of them they chose.* Thus, also in this place his statement *the firstborn of the whole creation* means "held in honor above all creation." If indeed he had said *firstborn* by itself, he would only have meant "held in

upon me, *"You are my Father"* ... *and I will place him as firstborn,* since God was not saying, "I will make each of them earlier in time than the rest," but "I will make of great value." David says this when he is relating God's promises to him, since he promised that he would adopt David's successors as members of his own household.

And the apostle says (Heb 12:22–23): *but you have come to Mount Sion and to the city of the living God, to the heavenly Jerusalem, and to the throng of ten thousand angels and to the church of the firstborn who have been enrolled in the heavens,* meaning "of those held worthy of very much honor."

Also it says (Exod 4:22): *my firstborn son, Israel,* instead of "held in honor by me."

In this way he also says here *the firstborn of all creation,* instead of "held in honor by all creation."

gnauit qui ab omni honoratur
creatura.*

nam is qui secundum carnem est Christus, et tempore primogenitus dicitur ueraciter totius creaturae quae in illum facta est, de
5 qua beatus Paulus hoc in loco uidetur dixisse. unde et illud quod
dixit: *primogenitus totius creaturae* interpretans adiecit:
  quoniam in ipso creata sunt omnia.

†non dixit *per ipsum,* sed *in*　　οὐκ εἶπεν δι᾽ αὐτοῦ, ἀλλ᾽ ἐν αὐ-
ipso. nec enim de prima dicit　　τῷ· οὐ γὰρ τὴν πρώτην λέγει κτί-
10 creatura, sed illam creaturae re-　　σιν, ἀλλὰ τὴν ἐν αὐτῷ γενομένην
parationem quae in eo facta est,　　ἀνάκτισιν, καθ᾽ ἣν τὰ πάντα δια-
secundum quam omnia dudum　　λελυμένα εἰς συμφωνίαν ἤχθη μίαν,
dissoluta in unum sunt consen-　　ὡς καὶ ἀλλαχοῦ φησίν· ἀνακεφα-
sum perducta; sicuti et alibi di-　　λαιώσασθαι τὰ πάντα ἐν Χριστῷ,
15 cit: *recapitulare omnia in Chri-*　　τά τε ἐν τοῖς οὐρανοῖς καὶ τὰ ἐπὶ
sto, quae in caelis sunt et quae su-　　τῆς γῆς.
*per terram.**

propter hominum etenim malitiam omnis, ut ita dixerim, creatura disrumpi uidebatur. auertebant enim se a nobis angeli et om-
20 nes inuisibiles uirtutes, propter indeuotionem nostram quam erga
Deum exercebamus. insuper etiam et nos ipsi morte soluimur, ex
qua accidebat animam separari a corpore; etenim et omnis connexio creaturae hinc soluebatur. fictus est enim a principio homo
quasi aliquod animal cognatione omnibus iunctum, eo quod cor-
25 pus quidem generaliter ex omnibus consistebat, id est, ex quattuor elementis; anima uero ad inuisibiles uirtutes propinquitatem
habere uidebatur. una uero quaedam uniuersorum copulatio exhinc fieri uidebatur, propter eam propinquitatem quam ad hominem cuncta habere uidebantur, omnibus in idipsum concurrenti-
30 bus, ita ut et uno consensu Deo redderent debitam culturam cum

3 est *om H*　6 adicit *C* addit *r*　8 sq. Coisl. 204, f. 146 b [Cr. vi. 308,
Fr. 142] Θεόδωρος δὲ καὶ ταύτην πλημμελῶς ἐξηγεῖται τὴν ῥῆσιν φάσκων· οὐκ
εἶπεν, κ.τ.λ.......ὅτι δὲ ταῦτα παύλου τοῦ σαμοσατέως φησὶν εἶναι ὁ μακάριος
ἰωάννης, φθάσαντες παρεθέμεθα.　10-11 separationem *C* H r*　15 recapitulari *r*　21 ipse *C*: corr.* ipsa　22 accedebat *C*　‖ separare *C* r*　24
coniunctum *H*　25 consistebant *C* H*　28-29 propter ... uidebantur *om r*
29 in unum (*for* in idips.) *H*

honor." But because he added *of all⁴ creation,* he pointed out him who is held in honor by all creation.*

Indeed, he who according to [267] the flesh is Christ is also truly said to be with respect to time the firstborn of the whole creation that was made in him, and it is about this creation that blessed Paul plainly has been speaking in this place. That is why, to interpret his statement *the firstborn of the whole creation,* he added:

1:16a *because in him all things were created,*

†He did not say "through him" but *in him.* For he is not speaking of the first creation but of the restoration of creation that took place in him, by which all things that long ago had been loosed asunder were brought to a single harmony, as he also says elsewhere (Eph 1:10): *to recapitulate all things in Christ, things that are in the heavens and things on earth.**

He did not say "through him" but *in him.* For he is not speaking of the first creation but of the restoration that took place in him, by which all the things that had been loosed asunder were brought to a single harmony, as he also says elsewhere (Eph 1:10): *to head up all things in Christ, things in the heavens and things on the earth.*

For indeed, because of the wickedness of human beings, if I may say so, the entire creation was seen to be broken apart. For the angels turned their backs on us, as well as [268] all the invisible powers, because of our failure to practice devotion to God. Furthermore, we ourselves were loosed asunder by death, by which it came about that the soul was separated from the body; and indeed, from this cause the entire joining together of creation was loosed asunder. For from the beginning man was made as some kind of living being joined to all by kinship, because the body was, generally speaking, composed of all, that is, of the four elements, but the soul was seen to have close association with the invisible powers. From this there was seen to come about a certain single linking of the entire universe because of the close association all things were seen to have to humanity, since all things flowed together to the same place, so that in single concord they might render to God with great and prudent care the observance due

---

⁴Here the Latin has *omnis* rather than *totius.*

cauta sollicitudine; omnes etiam illis quae illius legibus consentanea erant obtemperare properabant. quia propter peccatum facti sumus mortales, anima etiam a corpore separabatur, soluebatur
hinc propinquitatis copulatio, ita ut nec ultra existimarent inuisi-
5 biles uirtutes aliquam sibi nobiscum esse communionem secundum corporis nostri diligentiam; adiecto illo quod et odibiles Deo
eramus contemplatione peccati, qui etiam et auertebat se a nobis.
unde et hi, qui insistebant uisibilibus naturis, et commouebant eas
pro nostra utilitate secundum positum sibi terminum, nolebant
10 ultra ea implere, si non promissione Dei percepissent quod omnia aspera soluerentur. cessabit etiam mors et corruptio, omnibus
ad unum consensum redintegratis, sicuti ad Romanos scribit: *ua-*
nitati enim creatura subiecta est non uolens, sed propter eum qui subie-
cit, in spe quoniam et ipsa creatura liberabitur a seruitute corruptionis
15 *in libertatem gloriae filiorum Dei.* in nostra igitur renouatione secundum quam et omnium redintegratur connexio, cuius primitiae
sunt is qui secundum carnem Christus, in quo optima quaedam et
ut ita dixerim compendiosa omnium recreatio efficietur (sicut beatus Paulus dicit, *si qua in Christo noua creatura, antiqua transierunt,*
20 *et ecce omnia facta sunt noua); omnium enim ultra existentium in
incorruptibilitatem omnibus saluabitur consensus et concordia et
connexio, et ultra diligent nos etiam inuisibiles uirtutes utpote familiares Dei. bene ergo dixit: *in ipso creata sunt omnia*, non solum
quia per illa, quae erga eum facta sunt, futurorum adsecuti sumus
25 promissionem; sed quoniam et perfecta omnibus copulatio in illo custodietur propter inhabitationem diuinae naturae, ita ut nihil possit scissum ultra habere ex illis, quae communia nobis sunt.
una quidem ex parte diligentibus eum omnibus propter familiaritatem illam quam ad eum habere poterunt quasi ad hominem, ex
30 uisibili natura et inuisibili consistente eo; altera uero, cum mul-

1 illas *H r*   4   exhinc (*for* hinc) *H*   ‖   propinquitas *C*   11   cessauit *C H*
r   13   eum (*aft.* subi.) *add r*   19   his, Christi *r*   27   scisum (*sic*) *C* (*corr.*)
‖   haberi *C* (*corr.*)   29   potuerunt *r*   30   Deo (*for* eo) *r*

him. For all were eager to submit themselves to what accorded with his laws. Because we became mortal on account of sin and the soul was separated from the body, from this cause the linking of close association was loosed asunder, so that the invisible powers no longer thought they had any fellowship with us by way of caring for our bodily wants. In addition, we were also hateful to God because we fixed our sight on sin; he, too, turned his back on us. From this also those who used to preside over visible natures and move them for our benefit according to the end appointed for them would no longer have been willing to fulfill their tasks, if they had not perceived by God's promise that all harsh adversities would be loosed. For death will cease and corruption, when all things [269] are restored to a single concord, just as Paul writes to the Romans (Rom 8:20): *for the creation was subjected to vanity not willingly but because of him who subjected it, in hope that also the creation itself will be freed from slavery to corruption into the freedom of the glory of the sons of God*. Therefore, in our renewal in accord with which also the joining together of all things will be restored, it is he who is Christ according to the flesh who is the firstfruits. In him a certain best and, so to speak, concise new creation of all things will be brought about, just as blessed Paul says (2 Cor 5:17): *if there is a new creation in Christ,*[5] *the old things have passed away, and see, all things have been made new*. For from then on, the agreement and concord and joining together of all things will be preserved in incorruption for all things, and from then on, as well, the invisible powers will take diligent care of us as, indeed, members of God's household. Therefore, he rightly said *in him all things were created*, not only because it is by what came about with respect to him that we have attained the promise of the things to come, but also since the perfect linking together of all things will be kept in him because of the indwelling of the divine nature, so that there can no longer be any division from the things that are in common with us. From one perspective this has to do with all who love him because of that familial intimacy they are able to have with him insofar as he is a man, since he consists of a visible nature and an invisible one.[6] But from another perspective it has to do with all who have

---

[5] For this punctuation and reading, see Theodore's comments on Eph 2:10 and 219 n. 33.

[6] Since Theodore is speaking here of the Man, it would seem more likely that

to timore ad eum conuersis omnibus propter inseparabilem Deum Verbum qui inest ei unitus. unde dicens *omnia* adiecit:

quae in caelis sunt et quae super terram.

et quia incertum erat illud quod in caelis erat, et quod super
5 terram, utrum de uisibilibus diceret aut de inuisibilibus, eo quod sunt et in caelo quae uidentur, utpote sol et luna et stellae (*posuit* enim *illa in firmamento caeli*), manifestam faciens ipsam diuisionem adiecit:

uisibilia et inuisibilia.

10 hoc est, illa et ista omnia coniuncta sunt ulterius et conligata in ipso, siue uero propter cognationem, siue et propter dignitatem. et quoniam illa quae uisibilia erant magis certa esse uidebantur, utpote manifesta extante familiaritate illa quae erat ad ipsum hominem, qui uidetur, praetermittens hoc ad inuisibilia transit, eo
15 quod de illis dictum maius esse uidebatur; euidenter habens hic magnitudinis illorum probationem quae per Christum sunt directa, [eo quod] et inuisibiles naturae in illo acceperunt recreationem:

sedes siue dominationes, principatus siue potestates.

unde non est memoratus 'angelorum,' eo quod hoc nomen mi-
20 nistrationis magis significantiam habere uideretur; sed 'sedes et dominationes et principatus et potestates' dixit, quae et ipsae uocantur quidem sic a functione illa quam implere uidentur; habent autem et aliquam significationem dignitatis illius quae est ad illos, eo quod susceperunt ut inuisibiles immineant. et alii quidem
25 imminent aeri, alii uero soli, alii autem lunae, alii uero stellis, alii etiam aliis aliquibus, ut commoueant omnia secundum inpositum sibi a Deo terminum ad hoc ut omnia consistere possint. *principatus* et *potestates* hinc dicebantur, eo quod principare et potestatem exercere alicuius negotii acceperant potestatem; sicut et Ephesiis
30 scribens de diabolo dicit: *secundum principem potestatis aeris spiri-*

1-2 Dei V. quod i. eis iunctum *r*   5   uti cum (*for* utrum) *C H r*   11   cognitionem *H r*   17   eo quod *om C H r*   18   siue (1°) *om H*   19   minoratus (*for* mem.) *H*   20   magis *om H*   ‖   uidetur *H**   21   quia et ipse *r*   23   qui (*for* quae) *C**   24   emineant *r*   25   eminent *r*   26   stellis (*for* aliis) *r*   ‖   aliiquibus *C* reliiquibus *H*   30   dicens *C* *H r*

turned to him with much fear because he is inseparable from God the Word, who, united to him, is within him. Then, after saying *all things,* he added:

[270] 1:16b *which are in the heavens and which are on the earth,*

And because it was unclear what was in the heavens and what on the earth, whether he was speaking about visible or about invisible things—because even in heaven there are things that are seen, for example, the sun and the moon and the stars, for (Gen 1:17) *he put them in the firmament of heaven*—to make the distinction itself obvious, he added:

1:16c *visible things and invisible,*

That is, the latter and the former are all from now on joined and bound together in him, whether because of kinship or because of worth. And since the visible things seemed more certain because human familiarity with them made them obvious, he passes over this and goes on to the invisible things because what was said about them seemed more important. Here he clearly has proof of the greatness of Christ's dispensations because even the invisible natures received the new creation in him:

1:16d *thrones or dominions or rulers or authorities,*

The reason he did not mention angels is because this name appears to have more the meaning of ministering. But he said "thrones and dominions and rulers and authorities" because these names are so given from the service they are seen to fulfill.[7] And they have also another meaning that belongs to the worth attaching to them because they have undertaken the task of presiding as invisible beings. And some [271] preside over the air, while others over the sun and others over the moon, but others over the stars, and still others over some other things, so that they may move everything in accord with the end appointed for them by God in his purpose that all things may be able to hold together. They were called *rulers* and *authorities* because they had received authority to rule and to exercise authority over some kind of activity, just as Paul also says to the Ephesians, when writing about the devil (Eph 2:2): *according to the ruler of the*

---

the visible and invisible natures are the body and the soul rather than the two natures of Christ.

[7]Swete (1:270) points out the allusion to Heb 1:14 implied by "ministering," then says: "The title ἄγγελοι denotes a διακονία (*ministratio*); θρόνοι κ.τ.λ., sets forth a λειτουργία (*functio*)."

talis; et apud Daniel: *princeps Persidis restitit mihi,* et *princeps ue-*
ster—illum angelum qui pro illis sollicitudinem expendit sic euo-
cans. unde dilatauit sensum, *sedes dominationes* et *principatus* et
potestates dicens, idem ipsud uarie dicens. 'si (inquit) est aliquid
5 quod dominetur, siue dominium sibi uindicet, siue principatum
teneat, siue potestatem exerceat, quomodocunque quis dicere uoluerit de tributa illis a Deo potestate, *in ipso sunt omnia creata.* tae-
diantes etenim primum propter homines et suum opus pro nobis perficere nolentes, nunc cum alacritate omnia proficiunt, pro-
10 prietatem illam naturae nostrae quae ei unita est uenerantes, quam
neque adorare dubitant propter eam quae inest ei naturam in futuro saeculo, eo quod omnia copulatione quadam in se redigens
conligauit, eo uel maxime tempore quo omnis soluetur corruptio
et mors.' et quoniam uidebatur insuadibile esse quodammodo de
15 homine dicto, quod in eo sint creata omnia, confirmans illud adiecit:

    omnia per ipsum et in ipso creata sunt.

    'nolite mirari (inquit); non enim ex se illi est ista dignitas, sed
propter inhabitantem naturam, per quam omnia facta sunt, ad
20 quam etiam omnia respiciunt quaecunque facta sunt, suum eundem dominum esse existimantes.' et amplius illud augens:

    et ipse est ante omnes, et omnia in ipso consistunt.

    ut dicat: 'ipse ante omnes extans omnia produxit, et in eius uir-
tute omnia ut consistant habere uidentur.' non est autem demi-
25 randum, si quasi de homine disputans ab humanis rebus ad doctrinam deitatis transiuit. hoc enim ostendimus fecisse apostolum
et Philippensibus scribentem, ubi dicit *qui in forma Dei extans* et

---

1 Danihel *H*   4 id est (*for* idem) *r* || ipsum *C**   7 Dei *r*   9 uolen-
tes *C**   11 in *om r*   12 copulationem quandam *C H* || rediens *C* H r*
13 solueretur *r*   15 creata sint *H*   15-16 adicit *C r*   18 mirare *C**   20
quaeque *C r*   24-25 mirandum *r*   26 ostendemus *C H r*

authority of the windy air, and in Daniel (see Dan 10:13, 21): *the ruler of Persia stood against me* and *your ruler*[8]—the angel who spent great care for them by summoning them this way. The reason Paul expanded his meaning by saying *thrones, dominions* as well as *rulers and authorities* is to say the same thing in various ways. "If (he says) there is something that would have dominion, whether it would claim dominion for itself, whether it would hold rulership, whether it would exercise authority, in whatever way anyone would wish to speak of the authority bestowed on them by God, *in him all things were created*. And indeed, though they were at first reluctant because of humans and unwilling to accomplish their work for us, now they accomplish all things with enthusiasm because of their reverence for the special property united to our nature.[9] Nor do they hesitate in the age to come to worship him because of that nature present within him, because by renewing all things he has bound them all together in himself by a kind of linking, and especially at that time when all corruption and death will be loosed." And since to say that all things were created in the Man [272] seemed somehow unpersuasive, to establish the point he added:

1:16e *all things were created through him and in him,*

"Do not be astonished (he says), for that worth is his not of himself but because of the indwelling nature through which[10] all things were made and to which whatever has been made looks, supposing him to be their common Lord." And to amplify the point:

1:17 *and he is himself before all things, and all things in him hold together,*

He means: "Because he [the Word] exists before all, he himself brought forth all things, and by his power all things are seen to be placed so as to hold together." And it should not be a matter of surprise if when he is reasoning as though about the Man on the basis of human realities, he passed over to teaching about the divinity. For we have shown that the apostle also did this when he was writing to the Philippians, where he said (Phil 2:6): *who*

---

[8] That is, the archangel Michael; consequently, the "ruler of Persia" must be an opposing power.

[9] Theodore must mean the union of the divine Word with the assumed Man.

[10] "*Through* him" refers to the Word as the agent of creation, "*in* him" to the Man as the proximate agent of the new creation.

cetera; euidenter ibi apostolus a diuinis ad humanam transiuit, et quidem quasi de uno eodemque omnia dicens. sed ad Hebraeos itidem dicens: *locutus est nobis in filio quem posuit heredem omnium,* euidenter de homine id dicens, cuius et loquelam audiuimus, qui

5 suscepit eorum quae erant dominationem, quam ante non habebat. transiit uero ad diuinam ut exinde horum confirmaret magnitudinem; et iterum recurrit ad humanam, et quidem quasi de uno omnia in illa parte epistolae dicens. hoc et in euangeliis eundem Dominum saepe fecisse inueniet quis, in illis sermonibus quae de

10 se dixisse uidetur; quod et cautius quis recognoscere poterit, si interpretationem nostram decurrere uoluerit in illam partem euangelii Iohannis, quam super paralytico curato ad Iudaeos locutus fuisse uidetur. sic et hoc in loco memoratus est diuinae naturae, ut ab illa magnitudinem illorum confirmet quae erga hominem sunt.

15 exinde uero iterum recurrit ad hominem dicens:

et ipse est caput corporis ecclesiae.

hoc est: 'istum in quo omnia creata sunt, caput adscribit sibi in commune ecclesia, corpus eius per spiritalem regenerationem effecta, quae formam habet futurae resurrectionis, secundum

20 quam communicare ei sperantes et participes eius fieri inmortalitatis baptizati [sumus], quasi formam quandam illorum implentes, quorum princeps ipse nobis extitit. ea ergo ratione et caput illum adscribimus nobis.' unde adicit:

qui est [principium,] primogenitus ex mortuis,

25 hoc est; 'ante omnes resurgentes primus in illa uita renatus.' nam quoniam 'primogenitum ex mortuis' susceptum hominem uocat, manifestum est; sed et quia quasi de uno disputat et illa quae in superioribus sunt, et ista dicta. et hoc euidenter ex ipsis

5 suscipit *C* H r* 9 inuenietur *r* ‖ qui (*for* quis) *r* 13 in hoc in loco *C** 14 magnitudine *C H r* ‖ erga hominum *C H* ergo hominum *r* 18 in communi *C* (*corr.*) 21 sumus *om C H r* 27 sed quia quasi *C*: corr.* sed quia et quasi: *txt r* 28 hic *r*

was found in the form of God and the rest. Clearly there the apostle passed over from divine things to human and yet said everything as though of one and the same. Moreover, in the same way he says to the Hebrews (Heb 1:2): *he has spoken to us in the Son whom he appointed the heir of all things.* Clearly he says this of the Man, whose speech we have heard, who assumed the lordship of the things that existed, a lordship that he did not previously have. But Paul then passes over to the divine nature, so that on this basis [273] he may confirm the greatness of these things. And again he goes back to the human nature and yet says everything in this part of the letter as if of one.[11] Anyone will find that even in the Gospels the Lord has often done the same thing in those discourses he is seen to have spoken about himself. And he would be able to recognize this more clearly, if he were willing to track down our commentary on that passage in the Gospel of John where he may be seen to have spoken to the Jews about the paralytic who was healed (John 5:18, 23, 26–27). So, too, in this place he mentioned the divine nature so that from it he might confirm the greatness of what has to do with the Man. And from this point he turns back again to the Man, saying:

1:18a *and he is the head of the body, the church,*

That is, "the church assigns that one in whom all things have been created as its head in common, since it has been made his body by spiritual rebirth, which possesses the type of the future resurrection. Hoping to have fellowship with him and to become partakers of his immortality, we have been baptized according to this type, fulfilling, as it were, a certain type of those things of which he has come to be for us the first founder. Therefore, it is for this reason that we assign him as our head." Then he adds:

1:18b *who is the beginning,[12] the firstborn from the dead,*

[274] That is, "rising again before all as the first to be born again in that life." For it is obvious that he is calling the assumed Man "the firstborn from the dead," but it is also because he is reasoning as though about a single one both in what precedes and in these words. And it is clearly possible to perceive this on the

---

[11] Presumably, Heb 1:2, 3, 8, 10 refer to the divine nature, Heb 1:1, 4, 6, 9, 13 to the human nature.

[12] Swete (1:293–94) has restored *principium* to the text. It was apparently accidentally omitted because of the similarity of the next word, *primogenitus*. He also notes that it is surprising Theodore does not comment on *principium* (ἀρχή).

est perspicere sermonibus.

†qui autem uerba apostoli non recte interpretari adtemptant, et illud quod dixit: *qui est imago Dei inuisibilis, primogenitus totius creaturae* in diuinam suscipiunt naturam, nullomodo nostram interpretationem calumniis poterunt innodare, [pro] quibus diximus eum a diuina natura ad humanam transire, aut iterum ab humana ad diuinam; idipsum enim eos facere necessitas conpellit. illa enim quae in superioribus dicta sunt in diuinam accipere eos naturam res ipsa conpellit. nam hoc quod dixit *primogenitus ex mortuis*, licet ad omnia improbi contendere sciant, nequaquam id in diuinam poterunt suscipere naturam.*

οἱ δέ γε παρερμηνεύειν βουλόμενοι τὰ ῥητὰ καὶ τό ὅς ἐστιν εἰκὼν τοῦ θεοῦ τοῦ ἀοράτου, πρωτότοκος πάσης κτίσεως ἐπὶ τῆς θείας ἐκλαβεῖν ἐπιχειρήσαντες φύσεως, οὐδαμῶς συκοφαντῆσαι τὴν ἑρμηνείαν ἡμῶν δυνήσονται ἀπὸ τῆς ἀπὸ τῶν θείων ἐπὶ τὰ ἀνθρώπινα μεταβάσεως, ἤτοι τῆς ἀπὸ τῶν ἀνθρωπίνων ἐπὶ τὰ θεῖα· τὸ γὰρ αὐτὸ καὶ αὐτοὺς ποιῆσαι ἀνάγκη, τὰ μὲν ἀνώτερα ἐπὶ τῆς ἄνω ἐκλαμβάνοντας φύσεως, τὸ δέ· πρωτότοκος ἐκ τῶν νεκρῶν, εἰ τὰ πάντα ἀναισχυντοῖεν, οὐδαμῶς ἐκλαβεῖν ἐπὶ τῆς θείας δυναμένους φύσεως.

apostolus uero euidenter ostendens, quoniam et in superioribus dixerat: *primogenitus totius creaturae*, de hoc ipso iterum dixit: *primogenitus ex mortuis;* unde et adiecit:

ut fiat in omnibus ipse primatum tenens.

nam quod dixit *ut*, non causam dixit, sed illa quae sequebantur consuete sibi edixit. uult enim dicere quod est per omnia ipse primus, non solum quia inchoasse resurrectionem uidetur, sed quod sit et per omnia primatum tenens. 'omnia' enim, illa quae in creaturis nominantur, quasi maiorem honorem tribuens. et quasi

---

2 sq. Coisl. 204, f. 146 b [Cr. vi. 309, Fr. 142] ἐναντιούμενος δὴ συνηθῶς πᾶσιν τοῖς ἁγίοις πατράσιν, καὶ ταῦτα ἐπιφέρει· οἱ δέ γε, κ.τ.λ. προφανῶς τοίνυν κἂν τούτοις ἀπεδείχθη Θεόδωρος τὴν πρὸς τοὺς ἁγίους πάντας ἀράμενος μάχην. 3 interpretare C* 9 pro *om* C H r: *for. leg.* qua 13 accipere (*for* facere) H 15 εἰ μή Fr.: txt cod. Cr. 18 haec H 20 consciant r 25 unde et adicit C r unde adiecit H 27 ut non ut causam C (*corr.*) H

basis of the language itself.

†But those who attempt to misinterpret the apostle's words and take the statement (1:15) *he is the image of the invisible God, the firstborn of the whole creation* as a reference to the divine nature will be able in no way to tangle up our interpretation with false objections, because we have said that he passes over from the divine nature to the human or again from the human to the divine, for necessity compels him to do this very thing. For the very fact of the matter compels them to accept what is said above in reference to the divine nature.[13] Surely they will by no means be able to take his statement *the firstborn from the dead* as a reference to the divine nature, though shameless people know how to dispute everything.*

But those who wish to misinterpret what is said and who attempt to take (1:15) *he is the image of the invisible God, the firstborn of the whole creation* as a reference to the divine nature will be able in no way to make false objections to our interpretation because of the shift from divine things to human or that from human to divine. For it is necessary even for them to do the same thing. They take the verses above in reference to the nature above, but they can in no way take *the firstborn from the dead* as a reference to the divine nature, even if they were to be entirely shameless.

But the apostle clearly shows that what he had said above—*the firstborn of the whole creation*—is the same thing he has said again here—*the firstborn from the dead*. Then he also added:

1:18c *so that he might be made in all things, himself holding first place,*

[275] Indeed, he did not say *so that* to introduce a purpose clause, but he declared, as is his habit, those things that resulted. For he means that he [the Man] is the first throughout all things, not only because he is seen to have initiated the resurrection but also insofar as he is the one holding first place through all things. Indeed, he says "all things," that is, those named in what is created, as though he is attributing greater honor to them and as

---

[13] Unless the Latin misunderstands the Greek, Theodore must mean verse 17, since this is the only verse where he refers to the divine Word.

interpretans illa quae superius dixerat, et aperte illud quod dixerat ostendere cupiens ait, *quoniam in ipso creata sunt omnia* et cetera, quia in illa parte epistolae de humanitate fuerant dicta; unde
et adicit:

5   *quoniam in ipso complacuit omnis plenitudo inhabitare.*

'plenitudinem Dei' et ecclesiam uocat, necnon et omnia, quasi
quia et in omnibus sit et omnia impleat; et hoc est euidenter discere ex illis quae ad Ephesios scribens dixisse uidetur: *et ipsum dedit caput super omnem ecclesiam, quae est corpus eius, plenitudo eius*
10   *qui omnia in omnibus adimplet.* hoc ergo dicit, quoniam complacuit
Deo in eo, hoc est in Christo, omnem habitare plenitudinem—ut
dicat: 'omnem creaturam quae ab eo repleta est probauit illi coniungere.' et hoc idem latius dicens:

et per eum reconciliare omnia in ipso, pacem faciens per sanguinem
15   *crucis eius; per ipsum, siue illa quae in terris sunt, siue illa quae in*
caelis sunt.

'omnia (inquit) in sua morte (hoc enim dicit 'sanguinem' et
'crucem'), reconciliauit, et coniunxit et illa quae super terram
erant et quae super caelos, eo quod et mortuus est et resurrexit;
20   exsurgens uero commune omnibus praestitit promissum resurrectionis et inmortalitatis. omnia autem hinc connectuntur ad concordiam, sicut et in superioribus diximus, et ad illum inspiciunt,
ut puta concordiae auctorem;' hoc enim dicit *in eum.* optime dixit
quoniam per mortem eius omnia coniunxit, et in pace constituit
25   per eam quae erga se est copulationem. euidenter illud quod dixerat: *in ipso creata sunt omnia, quae in caelis sunt et quae super terram,*
hoc in loco iterasse uidetur; et caute comprobauit quoniam de eodem etiam illic uerbum fecisse uidetur, de quo etiam et hoc in loco
dixisse uisus est, quem et *primogenitum ex mortuis* nominans, ma-

---

1   perte (*sic*) *C*   3-4   quia—adicit om *r*   6   et (1°) om *r*   7   qui *r*   10   implet
H*   ‖   placuit Deo meo *H*   14   reconciliari *C* (*corr.*)   20   communem *C*   22
incipiunt *C H r*   23   ut puto *C H*   27   comprobabit *C**

though he is interpreting what he had said earlier and wishing to show clearly what he had meant by saying (1:16) *because in him all things were created* and the rest, namely, that what had been said in that part of the letter referred to the humanity. This is why he adds:[14]

1:19 *because in him the entire fullness was well pleased to dwell,*

He also calls the church "the fullness of God," and, indeed, also "all things," inasmuch as he is in all things and fills all things. And it is possible to learn this from what he plainly said when writing to the Ephesians (Eph 1:22): *and he gave him to be the head above all the church, which is his body,* [276] *the fullness of him who fills[15] all in all.* Therefore, he means that it was God's good pleasure that the entire fullness should dwell in him, that is, in Christ— so as to mean "he gave his approval of joining to him the entire creation that was replenished by him." And saying the same thing at greater length:

1:20 *and through him to reconcile all things in himself, making peace through the blood of his cross, through himself, whether those things that are in earth or those things that are in the heavens.*

"He has reconciled (he says) all things by his death (for this is what *blood* and *cross* mean), and he has joined together both things that were above earth and things above the heavens, because he both died and rose again. And by rising again he has bestowed on all in common the promise of the resurrection and immortality. And from this all things are linked together in concord, just as we have said earlier, and they fix their sight on him as the founder of concord." For he says that this is what "in him" means. Quite effectively he said that he joined all things together through his death and established them in peace by linking them together with himself. Clearly [277] he is seen to have repeated in this place what he had said (1:16): *in him all things were created, which are in the heavens and which are on the earth.* And he has carefully proved that he plainly also wrote there about the same thing he is seen to have spoken of in this place. And by designating him *the firstborn from the dead* (1:18) it is obvious that he called

---

[14]Swete (1:275) points out that the Latin has somehow been thrown "into confusion" but that "Th. wishes to say that verse 19, rightly explained, corroborates his view as to the reference of v. 16 to the *homo susceptus*."

[15]In the commentary on Ephesians the verb is passive rather than active.

nifestum est hominem susceptum a Patre sic uocasse. in his igitur
et illa quae erga Christum sunt ostendens magna et supereminen-
tia et multo maiora quam humana sibi uindicat natura, et quidem
et magnitudinem illorum quae per eum sunt confecta ex illis quae
5 generalia sunt sufficienter edocuit. conuertit uero ultra uerbum ad
eorum personam, eo quod potiti fuissent illud beneficium quod in
commune omnibus conlatum est, ita ut non solum ex communione eos ad reuerentiam adduceret ut ab illa fide quae in Christo est
non discederent, sed et de illis quae secundum eos sunt, siquidem
10 et ipsi magnis sunt beneficiis cum ceteris sublimati:

et uos aliquando cum essetis alienati et inimici intellectu in operibus
malis, nunc uero reconciliauit in corpore carnis suae per mortem, ut
exhiberet uos sanctos et immaculatos et inreprehensibiles coram se.

similiter sequentiam illorum quae in Ephesiorum epistola
15 scripserat, etiam hic seruasse uidetur; nam et in illis illa quae de
Christo sunt primitus magnifice referens, dein adiciens illam ecclesiae copulationem quae ad eum facta est, ad illa quae specialia
sunt transiens, memoratus est personas illorum ad quos epistolam
scribebat, dicens: *et uos mortui cum essetis delictis et peccatis uestris,*
20 *in quibus aliquando ambulastis secundum saeculum mundi huius*, et
cetera. sic et hoc in loco referens illa quae secundum Christum
sunt, sicuti et referri conueniebant, deinde adiciens illam ecclesiae
copulationem quae ad eum facta est, ad specialia transit, id est, ad
personam Colossensium, hoc dicens, quoniam 'talia quidem sunt
25 illa quae erga Christum facta sunt; magna etiam bona et uos potiti estis. alienos enim uos extantes a Deo et in parte inimicorum
illi constitutos, ob illam quam erga prauitatem habebatis diligentiam, reconciliauit uos Deo per suam mortem, auferens quidem
a uobis mortalitatem, inmortalitatem uero uobis donans; in qua
30 ultra constituti ab omni estis peccato securi effecti, et nihil agere
potestis ex illis quae non conueniunt. permanetis autem nullam
sustinentes incusationem, sed secundum omnem scrupulositatem
illi placite conuersamini.' hoc enim in omnibus epistolis notaui-

---

3 multa *C** ‖ et (2°) *om C* (*corr.*) 10 magni *C** 21 in hoc loco *r* 24
et (*for* sunt) *C* (*corr.*) 25 sunt facta *r* 27 illic *C H r: txt conj. Jacobi*

the Man assumed by the Father[16] by this name. Therefore, in these verses by demonstrating that the things to do with Christ are great and highly excellent and greater than human nature could claim for itself, he also sufficiently taught the greatness of those things accomplished through him on the basis of what has universal application, But from here on Paul turns his address to the Colossians, since they had acquired the benefit conferred on all in common, so that he may lead them to an awe that would prevent them from abandoning faith in Christ not only because of what they shared in common but also because of those things particular to them, if indeed they, too, along with the rest, were exalted by great benefits:

1:21–22 *And you, when you were once estranged and hostile in mind in evil deeds, now, indeed, he has reconciled in the body of his flesh through death, so that he might present you holy and blameless and without reproach in his sight,*

Here he seems to have preserved in a similar way the logical order of what he had written in the letter to the Ephesians. For also in Ephesians he referred first of all in fine language to what had to do with Christ and then added the linking that took place of the church to him, and passing over to what was particular to them, he mentions the persons of those to whom he was writing the letter, saying (Eph 2:1): *and when you were dead in transgressions and your sins in which you once walked according to the age of this world,* and the rest. So, too, in this place, referring to what concerned Christ as it was right for reference to be made, then adding the linking that came about to him of that church, [278] he passes over to particular considerations, that is, to the person of the Colossians, saying this: "Such are the things that came about because of Christ, and you have yourselves also acquired great good things. For when you were held estranged from God and placed in the position of enemies to him because of the care you used to have for vicious behavior, he reconciled you to God through his death, indeed removing mortality from you and giving you immortality. Established in this from now on, you have been made safe from all sin and can do no one of those things that are not right. And you persevere, incurring no blame, but you live your lives with all exact care well-pleasing to him." In all the letters we have

---

[16] This must be a mistake, since it is the Word that assumed the Man.

mus, quoniam de futuris apostolus magnitudinem illorum ostendit quae erga nos a Christo facta sunt; et quoniam omnis eius correctio in promissionibus posita est, quae est renouatio futura in futuro saeculo, idipsum et Ephesiis scribentem dixisse ostendimus.
et quoniam transiuit ulterius ad suam personam, designans quod
suasi fuissent ab illis qui suadebant eis diligentiam adhibere super
custodiam legis:

si tamen permanetis in fide fundati et stabiles et non commoti a spe
euangelii quod audistis, et reliqua.

et sicut in illis in quibus firmiter eos credere hortabatur, gratias
agens pro illis commemoratus est quoniam et per omnem orbem
euangelii gloria uim suam uindicat; sic et hoc in loco designans
quasi quia seducti fuerant ab illa gloria, quae apud omnes firma
esse uidetur. quod et memoratur, ut maius eos erubescere faciat:

quod praedicatum est in omni creatura quae sub caelo est.

graue admodum erat ut discederent ab illa re, quae in communi
ab omnibus bona esse conclamabatur. euidentius facere cupiens
illud quod dicit, adiecit:

cuius factus sum ego Paulus minister.

†hoc enim erat opus eius, ut   τοῦτο γὰρ ἦν ἔργον αὐτοῦ, τὸ
praedicaret euangelium in gen-   κηρύττειν εἰς τὰ ἔθνη τὸ εὐαγγέ-
tibus, excepta legitimorum ob-   λιον ἔξω τῆς τῶν νομικῶν παρατη-
seruantia*;   ρήσεως.

sicut beato Petro ceterisque diuidit praedicationem, sicut ipse Galatis scribens memoratus est. et ostendens quemadmodum con-
scius sibi sit quod bona doceat:

nunc gaudeo in passionibus pro uobis et suppleo minorationes tri-
bulationum Christi in carne mea, pro corpore eius quod est ecclesia;
cuius factus sum ego minister.

---

4 Efesis *C*   6   essent *H*   8   permanentis *C**   10   inquit (*for* in quibus) *H*
12 designat *C* (*corr.*)   13   reducti *H*   ‖   fuerint *r*   16   commune *r*   17
clamabatur *l* conclamatur *b*   18   adicit *C r*   19   minister *om H*   20   sq. Coisl. 204, f. 148 b [Cr. vi. 312, Fr. 142]. θεόδωρος φησίν· τοῦτο, κ.τ.λ.   22-23
obseruantiam *C**   26   edoceat *H*   27   nam *H* qui nunc *r*   29   ego *om H*

pointed out that it is on the basis of the things to come that the apostle demonstrates the greatness of what Christ has done for us and that all his reforming guidance has been placed in promises concerned with the future renewal in the age to come. And we have demonstrated that he has said the same thing when writing to the Ephesians. And since further on he passed over to his own person, pointing out that they might have been persuaded by those who were trying to persuade them to display diligence in keeping the law:

1:23a *if at any rate you persevere founded in faith and steadfast and not moved from the hope of the gospel that you have heard,* and the rest,[17]

Just as in those verses (1:3–6) in which he was exhorting them to believe with steadfast faith, he gave thanks for them and mentioned that even through the whole round world the glory of the gospel is claiming its strength, so also in this place he points them out as though it were the case that they had been led astray from that glory that seemed to be steadfast among all.[18] And this is mentioned to make them blush all the more:

[279] 1:23b *which has been preached in every creature that is under heaven,*

It would have been extremely serious for them to have gone astray from that practice that was acclaimed to be good by all in common. Wishing to make his meaning clearer, he added:

1:23c *of which I, Paul, was made a minister.*

†For it was his work to preach the gospel to the Gentiles, apart from observing the law's ordinances,*	For this was his work, to preach the gospel to the Gentiles, apart from observing the law's ordinances.

as he divided the preaching with blessed Peter and the others, just as he himself mentioned when writing to the Galatians (Gal 2:9). And to show how conscious he is that he is teaching good things:

1:24–25a *Now I am rejoicing in sufferings for you, and I am filling up the lacks of the afflictions of Christ in my flesh for his body, which is the church, of which I have been made a minister,*

---

[17] Swete (1:278) points out that this is "a superfluous gloss," since the rest of the text does follow.

[18] That is, both his hopes and fears for them are grounds for exhorting them to persevere in faith.

†'itaque et delector patiens pro uobis; [et] quoniam praeueniens ad conferendum uobis beneficium passus est Christus, ut corpus suum uos per resurrectionem esse pronuntiaret, illa quae deerant tribulationum eius ab illis quae pro uobis erunt adimpleo ego. quid erat quod deerat? ut discentes, quae sunt illa quae correcta sunt pro uobis, suscipiatis de illis promissionem. hoc autem sine labore et tribulationibus fieri nequaquam potest. pro his ergo patior circumiens et praedicans omnibus illa quae sunt directa, ita ut uos credentes affectu animi propinquitatem illam quae ad eum est accipiatis; horum enim ego extiti minister*.'

ὥστε (φησὶν) ἥδομαι καὶ πάσχων ὑπὲρ ὑμῶν· καὶ ἐπειδὴ προλαβὼν ὑπὲρ τῆς ὑμετέρας εὐεργεσίας ἔπαθεν ὁ Χριστός, ὥστε σῶμα ἑαυτοῦ ὑμᾶς ἀποφῆναι διὰ τῆς ἀναστάσεως, τὰ προσλείποντα ταῖς θλίψεσιν αὐτοῦ ταῖς ὑπὲρ ὑμῶν ἀναπληρῶ.' τί δὲ ἦν τὸ προσλεῖπον; τὸ μαθόντας ὑμᾶς τίνα ἐστὶν τὰ ὑπὲρ ὑμῶν κατορθωθέντα παρ' αὐτοῦ, δέξασθαι τὴν περὶ αὐτῶν ἐπαγγελίαν· τοῦτο δὲ ἄνευ πόνων καὶ θλίψεως γενέσθαι οὐδαμῶς οἷόν τε ἦν· ὑπὲρ δὴ τούτων πόσχω, περιιὼν καὶ κηρύττων ἅπασιν τὰ κατορθωθέντα, ὥστε ὑμᾶς πιστεύσαντας τῇ διαθέσει τῆς ψυχῆς τὴν τρὸς αὐτὸν οἰκείωσιν δέξασθαι· τούτων γὰρ ἐγὼ κατέστην διάκονος.'

et ut ne uideatur alta sapiens sibi ipsi ministerii adscribere directionem:

secundum dispensationem Dei quae data est mihi in uobis, adimplere uerbum Dei, mysterium quod absconditum est a saeculis et a generationibus; nunc uero manifestum est sanctis eius, quibus uoluit Deus notum facere quae sunt diuitiae gloriae mysterii huius in gentibus.

haec quidem etiam ipsis sermonibus in illam epistolam quam Ephesiis scripserat posita esse quis inueniet, eo quod et illam et istam ad illos qui se non uiderunt scribebat; ideo et multos sensus et in illa epistola et in ista similiter posuisse uidetur. dicit ergo quoniam 'ministerium hoc commissum est mihi a Deo ita ut omnes doceam illud quod olim omnibus erat incertum, nunc uero sanctis eius est cognitum.' quid illud tale? quod ob multam suam bonitatem et gloriae liberalitatem etiam et gentibus similiter eo-

---

1 et om C H r: txt jacobi ‖ sq. Coisl. 204 l. c. [Cr. Fr.] 5 uobis C H r: txt conj. Jacobi 10 discente C* H 11 sunt correcta r 24 inquit (aft. disp.) add r 28 illa epistola C (corr.) r 29 quis om C H ‖ inuenies C (corr.) 31 et in illa et in ista epistola r 34 cogn. est r ‖ quod (for quid) C r

†"And so I am even glad when I suffer for you. Since Christ, coming before, suffered to bring you benefit, so that he might proclaim you to be his body through the resurrection, I am filling up what was lacking in his afflictions by those that will be for you. What was it that was lacking? That by learning what are [280] those things that have been accomplished for you, you may receive the promise of them. But this can by no means be done without toil and afflictions. Therefore, I suffer for this, going about and preaching to all, those things that have been accomplished, so that by believing with the soul's affection you may gain familial intimacy with him. For it is of these things that I have taken my place as a minister."*

"So that (he says) I am glad even when I suffer for you. And since Christ in anticipation suffered for your benefit to declare you his own body through the resurrection, I am filling up what is lacking in his afflictions for you. What was it that is lacking? For you, by learning what was achieved for you by him, to receive the promise concerning them. It would not be possible in any way for this to come about without toils and afflictions. So for these things I suffer, going about and preaching to all what has been accomplished, so that by believing with the soul's affection you may receive familial intimacy with him. For it is of these things that I have been established a minister."

And to assign what directs his own ministry, so that he may not seem to think highly of himself:

1:25b-27a *according to the dispensation of God that was given to me among you, to fulfill the word of God, the mystery that was hidden from ages and from generations but has now been revealed to his saints, to whom God willed to make known what are the riches of the glory of this mystery among the Gentiles,*

Indeed, anyone will find this also placed in the very discourses in the letter he had written to the Ephesians (Eph 3:2–6), because he wrote both that letter and this one to people he had not seen. And so there are many ideas [281] that he seems to have put down in a similar way both in that letter and in this one. Therefore, he says that "this ministry has been entrusted to me by God, so that I might teach everyone what was once unclear to all but is now known to his saints." What is such a thing? That because of his great kindness and his glorious generosity he has bestowed the

rum praebuit fruitionem. nam antiquis temporibus omnis pietas
in Iudaeorum genere circumscripta habebatur, gentibus uero nulla ad eos erat societas; euangelium uero communem omnibus futurorum promisit donationem, quod et *mysterium* uocat, eo quod
olim erat occultum, nunc autem est manifestum. nam quia dixit:
sanctis eius quibus uoluit Deus, de apostolis dixit et illis qui tunc
erant praepositi; de quibus et Ephesiis scribens euidenter dixisse uisus est. et quoniam dixit: *quae sunt diuitiae gloriae mysterii,*
adiecit:

quod est Christus in uobis spes gloriae.

†hoc est magnae diuitiae, id   οὗτος ὁ μέγας πλοῦτος, ὁ Χρισ-
est, Christus, et ut in illum   τὸς καὶ τὸ ἐπ᾽ αὐτῷ πιστεύειν· οὗ-
credamus; hic enim est futurae   τος γὰρ ἡ τῆς μελλούσης δόξης ἐλ-
gloriae spes, qui et causa nobis   πίς, ὁ καὶ τὴν αἰτίαν ἡμῖν τοῦ προσ-
bonorum extitit, donans nobis   δοκᾶν ἐκεῖνα χαρισάμενος.
ut illa expectemus.*

quem nos adnuntiamus, admonentes omnem hominem, et docentes
omnem hominem, in omni sapientia, ut exhibeamus omnem hominem
perfectum in Christo Iesu.

'hunc (inquit) praedicamus, omnem hominem docentes ut in
eum affectum habeant, ut in futurum adsequi possint perfectionem per illam quae in eo est fidem.' 'perfectionem' etenim futurum statum uocat et in illa epistola quam ad Galatas, et in ista
quam ad Ephesios scripsisse uidetur; cui statui nihil boni deesse
uidebitur. et quoniam omnia ista ad illud retitulat quod dixerat:
nunc gaudeo in passionibus pro uobis, resumit iterum illud:

in quo et laboro in agone positus secundum operationem eius, quam
operatus est in me in uirtute.

'pro his (inquit) et laborare cupio, omnimodo decertans propter tributam mihi ad hoc uirtutem de caelo.' inueniet autem quis et
hoc per omnia simile esse secundum sensum illius epistolae, quam
ad Ephesios scripsisse uidetur, ubi dixit: *huius rei gratia ego Pau-*
lus uinctus Christi Iesu, et cetera. et quoniam ostendit euidenter
sibi competere pro his doctrinam, siquidem gentium ministerium
commissum habere uidetur et in hoc a Deo creatus est, satisfacere

5   manifestatum *C* (*corr.*)   9   adicit *C r*   11   sq. Coisl. 204, f. 150 a [Cr.
vi. 316, Fr. 143]. Θεόδωρος. καὶ ἄλλος ὁμοίως· οὗτος, κ.τ.λ.   13   hinc *H*   21
effectum *C* H*   25   retulit (*for* retit.) *r*   27   et *om H*   28   operatur esse (*for*
operatus est) *H* operatur *r*

enjoyment of these things likewise even on the Gentiles. For in the times of old all true religion was kept restricted to the Jews, while the Gentiles had no association with them. But the gospel has promised to everyone the common gift of the things to come. Paul also calls this a *mystery*, because it was once hidden but now has been revealed. For when he said *to his saints, to whom God willed*, he spoke of the apostles and those who were placed in charge at that time. He is also seen to have spoken clearly about them when writing to the Ephesians (Eph 3:5). And when he said *what are the riches of the glory of the mystery*, he added:

1:27b *which is Christ among you, the hope of glory,*

†This is the great riches, that is, Christ and that we may believe in him. For this is the hope of the glory to come, which also has come to be the cause of good things for us, giving us our expectation of them.*

This is the great riches, Christ and to believe in him. For this is the hope of the glory to come, which gives us the cause of expecting those things.

1:28 *whom we proclaim, admonishing every person and teaching every person in all wisdom, so that we may present every person perfect in Christ Jesus,*

"It is him (he says) that we preach, teaching every person so that they may have affection for him, so that they may be able in the future to acquire perfection [282] through faith in him." Indeed, he calls the future condition "perfection" also in the letter to the Galatians (Gal 3:26; 4:1–7) and in what he is seen to have written to the Ephesians (Eph 4:13). Nothing of the good will be seen lacking in that condition. And since he is summing up all these things back to where he said (Col 1:24): *Now I am rejoicing in sufferings for you,* he repeats the idea:

1:29 *in which also I toil, placed in a contest according to his working that has been worked in me in power.*

"For these things (he says) I want also to toil, contending in every way because of the power bestowed on me from heaven for this." And anyone will find this, too, to be similar in all respects to the sense of the letter he is seen to have written to the Ephesians, where he said (Eph 3:1): *For this reason I, Paul, a prisoner of Christ Jesus,* and the rest. And since he showed clearly that teaching on behalf of these things belonged to him, if indeed he is seen to have been entrusted with the ministry to the Gentiles and if indeed

properat eis, quoniam nondum uenerat ad eos:

uolo enim uos scire, qualem agonem habeam pro uobis et illis qui in Laodicia sunt, et quotquot non uiderunt faciem meam in carne.

'nec enim illud uolo (inquit) uos ignorare, quoniam etsi non ui-
di uos, sed ualde et de uobis agonem sustineo; nec enim minus de uobis sum sollicitus, quam de illis quos uidi.' quid autem est illud, quoniam agonem pro illis pateris?

ut consolentur corda eorum instructa in caritate et in omnibus diui-tiis perfectionis prudentiae.

'ut et uos in illam caritatem quae erga Christum est conuenien-tes, firmo intellectu illorum bonorum quae expectantur adsequa-mini fruitionem.'

in cognitionem mysterii Dei Patris et Christi, in quo sunt omnes thesauri sapientiae et scientiae absconditi.

'et ut inenarrabilibus bonis communicetis, quae a Deo donata sunt nobis, quae etiam absconsa sunt nunc in Christo; cum quo, cum adparuerit in futuro saeculo, et illa quae erga nos est liberali-tas in ipsis tunc uidebitur operibus.'

†'mysterium' etenim, sicut fre-quenter diximus, uocat illam gratiam quae erga gentes est, eo quod et ignota erat primitus; *co-gnitionem* uero *mysterii* partici-pationem eius edicit esse. ab-sconsos uero omnes thesauros sapientiae et scientiae esse in Christo edicit, utpote cum mul-ta prudentia institutos esse per Christum pro nostra utilitate, quia nunc quidem sunt incer-ti, uidebuntur autem tunc, cum adparuerit et ipse.*

μυστήριον δὲ καλεῖ τὴν περὶ τὰ ἔθνη χάριν, ὡς ἂν ἄδηλον οὖσαν τοῖς πρὸ τούτου, ἐπίγνωσιν δὲ μυστηρίου τὴν μετουσίαν αὐτῆς. ἀποκρύφους δὲ πάντας τοὺς θησαυροὺς τῆς σοφίας καὶ τῆς γνώσεως εἶναι ἐν τῷ Χριστῷ λέγει, ὡς ἂν τῶν μετὰ πολλῆς κατορθωθέντων συνέσεως διὰ τοῦ Χριστοῦ ὑπὲρ τῆς ἡμετέρας εὐεργεσίας νῦν μὲν ὄντων ἀδήλων, φανησομένων δὲ τότε ὁπότ' ἂν φαίνηται καὶ αὐτός.

edicens agonem quem habet pro illis, adiecit:

hoc dico, ut ne quis uos circumueniat in uersutia uerborum.

---

15 dona C* 19 sq. Coisl. 204 *l.c.* (p. 281) 22 erant C r ‖ sq. Coisl. 204, f. 150 b [Cr. vi. 317, Fr. 143] θεόδωρος. ἄλλος δέ φησιν. ἀποκρύφους, κ.τ.λ. 30 qui (*for* quia) C r ‖ φαίνεται Cr. Fr.: txt cod. 33 edicens—adiecit *om* r ‖ adicit C

he was appointed by God for this purpose, he is eager to make amends to them for the fact that he had not yet come to them:

2:1 *For I want you to know what kind of contest I have for you and those who are in Laodicea and as many who have not seen my face in the flesh,*

[283] "For neither do I want you to be ignorant (he says) of the fact that, though I have not seen you, yet I am undergoing a contest even about you, for I have been no less concerned about you than about those I have seen." So why is it that you should suffer a contest for them?

2:2a *so that their hearts may be encouraged, drawn up in love and in all the riches of the perfection of understanding,*

"So that you, too, agreeing together in the love of Christ, may acquire with steadfast understanding the enjoyment of those good things that are awaited."

2:2b-3 *in the comprehension of the mystery of God the Father and of Christ, in whom are all the treasures of wisdom and knowledge hidden.*

"And so that you may share in the ineffable good things that have been given us by God, which also are now hidden in Christ. When he shall appear in the age to come, with him at that time his generosity toward us will also be seen in the works themselves."

†And, as we have often said, he calls the grace toward the Gentiles a *mystery* because it was unknown at first, but he declares their sharing it *the comprehension of the mystery*. And he declares that *all the treasures of wisdom and knowledge* are *hidden* in Christ—as, of course, [284] to be established with much understanding through Christ for our benefit—because they are now, indeed, unclear, but they will be seen at that time when he will also appear himself.*

And he calls the grace concerning the Gentiles a *mystery* since it was unclear to those before this time, but he calls sharing it *the comprehension of the mystery*. And he says that *all the treasures of wisdom and knowledge* are *hidden* in Christ, since the things accomplished with much understanding through Christ for our benefit are now unclear but will appear at the time when he also appears.

Declaring the contest he has for them, he added:

2:4 *I am saying this so that no one may cheat you in the cunning of words.*

quid est autem *hoc dico?* 'et qua ratione hunc habeo de uobis agonem? timeo enim, ne quando mutabilitatem aliquam sustineatis suasoribus intendentes. tunc enim poteritis, ut dixi, adsequi uobis promissa, quando permanseritis erga pietatem firmi.'
5 et ostendens quoniam et laetitiae illorum participatur, si bene se
illa quae erga illos sunt habuerint:

si enim et carne absens sum, sed spiritu uobiscum, gaudens et uidens
uestrum ordinem et firmamentum fidei quae in Christo est.

'licet absens sim, sed uobiscum sum affectu animi, gaudens in
10 uobis, si tamen firmo cogitatu in Christi fide permanere uolueritis.' et ultra incipit exhortationem facere euidenter:

sicut ergo accepistis Christum Iesum Dominum, in ipso ambulate,
radicati et superaedificati in ipso, et confirmati in fide, sicut docti estis,
abundantes in ea in gratiarum actionem.

15 per omnia haec illa dicere uoluit: 'in illis manete quae accepistis, secundum illa conuersantes'; ita ut manifestum sit, quoniam extra obseruantiam legitimorum illa ab Epaphra susceperunt. propterea et laudauit traditionem eius in principio. bene autem quia et *in gratiarum actionem* adiecit, ostendens quoniam sic
20 bona est doctrina ita ut gratias agere conueniat eos, pro quibus eam
cognouerunt. deinde et aduersarios improbans dicit:

uidete ne quis uos depraedetur per philosophiam et inanem seduc-
tionem.

philosophiam dicit uerborum pomposam doctrinam, quae ab
25 aduersariis cum quadam simulatione fieri solebat ad seductionem
audientium. inde et ostendens quoniam non uera erat philoso-
phia, sed seductionis uerba ad deceptionem auditorum et excogitata erant et adinuenta:

secundum traditionem hominum, secundum elementa mundi et non
30 *secundum Christum.*

secundum elementa mundi dicit dierum et temporum obseruan-

---

6 ait (*aft* hab.) *r*   7 carnem *C* r*   9 sum *om H*   10 Christo *C**   14
habundanter *C H*   15 quoniam (*aft.* uoluit) *add r*   16 illam *C* r*   17 leg.
obs. *H*   18 laudabit *C*   21 docuit (*for* dicit) *C r*   25 aduersarios *H*

What, then, is *I am saying this*? "And for what reason do I have this contest for you? Because I am afraid that there may be a time when you may undergo some inconstancy by paying attention to those trying to persuade you. For you will be able, as I have said, to attain the things promised to you at that time when you will have persevered steadfast in true religion." And showing that he was also sharing in their gladness if they were content with their circumstances:

2:5 *For if even in the flesh I am absent, yet in the spirit I am with you, rejoicing and seeing your order and the firmness of faith*[19] *that is in Christ.*

"Even though I may be absent, yet I am with you in the soul's affection, rejoicing in you, if indeed with steadfast consideration you will prove willing to persevere." And from this point on he clearly begins to compose an exhortation:

2:6–7 *Therefore, as you have received Christ Jesus the Lord, walk in him, rooted and built up in him, and established steadfast in faith, as you have been taught, abounding in it for thanksgiving.*

[285] By all this he meant: "Remain in those things you have received, living your lives according to them." This is so that it may be obvious that they received those things from Epaphras apart from the observance of the law's ordinances. Because he also praised Epaphras's handing over of the faith in the beginning (Col 1:7–8), he also rightly added that it was *for thanksgiving,* showing that the teaching was so good that it was right for them to give thanks for having learned it. Then, also to condemn the opponents he says:

2:8a *See that no one plunders you by philosophy and empty seduction,*

By *philosophy* he means teaching made ostentatious by words, the kind that was usually composed with some kind of pretense by the opponents for the seduction of the hearers. Then, to show that the philosophy was not true but that words of seduction designed to deceive those who heard them had been both contrived and invented:

2:8b *according to the tradition of humans, according to the elements of the world and not according to Christ.*

By *according to the elements of the world* he means the observa-

---

[19]The text should read "your faith," but the second "your" has been omitted.

tiam, eo quod ab elementis mundi perficiuntur ista. 'elementum'
enim 'mundi' solem dicit et lunam, ex quibus dierum quoque et
temporum cursus effici uidentur; sic enim illud et Galatis scribens dixit. *traditionem* autem *hominum* non ipsam legem uocauit,
sed illam doctrinam illorum qui tunc erant; humanam dicens esse
eo quod nec secundum Dei sententiam fiebat. unde et ostendens
prauitatem eius adiecit: *et non secundum Christum.* Christi personam contrasistit ut ostendat prauitatem doctrinae, si tamen et ad
alia eos adducit qui discunt, praeterquam ad Filium.

   quoniam in ipso inhabitat omnis plenitudo diuinitatis corporaliter.
   omnem plenitudinem deitatis hoc in loco iterum dicit uniuersam
creaturam repletam ab eo; dicit enim illum sensum quem in superioribus posuisse uisus est, quoniam omnis creatura in eo inhabitat, hoc est, ipsi coniuncta est, et quasi quoddam corpus in
se retinet aptatum, propter illam copulationem quae ad eum est.
quemadmodum ergo inconueniens est intendere illi qui alia docet,
praeterquam quod ille docuit, in quem omnia coaptata sunt et co-
pulata! hoc enim est a communi consensu se ipsum extraneum facere. et euidentiorem ipsam inconuenientiam faciens adiecit:
   et estis in illo repleti, qui est caput omnis principatus et potestatis.
   euidenter illa, quae in superioribus dicta fuerant, compendiose
iterum ait: 'etenim et uos eum habentes in uobis, digni estis habiti
eius copulationi, qui et omnibus inuisibilibus uirtutibus in ordine capitis consistit, eo quod omnia ob cognationem ad illum sicut
corpus coniuncta sunt.' deinde et magnitudine donationum ad uerecundiam eos adducens dicit:
   in quo et circumcisi estis circumcisione non manu facta in exspolia-
tionem corporis peccatorum carnis, in circumcisione Christi.
   'in ipso (inquit) et ea quae in eo est fide ab inposita uobis mortalitate estis eruti, cum qua mortalitate etiam peccata uestra su-

8 et ostendit *r*   8-9 si tamen—filium *om r*   13 in eum *C**   13-14 habitat *r*   16 quia (*for* qui) *r*   17 coapta *C**   19 adicit *C*   22 aiunt *r*   23
uirt. inuis. *H*   24 cognitionem *H*   25 magnitudinem *C** magnitudo *r*   27
manifesta *H*   29 ab impositam *H*   29-30 mortalitatem estis eruditi *C* H r*

tion of days and seasons, because they are accomplished by the elements of the world. For by "elements of the world" he means the sun and the moon, from which the courses of days and seasons are seen to be brought about; for so he said also when writing to the Galatians (Gal 4:3). And he did not call the law itself *the tradition of humans*, but the teaching of those people who existed at that time, saying that it was human because it did not come about in accord with God's judgment. Then, to demonstrate its perversity he added *and not according to Christ*. He made the contrast with Christ's person to demonstrate the perversity of the teaching, if at any rate it led those who learned it to things other than the Son.

[286] 2:9 *For in him the entire fullness of divinity dwells bodily,*

By *the entire fullness of deity*[20] in this place he again means the entire creation filled by him. For he is giving the same meaning he is seen to have put down above (Col 1:19), that the entire creation dwells in him, that is, is joined to him, and he holds it fast like a body fitted to himself because of the linking that binds it to him. Therefore, how wrong it is to pay attention to that person who teaches things other than he taught, the one in whom all things are fitted and linked together! For by general agreement this would be for someone to make himself a stranger [to the faith]. And to make what is wrong with this clearer he added:

2:10 *and you have been filled in him who is the head of every ruler and authority,*

Clearly he is succinctly repeating what had been said above (Col 1:16): "Indeed, since you also possess him in yourselves, you have been held worthy of being linked with him, who for all the invisible powers [287] is also established in rank as the head, because all things have been joined together as his body on account of their kinship with him." Then, also to induce them to shame by the greatness of the gifts, he says:

2:11 *in whom also you have been circumcised with the circumcision not made with hands, in the stripping off of the body of the sins of the flesh, in the circumcision of Christ,*

"In him (he says) and by faith in him you have been uprooted from the mortality imposed on you, and with mortality he has

---

[20] See Swete's note (1:286): "Our translator follows the Latin authorities in the text, but in the comment throws off their trammels, and represents τῆς θεότητος by its more precise equivalent."

stulit.' uult enim dicere quoniam 'inmortalitatem adsecuti estis,
in qua constituti ultra non peccabitis, quod ex mortalitate sustinebatis necessitatem; itaque conuenit et propter hoc non ingratos
uos uideri erga illum, qui tantorum uobis bonorum extitit proui-
5 sor.' bene autem 'circumcisionem' nominauit mortalitatis ablationem, ita ut ex comparatione ostendat eius differentiam; siquidem
ibi corporis ablatio exigua est nullam habens prodificationem, hic
uero tanta mortalitas aufertur in melius corpore nostro transfor-
mato. unde et 'non manu factam circumcisionem' uocauit eam, ita
10 ut ex eo modo inoperationis eius ostendat differentiam; siquidem
illic humana manus est, quae perfecit circumcisionem, hic uero
diuina est gratia, quae inoperatur mortalitatis ablationem. necessaria uero est et adiectio quam adiecit dicens *in circumcisione Chri-*
sti, ut dicat quia 'hanc circumcisi estis circumcisionem, cuius pro-
15 missum uobis praestitit Christus.' et quoniam magna erant quae
dicta fuerant, necdum uero in opere erant effecta:
     consepulti (inquit) *illi in baptisma, in quo et consurrexistis per fi-*
dem operationis Dei, qui suscitauit eum ex mortuis.
     'si autem necdum negotio id potiti estis, tamen iam in forma il-
20 lorum effecti estis, commortui in baptismate et conresurgentes ei.
euidens est quoniam baptisma adsecuti estis credentes primitus,
quod potens sit ista facere Deus; et fecerit iam, ex quibus et suscitauit ex mortuis Christum, in illo communis resurrectionis primitias operatus.' multis uero in locis in apostolica doctrina ines-
25 se docuimus, quoniam probationes illorum quae secundum Christum sunt de futuris semper facere consueuit. commemoratur uero et forma illa quae ad praesens impletur, ita ut uideantur illorum
quae expectantur pignora aliqua in praesente habere; hinc etenim
sancti Spiritus primitias in baptismate percipimus. quoniam au-
30 tem dixit formam, resumit illum quod dictum fuerat a se, ut latius
illam, quasi exinde est, gratiam explicet:
     et uos, cum essetis mortui delictis et praeputio carnis uestrae, co-
nuiuificauit cum ipso, donans uobis omnia delicta.

---

2 sustinebitis *r* ‖ ex mortalitatis sustinebatis necessitate *C* (*corr.*) 8 nostro *om H* 14 hac, circumcisione *r* 17 qua *C H* 18 eum *om C** 20
consurgentes *r* 28 in praesenti *C* (*corr.*) *r* 30 illud *C* (*corr.*) 31 quae (*for*
quasi) *C* (*corr.*) quam *r* ‖ inde *r*

also taken away your sins." For he means that "you have drawn
near to immortality; once established in it you will no longer sin
to the extent that you used to submit to its necessity because of
mortality. And so it is right also for this reason that you should
not seem ungrateful toward him who has come to be your provider
of such great good things." And he rightly called the removal
of mortality *circumcision*, so that by the comparison he might
demonstrate its difference—assuming that there the removal from
the body is small, having no profit, but here such great mortality is
removed when our body is changed for the better. That is why he
called this removal *the circumcision not made with hands*, so that he
might demonstrate its difference by the method of its operation—
assuming that, there, it is the human hand that [288] completes
circumcision, but here it is divine grace that works the removal of
mortality. But the addition he made by saying *in the circumcision
of Christ* is also necessary, so that he may mean "you have been
circumcised with this circumcision, the promise of which Christ
has bestowed on you." And since what had been spoken of was
great but had not yet been brought about in actuality:

2:12 *buried* (he says) *with him in baptism, in which you have also
been raised with him through faith in the working of God who raised
him from the dead.*

"Even if you have not yet acquired this as a matter of fact,
nevertheless, you have been fashioned in the type of those things,
since in baptism you have died and been raised together with him.
It is clear that you have drawn near to baptism first of all because
you believe that God has the power to do those things and has
already done them, because he has raised Christ from the dead,
having worked in him the firstfruits of the general resurrection."
And in many places we have taught that this claim is present in the
apostle's teaching, since he had the habit of always giving proofs of
what has to do with Christ from the things to come. But that type
which is fulfilled in the present is also mentioned, so that they may
be seen to have in the present certain pledges of those things that
are awaited. Indeed, from this consideration it is the firstfruits of
the Holy Spirit [289] that we reap in baptism. And since he has
spoken of the type, he takes up what he had said so that he may
explain more fully that grace as follows:

2:13 *And you, when you were dead in transgressions and in the
uncircumcision of your flesh, he made alive with him, pardoning all*

†'praeputium' hoc in loco non corporis dicit, sed sicut circumcisionem ablationem uocauit mortalitatis, sic 'praeputium' illud uocauit quod adhuc circumfert mortalitatem. hoc ergo dicit, quoniam 'mortificatos uos peccatis propter circumpositam uobis mortalitatem conresuscitauit Christo, in ipso communem resurrectionem efficiens, ex qua omnis species peccati uestri exterminabitur.'*

ἀκροβυστίαν ἐνταῦθα οὐ τὴν τοῦ σώματος λέγει, ἀλλ' ὥσπερ περιτομὴν τὴν ἀφαίρεσιν ἐκάλεσεν τῆς θνητότητος, οὕτως ἀκροβυστίαν τὸ περικεῖσθαι ἔτι τὴν θνητότητα. τοῦτο οὖν λέγει, ὅτι 'νενεκρωμένους ὑμᾶς τοῖς ἁμαρτήμασιν διὰ τὴν περικειμένην θνητότητα συνανέστησεν τῷ Χριστῷ, ἐν αὐτῷ τὴν κοινὴν ἀνάστασιν κατεργασάμενος, ἀφ' ἧς πᾶν εἶδος ἁμαρτίας ὑμῶν ἀφανίσθησεται.'

hoc enim dicit *donans uobis omnia delicta*, eo quod constituit nos extra facilitatem peccandi per resurrectionem; etenim postquam inmortales natura extiterimus, peccare ultra nequaquam poterimus. deinde coniungit et aliud bonum, quod hinc nobis adquisitum est, quod et ad praesens argumentum sibi conuenire existimabat:

   delens cautionem decretis quae erat aduersus nos, quae erat contraria nobis, et ipsam tulit de medio, configens eam cruci.

cautionem legem dicit, cuius omnes actus implere debemus, utpote positae a Deo. quod erat durum, immo inpossibile, ut secundum legis scrupulositatem iustificaremur, quia lex qualitercumque et quandocumque peccantem punire praecepit; non peccare uero ad plenum hominem existentem ualde erat inpossibile. ex quibus fiebat ut illos qui sub lege conuersabantur securos a poena efficere minime posset. *cautionem* ergo *aduersus nos* legem uocat, eo quod *erat contraria nobis*, hoc est, non permittens iustificationem adsequi propter suam scrupulositatem; et hanc cautionem deleuit *decretis*, ut dicat 'resurrectionem et inmortalitatem'—

1-2 sq. Coisl. 204, f. 152 b [Cr. vi. 321, Fr. 143] θεόδωρος. ἀκροβυστίαν, κ.τ.λ.
7 mortificatis r   ‖ ἡμᾶς cod. edd.   9-10 conresusc. Christum C H cum resusc. Christum r   22 actum C r   27 illi C* H r   28 effici r   ‖ possit C* H possint r   ‖ chirographum (for caut.) l

your transgressions,

†In this place he does not mean the *uncircumcision* of the body, but just as he called the removal of mortality "circumcision," so he called what still spreads mortality round about *uncircumcision,* Therefore, he means this: "When you were made corpses in sins because of the mortality placed around you, he raised you up with Christ, bringing about in him the general resurrection by which every form of your sin will be removed."*

Here he does not mean the *uncircumcision* of the body, but just as he called the removal of mortality "circumcision," so he called the fact that mortality still encompasses us *uncircumcision.* Therefore, he means this: "When you were made corpses in sins because of the mortality that lay about you, he raised you up with Christ, working in him the general resurrection by which every form of your sin will be removed."

For he says *pardoning all your transgressions* because he has established us outside the easy tendency to sin by the resurrection. In fact, after we shall have come to exist immortal in nature, we shall in no way be able any longer to sin. Then he joins also another good acquired for us from this, and one that he thought suitable for his present argument:

2:14 *erasing the document, with the decrees,*[21] *that was against us, which was contrary to us, and he took it from the midst, nailing it to the cross.*

[290] He calls the law *the document,* all the duties of which we must fulfill, since they have been put down by God. But it was hard, indeed impossible, for us to be justified by exact care for the law, because the law decreed the punishment of whoever sinned, however, and whenever. But it was quite impossible that any existing person should completely refrain from sin. From these considerations it came about that it is by no means possible to make those who lived their lives under the law safe from punishment. Therefore, he calls the law *the document against us,* because it *was contrary to us,* that is, not permitting the acquisition of justification by exact care in keeping it. And he erased this document *with the decrees,* meaning "the resurrection

---

[21] *Delens cautionem decretis. Cautio* can mean a written stipulation or proviso, and the translator has used the word to render χειρόγραφον.

dogmata enim ista esse et Ephesiis scribens dixit, *legem praecepto-*
rum in decretis destituens. quare? quoniam lex necessaria erat illis
qui subiacebant peccato, retinens ac prohibens eos a peccato; quia
autem resurgentes effecti sunt inmortales, peccare ultra non pote-
5 runt. itaque et lex superflua est illis qui huiusmodi sunt; et 'in hoc
(inquit) nos securos facit, ut ne ulterius sub lege conuersemur, unde uel maxime sub poena facile incurrebamus.' bene autem dixit,
configens illam cruci, eo quod secundum praesentem uitam lex utilis est nobis, quando et peccare possumus; finis uero huius uitae
10 mors est. 'confixit (inquit) illam cruci, mortuus enim finem legi
dedit. nec enim in illis qui resurrexerunt locum aliquem ultra habere poterit lex. nam et nos secundum hoc extra legem efficimur,
secundum quod illis quae futura sunt transimus per formam baptismatis, secundum baptisma nostram conuersationem ordinan-
15 tes.' et quod maius est:

exuens se principatus et potestates traduxit cum fiducia, trium-
phans eos in se.

†*principatus et potestates* hoc   αἱ ἀντικείμεναι δυνάμεις οὐκ ἄν
in loco contrarias dicit esse uir-   ποτε ἔσχον τινὰ ἰσχὺν μὴ ἐπιδεχο-
20 tutes, quae aduersus nos nullam   μένων ἡμῶν ἁμαρτάνειν. 'τῷ οὖν
aliquando habuissent uirtutem,   ἀποθέσθαι (φησὶν) τὴν θνητότητα,
si nos peccare minime potuis-   ἣν ὑπὲρ τῆς κοινῆς ἀφεῖλεν εὐεργε-
semus. 'nam deponere (inquit)   σίας, ἀπεδύσατο κἀκείνων τὴν αὐθ-
mortalitatem, quam pro com-   εντείαν, ἧπερ ἐκέχρηντο καθ' ἡμῶν,
25 muni omnium abstulit utilitate,   μεγίστην καὶ ἀναμφίβολον τὴν κατ'
exuit et illos auctoritatem illam   αὐτῶν ἐργασάμενος νίκην, ὡς αἰσ-
qua abutebantur aduersus nos,   χυνθῆναι κἀκείνους μάτην τοσοῦτον
magnam et indubiam aduersus   ἐπιδειξαμένους καθ' ἡμῶν τὸν πό-
eos proferens uictoriam; ita ut   νον, ἀφ' οὗ μηδὲν αὐτοῖς ἐγένετο
30 confundantur et illi uane aduer-   ὄφελος, ἐν κρείττονι τῇ καταστάσει
sus nos tantum sustinuisse labo-   γεγονότων ἡμῶν, ὡς μηδὲ ἁμαρτεῖν
rem, ex quo nullum profectum   ἡμᾶς ἐπιδέχεσθαι ἔτι.'
habere potuerunt, in meliorem
statum transeuntibus nobis, ita

---

1 Efesis *C** 4 sunt eff. *r* 7 facile sub poena *H* 10 mortuos *C** 13 in
(*bef.* illis) *add C* (*corr.*) 18 sq. Coisl. 204, f. 153 b [Cr. vi. 223, Fr. 143]. ἄλλος
δὲ οὕτως φησίν· αἱ ἀντικ., κ.τ.λ. 23 deponens *C* (*corr.*) 25 utilitatem *C**
27 quae *C** 30 ille *C** illae uanae *r* ‖ ὄφειλος Cr. 31 ἁμαρτάνειν edd.
33 in melioris tantum *C** *r*

and immortality"—for also writing to the Ephesians he said that those things were the doctrines decreed (Eph 2:15): *destroying the law of commandments by decrees*. How so? Since the law was necessary for those who were subject to sin, holding them back and keeping them away from sin, but because when they are made immortal by rising again, they will no longer be able to sin. And so, as well, the law is useless for those who are like this. "In this way (he says) he makes us safe, so that we may no longer live our lives under the law from which we were especially liable easily to meet with punishment." And he rightly said *nailing it to the cross*, because the law is useful for us in the present life, when we are able to sin, and the end of this life is death. "He nailed it (he says) to the cross, for when he died, he put an end to the law. Nor, indeed, will the law any longer have a place among those who have risen again. For in accord with this we are made to be outside the law, because we pass over to those things that are to come by the type of baptism, [291] ordering our way of life by baptism." And something that is greater:

2:15 *Divesting himself of the rulers and authorities, he led them in procession, triumphing over them in himself.*

†In this place he means that *the rulers and authorities* are the opposing powers, which would never have had any power against us if we had been able not to sin in any way. "For (he says) by putting off mortality, which he took away for the common benefit of all, he also divested himself of those who used that full power against us, displaying a victory over them great and undoubted, so that even those are put to confusion for having undertaken such great toil against us in vain. From it they have been able to gain no profit, since we have passed over to a better condition so that we can no longer sin."*

The opposing powers would never have had any power if we had not admitted sinning. "Therefore, by putting off (he says) mortality, which he took away for the common benefit, he also divested himself of their full power that they used against us, working against them a victory great and undoubted, so that even those who displayed so much toil against us in vain have been put to shame. From it they had no profit, since we have come to be in a better condition, so that we no longer admit sinning."

ut ultra nec peccare possimus.'*

omnia enim coniunxit resurrectione. postquam ablati a mortalitate in incorruptione sumus effecti, efficimur quidem extra peccatum, liberamur uero et a seruitute legis; securi etiam efficimur et
5 ab omni daemonum impressione. quae cuncta sequuntur necessarie illos qui inmortales fuerint effecti, et ab omni facti fuerint
peccandi conditione securi, qui etiam diuinam gratiam custodiunt
in perpetuum in bonitatis affectum. et quoniam ostendit per illa
quae per Christum facta sunt et a legis conuersatione nos securos
10 effectos, adiecit:

> *ne ergo quis uos iudicet in esca aut potu aut parte festiuitatis aut*
> *neomeniae aut sabbatorum.*

et ostendens obseruationis horum differentiam aduersus illam
conuersationem quae secundum Christum est:

15 > *quae est umbra futurorum, corpus uero Christi.*

propemodo nihil illud esse ostendit comparationis exemplo; in
tantum illa illis quae secundum Christum sunt infirmiora esse dixit, in quantum a corpore infirmior est umbra. corpus equidem
est substantia, umbra uero solummodo solet adparere; sed et ip-
20 sa umbra, si non corpus fuerit, adparere nequaquam poterit. nam
ut fiat umbra aut uideatur, corpus id solet praestare. omnia ergo
quae in praesenti sunt et horum obseruantia, umbra sunt, si ad illa quae Christi sunt comparentur; quoniam illa quae Christi sunt
stabilita sunt, finem nullum sustinentia, eo quod inmortales et in-
25 corrupti post resurrectionem efficiemur; illa uero quae legis sunt,
in comparatione futurorum tamquam umbra sunt aliqua, eo quod
in praesentem uitam statum suum tantum obtinent. nam esca et
potus et festiuitas et neomeniae et sabbatum ad modicum tempus
custoditum pertransibit, eo quod illi qui semel mortui sunt ulte-
30 rius hanc non indigent obseruantiam; Christi uero donatio, atubi
semel coeperit, manet immobilis, nullam uertibilitatem umquam
sustinens. quod enim dixit *umbra futurorum*, hoc dicit, quoniam in
comparatione futurorum umbrae sunt ista omnia; unde ad signi-

---

2   resurrectioni *C* (*corr.*) *r*   5-6   necessario *r*   6   facti *H*   8   in (*bef.* bon.) *om*
r   10   effectos *om H*   ‖   adicit *C r*   12   neomenae *C**   16   propemodum *C*
(*corr.*) *r*   ‖   aliud (*for* illud) *H*   17   qui *C**   19   uero *om H*   ‖   solomodo *C*
24   sustinentes *C H r*   27   in praesente uitam *C** (praesenti *C* (*corr.*))   29
pertransiuit *C* H* pertransiit *r*   30   hac, obseruantia *C* (*corr.*) *r*   ‖   ut ubi *H*
r   33   ita (*for* ista) *C**

[292] For he has joined everything to the resurrection. After we have been taken away from mortality and fashioned in incorruption, we are indeed made outside sin, and we are freed also from slavery to the law. We are also made safe from every assault of the demons. These are all necessary consequences for those who will have been fashioned immortal and will have been made safe from every occasion for sinning, and they perpetually keep the divine grace in their affection for its generosity. And since Paul demonstrated by what Christ accomplished that we have been made safe from living our lives by the law, he added:

2:16 *Therefore, let no one judge you in food or drink or in a share of a feast or new moon or Sabbaths,*

And to demonstrate the difference between observing these things and their contrast to living the life that accords with Christ:

2:17 *which are the shadow of the things to come, but the body is Christ's.*

He demonstrated the former things to be all but nothing by his comparative example. Those things are as much weaker than what has to do with Christ as a shadow is weaker than a body. In fact, a body is a substance, but a shadow ordinarily merely appears. Moreover, the shadow could by no means appear by itself, if there were not a body, for the body ordinarily supplies the possibility for the shadow to come into being or be seen. Therefore, everything in the present and what we see of them are shadows, if they are compared to what has to do with Christ, since what has to do with Christ is firmly established, undergoing no end because we shall be made immortal and incorruptible after the resurrection. But what has to do with the law is like a shadow by comparison with the things to come, because it gains its position only in the present life. [293] For food and drink and feast and new moons and Sabbath, though kept for a short time, will pass away, because those who have once died will no longer need their observance. But the gift of Christ, once it shall have begun, remains unmoved, undergoing no change at all. For when Paul said *the shadow of the things to come*, he means that all those things are shadows by comparison with the things to come. Then he added *body* in connection with

ficantiam umbrae *corpus* adiecit, hoc dicens, quoniam apud Christum ueritas est perpetuitatem habens.

    nemo uos decipiat.

    hoc est, 'nemo brauium uestrum tollat.' brauium tollere dici-
tur, si is qui uictor extitit inter illos qui uicti sunt, fuerit contra
ueritatem statutus; illa ratione, quod illi qui brauia luctatoribus
dare sunt directi, id soleant facere. quasi ergo in confessionem id
deductum, quoniam hi qui in melioribus sunt tunc solent brauiis
nudari, quando a melioribus ad deteriora deferuntur.

    volens in humilitate et cultura angelorum, quae non uidit incedens,
frustra inflatus ab intellectu carnis suae.

    †eo quod per angelos lex di-
cebatur data esse, quasi ministrantibus illis in tempore quo
lex dabatur, sicut beatus Paulus dicit: *si enim quod per ange-*
los narratum est uerbum fuit fir-
mum. illi ergo qui legem custodire eos suadebant, proponebant etiam angelos indignari, si non lex fuerit custodita. deinde et humilitatem quandam simulantes ostendere properabant, quasi qui ob timorem ab obseruantia legis [non
discederent, eo quod neque angeli sustinerent legis] contemptu[m]. 'nolite (inquit) intendere illis, qui humilitatem hanc
ostendunt et uolunt angelos proponere; elatione tamen sensus
sui illa dicunt quae nesciunt,*

ἐπειδὴ δι' ἀγγέλων ὁ νόμος ἐλέγετο δεδόσθαι, ὡς ἂν διακονησα-
μένων αὐτοῦ πρὸς τὴν δόσιν (καθὼς καὶ ὁ μακάριος Παῦλος φη-
σίν· εἰ γὰρ ὁ δι' ἀγγέλων λαληθεὶς
λόγος ἐγένετο βέβαιος)· οἱ τὸν νόμον φυλάττειν αὐτοὺς ἀναπείθοντες
προεβάλλοντο τοὺς ἀγγέλους, ὡς ἂν
καὶ ἐκείνων ἀγανακτούντων, εἰ μὴ
ὁ νόμος φυλάττοιτο· εἶτα καὶ με-
τριότητά τινα δῆθεν ἐπεδείκνυντο,
ὡς ἂν δέει τῆς τοῦ νόμου φυλακῆς
οὐκ ἐξιστάμενοι τῷ μηδὲ τοὺς ἀγγέλους περιορᾶν τοῦ νόμου τὴν κατ-
αφρόνησιν. 'μὴ τοίνυν (φησὶν) τοῖς
τὴν μετριότητα ταύτην ἐπιδεικνυ-
μένοις καὶ βουλομένοις τοὺς ἀγγέλους προβαλέσθαι προσέχητε· ὑπὸ
γὰρ τύφου διανοίας λέγουσιν ἃ μὴ
ἴσασιν.'

4 aut brauium uestrum tollat (*aft* decipiat) *add C H l*   4-9 hoc est—
deferuntur *om r*   6 luctoribus *C**   9 nudare *C* H*   12 sq. Coisl. 204,
f. 154 b [Cr. vi. 325, Fr. 144] θεόδωρος. ἢ ἐπειδή, κ.τ.λ.   14 eo ... quo (*for* in
... quo) *r* ‖ qua (*for* quo) *C* quae *H*   19 eis *C* (*corr.*): *om r* ‖ προσεβάλλον-
το cod.   20-21 indignare *C* (*corr.*)   23 ὡς ἂν δὲ Cr. Fr.: txt cod.   25-28 ab
obseruantiam legis contemptu *C** et obseruantiam legis contempti *C* (*corr.*) ab
obseruantia legis contemptu *H* ad obseruantiam legis contemptae *r*   31 sensu *r*
32 nec sunt (*for* nesc.) *C* r*

the meaning of shadow, to say that the truth that has permanence is with Christ.

2:18a *Let no one deprive you,*

That is, "let no one take away your prize."[22] To take away a prize is said if one who has taken his stand as a victor should be placed contrary to the truth among those who were defeated, on the grounds that those who are appointed to give prizes to contestants have a habit of doing this. Therefore, this has been treated as an acknowledged fact, since those who are better off are usually stripped of their prize at the time when they are brought down from better to worse.

2:18b *insisting on humility and on the cult of angels, which he has not seen when advancing, puffed up to no purpose by the understanding of his flesh,*

[294] †Because the law was said to have been given through angels, inasmuch as they were ministering at the time when the law was given, as blessed Paul says (Heb 2:2): *for if the message declared through angels was valid.* Therefore, those who were trying to persuade them to keep the law were also suggesting that the angels would take offense if the law were not kept. Then they were also eager to show a kind of pretended humility, as though they were refusing to abandon the observance of the law because they were afraid to do so, since not even the angels would put up with despising the law. "Do not (he says) pay attention to those who show this humility and wish to set forth the angels; [295] yet it is by the exaltation of their un-

Since the law was said to have been given through angels, as they were ministering when it was given, as blessed Paul also says (Heb 2:2): *for if the word spoken through angels was valid.*

Those who were trying to persuade them to keep the law were setting forth the angels as though they would be vexed if the law were not kept. Then they also displayed a kind of pretended modesty, as though they were refusing to abandon the observance of the law because they were afraid to do so, since not even the angels would overlook despising the law. "Therefore, (he says) do not pay attention to those who display this modesty and wish to set forth the angels, for it is by the arrogance of their under-

---

[22] The comment more clearly reflects the Greek, καταβραβευέτω.

et ostendunt quia non iuste dicunt.'

et non tenens caput, ex quo omne corpus per tactus et connexus sub-
ministratum et coaptatum crescit incrementum Dei.

'cum conueniat uos illa sectari, quae Christi sunt; in cuius af-
5 fectum [dum] commune corpus continetur secundum submini-
stratam illis illam gratiam, illud quod secundum Deum est potestis facere incrementum.' et dein ab illis quae ante erant ostensa
facere properat exhortationem:

si mortui estis cum Christo ab elementis huius mundi, quid tam-
10 *quam uiuentes in mundo decernitis: 'ne tangas neque gustaueris neque*
contrectes'?

'si ergo sic instituti estis, quasi qui iam et commortui estis Christo et consurrexistis et extra statum istius uitae estis effecti (hoc
enim dicit *ab elementis mundi huius*); qua ratione quasi in praesenti
15 uita conuersantes patimini illos qui leges uobis statuunt et dicunt:
hoc manduca, hoc noli tangere, et alia quae huiusmodi sunt?' et
arguens uanitatem traditionis eorum:

quae sunt omnia in corruptione per abusionem, secundum mandata
et doctrinas hominum.

20 'quorum finis (inquit) corruptela est et degestio, hoc enim solet fieri in omnibus escis.' haec sunt hominum traditiones, sicut et
in superioribus dixit; non legislationem dicit *mandata et doctrinas*
hominum, sed nuperrima illorum.

quae sunt rationem quidem habentia sapientiae in religione simu-
25 *lata et humilitate, et non in parcitate corporis, non in honore aliquo*
ad satietatem carnis.

†obscurum quidem est dic-
tum. uult autem dicere, quoniam ut haec tradantur uidetur
30 quidem quod aliquam ostensionem scientiae doctorum habeat,
et quasi qui humilitatem uelint
studere eos qui erga talia oppor-

ἀσαφὲς μέν ἐστιν, βούλεται δὲ
εἰπεῖν, ὅτι τὸ ταῦτα παραδιδόναι
δοκεῖ μέν τινα τῶν διδασκόντων ἔν-
δειξιν ἔχειν γνώσεως· καὶ δῆθεν καὶ
μετριοφροσύνης βουλομένους ἐπιμελεῖσθαι τοὺς περὶ ταῦτα ἔχοντας
ἐπιδείκνυσιν, ὡς ἂν καὶ τοῦ σώμα-

---

3 in (*bef.* incr.) *add C* (*corr.*)   4-5 effectum *C H r* dum *om C H r*   10 in
mundo *om H*   12 constituti *l*   15 conuersamini *H*   18 abusione *H*   20
digestio *C* (*corr.*) *r*   21 hae *r*   22 dixit *om H*   23 nuperrimam *C** ‖ nup.
illorum *om r*   24 sed quae *r*   27 obscure *r* ‖ sq. Coisl. 204, f. 155 a [Cr.
vi. 327, Fr. 144] Θεόδωρος. ἄλλος φησίν· ἀσαφές, κ.τ.λ.   29 uidentur *C H r*
‖ τινας cod. edd.   31 habeant *C H r*

derstanding that they speak of standing that they say what they
things they do not know,* do not know."
and demonstrate that they are not speaking rightly."

2:19 *and not holding fast to the head, from which the whole body,
supplied and fitted together through sinews and joints, grows the
increase of God.*

"Since it is right for you to pursue the things that are Christ's,
by whose affection the common body is held together according
to the grace supplied to them, you are able to make that increase
that is in accord with God." And then he is eager to compose an
exhortation from what he had previously demonstrated:

2:20–21 *If you have died with Christ from the elements of this
world, why do you make determinations as though living in the world:
"You shall not touch, and you shall not taste, and you shall not
handle"?*

"If, therefore, you have been so established as though in some
way you have already both died with Christ and have risen again
with him, and have been fashioned outside the condition of that
life (for this is what *from the elements of this world* means), for what
reason do you put up with those who set up laws for you as though
you were living in the present life [296] and who say: eat this, do
not touch this, and other things of this kind?" And to condemn
the vanity of their tradition:

2:22 *which are all in corruption through abuse, according to the
commandments and teachings of humans.*

"The end of which (he says) is corruption and assimilation, for
this usually happens in all foods." These are the traditions of
humans, as he has also said above (Col 2:8). By *the commandments
and teachings of humans* he does not mean those of the law but their
more recent ones.

2:23 *These are indeed having an account of wisdom in pretended
religion and humility and not in the sparing of the body, not in any
honor for the satiety of the flesh.*

†What is said is indeed ob- This is unclear, but he wants
scure.[23] But he wants to say to say that the fact that these
that [297] the fact that these prohibitions are handed down

---

[23] So, too, is the Latin translation, which must be corrupt. Swete suggests two
ways of emending the text, and I am, in general, following the second, which
does not quite conform to the Greek.

tune habent; ostendit uero quasi quia et corpori suo parcere
nolint, et nihil honoris dignum
existiment, ut ex omnibus re-
5 pleant corpus, sed magis continent se a multis propter legis
traditionem.*

τος ἀφειδοῦντας καὶ οὐ τίμιον νομί-
ζοντας τὸ διὰ πάντων πληροῦν τὴν
σάρκα, ἀλλὰ γὰρ μᾶλλον αἱρουμέ-
νους ἀπέχεσθαι τῶν πολλῶν διὰ τὴν
τοῦ νόμου παράδοσιν.

haec autem dicebat, eo quod magna sapiebant illi super abstinen-
tia et quasi qui propter legem etiam escas contempnant. in subse-
10 quentibus arguit negotii ipsius miserabilitatem:

*si ergo consurrexistis Christo, quae sursum sunt quaerite; ubi est
Christus in dextera Dei sedens.*

†hoc est: 'miserabilis est in
comparatione uestra illa quae
15 erga ista est sollicitudo, qui iam
Christo secundum promissio-
nem consurrexistis, quos conuenit expletis his omnibus sollicitos esse de caelestibus et illam
20 quae in caelis est commorationem imitari,*

ἀντὶ τοῦ· 'ταπεινὸν πρὸς ὑμᾶς
κρινομένη ἡ περὶ τὰ τοιαῦτα σπουδή, τοὺς ἤδη τῷ Χριστῷ κατὰ
τὴν ἐπαγγελίαν συναναστάντας· οὓς
προσήκει μικρὰ τούτων ἁπάντων
φροντίζοντας τὰ ἄνω φαντάζεσθαι
καὶ τὴν ἐν οὐρανοῖς ἀπομιμεῖσθαι
δίαιταν.'

ubi Christus in dextera Dei residere dignatus est;' ut dicat: 'magnum adsecutus est honorem.' et persistens in exhortatione ipsa
adiecit:

25 *quae sursum sunt sapite, non quae super terram.*

et quoniam contrarium quodam esse modo uidebatur illis qui
super terram commorabantur dicere, ut illa saperent quae in caelis
sunt:

mortui enim estis et uita uestra abscondita est cum Christo in Deo.

---

1 instant (*for* habent) *C* (*corr.*) 2 corpore *C* 3 uoluit *r* 5-6 continens
ea multis *C* H r: txt C* (*corr.*) *g* 9 escas etiam *r* 13 sq. Coisl. 204 *l. c.* 15
istis *C* H* 18 expleto haec omnia *C H* expleta hoc o. *r* 20-21 commemorationem *C* H r* 22 habitus (*aft.* est) *add C H* 23-24 et—adiecit *om r* 24
adicit *C* 26-28 et quoniam—sunt *om H* 26 quodam ... modum *C** quendam ... modum *r* ‖ contrarium *om C* 27 esse (*bef.* comm.) *add C** ‖
dicit *r*

prohibitions are handed down seems as though it may have some demonstration of the teachers' knowledge and as though the people who are taking advantage of such things were desirous of cultivating humility. But it shows them as though they were unwilling to spare their own body and were thinking it worthy of no honor so as to satiate the body with everything, but rather were keeping themselves from many things because of the tradition of the law.*

seems to hold some proof of the teachers' knowledge. And supposedly it exhibits those who were occupied with these prohibitions to be people who want to cultivate modesty, since they do not spare the body and do not think it honorable to satiate the flesh in all respects, but rather choose to abstain from many things because of the tradition of the law.

And he said these things because they thought highly of abstinence and also somehow despised foods on account of the law. In what follows he condemned the baseness of the matter itself:

[298] 3:1 *If, therefore, you have been raised with Christ, seek those things that are above, where Christ is, sitting at the right hand of God.*

†That is, "care for those things is something base in your judgment, you who have already risen with Christ by promise, for whom it is right, since all these things have reached their end, to set your mind on heavenly things and to imitate that dwelling in the heavens,*

Instead of "zeal for such things is something base by comparison with you, who have already risen with Christ by promise, for whom it is right, having little regard for all these things, to imagine[24] the things above and to imitate the way of life in the heavens."

where Christ has been made worthy to sit at God's right hand," meaning, "has acquired great honor." And persisting in the exhortation itself, he added:

3:2 *Mind the things that are above, not the things on earth,*

And since it seemed somehow contradictory to tell those who were dwelling on earth to mind what was in the heavens:

3:3 *for you have died, and your life has been hidden with Christ in God.*

---

[24] φαντάζεσθαι, which the translator seems to have understood as φροντίζειν.

†'mortui (inquit) estis praesenti huic uitae;' hoc enim natura sustinebit. 'sed et surrexi-
stis.' etenim et hoc in Christo
5 effectum est, ut et in nobis fiat;
de quibus nulla poterit esse ambiguitas. sed incertum est hoc
interim, eo quod nec ipsum uidemus Christum. in Dei ergo
10 uirtute, qui et hoc ipsud perficiet, cum ipso Christo, qui horum est primitiae, qui interim
non uidetur; sed nec illud uidetur, quod futurum est.*
15 quid ergo?

'τεθνήκατε (φησὶν) ἤδη τῷ βίῳ
τούτῳ·' τοῦτο γὰρ ἡ φύσις δέξεται.
'ἀλλὰ γὰρ καὶ ἠγέρθητε·' καὶ γὰρ
καὶ τοῦτο ἐπὶ τοῦ Χριστοῦ, καὶ
ἀμφιβάλλειν ἔσεσθαι καὶ ἐπὶ ἡμῶν
οὐδαμῶς οἷόν τε. ἀλλὰ ἄδηλον
τέως τοῦτο ἐπεὶ μηδὲ αὐτὸν ὁρῶμεν
τὸν Χριστόν. ἐν οὖν τῇ τοῦ
θεοῦ δυνάμει τοῦ κατεργαζομένου
τοῦτο σὺν αὐτῷ τῷ Χριστῷ τῇ
τούτων ἀπαρχῇ τέως ἐστιν ἀφανὲς
τὸ ἐσόμενον.

cum Christus adparuerit uita uestra, tunc et uos cum ipso adparebitis in gloria.

'sed atubi ille de caelo adparuerit, qui est principatus inmortalis uitae uestrae, adparebitis et uos in iisdem, aeternae uitae et
20 futurae gloriae fruitionem adsecuti.' sic et eiciens illam conuersationem quae sub lege est per illa quae futura sperantur, egreditur
iterum ad exhortationem; et ostendens quoniam non solum inconueniens illis sit peccare, eo quod non sint sub lege, sed multo magis eis aptum sit illa quae ueritatis sunt perficere, si tamen conse-
25 quentia illis agere uoluerint quae per Christum fieri sperantur:
mortificate ergo membra uestra quae sunt super terram.

quia inmortales post resurrectionem effecti, peccare ultra non
poterimus; mortales uero sequitur ut peccent. sicuti ergo ex diuersis membris peccatorum compositum mortalem hominem subpo-
30 nit, propter quod et mortales talia agere possint. nam quod dixit:
membra quae sunt super terram, ut dicat 'actus prauos, qui solent

1-2   sq. Coisl. 204 l. c.   3   sed resurrexistis r   5   in om H   12   in (bef. Chr.)
add C H (corr.) r: v. Gk.   18   adubi C H ait ubi r   18-19   immortalitatis r
19   eodem (for iisdem) C (corr.)   30   possunt C*   31   quo (for qui) C* quos
C (corr.) H r b

†"You have died (he says) to this present life," for nature will undergo this. "But you have also risen." Indeed, even this has been brought about in Christ, [299] so that it may also be brought about in us. About this there will be no possibility of doubt. But it is for the time being unclear because we do not see Christ himself. Therefore, it is in the power of God, who will also perfect this, together with Christ, who is the first-fruits of these things and who is not seen, that what is to come is for the time being invisible.*[25] What then?

"You have already died (he says) to this life," for nature admits of this. "But you have also been raised." For indeed, even this is the case for Christ, and it is in no way possible to doubt that it will come to be also for us. But this is unclear for the time being, since we do not see Christ. Therefore, it is in the power of God, who brings this to completion with Christ himself by the firstfruits of these things, that what will be is for the time being not apparent.

3:4 *When Christ shall appear, your life, then you also shall appear with him in glory.*

"But when he who is the first principle of your immortal life shall appear from heaven, you shall also appear in the same things, having acquired the enjoyment of eternal life and of the glory that is to come." And so, discarding that way of life that was under the law by the things to come that are hoped for, he again digresses to exhortation. And showing that it is not right for them to sin not only because they are not under the law, but that it is much more suitable for them to accomplish what belongs to truth, if indeed they should be willing to act in accord with what is hoped will take place through Christ:

3:5a *Therefore, put to death your members that are on earth,*

Because we shall be made immortal after the resurrection, we shall no longer be able to sin. Therefore, in place of this he sets forth a mortal human as composed of sins, just as though of different members, [300] because mortals could do such things. For his statement *members that are on earth* means "perverse deeds,

---

[25]Swete (1:299) notes that the "translator has again missed the idea and construction of the Gk." The translation given here follows Swete's conjectural reconstruction of the Latin.

mortales sequi, et secundum praesentem hanc uitam, dum in terra
conuersamur, adnasci.' quae sunt ergo haec membra?

fornicationem, immunditiam, passionem, concupiscentiam malam
et auaritiam, et idolorum custodiam.

5 notandum quoniam et 'idolorum culturam' *auaritiam* uocauit,
quasi quia ad similitudinem eius a Deo possit diuellere. nec enim
possibile est, ut quis se a prauis abstineat negotiis qui plus habendi
cupiditate tenetur. et ostendens quoniam non potest quis ista sine
noxa facere:

10 *propter quae uenit ira Dei super filios diffidentiae.*

'non solum peccare nos absurdum est, sed et resurgentes, si de-
liquerimus, poenam necessariam expectabimus.'

in quibus et uos ambulastis aliquando, quando uiuebatis in iisdem.

'dudum quidem agebantur ista a uobis, quando cum praesenti
15 uita totam spem uestram demetiebatis, nihil amplius expectantes.'

nunc uero deponite et uos omnia.

'iam ultra secundum illa uiuere uos non conuenit, qui maxime
in inmortalitate eritis, in qua consistere nunc in forma existima-
mini; sed discedendum nobis est ab his omnibus.' a quibus? illis:

20 *iram, indignationem, malitiam, blasphemiam, turpiloquium ex ore*
uestro. nolite mentiri in inuicem.

non dixit 'alterutrum,' sed *in inuicem;* hoc enim uult dicere,
quoniam 'non est iustum, ut cum simulatione uobis narretis, sed
sincera mente.' et quoniam *membra* nominauit actus seipsum se-
25 quentes, adiecit:

exspoliantes uos ueterem hominem cum actibus suis.

'ex integro (inquit) conuenit uos mortalem deponentes hominem deponere etiam et actus consequentes illum.'

et induentes uos nouum, qui renouatur in agnitionem secundum
30 *imaginem eius qui creauit eum.*

5   et *om r*   6   quasi quae a similitudine Dei eos *r*   ‖   diuelli *C (corr.)*   7
abst. *om H*   ‖   negotiis abst. *r*   8   ut ostenderet *r*   ‖   istam *C*   11   nos
pecc. *r*   11-12   derelinquerimus *C* H delinquerimus *C (corr.)*: txt *r*   14   ista
om r   15   dimetiebatis *C (corr.) r* demecieratis *H (corr.) r*   16   deponere *H*   19
a quibus illis *om r*   21   mentire *C*   ‖   in *om H*   23   simulationem *C*   24
sed ipsum sequens *C* id ipsum persequens *C (corr.)*: txt *H r*   25   adicit *r*   29
et *om H*

which habitually follow mortals and arise in this present life while we are living on earth." What, then, are these "members"?

3:5b *fornication, impurity, passion, evil desire, and avarice and the keeping of idols.*

It should be noted that he called *avarice* also "the cult of idols," inasmuch as it can similarly drive people away from God. For it is impossible that anyone should keep himself from perverse occupations who is held fast by greed. And to demonstrate that no one can do those things without punishment:

3:6 *Because of these things the wrath of God comes upon the sons of disobedience,*

"Not only is it out of place for us to sin, but we shall also expect the necessary punishment when we rise again, if we have transgressed."

3:7 *among whom you also walked once when you were living in the same things,*

"Those things, indeed, used to be done by you formerly, when [301] you used to measure your entire hope by this life, expecting nothing more."

3:8a *But now put off also yourselves all these things,*

"It is no longer right for you to live in accord with those things, especially because you will exist in immortality in which you are considered now to stand in type. Rather, we must withdraw from all these things." From what things? These:

3:8b-9a *wrath, anger, malice, slander, foul language from your mouth. Do not lie to one another,*

He did not say "tell one or another lie," but *do not lie to one another.*[26] For he wants to say this: "it is not right for you to talk to one another falsely, but you should do so with a genuine mind." And since he gave the name *members* (3:5) to deeds, following his own logic, he added:

3:9b *since you are stripping off the old man with its deeds,*

"Renewed, (he says) it is right for you in putting off the mortal man also to put off the deeds that accord with him."

3:10 *and since you are clothing yourself with the new man, who is being renewed in knowledge according to the image of him who created him,*

---

[26]The Latin fails to make this meaning clear, but see Swete's comment (1:301).

'consentanea agere debetis huic nouo quem induti estis, renouati et facti secundum imaginem eius, qui istius recreationis uobis auctor extitit;' ut dicat, 'Christi.'—'itaque enim inconuertibi-
les manere uos in bono per omnia conuenit, hoc enim uobis in futuro aderit, pro possibilitate in praesenti uita.' deinde et ostendens
huius recreationis bonum:

ubi non est gentilis et Iudaeus, circumcisio et praeputium, barbarus
et Scytha, seruus et liber, sed omnia et in omnibus Christus.

'atubi (inquit) in illa transformatione constiterimus, ultra non
erit discretus Iudaeus et gens. nam circumcisionis et praeputii discretio interempta est, eo quod inmortales sumus effecti, ita ut neque barbarus neque liberi neque serui poterint ulterius perspici,
Christo in omnibus adparente, ad cuius similitudinem inmortalitate potiemur.' illos ergo qui hunc modum induti sunt hominem et
in illo sunt effecti secundum formam, quae conueniunt obseruare?

induite ergo uos ut electi Dei, sancti et dilecti, uiscera misericor-
diae, benignitatem, humilitatem, mansuetudinem, patientiam.

per omnia ista suasit, ut illam quae inuicem est caritatem in nobis custodiamus; caritatis enim opera sunt ista. et permanens in
hisdem adicit:

sufferentes in inuicem et donantes uobis ipsis, si aliquis ad aliquem
habet querelam.

et hoc exemplo illis suadere cupiens adiecit:
sicut et Christus donauit uobis, ita et uos.

deinde ad instaurationem dictorum:
super omnia haec caritatem.

compendiose dicere uult: 'caritatis habete diligentiam, ex qua
horum directio efficitur.' et ostendens caritatis utilitatem adiecit:
quae est uinculum perfectionis.

4   hic *C* H*: *txt C (corr.)*   8   scitta *C* schita *H*   10   gentilis *C (corr.) r*   14   hoc
modo *C (corr.)* huiusmodi *r*   15   obseruare *om H* conuenit obseruari *C (corr.)*:
txt C* r   18   in *om H**   23   hoc *om r*   ‖   adicit *C* ait *r*   25   staurationem *H*
confirmationem *r*   26   omnem hanc *C H r*   27   hebete *C**   ‖   et (*aft.* dilig.)
add C* H   28   caritatem *H*   ‖   adicit *C r*

"You ought to do what accords with this new man you have put on, [302] since you have been renewed and made according to the image of him who has come to be the founder for you of that new creation"—meaning Christ. "And so it is surely right for you to remain unchangeable in the good in all respects, for this will be actually present to you in the future in proportion to its possibility in the present life." Then also to demonstrate the good of this new creation:

3:11 *where there is not Gentile and Jew, circumcision and uncircumcision, barbarian and Scythian, slave and free, but Christ is all things and in all.*

"When (he says) we shall have been established in that transformation, there will no longer be a difference between Jew and Gentile. For the difference between circumcision and uncircumcision has been done away with because we have been made immortal, so that neither barbarian nor free people nor slaves may be capable any longer of being discerned, since Christ appears in all of them, Christ in whose likeness we shall acquire immortality." Therefore, what practices should those observe who have put on this kind of man and have been fashioned in him in type?

3:12 *Put on, therefore, as the chosen of God, holy and beloved, the innermost parts of compassion, kindness, humility, meekness, patience,*

In all respects he recommended those things so that we might keep among us love for one another. For those things are the works of love. And continuing with the same points, he adds:

3:13a *bearing with one another and pardoning each other if anyone has a complaint against someone,*

And wishing to persuade them by the following example, he added:

3:13b *just as Christ has pardoned you, so you, as well.*

[303] Then to bind up[27] his words:

3:14a *above all these things [put on] love,*

He wants to say succinctly: "Be diligent in love, by which guidance in these things is brought about." And to show the benefit of love he added:

3:14b *which is the bond of perfection.*

---

[27] The Latin is *instaurationem* (repetition or renewal). Swete (1:303) suggests that the gloss in the manuscript (*confirmationem*) is "probably correct" and that the Greek original may have been ἐπισφίγγων.

'etenim in future (inquit) saeculo atubi constiterimus, in illud quod praeceptum est adhuc (id est, caritatem) conligati in inuicem permanebimus, nullam separationem ulterius sustinentes; tenebimur uero in concordia illa quae erga alterutrum est.' idipsum aliter:

et pax Dei uigeat in cordibus uestris.

sciens enim beatus Paulus quoniam caritate manente omnia facile diriguntur, illis uero quae contraria sunt tenentibus nihil efficitur ex illis quae conueniunt; omni loco de caritate multum facere uidetur sermonem. et ostendens exhortationis utilitatem adiecit:

in qua et uocati estis in uno corpore; et grati estote.

'unum quoddam corpus per regenerationem facti sumus; euidens est autem quoniam in pace sumus uocati, eo quod nec corpus sibi ipsi umquam scit dissentire. ita conuenit uos, ob hanc ipsam uocationem operibus gratos habitu uos ostendi, custodientes illam erga alterutrum integram uocationem'

uerbum Dei inhabitet in uobis ditissime.

'sit (inquit) in uobis larga Christi doctrina.' quemadmodum?

in omni sapientia docentes et admonentes uos ipsos.

'sic illorum assiduam habete memoriam, ut semper uideamini uos ipsos docere et admonere, consequentem ei[u]s doctrinae conuersationem ostentantes. sic enim erit ditissima in uobis eius doctrina, si semper haec eadem cogitantes in uestro sensu eam custodire uolueritis.' nam quod dixit, *in omni sapientia,* 'sapientiam' uocauit illum intellectum qui de istis est.

psalmis hymnis et canticis spiritalibus, in gratia cantantes in cordibus uestris Deo.

'semper (inquit) in sensu uestro gratias agite Deo pro quibus talia praestitit uobis.'

et omne quodcumque facitis in uerbo aut in opere, omnia in nomine domini Iesu, gratias agentes Deo et Patri per ipsum.

1 inquit in fut. *r* ‖ adubi *C*H* ubi *C (corr.) l* 2 caritati *C* 4-5 alterutrum (*for* aliter) *r* 10 uidetur *om H* ‖ adicit *C r* 14 uos *om C (corr.)* 17 domini *C* Christi *r* ‖ habitet in u. abundanter. Ditissime sit, &c. *r* 19 ipsos *om H* 21 eis *C H r* 28 qui (*for* pro quibus) *C (corr.)*

"Indeed, in the age to come (he says), when we shall have been established in what has been prescribed at the present time, that is, love, we shall remain continually bound together with one another, undergoing no longer any separation, but we shall be held fast in concord with one another." Putting the same thing another way:

3:15a *And may the peace of God flourish in your hearts,*

For since blessed Paul knows that when love remains all things are easily guided, but that when contrary things hold sway nothing of what is right is accomplished, he plainly everywhere composes long discussions of love. And to show the benefit of the exhortation he added:

3:15b *in which also you have been called in one body; and be thankful.*

"We have been made, as it were, one body through rebirth, and it is clear that we have been called in peace, because [304] no body exists that ever can be in disagreement with itself. So it is right for you because of this very calling to be shown thankful in works by your manner of life, keeping that calling unimpaired with respect to one another."

3:16a *Let the word of God*[28] *dwell in you richly*

"Let the teaching of Christ (he says) be bounteous among you." How?

3:16b *in all wisdom, teaching and admonishing one another*

"Have so constant a memory of those things that you may always be seen to teach and admonish one another, displaying a way of life that accords with his teaching. For in this way his teaching will be extremely rich among you, provided you are willing to keep it in your mind by always pondering these same things." For when he said *in all wisdom*, he meant by "wisdom" that understanding that comes from those things.

3:16c *with psalms, hymns, and spiritual songs, singing in thanks to God in your hearts.*

"Always (he says) give thanks to God in your mind, because he has bestowed such things on you."

3:17 *And everything whatsoever you do in word or in deed, all things in the name of the Lord Jesus, giving thanks to God and the Father through him.*

---

[28]Swete argues that this is the correct reading, but Theodore's comment might suggest that he has adopted the other manuscript reading, Χριστοῦ.

'et quodcumque (inquit) aut dicitis aut agitis, intuentes in Christo, debitam gratiarum actionem Deo et Patri referre prope-rate pro illis quae per Christum uobis sunt praestita.' etenim *psal-mis et hymnis et canticis spiritalibus* gratiarum actionem uocauit,

5 hoc dicens quoniam 'in cordibus uestris gratias agite Deo;' aut 'quodcumque aut dicitis aut agitis, sic et dicite et agite, sicut iu-stum est dicere illos qui talia adsequi digni sunt habiti.' haec enim est uera gratiarum actio. deinde et in hac parte imitans illa quae ad Ephesios scripserat, uertitur ad specialem consolationem, dicens:

10 *mulieres, uestris subditae estote uiris, sicut conuenit, in Domino.*

uxores iubet subditas esse maritis.

uiri, diligite uxores uestras et nolite exacerbari ad illas.

uiros admonet diligere suas uxores, nec moleste erga illas uer-sari.

15 *filii, oboedite parentibus per omnia; hoc enim est beneplacitum in Domino.*

suadet filiis ut audiant parentibus.

patres, nolite exacerbare filios uestros, ut ne animo deficiant.

patribus suadet, ut non ex superfluo tristent filios suos.

20 *serui, oboedite per omnia dominis uestris qui sunt secundum car-nem, non ad oculum seruientes sicut hominibus placentes, sed in sim-plicitate cordis timentes Dominum; omne quodcumque facitis ex animo operamini quasi Domino et non hominibus, scientes quoniam a Domino accipietis retributionem hereditatis; Domino enim Christo seruientes.*

25 iubet et seruos oboedire suis dominis, inspicientes in illam mer-cedis remunerationem, quae a Deo illis tribuetur pro fideli serui-tio. 'et ita facite sicut et iustum est facere eos qui a Deo mercedem sibi tribui expectant, non sicut hominibus seruientes sed sicut illi, a quo et mercedum uicem sibi tribui expectant.' quibus adicit:

30 *qui enim nocuerit, recipiet quodcumque nocuit; et non est persona-rum acceptio apud eum.*

quoniam etsi aliqua ratione iniuste eos domini adfligere uolue-rint, non erunt innoxii, Deo scilicet nullius personam aut acci-

---

2 Christum *C (corr.)*   3 in (*aft* etenim) *add r*   3-4 psalmos et hymnis et canticis spiritalibus *C* H* psalmos et hymnos et cantica spiritalia *C (corr.)*   10 uestrae *C H*   ‖ conueniat *H*   12 exacerbare *C* H*   15 fili *C**   ‖ est *om H*   17 obaudiant *C (corr.) r*   18 exaceruare *C**   19 superflue (*for* ex superfluo) *r*   24 enim *om C (corr.) H (corr.)*   26 remunerationum *C (corr.)* ‖ retribuetur *H*   29 mercedem uicissim *r*

"And whatever (he says) you either say or do, fixing your gaze on Christ, be eager to render due thanks to God and the Father for what has been bestowed on you through Christ." In fact, [305] he called the giving of thanks *psalms and hymns and spiritual songs*, meaning "in your hearts give thanks to God" or "whatever you either say or do, both say and do it in such a way as is right for those who have been held worthy of acquiring such things." For this is the true giving of thanks. Then also copying in this part of the letter what he had written to the Ephesians, he turns to specific exhortations, saying:

3:18 *Wives, be subject to your husbands, as is fitting, in the Lord.*

He orders wives to be subject to husbands.

3:19 *Husbands, love your wives, and do not provoke*[29] *them.*

He admonishes husbands to love their wives and not to behave toward them in a troubling way.

3:20 *Children, obey parents in everything, for this is well-pleasing in the Lord.*

He urges children to listen to parents.

3:21 *Fathers, do not anger your children, so that they may lose heart.*

He urges fathers not to treat their children too harshly.

3:22–24 *Slaves, obey in all things your masters who are according to the flesh, not serving for the eye as pleasing humans, but in singleness of heart fearing the Lord; everything whatsoever you do, [306] work from the mind as to the Lord and not to humans, knowing that you will receive from the Lord the recompense of inheritance, for you are serving the Lord Christ.*

He also orders slaves to obey their masters, while having regard to that rewarding payment bestowed by God for faithful service. "And so act as is right for those who do so expecting the reward to be bestowed on them by God, not serving as though for humans, but as though for the one from whom they are also expecting the requital of rewards to be bestowed on them." To which he adds:

3:25 *For whoever harms will receive whatever harm he did, and there is no acceptance of persons with him.*

Since if the masters even for some reason will have been willing to injure them unjustly, they will not be blameless, since

---

[29] *Exarcerbari*, used here to translate πικραίνεσθε, but the same verb is used in verse 21 to translate ἐρεθίζετε.

piente aut reuerente.

domini, quod iustum est et aequum seruis praebete, scientes quia et uos habetis dominum in caelis.

et dominis suadet, ut illud quod condecet seruis tribuant, humane erga eos agentes et in opere dilectionem illis praebentes, et
diligentiam illorum adhibentes prout potest; et ueniam illis delinquentibus tribuant, cum eos peccare acciderit. hoc enim dicit *iustum et aequum*, non ut aequales sibi eos esse existiment; qui fieri enim potest, quando, ut seruiant serui et cum integro seruiant
affectu, tanta scripsit? suadet autem et his haec custodire illa memoria, quia et ipsi sint sub domino illo qui in caelis est. et iterum
ad commune uertitur:

orationi insistere, uigilantes in ea cum gratiarum actione.

praecepit sobria mente assidue orare, atque gratias agere pro illis bonis quae sibi sunt a Deo tributa.

orantes simul et pro nobis, ut Deus aperiat nobis ostium uerbi loqui mysterium Christi, propter quod et ligatus sum; ut manifestem illud, sicut conuenit me loqui.

'sed et pro nobis (inquit) orate ut cooperetur nobis Dominus et
docere omnes possimus illam quae in Christum est ueritatem, pro
quo et adligatus sum ad praesens.'

in sapientia ambulate ad eos qui foris sunt, tempus redimentes.

'cum prudentia (inquit) illis qui extranei sunt a fide discepta-
mini, praesens tempus, prout conueniens est, probe uobis aduten-
tes;' eo quod ille qui comparat aliquid, ad usum suarum utilita-
tum illud comparat. hoc uoluit dicere, quoniam 'praesenti tempore, in quo mala abundant, pro uirium uestrarum qualitate illud
agere properate quod uobis expedire cognoscitis; ut et mercedes
uobis in futurum pro hac conuersatione prouideatis, pro quibus
ita in praesenti saeculo commoramini.'

sermo uester semper in gratia sale sit conditus, scire quemadmodum uos conueniat unicuique respondere.

'properate (inquit) illa quae prudentiae semper plena sunt proloqui, considerantes quod oporteat unicuique dare responsum;

---

1   reuertente *C**   6   possit *C (corr.)*   7   accederit *C**   ‖   dicit *om H*   8
qui *om r*   10   effectu *C**r   12   exhortationem *(bef.* uertitur) *add C (corr.)* ad
communionem u. et ait *r*   17   manifestum *H*   23   cum prudentiam quit *C**
24   probe *om r*   29   pro hanc conuersationem *C**

it is obvious that God neither accepts nor respects the person of anyone.

4:1 *Masters, furnish what is just and fair to slaves, knowing that you also have a Master in the heavens.*

And he urges masters to bestow what is fitting on slaves, acting humanely toward them, bestowing affection on them in deed, and displaying care for them as far as possible. And let them bestow pardon on them when they transgress, since it will fall to their lot to sin. For he says *just and fair* not so as to think that the slaves are equal to the masters, for how could this be when he wrote that slaves should serve and should serve with complete affection? But he urges the masters, too, to keep in their memory the fact that they are themselves under that Master who is in the heavens. And again he turns to a general exhortation:

[307] 4:2 *Concentrate attention on prayer, being vigilant in it with thanksgiving,*

He instructed them to pray constantly with a sober mind and to give thanks for those good things God has bestowed on them.

4:3–4 *praying at the same time also for us, that God may open for us a door for the word, to speak the mystery of Christ, because of which I have also been bound, that I may reveal it, as it is right for me to speak.*

"But pray (he says) also for us that God may work with us and that we may be able to teach everyone the truth that is in Christ, for which I have also been bound at present."

4:5 *Walk in wisdom toward those who are outside, purchasing the time.*

"With intelligence (he says) dispute with those who are foreign to faith, using the present time for yourselves honestly, as is right." This is because the person who buys something buys it for the benefit of his own needs. He meant that "in the present time in which evils abound, be eager to do what you recognize to be profitable for you in accord with the character of your powers, so that by this way of life you may provide for yourselves for the future also the rewards for which you dwell this way in the present age."

4:6 *Let your speech always be in grace, seasoned with salt, to know how it is right for you to answer each one.*

"Be eager (he says) to utter words always filled with wisdom, keeping in mind what answer you ought to give to each one,

conuenienter disputantes, ita ut magis donum aliquod ex uestris sermonibus perfici uideatur.' his adiecit:

illa quae circa me sunt omnia nota uobis faciet Tychicus, carissi-
mus frater et fidelis minister et conseruus in Domino; quem misi ad uos
5 *ad hoc ipsum, ut cognoscat ea quae circa uos sunt et consoletur corda*
uestra, cum Onesimo fideli et carissimo fratre qui est ex uobis. omnia
uobis nota facient, quae hic aguntur.

'quoniam omnia uobis nota faciet Tychicus illa quae erga me sunt, propterea a me directus est cum Onesimo fratre, qui a uo-
10 bis uenerat, ita ut nota uobis faciant quae erga nos sunt, et oblec-
tent uos per suum aduentum, omnia quae hic aguntur manifesta facientes uobis.'

salutat uos Aristarchus concaptiuus meus, et Marcus, nepos Bar-
nabae, de quo mandatum accepistis ut, si uenerit ad uos, suscipiatis
15 *illum.*

deinde salutat eos ab Aristarcho, quem et captiuum suum edicit esse, utpote conligatum sibi; et a Marco quem nepotem dicit esse Barnabae, de quo etiam mandatum eos accepisse edicit ita ut ue-
nientem eum recipiant. dicit autem eos accepisse mandatum non
20 ab alio aliquo, neque a se, sed ab illo qui praedicauerat eis euangelium; neque a se, quod fieri non poterat eo quod necdum uiderat eos.

et Hiesus qui dicitur Iustus, qui sunt ex circumcision; hi soli sunt
cooperarii mei in regnum Dei, qui facti sunt mihi solatium.
25 salutat eos et ab Hiesu, qui cognominatur Iustus. hos solos di-
cit de illis qui ex circumcisione crediderunt cooperarios sibi esse in euangelio; quos et solatium sibi praebuisse dixit.

salutat uos Epaphras qui ex uobis est, seruus Christi, semper sol-
licitus pro uobis in orationibus, ut stetis perfecti et repleti in omni uo-
30 *luntate Dei. testimonium* (inquit) *perhibeo ei, quoniam habet multum*
zelum pro uobis et pro his qui in Laodicia sunt et eis qui in Hierapoli.

1 aliquid C* r aliquot H 2 adicit C 8-9 quoniam—sunt *om* r 10 faciet
C* faciat H: *txt* C (*corr.*) r [faciet—adventum *ad calc.* C] 13 nepus H 16
concaptiuum C (*corr.*) 20 ab (*bef.* alio) *om* H* ‖ enim *add* C H r 21 non
om C* 23 Iesus, Iesu r 30 haberet r 31 eorum C H

disputing rightly so that some gift may all the more be seen accomplished by your words." To this he added:

[308] *4:7–9 Tychicus, dearly beloved brother and faithful minister and fellow servant in the Lord, will make known to you all those things that concern me. I have sent him to you for this very purpose, so that he may let you know the things that concern us and may encourage your hearts, along with Onesimus, the faithful and dearly beloved brother, who is from you. They will make known to you all the things that are done here.*

"Tychicus will give you all the news concerning my affairs, because I have directed him together with the brother Onesimus, who had come from you, to give you news concerning our affairs and to make you glad by their coming, making clear to you everything that is happening here."

4:10 Aristarchus, my fellow prisoner, greets you, as does Mark the nephew of Barnabas, concerning whom you have received the command that if he should come to you, you should welcome him.

Then he gives them greetings from Aristarchus, whom he also declares to be his fellow prisoner, since he is in bonds together with him—and also from Mark, who he says is Barnabas's nephew and about whom he declares that they have received a command to welcome him if he comes. And he says that they have received the command not from someone else and not from him but from that person who [309] had preached the gospel to them—not from him, because that could not have happened, since he had not yet seen them.

4:11 Also Jesus who is called Justus [greets you]; they are from the circumcision. They alone are my fellow workers for the kingdom of God, who have been an encouragement to me.

He sends them greetings also from Jesus, who is named Justus. He says that only these from those of the circumcision who have believed are his fellow workers in the gospel. He also said that they furnished him with encouragement.

4:12–13 Epaphras greets you, who is from you, a servant of Christ, always anxious for you in prayers that you may stand perfect and fulfilled in every will of God. I bear witness (he says) *to him that he has much zeal[30] for you and for those in Laodicea and for those in Hierapolis.*

---

[30] "Zeal" (ζῆλον) instead of πόνον.

deinde salutat eos ab Epaphra qui praedicauit eis, dicens multam sollicitudinem habere eum de eis, ita ut oret ut firmi per-
maneant in fide. dicit enim apostolus testimonium perhibere ei,
quam multam sollicitudinem de illis habet, necnon et illis qui in
5 Laodicia sunt et in Hierapoli.

salutat uos Lucas, medicus carissimus, et Demas.

salutat eos et a Luca medico, qui euangelium conscripsit, necnon et Dema. deinde scribit eis:

salutate eos qui in Laodicia sunt fratres, et Nympham, et eam quae
10 *in domo eorum est ecclesiam.*

'salutate (inquit) illos qui in Laodicia sunt, et Nympham cum
omnibus suis, qui in domo eius sunt.' et adiecit:

et cum lecta fuerit epistola apud uos, facite ut et in Laodicensium
ecclesia legatur; et quae ex Laodicia est, ut et uos legatis.
15 itaque hanc epistolam, postquam ab illis fuerit lecta, legi et in
Laodicensium ecclesia praecipit. dicit autem eis, ut et illam quae
ex Laodicia est legant; non quia ad Laodicenses scribit. unde quidam falsam epistolam ad Laodicenses ex nomine beati Pauli con-
fingendam esse existimauerunt; nec enim erat uera epistola. aesti-
20 mauerunt autem quidam illam esse, quae in hoc loco est significa-
ta. apostolus uero non 'ad Laodicenses' dicit, sed 'ex Laodicia,'
quam illi scripserant ad apostolum, in qua aliqua reprehensionis
digna inferebantur; quam etiam hac de causa iussit apud eos legi,
ut ipsi reprehendant se ipsos discentes quae de illis sunt scripta. et
25 propter hoc, ut datur intellegi, neque scribere eis dignum existimauit, sed illam quae ad Colossenses scripta erat legi et apud illos
praecepit, ut bonorum pariter suscipiant monitionem et in melius
conuertantur; eo quod sic reprehensi sunt a Paulo, ut neque scripta ab eo percipere digni fuissent existimati. deinde dicit ad eos:

3 eis *C H r* 5 Laodecia *C (corr.)* 9 et *(aft.* sunt*) add C H* ‖ Nimpham
C Nymfam *H* 12 in do *(for* in domo*) C** ‖ adicit *C r* 16 ecclesiam *C**
22 scripserunt *r* ‖ reprehensione *l b* 24 dicentes *C* H r* 26 scripserat
C (corr.) 27 praecipit *C* r* 28 sint *H* ‖ et *(for* ut*) C* H r*

Then he sends them greetings from Epaphras, who preached to them, saying that he had so much anxiety about them that he is praying for them to persevere steadfast in the faith. Indeed, the apostle says that he bears witness to him as to how much anxiety he has for them, and for those in Laodicea and Hierapolis:

4:14 *Luke, the dearly beloved physician, greets you, and Demas.*

He sends them greetings also from Luke the physician, who composed the Gospel, and also from Demas. Then he writes to them:

4:15 *Greet those who are brothers in Laodicea, and Nympha, and the church which is in their[31] house.*

[310] "Greet (he says) those who are in Laodicea and Nympha together with all her people in her house." And he added:

4:16 *And when the letter will have been read among you, have it read also in the church of the Laodiceans, and the letter from Laodicea, see that you also read it.*

And so he orders that this letter, after they have read it, be read also in the church of the Laodiceans. And he tells them that they should read also the letter from Laodicea, but not because he is writing to the Laodiceans. [311] This is why some people have thought that a spurious letter to the Laodiceans was forged in the name of blessed Paul, for that was not a genuine letter. And there are some people who think that this is the letter indicated in this verse. But the apostle does not speak of a letter *to* the Laodiceans but of one *from* Laodicea, which they had written to the apostle. In it there were set forth some things deserving censure, and it was for this reason that he ordered it to be read by them, so that by learning for themselves what the Laodiceans had written they might censure the letter themselves. And because of this, granted this understanding, he did not think it appropriate to write to the Laodiceans but ordered that the letter he had written to the Colossians should be read also by the Laodiceans, so that they likewise might be put on warning and undergo a change for the better. The fact is that they were so censured by Paul that they had not been thought worthy even to earn a letter from him. Then he says to the Colossians:

---

[31]This appears to be a mistake of the copyist. The text should read "her house."

dicite Archippo: 'uide ministerium quod accepisti in Domino, ut illud impleas.'

deinde dicit eis dicere Archippo, ut ministerium quod accepit, impleat.

5   †ut autem est ex litteris exi-   ὡς ἔστιν ἐκ τῶν προγεγραμμέ-
stimare, apud Laodicenses idem   νων εἰκάσαι, παρὰ Λαοδικεῦσιν ὄν-
degens ministerium doctrinae   τι καὶ τὴν διακονίαν ἐγκεχειρισμέ-
commissum habere uidebatur.*   νῳ τῆς διδασκαλίας.

his adiecit:

10   *salutatio mea manu Pauli.*

quoniam sua manu salutationem scripsit, dicens:

memores estote uinculorum meorum.

hoc est: 'ad meam imitationem etiam pro ueritate pati nolite pigere.' adiecit consuete conclusionem:

15   *gratia uobiscum. amen.*

in hac designatione epistolae consummationem fecisse uidetur.

---

3   dicite (*for* dicere) *r*   5   eis (*for* est) *r*   5-6   existimari *C (corr)*   5   Coisl. 204, f. 161 a [Cr. vi. 339, Fr. 144] Θεόδωρος. ἄλλος δέ φησιν· ὡς ἔστιν, κ.τ.λ.   6 id est (*for* idem) *C* H r*   8   διακονίας (*for* διδασκ.) cod. edd.   9   adicit *C r*   14 consuetam *r*   16   explicit ad Colosenses incipit ad Tesalonicenses [Thesal. *H*] (*aft* uidetur) *add C H*

4:17 *Tell Archippus: "See to the ministry that you have received in the Lord, that you may fulfill it."*

Then he tells them to say to Archippus that he should fulfill the ministry that he received.

†And, as it is possible to suppose from what is written, he seemed to be living with the Laodiceans and to have the ministry of teaching entrusted to him.*	As can be conjectured from what was written above, he is with the Laodiceans and entrusted with the ministry of teaching.

To this he added:

4:18a *Greetings with my hand, Paul's.*

Since he wrote the greetings with his own hand, saying:

4:18b *Be mindful of my chains.*

[312] That is, "do not be displeased even at suffering for the truth by imitating me." He added his customary ending:

4:18c *Grace be with you. Amen.*

With this conclusion he is seen to have ended the letter.

THEODORUS MOPSUESTENUS IN EPISTOLAM B. PAULI AD THESSALONICENSES I

ARGUMENTUM

BEATUS apostolus Paulus peragrabat diuersas ciuitates praedicans fidem quae in Christo est. diuina uero monitus reuelatione
uenit ad ciuitates Macedoniae, exinde uero uenit et Thessalonicae,
sicut est cautissime discere ex libro Actuum apostolorum; prae-
5 dicauit ergo inter ceteras etiam Thessalonicensibus pietatis doctrinam. aduersariis uero super hoc indignantibus, euenit ut multa
pateretur idem apostolus in eadem ciuitate Thessalonicensium; in
qua et illi qui crediderunt Christo multa sustinuerunt mala a contribulibus suis, ita ut cogeretur beatus Paulus a Thessalonica di-
10 scedens Athenis proficiscere. pertimescens uero de illis qui crediderant, ne forte atrocitate aduersariorum inpulsi a suo deuia-
rent proposito, coactus Timotheum misit ad eos, simul ut et illa
quae gesta fuerant disceret, et fidelium animos tam sua praesentia confirmaret, quam etiam exhortatione salubri moneret in fide
15 persistere; qui etiam cuncta illa implens quae sibi a beato apostolo fuerant iniuncta, reuersus ad eum nuntiabat ei quoniam multa
ab aduersariis perpessi mala sustinuerint, nec a fide discesserint.
inter cetera uero nuntiauit ei esse aliqua apud illos quae corrigi de-

2 munitus *H* 3 Thessalonicam *r* 6 et uenit (*for* euenit) *r* 7 id est (*for*
idem) *C* r* 10 Athenas *r* ‖ proficisci *r* 14 ex oratione (*for* exhort.) *r*
15-16 Paulo (*for* ap.) *H* 16 nuntiauit *H r* 17 in aduersariis *C** in aduersis
C (*corr.*)

THEODORE OF MOPSUESTIA ON BLESSED PAUL'S FIRST LETTER TO THE THESSALONIANS

THE SETTING

[1] The blessed apostle Paul used to travel through different cities preaching faith in Christ. But it was when he was advised by divine revelation that he came to the cities of Macedonia and in this way came also to Thessalonica, as one can quite accurately learn from the book of the Acts of the Apostles (Acts 16:10; 17:1). Thus, he preached the teaching of true religion to the Thessalonians as well as in other cities. But since there were opponents indignant because of this, it came about that the apostle suffered many things in the city of the Thessalonians. There, too, those who believed in Christ endured many evils from their compatriots, so that blessed Paul was compelled to leave Thessalonica and set out for Athens (Acts 17:1–15). And since he feared [2] for those who had believed, that they might perhaps be driven by the fury of the opponents to stray from the message he had set forth, he was compelled to send Timothy to them both to find out what had happened and to strengthen the souls of the faithful as much by his presence as by his admonition with sound exhortation that they should persevere in faith (1 Thess 3:2). And when Timothy fulfilled all the tasks the blessed apostle had enjoined upon him, he returned and reported to Paul that the Thessalonians, suffering at the hands of the opponents, were still enduring many evils and yet would not depart from faith. But among other things Timothy reported to Paul that there were some things among them that ought to be put right. Learning

beant. haec a Timotheo discens apostolus scribit ad Thessalonicenses primam hanc epistolam, laudans eos, quod in aduersis rebus ita fideliter sustinuerunt pro fide decertantes; instruit uero eos
et de illis quae apud eos inconuenienter geri cognouerat. omnia
5 uero euidentissime ex illa interpretatione quae per partes fit, melius agnoscere poterimus.

　　*Paulus et Siluanus et Timotheus ecclesiae Thessalonicensium in
Deo Patre et domino Iesu Christo; gratia uobis et pax.*

　　hoc in loco uel maxime ostendit quoniam

10 †*gratia uobis* sic ponit, sicuti nos　τὸ χάρις ὑμῖν οὕτως τίθησιν ὥσπερ
in praescriptione epistolae sole-　ἡμεῖς τὸ χαίρειν ἐν ταῖς προγραφαῖς
mus 'salutem' ponere ; posuit　τῶν ἐπιστολῶν εἰώθαμεν· τὸ ἐν θεῷ
uero et *in Deo Patre*, sicut et nos　πατρὶ τεθεικώς, ὡς καὶ ἡμεῖς τὸ ἐν
scribere consueuimus 'in Do-　κυρίῳ γράφομεν.
15 mino.'*

　　*gratias agimus Deo semper pro omnibus uobis, memoriam uestri
facientes in orationibus nostris sine intermissione, memores operis fidei uestrae et laboris et caritatis et patientiae spei domini nostri Iesu
Christi coram Deo et patre nostro.*

20 　　'et *gratias* (inquit) *agimus pro uobis*, et sine intermissione pro
uobis oramus; memores enim sumus illa quae pro fide estis operati, et laborem illum quem pro caritate Christi sustinuistis, et tolerantiam quam in tribulationibus ipsis operibus ostendistis, propter illa quae sperantur uobis adesse pro illa quam in Christo habe-
25 tis fide.' bene autem adiecit *coram Deo et patre nostro;*
†ut dicat quoniam 'placite Deo　ἵνα εἴπῃ ὅτι 'ἀρέσκοντες τῷ θεῷ
ista facitis;' ita ut uideatur fides　ταῦτα ποιεῖτε·' ὥστε φανῆναι θεοῦ
illa quae erga Christum est et　ἀρέσκειαν τὴν ἐπὶ τὸν Χριστὸν
affectus ille secundum Dei fieri　πίστιν καὶ τὴν περὶ αὐτὸν διάθεσιν.
30 uoluntatem.*

　　et docens eos quoniam iuste omnia pro fide sustinent:

---

5 auitissime *C** aptissime *C* (*corr.*) auidissime *H r*　10　in (*bef.* gratia) *add*
C* H　‖　aq. Coisl. 204, ff. 161 a, 162 a [Cr. vi. 340, 344, Fr. 145 : cf. note]
Θεόδωρος. τὸ δὲ χάρις, κ.τ.λ. (f. 161).　11　ἐπιγραφαῖς (f. 162).　12–14　τὸ
δὲ ἐν θ. π. (om. τεθεικώς), ἐν κυρίῳ (om. τὸ) (f. 161).　16 uestram *H*　24
sperant *r*　26　placita *l*　‖　Coisl. 204, f. 162 b [Cr. vi. 345] ἔμπροσθεν, κ.τ.λ.
ἵνα εἴπῃ, κ.τ.λ.　27　faciatis *r*

these things from Timothy, the apostle writes this first letter to the Thessalonians, praising them because they so faithfully endured in adverse circumstances by contending for faith.[1] But he also instructed them about those things he had discovered were not being fittingly managed among them. And we shall be better able to recognize all these things with full clarity from the detailed interpretation.

1:1 *Paul and Silvanus and Timothy, to the church of the Thessalonians, in God the Father and the Lord Jesus Christ. Grace to you and peace.*

In this place especially he shows that

†he puts down *grace to you* just as we are accustomed to put down "greetings" in the salutation of a letter. And he also put down *in God the Father*, just as we have become accustomed to write "in the Lord."*	He puts down *grace to you* just as we are accustomed to put down "greetings" in the salutations of letters. And he put down *in God the Father*, just as we, too, write "in the Lord."

[3] 1:2-3 *We give thanks to God always for all of you, making mention of you in our prayers without ceasing, mindful of the work of your faith and toil and love and endurance of hope in our Lord Jesus Christ before God and our Father,*

"And (he says) *we give thanks for you*, and we pray for you without ceasing. For we are mindful of those things you have done for faith and that toil you have endured for the love of Christ and the fortitude in afflictions you have displayed by your very deeds, because what you are hoping for is present to you in return for your faith in Christ." And he rightly added *before God and our Father*

†to mean, "you are doing these things in a way pleasing to God," so that faith in Christ and affection for him may be seen to come about in accord with the will of God.*	To mean that "you are doing these things as those who are pleasing God," so that faith in Christ and affection for him may appear pleasing to God.

And teaching them that they should endure all things justly for faith:

---

[1] We might translate "for *the* faith," but it is not clear that Theodore distinguishes between the faith *that* Christians believe and the faith *by which* they believe.

scientes fratres dilecti a Deo electionem uestram, quoniam euange-
lium nostrum non fuit ad uos in uerbo tantum, sed in uirtute et Spiritu
sancto et in satisfactione multa.

'scitis (inquit) quemadmodum electi estis (hoc est, quemadmodum ad fidem accessistis), non puris sermonibus nostris credentes;

†nec enim dicebamus tantum, οὐκ εἴπομεν μόνον, ἀλλὰ καὶ θαύ-
sed et miracula ostendebamus* ματα ἐπεδειξάμεθα.

magna et gloriosa per uirtutem Spiritus effecta, ex quibus con-
firmabimini de his quae a nobis ad uos dicebantur. itaque ergo
quae cognouistis cautissime, illa cum iustitia retinete, neque ab illis quae uobis accidunt malis a uestro discedatis proposito.' deinde
et ex illis quae erga se erant suadens illis adiecit:

sicut scitis quales fuerimus in uobis propter uos.

'sed et illa quae erga nos sunt optime recognoscitis, in quibus et
ipsi fuerimus pressuris, et quanta fuerimus uestri causa perpessi.'
bene quia posuit *propter uos*, ut eos magis ad reuerentiam inuitaret; si enim ipsi pro illis patiebantur, multo magis illi ipsi pro se
pati iusta ratione debebant. quod et cum ueritate dictum maius
eos adhortare uidebatur; amabilis etenim tunc est uel maxime laus,
quando non fuerit gratis alicui tributa, sed ex praecedentibus negotiis animum ad uirtutes soleat excitare.

et uos imitatores nostri facti estis et Domini.

nam quia dixerat et illa quae ab illis erant similiter extitisse,
ualde poterat suadere eos ut in hisdem permanerent. unde optime et *Domini* faciens commemorationem maiorem fecisse uidetur
exhortationem, siquidem in pressuris non solum imitare apostolos
uidentur, sed et ipsum Dominum. deinde et manifestam faciens
imitationem quam dicit:

suscipientes (inquit) *uerbum in tribulatione multa cum gaudio*
Spiritus sancti.

'passus (inquit) est Dominus pro nobis, per crucem salutem
nobis expediens. et ipsi pro illa fide quae in eum est tribulationem
sustinentes, ut sciatis et nos et Deum imitasse; quoniam illa quae

---

5 ad deum (*for* ad f.) *r* 7 Coisl. 204, f. 163 a [Cr. vi. 346] οὐκ εἴπ. φησὶν μ.,
κ.τ.λ. 8 ostend. *om r* 11 retinere *C** ‖ pro (*for* ab) *C* (*corr.*) 13 adicit
C r 20 adhortari *r* 24 sim. erant *r* 25 inde iidem (*for* in hisd.) *r* 28
uidetur *C H r* ‖ facit *r* 29 cum (*for* quam) *r* ‖ dicat *C* 30 in m.
trib. *H* 32 p. est inquit *C* 34 et (*bef.* Deum) *om C* (*corr.*)

1:4–5a *knowing, brothers beloved of God, your choice, that our gospel was not with you only in word but in power and in the Holy Spirit and in much assurance,*

[4] "You know (he says) how you have been chosen, that is, how you have drawn near to faith, not merely by believing our words; †for we not only spoke, but we also displayed miracles,* We not only spoke, but we also displayed miracles. great and glorious, accomplished by the power of the Spirit. By them you were confirmed in what we were saying to you. And so, then, hold fast with righteousness to those things you have come to know quite accurately, and may you not depart from your purpose because of those evils that have happened to you." Then, persuading them also on the basis of his own conduct, he added:

1:5b *just as you know what kind of people we were among you for your sake.*

"Moreover, you recognized quite well our circumstances, by which we were ourselves hard pressed, and how much we suffered for your sake." The reason he rightly put down *for your sake* was to induce them all the more to respect. For if Paul and his companions were suffering on their behalf, they were much more themselves obliged for good reason to suffer for Paul and his companions. The fact that what he said corresponded with the truth would have appeared to encourage them all the more. For praise is especially welcome when it is given someone not for nothing but on the basis of things that have actually happened, and it usually rouses the soul to virtues.

1:6a *And you became imitators of us and of the Lord,*

For because he had said that their attitude stood out in a similar way, he was quite able to persuade them to persevere in the same behavior. For this reason, quite effectively also mentioning *of the Lord*, he is seen to have composed a greater [5] exhortation, if indeed when hard pressed they are seen to imitate not only the apostles but also the Lord himself. Then to make the imitation of which he is speaking obvious:

1:6b *receiving* (he says) *the word in much affliction with much joy of the Holy Spirit,*

"The Lord (he says) suffered for us, achieving salvation for us by the cross. And you are yourselves enduring affliction for faith in him, so that you may know that you have imitated both us and God, since you have endured those distressing sufferings this way

tristia erant ita sustinuistis cum gaudio, non grauiter illa ferentes
quae uobis accidebant, sed bono animo fuistis ob illa bona quae
hinc uobis retribui expectantur.'

†et bene adiecit dicens *Spiritus*　καλῶς δὲ προσέθηκεν τὸ πνεύματος
5 *sancti;* nec enim erat aliter gau-　ἁγίου. οὐ γὰρ ἦν ἑτέρως ἐνταῦ-
dere illos qui ad praesens trista-　θα λυπουμένους χαίρειν ὑπὲρ τῶν
bantur pro illis quae necdum ui-　οὐ φαινομένων, εἰ μὴ τὰ ὑπὸ τοῦ
debantur, nisi illa miracula quae　πνεύματος γενόμενα θαύματα βε-
a Spiritu fiebant firmam illis fi-　βαίαν αὐτοῖς παρεῖχεν τῶν μελλόν-
10 dem de futuris praepararent*;　των τὴν πίστιν.

ut ad illas uirtutes inspicientes facile possint ferre illa, quae in
praesenti tristitiae plena esse uidebantur. et augens in laudem eorum illa quae ad exhortationem illorum illis ipsis poterunt conuenire:

15　*ita ut fieretis forma omnibus credentibus in Macedonia et Achaia.*
'uos enim inspicientes illi qui in Macedonia sunt et Achaia,
et credunt et sustinent persecutionem, erubescentes ne dissimiles
uobis in hoc saeculo uideantur.' et quemadmodum formae extiterunt illorum qui se non uiderant?

20　*a uobis enim diffamatum est uerbum Domini non solum in Mace-*
donia et Achaia, sed et in omni loco fides uestra quae ad Deum exiuit.

†uerbum Dei hoc in loco non　λόγον κυρίου ἐνταῦθα οὐ τὴν
fidem dicit, nec enim fides ab il-　πίστιν λέγει, οὐ γὰρ ἡ πίστις ἀπ'
lis accepit principium ; 'sed om-　αὐτῶν ἔλαβεν τὴν ἀρχήν· ἀλλ' ἀντὶ
25 nes (inquit) cognouerunt quan-　τοῦ 'πάντες ἔγνωσαν ὅσα ὑπὲρ τῆς
ta pro fide passi estis, et omnes　πίστεως ἐπάθετε, καὶ πάντες ὑμῶν
fidei uestrae firmitatem miran-　τὸ βέβαιον θαυμάζουσιν τῆς πίσ-
tur, ita ut et alteros adhorten-　τεως, ὥστε καὶ προτροπὴν ἑτέροις
tur.*'　γενέσθαι τὰ ὑμέτερα.'

30　et abundantius illa ipsa constringens, ait:
ita ut non necesse habeamus loqui aliquid; ipsi enim de nobis ad-
nuntiant qualem introitum habuimus ad uos, et quomodo conuersi estis
ad Dominum a simulacris seruire Deo uiuo et uero et expectare filium

---

1 tristitia *C**　4 sq. Coisl. 204, f. 163a [Cr. vi. 346] καλῶς δέ, κ.τ.λ.　5
erit *H*　7　qui (*for* quae) *r*　‖　ὑπὸ πνεύματος Cr.　11　facile ferre p. *C r*　20
defamatum *C H*　22　sq. Coisl. 204, f. 163 b [Cr. vi. 348, Fr. 145] Θεόδωρος.
ἄλλος φησίν· λόγον, κ.τ.λ.　31　non *om C**　32　habuerimus *C r*

with joy, not bearing what happened to you heavily; rather, you were of good cheer because of those good things expected to be bestowed on you for this reason."

†And he rightly added *of the Holy Spirit*, for there was no other way those who were distressed in the present for the sake of those things not yet seen could rejoice, unless those miracles accomplished by the Spirit should provide them with a steadfast faith in the things to come,*	He rightly added *of the Holy Spirit*, for there was no other way those who were distressed in the present for the sake of things unseen could rejoice, unless the miracles that took place by the Spirit should provide them with a steadfast faith in the things to come.

so that by looking at those works of power they might be able easily to bear what in the present seemed filled with distress. And by praising them, elaborating the points that by the facts themselves were able to suit the exhortation he was giving them:

1:7 *so that you became an example to all the believers in Macedonia and Achaia.*

[6] "For, by looking at you, those in Macedonia and Achaia both believe and endure persecution, blushing lest they should appear unlike you in this age." And how did they come to be examples for those who had not seen them?

1:8a *For from you the word of the Lord has been published abroad not only in Macedonia and Achaia but also in every place your faith that is in God has gone forth,*

†By *word* of God in this place he does not mean the faith, for the faith did not receive its beginning from them. "But everyone (he says) has come to know how much you have suffered for faith, and everyone marvels at the steadfastness of your faith so that your example encourages others."*	By *word of the Lord* here he does not mean the faith, for the faith did not receive its beginning from them. But this is instead of "Everyone has come to know how much you have suffered for faith, and everyone marvels at the steadfastness of your faith so that your affairs are also an encouragement to others."

And binding these points together at greater length, he says:

1:8b-10 *so that we do not have the need to say anything. For they proclaim of us what sort of entrance we had to you and how you turned to the Lord from idols to serve the living and true God and to await*

eius de caelis, quem suscitavit ex mortuis, Iesum, qui eripiet nos ab ira uentura.

'nec enim indigemus ubicumque fuerimus aliquid de uobis dicere, eo quod cognita sunt omnibus illa quae erga uos facta fuerunt, ita ut nulla sit inuidia referentibus, quemadmodum suscepti sumus a uobis cum celeritate (hoc enim dicit *qualem introitum habuimus ad uos*); et quemadmodum nostris placitis doctrinis, discessistis quidem a simulacrorum cultura, recognouistis uero uestrum dominum, qui et uere uiuit et est Deus uerus; credidistis autem et illis quae de Iesu dicta sunt uobis, quoniam et a mortuis resurrexit ut omnes nos, qui in eum credimus, ab expectata liberet poena, et quoniam de caelo ueniet omnia nobis beneficia praestans.' bene autem primum dixit aduentum eius de caelo, deinde resurrectionem, et quidem cum ordine id secundum esse uideretur, eo quod ad fidei confirmationem illud uel maxime erat dignum, quod de caelo sit in fine saeculi cum magna adpariturus gloria.

†notandum est autem, quoniam in simulacrorum abdicatione Deum et 'uiuum' et 'uerum' esse adseruit, ut e contrario ostendat simulacra neque uiuorum neque uerorum esse deorum, sed tantum quia falso nomine id dicatur. igitur ubicumque uocem hanc inuenerimus, scire nos conuenit quoniam neque de Patre ad interceptionem dici possit Filii, neque de Filio ad interceptionem dici possit Patris; similiter et Patrem et Filium Deum apud omnes pios esse creditum.*

ἐπισημαντέον δὲ ὅτι ἐν τῇ τῶν εἰδώλων ἀναχωρήσει τὸν θεὸν καὶ ζῶντα καὶ ἀληθινὸν προσεῖπεν, πρὸς ἀντιδιαστολὴν ἐκείνων· ὥστε ὅπου ποτ' ἂν τὴν φωνὴν εὑρίσκομεν ταύτην, εἰδέναι χρὴ ὅτι μήτε ἐπὶ πατρὸς εἰς ἀναίρεσιν λέγει υἱοῦ, μήτε ἐφ' υἱοῦ εἰς ἀναίρεσιν πατρός, ὁμοίως ἀληθινοῦ πατρὸς καὶ υἱοῦ παρὰ τοῖς εὐσεβέσιν.

dicens autem ista ad exhortationem eorum, memoratur ultra et illa quae secundum se sunt; illa uel maxime dicens quae illi ipsi apud

---

10 qu. res. a mort. *r* 12 omnibus *C r* 16 cum magna *om r* 17 ἐπισημαντέον δὲ φησὶν ὅτι cod. edd. 29 interceptationem *r*

his Son from the heavens, whom he raised from the dead, Jesus, who will rescue us from the wrath to come.

"For we do not need to say anything about you, wherever we go, because everyone has come to know what you have done, [7] so that there is no envy of those who report[2] how we were quickly received by you (for this is what he means by *what sort of entrance we had to you*) and how, when our teachings found favor, you indeed left the worship of images behind, and you recognized as your Lord the one who both truly lives and is the true God. And you also believed in what was told you about Jesus and that God raised him from the dead so that all of us who believe in him might be freed from the punishment we expected and that he will come from heaven to bestow all benefits on us." And he rightly spoke first of his coming from heaven, then of the resurrection—even though, of course, his coming from heaven is plainly second in order—because the former was especially fitting to confirm faith, since he will appear with great glory from heaven at the end of the age.

†And it must be noted that in the abandonment of images he asserted that God is both *living* and *true*, so that by contrast he might demonstrate that the images are of gods neither living nor true but are only said to be gods by a false name. [8] Therefore, whenever we find this word, it is fitting we should know that it cannot be said of the Father to the exclusion of the Son, nor of the Son to the exclusion of the Father, but that it is believed by all godly people that both the Father and the Son alike are God.*

And it must be noted that in the abandonment of idols he declared God to be both *living* and *true* by contrast with them, so that wherever we find this word, it is necessary to know that it means neither the Father to the exclusion of the Son, nor the Son to the exclusion of the Father, since the Father and the Son are alike true according to godly people.

And in saying these things to exhort them, he goes on to mention also what concerns himself. And he speaks especially of what they

---

[2]Theodore apparently means that they are reporting what is already known and so are of no importance and cannot be the object of envy.

se facta esse sciebant, ut et illa quae de se erant cum illis commemorans, suaderet illis non cedere tristitiae:

*ipsi enim nostis, fratres, introitum nostrum qui fuit ad uos, quoniam
non inanis fuit, sed ante passi et contumeliis affecti, sicut nostis, in*
5 *Philippis, fiducialiter egimus in Deo nostro loqui ad uos euangelium
Dei in multo agone.*

'scitis (inquit) quoniam non absolute nec fortuitu ad uos uenimus; sed licet multa mala Philippis passi fuerimus, tamen non de-
fuimus ad uos uenientes cum fiducia praedicare uobis pietatem, et
10 quidem cum multa nobis ab exteris incumberet necessitas.' bene
autem dixit quia *in Deo fiducialiter gessimus;* ut ne sibi uideretur
ipsam fiduciam adscribere, ideo eam cooperationi diuinae adscripsit. demirandum est autem et illud quod dixit apostolus: *quoniam
non fuit inanis introitus noster,* eo quod multa erat ante passus; qua-
15 si ergo qui in passionibus ipsis lucrum sibi conlocet, dum nihil existimat se inane facere, quando et pati eum contigerit ob pietatem.
et quoniam dixit passiones, dicit etiam et doctrinae modum:

*consolatio enim nostra non ex errore, neque ex immunditia, neque
ex dolo; sed sicut probati sumus a Deo ut crederetur nobis euangelium,*
20 *sic loquimur, non tamquam hominibus placentes, sed Deo, qui probat
corda nostra.*

'consolationem' hoc in loco uocat doctrinam. 'sic enim uos (inquit) docuimus,—non sicut illi solent docere, qui seducere uolunt
illos quos docent, aut aliquid illis referre non uerum, qui et do-
25 lo saepe illa quae dicunt occultant—sed dogma uerum et plurima praeditum cautela et munditia, quod et probatis nobis creditum esse uidetur; unde et ipsi probatione consequenter persteti-
mus agentes, sicque illud cum fiducia dicentes, sicuti conueniebat
eos facere, qui non hominibus placere student, sed Deo, qui men-
30 tem cautissime cognoscit.' haec uero uniuersa coniunxit, ut ostendat quoniam iusta ratione fiducia est abusus; persistens uero referre illa quae secundum se sunt ad edocendos eos edicit:

---

3 quod (*for* qui) *C* H* 4 tanta (*for* ante) *H* (*corr.*) 6 sollicitudine (*for* agone) *r* 8-9 destimus *C** destitimus *C* (*corr.*) desumus *H*: *txt r* 10 a dextris
(*for* ab ext.) *r* 18 consolatione enim nostra non ex sermone *H* 22 consolationem uel exhortationem *r* 23 docuimus inquit *H** 26 quod et probabitis
nobis cr. nobis e. u. *C* H* quod et probabiliter nobis cr. e. u. *C* (*corr.*) quod
et probabitis et nobis cr. e. u. *r* 27 probationem *C* 27-28 perstitimus *C*
(*corr.*) 31-32 docere (*for* referre) *H*

knew for themselves took place with respect to him, so that by mentioning what happened to him with them he might persuade them not to give way to their distress:

2:1–2 *For you yourselves know, brothers, our entrance that was to you, that it was not in vain, but though we had before suffered and been treated with insults, as you know, at Philippi, we acted boldly in our God to speak to you the gospel of God in much struggle.*

"You know (he says) that it was not simply or accidentally that we came to you, but, granted that we had suffered many evils at Philippi, we did not fail to come to you with boldness to preach true religion to you, even though much difficulty pressed hard upon us from those outside." And he rightly said *we acted boldly in God*, lest he should seem to assign that boldness to himself, since, indeed, he assigned it to divine cooperation. Also to be admired is the fact that [9] the apostle said *our entrance was not in vain*, because he had previously suffered many things. Therefore, it is as though he placed his gain in the sufferings themselves, since he thought he was doing nothing in vain when it happened that he also suffered on behalf of true religion. And since he spoke of sufferings, he also speaks of the manner of his teaching:

2:3–4 *For our encouragement is not from error, nor from impurity, nor from deceit, but just as we have been approved by God so that the gospel might be entrusted to us, so we speak, not as those pleasing humans, but God, who tests our hearts.*

In this place he calls his teaching *encouragement*. "For (he says) we taught you this way—not as those usually teach who want to lead their pupils astray or to tell them something not true, and who often disguise what they say with deceit—but it is true doctrine provided both with extreme exactness and with purity that is seen to have been entrusted to us, since we have been tested. This is why as a consequence of the testing we have ourselves also remained steadfast in what we do and so speak our message with boldness, just as it should be fitting for those to do who are eager not to please humans, but God, who knows the mind with the greatest exactness." And he joined the whole of this together so that he might show that he employed boldness with good reason. And continuing to report his own circumstances to teach them, he declares:

nec enim aliquando in uerbo adulationis fuimus, sicut ipsi scitis.

'e contrario etenim dicebamus quod illi qui pie uiuere cupiunt, tribulationes praesentis uitae sunt passuri.' bene autem adiecit *sicut scitis;* illos ipsos testes suorum uerborum producere properat.

5 *neque in occasione auaritiae.*

'neque ad quaestum respeximus.' et hoc dicens non adiecit ultra *sicut scitis*, sed

Deus testis.

iusta ratione uitae suae Deum testem est abusus quasi plus ido-
10 neum.

neque quaerentes ex hominibus gloriam, neque a uobis neque ab aliis.

'sed neque respeximus aliquando qualiter adquiramus laudem, aut a uobis aut ab aliis aliquibus.' cautissime enim posuit *non quae-*
15 *rentes;* hoc est, 'non auspicantes hoc, nec hanc habentes actus nostri intentionem; hoc enim est quod a nobis fieri conuenit, ut ne intuitu gloriae humanae aliquid faciamus. nam nec ad nostrum crimen poterit peruenire, cum illa faciamus quae conueniant cum lege diuina, si nos ab hominibus gloria fuerit subsecuta.'

20 *cum possimus oneri esse, sicut Christi apostoli.*

†hoc ad illud reddidit quod dixerat, *neque in occasione aua-ritiae;* magis enim erat ut et habentes potestatem quasi aposto-li illa quae ad usus necesse habebant sibi acciperent, nec hoc uoluissent accipere.*	τοῦτο πρὸς τὸ οὔτε ἐν προφάσει πλεονεξίας ἀπέδωκεν· μεῖζον γὰρ ἦν τὸ καὶ ἔχοντας ἐξουσίαν ὡς ἀποστόλους τὰ πρὸς τὴν χρείαν λαμβάνειν, μηδὲ τοῦτο ἑλέσθαι.

sed facti sumus quieti in medio uestro.

hoc est, 'omni mediocritate et humilitate sumus abusi, nolentes
30 graues aliquibus uideri.'

sicuti si nutrix foueat suos filios, sic desiderantes uos complacemus participare uobis non solum euangelium Christi, sed nostras ipsorum

---

8 testis est d. *r* 9 testem deum *C* teste deo *r* ‖ usus *r* 9-10 idoneo *r* 11 omnibus (*for* hom.) *C** 12 illis (*for* aliis) *C* H* 14 a, ab *om C* H* ab *bef.* al. *add C* (*corr.*): *txt r* 15 hoc ausp. *C r l* 21 sq. Coisl. 204, f. 164 b [Cr. vi. 349] τοῦτο πρός, κ.τ.λ. 22 occansione *C** 28 uestri *C* (*corr.*) *H* uestrum *r* 29 usi *r* 32 participari *C* (*corr.*)

2:5a *For we were not at any time in a word of flattery, as you yourselves know,*

[10] "Indeed, on the contrary we were speaking because those who desire to live a godly life are destined to suffer the afflictions of the present life." And he rightly added *as you know*; he is eager to bring them forward as witnesses of his words.

2:5b *nor for an opportunity for greed,*

"Nor have we looked for financial gain." And in saying this he no longer added *as you know*, but

2:5c *God is the witness,*

With good reason he employed God as a witness to his life, as more suitable.

2:6 *nor seeking glory from humans, neither from you nor from others,*

"Moreover, we never looked for how we might gain praise either from you or from anyone else." Indeed, he quite carefully put down *not seeking*, that is, "not undertaking this, nor having this as the motive for what we did. For this is what is right for us to do, so that we may do nothing by considering human glory. For when we do what accords with the divine law, no accusation could consequently be made against us if glory from humans should follow us."[3]

2:7a *although we could have been for a burden as apostles of Christ,*

†He referred this to what he had said (2:5), *nor for an opportunity* [11] *for greed*. For it was greater that those who had authority as apostles to receive for themselves what they necessarily held to be for their needs should be unwilling to receive this.*

He referred this to (2:5) *nor by a pretext for greed.* For it was greater that those who had authority as apostles to receive what was for their needs not to choose this.

2:7b *but we became gentle*[4] *in your midst,*

That is, "we employed all moderation and humility, unwilling to seem a burden to any."

2:7c-8 *just as if a nurse should cherish her own children, so longing for you, we are well pleased to share with you not only the gospel of*

---

[3] See Swete's note (2:10): "The Ap. disclaims merely the *desire* of popularity."
[4] Reading ἤπιοι rather than νήπιοι.

animas, quoniam carissimi nobis facti estis.

uult equidem dicere quoniam 'tantum longe sumus ut pondus tribulationum grauiter feramus, ita ut in illis malis cum multo desiderio uos docere festinaremus; libenter pro uobis supponentes etiam animas nostras, eo quod fortiter uos diligebamus et affectu integro erga uos tenebamur.' demiratione uero dignum illud quod uolebat comprobauit prolati exempli qualitate; nam et matribus consuetudo est ut suis filiis suum lac cum multa celeritate praebeant, existimantes se adiuuare, cum filios suos lactare potuerint. 'nutricem' uero hoc in loco matrem dixit quae filios suos nutrit, et hoc euidenter ostendit per illa quae adiecit dicens, *si foueat filios suos.* deinde et quod magis augere eius poterat intentionem, eo quod nihil ab illis accipere uoluerit:

memores enim estis, fratres, laboris nostri et lassitudinis; nocte enim et die operantes ad hoc, ut ne grauemus quemquam uestrum, praedicauimus [in uobis] euangelium Dei.

'scitis et ipsi quantum sustinuimus laborem, ut ne graues uobis esse uideremur pro nostra necessitate. persistebamus enim, et non solum in die erga uestram doctrinam occupari uidebamur, nec poteramus per totum diem operi insistere, ita et ut sufficere nobis potuissemus.' et pro omnibus his illorum ipsorum utitur testimonio et Dei:

uos (inquit) *testes estis et Deus, quam sancte et iuste et sine querela uobis qui credidistis fuimus; sicut nostis, quomodo unumquemque uestrum tamquam pater filios suos obsecrantes uos et consolantes.*

utitur quidem illorum ipsorum testimonio, eo quod ipsi sciebant qualiter eos ad instar patris patienter obsecrabat, et consolabat super accidentibus illis tristitiis, deprecans eos non discedere a fide. memoratus est autem et Dei, quia dixit, *sancte et iuste et sine querela uobis qui credidistis;* apud quem maxime de his cauta cognitio haberi uidebatur.

1 facti *om* H   6 digna *r*   7 qualitatem *C* r*   9 adiuvari *C (corr.)*   11 illam *C (corr.) r*   ‖ sicut (*for* si) *r*   15 grauaremus *C (corr.) H r*   16 in uobis *om C H r*   18 uidemur *C** uideamur *r*   ‖ et *om C*   19 occupare *C* H*   20 et (1°) *om r*   ‖ sufficeret *C* H*   22 et *om C* r*   24 adfuimus *r*   27 ab (*for* ad) *H*   ‖ obsecrabatur *C**   27-28 consolabatur *C (corr.) r*   28 accedentibus *C r*   31 habere *C H r*

Christ[5] but our own souls, since you have become dearly beloved to us.

Surely he wants to say "we are so far from bearing the weight of afflictions heavily that in those evils we were hastening with much longing to teach you, gladly placing even our own souls at your disposal because we loved you intensely and were held fast by pure affection for you." And because of the character of the example he set forth, the proof he wanted to make is worthy of admiration. For mothers usually furnish milk to their children quite quickly, supposing they are helping when they can nurse their own children. In this place he called a mother *a nurse* [12] who nurses her own children, and he clearly demonstrated this by what he said in addition: *if she should cherish her own children.* Then, as well, what could all the more reinforce his motive for being unwilling to receive anything from them:

2:9 *For you are mindful, brothers, of our toil and weariness; for working night and day for this, that we might not burden any one of you, we preached [among you] the gospel of God.*

"You know even yourselves what great toil we underwent so that we might not appear to burden you with our needs. For we kept on working not only by day but also by night, for by day we were seen working at teaching you.[6] And we were unable to keep on working all day in such a way as to be able to provide enough for ourselves." And for all of this he employs their own witness and that of God:

2:10–12a *You* (he says) *are witnesses and God, how holily and justly and without blame we were to you who believed, as you know, each one of you, as a father his own children, beseeching you and encouraging.*

He surely employs their own witness because they knew how he patiently besought them like a father and encouraged them with respect to the distressing experiences that happened, begging them not to depart from faith. And he also mentioned God, because he said *holily* [13] *and justly and without blame to you who believed.* Accurate knowledge of these things was seen to be held especially by God.

---

[5] Instead of the correct reading, "of God."

[6] Following Swete's suggestion (2:12). He interprets the text by saying: "S. Paul, Th. meant to say, made up by night work for the loss of time in the day which was occasioned by his preaching."

et testificati sumus ut ambuletis digne Deo, qui uocauit uos in re-
gnum suum et gloriam.

bene quia posuit *testificati sumus,* ita ut ostendat quoniam in
principio haec ipsa illis loquebatur, quod conueniat eos dignos ha-
5 bere actus, quibus placere possint illi qui eos uocauit in suam cognitionem cum magna futurorum promissione; pro honoris magnitudine etiam paria eos agere conuenit. et dicens sua iterum ad
illorum transit personam, quando quidem illa quae et erga se sunt
commemorans, ut eos ad reuerentiam adducat; quando uero ad
10 laudem eorum sese aptat, ut eorum alacritatem tali studio magis
suscitare uideatur:

et propter hoc et nos gratias agimus Deo sine intermissione, quo-
niam cum suscepissetis a nobis uerbum auditus Dei, suscepistis non si-
cut uerbum hominum, sed sicut est uere, uerbum Dei, qui et inoperatur
15 *in uobis qui credidistis.*

'et talia quidem erant nostra; non deerant autem et illa quae
a uobis sunt. unde et gratias agere Deo pro uobis non cessamus,
quoniam suscipientes a nobis Dei doctrinam, non sicut hominibus uobis loquentibus suscepistis, sed sicut conueniens erat susci-
20 pere eos qui diuinam suscipiebant doctrinam, quae etiam et ipsis
operibus ostenditur esse apud uos.' et quemadmodum in operibus
ostendatur dicens:

uos (inquit) *imitatores facti estis, fratres, ecclesiarum Dei quae sunt*
in Iudaea in Christo Iesu, quoniam eadem passi estis et uos a propriis
25 *contribulibus, sicut et ipsi a Iudaeis.*

'similia (inquit) passi estis illorum, qui in Iudaea crediderunt
Christo; sicut enim illi a Iudaeis multa sunt perpessi mala, sic et
uos a propriis contribulibus'—ut dicat, 'gentibus.' bene autem eos
est adhortatus, commemorans illos qui in Iudaea crediderunt, ut
30 sustineant et ipsi magnanimiter laborent, siquidem non soli contemplatione pietatis patiuntur. nam et ecclesiae integrae quae per
totam sunt Iudaeam diuersis fluctuabantur persecutionibus. unde et latius Iudaeorum explicans malitiam, ostendit hinc, quanta

---

3 quippe (*for* quia) *r* 4 principium *C** 6 onus (*for* honoris) *C* H* oneris *C*
(*corr.*) omnis *r* 9 ad hoc commemorat (*for* commemorans) *r* ‖ reuelationem
(*for* reuer.) *r* ‖ quando quidem uero *C* (*corr.*) ‖ et (*for* ad) *C*H: txt r* 10
se *r* 14 operatur *r* 16 et alia *C H* et aliorum *r: txt conj. Jacobi* 24 in (2°)
om r 27 quae (*for* sicut) *C* (*corr.*) 30 et ipsi sust. *l* ‖ ne (*for* et) *C H r* [et,
laborem *ed. Migne*]

2:12b *And we bore witness that you should walk worthily of God, who has called you to his own kingdom and glory.*

He rightly put down *we bore witness* so that he might show that he spoke these very things to them at the beginning, because it was right for them to have worthy deeds by which they could please the one who called them to knowledge of himself together with the great promise of the things to come. It was also right for them to accomplish deeds matching the greatness of the honor. And while speaking of his own affairs he passes over to their person, sometimes calling to mind his own circumstances in order to lead them to respect, sometimes applying himself to praising them in order to be seen all the more rousing their eagerness for such zeal:

2:13 *And because of this we also give thanks to God without ceasing, that when you received from us the word of the hearing of God, you received it not as the word of humans, but as it truly is, the word of God, who is also at work in you who have believed.*

"And such, indeed, were our affairs, but yours were not lacking. For this reason we do not cease also to give God thanks for you, since when you received from us the teaching of God, [14] you received it not as though humans were speaking to you but as it was right for those who were receiving divine teaching to receive it, a teaching that is shown to be among you also by the works themselves." And to say how it was shown by works:

2:14 *You* (he says) *became imitators, brothers, of the churches of God that are in Judea in Christ Jesus, since you have suffered the same things, and you from your own compatriots, just as they also from the Jews,*

"You have suffered (he says) things just like the sufferings of those in Judea who have believed in Christ. For just as they suffered many evils from the Jews, so, too, you have from your own compatriots," meaning "the Gentiles." And he rightly exhorted them, reminding them of those in Judea who believed, so that they might endure and might toil bravely, if indeed they were not the only ones suffering for observing true religion. For whole churches throughout all Judea were being driven about by various persecutions. For this reason by explaining more fully the

et qualia patiebantur ab illis qui inter illos habitabant:

qui et dominum (inquit) *occiderunt Iesum et suos prophetas, et nos persecuti sunt.*

bene in medio posuit *prophetas*, ex quibus comprobatur eo quod et Dominum sola malitia interimere usurpauerunt et apostolos; siquidem et erga suos prophetas tales extitisse uidentur. et quod his maius est:

et Deo non placent.

dein et quod odiri magis erant digni:

et omnibus hominibus sunt contrarii, prohibentes nos gentibus loqui ut saluentur.

et quidem ex hoc factum est

ut impleantur eorum peccata semper; peruenit enim super eos ira in fine.

'nihil (inquit) mirum quodcumque facere adnituntur, ita ut nihil illis deesse uideatur mali. perfectam ergo pro quibus agunt poenam ab aeterno iudice excipiant.' haec autem omnia coniunxit in personam Iudaeorum, maximeque eos iusta ratione accusans; necessarie uero in praesenti memoriam eorum faciens simul et ut ostendat quanta patiuntur fideles qui sunt in Iudaea, qui in certamine quasi medio conuersantes; scilicet ut ostendat Thessalonicenses nihil tam durum a gentibus sustinuisse, si tamen illa quae patiuntur cum illis quae in Iudaea geruntur comparare uoluerint. haec igitur omnia exhortationem Thessalonicensium posuit. quoniam uero inter cetera dixerat de suo ad eos aduentu, hinc incipit illa quae post profectionem sunt dicere, publicans pariter in his etiam suum affectum quem habet erga illos:

nos autem, fratres, desolati a uobis ad instar orphanorum ad tempus horae, facie non corde, abundantius adcelerauimus faciem uestram uidere in multo desiderio.

bene per omnia auxisse uisus est suum erga illos affectum, in eo quod dixit '*non corde* a uobis discessimus sed *facie;*' et quod ab illis ad tempus segregatus, statim cupierit eos iterum uidere. su-

1 illis (*om* ab) *C* H* illi *C* (*corr.*): *txt r*   2   uos (*for* suos) *r*   8   non deo *r*   9 odere *C* H* odire *C* (*corr.*): *txt conj. Jacobi*   13   perueniet *C* (*corr.*)   16   uero (*for* ergo) *C r*   17   excipient *C* (*corr.*) accipiant *r*   19   necessario *r*   21   quasi in m. *H*   24   omnia ad *r*   ‖   in ex. *C* (*corr.*): *txt r*   25   uero *om H*   27   quam *C**   28   autem *om r*   33   ad temp. ab illis *C r*   ‖   interim (*for* iterum) *H*

wickedness of the Jews, he shows the extent and the character of the sufferings they were experiencing from those among whom they dwelt:

2:15a *who killed* (he says) *both the Lord Jesus and their own prophets and have persecuted us;*

He rightly put down in the middle the *prophets*, from whom it is proved that they asserted their right to kill both the Lord and the apostles out of sheer malice, since they are seen to have taken such a stand toward their own prophets. And what is greater than this:

2:15b *and they are not pleasing to God;*

And then that they were all the more worthy of being hated:

[15] 2:15c-16a *and they are opposed to all people, preventing us from speaking to the Gentiles so that they may be saved,*

And, indeed, from this it came about:

2:16b *so that their sins are always being filled up; for wrath overtakes them in the end.*

"It is no wonder (he says) that whatever they strive to do is so that nothing of evil may seem to be lacking them. Therefore, they will face complete punishment for what they do from the eternal judge." And he joined all this together in the person of the Jews, condemning them as greatly as possible with good reason. And he necessarily mentions the Jews here, at the same time to show how much the faithful in Judea are suffering as though they were living in the midst of a contest and, obviously, to show the Thessalonians they had undergone nothing so harsh at the hands of the Gentiles, if at any rate they were willing to compare what they were suffering with what was being done in Judea. Therefore, he put down all these things in order to exhort the Thessalonians. And since among other things he had spoken of his coming to them, he begins from here on to speak of the events after his departure, proclaiming at the same time in his words also his own affection for them:

2:17 *But as for us, brothers, deprived of you like orphans for the time of an hour, in face not in heart, we have hastened more fully to see your face in much longing,*

In every way he is rightly seen to have magnified his affection for them, by having said we have left you *not in heart* but *in face*, and by the fact that, though separated from them for a time, he immediately wished to see them again, [16] and above all he

per omnia autem quod segregatum se *ad instar orphanorum* dixit, multum suum affectum ostendit. et quidem in superioribus dixerat quoniam 'sicut pater unumquemque uestrum obsecrabam;' sed ibi quidem paterna imago aptata esse uidebatur, in absentium uero exquisitione illud quod dixerat separatum se *ad instar orphanorum.* nam huiusmodi uel maxime absentia etiam ab ipsa necessitate coartatur, ut patrem filii requirant. et quae est huius concupiscentiae probatio?

propter quod uoluimus uenire ad uos.

et quia dixit *uoluimus,* pluraliter de se dicens, adiecit:

ego quidem Paulus et semel et bis.

et quid obstitit ?

sed impediuit nos Satanas.

†eo quod erant adiuuandi Thessalonicenses ex eius praesentia; ergo necessarie omnem nociuitatem Satanae adscripsit.* τῷ μέλλειν ὠφελεῖσθαι Θεσσαλονικέας ἀπὸ τῆς αὐτοῦ παρουσίας· ὡς ἂν ἀναγκαίως πάντων τῶν βλαβερῶν ἀνατιθεμένων τῷ Σατανᾷ.

et quoniam non uane in eorum haberetur affectu ostendit:

quae est enim spes nostra aut gaudium aut corona gloriandi? nonne uos coram domini nostri Iesu Christi estis in eius aduentu? uos enim estis gloria nostra et gaudium.

'et omne quicquid illic boni in futura expectamus die tunc quando adueniet dominus noster Iesus Christus ad examinanda uniuersa; tunc ab illis laboribus quos pro uobis sustinemus mercedem nobis ab eodem finiri expectamus.'

propter quod ultra non sustinentes, complacuimus enim nobis relinqui Athenis solis, et misimus Timotheum fratrem et ministrum Dei in euangelio Christi.

hoc ad illud reddidit quod dixerat, *uolui uenire ad uos;* 'quoniam ergo illud implere minime potui, elegi relinqui ipse solus Athenis, et mittere Timotheum ad uos.' qua ex causa?

1 autem *om r* ‖ se *om r* 4 absenti *C H r* 5 ab (*for* ad) *C* H* 6 ad (*for* ab) *C** ad ipsam necessitatem *r* 7 coartantur *C* (*corr.*) 10 adicit *C r* 14 sq. Coisl. 204, f. 166 a [Cr. vi. 352] Θεοδώρου. τῷ μέλλειν, κ.τ.λ. 20 corona (*for* coram) *C H* ‖ Christi estis *om C* 22 illi (*for* illic) *C* H: om r* 24 ob (*for* ab) *C H* ob illos labores *r* 26-27 reliqui *C** 27 soli *C* (*corr.*) 29 addixerat *r* 30 solis *C**

showed how much affection he had for them by having said that
he was separated from them *like orphans*. Of course, he had said
above (2:11) that "as a father I besought each one of you." But
there it was plainly the image of a father that was applied, while in
his consideration of them when they were absent what he said was
that he was separated from them *like orphans*. For it is especially
an absence of this kind that even from the necessity itself compels
the children to try to find their father. And what is the proof of
this desire:

2:18a *because of the fact that we wanted to come to you,*

And because he said *we wanted*, speaking of himself in the
plural, he added:

2:18b *I, indeed, Paul, both once and twice;*

And what stood in his way?

2:18c *but Satan hindered us*

He says that the hindrances of his affairs are hindrances of
Satan,[7]

| †because the Thessalonians would have been helped by his presence. Therefore, he necessarily attributed every harmful thing to Satan.* | because the Thessalonians would be helped by his presence, since all harmful things are attributed to Satan. |

And he shows that it was not for nothing that he is held fast by
affection for them:

2:19–20 *For what is our hope or joy or crown of boasting? Is it not
that you are before our Lord Jesus Christ at his coming? For you are
our boast and joy.*

[17] "And there we are awaiting everything whatsoever is good at
the day to come when our Lord Jesus Christ will come to examine all
without exception. At that time we expect the reward to be determined for us from those toils we are undergoing on your behalf."

3:1–2a *Because of this, bearing it no longer, for we agreed to be left
alone in Athens, and we have sent Timothy, the brother and minister
of God in the gospel of Christ,*

He referred this to what he had said (1:18): *I wanted to come to
you.* "Therefore, since I was by no means able to fulfill this wish,
I chose myself to be left alone in Athens and to send Timothy to

---

[7]Swete (2:16) conjecturally restores this beginning of the sentence and calls
attention to Theodore's comment on 3:4.

ad confirmandos uos et consolandos pro fide uestra, ut nemo mouea-
tur in tribulationibus uestris.

'ita ut uos confirmet exhortatione suorum uerborum et animaequiores sua praesentia faciat, ita ut non cedatis tribulationibus uicti.' 'commoueri' dicit cedi. et ostendens quoniam iusta sunt quae
dicit:

ipsi enim scitis quoniam in hoc positi sumus.

et unde sciunt?

nam quando eramus apud uos, praedicebamus uobis passuros nos
tribulationem, sicut et factum est et scitis.

'ex quibus et praedixi uobis, quando
†negotiorum impedimenta Sa-   τὴν ἀπὸ τῶν πραγμάτων ἐγκοπὴν
tanae esse impedimenta dicens*   τοῦ Σατανᾶ ἐκάλεσεν.
illorum.' et quidem et opus subsecutum est:

propter hoc et ego iam ulterius non sustinens—

iterum adsumit, illam causam dicens ob quam Timotheum miserat:

misi ad cognoscendam fidem uestram, ne forte temptauerit uos is
qui temptat, et inanis fiat labor noster.

quid ergo cognouisti illo reuertente?

nunc autem ueniente Timotheo ad nos a uobis et euangelizante no-
bis fidem et caritatem uestram, et quoniam habetis memoriam nostram
bonam, semper desiderantes nos uidere, sicut et nos uos; propter hoc
consolati sumus, fratres, in uobis in omni tribulatione et necessitate no-
stra per uestram fidem.

'quoniam autem ueniens nuntiauit nobis firmitatem quam erga
nos habetis, et quoniam memores estis nostri, semper desiderantes nos sicut et nos uos, sufficientem omnis tribulationis nostrae
habemus consolationem, nuntium illum quem de uobis cognosci-
mus.' et quemadmodum oblectabant eum illa bona quae de illis
sunt cognoscere ostendens adiecit:

quoniam nunc uiuimus, si uos statis in Domino.

'nunc uiuere nos existimamus, si uos in fide perstiteritis, uitam
nostram.' et augens illud:

---

2 istis (*for* uestris) *r*   4 faciat *om C H: txt r*   ‖ ita *om r*   5 enim (*bef.* dicit)
add *r*   10 et (1°) *om H*   12 Coisl. 204, f. 166 a [Cr. vi. 352] Θεοδώρου. τὴν
οὖν ἀπό, κ.τ.λ. (cf. notes).   14 et (*bef.* quidem) *om C* (*corr.*)   19 uester *H r*
23 et nos et uos *H**   30 oblectabantur *C* (*corr.*)   31 adicit *C r*   33 uitam
nostram *om C* (*corr.*)

you." For what purpose?

3:2b-3a *to strengthen you and to encourage you for the sake of your faith, so that no one would be shaken in your afflictions.*

"So that he may strengthen you by the exhortation of his words and may make you calm by his presence, so that you may not yield, conquered by afflictions." By being *shaken* he means yield. And to show that what he says is just:

3:3b *For you yourselves know that we have been placed for this.*

And from what do they know it?

3:4 *For when we were with you, we foretold you that we would suffer affliction, as it has both happened and you know.*

[18] "From what I foretold you when [I was with you], †meaning that the hindrances   He called the hindrance of af- of his affairs are hindrances of   fairs that of Satan.
Satan.*

And, indeed, the actual fact followed close after:

3:5a *Because of this even I, no longer bearing it,*

He repeats his statement about the reason he had sent Timothy (3:1-2):

3:5b *I sent to find out about your faith, lest by chance he who tempts should have tempted you, and our toil should become in vain.*

Therefore, what did you find out when Timothy returned?

3:6-7 *But now since Timothy has come to us from you and has told us good news of your faith and love and that you have our good memory, always longing to see us, just as we do you, because of this we have been encouraged, brothers, in you in every affliction and difficulty of ours through your faith,*

[19] "And since, when he came, Timothy reported to us the steadfastness you have toward us and that you are mindful of us, always longing for us as we for you, we have sufficient encouragement in all our affliction—the news we have found out about you." And to show how finding out those good things about them delighted him, he added:

3:8 *since now we live, if you are standing firm in the Lord.*

"Now we think we live, if you should stand unchanged in faith. This is our life." And to elaborate this:

quam (inquit) *gratiarum actionem possumus Deo retribuere pro uobis super omni gaudio quo gaudemus propter uos coram Deo uestro?*

'sic enim nostra existimamus illa bona quae uestra sunt, ut quia talia audiuimus de uobis Timotheo deferente, magnum quoddam
5 de uobis gaudium habeamus, ita ut nec condigne pro his gratias agere Deo nos posse existimemus.' et ut ne uideatur ista dicens dixisse ab illo desiderio quo desiderabat ad eos uenire:

nocte et die superabundantius deprecantes, ut uideamus faciem ue-stram, et suppleamus ea quae desunt fidei uestrae.

10 'persistimus (inquit) orantes ut et uideamus uos et suppleamus, etiam si et deesse uobis aliquid uidetur.' et desiderium explicans suum adiecit:

ipse autem Deus et pater noster et dominus noster Iesus dirigat uiam nostrum ad uos.

15 hoc uel maxima desiderat, ut et oratione postularet id fieri, sic et ad tolerantiam durissimarum tribulationum adhortans eos, ora-tione dicta sua confirmat:

uos autem Dominus multiplicet, et abundare faciat caritatem in inuicem et in omnes, sicut et nos in uos, ad confirmanda corda uestra
20 *sine querela in sanctificatione coram Deo et patre nostro in aduentu domini nostri Iesu cum omnibus sanctis eius.*

'adiciat (inquit) uobis et in inuicem et erga omnes caritatem, ta-lem illam in uobis efficiens, qualis et in nobis de uobis est; et con-firmet in fide mentem uestram, ita ut permaneatis sine crimine, ab
25 omni uos cohibentes inconuenienti actu'—hoc enim dicit *in sanc-titate.* 'per quam poteritis etiam in future die fiduciam ad Deum adsequi, cum ceteris omnibus qui placite conuersantur in uirtute.'

de cetero, fratres, rogamus uos et obsecramus in domino Iesu, sicut accepistis a nobis quemadmodum conueniat uos ambulare et placere

---

3 ut *om r* 4 differente *C** referente *C* (*corr.*) *r* 5 habemus *C H r* ita *om r*
6 nostro (*for* nos) *r* 7 quod *C* 11 expleri (*aft.* uid.) *add in marg C* (*corr.*)
12 adicit *C r* 15 orationem *C* r* 16 ad *om r* 18 caritate *C* (*corr.*) 22
in (*bef.* inu.) *om r* 25 inconuenientu *H* 26 etiam *om r*

3:9 *What thanksgiving* (he says) *can we return to God for you in return for all the joy with which we rejoice because of you before your*[8] *God?*

"For we so thought those good things that are yours our own that, because we heard such things about you from Timothy's report, we have such great joy about you that we think we cannot worthily enough give God thanks for them." And lest he should seem by saying this to have spoken to one side of the longing[9] by which he was longing to come to them:

3:10 *Night and day we are praying more than abundantly that we may see your face and may complete those things that are lacking to your faith.*

"We are constant (he says) in praying that we may both see you and may complete anything you may seem to be lacking." And to explain his longing, he added:

[20] 3:11 *And may God himself and our Father and our Lord Jesus direct our way to you.*

He longs for this most of all, so that in his prayer he asks that it may take place. And so, exhorting them to bear patiently the harshest afflictions, he confirms what he has said by prayer:

3:12–13 *And may the Lord increase you and make you abound in love toward one another and toward all, just as also we toward you, to strengthen your hearts without blame in holiness before God and our Father at the coming of our Lord Jesus with all his saints.*

"May he give you in addition (he says) love both toward one another and toward all, forming it in you just as love for you is in us. And may he confirm your mind in faith so that you may persevere without fault, keeping yourselves away from every wrong act"—for this is what he means by *in holiness*. "By love you will also at the day to come be able to gain confidence toward God, together with all the others who live their lives well pleasing in virtue."

4:1 *For the rest, brothers, we ask you and we beseech in the Lord Jesus, just as you have received from us how it is right for you to walk and to please God, that you may all the more abound.*[10]

---

[8] An error; the text should read "our God."

[9] *Dixisse ab illo desiderio.* Swete's note (2:19) reads in part: "The sense seems to require the substitution of *discessisse* for *dixisse*, unless *ab* may possibly mean here 'at variance with,' as ἀπό in the phrase οὐκ ἀπὸ σκοποῦ.

[10] Note that "as, in fact, you are doing" is omitted from the text. Swete notes

Deo, ut abundetis magis.

    diximus et in argumento dudum, quoniam Timotheo a Thes-
salonica reuerso et nuntiante sibi firmitatem fidei eorum, quam
in persecutionis necessitate incurrentes inuiolatam seruauerunt,
5 necnon et quod sint aliqua apud illos quae correctionem indigeant;
scribit ergo hinc epistolam apostolus ad illa quae sibi nuntiata fuerant a Timotheo, illa quae conueniebant dicere ad laudem eorum,
pro quibus in aduersis firmi perstiterunt, simul et exhortans eos in
eadem perseuerare sententia. quae et in illis quae ante dicta sunt a
10 nobis consummasse uisus est, oratione suum cludens sermonem.
hinc uero incipit de illis disputare, quae inconuenienter ab illis agi
didicerat. hoc ergo dixit: 'obsecramus uos ut consequentem uitam uestram exhibeatis illius doctrinae quam adsecuti estis a nobis; festinantes placere Deo, et promouere ad legis eius directio-
15 nem.' optime autem inchoauit ab illo dicto quo dixit *de cetero fratres*, postquam laudes consummauit quas super fidei eorum dixerat firmitate. hoc uult dicere quoniam 'illam quam conuenit habere sententiam contemplatione pietatis ipsis negotiis demonstra-
stis. agite igitur et de cetero uitae uestrae diligentiam adhibeatis,
20 ut nihil uobis deesse uideatur ex illis, quae ad perfectionem uidentur uobis esse utilia.' necessaria uero et hoc in loco adiecit *sicut
accepistis a nobis;* demonstrauit enim eo quod non nunc inprimis
haec audire a se uideantur, sed et dudum de his fuerint instructi.
unde et augens illud:
25   *scitis* (inquit) *quae mandata dederim uobis per dominum Iesum.*
    omni in loco ostendens, quoniam nihil noui illis hodie scribit.
    haec est enim uoluntas Dei, sanctificatio uestra.
    necessarie dixit *haec est enim uoluntas Dei;* agere enim conue-
nit illa quae Deus fieri uult, eo quod *sanctificatio* ad plenum di-
30 citur omnium inconuenientium abdicatio. euidentius uero explicans, de quibus sit illi ad praesens sermo, adicit:
    abstinete uos ab omni fornicatione.

5   correctione *C (corr.) r* 10 concludens *C (corr.) r* 15-16 ergo (*aft.* de cet.)
add C 18-19 demonstratis *r* 19 adhibeamus *C* r* adhibeates (*sic*) *C (corr.)*
20 uobis uidentur *r* 23 ea se *C** ea a se *r* 24 agens *H* 25 Christum (*aft*
Ies.) *add r* 28 necessario *r* 29 uult f. *r*

We have said before in discussing the setting that Timothy [21] returned from Thessalonica and reported to Paul the Thessalonians' steadfastness in faith, which they had preserved unimpaired even though they met with the difficulty of persecution. But he also, in fact, reported that there were some things among them that needed to be set right. Therefore, it was at this time that the apostle wrote his letter in response to the news Timothy had brought, writing what was fitting to say by way of praising them for remaining steadfast in adversities and at the same time exhorting them to persevere in the same purpose. And we have seen that he completed these points in what he said before this place in the letter, concluding his words with a prayer. But from here on he begins to argue about those things he had learned they were doing unfittingly. Therefore, he said: "We beseech you to display your life in accord with that teaching you acquired from us, making haste to please God and to move forward toward the guidance of his law." And quite effectively he began by making the statement, *for the rest, brothers*—after he had finished the praises he had spoken concerning their steadfastness in faith. He wanted to say this: "You have shown by the very things that have taken place that purpose that is right to have in observing true religion. Therefore, be active for the rest in applying diligent care to your life so that you may be seen lacking none of those things that are plainly beneficial to you for perfection." And he added also in this place the necessary words, *just as you have received from us*, for he demonstrated that they were not hearing these things from him for the first time but had been previously instructed about them. Then, to elaborate the point:

4:2 *You know* (he says) *what instructions I gave you through the Lord Jesus.*

Showing in every place that he is writing nothing new to them at the present time.

4:3a *For this is the will of God, your sanctification.*

He necessarily said *for this is the will of God*, for it is right to do what God wills to be done, because complete *sanctification* [22] is the renunciation of everything unfitting. But to explain more clearly what he is now talking about, he adds:

---

that Theodore is simply following all the Greek commentators.

nuntiauit enim ei Timotheus inter cetera, quoniam indifferentes sunt erga permixtionem, lasciue uiuentes, ita ut quidam eorum etiam uxores habentes, non sint contenti suis uxoribus; quosdam uero eorum etiam alienis uxoribus permiscere nuntiauit. de quibus scribit nunc ad eos, correctioni optime conuersationis hoc principium sumens. nam dum dicit *ab omni fornicatione*, differentes fornicationis species euidentius ostendere uoluit; nec enim erat aliter possibile adiuuare eos qui delinquebant, si non specialiter dixisset de illis quae corrigi conueniebant.

scire unumquemque suum uas possidere in sanctitate et honore, non in passione concupiscentiae.

hoc quidem de illis dicit, qui uxores habentes non erant illis contenti.

†dixit *suum uas*, propriam eius uxorem sic nominans; *in sanctitate possidere* illud dicens tunc, quando non ut adultera sordidatur; *in honore* autem dixit, eo quod non despecta sua uxore ad alteram ulterius intueatur. apertius uero dixit *non in passione concupiscentiae*, eo quod ista agens non quasi uxori suae iunctus esse uidetur, sed propter permixtionem solam id agitur absolute, quam 'passionem concupiscentiae' nuncupauit.*

σκεῦος τὴν ἰδίαν ἑκάστου γαμετὴν ὀνομάζει· ἐν ἁγιασμῷ κτᾶσθαι αὐτὸ εἰρηκώς, ὅταν μὴ πρὸς ἑτέραν ῥυπαίνηται. ἐμφατικώτερον δέ τὸ μὴ ἐν πάθει ἐπιθυμίας, ὡς ἂν τοῦτο ποιοῦντος οὐκέτι ταύτῃ ὡς γυναικὶ συνόντος, ἀλλὰ διὰ μίξιν μόνην ἁπλῶς· ὅπερ πάθος ἐπιθυμίας ἐκάλεσεν.

concupiscentia enim in crimine uocari non potest, eo quod naturae

1-2 differentes *C** 4 permisceri *H* 5 correctione optime conu. *C H r*: *conj. Jacobi* correctioni conuersationis optime 14 Coisl. 204, f. 168 b [Cr. vi. 358, Fr. 145] θεόδωρος. ἄλλος φησίν· σκεῦος, κ.τ.λ. 25-26 agit *r* 28 in crimen euocari *C (corr.)*

4:3b *Keep yourselves from all fornication,*[11]

For among other things Timothy reported to Paul that the Thessalonians were making no distinctions regarding sexual intercourse, living licentiously, so that some of them, even though they had wives, were not satisfied with their wives. And Timothy reported that some of them were having sexual intercourse with other men's wives. Paul now writes to them about these people, quite effectively taking this as the beginning for his setting right their way of life. For since he says *from all fornication,* he wanted to show quite clearly that there were different forms of fornication. Nor, indeed, was it possible in any other way to help those who were transgressing, if he had not spoken individually about those things that were suited for being set right.

4:4–5a *to know each one of you how to possess his own vessel in holiness and honor, not in the passion of desire,*

He surely says this about those who, though they had wives, were not satisfied with them.

†He said *his own vessel,* giving this name to a man's own wife. By *to possess in holiness* he means the time when the wife is not defiled as an adulteress. And he said *in honor* because when a man's own wife is not scorned, [23] he does not look further away to another woman. But he said more clearly, *not in the passion of desire,* because when someone acts this way, he seems as though not joined to his own wife but acts this way simply for sexual intercourse, which he called *the passion of desire.*[*12]

He calls each man's own wife a *vessel,* having said *to possess* it *in holiness* of the time when he is not defiled with another woman.

And *not in the passion of desire* is more expressive, since whenever a man acts this way, he is no longer united with that woman as his wife but simply for sexual intercourse alone, which he called *the passion of desire.*

---

[11] Note that the imperative is used rather than the infinitive and that "all" is added.

[12] The Greek envisages only the male adulterer, whereas the Latin envisages the wife's adultery as well as the husband's. *In holiness* counters the first; *in honor,* the second. Swete points out (2:22) that Theodore parts company with most of the Greek commentators, who interpret "vessel" to mean one's own body.

motum in suam explere uidetur uxorem. 'passionem' uero 'concupiscentiae' dixit, quod aliis feminis permixti etiam suas uxores
ad similitudinem earum abuti uelint. deinde comparatione contrarium opus ipsum sufficienter derogauit:

5   *sicut et gentes quae nesciunt Deum.*

haec dicens de illis dixit, qui uxores habentes aliis mulieribus permiscebantur; in subsequentibus uero disputat et de illis
qui usurpabant permiscere illis mulieribus, quae legitime maritali
erant iunctae affectu:

10   *ut non supergrediatur et fraudet in negotio fratrem suum.*

pudicissime quidem dixit *in negotio;* per omnia uero iniquitatem operis enixus est arguere. nam dum dicit *non supergredi,* quasi
terminos quosdam positos inuadentem arguit. eo quod dixit *frau-
dare,* quasi qui alienam auferat possessionem. et quod dixit *fra-
15   trem,* maius crimen aggerauit, si et cum uxore illius qui per fidem frater est permisceatur; quem et fratrem nuncupauit, ut maius ostenderet usurpationis ipsius crimen, eo quod et apud omnes in confessione deductum est; ita ut nec demortuorum fratrum
uxorem quemquam ulterius accipere liceat. deinde et in timorem
20   redigere cupiens eos adicit:

       eo quod uindex sit Dominus et de omnibus istis.

bene *de omnibus* adiecit, ita ut et primis illud aptasse uideatur.
et iterum quasi contestans, quoniam et dudum haec eadem dixerat
illis, adiecit:

25   *sicut et praediximus uobis et contestati sumus.*

et ostendens quoniam necessarius sit illis et de his sermo:

       *non enim uocauit nos Deus in immunditiam, sed in sanctificatio-
nem.*

       'itaque si ab his nos continemus, tunc illa agimus quae nostram
30   agere conueniens est uocationem; uocauit enim nos ad sanctifica-

---

3   comparationem C^*H 4   ipsud C^* 12   enisus C (*corr.*)   15-16   fide C
(*corr.*)   16-17   maiorem C^*H 17   et (*bef.* usurp.) *add* C^* ‖   et *om* H 18
confusione r ‖   mortuorum C (*corr.*)   19   uxore C^* (*corr.*)   ‖   alterius r
‖   timore (*for* timorem) H in timore C 21   et *om* H 29   egimus r

Now desire cannot be summoned for accusation, because a man is seen to satisfy the movement of nature in his own wife. But he said *the passion of desire* because when they had sexual intercourse with other women, they would be willing to use even their own wives in a way similar to their use of the others. Then by a comparison with contrasting people he sufficiently denigrated the behavior itself:

4:5b *as also the Gentiles, who do not know God,*

He said this about those who, though they had wives, were sexually involved with other women. But in what follows he argues also about those who usurped the right to have sexual intercourse with those women who had been joined in lawful marriage:

4:6a *that he may not go beyond and defraud his own brother in the matter,*

Of course, he said *in the matter* as decently as possible, but in all respects he strived to condemn the wickedness of the behavior. For while saying *not to go beyond*, he condemned the one who pressed beyond, as it were, certain boundaries set in place, because he said *defraud* as though someone had carried off another's possession. And the fact that he said *brother* heaped the accusation higher, supposing that a man were to have intercourse with the wife of someone who is his brother in faith. And he called him *brother* [24] so that he might all the more make clear the accusation against this usurped right, because it is accepted by all as an acknowledged fact, that it is not permitted for anyone to take later on the wife of deceased brothers.[13] Then in his wish to bring them back to fear, he added:

4:6b *because the Lord is the avenger also of all those people,*

He rightly added *of all* so that he might be seen to have applied this also to the people first mentioned. And again, as though he were in a lawsuit, since he had previously told them these same things, he added:

4:6c *as we also told you before and bore witness.*

And showing that his words even about these things were necessary for them:

4:7 *For God has not called us to impurity, but to holiness.*

"And so if we restrain ourselves from these deeds, then we are

---

[13] Swete (2:24) points out that in Theodore's time both the church and Roman law prohibited marriage with a deceased brother's wife.

tionem possessionis in qua et existere in futuro speramus saeculo, quando exsurgentes et incorrupti effecti neque peccare ulterius
poterimus, quam et imitari nos secundum possibilitatem in praesenti conuenit uita.' deinde adicit:

5   *itaque qui haec spernit non hominem spernit sed Deum, qui et dedit*
Spiritum suum sanctum in uobis.

'itaque qui haec agit, ipsum spernit Deum, dum ad altera uocatus altera agit' necessaria est autem hoc in loco adiectio quam
adiecit de Spiritu dato, eo quod ab illo nobis futura tribuentur bo-
10   na; *seminatur* (inquit) *corpus animale, surgit corpus spiritale.* accipientes ergo hanc arram futurorum, id est primitias Spiritus, si fe-
cerimus alia praeter illa in quorum spe sumus uocati, spretio est
euidens Dei, qui nobis arram dedisse uidetur. haec de naturalibus
permixtionibus disputans transit ad aliud:

15   *de caritate autem fraternitatis non necesse habemus scribere uobis,*
ipsi enim a Deo docti estis, ut diligatis inuicem; etenim facitis illud in
omnes fratres qui in tota sunt Macedonia. obsecramus autem uos, fra-
tres, abundare magis, et stadium habere quietos esse, et agere propria
et operari manibus uestris, sicut et praecepimus uobis, ut ambuletis ho-
20   *neste ad eos qui foris sunt, et nullius necesse habeatis.*

cognouit quosdam esse et apud illos, qui ualde uidebantur esse indisciplinati, qui nihil operantes ex illis quae ad aliorum pertinebant utilitatem, insuper otiose uiuentes aliorum discutiebant
uitam et turbelas quasdam ex tali commouebant ratione. de qui-
25   bus et apertius in secunda disputauit epistola; et hoc in loco de illis scribit, eo quod ipsa otiositas et operum securitas faciebat eos
in nihil utile ipsam abuti otiositatem. etenim dum bonitas aliorum sine discussione cunctis indigentibus solatia praebebat, tantum si eiusdem fidei esse existimarentur; laudat quidem primitus
30   illos, qui praebebant ob tale propositum, et quod necessarie illud
explebant; simul etiam et conlaudat eos, quoniam non solum erga

---

4 uita conu. *r*   7 ad *om H*   8 est (*aft.* necess.) *om r* (*add aft* adiectio)   9
tribuantur *C* (*corr.*) tribuuntur *r*   10 surget *C* (*corr.*)   12 despectio (*for* spretio) *r*   18 uestrum negotium (*for* propria) *r*   24 turbas *r*   27 ipsa, ociositate
C (*corr.*) *H*   ‖   imbuti *H*   30 ob tali propositu (-o *H*) *C** *H*   ‖   necessario *r*
31-472.1 erga (*bef.* alios) *add C* (*corr.*)

doing what is right for our calling to do. For God has called us to the holiness of continence in which we also hope to exist in the age to come, when rising again and made incorruptible we shall no longer be able to sin—a sanctification that it is right for us also to imitate as much as possible in the present life." Then he adds:

4:8 *And so whoever spurns these things spurns not man but God, who also gave his Holy Spirit to you.*

[25] "And so whoever does these things spurns God himself, since he does one thing when called to another." And the addition he made in this place concerning the giving of the Spirit is necessary, because it is from the Spirit that the good things to come will be bestowed on us (1 Cor 15:44): *it is sown* (he says) *a physical body, it rises a spiritual body.* Therefore, since we receive this pledge of the things to come, that is, the firstfruits of the Spirit, if we should do anything other than those things in whose hope we have been called, the scorn of God, who has plainly given us the pledge, is clear. Arguing these points about natural intercourses, Paul passes over to another point:

4:9-12 *And concerning the love of the brotherhood we have no necessity to write to you, for you yourselves have been taught by God so that you might love one another. Indeed, you do this to all the brothers who are in the whole of Macedonia. And we beseech you, brothers, to abound all the more and to have zeal to be quiet and to do your own things and to work with your hands, just as we also instructed you, so that you might walk decently toward those who are outside and might have need of no one.*

He knew that there were some of them who seemed to be quite undisciplined, who were doing none of those things that pertain to the benefit of others. Besides, by living idly they were disturbing the life of others and were stirring up certain disruptions for such a reason. Paul argued about them more openly in his second letter, but even in this [26] place he writes about them, because their very idleness and their complacent negligence of working was making them of no benefit, since they were taking advantage of that very idleness. To be sure, as long as the kindness of others was furnishing relief without disturbance to all who were in need, at least if they were thought to be of the same faith, Paul indeed praises first of all those who were giving provisions for such a purpose, because they were fulfilling this task necessarily. At the same time, he also praises them since they were quick to fulfill such

suos, sed et alios fideles, qui in aliis locis commorare uidebantur,
tale adcelerarent studium adimplere. praecepit uero ceteris ut non
abutantur illorum liberalitatem ad illa quae non conueniunt, qui
neque ullum opus facere uolebant et otiositate ipsa ad illa quae non
conueniebant sese exercere properabant. 'sicut enim laudamus illos qui indigentibus ministrant et tale propositum erga fideles fratres suos ostendunt, sic et ceteros uolumus adsequi incrementum
ut quieti sint, et illa quae sua sunt agant, operantibus manibus
suis; ex quibus possibile sit eos non indigere alterius solatium, et
apud exteros minime confundi pro opere indecente.' et hoc in loco
similiter adicit: *sicut praecepimus uobis*, et reliqua, ostendens quoniam nec hoc nouum illis nunc indicit. transit uero ulterius ad illa
quae dici conueniebant, suadens ut non inhoneste ferant de his qui
ab hac uita excedunt; quamobrem et de futuro statu illis disputat,
et gloriam illam quae erga sanctos tunc erit explicat, et ob necessitatem doctrinae illa quae competere sibi existimabat ad praesens
argumentum enarrat. nam in quantum magna erant illa quae ex-
pectabantur, in tantum consolari magis poterant hi, qui profundo
luctu tenebantur.

nolumus autem uos ignorare, fratres, de dormientibus, ut non sitis
tristes, sicut et ceteri qui spem non habent.

bene quia non tristitiam ademit, sed inmensam eam esse pro-
hibuit comparatione uel maxime aduersariorum, ad uerecundiam
eos deuocans, eo quod illi non habent spem. etenim erat inconueniens, ut illi qui post mortem meliora praesenti statu expectant ad
similitudinem illorum tristentur qui nihil amplius post mortem
expectant. deinde et de illis qui in spe sunt dixit:

si (inquit) *credimus quod Iesus mortuus est et resurrexit, sic et Deus*
eos qui dormierunt per Iesum adducet cum eo.

'si etenim resurrectionem Iesu credimus, necessario debemus
et de dormientibus credere, quoniam et illos suscitabit per Iesum,
ita ut et sint cum eo'—hoc enim dicit *adducet cum eo*. nam quod
dixit *per Iesum*, sequentibus est reddendum, ubi dixit *adducet cum*

1 commemorari *C* (*corr.*) 2 accelerare *r* ‖ ergo (*for* uero) *r* 3 liberalitate
C (*corr.*) libertate *r* 5 conueniebat *C** 9 solatio *C* r* 10 indicente *C**
H r 11 praecipimus *H* ‖ et c. (*for* et rel.) *r* 20 contristemini (*for* sitis
tr.) *H* 23 comparationem *C* r* 24 deuotans *C H r*: *txt l* ‖ haberent *C*
(*corr.*) 25 statui *r* ‖ expectabant *C* (*corr.*) 26 tristarentur *C* (*corr.*) 27
expectabant *C* (*corr.*) 28 inquit *om r* 29 eos *om r* 33 redendum (*sic*) *C**
H

zeal not only for their own people but also for other of the faithful
who were seen to dwell in other places. But he instructed the
others not to use the generosity of the former people for things that
were not fitting. These others were unwilling to do any work and
in their very idleness were eager to busy themselves with things
that were unfitting. "For just as we praise those who minister
to the needy and display such a purpose toward their faithful
brothers, so we wish the others to get nourishment so that they
may be peaceable and may mind their own business, working with
their own hands. It may be possible that some of them do not
need relief from someone else and are at least mingled with the
outsiders because of their unseemly behavior." And in this place
he likewise adds *just as we instructed you* and the rest, showing
that he was pointing even this out to them not as something new.
But he passes over in what follows to what was suitable to be
said, urging them not to carry on about those who have departed
this life in an unseemly fashion. Because of this he reasons with
them also about the future condition, explains the glory that will
then be for the saints, and declares what he supposed relevant to
his present subject because of the necessity of teaching. For to
the degree that [27] those things awaited were great, to such a
degree were those held fast by deep grief capable of being the more
consoled.

4:13 *And we do not want you to be ignorant, brothers, concerning
those who have fallen asleep, so that you may not be grieving, as also
the rest who do not have hope.*

He was right not to deny grief, but he did prevent it from
being too great, especially by his comparison with the opponents,
summoning them to shame because they did not have hope.
Indeed, it would have been unfitting for those who await better
things than their present condition after death to grieve like those
who await nothing more after death. Then he spoke also of those
who exist in hope:

4:14 *If* (he says) *we believe that Jesus died and rose again, so, too,
God will bring those who have fallen asleep through Jesus with him.*

"If, indeed, we believe the resurrection of Jesus, we necessarily
ought also to believe concerning those who have fallen asleep that
God will also raise them up through Jesus, so that they may also
be with him"—for he says *he will bring with him*. His statement
through Jesus must be referred to what follows, where he said *he*

eo; ut sit simile illi dicto: *eo quod per hominem mors, et per hominem resurrectio mortuorum.* sic intellegi debet quoniam per Iesum
praestabit et nobis resurrectionem, utpote horum nobis causa existente.

5 †intendendum uero est illi rei, προσεκτέον δὲ ὅτι ἐπὶ μὲν τοῦ
quoniam de Iesu dicens [*mor-* 'Ιησοῦ τὸ ἀπέθανεν εἶπεν, ἐπὶ
tuus est dixit, de ceteris uero δὲ τῶν λοιπῶν τοὺς κοιμηθέντας·
dicens] 'dormientes' dixit; eo ὡς ἐκεῖ μὲν θανατου ὄντος διὰ
quod ibi quidem adhuc mors τὸ μηδέπω λελύσθαι· ἐνταῦθα δὲ
10 erat, nec enim fuerat soluta; hoc κοιμήσεως, διὰ τὸ ἤδη λελύσθαι.
uero in loco dormitionem dixit,
eo quod iam erat mors ipsa soluta*,

siue secundum promissionem, siue secundum opus, quando ta-
15 men quis illud secundum Christum examinare uoluerit ex mortuis
resurgentem. et ad maiorem dictorum confirmationem posuit uoces: 'si (inquit) mortuus Christus surrexit et nihil ei obsistit ad resurrectionem, quia hoc uoluit Deus, et quidem primitus, necdum
erat soluta mors; multo magis in nobis illud esse post solutionem
20 iusta credimus ratione.' etiam et illud intendendum est, quoniam
de resurrectione disputans Christi, dormientium resurrectionem
relinquens dicere, de assumptione disputat; euidens quidem est
quoniam assumptioni etiam resurrectionis confessio sit coniuncta.
nam de illis quae supereminere uidebantur magis eos in praesen-
25 ti negotio suadere deproperat; quod et latius explicans futurorum
ostendit magnitudinem:

 hoc enim uobis dicimus in uerbo Domini.

---

2 et (*for* sic) *r* 3 et *om H* 3-4 existentem *C* (*corr.*) 5 Coisl. 204, f. 170
a [Cr. vi. 361] προσεκτέον δέ, κ.τ.λ. 6-8 mortuus ... dicens *om C H r* (*per
homoeotel.*) 16 maiorum *C H* 16-17 uobis (*for* uoces) *C* (*corr.*) 19 post
om C* H 27 uobis *om H**

will bring with him, so that it may be like his statement (1 Cor 15:21): *because death is through a man, also through a man is the resurrection of the dead.*[14] Thus, it ought to be understood that it is through Jesus that God will bestow also on us the resurrection, since he exists as the source for us of these things.

†And it must be noticed in this connection that when speaking of Jesus [he said *he died*, but in speaking of the others],[15] he spoke of their "sleeping," [28] because there, indeed, death still existed, for it had not been destroyed. But in this place he spoke of sleeping, because death itself no longer existed because it was destroyed,*

And it must be noticed that in reference to Jesus he said *he died*, but in reference to the others, *those who have fallen asleep*, because there death existed because it had not yet been destroyed, while here it is sleep, because it has already been destroyed.

whether by promise or in actual fact, at least when someone proves willing to consider the point by reference to Christ's rising from the dead. And for a greater confirmation of his words he put them down as pronouncements:[16] "If (he says) Christ, though dead, has risen, and nothing stood in the way of his resurrection because God willed it, and if this was for the first time while death was not yet destroyed, how much more do we believe with good reason that this will be ours after death's destruction." It must also be noticed that when he is reasoning about Christ's resurrection and stops speaking about the resurrection of those who are asleep, he reasons about the taking up [of those who are still alive]. Of course, it is clear that the acknowledgement of the resurrection is joined together with the taking up. For he hastens to persuade them all the more in the present connection about what seemed to be standing out as important.[17] And to explain this more fully, he demonstrates the greatness of the things to come:

4:15a *For this we say to you in the word of the Lord,*

---

[14]That is, we should not read "those who have fallen asleep through Jesus" but rather "God will bring them [to the resurrection] through Jesus and with him." Thus, the Man is both the proximate agent of the general resurrection and its first instance.

[15]Swete has emended the Latin on the basis of the Greek.

[16]*Uoces.* Is there a possible allusion to credal pronouncements?

[17]Presumably, the Thessalonians' doubts about the resurrection.

bene posuit *in uerbo Domini,*
†hoc est, 'secundum reuelationem quae inoperatione diuina
in nobis facta esse uidetur.' nec
5 enim erat de futuris dicenti ei
credere, si non inde fuisset edoctus.*

ἀντὶ τοῦ κατὰ ἀποκάλυψιν· οὐ
γὰρ ἦν περὶ μελλόντων πιστεύεσθαι
λέγοντα, μὴ ἐκεῖθεν μαθόντα.

quoniam nos qui uiuimus, qui subrelinquimur in aduentu Domini.

†quod dixit *nos,* non de se
10 neque de illis qui in praesenti
uita tunc habebantur dicit, sed
de illis fidelibus qui tunc uicturi sunt quando resurrectio est
futura. *nos* dixit, hoc est 'fide-
15 les,' eo quod et ipse talis erat et
ad tales scribebat. unde et adiecit: *qui subrelinquimur in aduentu Domini*;

τὸ δὲ ἡμεῖς οὐ περὶ ἑαυτοῦ φη-
σίν· ἀλλὰ τοὺς πιστοὺς λέγει. διὰ
τοῦτο προσέθηκεν οἱ περιλειπόμε-
νοι εἰς τὴν παρουσίαν τοῦ κυρίου.

ostendens quoniam non de illis qui eius tempore uiuebant dicit,
20 sed de illis qui in consummatione sunt uicturi.

non praeueniemus dormientes.

uult dicere quoniam tempore assumptionis illos fideles qui iam
sunt mortui illi qui tunc in uita inuenientur non praeuenient.
quod euidentius indicans adicit:

25 *quoniam ipse Dominus in iussu, in uoce archangeli, et in tuba Dei descendet de caelo; et mortui qui sunt in Christo resurgent primum, deinde
nos qui uiuimus, qui subrelinquimur, simul cum illis rapiemur in nubibus
in obuiam [Domini] in aerem, et sic semper cum Domino erimus.*

'mortuos in Christo' illos dicit qui et crediderunt in Christum
30 et pro Christo mortui sunt; quos resurgere dixit primos, sicuti
et Corinthiis scribens dixit: *primitiae Christus, deinde hi qui sunt*

2 Coisl. 204, f. 170 b [Cr. vi. 362] ἀντὶ τοῦ, κ.τ.λ. 3 operatione *C* (*corr.*) 6-
7 et datus *C* H* et dictum *r* 9 Coisl. 204, f. 170 b [Cr. vi. 362] τὸ δέ, κ.τ.λ.
25-26 descendit *C** 26 in Chr. sunt *r* ‖ resurgunt *r* 28 in (*bef.* obu.)
om *C* (*corr.*) *r* 29 Christo (*for* Christum) *H r* 30 dixit om *H*

He rightly put down *in the word of the Lord,*

†that is, "according to the revelation that is seen to have taken place in us by divine working." For it would not have been right to believe him when speaking of the things to come, if he had not been taught from there.*

Instead of "by revelation." For it would not have been right for the one speaking of the things to come to be believed, if he had not learned them from there.

[29] 4:15b *that we who are alive, who are left at the coming of the Lord,*

†When he said *we,* he does not mean himself or those who were at that time kept in the present life, but those faithful who will be living when the future resurrection takes place. He said *we,* that is, "the faithful," because such he was and to such he was writing. That is why he added, *we who are left at the coming of the Lord,**

He says *we* not about himself; rather, he means the faithful. That is why he added *who are left for the coming of the Lord.*

showing that he does not mean those who were living in his time but those who would be living at the end of the world.

4:15c *we shall not precede those who are sleeping,*

He wants to say that, at the time of the taking up, those who will then be found living will not precede those faithful who have already died. To point this out more clearly he adds:

4:16–17 *since the Lord himself, with a command, with the voice of the archangel and with the trumpet of God, will come down from heaven. And the dead who are in Christ will rise again* [30] *first, then we who are alive, who are left, at the same time with them will be caught up in the clouds to meet the Lord in the air, and so we shall always be with the Lord.*

By *the dead in Christ* he means both those who have believed in Christ and those who have died for Christ. He said that they would rise again first, just as he also said in writing to the Corinthians (1 Cor 15:23–24a): *Christ the firstfruits, then those who are Christ's, who have believed in his coming, then the end.*[18] And he

---

[18] The citation includes what Swete (2:30) calls "the remarkable gloss" found

Christi, qui aduentum eius crediderunt; deinde finis. uelocitatem uero resurrectionis ostendit euidenter in illa epistola dicens: *in mo-
mento, in ictu oculi, in nouissima tuba; tubicinabit enim, et mortui
resurgent incorrupti et nos immutabimur.* hoc ergo et hoc in loco di-
5 cit, quoniam descendet quidem de caelo Christus cum tuba terribili, et uoce quadam magna tunc perstrepente, secundum diuinam inoperationem, ut moris est. 'tubam' nuncupat archangelum
praecipientem omnibus, 'surgite.' 'iussum' uero uocat uocem eiusdem archangeli, quia dicet 'surgite.' his autem ita effectis om-
10 nia erunt compendiosa, ita ut illi qui pro fide mortui sunt priores
ceteris resurgant, et cum illis fidelibus qui tunc in uita hac inueniuntur super nubes quasi quibusdam uehiculis rapti ducantur in
aërem obuiam Domini, ita ut sint semper cum Domino. ualidam
autem et nimiam illorum esse uelocitatem insinuauit quae tunc
15 erunt; siquidem domino Christo adparente de caelo, et tuba so-
nante et angelo clamante 'surgite,' sic omnia expedientur compendiose, ut pariter et mortui resurgant et uiui cum illis rapiantur; neque praeuenire illos ultra poterunt, sic omnibus simul in idipsum
diuina quadam et terribili inoperatione effectis.
20 †euidens est autem et illud, quo-   δῆλον μέντοι κἀκεῖνο, ὅτι ὅταν εἴπῃ
niam quando dicit: *mortui in*   οἱ νεκροὶ ἐν χριστῷ ἀναστήσονται
Christo resurgent primum, non   πρῶτον, οὐκ ἀναιρῶν τοὺς πρὸ τῆς
ad interceptionem illorum di-   Χριστοῦ παρουσίας δικαίους λέγει·
cit iustorum, qui ante Christi   πῶς γάρ; ὅ γε σαφῶς ἐν τῇ πρὸς
25 aduentum uenerunt. qui fieri   Ἑβραίους λέγων· καὶ οὗτοι πάν-
enim potest, ut is qui euidenter   τες μαρτυρηθέντες διὰ τῆς πίσ-
de illis Hebraeis scribendo dixe-   τεως οὐκ ἐκομίσαντο τὰς ἐπαγγε-
rat: *et isti omnes testimonium ad-*   λίας, τοῦ θεοῦ περὶ ἡμῶν κρεῖτ-
secuti per fidem non perceperunt   τόν τι προβλεψαμένου, ἵνα μὴ χωρὶς
30 *promissionem,* Deo scilicet de no-   ἡμῶν τελειωθῶσιν· ὡς δῆλον ὅτι
bis melius quid deliberante, ut ne   σὺν αὐτοῖς τελειοῦσθαι μέλλουσιν.
sine nobis consummarentur? ex   ἀλλ' ἐπειδὴ μετὰ τὴν τοῦ Χριστοῦ

---

1   in (*bef.* adu.) *add* H   2-3   memento (*sic*) H   3   tuba canet e. C (*corr.*) canit
e. tuba *r*   4   et *om* C (*corr.*)   5   descendit *r*   8   percipientem et (*bef.* praec.)
add C H percipientes et *r*   9   affectis C* H *r*   13   Domino (*for* Domini) *r*   15
de (*bef.* domino) *add* C*   17   uiue C*   19   diuinam quamdam et terribilem
inoperationem C* H *r*: conj. *Jacobi* per, &c.: *txt* C (*corr.*)   20   Coisl. 204, f. 172
a [Cr. vi. 365] δῆλον μέντοι, κ.τ.λ.   23   interceptationem *r*   25   quia (*for* qui
1°) C*: *om* H* *r*   29   receperunt (*for* perc.) *r*

clearly shows the rapidity of the resurrection in that letter, when he says (1 Cor 15:52): *in a moment, in the twinkling of an eye, at the last trumpet; for the trumpet will sound, and the dead will rise again incorruptible, and we shall be changed.* Thus, this is what he also says in this place—that Christ will surely come down from heaven with a fearful trumpet and some great voice resounding at that time, according to the divine working as usual. "Trumpet" is the name he gives the archangel, who orders everyone, "Rise!" And he calls the voice of the same archangel "a command," because he will say, "Rise!"[19] And when these things have taken place this way, everything will happen quickly, so that those who have died in accord with faith will rise before the rest; and caught up as though by certain vehicles together with those faithful found then still living, they will be led above the clouds into the air to meet the Lord, so that they may always be with the Lord. [31] And he implied the powerful and extreme rapidity of those things that will then take place, if indeed when the Lord Christ appears from heaven and the trumpet sounds and the angel cries out "Rise!" all these things will be accomplished so quickly that at the same time both the dead will rise and the living will be caught up with them. Nor will the dead be able to precede the living by much, since all these things will so take place at the same time and in the same way for all by some divine and fearful operation.

†And this, too, is clear, that when he says *the dead in Christ will rise again first,* he does not mean to make an exception of those righteous people who came before the coming of Christ. For how could it possibly happen that Paul would say this, when he had clearly said in writing of those Hebrews (Heb 11:39–40): *And all these, having attained testimony through*

Nevertheless, it is also clear that when he said *the dead in Christ will rise first,* it was not to exclude those before the coming of Christ whom he calls righteous. For how could this be? Paul says clearly in the letter to the Hebrews (Heb 11:39–40): *And all these, attested through faith, did not receive the promises,*[20] *since God on our behalf provided something better, so*

---

in some of the manuscripts and versions: "who have believed."

[19] Swete (2:30) points out that, while Theodore identifies both the trumpet and the command with the archangel, Chrysostom thinks of the command as Christ's.

[20] Is the plural a scribal mistake?

quibus patet quoniam cum illis   παρουσίαν ταῦτα ἔγραφεν, ὡς πρὸς
et ipsi habent consummari. sed   τοὺς μὴ πεπιστευκότας τὸ ἐν Χρισ-
quoniam post Christi aduentum   τῷ διαστέλλων λέγει.
ista scribebat, ad distinctionem
5   illorum qui non crediderunt [in]
Christum istud dixit;*
eo quod iusti qui ante eius aduentum fuerant, quantum attinet ad
eos, secundum proprium tempus laborauerunt, et propter hoc iusta ratione cum illis deputabuntur. tamen quia memoria dictorum
10 sufficienter eos ad uerecundiam induxit, instruens eos pariter ut
talia expectantes bono animo pro illis non deficiant qui ab hac uita discedunt, nisi quantum debent compati propter amicitiam et
solitam consuetudinem; unde et adicit:
     itaque consolamini in inuicem in uerbis istis.
15   'haec (inquit) in tribulationibus positi inuicem uobis referte;
sufficiet enim eorum memoria audientibus ferre solatium, si tamen
domestici sunt fidei et non dubitant de futuris.'
     de temporibus uero et momentis, fratres, non necesse habetis scribe-
re uobis; ipsi enim cautissime scitis, quoniam dies Domini sicut fur in
20 *nocte sic uenit.*
     alterum iterum hic incipit capitulum. requirebatur enim ab il-
lis, 'quando erit huius saeculi finis?' bene ergo illis scribit ut non
requirant, neque existiment se posse discere qui semel audierunt
quoniam incertum est tempus aduentus dominici. hoc enim dicit:
25 *tamquam fur in nocte*, eo quod et fur non praedicens uenit. et quia

2 consummare *C H r*   5   in (*bef.* Chr.) *om C* H r*   6   iste *C** isti *C* (*corr.*)
ista. *H*   7   adu. eius *r*   10   instruit *C* (*corr.*)   11   hanc *C**   12   tantum (*for*
quant.) *C r*   14   in (*bef.* inu.) *om H*   15   uobis uobis referte *H*   16   suffici
etenim eor. memoriam *C** sufficiet enim eor. memoriam *r*   18   et mom. uero *r*
20   sic *om r*   21   tunc (*aft.* enim) *add H**   24   domini (*for* dominici) *r*

faith, have not received the pro- *that they might not be perfected*
mise, since God on our behalf was *apart from us*, so that it is clear
surely resolving something better, that they are going to be perfec-
so that they might not be perfected ted together with them ["us"].
without us? From these words it
is obvious that the latter have
to be perfected with the for-
mer. But since he was writing But since he wrote these things
after Christ's coming, he said after the coming of Christ, he
in Christ by way of distinction says *in Christ* by way of distinc-
from those who have not belie- tion from those who have not
ved.* believed.

This is because the righteous who had existed [32] before Christ's
coming toiled as much as was appropriate for them in accord with
their own time and because of this were with good reason given
the same rank as those who believed in Christ. Then, because
the memory of his words was enough to shame them, he instructs
them at the same time so that, since they are awaiting such things,
they should not fail to be of good cheer for those who have
departed this life, save so far as they ought to be compassionate
because of friendship and ordinary custom. For this reason he also
adds:

4:18 *And so comfort one another with these words.*

"These things (he says) repeat to one another when you are
placed in sorrows, for calling them to mind will be enough to bring
comfort to those who hear them, if at any rate they are of the
household of faith and are not in doubt about the things to come."

5:1-2 *And concerning times and moments, brothers, you have no*
need of writing to you, for you yourselves know quite accurately that
the day of the Lord so comes as a thief in the night.

Here again he begins another section. For they were asking
him, "When will the end of the world take place?" Therefore, he
rightly writes that they should not ask, nor should they think they
can find out, since they once heard that the Lord's coming is at
an uncertain time. For he says like *a thief in the night* because
it is without forewarning that a thief comes. And because the
opponents were making fun of the very thing they were saying,
claiming that it could in no way take place, he adds:

5:3 *When they say "peace and safety," then suddenly destruction*
comes upon them, as the pain of birth on a woman with child, and they

inridebant aduersarii hoc ipsum quod ab illis dicebatur, dicentes
nequaquam fieri posse, adicit:

cum dixerint: 'pax et securitas,' tunc repente illis instat extermi-
nium, sicuti dolor partus in utero habentis, et non effugient.

5   'nam conuenit (inquit) prospicere infideles, eo quod necessario
erunt ea quae a nobis dicuntur, etiamsi millies nihil tale fieri existiment; sed etsi aestiment se esse securos et libertate arbitrii agere
quae uelint, sed subito illis instabit iudex, sicuti et dolores prae-
gnantibus, ita ut nec possibile sit eos euadere poenam.' ad omnia
10   ergo optime hoc abusus est exemplo, eo quod et graui subdentur
poenae (grauis enim est partus praegnanti); et ut ostendat quoniam praefinitum est a Deo tempus consummationis, licet nobis,
dum subito fit, incerta esse uideatur. nam et mulieribus tempus
partus definitus esse uidetur, secundum mensium enim curricula
15   partum solent expectare mulieres; uero tamen partus ipsius dies
est illis incertus, nec enim scire possunt, nisi cum repente dolor
partus illis institerit. deinde et ad exhortationem uertitur, ex praecedentibus consiliis sumens occasionem:

uos autem, fratres, non estis in tenebris, ut dies illa uos tamquam
20   *fur comprehendat. omnes enim uos filii luminis estis et filii diei; non*
sumus noctis neque tenebrarum.

quoniam dixit: *sicut fur in nocte sic ueniet*, hoc in loco dicit quoniam 'non estis in tenebris, cognouistis enim ueritatem. itaque etsi
repente dies instat, sed non erga uos ordinem sibi uindicat furis,
25   qui iuuandi estis ex eius aduentu; sed illis qui noxam expectant
poenalem.' et ut recognitionem sufficere sibi existiment, adicit:

igitur non dormiamus, sicut et ceteri; sed uigilemus et sobrii simus.
qui enim dormiunt, nocte dormiunt, et qui inebriantur, nocte inebrian-
tur; nos autem, qui diei sumus, sobrii simus, induti loricam fidei et ca-
30   *ritatis et galeam spei salutis. quoniam non posuit nos Deus in iram,*
sed in adquisitionem salutis per dominum nostrum Iesum Christum,
qui mortuus est pro nobis, ut siue uigilemus, siue dormiamus, simul cum
illo uiuamus.

conuenit igitur nos tali remuneratos scientia uigilare et sobrios

---

5   non (*for* nam) *C H r*   6   erant *C**   8   et subito *C** et s. tunc *C* (*corr.*)   11
poena *H r*   ‖   praegnantis *H*   13   uidetur *H*   15   uero tam *H* uerum tamen *r*
16   illis *om H*   17   et *om C* (*corr.*)   18   cum filiis (*for* cons.) *r*   ‖   ait (*aft*
occ.) *add H r*   20   non (*bef.* compr.) *add H*   25   erga illos (*for* illis) *C* (*corr.*)

will not escape.

[33] "For it is right (he says) to look out for the faithless, because what we say will of necessity come to pass, even if they suppose a thousand times no such thing will happen. But even if they think they are safe and can do what they want by freedom of choice, yet without warning the judge will come upon them, as labor pangs upon pregnant women, so that it is impossible for them to escape punishment." Thus, in all respects he quite effectively used this example, both because they will be subject to grave punishment (for giving birth is grave for the pregnant woman) and to show that God has fixed the time of the world's end beforehand, granted that to us it seems uncertain in time, since it takes place without warning. Indeed, even the time of giving birth seems to be fixed, for women usually expect the birth according to the elapse of months. And yet the day of the birth itself is uncertain to them, for they are unable to know it except when suddenly the birth pangs come upon them. Then he turns to an exhortation, taking his occasion from what precedes:

5:4–5 *But you, brothers, are not in darkness, so that that day should catch you like a thief. For you are all children of light and children of day; we are not of the night nor of darkness.*

Since he said (5:2) *it will come*[21] *as a thief in the night*, in this place he says: "You are not in darkness, for you have come to know the truth. And so even if the day comes suddenly, yet it would not claim the role of a thief toward you who are to be benefited by its coming, but rather for those who are awaiting the harm of punishment." And so that they may suppose this consideration to be enough for them, he adds:

5:6–10 *Therefore, let us not sleep as also the rest, but let us be awake and be sober.* [34] *For those who sleep, sleep at night, and those who are drunk are drunk at night. But we who are of the day, let us be sober, putting on the breastplate of faith and love and the helmet of the hope of salvation, since God has not placed us for wrath but for the gaining of salvation through our Lord Jesus Christ, who died for us so that, whether we are awake or are sleeping, we may live together with him.*

Therefore, it is right for us, rewarded with such knowledge, to be awake and to be sober by carefully observing what is right for

---

[21] *Veniet* instead of *venit*, as in the text of 5:2.

esse erga illorum diligentiam, quae nobis conueniunt. ad [dor-
mien]dum [quidem] nocturnum tempus nobis magis est necessarium et ad ebrietatem; latere enim poterit facile is qui talis est. illos
uero qui per cognitionem tamquam in die iam consistunt, sobrios
5 esse conuenit et uigilantes erga studia uirtutum, quasi qui et in diei
tempore conuersantur, in quo neque latere quemquam sit possibile, si tamen aliquid ex illis quae non conueniunt perfecerit. quae
sunt autem illa opera, quae nobis ut in die conuersantibus depu-
temus? fidem inquio et caritatem, ex quibus spes nobis adquiritur
10 salutis; quod et Dominus Deus per Christum, qui pro nobis suscipere uoluit mortem, salutem nobis praeuidit, non poenam; ut
licet secundum praesentem hanc uitam habeamur— hoc enim dicit *uigilemus*—etiamsi egressi fuerimus a uita hac —hoc enim dicit *dormiamus* (uult enim dicere, et illi qui tunc uiuunt in Christi
15 aduentu et qui iam sunt mortui), omnes aeternam uitam et incor-
ruptam adquiramus; dum illi qui praecesserunt dudum in mortem
ita resurgunt, et illi qui tunc uiuunt in incorruptibilitatem mutan-
tur, sicut idem apostolus alio in loco dicit quoniam *omnes immu-*
tabimur. igitur nihil est quod prohibeat salutem nos frui futuram,
20 si tamen illa quae ex nobis sunt minime nobis obstiterint. et hinc
dicens adicit:

    propter quod consolamini in inuicem, et aedificate unus unum, sicut
et facitis.

    eo quod ad propositam exortus est exhortationem ab illo loco
25 quo dixit non debere eos de consummatione saeculi et eius tempore curiose agere, necessarie hoc in loco istud adiecit, hoc est:
'relinquentes illa, haec agite et de his estote solliciti, et de illis ad
alterutrum disputate pro communi utilitate.' post hoc uero exhortatur eos dicens:

30   *rogamus autem uos, fratres, scire eos qui laborant in uobis et prae-*

---

1 eorum (*for* illorum) *r* ‖ ad............dum *C* H* ad dormiendum *C corr.*
(*but without completely filling up the lacuna*) ad custodiendum *r*   6-7   poss. sit *r*
7 aliquot *H* ‖ non (*aft.* si) *add C* (*corr.*) ‖ perficere *H*   9 inquam et
c. *H* ait in quo et c. ponit *r*   10 et quod et *C* H*   11 peruidit *C** prodidit
[*sic*: prouidit?] *r*   14 ut et illi tunc uiuent *C* (*corr.*)   16 adquiremus *C* (*corr.*)
17 resurgent *C* (*corr.*) ‖ incorruptibilitate *H*   17-18 mutabuntur *C* (*corr.*)
19 salute, futura *C* (*corr.*)   20 nobis *om H*   22 in *om H* ‖ alterutrum (*for*
unus u.) *r*   23 illud (*aft* fac.) *add C*   24 eo quid *C* H* eo ... exhortationem
om r   26 necessario *r*   28 post haec *C* (*corr.*)

us; nighttime for us, of course, is more necessary for sleeping and for sobriety. For the person "of the night"[22] could then easily be able to escape notice, while for those who by knowledge already stand as though in the day, it is right to be sober and awake for the pursuit of virtues, as though they were living in the daytime when it is impossible for anyone to escape notice, if indeed he should do anything unfitting. What, then, are those deeds we assign to ourselves as people who live our lives in the day? He says faith and love, by which we acquire the hope of salvation, because the Lord God provided us with salvation—not punishment—through Christ, who was willing to accept death on our behalf, no matter whether we are held in this present life [35]—for this is what *should we be awake* means—or even if we should have departed from this life—for this is what *should we sleep* means. For Paul wants to speak both of those who are alive at the time of Christ's coming and of those who have already died. All of us will gain life eternal and incorruptible, since those who have previously departed accordingly rise again, and those living at that time are changed into incorruption, just as the apostle says the same thing in another place (1 Cor 15:51): *we shall all be changed*. Therefore, there is nothing to prevent us from enjoying the salvation that is to come, if indeed what we do should by no means stand in our way. And speaking on the basis of this, he adds:

5:11 *Because of this encourage one another, and each one of you build up each one, just as you are also doing.*

Because this came up in reference to his previous exhortation (4:18), from the place where he said they ought not be inquisitive about the end of the world and its time (5:1–10), in this place he necessarily added this point, that is, "leaving those things behind, do these things, and take great care about them and reason with one another about them for the common benefit of all." And after this he exhorts them, saying:

---

[22] Literally "such" (*is qui talis est*). The Latin is quite obscure at this point.

*sunt uobis in Domino et admonent uos; aestimate eos superabunde in
caritate propter opus eorum; pacem habete in eos.*

'itaque illos qui doctrinae iniunctum opus habere uidentur plurimo honore dignos existimate, non resultantes illis, quando uos
5 corrigere cupiunt.' hoc enim dicit: *pacem habete in eos.* nam et fieri
hoc solebat ab illis qui indisciplinate uiuebant, ad quos scribens in
superioribus uidetur contumaciam eorum signasse, quoniam dum
delinquentes corrigere cupiebant doctores qui illa faciebant quae
non conueniebant, etiam grauari se doctorum arguitione existima-
10 bant. sicque ad illos disputans uertit suum sermonem ad doctores,
dicens:

*obsecramus uos autem, fratres, instruite indisciplinatos, consolami-
ni pusillanimes, sustinete infirmos, patientes estote ad omnes.*

necessarium enim erat et hos exhortari ut non discederent ab
15 opere propter quorundam contumaciam. omnia uero consequenter de illis, quae ipse praedixerat, praecepit etiam doctores facere; de quibus et ipse in epistola sua scripserat, ut de his diligentiam adhiberent et illis praecipiens compendiose ut 'instruerent
indisciplinatos,' ad quos et ipse uidetur scripsisse; *consolamini* ue-
20 ro *pusillanimes*, qui ob illos qui decedebant flebiliter eorum separationem ferebant; *sustinete infirmos*—dicit autem de illis qui fornicatione deturpabantur, docens non abdicare eos propter peccati
ipsius exprobrationem, sed et diligentiam erga illos debitam adhibere, et curam magis illis facere ut conuertantur. sic et alio in
25 loco scribens: *quis* (inquit) *infirmatur et non ego infirmor?* hoc est,
'mea esse aliorum existimo peccata.' bene autem adicit *patientes
estote ad omnes*, eo quod hoc necessarium ualde est magistris, ita
ut non facile desperent propter peccata, patienter uero suam impleant doctrinam, expectantes semper ut discipuli meliores sui ef-
30 ficiantur, lucrumque proprium esse existiment, etiamsi et serius
aliquando eos potuerint ad id quod honestum est reuocare. et ite-

1 in eis *C* (*corr.*) 4 aestimate *r* 5 etsi (*for* et) *H* 6 solebat h. *r* 7
significasse *l* 8 eos (*aft.* del.) *add H* ∥ doctores eos *C* H* docturus eos *r*
9 conueniebat *C** ∥ qui (*bef.* etiam) *add C* r* ∥ arguitionem *C* r* 10 ad
doctores *om H* 11 docens (*for* dicens) *r* 12 autem uos *r* 14 enim, et *om r*
∥ discederint *C** 15 corundam *H* 16 praecoepit *C* 18 praecipiens *om r*
∥ instruerit *C** 20 decidebant *C* r* 21 sustinere *C** 22 deturpebantur
H deturbabantur *r* 23 abdicationem (*for* exprobr.) *H* 24 in alio *l. H* 25
scribis *C** scribit *C* (*corr.*) ∥ inquit *om H* ∥ ego non *H r* 26 pecc. exist. *r*

5:12–13 *And we ask you, brothers, to know those who toil among you and preside over you in the Lord and admonish you; take consideration of them more than abundantly in love because of their work; have peace in them.*

[36] "And so consider those who are seen to have their work bound up with teaching, worthy of special honor, not springing back at them when they want to set you right." This is what *have peace in them* means.[23] For this was habitually taking place from those who were living undisciplined lives. Paul, writing to them earlier in the letter,[24] seems to have pointed out their defiant behavior, since while the teachers wanted to set right those who transgressed because they were doing what was not right, they thought they were being oppressed by the accusations of the teachers. And so, reasoning with them, Paul turns his address to the teachers, saying:

5:14 *And we beseech you, brothers, instruct the undisciplined, encourage the fainthearted, support the weak, be patient with all.*

For it was necessary also to exhort these people not to abandon their work because of the defiant behavior of some. And it was in accordance [37] with what he had said himself before, that he instructed also the teachers to do all these things. And he had written about them in his letter so that they might apply diligent care to them. He instructs them succinctly to *instruct the undisciplined,* to whom he seems to have written. And he says *encourage the fainthearted*, who because of the departed were bearing their separation from them tearfully. And by *support the weak* he means those who were being defiled by fornication, teaching them not to abandon them because of the reproach of their sin but to apply due diligence toward them and greater care for them, so that they may be converted. So he also writes in another place (2 Cor 11:29): *who* (he says) *is weak, and I am not weak?*—that is, "I think my sins those of others." And he rightly adds *be patient with all*, because this is quite necessary for professional teachers, so that they may not easily lose heart because of mistakes but may faithfully accomplish their teaching, always expecting that their students will be improved and may

---

[23] That is, "be peaceable with your teachers," rather than "be peaceable with one another."

[24] Theodore may be thinking of 3:5, 8, 10.

rum ad generalem exhortationem progrediens praecipit:

uidete ne quis malum pro malo alicui reddat, sed semper quod bo-
num est sectamini in inuicem et in omnes.

nulli malum pro malo debere retribuere dicit, [bonum sectari]
5   uero in quantum uirtus opitulatur, ut magis in inuicem sibi beneficia praebeant, cum illis qui externi nobis esse uideantur. deinde
adicit:

semper gaudete.

hoc est: 'pro omnibus tristitiis quae uobis accidunt bono animo
10   estote, futurorum expectatione animaequiores effecti.' et post hoc
praecipit:

sine intermissione orate, in omnibus gratias agite; haec enim est uo-
luntas Dei in Christo Iesu in uobis.

praecipit orare incessanter, gratias autem semper agere in ora-
15   tionibus; eo quod ista Deus uelit, et ista a nobis uel maxime depo-
stulet, ut grati illi simus, et ut gratias illi debitas agamus pro illis
bonis, quae nobis ab ipso sunt donata.

Spiritum nolite exstinguere, prophetias nolite spernere; omnia au-
tem probate, quod bonum est tenete.

20   multis existentibus qui tunc spiritales gratias habebant, erant
etiam et alii, qui et ad suasionem aliqua proponebant, quasi qui
et ipsi ex diuina reuelatione illa esse simulantes quae a se fiebant,
sicuti et Iudaeos exorcizare et daemoniacos in nomine Christi
usurpasse per Actus didicimus apostolorum. quoniam ergo apud
25   Thessalonicenses quidam erant, qui non suscipiebant illa quae secundum inoperationem spiritalem profitebantur, qui et confinge-
bant seductorum se causa studio cautelae id declinare,—fiebant
autem ista ab indisciplinatis, eo quod saepe indisciplinatio eorum
arguebatur ex illis quae a prophetis dicebantur—ideo dixit: 'pro-
30   phetas nolite reprobare, neque spiritalem inoperationem prohibere.' nam quod dixit 'reprobare prophetas' et illa nolle suscipere
quae ab illis dicebantur, hoc dicit spernere Spiritus inoperationem. 'sed si (inquit) seductores timetis, accipite illa quae dicuntur,

---

4   retribuere dicit *om C**   ‖   bonum sectari *om C* H*: reddere dicit sectare
C (*corr.*) [*both C * and H shew a lacuna*] retribui d. bonum sectare *r*   6   etiam
(*aft.* praebeant) *add C* (*corr.*)   ‖   quae ex terrena materia (*for* qui externi) *r*   10
post *om H*   17   ab ipso s. d. nobis *r*   20   multum existimantibus *C* H r*: txt
C (*corr.*)   23   et (2°) *om C*   25-26   in oper. (*for* sec. inop.) *l*   27   declinantes *r*
29   prophetias *C* (*corr.*)   30   operationem *r l*   32   spiritus spern. *r*

suppose this to be their own gain, when they are able to call them back to what is virtuous, even if it is at a later time. And proceeding once more to a general exhortation, he gives instruction:

5:15 *See that no one repays evil for evil to anyone, but always pursue what is good with one another and with all.*

He says that no one ought to give back evil for evil but should aim at good so far as virtue is of service, so that they may the more bestow benefits on one another, as well as on those who are seen foreign to us. Then he adds:

5:16 *Always rejoice.*

That is, "for all the misfortunes that happen to you [38] be of good cheer, since you have been made calm-minded by awaiting the things to come." And after this, he gives the instruction:

5:17–18 *Pray without ceasing, give thanks in all things, for this is the will of God in Christ Jesus for you.*

He instructs them to pray unceasingly and always to give thanks in their prayers, because God wills those things and especially asks them of us, so that we may be grateful to him and so that we may give him due thanks for those good things he has given us.

5:19–21 *Do not quench the Spirit; do not despise prophesies; and test all things; hold fast to what is good;*

Though there were many people who at that time had spiritual gifts, there were also others who were setting forth other things to recommend themselves, inasmuch as they, too, were pretending that what they were doing was by divine revelation. For example, we have learned by the Acts of the Apostles (Acts 19:13) that the Jews, as well, claimed the power to exorcize in the name of Christ even those possessed by demons. Therefore, since among the Thessalonians there were some who did not receive what was promised according to spiritual working and who were pretending that they had refused this by zealous caution because of those who were leading them astray—and that came about from the undisciplined, because their lack of discipline was often condemned on the basis of what was being said by the prophets—for this reason he said, "do not reject the prophets nor prevent

probantes illa, et si inuenta fuerint aliqua diuinis legibus contraria
de illis quae dicuntur, illa sola reicite, tenete uero meliora.' deinde
adicit:

ab omni specie mala abstinete.

5   quasi qui et hoc ipsum uersute facerent, dicens:

*ipse autem Deus pacis sanctificet uos perfectos; et integer uester
spiritus et anima et corpus sine querela in aduentum domini nostri Iesu
Christi seruetur.*

orat pro illis ita ut sancti per omnia custodiantur et sine querela
10   animo quoque sint et corpore, ita ut et tributa Spiritus gratia integra in illis custodiatur, nullam sustinens minorationem propter
eorum malitiam, ita ut in Christi aduentu adsequi possint aeternas
mercedes. et ut non de oratione dubii habeantur, adicit:

fidelis qui uocauit uos, qui faciet.

15   hoc est: 'uerus est qui uocans uos bona uobis promisit, qui et
replebit uos sua benedictione.'

fratres, orate et pro nobis.

scribit et post hoc ita ut et pro se orent, simul in caritate sua
eos constringens; nam et ut pro alterutro orent, lex defigit carita-
20   tis, nec enim umquam orare patiemur pro illis quos non diligimus.
simul et instruit nos idipsum etiam ab inuicem debere depostulare
et facere pro alterutro.

salutate fratres omnes in osculo sancto.

deinde et praecepit eis omnes fratres salutare *in osculo sancto,*
25   'sanctum osculum' dicens quod cum perfecta efficitur caritate.

*adiuro uos per Dominum, ut legatur epistola omnibus sanctis fra-
tribus.*

---

1   si inu. al. f. diuinibus [*sic*] leg. *H*   4   uos (*bef.* abst.) *add C* (*corr.*)   5   dicit
C (*corr.*)   10   sancti (*aft* sp) *add r*   14   et (*aft.* qui) *add C* (*corr.*) etiam *add r*
‖   eos (*for* uos) *C* H*   19-20   caritatem *C H r*

spiritual working." For when he spoke of [39] "rejecting the prophets" and not accepting what they were saying, he means despising the working of the Spirit. "But if (he says) you are afraid of those who lead you astray, accept what is said, testing it; and if anything should be found in what is said contradictory of the divine laws, reject only this, but hold fast to what is better." Then he adds:

5:22 *keep away from every evil appearance.*

As if they might do this very thing craftily, saying:

5:23 *And may the God of peace himself sanctify you entirely, and may your spirit and soul and body be preserved without fault for the coming of our Lord Jesus Christ.*

He prays for them that they may be kept holy in all respects and without fault also in soul and in body, so that, as well, the gift of the Spirit [40] that was bestowed may be kept unimpaired in them, suffering no diminution because of their wickedness, so that at the coming of Christ they may be able to gain eternal rewards.[25] And so that no doubts should be held about prayer, he adds:

5:24 *The one who called you is faithful, who will do it.*

That is, "true is the one who by calling you promised you good things, and he will fill you with his blessing."

5:25 *Brothers, pray also for us.*

He writes also this afterwards, so that they may pray for him, at the same time binding them together in his love. For the law of love declares authoritatively that they should pray for one another, nor, indeed, should we ever put up with praying for those whom we do not love. At the same time he has also instructed us that we ought to ask the same thing from one another and to do it for one another.

5:26 *Greet all the brothers with a holy kiss.*

Then he also instructs them to greet all the brothers *with a holy kiss*, meaning by "holy kiss" what is brought about by perfect love.

5:27 *I command you by oath through the Lord that the letter be read by all the holy brothers.*

---

[25]Theodore and the other Antiochenes refer "spirit" in the text to the Holy Spirit and do not understand the verse as a reference to a trichotomous account of a human as body, soul, and spirit.

adiurat, ut epistola omnibus legatur sanctis fratribus, suspicans
ex aliquibus quae sibi fuerant delata, quoniam non ad omnium notitiam scripta eius deferrentur. et post hoc adiciens:

gratia domini nostri Iesu Christi uobiscum. amen.

consummasse uidetur epistolam.

2 delatae *r* 3 deferentur *C** 4 Iesu Chr. *om H* 5 confirmasse (*for* consummasse) *H* hoc enim uerbo cons. apostolus uidetur suam ep. *r* ‖ explicit
epistola ad thessalonicenses prima incipit argumentum in epla scda ad thessalonicenses (*aft.* epistolam) *add C* (*corr.*) explicit ad thesal. 1. incipit secunda ad
eosdem *H*

He commands by oath that the letter be read by all the holy brothers, because he suspects on the basis of some of the things that had been reported to him that what he wrote might not be brought to everyone's attention. And adding after this:

5:28 *The grace of our Lord Jesus Christ be with you. Amen.*

He is seen to have finished the letter.

THEODORUS
MOPSUESTENUS
IN EPISTOLAM B. PAULI
AD THESSALONICENSES II

ARGUMENTUM

BEATUS apostolus Paulus, postquam primam ad Thessalonicenses scripserat epistolam, cognouit quod quamquam aduersariorum pertinacia in eadem perstiterit saeuitia, uariis temptationibus adgressa eos qui crediderant, tamen ad omnia illa aspera quae
5 isdem fuerant [inlata, uirtute] Dei in fide persistentes, superiores omni temptatione fuerint demonstrati. cognouit uero quod a quibusdam suasi aestiment finem praesenti incumbere saeculo, hocque aliqui quasi ab ipso apostolo edocti ceteris nuntiabant; adiecto illo, quod illi qui indisciplinate uersabantur nulla ex parte ex litteris
10 prioribus apostoli meliores sui fuerant effecti, sed perseuerauerint in pristino suo prauo proposito. scribit igitur secundam hanc epistolam, primum quidem conlaudans eos, eo quod contra omnes impetus aduersariorum decertantes non fuerant superati; adhortatur uero eos etiam currenti tempore in eodem persistere proposito,
15 omnemque tempestatem ab aduersariis inlatam per patientiam superare. deinde instruit eos, ut non existiment incumbere sibi consummationes temporum. inter cetera uero instruit eos

---

3 prestiteret *C** 5 eisdem *C* (*corr.*) ‖ inl. uirt. *om C* H r* [*a lacuna follows* fuerant *in C** (*apply*) *H*] *add* in lata *C* (*corr.*) ‖ di in (*for* dei in) *C** dein *H* in *C* (*corr.*) *r* 7-8 hoc qui *C* (*corr.*) 9 quo (*for* quod) *C** quae *H* quod illi *om r* 10 sui *om C* (*corr.*) 11 propositu *C** 12 eo (*bef.* quod) *om r* 14-15 propositu *C** 16 superari *C*H* 17 consummationem *l* ‖ temporam (tempora?) *C** ‖ uero instruit *bis H*

THEODORE OF MOPSUESTIA ON BLESSED PAUL'S SECOND LETTER TO THE THESSALONIANS

THE SETTING

[41] The blessed apostle Paul, after he had written his first letter to the Thessalonians, found out that, although the stubbornness of the adversaries persisted with the same ferocity and assaulted those who had believed with many different trials, nevertheless, by persisting by God's power in faith in the face of all those harsh measures that had been inflicted on them, they had proved stronger than every trial. But Paul found out that they had been persuaded by some people to believe that the end of the present age was at hand and that some of them, claiming to be taught by the apostle himself, [42] were proclaiming this to the rest. In addition, he found out that those who were living undisciplined lives had in no way been improved by the apostle's earlier letter but had persisted in their previous misguided behavior. Therefore, he writes this second letter first, of course, to praise them because they had not been conquered in struggling against all the attacks of their adversaries. And he exhorts them even as time goes on to persist in the same purpose and to prevail by endurance over every storm inflicted by the adversaries. Then he instructed them not to suppose the times of the end of the world[1] were at hand for them. And among other things he instructed them also about the coming

---

[1]*Consummationes temporum*. Swete (2:42) calls attention to 1 Cor 10:11 and Heb 9:26 and suggests that the original reading may have been *consummationis tempora*.

et Antichristi aduentum, et qualiter uel quomodo sit adpariturus;
dein indisciplinatis scribit, uehementer eos corripiens, eo quod nihil ex illis prioribus scriptis fuerint adiuuati, in quibus consilium
illis dederat de illis quae eos agere conueniebant. cautius uero de
omnibus instruemur ex illis quae in subsequentibus habentur.

*Paulus et Siluanus et Timotheus ecclesiae Thessalonicensium in
Deo patre nostro et domino Iesu Christo. gratia uobis et pax a Deo
patre nostro et domino Iesu Christo.*

hanc praescriptionem epistolae faciens, incipit sic:

*gratias agere debemus Deo semper pro uobis, fratres, sicut dignum
est.*

a gratiarum actione incipere idem apostolus saepe est consuetus. hoc uero in loco etiam dilatasse ipsam gratiarum actionem uidetur, non absolute dicens 'gratias agimus,' sed quoniam *gratias
agere debemus*, quasi qui et incusari sit dignus, si non debitum redderet pro illis, pro quibus et debent gratiarum actionem, eo quod
et necessarie debere illam uideatur. et adiectio est perspicua quam
adiecit dicens *sicut dignum est;* quod et ipsum augmentum habet
gratiarum actionis, siquidem talia sunt quae secundum eos sunt,
ut iuste Deo pro illis gratiarum actio referatur. unde ostendens
quia iure ista dicit, eo quod magna erant illa quae secundum eos
erant, ait:

*quoniam supercrescit fides uestra, et abundat caritas uniuscuiusque
omnium uestrum in alterutrum.*

etenim per omnia ostendit quoniam magna erant illa quae secundum eos erant, ex quibus dixit fidem eorum augere, quod habebant aliquid amplius a firmitate; firmitas enim dici potest, etsi
in eodem statu maneat. nam quod dixit *supercreuit,* ostendit quod
et in ipsa fide augmentum sumpserint; et 'in alterutrum caritatem
eorum abundare' dicens, quod et ipsum ostendit in dies singulos
meliorem illorum fuisse profectum. quod etiam maius adserere
cupiens dixit: *uniuscuiusque omnium uestrum in alterutrum;* omnes

1 A. aduentu *C** de A. aduentu *C* (*corr.*) 2 deindisc. scribi *C** de in disci-
plinatis scribens *r* 3 adiuti *r* 4 qui (*for* quae) *C** ‖ conueniebat *C* (*corr.*)
‖ uere *r* 5 instr. de omn. *H* 9 hac praescriptione epistolae facta *r* 12-13
a *om C** solitus (*for* consuetus) *r* 16 pro quibus debet *C* (*corr.*) 17 et (*bef.*
necess.) *om C* (*corr.*) *r* 18 habet grat. *om r* 20 ualde (*for* unde) *H* 21 eo
et quod *r* ‖ erunt *r* 24 omnium *om H* 25 quon. magna er. *om C** 27
si (*for* etsi) *C* (*corr.*) 29 in (*bef.* ipsa) *om H* 31 meliorum *C** 32 dicit *H*
‖ uestrum omn. *r*

of Antichrist and in what way or how he would appear. Then he writes to the undisciplined, strongly rebuking them because they had profited not at all by his earlier letter in which he had given them advice about what they should rightly do. But we shall explain all these things more carefully in what follows.

1:1–2 *Paul and Silvanus and Timothy to the church of the Thessalonians in God our Father and the Lord Jesus Christ. Grace to you and peace from God our Father and the Lord Jesus Christ.*

Composing this salutation of the letter, he begins as follows:

1:3a *We ought to give thanks to God always for you, brothers, as is worthy,*

The same apostle often had the habit of beginning with a thanksgiving. But in this place he has also plainly expanded the thanksgiving, since he does not simply say "we give thanks," but [43] *we ought to give thanks,* as though he might deserve blame if he should not render what was due for those things for which they, too, ought to give thanks, because it seemed that this was necessarily owing as well. And the addition he made by saying *as is worthy* is perfectly clear, because it elaborates the thanksgiving, if indeed their affairs are such that thanksgiving may be justly rendered to God for them. Showing from this that he is saying these things with good reason because their conduct was great, he says:

1:3b *since your faith grows abundantly and the love of each one of all of you for one another abounds,*

Indeed, in all respects he shows that their affairs were great, among which he said that their faith was increasing because they were gaining something more by their steadfastness; for one can speak of steadfastness even if it means remaining in the same condition. For the fact that he said *has grown abundantly*[2] shows that they gained an increase even in faith itself. And by speaking of "their love for one another abounding" he shows that their progress was itself also better day by day. Wishing to assert this still more, he said *of each one of all of you for one another.* For he

---

[2] Swete (2:43) suggests that the change of tense is Theodore's mistake.

enim similiter dixit tales esse. et quae est istius rei probatio?

ita ut nos ipsi in uobis gloriemur in ecclesiis Dei, pro patientia ue-
stra et fide in omnibus persecutionibus uestris et tribulationibus quas
sustinetis.

5 'denique et nos omni in loco de uobis gloriantes referimus fidei
uestrae firmitatem, laudantes, eo quod et tormentis uariis affecti
in eodem statu permansistis.' bene autem dixit *quas sustinetis*, eo
quod hoc demiratione dignum erat, quod forti animo sustinerent
inlata sibi tormenta. deinde dicit et ipsius passionis utilitatem:

10 *demonstrationem iusti iudicii Dei, ut digni habeamini regno Dei,*
pro quo et patimini.

'adparebitis etenim ob ista in futuro saeculo iusta ratione regnum caelorum fruentes, si tamen et pro illo pati adquiescitis,
magnum quoddam bonum existimantes eius esse fruitionem.' et
15 ostendens quoniam nec aduersariis talia in illis facientibus erit im-
pune, adicit:

si tamen iustum est apud Deum retribuere his qui tribulant uos re-
tribulationem, et uobis, qui tribulamini, requiem nobiscum.

nam quod dicit *si iustum est*, hoc dicit: *si tamen iustum est*. uult
20 enim dicere quia 'iusta tunc ratione Deus illos quidem qui talia in
praesenti uita erga uos gesserunt subdet poenae; uobis uero, pro
quibus patimini, magnam praebebit remunerationem largitatis.'
et poenae ipsius publicans pondus, dicit etiam qualis sit aduentus
ipsius iudicis:

25 *in reuelatione domini Iesu de caelo cum angelis uirtutis eius, in*
flamma ignis dantis uindictam his qui non nouerunt Deum et qui non
obaudiunt euangelio domini nostri Iesu.

terribilem per omnia eius aduentum esse ostendit, et loci natura, siquidem de caelo uidetur; et ministrorum fortitudine, cum an-
30 gelis enim uirtutis uenturum dicit; et tormentorum specie, flam-

---

2   domini (*for* dei) *r*   9   in (*bef.* torm.) *add C**   10   in (*bef.* demonstr.) *add r*
12-13   regno *C* (*corr.*)   14   eius *om r*   ‖   fruitione *r*   18   tribulationem *C r*
19   nam quod d. si iustum e. h. d. si tamen iustum est *om H*   21   pro *om C*
(*corr.*)   27   Christi (*aft* Iesu) *add r*   29   min. uidetur fortitudinem *C* H* min.
uid. fortitudo *r*: txt *C* (*corr.*)   30   eorum (*for* enim) *r*   ‖   speciem *C* H r*

said that all are alike in this way. And what is the proof of that fact?

1:4 *so that we ourselves may boast of you in the churches of God for your endurance* [44] *and faith in all your persecutions and the afflictions you are enduring,*

"And then we also in every place, boasting about you, report the steadfastness of your faith, giving praise because even though weakened by many different torments, you have stood fast in the same condition." And he rightly said *that you are enduring,* because it was worthy of admiration that they endured the torments inflicted on them with a brave mind. Then he speaks also of the benefit of the suffering itself:

1:5 *the demonstration of the just judgment of God, so that you may be held worthy of the kingdom of God, for which you are also suffering,*

"Indeed, because of those things you will appear in the age to come as people enjoying for good reason the kingdom of the heavens, if indeed you bear up with suffering for it, supposing its enjoyment to be some great good." And to show that not even when their adversaries do such things to them it will go unpunished, he adds:

1:6–7a *if indeed it is just for God to repay those who afflict you with affliction, and to you who are afflicted, relief with us,*

For when he says *if it is just,* he means *if indeed it is just.*[3] [45] For he means that, "with just reason God at that future time will subject to punishment those who have dealt with you in such ways in the present life, but he will bestow on you in return for what you have suffered the great recompense of his generosity." And to proclaim the weight of the punishment itself, he says also what the coming of the judge himself may be like:

1:7b–8 *at the revelation of the Lord Jesus from heaven with the angels of his power, with a flame of fire, giving vengeance on those who have not known God and who do not obey the gospel of our Lord Jesus,*

He shows that his coming is in all respects fearful, both by the nature of its place, since it is seen to be from heaven, and by the strength of its ministers, for he says he will come with angels of

---

[3] Theodore's comment is intelligible only on the basis of the Greek. The text of 1:6 reads εἴπερ, which could imply doubt, and Theodore is arguing that the word must be understood as εἴγε. The Latin here represents the first of these words by *si tamen,* which is the usual way the translator has rendered the second of the Greek words. The basic point is that "if" does not express any doubt about God's just retribution. See Swete's notes, 2:44 and 1:172.

mam enim ignis dixit. adserens uero et de illis qui sunt tormentis subiciendi, ait eos *qui non nouerunt Deum, et qui non obaudie-*
runt euangelio; maiorem tormentorum eorum praebuit probationem. siquidem et illos, si solummodo non obaudierint fidei, poena
5 maneat, quanto magis illos, qui credentibus calumnias impressio-
nesque irrogant? deinde et tormentorum speciem exaggerat prout
potis est, dicens:
  qui poenas luent interitus aeternos.
  nam ex qualitate ipsa grauia tormenta esse ostendit, siqui-
10 dem interitus sunt exterminii perditionem perficientes ex tempore, quod non ad tempus, sed aeterno sunt. et iterum ad personam
recurrit iudicis, poenae ipsius magnitudinem exinde ostendens:
  a facie Domini et gloria fortitudinis eius.
  et quia per omnia magna ostendit esse tormenta quae in aduer-
15 sarios sunt depromenda, dicit in quibus tunc erunt hi qui crediderunt:
  cum uenerit glorificari in sanctis suis et mirificari in omnibus qui
  crediderunt, quoniam creditum est testimonium nostrum in uobis, in
  die illo.

20 †quod dixit *in die illo* ad illud reddendum est quod dixerat
et mirificari in omnibus qui credi-
derunt, ut sit in medio positum
quoniam creditum est euangelium
25 *nostrum in uobis,* et[si] secundum sensum nouissimum iace-
re uideatur. uult enim dicere
quoniam 'secundum illum diem
gloriosus et mirabilis uidebitur
30 in his qui sibi crediderunt, per
illa bona quae erga illos faciet,
quae etiam et uos estis fruituri,

τὸ ἐν τῇ ἡμέρᾳ ἐκείνῃ πρὸς τὸ
καὶ θαυμασθῆναι ἐν πᾶσιν τοῖς πισ-
τεύσασιν ἀποδοτέον· ἵνα ἡ διὰ μέ-
σου κείμενον τὸ ὅτι ἐπιστεύθη τὸ
μαρτύριον ἡμῶν ἐφ' ὑμᾶς, τελευ-
ταῖον ὂν τῇ τῆς ἐννοίας ἀκολουθίᾳ.
βούλεται γὰρ εἰπεῖν ὅτι 'κατ' ἐκείνην τὴν ἡμέραν ἐπίδοξος καὶ θαυ-
μαστὸς ἐν τοῖς πεπιστευκόσιν φανήσεται διὰ τῶν περὶ αὐτῶν ἀγα-
θῶν· ὧν δὴ καὶ ὑμεῖς ἀπελαύσατε,
ἅτε δὴ τὴν διδασκαλίαν ἡμῶν πα-
ραδεξάμενοι.'

---

1 esse (*for* enim) *r* 2 subiecendi [subiac. *r*] aut eos *C* r* 4 et siquidem
(*for* siqu. et) *r* 7 potens e. *H* potest *r* 8 in (*bef.* int.) *add C* (*corr.*) 10 ex
ext. perditione *C*H* et ext. p. *r* ‖ praeficientes *C*H* prof. *C* (*corr.*): *txt r* 11
aeterne *C* (*corr.*) aeterna *r* 12 ostendit dicens *H* 13 eius *om r* 20 dixerant
C* ‖ sq. Coisl. 204, f. 180 a [Cr. vi. 384] ἄλλος φησίν· τὸ ἐν τῇ, κ.τ.λ. Cr.:
"hoc scholion uidetur esse Origenis." 21 redendum *H* ‖ quoniam (*for*
quod) *H* 25 si *om C H r* 28 quoniam *om r* 31 eos (*for* illos) *r*

power, and by the kind of torments, for he spoke of a flame of fire. And in his assertions about those who are to be subjected to torments he says that they are those *who have not known God and who* have not obeyed *the gospel.* He has furnished a greater proof of their torments. Indeed, if a punishment remains for those who have only failed to obey the faith, how much more for those who call down false accusations and assaults on those who believe? Then he also piles up the kind of torments as much as possible, saying:

1:9a *who will suffer the punishments of eternal destructions*

For he shows how heavy the torments are by what they are like, [46] since the destructions are exterminations that accomplish ruin in time, yet are not temporal but for eternity. And again he turns back to the person of the judge, showing on this basis the magnitude of the punishment itself:

1:9b *from the face of the Lord and the glory of his might,*

And because he is showing that the torments to be brought forth upon the adversaries are great in all respects, he says in what condition those who have believed will be at that time:

1:10 *when he comes to be glorified in his saints and to be marveled at among all who have believed, since our testimony among you has been believed, on that day.*

†His statement *on that day* must be referred to what he had said, [47] *and to be marveled at among all who have believed,* so that what is placed in the middle—*since our gospel among you has been believed*—may appear to stand in last place according to the meaning. For he wants to say, "at that day he will appear glorious and marvelous among those who have believed in him through those good things he will do for them, which you also are destined to enjoy, because you have accep-

On that day must be referred to *and to be marveled at among all who have believed,* so that what lies in the middle—because our testimony to you has been believed—may be last in the logical order of the sense. For he wants to say, "at that day he will appear glorious and marvelous among those who have believed through the good things concerning them, which you also have enjoyed, since you have accepted our teaching.

eo quod doctrinam nostram re-
cepistis.*'

sic per omnia adhortans reuelatione eorum quae expectantur, eo
quod aduersariis magna inferentur tormenta, et quod magnorum
5 bonorum fruitionem expectent potire credentes, adicit:

*in quod et oro semper pro uobis, ut uos dignos uocatione sua Deus
habeat, et impleat omne placitum bonitatis et opus fidei in uirtute; ut
glorificetur nomen domini nostri in uobis et uos in ipso, secundum gratiam Dei nostri et domini Iesu Christi.*

10 'pro his quae talia sunt perseueramus pro uobis orantes, ita ut
dignos uos bonorum illorum exhibeat Deus, in quorum et uocati
estis fruitionem; implens uos omni bono et confortans, ita ut et in
operibus ostendatis fidem, et illa quae ab aduersariis inferuntur facile sustineatis. sic enim et Christus in uobis gloriosus secundum
15 praesens saeculum uidebitur, quando cum alacritate adquiescitis
pati pro eo; uosque qui sic firmiter in eo credidistis, futuram frue-
mini gloriam, quam sua gratia sibi credentibus repromisit.' quae
ergo conueniebant dici ad laudem eorum qui in aduersis firmi perstiterunt, et ad exhortationem ut in eadem persisterent sententia,
20 in hisce uisus est consummasse. hinc uero incipit de consummatione saeculi disputare, docens eos non existimare sibi finem mun-
danum imminere:

*rogamus autem uos, fratres, per aduentum domini nostri Iesu Chri-
sti et nostram congregationem in eum, ut ne cito moueamini a sensu
25 uestro, neque terreamini neque per spiritum, neque per uerbum, neque
per epistolam quasi ex nobis, quasi quia instet dies Domini.*

adueniente Domino iustos omnes debere rapi super nubes in
obuiam eius ut et simul sint semper cum eo, apostolus uero in pri-

---

1-2 suscepistis *l*   5 potiri *C (corr.) r*   6 in quo *r*   7 omnem *H*   9 in
uobis et uos in illo (*aft* Christi) *add C H r: see note*   16-17 futura, gloria *C*
(*corr.*)   ‖ fruimini *C* H*   19 perstiterent *r*   20 hic *H*   21-22 mundi *C*
(*corr.*)   24-25 a sensu u. neque terr. *om r*   27 in (*for* super) *om r*   28 et ut
(*for* ut et) *r*   ‖ uero *om r*

ted our teaching."*4

So, in all respects exhorting them by the revelation of those things that are awaited, because they are being afflicted with great torments by the adversaries and because they are awaiting the actual enjoyment of great good things by believing, he adds:

1:11–12 *For this also I[5] pray always for you, that God may hold you worthy of his calling and may fulfill every good pleasure of goodness and work of faith in power, so that the name of our Lord[6] may be glorified in you and you in him, according to the grace of our God and the Lord Jesus Christ.*

"For such reasons we persevere in praying for you, so that God may display you worthy of those good things to the enjoyment of which [48] you have been called, filling you with every good and strengthening you, so that you may both show your faith in deeds and endure easily what is inflicted by the adversaries. For in this way Christ will also appear glorious in you in the present age, when you are content to suffer for him eagerly. And you who have so steadfastly believed in him will enjoy the glory to come, which by his grace he has promised to those who believe in him." With these words he seems to have finished what was suitable to be said for praising them because they have stood fast in adverse circumstances and for exhorting them to continue to stand fast in the same purpose. But from here on he begins to reason about the consummation of the age, teaching them not to suppose that the end of the world is at hand for them:

2:1–2 *And we ask you, brothers, as far as the coming of our Lord Jesus Christ and our gathering with him are concerned, that you not be quickly disturbed from your sense, nor terrified either by spirit or by word or by letter as though from us, on the grounds that the day of the Lord may be at hand.*

Now in his first letter (1 Thess 4:17) the apostle clearly asserted that when the Lord comes, all the righteous must be caught up above the clouds to meet him, so that at the same time they may be

---

[4] Note that the Latin translation substitutes "gospel" for testimony. As well, it locates the enjoyment of good things in the age to come, contradicting the Greek: "which you also have enjoyed." There is no difficulty in supposing that Theodore can accept a *present* enjoyment of the good things to come.

[5] The Greek text has the first-person plural, and in the commentary the Latin translation follows this.

[6] The Latin translation omits "Jesus."

ma epistola euidenter adseruit. hoc ergo dicit: *et nostram congre-*
gationem ad eum,

†dicit etenim Christi aduentum	ὅτι περὶ τῆς Χριστοῦ παρουσίας καὶ
et congregationem nostram tunc	τῆς ἡμῶν ἐπ' αὐτὸν ἐκείνης ἐπισυ-
ad eum futuram. 'nolite suade-	ναγωγῆς, μὴ πείθεσθε τοῖς βουλο-
ri illis qui uos seducunt, quasi	μένοις ἀπατᾶν ὑμᾶς, ὡς ἂν ἐγγύ-
quia prope sit illud tempus; sed	θεν παρόντος ἐκείνου τοῦ καιροῦ·
siue quis se de spiritali id ino-	ἀλλ' εἴτε ὡς ἀπὸ πνευματικῆς ἐνερ-
peratione promittat dicere, siue	γείας λέγειν τις ἐπαγγέλλεται, εἴτε
quasi ex uerbo et epistola nostra	ὡς ἀπὸ λόγου ἢ ἐπιστολῆς ἡμετέ-
sit edoctus, nolite suaderi ei.*'	ρας τοῦτο μαθών, μὴ πείσεσθε.'

et uehementius eos cautos facere uolens adicit:

   ne quis uos seducat ullo modo.

   'qualitercumque ista quis dixerit uobis, nolite ei credere.'

   quoniam [ni]si uenerit apostasia primum et reuelatus fuerit homo
peccati, filius perditionis, qui aduersatur et superextollit se super omne
quod dicitur deus aut quod colitur, ita ut in templo Dei ut Deus sedeat,
ostendens se quoniam est Deus.

uult quidem dicere, quoniam non possunt illa fieri priusquam
Antichristus ueniat. oportet enim primum illum uenire; deinde
consequentur illa quae dicuntur. 'apostasiam' uero uocauit tempus illud, eo quod paulo minus omnes tunc discedent a pietate, et
adcurrent ad eum. 'hominem' equidem eum nominauit iusta ratione, eo quod et homo erit, daemone in eo omnia inoperante, sicut et in illum hominem qui pro nostra salute sumptus est, Deus
Verbo omnia perfecisse uidetur. temptat enim ille per omnia illa, quae Christi sunt, imitari, utpote et Christum se esse dicens.
'peccati' uero 'hominem' eum dixit, eo quod peccatum ministra-
bit, et multis hominibus huius causa existet. et 'filium' eum 'perditionis' dicit, utpote perditioni subdendum post hoc, sicut et in
subsequentibus euidentius dicit. uocat autem eum 'aduersarium'

---

3 aduentu (*om* et) *l* ‖ sq. Coisl. 204, f. 180 b [Cr. vi. 386, Fr. 146] Θεοδώρου.
ὅτι περὶ τῆς, κ.τ.λ. 4 nostram *om* r 5-6 suadere illos *C* H* suadere illis *C*
(*corr.*) persuaderi ab illis *r* 7 quia *om* r 8 quis de (*om* se) *H* qui spe (*for*
quis se) *r* quis (*om* se de) *l* ‖ se dicere *l* 11 suadere ei *C H* persuaderi ei *r*
14 qui taliter cumque *C* H* qui taliter utcumque *r*: txt *C* (*corr.*) 15 quo si
uenerit *C** quoniam si u. *H r*: txt *C* (*corr.*) 19 quo (*for* quoniam) *C** 21
consequuntur *H** consequenter *r* 24 et *om* r 24-25 sicuti *r* 25 in illo
homine *C* (*corr.*) 26 omnia *om* r ‖ temptabit *C* (*corr.*) 27 dicens *om* H
29 multi *C* H* 31 consequentibus *H*

always with him. Thus, this is what he means by *and our gathering with him,*

†For he is speaking of Christ's coming and [49] our future gathering with him then. "Do not be persuaded by those who are leading you astray, as though that time were near. Rather, whether someone professes to say this from a spiritual working or has been taught it as though by word and our letter, do not be persuaded by him."*

[He says] that "concerning Christ's coming and that gathering of us to him, do not be persuaded by those who want to deceive you, as though that time were present near at hand. Rather, whether someone professes to be speaking as from a spiritual working or to have been instructed as from a word or a letter of ours, do not be persuaded."

And wishing more strongly to make them cautious, he adds:

2:3a *Let no one lead you astray in any way,*

"No matter in what way anyone should say those things to you, do not believe him."

2:3b-4 *since unless the apostasy comes first and there has been revealed [50] the man of sin, the son of destruction, who opposes and highly exalts himself above everything that is said to be god or that is worshiped, so that he may sit in the temple of God as God, showing himself that he is God.*

He surely means that those things cannot happen before Antichrist comes.[7] For he must come first, and then in following order what is being discussed. And Paul calls that time *apostasy,* because nearly all people will then abandon true religion and hasten to Antichrist. And he certainly named him *the man* with good reason, because he will be a man, with a demon working in him, [51] just as also in that Man assumed for our salvation God is seen to have accomplished everything by the Word.[8] For Antichrist tries to imitate Christ in all those things that belong to Christ, since he even says that he is Christ. And Paul spoke of him as *the man of sin,* because he will minister to sin and will come to be its cause for many people. And he says he is *the son of*

---

[7]That is, something needs to be supplied in the verse before "unless." According to Theodore the sense is: "since these things cannot happen unless the apostasy comes first, etc."

[8]That is, the spiritual working in the man Antichrist is demonic, a parody of the divine working of the Word in the assumed Man.

quidem, quasi qui et aduersa agat diuinae uoluntati et omnes ad
se transducere adnitatur. 'superextollentem' uero 'se super omne quod dicitur deus aut quod colitur,' eo quod omnes homines
a propria eorum secta discedere suadens, sibi faciet adorare, seipsum dicens esse Christum, cui et ab omnibus honorem Dei tribui
ut iustum uindicabit. sic enim et 'in Dei templis,' hoc est, et in
domibus orationum, ingrediens sedebit, quasi quia ipse sit Christus et propter hoc debeat ab omnibus adorari in ordinem Dei. et
ostendens quoniam nihil nunc noui dicit ad eos:

non estis (inquit) *memores, quoniam cum adhuc essem apud uos,
haec dicebam uobis?*

deinde adicit:

et nunc quid detinet scitis, ut reueletur in suo tempore.

quidam dixerunt Spiritum gratiarum hoc in loco dixisse apostolum *et nunc quod detinet;* eo quod 'tunc (inquit) ille uidebitur,
atubi Spiritus gratiae ad plenum destiterit, et perficere inoperatio-
nes in aperto cessabit.' sed

†hoc mihi non uidetur esse ap-	οὐ πιθανὸν ἔμοιγε φαίνεται τοῦτο,
te dictum, eo quod et cessaue-	ἐπεὶ καὶ ἐπαύσαντο ἐκ πλείονος ἤδη
runt ex multo iam tempore ino-	τοῦ χρόνου [αἱ τοῦ πνεύματος ἐν-
perationes Spiritus. si uero quis	εργεῖαι]. εἰ γάρ τις μὴ πεπαῦσθαι
uoluerit dicere non cessasse, eo	βούλοιτο λέγειν διὰ τὸ παρά τινων
quod et ab aliquibus adhuc per	[κατὰ] προσευχὴν γίνεσθαι κατὰ τὸ
orationem fiant aliqua, licet si	σπάνιον ἔνια, οὐδὲ παυθήσεται κατά
et rare; secundum igitur hunc	γε τοῦτον τὸν τρόπον, ἐπεὶ μηδὲ
modum neque cessare adsero,	ἐπιλείπειν πάντῃ τοὺς ἁγίους οἷόν
eo quod neque deficere ad ple-	τε, ἐσομένων καὶ τότε τῶν οὐ προσ-
num sancti umquam poterunt.	ιεμένων τὴν ἐκείνου διδασκαλίαν, οἳ
erunt enim et tunc qui non su-	καὶ διαλάμψουσιν ἐν τοῖς ὑπὲρ εὐ-

2 extollentem *C* ‖ se *om C** 4 sibi *om C (corr.)* se (*for* sibi) *r* [*cf. Rönsch,
Itala, p.* 439] 5 hominibus (*for* omn.) *H* 6 et (*bef.* in dom.) *om r* 7 quia *om
r* 8 hominibus (*for* omn.) *r* ‖ ordine *C (corr.)* 9 noui nunc *H* 10 cum
om H ‖ adessem (*for* adhuc essem) *r* 13 quod *C (corr.) r* 14 quidam ...
aduersus eum *om r* ‖ spiritus *H* 16 adubi *C** ubi *C (corr.)* 18 Coisl. 204,
f. 182 a [Cr. vi. 388–9, Fr. 147–8] σευηριανὸς δὲ τὸ κατέχον φησὶν τὴν τοῦ ἁγίου
πνεύματος χάριν. θεόδωρος δὲ ὁμοίως τῷ μακαρίῳ ἰωάννῃ ταύτην οὐ προσίεται
τὴν ἐξήγησιν, φάσκων· οὐ πιθανόν, κ.τ.λ. 19 et *om C (corr.)* 20 αἱ τ. πν.
ἐν om. cod. edd. 21 si quis uero uoluit *H* 23 κατὰ om. cod. edd. 24
fiet (*for* si et) *C* 25 raro *C (corr.)* ‖ sec. hunc igitur *C* 28 potuerint *H**
poterint *H (corr.)* 29 erant *C**

destruction, since afterwards he must be subjected to destruction, just as Paul says more clearly in what follows. And he calls him "the adversary,"[9] inasmuch as he does things adverse to the divine will and strives to draw all people over to himself. And he is the one "highly exalting himself *above everything that is said to be god or that is worshiped*," because by persuading all people to depart from their own sect, he will make them worship him, saying that he is himself Christ, to whom he will claim the honor of God should be bestowed by all, as is right. For in this way even "in God's temples," that is, even [52] in the houses of prayer, he will enter and take his seat as though he were Christ and for this reason should be worshiped in the rank of God by all. And to show that he is now saying nothing new to them:

2:5 *Do you not remember* (he says) *that when I was still with you, I told you these things?*

Then he adds:

2:6 *And now what is restraining him you know, so that he may be revealed in his own time.*

There are some who have said that it was the Spirit of gifts of which [53] the apostle spoke in this place by saying *and now what is restraining*, on the grounds that "then (he says) Antichrist will appear when the gifts of the Spirit have completely failed, and their workings will openly cease to have any effect." But

†this does not seem to me to have been said appropriately, because the workings of the Spirit have already ceased for a long time. But perhaps someone would want to say they have not ceased because some things are still done by some people by prayer, even though seldom. In that case neither do I assert they have ceased in this way, because saints can never completely fail. For even then there will be those who	This does not seem persuasive to me, since the workings of the Spirit have already ceased for a long time. Someone might wish to say that they have not ceased because some of them happen rarely from some people by prayer and that they will not cease at least in this way, since it is impossible that saints should ever be completely wanting, because even at that time there will be those who do not go over to the teaching of Antichrist,

---

[9] *Adversarium*, referring to "who opposes" in 2:4 (*qui aduersatur* = ὁ ἀντικείμενος).

scipient eius doctrinam, qui et
clari erunt contemplatione pietatis decertantes aduersus eum.
dicit autem *quod nunc detinet*
5 eo quod diabolus quidem dudum uoluerit hoc idem facere,
Deus uero interim retinet eum,
eo quod tempus statuit consummationis saeculi istius, secun-
10 dum quam uideri concedit eum.
hoc apostolus nominauit *quod
nunc detinet*, Dei dicens definitionem detinere eum. unde et
adicit: [*ut*] *reueletur* idem *in suo*
15 *tempore*,*

σεβείας ἀγῶσιν. λέγει δὲ τὸ κατέχον, ὡς ἂν τοῦ διαβόλου μὲν ἐθέ-
λοντος καὶ ἤδη τοῦτο ποιῆσαι, τοῦ
θεοῦ δὲ κατέχοντος αὐτὸν τέως διὰ
τὸ καιρὸν ὁρίσαι τῇ συντελείᾳ τοῦ
αἰῶνος, καθ' ὃν ὀφθῆναι συγχωρεῖ
κἀκεῖνον. τοῦτο [τὸ] κατέχον ὁ
ἀπόστολος ὀνομάζει, τοῦ θεοῦ [λέ-
γων] τὸν ὅρον, ὅθεν καὶ ἐπήγα-
γεν· εἰς τὸ ἀποκαλυφθῆναι αὐτὸν
τῷ ἑαυτοῦ καιρῷ.

quasi qui prohibeatur nunc uideri usque tunc, eo quod diuina definitione ad praesens teneatur. uidebitur uero tunc in saeculi fine,
quando et concedet illi Dominus suam ostendere malitiam; propter quod bene adicit:

20   *mysterium enim iam inoperatur iniquitatis.*

†hoc est: 'etsi non aperte
apostasiam operatur diabolus,
sed quasi in mysterio nunc peragit, per singula momenta per
25 suos a pietate temptans diuellere eos qui ad fidem accedunt.*'

ἀντὶ τοῦ· 'εἰ καὶ μὴ κατὰ
τὸ σαφὲς ἤδη τὴν ἀποστασίαν
ἐργάζεται ὁ διάβολος, ἀλλ' οὖν
γε ὡς ἐν μυστηρίῳ πλεῖστα καὶ
νῦν διαπράττεται, ἑκάστοτε διὰ
τῶν οἰκείων τῆς εὐσεβείας ἀφιστᾶν
πειρώμενος τοὺς προσιόντας τῇ
πίστει.'

et hoc ipsum iterum resumens:

tantum qui tenet nunc, usquedum de medio fiat; et reuelabitur ille
iniquus. hoc est: 'atubi definitio Dei quae eius prohibet aduentum
30 cessabit, tunc adparebit ille.'

---

3 decertantis *C** 5-6 dudum quidem *r* 7 eum *om r* ‖ τό, λέγων om.
cod. edd. 10 concedet *C* (*corr.*) 13 et *om r* 14 ut *om C H* ‖ id est (*for*
idem) *C** ‖ in *om r* 18 concedit *C* *r* 21 Coisl. *l.c.* τὸ γὰρ μυστήριον
ἤδη ἐνεργεῖται ἀντὶ τοῦ κ.τ.λ. 28 usque nunc dimidio *C* *H* teneat usque de
medio *C* (*corr.*) usque tunc dimidium *r* 29 hoc enim adubi *C* *H* h. e. ait ubi
C (*corr.*) hoc est ubi *l* ‖ hoc … ille *om r*

will not accept the teaching of Antichrist and who will be distinguished in their observance of true religion, contending against him. [54] And he says *what is now restraining*, because the devil has wanted to do this very thing for a long time, but God restrains him for the time being because he has established a time for the consummation of that age, when he has permitted him to appear. This is what the apostle has named *what is now restraining*, meaning that the time fixed by God restrains him. This is why he also adds, *so that he may be revealed in his own time,**

and they will be distinguished by their contests for true religion. And he says *that which restrains*, since the devil even now wants to do this, but God restrains him for the time being because he has fixed the time for the consummation of the age, when he permits even him to appear.

The apostle names this *that which restrains*, meaning the time set by God, which is why he also continued *for his being revealed in his own time.*

inasmuch as he is now prevented from appearing until that time, because for the present he is held fast by the time fixed by God. But then he will appear at the end of the age, when the Lord will permit him to display his wickedness. Because of this he rightly adds:

> 2:7a *For the mystery of wickedness is already at work,*

†That is, "even though the devil is not openly working apostasy, yet he is now carrying on his work in a mystery, moment by moment through his own people trying to tear away from true religion those who have drawn near to faith."*

Instead of "even though the devil is not already openly working apostasy, yet even now he is working a great many things as in a mystery, at every moment trying through his own people to remove from true religion those who have drawn near to faith."

And repeating the same point:

> [55] 2:7b-8a *only he who restrains now, until he comes to be from the midst, and then that unjust one will be revealed,*

That is, "when the time set by God that prevents his coming will come to an end, then he will appear."

†intendendum uero est illi par-
ti, quoniam 'reuelationem' Antichristi manifestationem
uocauit, et in superius dicens:
5 *cum reuelatus fuerit homo*, et hoc
in loco: *reuelabitur iniquus;* eo
quod diabolus semper quidem
ab aduentu Domini meditatur
illud facere ad nociuitatem ho-
10 minum, et utique illud fecisset,
si non secundum inenarrabilem
suam prouidentiam continuis-
set eum Deus. operabitur uero
tunc et perducet illud in aper-
15 to, quod dudum sibi uidebatur,
cum illi fuerit concessum suam
uoluntatem in opere producere.*

προσεκτέον ὅτι 'ἀποκάλυψιν' τοῦ
ἀντιχρίστου ἐκάλεσεν τὴν φανέρω-
σιν, ἔν τε τοῖς ἀνωτέροις ἀποκαλυ-
φθῇ ὁ ἄνθρωπος εἰπών, κἀνταῦθα,
ἀποκαλυφθήσεται ὁ ἄνομος· ὡς ἂν
τοῦ διαβόλου πάντοτε μὲν ἀπὸ τῆς
τοῦ κυρίου παρουσίας μελετῶντος
αὐτὸ ἐπὶ τῇ τῶν ἀνθρώπων βλάβῃ,
καὶ ἤδη γε αὐτὸ καὶ ποιήσαντος ἄν,
εἰ μὴ κατὰ τὴν ἀπόρρητον αὐτοῦ
βουλὴν κατεῖχεν αὐτὸν ὁ θεός· ἐρ-
γασομένου δὲ τότε καὶ οἴσοντός γε
εἰς φανερὸν τὸ πάλαι δοκοῦν αὐτῷ,
ὅταν συγχωρηθῇ τὴν οἰκείαν γνώμην ἐκβαλεῖν εἰς ἔργον.

et ostendens quoniam nec ille sine poena erit, adicit:
20 *quem dominus Iesus interficiet spiritu oris eius et destruet in appa-
ritione aduentus sui.*

euidens est quoniam de homine id dicit; nec enim Satanan ex-
pedit, quem aeternae poenae est traditurus, sed illum, eo quod or-
ganum sibi illum ad tantam explendam malitiam daemon oppor-
25 tunum cogitationibus suis esse repperit. et hoc in subsequentibus
apertius manifestauit dicens: *cuius est aduentus secundum inoperationem Satanae.* alium quendam insinuauit eum esse praeter Satanan, cuius inoperatione se ipsum demonstrabit. terribile est autem quod dicit;
30 †illo enim talia agente et per totum orbem omnes homines discedere a pietate suadente, subito de caelo adparens Christus et

ἐκείνου [γὰρ] τοιαῦτα διαπραττο-
μένου κατὰ τῆς οἰκουμένης καὶ
πάντας ἀνθρώπους ἀφιστῶντος τῆς
εὐσεβείας, ἐξαίφνης ἀπ' οὐρανῶν

1-2 Coisl. *l. c.* προσεκτέον ὅτι, κ.τ.λ.   2 quo (*for* quoniam) C*   4 in (*bef.*
sup.) *om* C (*corr.*) r   ‖ in hoc loco r   11-12 ἐργασαμένου Cr.   13 deus
eum r   19 addit r   20 Iesus *om* r   ‖ oris sui C r   ‖ in apparitionem C
illustratione r   22 Satanam r   23 que C* qui C (*corr.*)   ‖ est poenae r   24
maliticiam C   ‖ daemonum H   27 Satanam r   28 inoperationem H r   ‖
illum r   30 Coisl. 204, *l. c.* ἐκείνου (φησὶν) τοιαῦτα, κ.τ.λ. γὰρ om. cod. edd.

†And it must be noted in that verse that Paul called the appearance of Antichrist his "revelation." Above (2:3) he says, *when*[10] *there has been revealed the man,* and in this place *the unjust one will be revealed.* This is because the devil always takes thought from the coming of the Lord for doing what harms people, and he certainly would have done that, if God had not held him back in accord with his ineffable providence. But he will then work and will bring into the open what long ago seemed good to him, when God allows him to bring forth his wish to deed.*

And it must be noted that Paul called the appearance of Antichrist his "revelation." Above (2:3) he said *the man has been revealed,* and here *the lawless one will be revealed.* This is because the devil always takes thought from the coming of the Lord for what will harm people, and he would already have done this, if God had not restrained him in accord with his ineffable purpose. But he will then work and bring into the open what he decided long ago, when he is allowed to bring forth his own intent to deed.

And to show that Antichrist will not be unpunished, he adds:

2:8b *whom the Lord Jesus will slay with the breath of his mouth and will destroy with the appearance of his coming,*

[56] It is clear that he says this of a man, for God is not releasing Satan,[11] whom he destines for eternal punishment, but that one, because a demon has found him as an instrument fit for his own designs to fulfill such great wickedness. And Paul made this clear more openly in what follows (2:9) by saying, *whose coming is according to the working of Satan.* He implied that he is someone other than Satan, by whose operation he will reveal himself. And what he says is frightening;

†for when Antichrist does such things and tries to persuade all people throughout the whole world to draw away from true religion, suddenly Christ, appearing from heaven and only

For when Antichrist does such things throughout the world and tries to draw all people away from true religion, suddenly Christ, having appeared from heaven and only having cried

---

[10] See Swete's note (2:55): "The translator has carelessly added *cum* instead of *nisi* to complete the sense.

[11] This view contradicts Rev 20:7, but it is likely that Theodore does not accept Revelation and certain that he does not accept a millennial reading of it.

solummodo clamans cessare faciet ab opere, totum illum ex-
pendens. hoc enim dicit: *spiritu oris*, hoc est, uoce; ex illis
5 quae apud nos sunt sumens illud et dicens, eo quod nos spiritu cooperante abutimur ad ar-
ticulatam loquelam.*

φανεὶς ὁ Χριστὸς καὶ μόνον ἐπιβοή-
σας παύσει τῆς ἐργασίας, ὅλον αὐτὸν ἀναλώσας· τοῦτο γὰρ λέγει τὸ
τῷ πνεύματι τοῦ στόματος αὐτοῦ,
ἀντὶ τοῦ 'τῇ φωνῇ,' ἀπὸ τοῦ παρ'
ἡμῖν αὐτὸ εἰρηκώς, ἐπειδὴ ἡμεῖς τῷ
πνεύματι συνεργῷ κεχρήμεθα πρὸς
τὴν ἔναρθρον λαλιάν.

quae secundum illum sunt, referre incipit:
10 *cuius est aduentus secundum inoperationem Satanae.*
hoc est: 'adparebit ille Satana sibi inoperante omnia.' deinde
adicit et quid illud operatur in eo:
in omni uirtute et signis et prodigiis mendacibus.
'multa (inquit) et magna signa quoque et prodigia demonstra-
15 bit per eum.' bene autem adicit *mendacibus*, ostendens quoniam
in phantasmate magis quam in opere facit ea. qua autem ratione
hoc operatur?
et in omni seductione iniustitiae in his qui pereunt.
ut omne quicquid iniustitia plenum est operetur, et seducat eos
20 qui perditione digni sunt. sic autem uocat eos, qui sunt ei adpo-
nendi.
pro quibus caritatem ueritatis non susceperunt ut saluentur.
'cum conuenerit (inquit) eos permanere in ueritate caritatis, et
non discedere ab ipsa ex qua et saluari poterant.'
25 *et propter hoc mittit eis Deus inoperationem erroris, ut credant
mendacio; ut iudicentur omnes qui non crediderunt ueritati, sed complacuerunt iniquitati.*

†euidens est, quoniam concessionem Dei quasi opus eius
30 esse adscripsit; uult enim dicere, quoniam non permanentes
in ueritate intendent seductio-
ni et credent mendacio, iustam

τὴν συγχώρησιν δηλονότι ὡς
ἔργον τῷ θεῷ περιῆψεν· βούλεται
γὰρ εἰπεῖν, ὅτι μὴ μείναντες ἐπὶ τῆς
ἀληθείας προσέξουσιν τῇ πλάνῃ καὶ
πιστεύσουσιν τῷ ψεύδει, δικαίαν
δεχόμενοι τὴν τιμωρίαν ὑπὲρ ὧν

6-7 spiritum cooperante *C*   11   illi Satana sibi *C H* illi Satanas sibi *r*: *txt conj.*
Jacobi   12   ille (*for* illud) *r*   14   et prodigia *om H*   19   ut omne ... digni
sunt *om r*   20-21   accipiendi (*for* apponendi) *r*   25   mittet *C* (*corr.*)   28-29
concessione *C H r*: *txt g*   28   Coisl. 204, f. 183 a [Cr. vi. 391, Fr. 148] θεόδωρος
δέ φησιν εἰς τὸ 'διὰ τοῦτο πέμψει αὐτοῖς ὁ θεὸς ἐνέργειαν πλάνης'· τὴν συγχ.,
κ.τ.λ.   33   iustam p. sub. *r*

by crying out, will make him cease his work, inflicting total punishment on him. For what he means by *the breath of his mouth* [57] is his voice, taking this and saying it from what applies to us, because we use the help of breath to articulate speech.*

out, will stop his working, having destroyed him totally. For he says *by the breath of his mouth* instead of "by his voice," having found the expression from what applies to us, since we use the help of breath to articulate speech.

Paul begins to record what has to do with Antichrist:

2:9a *whose coming is according to the working of Satan*

That is, "he will appear, while Satan works everything in him." Then he adds also what it is that is worked in him:

2:9b *in all power and signs and lying wonders,*

"He will display (he says) many and great signs as well as wonders through him." And he rightly adds *lying*, to show that he does them in fantasy rather than in deed. And for what reason is this done?

2:10a *and in every leading astray of injustice in those who are perishing*

So that he may work everything whatsoever that is filled with injustice and may lead astray those who are worthy of perishing. So he calls those who are to be placed under him.

[58] 2:10b *because they have not received the love of truth so that they might be saved.*

"Although it would have been right (he says) for them to persevere in the truth of love and not to turn away from that by which they could have been saved."

2:11–12 *And because of this God sends to them the working of error, so that they may believe a lie, so that all who have not believed the truth but have been well-pleased with iniquity may be judged.*

†It is clear that he assigns the permission to God as though it were his work, for he wants to say that those who pay attention to the one leading them astray, by not remaining in the truth, and who believe a lie are those who undergo just punishment because, leaving the truth, they

Obviously, he assigned permission to God as though it were his doing. For he wants to say that they will cleave to error and will believe the lie, if they do not remain in the truth, receiving just punishment because by deserting the truth they turned aside to injustice.

subeuntes poenam pro quibus relinquentes ueritatem ad iniustitiam declinauerunt; ut dicat 'diabolum adorauerunt,' 'iniu-
5 stitiam' eam uocans, eo quod nec in iusta fiat ratione ab illis qui ea faciunt.*

καταλιπόντες τὴν ἀλήθειαν πρὸς τὴν ἀδικίαν ἔκλιναν· ἵνα εἴπῃ τοῦ διαβόλου τὴν προσκύνησιν, ἀδικίαν αὐτὴν καλέσας, ὡς οὐ δικαίως γινομένην παρὰ τῶν ποιούντων.

et quoniam de illis qui tunc increduli erunt dixit, bene adicit:

nos autem debemus gratias agere Deo semper pro uobis, fratres di-
10 *lecti a Domino, quoniam praeelegit uos Deus ab initio in salutem in sanctificatione Spiritus et fide ueritatis, in quod et uocauit uos per euangelium, in adquisitionem gloriae domini nostri Iesu Christi.*

'itaque et propter hoc (inquit) pro uobis gratias agimus Deo, quoniam uos elegit ita ut expectatam fruamini salutem, partici-
15 pans quidem uobis gratiam Spiritus, donans uero uobis ueritatis fidem. hoc enim uobis euangelii praebuit uocatio, futuram gloriam per illam fidem quae in Christo est repromittentis.' et post hoc:

itaque, fratres, state et tenete traditiones quas didicistis sine per
20 *uerbum, siue per epistolam nostram.*

hoc enim ad totum reddidit, hoc est: 'nolite suaderi illis qui uos seducere uolunt, sed manete in illis quae uobis tradidimus, siue per uerbum praesentes, siue et absentes per litteras.' deinde iterum orat pro eis:

25 *ipse autem dominus noster Iesus Christus, et Deus et pater noster, qui dilexit nos et dedit nobis consolationem aeternam et spem bonam in gratia, consoletur corda uestra et constabiliat in omni uerbo et opere bono.*

'qui gratia (inquit) sua aeternam illam consolationem nobis do-
30 nauit (id est, futurorum bonorum spem), ipse et secundum praesentem uitam hanc prosperet corda uestra, confirmans uos, ut omne quicquid illi boni est et dicere et facere possitis.' post hoc scribit eis:

---

3 declinauere *H* 9-10 di (*bef.* dilecti) *add H* 10 nos *r* ‖ in quo (*for* in quod) *H* 17 repromittentes *C* H* repromittans *C* (*corr.*) *r* 21 suadere illis *C H* persuaderi ab illis *r* 27 constabiliet *H* 29-30 donabit *C H* 31 prospere et corda uestra conf. uos ut *C** prospere consoletur a. u. conf. uos ut *C* (*corr.*) prospere et c. u. conf. ut *H* prosperet et c. u. uos conf. ut *r* 32 illud *C r*

have turned aside to injustice. He means "they have worshiped the devil," calling it "injustice" because it is not done with just reason by those who do these things.*

He means the worship of the devil, having called it injustice since it takes place unjustly by those who do it.

And since he has spoken of those who at that time would be unbelievers, he adds:

2:13–14 *And we ought to give God thanks for you, brothers beloved by the Lord, since God has chosen you from the beginning*[12] *[59] for salvation in the sanctification of the Spirit and the faith of truth, to which he has also called you through the gospel, to the possession of the glory of our Lord Jesus Christ.*

"And so also because of this (he says) we give God thanks for you, since he chose you so that you might enjoy the salvation awaited, surely sharing with you the grace of the Spirit and giving you faith in the truth. For the calling of the gospel has bestowed this on you, since it promises the glory to come through faith in Christ." And after this:

2:15 *And so, brothers, stand and hold fast to the traditions that you have learned, whether by word or by our letter.*

Now he referred this to the whole discussion; that is, "do not be persuaded by those who want to lead you astray, but remain in what we have handed down to you, whether by word when we were present or by letter when we were absent." Then once more he prays for them:

2:16–17 *And may our Lord Jesus Christ himself and God and our Father, who loved us and gave us eternal encouragement and good hope in grace, encourage your hearts and establish them in every word and good work.*

"May he who by his grace (he says) has given us that encouragement (that is, the hope of the good things to come), himself prosper your hearts in this present life, strengthening you [60] so that you may be able both to speak and to do everything whatsoever that belongs to that good." After this he writes to them:

3:1–2a *For the rest, brothers, pray for us that the word of God may*

---

[12] *Ab initio*, presumably reading ἀπ᾽ ἀρχῆς instead of ἀπαρχήν.

de cetero orate, fratres, pro nobis, ut uerbum Dei currat et glorifi-
cetur sicut apud uos, et ut eripiamur a prauis et pessimis hominibus.

ita ut orent pro eo, ut pro eius desiderio doctrina ubique profectum accipiat, sicuti et apud illos; ita ut ab omnibus insidiis aduersariorum eripiatur. quibus adicit:

non enim omnium est fides.

hoc est, quia non omnes credunt, sunt uero qui et contrasistunt
ueritati. ut ergo ab insidiis horum eripi possit, dignum existimat
esse orationes.

fidelis est autem Dominus, qui confirmabit uos, et custodiet a ma-
ligno.

hoc ad uerba orationis quam fecerat reddidit, fidei firmitatem
adesse illis optans, simulque et dicens quoniam 'uerus est Deus,
qui uocauit uos in spe bonitatis; ipse uos confirmabit in fide, ita
ut adsequi possitis illa bona, ab omni discedentes inconuenienti
actu.' quibus et adiungit:

confidimus autem in Domino de uobis, quoniam quae praecipimus
et facitis et facietis.

nam dum dicit, se de eis bonam habere confidentiam quoniam
omnem eius doctrinam cum sollicitudine efficient, sufficiens est et
exhortare illos, ut opinionem suam opere firmam esse ostendant.
et iterum orat pro illis dicens:

Dominus autem dirigat corda uestra in caritate Dei, et in patientia
Christi.

'contingat uobis in ea permanere caritate quae erga eum est, to-
lerantes etiamsi et aliquid conueniat pro eo pati.' nam quod dixit
Dei et Christi, in commune id positum esse uidetur, id est, 'in caritate et patientia.'

praecipimus autem uobis, fratres, in nomine domini nostri Iesu

---

7   contrasistant *r*   9   orationes esse *r*   10   est *om r*   ‖   confirmauit *C* r*   10-
11   malo *r*   12   est (*aft.* hoc) *add* H   ‖   quae (*for* quam) *l*   14   confirmauit
C*   18   et facitis et facitis *C**   19   et (*bef.* quoniam) *add C r*   20   efficiens
(*for* efficient) *C* H r* efficiant *C* (*corr.*)   21   exhortari *C* (*corr.*)   23   in (*bef.* pat.
Chr.) *add r*   25   perm. in ea car. *C r* perm. in illa c. *l*   29   denuntiamus (*for*
praecipimus) *r*

run swiftly and may be glorified just as among you and that we may be rescued from perverse and most wicked people;

So that they may pray for him that according to his desire the teaching may gain completion everywhere, just as it has among them, and that he may be rescued from all the plots of his adversaries. To this he adds:

3:2b *for not all have faith.*

That is, because not everyone believes, there are even some who have taken a stand against the truth. Therefore, he thinks it worthwhile that there be prayers so that he can be rescued from their plots.

3:3 *And the Lord is faithful, who will strengthen you and will guard you from the malignant one.*

He referred this to the words of the prayer he had composed (2:17),[13] asking that steadfastness in faith be present to them and at the same time saying that "God[14] is true, who has called you in the hope of his goodness. He himself will strengthen you in faith so that you may be able to attain those good things by refraining from every unfitting act." To which he joins:

3:4 *And we are confident in the Lord concerning you, that what we have instructed, you both do and will do.*

[61] For as long as he says that he has good confidence about them, that they will accomplish all his teaching with great care, it is enough also to exhort them to show that their intent is steadfast in deed. And once more he prays for them, saying:

3:5 *And may the Lord direct your hearts in the love of God and in the endurance of Christ.*

"May it be granted you to persevere in love toward him, bearing up even if it may be right, as well, to suffer something for him." Now when he said *of God* and *of Christ*, he seems to have put down the expressions in common with one another, that is, "in love and endurance."[15]

3:6 *And we instruct you, brothers, in the name of our Lord Jesus*

---

[13] "Strengthen" (*confirmabit*) here and "establish" (*constabiliat*) in 2:17 both translate the same Greek word (στηρίζω), thus obscuring the connection Theodore wishes to make between the two verses.

[14] Instead of "the Lord," as in the text of verse 3.

[15] See Swete's note (2:61): "The meaning seems to be that S. Paul's words are in effect the same as if he had written εἰς τὴν ἀγάπην καὶ ὑπομονὴν τοῦ θεοῦ καὶ τοῦ Χριστοῦ."

Christi, ut subtrahatis uos ab omni fratre inordinate ambulante, et non secundum traditionem quam acceperunt a nobis.

manifestus est hic euidenter de indisciplinatis dicere, quos et uehementer corripit, praecipiens etiam ut a conloquio eorum se-
5 se cohibeant. hoc enim est quod dicit: *separate* uel *subtrahite uos;* hoc est, 'adcelerate secernere uos ab illis qui tales sunt.' et ut ne uideretur uerbo tantum id tradere:

ipsi enim scitis quemadmodum oporteat imitari nos; quoniam non inquieti fuimus in uobis.

10 et quoniam ista adhuc non erant magna, adicit:

neque gratis panem manducauimus apud aliquem.

et quod his maius est:

sed in labore et lassitudine nocte et die operantes, ut non grauaremus quemquam uestrum.

15 et quod maius extolli potest, adicit:

non quia non habemus potestatem, sed ut nos formam demus uobis, ut imitemini.

'et quidem nobis licet accipere, eo quod erga doctrinam uacare uidemur; sed noluimus, ut ipso opere uos doceamus quemadmo-
20 dum conuenit facere.' et ostendens quoniam talia agens apud illos permansit, memoratur iterum traditionem suam:

nam et cum eramus apud uos, hoc praedicabamus uobis, quoniam 'qui non uult operari, neque manducet.'

'haec et praesentes dicebamus, quod pigri neque manducare
25 sint digni.' non generaliter hoc dicens, quod ille, qui non opera-tur, non debet manducare; uidetur enim ipse Corinthiis scribens longa prosecutione id explicasse, quoniam illis debetur qui doc-trinae uacant, ut a discipulis corporalium percipiant ministerium. sed illum dicit non esse operarium, qui neque de melioribus sol-
30 licitus est, neque corporale aliquid uult operari, otiosus uero exi-stens aliorum uitam curiose discutit; de indisciplinatis etenim illi

---

3 manifestus est hinc *C** manifestum est hic *C (corr.)* manifestum est hinc *H r* 4 etiam et (*aft.* ut) add *C H* 5 hoc est enim *r* 7 ait (*aft* tradere) *add r* 11 enim (*aft.* neque) *add r* 16 habuerimus *r* ‖ daremus *r* 19 nos (*for* uos) *r* 22 praedicebamus *C* 28 accipiant (*for* perc.) *H* ‖ mysterium (*for* minist.) *C** 30 operare *H* 30-31 extans (*for* exist.) *C r*

Christ, that you withdraw yourselves from every brother who walks
disorderly and not according to the tradition that they have received
from us.

It is obvious that here he is clearly speaking of the undisciplined, whom he also vigorously rebukes, even ordering them to keep
themselves from speaking with them. For this is what he means by
separate or *withdraw yourselves*; that is, "be quick to disassociate
yourselves from people who are like this." And, so that he might
not seem to be handing this over only by word:

3:7 *For you know yourselves how it is necessary to imitate us, since*
we were not disorderly among you,

[62] And since that was still not a very great thing, he adds:

3:8a *nor did we eat bread with anyone without payment,*

And what is greater than this:

3:8b *but in toil and weariness, working night and day so that we*
might not burden any one of you,

And he adds what can be extolled still more:

3:9 *not because we do not have authority, but so that we might give*
you an example that you might imitate it.

"Indeed, we are permitted to accept provision because we are
plainly left free for teaching. But we said no to this so that we
might teach you by our very work how it is right to act." And
showing that he remained with them doing such things, he again
mentions what he had handed over:

3:10 *For also when we were with you, we kept on preaching*[16] *this*
to you, that "whoever is unwilling to work should neither eat."

"And when we were present, we kept on saying this, that the
idle are not worthy even of eating." He is not making a universal
statement that the person who does not work ought not to eat, for
when writing to the Corinthians (1 Cor 9) he plainly explained
this himself in a lengthy discussion, saying that those who are free
for teaching have the right to accept the ministry of bodily things
from their disciples. Rather, he means that the person who does
not work is someone who is neither concerned about better things
nor willing to work for any bodily thing, but by living idly stirs up
the life of other people inquisitively. Indeed, his words concern

---

[16]See Swete's note (2:62): "*praedicabamus*] = παρηγγέλλομεν. In every other
instance except 1 Tim. i. 3 ... our translator renders παραγγέλλειν by
praecipere."

est sermo. quod et apertius indicans, dicit:

audiuimus enim quosdam ambulantes in uobis inquiete, nihil ope-
rantes, sed curiose agentes.

'curiose agere' dicens, quasi qui otio abusi, ad hoc uacant, ut
5   aliorum examinent uitam. quod fieri quasi inconueniens abdi-
cauit, praecipiens quidem illis, ut separent se a talibus; dicens quoniam nec manducare sint digni, si non operari uoluerint. et abundantius illud pandens adicit:

illis autem qui huiusmodi sunt, praecipimus et obsecramus per do-
10   *minum nostrum Iesum Christum, ut cum modestia operantes suum pa-*
nem manducent.

non absolute dicens, 'ut operentur,' sed adiecit *cum modestia,*
quod erant adimentes, ut ne uitam alienam curiose agerent. uolebat enim, ut sine ulla curiositate illa operentur quae poterant si-
15   bi ipsis sufficere ad sustentationem. et quoniam illi qui huiusmodi erant et operari minime uolebant, seditiose quae non conueniebant illa perficiebant, occasione ea quia ceterorum liberalitas praestabat illis cum omni celeritate illa quae erant necessaria, quasi
eiusdem fidei constitutis—quod et in prima epistola interpretan-
20   tes signasse uisi sumus; adicit ad illos qui praebebant:

uos autem, fratres, ne deficiatis bonum facientes.

hoc est, 'uos exequimini proprium opus, et ne propter aliorum
malitiam discedatis a bono opere; licet illi praui sint suo proposito, sed uobis merces similis erit ob uestrum propositum, cum quo
25   tribuitis.' et iterum ad illos uertit suum sermonem:

si quis uero non obaudit uerbo nostro per epistolam.

ut dicat, 'uerba quae per epistolam loquimur;' hoc est, per litteras [has].

hunc notate, et nolite commiscere ei, ut erubescat.

1   et (*bef.* apert.) *om r*   5   examinant *C**   5-6   abdicabit *C** abdicans abdi-
cauit *H*   9   eius modi *H*   10   cōmodestia *C**   13   uita aliena *C* r* de u. a.
C (*corr.*): txt *H*   14   curiose (*for* curiositate) *H*   ‖   operarentur *C* (*corr.*)   17
quae (*for* quia) *C* r* quod *C* (*corr.*)   20   ad *om H*   24   propositu *C**   ‖   quo
om r   25   et iterum … fratrem *om r*   28   has *om C H*

the undisciplined. To point this out more openly he says:

[63] 3:11 *For we have heard that there are some walking among you in a disorderly way, doing no work but acting inquisitively.*

He says *acting inquisitively* inasmuch as those who have the use of leisure are free to inquire about the life of other people. Paul forbade them to do this, as it was unfitting, and even ordered them to separate themselves from such people, saying that they were not even worthy of eating if they were unwilling to work. And to disclose this more fully, he adds:

3:12 *And to those who are of this kind we order and beseech through our Lord Jesus Christ, that working with modesty they may eat their own bread.*

He does not say that they should work without qualification, but he added *with modesty,* which they had taken away. He added this so that they might not be inquisitive about someone else's life; for he wanted them without any inquisitiveness to do what work they could so as to have enough to support themselves. And since people like this were by no means willing even to work, they were bringing about what was unfitting in a way calculated to create discord. This was occasioned by the fact that the generosity of the rest with all eagerness was supplying them with their needs, as people established in the same faith—something we have plainly pointed out in our interpretation of the first letter. Paul adds an instruction addressed to those who were supplying their needs:

3:13 *But you, brothers, may you not grow weary in doing good.*

[64] That is, "pursue your own work and do not abandon good work because of the wickedness of others. Even though those people are perverse in their own purpose, you will have an appropriate reward because of your purpose in supplying their needs."[17] Once more he turns his discourse to the undisciplined:

3:14a *But if anyone does not obey our word through the letter,*

Meaning "the words we are speaking by the letter," that is, by this letter.

3:14b *take note of him and do not associate with him, so that he may be ashamed.*

---

[17] Theodore's comment is somewhat obscure. Perhaps he means that even though the idle will be punished, those who care for them will be rewarded. Good works may be done to the undeserving. In any case, they should continue to supply the needs of those who cannot or need not work.

hoc dicit, quod et in superioribus dixit, 'excludite eum et a conloquio uestro.' et docens eos cum modestia id facere et non odio:
et non tamquam inimicum illum habeatis, sed admonete ut fratrem.
'hoc (inquit) uolo facere uos, ut non in parte inimici eum ha-
5 beatis, sed ut modis omnibus increpatione, obsecratione, doctrina
reducatis eum ad id quod honestum est.'
ipse autem Deus pacis det uobis pacem semper in omni modo. Do-
minus cum omnibus uobis. amen.
deinde orat tribui eis pacem a Deo, ita ut semper eam habeant,
10 et ut modis omnibus semper illis adsit a Deo.
salutatio mea manu Pauli.
'salutationem' uocauit subscriptionem; pro illo enim quod nos
solemus ponere, 'incolumem,' ille semper ponit: *gratia domini no-*
stri Iesu Christi. hanc ergo 'salutationem' uocat; nec enim uidetur
15 aliquos in epistola sua salutasse.
quod est signum in omni epistola; sic scribo. gratia domini nostri
Iesu Christi cum omnibus uobis. amen.
'hoc igitur quasi signaculo abutor in omni epistola, scribens illud mea manu; quod et in hac epistola feci, ita ut nemo dubitet
20 meas esse litteras.' hoc autem uidetur hoc in loco adiecisse non
absolute, sed quia illi qui de consummatione saeculi loquebantur
et dicebant eam esse propinquam, persuadebant eis, quasi qui et
ex epistola apostoli hoc idem significantes dicerent; quodque et
ipse in superioribus significauit, scribens eis non suaderi illis qui
25 per epistolam apostoli haec se dicere promittebant. necessarie ergo hoc in loco significauit in quibus scripserat de his ad eos, quoniam eius est epistola hoc salutatione sufficiente ostendere, quod
et hoc illi sit in consuetudine, et quod sua manu consuete subscri-
bat; ut nihil contrarium recipiant illis quae hic scripta sunt ad eos,
30 si a quolibet hisdem suadeatur.

10 assit *H*   16 sic scribit *H* ita scribo *r*   18 utor (*for* abutor) *r*   19 ma-
num *r*   22 eis *om H* suadebant hoc *l*   23 id est (*for* idem) *r*   24 suadere
illis *C H* persuaderi ab illis *r*   25 promittebat *C* H*   ‖ necessario *r*   27
hoc salutationem *C* ob salutationem *i*   ‖ sufficientem *r*   29 illic (*for* illis) *r*
30 isdem *C* iisdem *r*: txt *H*   ‖ explicit secunda ad thesalonicenses. incipit
argumentum ad timotheum (*aft* saud.) *add H*

He is saying what he also said above (3:6), "shut him out even from your conversation." And to teach them to do this with restraint and not with hate:

3:15 *And may you not hold him as an enemy but admonish him as a brother.*

"This (he says) is what I want you to do, so that you may hold him not as taking the part of an enemy but so that in all ways, by reproof, by entreaty, by teaching, you may lead him back to what is honorable."

3:16 *And may the God of peace himself give you peace always in every way. Amen.*

[65] Then he prays that peace be bestowed on them by God, so that they may always have it and that in all ways it may be theirs from God.

3:17a *The greeting by my own hand, Paul's.*

He called the subscript a greeting. For instead of what we usually put down—"May God keep you unharmed"—he always puts down *the grace of our Lord Jesus Christ.* Thus, he calls this "the greeting," though he does not appear to have greeted anyone in this letter.

3:17b-18 *This is the mark in every letter; thus I write. The grace of our Lord Jesus Christ be with all of you. Amen.*

"Therefore, I use this as a seal in every letter, writing it with my own hand. And this is what I have done in this letter, so that no one may doubt it is my letter." And he seems to have added this here not without reason, but because those who were speaking about the consummation of the age and saying that it was near were trying to persuade them as though they said this by pointing to the same conviction in one of the apostle's letters. Paul indicated this himself above (2:2), when he wrote them not to be persuaded by those who claimed they were saying these things because of a letter of the apostle's. Therefore, in this place he necessarily pointed out in what he had written them about these matters, that this is his letter, since the "greeting" is enough [66] to prove it, because this is his custom and because he usually wrote the subscription in his own hand. He did this so that they might accept nothing that contradicted the letter here written to them, no matter who tried to persuade them.

THEODORUS MOPSUESTENUS IN EPISTOLAM B. PAULI AD TIMOTHEUM I

ARGUMENTUM

Sanctus apostolus Paulus beatum Timotheum Ephesi reliquit, scilicet ut omnem peragrans Asiam uniuersas quae illo sunt
ecclesias gubernaret. scribit igitur ad eum in prima epistola quam
ad praesens interpretare adnitimur, in principio quidem epistolae
5 statim commonens eum, ut suos cautissime instruat non intendere illis qui legis custodiam christianis modo subintroducere uolunt; docet uero eum in subsequentibus, quae conueniat eum facere ecclesiarum dispensationem indeptum. unde et de omnibus
illum instruit, docens eum qualem esse unumquemque conueniat
10 eorum qui quolibet modo in ecclesiastico ordine deputantur, uel
ministerio fungere uidentur. quod et cautissime explicans instruxit eum de illis quae presbyterum agere, quae uel diaconum, quales etiam conueniat esse uiduas; et de ceteris similiter omnibus ea
quae conueniebant instruens eum, perfectam in ipsa epistola doc-
15 trinam uisus est deprompsisse. memoratus uero est et quaedam
de dogmate in media parte epistolae, de quibus uel maxime necessarium sibi doctrinam esse perspiciebat. nihil uero ex illis reliquit quae ad commune ornamentum pertinere poterant, si tamen
quis scripta eius cum competenti cautela uel legere uel custodi-
20 re uoluerit. hanc igitur epistolam meo iudicio omnes cautissime
episcopos ediscere conueniebat; sic enim diligenter instructi co-

---

1 effisi C   2 illic r   4 interpretari C (corr.) r   7 uere r   8 adeptum H
11 fungi C (corr.) r   11-12 instruit r   12 quae deceant presb. quaeue diac. r
13 conueniant C*   14 eum om r   ‖ perfectum C*   18 communem C H
19 qui H   20 eo (for meo) H

THEODORE OF MOPSUESTIA ON BLESSED PAUL'S FIRST LETTER TO TIMOTHY

THE SETTING

[67] The holy apostle Paul left blessed Timothy at Ephesus, evidently so that by traveling about all of Asia he might govern all the churches there. Thus, he writes him the first letter, which we are presently striving to interpret. At once at the beginning of the letter he reminds Timothy to instruct his own people as carefully as possible not to pay attention to those who want now to introduce the keeping of the law to Christians. And in what follows Paul teaches Timothy what he ought to do now that he has entered upon the administration of the churches. For this reason he gives him complete instructions, teaching him what sort of character is suitable for each one of those who in whatever way [68] are appointed to ordination in the church or are seen to exercise ministry. Expanding his discussion as carefully as possible, he instructed him about what a presbyter should do or what a deacon, and also about what sort of women were suitable for the order of widows. And instructing him likewise about everything else that was necessary, he has plainly produced in the letter a complete body of teaching. And in the middle section of the letter he also mentioned certain points of doctrine, the teaching of which he recognized as especially necessary. And he omitted nothing that could pertain to the adornment of the community, if at any rate someone is willing either to read or to keep his writings with suitable carefulness. Therefore, in my judgment it would be fitting for all bishops to study this letter thoroughly as carefully as possible. For diligently instructed in this way, they would be

gnoscere poterant ecclesias Domini Dei secundum ut decens est
uel regere uel dispensare, beati Pauli legibus inseruientes. ea enim
quae ad Timotheum tunc scripsit relinquens eum Ephesi, omnibus eum ecclesiis quae secundum Asiam esse uidebantur praepo-
5　　nens, haec omni episcopo qui ecclesiam Dei creditus est gubernare
aptari posse nemo dubitet. incipienda ergo est illa expositio quam
per partes expedire nos conuenit, eo quod argumentum in hisce
sufficienter a nobis expressum uidetur esse.

Paulus apostolus Christi Iesu secundum imperium Dei saluatoris
10　　*nostri, et Christi Iesu, spei nostrae: Timotheo carissimo filio in fide,*
gratia, misericordia, pax a Deo patre nostro et Christo Iesu domino
nostro.

uidetur beatus Paulus in praescriptione praesentis epistolae
contra suam consuetudinem adiecisse [ad] gratiam et pacem 'mi-
15　　sericordiam,' ab affectu maiori quem erga Timotheum habere uidebatur hanc uocis adiectionem abusus. consummans uero praescriptionem in his incipit sic:

sicut rogaui te ut sustineres Ephesi, cum irem in Macedoniam, ut
denuntiares quibusdam non aliter docere neque intendere fabulis et ge-
20　　*nealogiis infinitis, quae quaestiones praestant magis quam dispensatio-*
nem Dei, quae est in fide.

ante omnia beati Pauli humilitas digna est demirationem, quoniam discipulo suo scribens non dixit: 'sicut praecepi,' aut 'probaui,' aut 'dixi;' sed simpliciter *sicut rogaui*, uel 'obsecratus sum.'
25　　sic sanctis illis studium erat uniuersos obsecratione ad opus pietatis inuitare, ita ut et alacritatem hisdem cum quadam animi oblectatione inponerent; eo quod obsecratio quidem etiam ualde desi-
diosos scit animare, praecepti uero pondus et illum qui alacritate tenetur pigrum saepe fecisse uidetur. intendendum est autem
30　　et sensui dictorum. nec enim hoc uult dicere, sicut sensus qui in
promptu est significare uidetur, quoniam rogauit eum ut sustineret Ephesi, ita ut praeciperet quibusdam ut ne aliter docerent;
†nec enim pro hoc solo reliquit　οὐ διὰ τὸ παραγγέλλειν μόνον τι-

---

4　uidebantur esse *r*　4-5　proponens *r*　6　altari *C* H*　‖　est ergo *r*　8
esse uidetur *r*　11　gratiae *C* gratia e *H*　14　ad *om C H r*　‖　gratiam et pacem
atque mis. *r*　15　ob affectum maiorem *C* ob affectum maiore *r*　16　hanc u.
adiectione fuisse abusum *r*　18　in *om C**　22　demiratione *C* (*corr.*) *r*　24
sed dixit simpl. *r*　26　isdem *H* iisdem *r*　32　ut *om r*　33　Coisl. 204, f. 188
a [Cr. vii. 5, Fr. 149] θεόδωρος. ἄλλος δέ φησιν· οὐ διά, κ.τ.λ.

able to know how either to rule or to administer the churches of the Lord God as is right, by devoting themselves to Paul's laws. For what Paul wrote to Timothy when he left him at Ephesus and put him in charge of all the churches in Asia are rules no one may doubt can be applied to every bishop entrusted with the governance of the churches of God. So, the interpretation we must work out in detail can begin, since we have sufficiently described the setting by these points.

1:1–2 *Paul, an apostle of Christ Jesus by the command of God our Savior and of Christ Jesus, our hope. To Timothy, dearly beloved son in faith: grace, mercy, peace from God our*[1] *Father and Christ Jesus our Lord.*

In the salutation of the present letter blessed Paul, contrary to his custom, plainly has added *mercy* to grace and peace. It is out of the great affection he seems to have had for Timothy [69] that he employed the addition of this word. And finishing the salutation with these words, he begins as follows:

1:3–4 *As I have asked you that you might stay at Ephesus, when I go to Macedonia, so that you may give orders to certain people not to teach false doctrine*[2] *or to pay attention to myths and boundless genealogies, which furnish speculations more than the dispensation of God, which is in faith.*

Above all blessed Paul's humility is worth admiring, since in writing to his disciple he did not say "as I have commanded" or "I have approved" or "I have said," but simply *as I have asked* or "as I have entreated." In this way those saints were zealous to summon all people to the work of true religion by entreaty, so that they might produce eagerness in them together with a certain delight of the mind. This is because an entreaty surely can animate even those who are quite indolent, while the weight of a command seems often to have made sluggish even the person grasped by eagerness. Attention must also be paid to the meaning of the words. For he does not want to say just what the obvious meaning seems to suggest—that Paul has asked Timothy to stay at Ephesus to command certain people not to teach false doctrine. †For he left him there not just   He left him in Ephesus not only

---

[1] Chrysostom and Theodoret also add "our" before "Father."

[2] Literally, "to teach another way" (*aliter docere*), translating ἑτεροδιδασκα-λεῖν.

eum illic, sed ut omnia pro illa   σὶν μὴ ἑτεροδιδασκαλεῖν κατέλιπεν
faceret sollicitudine quam erga   αὐτὸν ἐν Ἐφέσῳ, ἀλλὰ καὶ πά-
ecclesias Dei expendere fuerat   σης ἐπιμελεῖσθαι τῆς ἐκκλησιαστι-
ordinatus. de quibus etiam om-   κῆς καταστάσεως, περὶ ἧς αὐτῷ
5 nibus scripsisse uidetur ad eum   καὶ γεγράφηκεν.
in epistola.*

 sunt autem sensus duo complexi sibi inuicem, primo sensu secundum exclamationem inperfecte expresso, ut tali ratione etiam
unum esse quod dictum est uideretur. uult enim dicere: 'sicut te
10 rogaui, Macedoniae proficiscens, ut sustineres Ephesi, diligentiam
illis adhibens qui illo sunt; quod et facito, commissum tibi opus
expediens, et omnia sollicite implens quae ad communem pertinent correctionem.' hoc igitur est, quod uult significare per illud
quod dixit: *sicut rogaui te ut sustineres Ephesi, cum irem in Macedo-*
15 *niam;* quod et inperfecte dictum esse adstruxi, beato Paulo consuete nullum loquelae studium adhibente, illud autem quod sibi
uidebatur pro sua uirtute ut poterat explicante. nam nec disciplinam dicendi studuerat, sed nec pro hoc studium adcommoda-
re conueniens sibi esse existimabat. deinde adicit: *ut denuntiares*
20 *quibusdam* et reliqua; hoc dicens quod uel maxime ante omnia eum
procurare uolebat. quid ergo illud est? 'uolo te (inquit) ante omnia
ut dehorteris illos qui in ecclesia alia cupiunt docere praeterquam
pietatis postulat ratio.'

 †euidens est enim quod dixit,   δῆλον δὲ ὅτι τὸ ἵνα παραγγείλῃς
25 *ut denunties quibusdam;* de suis   τισὶν περὶ τῶν οἰκείων λέγει· οὐ γὰρ
enim id dicit et non de alie-   δὴ τοῖς ἀλλοτρίοις παραγγέλλειν
nis. nec enim exteris denuntia-   ἠδύνατο, τοὐναντίον γὰρ καὶ πολλὰ

---

8 inperfecto *H*   11 illic *r*   ‖ facite *r*   15-16 consuetae *r*   16 illud (*for*
nullum) *C* in illum *H r*   ‖ adhibentem *r*   17 explicare *H*   19 adiecit *r*   20
autem (*for* eum) *C r*   24 Coisl. 204, *l. c.*

for this, [70] but so that he might do everything in accord with that great care he had been appointed to furnish to the churches of God. It is about all these things that Paul plainly wrote him the letter.*

to give orders to certain people not to teach false doctrine but also to take care of the entire ecclesiastical administration, concerning which he has also written to him.[3]

So there are two meanings intertwined with one another, with the first meaning incompletely expressed by an exclamation so that for such a reason there seems to be only one meaning mentioned.[4] For he wants to say, "just as I asked you, when I was setting out for Macedonia, to stay at Ephesus to apply diligent care to those who are there; do this by accomplishing the work entrusted to you and by fulfilling with great care everything that pertains to setting things right in the community." This, then, is what he wants to indicate by having said *as I have asked you that you might stay at Ephesus, when I go to Macedonia.* I have added that this is said incompletely, since blessed Paul usually pays no attention to grammar but expounds the idea that appears to him according to his own power, so far as he could. For he had not studied the discipline of rhetoric, nor did he think it suitable to devote himself to this study. It is then that he adds *so that you may give orders to certain people* and the rest. He says this because he wanted Timothy to pay special attention to this responsibility above all. What, then, is it? "I want you (he says) above all to dissuade those who want to teach in the church things different from what the account of true religion [71] demands."[5]

†For it is clear that he makes his statement, *so that you may give orders to certain people,* about his own people and

And it is clear that he says *so that you may give orders to people,* about his own people, for they were not able to instruct

---

[3] Swete points out (2:70) that the catenist has apparently "cropt" the text.

[4] Swete (2:70) suggests that the first meaning is incompletely expressed "after the manner of an exclamation" by Paul's request that Timothy remain at Ephesus in 1:3. But could "by an exclamation" (*secundum exclamationem*) mean "in the declarative part of the sentence" and not in the purpose clause? Only one purpose is fully expressed (forbidding the false teaching), but staying at Ephesus can include all the instructions Paul gives Timothy about church order.

[5] *Praeterquam pietatis postulat ratio.* This reflects 1:3, "not to teach false doctrine."

re erat Timothei, tunc uel maxime magistris pietatis non solum increpare contrariis minime usurpantibus, sed e contrario plurima ab illis mala susti-
nentibus. dicit autem non debere *aliter docere*, de illis dicens
qui ex circumcisione crediderant, qui et multa quasi pro lege loquentes eos qui ex gentibus
erant docere adnitebantur contra christiani dogmatis ritum.*

κακὰ ὑπέμενον παρ᾽ ἐκείνων. λέγει δὲ περὶ τῶν ἐκ περιτομῆς,
οἳ πολὺν ὑπὲρ τοῦ νόμου δῆθεν ποιούμενοι λόγον, τοὺς ἀπὸ
ἐθνῶν ἐπεχείρουν διδάσκειν ἐναν-
τία τοῦ χριστιανικοῦ δόγματος.

nam et in omnibus epistolis propemodo beatum quis inueniet Paulum de illis plurima scribentem, eo quod et multi tunc erant, qui
huiusmodi proponebant doctrinam; quod et melius cognoscere
quis poterit, si interpretationem nostram, quam propemodum per
omnes epistolas explicasse uidemur, decurrere uoluerit, in quibus
ostendimus beatum Paulum multa de his fuisse locutum.

†nam quod dixit: *non inten-*
dere fabulis et genealogiis infini-
tis, in commune quidem de omnibus dixit, maxime his qui ex
gentibus sunt; qui intendentes
illis quae a Iudaeis dicebantur,
saepe in dogmate pietatis noceri uidebantur. quod et Galatae perpessi fuisse inueniuntur, qui cum obseruantia ceterorum quae in lege fuerant de-

λέγει τοίνυν· ʽπᾶσιν μὲν παράγ-
γελε, προηγουμένως δὲ τοῖς ἀπὸ
ἐθνῶν, μὴ προσέχειν τοῖς μύ-
θοις τοῖς ὑπ᾽ ἐκείνων λεγομένοις
καὶ ταῖς γενεαλογίαις.ʼ πολλὴν γὰρ
ἐποιοῦντο τὴν σπουδὴν τοῦ δεικνύ-
ναι τὸν Χριστὸν οὐκ ἀκολούθως
ταῖς ἐπαγγελίαις ἐξ ᾽Αβραὰμ καὶ
Δαβὶδ γεγονότα, καὶ διὰ τοῦτο ἐπεχείρουν καὶ τὰ γένη τὰ παλαιὰ
διηγεῖσθαι δῆθεν· ἀφ᾽ ὧν δὴ πολ-

5　male *C H r: txt g (conj. Jacobi)*　19　Coisl. 204, *l. c.*　22　max. his de illis
C* H max. autem de illis *C (corr.)* max. de illis *r: see note*　23　intendentibus *r*
25-26　nocere *C H r: txt conj. Jacobi*　28　observantiam *C r*

not about strangers. For it was strangers.
not Timothy's job to give no-
tice to outsiders, since at that
time especially, the teachers of
true religion by no means claimed the right to reprove their
rivals, but on the contrary en- Indeed, on the contrary, they
dured a good many evils from even endured many evils from
them. And he says they ought them.
not to *teach false doctrine* in refe-
rence to those from the circum- And he is speaking about those
cision who had believed, since from the circumcision, who by
by speaking much as though speaking much at that time on
for the law, they were striving behalf of the law were trying
to teach the Gentile Christians to teach the Gentile Christians
what contradicted the establi- things that contradicted Chri-
shed teaching of Christian doc- stian doctrine.
trine.*

Indeed, in almost all his letters one will find Paul writing a good
deal about those people, because there were many of them at that
time who were setting forth teaching like this. Someone could find
this out better if he were willing to track down our interpretation,
which we have plainly expounded throughout almost all the letters
and where we have demonstrated that blessed Paul spoke a great
deal about these matters.

†Now he made his statement Therefore, he says, "give orders
nor to pay attention to myths to all, but especially to the Gen-
and boundless genealogies to all in tile Christians, not to *pay atten-*
common but especially to Gen- *tion to the myths* they tell and the
tile Christians, [72] who by pay- *genealogies*."[6]
ing attention to what the Jews
were saying often were plainly
harmed regarding the doctrine
of true religion. The Galatians
were found to have experienced this, since together with the
observance of other commandments defined in the law, they

---

[6] Swete has reconstructed the beginning of this passage from the catenae.

finita, etiam nec a circumcisione se cohibuerunt. genealogiis
uero eos intendere minime conuenire edixit, eo quod Iudaei
tunc multam expendebant sollicitudinem ut ostenderent Christum non promissorum sequentia ex Abraham et Dauid descendisse, et propter hoc adnitebantur etiam progenies ueteres memorari, dicentes quemadmodum ille ortus est ex illo, quemadmodum uero ille ab
illo natus est; ex quibus etiam
multos conturbari eueniebat ex
illis uel maxime qui ex gentibus crediderant, qui nihil cautissime ex antiquis libris scire
potuerant 'his ergo praecipito
(ait), ut genealogiis non intendant.' quas bene et 'infinitas'
esse edixit, eo quod illi qui talia explicant poterant modo hic
modo illic suum uertere sermonem, et nunc quidem huius dicere progeniem, nunc uero alterius, et iterum ab isto transire ad alterum, quod in genealogiis fieri solet necessarie,*
quando quis progeniem ex multis descendentem uoluerit interpretari; 'infinitas' nominans eo quod nullum finem habeant, sed
nec deficere possint occasiones uerborum in talibus uel maxime
quaestionibus, quas etiam occasiones narrationum et

λοὺς τῶν ἀπὸ ἐθνῶν πεπιστευκό
των παρετάραττον, οὐδὲν τῶν πα
λαιῶν ἀκριβῶς ἐπισταμένων. κα
λῶς δὲ αὐτὰς καὶ 'ἀπεράντους' ἐκά
λεσεν, ὡς τῶν ἐπὶ τὰ τοιαῦτα ἐκ
φερομένων δυναμένων τῇδε κἀκεῖ
σε περιάγεσθαι τῷ λόγῳ· ὅπερ ἐν
ταῖς γενεαλογίαις γίνεσθαι ἀνάγκη,
νῦν μὲν τούτου λεγόντων τὸ γένος,
αὖθις δὲ τὸ ἑτέρου, καὶ πάλιν ἀπὸ
τούτου μεθισταμένων εἰς ἕτερον.

---

4 dixit r　12 natus (for ortus) H　19 poterant r　‖ praecipio H　22
dixit r　27-28 transisse r　29 necessario r　31 habent r

even failed to keep themselves apart from circumcision. And he declared that it was by no means right for them to pay attention to genealogies because the Jews were at that time spending much care to demonstrate that Christ himself traced his descent from Abraham and David, not by the sequence of promises; and for this reason they were striving to call to mind the old lineages, saying how Christ was descended from that one and how he was born from that other one. Because of this it also happened that many people were disturbed, especially the Gentile believers who had been able to find out nothing with great accuracy from the ancient books. "Therefore, (he says) let him instruct them to pay no attention to genealogies." And he rightly declared that the genealogies were *boundless*, because those who were expounding such things were able to turn their argument now one way, now another, now [73] speaking of one person's lineage, now of another's, and again passing over to another's—which is necessarily what usually happens in genealogies,*

For they were taking great pains to show that Christ descended from Abraham and David, not according to the promises, and for this reason they were trying also to explain the ancient generations.

Because of this they were disturbing many of the Gentile believers, since they knew nothing of the ancients accurately.

And he rightly called the genealogies *boundless*, since those who were setting forth such things were able to turn themselves here and there in their argument—which necessarily happens in genealogies—now speaking of the family of this one, and then that of another, and again turning from this one to another.

when someone wants to explain a lineage that comes down from many people. He names them *boundless* because they have no end, nor could there be lacking occasions for words, especially in such speculations, which are also occasions for discussions.

† 'fabulas' esse dixit, eo quod
nec aliquid habeant in se necessarium, sed solam narrationem
contineant*

'μύθους' δὲ αὐτοὺς ὠνόμασεν ὡς μὴ
ἔχοντας ἀναγκαίαν διήγησιν.

5 uanam quandam et fabulosam, quoniam 'ille illum ex illa genuit.'
et interpretans quid 'infinitum' esse dicit, optime adiecit: *quae
quaestiones praestant magis quam dispensationem Dei in fide.*

† 'talium (inquit) narratio, et sollicitudo quae de talibus est,
10 quaestiones quidem copiosas
quasdam et infinitas praestare
uidetur; prohibet uero diuinam
cognoscere dispensationem, secundum quam Deus nostram
15 salutem per Christum operari
dignatus est, cui uel maxime
cum omni fide intendere conuenit illos qui audiunt, qui et ipsis rebus ueritatis habere pos-
20 sunt probationem.*

ἡ γὰρ περὶ ταῦτα σχολὴ καὶ ζή-
τησις οὐκ ἐᾷ γνῶναι τοῦ θεοῦ τὴν
οἰκονομίαν, καθ' ἣν τὴν ἡμετέραν
διὰ Χριστοῦ εἰργάσατο σωτηρίαν·
ἣ μᾶλλον προσέχειν ἔδει μετὰ πίστεως, ἀπὸ τῶν πραγμάτων ἔχοντας
τῆς ἀληθείας τὴν ἀπόδειξιν.

quorum doctrina minime praetermissa, successiones non conuenit discutere generum.' nam quia tunc mala erant de hisce uerba,
liquido id probatur ex Matthaei et Lucae euangelistarum narratione. utrique etenim explicauerunt quemadmodum Christi genera-
25 tio ex antiquo descendit, non tamen per illam ipsam generationem
a Dauid utrique uenerunt; sed Matthaeus ad aliam genealogiam ex
Dauid descendisse uidetur, Lucas uero ad aliam coactus est uenire
narrationem, ab illis quaestionibus quae tunc uel maxime moue-
ri uidebantur. quod etiam cautissime quis scire poterit interpre-
30 tationem nostram decurrens, quam de euangeliis expressisse uisi
sumus. et dicens illa quae conueniebant praecipere eis, et a quibus se cohibere deberent, dicit compendiose quae emendare eum
[in] fidelibus uidebatur, ita ut diligentiam eorum adhiberet:

finis (inquit) *praecepti est caritas, ex mundo corde et conscientia*
35 *bona et fide non ficta.*

---

8   Coisl. 204, *l. c.*   12   prohibent *r*   22   uerbis *r*   24   utr. expl. enim *r*   25
per illa ipsa generatione *C H* pro &c. *r*   26   ad D. utique *r*   32   emendare eum
fid. uidebat *C H* em. cum fid. uid. *r*: txt *conj. Jacobi*

†And he said that they were *my-ths*, because they have nothing compelling in themselves but contain only a narrative*

And he named them *myths*, since they do not have a cogent narrative.

that is somehow vain and legendary, on the grounds that "he begat him from her." And to explain what *boundless* means, he quite effectively added, *which furnish speculations more than the dispensation of God in faith.*

†"A narrative of such things (he says)—and great care about such things—plainly furnishes certain speculations that are, indeed, countless and bound-less. But it prevents knowing about the divine dispensa-tion by which God saw fit to work out our salvation through Christ. Attention must be paid to this, especially with entire faith, by those who hear, who also are able to have proof of the truth by the facts themselves.*

For study and speculation about these things

does not permit knowledge of God's dispensation, by which he worked out our salvation th-rough Christ. Attention must be paid all the more with faith to it by those who have proof of the truth from the facts.

When teaching these things is by no means disregarded, it is unnecessary to waste time on the successions of generations." For the fact that talk about these matters was harmful is proved with utter clarity by the narratives of the Evangelists Matthew and Luke. For both of them have explained how Christ's generation comes down from ancient time. [74] Nevertheless, the two of them did not trace his descent from David through the same generations. Rather, Matthew plainly has traced his descent from David by one genealogy, while Luke was compelled to resort to another narration by those speculations that in his time seemed to be in circulation. As well, someone can find out about this more accurately by turning to our interpretation that we are seen to have published on the Gospels. And, speaking of what was fitting to advise them and from what they ought to hold themselves back, Paul says succinctly what seemed necessary to set right among the faithful in order to introduce his diligent care for them:

1:5 *The aim* (he says) *of instruction is love from a pure heart and a good conscience and faith unfeigned,*

'praecipere autem te uel maxime cupio illis, quod et finis est nostrae doctrinae, ut discedant ab omni quaestione uana, non intendant uero illis qui fabulosa quaedam narrare cupiunt; saluam uero
atque integram caritatem erga communem Dominum custodiant,
5   mundo corde et perfecta conscientia.' et ostendens quanta nociuitas adnascitur illis qui non ita erga dogma pietatis consistunt, adicit:

a quibus quidam excidentes conuersi sunt in uaniloquium, uolentes
esse legis doctores, non intellegentes neque quae dicunt, neque de quibus
10 *adfirmant.*

'horum (inquit) diligentiam quidam sic facientes a pietate quidem exteri sunt facti, erga uaniloquium uero uacantes confingunt
se illa quae legis sunt docere; qui etiam quae a se dicuntur minime
intellegunt.' et quia non uerisimile esse uidebatur, ut non intelle-
15 gerent ipsi de quibus dicunt, optime adicit: *neque de quibus adfir-*
mant. nam qui minime sciunt pro quibus loqui eos conueniat, hi
propria uidentur ignorare. et ut ne uideretur legem incusare, adicit:

scimus quoniam bona est lex, si qui eam legitime utatur.
20 'haec autem adsero non legem incusans, sed insipientiam illorum arguens, qui nesciunt eam abuti; si uero quis eam abusus fuerit sicut conuenit, ualde et laude dignissimam et uenerabilem legem esse recipio.' et ut ne uideatur conuersationem legis iterum
subintroducere quasi usu aliquo, adicit:
25 *sciens hoc quoniam iusto lex non est inposita, iniquis autem et in-*
subditis, impiis et peccatoribus, sceleratis, contaminatis, patricidiis
et matricidiis, homicidis, fornicatoribus, masculorum concubitoribus,
plagiariis, mendacibus, periuris.

'illud autem scio, quoniam autem lex actuum inconuenientium
30 abdicationem continet; posita est enim, ut prohibeat omnes ini-
quitates. ergo illis qui peccant necessaria est legis definitio, docet
enim eos minime illa facere; qui autem semel sunt iustificati et ab
omni peccato superiores effecti, superflua est illis lex, qui uel maxime legis possident directionem. hoc autem est apud nos, qui ex-

---

8   aberrantes (*for* exc.) *C r*   12   ext. f. s. *r*   14   quoniam (*for* quia) *r*   ‖   non
om r   16   conueniant *C H* (*corr.*)   19   si quis ea *C r* his qui eam *H*   21   ea
uti *r*   ‖   abusus eam *C* usus ea *r*   25   uero (*for* autem) *H*   27   parricidis (*for*
homic.) *H*   28   periuriis *C*   29   autem *om r*   31   erga illos *r*   34   peccamus
· (*for* expect.) *C H r*

"And I especially want you to instruct them that the aim of our teaching is that they should depart from every vain speculation and should pay no attention to those who want to narrate certain legendary stories, but that they should, as well, keep love for their common Lord unimpaired with a pure heart and a perfect conscience." And showing [75] how much harm arises for those who do not so stand fast in the doctrine of true religion, he adds:

1:6–7 *from which some people, falling away, have turned to vain speech, wishing to be teachers of the law, not understanding either what they are saying or about what they are making affirmations.*

"Some people (he says) by taking diligent care for these things, have in fact become outsiders to true religion, and by being free for vain speech they imagine they are teaching what belongs to the law. They by no means even understand what they are saying." And because it did not seem plausible that they would not themselves understand what they were saying, quite effectively he adds, *or about what they are making affirmations.* For those who by no means know what they ought to speak about are plainly ignorant of their own words. And so that he may not seem to find fault with the law, he adds:

1:8 *We know that the law is good if one uses it lawfully,*

"And I am making these assertions not to find fault with the law but to condemn the folly of those who do not know how to use it. But if anyone were to use it as he ought, I strongly admit that the law is both worthy of the highest praise and venerable." And so that he might not seem to be introducing once more the law's way of life as though for some use, he adds:

1:9–10a *knowing this, that the law is not put down for the just person but for the wicked and* [76] *insubordinate, for the ungodly and sinners, for the accursed, for the profane, for patricides and matricides, for murderers, for fornicators, for those who lie with men, for kidnappers, for liars, for perjurers,*

"And I know that the law includes the condemnation of unfitting acts, for it has been put down to prohibit every kind of wickedness. Therefore, the ruling of the law is necessary for those who sin, for it teaches them by no means to do those things. But once they have been justified and made superior to all sin, the law is useless for those who in a special way possess the guidance of the law. This is how it is with us, who await the resurrection and

pectamus resurrectionem et incorruptionem, cum qua et in inuertibilitate perpetua persistemus, peccare minime ultra ualentes, et
propter hoc legem non indigemus. itaque nobis qui credidimus et
per formam baptismatis in illis iam extitimus, superflua est legis
5 definitio; qui ultra a peccatis nos abstinere non ex lege instruimur,
sed docemur imitari illas res in quarum formam iam nunc consistimus.' et euidentius post enumerationem peccatorum adicit:

et si quid aliud sanae doctrinae aduersatur, secundum euangelium
gloriae beati Dei, quod creditum est mihi.

10 ut dicat quoniam 'omnia quae praua sunt, contraria sunt nostrae doctrinae, quam consequenter euangelio gloriae facimus.'
'gloriam' quidem dicens, illam dicit quae in futuro saeculo post
resurrectionem aderit hominibus, quasi qui et in meliorem tran-
situri sunt statum; *seminatur* enim (ait) *in corruptione, surgit in in-*
15 *corruptionem; seminatur in infirmitate, surgit in uirtute; seminatur*
in ignobilitate, surgit in gloria. euangelium uero *gloriae* uocat illam
praedicationem quae de euangelio est, quod et consequenter 'creditum sibi' esse edixit, ut doceret omnes homines debere expectare illa per eam fidem, quae in Christo est. gloriam uero *beati Dei*
20 dixit, ut dicat 'quae ab illo nobis tribuitur.'

†iure 'beatum' Deum hoc in lo- εἰκότως δὲ 'μακάριον' αὐτὸν ἐνταῦ-
co uocat, eo quod idem in na- θα καλεῖ, ὡς ἂν αὐτοῦ μὲν τὸ μα-
tura beatitudinem habeat prop- κάριον ἔχοντος ἐν τῇ φύσει διὰ τῆς
ter suam inuertibilitatem, nobis ἀτρεπτότητος, ἡμῖν δὲ χάριτι τοῦτο
25 uero gratis id tribuat.* περιποιοῦντος.

haec ergo praedicatio est de futuris quae expectare omnes do-
cemus, consequentem ei facientes doctrinam; praeparamus enim
omnes illam uitam in praesenti saeculo imitari, prout potest
cauentes a peccato, eo quod licet eis credentibus per baptismatis
30 formam consortes illorum fieri bonorum. talibus uero extantibus
superflua est illis lex, unum quidem, quia rebus ipsis frui illa expectant in quibus existentes non habent necessariam legis defini-

---

1 in *om C* r* 2 ultra min. *r* 3 lege *r* 5 nos a peccatis *H* || instrui-
mus *C* 6 quorum *r* 7 adiecit *r* 12 illum *C** 14 surget *H r* 14-15
incorruptione *r* 15 surget *H r* 16 surget *H r* || gloriae *om r* 18 dixit *H*
r 19 illam (*for* illa per eam) *H* || gl. autem dixit b. D. *C r* 21 Coisl. 204,
f. 189 b [Cr. vii. 9, Fr. 150] Θεόδωρος. εἰκότως, κ.τ.λ. 26 quae (*for* est) *H r* ||
quam et (*for* quae) *H* quam (*om* et) *r* 26-27 docemur *C r* 27 doctr. fac. *H*
28 potestis *C* 29 peccatis *r* || per baptismate *H* 30 consortes *om C H*:
txt r 32 diffinitionem *r*

the incorruption with which we shall also continue to stand in perpetual changelessness. We shall by no means any longer have the power to sin, and for this reason shall have no need of the law. And so for us who have believed and by the type of baptism have already come to exist in those things, the ruling of the law is useless. We are no longer instructed by the law to abstain from sins, but we are taught to imitate those things in whose type we already now stand fast." And after the list of sins he more clearly adds:

1:10b-11 *and if anything else is opposed to sound teaching, according to the gospel of the glory of the blessed God, which has been entrusted to me.*

He means that "everything perverse is contradictory of our teaching, which we compose by following the gospel." When he says *glory*, he means that glory that in the age to come after [77] the resurrection will be present to people, inasmuch as they will be transformed to a better condition. For he says (1 Cor 15:42–43): *it is sown in corruption, it rises in incorruption; it is sown in weakness, it rises in power; it is sown in dishonor, it rises in glory.* And he calls the preaching based on the gospel *the gospel of the glory,* which he consequently declares "has been entrusted to him," in order to teach all people that they ought to await those things by faith in Christ. And he said *the glory of the blessed God* to mean "the glory he bestows on us."

†He rightly calls God *blessed* in this place because he freely bestows on us the same blessedness he has by nature because of his own changelessness.*

He rightly calls him *blessed* here, since he has blessedness by nature through changelessness and procures it for us by grace.

Therefore, this preaching is about the things to come that we teach everyone to await by composing our teaching in accordance with it. For we make everyone ready to imitate that life in the present age, by guarding against sin as far as possible, because it is permitted for those who believe to become participants through the type of baptism in those good things. And when they are like this, the law is useless for them, for one thing because by existing in the very things they expect to enjoy [78] they have no need of the law's ruling, and for another since faith that comes from those

tionem; alterum uero quoniam omnem omnis legitimae doctrinae formam praecellere uidetur illa fides quae de illis est, et ad omnem uirtutum cautelam eos perducere potest.

deinde quasi ex dictorum sequentia uertitur, ut gratias agat Deo, quoniam commissum est sibi euangelium, cum non esset dignus. abutitur uero illa quae erga se erant, referens ad ostensionem dictorum, simulque demonstrans quoniam misericordia uniuersos Christus saluauit, in futuris illos constituens bonis, in quibus et persistentes inuertibiles ultra sine peccato; ita ut et superflua illis necessario lex esse uideatur. quod ex ipsis magis ostenditur uerbis; dicens enim *secundum euangelium gloriae beati Dei, quod creditum est mihi*, adicit:

et gratias ago et qui me confortauit in Christo Iesu Domino nostro, quoniam fidelem me existimauit, ponens in ministerium, qui primum eram blasphemus et persecutor et contumeliosus.

'gratias (inquit) multas refero pro his Christo, qui in tali me opere confortauit, ita ut uniuerso orbi euangelium praedicarem (nec autem erat possibile hoc posse, si non eius cooperatione dignus fuissem effectus); et quoniam sua reuelatione ad pietatem me tradens, [in] ministerium ali[or]um saluti ponere est dignatus, dignum me existimans ad hoc, equidem cum studio tenerer persequendi et blasphemandi et contumeliis afficiendi eos qui in illum credebant.' et exaggerans illud adicit:

sed misericordiam consecutus sum, quoniam [ignorans] feci in incredulitate; superabundauit autem gratia Domini nostri cum fide et caritate, quae est in Christo Iesu.

'sed talis quidem eram ego; misericordiam uero adsecutus, dignus habitus sum magnorum, Deo scilicet peccata quidem mea ignorantiae meae deputante, bonitate uero sua in fidem et caritatem recipiente.' et postquam de se gratias [agens] ad demonstrationem praedictorum, sicut dixi, illa quae de se fuerunt uisus est

1 omni *C H r*   2 et (*bef.* illa) *add* (*bef.* ad) *om C H r*   4 uertititur (*sic*) *C** 6 utitur u. illis *r*   7 misericordia *om r*   10 necessaria *C r*   ‖ et (*for* ex) *r*   13 in (*bef.* Chr. I.) *om r*   17 orbe *C**   18 nec erat autem *r*   19 suam reuelationem *C H*   20 tradens min. alium s. p. *C H*. tradens min. aliud s. imponere *r*   21 existimas *r*   ‖ quamuis adhuc (*for* ad hoc, equidem cum) *r*   22 efficiendi *C*   23 ait (*for* adicit) *r*   24 ignorans *om C H*   24-25 incredulitatem *C*   27 uero *om H*   28 Dei *H*   29 deputanti *C H*   ‖ bonitate u. suam *C* bonitatem u. s. *H* bonitate u. suae *r*   ‖ in fide et caritate *H*   31 dixit *C r*

things plainly excels every kind of every legal teaching and has the power to lead them to an entire carefulness about virtues.

Then, it is as though he turns aside from the logical order of what he is saying to give God thanks that the gospel has been entrusted to him, although he is not worthy. Indeed, he makes use of what had happened to him, referring it to what he has said and at the same time showing that Christ has saved everyone by his mercy, establishing them in the good things to come in which they will also persist unchangeable from then on without sin, so that the law may necessarily be seen useless for them. This is all the more shown by his very words, for when he says *according to the gospel of the glory of the blessed God, which has been entrusted to me*, he adds:

1:12–13a *And I give thanks to the one who has strengthened me in Christ Jesus our Lord, since he has considered me faithful, appointing me for ministry, who was at first a slanderer and persecutor and insolent.*

"I render (he says) Christ much thanks for these things. He has strengthened me for such a work, so that I might preach the gospel to the whole world, and this could not have been possible had I not been made worthy of his cooperation. And since he handed me over to true religion by revealing himself, he saw fit to appoint me to a ministry for the salvation of others, thinking me worthy of this,[7] although for my part [79] I was possessed with zeal for persecuting and slandering and afflicting with insults those who believed in him." And to amplify this he adds:

1:13b–14 *But I received mercy, since I acted ignorantly in unbelief. And the grace of our Lord with faith and love that is in Christ Jesus has superabounded.*

"But this is what I was like. Yet I attained mercy and was held worthy of great things, since God obviously assigned my sins to my ignorance and by his own kindness received me into faith and love." And after giving thanks about himself in reference to his previous remark (1:11), as I have said, he plainly referred to his

---

[7] Following Swete's suggested reconstruction (2:78).

retulisse, adiciens:

fidele uerbum et omni acceptione dignum, quoniam Christus Iesus uenit in mundum peccatores saluos facere; quorum primus sum ego.

'uerum est ergo, quoniam Christus pro peccatorum uenit salu-
5 te, sicut ex me est id perspicere.' *fidele* autem *uerbum* dicens, uerum dicit uerbum; *acceptione* uerum *dignum* ideo dixit, eo quod
omnis quicumque fuerit ille recipiet, credens quia Deus homines
misericordia saluat, cum sint peccatores propter suam infirmitatem. acceptabilis uero est omnibus bonitas maxime Dei, quae ual-
10 de est magna et multo copiosior erga nos effecta; omnis autem quicumque ille delectatur in hisce sermonibus, cum sit ipse homo, et
bona de hominibus audire cupiat. et latius hoc idem dicens adicit:

*sed propter hoc misericordiam consecutus sum, ut in me primum
ostendat Christus Iesus omnem patientiam ad informationem eorum
15 qui sunt credituri illi in uitam aeternam.*

'ideo me ministrum uocationis gentium de talibus elegit, ut ex
me manifestum omnibus faciat, quoniam clementia Dei et bonitate omnes qui credunt in eum saluabuntur, aeternam potituri uitam. si autem doctrinae minister talis sumptus est, quales erunt
20 illi, qui per eum ad pietatem uocantur?' et quasi qui ostenderit
per haec, quoniam uera ratione misericordia tunc omnes saluaban-
tur, quando a peccato exteri facti legem ultra minime indigere uidebuntur; ut ex hoc confirmet illud, quod propositum sibi fuerat,
quoniam non conuenit per legem litigare, credentes uero in Chri-
25 stum expectare futura et secundum illa pro uirium suarum possibilitate in praesenti saeculo suam regere uitam, ita ut nec sit illis ad
praesens adeo necessaria lex, si tamen ad futura respicientes uirtutis uoluerint curam habere; gratiarum actione suum conclusit sermonem, eo quod et magna adesse nobis bona ostendit. quapropter
30 et dicit:

*regi autem saeculorum incorrupto, inuisibili soli Deo, honor et glo-
ria in saecula saeculorum. amen.*

hoc est:

---

1 ait (*aft* adiciens) *add r*   2   quia (*for* quoniam) *H r*   3   in hunc mund. *r*   ‖
ego sum *r*   6   dicitur (*for* dicit) *C H* dicetur *r*   8   sinit (*for* sint) *r*   11   illi *C H*
r   13   consecutus sum (*aft.* hoc) *add r*   18   petituri *r*   19   miser (*for* minister)
H*   20   uocatur *C**   ‖   ostendit *r*   22   lege *r*   24   credente *C* credenti *H*
r   26   uitam regere *r*   27-28   uirt. habere curam uol. *r*   31   immortali (*for*
incorrupto) *r*

previous life, adding:

1:15 *Faithful is the word and worthy of all acceptation, that Christ Jesus came into the world to save sinners, of whom I am the first.*

"Therefore, it is true that Christ came for the salvation of sinners, just as it is possible to discern this in my case." And when he says *faithful word, he means true word.* And he surely said *worthy of acceptation* because everyone, whoever he may be, will receive it if he believes that God [80] saves people by mercy, since they are sinners because of their weakness. And God's kindness is especially acceptable to all because it has forcefully been made great and much more ample toward us. And everyone, whoever he is, delights in these words, since he is himself a human being and wants to hear good things about humans. And saying the same thing at greater length, he adds:

1:16 *But because of this I received mercy so that in me as the first Christ Jesus might show all patience for the formation of those who are going to believe in him for eternal life.*

"For this reason he chose me as a minister of such things for the calling of the Gentiles, so that he might from me make manifest to all that by the clemency and kindness of God all who believe in him will be saved, destined to acquire eternal life. And if such a person has been taken as a minister of teaching, what kind of people will those be who are called by him to true religion?" And inasmuch as he showed by these things that with true reason all will be saved at that time by mercy, they will be seen by no means to have any further need of the law once they have been made strangers to sin. This is so that he might confirm the point he had set forth, since it is not fitting to argue for the law, but by believing in Christ to await the things to come and by them in accordance with the possibilities of their own strengths to live their life in the present age, so that the law for this reason would be unnecessary for them in the present, if at any rate by looking to the things to come they were willing to take care for virtue. He finished his discourse with a thanksgiving, because he has shown that great good things are present to us. For this reason he also says:

[81] 1:17 *And to the King of the ages, incorruptible, invisible, the only God, honor and glory to the ages of ages. Amen.*

That is,

†'pro omnibus bonis illum laudari iustum est a nobis, qui
tantorum nobis bonorum auctor extitisse uidetur.' tamen et
5 hymnis nullum nomen absolute posuit, sed 'regem' quidem
'saeculorum' uocauit Deum,
propter futurorum aeternita-
tem; 'incorruptibilem' uero di-
10 xit, propter illam incorruptibilitatem quam nobis adesse expectamus; 'inuisibilem' uero ait,
eo quod non uideantur illa bona quae expectantur. ergo ab il-
15 lis quae Deo adsunt, illa quae
nobis ab eo aderunt credi bene
reinsinuauit,*

ὑπὲρ ἁπάντων ἐκεῖνον ὑμνεῖσθαι
δίκαιον παρ' ἡμῶν, τὸν τοσούτων
ἡμῖν αἴτιον γεγονότα ἀγαθῶν.' καὶ
'βασιλέα' μὲν 'τῶν αἰώνων' ἐκάλεσεν τὸν θεόν, διὰ τὸ τῶν μελλόντων ἀτελεύτητον. 'ἄφθαρτον' δέ,
διὰ τὴν προσδοκωμένην περιέσεσ-
θαι ἡμῖν ἀφθαρσίαν· 'ἀόρατον' δέ,
διὰ τό μὴ φαίνεσθαι τὰ προσδοκώμενα. ὥστε ἀπὸ τῶν τῷ θεῷ προσ-
όντων τὰ ἡμῖν περιεσόμενα παρ'
αὐτοῦ πιστευθῆναι.

sicuti et in superioribus 'beatum' eum dixit ad confirmationem
beatitudinis illius quae nobis aderit. uerum quia nihil ex his apo-
20 stolus definitum pro suo posuit arbitrio, sed omnia (sicut in interpretatione ostendimus) congregauit aduersus eos qui pro legis
doctrina corrumpere dogmatis adnitebantur simplicitatem; unde
et scripsit illi, ut praeciperet suis non debere sustinere illos qui docentes, neque debere intendere illis qui talia docere uolunt. quod
25 euidentius in subsequentibus ostendit. postquam autem reddidit
hymnos, adiecit:

   hoc praeceptum tibi commendo, fili Timothee.

   'hoc (inquit) tibi commendaui, id est praeceptum;' ut dicat:
'iniunxi tibi, ut de his doceas, ut praecipias tuis, ita ut non in-
30 tendant illis qui seducere eos uolunt, et transducere ad legis sec-
tam.' et ostendens quoniam non absolute ista illi iniungere uisus
est, adicit:

   secundum praecedentes in te prophetias.

   hoc est: '[secundum] reuelationem diuinam tui faciens electio-

---

1-2 laudare C H: txt r g   1   Coisl. 204, f. 191 a [Cr. vii. 13] ἄλλος δέ φησιν·
ὑπέρ, κ.τ.λ.   5 hymnus r   15 assunt H adsint r   23-24 docent r   25 postquam addidit (for postquam ... adiecit) r   26 adicit C   27 filii C   29 iniuxi
C*   31 non om H   33 praecendentes C*   34 est om r l   ‖ secundum om
C H r: txt l

†"It is right for him to be praised by us for all good things,
since he is seen to have become
the source of such great things
for us." Nevertheless, he put no
name down in his doxology to
no purpose, but he called God
King of the ages because of the
eternity of the things to come;
and he said he is *incorruptible*
because of the incorruption we
expect to be ours; and he says
he is *invisible* because the good
things to come are not seen.
Therefore, from what belongs
to God he rightly implied belief
in what will belong to us from
him,*

"It is right for him to be praised
by us for all good things, since
he has become the source of
such great things for us."

And he called God *King of the
ages* because there will be no
end of the things to come; and
incorruptible because of the incorruption we expect to be ours;
and *invisible* because the things
awaited are not apparent. Consequently, from what belongs
to God, what will belong to us
from him is believed.

just as above (1:11) he called God "blessed" to confirm the
blessedness that will be ours. It is true that the apostle put down
nothing clearly defined by these words on behalf of his judgment,
but (just as we have demonstrated in our interpretation) he has put
everything together against those who were striving to adulterate
the simplicity of doctrine on behalf of the teaching of the law.
This is why he wrote to Timothy, so that he might instruct his
own people that they ought not [82] put up with those teachers
or pay any attention to people who want to teach such things. In
what follows he shows this more clearly. So, after he offered his
doxology, he added:

1:18a *I commit this instruction to you, son Timothy,*
"I have committed (he says) this to you, that is, the *instruction*,"
meaning "I have enjoined upon you the tasks of teaching about
these things and of instructing your own people so that they may
pay no attention to those who want to lead them astray and bring
them over to the sect of the law." And to show that he is plainly
not simply enjoining these things on him, he adds:

1:18b *according to the prophecies that came before to you,*
That is, "according to divine revelation, I ordained your

nem commisi tibi doctrinae opus.' deinde ut non uideatur uane illi post prophetias consilium dare, quasi qui ulterius non indigeat, addit:

ut milites (inquit) *in illis bonam militiam, habens fidem et bonam*
5 *conscientiam.*

'prophetia quidem eliganter gratiam ostendit; erit uero tuo in opere ipsam electionem firmare.' nec autem electio uim inferre nostro consueuit arbitrio, eo quod nec Iudam praui arbitrii extantem electio aliquid potuit adiuuare. 'permane ergo firmus in
10 dogmate—hoc autem dicit, *habens fidem cum bona conscientia*—in illis conuersans, ita ut nec tu ipse transducaris et alios docere non pigeas, etiamsi te aliquid pati pro illis conuenerit. hoc enim magnum tibi prouidebit iuuamen et consequenter eligenti istae gratiae.' et ostendens quanta sit nocibilitas, si non bonam erga dog-
15 mata habuerit conscientiam, ait:

quam quidam repellentes erga fidem naufragauerunt.

inconuenientem quidem de illis conscientiam habentes, suscipientes uero aduersariorum doctrinam, extra fidem sunt effecti; per partes autem dubii extantes, ab omni sunt pietate exteri de-
20 monstrati. et ut maius eum in timore redigat, nominatim memoratus est eorum qui tales fuerunt, quos uel maxime sciebat praeter ceteros in deterius serpsisse:

ex quibus est (inquit) *Hymenaeus et Alexander.*
et quid de illis gestum est?
25 *quos tradidi Satanae ut discant non blasphemare.*

nam quod dicit: *tradidi Satanae,* hoc est, 'abalienaui eos ab ecclesia;' sicuti et Corinthiis scribens dixisse uidetur: *tradere eum qui talis est Satanae,* eo quod illi qui ab ecclesia excluduntur sub Satanae potestate positi esse uidentur—ecclesiae alienationem 'tra-
30 ditionem Satanae' uocans, ostendens per hoc quantum mali sit de ecclesia excludi. et ut ne uideretur seueritate quadam eos tradidisse et quod nolit eorum recipere correctionem, adicit: *ut discant non blasphemare.* non *ut* causam posuit, sed consequenter secun-

---

3   id est (*for* addit) *C H*   9   permanere *r*   13   inuanem *C* * *H*   ‖   consequentem *H*   ‖   eligent *C H r*   14   nobilitas *C H* ignobilitas *r*   14-15   dogmate *C* * *H*   22   scripsisse *C H r*   23   Hymenius *C*   26   alienaui *C r* [1. *p.* 149, *l.* 7, *note*]   29   potestatem positi *C* * positi potestate *r*: *txt C* (*corr.*) *H*   30   sint *C* *   31   quosdam (*for* quadam) *C* * *H* quodam *C* (*corr.*): *txt r*   32   nollet *r*

election and committed the work of teaching to you." Then, so that he might not seem to be giving him advice in vain after the prophecies, as though he needed nothing more, he adds:

1:18c-19a *so that you may fight* (he says) *the good fight in those things, having faith and a good conscience,*

"Prophecy, indeed, demonstrates grace in a preeminent way, but it will be your task to confirm that very election." And not even election [83] has usually brought strength to our choice, because election could not bring any help to Judas once he came to have a perverse purpose. "Therefore, persevere steadfast in doctrine—and this is what he means by *having faith with a good conscience*—living your life in those things so that you may not be led astray yourself and may not be reluctant to teach others even though you must suffer something for them. For this will provide you with help that is great and in accord with that electing grace." And to show how much harm there would be if he were not to have a good conscience with respect to doctrines, he says:

1:19b *which some people by rejecting have made shipwreck regarding faith,*

By having an unfitting conscience about those things and by accepting the teaching of the adversaries, they have come to be outside faith. And by being doubtful in particulars, they have been shown to be outsiders to all true religion. And so that he might all the more reduce Timothy to fear, he mentioned by name those who were like this, whom he especially knew had crawled into what was worse more than the rest:

1:20a *among whom* (he says) *are Hymenaeus and Alexander,*

And what was done about them?

1:20b *whom I have handed over to Satan, so that they may learn not to slander.*

For when he says *I have handed over to Satan,* he means "I have excommunicated them [84] from the church, just as he also plainly said when writing to the Corinthians (1 Cor 5:5): *to hand over him who is like this to Satan.* This is because those who are excluded from the church are seen to be placed under the authority of Satan. He calls excommunication from the church "handing over to Satan," showing by this how much an evil it is to be excluded from the church. And so that he may not seem to have handed them over by some kind of severity and was unwilling to accept their being set right, he adds *so that they may learn not to slander.*

dum suam proprietatem illud est abusus. 'exclusi (inquit) eos ab
ecclesia, non intercludens eorum correctionem, sed et ualde id fieri
expectans, si quo modo ab increpatione meliores effecti didicerint
non blasphemare sed reuerti ad ueritatem.' sic et Corinthiis scribens adiecit: *in interitum carnis, ut spiritus saluus fiat;* hoc dicens
quoniam 'ideo eum ab ecclesia reppuli, si quo modo per poenitentiam secundum praesentem uitam se ipsum adfligens dignus fieri
uideatur, ut futuram salutem adsequi possit'

    hucusque dicens illa quae secundum praesentem uitam multis
necessaria esse ad dogmatum existimabat cautelam, incipit ulterius de illis dicere quae ad ornamentum commune pertinere uidebantur, et de illis quae debent necessarie in ecclesia impleri, hoc
est, orationes. et inprimis quidem ista dicit, eo quod necessarium
existimabat primum debere docere illa, quae eos conuenienter facere decebant; dein de proposito uitae disputat illis, incipiens tali
modo:

    *obsecro primum omnium fieri orationes, obsecrationes, postulatio-
nes, gratiarum actiones.*

    'ante omnia (inquit) illud obsecro quod uel maxime uos scire
operis esse debet, ut conuenienter scire possitis quid fieri conueniens sit.' dicit autem *orationes, obsecrationes, postulationes;* secundum uarietatem postulationum etiam nominum abusus est mutabilitatem. aut enim bona nobis a Deo dari postulamus, quod *orationes* uocauit; aut malorum solutionem, quod *obsecrationes* nuncupauit. nam et quod dixit, *postulationes,* ualde consequenter dixit prae omnibus. etenim adcelerare nitimur ad uirtutum opera,
illa uero quae ad hoc nobis sunt contraria multa sunt et adsidua;
unum quidem, daemonum subreptio uarie nos a bono auertere cupit; alterum uero, molestia passionum quae nobis inesse uidetur.
a quibus et a bonis exclusi contra nostrum propositum saepe in illis quae nobis non conueniunt concludimur. sed necessarium est

1   illo est usus *r*   3   sui (*aft.* meliores) *add r*   5   adicit *r*   8   uidetur *C H*
9   illam *r*   12   necessario *r*   15   decebat *C* (*corr.*) *r* ‖ deinde propositu *C**
deinde propositum *H** deinde de propositum *H* (*corr.*) deinde de proposito *r*
17   obs. igitur primo omn. f. obsecr. orat. &c. *r*   17-18   postulationes …
obsecrationes *om H* (*per homoeotel.*)   20   conuenientes (*for* conuenienter) *r*   22
postulationem (*for* postulationum) *C H*   22-23   mutabilitate *r*   23   dare *C H*
‖ postulatus *a*   25   nam quod et d. *r*   28   quia (*bef.* daem.) *add r a*   29
molestiam *H*

He did not put down *so that* to indicate purpose, but he used the word to mean result, in accord with his own peculiar style. "I have excluded them (he says) from the church, not to preclude their being set right, but quite expecting this to happen, if in any way improved by rebuke they may learn not to slander, but may be turned back to the truth." In this way also, when writing to the Corinthians, he added (1 Cor 5:5): *for the destruction of the flesh, so that his spirit may be saved.* He means: "For this purpose I have driven him away from the church, supposing that in some way by afflicting himself through repentance in the present life he may appear to become worthy of being able to gain the salvation that is to come."

Speaking up to this point of what he thought in many respects necessary in this life for the exactness of doctrines, in what follows he begins to speak of those matters that appeared to pertain to the adornment of the community and of what ought necessarily be fulfilled in the church, [85] that is, prayers. And first of all he speaks of that, because he thought it necessary first to teach them what they ought to do. Then he reasons with them about the conduct of life, beginning like this:

2:1a *I make entreaty first of all that there be made prayers, entreaties, requests, thanksgivings*[8]

"Before all (he says) I make entreaty about what you especially ought to know is part of your work, so that you may be able to know fittingly what ought to be done." And by saying *prayers, entreaties, requests* he used the change of names in accord with different sorts of requests. For we ask either that good things be given us from God—which he called *prayers*—or release from evils—which he named *entreaties.* Now when he said *requests,* he surely meant it to come in logical order before all. We do strive to be quick to accomplish virtuous deeds, but many and persistent are the obstacles that stand in our way for this. For one thing the stealth of demons in various ways wants to turn us away from good, while for another it is the disturbance of the passions that are plainly within us. Shut out by them from good things against our will, we are often confined in what is not fitting for us. Yet it is necessary for us who endure much struggle for this [86] to

---

[8] Swete (2:85) points out that the order is unusual and alerts the reader to Eph 6:18.

nos qui multam super hoc pugnam sustinemus ad Deum recurrere, qui potens est suo auxilio sedare uniuersa illa quae ad nostram
pertinent molestiam. hoc 'postulationem' dixit, eo quod pro illis
quae nobis repugnant Deo orationem adsidue factam uiduae ad-
similauit, quae ab aduersarii potentia se liberari postulabat. nam
quia dixit 'gratiarum actionem,' euidens est quoniam habere possit differentiam ab oratione, quoniam aliter quidem postulationem
habet illorum quae desunt in usu; gratiarum uero actio pro his
quae iam praestita sunt efficitur. et pro quibus haec fieri conueniant docens:

  pro omnibus hominibus.

in commune *pro omnibus hominibus* debere eos sollicitos esse
praecipit. nam is qui pro omnibus hominibus hoc facere iubetur, euidens est quoniam et pro omnibus sollicitudinem expendere iubetur. deinde ad illa quae summa esse uidentur inter homines
transit:

  pro regibus (inquit) *et omnibus qui in sublimitate sunt.*

et ostendens quoniam et hoc lucrum sit eorum:

  ut quietam (inquit) *et tranquillam uitam agamus cum omni pietate
  et sobrietate.*

'si enim ut conueniens est in pace illi deguerunt, possibile est
et nos tranquillitatem fruentes pietati intendere et uitae sobrietati.' et suadens illi ista sic facere sicut ipse, praecepit communem
pro omnibus hominibus sollicitudinem qui per totum orbem esse
uidentur expendere, et communia bona debere existimari ea quae
uniuersorum sunt:

  hoc autem est bonum et acceptum coram saluatore nostro Deo.

sufficienter suasit eos sic sapere, siquidem et Deo sic placet.
unde et probationem faciens quod Deo ista placent, adicit:

  *qui omnes homines uult saluos fieri et ad cognitionem ueritatis ue-
  nire.*

nam quia Deus de omnibus hominibus ista uelit, nemo poterit
contradicere; euidens autem est quoniam omnes uult saluari, quia
et omnes tuetur. necessarium est ergo ut nos eius tuitionem erga

---

1 super hoc *om H* ‖ dominum (*for* deum) *a* 3 dixit postulationes *a* 4
faciamus quod factum (*for* factam) *r* 5 aduersariis *H* ‖ postulabit *C** 9-10
conueniat *C* (*corr.*) *r* 10 doceris *r* 12 hominibus *om r* 13 praecepit *r* 18
et (2°) *om H* 21 deguerint *C* (*corr.*) *r* 22 faciens (*for* fruentes) *r* 22-23
sobrietate *C H* 23 illis *H* 30 agnitionem *H*

hasten back to God, who is able by his help to calm everything that pertains to our disturbed emotions. Paul called this "request" because he compared a prayer to God because of those things that fight against us to the prayer made persistently by the widow who requested that she be delivered from the authority of her adversary (Luke 18:3). Now because he said "thanksgiving," it is clear that it is a different sort of prayer, since it is something other than a request for what is usually lacking; a thanksgiving is made for what has already been bestowed. And to teach for whom this ought to be done:

2:1b *for all people,*

He instructs them that they ought to have great care generally *for all people.* For it is clear that the person ordered to do this for all people is ordered to expend great care for all people. Then he goes on to what seems of greatest importance among humans:

2:2a *for kings* (he says) *and all who are in high position,*

And to show that this is profitable for them:

2:2b *so that* (he says) *we may live a quiet and tranquil life with all godliness and sobriety.*

"For if they live in peace, as is right, it is possible for us by enjoying tranquility to attend to godliness and [87] a sober life." And urging Timothy to do these things in such a way as he himself does them, he instructs him to expend great care generally for all people seen throughout the whole world and that common goods ought to be considered as belonging to everyone:

2:3 *And this is good and acceptable before God our Savior,*

He has sufficiently urged them to be so minded, assuming it so pleases God. For this reason, to prove that those things please God, he adds:

2:4 *who wishes that all people be saved and come to the knowledge of the truth.*

Now no one could deny that God wishes this for all people. And it is clear that he wants all to be saved because he oversees all. Therefore, it is necessary that we should imitate his oversight regarding all people, if indeed we are fully eager to mind things

omnes imitemur, si tamen ad plenum adceleramus similia sapere
Deo. et omni ex parte id ostendens, adicit:

unus autem Deus est.

hoc est, 'quia est omnium Dominus, non aliorum quidem est
5   Dominus, aliorum uero non est; itaque non est possibile eum despicere aliquos quasi alienos sibi existentes.'

unus et mediator Dei et hominum, homo Christus Iesus.

'sed et ille mediator qui nos homines Deo adnititur copulare
unus est et iste, et hinc *homo* secundum naturam existens.' oppor-
10   tune uel maxime hoc in loco 'hominem' eum uocauit, ut et a natura ostenderet donationis communionem; omnibus necessario id
confitentibus quoniam uniuersitatis pars existens secundum naturam communem omnibus potest per similitudinem naturae donationem praestare. unde illud quasi iam in confessionem deductum
15   hinc accipiens, adicit:

qui dedit seipsum redemptionem pro omnibus, testimonium tempo-
ribus suis.

nam et *pro omnibus dedit seipsum;* nec autem pro aliquibus mortem subire adquieuit, sed omnibus uolens in commune confer-
20   re beneficium, passionem suscipere est dignatus secundum illud
tempus quo passus est; *testimonium* enim uocat passionem ipsam,
temporibus uero *suis* dicit ut adserat secundum illud tempus quo
passus est. et quia per omnia necessarium esse ostendit illis quod
conueniat in commune de omnibus hominibus sollicitudinem im-
25   pendere, eo quod et Deus omnibus curam adhibet (nam et quod
in commune sit omnium dominus, et, quod maius est, quia et ipse Christus similiter omnibus adpropinquare uidetur proprietate
naturae; nam et omnibus praebuit beneficium, *pro omnibus* passionem suscipiens); comprobat uero illud de cetero etiam et de illis
30   quae secundum se sunt:

in quo positus sum (inquit) *ego praedicator et apostolus—ueritatem*
dico, non mentior—doctor gentium in fide et ueritate.

'pro his ergo et ego constitutus sum apostolus, ut et ipsam doctrinam ad omnium hominum notitiam deferam et omnes ad fidem

---

2 id *om r*   6   existantes *C* H* exstantes *C* (*corr.*)   9   et iste est *r*   ‖   existans *C* H* exstans *C* (*corr.*)   11   communitionem *H*   12   existans *C H*   14
confessione *H*   ‖   deductam *r*   16   que (*for* qui) *H**   18   enim (*for* autem) *r*
23   necessariam *C* H r*   24   communi *C**   26   qui (*for* quia) *C H r*

similar to God. And demonstrating this in every particular, he adds:

2:5a *And God is one,*

[88] That is, "because he is Lord of all, he is not Lord of some but not of others. And so it is impossible for him to despise some as though they were strangers to him."

2:5b *and there is one mediator of God and humans, the man Jesus Christ,*

"Moreover, that mediator who strives to link us humans to God is one and the same and exists as this,[9] *man* by nature." And it was in an especially suitable way that in this place he called him *the man*, so that he might demonstrate from nature the common character of the gift, since everyone necessarily admits that when a part of the whole exists by a nature common to all, it can bestow a gift by the similarity of nature. This is why, accepting this point as though already deduced as an acknowledged fact, he adds:

2:6 *who gave himself a ransoming for all, the testimony in his own times,*

Now *he gave himself for all* does not mean it was for some [89] that he allowed himself to undergo death; rather, it was in his wish to confer benefit on all in common that he saw fit to undergo the passion at the time he suffered. For Paul calls the passion itself *the testimony*, and he says *in his own times* to assert that it was at a favorable time that he suffered. And since it is in all respects necessary, he shows them that it is right to expend great care for all people in common, because God, as well, applies care to all, both because he is Lord of all in common and because Christ himself likewise plainly drew near to all by his own nature and bestowed benefit on all, since he underwent the passion *for all*. And Paul proves this in another way and from his own affairs:

2:7 *for which I have been appointed* (he says), *I, a preacher and apostle—I am speaking the truth, I am not lying—a teacher of the Gentiles in faith and truth.*

"For these things, therefore, even I have been appointed as an apostle, so that [90] I might bring this teaching to the attention of all people and might make everyone draw near to faith in Christ, by whom those things have been bestowed on us. Indeed, I have

---

[9]Correcting *hinc* to *hic*, as Swete suggests (2:88).

Christi accedere faciam, per quem nobis ista retributa sunt. et quidem ad horum doctrinam et insinuationem gentium creatus sum
apostolus'—ut dicat, 'omnium hominum qui in omni loco sunt.'
bene autem interposuit dicens *ueritatem dico, non mentior;* ita ut
5　et confirmatione sua credi faceret id quod dicebat. nam quod dixit *in fide et ueritate,* ut dicat quoniam 'pro his constitutus sum
magister gentium, ita ut et fidem eos doceam et ueritatem.' sicque comprobans per omnia quod necessarie conueniebat illis in
idipsum uenientibus pro omnibus facere orationem communem,
10　omnibus prouisionem ad similitudinem Dei facientibus, incipit de
cetero disputare quale eorum uult esse institutum, discernens eos
secundum sexum, in quem uiros diuidens et mulieres. et primum
quidem secundum ordinem conuenientem de uiris loquitur, causam explicans ob quam discreuit eos, et quidem communes illis le-
15　ges uirtutum statuere adnitescens; sicut ex subiectione poterimus
id melius discere:

　　uolo (ait) *orare uiros, in omni loco extollentes manus sanctas sine
ira et disceptatione.*

　　nam quod dixit *in omni loco,* reddendum est illi dicto quod di-
20　xit *extollentes sanctas manus;* hoc enim dicit quoniam 'uolo eorum
tale esse institutum ita ut semper orantes, in quocumque loco orationem facere uidentur, sanctas ad Deum extollant manus.' nam
sanctas manus ab arbitrio euidens est eum dixisse; unde et interpretans quemadmodum extensio manuum possit esse sancta, adi-
25　cit: *excepta ira et disceptatione.* compendiose perfectam in his de-
finiuit uirtutem. nam quod dicit *excepta ira,* hoc est, 'neminem
hominum odientes;' quod autem dixit *disceptatione,* ut dicat 'fideli mente minime dubitantes illa accipere quae postulant.' ex altero enim caritatem quae erga proximum est uisus est confirmasse,
30　ex altero uero erga Deum. siquidem ille qui firmiter credit Deo
quoniam dat nobis sine inuidia quaecumque postulauerimus ab
eo, consequens est et ut diligat illum utpote bonorum largitorem.
deinde, dicens de uiris, adicit:

1　ista nobis *r*　‖　retributio *H*　2　doctrina et insinuatione *H*　4　ergo (*for*
autem) *C r*　‖　ut *om r*　5　confirmationem suam *r*　8　per omnia comprobans *r*　‖　necessario *r*　‖　conueniat *C r*　13　conuenienter *r*　14-15　legis
C * *r*　16　dicere *H*　19　quo (*for* quod 2°) *H*　25-26　definit *C r*　28　quae
postulant acc. *H**　30　sic quidem *C r*　33　mulieribus (*for* uiris) *r*

been made an apostle for the teaching of these things and for the inclusion of the Gentiles," meaning "all people who are in every place." And he rightly inserted *I am speaking the truth, I am not lying*, so that he might make what he was saying credible by his own confirmation. Now when he said *in faith and truth*, he means that "for these things I have been appointed as a teacher of the Gentiles, so that I might teach them faith and truth." And thus proving in all respects that it was necessarily right for them when they came together to make a common prayer for all people, since they were making provision for all in imitation of God, he then begins to reason about something else—how he wants them to be organized, distinguishing them by sex to separate the men and the women. And he speaks first about the men in accord with the right order, explaining the reason he has separated them, enlightening them by establishing general laws about virtues, just as we shall be able to learn better in what follows:

2:8 *I want* (he says) *the men to pray, lifting up in every place holy hands without anger and argument,*

[91] Now the phrase *in every place* must be referred to his statement, *lifting up holy hands.*[10] For he means that "I want them to be organized in such a way that when they pray, in whatever place they are seen to make their prayer, they may always lift up holy hands to God." Then, it is clear that he said *holy hands* by reference to moral judgment. That is why in explaining how the extension of hands can be holy, he adds *with anger and argument set aside.*[11] By these words he succinctly defined perfect virtue. For when he says *anger set aside*, he means "hating no single person." And he spoke of *argument* to mean "with a faithful mind, by no means doubting they will obtain what they ask for." For by one of the words he appeared to have confirmed the love of neighbor, while by the other, the love of God. This is assuming that the person who firmly believes in God, trusting that he gives us without envy whatever we ask of him, consequently loves him as the one who generously bestows good things. Then, after speaking of the men, he adds:

---

[10]That is, they are to lift up their hands wherever they pray, but not to pray everywhere.

[11]The Vulgate reading, used in the text, is here abandoned.

similiter autem et mulieres.

bene autem dixit *similiter,* ostendens quoniam discreuit eas non hac ratione, nam ista similiter et uiris adesse et mulieribus cupit; sed et ceterorum causa de quibus uel maxime exhortare mulieres necessarie uidebatur. unde et adicit:

in habitu ornato cum uerecundia et pudicitia ornare se ipsas, non in flexis crinibus [aut] auro aut margaritis aut ueste pretiosa, sed quod decet mulieribus promittentibus Deum colere, per bona opera.

per omnia haec uult dicere quoniam 'conuenit et mulieres illorum ipsorum diligentiam adhibere;' docentem mulieribus quae Deum colere nituntur ita ut in ipsa specie uestimentorum et uerecundiam et pudicitiam simul ostendant. hoc enim dicit *in habitu ornato cum uerecundia et sobrietate;* 'non sibi a foris ornamentum inponere properent ita ut solet fieri, ex auro aut margaritis aut flexu crinium aut pretiosa ueste.' quoniam autem super hoc necessarium erat exhortare mulieres magis quam uiros euidens est. nam quod dixit, *per opera bona,* illi loco reddidit quod dixerat, *ornare seipsas;* ut sit dictum non illis se debere ornari quae superius sunt memorata, sed bonis operibus; quod ornamentum decens est illis qui Deum colere promittunt. bene illi ornamento *bona opera* contrasistit, euidenter multam habentia differentiam ad illa ornamenta, siquidem illa ornamenta uituperatione magis digna sunt, hoc uero ornamentum necessario laudem adquirit. intendendum est autem in apostoli sermonibus quoniam in abdicationem contrariorum illud quod deterius erat primum posuit, dicens *non in tortis uel plexis crinibus;* et tunc adiecit, cetera dicens, *auro aut margaritis aut ueste pretiosa.* hoc autem et propter inconuenientem uanitatem interea euenit fieri, illud uero propter solum ornatum. dicens uero hoc quod uel maxime proprie ad exhortationem mulieribus pertinere existimabat, adicit et aliud quod illis quidem poterat dicere, uiris autem nequaquam in earum similitudinem:

mulier in silentio discat cum omni subiectione.

---

1   de (*bef.* mulieres) *add H**   4   causam *H r*   6   ornatu *C * r*   7   inflexis (*for* in fl.) *r*   10   dicentem *r*   11   et (*for* in) *H*   13   ornatu *C * r*   16   exhortari *r* 17   per opera in bonis operibus bona (*for* per op. b.) *H r*   ‖   dixit *C r*   18   et (*for* ut) *r*   20   se repromittunt *r*   21   habentem *C H: txt r*   24   abdicatione *H* 26   plexibus *H*   29   ad *om H**

2:9a *and likewise also the women*

And he rightly said *likewise,* showing that he separated them not for this reason,[12] for he wants those things to be present likewise both to men and to women; rather, it was because of other things about which he is seen necessarily to exhort the women in particular. This is why he adds:

[92] 2:9b-10 *in clothes adorned with modesty and to adorn themselves with chastity, not with curled hair, with gold, or with pearls or with a costly garment, but what becomes women promising to worship God, through good works.*

By all this he wants to say that "it is right for women to apply diligent care to these very things." He is teaching the women who are striving to worship God so that they may show both modesty and chastity at the same time in the appearance of their clothes. For this is what he means by *in clothes adorned with modesty and sobriety.* "Let not those from outside be eager to put adornments on you, as usually happens, of gold or pearls or the curling of hair or a costly garment." It is clear that it was necessary to exhort the women about this more than the men. Now when he said *through good works,* he referred to the place where he had said *to adorn themselves,* so that what is meant is that they ought not to be adorned with the things he mentioned but with good works. He rightly contrasted *good works* with that adornment, [93] since they clearly are quite different from those adornments, assuming that those adornments are more worthy of blame, while this adornment necessarily gains praise. It must also be pointed out in the apostle's words that in rejecting the harmful adornments, he put what was worse first, saying *not with braided or curled hair,*[13] and then he added, speaking of other things, *with gold or with pearls or with a costly garment.* The latter happen to be done from time to time also because of unfitting vanity, while the former only for adornment.[14] And saying what he supposed especially appropriate as pertaining to his exhortation of the women, he adds also something else he could say to them but by no means to the men as to them:

2:11 *Let a woman learn in silence with all submission;*

---

[12] That is, not for prayer. Men and women pray "likewise."

[13] The translator uses two words for the single one in the text.

[14] A puzzling comment. Is the point that braids and curls have to do with the woman herself, while jewelry and clothes are external vanities?

et euidentius dictum suum interpretans, adicit:

mulierem autem docere non permitto neque dominari super uirum suum, sed esse in silentio.

†euidens est quoniam hoc de statu illo adicit qui in commune fiebat, eo quod non conueniat eas in ecclesia docere.*

δηλονότι περὶ τῆς ἐν κοινῷ καταστάσεως λέγει, ὡς ἂν οὐ δέον ἐν ἐκκλησίᾳ αὐτὰς διδάσκειν.

necessaria autem erat illo in tempore huiusmodi praeceptio, quando et prophetasse diuinae gratiae digne existimabantur; ex quibus non modicam dicendi fiduciam in commune adsequi uidebantur. unde et instruebantur necessario ut non ad deturbationem ecclesiae spiritalem gratiam abuterentur, quae intra domesticos parietes illud ostendere ad aliorum utilitatem debebant.

†de domestica enim conuersatione earum haec statuere nequaquam patiebatur Paulus; neque uetabat mulieres ut impios maritos suos ad pietatem uel inuitarent uel docerent, aut pios inconuenienter conuersantes ad opera inuitarent uirtutum.*

περὶ γάρ τοι τῆς κατ' οἶκον ἀναστροφῆς αὐτῶν ταῦτα νομοθετῆσαι οὐκ ἄν ποτε ἠνείχετο Παῦλος, οὐδ' ἂν ἐκώλυσεν γυναῖκας ἢ ἀσεβοῦντας τοὺς ἄνδρας παιδεύειν τὴν εὐσέβειαν, ἢ μὴ δεόντως πολιτευομένους ἐπὶ τὰ τῆς ἀρετῆς ἔργα προάγειν.

nam ubi erit quod dictum est, *unde enim scis, mulier, si uirum saluum facias?* dicit ergo illa ad communem, ut dixi, ornatum; nam ad plenum illa quae in commune conueniunt plurima in epistolae parte uisus est dixisse. unde et copiose intendens quod in communi congregatione non deceat mulieres *docere, sed esse in silentio*, et primam quidem probationem facit ex natura, adserens:

Adam enim primus plasmatus est, deinde Eua.

secundo de illis quae acciderant:

et Adam non est seductus; mulier autem seducta in praeuaricationem facta est.

et quidem seductus est et ille; sed quoniam in commune dispu-

---

4 Coisl. 204, f. 195 b [Cr. vii. 20, Fr. 150] θεόδωρος. ἄλλος δὲ εἰς τὸ 'γυναικὶ δὲ διδάσκειν ἐν ἐκκλησίᾳ (sic) οὐκ ἐπιτρέπω' φησίν· δηλονότι, κ.τ.λ. 9 prophetase d. gr. digne C * H prophetissae *l b* (*see note*) prophetiae diuina gratia dignae *r* 11 deturpationem C 12 spiritalem gratiarum C* spiritale gratia C (*corr.*) spirituali gratia *r*: txt H ‖ infra domesticis parietibus C* H [paries C (*corr.*)] infra domesticis parietis *r* 14 Coisl. 204, *l. c.* 15 eorum C H *r*: cf. g 21 inuitare C H: txt *r* 22 enim *om* H 23 ob (*for* ad) C *r* 32 disputabant H

And to explain more clearly what he said, he adds:

2:12 *and I do not permit a woman to teach or to exercise authority over her husband, but to be in silence.*

†It is clear that he adds this from the arrangement made in the community, because it would not be fitting for them to teach in the church.*

Obviously, he is speaking of the arrangement in the community, so that it would not be right for them to teach in the church.

And a command of this kind was necessary at that time, when even prophetesses were thought worthy of divine grace, from which [94] they plainly gained no small confidence for speaking in the community. For this reason they were necessarily instructed not to use spiritual grace for the disturbance of the church, a grace that they were obliged to display for the benefit of others within the walls of their own houses.

†For Paul was by no means content to put down these rules to apply to their life in the household, nor did he forbid women either to induce their godless husbands to true religion or to teach them, or to induce godly people who were living in an unfitting way to the deeds of the virtues.*

For Paul would never have been content to put down these rules to apply to their conduct in the household, nor did he prevent women either from instructing their godless husbands in true religion or from leading those who were not living as they should to the deeds of virtue.

For where would be his statement (1 Cor 7:16): *for how do you know, woman, whether you might save your husband?* Thus, he is speaking, as I have said, about what adorns the community; for in the greater part of the letter he has plainly spoken entirely of what is fitting for the community. This is why he points out at length that it is not becoming for women in the common assembly *to teach, but to be in silence.* And he makes his first proof from nature, asserting:

2:13 *For Adam was fashioned first, then Eve.*

Secondly, from what happened:

[95] *And Adam was not led astray, but the woman, led astray, came to be in transgression.*

Indeed, Adam was also led astray. But since Paul was reasoning

tabat discernens quae quidem a mulieribus fuissent peccata ad-
missa, quae uero a uiris, bene illum quidem non fuisse seductum,
hanc uero seductam,

†eo quod illius seductionis mu-
5 lier causa extitisse uidebatur,
quia ea in illum causam uertere
nequaquam poterat.*

ἐπειδὴ ἐκείνου μὲν τῆς ἀπάτης τὴν
αἰτίαν εἶχεν αὕτη, αὐτὴ δὲ ἐπ᾽
ἐκεῖνον τῆς αἰτίαν στρέφειν οὐκ
ἠδύνατο.

et ut ne uideretur de genere mulierum pronuntiare quasi inutile
ad pietatem, quia ritus ille et ius in omni genere mulierum perti-
10 nere uidetur, 'seducta est illa, idipsum iustitia et ratio depostulat
in omnibus uideri mulieribus':

*saluabitur autem per filiorum procreationem, si manserit in fide et
caritate et sanctificatione cum pudicitia.*

'sed non origo est repellenda'; *per filiorum* enim dicens *procrea-*
15 *tionem*, in subsequentibus id demonstrauit, mulieribus ostendens
quod salute digna esse uidetur progenies per eas mulieres quae
ad pietatem respiciunt et permanent in fide et caritate, necnon et
sanctificatione uiuentes cum pudicitia, et diligentiam suae adhibentes uitae. nam quod dixit, *saluabitur per filiorum generationem*,
20 non de Eua dicit, sed de genere loquitur; eo quod et de genere disputans ad personas recurrit Adam et Euae, inde probans quod
non conueniat ad instar uirorum etiam has sibi actum in commune uindicare. et ne incusatio generis esse uideretur illud quod de
personis dicebatur, bene ostendit non esse adiectum genus, ne-
25 que reprobandas ad pietatem esse mulieres quae uolunt diligentiam adhibere conuenientium; ut dicat quoniam 'ad pietatem similiter recipiendae sunt sicut uiri, in communi uero congregatione posteriorem eas oportet locum tenere.' et quod ita debeat fieri, ex multis id negotiis comprobauit. sicque [in] sexus ecclesiam
30 diuidens, memoratus est semotim quidem uirorum, semotim uero mulierum; ubi uisus est communi exhortatione etiam ea dixisse

4 Coisl. 204, *l. c.*   5 causam ext. scribebantur *C** causam ext. uidebantur
H: *txt r*   6   qui ea in illum c. *C H* quia in illam c. *r*   7   poterant *r*   8   inutilem
C H   10   illas *r*   15   demonstrabit *C H r*   22   ad (*bef.* instar) *om C* (*corr.*)
25   reprobans *C H r*   26   quod (*for* quoniam) *r*   26-27   sim. ad p. *H**   27
sicut et u. *r*   29   in *om C H r*   30   seorsum, seorsum (*for* sem., sem.) *r*   31
eam *H*

generally by distinguishing what sins would be committed by women and what by men, he rightly said that Adam had not been led astray but that Eve had been,

†because the woman was seen to have become the cause of leading him astray, since she was in no way able to turn the cause back to him.* since she was the cause of his deception, and she was not able to turn the cause back to him.

And so that he might not seem to be pronouncing a judgment about the gender of women, that it was useless for true religion, as though Eve's practice and sentence should be seen pertaining to the entire gender of women and as though he were saying "since Eve was led astray, justice and reason demand that the same thing be seen in all women":

2:15 *But she will be saved through the procreation of children, if she remains in faith and love and sanctification with chastity.*

"But the source must not be spurned." For Paul has demonstrated what he means by *through the procreation of children* in the following words, when he shows with reference to women [96] that their offspring are plainly worthy of salvation through those women who fix their sight on true religion and persevere in faith and love, living furthermore in sanctification with chastity and applying diligent care to their life. For when he said *she will be saved through the begetting*[15] *of children,* he does not mean Eve but is speaking of the gender, because it is when he is reasoning about the gender that he turns to the persons of Adam and Eve, proving from them that it is not fitting for these women, as well, to claim for themselves an active part in the community, like men. And lest what he was saying about Adam and Eve should be seen as a condemnation of the female gender, he rightly shows that the gender is not rejected, nor are women who are willing to apply diligent care to what is right to be excluded from true religion. What he means is that "women must be accepted for true religion in just the same way as men, but in the common assembly they must take a lower place." And he proved from many considerations that this is the way it should be done. And so, dividing the church by sex, he mentioned separately now the men and now the women, even in his general exhortation where he is seen to have said what [97]

---

[15] *Generationem* instead of *procreationem,* which is used in the text of 2:15.

quae proprie mulieribus aptari possent. sicque communi exhortatione comprehendit omnes qui ecclesiae pertinent; qui enim uirorum memoratus est et mulierum, euidens est quoniam omnes
in idipsum conclusit. exinde uero pergit ad ordinum diuisiones,
5   quia, ut dixi, pro communi omnia disputat utilitate, et ordinum ipsorum secundum diuisionem memoratus est, ostendens quae quidem sunt quae hunc agere deceant, quae uero illum; ita ut nihil
minus esse uideatur ex illis quae pro communi utilitate fieri debent.

10   *fidele verbum.*

simile est dictum quod in euangelio est expressum: *amen, amen
dico uobis.* sicut enim illum adfirmatione dictum et ob maiorem
positum firmitatem, sic et hoc est ut dicat 'uera [res] est et credi
digna est;' *fidele* dicens,

15   *si quis episcopatum desiderat, bonum opus concupiscit.*

bene *opus* dixit et non 'dignitatem,' nec enim dignitates sunt
ecclesiasticae functiones, sed opus; eo quod unumquodque horum pro communi est utilitate constitutum, siue episcopatus, siue
diaconia, siue et aliquid aliud. qui enim in hoc creatur, euidens
20   est quoniam in opere sancto producitur in medium, pro aliorum
necessitate et utilitate functionem adsequens hanc. demirationem autem digna est hoc in loco prouidentia beati Pauli, quoniam
non dixit 'nemo concupiscat,' ut ne uideretur negotium ipsum fu-
giendum insinuare, aut iterum aestimaretur uolentibus inuidere;
25   e contrario uero non dixit 'concupiscat,' ut ne alia ratione omni
reuerentia dampnata omnes ad id currere hortaretur. mediam uero
emisit uocem: *si quis episcopatum desiderat, bonum opus concupiscit;*

---

2   ad ecclesiam *r*   4   ordinem *C H r*   6   quia quaedam (*for* quae quidem) *r*   12
illud *H r*   ‖   ad confirmationem *C* (*corr.*)   13   scio (*for* sic) *H*   ‖   dictum (*aft.*
hoc est) *H r*   ‖   res *om C* H r*   14   uerbum (*aft.* fidele) *add r*   15   desiderat
(*for* conc.) *H r*   19   et *om r*   ‖   creatur in hoc *r*   20   indicium operis cum
(*for* quon. in op. sancto) *r*   ‖   operi (*for* opere) *H*   21   est (*aft.* alior.) *add r*
21-22   demiratione *H*: *om r*   22   in hoc loco *r*   23   non *om r*   ‖   concupiscit
H r   ‖   ut ne uideretur ... concupiscat *om r* (*per homoeotel.*)   ‖   uiderentur
C H   24   aestimarentur *C H*

can be particularly applied to women.[16] And so in his general exhortation he includes everyone who belongs to the church, for the way he mentioned men and women makes it clear that he includes everyone in the same thing. But from there he moves on to the division of the orders,[17] because, as I have said, he is discussing everything for the benefit of the community. And he mentioned the orders themselves according to their division, demonstrating the duties this one or that one should accomplish, so that nothing might appear lacking in what should be done for the benefit of the community.

3:1a Faithful is the word;

What he says resembles the expression in the gospel, *amen, amen, I tell you.*[18] For just as that was said by way of affirmation and put down for greater confirmation, so here, too, it means "it is a true thing and worthy of belief." Saying *faithful:*[19]

3:1b if anyone wants to be a bishop, he desires a good work.

He rightly said *work* and not "office." For [98] ecclesiastical services are not offices but a work,[20] because each one of them is appointed for the benefit of the community, whether it is the episcopate or the diaconate or anything else. For it is clear that the person appointed for this is brought forward[21] for a holy work, acquiring this service for the needs and benefit of others. And blessed Paul's foresight in this place is worth admiring, since he did not say "let no one desire." This is so that he might not seem to imply that the occupation itself should be avoided or again should be thought to begrudge those who want it. But, on the other hand, he did not say "let him desire it," so that for another reason no one should be exhorted to run for it with all restraint renounced. He pronounced a middle view: *if anyone wants to be a bishop, he desires a good work.* He all but says: "I do not forbid the person

---

[16] See Swete's note (2:96): "The reference appears to be to c. ii. 9, 10; cf. p. 93, ll. 8–11. 'Some of the Ap.'s directions with regard to the conduct of women are in a less degree applicable to men; others (e.g. c. ii. 11, 12) belong exclusively to the female sex.'"

[17] That is, the discussion of bishops/presbyters and deacons. The "orders" include the widows as well.

[18] See, e.g., John 1:52.

[19] That is, the "word" in question is what follows and not, as Chrysostom supposed, what precedes (see Swete, 2:97).

[20] *Nec enim dignitates sunt ecclesiasticae functiones, sed opus.*

[21] Literally, "advanced to the midst" (*producitur in medium*).

solum hoc non dicens, quoniam 'ego desiderantem non prohibeo,
nam et optimum adnititur opus qui hoc concupiscit; ostendo uero
qualem esse conuenit illum qui ista adsequi cupit.' protinus etenim et ab ipso primordio sollicitos faciens eos et hoc ipsud quod
5 dixit, quoniam operam concupiscit bonam; docuit enim eos interim scire quoniam *opus* episcopatus, et ad opus quoddam uocatur
qui ad hoc uocatur, quod et necesse est eum cum sollicitudine implere. in timorem uero redigit maiorem ex illis dictis quae subsequuntur, eo quod et singillatim ea expressit, insinuans quibus uir-
10 tutibus uitae ornatus debet concupiscere episcopatum; hoc enim
erat suadere ut intellegerent non esse concupiscendum, debere uero scire quemadmodum conueniat concupiscere pro eius doctrina.
quid ergo?

oportet autem episcopum inreprehensibilem esse.

15 euidens quoniam

†*inreprehensibilem* dicens non ad | τὸ ἀνεπίληπτον, οὐ τῇ ἑτέρων συ-
calumniatorum respiciens in- | κοφαντίᾳ, ἀλλὰ τῷ ἐκείνου βίῳ·
tentionem dixit, sed ad eius in- | ἐπεὶ μηδὲ ἄλλως ὁ Παῦλος τὰς
tuens uitam; nam nec ipse Pau- | τῶν συκοφαντούντων διαβολὰς ἐξ-
20 lus calumniatorum poterit eua- | έφυγεν.
dere accusationem.*

unius uxoris uirum.

hoc differenter quidam acceperunt.

†*ridiculum* uero est illud quod | γελοιότατον παρὰ τοῖς πολλοῖς ἐσ-
25 quasi a pluribus obseruatur. si | τιν αὐτὸ φυλαττόμενον δῆθεν εὑ-
enim quidam pudice uiuens se- | ρεῖν· εἰ μὲν γάρ τις εἴη σώφρων ὡς
cundam acceperit uxorem, ta- | δευτέραν ἀγόμενος γυναῖκα, τοῦτον
lem in clero non recipiunt; si | οὐ προσίενται εἰς κλῆρον· εἰ δὲ βιώ-
autem quidam uiuens luxurio- | σας τις ὡς οὐ προσῆκεν μίαν ἠγά-
30 se unam legitime acceperit uxo- | γετο κατὰ νόμον, οὗτος εἰς μέσον
rem, is in clero et recipitur et | παράγεται, καίτοι τὸν μὲν δεύτε-
producitur, et quidem cum bea- | ρον γάμον τοῦ μακαρίου Παύλου

---

3 iusta (*for* ista) *H* 4 eos f. *H* ‖ ipsum *C* (*corr.*) *r* 6, 7 uocatus (*for* uocatur) *r* 7 quia (*for* qui) *C H r* 8 timore *H* 9 et quod *r* 16 Coisl. 204,
f. 196 a [Cr. vii. 22] θεόδωρος μοψουεστίας. τὸ ἀνεπίληπτον δέ, οὐ τῇ ἑτέρων,
κ.τ.λ. 17 calumniatorem *C* H* 18 ἐπειδὴ Cr. 23 differentes *C r* 24
uere *r* ‖ Coisl. 204, f. 197 a [Cr. vii. 23, Fr. 150] θεόδωρος δέ φησιν· γελοιό-
τατον, κ.τ.λ. 25 pruribus (*for* pl.) *C** 28 recipiant *C* (*corr.*) 31 clerico *C*
32 equidem *H* ‖ in ceteris (*aft.* cum) *add r*

who desires this, for the one who desires it is striving for the best work. But I want to make it clear what sort of person that man who wishes to attain those things ought to be." Indeed, right away even from the beginning he is making them take great care even about the very thing he said, that *he desires a good work*. For he taught them at the same time that being a bishop is a *work*, and the person called to this is called to a certain work that he must fulfill with great care. And he reduced them to greater fear by what he went on to say, because he portrayed one by one the qualifications so as to make known with what virtues of life the person should be adorned who ought to desire the episcopate. This was to persuade them that the episcopate must not be desired by all but that [99] they ought to know how to desire it in accord with his teaching. What, then, is that?

3:2a *And a bishop ought to be above reproach,*

It is clear that

†by saying *above reproach* he did not speak in reference to the aim of slanderers but was considering his life. For not even Paul himself could have escaped the accusation of slanderers.*

Above reproach does not refer to the slander of other people but to his own life, since not even Paul in any way escaped the charges of slanderers.

3:2b *the husband of one wife,*

People have understood this in different ways.

†But ludicrous is [100] the practice now observed by a great many. For if someone living chastely should take a second wife, they do not admit such a person to the clerical order. But if someone living licentiously should lawfully take a single wife, he is received in the clerical order and advanced, even though blessed Paul clearly would allow that second marriages should take place, while all sexual intercourse outside lawful marriage is clearly held to be fornication. And

It is quite ludicrous to find the practice observed by many. For if someone living chastely should take a second wife, they do not admit him to the clerical order. But if someone who has lived in an unfitting way has lawfully married one wife, he is advanced, even though blessed Paul clearly allows a second marriage to take place, while all sexual intercourse outside lawful marriage is clearly fornication.

tus Paulus euidenter adnuerit
secundas debere nuptias fieri,
omnis uero permixtio quae
praeter legitimas nuptias habetur euidens fornicatio est. et interim praetermitto illud, quod
et duas uxores legitimas palam
accipientes et baptizant et in
clero eos indiscrete producunt,
et quidem cum in ceteris id
obseruare existimentur; quasi
quia baptisma faciat eum non
habuisse duas uxores. frequenter autem hoc idem agunt et
de illis qui sunt praui arbitrii,
existimantes se optime facere si
baptizantes illum qui uita uixit
luxuriosa ad functionem cleri-
catus produxerint, qui nulla nec
uirtutum nec pietatis diligentia
praeditus umquam fuisse uidetur. ut autem silentio praete-
ream baptismi causam ob quam
datur, ad quam rationem plurimi neque inspicere uolunt, illud
uero conueniebat eis scire, quoniam beatus Paulus de uita illa disputat secundum quam (ut
idem: opinatur) oportet uixisse
episcopum, non de concessione
peccatorum disputat quae per
gratiam gignitur illis qui bap-

σαφῶς ἐπιτρέψαντος γίνεσθαι, πάσης δὲ τῆς παρὰ τὸν νόμιμον γάμον κοίτης πορνείας οὔσης σαφῶς.
καὶ παρίημι τέως ἐκεῖνο, ὅτι καὶ
δύο γυναῖκας εἰληφότα σαφῶς (νομίμους λέγω), βαπτίσαντες ἐπὶ τὸν
κλῆρον παράγουσιν ἀδεῶς, καίτοι
γε ἐπὶ τῶν λοιπῶν αὐτὸ φυλάττεσ-
θαι δοκοῦντες, ὡς ἂν τοῦ βαπτίσματος ποιοῦντος αὐτὸν οὐκέτι εἶναι
συνῳκηκότα δυσὶν γυναιξίν· πολλάκις δὲ τοῦτο καὶ ἐπὶ τῶν καθόλου
μοχθηρῶν διαπραττόμενοι, οἴονται
κάλλιστα ποιεῖν, εἰ δὴ βαπτίζοντες
τὸν ὅπως ποτὲ ἐζηκότα ἐπὶ τὴν τοῦ
κλήρου λειτουργίαν παράγοιεν, μηδὲν ἀρετῆς καὶ τῆς περὶ τὴν εὐσέβειαν ἐπιμελείας γνώρισμα ἐπαγό-
μενον. ἵνα γὰρ σιωπήσω τοῦ βαπτίσματος τὴν αἰτίαν, ἐφ' ᾗ δίδο-
ται, πρὸς ἣν οὐδὲ ἀφορᾶν ἐθέλουσιν
οἱ πολλοί· ἐκεῖνο γοῦν εἰδέναι αὐτοὺς ἐχρῆν, ὅτι ὁ μακάριος Παῦλος
περὶ βίου νομοθετεῖ, καθ' ὃν νομί-
ζει δεῖν ἐζηκέναι τὸν ἐπίσκοπον, οὐ
περὶ συγχωρήσεως διαλέγεται τῆς
[διὰ] χάριτος προσγινομένης τοῖς
τὸ βάπτισμα εἰληφόσιν· εἰ γὰρ δὴ
τοῦτο γίνεσθαι οὕτως καλόν, περιττὴ πᾶσα ἡ νομοθεσία τοῦ Παύλου, συγχωρήσαντος καὶ τὸν ὁπώ-
σποτε βιώσαντα βαπτίζοντα εὐθὺς

---

3 queretur (for quae praeter) C* ‖ οὔσης. σαφῶς edd.; for. leg. οὔσης σα-
φοῦς. 4 legitimis nuptiis C* H 7 post (bef. duas) add r 8 accipites C*
accipitis H acceptas r 11 existimantur r 12 quae (for quia) C H 14 βαπτί-
ζοντας Cr.; txt., cod. Fr. (who however suggests βαπτίσαντες) 19-20 nullam,
diligentiam H 23 baptisma C* 26 eos H 27 ciuiate C H ciuilitate r (for
de uita) ‖ διὰ om. cod. edd. ‖ προγινομένης Cr. 29 opinantur C (corr.)
32 βαπτισθέντα Fr.

for the time being I pass over the fact that they both baptize those who publicly take two lawful wives and [101] advance them to the clerical order without scruple, even though afterwards they are thought to observe this rule—as though baptism made him not to have had two wives. And often they do the same thing for those perverse in their conduct, supposing they are acting for the best if, baptizing the one who has lived a licentious life, they should advance to the service of the clerical order someone who seems never to have been endowed with any diligence either for virtues or for true religion. And let me pass over in silence the purpose for which baptism is given, which reason a great many people are unwilling even to examine. But they ought to have known that blessed Paul is discussing that life according to which he supposes the bishop ought to have lived; he is not discussing the pardon of sins, which takes place by grace for those who have received baptism. And if they suppose it best for this to be done this way, Paul's entire legislation is useless, as long as practice admits someone to baptism no matter how he has lived and to be advanced to the clerical order [102]—something Paul surely

And for the time being I pass over the fact that, baptizing even someone who has clearly taken two wives (I mean lawful ones), they introduce him to the clerical order without scruple, even though afterwards they think this rule should be observed—as though baptism made him no longer someone who had lived with two wives. And often, when they do this in the case of those who are completely immoral, they think they are acting for the best if, baptizing someone no matter how he has lived, they should introduce him to the service of the clerical order, even though he has provided no proof of virtue and a concern for true religion. Let me pass over in silence the purpose for which baptism is given, which many people are unwilling even to keep in view. They ought at least to have known that blessed Paul is legislating about the life according to which he supposes the bishop ought to have lived; he is not discussing the pardon that takes place by grace for those who have received baptism. For if it were good for this to be done this way, Paul's entire legislation would be useless, since he would be permitting them to baptize someone no matter how he lived and right away to bring him into the cle-

tisma perceperunt. si autem
hoc ita fieri optimum esse existimant, superflua est omnis le-
gislatio Pauli, dum res admittat
5 illum qui qualitercumque uixit
baptizari et protinus in clerum
produci; quod a Paulo quidem
abdicatum est. uult enim ut ille qui in episcopatum adducitur
10 testimonium suae bonitatis ex
praeterita uita habere uideatur,
qui et per omne tempus uitae
suae uirtutum studiis inhaesit,
aut certe poenitentia mediante
15 ostendit quoniam a deteriori uita ad meliorem statum transiit.
quod et melius cognoscere poterimus ex illis quae subsequuntur. fit etiam id et ad praesens a
20 plurimis, qui ita id faciunt quasi
qui magnum aliquid agunt bonum.

quod ergo dixit, *unius uxo-*
ris uirum, quidam sic intellexe-
25 runt, quod et ego magis uerum
accipio, eo quod illo in tempore multi erant qui in idipsum duas uxores habebant legitimas; quod et Moysaica le-
30 ge facere eos licenter eueniebat.
multi uero unam legitimam habentes uxorem non erant ei contenti, permiscebantur uero et
aliis siue ancillis suis siue et aliis
35 mulieribus absolute lasciuien-

εἰς κλῆρον ἄγειν. ὅπερ ἀπηγόρευ-
ται μὲν παρὰ τῷ Παύλῳ, βουλο-
μένῳ τὸν εἰς ἐπισκοπὴν ἀγόμενον
μαρτυρίαν τινὰ τῆς ἑαυτοῦ καλο-
κἀγαθίας ἀπὸ τοῦ παρελθόντος ἐπ-
άγεσθαι βίου, ἤτοι πάντοτε γεγονότα τοιοῦτον, ἢ μεταμελείᾳ γοῦν
δεικνύμενον ὅτι δὴ ἀπὸ τοῦ χείρο-
νος ἐπὶ τὸν κρείττονα μετελήλυθεν
βίον, ὃ καὶ ἄμεινον εἰσόμεθα ἀπὸ
τῶν ἑξῆς· γίνεται δὲ παρὰ πολλοῖς
νυνί, ὥς τι καὶ μέγιστον διαπρατ-
τομένοις καλόν.

τὸ οὖν *μιᾶς γυναικὸς ἄνδρα* τινὲς οὕτως ἐξέλαβον, ὃ καὶ ἔγωγε
μᾶλλον ἀληθὲς εἶναι πείθομαι· ἐπειδὴ τότε πολλοὶ μὲν κατὰ ταὐτὸν
δύο νομίμους εἶχον γυναῖκας, ὃ καὶ
ἀπὸ τοῦ Μωσαϊκοῦ νόμου ποιεῖν
αὐτοῖς ἐπετέτραπτο· πολλοὶ δὲ νο-
μίμην ἔχοντες μίαν, ταύτῃ μὲν οὐκ
ἠρκοῦντο, ἐκέχρηντο δὲ καὶ ἑτέραις
ἤτοι παιδίσκαις ἑαυτῶν, ἢ καὶ εἰς
τὰς τυχούσας πολλάκις ἀδεῶς ἁμ-
αρτάνοντες· ὃ καὶ μέχρι τῆς δεῦρο
γίνεται παρὰ τῶν οὐκ ἐπιμελομένων

---

1 sicut (*for* si) *C* H r* 2 est (*for* esse) *C** est ut *C* (*corr.*) 6 baptizare *H*
8 δεῖ (for δή) cod. 12 et qui et *C** 14 meditante *C* H* 20 ita *om r* 21
aliquod *r* 23 ego dixi (*for* ergo dixit) *C* 26 accipit *H* 31 ἑταίραις (for
ἑτέραις) cod. (corr.) 32 ea *r*

renounced. For he wants the man brought to the episcopate to be seen having testimony of his goodness from his previous life, someone who even through the whole time of his life has adhered to the pursuits of the virtues, or, if repentance has intervened, has without doubt demonstrated that he has passed over from a worse life to a better condition. We shall be able to recognize this better in what follows. Even this is done at the present time by a great many people, who do this as though they were accomplishing some great good.[22]

Then there are some who have understood *the husband of one wife* the following way—which for myself I prefer to accept as true. At that time there were many who at the same time [103] had two lawful wives, something it turned out they were doing by permission, even by that of the Mosaic law. But many who had one lawful wife were not satisfied with her but were sexually involved with other women, acting licentiously whether with their own servants or simply with other women. This continues to be done up to the present time by those unwilling to apply any diligent

rical order. Paul forbade this, since he wants the man brought to the episcopate to introduce some testimony of his own good character from his previous life, that he was always like this or at least could demonstrate by repentance that he has passed over from a worse to a better life.

We shall know this better by what follows. But this takes place now with many people, who do this as though it were some greatest good thing.

Then there are some who have taken *the husband of one wife* the following way—which for myself I am more persuaded is true. At that time there were many who at the same time had two lawful wives, something they were permitted to do even by the Mosaic law. And there were many who, though they had one lawful wife, were not satisfied with her but used other women, as well, whether they were sinning with their own servant girls or often without scruple with those they chanced to meet. This happens up to the present time on the part of those who have no

---

[22] See Swete's note (2:102): "I.e., the promotion to holy orders of persons who before their baptism had been not only digamists, but unchaste."

tes; quod et usque ad praesens
fit ab illis qui pudicitiae diligentiam nullam uolunt adhibere. aiunt ergo Paulum id dixisse, ita ut ille qui eiusmodi
est [ad] episcopatum produca-
tur, qui uxorem accipiens pudice uiuebat cum ea, contentus ea tantum et usque ad illam naturae motus sistens. qui
si sic uiuens post amissionem
primae secundam legitime acceperit, eodemque modo et cum
illa uiuere perstiterit, non debere prohibere eum ad episcopatum transire, secundum Pauli definitionem. hoc dixerunt
quidam a beato Paulo et definitum esse et statutum; quorum ego dictum ualde respuo,
nec suadeor illis quod is qui secundas nuptias similiter praecipit, illum qui post amissionem
primae secundam uxorem suo
ordine accipit ad episcopatum
produci prohibeat. qui enim dixit: *dico autem innuptis et uiduis*, et simul coniungens utriusque unam legem uisus est deprompsisse, euidens est quod
unum esse utrisque existimabat. quid enim differt secundum naturae motum aut ad plenum non habuisse, aut habuis-

σωφροσύνης· τοῦτο εἰρηκέναι τὸν
Παῦλον ἔφησαν, ὥστε τὸν τοιοῦτον εἰς τὴν ἐπισκοπὴν παράγεσθαι,
ὃς ἀγαγόμενος γυναῖκα σωφρόνως
ἐβίω μετὰ ταύτης, προσέχων αὐτῇ
καὶ μέχρις αὐτῆς ὁρίζων τῆς φύσεως τὴν ὄρεξιν. ὡς εἴτις οὕτως
ζήσας, ἀποβαλὼν τὴν προτέραν νομίμως ἀγάγοιτο δευτέραν, τὸν αὐτὸν δὴ τρόπον βιοὺς καὶ μετὰ ταύτης, μὴ εἴργεσθαι αὐτὸν κατὰ τὴν
τοῦ Παύλου νομοθεσίαν τῆς εἰς τὴν
ἐπισκοπὴν παρόδου. τοῦτο εἰρῆσ-
θαι παρὰ τοῦ μακαριωτάτου Παύλου νενοηκότας τινὰς πάνυ γε ἀπο-
δέχομαι, μάλιστα πάντων οὐ πειθό-
μενος ὅτι ὁ τὸν δεύτερον γάμον ὁμοίως ἐπιτρέψας τῷ πρώτῳ, εἰ νομίμως γίγνοιτο, εἰς ἐπισκοπὴν παριέ-
ναι τὸν τοιοῦτον ἐκώλυσεν. ὁ γὰρ
εἰπών· *λέγω δὲ ταῖς ἀγάμοις καὶ*
ταῖς χήραις, καὶ ὁμοῦ συνάψας αὐτοὺς καὶ ἕνα νόμον ἐξενεγκών, δῆ-
λος ἦν ἕν τι ἀμφοτέρους ἡγούμενος.
εἰκότως· τί γὰρ διαλλάττει κατά
γε τὴν τῆς φύσεως ὄρεξιν ἢ καθόλου μὴ ἐσχηκέναι, ἢ ἐσχηκέναι μέν,
ἀποβεβληκότα δὲ οὐκ ἔχειν; ἐπεὶ
καὶ συντυχίας τὸ τοιοῦτο μᾶλλόν
ἐστιν ἢ γνώμης. ὁ μὲν γὰρ ἐσχη-
κὼς ἐπὶ πολὺ τὴν ἑαυτοῦ βιώσασαν
γυναῖκα, ἀπέλαυσεν αὐτῆς ἐφ' ὅσον
ἐβούλετο, ὁ δὲ μετὰ βραχὺ πολλάκις αὐτὴν ἀποβαλὼν ἐξ ἀνάγκης ἐπὶ

---

2 ab illis *om* C r   6   ad *om* C* H   10   sitens (*for* sistens) C* H sit eius r   13
eoque (*for* eodemque) r   15   prohiberi r   17   diffinctionem C* deffinitionem
C (*corr.*) difinitionem H diffinitionem r   18-19   definctum C* H   19   fuisse H   21   ab (*aft.* suadeor) *add* r   22-23   praecepit r   24   uxorem *om* H   26
prohibeor H   31   inquit (*aft.* unum) *add* r

care to chastity. Since all this is so, they claim that Paul said this so that there should be advanced to the episcopate someone who, taking a wife, was continuing to live chastely with her, kept together with her and confining the activity of nature to her. If someone living this way should lawfully take a second wife after the loss of the first and should continue living with her in the same way, this should not prevent him from passing on to the episcopate, according to Paul's ruling. Some have said that this is what blessed Paul both ruled and established. I strongly reject their opinion,[23] nor am I persuaded by them that he who in a similar way advised second marriages [104] would prohibit from advancement to the episcopate the man who after the loss of his first should take a second wife in order. For when Paul said (1 Cor 7:8), *and I say to the unmarried and the widows*, by joining them together he has plainly brought forth a single law for both, and it is clear that he thought both to be in one condition. For what difference is made with respect to the activity of nature whether it has not been exercised at all or has been exercised and lost and

care for chastity. Since all this is so, they have said that Paul made his statement so that the kind of man to be brought to the episcopate would be one who, marrying a wife, continued to live chastely with her, keeping to her and limiting the appetite of nature to her. So, if someone who lived this way were to marry a second wife lawfully after losing the first, and lived the same way with her, according to Paul's legislation he should not be barred from entrance to the episcopate. I certainly accept what they have understood most blessed Paul to have said, and most of all I am not persuaded that the one who in a similar way permitted a second marriage after the first, provided it took place lawfully, would have prevented such a man from entering the episcopate.

For since Paul said (1 Cor 7:8), *and I say to the unmarried and the widows*, both joining them together and bringing forth a single law, it was clear that he considered both to be in one condition. He was quite right. For what difference is made with respect to the appetite of nature whether it has not been exercised at all or whe-

---

[23] The translator has clearly misunderstood Theodore and imposed his own view, as the rest of the translation shows.

se quidem et amisisse et non habere? nam huiusmodi ratio magis in euentu consistit quam ad propositum respicit. nam is qui habuit multo tempore conuiuentem sibi uxorem, potitus utique est eam in quantum uoluit; qui uero post exiguum tempus eandem amisit, necessarie ad secundas accedit nuptias. accidunt autem ista euentu potius quam directione arbitrii. quae discutiens ad plenum beatus Paulus, eum qui uel maxime in episcopatum producitur de tali uita cognosci debere intulit. nam et ridiculum est beatum Paulum legem statuere non arbitrium uel propositum probantem, sed ex euentu et ex accidente discretionem statuere. si autem quis dicat quoniam de euentu et de accidente exiguum quid curans apostolus, cum magna diligentia et scrupulositate de episcopis uoluit statuere quod debent uni tantum coire uxori; audiant quoniam secundum hanc rationem neque post baptisma illum qui talis est produci iusta ratione patietur. nec enim baptisma facit illum non duabus coisse uxoribus, aut apud omnes facit exi-

τὸν τῆς δευτέρας ἔρχεται γάμον· ἔστιν δὲ ταῦτα συντυχίας οὐ γνώμης κατορθώματα, ἅπερ ἐξετάζων ὁ μακάριος δι᾽ ὅλου φαίνεται Παῦλος, τὸν εἰς ἐπισκοπὴν παραγόμενον μάλιστα ἀπὸ τοιούτων γνωρίζεσθαι δεῖν ἡγούμενος· ἐπεὶ καὶ γέλοιον νομίζειν Παῦλον νόμους τιθέναι μὴ γνώμην δοκιμάζοντα, ἀλλ᾽ ἀπὸ τῆς συντυχίας τὴν διάκρισιν ἐργαζόμενον. εἰ γάρ τις ἐκεῖνο λέγοι, ὅτι μικρὰ καὶ τῆς συντυχίας φροντίσας, πλείονος τῆς ἀκριβείας ἐπιμελόμενος ἐπὶ τοῦ ἐπισκόπου, ἐνόμισεν αὐτὸν ὅπως ποτὲ μιᾷ δεῖν κεκοινωνηκότα γυναικί· ἀκουέτω, ὅτι κατὰ τοῦτον τὸν λόγον οὐδὲ μετὰ βαπτίσματος τοιοῦτον παράγεσθαι δίκαιον ἦν. οὐ γὰρ δὴ τὸ βάπτισμα ἢ οὐκ εἶναι αὐτὸν δυσὶν κεκοινωνηκότα ποιεῖ γυναιξίν, ἢ παρὰ πᾶσιν ὡς μιᾷ κεκοινωνηκότα ὑπολαμβάνεσθαι· πολλῷ δὲ πλέον τὸν μιᾷ μὲν συγγεγονότα κατὰ τὴν νόμιμον συνάφειαν, πολλαῖς δὲ ἑτέραις ἀκολάστως συμπλακέντα, καὶ πρόδηλον ἐπὶ τῷ τοιούτῳ γεγονότα βίῳ εἰς τὴν ἐπισκοπὴν παράγεσθαι οὐχ ὅσιον, κατά γε τὸν αὐτὸν λόγον, διὰ τὸ τοῦ βαπτίσματος τετυχηκέναι. εἰ γὰρ δὴ τὸν νομίμως δυσὶν συμπλακέντα, σωφρόνως τε αὐταῖς συνεζηκότα, προθέσει γνώμης φάσκοιεν δι᾽ ἀκρίβειαν

1 quidam C * H quiddam C (corr.) ‖ et om H 2 non (for nam) r 5-6 conuenientem C r 6-7 potius H* 9-10 necessario r 13 b. P. ad pl. H 14 eum om r 18 constituere (for stat.) r 19 παραγενέσθαι cod. edd. 20 ex accidenti discretione H 21 accedente C* (bis) 23 accidenti H 24 exiguam C* H 27 deberent r ‖ in (for uni) r 34 homines (for omnes) r 34 existimare r

so not exercised? For an affair of this kind consists in the circumstances and does not regard moral purpose. For he who has had for a long time a wife suitable for him has certainly possessed her as much as he has wanted, but he who has lost his wife after a short time necessarily goes on to a second marriage. And those things happen by circumstance rather than by the guidance of free choice. In his complete examination of the subject [105] blessed Paul has set forth the view that the man advanced to the episcopate ought especially to be recognized for this kind of life. For it is ludicrous to say that blessed Paul is establishing a law not to sanction choice or purpose but is establishing one that makes a determination on the basis of circumstance and chance. And if someone were to say that the apostle with little concern for circumstance and chance wanted with great diligence and strictness to establish concerning bishops the rule that they ought to have intercourse only with one wife, let them hear that by this reasoning he would neither have allowed someone like this to be advanced with just reason after baptism. For baptism does not make him not to have had intercourse with two wives or make him thought by all to

ther it has been exercised but cast away is not exercised, since such a thing belongs to chance rather than to will? For the man who has had a wife living with him for a long time has enjoyed her as much as he wanted, but often the one who has lost her after a short time necessarily goes on to marry a second wife. These things belong to chance rather than to the achievements of purpose. In completely examining the subject, blessed Paul appears to consider that the man advanced to the episcopate ought to be especially recognized from such things, since it would be ludicrous to suppose that Paul is setting down laws not to sanction purpose but to make a determination from chance.

For if someone were to say that, with little thought for chance, it was because he was concerned with greater strictness regarding the episcopate that he made the law that the bishop should have intercourse only with one wife, let him hear that by this reasoning it would not be right for someone like this to be advanced even with baptism. For baptism does not make it the case either that he has not had intercourse with two wives or that he is supposed by all to have had intercourse

stimari quasi qui unam habuerit uxorem; multo uero amplius
eum qui unam legitimam habet uxorem et multis aliis luxu-
5 riose uiuendo permixtus est et
manifestatus est talis uitae fuisse, ad episcopatum non debere produci, licet etsi secundum
eorum uerbum baptisma fuerit
10 adsecutus. si enim ille qui legitime duabus iunctus uxoribus
et proposito sui arbitrii pudice cum illis conuixit, non debet
in episcopatum recipi ob scru-
15 pulositatem uero uitae; multo
amplius eum qui luxuriose uixit, indecens est ad hoc produci eum ea ratione qua baptisma
adsecutus est. haec quidem dic-
20 ta sufficiunt de illo quod dixit
unius uxoris uirum; cuius interpretationem euidentius dicere
ipsa sumus necessitate inpulsi,
consuetudinem illam quae apud
25 plurimos teneri uidetur despicientes.*
nam plenarie sensum apostoli in subsequentibus manifestabimus
ex ipsis sermonibus, uel maxime dictorum facientes probationem;

ἐπὶ τὴν ἐπισκοπὴν οὐκ εἶναι δεκ-
τόν, πολλῷ πλέον τὸν καὶ ἀκολάστως βιώσαντα οὐ θεμιτὸν ἐπὶ τοῦτο
προάγεσθαι, ἐπειδὴ τοῦ βαπτίσματος αὐτῷ τυχεῖν ἐγένετο. καὶ ταῦτα μὲν εἰρήσθω περὶ τοῦ μιᾶς γυ-
ναικός ἄνδρα· οὗ δὴ τὴν ἑρμηνείαν
σαφέστερον εἰπεῖν ἀναγκαῖον ἡγη-
σάμεθα, μικρὰ τῆς κρατούσης παρὰ τοῖς πολλοῖς φροντίσαντες συνηθείας.

2 multo a. uero r 4 et om C* H 8 etsi om r 9 uerborum C H r 11
The catenist adds: καὶ ταῦτα μὲν θεόδωρος ἄντικρυς τοῖς ἐναργέσιν μαχόμενος,
τῇ τε ἐκκλησιαστικῇ παραδόσει καὶ πάσαις ταῖς συνόδοις· πρὸς ἃ δυνήσεταί τις
ἀντειπεῖν, καιροῦ καλοῦντος. 12 propositi H r 19 est om H 20 sufficiant r
23 compulsi H 27 pleniorem C* r plena re C (corr.) plenere r

be as though he had only one wife.[24] And how much more must the man not be advanced to the episcopate who has one lawful wife but by living licentiously has had sexual intercourse with many other women and has been conspicuous for living such a life, even though it is granted according to their argument that he would have received baptism. [106] For if the man who, lawfully joined to two wives, has also lived together with them chastely by the purpose of his own choice should not be accepted into the episcopate truly on account of strictness of life, how much more in the case of the man who has lived licentiously is it improper that he should be advanced to it on the grounds that he has received baptism. This is enough to say about *the husband of one wife*. Quite clearly we have been driven by very necessity to give our interpretation, because we disdain that custom seen to be held by a great many.*

only with one. And how much more is it not sanctioned that there should be advanced to the episcopate a man who has been lawfully joined to one wife but who has been sexually involved with many other women licentiously and has become conspicuous for such behavior, even though according to the same argument he had received baptism. For if they should say that the man who has been sexually related to two wives and has lived chastely with them by the purpose of his will should not be accepted into the episcopate because of strictness, how much more is it not right that the man who has lived licentiously should be advanced to this since he happens to be baptized. So much for what should be said about *the husband of one wife*. Quite clearly we have considered it necessary to give an interpretation of this, because we disdain the custom that prevails with many.[25]

Now we shall make the apostle's meaning completely clear in what follows, on the basis of his discussion and by examining his

---

[24] That is, strictness must apply to the candidate's life before baptism. What Theodore wants to deny is that baptism cancels out one's previous life, and his argument with the view he rejects is that those who hold it are inconsistent in that they insist on the rule of one wife only after baptism and suppose this a rigorous rule.

[25] The catenist adds: "Theodore is making these polemical remarks against obvious authorities, both the ecclesiastical tradition and all the synods. Someone will be able to refute what he says, if occasion calls for this."

nam uirtutis et aequitatis ratio postulat ut is qui de tali negotio
loquitur non consuetudinem aequitati anteponat, sed Pauli leges
discutiat, et illa Deo aptet quae ei decent aptari qui semper cum
iustitia et non euentu aut accidenti uniuersa solet probare, sed se-
5　cundum propositum et arbitrium hominum unumquemque scit
iudicare. nam et illa quae baptismi sunt frequenter euentus fieri solent; aliter adsecutus ob infirmitatem aut ob aliam aliquando
occasionem in infantiam baptismi gratiam, aliter uero post senectutem longaeuam, qui et per omne tempus uitae suae uixit luxu-
10　riose, tempore uero mortis baptismi gratiam adsecutus. ille uero qui ab infantia baptisma fuerit adsecutus, diligentiam uirtutibus adhibuit plurimam, deliquit uero et aliqua utpote homo, et ut
adsolet fieri, incurrit etiam et in graue peccatum infirmitate magis lapsus quam affectu animae; ridiculum dignum erit, si idem
15　ex euentu noceatur, nullum iuuamen ob bonorum adsequens diligentiam eo quod in infantia baptismatis gratiam est adsecutus;
iste uero, quamquam nihil sustinuerit pro quibus peccauit, adhuc
et clarus in futura uidebitur uita, et hoc cum nullam bonitatis habuerit diligentiam, quia ita euenit ut in finem uitae suae baptisma
20　adsequeretur. sed haec ab illis intellegi debent qui nesciunt rationem ob quam baptisma datur. sed nec diuinas uoluerunt examinare scripturas, ex quibus discere poterant quoniam Simonem nihil
adiuuauit baptismi donum propter propositi prauitatem, Spiritu
sancto in eo non requiescente; latroni uero ut in paradisi habita-
25　tionem transiret nullum adtulit impedimentum, ob propositi eius
uirtutem, ea ratione qua non fuerat baptisma adsecutus. dico autem haec non ad destructionem baptismatis, sed propter eos qui
sub occasionem baptismatis incuriam multam inducere adnituntur iudicio iusti Dei. nam et baptisma magnum, eo quod tanto-
30　rum bonorum continet largitatem; et propositum uniuscuiusque
necessarie iudicatur ex Domino Deo, a quo uel maxime et baptismi donatio multum suscipientibus illum potest conferre iuuamen. nec aquae natura sed suscipientium fides perfectam Dei li-

---

2　lege *H*　4　euentus *C* H*　7　firmitate *H* firmitatem *r*　8　in *om C* H r*　9
longaeuum *r*　10　gratia *H*　13　solet *C r*　14　dignum *om r*　15　honorem
(*for* bonorum) *H*　16　est *om C H*　17　sit (*aft.* ads.) *add C* (*corr.*): *txt r*　18
nulla *H*　19　in *om H*　21-22　eximinare *H*　23　adiuuabit *r*　25　adtullit *C*
26　quam *H*　31　necessario *r*　‖　Dom. et Deo *H*

words as carefully as possible. For the principle of virtue and impartiality demands that the person who speaks of such a matter should not place custom before impartiality but should discuss Paul's laws and should apply to God what ought to be applied to him, since he customarily examines all things with justice and not by circumstance or chance; rather, he knows how to judge each individual human being in accord with his purpose and choice.

For even those things that have to do with baptism usually happen as chance events. In one case someone receives baptism because of sickness or sometimes because of some other [107] circumstance for the grace of infant baptism. But in another case it is at the end of extreme old age that someone who has lived his entire life licentiously at the time of his death receives the grace of baptism. But suppose someone who received baptism from his infancy has applied very great diligence for the virtues, yet has committed some transgressions, as he is human and as usually happens, and has even run into serious sin because he has fallen more by weakness than by the disposition of his soul. It would be ridiculous if he were harmed by circumstance, gaining no help from his diligent care for good things, because he received the grace of baptism in infancy, while that other person, though he suffered nothing because he sinned, still would appear illustrious in the life to come—and this although he had no diligent care for goodness—because it so happened that he received baptism at the end of his life. Now these considerations ought to be recognized by those who fail to know the reason for which baptism is given. Yet they have been unwilling to examine the divine scriptures from which they could have learned that the gift of baptism gave Simon nothing by way of help because of the perversity of his purpose, since the Holy Spirit did not rest in him (Acts 8:14–24). On the other hand, no obstacle on the grounds that he had not received baptism prevented the thief from passing over to the dwelling of paradise because of the virtue of his purpose (Luke 23:40–43). But I am saying these things not to demolish baptism but because of those who [108] take baptism as an occasion for striving to introduce much negligence into the judgment of God, who is just. Indeed, baptism is a great thing because it includes the liberal distribution of such great good gifts; as well, the intention of each individual is necessarily judged by the Lord God, from whom especially the gift of baptism is able to contribute much help

beralitatem in baptisma adtrahere solet. uideamus autem et cetera quae de episcopo dicit:

sobrium.

ita ut cum sollicitudine prospiciat illa quae geri conueniunt.

5 *pudicum.*

necessarie, eo quod in commune et uirorum et mulierum constituitur doctor.

ornatum.

conuersatione, motu, specie; per omnia ostendit qualem co-
10 nueniat esse episcopum.

hospitalem.

conuenit esse episcopum *hospitalem*, non absolute dicit pere-grinorum omnium, sed illorum qui eiusdem fidei sunt; quos notos extantes sibi ut suos suscipere debet cum summa diligentia.

15 *docibilem.*

hoc eius opus ut doceat homines et uirtutem et pietatem; si autem docere ista nescierit, ignorare uidetur illud quod profite-tur edocere. sed non illum dicit *docibilem* qui longam potest pro-secutionem uerborum in ecclesia facere—hoc et perpauci solent
20 implere—sed qui potest qualicumque sermone et in commune et singillatim unumquemque dogmata pietatis instruere, tam pieta-tem quam uirtutem, et quibus modis implere debent ista ex qui-bus uel maxime augmentum illa adsequi poterunt. si ista episco-pus nescierit, nihil a ceteris differre uidebitur, superfluam speciem
25 doctoris in se simulans. denique et cito scribens inter cetera quae de episcopo dicebat, ait quoniam oportet eum retinere *id quod se-cundum doctrinam fidele uerbum, ut potens sit exhortare in doctrina sana et eos qui contradicunt arguere;* sic uult nihil deesse episcopo illorum quae ad doctrinam pertinent.

30 *non uinolentum.*

iure id dicit; si enim et omni homini hoc necessarium est, multo magis episcopo, qui omni in tempore paratus debet esse ad actum illorum quae fieri conueniunt.

---

16   est (*aft.* hoc) *add* C (*corr.*)   17   ista docere H r   18   solum (*bef.* illum) *add* r   20   qui *om* H   22   debeant r   23   poterant C * H r   27   exhortari C (*corr.*) r   32   in *om* C r

to those who receive it. It is not the nature of water but the faith of those receiving it that is fitted to draw the perfect generosity of God into baptism.

But let us see what else Paul says about a bishop:

3:2c *sober,*

So that with great care he may be attentive to what ought to be done.

3:2d *chaste,*

Necessarily, because he is appointed in the community as a teacher of both men and women.

3:2e *adorned,*

In way of life, in gait, in appearance. By all this he shows what sort of person ought to be a bishop.

3:2f *hospitable,*

He says that a bishop must be *hospitable* not simply to all foreigners but to those of the same faith, whom he ought to receive as his own, when they are known to him.

3:2g *an apt teacher,*

His work is to teach people both virtue and true religion. [109] And if he should not know how to teach these things, he would appear to be ignorant of what he professes to teach. But Paul does not mean that an *apt teacher* is someone who can make a long procession of words in the church—very few usually accomplish this—but someone who by whatever speech, both in the community and with individuals, is able to instruct each person in the doctrines of true religion. And since it is as with true religion so with virtue, he should be able to instruct them in what ways they ought to fulfill those duties by which true religion and virtue can especially gain increase. If a bishop should not know these things, he will appear to differ in no way from the rest, feigning in himself the useless appearance of a teacher. Soon afterwards, writing among other things what he had to say about a bishop, Paul says that he must hold fast to (Titus 1:9) *that word which is faithful according to teaching, so that he may be able to exhort with sound teaching and to refute those who contradict it.* Thus, he wants a bishop to lack nothing that pertains to teaching.

3:3a *not a drunkard,*

He rightly says this. For if this is necessary even for everyone, how much more it is for a bishop, who ought to be ready at every time for doing what ought to be done.

non percussorem.

ne absolute aut sine causa, aut adsidua increpatione, feriat quemquam. uult eum cum modestia magis de singulis agere, sicut et in secunda epistola dicit: *modestum* eum *oportere ad omnes, non*
5 *recordantem malitiam, in mansuetudine docentem eos qui resistunt;* licet si et increpare aliquando sit necessarium, uideatur ab ipsa necessitate illud facere, et non arbitrii sui ferocitate. denique dicit:

sed modestum esse, non litigiosum.

his adicit et aliud:

10 *non cupidum pecuniarum.*

hoc prae ceteris omnibus necessarium est episcopo, quod si illi hoc non adfuerit, numquam diligentiam adhibet conuenientium, eo quod cupiditas pecuniarum multa eum facere inpellit ex illis quae fieri non conueniunt.

15 *domum suam bene regentem.*

hoc est, 'dispensantem et diligentiam adhibentem.' denique et ipsum regimen ostendens quid dicat, adiecit:

filios habentem in subiectione cum omni pudicitia.

et his consequenter adicit:

20 *si autem quis domui suae praeesse nescit, quomodo ecclesiae Dei diligentiam adhibebit?*

qui suos conuenienter regere nescit, multo magis ecclesiam regere uel docere minime poterit. nam quod dixit: *filios habentem in subiectionem,* non de arbitrio filiorum dicit sed de patris sollici-
25 tudine, ita ut ipse adceleret eos pudice instituere et subditos eos habere, obtemperantes sibi in quibus de conuenientibus dat illis consilium. si autem patris tali existente arbitrio, filii in deterius persistere uoluerint arbitrii sui prauitate, non patris culpa est. eo quod ad praesens de eius proposito loquitur ita ut erga suos sollici-
30 tudinem expendat ut cum modestia et disciplina et grauitate instituentur; ex hoc ostendi potest quoniam eodem modo et de omni-

3:3b *not a striker,*

Let him not beat anyone simply or without cause or with constant loud reproach. Paul wants him to behave gently all the more with individuals, just as he also says in the second letter (2 Tim 2:24–25): *he ought to be gentle* [110] *to all, not remembering wickedness, teaching those who offer resistance with mildness.*[26] Granted that it is sometimes necessary to reproach, let him be seen to do this from the very necessity and not by the ferocity of his own choice. Then he says:

3:3c *but to be mild, not quarrelsome,*

He adds another point to these:

3:3d *not greedy for money,*

Above all the rest this is necessary for a bishop, because if this were not characteristic of him, he would never apply diligent care to what is right, because greed for money would drive him to do many things that ought not to be done.

3:4a *rightly ruling his own household,*

That is, "administering it and applying diligent care to it." And then to show the very ruling he means, he added:

3:4b *having children in subjection with all decency.*

And in accord with this he adds:

3:5 *And if anyone does not know how to take charge of his own household, how will he apply diligent care to the church of God?*

The one who does not know how to rule his own people fittingly will much more be incapable by any means of ruling the church or teaching. For when he said *having children* [111] *in subjection,* he is not speaking of the free choice of the children but of the great care of the father, so that he may be quick to train the children decently and to keep them obedient, submitting to his advice about what is right. But if, when the father makes such a choice, the children wish to persist in what is worse by the perversity of their own choice, it is not the father's fault. This is because at present Paul is speaking of the father's own purpose, so that he may expend great care on his own people that they may be established with modesty and discipline and seriousness. From this it can be demonstrated that he will have great care for all in

---

[26] The text is cited loosely. "Not remembering wickedness" suggests a textual variant or a misremembering of the text. See Swete (2:110): "for ἀνεξίκακον the translator seems to have had before him ἀμνησίκακον.

bus erit sollicitus. nam et filii Samuelis perspiciuntur, quod amore pecuniae iustitiam prodiderint; et non utique Samuelem incu-
samus ob eorum tale propositum.

non neophytum, ut ne in superbiam elatus in iudicium incidat dia-
boli.

ualde fatue quidam hoc in loco existimauerunt *neophytum* dicere apostolum illum qui secundum aetatem est iuuenis. quos conueniebat etiam etsi nihil aliud saltem illud perspicere, quoniam
ipse Timotheus cui haec scribebat non modo iuuenis erat, uerum
etiam et nimium iuuenis, ita ut per hoc contempni posse uideretur; scripsit ergo ei: *nemo iuuentutem tuam contempnat.* nam et ipse
iuuenis cum esset in apostolatum electus est sicut in Actibus apostolorum Lucas insinuat. sed *neophytum* dixit aut illum qui nuper
credidit, aut illum qui nuper baptismum est adsecutus. nam fidem
'plantationem' uocat, sicut et scribens dixit *ego plantaui*, hoc est,
'ad fidem adduxi.' et de baptismate similiter scribit: *si enim con-*
plantati facti sumus similitudini mortis eius, de baptismate dicens.
etenim non adeo erant ista apostolorum tempore diuisa ut et crederent et baptizarentur, eo quod illi qui non baptizati erant nec fideles tunc nuncupabantur; unde et ex eadem consuetudine adhuc
et praesens illi qui baptizati sunt 'fideles' uocantur. plurimis uero in partibus neque christianos uocant eos qui non perceperunt
baptisma. nam et apostolus sic dicit: *si quis autem Christi Spiritum*
non habet, hic non est eius. euidens est quoniam Spiritum non habet qui baptisma non percipit. uult ergo eum qui in episcopatum
producitur ex multo tempore fidelem esse et baptizatum; unde et
multas causas dicit huic rei necessarias et ualde dignas. adiecit uero primam causam dicens: *ut ne elatus in iudicium incidat diaboli.*
elatio enim dicitur qui in illis quae sibi non adsunt extollitur, magna de se sapiens. nuper ergo credens et baptismi gratiam potitus

---

2 perdiderint iust. *r*   3 talem *C* H*   4 neofitum *C H*   8 saltim *C*
‖ praespicere *C* prospicere *r*   15 hoc est ego pl. *C* H*   16 induxi *H*   17
similitudi *H*   19 erant bapt. *H*   20 nunc cupabantur *C** ‖ consuetudinem
C* H ‖ ad praes. *C (corr.)*   21 illos *H*   22 uocans *H r*

the same way. For even Samuel's children are singled out because they handed down justice for the love of money (1 Sam 8:3), and we certainly do not blame Samuel for such a purpose as was theirs.

3:6 *Not a neophyte, so that he may not, lifted up in pride, fall into the condemnation of the devil.*

Some people have quite foolishly supposed that the apostle in this place says *neophyte* of someone who is young in age. Even if nothing else, they ought at least to recognize that Timothy himself, to whom Paul was writing this letter, was not only young but even so extremely young that because of this he seemed capable of being despised. Therefore, Paul wrote to him (1 Tim 4:12): *let no one despise your youth*. Even Paul himself was young when he was chosen to be an apostle, as Luke implies in the Acts of the Apostles (Acts 7:58). Instead, Paul said *neophyte* either of the person who had recently believed or the person who had recently [112] received baptism. For he calls faith "a planting," just as in writing to the Corinthians he said (1 Cor 3:6): *I have planted*;[27] that is, "I have brought forth." And in a similar way he writes of baptism (Rom 6:5): *for if we have been planted together in the likeness of his death*, speaking of baptism. Indeed, in the time of the apostles those two things were not separated to such an extent, so that they both believed and were baptized, because those who were not baptized were not at that time named "faithful." And so by the same custom those who have been baptized are still called at the present time "the faithful." And in a good many places they do not even call those who have not received baptism Christians. Indeed, the apostle speaks this way (Rom 8:9): *but if someone does not have the Spirit of Christ, he is not his*. It is clear that whoever has not received baptism does not have the Spirit. Therefore, Paul wants the person advanced to the episcopate to be faithful and baptized for a considerable time. And then he also says there are many and quite worthy reasons for this practice. And he added the first reason by saying *that he may not, lifted up,* [113] *fall into the condemnation of the devil*. For "lifting up" refers to someone who is exalted in those things that are not his, thinking highly of himself. Therefore, someone who is a recent believer and has received the grace of baptism and has not yet furnished

---

[27] Here ἐφύευσα; thus, the "neophyte" is the one newly planted by faith or baptism.

et necdum sui propositi probationem praebens neque secundum
ordinem doctus de illis quae ad se conueniunt, si productus fuerit ad hoc ut alios ipse doceat, ab ipsa ordinatione elatus magna
desipiet. qui et quasi magister discere ab aliquo interdum non pa-
5 tietur, eo quod doctor sit ipse constitutus; docere autem nescit, eo
quod primitus non didicit. elatus uero extitit in illis quae sibi secundum ueritatem minime adsunt; uane uero extollens se propter
inpositam magisterii speciem, nihil differre uidebitur diabolo, qui
minister Dei creatus quae magna de se sapere est adnisus, Dei si-
10 bi adsciscens et nomen et honorem; in illis se extollens quae sibi
non adhaerent iustam iudicis poenam expectat. ita ut manifestum
sit ex his illud quod [in] superioribus dicebamus, quoniam Paulus per omnia propositi probationem requirit, talem esse et episcopum uolens qui in opere propositi sui documenta praestare pos-
15 sit. quod baptismati adesse nequaquam potest, remissionem enim
peccatorum baptisma praestat—si sic absolute excepto proposito et hoc pronuntiare sit cautum—uirtutem uero non gestam non
inoperatur. deinde et aliam dicit causam quod oporteat uirtutibus
exercitatum eum esse per omnia erga pietatem qui in episcopatum
20 est producendus:

oportet autem eum et bonum testimonium habere ab his qui foris
sunt, ut non in obprobrium incidat et laqueum diaboli.

ab his qui foris sunt edicens, illos putat qui extra ecclesiam sunt,
apud quos necessarie conuenit integram eum debere opinionem
25 habere prout potest; docens pariter ut opinionis suae diligentiam
habeat. nam quod dicit tale est. sunt aliquae professiones quae secundum se illum qui eam profitetur reprehensioni subdi efficiunt,
ut puta publicanus aut caupo aut leno, aut et aliud aliquid quod
a plurimis uel reprehendi posset uel uituperari. uidemus etenim
30 frequenter homines de aliquibus non bonum habere existimare, ea
ratione [qua] uitae suae opinionem maculis inusserunt, et ad plurimorum peruenit notitiam quia aut luxuriose uixerunt aut erga pecunias auari extiterunt, aut mercatum exercere uoluerunt ob iniu-
stos et turpes lucres. hoc ergo uult dicere: 'si aliqui fuerint tales,

---

2 non (bef. ad se) add H   4 desipiat H   6 non prim. r   12 in (bef. sup.) om
C H r   24 necessario r   27 quidem (aft. illum) add r   28 utpote H   ‖   et
om r   29 possit r   30 bonam h. existimare H bonam h. existimationem r   31
qua om C H r   ‖   maculis iniusserunt C* [inserunt C (corr.)] macu inuiserunt
(sic) H   32 qui (for quia) H   34 turpia lucra r

proof of his own purpose or been taught in order about what is fitting for him, if he should be advanced to this position so that he would himself teach others, lifted up by this very ordination, he will greatly lose his senses. And as an official teacher he will not for the time being put up with learning from someone else, because he has been appointed as a teacher. But he does not know how to teach, because he has not first learned. And, lifted up, he has taken a prominent position in those matters that in truth by no means belong to him. And vainly exalting himself because of the outward show of a teacher placed upon him, he will appear to differ in no way from the devil, who, though created as God's minister, strived to think highly of himself, arrogating to himself both the name and honor of God. By exalting himself in what does not apply to him he is waiting for the just judgment of the judge. And so these remarks are aimed at showing that what we were saying above is obvious—that Paul in all respects demands proofs of someone's intention, wishing that a bishop should be such a person as is capable of setting forth instances of his intention in what he has done. The fact that he has been present at baptism is of no avail at all, for baptism bestows the remission of sins—if without qualification and with intention set aside, [114] it may be safe even to affirm this—but it does not bring about virtue carried out in deed. Then Paul speaks of another reason why the one to be advanced to the episcopate must be trained in all respects in the virtues that have to do with true religion:

3:7 *And he must also have good testimony from those who are outside, so that he may not fall into reproach and the snare of the devil.*

By declaring *from those who are outside*, he is thinking of those who are outside the church, among whom the candidate ought necessarily to have an unblemished reputation as far as possible, and he is teaching that the candidate should have diligent care for his reputation. For what Paul means is like this. There are some occupations that of themselves cause the person who practices it to be subject to reproach, for example, a tax collector, or an innkeeper, or a brothel keeper, or any other occupation that could be censured or criticized by many people. Moreover, we often see people who do not have a good opinion from others on the grounds that they have branded the reputation of their life with stains, and it has come to the notice of a good many people that either they have lived licentiously or have been miserly with regard to

qui ex antiqua uita et professione apud homines existimati sunt
prauissimi extitisse arbitrii, eiusmodi homines conuenit deiecta-
re ne in episcopatum producantur, licet si et uideantur fideliter
accessisse et uitam suam studio meliorum inlustrasse, donec per
5   longum tempus uitae suae et conuersationis documenta demon-
strarent, ita ut opinionem suam in melius inlustrasse apud illos
qui extra ecclesiam sunt uideantur. quare? eo quod licet tibi fideli contemplatione fidei uel baptismatis uideatur esse dignus, tamen praecedens uita adimit ei fiduciam apud eos qui extra eccle-
10 siam sunt, ita ut non modo iuuare possit exteros, sed exprobrari ob uitae suae turpitudinem.' nam quod dixit: *ut ne in obpro-*
brium incidat, adicit et tertiam causam dicens: *et in laqueum dia-*
boli. haec causa prae ceteris alia est, nulla ex parte infirmior illorum quae ante dicta sunt, eo quod non est cautum tali homi-
15 ni aliorum committere diligentiam et tantam ei repente praebere
potestatem. quare? quia adhuc uitae et morum suorum necdum
cautum praebuit documentum, et incertum est utrum nihil simile pristinae perficiat uitae, diabolo multas aduersus eum machi-
nas inueniente ut iterum eum in antiquis praecipitet delictis; eo
20 quod nuper adhuc a deterioribus recessisse uidetur, et non potest sub alterius cura non pertinens in melius corrigi, eo quod ipse uidetur aliorum potius sollicitudinem habere commissam. sic
per omnia ostendit illum qui in episcopatum producitur probabilem debere esse et uirtutibus illis quae secundum pietatem sunt
25 ornatum; nec enim ob solam fidem aut baptismi gratiam dignum
habere eum existimari istius esse loci, nisi et uitae et conuersationis suae fultus fuerit testimonio. tres causas necessarias exposuit
quod ita conueniat fieri—unam quidem eo quod facile extollatur
ab illa potestate qua docere ceteros statuitur; alteram uero quod
30 oporteat eum bonum testimonium habere ab illis qui foris sunt; et
tertiam, quod non caute de eo possent conicere eo quod incertum

---

2-3 deuitare (*for* deiect.) *H r*   3   licet etsi *H* licet *r*   4   arcessisse *C H*   8
fide *C H r* ‖ baptismate *r* 14 a me (*for* ante) *H* ‖ eo quod est cautum non
est tali *r* 19 et (*aft.* ut) *add r* 21 corrige *C** corrigere *H* 26 existimare *H*

money or have been willing to engage in trade for unjust and sordid profits. Therefore, this is what Paul means: "If any should be like this, who from their former life and occupation have been thought by people to have been noted for a perverse choice of life, it is necessary to reject people of this kind, so that they may not be advanced to the episcopate, even though they may seem to have drawn near faithfully and to have illumined their life with zeal for better things. They should not be accepted until by a lengthy time [115] they show instances of their life and behavior, so that they may be seen to have illumined for the better their reputation among those outside the church. Why? Because, granted that he may seem to you who are faithful worthy of baptism by his observance of the faith, nevertheless, his previous life takes away confidence in him among those outside the church, so that he cannot help outsiders in any way but is held in reproach because of the shameful reputation of his life." Now when he said *so that he may not fall into reproach*, he added a third reason by saying *and into the snare of the devil*. This reason is different from the others but in no respect weaker than those mentioned before, because it is not safe to entrust the diligent care of others to such a person and to bestow such great authority on him suddenly. Why? Because up to now he has not yet furnished a safe instance of his life and character, and it is unclear whether he may accomplish what is in nothing similar to his former life, since the devil contrives many devices against him so that he may hurl him once more into his former transgressions. Because he is seen to have withdrawn from worse things quite recently and is unable to be set right for the better, since he does not belong to someone else's care because, instead, he is seen himself to have the great care of others. Thus, in all respects Paul demonstrates that the person advanced to the episcopate ought to be tried and true and adorned with those virtues that have to do with true religion; nor should one hold him deemed worthy of that position because of faith alone or the grace of baptism, unless he is supported by testimony both to his life and to his behavior. Paul has set forth three necessary reasons why it must be done this way: one, because the neophyte is easily exalted by the authority by which he is appointed to teach others; another, because he ought to have good testimony from those who are outside; [116] and third, that they are unable to make conjectures about him safely, because it is unclear whether he will

est an in proposito meliore persistat necne ad antiqua recurrens
sui deterior existat, sed studio meliorum inlustretur. haec quidem
dicta sunt a Paulo qua a uiro diuina credito gratia dici debuerant.
hi uero qui Pauli decretis superiores se esse existimant, nihil horum perpendere uolunt, sed plurimos in episcopatum producunt
nec uitam eorum antiquam nec propositum examinare suadentes,
sed ad defensionem suam hoc solum proferunt, quod aut nuper
crediderit aut nuper sit baptizatus. sed siquis uult differentiam recognoscere illam quae inter Pauli decreta interque horum habetur
prudentiam, intendat causas ob quas non sic fieri oportere Paulus
instruxit, et tunc perspiciet decreti eius utilitatem; examinet uero
iam ipsis negotiis, et perspiciat si non de illis qui hoc modo facti
sunt episcopi aut omnes causas istas inueniet aut saltem unam ex
illis repperiet; aut inueniet eos elatione immensa extolli ita ut eos
qui in eandem sunt gratiam accersiti nec similes sibi nec dignos esse existiment, et hoc de illis qui semper uitam suam studiis optimis
inlustrauerunt et non discesserunt ab illo optimo proposito quod
in anteriorem uitam expendisse uidebantur; et maxime ob cupiditatem pecuniarum et quod omni ex parte coadunare properent
pecunias, si tamen tales antea fuerunt. aut certe ab illis qui extra
ecclesiam sunt inproperiis pulsentur, pro quibus ante non multum
temporis cum professionis essent talis aut talis, nullum uitae suae
uel integritatis testimonium habentes quod possent talia augere,
aliis diligentiam adhibere sunt praepositi. euidens uero illud ex
his quae a nobis ante dicta sunt quoniam beatus Paulus eum qui
de praua uita ad meliorem uitam transiit et opere ipso uitae suae
documenta praebuerit, in ecclesiasticam recipit functionem, non
ob primam conuersationem reprobans eum, sed pro secunda dignum esse existimans. nam illum qui huiusmodi fuerit, necessario
testimonium bonum subsequitur ob uitae eius correctionem, quia
in melius se sponte transtulit, et obprobrium pristinae uitae suae a
se dispulit. et non est pertimescendum ne facile redeat in deterius
qui arbitrio suo ab illis sponte discedere praehonorauit, optimum

1 si *(for* an) *H* ‖ et in *(for* ad) *r* 3 quia uero *C * H* quae uiro *r* 4 sa-
pientiores *C* ‖ se *om C * r* 11 examine *C r* 13 saltim *C* 17 quem
(for quod) *H* 20 antea t. *r* 22 esset *C H r* 23 habens *H* ‖ quo *C*
(corr.) ‖ alia *(for* talia) *H* 24 aut aliis *C (corr.)* aliis et *r* ‖ sui *(for* sunt) *r*
‖ euidens ... dicta sunt *om H* 32 interius *(for* in det.) *C* H* ulterius *r* 33
discere *(for* discedere) *C**

persist in a better intention and not become worse by turning back to his old way of life rather than being illumined by his zeal for the better. Paul has said these things as a man entrusted with divine grace ought to have said them. But those who think they are superior to Paul's commands are willing to put in the balance nothing of this. Instead, they advance a great many people to the episcopate without urging an examination either of their old life or of their intention, but offer in their own defense only this—that he either has recently believed or has recently been baptized. But if someone is willing to recognize the difference between Paul's commands and the sagacity held by these people, let him pay attention to the reasons why Paul has given instructions that it not be done this way, and then he will see the benefit of Paul's command. And let him examine the very affairs that take place now, and let him see whether he will not find in the case of those who have been made bishops this way either all those reasons or at least will discover one of them. For one thing he will find them so exalted by immense elevation that they consider those who have been summoned to the same grace neither like themselves nor worthy—and this about those who have always illumined their life with the best pursuits [117] and have not departed from that best intention they plainly expended in their previous life. And he will find others, most of all, who because of greed for money hasten to gather money from every quarter, if at least they have been like this before. Or he will find those who without doubt are assailed by reproaches from those outside the church, because not long ago they were of such or such an occupation. Although they have no testimony to their life or moral integrity that could promote such things, they have been put in charge of applying diligent care to others. But it is clear from what we have previously said that blessed Paul accepts for ecclesiastical service the person who has passed over from a perverse life to a better life and who furnishes instances of his life in its very activity, not condemning him for his first way of life, but considering him worthy because of his second. Now for the person who might fit these requirements there must necessarily follow him good testimony that his life has been set right—that he has passed over to the better by his own free choice and has driven away from himself the shame of his former life. And it is not greatly to be feared that someone would easily return to the worse who has by his own choice made it a matter of first

esse existimans ut meliorum curae studeat. secundum hunc modum etiam beatum Matthaeum ex publicano electum fuisse inue-
niemus, et ipsum apostolum inuenimus transisse, eo quod pristina
uita eorum nullum illis adtulit impedimentum quin hoc officium
5 sumerent, eo quod et perfecto affectu meliorum studiis sese inlustrauerunt

diaconos similiter.

opinabatur quisquis usum diuinarum non habet scripturarum
beatum Paulum presbyteros praetermisisse. sed non ita se res ha-
10 bet; illa enim quae de episcopo in anterioribus dixit, etiam et de
illis dicit qui nunc nominantur presbyteri, eo quod

†antiquis temporibus utrisque
his nominibus uocabantur presbyteri. et hoc notauimus [in
15 epistolam ad] Philippenses scribentes; in ea epistola scribens
apostolus *coepiscopis et cumdia-
conibus* dixit. euidens quia non
erat possibile ut multi essent
20 episcopi in una ciuitate. melius autem quis cognoscere poterit illud ex illis quae ad Titum
scripsit apostolus; dixit etenim:
ut constituas per singulas ciuita-
25 *tes presbyteros sicut ego tibi prae-*
cepi, et dicens quales debeant
ordinari adicit: *oportet enim epi-*
scopum inreprehensibilem esse si-
cut Dei dispensatorem. cum co-
30 nueniret utique illi ut 'presbyterum' eum diceret; sed euiden-

τὸ παλαιὸν δὲ ἀμφοτέραις ταύ-
ταις ἐκαλοῦντο ταῖς προσηγορίαις
οἱ πρεσβύτεροι. καὶ τοῦτο ἐπεση-
μηνάμεθα καὶ ἐν τῇ πρὸς Φιλιπ-
πησίους, ἔνθα γράφων φησίν· συνεπισκόποις καὶ διακόνοις. δῆλον
γὰρ ὡς οὐκ ἐνῆν ἐπισκόπους μιᾶς
πόλεως πλείους εἶναι. ἄμεινον δὲ ἐν
τοῖς πρὸς Τίτον γεγραμμένοις αὐτὸ γνοίη τις ἄν. εἰπὼν γάρ· ἵνα
καταστήσῃς πρεσβυτέρους, ὡς ἐγώ
σοι διεταξάμην, καὶ προστεθεικὼς
οἵους, ἐπάγει· δεῖ γὰρ τὸν ἐπίσκοπον ἀνέγκλητον εἶναι ὡς Θεοῦ οἰ-
κονόμον· δέον εἴπερ ἄρα τὸν πρεσ-
βύτερον εἰπεῖν, ἀλλὰ σαφῶς τὸν
αὐτὸν 'ἐπίσκοπον' καὶ 'πρεσβύτε-
ρον' ὀνομάζων. τί δὴ τοῦτό ἐστιν; ἄξιον γὰρ μὴ παραλιπεῖν τὴν
αἰτίαν τῆς ἐναλλαγῆς τῶν ὀνομά-

3 in apost. *C r* 4 qui in (*for* quin) *C H* qui (*om* in) *r* 5 se (*for* sese) *r* 12
sq. Coisl. 204, f. 199 a [Cr. vii. 27] τὸ παλαιὸν δέ, κ.τ.λ. 13 uocantur *C H r*:
txt a ‖ ἐκαθοῦντο Cr. 14 notabimus *C H* notabamus *r* ‖ filipenses (*for* in
ep. ad Ph.) *C* H* de Philippensibus *r* 15-16 scripta (*for* scribentes) *C* (*corr.*)
16 in ea ep. scribens ap. coepisset et coepiscopis et cum diaconibus *C * H* in ea
ep. cum scribens ap. coepisset et coepiscopis et cum diaconis *r* quibus scribens
ap. coepiscopis et diaconibus *C* (*corr.*) 21-22 illud poterit *H* 23 enim *H*
a 27 ordinare *C* H r* ‖ addidit *a* 29-30 conuenerit *C H r* conueniat *C*
(*corr.*): *txt a* 30 illum *C*: om *a*

importance freely to depart from those things so that he may be zealous in caring for better things. In this way we shall also find that blessed Matthew was chosen from being a tax collector, and we find that the apostle Paul himself changed his life. Because of this their former life afforded them no obstacle to taking up their duty, since they distinguished themselves by a perfect disposition for the pursuits of better things.

3:8a *Deacons likewise*

Anyone who is not used to the divine scripture would suppose [118] that blessed Paul has left out the presbyters. But this is not the case, for what he said above about the bishop he means also to refer to those who are now named presbyters, because

†in ancient times presbyters were called by both these names. And we have noted this when writing about the letter to the Philippians. In this letter the apostle said he was writing (Phil 1:1) *to the fellow bishops and fellow deacons.*[28] It is clear that it was not possible for there to be many bishops in a single city. And someone could recognize this better on the basis of what the apostle wrote to Titus. Indeed, he said (Titus 1:5): *so that you may appoint presbyters in each city, as I have instructed you.* And when he said what sort of people ought to be ordained, he adds (Titus 1:7): *for the bishop ought* [119] *to be above reproach, as the administrator of God.* Although it was certainly right for Paul to speak of him as a presbyter, yet he clearly named the same person both "bi-

Of old presbyters were called by both these names. And we have noted this also in the letter to the Philippians, where Paul writes and says (Phil 1:1): *with the bishops and the deacons.* For it is clear that it would not have been possible for there to be more than one bishop in a single city. And someone could recognize this better in what was written to Titus. For when Paul said (Titus 1:5): *so that you may appoint presbyters, as I have instructed you,* after setting forth what kind, he continues (Titus 1:7):

for the bishop must be blameless, as the steward of God. Even though it was certainly right to speak of a presbyter, yet Paul is clearly naming the same person "bishop" and "presbyter."

---

[28]This mistranslation compounds the mistake made in the commentary on Philippians.

ter eundem et 'episcopum' et
'presbyterum' nominauit. quae
autem sit causa non est iustum
eam silentio praeterire ob illam
5 immutationem nominum quae
ad praesens esse uidetur, et qua
ex causa discreta sunt nunc nomina, et neque episcopus dici
potest 'presbyter' neque 'pre-
10 sbyter' umquam 'episcopi' nuncupationem poterit sibi uindicare, usquedum presbyter esse sistit. antiquis etenim temporibus quando pietati [pauci]
15 studebant, presbyteri omni in
loco ordinabantur, hoc quidem
nomen contemplatione honoris
accipientes, sicut et apud Iudaeos presbyteri dicebantur qui
20 populo praeerant. uocabantur
autem et 'episcopi' ab illo opere
quod et implere uidebantur, eo
quod considerate omnia quae ad
cultum pertinent pietatis fue-
25 rant constituti, ita ut uniuersorum dispensationem haberent
commissam. nam et perfectam
dispensationem et auctoritatem
ecclesiastici ministerii ipsi tunc
30 commissam habebant, et omnia regebantur pro eorum arbitrio. hoc autem poterit quis
et a Luca discere manifestius,
qui in Actibus apostolorum in-
35 ter cetera dicit misisse Paulum
Ephesi et euocasse presbyteros

των, καὶ τίνος ἕνεκεν τὰ ὀνόματα
διακέκριται νῦν, καὶ οὔτε ὁ ἐπίσ-
κοπος λεχθείη ἂν πρεσβύτερος, οὔτε ὁ πρεσβύτερος δέξεται ἄν ποτε
τὴν τοῦ ἐπισκόπου ὀνομασίαν, μέχρις ἂν πρεσβύτερος ᾖ. τὸ παλαιὸν
ὀλίγων ὄντων τῶν εὐσεβῶν πρεσβύτεροι ἀπανταχόσε καθίσταντο, τοῦτο μὲν ἀπὸ τῆς τιμῆς ὀνομαζόμε-
νοι, ὡς καὶ παρὰ Ἰουδαίοις 'πρεσβύτεροι' οἱ τοῦ λαοῦ προηγούμενοι
ἐλέγοντο· καλούμενοι δὲ καὶ ἐπίσκοποι ἀφ' οὗπερ μετῆσαν καὶ ἔρ-
γου, τῷ μάλιστα πᾶσιν ἐπισκοπεῖν
καὶ τὴν ἁπάντων οἰκονομίαν ἐγκε-
χειρίσθαι. καὶ γὰρ ὁλοτελῆ τῆς ἐκκλησιαστικῆς διοικήσεως τὴν αὐθ-
εντείαν εἶχον τότε, καὶ πάντα ἀπήρ-
τητο τῆς αὐτῶν γνώμης. τοῦτο δὲ
ἔνεστιν καὶ παρὰ τῷ Λουκᾷ μαθεῖν
ἀκριβῶς, ὃς ἐν ταῖς Πράξεσιν τῶν
ἀποστόλων λέγει μὲν ἀποστείλαν-
τα τὸν Παῦλον εἰς τὴν Ἔφεσον κε-
κληκέναι τοὺς πρεσβυτέρους, τίθησιν δὲ αὐτοῦ πρὸς τοὺς παραγεγο-
νότας διάλεξιν· ἐν οἷς ὁ Παῦλος οὕτως φησίν· προσέχετε οὖν ἑαυτοῖς
καὶ παντὶ τῷ ποιμνίῳ, ἐν ᾧ ὑμᾶς
τὸ πνεῦμα τὸ ἅγιον ἔθετο ἐπισκόπους ποιμαίνειν τὴν ἐκκλησίαν τοῦ
Θεοῦ. προδήλως οὓς αὐτὸς ὠνόμασεν πρεσβυτέρους, τούτους ἐπισκόπους εἰπὼν ὑπὸ τοῦ Παύλου κε-
κλῆσθαι. οἱ δὴ τὴν τοῦ χειροτονεῖν
ἐξουσίαν ἔχοντες, οἱ νῦν ὀνομαζό-
μενοι ἐπίσκοποι, οὐ μιᾶς ἐκκλησίας

1 eundem om C r 4 ob illa immutatione H 7 nunc om H nec nunc r 13
desistit a 14 pauci om C H r: txt a g 17 contemplationis H r 20 populum
C* 24 pertinet C H

shop" and "presbyter." But it is not right to pass over in silence the reason for that change of names that is seen to exist at the present time and why the names are now distinguished— neither can a bishop be spoken of as a presbyter, nor could a presbyter ever claim for himself the title of bishop, as long as he stays a presbyter. In ancient times, however, when few were zealous for true religion, presbyters were appointed in every place, receiving this name [120] in consideration of honor, just as even among the Jews those who presided over the people were said to be "presbyters." And they were also called "bishops" from the work they were seen to fulfill, because they had been appointed to oversee everything that pertained to the observance of true religion, so that they had entrusted to them the management of everything. Indeed, at that time they had entrusted to them both complete management and authority over the church's ministry, and everything used to be ruled by their judgment. And anyone could learn this more clearly from Luke, who in the Acts of the Apostles says among other things that Paul sent to Ephesus and summoned the presbyters to him (Acts 20:17). He also put down the exhortation Paul

Why, then, is this? Indeed, it is right not to pass over the reason for the interchange of the names and why the names are now distinguished—

neither would a bishop now be said to be a presbyter, nor would a presbyter ever receive the title of bishop, as long as he is a presbyter. Of old, when there were few godly people, presbyters were appointed in every place, named this from honor, since even among the Jews those who presided over the people were said to be "presbyters." And they were also called bishops for the work they were pursuing by overseeing everyone as much as possible and undertaking the management of everything.

For they had complete authority to manage the church at that time, and everything depended on their judgment.

And it is possible to learn this accurately from Luke, who in the Acts of the Apostles says that Paul sent to Ephesus to summon the presbyters (20:17). And he puts down Paul's address to them when they had assembled.

ad se. cuius etiam et exhortationem ad eos factam exponit, quam hisdem aduenientibus fecisse uidetur; in quibus Paulus ita disserit: *adtendite uobis et omni gregi, in quo uos Spiritus sanctus posuit episcopos ad regendam ecclesiam Dei.* euidens est quia quos ipse nominauit 'presbyteros,' hos a Paulo *episcopos* arcessitos denuntiauit; ii uero qui ordinationis nunc habent potestatem, qui nunc nominantur 'episcopi,' non unius ecclesiae creabantur episcopi sed prouincias integras eo in tempore regebant, apostolorum nomine nuncupati. sic uniuersae Asiae Timotheum praeposuit beatus Paulus et Cretae Titum. euidens autem est quoniam et alios aliis prouinciis per partes itidem praeposuit, ita ut unusquisque eorum integrae prouinciae sollicitudinem indeptus percurrat ecclesias uniuersas, et ad ecclesiasticam functionem, ubi deerant clerici, ordinaret; et quaecumque causae durae apud illos accidebant, dissoluebat eas, simul et uerborum doctrina corrigens eos, et durissima peccatorum delic-

γινόμενοι ἀλλ' ἐπαρχίας ὅλης ἐφεστῶτες, τῷ τῶν ἀποστόλων ἐκαλοῦντο προσηγορίᾳ. οὕτως ἀπάσῃ τῇ Ἀσίᾳ τὸν Τιμόθεον ἐπέστησεν ὁ μακάριος Παῦλος, καὶ τῇ Κρήτῃ τὸν Τίτον. δῆλον δὲ ὅτι καὶ ἑτέρους ἐπαρχίαις ἑτέραις κατὰ μέρος ἐπέστησεν, ὡς ἕκαστος ὅλης τῆς ἐπαρχίας τὴν φροντίδα ἀναδεχόμενος ἐκπεριήει τὰς ἐκκλησίας ἁπάσας, τοὺς πρὸς τὴν ἐκκλησιαστικὴν λειτουργίαν λείποντας προχειριζόμενος, τὰ χαλεπώτερα τῶν παρ' αὐτοῖς διαλύων, λόγοις διδασκαλίας αὐτοὺς ἐπανορθῶν, τὰ βαρύτερα τῶν ἁμαρτημάτων ἐξιώμενος, καὶ ὅλως ἅπαντα ποιῶν ὅσα εἰκὸς ἦν ἄνδρα ποιεῖν ἡγούμενον, ἀπασῶν τῶν πόλεων τότε ἐχουσῶν τοὺς πρεσβυτέρους, ὡς ἔφην, οἳ τὰς ἑαυτῶν διεῖπον ἐκκλησίας· ὡς εἶναι τότε τοῦτο τῇ ἐπαρχίᾳ τοὺς νῦν ὀνομαζομένους ἐπισκόπους, τότε δὲ ἀποστόλους, ὅπερ εἰσὶν νῦν τῇ πόλει καὶ τῇ χώρᾳ ἐφ' ᾗπερ τὴν κατάστασιν δέχονται. καὶ τότε μὲν τοῦτον εἶχεν τὸν τρόπον τὰ κατὰ τὴν ἐκκλησίαν. ἐπειδὴ δὲ πολλὴ μὲν ἡ τῆς εὐσεβείας ἐπίδοσις ἐγένετο, μέγισται δὲ οὐ πόλεις μόνον ἀλλὰ καὶ χῶραι τῶν πεπιστευκότων ἦσαν, τῶν τε μακαρίων ἀπογενομένων ἀποστόλων, οἱ

---

3 iisdem *r* 5 deserit *C* H** 6 uniuerso *H* 9 quod (*for* quia quos) *C H*: txt *r* 11 accessitos *r* ‖ hi *r* 14 huius (*for* unius) *C H r* 15 creabuntur *C * H r* 16 et (*for* eo) *C H r* 18 nunccupati *C** 18-19 uniuersi *H* 20-22 τοὺς πρεσβυτέρους... τῇ ἐπαρχίᾳ om. Cr. 23 ita et *r* 26 percurret *C** curet *C* (*corr.*) percurreret *r* 27 εἶχον Cr. 29-30 a se dure (*for* causae durae) *H* 30 accedebant *C* r* 31 eos (*for* eas) *r* 31-32 uerbo doctrinae *C r* 33 peccarum *C**

is seen to have made to them when they assembled. [121] In it Paul uses the following words (Acts 20:28): *watch over yourselves and the whole flock in which the Holy Spirit has put you as bishops to rule the church of God.* It is clear that those Luke named presbyters, Paul pronounced bishops once they were assembled. And those who now have authority to ordain and are now named bishops used not to be made bishops of a single church but at that time used to rule over whole provinces, designated by the name of apostles. [122] Thus, blessed Paul put Timothy in charge of all Asia and Titus of Crete. And it is clear that he also put other people in charge of other provinces throughout the regions in the same way so that each one of them, when he had entered upon the care of a whole province, might travel to all the churches and might ordain people to the service of the church, wherever clergy were lacking. And he used to resolve whatever hard cases happened among them, at the same time setting them right by the words of teaching; and he plainly used to loose by grace the most serious faults of sins by propitiating God, doing fully all those things that the one placed in charge for this purpose ought to do. Now

In it Paul says the following (Acts 20:28): *therefore, watch over yourselves and the whole flock in which the Holy Spirit has put you as bishops to shepherd the church of God.* Obviously, those whom Luke has named presbyters, these, he says, were called bishops by Paul. Indeed, those who have the authority to ordain, who are now called bishops, used to preside not over a single church but over a whole province, and they were called by the name of apostles. Thus, blessed Paul put Timothy in charge of all Asia and Titus of Crete. And it is clear that he also put other people in charge of other provinces individually, so that each one receiving the care of a whole province would travel about all the churches, ordaining those needed for the service of the church,

resolving the more difficult matters among them, setting them right by the words of teaching, healing the more serious of sins, and on the whole doing everything right for a man who was governing to do,

ta, repropitians Deum, disso-
luere per gratiam uidebatur; ad
plenum etiam omnia faciens illa quae conueniebat facere eum
5 qui praepositus idem ad hoc
fuerat. nam et uniuersae ciuitates tunc presbyteros (ut dixi) habebant, qui suas ecclesias
singuli gubernabant; ita ut es-
10 sent tunc per singulas prouincias singuli qui nunc 'episcopi'
nominantur, qui tunc 'apostoli' dicebantur, quod nunc uero
per singulas ciuitates aut pos-
15 sessiones qui ordinationem episcopatus susceperunt. et tunc
quidem hoc modo ecclesiae regebantur. quoniam uero pietas incrementum sumpsisse ui-
20 detur, repletae autem sunt non
modo ciuitates credentium, sed
regiones. beatis uero apostolis decedentibus, illi qui post illos ordinati sunt ut praeessent
25 ecclesiis illis primis exaequari
non poterant neque miraculorum testimonium par illis habere, sed et in multis aliis infirmiores illorum esse uideban-
30 tur, graue existimauerunt apostolorum sibi uindicare nuncupationem. diuiserunt ergo ipsa nomina, et hisdem (id est,
presbyteris) presbyterii nomen

μετὰ τοῦτο εἰς τὴν καθόλου προ-
βαλλόμενοι ἐπιστασίαν οὐκέτι τοῖς
προτέροις ἐγίνοντο ὅμοιοι, οὐδὲ τὴν
ἀπὸ τῶν θαυμάτων μαρτυρίαν ἴ-
σην ἔχειν ἠδύναντο, τυχὸν δὲ καὶ
ἐν ἑτέροις πλείστοις ἐλαττούμενοι
ἐκείνων ἐφαίνοντο, βαρὺ νομίσαν-
τες τὴν τῶν ἀποστόλων ἔχειν προσηγορίαν, διείλαντο τὰς ὀνομασίας·
καὶ τὸ μὲν τοῦ πρεσβυτέρου κατ-
αλελοίπασιν τοῖς πρεσβυτέροις, τὸ
δὲ τοῦ ἐπισκόπου τεθείκασιν τῷ
τὴν τοῦ χειροτονεῖν ἐχουσίαν ἔχον-
τι, ὡς ἂν τὴν καθόλου ἐπιστασίαν
ἐγκεχειρισμένου. ἐγένοντο δὲ καὶ
πλείους διὰ μὲν τὴν χρείαν τὸ πρῶ-
τον· ὕστερον δὲ καὶ ὑπὸ φιλοτιμίας
τῶν ποιούντων, ἐν ἀρχῇ μὲν δύο
κατ' ἐπαρχίαν γινομένων ἢ τριῶν τὸ
πλεῖστον (τοῦτο δὲ ἐπὶ τῆς δύσεως
οὐ πρὸ πολλοῦ μὲν ἐν πλείσταις ἦν,
ἐν ἐνίαις δὲ καὶ ἄχρι τῆς δεῦρο πε-
φυλαγμένον εὕροι τις ἄν)· τοῦ δὲ
χρόνου προβαίνοντος οὐ κατὰ πόλιν
γινομένων μόνον ἀλλὰ καὶ κατὰ τό-
πον, ἐν ᾧ μηδὲ χρεία ἦν εἰς ταύτην
τινὰ τὴν λειτουργίαν προβάλλεσθαι
καταναγκάζουσα.

---

8 habent C* H 9 gubernabant ... singuli om C H r [see note to l. 1 below] ||
διείλοντο cod. (corr.), Cr. 11 qui uero nunc epī nom. illi, &c. r 13 quoniam
(for quod nunc) C H r 20 et repl. runt (for repl. autem s.) r 25 γινομένου
cod. 27 parem C H [cf g] 28-29 inferiores illis a 32 erga C* 33 ab
isdem C ab hisdem H et illis r

the cities everywhere, as I have said, at that time used to have presbyters, [123] who individually used to govern their own churches, so that there were at that time in the individual provinces those who are now named bishops but then were said to be apostles. But now those who have received ordination to the episcopate are in individual cities or country estates. At that time the churches used to be ruled in this way. But since true religion appears to have gained increase, not only cities but also country districts have been filled with believers. [124] But when the blessed apostles departed this life, those who were ordained after them to preside over the churches were unable to equal those first ones nor to have the testimony of miracles like them. Moreover, in many other respects they appeared to be weaker than they were, and so they thought it too weighty to claim for themselves the title of apostles. Therefore, they separated the names, and they left the name of presbyter to these, that is, to the presbyters, but others were titled bishops—those endowed with the authority of ordination, so that people might recognize that they were most completely in charge of the churches. And still more were made

since all the cities at that time had presbyters, as I have said, who managed their own churches, so that there were at that time in the province for this purpose those now called bishops but then apostles, although now bishops are in the city or country district where they have settled.

At that time this is the way church affairs were managed, but when true religion increased in numbers, and not only the largest cities but also the country districts were filled with believers, when the blessed apostles were taken away by death, those who were advanced after this for the office of exercising general authority were no longer like the former people, nor were they able to have equal testimony from miracles. And it happened that in most other respects they appeared inferior to those people. Since they thought it too weighty to have the title of apostles, they divided the names, and they applied the name presbyter to the presbyters who had been left and that of bishop to the one who had authority to ordain, since he was entrusted with general authority.

And at first there were more

reliquerunt; alii uero episcopi
sunt nuncupati, ii qui et ordinationis praediti sunt potestate, ita
ut plenissime idem praepositos
5 se ecclesiarum esse cognosce-
rent. facti sunt uero et ampliores episcopi, causa sic depostu-
lante; postea uero et illis adiecti sunt alii liberalitate eorum qui
10 ordinationes faciebant. inprimis enim per singulas prouincias duo aut (ut multum) tres
fiebant episcopi; quod etiam et
in partibus occiduis non ante
15 multi temporis spatium in plurimis prouinciis custodire uidebantur, in aliquibus uero et
usque ad praesens id inueniet
quis custoditum. tempore ue-
20 ro promouente non solum per
ciuitates ordinati sunt, sed et
per singula loca in quibus nec
adeo necessitas flagitabat ut ad
hanc functionem explendam or-
25 dinarentur*.

et haec quidem ad manifestationem sensus apostolicae scripturae
a nobis sunt dicta, ut et illa quae dudum fuerat uel consuetudo uel
demutationis causa in apertum consisteret. intendendum uero est
de cetero illis quae de diaconibus dicit, cum euidens sit illud, quo-
30 niam illa quae de episcopis dicta sunt, de illis qui nunc presbyteri nuncupantur uoluit significari. quae uel maxime conueniunt ad
praesens ut cum omni diligentia obseruentur ab illis qui nunc epi-

---

2 hii *C* hi *H r*   2-3 ordinationes *C* H*   4 iidem *r*   6 facta *H r*   ‖ sunt *om H**   9 liberalitatem *C H*   12 ut *om C r*   13 et in p. etiam *r*   15 in (*bef.* plurimis) *om C H*   16-17 uidebatur *C* (*corr.*)   21 sed *om C r*   23 et (*for* ut) *C H*   24 hunc *H*   28 consistere *H*   30 tunc (*for* nunc) *C* (*corr.*) *r*   30-31 presbiteros *C r* presbiteris *H*   31 gubernabant ita ut essent tunc per singulos prouincias singuli (*aft.* presbyteri) *add C H r: see p.* 123, *l.* 1, *note*   ‖ nuncupantes *C r* nuncupanter *H*   32 et, obseruantur *r*

bishops, since the case so required. But later on still others
were added to them because of
the liberality of those who performed ordinations. For at first
in individual provinces there
were made two or at most three
bishops. [125] And in the West
not long ago they were seen to
observe this custom in a great
many provinces, and in some of
them one will find this observed
up to the present time. But as
time moved on, not only were
bishops ordained throughout
the cities but also in particular
places where no necessity demanded to such an extent that
bishops should be ordained to
fulfill this service.*

bishops because of need, but
later on this was also because of
the ambition of those who were
appointing them.

In the beginning there were two
or at most three in each province. Not long ago this was the
case in the West in most provinces, and in some one may find
that this has been kept up to the
present time.

But as time went on there were
bishops not only in each city
but also in each country district
where there was no compelling
need that anyone should be advanced for this service.

Now we have said this to make the meaning of the apostolic scripture clear, so that even what had been long ago either by way of
custom or by way of a reason for change [126] might be placed
in the open. But attention must be paid, furthermore, to what
Paul says about deacons, since it is clear that he wanted what was
said about bishops to be referred to those who are now called presbyters. What is especially fitting at the present time for those

scopi nuncupantur, tanto intentius quanto et maiorem functionem
commissam habere uidentur. quid ergo dicit: *diaconos similiter?*
illum ordinem propemodum et hoc in loco seruasse uidetur quem
de mulieribus dixerat et uiris. nam et illa quae de uiris primitus
5　dicens, adiecit: *similiter autem et mulieres;* ostendens quoniam illa quae uirtutum sunt, commune ad eos uult pertinere. hoc idem
uero fecit et hoc in loco; dicens illa quae tunc de episcopis dixerat
qui nunc nominantur 'presbyteri,' adicit: *diaconos similiter;* hoc
est, 'uniuersa quae ad uirtutem pertinent, similiter et his adesse
10　cupio.' deinde adicit:
　　pudicos.
　　iusta ratione, eo quod mediatores quidem et ministri functionis sacerdotalis non solum erga uiros erant sed et erga mulieres;
necessarie ergo eos tales esse conueniebat.
15　　*non bilingues.*
　　et hoc iusta dicit ratione; si enim deferunt illa quae mandantur a
presbyteris siue uiris siue mulieribus ad quos et mittuntur, iustum
est eos sincero arbitrio sicut conuenit implere quae sibi [mandan-
tur] quae per eos mandantes audiunt. nam utilitatem decretorum
20　beati Pauli unusquisque tunc euidenter perspicere poterit, si rebus
ipsis una examinare uoluerit.
　　non uino multo deditos, non turpilucres.
　　utraque enim haec necessaria sunt diaconibus sicut et presbyteris. nam et in persona presbyterorum idipsum posuit, dicens *non*
25　*uinolentum, non cupidum pecuniarum.* in eo autem dum dicit *simili-*
ter, sufficienter uisus est hoc ipsum significasse, quoniam per omnia illis communia esse illa quae uirtutum sunt oportere existimat;
adiecit uero et aliqua specialiter dicens, ut magis magisque ipsius
rei fecerit confirmationem. deinde adicit generaliter:
30　　*habentes mysterium fidei in munda conscientia.*
　　compendiose illa quae deceant diaconos obseruare dixit. 'iustum est (inquit) eos fidei mysteria ministrantes—ut dicat 'dogmata pietatis,' mysterium enim saepe uocat illud dogma quod

---

3　in hoc loco *H r*　6　uirtutem *C (corr.)*　7　in hoc loco *C r*　15　bilinguos *C**
16　iusta r. d. *C*　17　admittuntur *(for* et mitt.*) C r*　18-19　mandantur *om C H*
(but with lacuna) dicuntur et *r*　22　turpe lucrum spectantes *r*　24　ad idipsum
C adipsum *H* et ipsum *r*　27　existimet *r*　28　adicit *C H r*　29　faceret *r*　30
ministerium *C r*　‖　in consc. pura *r*　32　mysterio *C H* ministerio *r*　‖
dicant *C (corr.)*

who are now called bishops to observe with all diligence is as much stricter for them as they are seen to have a greater service entrusted to them. Thus, what does Paul mean by *the deacons likewise*? He almost seems in this place, as well, to have kept the order in which he had spoken of men and women; for speaking first of what had to do with the men, he added (2:9) *and likewise also the women*, showing that he wants what belongs to the virtues to apply to them in common. And he has done the same thing in this place. Saying what he had said about bishops at that time (who are now called presbyters), he adds *the deacons likewise*, that is "everything that pertains to virtue I want them to have *likewise*." Then he adds:

3:8b *chaste,*

With just reason, because the mediators and ministers of priestly service dealt not only with men but also with women. Therefore, it was necessarily fitting they should be such people.

3:8c *not double-tongued,*

This, too, he says with just reason. For if they carry out the orders of the presbyters, whether it is to men or to women that [127] they are sent, it is right for them to fulfill with a sincere judgment the orders given them that they hear through those giving the orders. Now each person will be able to discern the benefit of blessed Paul's commands at that time when he is willing to examine them together with the circumstances themselves.

3:8d *not given to much wine, not greedy for dishonest gain,*

For both these qualifications are necessary for deacons just as for presbyters. Indeed, he put the same thing down in characterizing the presbyters, by saying (3:3): *not a drunkard ... not greedy for money.* By the fact that he says *likewise* he is sufficiently seen to have pointed out the same thing, since he thinks that what belongs to the virtues ought to be in all respects common to them. But he added some other words so that more and more he might make a confirmation of his very point.[29] Then he adds in general terms:

3:9 *holding the mystery of faith in a pure conscience.*

He has said succinctly what it becomes deacons to observe. "It

---

[29] That is, 3:3 and 3:8 make the same points, but 3:8 uses more words.

de Christo est, sicut et in hac epistola ex subsequentibus melius cognoscere poterimus—ut mundam conscientiam habeant in ea functione qua implere uidentur.' inde adicit:

et hi probentur primum, et sic ministrent, sine crimine constituti.

5   nam quod dixit *ministrent*, hoc est, 'producantur in diaconia.' eo quod nec poterat fieri ut ministrarent, si non primum fuerint ordinati. sic uidetur per omnia beatus Paulus de illo qui in ministerio est producendus scribere, ut bonum testimonium habeat ex praeterita uita; non tamen absolute et fortuito in ministerio pro-

10   ducatur. deinde quia *diaconos* dixit, commune uero hoc nomen est etiam et mulieribus quae in hoc opere producuntur, optime adicit:

mulieres similiter pudicas.

non hoc uult dicere in hoc loco quoniam conuenit eos tales habere uxores, sed quoniam et mulieres quae diaconis officium im-

15   plere statuuntur similes esse conuenit, ut uirtutis studio aeque sint inlustratae. nam et in loco hoc ideo adiecit:

non accusatrices.

eo quod necessarie fieri soleat ut ceterae mulieres confidenter illis ea quae de se sunt referant, necessarie ergo dicit non debere

20   eas esse accusatrices, ita ut non publicent illa aliis quae a quibusdam illis dicuntur, ne ex hoc contentiones aliquas adnasci faciant aut diuortia.

sobrias.

hoc est, 'argutas,' ita ut impleant cum uelocitate omnia illa quae

25   a se fieri conueniunt. deinde plenarie dicit:

fideles in omnibus.

media uero interponens illa quae de mulieribus diaconiae officium fungentibus propter nominis dixerat communionem, ita ut ostenderet quod uult similiter et istas studiis uirtutum intendere.

---

1   et subseq. *C* H* in subseq. *C (corr.)*   2   munda conscientia *H*   3   quam *(for* qua*) r*   4   constituto *H*   5   in *om r*   10   communi *H*   16   hoc *om H*   18 necessario *r*   20   duplicent *r*   27   diaconia *C* H*   27-28   officia *H* officio *C* *(corr.)*   29   ostendere *H*

is right (he says) for those who minister the mysteries of faith—
meaning 'the doctrines of true religion,' for he often calls the
doctrine concerning Christ the mystery, as we shall be able to
recognize better in this letter by what follows—to have a pure
conscience in the service they are seen to fulfill." Then he adds:

3:10 *And let these be tested first, and so let them minister,*[30]
appointed without fault;

[128] Now his statement *let them minister* means, "let them be
advanced to the diaconate." This is because it was not possible
for it to happen that they should minister, if they had not first
been ordained. Thus, blessed Paul is seen in all respects to write
about the person to be advanced in the ministry that he should
have good testimony from his past life and should not be advanced
in the ministry merely without qualification and by chance. Then,
because he said *deacons*, but this name is common also to the
women who are advanced for this work, he quite effectively adds:

3:11a *the women likewise chaste,*

He does not mean in this place that the male deacons ought to
have wives like this but that the women who are appointed to fulfill
the duty given deacons ought to be like the men, so that they may
be equally distinguished by the pursuit of virtue. Indeed, for this
reason he also added in this place:

3:11b *not slanderers,*

Because necessarily it usually happens that other women
with assurance [129] tell them their concerns. Therefore, he
necessarily says that they ought not to be slanderers, so that they
may not make public to others what is told them by any one of
them, lest by doing so they cause any quarrels or divorces to arise.

3:11c *sober.*

That is, "quick-witted," so that they may fulfill speedily
everything they ought to do. Then, summing up, he says:

3:11d *faithful in all things.*

And he places in the middle of his discussion what he had said
about the women who perform the duty of the diaconate because
of the name they hold in common with the men, so that he may
show that he wants the women likewise to pay attention to the
pursuits of the virtues. Then he takes up again the logical order

---

[30] *Ministrent*, as a translation of διακονείτωσαν. "To minister" refers to the
work of the deacon.

deinde resumit prosecutionem illam quam de diaconibus in praecedentibus dixerat, residua adiciens:

diaconi (inquit) *sint unius uxoris uiri, filios bene regentes et suas*
domos.

5   compendiose idipsum dicit quod in superioribus et de presbyteris dixerat, per omnia ostendens quoniam commune illis uult
adesse studium uirtutis. deinde quia infirmiores esse uidentur
presbyteris secundum gradum, ostendens quia in nulla parte mi-
norantur ab illis si secundum ut conueniens est suum officium im-
10   plere uoluerint, adicit:

qui enim bene ministrauerint, gradum sibi bonum adquirunt et mul-
tam fiduciam [*in fide*] *quae est in Christo Iesu.*

'qui enim conuenienter functionem suam impleuerint, licet si
in praesenti infirmioris gradus esse uideantur, sed prouisores sibi
15   in futuro optimi gradus existunt, fiduciam plurimam adsecuturi a
Christo.' *bonum gradum* non in praesenti saeculo dicit. nec dixisset
gradum sibi ipsi bonum adquirent—nam et diaconiae gradus bonus
est—sed dixisset utique 'maiorem;' nunc autem adiciens *bonum,*
non quia non bonus gradus diaconiae, sed quoniam illum quidem
20   gradum confitetur esse bonum, et iuuans eos qui eum adsequi uoluerint. hunc uero ait diaconiae gradum iam non posse quemquam
iuuare, si non et illa quae conscientiam nostram possent integram
reseruare concurrerint nobis. et adiecit: *et multam fiduciam in fide*
quae est in Christo Iesu. euidenter ostendit quoniam de illis quae
25   tunc erunt dicit, uult enim eos docere quia nullum detrimentum
adferre poterit infirmior gradus illis qui digni inueniuntur magna
et perfecta adsequi bona, si tamen conscientia eorum prout conuenit inlibata ab illis ipsis fuerit custodita. percurrens uero hoc modo etiam illos ordines qui in functione habentur ecclesiastica, adi-
30   cit:

haec tibi scribo, sperans uenire ad te cito; si autem euenerit me re-
tardare, ut scias quemadmodum conueniat te in domum Dei conuersa-
ri, quae est ecclesia Dei uiui, columna et firmamentum ueritatis.

---

4   domos suas *r*   5   dixit *r*   ‖   et (*aft.* quod) *add H*   11   ministraverit *H**
12   in fide *om C H*   14   si (*for* sed) *r*   15   assequitur *H*   17   ipsum *H*: *om r*
‖   acquirere *r*   20   adiuuans (*for* et iuuans) *C* (*corr.*)   21   hunc … gradum *om*
r   ‖   nam (*for* iam) *r*   23   concumpserit *C** contulerit *C* (*corr.*) concupserint
H consenserit *r*   29   illis ordines qui funct. *r*   31   tardauero (*for* euenerit me
ret.) *r*   32   domo *r*

of his discussion about the deacons in what preceded, adding what was left out:

3:12 *Let the deacons* (he says) *be husbands of one wife, rightly ruling their children and their own households;*

He says succinctly what he had said above also about the presbyters (3:2–5), showing that he wants their pursuit of virtue to be in common with that of the presbyters. Then, because the deacons seem to be lower than the presbyters in rank, to show that in no respect are they less than the presbyters if they are willing to fulfill their duty as they should, he adds:

3:13 *for those who will have ministered well acquire for themselves a good rank and much confidence in the faith that is in Christ Jesus.*

[130] "For those who will have fulfilled their service fittingly, even though in the present they seem to be of a lower rank, yet in the future they will be their own providers of the best rank, since they will acquire very great confidence from Christ." By *good rank* he does not mean in the present age; nor would he have said *they will acquire*[31] *for themselves a good rank*—for the rank of the diaconate is good—but he would have said a "better" rank. But as it is, he adds *good,* not because the rank of the diaconate is not good, but since he acknowledges that rank to be good and advantageous to those who want to acquire it. But he says that this rank of the diaconate cannot now help anyone, if those things that can keep our conscience unimpaired should not join forces in us. And he added *and much confidence in the faith that is in Christ Jesus.* He clearly shows that he is speaking of what will be at that future time, for he wants to teach them that a lower rank can bring no diminishment to those found worthy of acquiring great and perfect good things, if indeed their conscience, as is right, should be kept intact by these very things. And going through in this way those orders held in ecclesiastical service, he adds:

3:14–15 *I am writing these things to you, hoping to come to you soon. And if it should turn out that I am delayed, so that you may know how it is necessary for you to behave in the house of God, which is the church of the living God, the pillar and support of truth.*

---

[31] Here the future is substituted for the present, possibly because of Theodore's interpretation.

'de his (inquit) scripsi tibi, sperans uel maxime cito uenire ad
te; si uero euenerit me retardare, ut scias quae te agere conueniant
et quomodo debeas ecclesiam Dei regere.' optime autem adiecit
Dei uiui, ita ut ostendat ex hoc ecclesiae dignitatem. illud uero est
cognoscendum quoniam *domum Dei*

†ecclesiam, non domos oratio- [οἶκον θεοῦ] ἐκκλησίαν οὐ τοὺς
nis dicit secundum plurimorum οἴκους λέγει τοὺς εὐκτηρίους κατὰ
opinionem, sed fidelium con- τὴν τῶν πολλῶν συνήθειαν, ἀλλὰ
gregationem; sicuti et Hebraeis τῶν πιστῶν τὸν σύλλογον. ὅθεν καὶ
scribens dicit: *quae domus su-* 'στύλον' αὐτὴν καὶ 'ἑδραίωμα τῆς
mus nos. unde et 'columnam' il- ἀληθείας' ἐκάλεσεν, ὡς ἂν ἐν αὐτῇ
lam et *firmamentum ueritatis* uo- τῆς ἀληθείας τὴν σύστασιν ἐχούσης.
cauit, eo quod in ea ueritatis fir-
mitas habeatur.*

eo quod ecclesia fidelium est congregatio, in hac pietatis est necesse dogma saluari. qui si secundum ut conueniens est in fide per-
manserint, inlibatum utique permanet dogma pietatis; si autem ii
qui ecclesiae sunt a suo proposito auersi fuerint, necessarie uacil-
labit et dogmatis scrupulositas, eo quod secundum praesentem uitam ueritatis cognitio apud homines esse perspicitur.

†illud uero dictis nostris adi- ἐκεῖνο δὲ προσθεῖναι ἄξιον, ὅτι
ci dignum est, quoniam non co- μὴ δεῖ θαυμάζειν εἰ μήτε ὑποδια-
nuenit demirari si neque sub- κόνων ἐμνήσθη, μήτε ἀναγνωστῶν.
diaconum neque lectorum me- τῶν γὰρ ἐν τῇ τῆς ἐκκλησίας λει-
moriam apostolus fecisse uide- τουργίᾳ βαθμῶν ἔξωθεν μᾶλλον οὗ-
tur. illis etenim gradibus func- τοί εἰσιν, διὰ τὴν χρείαν ἐπινοη-
tionum qui in ecclesiis necessa- θέντες ὕστερον, ἣν διὰ τὸ τῶν πε-
rium habentur, isti postea magis πιστευκότων πλῆθος λοιπὸν δι' ἑτέ-
sunt adiecti propter utilitatem ρων πληροῦσθαι ἠναγκάσθη· ὅθεν
ministerii, quod propter multi- οὐδὲ νενόμισται αὐτοὺς πρὸ τοῦ θυ-
tudinem credentium per alteros σιαστηρίου τὴν χειροτονίαν δέχεσ-
postea impleri debere necessi- θαι, ἐπεὶ μηδὲ αὐτῷ ὑπηρετοῦν-

2 retardere *C* H* tardare *r* 4 ostendit *C** 5 donum *C** 6 domum (*for*
domos) *C r* ‖ sq. Coisl. 204, f. 201 a [Cr. vii. 31, Fr. 153] θεόδωρος. ἄλλος
δέ φησιν· ἐκκλησίας, κ.τ.λ. 15 est fid. congr. *C r* ‖ est *om H* 17 hii *C*
hi *H r* 18 necessario *r* 18-19 uacillabitis *C H* 19 scrupulositatis *H* 20
cognatio *C* 21 sq. Coisl. 204, f. 200 b [Cr. vii. 30, Fr. 153] θεοδώρου. ἐκεῖνο
δέ, κ.τ.λ. 22-23 ὑπὸ διακόνων cod. (1ᵃ.m.). 23 se (*for* si) *C** se quod *r* 23-
24 subdiaconorum *a* 24 electorum (*for* lect.) *H r* 27 ecclesia *H a* 27-28
necessario *r a* 32 implere *C H r: txt a*

[131] "I have written to you (he says) about these things, hoping to come to you as quickly as possible. But if it should turn out that I am delayed, it is so that you may know what you ought to do and how you ought to rule the church of God." And he quite effectively added *of the living God* to show by this the excellence of the church. But it must be recognized that by calling

†the church *the house of God,* he does not mean the house of prayer, as a great many people think, but the assembly of the faithful. For example, when writing to the Hebrews, he says (Heb 3:6): *which house we are.* And so he called the church *the pillar and support of truth,* because in it the confirmation of truth is held.*

He does not mean by saying the church is *the house of God* the houses of prayer according to the customary usage of many people, but the assembly of the faithful.

And so he called the church *the pillar and support of truth,* since it has in it the confirmation of truth.

Because the church is the assembly of the faithful, it is necessary that the doctrine of true religion be preserved in it. If they persevere in faith as they ought, undoubtedly the doctrine of true religion remains unimpaired. But if those who belong to the church should go astray from their purpose, necessarily careful attention to doctrine will also waver, because in the present life knowledge of the truth is discerned among human beings.

†[132] And it is worth adding to what we have said that it is not necessary to be astonished if the apostle plainly has made no mention either of subdeacons or readers. They were added later to the ranks of service held necessary in the churches for the benefit of ministry, because necessity demanded later on that ministry should be fulfilled by some other services on account of the multitude of believers. That is why they do not receive ordination before the altar, [133] because they are

It is worth adding that there must be no astonishment if he mentioned neither subdeacons nor readers. For these are somewhat outside the ranks of the church's service, since they were devised later on because of the need that became necessary on account of the multitude of the believers for the service thereafter to be fulfilled by other offices. This is why it has not been the custom for them to receive ordination before the altar, since they do not serve the mystery itself;

tas flagitauit. unde nec ordinationem ante altare adsequuntur,
eo quod nec mysteriis ministrare statuuntur, sed alii quidem
5 eorum lectionum officium implent; alii uero intra diaconicum
illa praeparant quae ad diaconum pertinent ministeria, necnon sollicitudinem implent lu-
10 minariorum.*

ται τῷ μυστηρίῳ, ἀλλ᾽ οἱ μὲν τὴν
ἀνάγνωσιν ἐκτελοῦσιν, οἱ δὲ ἔνδον
τὰ πρὸς τὴν τῶν διακόνων ὑπηρεσίαν εὐτρεπίζουσιν, ἐπιμελόμενοι
καὶ τῶν ἐκκλησιαστικῶν φώτων.

nam mysterii ministerium presbyteri implent et diaconi soli; alii
quidem eorum sacerdotale opus implentes, alii uero sacris ministrantes. et hoc quidem signauimus ut nec aliquis existimet Paulum obliuione quadam eos minime memorasse quos memorem es-
15 se conueniebat. intendendum uero est et sequentiae narrationis.
nam apostolus eo quod ecclesiam 'columnam et firmamentum ueritatis' uocauit, optimum esse existimauit etiam dogmaticos inter-
serere sermones, ut ostendat ipsam ueritatem quae sit, praeparet
uero Timotheum etiam et de illis disputare ad illos. dogmatico-
20 rum uero memoratus est uerborum illorum quae uel maxime tunc
memorari necessitas ipsa flagitabat; propter quod et ait;

> et manifeste magnum est pietatis mysterium.

ut dicat 'dogma'; hoc erat quod in superioribus significauimus,
quoniam mysterium saepe illud dogma dicit quod de Christo est;
25 eo quod deitas Unigeniti inerat in homine, et propter hoc facile
non ad cognitionem poterat uenire multorum. nam et mysteria
consueuerunt non ab omnibus cognosci similiter. sic etiam et Corinthiis scribens dixit: sed loquimur Dei sapientiam in mysterio quod
absconditum est; euidenter de praedicatione illa quae secundum
30 Christum est dicens. et post pauca adicit quoniam si cognouissent,
numquam dominum gloriae crucifixissent. etiam hoc in loco, manifeste (inquit) magnum pietatis mysterium. hoc est, 'indubium;' nam

---

1-2 inordinationem *a*   3   nec *om H*   6   infra diaconiam *C** infra diaconium
C (*corr.*) infra diaconicum *H* infra diaconum *r* intra diaconium *a*   7-8   diaco-
norum *r* diaconi *a*   11   presb. soli impl. et d. *a*   12   sacerdotalem *C**   13
ne (*for* ut nec) *r*   14   obliuionem *H*   ‖   memores *C H r*   ‖   quorum (*for*
quos) *r* [*cf.* 11. *p.* 3, *l.* 6, *note*]   16   eo quod *om H*   18   praeparat *C r*   19   et
om r   21   et *om r*   24   sacramentum siue myst. *r*   26   mysterii *C**   29   de
precatione *H*   31   non utique (*for* numquam) *r*   32   hoc non est dubium *r*

not appointed to minister in the mysteries, but some of them fulfill the duty of readings, while others within the diaconate prepare what pertains to the ministries of the deacons, and, indeed, they fulfill the care of the lamps.*

but some accomplish the reading, while others within prepare what is needed for the service of the deacons and are in charge of the church lamps.

For only the presbyters [134] and the deacons fulfill the ministry of the mystery. Some of them fulfill the priestly work, while others minister to the holy things. We have indicated this so that no one would think that Paul by some kind of forgetfulness failed to mention at all those whom he ought to have remembered. But attention must also be paid to the order of the discourse. Now because the apostle called the church *the pillar and support of truth*, he thought it best to interpose some doctrinal statements to show what that truth is and also to prepare Timothy to reason about them with those people. And he called to mind those doctrinal words that, especially at that time, necessity itself demanded should be remembered. Because of this he says:

3:16a *And obviously, great is the mystery of true religion:*

He means "doctrine." This is what we have pointed out above,[32] since he often calls the doctrine about Christ a mystery, because the divinity of the Only Begotten was present in the Man and for this reason could not come easily to the understanding of many. Indeed, mysteries are not usually known by all alike. So, as well, when writing to the Corinthians, he said (1 Cor 2:7): *but we speak the wisdom of God in a mystery that is hidden,*[33] clearly speaking of the preaching that has to do with Christ. A little later he adds (1 Cor 2:8): *if they had known, they would never have crucified the Lord of glory.* Also, in this place *obviously,* (he says)

---

[32] In his comments on 3:9. See Swete, 2:127.

[33] In the Greek text, "hidden" modifies "wisdom" rather than "mystery." Swete (2:134) suggests: "The error, if it be such, is perhaps due to Th. himself."

et habebat ex ipsis rebus indubiam probationem. unde et adicit:
qui manifestatus est in carne.

hoc est, 'pietatis delector mysterio eo quod sit magnum et supereminens; quoniam is qui inuisibilis est Deus Verbum, Unigenitus
5 Patris, manifestauit se hominibus, in carne adparens pro communi omnium salute.' optime autem hoc in loco non dixit 'in homine' sed *in carne*, et quidem in superioribus euidenter dixerat quoniam *mediator Dei et hominum homo Christus Iesus*, eo quod hoc
erat quod tunc dubie suscipiebatur, et hac de causa ad ista uer-
10 ba descendere est compulsus. nam illo in tempore contra pietatis
doctrinam dogma Simonis magi pullulare uidebatur; quod dogma
uniuersa ista quae uidentur ab opificatione Dei alienare tempta-
bat. propter hoc etiam carnis denegabat factam fuisse adsumptio-
nem; dicebat enim phantasmate solo dominum adparuisse in car-
15 ne, ita ut non uideretur caro tali ratione honore et diligentia digna
uideri, siquidem et inhabitatione diuina digna fuerit. deinde dicens *qui manifestatus est in carne* (quod de Deo dici iure uidebatur,
nam illa erat diuinitas quae in carne Christi fuerat uisa), transit et
ad illa quae de homine dici poterant, ut ampliore sermonum pro-
20 secutione confirmaret illud quod tunc uocabatur in dubium:
iustificatus in Spiritu.

euidens hoc quoniam ad deitatem nequaquam potest pertinere; humanae uero naturae euidenter potest aptari, qui et Spiritus
inhabitationem in baptismate accepit, quando et in specie colum-
25 bae insuper illum uenit. sed a Spiritu in solitudinem ductus est
ut contra diabolum in agone decertaret, et in Spiritu Dei eicie-
bat daemones, sicut ipse in euangeliis dicit; et ad plenum omnia
illa quae secundum inhabitantem in se Spiritum gratiae pro nostra expediebat salute. primitiae quidem nostrae salutis erant illa
30 quae secundum Christum celebrantur; unde et Spiritus ad perfectionem omnium suscepit bonorum inhabitationem Dei Verbum,

1   et *om H*   2   qui manifestus *C* quod manifestum *r*   3   delectus *C* r* dilec-
tus *H* ‖ ministerio *r*   3-4   super est eminens *C**   9   suscipiebamus *C H r*
11   siminus magis *C* H r* ‖ pulurare *C**   12   ob opificationem *r*   13   in
(*bef.* carnis) *add C* H*   14   sola *C H: txt r*   18   diuinitas erat *H* ‖ causa
(*for* uisa) *H*   19   ad *om H*   21   iustificatur *C* iustificatum est *r*   23   quae
et *H* quia *l*   24   habitationem *l* ‖ accipit *C**   25   super (*for* insuper) *r*
27   dixit *H*   28   Spiritus *C* H r*   29   salutis nostrae *r*   30   celebratur *H*
celebrabantur *C* (*corr.*)   31   suscipit *C* H r* ‖ uerbi *C H r*

great [135] *is the mystery of true religion*, that is, "undoubted." For he had from the facts themselves undoubted proof. That is why he adds:

3:16b *who was manifested in flesh,*

That is, "I take delight in the mystery of true religion because it is great and highly exalted, since he who is invisible, God the Word, the Only Begotten of the Father, has manifested himself to humans, appearing in flesh for the common salvation of all." And quite effectively in this place he did not say "in the Man" but *in flesh*, even though above he had clearly said (2:5): *the mediator of God and humans, the man Christ Jesus*. This was because at that time Christ's humanity was being doubtfully received, and for this reason Paul was compelled to stoop to those words. For at that time [136] the doctrine of Simon the Magician was seen to be springing forth against the teaching of true religion, a doctrine that was trying to alienate everything that is seen from God's creation. Because of this Simon was even denying that an assumption of flesh had taken place, for he was saying that the Lord had appeared in flesh only as a phantom, so that it might seem for such a reason that the flesh did not seem[34] worthy of honor and care, had it been worthy of divine indwelling. Then, saying *who was manifested in flesh*—which seems rightly said of God, for it was the divinity that had been seen in Christ's flesh— he goes on to what could have been said of the Man, so that by a fuller sequence of statements he might confirm what was at that time called into doubt:

3:16c *justified in the Spirit,*

It is clear that this can in no way pertain to the divinity but can clearly be applied to the human nature, which, as well, [137] received the indwelling of the Spirit in baptism, when he came upon him in the form of a dove. Moreover, it was by the Spirit that he was led into the wilderness to struggle in the contest against the devil, and it was by the Spirit that he used to cast out demons, as he says himself in the Gospels (Matt 12:28). And he accomplished completely everything for our salvation in accord with the Spirit of grace that indwelt him. Those things celebrated with respect to Christ were the firstfruits of our salvation. And

---

[34] Swete's comment on the repetition of "seem" (*videretur ... videri*) is (2:136): "A singular instance of the laxity of our translator's Latin style."

eo quod et nobis participatione Spiritus omnium bonorum causa
adquiritur siue in praesente saeculo siue in futuro. et illud non est
mirandum si qua de eodem ipso disputans de deitatis sermonibus
ad humanitatem transisse uideatur. consuetudo haec est diuina-
5   rum scripturarum; sicut non solum in apostolica interpretatione
id ostendimus, sed et in euangeliorum interpretatione identidem
id demonstrauimus.
     adparuit angelis.
     hoc est, 'perspicuus et angelis factus est'—hoc enim dicit *ad-*
10   *paruit;* ut ostendat quemadmodum magnitudo eius et angelis exi-
steret mirabilis.
     praedicatus in gentibus.
     'adnuntiatus (inquit) est hominibus.' deinde, quod maius est:
     creditus est in mundo.
15   nihil enim magnum erat quod praedicabatur secundum se, si
non et fides auditorum subsecuta fuisset. hoc autem dicebat magnitudinis eius sufficientem probationem, eo quod homines qui in
omnibus locis erant susciperent de eo fidem; qui numquam pa-
terentur cum consensu credere de illis quae de eo dicebantur, si
20   non rebus ipsis de his quae dicebantur testimonium satisfactionem
percepissent.
     adsumptus in gloria.
     dicit enim de illa adsumptione qua de hominibus adsumptus
est. in ultimo autem illud posuit, quasi quia sufficiens esset ad fi-
25   dem eos inuitare, eo quod et angelis fuerit factus perspicuus, et hominibus praedicatus, fide sit ab illis susceptus. haec de Christo dicens, quasi quia et necessarie et cognosci et custodiri debeant, nec
a ueritate dimoueri, si tamen firma et non absolute horum confessio apud fideles permanserit. adiecit et aliud:
30   *Spiritus autem manifeste dicit quoniam in nouissimis temporibus*
discedent quidam a fide, adtendentes spiritibus erroris et doctrinis dae-
moniorum in hypocrisin mendaci[loqu]orum, cauteriatam habentium

---

3   quasi (*for* si qua) *C r*   ‖   ipse *H*   5   non solum *om H*   6   identibus is
(*for* identidem id) *C* uidentibus his *H r*   12   praedicatum *r*   13   est inquit *r*
14   creditum *H r*   16   adiutorum *C**   19   de *om r*   20   satisfactione *r*   22
assumptus est *r*   27   quia *om C**   ‖   necessario *r*   ‖   custodire *C H: txt r*   28
obsolute *H*   29   adiecit et aliud *om r*   30   dat (*for* dicit) *C* H*   31   discendent
C*   ‖   doctoris *C**   32   hipocrisint (*sic*) *C* hypocrisi *r*   ‖   mendaciorum *C*
H loquentium mendacium *r*

so the Spirit supported the indwelling Word of God, to perfect all good things, because even for us it is by sharing in the Spirit that the source of all good things is acquired, whether in the present age or in the one to come. And we should not be astonished if where Paul is reasoning about the same point he is seen to pass from words about the divinity over to the humanity. This is the custom of the divine scriptures, as we have demonstrated not only in interpreting the apostle [138] but have also demonstrated repeatedly in interpreting the Gospels.

3:16d *he appeared to angels,*

That is, "he was made clearly visible even to angels"—for this is what he means by *he appeared.* This was to show how his greatness came to be marvelous even to angels.

3:16e *preached among the Gentiles,*

"He was proclaimed (he says) to humans." Then, what is greater:

3:16f *he was believed in the world,*

For there would have been nothing great of itself about the preaching that took place, if the faith of those who heard it had not followed. And Paul was saying this as a sufficient proof of his greatness, because people in all places received faith in Christ. They would never have admitted unanimous belief in what was being said about him, if they had not received satisfactory testimony about what was being said by the facts themselves.

3:16g *taken up in glory.*

For he is speaking of the ascension by which he was taken up from humans. And he put this last inasmuch as it would have been enough to draw them to faith that he was made clearly visible to angels and when preached to humans was received by them in faith.[35] He says these things of Christ, inasmuch as they ought necessarily both be recognized and be kept, [139] nor be set aside from truth, if indeed the confession of these things among the faithful is to remain steadfast and not lightly held. He added another point:

4:1–3a *And the Spirit clearly says that in the last times some will depart from faith, paying attention to the spirits of error and the teachings of demons in the hypocrisy of false speakers, having their*

---

[35] Does he mean that it is the ascension that made Christ visible to the angels and marked the beginning of the Christian preaching?

suam conscientiam, prohibentium nubere, abstinere a cibis.

euidens quidem quoniam haec dicit beatus Paulus non quia tunc iam apud aliquos coeperant ista profiteri, sed quod postea ista erant ab hominibus principium sumptura. nam et ista eo Spiritu cognouisse designauit, et quod in nouissimis temporibus sint futura pronuntiauit.

†coniunxit uero ea illis sermo- ἐπισυνῆψεν ταῦτα τοῖς περὶ τοῦ
nibus quae de Christo fuerant Χριστοῦ λόγοις, οὐχ ἁπλῶς, ἀλλ᾽
dicta, non absolute, sed quo- ἐπειδὴ τοὺς αὐτοὺς ἠπίστατο ἔσεσ-
niam illos ipsos sciebat tales es- θαι τοὺς περί τε γάμων καὶ βρω-
se futuros qui et nuptias et escas μάτων ἐκεῖνα ἀναιροῦντας, καὶ τὸ
erant adempturi, simul negan- ἀνειλῆφθαι σάρκα παρὰ τοῦ θεοῦ
tes et quod suscepta fuerit caro a λόγου μέλλοντας ἀναιρεῖν, εἰκότως
Deo Verbo; optime ergo ea cum αὐτὰ ἐκείνοις συνέπλεξεν.
illis complexus est*,

ut uideretur insistere ex utroque latere quasi aduersus unum propositum. nam et Manichaeos et Marcionistas et eos qui de Valentiniana sunt haeresi et omnes qui eiusmodi sunt, similiter quis perspiciet et nuptias dampnare et escarum usum quasi inhonestum criminare; et quod adnitantur ostendere carnem a Domino non fuisse susceptam. intendendum uero quemadmodum amarissime memoratus eorum, et ut uehementer instituat de illis qui ista docere in nouissimis temporibus incipient, spirituum alienorum seductiones eas esse dicens, et 'doctrinas daemoniorum' uocans illas; sic grauem horum professionem esse existimabat. bene autem quoniam dixit *hypocrisin* mendacium. omnes isti Christianos se esse simulant et doctrina sua maiorem se tenere promittunt castitatem, multum uero pietatis contraria eos qui sibi obtemperant de Christo docere adnituntur; omnia uero illa quae luxuriae sunt plena, quae et omnem in se continent prauitatem, ipsi inter se agere cum omni properant sollicitudine. quae inprimis ad plenum silere uidentur; atubi uero per illam quam ineunt simulationem ali-

1 suam *om* r ‖ et reliqua (*aft* cibis) *add* C H et cetera r 2 et uidens (*for* euidens) C* 7 ex (*for* ea) H ‖ sq. Coisl. 204, f. 201 b [Cr. vii. 32] ἐπισυνῆψεν, κ.τ.λ. 13 λόγον Cr. 17 Marcianistas C H 17-18 Valentiniani C H r 18 quos perspicit C (*corr.*) 20 criminari C (*corr.*) r 23 malignorum (*for* alien.) r 26 in hypocrisi mendaciorum C (*corr.*) in hypocrisi loquentium mendacium r ‖ nam (*bef.* omnes) *add* r 28 pietati C (*corr.*) 29 adnititur C*H 30 agere (*aft.* inter se) *om* C 31 omnia H 32 adubi C*H ‖ ad illam quae H

own conscience cauterized, forbidding to marry, to abstain from foods,

It is clear that blessed Paul is saying these things not because at that time there were some who had begun to profess them[36] but because later on people were going to take their beginning from them. For Paul has pointed out that he knew those things by the Spirit, and he has affirmed that they were going to take place in the last times.

†And he has joined these remarks to the words that had been spoken about Christ, not lightly, but since he knew that the very people who were going to do away with marriage and foods would be such as to deny at the same time that flesh would have been assumed by God the Word. Therefore, he quite effectively bound the two points together,*

He has joined these remarks to the words about Christ, not lightly, but since he knew that the same people would be those who would do away with what concerned marriage and foods and who were going to do away with the assumption of flesh by God the Word, he quite rightly bound the two points together.

so that he might be seen to stand on both sides as though against a single assertion. For as to the Manichees and the Marcionites and those from the Valentinian heresy, [140] and all those who are like this—anyone will perceive that they alike both condemn marriage and denounce the use of foods as shameful and that they strive to demonstrate that flesh was not assumed by the Lord. And it must be noticed how Paul has mentioned them with the greatest bitterness, and, so that he may vigorously give instruction about those who will begin to teach those things in the last times, he says that their seductive errors are those of alien spirits and calls them *the teachings of demons*, so serious did he consider the profession of these things to be. And he rightly said that lying was *hypocrisy*. All those people pretend that they are Christians, and they promise in their teaching that they hold themselves to a greater chastity, but they strive to teach those who submit to them much about Christ that is contradictory of true religion. And everything that is filled with indulgence and that includes every perversity in itself—these

---

[36] Swete (2:139) cites Chrysostom's view that it was not the Jews who said these things. Theodore appears to follow this interpretation, arguing that the gnostics and others partly base their heresies on Jewish teachings.

quem instanter suaderi sibi per omnia fecerunt, tunc illa sermonibus quibusdam adducunt ad medium, suadentes ut illa peragant
quasi pietatis opera perficientes quae omnis sunt spurcitiae plena.
et hoc inueniet quis si illa omnia quae praedicta sunt cautissime
5 considerare uoluerit, licet non facile possint deprehendi, eo quod
latere plurimos super talibus operibus adnituntur. consequenter
autem adiecit: *cauteriatam habentium suam ipsorum conscientiam;*
qui enim de castitate se disputare simulant, omnem spurcitiam in
se perpetrare inueniuntur. euidens quoniam talia facientes non in-
10 tegram possunt habere conscientiam; contraria enim specie suorum sermonum sibi ipsi conscii sunt, quae et in se exercent et alios
docent. euidens autem quod dixit: *prohibentium nubere, abstinere a*
cibis, [non] ostendens quoniam non nubere aut non sumere escas
crimine dignum est, sed quod lege ista prohibere adnitantur; ex
15 arbitrio enim continere se aliquem ab istis non est inconueniens.
nam prohibere de his necessitatis est potius, non propositi, quod
similiter dicere non potest, quoniam ubi propositum est, ibi continentia; ista uero euidens execratio est. notandum uero est in eo
quod dixit *abstinere a cibis,* sicuti et in praefatione notauimus, eo
20 quod nullam diligentiam eloquentiae faciat, multa dicens inperfecte. nam et hoc in loco quod dixit *prohibentium,* quasi per necessitatem illud fieri accipiens, sequentiam dictorum reliquit inper-
fectam, quasi quia hinc possit etiam illud cognosci quoniam incu-

1 fecerint *C* (*corr.*)   2   in (*for* ad) *r*   3   omni (*for* omnis) *C* H r*   7   habentes *H*   8   se disputare *om r*   9   euid. est *r*   9-10   integra *H*   10   conscientiam
(*aft.* habere) *om C* H*   11   serm. suor. *H**   12   euid. a. est *H*   13   non (1°)
om C H r   19   imperfectione (*for* in praefat.) *C* inperfectione *H* imperfectio-
nem *r*   23   quae (*for* quia) *C* H* quod *C* (*corr.*): *om r*   ‖   quo (*for* quoniam) *r*

things they are eager to practice among themselves with entire care. At first they seem to be completely silent about these things, but when by the deceit they embark upon they have managed to make someone urgently persuaded by them in all respects, then they bring these things forward by certain speeches, persuading them to perform those things that are filled with all filth as though they were accomplishing the works of true religion. And anyone will discover this [141] if he is willing to consider as carefully as possible everything that has been predicted, even though these people cannot easily be caught because most of them strive to stay hidden with respect to such deeds. And in accord with this Paul added *having their own conscience cauterized*. For while they pretend to reason about chastity, they are found to carry out every filth among themselves. It is clear that because they do such things they cannot have a pure conscience, for they are conscious in themselves that what they practice among themselves and teach others contradicts the show of their own words. And it is clear that Paul said *forbidding to marry, to abstain from foods*, not to show that not marrying or not taking foods is worthy of blame but because they strive to forbid those things by law.[37] For it is not unfitting for someone to keep himself from those things by choice. Certainly, to forbid these things claims its power from necessity and not from intention, because it is not possible to say in the same way that where there is an intention, there is continence. Such a prohibition amounts to an anathema.[38] And it must be noted that in his statement *to abstain from foods*, as we have noted in the introductory part of the letter,[39] that Paul takes no care for effective speech, saying many things incompletely. For even in this place when he said *forbidding*, understanding this to be done by necessity, [142] he leaves the sequence of words incomplete, inasmuch as from this word it could also be recognized that he is

---

[37] That is, celibacy and extreme fasting are not to be blamed but should not be required.

[38] Swete paraphrases the meaning as follows (2:141): "*evidens execratio est*] 'A prohibition of this kind amounts to an anathema, such as Saul's (1 Sam. xiv.24), or that of the conspirators (Acts xxiii.12)....' Perhaps however *execratio* merely represents some such word as ἀπαγόρευσις, and the meaning is: 'in such a case no choice is left; there can be no exercise of προαίρεσις, and therefore no virtue in the act of abstaining.'"

[39] See Swete, 2:70.

sat eos qui cogunt abstinere a cibis. deinde dicens eam sententiam
quam et accusat quia in ultimo erit apud homines, adicit probationem quod non conuenienter ista proponant:

quae Deus creauit ad fruitionem cum gratiarum actione.

5   nam et ualde inconueniens erat, Deum illa ad hoc facientem, lege ab eorum usu homines prohibere. necessario uero adiecit, *cum
gratiarum actione* dicens, ita ut et modum adiciens esse uideatur
ipsius usus secundum quem facta sunt, sufficienter comprobans
prauitatem prohibentium. si enim gratias agere Deo bonum pro
10 escis, impium est incusare eas, nullam de cetero gratiarum actionem subrelinquentes illis qui ita eas sibi tributas esse existimant.
nam is qui ad hoc facta illa a Deo confitetur, licet contineat se
suo proposito, tamen cognoscit quod conueniat de illis Deo gratias agere. et arbitrio eorum prauitatem latius subplicans, adiecit:

15   *fidelibus et qui cognouerunt ueritatem.*

non dixit absolute 'hominibus,' et quidem omnibus hominibus
similiter usus escarum propositum esse uidetur, eo quod ita eos
uniuersitatis fecerit Deus; sed ut maiorem ostendat prauitatem eorum qui ita de escis sentiunt, siquidem et alia dicere usurpant de
20 illis quorum uel maxime usus omnibus uidetur esse et necessarius
et aptus. accusat uero eos grauius, adiciens *cum gratiarum actione*,
nam ideo factae sunt escae ut cum gratiarum actione unusquisque
eas insumat, etenim iustum est eos qui fruuntur illas, gratias agere
ei qui eas largire dignatus est. sed hoc non de omnibus dicit, sed
25 de solis fidelibus loquitur; nam infideles nec gratiaram actionem
reddere sciunt. itaque etsi pro ratione opificationis in commune
omnibus usus escarum propositus esse uidetur, sed ut oportet conuenienter fieri fidelibus magis uidetur posse aptari. multam ergo
prauitatem eorum per hoc ostendit qui cum gratias agere deberent
30 pro largita sibi requie, utrum insumant eas utrum se ab eis conti-

---

1 etiam (*for* eam) *r* 2 incusat *C* (*corr.*) 4 ad percipiendum (*for* ad fruit.) *r*
7 modus adiectus (*for* modum adiciens) *r* 8 quae (*for* quem) *r* 9 est (*aft.*
enim) *add C* 10 est *om C* || incausare *C** || nullum *r* 11 subreliquentes
C* 14 arbitrii *C* (*corr.*) *r* || explicans *r* || et (*aft.* subpl.) *add CH: txt r*
16 et quidem, hominibus (2°) *om r* 17 de usu (*for* usus) *r* || propositus
C (*corr.*) 19 de illis usurpant *H* 21 adicens *H* 23 illis *C r* 24 largiri
C (*corr.*) *r* 25 actionum *C** actione *H* 26 opificationes *C** 27-28 fieri
conu. *H* 30 require *C H: txt r*

condemning those who compel abstinence from foods.[40] Then, speaking of that opinion that he also condemns because it will be current among people at the last day, he adds proof that they are not setting forth these views fittingly:

4:3b *which God created for enjoyment with thanksgiving*

For it would have been quite unfitting for God, who made foods for this purpose, to forbid people their use by law. And he necessarily added *with thanksgiving* so that he might be seen to be adding the manner in which their use should be made, sufficiently proving the perverseness of those who were forbidding. For if it is good to give God thanks for foods, it is ungodly to find fault with them, besides leaving no place for thanks to those who think that foods have been bestowed on them this way. For the one who confesses that foods were made by God for this reason, granted that he remains continent by his own purpose, yet knows that it is right to give God thanks for them. And to underline more fully the perverseness in their judgment, he added:

4:3c *for the faithful and who have known the truth,*

He has not said simply "for humans," even though he seems to have argued that the use of foods is for all people alike, because the God of the universe made them this way. But this is to demonstrate the greater perversity of those who have this opinion about foods, inasmuch as they take it upon themselves to say strange things about them, the use of which seems to everyone for the most part [143] both necessary and suitable. And he condemns them quite sternly by adding *with thanksgiving*. For foods have been made for this reason, that each person might consume them with thanksgiving; and it is, indeed, right for those who enjoy them to give thanks to the one who saw fit to lavish them. Yet he does not say this of everyone, but he speaks only of the faithful, for the faithless do not even know how to render thanks. And so although because of creation he has plainly argued that the use of foods is common to all, yet that it should be done rightly plainly can be applied more to the faithful. Therefore, by this he shows the extent of the perversity of those who, though they ought to give thanks for the relief lavished on them, whether they consume

---

[40]That is, *forbidding marriage, to abstain from foods* should not be read "forbidding marriage and abstinence from foods" but "forbidding marriage and requiring abstinence from foods."

neant, utpote fideles, e contrario incusant escas quod non sint bene
factae et usum earum lege adnituntur abdicare. deinde dicens quia
a Deo factae sunt, consequenter adiecit:

    quia omnis creatura Dei bona, et nihil reiciendum.

5   'quemadmodum (inquit) incusatione dignum possit uideri illud, a Deo factum?' bene autem illud generaliter dixit, quoniam
omnis creatura Dei bona est, et nihil est reiciendum. omnia autem
utilia sunt; itaque et illa quae in usum escae data sunt non sunt
reicienda, sed potius recipienda, eo quod a Deo sint ad hoc facta.

10 adiecit autem iterum et modum secundum quem oportet eosdem
escas insumere:

    quoniam cum gratiarum actione percipitur.

    deinde adicit et quod ex illis lucrum possit adnasci:

    sanctificatur autem per uerbum Dei et orationem.

15   'nam insumptio escarum, quando cum gratiarum efficitur actione, iam non communem escam facit participare, sed sanctam;
in eo etenim dum gratiae aguntur Deo, etiam escae sanctificantur.'
sic ad dogmaticos egressus sermones, ad confirmationem ueritatis illos interserens quorum et *firmamentum* ecclesiam esse adse-

20 ruit; dicens autem illa uel maxime quae tunc dici oporterent pro
commotis tunc quaestionibus, ita ut Timotheus frequentem de his
doctrinam faceret ad fideles, adicit:

    haec proponens fratribus, bonus eris minister Iesu Christi.

    'eris (inquit) minister Christi probabilis, si haec cum sollicitu-

25 dine eos qui fide nobis iuncti sunt docueris.' et ostendens quia et
ipsi utilis sit huiusmodi sollicitudo:

    *enutritus (inquit) uerbis fidei et bonae doctrinae quam subsecutus
es.*

    'proficiet (inquit) hoc et tibi in melius; nam dum cum debita

---

1   et (*bef.* quod) *add r*   2   adnitantur *C* H r*   4   quoniam (*for* quia) *r*   ‖
reiecientem *C** reicientem *H*   5   non (*bef.* possit) *add r*   5-6   illud enim *C*
illud quod *r*   6   est (*aft* factum) *add C r*   ‖   generaliter illud *r*   7   est (*aft.*
nihil) om *r*   ‖   reiciendum *C**   10   easdem *r*   12   quod (*for* quoniam) *C*
(*corr.*) *r*   13   adiecit *r*   15   in sumptione *C r*   16   participari *C* (*corr.*)   20
dixitque (*for* dicens autem) *r*   21   maxime (*aft.* tunc) *add r*   ‖   frequenter *r*
22   ideo illum his uerbis admonet (*for* adicit) *r*   23   Chr. I. *r*   25   simul (*aft*
ost.) *add r*   ‖   quae (*for* quia) *C** quod *C* (*corr.*) que *H*   26   ipsa *C*   ‖
huiusmodi *om H*   27   assequutus *r*   29   necdum (*for* nam d.) *C** nam nudum
H nam quando *r*: *txt C* (*corr.*) *l*   ‖   cum *om l*

the foods or abstain from them, as faithful people should, quite the contrary find fault with the foods because they have not been rightly made and so strive to repudiate their use by law. Then, saying that they have been made by God, he added in logical order:

4:4a *because every creature of God is good, and nothing must be rejected,*

"How (he says) could what has been made by God be seen worthy of condemnation?" And he rightly said as a general statement that *every creature of God is good, and nothing must be rejected.* And all things are useful, and so, as well, what has been given to use as food must not be rejected but instead must be accepted, because it has been made by God for this purpose. And again he added also the way in which it is right for them to consume foods:

4:4b *since it is received with thanksgiving,*

Then he adds also what gain can arise from thanksgiving:

4:5 *and it is sanctified by the word of God and prayer.*

"For the consumption of foods, when it takes place with thanksgiving, [144] already makes it a sharing not in common food but in holy. When eating, as long as thanks are given to God, even foods are sanctified." Thus, having digressed to doctrinal statements, inserting them to confirm the truth of those things of which he asserted the church to be the *support* (3:15), and speaking especially of what ought to be said at that time with respect to the disputes that were then being stirred up, so that Timothy may give the faithful frequent teaching about these things, he adds:

4:6a *Putting these things before the brothers, you will be a good minister of Jesus Christ,*

"You will be (he says) a minister of Christ tried and true, if you teach these things with great care to those who have been joined to us in faith." And to show that care of this kind is beneficial to him:

4:6b *nourished* (he says) *by the words of faith and the good teaching that you have followed.*

"This (he says) will advance even you to what is better, for as long as you strive with due care to teach others what belongs to

sollicitudine docere alios illa quae fidei sunt adniteris, maiorem firmitatem ipse eorum adquiris, quasi qui et adsidua meditatione nu-
triaris.' illis ostendere uolens quod aptum sit illi ut adsidue alios
doceat; adiciens *quam subsecutus es*, hoc est, 'quae frequenter et au-
5   disti et didicisti semper mecum degens, haec iustum est te docere
et alios.' exhortans uero eum in hisce dictis sufficienter ut doctrinae inmineat cum omni sollicitudine, dehortatur eum pariter ne
illis quae contraria sunt uel leuiter intendat, dicens:
    profanas autem et aniles fabulas deuita.
10   hoc uel maxime prae ceteris commodo dictum est ab apostolo.
si igitur quis libris apocryphis intendere uoluerit, illis quos habere
uidentur illi qui ista dogmata profitentur, nomine quidem beatissi-
morum editos apostolorum, daemoniacorum uero hominum con-
scriptione repletos, perspiciet dictorum Pauli commoditatem. ita
15   autem et omnes profani sunt sermones illi et aniles fabulae quae in
hisdem libris inseruntur; immo et a fabulis anilibus plus sunt exe-
crabiliores, spurcitias enim et immunditias continent quae nec aures hominum sustinere potuerunt. haec uero super dehonoratio-
nem illorum quae ab aduersariis confincta sunt commode dicens,
20   et consequenter praecedentibus adiecit iterum:
    exerce teipsum ad pietatem.
    et in prioribus dicens quoniam 'doce ista cum debita sollicitu-
dine; adiuuabit autem frequens eorum meditatio non solum eos,
sed et te.' et quia interiecit illa in illis sermonibus quos in dehorta-
25   tionem aduersariorum fecerat, ad illa ipsa rediit. bene uero exercitationem pietatis diligentiam dixit esse doctrinae, quae alios ita instruere deproperat ita ut sit exercitatio pietatis ei qui pietatis exequitur opera. 'exercitationem' uero dicit ut alios cum omni diligentia ista instruat; frequens autem meditatio pietatis laborem so-
30   let exercere. et quoniam exercitationem illam quasi ad corporalem
agonem dixit, ex comparatione illius ostendit istius differentiam:

1   illa *om H*   4   quod secutus est quasi diceret haec quae (for adiciens … hoc
est) *r*   ‖   haec quae *C*   5   docere te *H*   7   inmineant *C* H r*   8   intendant (*om
dicens*) *r*   9   ineptas (*for* prof.) *r*   10   quomodo (*for* comm.) *H*   11   apocrisin
C* apocrysin *H*   ‖   illos *C r*   13   apost. ed. *H*   16   illis (*for* hisdem) *r*
‖   animalibus (*for* anil.) *C H*   16-17   exacrabiliores *C** execrabiles *H r*   19
conficta *H r*   20   et *om C* (*corr.*)   22   in deterioribus *C** in posterioribus *C*
(*corr.*) de interioribus *H*: *txt r*   23   adiuuauit *H*   25   reddidit *C*   26   qua *r*
29   labore *C* H r*   30   exerceri *r*   31   illius (*for* istius) *r*

faith, you will gain their greater steadfastness, inasmuch as you are nourished by constant reflection." Paul wants to show by this what is suitable for Timothy, so that he may teach others constantly. He adds *that you have followed*, that is, "what you have often both heard and learned while you were always living with me, these things [145] it is right for you to teach also to others." And exhorting him sufficiently by these words to be intent on teaching with all care, he equally dissuades him from paying attention to contradictory views or those said groundlessly, saying:

4:7a *And avoid profane and old wives' myths.*

The apostle said this especially before the rest appropriately. Therefore, if someone were willing to look into the apocryphal books, those that the people who profess these doctrines appear to possess—published, of course, in the name of the most blessed apostles but filled with the records of demon-possessed people— he will see how appropriate Paul's words are. And so all those discourses and old wives' myths sown in these books are profane; indeed, they are even more accursed than old wives' myths, for they contain filths and impurities that not even the ears of humans could bear. And saying these things appropriately to dishonor those books fabricated by the adversaries, he again added in accord with what preceded:

[146] 4:7b *Train yourself for true religion.*

Just before this he says,[41] "teach those things with due care, and constant reflection about them will help not only them, but also you." And because he inserted into his discourse what he had composed to dissuade Timothy from the adversaries,[42] he returns to the very points he was making before the insertion. And he rightly said that the training of true religion is diligent care for teaching, which is eager to instruct others in such a way that the training of true religion belongs to the person who pursues the works of true religion. And he says "training" so that he may instruct others in those things with all diligence, and constant reflection customarily trains the toil of true religion. And since he used the word "training" as though it might refer to a bodily contest, he shows by comparison how this training differs from that:

---

[41] See Theodore's comment on 4:6b.
[42] Theodore seems to mean 4:7a.

corporalis (inquit) *exercitatio ad modicum est utilis; pietas uero ad omnia est utilis, promissiones habens uitae praesentis et futurae.*

'qui enim in agone sunt corporali et ad hoc seipsos exercent usque in praesentem uitam, inde solent habere solatium. nam
5 pietatis agon et istius exercitatio ex multis partibus nobis magnum praebet iumentum, promittens nobis in futuro saeculo magna praebere; nam secundum praesentem uitam conferre nobis non minima potest.' nam quod dixit 'uitam praesentem,' sic dicit quod pii, si etiam aliquando necessitatem sustinuerunt, plurimum
10 iuuamen etiam secundum praesentem uitam adsequuntur. et dictum suum confirmans adiecit:

fidele uerbum et omni acceptione dignum.

hoc est, uera haec dixit quae nullam dubitationem suscipere poterant, eo quod pietas suis sectatoribus multorum bonorum lar-
15 gitatem praestare uidetur. et post confirmationem suorum dictorum iterum ad sequentiam exhortationis suae conuertitur:

in hoc (inquit) *laboramus et exprobramur, quoniam sperauimus in Deum uiuum, qui est saluator omnium hominum, maxime fidelium.*

'itaque cum pietas multa bona possit prouidere, nec mirum est
20 nos qui credimus Deo semper extanti pro eo et laborare et exprobrari pro quo et pati optimum est, eo quod scit omnes saluare sua bonitate; fidelibus uero ob alacritatem animae eorum etiam multas scit praestare mercedes.' et quoniam per omnia ostendit necessarium esse horum studium et ut exerceantur ad pietatem ceteros
25 docentes, resumit praepositam exhortationem, adiciens:

praecipe haec et doce.

non absolute posuit *praecipe*, sed quod conueniat eum instanter insistere, si quando res ipsa eum id facere compellerit. deinde quia iuuenis erat, et uidebatur aetas ipsa a plurimis contempni, adiecit:
30 *nemo iuuentutem tuam contempnat.*

---

1 nam corp. (*for* corp. inquit) *r* ‖ est *om C** 1-2 utilis est *r* 1 autem (*for* uero) *C r* 6 adiumentum *C* (*corr.*) iuuamentum *r* ‖ promittent *C** *H* promittitque *r* 8 quod uero (*for* nam quod) *r* ‖ dixit *r* 9 si pii *r* 10 et … adiecit *om r* 12 fidelis sermo, dignus *r* 16 et ait (*aft* conuertitur) *add r* 17 inquit *om r* ‖ maledicimur (*for* exprobr.) *r* ‖ quia (*for* quoniam) *C r* 20 pro ea *H r* 21 pro quod *C H* ‖ bonum (*for* opt.) *H* 23 ost. per omnia *H* 24 est (*for* esse) *C H r* ‖ et *om C* (*corr.*) 25 resumens *C* (*corr.*) ‖ propositam *H* ‖ adicit *C* et ad. *r* 29 eatas *C** 30 adolescentiam *r*

4:8 *Bodily training* (he says) *for a little is useful, but true religion is useful for all things, having the promises of the present life and the one to come.*

"For those who are in a bodily contest and train themselves for this so far as the present life is concerned usually have comfort from this. Now the contest of true religion and its training in many respects bestows on us great help, since it promises to bestow great things on us in the age to come; indeed, in the present life [147] it can confer on us no trifling things." For when he said the present life, he means that godly people, even if they sometimes endure difficulty, gain a great deal of help even in the present life. And confirming what he said, he added:

4:9 *Faithful is the word and worthy of all acceptation.*

That is, he has spoken these true words,[43] which could admit of no uncertainty, because true religion plainly bestows upon its followers the largess of many good things. And after confirming his words, he again turns to the logical order of his exhortation:

4:10 *For that (he says) we toil and are reproached,[44] since we have hoped in the living God, who is the Savior of all humans, especially of the faithful.*

"And so, since true religion is able to provide many good things, it is no wonder that we who believe in God, who always exists, should both toil and be reproached for him, for whom it is also best to suffer, because he knows how to save everyone by his kindness. And he also knows how to bestow many rewards on the faithful because of the eagerness of their soul." And since he has showed in all respects that zeal for these things is necessary and that they should be trained for true religion by teaching the rest, he takes up once more the exhortation he is setting forth, adding:

4:11 *Give instruction about these things and teach.*

He did not put down *give instruction* without reason, but because it would be right for him [148] to set about this insistently whenever the circumstance itself might compel him to do it. Then, because he was a young man, and his age itself seemed to be despised by a great many people, he added:

4:12a *Let no one despise your youth,*

---

[43] That is, the verse refers to what precedes rather than to what follows it.
[44] Theodore's reading is ὀνειδιζόμεθα rather than ἀγωνιζόμεθα.

'noli autem propter aetatem pusillanimis esse, neque caueas quin cum auctoritate doceas, eo quod ad hoc sis in iuuentute electus.' admirabilis uere est adiectio quam adiecit, dicens:

sed forma esto fidelium in uerbo, in conuersatione, in caritate, in 5 *fide, in castitate.*

'ad aetatem (inquit) tuam noli respicere, diligentiam uero adhibe horum, ut dicas et agas illa quae dici oportent, quo secundum ut condecens est conuersentur; ut caritatem eam quae erga omnes est teneant, ut firmi sint in fide, ut pudicitiae diligentiam 10 adhibeant; ita ut et ipse formam te praebeas fidelibus pro quibus uitam regis tuam, instruens quemadmodum conueniat conuersari, ita ut ex ipsis actibus tuis testimonium uitae tuae hisdem praebeas. noli doctrinae dignitatem aetate dimittere tua; cum fiducia uero omnia dicere properato.' deinde ex generalitate eum exhor- 15 tans de his quae ei conueniunt, adicit:

usque dum ueniens, intende lectioni, [exhortationi,] doctrinae.

'et sollicitudinem impende erga lectiones, ut discere possis quae te et facere et alios docere conueniat; ut assiduitate lectionum teipsum instruens, insistere possis doctrinae et exhortationi.'

20 †dicit enim ['doctrinam'] abso-	'διδασκαλίαν' φησὶν τὴν ἀπόλυτον
lute narrationem; 'exhortatio-	ἐξήγησιν, 'παράκλησιν' δὲ τὴν ἀπὸ
nem' uero siue 'consolationem,'	τινῶν συμβεβηκότων νουθεσίαν τε
illam commonitionem quae ex	καὶ ὑπόμνησιν, ἣν ἐνίοτε μὲν καὶ
aliquibus accidentibus fieri so-	ἐπὶ τοῦ κοινοῦ γίνεσθαι ἀνάγκη,
25 let, quam interdum et in com-	μάλιστα δὲ καὶ ἐν ταῖς πρὸς τὸν
muni facere est necesse, uel ma-	καθ' ἕνα διαλέξεσιν.
xime cum in illam narrationem	
inciderimus quam singulis ex-	
ponere res ipsa compellat.*	

1   idem [id est?] (*bef.* noli) *add* r   ‖   pro pietate (*for* propter aetatem) *H*   ‖   paueas (*for* caueas) *C* (*corr.*)   3   uero   4   exemplum (*for* forma) *r*   7   ut secundum quod decet conu. *r*   ‖   oporteant *C* (*corr.*)   ‖   quae (*for* quo) *H*   12   illis (*for* hisdem) *r*   13   dign. doctr. *r*   ‖   aetatem d. tuam *C** propter aet. &c. *C* (*corr.*) aetate d. tuam *H*: txt *r*   16   ueniam *C* (*corr.*)   ‖   exhort. *om C H*   18   lectionem *r*   20   dicit e. abs. narr. non exort. uero siue cons. illam commonitione (*corr.* commonitionum) *C* dicit e. abs. narr. non exort. si uero cons, illam commonitionem *H* non dicit e. abs. narr. sed exhort. siue collationem illam commotionem *r*: cf. *g and note*   ‖   sq. Coisl. 204, f. 203 a [Cr. vii. 36, Fr. 153] Θεόδωρος. διδασκαλίαν, κ.τ.λ.   24   accedentibus *C* r*   27   illa (*om* in) *C** illam *r*

"And do not be discouraged because of your age or avoid teaching with authority because you have been chosen for this in your youth." The addition he makes is truly admirable, saying:

4:12b *but be an example of the faithful in word, in way of life, in love, in faith, in chastity.*

"Do not be concerned (he says) about your age but apply diligent care to these people so that you may speak and do what ought to be said, whereby they may live their lives in a proper way, so that they may hold fast to love toward all, so that they may be steadfast in faith, so that they may apply diligent care to chastity. Do this in such a way that you may furnish yourself as an example to the faithful for whom you are ruling your life, instructing them how they ought to live in such a way that by your very deeds you may furnish them with the testimony of your life. Do not give up the honor of teaching because of your age, but be eager to say everything with confidence." Then, exhorting him in general terms about what he ought to do, he adds:

4:13 *Until I come, pay attention to reading, to exhortation, to teaching.*

"Expend great care in readings, so that you can learn [149] what is right for you both to do and to teach others, so that instructing yourself by application to readings you may be able to press on with teaching and exhortation."

†For by *teaching* he means general exposition,[45] and by *exhortation* or consolation that reminder that usually takes place because of certain circumstances and that sometimes must be made in the community or especially when we fall into that exposition that the circumstance itself compels us to make to individuals.*

By *teaching* he means general exposition, and by *exhortation* the admonishment and reminder from certain circumstances that sometimes must take place in the community, but also especially in conversations with an individual.

---

[45] See Swete's note (2:149): "*absolute*] I. q. *absolutam* (see Gk.), 'general, without reference to the circumstances of the individuals addressed.'"

permanere uero doctrinae et exhortationi diligenti suadens placabilitate, adicit:

noli negligere gratiam quae in te est.

nam et sufficienter poterat eum persuadere ut cum sollicitudine doctrinae opus impleret, eo quod ad diuinam donationem ab
hac ipsa causa dignus fuerit adsequi. unde et mirum probate datum ipsum augere cupiens, ut magis magisque eum adhortaretur,
adicit:

quae data est tibi per prophetiam cum inpositione manus presbyte-
rii.

'nam et donum diuinum propter hoc adsecutus es, per reuelationem illud accipiens perque inpositionem manuum plurimorum
et hoc non uilissimorum, qui in tua ordinatione ipsi gratiae uisi
sunt ministrasse. itaque omni ex parte non est cautum tibi ut ne-
glegas illa quae tibi sunt iniuncta, siue propter reuelationem cum
qua adsecutus es, siue ob dignationem eorum qui ob hoc ipsum
ministrantes manus tibi inposuerunt.' *presbyterii* uero hoc in loco non eos nunc nominauit qui nunc nominantur presbyteri—nec
autem res admittebat istos manus inponere ad ordinationem ipsius
functionis; sed

†apostolorum dicit conuentum	τὸν τῶν ἀποστόλων σύλλογον φη-
qui aderat apostolo Paulo et cum	σίν, οἳ συνῇεσάν τε αὐτῷ καὶ συν-
eo manus inponebant in eius or-	εφήπτοντο ὡς εἰκὸς ποιουμένῳ τὴν
dinationem. 'presbyterium' au-	ἐπ' αὐτῷ χειροτονίαν, 'πρεσβυτέ-
tem illud nominauit contempla-	ριον' αὐτὸ ὀνομάσας ἀπὸ τοῦ ἐντί-
tione honoris. ista uero consue-	μου. τοῦτο δὲ καὶ νῦν ἔθος ἐν ταῖς
tudine etiam nunc agunt usque	τῶν ἐπισκόπων γίνεσθαι προβολαῖς,
huc, ut in episcoporum ordi-	τὸ μὴ ὑφ' ἑνός, ἀλλ' ὑπὸ πλειόνων
natione non unus sed plurimi	τὰς τοιαύτας ἐν τῇ ἐκκλησίᾳ χειρο-
et huiusmodi ordinationem im-	τονίας πληροῦσθαι.
pleant.*	

deinde et persistens in praebendo consilio adicit:

---

4 ei *r*   5 implere *C**   6 amplius (*for* mir. prob.) *r*   7 adhortare *H*   9
impositioni *H*   12 per quem *C* H* per inquam *r*   14 auctum (*for* caut.) *H*
16 ea (*aft.* qua) *H r*   17 presbyteros *C* (*corr.*) *r*   18 tunc (*for* nunc) *C* (*corr.*):
om r   21 sq. Coisl. 204, *l. c.* Θεόδωρος. ἢ καὶ τὸν τῶν, κ.τ.λ.   27 agunt *om*
C agunt ut *om H*   28 agitur (*aft.* usque) *add C* (*corr.*): *txt r*

And gently[46] urging him to persevere in teaching and in diligent exhortation, he adds:

4:14a *Do not neglect the grace that is in you,*

Now Paul was able sufficiently to persuade Timothy to fulfill the work of teaching with great care because he was worthy of attaining the divine gift from this very source. Then, wishing by his approval to increase the marvel of what had been given him, so that he may more and more exhort him, he adds:

4:14b *which was given to you by prophecy with the laying on of hand of the presbyterate.*

"Now you have attained the divine gift because of this, [150] receiving it by revelation and by the laying on of a great many hands, and those not of smallest account, which plainly have themselves ministered the grace in your ordination. And so in every respect it is not safe for you to neglect what has been enjoined on you, whether on account of the revelation by which you attained it or because of the worth of those who, ministering because of this very thing, laid hands on you." And in this place he has not used the name *presbyterate* to mean those who are now called presbyters—nor would the matter have permitted the laying on of those hands for the appointment to this very service.[47] Rather,

†he means the meeting of the apostles present with the apostle Paul and who with him laid hands on Timothy for his ordination. And he named this the *presbyterate* with regard to honor. And even now, up to this time, they act by that custom so that in the ordination of bishops not one but several fulfill an ordination of this kind.*	He means the meeting of the apostles who came together with him and apparently joined with Paul in laying hands on Timothy, having named it the *presbyterate* from its honored character. Even now this custom takes place in the advancement of bishops, that such ordinations in the church are fulfilled not by one but by several.

Then, continuing to furnish advice, he adds:

---

[46] See Swete's comment (2:149): "*Placabilitate* = ἠπίως?"

[47] Theodore's point is that presbyters, while they join the bishop in ordaining a presbyter, have no part in ordaining a bishop. Since Timothy is being regarded as a bishop, the "presbyterate" of the text must refer to other bishops, that is, the apostles.

haec meditare, in illis esto, ut profectus tuus manifestus sit omni-
bus; intende tibi ipsi et doctrinae, permane in illis. hoc enim faciens et
te ipsum saluum facies et eos qui te audiunt.

et per omnia illud dicit quoniam 'conueniat te tuam ipsius diligentiam habere ac uirtutibus inlustrare, ita ut et omnia ante lectio-
nibus intendas, et doctrinae opus cum omni expedias sollicitudine;
sic enim tibi ipsi et aliis multis eris bonitatis prouisor.' et quoniam
de his consummauit exhortationem plurimis eam sermonibus ex-
plens, scribit de cetero et qualem eum esse erga singulos conueniat:

seniorem ne increpaueris, sed obsecra ut patrem.

seniorem dicit non secundum ordinationis rationem, sed secundum aetatem, hoc est, senem; ut dicat: 'senibus noli acerbus uideri, sed cum modestia illis loquere quasi patribus tuis.'

iuueniores ut fratres.

in commune posuit illud quod dixerat, *obsecra;* uult enim dicere: 'nulli inuehas te, neque sis acerbus aut amarus; clementer uero erga omnes tuum exhibe affectum, longaeuos quasi patres diligens, iuniores ut fratres.' et quia ista de uiris dixerat, uolens ostendere quoniam parem affectum conuenit eum habere erga uiros et
erga mulieres, transit ad illam partem paria dicens:

anus ut matres.

est: 'erga mulieres (inquit) talem te exhibe ut seniores earum
matres tuas esse existimes.' deinde et de nouellis similia adiciens,
dicit:

adolescentulas ut sorores in omni castitate.

est: 'et has (inquit) sicut sorores proprias dilige.' diuisionem
sexuum et aetatum fieri debere probauit, et quidem cum possis illa
magis et absolute et in commune dicere. sed nec fecit; ut per par-

---

1 istis (*for* illis) *H* his *r* ‖ prouectus *H* 2 attende, insta (*for* int., perm.) *r*
‖ ipsi *om C r* ‖ permanens *H* 3 saluans (*for* saluum) *C* H* saluas *C*
(*corr.*) 4 te tum *C* H* totam *C* (*corr.*): *txt r* 5 hac (*for* ac) *C** ‖ ante
omnia *C* (*corr.*) *r* 7 multis aliis *H* 11 increpueris *r* 13 aceruus *C H* 15
iuniores *H* iuuenes *r* 17 inueas *H* inueharis *r*: *txt C l* ‖ aceruus *C H* 18
et benigne (*aft.* uero) *add H* 18-19 diligens *om H* 20 patrem (*for* parem) *C*
H paternum *r* 23 esto (*for* est) *H*: *om r* 1 exhibere *C** 24 adiciens adicit *H*
dicens adicit *r* 26 iuuenculas, cum (*for* adol., in) *r* 27 esto (*for* est) *H* 28
et aetatem *H* per aetatem *r* ‖ probabunt *C* H* ‖ possit *C* (*corr.*) *r* 29 in
communi *r* ‖ hoc (*for* nec) *C r* 29 patres (*for* partes) *C H*

[151] 4:15–16 *Reflect on these things, be in those things, so that your progress may be manifest to all. Pay attention to yourself and to teaching, persevere in those things. For doing this you will save both yourself and those who hear you.*

And by all this he means: "May it be right for you to have diligent care for yourself and to shine with virtues so that before everything you may pay attention to readings and may get ready for the work of teaching with all care. For in this way you will provide goodness for yourself and for many others." And since he has finished his exhortation about these matters, completing it with a great many words, he writes in what remains how Timothy ought to conduct himself toward individuals:

5:1a *Do not speak harshly to an elder, but beseech as a father,*

He says *an elder* not in reference to the principle of ordination but in reference to age, that is, old. He means: "Do not appear harsh to old men, but speak to them with mildness, as though to your fathers."

5:1b *to young men as brothers,*

He put down *beseech* to refer to both in common. For he wants to say: "May you attack no one with words, and may you not be harsh or bitter, but show your affection to all in a kindly way, loving the aged as fathers and the young as brothers." And because he had said this about men, in his wish to show that it was right for him to have equal affection for men and for women, he goes on to that sex, using equivalent words:

5:2a *to old women as mothers,*

[152] That is: "Show yourself toward women such that you may regard the older of them to be your own mothers." Then, adding similar words about the young ones, he says:

5:2b *to young girls as sisters, in all chastity.*

That is: "And love these (he says) as your own sisters." He has proved that a separation of sexes and ages ought to be made even when you may be able to speak of those things to a greater extent, without qualification, and in the community. Nevertheless,

tes ostenderet quoniam similiter eum uult erga omnes tam uiros quam mulieres affectum ostendere suum siue senes sint siue iuuenes. optime autem non solum secundum sexum uiros et mulieres diuisit, sed etiam et secundum aetates quae per proprietatem na-
5 turae accidere solent. unde et nomina secundum aetatem memoratus est, ita ut longaeuos quidem more parentum adfectarentur, iuuenes uero more fratrum. et ut augeret eius affectum in melius, simile aliquid dixit illorum quae Dominus dixerat ad illos qui sibi nuntiauerant quoniam 'mater tua et fratres tui expectant te foris';
10 respondit: 'mater (inquit) mea et fratres hi sunt qui faciunt uerbum meum.' sic et ipse in eodem ordine fideles eum habere praecipit. intendendum est ei cautelae, quemadmodum de adolescentibus mulieribus loquens posuerit *tamquam sorores*, et his adiecerit *in omni castitate*; simul et consilium suum erga personas memora-
15 tarum propter aetatem cautum ostendens, simul et illud instruens quoniam possibile est affectum habere uehementem contemplatione pietatis erga mulieres licet sint per aetatem nouellae, et non et hoc in actum deduci turpissimum. nam quod dixit *sicut sorores*, ex superiore sequentia etiam hoc in loco id posuit, consilium dans
20 ut non solum diligat eas (sicut et in superioribus dixerat); sed et ad ostensionem integritatis adiecit, ut ne ob affectum iura temerentur castitatis, si tamen non aliquis sponte meliora despiciens in deterius serpere uoluerit. siquidem et sorores sint mulieres et eandem habeant naturam et similia perpeti possint, et diligimus propter
25 naturae propinquitatem et cauemus aliquid inconueniens in illas agere, propinquitatem uenerantes naturae cum debita reuerentia.
  uiduas honora quae uere uiduae sunt.
  omnia quae in superioribus interiecisse uidetur beatus apostolus Paulus, ab illo loco quo dixit *et manifeste magnum est pietatis*
30 *mysterium*, usque ad hoc dictum quo dixit *adolescentulas ut sorores in omni castitate*. illa quidem quae dogmatica sunt ad probationem ueritatis posuit, eo quod ecclesiam dixit esse 'columnam et firma-

---

4 per *om C r* proprietate *C (corr.) r* 6 affectaret *r* 8 illum *r* 9 nuntiauerat *C* H r* 11-12 praecepit *r* 12 int. uero est illi *r* ‖ uero (*aft.* est) *add H* 13 melioribus (*for* mul.) *C* H* 14-15 memoraturum *C H r* 15 et *om C* r* 18 deducitur pessimum *C H r* 19 superiori *H* ‖ in hoc in l. *H* 20 sicuti *H r* 21 ab affectu *r* ‖ temeremur *C* uiolentur *r* 22 meliore *C** mulierem *C (corr.) H* ‖ dispiciens *C r* 24 diligemus *r* 25 cauebimus *r* 27 uerae *C* 30 et (*for* ut) *C r*

he composed his words so as to show by the different groups that he wants Timothy to show his affection alike to all, so to men as to women or whether they are old or young. And quite effectively he separated the men and the women not only by sex but also by the ages that usually come about by the special property of nature. That is why he mentioned their names by age, so that the aged might be held in affection like parents and the young like brothers and sisters. And to increase for the better his affection, he said something like what the Lord had said to those who had brought him the news that "your mother and your brothers are waiting for you outside." He answered, "My mother and brothers are those who do my word" (see Luke 8:20–21). So, too, Paul himself advises Timothy to hold the faithful in the same ordering. Attention must be paid to his caution, how, when speaking of young women, he put down *as sisters* and added to this *in all chastity.* At one and the same time he shows that his advice regarding the persons of those he has mentioned [153] is cautious because of age, and he gives the instruction that it is possible in the observance of true religion to have strong affection toward women, even if they are young in age, and not to be led by this to a most shameful act. Now when he said *as sisters*, he also put the phrase down placed in sequence with what is above,[48] giving advice that he should not only love them (just as he had said above), but he also added for the demonstration of moral purity that the rights of chastity should not be violated because of affection, if at least someone were unwilling of his own accord by despising better things to crawl down to what is worse. Even if sisters are women and have the same nature and can undergo the like experiences, we love them because of their natural close relationship to us, and we avoid doing anything unfitting to them, revering the close relationship of nature with due respect.

5:3 *Honor widows who are truly widows.*

The blessed apostle Paul seems to have inserted everything above from that place where he said (3:16): *and obviously, great is the mystery of true religion,* up to the place where he said (5:2): *to young girls as sisters, in all chastity.* In the insertion he put down doctrinal statements to prove the truth, because he said the church is "the pillar and support of truth" (3:15). And he said other things

---

[48]That is, "beseech" in 5:1. We must understand "beseech them as sisters."

mentum ueritatis'; alia uero ad instructionem beati dixit Timothei, quae et facere eum iustum existimabat, siue ob illius ipsius
causam siue ob ceterorum iuuamen. coepit autem ab illo loco quo
dixit *obsecro ergo primum omnium fieri orationes, deprecationes, po-*
5 *stulationes, gratiarum actiones*—quae uniuersa ad utilitatem [et] ad
ornamentum communis ecclesiae pertinere uidebantur. nam quod
dicit *ante omnia*, illud uel maxime designat quod in communem
congregationem ecclesiae ab illis fieri oportere existimabat, scilicet ut omnis cultus Deo debitus restituatur, cum debita gratiarum
10 actione, quae ei debetur pro illis quae ab eo data sunt nobis. et quidem orationem facientes non pro nobis ipsis solis facere debemus,
sed et pro omnibus hominibus. unde et in subsequentibus necessario adicit quales eos esse conueniat uel in uita uel in moribus uel
in conuersatione; et primum quidem in communi naturae adusus
15 est diuisionem, alia dicens ad instructionem uirorum, instruens
quales eos oporteat esse, alia uero ad mulieres. sicque commune
ad omnes super uirtutibus implendis consilium uisus est dedisse. deinde ad ordinem transit, illos qui ecclesiae ministerium implere uidentur reputans, quoniam priuatam hi indigeant exhorta-
20 tionem, eo quod in commune conueniens ecclesia eorum impletur
ministerio, et istis quidem bene agentibus multum possunt ceteri
adiuuari; e contrario etiam istis illa quae conueniunt minime pro-
curantibus, plurima detrimenta multis uideantur inrogari. unde
et de presbyteris primam uidetur fecisse disputationem, instruens
25 quales eos esse oporteat; dein de diaconibus, postea uero de uiris et mulieribus. post consummationem uero horum ad hoc instructionem suam produxisse uisus est, quam et interpositam et
interiectam esse diximus. conueniens autem erat post communem
exhortationem quam ad omnes fecisse uidetur, et proprie ad illos
30 qui ecclesiae functionem implere uidebantur, coniungere etiam illa quae de uiduis dici conueniebant; quas etiam in suo ordine memorare conueniebat ob illam prouidentiam quam erga eas implere

5 ad orn (*om* et) *C* H r* et orn. *C* (*corr.*)   7   communiter (*for* in comm.) *C r*
10   ei *om H*   10-11   quidam *C H*: *om r*   14   adorsus (*for* adusus) *C* (*corr.*)   15
diuisione *H r*   16   communiter *r*   17   usus (*for* uisus) *H*   18   illorum qui nec
eccl. *r*   ‖   nec (*bef.* eccl.) add *C* H*   19   priuata, exhortatione *C* (*corr.*)   25
eos quales *H*   ‖   deinde (*for* dein de) *H r*   26   hoc *om H*   29   uidebatur *H*   ‖
propriae *C*   30   fructionem *C** fruitionem *H*   ‖   implebant (*for* impl. uid.) *r*
31   etiam et *H*   31-32   memorari *C* (*corr.*)   32   par erat (*for* conueniebat) *r*

to instruct blessed Timothy as to what he thought he ought to do, whether for his own sake or for the help of others. Paul begins the instructions[49] from the place where he said (2:1): *Therefore, I make entreaty first of all that there be made prayers, intercessions, requests, thanksgivings*—all of which were seen to pertain to the benefit and common adornment of the church. Now by saying *before all* [154] he points out what he thought especially ought to be done by them in the common assembly of the church; that is, that entire worship owed to God should be rendered with due thanksgiving owed him for what he has given us. And we ought to pray not only for ourselves but also for all people. Then in what follows he necessarily adds what sort of people they ought to be either in life or in habits or in behavior. And at first he employs a natural separation in the community, saying some things for the instruction of the men, instructing them as to what sort of people they ought to be, and other things for the women. And in this way he has plainly given common advice to all concerning the virtues that must be implemented. Then he goes on to church order (3:1), considering those seen to fulfill the ministry of the church, since they need a particular exhortation. This is because when the church assembles together it is fulfilled by their ministry, and when they perform their tasks well, the rest can be much helped. On the other hand, when they attend to what is by no means fitting, they plainly inflict a great deal of damage on many people. And so he plainly composed his first discussion about the presbyters, giving instruction as to what sort of people they should be. Then he goes on to the deacons and afterwards to male and female deacons. And after completing these discussions up to this point (3:15), he seems to have introduced his instruction, which we have said has been both put in the middle and inserted. And it would have been fitting, after the general exhortation he plainly made to all, as well as his particular address to those who were seen to fulfill the service of the church, for him to join to this

---

[49]The insertion appears to be 3:16–5:2, and it includes the doctrinal material (3:16) and instructions to Timothy (4:1–5:2). But confusion results from Theodore's location of the beginning of Paul's instructions to Timothy at 2:1. Does this mean that the discussion of offices (3:1–15) interrupts the instructions to Timothy? The only point that seems clear is that Theodore supposes that the discussion of the order of widows in 1 Tim 5 ought to have followed the discussion of bishops and deacons in 1 Tim 3.

oportebat. hinc uero, ut dixi, ad propositam interiectionem ab illa
egressus est sequentia; post sequentiam autem dictorum consuetudo est illi etiam et interiectiones facere. sicque ad illos sermones
exiit qui super uiduis dici debebant: *honora* (inquit) *illas quae uere*
5 *sunt uiduae.* non absolutam promissionem earum intendere uoluit,
sed quando promissio ipso opere impleri uidetur. nam quod hoc
in loco dixit *honora*, hoc est, 'diligentiam illis adhibe;' quod euidens fit ex illis dictis quae sequuntur. quas quidem ita uera ratione
existimat esse uiduas, sicut in subsequentibus melius instruimur.
10 iterum uero de illis loquitur quae non debent ecclesiastico sumptu
aleri, adiciens de illis:

si qua uidua filios aut nepotes habet, discant primum propriam do-
mum colere, et uicem reddere parentibus; hoc enim est acceptum in
conspectu Dei.

15   †quod dixit *discant*, de filiis et nepotibus dixit, non de
uiduis; properabat enim docere quoniam illae solae debent
sumptu ecclesiastico nutriri,
20 quae aliunde alimoniam habere
minime possint. si igitur uidua
filios aut nepotes habet, discant
illi qui ex ea nati sunt alere matrem siue auiam;*

μανθανέτωσαν· 'τὰ τέκνα,' λέγει, 'καὶ τὰ ἔκγονα', οὐχ αἱ χῆραι.
σκοπὸς γὰρ αὐτῷ διδάξαι ὅτι ἐκεῖ-
ναι μόναι τῆς ἐκκλησιαστικῆς ἐπιμελείας ἀξιοῦσθαι ὀφείλουσιν, αἷς
οὐδεὶς κηδεμονίας ἑτέρωθεν ὑπολέ-
λειπται τρόπος. ἐὰν τοίνυν (φησὶν)
ἢ χήρα τέκνα ἔχουσα ἢ ἔκγονα, δι-
δασκέσθωσαν οἱ ἀπ' ἐκείνης τεχθέν-
τες ἐπιμελεῖσθαι τῆς μητρὸς ἤτοι
τῆς μάμμης.

25 quia hoc magis placitum est Deo ut ab illis nutriantur, et non ecclesiasticum indigeant solatium. deinde dicit de illis uiduis quas
uere uiduas esse existimat, dicens:

quae autem uere uidua est et desolata, speret in Deum et permaneat
in oratione et deprecatione nocte et die.

30   euidens est quod ueram uiduam duobus ab causis ecclesiastico

---

3 et *om* H   4 exigit (*for* exiit) H   ‖ uiduas H   6 implere C* H   7-8
uidens sit C* euidens sit H r: txt C (*corr.*)   9 existiment H   11 ali C (*corr.*) r
12 si qua autem r   ‖ domum suam regere r   13 coram Deo (*for* in consp.
Dei) r   15 sq. Coisl. 204, f. 204 a [Cr. vii. 38] ἄλλος φησίν· τὸ μανθανέτωσαν,
κ.τ.λ.   16 ἔγγονα cod. (but below, p. 156 l. 22, ἔκγ.).   18 ille sole C* H   22
aut (*bef.* fil.) add C r   25 nutrientur C*   25-26 ecclesiastico, solatio r   28
sperat r   29 instat obsecrationibus et orationibus r   ‖ ac (*for* et [2°]) r   30
duobus ob c. C* H duabus ob c. C (*corr.*) duabus ex c. r

also what ought to be said about widows. Still more, he ought to have mentioned them in his own logical order because of the provision that it was necessary to make for them. But from this point (3:15), as I have said, he digressed from the logical order to the insertion he set forth. [155] And he has a habit after following the logical order of his words also to make insertions. And so he ends his digression by turning to the discussion that should have been made concerning widows (5:3): *honor those who are truly widows.* He wanted to maintain their professed vow not without qualification, but when the vow is seen fulfilled in deed. Now when he said in this place *honor*, he means "apply diligent care to them." This becomes clear in what he goes on to say, as indeed we are better informed in what follows who the women are whom with true reason he esteems to be such widows. On the other hand, he speaks of those who should not be supported at the expense of the church, adding about them:

5:4 *If a widow has children or grandchildren, let them learn first to revere their own household and to give back in return to parents, for this is acceptable in the sight of God.*

†When he said *let them learn,* he spoke of children and grandchildren, not of widows, [156] for he was eager to teach that only those who could by no means have sustenance from any other source should be supported at the expense of the church. Therefore, if a widow has children or grandchildren, let these born from her learn how to support their mother or grandmother,*

Let them learn. He means the children and the grandchildren, not the widows. For his aim is to teach that only those for whom no means of care has been left from another source should be thought worthy of the church's support. Therefore, if (he says) a widow has children or grandchildren, let those who have been born from her learn how to support their mother or grandmother.

because it is more pleasing to God that they should be nourished by them and not need the relief of the church. Then he speaks about those widows he regards as truly widows, saying:

5:5 *But she who is truly a widow and left alone, let her hope in God and let her persevere in prayer and intercession night and day;*[50]

---

[50]The use of the subjunctive ("let her hope and persevere") departs from the Greek text.

sumptu uult nutriri; unum, ut et moribus sit ordinata et uirtutibus inlustrata; alterum, eo quod ad plenum neminem uidetur habere qui diligentiam ei adhibeat. haec autem est *uere uidua*, quae
propinquum non habet et per omne tempus uitae suae solis uacat
5   orationibus.

quae autem in deliciis est, uiua mortua est.

'si aliqua amisso uiro in uiduitate se persistere promittit et deli-
ciosam exercet uitam, mortua est magis quam uiua, licet si et uiuere uideatur. nec autem ultra maritali conscientia tenetur, neque
10   uirtutis studio inlustratur; sed solis epulis ac deliciis uacare properans, nihil ex illis quae sibi conueniunt facere poterit.' et uolens
Timotheum erga talem sollicitudinem incitare, adiecit:

et haec praecipe, ut inreprehensibiles sint.

hoc est, 'et his dicito ut optime uiuentes maneant inreprehen-
15   sibiles.' deinde adiecit:

si autem quis suorum et maxime domesticorum curam non habet,
fidem negauit et est infideli deterior.

hoc ad illud retulit: *si qua uero uidua filios aut nepotes habet, di-*
scant primum suam domum colere; eo quod dixit quoniam oportet
20   ut talis uidua a filiis et nepotibus nutriatur, ita ut nihil illis desit
de his quae eis necessantur. hoc de illis dixit, admonens eos ut erga parentum diligentiam sint solliciti, quoniam oportet omnibus
qui nobis propinquitate iunguntur diligentiam adhibere. *maxime*
domesticorum; ut dicat, 'eorum qui nobis nimia propinquitate ge-
25   neris iungi uidentur, ut puta mater, pater, auus, auia.' si quis uero hos despicit, manifestus est quod nec fidei curam habet ullam,
sed et *infideli sit deterior;* siue quia illam legem quae naturae posita
est ille qui se pietatem seruare promittit custodire noluerit. inci-

3   uera *H*   8   etsi (*for* si et) *H*   9   altera (*for* ultra) *r*   11   et ... adiecit *om r*
12   adicit *C*   13   hoc (*for* haec) *H r*   15   adicit *r*   18   refertur (*for* retulit) *l*
20   tales uiduae *H* (*corr.*)   ‖   uidua *om r*   ‖   nutriantur *C* H* (*corr.*)   21
necessaria sunt (*for* necessantur) *r*   24   nimia nobis *r*   25   iungere *C* H*   ‖
pater mater *H*   26   dispicit *C** despiciat *r*   ‖   manifestum *C r*   27   et *om r*
‖   illi *C** [?] *r: txt C* (*corr.*)

It is clear that for two reasons he wants the true widow to be supported at the expense of the church. For one thing, that she may be well-ordered in her habits and distinguished by virtues; for another, because she seems to have absolutely no one to care for her. And this is the woman who is *truly a widow*, the one who has no relative and is free to spend the whole time of her life in prayers alone.

5:6 *but the one who is in luxuries, living, is dead.*

"If any woman, when she has lost her husband, promises that she will remain a widow and indulges in a life of luxury, she is more dead than alive, even if [157] she seems to live. And she is neither bound any longer by her husband's knowledge of her nor enlightened by the pursuit of virtue. Instead, since she is eager to be free for delicacies and luxuries, she can do nothing of what she ought to do." And wishing to rouse Timothy to such care, he added:

5:7 *And give these instructions, so that they may be without reproach.*

That is, "And speak to them so that they may remain without reproach by living the best way possible." Then he added:

5:8 *And if someone does not have care for his own and especially for those of his household, he has denied faith and is worse than an unbeliever.*

He referred this to (5:4): *and if a widow has children or grandchildren, let them learn first to revere their own household.* This is because he said that it was right for such a widow to be nourished by children and grandchildren, so that they might lack nothing they needed. He said this about them, urging them to be caring by diligently supporting their parents, since it is right to apply diligent care to all who are joined to us as relatives. *Especially for those of his household* means "those who are seen joined to us by the special relationship of family descent, for example, mother, father, grandfather, grandmother." And if someone despises them, it is obvious that he has no concern for faith but is even *worse than an unbeliever*, whether because [158] he has despised the law set down for nature or because he who has promised to observe true religion has proved unwilling to keep the law itself.[51] And while he begins

---

[51] Following Swete's suggested emendation (2:157–58): "Perhaps a line has fallen out after *posita est*; add *despexerit, siue quia et ipsam legem divinam*, or

piens uero docere ab illo loco quo dixit *uiduas honora quae uere ui-*
duae sunt, quales conueniat esse illas quae sub ecclesiasticorum diligentia habentur, interposuit de illis uiduis quae filios uel nepotes
habent. ad quos hoc reddidit, implens illud quod in superioribus
5 minus dixerat; deinde ad suam recurrens sequentiam, manifeste
exponit quales uult esse uiduas quae et sub regula ecclesiastica et
prouidentia debent haberi, dicens:
  uidua eligatur non minus annorum sexaginta.
  ante omnia aetatem designandam esse credidit in qua constitu-
10 tae debent in ordinem recipi uiduarum. quidam uero non considerantes quam ob causam aetatem uoluerit significari, hoc statue-
runt, utrumnam mulieres diaconissas ante hanc aetatem ordinari
minime conueniat. erga quas uel maxime id debere obseruari existimauerunt, eo quod in maiori ordine a uiduis sint producendae;
15 neque illud intellegentes quoniam si in earum ordinatione id obseruare decreuit, sed multo magis erga presbyteros et episcopos id
custodire praecepisset; quod minime perspicere potuerunt. beatus autem Paulus qui numquam aetate functionem credidit esse
decernendam, denique Timotheum ipsum ualde iuuenem extan-
20 tem tantis praeposuit ecclesiis, magnum illi opus et quod omnibus praecellere uidetur committens— et hoc significatur per illas
litteras quas ad eum dirigit dicens, *nemo iuuentutem tuam contemp-*
nat—quid est ergo? uirtutis industriam non ex aetate cupit firma-
ri, cuius uel maxime probationem facere uidetur; sufficit enim illa
25 aetas quae ante haec tempora nimiam et cautam praeberet probationem uniuscuiusque propositi.
  †quia uero uiduae in ordine ἀλλ' ἐπειδὴ κατελέγοντο χῆραι διὰ
  constituebantur ecclesiastico ut   τὸ τῆς ἐκκλησιαστικῆς ἐπιμελείας

---

1 quod (*for* quo) *H r*   2 illos *H*   8 sex. ann. *r*   9 aetate *C* (*corr.*)   ‖
designatum *H**   10 ordine *H*   11 haec *r*   13-14 existimauerit *C** existi-
mauerint *C* (*corr.*) aestimauerunt *r*   15 eorum *C H r*   15-16 obseruari *C*
(*corr.*) *r*   17 custodiri *C* (*corr.*)   ‖ nemine (*for* min.) *H*   ‖ potuerit *C*   18
qui *om r*   ‖ aetati *C H* per aetatem *r*   19 nam (*for* denique) *r*   21 signa-
tur *H*   22-23 condemnat *r*   23 quid ergo est *H* qu. e. est hoc quod dicit *r*
25 ante his temporibus *C H*   ‖ praebuerit *r*   27 sq. Coisl. 204, f. 204 b [Cr.
vii. 39, Fr. 153] Θεόδωρος. καὶ ἄλλος φησίν· οὐ περὶ τῶν εἰς διακονίαν προαχ-
θῆναι ὀφειλουσῶν διαλέγεται, ἀλλὰ περὶ τῶν εἰς τὸ χηρικὸν ἐγκαταλεγῆναι· οὐδὲ
γὰρ ἡλικία (sic) τῶν εἰς κλῆρον προαγομένων ὁρίζεσθαι χρή, ὥσπερ οὐδὲ ἐπ' αὐτοῦ τιμοθέου ὁ ἀπόστολος τοῦτο παρεφυλάξατο, ἀλλὰ τῇ ἀρετῇ τὴν δοκιμασίαν
χαρακτηρίζειν. ἀλλ' ἐπειδή, κ.τ.λ.

his teaching from the place where he said (5:3): *honor widows who are truly widows*, and while he said what sort of women those held under the care of church officials ought to be, he has inserted his remarks about those widows who have children or grandchildren. It is to them that he refers this verse, completing what he had said briefly above. Then returning to his own logical order, he quite clearly sets forth what sort of widows he wants those to be who deserve to be kept under the rule and provision of the church, saying:

5:9a *Let a widow be selected not less than sixty years old,*

He believed that before all the age ought to be designated at which women who were appointed ought to be received into the order of widows. But some people, because they have paid no attention to the reason for which he wanted the age to be indicated, [159] have decided this means one should question whether it is in the least right that women should be ordained deaconesses before this age. They have thought that this ought to be especially observed in the case of deaconesses, because they are advanced to a higher rank than widows. They fail to understand that if Paul had decreed this observation in their ordination, he would have far more ordered its observation in the case of presbyters and bishops—something they could by no means discern. But blessed Paul, who never believed that a service was to be determined by age, did indeed put Timothy in charge of such great churches when he was still quite young, entrusting him with a good work and one plainly surpassing all—and this is indicated by the words he directed to him, saying (4:12): *let no one despise your youth.* What, then, shall we say? Paul does not wish purposeful activity for virtue—the proof of which age especially seems to make—to be established by age, for the age someone has lived up to this time furnishes more than enough and careful proof of each one's purpose.

†But because widows were appointed to an order in the church so that they might acquire the church's provision, there were many women who had lost their husbands who

But since widows were enrolled because they were considered worthy of the church's care,

---

words to the same effect."

ecclesiasticam potirentur prouidentiam, multae autem erant
quae uiros amiserant quae non
uirtutum studio inter uiduas se
5 connumerari uolebant, sed ut
ecclesiasticam fruentes prouisionem secure illa quae ad usum
pertinent corporalem habentes
uitam suam transigere possent,
10 ex hac uero ratione multa (ut
adsolent) mala adnascebantur;*

ἀξιοῦσθαι, οὐκ ἀρετῆς ἐπιθυμίᾳ
τὴν χηρείαν μετιοῦσαι, ἀλλ᾽ ὥστε
ἀμερίμνως τὰς σωματικὰς ἐκ τῆς
ἐκκλησίας πορίζεσθαι χρείας, ἐκ δὲ
τούτου πλεῖστα ὡς εἰκὸς ἐπετελεῖτο
κακά...

eo quod nec ut decebat [uiuere] studebant quae non contemplatione uirtutis sese adscribere uiduas cupiebant, sed solo securitatis
desiderio, et ut sine aliquo labore uel opere facile cotidianum uic
15 tum haberent. haec ergo beatus Paulus cautissime cupiens confirmare,

†aetate et uirtute statuit debere
probari illam quae inter uiduas
se cupit adscribi;*

... διὰ τοῦτο ἡλικίᾳ καὶ ἀρετῇ
ὡρίσατο τὴν εἰς τὸν κατάλογον τῶν
χηρῶν συντελεῖν ὀφείλουσαν.

20 aetate quidem, eo quod ante hoc tempus aetatis possent etiam per
opera manuum suarum sibi uictum adquirere; uirtute uero, eo
quod iustum esse existimabat ut non ecclesiastici sumptus absolute in quaslibet uiduas expenderentur, sed magis decere existimans
ut uirtute sint inlustratae quae ecclesiastica sunt tuendae diligen
25 tia. unde dicens de tempore, adiecit in subsequentibus etiam de
moribus earum, quo uellet eas instituto haberi. et primum dicit:

quae unius uiri uxor.

†non autem hoc in loco dicens 'unius uiri uxorem' illud
30 dicit 'quae non secundum accepit maritum'; ipse enim id
fieri dedit consilium, quod nequaquam aliqua ratione incusa

γεγονυῖα ἑνὸς ἀνδρὸς γυνή, [οὐκ]
ἀντὶ τοῦ 'μὴ δεύτερον ἀγαγομένη,'
ἀλλ᾽ 'ἐκείνῳ προσκαρτερήσασα καὶ
σωφρόνως βιώσασα, εἴτε ἕνα τοῦ
τον ἔσχεν, εἴτε καὶ δεύτερον ἠγά
γετο.'

---

5 commorari C* H r 9 possint C* H 10 rationem C* 12 dicebat H ‖
uiuere *om* C H 12-13 contemplationem C* 13 adscribuntur C* adscribi
inter C (*corr.*) r: *txt* H 17 sq. Coisl. 204, *l. c.* 22 non *om* H 22-23 obsolute H 23 expenderetur C* ‖ dicere H 25 adicit C r 26 eorum C
‖ quomodo r ‖ institutas r 27 est (*aft* uxor) *add* H 28 nunc (*for* non)
C H r ‖ sq. Coisl. 204, *l. c.* 30 non quae sec. r 32 εἶχεν Cr.

used to want to have themselves numbered among the widows, not for the pursuit of virtues, but so that they might pass their life enjoying the church's provision safely, having what pertained to bodily use. For this reason many [160] evils used to arise, as one might expect,*

not because they were pursuing widowhood by a desire for virtue, but so that their bodily needs would be provided by the church without anxiety, for this reason the greatest evils were brought about, as one might expect.

because the women who wanted to enroll themselves as widows, but not for the observation of virtue, were not eager to live as they ought, but wanted this only by a longing for security and so that they might have their daily food easily without any toil or work. Therefore, blessed Paul, wishing to confirm these things as carefully as possible,

†decided that the woman who wanted herself to be enrolled among the widows ought to be tested by age and virtue,*

For this reason he decided that the woman ought to be assigned to the list of widows by age and virtue.

by age because before this age [of sixty] they could acquire food for themselves even by the works of their own hands, and by virtue because he thought it right that the expenses of the church should not be spent on any widows whatsoever without qualification, but thought it more suitable that the women to be maintained by the care of the church should be distinguished by virtue. That is why in speaking of the time of life he added in what follows also qualifications concerning their habits by which he wanted them to be considered for appointment. First, he says:

5:9b *who is the wife of one husband,*

†And by saying in this place *the wife of one husband*, he does not [161] mean "who has not taken a second husband." For Paul himself gave advice that this should be done, because in no way for any reason did he allow this to be blamed as unbecoming. Instead, "if she has lived chastely with her own

Who has been the wife of one husband, not to mean "not married a second time,"

but to mean, "she has been faithful to him and has lived cha-

ri quasi indecens patiebatur; sed
'si pudice cum suo uixerit uiro, siue unum tantum habuerit,
siue et secundo fuerit nupta,'*

5 tantum si alteri numquam intendit eo tempore quo maritum habebat; pudicitiam etenim requirit ab eiusmodi uiduis. nam pudicitiam exequuntur etiam et illae quae in coniugio pudice suis uiris conuiuunt siue cum primo marito, siue cum secundo; inconueniens etenim erat illas quae secundis nuptiis iunctae uirtutum stu-
10 diis ut conuenit sunt adornatae, deinde ad profundam senectutem
sunt redactae, ab ecclesiastica eas excludi diligentia, ita ut egentes
penuria conterantur ea ratione qua secundo fuerint iunctae marito. quod nullo in loco prohibuisse uisus est Paulus; ex contrario
uero, excludens fornicationem, id fieri adnuerit. deinde adiecit:

15 *in operibus bonis testimonium habens.*

et hoc quidem summatim explicauit; in subsequentibus uero illud per partes egerit, dicens:

et si filios enutriit.

†illa autem quae suorum fi-   ἡ γὰρ τῶν οἰκείων μὴ ἐπιμελη-
20 liorum curam non habuit, eui-   σαμένη τέκνων, δήλη πάντως ἐσ-
dens est multam inhumanita-   τὶν πολλὴν ἐπὶ τῆς ψυχῆς τὴν ἀπαν-
tem in animum habuisse suum.*   θρωπίαν ἔχουσα.

si peregrinos hospitio recepit.

non de peregrinis quibuslibet loquitur, sed de fidelibus et fide-
25 libus qui uirtuti studeant. denique uolens et in subsequentibus ipsius hospitalitatis speciem explanare quam et maxime eas exequi
cupit, adiecit:

si sanctorum pedes lauit.

non 'peregrinos' absolute dixit, sed sanctos; ut suadeat etiam
30 pedes lauari eorum quos hospites recipit, memoriam faciens sanctorum. hoc ut dixi ad exhortandas eas

1 indicens *C** 7 et *om C** 11 eas *om r* 12 quae *r* 13 in loco *om C*
14 adicit *r* 18 educauit (*for* enutr.) *r* 19 sq. Coisl. 204, *l. c.* [Cr. vii. 40,
Fr. 154]. 22 animo, suo *r* 23 et (*bef.* si) *add H* 24 et iis fid. *r* 25 uirtute
C H ‖ studeant *H* 26 uel (*for* et) *H r* 27 adicit *C r* 29 obsolute *C*
‖ abs. d. per. *H* 30 hospitio *H*

husband, whether she may have | stely, whether she has had this
had only one or has also been | one or has married a second."
married to a second"—*
but only if she has never submitted to another man during the
time when she had a husband. For he requires chastity of this
kind from widows. For those women pursue chastity who live
together with their husbands chastely in marriage, whether with a
first husband or a second. Indeed, it would have been unfitting for
those women who, joined in a second marriage, were adorned by
the pursuits of the virtues, as is right, then reduced to deep old age,
to be excluded from the church's care, so that living in want they
would be ground down because they had been joined to a second
husband. Nowhere is Paul seen to have forbidden this, but, on
the contrary, he approves of its being done, though he excludes
fornication. Then he added:

5:10a *having testimony in good works,*

He has explained this in a summary fashion, but in what follows
he has worked it out in detail, saying:

5:10b *and if she has brought up children,*

†And the woman who has | For the woman who has not
not cared for her own children | cared for her own children is
is clearly one who had much | clearly one who in all respects
inhumanity in her soul.* | has much inhumanity in her
soul.

[162] 5:10c *if she has received strangers with hospitality,*

He is not speaking of any strangers whatsoever, but of the
faithful, and the faithful who are zealous for virtue. Then, since
he wishes in what follows to explain a form of hospitality that he
especially wants them to pursue, he added:

5:10d *if she has washed the feet of the saints,*

He has not said *strangers* without qualification but *saints,* so that
by mentioning the saints, he may urge her even to wash the feet of
those whom she receives as guests. As I have said, it was to exhort
these women that

†adiecit, ut ostendat quoniam summa diligentia conuenit eos hospitio recipi,*

τοῦτο προσέθηκεν ἐπὶ τὸ δεῖξαι ὅτι καὶ μετ᾽ ἐπιμελείας αὐτοὺς ὑποδέχεσθαι χρή.

nec aliquid ex his quae ad honestum pertinent obsequium despi-
5 cere.

si tribulationem patientibus subministrauit.

iterum summatim id dixit:

si omne opus bonum subsecuta est.

euidens est quoniam pro uirium qualitate ista fieri suadet. cer-
10 tum est autem ex his dictis quoniam illas quae in matrimonio sunt
fideles tales cupit esse [quales] uiduas. qui enim uiduas dicit talis uitae debere fuisse, eo in tempore quo erant in matrimonio paria cupit implere. alioquin quemadmodum potuerunt huius uitae
inueniri, si non in matrimonio constitutae tales fuerint? et osten-
15 dens quamobrem etiam aetatem designauit secundum quam illas
in ordine uiduarum recipi praecepit, adiecit:

iueniores autem uiduas deuita.

non quia non sit digna iuuentus et exequi uirtutem, sed quam
ob causam id dixerit in subsequentibus pandit:
20 *cum enim luxuriatae fuerint in Christo, nubere uolunt, habentes
dampnationem, quia primam fidem inritam fecerunt.*

bene 'luxuriatas in Christo' dixit; hoc est:

†'atubi inter uiduas fuerint re-
ceptae [et] ecclesiasticum adse-
25 cutae fuerint sumptum, securae
extantes super corporalibus necessitatibus, nihil aliud curant
nisi quae otiose uacent luxuriae
corporali, eo quod non habent
30 de quibus sollicitae sint; quae
etiam solent et intellectum humiliare humanum. otiosae uero
effectae, despicientes professio-

ἐπειδὰν ταῖς χήραις ἐγκαταλεγῶ-
σιν τῆς ἐκκλησίας καὶ ἀξιωθῶσιν
ἐπιμελείας, πρὸς στρήνους ἐντεῦθεν
χειραγωγηθεῖσαι τῷ μηδὲν ἔχειν
ὅπερ μεριμνῶσαι ταπεινοῦσθαι δύ-
νανται τὴν διάνοιαν, μακρὸν χαίρειν
εἰποῦσαι τῇ οἰκείᾳ ἐπαγγελίᾳ με-
λετῶσιν γάμον, ἀμερίμνως τὰ τῆς
χρείας ποριζόμεναι.

1 adicit *C r* ‖ sq. Coisl. 204, *l. c.* 11 tales *C* H r* ‖ esse c. *H* 12
quod *C* H* 13 poterint *C (corr.)* 15 designauerit *r* 16 praecepit *H* 17
iuniores *H* adolescentiores *r* 18 et *om C r* 23 sq. Coisl. 204, f. 205 b [Cr.
vii. 40] ἄλλος δέ φησιν· ἐπειδάν, κ.τ.λ. 24 et *om C H r: txt l* 24-25 conse-
cutae *l* 27 μεριμνῶσι Cr. 28 quod (*for* quae) *C (corr.)* ut *r* 30 after γάμον
the catenist adds καὶ τὰ λεχθέντα ἐφεξῆς διαπράττονται.

†he added this, to show that they ought to be received in hospitality with the greatest care*

and that they ought not despise anything pertaining to honorable deference.

He added this to show that they ought to welcome them with care.

5:10e *if she has assisted those suffering affliction,*

Again, he said in a summary fashion:

5:10f *if she has followed every good work.*

It is clear that he urges those things to be done according to the nature of their resources, and it is certain because of these words that he wants the widows to be faithful the way they are in marriage. For Paul, who says that widows ought to have lived such a life, wishes them to accomplish the same things they did when they were married. Otherwise, how could they be found [163] in this life, if they had not been settled as such women in marriage? And to show why he also designated the age at which he instructed them to be admitted to the order of widows, he added:

5:11a *But avoid the younger widows;*

Not because youth is not worthy also of pursuing virtue, but for the reason he discloses in what he goes on to say:

5:11b-12 *for when they have luxuriated in Christ, they want to marry, having condemnation, because they have made first faith ineffectual.*

He rightly said *luxuriated in Christ*, that is:

†"Whenever they were admitted among the widows and would acquire the expenditure of the church, existing freed from bodily needs, they would care for nothing else save to be free in idleness for bodily luxury because they would have nothing to be concerned about; and this usually lowers human understanding. And when they become leisured, despising their profession, they begin to think about marriage,*

Whenever they are put on the list of widows and considered worthy of the church's care, since they would be provided with their bodily needs without anxiety, they would be led for this reason to wanton behavior, because they would have nothing that could bring them in their anxiety to humble themselves in understanding. And becoming idle, they at length bid farewell to their own promise and think about marriage, since they are furnished their

nem suam, de nuptiis incipiunt
cogitare,*
grauissime se obnoxias facientes ea ratione qua promissum suum
quod Christum promiserunt spernendum esse existimauerunt,
5 primam duntaxat fidem inritam facientes.' nec autem de nuptiis
ista dixit, sicut quidam a multa desipientia suspicati sunt, sed de
professione dixit uiduitatis; quia nec fas erat ut dampnationi obnoxias diceret illas quae illud faciunt quod ille fieri uisus est ad-
nuisse. et otiositatis ipsius malitiam explanans adiecit:
10   *simul autem et otiosae discunt circuire domos, non solum autem
otiosae sed et uerbosae et curiosae, loquentes quae non conueniunt.*
hoc uult per ista omnia dicere, quoniam nullam habentes sollicitudinem corporalium dum securae adsequuntur illa quae usui
sunt necessaria, discunt et ex ipsa largitate studere otiositati; nec
15 autem est ulla res quae illas possit ultra ad opus cohortari. otiosae
uero extantes uacant erga uerbositatem, et properant horum dicta
ad illos deferre et illorum ad istos; et ex hoc adnascuntur tristitiae,
dum de alienis curiose agentes, loqui illa student quae loqui minime oportet. ob hanc igitur causam significauit in superioribus
20 et aetatem et mores, statuens ut quae erga studia uirtutum curam
non impendunt ecclesiastico sumptu minime nutriantur. nam illae quae in iuuentute adhuc tales sunt debent erga uictum corporis
sollicitudinem expendere, eo quod possit talis sollicitudo etiam erga studium pietatis illis multum prodesse, eo quod ipsa sollicitudo
25 alimentorum potest eas a nimia uanitate coercere, et ut cogitatum
suum humiliantes de se sint sollicitae. propter hoc neque de presbyteris neque de diaconibus dicens aetatis est memoratus, sed de
uiduis tantum, quae se ob illam causam quam dixi in ordine uiduarum adscribi deproperant. ostendit uero et causam ob quam
30 iuniores uiduas praeceperat minime recipi; non quia non sit fidelis et utilis iuuentus ad studia uirtutum, sed quia non competenter

---

4 quem (*for* quod) *C* H r* ‖ Christo *C* (*corr.*) ‖ promis. Chr. *r* 6
dissipientia *C* H* 8 illi *r* 9 ipsius *om H* ‖ adicit *C r* 10 autem *om*
r ‖ circumire *C r* 13 temporalium (*for* corp.) *l* ‖ diu (*for* dum) *C**
‖ sui (*for* usui) *C** 14 et *om r* 16 uerbositati (*for* erga u.) *r* 17 illas *C*
r ‖ istas *r* 18 ad (*for* de) *H** ‖ eloqui *r* 19 signauit *H* 22 in (*bef.*
iuuent.) *om C* ‖ tales *C** 23 sollicito *C** 27 aetates *H* 29 et *om C*
(*corr.*) *r* 30 uiduas *om r*

needs without anxiety.[52]

making themselves in the most serious possible way liable to punishment, on the grounds that [164] they have thought their own promise to Christ one to be spurned, making at least their first faith ineffectual." But he has not said these things about marriage, as some people quite foolishly have suspected; instead, he spoke of the profession of widowhood. This is because it would not have been right for him to say that those who did what he has plainly allowed done were liable to condemnation. And to explain the wickedness of idleness itself, he added:

5:13 And at the same time also being idle, they learn how to make a circuit of houses, and not only idle but also garrulous and inquisitive, speaking what is not fitting.

By all this he wants to say that because they have no anxiety about bodily needs as long as they are secure in gaining what is necessary for their use, they learn from the very largess how to occupy themselves with idleness; nor is there anything that can any longer encourage them to work. But since they are idle, they are free to be garrulous, and they are eager to retail what these said to those and what those said to these. Ill feelings arise from this as long as by behaving inquisitively about strangers they occupy themselves with speaking what by no means ought to be spoken. Therefore, it is for this reason that Paul has indicated above both the age and the habits, setting down the rule that women who devote no care to the pursuits of the virtues are by no means to be nourished at the expense of the church. Now the women who are still young are such as ought to expend care for the sustenance of the body, because such care can also be of much profit to them for the zealous pursuit of true religion, since care for provision can itself [165] restrain them from too much vanity, so that, as well, by humbling their thoughts they may be careful about themselves. For this reason neither in the case of presbyters nor in that of deacons has he mentioned age, but only in the case of widows, who for the reason I have mentioned are eager to be enrolled in the order of widows. And he has also shown why he had instructed that younger widows should by no means be accepted—not because youth may not be faithful and useful for the pursuits of the virtues, but because many of them are seen

---

[52] Following Swete's conjectural reconstruction of the Greek (2:163).

multae earum id exequi uidentur; simulant et autem se persistere
in uiduitate spe illa sola ut ecclesiastico sumptu nutriantur.

*uolo ergo iuniores uiduas nubere, filios procreare, matresfamilias es-
se.*

5   quare? ut iuuentutis impetus erga plurimam sollicitudinem,
sed occupatae, possit compescere. hoc autem erat non ut iuueniores uiduas a uirtutum studiis excluderet, sed ut magis eas inuitaret.
qui enim dixerat non oportere illas quae nec aetate nec uirtutibus
sunt uestitae in ordine recipi uiduarum illarum quae ecclesiasti-
10 co sumptu aluntur, ista uero dicens praeparabat eas ut id non adtemptarent. conuenienter—dicta enim illius illa cupit per omnia
confirmare ut illa quae oportent custodiant. unde ne uideretur ad
plenum deuitare iuueniores uiduas quae caute uitam suam insti-
tuunt, sequitur:

15   *nullam occasionem dare aduersario maledictionis gratia.*

'non enim uolo illas ob illam causam uiduitatem simulantes,
postea in aliis inueniri, et ex hoc dare occasionem illis qui nobis de-
rogare properant ob illam rationem qua uitae nostrae nullum studium adhibemus, sed specie tantum uirtutem nos exequi simula-
20 mus.' et ut ne uideatur ipse suspicione id colligere, causam ipsam
ponit et dicit:

iam enim quaedam conuersae sunt post Satanan.

sic uidetur modis omnibus illas quae non bene abutuntur ipsam uiduitatem excludere ab ordine uiduarum, omnem dissimu-
25 lationis occasionem ab ipsa adimens professione. nam et ridiculo
dignum uidetur [in] uirginitatem recipere, si quis eandem profiteri uelit, sicut est id perspicere ex epistola eius quam ad Corinthios scripsisse uidetur, illas uero adolescentulas quae uiris sunt
priuatae non recepisse, [si] tamen uiduitatem ut conuenit studere

---

3 autem (*for* ergo) *H*   6   sed (*bef.* occup.) *om r l*   ‖   occupatus *r*   ‖   possint *l*   6-7 iuniores *H r*   9   uirtute (*for* uestitae) *C* H* ornatae *C* (*corr.*) *r*
‖   ordinem *r*   11   illas (*for* illius) *H*   12   oportet *r*   ‖   non (*for* ne) *r*   13
iuniores *r*   14   adiecit (*for* sequitur) *H*   15   maledicti *r*   18   quia (*for* qua) *r*
22   conuersa est *C H* conuersae sunt retro Sathanam *r*   23-24   utuntur ipsa
uiduitate *r*   24-25   desim. occansionem *C**   25   risu (*for* ridiculo) *r*   26   in
om C H r   ‖   qua (*for* quis) *H*   27   exempla (*for* ex ep.) *H*   29   tamen (*om*
si) *C H* tamen si *r*

unsuitable for being placed on this level. And they pretend that they will persist in widowhood only in the hope that they may be nourished at the expense of the church.

5:14a *Therefore, I want the younger widows to marry, to beget children, and to be mothers of households,*

Why? So that the vigorous impulse of youth toward quite anxious care, at least when the young women are occupied in these pursuits, can be restrained. But this was not so that he might exclude the younger widows from the pursuits of the virtues, but so that he might all the more attract them to this. For he had said that it was not right for those women who were clothed neither with age nor with virtues to be admitted to the order of those widows supported at the expense of the church. But by saying those things he was preparing them not to attempt this unfittingly.[53] For he wants his words in all respects to confirm them in keeping what they ought to do. Then, so that he might not seem completely to avoid the younger widows who order their life carefully, he goes on:

[166] 5:14b *to give no opportunity to the adversary for the sake of abuse.*

"For I do not want them by making a pretense of widowhood for that reason[54] to be found afterwards in other things and by this to give an opportunity to those who are eager to slander us on the grounds that we apply no zeal to our life but only in appearance are pretending that we are pursuing virtue." And so that he may not seem to be deducing this himself by what he suspected, he puts down the cause itself and says:

5:15 *For already some women have turned away after Satan.*

Thus, in every way he plainly excluded from the order of widows those women who do not use their widowhood rightly, taking away from their profession every opportunity for dissimulation. Indeed, it would also seem ridiculous to admit to virginity anyone who should want to profess it, just as one can see this from the letter Paul is seen to have written to the Corinthians (see 1 Cor 7:8, 25–26), while not admitting those young girls deprived of a husband, if at least they were willing to occupy themselves with wi-

---

[53] Following Swete's suggested revision of the punctuation (2:165): "*adtemptarent. conuenienter, &c.*] Read perhaps *adtemptarent inconuenienter; dicta, &c.*"

[54] That is, in order to be supported by the church.

uoluerint. nec autem illae quae uirginitatem profitentur post senectutem erint uirginitatem professurae. iustum est hoc in loco
memorare illorum qui omne studium in eo ponunt ut a nuptiis ex-
cludant, qui et diuersa facere conantur ut aliquos in hac professio-
5 ne adducant. a quibus negotiis tantum uidetur Paulus distare, ut
et ab ipsa professione prohibeat tamdiu quamdiu quis [non] plurimam uirtutis diligentiam in conuersatione sua ostendit. deinde
adiecit et aliud:
   si quis fidelis habet uiduas, subministret eis, ut non grauetur eccle-
10 *sia.*
   est: sicuti enim in superioribus de illis dixit quae habent filios
aut nepotes, ut ab illis nutriantur; sic et hoc in loco eos qui fideles
habent in domibus suis uiduas uult ut diligentiam illis adhibeant,
ita ut ecclesia non multam sollicitudinem de talibus sustineret. et
15 ut ne uideatur hoc idem lege statuere, ut tali occasione hi qui praesunt ecclesiis pecunias possint colligere, securi extantes a multitudine et sollicitudine uiduarum quibus necessaria praestent, bene
adiecit:
   ut his quae uerae sunt uiduae sufficiat.
20 'ueras uiduas' dicit illas quae ex omni parte sunt desolatae et
neminem habent qui diligentiam illis adhibeat. sic enim poterat
illarum facere prouidentiam ecclesia quae desolatae sunt, quando
non multarum sollicitudinem [habebat] sed paucarum, auxilianti-
bus eis ad hoc fidelibus, si tamen praebere ualuerint ex opibus suis.
25 illis uero uiduis quas in domos proprias singuli habent, prouisionem illis facere adhortatur; si autem matrem habent aut auiam,
propter summam propinquitatem pro uirium suarum qualitate diligentiam illis adhibeant.
   tanta super alendis uiduis disputans, quia in superioribus dixe-
30 rat quales esse conueniat presbyteros, de obsequiis uero eorum uel
alimentis nihil fuerat memoratus, et quidem illis ipsis secundum
illud tempus sollicitudinem ecclesiarum implentibus; bene adiecit

---

3 omni studio *H*   5 Pauli sermo (*for* Paulus) *r*   6 donec (*for* quamdiu) *r*
‖ qui (*for* quis) *H* (*corr.*)   ‖ non *om C H r*   7 uirtutes *C** uirtutem *H r*   ‖
ostendat *C* (*corr.*) *r*   8 adicit *C*   9 si quis f. uel si qua f. *r*   ‖ illis (*for* eis) *r*
‖ et (*for* ut) *r*   11 etenim sicuti (*for* est sicuti enim in) *r*   12 nutrientur *C**
H   14 solitudinem (*for* sollic.) *C**   ‖ sustinere *C** H* sustinere cogatur *C*
(*corr.*)   18 adicit *C r*   19 uere *H*   ‖ uid. sunt *r*   20 desolutae *C**   23
habebat *om C H r*   26 aut (*for* autem) *r*   32 adicit *C r*

dowhood as is right.[55] And neither would those women who profess virginity have professed virginity after old age. It is right in this place to call to mind those people who put all their zeal in the effort to exclude people from marriage and who try different ways of leading some others to this profession of virginity. Paul plainly stands so far apart from these matters that he even forbids from this profession [167] anyone as long as he fails to show great care for virtue in his way of life. Then he added another point:

5:16a *If any faithful man has widows, let him assist them, so that the church may not be burdened,*

That is, just as above he spoke of those women who have children or grandchildren so as to be nourished by them (5:4), so also in this place he wants those who have faithful widows in their households to apply diligent care to them so that the church may not incur much care for such women. And lest he seem to be laying this down by law so that by such an opportunity those in charge of the churches might be able to collect money, since they would be freed from caring for a multitude of widows whose needs they would supply, he rightly added:

5:16b *so that it may provide for those who are true widows.*

By *true widows* he means those who are in every way left alone and have no one who may apply diligent care to them. For in this way the church was able to oversee those women who were left alone, since it had the care not of many but of few, because the faithful helped it in this task, at least if they were willing to give help from their own means. And he exhorts the individuals who have widows in their own households to make provision for them, and if they have a mother or grandmother, to apply diligent care to them so far as their resources permit because they are their closest relations.

While discussing important matters concerning the support of widows, because above (3:2–7) [168] he had said what sort of people ought to be presbyters but had made no mention of what was due them or of their support, even though they were fulfilling the care of the churches at that time, he rightly added about them:

---

[55] Theodore appears to be arguing that the age limit of sixty should not be regarded as a fixed rule but only as a caution against accepting the younger widows.

et de his:

qui bene praesunt presbyteri, duplici honore digni habeantur.

'duplicem' dicens multiplicem dicit. nam 'presbyteros (inquit) etiam maioris prouisionis dignos oportere existimare iusta depo-
5   scit ratio.' unde et adiecit: *qui bene praesunt.* sed nec de illorum prouidentia absolute dixit, qui in ordine et gradu tantum sunt pre-sbyterorum; sed de illis qui gradus sui functionem implere prout conuenit uidentur. unde et adiecit:

maxime qui laborant in uerbo et doctrina.

10   non absolute hos dignos esse prouidentia dixit, sed illa ratione qua plurimum laborem expendant, si tamen ut conuenit doctrinae opus implere uoluerint, ita ut in commune de omnibus sollicitu-dinem impendant, ac doceant eos illa facere quae fieri oportent; et ut de singulis solliciti, multum habeant agonem ut unumquem-
15   que consiliis optimis et exhortationibus ad illud quod decens est adducant. sic enim et beati apostoli uidentur doctrinae opus om-nibus operibus anteposuisse. unde et contemplatione uiduarum aliquando oborta controuersia, dixerunt 'non esse dignum relin-quentes se uerbum doctrinae ministrare mensis' uiduarum; quod
20   doctrinae opus sibi magis decere existimabant. uolens autem et scripturarum testimonio apostolus comprobare de presbyteris illa quae dixerat, adserens *qui maxime laborant in doctrina,* adiecit:

dicit enim scriptura, 'boui trituranti os non alligabis'; et, 'dignus est operarius mercede sua.'

25   haec diligentia debite praebenda illis dicens, adiecit:

aduersus presbyterum accusationem noli suscipere, exceptis duobus aut tribus testibus.

omni demiratione dignus est apostolus, quia et super hoc nego-tio sollicitus fuit. nam et dictum fuerat generaliter: *in ore duorum*
30   *et trium testium stabit omnis sermo.* sed hoc in loco contrario ab-dicans accusationem, dixit autem: *noli suscipere nisi coram duobus aut tribus testibus.* eo quod super ceteris interea res patitur ut et

---

3   intellegit (*for* dicit) *r*   4   existimari *C* (*corr.*)   5   adicit *r*   8   adicit *C r*   12
in communi *C* r*   13   oportet *r*   18   aborta *H* [*cf.* 1. p. 197, *l.* 7, *vv. Il.*]
|| contentione (*for* controuersia) *H r*   18-19   relinquere et ministrare *C* (*corr.*)
19   menses *H*   20   se (*for* sibi) *r*   21   testimonia *H*   22   laborent *C* H* ||
adicit *C r*   23   non infrenabis os boui trit. *r*   25   adicit *C r*   26   recipere *r*
|| nisi sub (*for* exc.) *r*   30   omne verbum *H*   31   autem *om C* (*corr.*) || nisi
om r

5:17a *The presbyters who preside well, let them be held worthy of double honor,*

By saying *double* he means multiple. For "just reason (he says) demands that we must think the presbyters worthy of still greater provision." This is why he added *who preside well.* He was not speaking without qualification of providing for those who are merely in the order and rank of presbyters but of those seen to fulfill the service of their rank as far as they ought. For this reason he added:

5:17b *especially those who toil in word and in teaching,*

He said that they were worthy of provision not without qualification, but because they expend a great deal of toil, if at any rate they are willing to fulfill the work of teaching fittingly, so that they may devote great care to all in common and may teach them what ought to be done, and so that in caring for individuals they may struggle hard to lead each one by the best counsels and exhortations to what is becoming. For in this way the blessed apostles plainly have put the work of teaching before all works. This is why when a controversy once arose with respect to widows, they said (Acts 6:1–2) that it was not right for them to leave the word of teaching to minister [169] to the tables of widows, because they thought the work of teaching more becoming to them. And the apostle, wishing to prove by the testimony of the scriptures what he has said about the presbyters by asserting *especially those who toil in teaching*, added:

5:18 *for scripture says* (Deut 25:4; 1 Cor 9:9) *"You shall not bind the mouth of a treading ox"* and *"the worker is worthy of his pay"* (Luke 10:7).

Saying that careful attention ought to be paid to these statements, he added:

5:19 *Do not accept an accusation against a presbyter, two or three witnesses excepted.*

The apostle is worthy of all admiration because he was concerned about this matter. For it had been said in a general way (Deut 19:15): *in the mouth of two or three witnesses every word will stand.* In contrast, in this place it is to refuse an accusation that he said: *do not accept it unless in the presence of two or three witnesses.*[56] This is because in other cases [170] the fact is in one way or

---

[56] See Swete's comment (2:169): "The rule is positive; the Apostle uses it

aliter de negotio iudicetur; hoc uero in loco non debere ita fieri ob
duas posuit causas. una, quoniam necesse est presbyterum utpote communem patrem tam uirorum quam mulierum curam adhibere; eo quod et similiter utriusque sexus sollicitudinem implens
indiscrete et mulieres cogitur uidere et loqui cum illis, prout ratio
exigit pietatis. altera uero causa, eo quod multis et uariis occasionibus diuerse contra eos exercebantur, ea ratione qua idem presbyteri coacti interdum increpant obnoxios pro admissis peccatis,
et arguunt eos pro quibus non competenter agunt. prospexit ergo apostolus quoniam facile aduersus presbyteros ab huiusmodi
hominibus accusationes adnasci possint, opitulante eis opere ipsorum ut id quod uolunt aduersus eos dicere uerissimum existimetur, propter quod licenter uel uideant uel loquantur cum mulieribus; quae res malignis hominibus occasionem accusationis dare
uidetur. quid ergo obseruari decernit? 'aliter (inquit) noli audire,
nisi duo aut tres uideantur testes esse negotii ipsius de quibus in-
tenditur accusatio.' et ut ne uideretur ista dicens delinquentium
peccata uelle contegere, adiecit:

    peccantes autem coram omnibus arguantur, ut et ceteri timorem
habeant.

    'examen negotii de illis cum omni scrupulositate uolo fieri, et
non absolute aduersus eos crimen adpinctum recipi. si uero aliqui uera ratione deliquisse fuerint detecti, aperte increpentur, ut
et ceteri eorum exemplo pudici efficiantur.' optime autem et ad
aliorum correctionem edixit; nec enim erat necessarium ut hoc ita
fieret, nisi ob aliorum id fieret emendationem. deinde omnibus illis dicens terribiliter adiecit:

    testificor in conspectu Dei et domini Iesu Christi et electorum ange-
lorum, ut haec custodias sine ullo praeiudicio, nihil faciens secundum
declinationem.

3 commune *H*   7 diuersae [accusationes] *r* (*edd*)   8 delictis [deliciis *ed.*]
(*for* peccatis) *l*   10 quam (*for* quoniam) *l* ‖ ad (*for* ab) *H*   11 operum *H*
12 uerissima existimatur *C* H* uerissime existimetur *C* (*corr.*) uerissima existimatur accusatio *r*   13 uid. mul. uel loquantur cum eis *r*   14 occansionem
occansionis *C* occasionem occasionem *H*: *txt r*   16 sine (*for* nisi) *H**   18 adicit *C r*   19 inquit (*for* autem) *C*: *om r* ‖ argue *r*   22 ad punctum *C* (*corr.*) *r*
[*cf. p.* 145, *l.* 15, *vv. ll. and note*]   24 efficientur *C* H* ‖ optimae *H* ‖ ad
om r   25 haec dixit (*for* edixit) *C* (*corr.*) esse dixit *r*   26 ab ... emendatione
C* H ob ... emendatione *C* (*corr.*) *r* ‖ id *om r*   27 adicit *C r*   29 ullo *om*
r ‖ praeiudicii *H*

another disclosed so that a judgment is made about the affair some other way. But in this place he affirmed it should not be done this way for two reasons. One reason is that it is necessary for a presbyter as the common father to apply care to both men and women, and because in fulfilling his care alike to both sexes without distinction he is obliged to see women and to speak with them so far as the principle of true religion requires. And the other reason is because in many different circumstances people were agitated in various ways against them on the grounds that now and then presbyters were compelled to reproach those accountable for sins they had committed and to rebuke them for unsuitable behavior. Therefore, the apostle anticipated that accusations from people of this kind could easily arise against presbyters, since their work served to make it thought that what those people wanted to say against the presbyters was quite true. This is because of the fact that presbyters either see or speak with women unrestrainedly, something that seems to give spiteful people an opportunity to make accusations. What practice, then, does he determine should be observed? "Do not listen (he says) in any other way, unless there are seen to be two or three witnesses of the matter concerning which the accusation is submitted." And lest he seem to be saying that he was willing to cover up the sins of transgressors, he added:

[171] 5:20 *And let those who sin be rebuked in the presence of all, so that also the rest may have fear.*

"I want the examination of the affair concerning them to be made with all exactness and the charges drawn up against them not to be accepted simply as such. But if some have for true reason been exposed as having transgressed, let them be openly reproached so that the rest may be brought to shame by their example." And quite effectively he declared this for setting other people right. For it would not have been necessary for this to be done this way unless it were to take place for the amendment of others. Then with words designed to strike fear in all of them, he added:

5:21 *I testify in the sight of God and the Lord Jesus Christ and the elect angels that you keep these things without any prejudice, doing*

---

here, however, to point a prohibition. In other cases it is expedient to have two witnesses at the least; in this case it is essential." Witnesses are necessary not merely to assess the charge but also for making it in the first place.

scilicet: 'ut non facile contemplatione odii aduersus aliquem pronunties, priusquam uera ratione conuincantur; neque e contrario contemplatione amicitiarum aliquorum occulta peccata'— hoc autem dicit *nihil faciens per declinationem.* nam huiusmodi conte-
5 statio in talibus negotiis admodum est necessaria. deinde aduertitur ad eum, dans ei consilium:

manus cito nemini inposueris.

'omnino non facile ad ordinationem quemquam producas sine plurima probatione.' et pondus ipsius negotii graue ostendens,
10 adiecit:

neque communicaueris peccatis alienis.

'si (inquit) te ut conuenit probante ille deliquerit, non est tuum crimen; si uero tu facile et non cum cauta probatione ad ordinationem producis, particeps efficeris eius delictorum. ille enim pro
15 quibus [peccauit], iusta ratione punietur; tu uero, pro quibus non caute gessisti, nec perfectam arbitrii eius colligens probationem ad ministerium eum produxisti.' et adhuc in timorem eum redigens adiecit:

teipsum castum custodi.
20 deinde et illa quae de eo erant dicit:

noli (inquit) *ulterius aquam bibere, sed uino modico utere propter stomachum tuum et frequentes tuas infirmitates.*

euidens est quoniam et super hoc consilium illi dat, eo quod ualde infirmum eum corpore esse perspiciebat; contemplatione
25 autem continentiae adhuc aquam bibere persistebat. et quia frequenter aliorum causa talia agimus ut ne uideamur indifferentes esse erga conuersationem, non ignorantes quoniam illa quae ad usum nobis uel facta sunt uel tributa nequaquam nos insumpta potuerint nocere, bene adiecit:
30 *quorundam hominum peccata manifesta sunt, praecedentia in iudicium; quosdam autem et subsequuntur. similiter et bona opera ma-*

---

2 conuincatur *r* ‖ e contr. *r*   3 amicorum *r* ‖ occulte *C** occultes *C* (*corr.*) *r*   5-6 uestitur *r*   6 dando *r* ‖ ei *om H* ‖ et ait (*aft* cons.) add *r*   8 omnium (*for* omnino) *C H*   10 adicit *C r*   15 peccauit *om C H r*   16 cauta egessisti *C** cautae egess. *C* (*corr.*) cautae gessisti *H* caute egisti *r* ‖ ne (*for* nec) *H*   17 timore *H*   18 adicit *C r*   19 cust. cast. *r*   21 inquit *om r* ‖ adhuc (*for* ult.) *r*   22 tuos *C**   25 autem *om H*   29 poterunt *r* ‖ adicit *C r*: txt *H l*   30 ad (*for* in) *r*   31 facta bona (*for* b. op.) *r*

nothing according to inclination.

Evidently, "that you may not render a verdict against anyone easily because of hatred before they have been convicted for true reason; nor, on the contrary, should sins be hidden for the sake of friendship for any." This is what he means by *doing nothing by inclination.* Indeed, a solemn declaration of this kind is still necessary in such matters. Then he turns his attention to Timothy, giving him advice:

5:22a *May you put your hands on no one hastily,*

"In no circumstance may you advance anyone easily to ordination [172] without a good deal of testing." And to show the weightiness of the matter, he added:

5:22b *nor may you share in alien sins.*

"If (he says) that person has transgressed, even though you examine him fittingly, it is not your fault. But if you advance him to ordination easily and without careful examination, you would become a participant in his transgressions. For he will be punished for his sins with just reason; but you, because you have not acted carefully, nor have you advanced him to the ministry by assembling a complete examination." And still further reducing him to fear, he added:

5:22c *Keep yourself chaste.*

Then he speaks of what particularly concerns Timothy:

5:23 *Do not* (he says) *any longer drink water, but use a little wine because of your stomach and your frequent ailments.*

It is clear that he gives him advice also about this because he saw that he was quite weak in his body. And he was still persisting to drink water for the sake of continence. And because we often do such things for the sake of others, so that we may not seem indifferent to their way of life, and not because we are unaware that what has been made or given for our use could by no means harm us by its consumption, he rightly added:

5:24–25 *The sins of some people are obvious, going before to judgment, but they also follow some people. Likewise, good works are*

nifesta sunt, et quae se aliter habent abscondi non possunt.

†uult dicere quoniam sicut
delinquentium hominum et non
recte uiuentium delicta manifesta sunt, quae necessarie illis
in futuro saeculo poenas sunt
prouisura, licet si et faciant aliqua quae multos latere poterunt; sic et de illis qui recte uiuere instituerunt, plurima
quidem illorum manifesta sunt
hominibus, sunt etiam et aliqua
quae lateant multos—haec enim
significat dicens *similiter et quae
se aliter habent*—nec enim possunt omnia incerta esse. 'itaque
ne hoc pertimescas ne quando
non bonam hinc opinionem ad-
quiras, teipsum aquae potu ex-
pendens; utere uero exiguo uino pro ipsa infirmitatis necessitate, ualde sciens quoniam et
illa quae homines coniciunt, si
tamen recte uiuamus, bona esse
plurima ex parte perspicientur;
nec ullam ex his nociuitatem su-
stinebimus, licet uideantur multi actus nostri a multis ignora-
ri.'*

post hoc adiecit et de seruis:

βούλεται εἰπεῖν ὅτι ὥσπερ τὰ
τῶν οὐκ εὖ βιούντων ἀνθρώπων
πταίσματα πρόδηλά ἐστιν ἀναγκαίως τὴν ἐπὶ τοῦ μέλλοντος αἰῶνος τιμωρίαν αὐτοῖς ἐπάγοντα, εἰ
καὶ (ὡς εἰκὸς) τινὰ παρ' αὐτῶν
λανθάνει τοὺς πολλούς· οὕτως καὶ
ἐπὶ τῶν εὐσεβούντων τὰ πολλὰ μὲν
πρόδηλα τοῖς ἀνθρώποις ἐστίν· ὅσα
δέ ἐστιν λανθάνοντα τοὺς πολλοὺς
(ταῦτα γὰρ λέγει τὰ ἄλλως ἔχοντα) οὐχ οἷόν τε πάντα ἄδηλα εἶναι.
'ὥστε (φησὶν) μὴ τοῦτο δεδιὼς μὴ
οὐ χρηστὴν ἐντεῦθεν παρὰ τοῖς ἀνθρώποις ὑπόληψιν κτήσῃ, τῇ ὑδρο-
ποσίᾳ σαυτὸν κατανάλισκε·' εἰδὼς
ὅτι καὶ ἡ παρὰ τοῖς ἀνθρώποις ὑπό-
ληψις, ἐὰν ἡμεῖς κατὰ τὸ προσῆκον βιῶμεν, κατά γε τὸ πλεῖστον
καλλίστη γίνεται, οὐδὲν ἀπὸ τούτων
παραβλαπτομένη, κἂν δοκῇ πολλὰ
τῶν καθ' ἡμᾶς τοὺς πολλοὺς λαν-
θάνειν.

1 ascendi *C** 2 sicut *om r* ‖ sq. Coisl. 204, f. 207 b [Cr. vii. 44] θεόδωρος.
ἄλλος δὲ πάλιν φησίν· βούλεται, κ.τ.λ. 4-5 manifestata *l* 4 δῆλα cod. Cr.
5 necessario *C* (*corr.*) necessaria *H* necessarias *r* 6 pene (*for* poenas) *C H*:
txt *r l* 8-9 poterint *C* (*corr.*) 11 manifestata *l* 25 prospicientur *r* 27
uideant *H* 28-29 ignorare *C** *H* 30 haec *H* ‖ adicit *C r*

also obvious, and the things that are otherwise cannot be hidden.

[173] †He wants to say that, just as the transgressions of people who transgress and do not live uprightly are obvious because they will necessarily provide them with punishments in the age to come, even though they do some things that can escape the notice of many, so, too, as to the deeds of those who have decided to live uprightly, a great many of them are obvious to people, while there are others that escape the notice of many (for he indicates this by saying *likewise … and the things that are otherwise*), yet not all of them can be unclear. "And so do not be afraid that you may acquire a bad reputation when you dispense yourself from drinking water, but use a small amount of wine for the very necessity of your weakness, knowing that people's conjectures, if at any rate we live uprightly, are perceived to be good for the most part; nor will we suffer any harm from them, even though much of what we do is ignored by many."*[57]

He wants to say that, just as the transgressions of people who do not live well are obvious because they necessarily bring punishment on them in the age to come, even if, as is likely, some of their deeds escape the notice of many, so, too, in the case of those who are godly many things are obvious to people. But whatever deeds escape the notice of many (for this is what he means by *the things that are otherwise*), it is impossible that all should be unclear. "So (he says), not fearing that you may acquire from this a bad reputation with people, dispense yourself from drinking water."

He knows that our reputation with people, if we live as we ought, is for the most part the best possible and brings us no harm from them, even if many of the things that have to do with us seem to escape the notice of many.

[174] After this he added comments about slaves:

[57]Theodore appears to be puzzled about 5:24–25, particularly because these verses seem to have little connection with the context. His unusual attempt to connect them with verse 23 revolves around the idea that bad and good deeds are in the present partly known and partly unknown. Perhaps what he means is that Paul is advising Timothy to take a little wine and not be afraid that this will offend people who fail to perceive doing so as a good deed.

si qui sub iugo sunt serui, dominos suos omni honore dignos esse exi-
stiment; ut non nomen Dei et doctrina blasphemetur.

haec de illis scribit qui infideles habent dominos, praecipiens
eis ut omne obsequium suis praebeant dominis, licet si sint a pieta-
5 te alieni; ut non hinc blasphemia aliqua Deo aut pietatis doctrinae
adpingatur, existimantibus illis quod ita eos instituamus ut contempnant dominos suos. quoniam autem de illis seruis dicit qui
infideles dominos habent euidens est et ex quibus dixit: *ut ne doc-*
trina Dei hinc blasphemetur. manifestius uero id ostenditur et ex
10 illis quae sequuntur; adiecit enim:

qui autem fideles habent dominos non contempnant, quoniam fra-
tres sunt; sed magis seruiant, quoniam fideles sunt et dilecti qui bene-
ficiorum sunt participes.

'iustum (inquit), est ut et hi non contemplatione pietatis suos
15 contempnant dominos qui benigne cum illis agunt, sed multo magis debent eis seruire quasi fidelibus, qui et diligi propter ipsud debent ab eis, et illa uel maxime causa qua benigne illis utuntur. hoc
enim dicit *qui beneficiorum sunt participes:* hoc est, 'qui beneficiis
eos subleuare properant contemplatione pietatis quam exequun-
20 tur.' igitur dominorum benignitas non debet seruis occasio fieri
contemptus, sed magis eos in affectu ampliori debet retinere. et
iterum adiecit:

haec doce et obsecra.

per omnia exsuscitans eum ut cum multa sollicitudine de omni-
25 bus his doctrinam proponere deproperet. et quoniam omnia per-
currit quae ad correctionem ecclesiae in commune conuenire existimabat, sicut scrupulosius significauimus in illis quae antea in-
terpretati sumus; memoratur iterum et de illis qui contraria pietatis docere conantur. dicit autem de illis qui ex circumcisione credi-
30 derunt, qui omnia agere adnitebantur uolentes legis custodiam fidelibus inponere; de quibus et in principio epistolae plurima dixe-

---

1 si quis *H* quicumque *r*   ‖   dign. o. h. exist, ne *i* (*see note*)   2   arbitrentur
ne n. domini *r*   4   si *om C r i*   5   aliquando (*for* al. Deo) *H*   ‖   uituperium
(*bef.* piet.) *add r*   8   nec (*for* ne) *C*   10   adicit *C r*   11-12   quia (*for* quoniam) *r*   12   dil. benef. sunt participes *C** d. b. qui sunt participes *C* (*corr.*) d.
b. participes sunt *H* d. b. sunt participes *r*   14   est et hos *C H* est ut et hos *r*   ‖
templatione (*for* cont.) *H*   ‖   ut (*bef.* suos) *add C* (*corr.*)   17   de (*bef.* causa)
add r   20   serui *C*   21   contemptibile *C H*   ‖   debent *H*   22   adicit *C r*
28   memoratus *H*   29   enim (*for* autem) *r*

6:1 *If there are slaves under the yoke, let them think that their own masters are worthy of all honor, so that the name of God and the teaching may not be slandered.*

He is writing this about those who have unbelieving masters, instructing them to furnish all obedience to their masters, even though they are strangers to true religion, so that in this way no slander may be drawn up against God or the teaching of true religion by people supposing we have instructed them to despise their masters. And the fact that he is speaking of those slaves who have unbelieving masters is clear because he said: *so that the teaching of God may not be slandered for this reason.*[58] And this is demonstrated more clearly by what follows, for he added:

6:2a *And those who have believing masters, let them not despise them since they are brothers, but let them serve all the more, since they are believers and loved who are sharers in the benefits.*

"It is right (he says) that for the sake of true religion they should not despise their masters who treat them kindly, but they ought much more serve them as believers whom they ought to love for that reason and especially because they are masters who use them kindly." For this is what he means by *who are sharers in the benefits,* [175] that is, "who are eager to raise them up with benefits for the sake of the true religion they follow." Therefore, the kindness of masters ought not to become an opportunity for the slaves to despise them but ought all the more bind them with fuller affection. And again he added:

6:2b *These things teach and entreat.*

In all respects he is rousing Timothy so that he may be eager to set forth his teaching with much care for all this advice. And since Paul has run through everything he thought fitting for setting the church right in common, as we have more carefully pointed out in our interpretation of what precedes this place in the letter, he once more mentions those trying to teach what is contradictory of true religion. And he speaks of those from the circumcision who have believed, who were striving to do everything in their wish to impose the keeping of the law on the faithful. He had said a good deal about them in the first part of the letter.[59] In this way, after he

---

[58] A rather loose rendering of the text.
[59] Swete (2:175) points out the "resemblance" between 1:4, 5, 18, 19 and 6:3, 4, 12, 20, 21.

rat. sicque ad sermones correctionis qui in commune conueniunt egressus, iterum de illis ipsis quae in principio dixerat dictum resumens, in illis ipsis etiam finem concludit, cetera in media parte epistolae intericiens.

5 *si quis* (inquit) *aliquid aliter docet, et non intendit sanis uerbis domini nostri Iesu Christi et doctrinae quae secundum pietatem est, elatus est, nihil sciens.*

bene elationi iunxit 'nihil scire.' elatio uera ratione dicitur illa esse quae homines magna sapere facit de illis quae sibi non adsunt.
10 et quidem maximum est illis opprobrium ut alios docere promittant, ipsi nihil sciant. nam et de hoc ipso derideri digni sunt, dum alios docere promittentes, ipsi nihil sciant. huius uero rei probatio ex praecedentibus apertius est manifesta. si enim non intendunt illi doctrinae quae secundum pietatem est, euidens est quoniam
15 nihil sciunt de illis quae scire conueniunt. ergo et uane se docere promittunt, illa ignorantes quae scire conueniunt. dein opus eorum incusans adiecit:

sed languescens erga quaesitiones et uerborum rixas est.

quia et plurimas eueniebat eos quaesitiones commouere, illa ra-
20 tione qua sua statuere cupiebant. bene autem posuit 'languescere' eos. languorem dicit cogitationem eorum, eo quod relinquentes pietatem ad quaesitiones inconuenientes euoluebantur. et ostendens ut alia multa inhonesta studio quaesitionum adnascebantur, adiecit:

25 *ex quibus fiunt inuidiae, contentiones, blasphemiae, suspectiones malae, contentiones hominum corruptam mentem habentium [qui] fraudati a ueritate sunt, existimantium quaestum esse pietatem.*

†efficiuntur hinc *inuidiae,*   [ἐντεῦθεν γίνονται] φθόνοι μὲν
unumquemque inuidentem il- ἑκάστου βασκαίνοντος τὸ ὅπως
30 li qui potest qualibet ratione ποτὲ εὐδοκιμεῖν ἐν τῇ διαλέξει

---

1 quae *C H r*   3 finem *om C**   4 interitiens est (*for* intericiens) *H*   5 si quis &c. [*as in Vulg.*] *r*   7 est (*aft.* sciens) *add H*   10-11 promittunt *C* H* 11 ipsum (*for* ipso) *H* ‖ deridere *H*   12 cum ipsi nihil faciant *r*   14 est (*aft.* piet.) *om H* ‖ quomodo (*for* quoniam) *H*   15 ut a me (*for* et uane) *H* inane *r*   17 adicit *C r*   18 est *om r*   19 quaestiones *H r* ‖ commoueri *C H*   22 ad *om r*   23 quoniam et (*for* ut) *H* ‖ quaestionum *r*   24 adicit *C r*   25 suspitiones *C* (*corr.*) [*r throughout verse as in Vulg.*]   26 qui *om C H* 28 inuidente *H* ‖ sq. Coisl. 204, f. 208 b [Cr. vii. 47, Fr. 154] θεόδωρος. ἄλλος φησὶν εἰς τὸ ἐξ ὧν γίνεται φθόνος καὶ ἔρις καὶ τὰ ἑξῆς· φθόνος μέν, κ.τ.λ.

digressed to discourses designed to set things right and that were suitable for the community, he draws the letter to a close by taking up again the points he had spoken of in the beginning of the letter, inserting the rest into the middle of the letter.[60]

6:3–4a *If anyone* (he says) *teaches anything otherwise and does not pay attention to the sound words* [176] *of our Lord Jesus Christ and to the teaching that is in accordance with true religion, he is lifted up, knowing nothing;*

He rightly joined the lifting up to *knowing nothing.* For true reason "lifting up" is said to be something that makes people think highly of what is not theirs. And, indeed, the greatest shame belongs to those who promise to teach others but know nothing themselves. Now for this very thing they are worthy of derision, since when promising to teach others they know nothing themselves. But the proof of this fact is more openly obvious from the preceding discussion. For if they pay no attention to the teaching that accords with true religion, it is clear that they know nothing about what they ought to know. Therefore, it is in vain that they promise to teach, since they are ignorant of what they ought to know. Then, to condemn their work he added:

6:4b *but he is falling sick with regard to speculations and quarrels about words,*

Because it happened that they were stirring up a great many speculations because of their desire to establish their own views. And he rightly put down that they were *falling sick.* He calls their thinking sickness, because by deserting true religion they were being rolled away to unfitting speculations. And to show that many other shameful things were arising by their zeal for speculations, he added:

6:4c–5a *from which there come about envies, conflicts, slanders,* [177] *evil suspicions, conflicts of people who have a corrupt mind, who have been defrauded from the truth, thinking true religion to be gain.*

†*Envies* come about from this, when each one envies the one who can be seen in teaching for whatever reason;	*Envies* come about from this, when each one begrudges anyone who has been enabled in whatever way to have

---

[60] That is, 2:1–6:2 can be regarded as an "insertion," while 1 Tim 1 and 6:3–5 deal with the adversaries.

in doctrina uideri; *rixae* etiam
[cum ad lites proferuntur; et
blasphemiae autem, cum] plurima loquuntur ex his quae loqui
5 non conueniunt, maxime cum
et illi qui nobis non sunt communes in fide blasphemant nos
et inquirunt aduersus nos causas otiose existentes. fitque ex
10 hoc necessarie ut malam de nobis habeant suspicionem maxime hi qui fide nobis exteri sunt,
illos uero diligant, oblectati uerbis suis; quos et imitari pro-
15 perant illa agentes quae ab illis
fieri uideant, homines corrupti
mente, nullam ueritatis habentes cupiditatem, qui et omnia
lucrorum causa et redituum fa-
20 cere adnituntur;*

δυνηθέντι· ἔριδες δὲ ἐκφερομένων
αὐτῶν εἰς μάχας, καὶ βλασφημίαι
δέ, πολλὰ μὲν καὶ αὐτῶν λεγόντων
οἷα μὴ προσῆκεν, μάλιστα δὲ τῶν
ἐκτὸς βλασφημούντων ἡμᾶς, ὡς
περὶ τὸ ζητεῖν τὴν σχολὴν ἔχοντας.
ἀνάγκη οὖν καὶ ὑπονοίας πονηρὰς
περὶ ἡμῶν ἐγγίνεσθαι τοῖς ἐκτὸς
ἀπὸ τούτων· ἄνθρωποι διεφθορότες
τὴν διάνοιαν καὶ οὐδεμίαν τῆς
ἀληθείας ἐπιθυμίαν ἔχοντες, πάντα
κέρδους ἕνεκεν ἐπιτηδεύοντες.

quaestum sibi *pietatem esse* existimantes inhonestum, ex quo et alia
plurima adnascebantur mala. optime adiecit:

    discede ab eiusmodi.

    postquam autem ostendit prauitatem hominum et illa quae in-
25 honesta ab illis efficiuntur, sufficiebat ut tantum consilium daret
separare ab eis. deinde relinquens cetera ad illam partem redit,
atque insistit qua pecunias colligere adcelerabant; inque hac parte
uel maxime suum sermonem latius exaggerat, eo quod nec facile
posse existimabat eos despicere pecunias. sciens uero et illud quia
30 cupiditas pecuniaria nihil ex illis quae fieri conueniunt facere per-
mittit, despectus etenim pecuniarius facile illa expedire facit quae
meliora sunt, ait:

2 cum ad lites &c. *om C H r* 3-4 plurimae *C H r* 4 quia (*aft.* plur.) *add r*
8 et uersus (*for* adu.) *C** 9 ex *om C* et (*for* ex) *H r* 10 necessario *r* 11
hab. de n. *r* 14 eoram (*for* suis) *H* 16 uident (*for* uideant) *H* uidentur *r* 19
et reditum *C* H: om r* 21 ex qua *C* H* qui *C* (*corr.*) ‖ in homines tamen
(*for* inhonestum) *C* in h. tam *H*: txt *r* 22 adicit *C r* 23 huiusmodi *H* 25
officiantur *C* H* officiuntur *C* (*corr.*): txt *r* 27 quae *H r* 30 pecuniae (*for*
pecuniaria) *H* 31 despectos, pecuniarios *r*

and *quarrels*,[61] when they are brought forward to contentions; and *slanders*, when they speak a great deal about what they ought not to speak, especially when those who do not share with us in faith slander us and seek charges against us that are ineffectual.[62] And from this it necessarily happens that they have an evil suspicion about us, especially those who are outside us in faith, but love those people because they are delighted with their words. They are eager to imitate them by doing what they see done by them. They are people corrupted in mind, having no desire for the truth, and they strive to do everything for the sake of material gain and revenue,*

a fine reputation for speaking; and *dissensions* are of those who are carried away to contentions; and *slanders* are of those who say many things that are not fitting, and especially of those outside who slander us as though we had leisure for speculation. Therefore, it is necessary that evil suspicions concerning us also come about from these things on the part of those outside.

They are people corrupted in their thinking, having no desire for the truth, practicing everything for the sake of gain.

because they think that *true religion* is shameful *gain* for themselves, from which, as well, a great many other evils arise. Quite effectively he added:

[178] 6:5b *Depart from people of this kind.*[63]

And after Paul demonstrated the perverseness of these people and the shameful things done by them, it was enough only to give Timothy the advice to withdraw from them. Then, leaving the other points to one side, he turns to one part of his argument and focuses attention on their haste to gather money. And on this point he especially amplifies his discourse to a considerable extent, because he thought it could not be easy for them to despise money. And since he also knows that greed for money allows people to do nothing of what ought to be done, while contempt for money easily assists what is better, he says:

---

[61] *Rixae* instead of *contentiones*, as in the citation of the text.

[62] The translator has clearly misunderstood the Greek.

[63] An addition to the text found in some manuscripts and versions.

est autem (inquit) *quaestus magnus pietas cum sufficientia.*

'magnum lucrum, magnae diuitiae, lucratiua negotiatio pietas est, ut erga eam solliciti simus, necessitatibus nostris sufficientes.' bene uero adiecit: *pietas cum sufficientia*, ita ut necessitatem non
5   uideretur intercipere, et nimietatis studium excluderet, et omni ex parte sollicitudinem pecuniarum adimeret.

nihil (inquit) *intulimus in mundum, uerum quia nec auferre possumus.*

multus ac potens sensus in compendio uerborum horum con-
10   tineri uidetur. illi enim qui erga pecunias studium habent pro illis quidem quae adsunt sibi laborant, ut permanere possint et custodiri; illa uero quae necdum habent quemadmodum adquirere possint. utrumque exclusit, ita ut pro illis quae sibi adsunt minime laborem expendant. nam quod dixit '*nihil intulimus*, sed nudi in
15   hunc mundum in hac uita uenimus,' de illis quae nobis adsunt laborem expendere [exclusit], quasi de propriis nostris quae quidem nos quando in hanc uitam ingredimur inuenimus. nam et pro illis laborem expendere uanum admodum esse ostendit, dicens: *quia nec auferre quid possumus.* quae enim est utilitas laborem expen-
20   dere ubi etsi omnia adquirere possumus, hic illa relinquemus quae congregauimus? quid ergo fieri debet, quoniam et illud necessarium est et hoc superfluum?

habentes autem alimenta et quibus tegamur, his contenti sumus.

sufficit illa habere quae ad usum nobis sunt necessaria. haec
25   enim effruemur sola; cetera uero, etiamsi cumulata fuerint, aliis relinquemus in mundo. 'superfluum est (inquit) nos qui *nihil intulimus*, [multa uelle conquirere ut hinc efferamus].' deinde ostendens quemadmodum nociua sit huiusmodi sollicitudo ei [qui] pietati studere cupit:

30   *qui autem uolunt diuites fieri, incidunt in temptationem et laqueum*

---

1   quaestum (*for* est autem) *C H* quaestus est magnus (*for* est ... magnus) *r*   3
ea *Hr*   4   adicit *C r*   5   excludere et ut *H*   6   adimere *r*   7   nihil enim &c.
[*as in Vulg.*] *r*   7-8   possimus *C**   9-10   continere *C H*   11-12   custodire
C* H   15   in hanc uitam *r*   16   expend ... *C** (?) expendere (*om* exclusit)
C (*corr.*) *H r*   17   ingredimur inuenimus *H r*   20   hinc *C* H*   23   simus *C*
(*corr.*)   24-25   his e. fruemur solis *r*   26   relinquimus *C r*   ‖   sup. enim est *r*
27   multa ... efferamus *om C H: txt r*   28   solitudo *C r*   ‖   qui *om C H: txt r*
29   studire *C**   ‖   adicit (*aft* cupit) *add r*   30   nam qui &c. [*as in Vulg.*] *r*

6:6 *And* (he says) *true religion is great gain with sufficiency.*

"Great profit, great riches, a lucrative business—this is true religion, so that we may exercise great care for it when we have enough for our needs." And he rightly added *true religion with sufficiency* so that he might not seem to cut off our needs, while excluding greed, and so take away the care for money in every respect.

[179] 6:7 *We have brought* (he says) *nothing into the world, true*[64] *because neither can we take anything out of it.*

An abundant and powerful meaning seems to be concisely included in these words. For those who occupy themselves with money toil for what is their own, so that it can remain and be kept, and for how they can acquire what they do not yet possess. Paul has excluded both aims, so that they may by no means expend toil for what is their own. Now when he said "*we have brought nothing*, but we have come naked to this world in this life," he has excluded expending toil for what is our own, inasmuch as we found what was suitable for us when we entered this life. Now he also showed that to expend toil for them is altogether vain, by saying *because neither can we take anything out of it.* For what is the use of expending toil when, even if we could acquire everything, we shall leave behind here what we have gathered together? Therefore, what ought to be done, since one thing is necessary and the other useless?[65]

6:8 *And having food and that by which we are sheltered, with these we are content.*

It is enough to have what is necessary for our use, [180] for we shall enjoy these alone, and the rest, even if they have been accumulated, we shall leave in the world for others. "It is useless (he says) for us, who *have brought nothing*, to want to collect many things so that we can carry them away from here." Then, to show how harmful care of this kind is to the person who wants to be zealous for true religion:

6:9 *And those who want to become rich fall into temptation and*

---

[64] *Verum.* This must be a scribal error. See Swete's note (2:179): "In the comm. below ... *verum* disappears. On the whole we may conclude that Th.'s text had no adjective before ὅτι, although in that case it differed from the text of Chrys. and the other Gk. commentators, who give δῆλον ὅτι, κ.τ.λ."

[65] That is, the necessities of life are freely provided, but we can take nothing with us when we die.

diaboli et desideria multa quae [*non*] *secundum intellectum sunt et no-*
ciua; quae mergunt homines in exterminium et perditionem.

necesse est eum qui cupit diuitias adquirere multis implicari
tribulationibus, multa enim [oportet eum] sustinere pericula et ad
5 desideria prorumpere nociua et stulta, ex quibus maxime augeri
solent et abundare; [quae commodum quidem praestare] poterunt
nullum, perditionem uero multam prouident illis qui semel occu-
pati fuerint eorum desiderio. et quis sufficienter poterit dicere illa
mala quae ex desiderio solent diuitiarum adnasci? unde et adiecit:
10 *radix enim omnium malorum est cupiditas pecuniaria.*

'et ut compendiose (inquit) dicam, nihil indecens est quod non
per concupiscentiam admittatur pecuniarum.' et ostendens quoniam experimento doctus ista dicit, sciens multos fuisse ex ipsa
concupiscentia non leuia nocitos, adiecit:
15 *quam quidem adpetentes oberrauerunt a fide et seipsos inseruerunt*
doloribus multis

'ex hac (inquit) concupiscentia multi a fide cecidisse uidentur,
et nec secundum praesentem uitam in melioribus poterant inueniri, sed e contrario deflentes ac dolentes persteterunt pro illis quae
20 sibi ex his acciderunt tristitiis.' et iterum ipsi Timotheo consilium
dans adiecit:
tu autem, homo Dei, haec fuge.

apte uisus est eum exhortasse ut ista fugiat, 'hominem' illum
dicens esse 'Dei.' aptum enim est ei qui talis est ut ab omni malo
25 sese superiorem custodiat. deinde scribit ei utpote carissimo discipulo, insinuans quae eum agere oporteant:
insequere autem iustitiam, pietatem, fidem, caritatem, patientiam,
mansuetudinem.

'erga ista sollicitudinem (inquit) expendere.' et quoniam labor

---

1 non *om C H* 2 perdictionem *C** 4 eum (*for* enim) *r* ‖ oportet eum
om C H r 5 augere *H* 6 quae … praestare *om C H r* ‖ poterant nullum
C H poterunt (*om* nullum) *r* 7 multa (*for* multam) *H* multam perd. uero *r*
‖ quae (*for* qui) *C** 8 fuerunt *C* H* 9 unde adicit *C* unde et adicit *r* 10
auaritia (*for* cup. pec.) *r* 11 malum nullum (*aft.* indecens) *add r* 12 per
concupiscentiae *C* H* [δὶ ἐπιθυμίας ?] 13 sit (*aft.* doctus) *add C H r* 14
leuiter *C r* ‖ deceptos (*for* nocitos) *r* ‖ adicit *C r* 15 oberrauerit *C*
errauerit *r* ‖ inser. se *r* 18 potuerint *r* 19 persteterit *C** persteterint *r*
20 acciderit *C** ‖ tristiis *H* ‖ et iterum … adiecit *om r* 21 adicit *C* 23
aperte (*for* apte) *l* 25 superiorem *om r* 26 oporteat *C* (*corr.*) *r* 27 sectare
uero (*for* inseq. aut.) *r* 29 istam *H* ‖ expende *C* (*corr.*) *r*

the snare of the devil[66] and many desires that are not according to understanding and harmful, which plunge people into ruin and loss.

It is necessary that the person who wants to acquire riches be involved in many afflictions, for he must endure many dangers and must burst forth into harmful and foolish desires, by which afflictions and dangers are usually increased to the greatest extent and abound. Riches will be able to furnish nothing advantageous, but provide much loss to those who have once been possessed by their desire. And who could say enough about the evils that usually arise from the desire for riches? For this reason he added:

6:10a *For the root of all evils is greed for money,*

[181] "And, that I may speak succinctly, (he says) there is nothing unseemly that is not admitted by the lust for money." And to show that he says this because he has learned it by experience, since he knows that many have suffered no light harm from this lust, he added:

6:10b *seeking which some have wandered away from faith and have pierced themselves with many pains.*

"From this lust (he says) many plainly have fallen away from faith and could not be found in better circumstances in the present life; but, on the contrary, they have persisted in weeping and suffering pain for those misfortunes that have happened to them because of this." And once more giving advice to Timothy himself, he added:

6:11a *But you, man of God, flee these things,*

Paul is seen to have exhorted Timothy appropriately to flee these things, by saying that he is a *man of God.* For it is appropriate for someone like this to keep himself having the upper hand over every evil. Then he writes to him as his dearly beloved disciple, introducing what he ought to do:

6:11b *and pursue justice, true religion, faith, love, endurance, gentleness.*

[182] "On those things (he says) expend great care." And since

---

[66] "Of the devil" has been added to the text.

est necessarius illis qui uirtutem exequi adnituntur, adiecit:

certa bonum certamen fidei.

necessarie adicit *bonum certamen* uel agonem, ut hoc loco uel maxime ostendat quod necessarius sit labor talibus qui pro multis expenditur bonis. deinde laboris ipsius lucra pandens adiecit:

adprehende (inquit) *uitam aeternam.*

'certaminum autem uel agonum horum merces uita aeterna est.' quibus poterit eam adsequi et suadens ei ut de his studiose agat:

in qua (ait) *uocatus es et con[fessus es bonam con] fessionem.*

'ob hanc enim et credidisti (hoc enim dicit *uocatus*); ob hanc uocationem confessus es pietatem—' ut dicat quoniam 'pro hac passus es.' nam quod dixit *confessus es*, hoc est, 'passus es' dicit. unde et plus eum adhortans ut pro hisce rebus sustineat laborem, adiecit:

coram multis [testibus].

†multi enim erant qui sciebant beatum Timotheum adiunctum fuisse Paulo contemplatione pietatis, utque is passus fuerat non pauca.*	πολλοὶ γὰρ ἦσαν οἱ τὸν μακάριον Τιμόθεον συνόντα τῷ μακαρίῳ Παύλῳ εὐσεβείας ἕνεκεν εἰδότες, καὶ μὴν καὶ πεπονθότα οὐκ ὀλίγα διὰ ταύτην.

'itaque necessarium (inquit) tibi est ut omni ex parte pro aeterna uita laborem sustineas pro qua et credidisti et confessus es pietatem, periculis frequenter adiectatus. iustum etenim est ut minime ex posteriori desidia illa exterminentur quae inprimis sunt adquisita.' deinde et plus eum adhortans adiecit:

praecipio in conspectu Dei qui uiuificat omnia, et domino nostro Iesu Christo qui testimonium reddidit sub Pontio Pilato [bonam] confes-

1 uirtutes *H* (*corr.*) ‖ adicit *C* 3 necessario *C* 4 ostendit *r* 5 labiis (*for* laboris) *H* ‖ adicit *C* 8 eam adsequi *om C H* 10 agit (*for* ait) *C** ‖ confessus es bonam *om C H r* 11 in qua u. es et confessus b. confessionem (*aft.* uocatus) *add r* 13 quotquot (*for* quod) *C** 14 adhortens *H** 14-15 adicit *C r* 16 testibus *om C H* 17 autem (*for* enim) *H* ‖ sq. Coisl. 204, f. 209 a [Cr. vii. 48, Fr. 154] θεόδωρος. τουτέστιν, μὴ καταισχύνῃς τὴν παρρησίαν ἐκείνην [Chrys., cf. Fr.] πολλοὶ γάρ, κ.τ.λ. Cr. notes: "deest verbum aliquod" [post Τιμόθεον], Nothing is wanting in the MS. 19-20 ἕνεκεν, εἰδότες καὶ Cr. 20 atque his *r* 22 tibi necess. *r* ‖ te (*for* tibi) *C** H* ‖ et (*bef.* aeterna) *add C* 24 adsectatus *C* ‖ est etenim *H* 26 adhortatus *r* ‖ adicit *C* subdit *r* 27 dom. nostro *om r* 27-28 Chr. I. *r* 28 bonam *om C H*

there is necessary toil for those who strive to pursue virtue, he added:

6:12a *Fight the good fight of faith;*

He necessarily adds *the good fight* or contest, so that in this place especially he may show that there is necessary toil to be expended by such people for abundant good things. Then, disclosing the profit of the toil itself, he added:

6:12b *take hold* (he says) *of eternal life,*

"The reward of these fights or contests is eternal life." And to urge him to act zealously about what could enable him to attain it:

6:12c *in which* (he says) *you have been called and have confessed the good confession*

"For it is because of this life that you have believed—for this is what he means by *called*—because of this calling you have confessed true religion," meaning that "you have suffered for this." Now when he said *you have confessed*, what he means is "you have suffered." And so, exhorting him further to endure toil for these things, he added:

[183] 6:12c *in the presence of many witnesses.*

†For there were many who knew that blessed Timothy had been joined with Paul for the sake of true religion and that he had suffered no few things.*	For there were many who knew that blessed Timothy was joined with blessed Paul for the sake of true religion and, indeed, suffered no few things because of this.

"And so it is necessary for you (he says) to endure toil in every respect for eternal life, for which you have both believed and confessed true religion and have often been thrust into dangers. It is, indeed, right that what had been at first acquired should by no means be ruined by a later slacking off." Then to exhort him further, he added:

6:13–14 *I charge you in the sight of God, who gives all things life, and of our Lord Jesus Christ, who rendered a good confession as testimony under Pontius Pilate, to keep the commandment without spot, blameless to the coming of our Lord Jesus Christ,*

By *the commandment* he means "those things that I have

sionem, custodire te mandatum sine macula inreprehensibile usque ad
aduentum domini nostri Iesu Christi.

est *mandatum* ut dicat, 'illa quae mandaui tibi.' bene hoc in loco
[dicit] ob quam rem etiam et in agone pro fide certare eum prae-
5 cipiebat. unde et memoratus Christi aduentum, confirmans atque
stabiliens quod necessarie utique erit adiecit:

quem temporibus suis ostendit beatus et solus potens rex regum et
dominus dominantium, qui solus habet inmortalitatem et lumen ha-
bitat inaccessibile, quem uidit hominum nemo nec uidere potest; cui
10 *honor et potestas aeterna. amen.*

ex magnitudine diuinae naturae et illa quae erga eum habentur
confirmauit futura. unde et ista quae erga Deum sunt posuit in
praesenti, quae confirmationem quandam futurorum habere poterant. hoc ipsum autem et [in] initium epistolae fecisse uidetur,
15 ubi dicit: *regi autem saeculorum, incorrupto, inuisibili, soli Deo ho-*
nor et gloria in saecula saeculorum. amen. unde etiam et hoc in loco

†'beatum' illum uocauit ad con-	'μακάριον' αὐτὸν ἐκάλεσεν ἐπὶ συσ-
firmationem futurae inuertibili-	τάσει τῆς μελλούσης προσέσεσθαι
tatis quae nobis aderit, quia ille	ἡμῖν ἀτρεπτότητος, 'δυνάστην' δὲ
20 talis est, in natura beatitudinem	ὅτι δὴ τὴν ἀνάστασιν ἐργάσασθαι
habens, nec autem ullam pote-	δυνατός, καὶ μὴν καὶ 'βασιλέα' καὶ
rit sustinere uertibilitatem. 'po-	'κύριον' ἐπὶ ἀποδείξει τοῦ πάντων
tentem' uero dixit eum, ut ne-	κρατεῖν καὶ δύνασθαι ὑποτάξαι καὶ
mo dubitet quoniam resurrec-	θάνατον ἀφελεῖν· διὰ τοῦτο καὶ 'μό-
25 tionem nobis poterit conferre.	νον ἔχοντα ἀθανασίαν,' ὡς ἂν ἱκα-
et quidem et 'regem' eum 're-	νὸν τοῦτο ἡμῖν παρασχεῖν· καὶ τὸ
gnantium' et 'dominum domi-	φῶς δὲ οἰκῶν ἀπρόσιτον, σύστασιν
nantium' dixit, ut ostenderet ex	ἔχον τοῦ ἐν ἀφάτῳ τινὶ καὶ ἀπροσί-
hoc quoniam omnes subiugat et	τῳ τυγχάνοντα φωτὶ ὄντως δὴ φω-
30 potens est etiam daemones su-	τεινὰ καὶ τῶν δικαίων ποιήσειν τὰ
biugare et mortem adimere et	σώματα· οὕτως καὶ τὸ ὂν εἶδεν οὐ-

1 ut serues (*for* custodire) *r* 3 in hoc loco *C* 4 dicit *om C H r* ‖ distare
(*for* certare) *H* 5 est (*aft.* memor.) *add r* 6 necessarium *C** necessario *r* ‖
erat et (*for* erit) *C* (*corr.*) ‖ adicit *C r* 8 lumen h. inaccessibilem *H* lucem
h. inaccessibilem *r* 9 nullus (*for* nemo) *r* 10 imperium sempiternum (*for*
pot. aeterna) *r* 11 eam *r* 14 ipsum *om H* ‖ initio *C* in initio *C* (*corr.*)
r initium *H* 15 est (*bef.* soli) *add C* H* 16 in hoc loco *r* 17 illo *C* H*:
txt r ‖ sq. Coisl. 204, f. 209 b [Cr. vii. 50, Fr. 154] Θεόδωρος. ἄλλος φησίν·
μακάριον, κ.τ.λ. 18-19 aduertibilitatis *r* 19 adherit *H* 20 est *om C* ‖
δεῖ (*for* δὴ) cod.

commanded you." In this place he rightly says why he was instructing him to fight the contest for faith. Then, since he mentioned the coming of Christ to confirm and establish what will necessarily doubtless come to pass, he added:

[184] 6:15–16 *which he shows in his own times—he who is blessed and the only powerful King of kings and Lord of lords, who only has immortality and dwells in light inaccessible, whom no one of humans has seen nor can see, to whom be honor and eternal power. Amen.*

He has confirmed from the greatness of the divine nature also those things that are held to take place because of him in what is to come. For this reason he has put down those statements concerning God in the present that could enable some confirmation of the things to come. And he is seen to have done the same thing at the beginning of the letter, where he says (1:17): *and to the King of the ages, incorruptible, invisible, the only God, honor and glory to the ages of ages. Amen.* So also in this place

†he called God *blessed* to confirm the changelessness of the future that will be ours, because God is like this, since he has blessedness by nature and could not suffer any change. And he said God is *powerful* so that no one would doubt that he has power to bestow the resurrection on us. And he said that he is *King of kings and Lord of lords* to demonstrate [185] by this that he makes all subject to him and is powerful even to make demons subject and to banish death and to take away what afflicts us in the present. And so he said that *he only has immortality*, because he is capable of bestowing on us what he alone possesses by nature, having acquired it from nothing else. And his statement *dwelling in light inaccessible* is a confir-

He called God *blessed* to confirm the changelessness to come that will be ours,

and *powerful* because he has power to cause the resurrection, and, indeed, *King and Lord* to demonstrate that he rules over all and is able to subject and take away death.

Because of this he is the one *who only has immortality*, since he is able to bestow this on us.

And *dwelling in light inaccessible* is a confirmation of the fact that,

omnia illa intercipere quae nos
ad praesens adfligunt. ideo et
'solum' dixit 'habere inmortalitatem,' eo quod sufficiens sit
5 nobis hoc praestare quod ipse solus possidet in natura, a
nullo alio adsecutus. et quod
dixit 'lumen habitans inaccessibile,' confirmationem habens,
10 quod in inmenso quodam lumine et inaccessibili persistat, qui
etiam et uera ratione iustorum
corpora lumine faciet inlustra-
ti. sed et illud quod dixit: *quem*
15 *uidet hominum nemo nec uidere*
potest, ut ostendat quoniam 'nihil demiratione dignum est si illa quae tunc erga uos erunt ad
praesens non uideantur; siqui-
20 dem et ipse qui nobis ista conla-
turus est inuisibilis nobis existat
per naturam.'*

δεὶς ἀνθρώπων οὐδὲ ἰδεῖν δύναται,
ὥστε δεῖξαι ὅτι οὐδὲν θαυμαστὸν μὴ
φαίνεσθαι νῦν τὰ τότε περὶ ἡμᾶς ἐσ-
όμενα, ὅπου γε καὶ αὐτὸς ὁ τούτων
αἴτιος ἀόρατος ἡμῖν πάντη τὴν φύσιν ἐστίν.

sicque suum sermonem futurorum confirmatione uisus est consummasse, ut magis suaderet Timotheo inuigilare de his quae si-
25 bi sunt scripta. adiecit uero et de diuitibus, perspiciens quoniam
hoc in media parte epistolae dicere praetermiserat ubi de ceteris
disputauerat ad eum:
　　diuitibus in [hoc] saeculo praecipe non altum sapere.
　　bene dixit *in hoc saeculo*, ut ostendat ipsas diuitias temporales
30 esse, pro quibus uel maxime non conueniebat ut alta saperent.
　　neque sperare in incerto diuitiarum.
　　et hoc adicit ut ostendat quoniam neque in hoc saeculo diuitiae
a diuitibus caute tenentur.
　　sed in Deo uiuo, qui praebet nobis omnia abunde ad fruitionem.
35 　　optime autem posuit de diuitiis temporalibus illam abundan-

---

5 nobis sit *r*　10　in *om C r*　11　inaccessibile *C* H*　12　et *om r*　14　quod
om C r　16-17　nulla (*for* nihil) *C r*　25　sunt *om H*　‖　adicit *C r*　27　et
ait (*aft* eum) add *r*　28　hoc *om C H*　34　fruendum (*for* fruit.) *r*　35　contra
(*for* autem) *r*

mation that he remains unchanged in some infinite and inaccessible light and will with true reason cause the bodies of the just to be glorified with light. Moreover, when he said *whom no one of humans sees*[67] *nor can see*, it is to show that "it is nothing worthy of astonishment if what will then be the case for us is not seen at present, since he who will bestow those things on us exists invisible to us by nature."✳ since he happens to be in some ineffable and inaccessible light, he will really make the bodies of the just also luminous. In this way also *whom no one of humans has seen nor can see* is to show that there is nothing astonishing about the fact that what will then be the case for us does not now appear, since he who is the cause of these things is altogether invisible to us by nature.

And so he has plainly completed his discourse to confirm the things to come, in order all the more to urge Timothy to be attentive to what he has written him. And he adds something about rich people, noticing that he had passed over saying this in the middle part of the letter[68] where he discussed other things for him:

6:17a *Instruct the rich in this age not to be high-minded,*

[186] He rightly said *in this age* to show that they are temporal riches that it would be especially unfitting for them to mind highly.

6:17b *nor to hope in the uncertainty of riches,*

And he adds this to show that neither should riches in this age be kept carefully by rich people.

6:17c *but in the living*[69] *God, who will furnish us with everything abundantly for enjoyment,*

And quite effectively on the subject of temporal riches he put down the abundance given us by God. For who is so foolish as to doubt that it is better to hope in God than in riches? And so

---

[67] *Videt* rather than *vidit*, as in the text of verse 16.

[68] Presumably, Theodore means 4:1–5:2.

[69] "Living" seems clearly to be in Theodore's text.

tiam quae a Deo nobis datur. quis enim sic stultus est ut dubitet
quin melius sit in Deum sperare quam in diuitiis? unde et adiecit
'uiuum,' ut magis illud exaggeret. comparauit enim cum Dei sem-
piternitate diuitiarum usum temporalem, et ipsum usum dixit esse
5 'incertum.' et quod dixit: *omnia nobis abunde praebet,* uerum esse
ab illo loco quo superius dixerat euidens est, quoniam omnia eius
fruimur. et ut ostenderet quia oportet magis Deo intueri, a quo
et omnium bonorum habemus fruitionem, despicientes illas opes
quae nobis in praesente adsunt; conuenit uero nos semper gratias
10 agere Deo qui omnium quae potimur bonorum auctor et donator
esse uidetur. deinde et quod necessarium erat post hoc facere illos
instruxit, dicens:

> *bonum opus facere, diuites esse in operibus bonis, facile tribuere,*
> *communicare.*

15 et quod erit ex hoc lucrum? dicito:

> *thesaurizantes* (inquit) *sibi ipsis fundamentum bonum in futuro, ut*
> *adprehendant uitam aeternam.*

percipient autem in futuro saeculo mercedes magnas pro quibus in hoc saeculo ista faciunt. nam et mercedes percipient ta-
20 les quae nullam umquam poterunt mutabilitatem sustinere. nam
quod dixit *fundamentum,* firmitatem eorum uoluit significare.
compendiose uero hoc uoluit dicere: 'praecipe illis ut non magna
sapiant propter illa quae possident; cognoscant uero Dominum
horum sibi esse largitorem, et huic semper pro omnibus sibi tribu-
25 tis gratias debent referre, in bonis operibus sollicitudinem expen-
dentes, quod parua dantes in praesenti uita magna in futuro saeculo recipiant.' et dicens de diuitibus iterum ad Timothei se uertit
personam, illis quae praedicta fuerant competenter adiciens:

> *o Timothee, commendatum custodi, deuitans profanas nouitates*
30 > *uocum et oppositiones falsi nominis scientiae, quam quidam promit-*
> *tentes a fide exciderunt.*

de illis enim hoc in loco dicit. 'tu (inquit) custodi fidem, omni uirtute declinans eos qui contraria docent et semper excogitant
aliquid nouius dicere et inconueniens; qui et controuersias con-

---

5 omnibus *r* 7 intueri Deum *r* 8 bon. omn. *r* 9 in praes. *om H r* 11
illis *C (corr.)* 16 tessaurizantes *H* || inquit *om r* || sibimet *C (corr.)*
19 mercedem p. talem *r* 20 numquam ullam *C r* 21 firmamentum *(for*
firmitatem) *r* 24 hunc *(for* huic) *C* H* 26 dates *H** 27 dicens autem *r*
29 o T. depositum &c. [*as in Vulg.*] *r* 30 quidem *C H r* 34 noui *r*

he added *living* so that he might all the more amplify the point.
For he compared the temporal use of riches with the eternity of
God, and he meant that the use of riches is "uncertain." And when
he said *he will furnish us with everything abundantly*, it is clear that
his statement is true because of the place above (4:3) where he had
said that we enjoy everything from God. And this is to show that
we ought all the more to fix our sight on God, from whom we
have the enjoyment of all good things, despising the wealth that
is ours in the present. And it is right for us always to give thanks
to God, who is plainly the source and giver of all the good things
we possess. Then Paul gave instructions after this about what it
was necessary for them to do, saying:

6:18 *do good work, be rich in good works, bestow easily, share,*

And what will be the profit from this? Let him say:

6:19 *treasuring up* (he says) *for themselves a good foundation for
what is to come, so that they may take hold of eternal life.*

[187] And they will earn in the age to come great rewards for
what they do in this age. Indeed, they will earn rewards such
as can never suffer any change. Now when he said *foundation*,
he wanted to indicate their steadfastness. And he wanted to say
succinctly: "Instruct them not to be high-minded because of what
they possess, and let them know that the Lord is the one who
lavishes these things on them and that they ought to render thanks
to him for everything bestowed on them, by expending great care
on good works, because those who give small things in the present
life will receive great things in the age to come." And speaking of
rich people, he once more turns his attention to Timothy's person,
suitably adding to what had been said before:

6:20–21a *O Timothy, keep what has been entrusted, avoiding the
profane novelties of words*[70] *and the contradictions of the knowledge
of a false name, which some by promising have fallen away from faith.*

For he says of them in this place: "You (he says), keep
faith, turning away with all your might from those who teach

---

[70]Theodore is reading χαινοφωνίας rather than χενοφωνίας.

tra ueritatem excogitant sub nomine scientiae quam mentiti insi-
mulant, promittuntque se scientiam habere, longe autem multum
distant a fide.' bene autem et 'commendationem' dixit dogmatum
scrupulositatem, ut ostenderet magis quia necessarium sit ei ut cu-
5 stodiat illa quae ab eo accepit, quia et exigendus est illa quae sibi
sunt commendata. consummans uero in his epistolam, consuetam
adiecit salutationem, in ultimam partem epistolae dicens:
    gratia tecum. amen.

1 scientia qua *H*   2   promittunt qui *H*   ‖   multumque *r*   4   scrupulositate
H r   ‖   quae (*for* quia) *C* H* quod *C* (*corr.*) *r*   ‖   necessitatem *H*   6   in
ultima parte *r*   7   adicit *C r*

contradictory things and are always thinking up something to say more novel and unfitting. They think up controversies against the truth under the name of the knowledge to which they pretend in their lies; they profess that they have knowledge but are standing a long way and far apart from faith." And Paul rightly called [188] the exactness of doctrines what had been *entrusted*, so that he might show all the more that it is necessary for Timothy to keep what he received from him, because what was entrusted to him must be enforced. Finishing his letter with these words, he added his customary greeting, saying at the end of the letter:

6:21b *Grace be with you. Amen.*

THEODORUS
MOPSUESTENUS
IN EPISTOLAM B. PAULI
AD TIMOTHEUM II

ARGUMENTUM

Epistolam Pauli ad Timotheum secundum sensum explicaturus, argumentum eius ut moris est nobis primitus explicabimus.

†euidens est enim illud quod
non post primam epistolam
5 etiam hanc protinus scripserit,
sed et nec de hisdem scripserit locis de quibus primam illam
scripserat epistolam. primam
enim scribens dicit: *sicut rogaui*
10 *te sustinere Ephesi;* ostendens
quoniam illic eum reliquerat,
et sic epistolam ad eum scribit
quasi adhuc in illis locis com-
morante eo. in hac uero epistola
15 in finem scribit: *Tychicum* (inquit) [*misi*] *Ephesi;* dixisset utique 'ad te,' si Ephesi adhuc Timotheus moraretur, quando et
hanc ad eum scribebat episto-
20 lam. et primam quidem sic se

ὅτι μὴ ἀκολούθως τῇ προτέρᾳ ταύτην γεγράφηκεν, μηδὲ ἐπὶ τῶν αὐτῶν διάγοντι τόπων δῆλον, ἀλλὰ
μετὰ πολὺν χρόνον ἄγαν· ἐκείνην
μὲν γὰρ ἀπέστειλεν αὐτῷ ἐν 'Εφ-
έσῳ διάγοντι, ἐν ταύτῃ δὲ πρὸς τῷ
τέλει φησίν· Τυχικὸν ἀπέστειλα εἰς
"Εφεσον· εἶπεν δ' ἂν ὅτι 'πρός σε,'
εἴπερ ἐπὶ τῆς 'Εφέσου διάγοντι καὶ
ταύτην ἔγραφεν τὴν ἐπιστολήν. κἀ-
κείνην μὲν οὕτω γράφων δῆλός ἐστιν ὡς ἂν μετ' οὐ πολὺ πρὸς αὐτὸν
ἐλευσόμενος, ταύτην δὲ ὡς μετ' οὐ
πολὺ διὰ τὴν τοῦ Χριστοῦ ὁμολο-
γίαν τὴν ἐκ τοῦδε τοῦ βίου μετάσ-
τασιν δέξασθαι προσδοκῶν· κελεύει
δὲ αὐτὸν καὶ θᾶττον πρὸς αὐτὸν ἀφ-
ικέσθαι. γράφει δὲ αὐτὴν ἀπὸ 'Ρώ-

---

3 sq. Coisl. 204, f. 211 a [Cr. vii. 52, Fr. 155] θεόδωρος. ἄλλος φησίν· ὅτι μή,
κ.τ.λ. 4 post *om* H ‖ τινὰ...τόπον (for τῶν αὐτῶν...τόπων) edd. 6 iisdem *r* 10 εἶπε δὲ ἂν edd. 11 reliquere *H* 13-14 commemorante *H*
commorantem (*om* eo) *r* 14 ὅταν (for ὡς ἂν) edd. 15 fine *r* 16 misi *om*
C* H Ephesi direxi ad te quasi (*for* m. E. dixisset utique ad te si) *r*

THEODORE OF MOPSUESTIA ON BLESSED PAUL'S SECOND LETTER TO TIMOTHY

THE SETTING

[189] Since we are about to explain the meaning of Paul's second letter to Timothy, we shall first explain its setting, as is our custom.

†Now it is clear that he did not write this immediately after the first letter and, further, did not write of the same places of which he had written the first letter. For when writing the first letter, he says (1 Tim 1:3): *as I have asked you to stay at Ephesus*, showing [190] that he had left Timothy there and so is writing to him while he is still dwelling there. But in this letter he writes at the end (4:12): *I have sent* (he says) *Tychicus to Ephesus*. He would have said "to you,"[1] if Timothy were still dwelling at Ephesus when he wrote him this letter. Indeed, he has made it obvious that

It is clear that he wrote this letter not immediately following the first, nor to Timothy when he was living in the same places, but after a quite considerable period of time. For he sent the first letter to Timothy when he was living in Ephesus, while in this one he says toward the end (4:12): *I have sent Tychicus to Ephesus*. He would have said "to you," if he were writing this letter to Timothy while he was still living in Ephesus.

---

[1] Swete (2:190) calls attention to Titus 3:12.

scripsisse ad eum manifestauit, μης, ἡνίκα...
ut et insinuaret quod non mul-
to post tempore sit ipse ad eum
uenturus; dicit enim: *haec tibi*
5 *scribo sperans me uenire ad te ci-*
to. hanc uero scribens designat
quia non multo post tempore ad
Christi confessionem istius uitae transitum expectet; ait nam-
10 que: *ego enim iam delibor, et*
tempus meae resolutionis instat.
iubet autem eum cito uenire ad
se, dicens: *festina* (inquit) *ueni-*
re ad me cito. scribit autem hanc
15 epistolam ad eum ex urbe Roma, in illo tempore quando*
Felicem adpellans uinctus Romae ex Iudaeae partibus fuerat ductus. duobus etenim annis tunc, sicut Lucas dicit, Romae commorans, quia ante Neronem ductus pro se satisfaceret, ex sententiae
20 eius laxatus est auctoritate, eo quod nihil ab eo crimine dignum
gestum fuisse Nero reppererat. qui dimissus protinus suum opus
implebat; percurrens enim orbem terrae pietatis rationem omnibus tradere properabat. post illud uero secundo Romae adueniens,
praecepto Neronis
25 †contemplatione pietatis capite   τῆς εὐσεβείας ἕνεκεν τὴν κεφαλὴν
plectitur,*   ἀποτέμνεται.
eo in tempore quando et hanc epistolam Timotheo ab urbe Roma
scripserat. et illud non incertum est quoniam ubicumque tunc Timotheus commorabatur, pro uoluntate beati Pauli ab aliorum uti-

---

10   delebor *C* H: txt C (corr.) r*   17   filicem *C* filice *H** Caesarem *H (corr.)*:
txt r   ‖   unctus (*for* uinctus) *C**   18-19   commemorans *C**   19   qui (*for*
quia) *C H r*   ‖   introductus *r*   ‖   sententia *C r*   20   aliud (*aft.* nihil) *add C*
r   23   *sq.* post illud ... scripserat *om r*   25   contemplationi *H*   ‖   Coisl. *l.c.*
28   quomodo (*for* quoniam) *H*   29   ob ... utilitate *C (corr.)* ad ... utilitatem *r*

he wrote him the first letter to make it known that after a short time he was going to come to Timothy, for he says (1 Tim 3:14): *I am writing these things to you, hoping that I shall come to you soon.* But in writing this letter he indicates that shortly after his confession of Christ he expects his departure from this life, for he says (4:6): *as for me, I am already poured out, and the time of my dissolution is at hand.*

And he writes the first letter in such a way that it is clear that in a short time he was going to come to him,

while in the second he is expecting soon to receive his departure from this life because of his confession of Christ.

And he orders Timothy to come quickly to him, saying (4:9): *make haste* (he says) *to come to me quickly.* And he writes this letter to him from the city of Rome at the time when*

And he orders Timothy to come quickly to him. And he writes it from Rome, when ...

[191] appealing to Felix he had been brought bound to Rome from the regions of Judea.[2] And then he dwelt at Rome for two years, as Luke says, because when brought before Nero he made his defense and was released by the authority of Nero's verdict, since Nero had found that he had done nothing criminal. Once freed he immediately began to fulfill his own work, for, traveling throughout the round world, he was eager to hand over to everyone the account of true religion. But after that, coming to Rome a second time, by Nero's command

†he suffered capital punishment for the sake of true religion.*

he is decapitated for the sake of true religion.

It is at that time that he wrote this letter to Timothy from the city of Rome. And what is [192] not uncertain is that wherever Timothy was dwelling at that time, he was dwelling according to

---

[2]This is clearly a mistake. The catena suggests that the passage must have read: "And he writes this letter to him from the city of Rome. Appealing to Felix he had been brought to Rome ... coming to Rome a second time. At that time..." Note that on 2:190 the Latin has "at the time when" (*in illo tempore quando*) and on 2:191 "at that time when" (*eo in tempore quando*). Presumably Theodore has summarized the entire story leading up to the eve of Paul's execution, which is when he is thought to have written the second letter.

litate commorabatur. nam nec erat possibile apostolum sic scribere ad eum, in quibus laudaret eum et opus eius reciperet et de
singulis quae erga illum erant adfectaretur, si contra uoluntatem
apostoli relinquens eum aliis locis ubi sibi placitum fuerat fuisset
5   commoratus. scribit igitur ad eum hanc epistolam. non sicut in
prima instruit eum quemadmodum conueniret eum de singulis illis facere quae ad commune ornamentum ecclesiae poterant pertinere; sed quasi qui sufficienter eum in prima epistola de omnibus
instruxerat quae eum instrui conueniebat, hanc ad eum fecit epi-
10   stolam, consilium dans ei simulque et

†commonens eum ut cum sum-   διεγείρων αὐτὸν εἰς τὸ μετὰ σπου-
ma diligentia ea quae ad alio-   δῆς τὰ ὑπὲρ τῆς ἑτέρων ὠφελείας
rum pertinent utilitatem expe-   ἐπιτελεῖν σὺν ἡδονῇ, καὶ τὸ πάσχειν
diret cum omni alacritate; et ut   ὑπὲρ τούτων αἱρούμενον.
15   pro ipsa praedicatione etiam, si
res exigit, nec periculis se dubitaret obiectare.*

nam et plurima pars huius epistolae hoc idem uidetur exprimere;
quamobrem etiam de se, qualia et quanta multis in locis fuerit per-
20   pessus, referre adnititur, ut ad similitudinem sui etiam illum hortaretur paria sustinere. in media uero parte epistolae in qua eum
uel maxime exhortare uidetur,

†memoratus est etiam illos qui   μέμνηται δὲ καὶ τῶν πρὸς τὸ χεῖρον
in deterius serpere adniteban-   βλεπόντων, οὐ μικρῶς αὐτῶν καθ-
25   tur, non leuiter arguens eos*;   απτόμενος.

adhuc etiam et illud significans, quod tempore proficiente inter
homines malitia plurimum sumat incrementum, docens eum non
discedere ab opere propter eos qui in deterius serpunt.

†in finem uero epistolae interea   πρὸς δέ γε τῷ τέλει τῆς ἐπιστολῆς
30   illa quae secundum se sunt insi-   τὰ καθ᾽ ἑαυτὸν δηλοῖ, ἡνίκα ἐγένετό
nuat, in quibus fuerit uel sit;*   τε καὶ ἔσται.

interea uero et mandat de illis de quibus mandare ei conueniebat,
utpote qui et ad carissimum scribebat discipulum suum. nam cau-

---

3 effectaretur *C H r*   4 fuisse *H*   6 conuenire *H*   7 facere illis *r*   ‖
communem *C* H*   11 Coisl. *l. c.*   12 quae aliis essent utilia (*for* quae ad
aliorum, &c.) *r*   14 et (*aft.* exped.) *add r*   16 exiit (*for* exigit) *C H*: txt *r*   19
fuerat *r*   20-21 hortetur *r*   22 exhortari *C (corr.) r*   23 sq. Coisl. *l. c.*   27
plurima *r*   ‖ incertum (*for* increm.) *C H*: txt *r*   30 sec. serunt (*for* sec. se
sunt) *C* H* secum ferat *r*   33 sed (*for* nam) *r*

blessed Paul's wish for the benefit of others. For it would not have been possible for the apostle to write him such a letter—in which he praises him and accepts his work and is moved by each one of Timothy's circumstances—if it had been against the apostle's wish that Timothy had left him and gone to dwell somewhere else as he pleased. Thus, Paul writes him this letter. He does not instruct him, as he did in the first letter, as to how he ought to perform each of his tasks pertaining to the common adornment of the church; but inasmuch as he had sufficiently instructed him in the first letter about everything concerning which he needed instruction, he composed this letter, giving him advice and at the same time

†admonishing him to accomplish with the greatest diligence what pertained to the benefit of others and to do so with all enthusiasm and, if the event required it, to have no hesitation in thrusting himself into danger on behalf of the preaching.*

urging him to accomplish with zeal what was for the help of others and to do so with pleasure, even if he were chosen to suffer for them.

Indeed, the greater part of this letter plainly expresses this same point. For this reason Paul also strives to give an account of himself—how, what sort, and how many things he had suffered in many places—so that he may exhort Timothy to endure similar sufferings following his example. But in the middle part of the letter [193], where he is seen especially to exhort him,

†he also mentions those who were striving to creep into what was worse, not lightly condemning them,*

And he also mentions those who were looking to what was worse, upbraiding them in no small way.

and still further pointing out that as time goes on wickedness among people all the more increases, and teaching Timothy not to abandon his work because of those who creep into what is worse.

†And at the end of the letter he at times introduces his own circumstances, as they would be and are.*

And at the end of the letter he makes clear his own circumstances, as they were and would be.

And sometimes he commands what he ought to command, since, of course, he was writing to his dearly beloved disciple. Now we shall learn about each of these points as carefully as possible on the

tissime de singulis cognoscebimus ex illa interpretatione quae per partes efficietur; quorum etiam interpretationem tempus nos facere admonet, sufficienter argumento in his explanato.

Paulus apostolus Christi Iesu per uoluntatem Dei, secundum pro-
5   *missionem uitae quae est in Christo Iesu: Timotheo carissimo filio gratia, misericordia, pax a Deo Patre et Christo Iesu domino nostro.*

quod dixit: *secundum promissionem uitae quae est in Christo Iesu,* ad illud reddit quod dixerat *apostolus;* hoc est: 'apostolus creatus sum ut praedicarem promissam omnibus in futuro saeculo uitam
10   inmortalem per Christum, qui et primus pro omnibus uisus est resurrexisse; et docere uniuersos homines qui per omnem sunt orbem terrarum, ita ut suscipientes de his doctrinam possint etiam promissorum bonorum adsequi fruitionem.' et ista quidem sunt in praefatione epistolae scripta. incipit uero sic:

15   *gratiam habeo Deo, cui seruio a proauis meis in munda conscientia.*

hoc est: 'cui adcelero seruire in conscientia munda.' nec enim quasi testimonium sibi ipsi perhibens ista dixit, licet ueraciter profitetur quod haec ita se haberent. unde et adiecit:

quemadmodum sine intermissione memoriam tui habeo in orationi-
20   *bus meis nocte et die, cupiens te uidere.*

hoc uero totum in inconsummato sensu interiectum esse uidetur. ad illud autem reddidit ista apostolus quod dixerat, *gratiam habeo Deo*, et cetera.

memor lacrimarum tuarum, ut gaudio implear.

25   uult autem dicere quia 'semper memoriam tui facio in oratione mea, siue in nocte orem, siue in die; multas pro te Deo gratias refero, memor lacrimarum illarum quas effundebas eo tempore quo a me discedebas. gaudium et autem mihi plurimum confertur memoria illarum lacrimarum.' nam quod dixit: *ut gaudio implear*, il-
30   lud *ut* non causam dicit, sed consuete illud significat quod sequitur. et ut ne uideretur absolute gaudere super lacrimas:

---

1   cognoscemus *C (corr.) r*   8   redit *C r*   9   sum *om H*   20   et *(bef.* cupiens) *add C* r*   22   illum *H r*   25   illud *(for* uult) *H*   ‖   quae *(for* quia) *C H*   28   et *om H*   29-30   illud *om H*   30   non ut *(for* ut non) *H*   ‖   consuere *(sic) H*

basis of the detailed interpretation that will be made. And time urges us to compose this interpretation, since the setting has been sufficiently explained by these words.

1:1–2 Paul, an apostle of Christ Jesus by the will of God according to the promise of life that is in Christ Jesus: to Timothy, dearly beloved son, grace, mercy, peace from God the Father and Christ Jesus our Lord.

His statement *according to the promise of life that is in Christ Jesus* refers to the fact that he had said *an apostle*. That is, "I have been made an apostle in order to preach the immortal life promised to everyone in the age to come by Christ, who is seen to have risen the first on behalf of all, and in order to teach all people [194] who are throughout the lands of the whole world, so that by receiving the teaching of this they may be able to attain the enjoyment of the good things that are promised." Those words were written in the salutation of the letter. And he begins this way:

1:3a I am grateful to God, whom I serve from my ancestors in a pure conscience,

That is, "whom I am eager to serve in a pure conscience." For he has not said this to claim a testimony for himself, even though he might truly profess that this was the case. Then he added:

1:3b-4a how without ceasing I remember you in my prayers night and day, wishing to see you,

All this seems to be inserted with the meaning left incomplete. But the apostle has referred it to what he had said: *I am grateful to God* and the rest.[3]

1:4b mindful of your tears so that I may be filled with joy,

And he wants to say: "I always remember you in my prayer, whether I pray at night or in the daytime. I return much thanks to God for you, mindful of those tears you shed when you were leaving me. And very great joy is conferred on me by the memory of those tears." Indeed, when [195] he said *so that I may be filled with joy*, he says *so that* not to indicate purpose but, as usual, the result that follows. And so that he may not seem without qualification to rejoice because of tears:

---

[3] See Swete's note (2:194): "Th. connects χάριν ἔχω ... μεμνημένος, regarding ὡς ἀδιάλειπτον ... ἰδεῖν as parenthetic." That is, the logical order would be "I am grateful to God, mindful of your tears."

memoriam (inquit) *accipiens eius fidei quae in te est sine simulatione.*

'excogito et autem hinc quemadmodum sinceram Deo exhibeas fidem ex illis uel maxime ex quibus tantum erga nos exhibeas affectum qui magistri tibi uerborum pietatis extitimus, ita ut nec separationem nostram magnanimiter ferre possis.' et ostendens quoniam necessaria sit ei multis ex partibus pietatis diligentia, adiecit:

quae inhabitauit primum in auia tua Loide et matre Eunice.

et quia hoc necdum ad laudem Timothei pertinere uidebatur, si aui uel parentes eius tales fuissent, adiecit:

certus sum autem quia et in te.

hoc est, 'talis es et ipse.' et ut omni ex parte doceret ei esse pietatis diligentiam, siquidem et ab auis et a parentibus ad eundem descenderat, et quia et ipse similia hisdem exequebatur:

quam ob causam magis commoneo te ut resuscites gratiam Dei, quae in te per inpositionem manuum mearum est.

'itaque omni ex parte competit mihi sermo is qui ad te fit, ita ut in opere ipsam gratiam ostendas quam per ordinationem manuum mearum adsequi dignus repertus es.' sufficienter uero eundem est adhortatus ut omni nisu aliis adiuuare deproperet, *gratiam* uocans ordinationem eius. nam nec iustum erat eum qui diuinam donationem fuerat hac de causa adsecutus neglegere commissam sibi gratiam. et quia sufficienter eum in his omnibus ad id quod ei conueniebat exhortatus est, memoria auorum et parentum et proprii eius propositi uel arbitrii, necnon et gratiae illius quam in ordinatione fuerat adsecutus; laboriosum uero negotium ipsum esse uidebatur, et maxime ea de causa quia multa pericula illis ab aduersariis eo in tempore inferebantur, adiecit:

non (inquit) *dedit nobis Deus spiritum timoris, sed uirtutis et caritatis et pudicitiae.*

est:

3-4 exhibens *C* H r*   6   positis (*for* possis) *C** possit *r*   8   adicit *C*   9 Euniche *C H*   11   adicit *r*   13   tulisse (*for* talis es) *C* H*   ‖   inesse *C (corr.)* 15   qui (*for* quia et) *C* quae et *r*   ‖   ait (*aft* exeq.) *add r*   17   mearum *om H*   19   ordinatione *H*   20   esse (*for* es) *C* H* es esse *C (corr.)* esses *r*   ‖   est *om r*   21   alios *H r*   ‖   deproperaret *r*   22   nec nam *H*   25   memoriam *H* 26   arbitri *H*   29   ideo (*bef.* adiecit) *add r*   30   enim (*for* inquit) *r*   30-31 dilectionis (*for* caritatis) *r*   32   est *om C (corr.) r*

1:5a *receiving the memory* (he says) *of the faith that is in you without pretense,*

"And I recognize how you display sincere faith in God, especially from the great affection you display toward us who came to be your teacher in the words of true religion, so that you could not bear our separation bravely." And to show that diligence for true religion is necessary for him from many considerations, he added:

1:5b *which dwelt first in your grandmother Lois and your mother Eunice,*

And because it would plainly not yet have pertained to Timothy's praise if his grandparents or parents were such people, he added:

1:5c *and I am certain that it is also in you.*

That is, "such you also are yourself." And so that in every respect he may teach him to have diligence for true religion, even though it had come down to him from his grandparents and parents, and that he was himself following a way of life like theirs:

[196] 1:6 *For this reason I admonish you all the more that you may renew the grace of God that is in you through the laying on of my hands.*

"And so in every respect the discourse I am composing for you is designed so that you may show in deed the grace you were found worthy of receiving by the ordination of my hands." And he sufficiently exhorted him to be quick in helping others by every effort, calling his ordination *grace.* Indeed, it would not have been right for Timothy, who had received the divine gift for this reason, to neglect the grace committed to him. And because Paul has sufficiently exhorted him regarding what was right for him by all these considerations—the memory of his grandparents and parents, and of his own purpose or judgment, to say nothing of the grace he had received in ordination—and because the task itself seemed toilsome, especially because many dangers were being inflicted on them by their adversaries at that time, he added:

1:7 *God* (he says) *has not given us a spirit of fear but of power and love and chastity.*

That is,

†'nec enim formidare nos conuenit de illis malis quae ab exteris nobis inferuntur.   quare?
quoniam illa gratia Spiritus, qui
est in nobis, sufficiens est per
omnia nos confortare et in Dei
constringere caritate, necnon et
pudicos nos etiam ipsis efficere
cogitationibus.'*

οὐ τοίνυν οὐδὲ δειλιᾶν προσήκει τὰ
παρὰ τῶν ἔξωθεν ἐπαγόμενα κα-
κά· διὰ τί; ὅτι ἡ ἐνοῦσα ἡμῖν τοῦ
πνεύματος χάρις ἱκανὴ καὶ ἐνισ-
χύειν ἡμᾶς, καὶ πρὸς τὴν ἀγάπην
ἐπισφίγγειν τοῦ θεοῦ, καὶ σωφρο-
νεστέρους ἐν τοῖς λογισμοῖς μένειν
τοῖς οἰκείοις ποιεῖν.

deinde ad uerecundiam eum inuitans, adiecit:

  *ne ergo erubescas testimonium domini nostri, neque me uinctum
eius.*

    nam ualde eum ad uerecundiam in hisce dictis adtraxit, dicens
ne erubescas; quasi qui erubescere deberet illa quae pietatis, si non
et aliqua contemplatione pietatis sponte perpeti uellet. unde non
dixit *ne erubescas* Dominum, sed *testimonium Domini;* hoc est, passionem. et non sufficit ut ista diceret, sed adiecit: *et me uinctum;*
sufficienter admonens ut memorans Christum et illa quae secundum se sunt non pigeret pati, si tamen et cum apostolo et cum
Christo communionem habere adfectaretur pro hisce passionibus.
unde et adiecit:

  sed conlabora in euangelio.

    'itaque quia per passiones ipsud euangelium est perfectum, ne-
cessarium est ut communices ei per passiones quas pateris pro
aliorum utilitate.' ostendens quoniam tale est euangelium ita ut
pati pro eo dignum sit:

  *secundum uirtutem Dei, qui saluos nos fecit et uocauit uocatione
sancta, non secundum opera nostra, sed secundum suum propositum et
gratiam.*

    similis est autem haec species narrationis qua dixit: *secundum
uirtutem Dei,* illi dictioni quam dixerat: *secundum promissionem uitae quae est in Christo Iesu,* quod in praefatione posuit huius epi-

---

1 sq. Coisl. 204, f. 212 a [Cr. vii. 57, Fr. 155] Θεόδωρος· οὐ τοίνυν, κ.τ.λ.   2
ab *om H*   4   quae (*for* qui) *r*   9   cogitionibus (*sic*) *C H*   10   adicit *r*   11   noli
itaque erubescere t. d. n. Iesu Christi *r*   13   non (*for* nam) *H*   14   sunt (*aft.*
pietatis) *add r* sin (*for* si non) *H*   17   adicit *C*   ‖   se (*for* me) *C H r*   19   est
(*for* sunt) *H*   ‖   et (2°) *om H*   20   affecteret *r*   21   adicit *r*   22   labora *H*
‖   in *om r*   23   quae (*for* quia) *C* H*   ‖   ipsum *r*   25   utilitatem *H*   31
propositionem *C* H r*

†"for it is not right for us to be afraid of those evils inflicted on us by those outside. Why? Since the grace of the Spirit who is in us is enough to strengthen us in all things and [197] to bind us together in the love of God, to say nothing of making us also chaste in our very thoughts."*

Therefore, neither is it right for us to be afraid of the evils inflicted on us by those outside. Why? Because the grace of the Spirit that is within us is enough both to strengthen us and to bind us to the love of God, and to make us remain more continent in our own thoughts.

Then, inducing him to shame, he added:

1:8a *Therefore, do not be ashamed of the testimony of our Lord nor of me who am bound as his prisoner;*

Indeed, by these words he has quite dragged him to shame by saying *do not be ashamed*, inasmuch as he ought to be ashamed of what belongs to true religion if he were unwilling freely to suffer anything for the sake of true religion. That is why Paul did not say *do not be ashamed* of the Lord but *of the testimony of the Lord*, that is, his passion. And it is not enough to say this, but he adds *and of me who am bound prisoner*. He sufficiently admonishes him not to be reluctant to suffer by reminding him of Christ and of his own situation, if at least he is moved to have fellowship with the apostle and with Christ for these sufferings. Then he added:

1:8b *but toil together[4] in the gospel*

"And so, because the gospel itself is made perfect through sufferings, it is necessary for you to share in it by the sufferings you experience for the benefit of others." Showing that the gospel is like this so that it is right to suffer for it:

1:8c-9a *according to the power of God, who has saved us and has called us* [198] *by a holy calling, not according to our works, but according to his own purpose and grace,*

And the way he has expressed his discourse by saying *according to the power of God* is similar to what he had said (1:1), *according to the promise of life that is in Christ Jesus*, which he put down in

---

[4]*Conlabora.* The Greek text is συγκακοπάθησον (NRSV: "join with me in suffering"). Theodore's comment reflects the Greek text. See also 2:3.

stolae. sicut autem illic *secundum promissionem uitae* dicit, hoc autem ait: 'promissam uobis uitam creatus sum apostolus ut hanc
praedicarem;' sic et hoc in loco *secundum uirtutem* (inquit) *Dei*—
hoc est, 'per uirtutem Dei'—*qui saluos fecit nos.* 'adnitere ergo et
5 labora et passionibus te subice, ut omnibus tu ad notitiam defe-
ras illa quae pro nobis sunt dispensata.' uult autem dicere quoniam 'magnum est euangelium; uirtus autem est Dei in eo, qui saluauit nos et uocauit in sanctificationem et in incorruptelam illam
quam expectamus; quod et fecit non ob nostrum meritum sed ob
10 suam misericordiam.' tale est illud quod dictum est ad Romanos:
nec autem erubesco euangelium, uirtus autem Dei est in salutem omni
credenti. 'labora ergo digne pro magnitudine promissorum bonorum.' deinde ostendens euangelii magnitudinem, etiam de anti-
quitate uult illud extollere; ait enim:
15   *quae data est nobis in Christo Iesu ante tempora aeterna, manife-*
stata autem [nunc] per reuelationem saluatoris nostri Iesu Christi.
    'si enim exitu negotiorum nouum esse perspicitur euangelium,
sed arbitrio donantis antiquum est. nam dudum haec in Christo
fieri probauerat Deus; nunc ergo quando ipse Christus nobis ad-
20 paruit in opere illud produxit.' et magnitudinem illorum bonorum quae pro nobis fuerant dispensata ad confirmationem euangelii [ostendens], adiecit:
    qui destruxit quidem mortem, inluminauit autem uitam et incor-
ruptionem per euangelium.
25   'hoc (inquit) fecit; destruxit quidem mortem, uitam uero quandam nouam nobis reuelauit, quoniam [pro] omnibus liberatus est
corruptela. talis enim est illa uita quam per resurrectionem nobis
tribui expectamus.' et quoniam sufficienter magnitudine dogma-

---

1   hoc autem ut *C H* hoc est ut *r*   3   in hoc loco *C r*   ‖   uirtutem (1°) *om*
H   5   subie (*sic*) *H*   ‖   te (*for* tu) *C* H*: *om r*   5-6   deferes *C** defferas *H*
8   in sanctificatione et in incorruptela illam *H* in s. et in inc. illa *r*   11   enim
(*for* autem *bis*) *r*   13   et etiam *r*   15   et gratiam (*bef.* quae) *add r*   ‖   da-
tis *H*   15-16   saecularia m. est a. nunc per illuminationem *r*   16   nunc *om*
C H   19   probauerit *H*   22   ostendens *om C H r*   ‖   adicit *C r*   26   nobis
nouam *r*   ‖   quae omnibus libera e. *C* r* quoniam omnibus liberatus est *H*
27   resurrectionis *H*   28   magnitudinem *C H r*

the salutation of this letter. And just as there he says *according to the promise of life* and affirms this, "I have been made an apostle to preach the life promised to you," so also in this place he says *according to the power of God*—that is, by the power of God—*who has saved us.*[5] "Therefore, strive and work and subject yourself to sufferings, so that you may bring to everyone's notice what has been dispensed on our behalf." And he wants to say that "the gospel is great, and in it is the power of God, who has saved us and called us to sanctification and to the incorruption we await; and he did this not because of our deserving, but because of his mercy." What was said to the Romans is like this (Rom 1:16): *and I am not ashamed of the gospel, and it is the power of God for salvation to everyone who believes.* "Therefore, work in a way worthy of the greatness of the good things that are promised." Then, since he is demonstrating the greatness of the gospel, he wants to extol it because of its antiquity, for he says:

1:9b-10a *which was given to us in Christ Jesus before the times of eternity, [199] and has now been manifested through the revelation of our Saviour Jesus Christ,*

"For if by the outward fulfillment of its affairs the gospel is perceived to be new, yet by the decision of its giver it is ancient. For God had long ago given his approval that these things should be done in Christ; therefore, when Christ himself has now appeared to us, he has brought the gospel forth in actual deed." And to show the greatness of the good things dispensed for us for the confirmation of the gospel, he added:

1:10b *who has, indeed, destroyed death and has brought to light life and incorruption through the gospel,*

"This (he says) he has done; he has, indeed, destroyed death and has revealed a certain new life to us, since he has been freed from corruption on behalf of everyone. For such is that life that we expect to be bestowed on us by the resurrection." And since he has sufficiently aroused Timothy by the greatness of the doctrines,

---

[5] Swete explains this obscure comment as follows (2:198): "'As in v. 1 ἀπόστολος ... κατ' ἐπαγγελίαν means "an apostle ordained to proclaim the promise," so here κατὰ δύναμιν is to be joined with εὐαγγελίῳ, the sense being: "the Gospel which is accompanied by and operates through the power of God."' Th.'s meaning is obscured by the translation.... That the point of his remark is what I have stated, seems clear from l. 13sq. All the other Gk. commentators prefer to connect κατὰ δ. with συγκακοπάθησον."

tum eundem incitauit, adiecit:

in quo positus sum ego praedicator et apostolus et doctor gentium.

et ut ad similitudinem incitaret Timotheum: 'pro his (inquit) ego constitutus sum, ita ut et tu haec agens particeps mihi esse ui-
5 dearis.' et ultra de suis eundem plenarie adhortans, adiecit:

quam ob rem et haec patior; sed non confundor.

bene posuit *non confundor*, quia et in superioribus dixerat ad eum: *non ergo erubescas.* et ostendens quoniam iusta ratione docet non erubescere:

10 *scio* (ait) *cui credidi et certus sum quoniam potens est commendatum meum custodire in illum diem.*

'nam et ualde (inquit) supplicatus quoniam

†qui spe futurorum arram Spiritus quasi quandam commendationem mihi dedit, custodiet hoc inuiolatum, ut perfectam tunc Spiritus gratiam adsequi possimus; in qua spe ad praesens hanc Spiritus gratiam ut arram adsecuti sumus.'*	'[ὁ νῦν τὸν ἀρραβῶνα τοῦ πνεύματος] ὥσπερ τινὰ παρακαταθήκην μοι δεδωκὼς ἐπ' ἐλπίδι τῶν μελλόντων, διαφυλάξαι τοῦτο ἀκέραιον, ἐπὶ τῷ τὴν ὁλοτελῆ με τότε τοῦ πνεύματος κομίσασθαι χάριν, ἧς ἐπ' ἐλπίδι νυνὶ κεκόμισμαι ταύτην.'

formationem habe sanorum uerborum quae a me audisti in fide et caritate quae est in Christo Iesu domino nostro.

'memor esto doctrinae meae et ea quae a me saepe audisti dicente tibi de fide illa quam Deo exhibere debemus, et caritate illa
25 quae secundum Christum est.' bene autem dixit: 'formationem habe doctrinae meae.' deinde quod dixerat de se, hoc etiam et illi suadet, consilium dans ei:

bonam commendationem custodi per Spiritum sanctum, qui habitat in nobis.

30 'quam (inquit) accepisti gratiam Spiritus, hanc inlibatam cu-

1 in (*bef.* eundem) *add C H* ‖ adicit *C r* 2 et *om r* ‖ magister (*for* doctor) *r* 4 apostolus (*aft.* sum) *add r* ‖ ita (*bef* agens) *add H* 5 adicit *C r* 6 quam ob causam *H* ob quam causam h. p. *r* 7 superibus (*sic*) *H* 9 ait (*aft* erubescere) *add r* 10 ait *om r* 10-11 quia p. e depositum meum seruare *r* 13 arrha *r* ‖ sq. Coisl. 204, f. 213 b [Cr. vii. 60, Fr. 156] Θεόδωρος· ἄλλος δὲ πάλιν φησὶν παρακαταθήκην λέγεσθαι νῦν τὸν ἀρρ. τοῦ πν. ὃν ὥσπερ, κ.τ.λ. 21 formam habes *r* 22 dilectione in Chr. I. *r* 23 uidisti (*for* aud.) *C H r* 24 a deo *H* 25 formationem habet *C* H* formam habes *r* 26 dixit *r* 28 bonum depositum *r* 30 inquit *om r*

he added:

1:11 *in which I have been placed as a preacher and an apostle and a teacher of the Gentiles.*

And so that he may arouse Timothy to follow his example: "it is for these things (he says) that I have been appointed, so that you also by doing these things may be seen to share with me." And to exhort him fully and further from his own affairs, he added:

1:12a *For this reason I also suffer these things, but I am not dismayed.*[6]

He rightly put down *I am not dismayed*, because above he had said [200] to Timothy (1:8): *therefore, do not be ashamed.* And to show that it was with just reason he is teaching him not to be ashamed:

1:12b *I know (he says) in whom I have believed, and I am certain that he is mighty to keep my trust for that day.*

"Indeed, I have greatly implored (he says) that

†he who has given me in the hope of the things to come the pledge of the Spirit as a kind of *trust* will keep it unstained, so that we can acquire at that time the complete grace of the Spirit, in which hope we have acquired in the present this grace of the Spirit as a pledge."*	The one who now has given me the pledge of the Spirit as a kind of *trust* for the hope of the things to come may keep it unstained for my acquiring at that time the complete grace of the Spirit, which I have now acquired in hope.

1:13 *Hold fast the pattern of sound words that you have heard from me in the faith and love that is in Christ Jesus our Lord.*[7]

"Be mindful of my teaching and what you have often heard from me when I was speaking to you about the faith we ought to display to God and the love that accords with Christ." And he rightly said [201], "*hold fast the pattern* of my teaching." Then he also urges upon him what he had said about himself (1:12), giving him the advice:

1:14 *Keep the good trust through the Holy Spirit who dwells in us.*

"You have received (he says) the grace of the Spirit. Be quick by

---

[6]*Non confundor.* As the following comment shows, the translator should have used *erubesco* to translate ἐπαισχύνομαι. Swete comments (2:199): "The translator is here so tied to the Latin versions, that the requirements of the sense have not induced him to substitute 'erubesco,' even in the comm."

[7]"Our Lord" is added without support in the manuscripts or versions.

stodire depropera, sollicitudine et diligentia eorum quae conueniunt.' et iterum sua memorans suadet ei ut inpigre doctrinam
impleat, nullius momenti existimans illas esse tristitias quae per
singulos dies accidere ei uidentur:

5   *scis hoc quoniam auersi sunt a me omnes qui in Asia erant, ex quibus*
est Figelus et Hermogenes.

hoc in loco commemoratus esse existimatur qui et simulabant
se fidem tenere, qui etiam in Asia eo degente auersi sunt ab eo.
nam et omnis pugnae exterioris grauior est interior, hoc est, ut sui
10   se relinquant 'nihil (ait) debet te tristem facere ex illis quae accidunt tristitiis. reputa autem illa quae erga me fiunt, et quoniam
qui uidentur communes nobis esse in fide omnes me in Asia reliquerunt, ex quibus Figelus est et Hermogenes.' memoratus est
autem horum memoratim eo quod forte omnium deterius arbi-
15   trium erga apostolum in Deum ostenderunt. hoc quidem ad consolationem et instructionem dixit Timothei, ut non grauiter ferat
super illis tristitiis quae sibi accidunt; adhortans uero eum ad meliora memoratus est etiam illum qui dissimile arbitrium habuit:

det (inquit) *Dominus misericordiam Onesifori domui, quoniam*
20   *frequenter me refrigerauit et catenam meam non erubuit, sed cum ue-*
nissem Romae sollicite me exquisiuit et inuenit. det ei Dominus miseri-
cordiam inuenire a Domino in illa die. et quanta Ephesi ministrauerit
mihi, melius tu cognoscis.

nam dum memoratur Onesiforum, hortatur et Timotheum er-
25   ga pietatem diligentiam adhibere. unde et hoc in loco posuit: *et*
catenam meam non erubuit. consequenter ista iunxit illis quae ad
eius exhortationem dixerat: *ne ergo erubescas testimonium Domini.*
confidens uero de praecedenti exhortatione adiecit:

tu ergo, fili mi, confortare in gratia quae est in Christo Iesu; et quae
30   *audisti a me per multos testes haec commenda fidelibus hominibus, qui*
idonei sint etiam alios docere.

---

1 deproperat *C* H** 5 quod (*for* quoniam) *r* 6 Philetus *r* ‖ Hermogenis *H* 7 comm. est existimant *C** memoratus est existimabantur *H* memorati
esse existimantur *r*: txt *C* (*corr.*) ‖ et *om r* 9 omni p. exteriori *r* 11 re-
putat *H* 12-13 relinq. *H* 13 Philetus *r* ‖ Hermogenis *H* ‖ meminit
(*for* mem. est) *r* 14 nominatim (*for* memoratim) *r* ‖ deteriorem *C* H* 16
et *om r* ‖ et (*bef.* ut) *add r* 18 meminit (*for* mem. est) *r* ‖ et ait (*aft*
habuit) *add r* 19 det &c. [*as in Vulg.*] *r* ‖ inquit *om r* ‖ Onesiferi *H* 24
memoratus Onesiferum *H* 27 nec (*for* ne) *H* 28 procedente *r* ‖ adicit
C r 31 erunt et (*for* s. etiam) *r*

care and diligence for what is right to keep it undiminished." And
calling to mind once more his own situation, he urges him to fulfill
his teaching energetically, considering those misfortunes that were
plainly happening to him day by day to be of no importance:

1:15 *You know this, that all who were in Asia have turned away
from me, among whom are Phigelus and Hermogenes.*

In this place he is thought to have mentioned those who
pretended to hold the faith and who also turned away from him
while he was living in Asia. Indeed, every conflict among insiders
is more serious than one with outsiders; that is, it was his own
people who deserted him. "Nothing (he says) ought to bring
sorrow upon you, [202] none of the sorrowful misfortunes that
chance to happen. And consider what took place regarding me,
and that everyone in Asia, those who seemed to share with us in
faith, all deserted me, including Phigelus and Hermogenes." And
he mentioned them by name perhaps because they, worst of all,
showed their attitude toward God by the way they treated the
apostle. Paul said this to console and instruct Timothy, so that
he would not take too seriously the misfortunes that happened
to him. And to exhort him to better things he also mentioned
someone who had a different attitude:

1:16–18 *May the Lord* (he says) *give mercy to the household of
Onesiphorus, since he often refreshed me and was not ashamed of my
chain, but when I came*[8] *to Rome, he carefully sought me out and found
me. May the Lord grant him to find mercy from the Lord at that day.
And how much he ministered to me at Ephesus, you know better.*

Now while he mentions Onesiphorus he is also urging Timothy
to apply diligence for true religion. That is why he put down in
this place: *and he was not ashamed of my chain.* In logical order he
has joined these words to those he had spoken in his exhortation
(1:8): *therefore, do not be ashamed of the testimony of the Lord.*[9] And
confident about his preceding exhortation, he added:

2:1–2 *You, therefore, my son, be strong in the grace that is in Christ
Jesus,* [203] *and the things you have heard from me through many
witnesses, these entrust to faithful people, who may be fitted also to*

---

[8]*Cum venissem.* The text should probably read "when he came." Swete
points out (2:202) that "when I came" would represent γενόμενον rather than
γενόμενος, a reading that has no warrant.

[9]"Be ashamed" also occurs in 1:12.

'omni ergo ex causa gratiam illam quae data est tibi a Christo ob aliorum utilitatem rebus ipsis ostende; studium tuum ut omne quodcumque magnum est cum sollicitudine illud agas, et quae a me audisti frequenter dum alios docerem —hoc enim dicit: *per*
5 *multos testes*—haec propera et ipse docere, non quoslibet, sed quos discere ista idoneos esse existimas, qui poterint lucrum horum et in alios proferre.' deinde et exemplo eum adhortans dicit:

tu ergo conlabora, quasi bonus miles Christi Iesu.

'imitare milites istius saeculi, et militem te Christi existimans,
10 omne quod durum est et laboriosum contemplatione pietatis ferre depropera.' et ipso exemplo dans ei consilium adiecit:

nemo militans Deo implicat se negotiis saecularibus; ut ei possit placere cui se probauit.

'scito (inquit) quoniam qui uolunt ante omnia in militia sua
15 probabiles inueniri ab omni negotiatione saeculari seipsos cohibent, opere suo tantum intendentes.' bene autem dixit 'implicantur' et ualde proprie illud dixit eo quod ille qui talis est et de his studium habet, nec adtendere potest in melius, eo quod semel saecularibus implicatus est. deinde et ad aliud transit exemplum:

20 *si autem et in agone quis decertat, non coronatur nisi legitime certauerit.*

'et quidem athletas coronas adsequi inpossibile est si non solae athletitiae disciplinae intenderint et in eius perstiterint legibus. sic multo magis decens est te siue quasi athletam siue quasi mili-
25 tem Christi cohibere a corporalibus negotiis, intendere uero solae pietati.' et quia exhortatus est eum ut nullam sollicitudinem de saecularibus habeat negotiis, sed ad illa tantum intendat quae ad

---

2 ab (*for* ob) *H*   ‖   ostendere *H*   ‖   sit (*aft.* tuum) *add r*   4   a. docere (*for* dum a. docerem) *H*   ‖   dicit *om H*   5   propterea (*for* propera) *r*   ‖   quoslibet sed *om H*   6   esse ex. quae *H* ex qui *r*   8   labora sicut b. m. in Christo Iesu *r*   11   adicit *C r*   12   saecularibus *om r*   ‖   placeat (*for* p. pl.) *r*   13   placare *H*   14   uoluntate (*for* uolunt ante) *C H r*   ‖   omni (*for* omnia) *C* (*corr.*) bona *r*   15   probabilis *H*   ‖   inuenire *C** inueniri desiderant *C* (*corr.*) inueniuntur *r*   16-17   impleantur *H*   17   de (*aft.* ualde) *add H*   ‖   dixi *H*   20   nam et &c. [*as in Vulg.*] *r*   22   et quidem ad letas coronas *C* et qui   ‖   as [*sic*] coronas beatas *H* et beatas coronas *r*   22-23   solae [*corr.*: soli] ad letae disciplinae *C* sole ad letitiae disc. *H* solum ad laetitiae disciplinam *r*   23   et in eius pertinerint [?] *C** et in e. perstiterunt *C* (*corr.*) et in e. perstiterint *H* sed etiam in e. persteterint *r*   24   adletam *C* athletam *H r*   25   ea (*for* a) *H*

teach others.

"Therefore, for every reason display by the facts themselves the grace given you by Christ for the benefit of others. Your eager pursuit should be to do with care everything whatsoever that is great. And what you have often heard from me while I was teaching others—for this is what he means by *through many witnesses*—these things be quick yourself to teach, not to just anyone, but to those you consider fitted to learn, who could profit by the teaching and bring it forth to others." Then to exhort him by an example, he says:

2:3 *You, therefore, toil together*[10] *as a good soldier of Jesus Christ.*

"Be quick to imitate the soldiers of this age, and by considering yourself a soldier of Christ to bear everything harsh and toilsome for the sake of true religion." And giving him advice by the same example, he added:

2:4 *No one who is a soldier for God*[11] *entangles himself in worldly affairs, so that he may be able to please him to whom he has commended himself.*

"Know (he says) that those who before everything want [204] to be found tried and true in their military service keep themselves apart from every worldly affair, so intent are they on their work." And he rightly said, "they are entangled." He said this quite appropriately because the person who is like this occupies himself with these things and is unable to pay attention to what is better, because he has once and for all been entangled in worldly things. Then he goes on to another example:

2:5 *And if also someone competes in a contest, he is not crowned unless he has competed lawfully.*

"Indeed, it is impossible for athletes to win crowns if they do not focus their attention solely on athletic training and continue to stand fast in its laws. Thus, it is far more fitting for you, whether as an athlete or as a soldier of Christ, to keep away from bodily affairs and to pay sole attention to true religion." And because he has exhorted him to have no concern for worldly affairs, but to pay

---

[10] See 1:8.

[11] "For God" appears in the Vulgate but was almost certainly not in Theodore's text.

utilitatem pertinent aliorum, necessitas flagitat humana etiam de
illis perquiri quae erga escas sunt et indumentum:

laborantem (inquit) *agricolam oportet primum de fructibus parti-*
cipare. intellege quae dico; dabit enim tibi Dominus intellectum de
5 *omnibus.*

uult ergo dicere quoniam 'quae ad usum tuum necessarie pertinent, indiscrete adsequere a fidelibus, qui praestant tibi.' suasit
uero ei ipso exemplo uel maxime: 'sicut enim agricola quidam, ipse tu tua doctrina instituis ac doces fidelibus uirtutis et boni operis
10 fructus Deo offerre; iustum est et ante omnes te adsequi, cuius labore etiam ceteri adsequi uidentur.' unde et adiecit: *intellege quae*
dico, quasi qui occultius illud dixerit. simul etiam et optat de omnibus ei tribui intellectum.

memor esto Iesum Christum surrexisse ex mortuis ex semine Dauid
15 *secundum euangelium meum, in quo laboro usque ad uincula quasi ma-*
lefactor.

bene memoratus est *ex semine*, ut corporis magis adsumptio-
nem factam insinuaret. nec autem absolute ista posuit, sed necessarie. eo uel maxime tempore ista docere adnitebantur. nam
20 Simon et qui ex eius sunt haeresi omnes tune inchoauerant dicere quoniam Christus non fuit in carne, sed in phantasmate quodam adparuit, ita ut nec resurrectio uera facta esse susciperetur;
qui enim fieri poterat ut uera crederetur resurrectio, si caro uera
ratione non fuisset sumpta? hoc ergo idem dicit: 'memor esto do-
25 cere pro uirium tuarum possibilitate quoniam ex semine natus est
Dauid Iesus Christus, homo uera ratione secundum naturam factus, qui et resurrexit a mortuis; quod etiam cunctis futurum esse
euangelizo. hac de causa adquiesco illa sustinere quae sustinent
malefactores, eo quod magnum lucrum scio ex hoc posse adqui-
30 ri.' et ut ostendat quoniam ex illis tristitiis quae ei accidunt pietas

---

2 qui *H* ‖ esca *C*H* escam *r* 3 inquit *om r* 3-4 particire (*sic*) *H* accipere
(*for* participare) *c* 6 autem (*for* ergo) *H r* ‖ quomodo (*for* quoniam) *H*
‖ necessario *r* 7 fidebus (*sic*) *r* fideles qui (*for* fidelibus) *r* 9 et *om H* 10
differe (*for* deo off.) *H* ‖ adsequere (*for* adsequi [1°.]) *C*H*r* 11 adicit *C*
dicit *r* 12 occultus *H** 13 et (*for* ei) *H* 14 resurrexisse a (*for* surr. ex) *r*
‖ quod (*for* Dauid) *C* H* 15-16 male operans (*for* malef.) *r* 17 autem
dixit (*for* mem. est) *r* 18-19 necessario *r* 19 annitebatur *r* 23 quia (*for*
qui) *r* 24 non *om C* H r* 28 euangelio *C* H* euangelium testatur *r* 29
et (*for* ex) *H* 30 accedunt *r*

great attention to what pertains to the benefit of others, human necessity demands that questions about food and clothing also be raised:

2:6–7 *The farmer who toils* (he says) *must be the first to share in the fruits. Understand what I am saying, for the Lord will give you understanding about all things.*

[205] Therefore, he wants to say: "those things that necessarily pertain to your needs, acquire them indifferently from the faithful who furnish them to you." And he urges him especially by the very example he uses: "for just like some farmer you set to work on your teaching, and you teach the faithful to offer to God the fruits of virtue and doing good, and it is right for you, by whose toil the rest also plainly acquire their share, to acquire your share before all." Then he added: *understand what I am saying*, as though he were speaking rather obscurely. And at the same time he also prays that understanding about all things may be bestowed on Timothy.

2:8–9a *Be mindful that Jesus Christ has risen from the dead, from the seed of David, according to my gospel, in which I toil up to chains as a criminal,*

He rightly mentioned *from the seed*, so that he might all the more imply that the assumption of the body took place. And he did not put those words down without purpose, but necessarily. Especially at that time people were striving to teach those things.[12] For Simon and all those from his heresy had begun at that time [206] to say that Christ did not exist in flesh but appeared in some kind of apparition, so that no true resurrection should be accepted to have taken place. For how could belief in a true resurrection have come about if flesh had not been assumed by true account? Thus, he is saying this very thing: "be mindful of teaching with all the might you can that Jesus Christ was born of the seed of David, made a man by true account according to nature, who also rose from the dead—this I also preach in the gospel will come to pass for all. It is for this reason that I am content to endure what criminals endure, because I know I can gain great profit from this." And to show that true religion can in no way be harmed by

---

[12]That is, docetic views of Christ.

nulla ex parte noceri potest, adiecit:

sed uerbum Dei non est alligatum.

hoc est: 'licet ego plurima sustineam mala, sed nulla ex hoc adnascitur nociuitas ueritati negotiorum; mansit etenim Dei promissio inlibata, si innumeris ego uidear subici tormentis.' consequenter uero praecedentibus adiungit:

*propter quod omnia sustineo propter electos, ut ipsi salutem adse-
quantur eam quae in Christo est Iesu cum gloria aeterna.*

'propter eos qui ad hoc sunt electi et segregati omnia pati sustineo, ita ut per Christum salutem adsequantur, in perpetua gloria
degentes.' et ad exhortationem Timothei dicens adiecit:

*fidele uerbum: 'si enim commortui sumus, et conuiuemus; si susti-
nemus, et conregnabimus'.*

'indubium (inquit) est hoc, quoniam nos qui communicamus
illis quae deteriora sunt, necessarie communicabimus ei et in illis
quae meliora sunt.' et ostendens lucra quae ex compassione solent
adquiri, dicit etiam illud detrimentum quod illis solet euenire qui
in fide persistere noluerunt:

si negabimus, et ille negabit nos.

deinde ne uideretur secundum aequam partem et ipse a nobis
negatus noceri, adiecit:

si non credimus, ille fidelis manet; negare seipsum non potest.

nam illa quae a nobis inconuenienter fiunt [nobis nocent], ille
uero nulla ex parte nocetur; manet etenim in sua gloria stabilis ac
firmus, nec autem possunt ista negari quae in ipsis perspiciuntur
negotiis.

haec commone, testificans coram Domino.

bene dixit *testificans*, ut in timorem eum redigat.

noli uerbis pugnare; in nihil utile est nisi in subuersione audien-

---

1   docere (*for* noceri) *C* H r* decidere *C* (*corr.*)   ‖   adicit *C r*   3   dicit (*for* licet) *H*   ‖   malam *C**   ‖   nulli *C H r*   4   maneret enim *C** manet *C* (*corr.*) *r* mansierat *H*   5   si *om H*   ‖   subieci *C** uideor subici *C* (*corr.*)   7   ideo &c. [*as in Vulg.*] *r*   11   adicit *C r*   12   fidelis sermo &c. [*as in Vulg.*] *r*   ‖   cummortui *C*   14   non est dubium inquit hoc nos *r*   15   necessario *r*   19   negauerimus *r*   20   ipse a nobis negastis [*sic*] noceri *C** ipsi nobis negantibus nocere *r*   21   adicit *C r*   23   nobis nocent *om C H: txt r*   ‖   illi *C r*   25   etiam (*for* autem) *r*   ‖   negare *C H r*   27   commune *r*   28   timore *C* H* in timore *C* (*corr.*): *txt r*   29   contendere (*for* pugnare) *r*   ‖   ad nihilum enim u. e. nisi ad subuersionem *r*   ‖   est *om C* (*corr.*)

the misfortunes that happen to him, he added:

2:9b *but the word of God is not bound.*

That is, "even though for my part I am enduring a great many evils, yet no harm to the truth of the matter arises from this. Indeed, God's power has remained undiminished no matter how numberless the torments are to which I am seen subjected." And in logical order with what precedes, he joins to it:

2:10 *Because of this I endure everything because of the elect, so that they may themselves gain the salvation that is in Christ Jesus with eternal glory.*

"Because of those who have been elected and separated for this I endure suffering all things so that they may gain salvation through Christ, living in perpetual glory." And speaking to exhort Timothy, he added:

2:11–12a *Faithful is the word: "for if we have died with him, we shall also live with him; if we endure, we shall also reign with him."*

[207] "There can be no doubt (he says) that we who have shared in what is worse shall necessarily share with him also in what is better." And to show the profits that are usually gained by suffering with him, he speaks also of the loss that usually comes about for those unwilling to continue steadfast in faith:

2:12b *If we shall deny, he also will deny us.*

Then, lest it should seem that in the same respect God should himself be harmed by our denial, he added:

2:13 *If we have not believed, he remains faithful, for he cannot deny himself.*

Indeed, what we do unfittingly harms us, but he is in no respect harmed. He surely remains immoveable and steadfast in his own glory, nor can those things perceived in these very matters be denied.

2:14a *Remind these things, testifying in the presence of God.*

He rightly said *testifying*, so that he might reduce him to fear.

2:14b *Do not fight with words, for there is nothing beneficial unless*[13] *in the overturning of the hearers.*

---

[13] See Swete's note (2:207): "*noli u. pugnare*] μὴ λογομάχει. The comm. (p. 208, l. 2) seems to shew that this, the reading of the Latin versions, was also followed by Th. *Pugnare* (Vulg., "contendere") finds place in Ambrstr.; in the rest of the verse our translator agrees with *Clarom.*, excepting that the latter authority, with the Latin versions generally, adds "enim," and omits *nisi. Nisi,* it will be observed, is omitted by *C* and *H* in the comm. (p. 208, l. 3). Th.

tium.

'commone (inquit) ut ista sectentur, Dei illis proponens iudicium. noli autem contentioni studere; ex contentione enim nihil adnascitur, quia mendacia confirmare cupiunt ad plurimorum su
5   buersionem.'

festina teipsum probabilem exhibere Christo, operarium inconfusibilem, recte tractantem uerbum ueritatis; profanas autem uocum nouitates deuita.

'cautelae dogmatum intende, et ea quae ueritatis sunt commo
10   ne; recto edoce instituto, et non pigeas laborem pro his subire. nam aduersariorum *nouitates uocum,* quae omni immunditia plenae sunt, ad nociuitatem multorum excogitatae, repelle.'

*multum autem proficiunt ad impietatem, et sermo eorum sicut cancer serpit; ex quibus est Hymenaeus et Filetus, qui a ueritate excide
15   runt, dicentes resurrectionem iam factam esse, et fidem quorundam subuertunt.*

uult dicere: 'noli nouum aliquid existimare etsi secundum impietatem prouectum eos ad praesens habere perspicias, eo quod multi eos subsequentur. ad similitudinem et autem passionis can
20   cer[is] qui solet serpere in gregem, etiam ipsi multos fidelium suis sermonibus inescantes adtrahunt ad impietatem; sicut Hymenaeus et Filetus, qui ueram Christi resurrectionem abnegantes, aliam quandam resurrectionem somniantur, quam et in successionem aiunt nostram constare.' necessarie et ista ad consolationem
25   eius dixisse uidetur apostolus, eo quod ualde consueuit tristes facere eos qui utilitatem aliorum prospicere sunt ordinati, si plurimos fidelium uiderint in deterius serpere. unde et persistens suadere ei ut non adflictus animo deficiat et ob aliorum malitiam in stuporem uertatur, adiecit:

---

2   commune *C* H*   4   quae (*for* quia) *C H* quod *r*   ‖   plurimo non (*for* plurimorum) *C* H**   6   sollicite &c. [*as in Vulg.*] *r*   7   ueritate *C* H*   ‖ profana a. inaniloquia *r*   9-10   commune *C H*   11-12   plena, excogitata *C H r*   12   sunt (*aft.* mult.) *add C* H r*   ‖   et (*aft.* sunt) *add r*   ‖   nouitatem (*for* nociu.) *C H*   15   esse *om r*   ‖   subu. fid. quor. *r*   17   et (*for* etsi) *r*   17-18   pietatem (*for* imp.) *C r*   18   prouectam *C* H*   19   subsequentur *C* H*   ‖   et *om r*   19-20   cancer *C H r*   20   serpiri *H*   21   adtrahant *C* H r*   23   somniant *r*   23-24   succensionem *C H r*   24   aiunt n. *om r*   ‖   necessario *r*   26   ad (*bef.* util.) *add r*   ‖   pro specie (*for* prosp.) *r*   26-27   plures nos (*for* plurimos) *H*   27   ifidelium (= inf.?) *H*

[208] "Remind them (he says) to follow those things, setting before them God's judgment. And do not be zealous for dispute, for nothing arises from dispute, because people want to confirm lies to overturn a great many people."

2:15–16a *Make haste to present yourself approved to Christ, a worker not put to shame, rightly handling the word of truth. And avoid profane novelties of words.*[14]

"Pay attention to accuracy of doctrines, and remind them of what belongs to truth. Instruct them in a right way of life, and do not be displeased at undergoing toil for them. Drive away, then, the adversaries' *novelties of words*, which are filled with every impurity, thought up for harming many."

2:16b-18 *And they go forward further to ungodliness, and their word creeps on like a cancer.*[15] *Among them are Hymenaeus and Philetus, who have fallen away from the truth, saying that the resurrection has already taken place, and they overturn the faith of some.*

He wants to say: "do not consider it something strange, even if you perceive that what has been brought forth in accord with ungodliness has taken hold of them for the present, because there are many who follow them.[16] And like a cancerous disease that usually creeps on into a gangrene,[17] they even [209] drag many of the faithful to ungodliness, enticing them with their words. Take, for example, Hymenaeus and Philetus, who deny the true resurrection of Christ and dream of some other resurrection that they say consists in our adoption." The apostle seems to have said this necessarily to console Timothy, because it was quite usual for those ordained to look out for the benefit of others to be despondent if they saw a good many of the faithful creeping on to what was worse. And so, continuing to urge Timothy, afflicted in his soul, not to lose heart and not to be bewildered because of the

---

was probably at one with Chrys. and Thdt. in reading εἰς οὐδὲν χρήσιμον, ἐπὶ καταστροφῇ, κ.τ.λ. So the Peshito."

[14] *Vocum novitates*, reflecting the reading καινοφωνίας rather than κενοφωνίας. Cf. 1 Tim 6:20.

[15] *Cancer* can mean not only "crab" but also various diseases, including gangrene.

[16] The reference of the two instances of "them" is unclear. What Theodore appears to mean is that the heresy has taken hold of many of the faithful (the first "them"), who follow the heretics (the second "them").

[17] Swete (2:208) suggests emending *in gregem* to *in gangraenam*.

firmum autem fundamentum Dei stat, habens signaculum hoc:
'nouit Dominus qui sunt eius.'

'hic et (inquit) te duo consolentur; primum quidem, quoniam
aliorum seductio non exterminat rerum ueritatem; secundo, quoniam suos qui ueri sunt eius olim cognouit Deus. itaque eos quos
nunc perspicis seduci, hos Deus olim reprobos esse sciebat; nihil
ergo fit nouum, ut in stuporem uertaris, sed illud fit quod olim fieri
sciebat Deus.' nam cuius rei curam habere debemus instruit, dicens:

et, 'discedat ab impietate omnis qui nominat nomen Domini.'

ut huiusmodi homines discedant ab omni impietate. et quia
hoc modo optimos magistros sciebat ualde his adfligi, qualis erat
et beatus Timotheus, ea ratione qua multos ex suis uidebat in deterius prorupisse; hac de causa adiecit et aliam ei consolationem:

in magna (inquit) *domo non sunt sola uasa aurea et argentea, sed*
et lignea et fictilia; et quaedam quidem sunt in honorem, alia uero in
contumeliam.

'magna (inquit) est domus Dei ecclesia, ex multis consistens
hominibus; necesse est ergo non omnes ibi esse aequos. nam et
in magna domo non possunt omnia uasa similia repperiri, licet sit
domus ualde magna; sed inter aurea et argentea uasa perspiciuntur et lignea et fictilia; et alia quidem multo digna sunt honore, alia
uero sunt contemptibiliora, et ad certum usum discreta.' deinde
quia et naturalis uasorum erat diuisio, ut ne quid tale apud nos existimaret, adiecit:

si enim qui se mundauerit ab his, erit uas in honore, sanctificatum
et optimum Domino, ad omne opus bonum praeparatum.

'sed quod illic materia naturalis, facit [hic] arbitrium—qui
enim se a deterioribus segregauerit est uas utile; hoc autem in nostro est positum arbitrio et potestate.' et ostendit illud esse pro-

1 primum (*for* firmum) *C H* ‖ sed firm. (*for* firm. autem) *r* 2 cognouit *r*
8 instituit *r* 10 et *om r* ‖ iniquitate *r* 12 homo (*for* hoc modo) *C H* ‖
de (*bef.* his) *add r* 14 ei *om C* 15 inquit *om r* 16 quidam (*for* quaedam) *H*
‖ honore *H* 17 contumelia *H* 18 domus est eccl. (*om* Dei) *r* 23 con-
temptibilia *r* 24 est (*for* et) *C**: *om r* ‖ erat uas. *r* 24-25 et estimaret *C**
exestimaret *H* 25 adicit *C r* 26 mund. se *r* 27 paratum *H* 28 hic *om*
C H ‖ est (*aft.* arb.) *add H* 29 ut ille (*for* utile) *H* 30 potestatem *C**
‖ esset *H*

wickedness of others, he added:

2:19a *And the firm foundation of God stands, having this seal, "The Lord knows who are his,"*[18]

"Here (he says) there are two things to console you: first, that the straying away of others does not destroy the truth of the facts; second, that God long ago recognized those who are truly his own. And so God long ago knew that those you now see being led astray would be reprobates. Therefore, nothing strange is happening to bewilder you, but what is happening is what God long ago knew would happen." So he instructs us about what we ought to be concerned, saying:

2:19b *and "Let everyone who names the name of the Lord depart from ungodliness."*[19]

That people of this kind may depart from all ungodliness. And because [210] he knew that the best teachers in this way were strongly afflicted by this, as was blessed Timothy on the grounds that he saw many of his own people breaking forth to what was worse, for this reason Paul added another consolation for him:

2:20 *In a great house* (he says) *there are not only gold and silver vessels but also wood and clay, and some, of course, are for honor, but others for dishonor.*

"The great house of God (he says) is the church, consisting of many people; therefore, it is necessary that not all of them there are equal. For, as well, in a great house not all the vessels can be found alike, granted that the house is quite great; but among the gold and silver vessels are seen also wooden and clay ones. And, of course, some are worthy of much honor, but others are less important and set aside for particular use." Then, because the distinction of vessels was a natural one, so that Timothy would not think such a thing the case with us, he added:

2:21 *For if someone should cleanse himself from these, he will be a vessel for honor, sanctified and best for the Lord, prepared for every good work.*

"But what there the natural material does, here free choice does—[211] for whoever has separated himself from the worse things is a useful vessel. And this has been placed in our free choice and authority." And he shows that this belongs to our

---

[18] See Num 16:5; John 10:14; 1 Cor 8:3.

[19] *Ab impietate.* In his comment Theodore has added "all"—*ab omni ipietate.*

positi; iterum uertit se ad eius exhortationem, paulo minus hanc
habens intentionem per omnem hanc epistolam. unde et adiecit:
    iuuenilia desideria fuge.
    'omnem delectationem et uanam uoluptatem quae tibi non co-
5 nuenit longe a te facito, quibus uel maxime rebus capi consueuit
iuuentus.'
    sectare uero iustitiam, fidem, caritatem, pacem, cum omnibus qui
inuocant Dominum ex mundo corde.
    'diligentiam adhibe iustitiae et eam quae in Deum est fidem et
10 caritatem et pacem, cum illis qui uitae uirtutibus student.' optime
dicens de his suadet ut in quibus et deceret et possibile esset pacem
seruare adnitatur:
    stultas (inquit) *et indoctas quaestiones deuita, sciens quoniam ge-*
nerant lites.
15   *stultas et indoctas* uocauit *quaestiones* quae non ob aliquam fiunt
utilitatem. 'declina (inquit) ab illis qui absolute solis quaestionibus operam suam expendere cupiunt. rixae autem ex his adnascuntur, quorum nec recta est intentio.' et quia res ista nec conueniat nec deceat ei ostendit:
20   *seruum* (inquit) *Domini non oportet litigare.*
    deinde et modum illi exponens quomodo debeat doctrinae in-
tendere:
    sed modestum esse ad omnes, docibilem, non litigiosum, cum mode-
stia docentem eos qui resistunt ueritati.
25   et utilitatem ipsius rei ostendens et quantum melius sit sic docere resistentes, adiecit:
    ne quando det eis Deus poenitentiam ad cognitionem ueritatis, et
resipiscant a diaboli laqueis, a quo capti tenentur ab eo in eius uolun-
tate.
30   ex contentione autem placari aduersarios inpossibile est; doctrina uero mansuetudine probata saepe scit suadere et duritiam

---

1 haec (*for* hanc) *C* H*   2 adicit *C* inquit *r*   3 autem (*aft.* iuuenilia) *add*
r   5 ad (*for* a) *C**   7 his (*for* omnibus) *r*   9 est *om C*   11 de his dicens
C r || suadit *C* H* || et (1°) *om r* || et (2°) *om H* || decertet (*for*
deceret) *C* (*corr.*) || est *H*   13 sine disciplina (*for* indoctas) *r* || quia (*for*
quoniam) *r*   17 spendere (*sic*) *C** splendere *r*   18 quae (*for* quia) *C H*   19
eum *r*   22 ait (*aft* intend.) *add r*   25 quanto *C r*   26 sistentes *C*: om H*
|| adicit *r*   27 agnitionem *r*   28 captiui *r* || tenenentur (*sic*) *C*   28-29
uoluntatem *H*   30 aduersariis *r* || est *om H*   31 in (*bef.* mans.) *add H*

purpose. Once more he turns his attention to exhortation, since he has this aim in almost all of this letter. And so he added:

2:22a *Flee youthful desires,*

"Keep far from you every delight and vain sensual pleasure that is not fitting for you; by these things especially youth has usually been taken captive."

2:22b *and pursue justice, faith, love, peace, with all who call upon the Lord from a pure heart.*

"Hold fast to diligence for justice and to faith in God and love and peace, together with those who are zealous for the virtues of life." Speaking quite effectively of these things, he urges Timothy to strive for preserving peace among those for whom it is both fitting and possible:

2:23 *Avoid* (he says) *foolish and uninstructed speculations, knowing that they generate disputes.*

He called *speculations* that do not take place for any benefit *foolish and uninstructed.* "Turn away (he says) from those who wish to expend their effort simply on speculations alone. It is from them that quarrels [212] arise; these people do not have a right aim." And he shows him that this practice is neither right nor becoming:

2:24a *The servant of the Lord* (he says) *ought not to dispute,*

Then, to set forth the way he ought to pay attention to teaching:

2:24b-25a *but to be modest to all, capable of teaching, not disputatious, teaching with modesty those who oppose the truth,*

Demonstrating both the benefit of this very thing and how much better it is to treat opponents this way, he added:

2:25b-26 *if at some time God may give them repentance to the knowledge of the truth and they may come to their senses from the snares of the devil by which they are held captive by him in his will.*

"It is impossible for adversaries to be conciliated by contention, but teaching with acceptable gentleness often can persuade and

animi mollire. praeparat enim ut et ad ueritatem perspicere possint, discedentes a praesumptione, a qua et anticipati quasi quodam laqueo diabolico constricti tenentur, protractum quidem in
deterius, correctionem uero in melius nullam uolentes suscipere.'
5   deinde et futurorum in nouissimis temporibus memoria consolatur beatum Timotheum ut non animo deficiat pro prauissimis
temporibus [et] hominibus:

    hoc (inquit) *cognosce quoniam in nouissimis diebus instabunt tempora periculosa.*

10   consueuit namque deteriorum memoria consolare eos qui in
moribus malis sunt. et quae sint tempora periculosa egerens adiecit:

    erunt (inquit) *homines*
†*seipsos amantes.*   Φίλαυτοί
15   omnia ad suam facientes uti-   εἰσιν οἱ πάντα πρὸς τὴν ἑαυτῶν
litatem uel prodificationem.*   ὠφέλειαν ποιοῦντες·

    cupidi pecuniarum.

    quia et studium omne expendunt in colligendis pecuniis.
†*elati.*   ἀλαζόνες,
20   qui iactant se illa habere quae   καυχώμενοι ἔχειν ἃ μὴ ἔχουσιν·
non habent.

    superbi.   ὑπερήφανοι,

    qui magna sapiunt pro illis   μεγάλα φρονοῦντες ἐπὶ τοῖς οὖ-
quae habere uidentur.   σιν·
25   *blasphemi.*   βλάσφημοι,

    derogationi studentes et om-   κατηγορίαις χαίροντες.
nem curam erga derogationem
habentes.*

    parentibus non oboedientes.
30   euidens est quod adiecit.

    ingrati.

    ad eos qui bene sibi faciunt; nam in parte prauorum ponit etiam

---

1 ut uer. prospicere p. *l*   2 quasi *om H*   3 quidem (*aft.* protractum) *om C*
4 correctione *H*   7 tempori *C* (*corr.*) ‖ et *om C H r* ‖ sicut sequitur in
subiecto capite (*aft* hom.) *add r*   10 immoribus (*for* in mor.) *H*   11 mali *C*
‖ egerans *C* H* exaggerans *C* (*corr.*) ostendens *r*   11-12 adicit *C r*   14 sq.
Coisl. 204, f. 218 a [Cr. vii. 71, Fr. 156] Θεόδωρος. φίλαυτοι, κ.τ.λ.   16 pro
defectione (*for* prodif.) *C H r*   20 qui *om H**   23-24 Fr.: "legendum uidetur
προσοῦσιν uel ὑπάρχουσιν."   30 adicit *C r*   32 tibi (*for* sibi) *C* H*

soften the hardness of the soul. For it prepares people so that they are able to look at the truth, departing from the stubbornness by which they are held fast bound in their presuppositions as though by some diabolic snare, willing to receive progress toward the worse but no correction for the better." [213] Then he also consoles blessed Timothy by mentioning the things to come in the last times, so that he may not lose heart in the face of the most perverse of times and people:

3:1 *Know this* (he says), *that in the last days perilous times will come about.*

To be sure, the mention of what is worse usually has consoled those who live in evil times.[20] And to express what the perilous times are, he added:

3:2a *There will be people*

†*loving themselves,*	*loving themselves,*
Doing everything for their own benefit or advancement.*	They are those who do everything for their own benefit.
3:2b *lovers of money,*	
Because they expend all their zeal in gathering money.	
†3:2c *lifted up,*	*pretentious,*
Who boast that they have what they do not have.	Boasting that they have what they do not have.
3:2d *proud,*	*arrogant,*
Who think highly of what they seem to have.	Thinking highly of their possessions.
[214] 3:2e *slanderers,*	*slanderers,*
Zealous for accusation and having entire concern for accusation.*	Taking pleasure in accusations.

3:2f *disobedient to parents,*
What he has added is clear.

3:2g *ungrateful,*
To those who treat them well; for he places in one group of

---

20 Reading, as Swete suggests (2:213), *in temporibus malis* instead of *in moribus malis.*

eos qui beneficio sunt subleuati, si non gratias agant illis qui beneficia contulerunt.

†scelesti.   ἀνόσιοι,

illos dicit qui iustitiae nullam   ἐπιμέλειαν τοῦ δικαίου μὴ ποιού-
5 adhibent diligentiam.   μενοι·

sine affectu.   ἄστοργοι,

illos dicit qui nullum erga   περὶ οὐδένα σχέσιν ἔχοντες·
quemquam affectum uolunt ha-
bere.

10 [sine fide.   ἄσπονδοι,

qui neque firmi sunt erga   οὐ βέβαιοι περὶ τὰς φιλίας, οὐδὲ
amicitias, neque ueraces super   ἀληθεῖς περὶ ἃ συντίθενται·
iis quae] spondent.

criminatores.   διάβολοι,

15 qui istorum uerba ad illos   ταῦτά τε ἐκεῖ κἀκεῖνα ἐνταῦθα
et aliorum ad istos referunt, ut   λέγοντες ἐπὶ τῷ κατεργάζεσθαι
lites inter eos commoueant.   μάχην·

incontinentes.   ἀκρατεῖς,

illos dicit qui passionibus in-   ἥττους τῶν παθῶν·
20 firmiores sunt.

inmites.   ἀνήμεροι,

illos dicit qui nullius boni   οὐδεμιᾶς χρηστότητος ἐπιμε-
diligentiam uolunt habere.   λούμενοι·

ingrati.

25 qui non libenter bonorum
studia exequuntur.

proditores.

ut dicat 'amicorum.'

proterui.

30 parati ad malum.

inflati.   τετυφωμένοι,

quoniam magna sapiunt in   μεγάλα φρονοῦντες ἐπὶ τοῖς μὴ
his quae sibi minime adsunt. est   προσοῦσιν· διαφέρει δὲ τοῦ ἀλαζό-
autem differentia inter 'elatum'   νος τῷ τὸν μὲν τετυφωμένον ἀπὸ
35 et 'inflatum,' quoniam inflatus   τῆς γνώμης λέγειν, ἀλαζόνα δὲ τὸν
ab arbitrio designatur, elatus ue-   ἐπὶ ῥήματι καυχώμενον.

---

3 sq. Coisl.*l. c.*   7 nullam *C* H*   10 sine fide … quae *om C H r: cf. g*   13
sponte (*for* spondent) *r*   15 ἐκεῖνα (*for* κἀκ.) cod. edd.   17 illos (*for* lites) *H*
19 in (*bef.* pass.) *add r*   34 deferentia *C**

perverse people even those who have been assisted by a benefit, if they do not thank those who have conferred the benefits.

†3:2h *profane,*
He means those who apply no diligence to justice.

profane,
Having no concern for what is just.

3:3a *without affection,*
He means those who are unwilling to have any affection for anyone.

without affection,
Having a relation with no one.

[3:3b *without trust,*
Who are neither steadfast in friendships nor truthful about the things] they pledge.[21]

implacable,
Not steadfast in friendships nor truthful in what they covenant to do.

3:3c *accusers,*
Who carry back the words of those to these and of others to those, so that they may stir up quarrels among them.

false accusers,
Speaking these things there and those things here to work up a quarrel.

[215] 3:3d *incontinent,*
He means those who are weaker than their passions.

incontinent,
Weaker than the passions.

3:3e *savage,*
He means those unwilling to have diligence for any good thing.

savage,
Caring for no goodness.

3:3f *ungrateful,*[22]
Who do not freely follow pursuits of good things.

3:4a *betrayers,*
Meaning "of friends."

3:4b *reckless,*
Ready for evil.

3:4c *puffed up,*
Since they think highly of what is by no means theirs. And

puffed up,
Thinking highly of what is not theirs. And this person

---

[21] Swete (2:214) restores the Latin between the brackets on the basis of the Greek and notes that *spondent* has "escaped" the copyist's omission.

[22] See Swete's note (2:215): "The copyists appear to have transcribed this word from v. 2, in place of 'bonorum inimici' (Ambrstr.), or 'sine benignitate' (*Clarom.*, Vulg.)."

ro qui in sermonibus se iactare
consueuit.*

amatores magis uoluptatum quam Dei.

qui uoluptates pietati praehonorandas esse existimant. haec
5 autem non de exteris dicit sed de domesticis ecclesiae, quia tales
erunt. nam et ab initio sermo illi de talibus fuit qui in deterius
solent serpere, ex illo loco quo dixit: *memor esto Iesum Christum
resurrexisse ex mortuis,* in exhortatione ea qua consilium dans ipsi
Timotheo aduersarios arguere est adnisus qui et multos ex illis qui
10 ecclesiae erant subuertere nitebantur; pro quibus eum et ad plenum consolatur ut non grauiter ferat ualde, sed intendat quidem
suo opere, segreget uero se ad plenum a prauis hominibus. unde
et nunc quasi qui de talibus dicat, quia 'erunt quidem aliquando
in nouissimis diebus uel temporibus, qui sub specie domesticorum
15 acturi sunt illa quae non oportent fieri.' unde optime adiecit:

habentes formationem pietatis, uirtutem autem eius negantes.

et simulantes quidem se tenere pietatem, a negotio uero ipso
multum distantes. et quia tales sunt illi qui tunc erunt, de quibus
ei sermo:

20 *et hos* (inquit) *deuita. ex his autem sunt qui se mergunt in domos et
captiuas ducunt mulierculas coaceruatas peccatis, quae ducuntur uariis desideriis, semper discentes et numquam ad scientiam ueritatis uenientes.*

'itaque talibus extantibus illis qui in nouissimis erunt diebus,
25 quorum in aenigma isti sunt, declinare ab eis pro uirium tuarum
possibilitate adcelera, qui sua prauitate in domibus sese aliorum
inmergunt, ut seducentes aliquas in deterius adtrahant; non illas
mulieres quae uere sunt piae et fideles—hoc enim fieri inpossibile est—sed illas quae aestimantur esse nostrae, repletae sunt ue-
30 ro omni prauitate et a nobis quidem semper discunt illa quae agere oportebant, iuuamen uero nullum ex doctrina nostra recipiunt

3 uoluntatum *H* ‖ uolupt. magis *r* 4 uoluntates *C H r* ‖ pietatis *r*
‖ est (*for* esse) *C** ‖ existimat *H* 5 tales erant *C** talis est *H* 7 quo
om H 8 a (*for* ex) *H* ‖ ipse *C H* 9 Timotheum *H* 10 erunt *C** sunt *r*
‖ nituntur *r* 11 ualde f. *C r* 12 operi *r* 13 dicit *H** ‖ erunt (*for*
quia e.) *C* quae sunt *H* qui s. *r* 15 oportet *H r* ‖ adicit *C r* 16 formam,
abnegantes *r* ‖ autem *om H* 17 uero *om H* 18 erunt (*for* sunt) *C r* 20
penetrant (*for* se m.) *r* 21 oneratas *r* 22-23 peruenientes *r* 26 domos *r*
29 non re (*for* nostrae) *H* 30 illas *C* H*

there is a difference between "lifted up" and "puffed up," since the person puffed up is so designated from his purpose, but the person who is lifted up is the one who has usually boasted of himself in words.*

differs from the braggart, because he means someone puffed up from his purpose, while the braggart is someone who boasts in his speech.

3:4d *lovers more of pleasure than of God,*

[216] They suppose that pleasures must be honored before true religion. And he says these things not of outsiders but of those belonging to the household of the church, because there were such people. Indeed, from the beginning his discourse was about such people who usually creep into what is worse, that is, from the place where he said (2:8): *be mindful that Jesus Christ has risen from the dead.* Giving Timothy advice in his exhortation, he made every effort to condemn the adversaries, who were striving to overturn many of those who belonged to the church. And he gives Timothy full consolation for those who were overturned, so that he would not bear it too heavily but would attend to his own work and separate himself completely from perverse people. That is why now, as though he were speaking of such people, he says (see 3:1): "there will, indeed, be a time in the last days or times when some who appear to belong to the household of faith will be driven to do what ought not be done." And so he quite effectively added:

3:5a *having the outward form of true religion but denying its power.*

Pretending that they are holding fast to true religion but standing far apart from its practice. And because this is what those who will come to be at that time are like, Paul's word about them to Timothy is:

3:5b-7 *And these people* (he says), *avoid them. And some of them are those who plunge themselves into houses and lead captive foolish women, heaped over by sins, who are led by all kinds of desires, always learning and never coming to the knowledge of the truth.*

"And so, since such people as those who will be in the last days now exist as their shadowy form, hasten to turn away from them with all the strength [217] you can muster. In their perversity they plunge themselves into other people's houses to lead astray and drag some women to what is worse—not those women who are truly godly and faithful, for this could not possibly happen, but those thought to be ours and yet filled with every perversity.

propter prauitatem propositi et arbitrii sui; quae hac uel maxime de causa intendunt illis, eo quod uerba eorum suis perspiciunt concurrere desideriis.' consolans uero eum memoria futurorum, consolatur etiam eum ex illis quae antea iam facta fuerunt:

5   *quemadmodum* (inquit) *Iamnes et Mambres restiterunt Moysi, sic et hi resistunt ueritati, homines corrupti mente, reprobi erga fidem.*

'memor esto (inquit) ea quae secundum Moysen olim facta fuerunt, cui malefici uiri restiterunt. itaque nihil demiratione dignum est, si et nunc homines corrupti mente ueritati resistunt, et quasi

10 quadam ratione hi qui eiusmodi sunt maxime in principio fidem simulantes latere multos uidentur, qui uel quales sint.'

    sed non promouerint (inquit) *amplius, insipientia autem eorum manifesta erit, sicut et illorum fuit.*

'non poterunt diu se occultare quicumque sunt illi. manifestos

15 autem faciet eos tempus, sicuti et illorum insipientiam manifestam faciet tempore subsequenti.' nam quod interrogant quidam unde poterit beatus Paulus cognoscere nomina illorum qui restiterunt Moysi, multae stultitiae est. ridiculum etenim est Moysen quidem [qui] tanta ante se facta uidebatur edixisse illa quae mul-

20 tis erant incerta, memorari etiam tantorum quos nemo tunc scire poterat; Paulum uero demirari si duorum hominum nomina qui antea fuerant ualuerit dicere. nam et secundum traditionem antiquorum ista illum scire nihil noui fuit. illud uero notari dignum est, quod uidetur apud multos quaestionem commouere, quemad-

25 modum in superioribus dixerit *multum proficiunt;* hoc uero in loco dixit, *sed non proficient amplius.* dicit autem ista non secundum unam eandemque rationem; illic enim dicit *proficient,*
†de illis dicens qui seducuntur, ἀνωτέρω ἐπὶ τῶν ἀπατωμένων λέ-

1 quia (*for* quae) *r*   3 terrens (*for* consolans) *r*   4 eum *om C* || facta *om* *H* || fuerant *H*   5 Iamnis *H* || Zambris (*for* Mambres) *H*   6 hii *C* isti *H*: *txt r*   8 nulla (*for* nihil) *r*   9 resistant *H* || quae (*for* quasi) *C r* etq: quasiam (*sic*) *H*   11 multis *r* || quali *C H*   12 promouerit *C* promouent *H* promouebant *r* || insipientiam *C**   14 poterant *C H*: *txt r* || duo *C** *H* denuo *r* || illi *om H*   15 fecit *C* facit *H*: *txt r* || et (*aft.* fecit) *add r*   16 facit *H* nam qui *C* namq: *H*: *txt r*   17 potuit *H r*   18 dignum (*aft.* stult.) *add C r* || Moyses *C H*: *txt r*   19 qui *om C H r* || uideatur *r* 19-20 multi *H*   20 scire *om H*   22 ante *r*   23 notatu *r*   24 multas *r* || mouere *r*   27 uanam eam denique (*for* unam eandemque) *C* H r* || dicent *H* 28 sequuntur (*for* seducuntur) *r* || sq. Coisl. 204, f. 219 b [Cr. vii. 73] ἄλλος δέ φησίν· ἀνωτέρω, κ.τ.λ.

They are, indeed, always learning from us what they ought to do, but they receive no help from our teaching because of the perversity of their purpose and judgment. The reason they pay special attention to those people is that they perceive that their words coincide with their desires." And consoling Timothy by mentioning what is to come, Paul also consoles him for what had already now happened:

3:8 *Just as* (he says) *Jamnes and Mambres opposed Moses, so, too, these people oppose the truth, people corrupt in mind, base regarding faith.*

"Be mindful (he says) of what took place long ago with respect to Moses, whom wicked men opposed. And so there is nothing to be astonished about if even now people corrupt in mind oppose the truth, and if as though for some reason those who are like this, by pretending faith especially to begin with, plainly escape the notice of many people as to who they are and what they are like."

3:9 *But they will not* (he says) *move forward further, but their folly will be manifest, just as that of those people was.*

[218] "They will not be able to hide themselves for long, whoever they are. And time will make them manifest, just as it made[23] the folly of those people manifest in the following time." Now some people ask where blessed Paul could have found out the names of those who opposed Moses, but the question is quite foolish. For it would be ridiculous that Moses stated so many things that plainly happened before his time that were unclear to many people and mentioned so many things that no one in his time could have known, but that we should be astonished at Paul if he was able to give the names of two men who had lived before him. Indeed, by the tradition of the ancients there would be nothing strange in his knowing that. But what is worth noting is what seems to stir up a question for many people: How is it that Paul said above (2:16) *they go forward further* but in this place has said *but they will not go forward further?*[24] But he makes the statement for different reasons. In the former passage he says "they will go forward,"

†speaking of those who are led   Above he is speaking of those

---

[23] Literally, "will make" (*faciet*). I have changed the tense in accordance with the sense.

[24] The Latin here uses *proficient* instead of *promoverint*, as in the citation of the text. The Greek text has προκόψουσιν both in 2:16 and 3:9.

eo quod numquam poterint deficere hi qui secundum dicta eorum faciunt. adicit denique dicens: *et sermo eorum sicut cancer*
5 *serpit.* hoc uero in loco apud eos
qui probare sufficiunt ueritatem
dixit non proficere eos, quia in
principio frequenter multi homines de illis nescientes spe-
10 cie eorum ac schemate solo ine-
scantur, qui tempore currenti necessario dogmatum eorum
subuersionem cognoscentes habere ab his poterunt.*

γει, ὡς ἂν οἰδεπότε ἐπιλειψόντων
αὐτοῖς τῶν πειθομένων οἷς λέγουσιν. ἐνταῦθα δὲ παρὰ τοῖς τῆς
ἀληθείας δοκιμασταῖς οὐ προκόπ-
τειν αὐτούς φησιν· οἱ γὰρ ἐν ἀρχῇ πολλάκις οὔπω τὰ κατ᾽ αὐτοὺς
εἰδότες, τῷ σχήματι δελεάζονται,
τῷ χρόνῳ μέντοι τὴν ἐνοῦσαν αὐτοῖς τῶν δογμάτων διαφθορὰν ἐπι-
γινώσκουσιν.

15 quod ergo dixit *non proficient*, secundum illud dixit quod latere
possint ad tempus; unde et adiecit: *insipientia enim eorum manifesta erit.* per omnia ergo ista consolatus est Timotheum ut ne nimium adfligeretur pro illis qui in deterius serpunt. suis uero consiliis incitat eum dicens:

20 *tu autem subsecutus es meam doctrinam, meum institutum, propositum, fidem, longanimitatem, caritatem, patientiam, persecutiones,
passiones.*

'semper (inquit) mecum commorans horum experimentum accepisti, docens qualia quidem ipse alios docere consueueram, que-
25 madmodum uero meipsum instituebam; uel quia illa per singulos
dies agere properabam erga fidem, quemadmodum in ea sine ulla
persistebam malitia, et diligens cunctos et sustinens; et quod cum
multa oblectatione persecutiones illas quas mihi aduersarii infere-
bant sustinuerim. haec ergo imitare, et erga ista sollicitudinem ex-
30 pende, nullius momenti aduersarios esse existimans.' deinde dicit
et passiones ipsas ad exhortationem Timothei:
*qualia mihi sunt facta in Antiochia, in Iconio, in Lystris; quales
persecutiones sustinui.*

---

2 dictis *C H*: *txt r*   4 ut (*for* sicut) *r*   5 οἱ cod. Cr.   6 prauare *C H*
deprauare *r*: *txt g*   9-10 speciem e. ac scema solum agnoscunt *r*   9 διαφορὰν
Cr.   10 sola *C H*   14 in (*for* ab) *r*   ‖ poterant *H*   15 ego dixi (*for* ergo
dixit) *H*   ‖ error eorum (*aft.* quod) add *r*   16 possit *C H r*   20 assecutus *r*
21 pietatem (*aft.* car.) *add r*   22 passiones *om H*   29 sustinuerimus *H*   30
mementi (*sic*) *H*

astray, [219] because there can who are deceived, since there never fail to be people who act can never fail to be people per- according to what they have suaded by them by what they said. And then he adds the sta- say. tement: *and their word creeps on like a cancer.* But in this place But here he says that they do he has said they do not go for- not go forward with those who ward among those who have examine the truth. a capacity sufficient for testing the truth. This is because often For often in the beginning in the beginning there are many some, because they do not yet who, since they know nothing know what has to do with them, about them, are enticed by their are enticed by appearance, but appearance and outward form, in time they recognize the cor- but who as time goes on, by ruption of the doctrines within recognizing the subversive cha- them. racter of their doctrines, are able to keep away from them.*

Therefore, when he said *they will not go forward*, he has spoken of the fact that they can lie hidden only for a time. That is why he added: *for their folly will be manifest.* Therefore, in all respects he has consoled Timothy about those things, so that he may not in the least be afflicted for those who creep into what is worse. And he rouses him with his own counsels, saying:

3:10–11a *And you have followed my teaching, my conduct, purpose, faith, longsuffering, love, endurance, persecutions, sufferings,*

"Always (he says) while you were dwelling with me, you accepted the example of these things, since you were teaching the sort of things I was accustomed to teach others myself, in fact just as I set myself to the task—for instance, just as I continued to stand fast in faith without any malice, both loving everyone and enduring, because I was eager to do what concerned faith day by day, and that I endured with much complaisance the persecutions the adversaries were inflicting on me. Therefore, continue to imitate these things and expend great care on them, considering the adversaries to be of no importance." Then he speaks also of the sufferings themselves to exhort Timothy:

[220] 3:11b *such as happened to me in Antioch, in Iconium, in Lystra, what sort of persecutions I endured;*

et quod magis poterat eum animaequiorem erga passiones to-
lerandas facere, adiecit:

et ex omnibus me liberauit Dominus.

'non ignoras (inquit) etiam in diuersis rebus Dei erga nos pro-
5 latam prouidentiam; a qua non debes discedere, si tamen haec ipsa
patiens persistere uolueris.'

et omnes qui uolunt pie uiuere in Christo Iesu persecutiones patien-
tur; mali autem homines et seductores proficient in deterius, errantes
et in errorem mittentes.

10 iterum hoc in loco 'proficere' dixit de illis qui seducuntur, eo
quod numquam deficere possint huiusmodi homines. nam et utraque quicumque uoluerit rebus ipsis examinare inueniet per omne tempus fieri; eo quod omnis haeresis inprimis adparens multis
fit in suspectatione, arguitur uero tempore, eo quod in aduentione
15 noui dogmatis non possunt minus inueniri qui seducantur.

tu uero permane in his quae didicisti et credidisti.

et suadens illum tenere ac permanere adiecit:

sciens a quo didiceris.

sufficiens autem est ad hortationem discipulorum magistri di-
20 gnitas. deinde et aliud dicit:

et quia a pueritia sacras litteras didicisti.

nam et hoc sufficiens erat exhortare eum. rubore autem dignum uidebatur ut is qui a pueritia in bonis fuerat enutritus, in
ultimo post longi temporis meditationem indigna uideretur agere.
25 nam et ipsam doctrinam admodum sublimem ostendit, dum dicit
sacras litteras diuinas esse scripturas, quibus omni ratione credi conuenit. unde et qualitate ipsam doctrinam cumulans adiecit:

quae te possunt instruere ad salutem per fidem Iesu Christi.

nam et ostendit necessarium esse ut maneat in doctrina pieta-
30 tis, una quidem ex causa ex magnitudine doctoris; altera uero, quia
et a pueritia illa didicerit, et quod ipsa doctrina sit diuina, et quod

---

1   animimquiorem *r*   3   inquid (*aft.* omn.) *add H*   4   nos *om H*   4-5   pro-
batam (*for* prolatam) *r*   5   in (*bef.* haec) *add r*   7   persecutionem *H*   7-8
pacienter *H*   12   in utroque *C r*   13   omnes haereses *C* H*   14   suspectio-
ne *H* ‖ suspectationem *r*   16   didisci (*sic*) *H*   17   ac *om H* ‖ adicit *C*   22
exhortari *r*   23   uideatur *C H* uidetur *r* ‖ hi (*for* is) *H*   24   meditatione *H*
 ‖ incipiat (*for* uideretur) *r*   27   ad (*bef.* ipsam) *add r* ‖ adicit *C r*

And he added what could make him all the more calm-minded in bearing sufferings:

3:11c *and the Lord freed me from all of them.*

"You are not unaware (he says) that in differing circumstances God's providence has also been brought forth to us, from which you ought not to depart, if indeed you are willing to continue steadfast suffering these very things."

3:12–13 *And all who want to live a godly way in Christ Jesus will suffer persecutions; and evil people and those who lead astray will go forward to the worse, erring and sending into error.*

Again in this place he has said "go forward" about those who are led astray, because there can never be any lack of such people. Indeed, someone willing to make a close investigation will find two facts in these matters that occur every time. At first every heresy that appears falls under the suspicion of many people, but it is condemned only in time, because when novel doctrine first arrives, it is impossible there should not be found some who are led astray.

3:14a *But you, persevere in those things that you have learned and believed,*

[221] And urging him to hold fast and to persevere, he added:

3:14b *knowing from whom*[25] *you learned*

And the worthiness of the teacher is sufficient for the encouragement of his disciples. Then he says something else:

3:15a *and that from childhood you have learned sacred letters,*

For this, too, was sufficient to exhort him. And it would have seemed shameful that he who had been brought up from childhood in good things should finally after a long time of reflection be seen to commit unworthy deeds. Indeed, he shows that the teaching is altogether lofty, since he says that the divine scriptures are *sacred letters*, which must be believed for every reason. Then, piling up praise of the teaching by its character, he added:

3:15b *which can instruct you to salvation through faith of Jesus Christ.*

He shows that it is necessary for him to persevere in the teaching of true religion, for one reason because of the greatness of the teacher, and for another that he had learned those things

---

[25] *A quo.* Chrysostom and Theodoret agree with Theodore in using the singular. The Greek text uses the plural.

magna possit praestare illis qui Christo credere uoluerint, dum illam salutem quae ex fide est adsequuntur. et quia dixit, *sacras lit-*
teras quae te possunt instruere, adiecit:

    omnis scriptura diuinitus inspirata utilis est ad doctrinam, ad ar-
5 *gutionem, ad correctionem, ad eruditionem quae est in iustitia; ut per-*
fectus sit homo Dei, ad omne opus bonum paratus.

    'talis est (inquit) omnis scriptura quae a diuino est data Spiritu,
ut sufficiens sit omnia prospicere utilitati; siue docere conueniat de
illis quae agi debeant, siue peccantes debeant argui, siue poeniten-
10 tibus debeat inferri aliqua correctio, siue erudire oporteat de illis
quae possunt adducere homines ad iustitiam. ita ut quicumque se
Deo uoluerit dicare, per scripturarum utilitatem per omnia possit esse perfectus.' et postquam de omnibus est eum exhortatus,
terribilem cupiens suam facere exhortationem, adiecit:

15   *testificor ergo ego in conspectu Dei et domini nostri Iesu Christi,*
qui iudicaturus est uiuos et mortuos secundum reuelationem suam et
regnum suum.

    hoc est: 'tune omnes est iudicaturus quando adparuerit secun-
dum suam dignitatem, in qua et consistit.'

20   *praedica uerbum, insta opportune, inportune.*

    non hoc dicit ut inportune instet, nam inportunum quodcum-
que est, illud nulla ratione agi debet. sed dicit: 'nullum tempus
relinquas doctrinae; omne tempus opportunum tibi ad hoc esse
existimes.' hoc quidem de illis dicit qui instrui debent. quoniam
25 autem euenit aliquos desidiae causa non permanere in doctrina:

    argue (ait), *increpa, obsecra.*

    '*argue* eos qui persistunt in peccatum, ut intellegere possint
suum peccatum; *increpa* sentientem (inquit) suum peccatum, sub

---

2   ex in est *C* ex in fide e. *H*: *txt r*   3   adicit *r*   5   in *om r*   7   est (2°) *om*
H   8   perspicere *H*   10   debet *C H*: *txt r*   ‖   correptio *l*   14   adicit *C r*
‖   in sequenti capite (*aft* adiecit) *add r*   19   et *om r*   21   inoportunum *r*   22
debeat *r*   27   peccatu *C* (*corr.*) peccato *r*   ‖   intellege *H*   28   et (*bef.* sub)
add r

from childhood, and also because the teaching itself is divine, and because it can bestow great things on those willing to believe in Christ, [222] since they attain the salvation that comes from faith.[26] And because he said *the sacred letters, which can instruct you*, he added:

3:16–17 *All scripture divinely inspired*[27] *is useful for teaching, for condemnation, for correction, for the instruction that is in justice, so that the man of God may be equipped for every good work.*

"All scripture (he says) that has been given by the divine Spirit is such that it is sufficient to provide for usefulness in all things, whether there ought to be teaching about what should be done, whether sinners should be condemned, whether any correction should be imposed on those who repent, whether it is necessary to give instruction about what can lead people to justice. This is so that whoever is willing to dedicate himself to God may be able to be perfect in all respects through the usefulness of the scriptures." And after he has exhorted him in all these ways, wishing to make his exhortation terrifying, he added:

4:1 *Therefore, I testify in the sight of God and our Lord Jesus Christ, who will judge both the living and the dead at his appearing and his kingdom,*

That is, "he will judge everyone at that time when he appears according to his own excellence in which he also remains fixed."

4:2a *preach the word, be persistent seasonably, unseasonably,*

[223] He does not mean that Timothy should be unseasonably persistent, for whatever is unseasonable should not be done for any reason. Rather, he means: "at no time abandon teaching; consider every time suitable to you for this purpose." He is saying this about those who ought to be instructed, since it happens that some people do not persevere in teaching because of laziness.[28]

4:2b *condemn* (he says), *rebuke, beseech*

"*Condemn* those who persist in sin, so that they can understand their sin. *Rebuke* (he says) the person who has a sense of his own

---

[26] See Swete's note (2:221): "Four reasons for steadfastness are conveyed in the phrases παρὰ τίνος, ἀπὸ βρέφους, τὰ ἱερὰ γράμματα, εἰς σωτήριον, respectively."

[27] Notice that the text appears to omit "and" before "useful."

[28] What Theodore seems to mean is that the "unseasonable" times are those when the teacher has lazy disciples and that some teachers give the task up for this reason.

definitione constitue; *obsecra*, reduc iterum ad antiquum statum
post poenitentiam.' et modum quo fieri hoc conueniat docens:

    in omni patientia et doctrina.

    'neque ad argutionem neque ad increpationem nulla utaris de
5 illis quae agi [non] conueniunt.' et quoniam eueniebat aliquos
haec non suscipere propter morum suorum prauitatem, iterum
memoratur de illis hominibus:

    erit (inquit) *tempus cum sanam doctrinam non admittent, sed se-
cundum sua desideria sibi ipsis coaceruabunt magistros, prurientes au-*
10 *ribus; et a ueritate quidem auditum auertent, ad fabulas autem co-
nuertentur.*

    †*fabulas* dixit illa uerba quae   μύθους εἶπεν τὰ ἐναντία τῆς
contraria sunt pietati.*   εὐσεβείας ῥήματα.

necessaria uero ei fuit in praesenti negotio horum memoria. po-
15 stquam enim exhortatus est eum arguere et increpare et obsecra-
re, ne animo deficeret ipse si haec facientem minime uellent aliqui intendere, in deterius prorumpentes, ideo insinuat quod horum multum deteriores erunt hi qui in ultimis erunt temporibus,
maiorem suis doctoribus prouidentes laborem. unde et adiecit:

20   *tu autem sobrius esto, in omnibus labora, opus fac euangelistae, ministerium tuum imple.*

    hoc est: 'si non adiuuentur aliqui, tu illa quae te oportent age-
re age; cum omni age sollicitudine, sustinens pro euangelio laborem, et illud quod ad te pertinet facito, pro hoc autem et rationem
25 redditurum non pro aliorum arbitrio.' bene autem dixit, *ministerium tuum imple;* hoc est, 'commissum tibi opus diligenter imple,
matura, contentus opere tuo, licet si illa quae discipulorum sunt
minime concurrere uideantur.' et quia testificatus est de his post
exhortationem, ostendere cupit quod tempus opportunum sit ei
30 ad contestationem; unde et adiecit:

---

2   quod (*for* quo) *H* ‖ hoc fieri *r* ‖ docet *r* 4 nulla utares *C* * *H* nulla
non ut. *C* (*corr.*) nullam omittas *r* 5 non *om C H r* ‖ aliquis *C H r* 8
summam (*for* sanam) *C H*: txt *r* 9 coaceruabant *H* 12 esse (*aft.* uerba)
add H r ‖ sq. Coisl. 204, f. 221 b [Cr. vii. 77, Fr. 156] Θεόδωρος. μύθους,
κ.τ.λ. 14 negotio (*for* memoria) *H* 15 autem (*for* enim) *H* 16 ne ficere
(*sic*) (*for* deficeret) *H**: corr. ficeret ‖ uelint *C r* 18 multo *C r* 19 adicit *C*
23 et (*bef.* cum) *add r* 24 a (*for* ad) *H* 25 redditurum *C** reddit *r* 30 a
contestatione *C H r* ‖ dicit (*for* adiecit) *C r*

sin; place him under a ruling. *Beseech*, bring him back again to his former status after penance."[29] And to teach the way this must be done:

4:2c *in all patience and teaching.*

"Employ no means that should not be used either for condemnation or for rebuke." And since it happened that some people would not accept these things because of the perversity of their habits, he again mentions those people:

4:3-4 *There will be* (he says) *a time when they will not put up with sound teaching, but according to their desires, itching in ears, they will pile up teachers for themselves, and they will turn hearing away from the truth and will turn to myths.*

[224] †He said that words contradictory of true religion are *myths.**

He said that words contradictory of true religion are *myths.*

It was necessary for him to mention these things because of his present concern. For after he exhorted Timothy to condemn and rebuke and beseech, lest he should lose heart if some others were by no means willing to pay attention to him when he was doing this, bursting forth into what was worse, for this reason he introduces the fact that in the last times there will be people much worse than these, providing greater toil to their teachers. Then he added:

4:5 *But you, be sober, toil in all things, do the work of an evangelist, fulfill your ministry.*

That is, "if some are not helped, for your part do what you ought to do; act with entire carefulness, enduring toil for the gospel, and accomplish what pertains to you, since you will render an account for this and not for the conduct chosen by others." And he rightly said *fulfill your ministry*, that is, "diligently fulfill the work entrusted to you, perform it in good time, energetic in your work, even if the response of your disciples by no means seems to concur with it." And because he testified about these matters after his exhortation, he wants to show that the time is seasonable for his own contest. That is why he added:

---

[29]This seems to mean that those who have committed serious sins must first be excommunicated, then placed under rule as penitents, and finally brought back to the communion of the church.

ego enim iam delibor, et tempus meae solutionis instat.

'propinquus mihi est exitus uitae praesentis, et iam ultra non habebo tempus commonere te de his quae fieri conueniant. unde et hanc feci ad te exhortationem sub teste Deo.' non absolute di-
5 xit *libor*, sed quia pro Christi confessione mortem erat subiturus, libationem dixit; nam libatio uini dicitur effusio quae fit in diuini honoris expiatione.

certamen bonum certaui, cursum consummaui, fidem seruaui.

non plaudens se ista dicit, sed ad exhortationem dicit Timo-
10 thei. hoc est, 'secundum tempus quod in hac uita habebam, omnia quae mihi pertinere uidebantur implebam.' et quae alia laborum merces?

de cetero reposita est mihi iustitiae corona, quam reddet mihi Do-
minus in illa die iustus iudex.

15 bene *iustitiae coronam* uocauit illam quae contemplatione laborum datur. et *iustum iudicem* nominauit, ad confirmationem illorum quae illi aderunt pro labore. et ostendens quoniam non solum ipse lucrum huiusmodi adsequatur, sed et omnes qui ad eius sollicitudinem laborare pro euangelio uoluerint—unde et dicit:
20 *non solum autem mihi, sed et omnibus qui diligunt aduentum eius.*

'itaque propositum est (inquit) et tibi coronae praemium, si tantum nunc ualueris elaborare.' miraculi uero dignum est quod non dixit 'illis qui laborauerunt, aut passi sunt,' sed dixit: *qui diligunt aduentum eius;* eo quod certaminum et passionum tempus
25 non semper est, caritatis uero tempus est, si nunc eam etiam in tempore pacis prout oportet saluare quis deproperauerit, nullam fraudem adsequens si tempus certaminum minime adfuerit. in hisce dictis suum consummans consilium, exhortationem suam sub testificatione concludens doctrinae quam ad eum fecisse uidetur,
30 scribit ultra de his rebus de quibus scribere eum ratio exigebat, ut-

---

1 delebor *C** ‖ resolutionis *r* 3 commouere *C** 5 delibor *r* ‖ ero *r*
7 expiationem *C (corr.)* 8 bon. certamen *r* 9 pludens *C H* ludens (*om* se) *l*
‖ sibi (*for* se) *C (corr.):* om *r* ‖ dixit *H l* ‖ dixit (*for* dicit [1°]) *H* 10
habebant *C** habebat *H r* 11 implebamus *H* ‖ et quae ... merces *om r*
‖ alium *C H* 13 corona iust. *H* 14 in *om C* 15 contemplatio *H (corr.)*
18 luctum (*for* lucrum) *C* H* luctam *r* 19 uoluerit *H* 20 autem *om H* 22
non (*for* nunc) *C H: om r* ‖ laborare *C** ‖ miraculo *r* 23 dixit [2°] *om r*
25 si non eam *C H* si ea *r* 26 salutare *C* H* 28 consumans *H* ‖ suum
H sua *r*

4:6 *For I am already poured out, and the time of my dissolution is at hand.*

[225] "My departure from the present life is near, and I shall no longer have time to admonish you about what ought to be done. This is why I have composed this exhortation to you, with God as my witness." He did not say without reason *I am poured out*, but because he was about to undergo death for his confession of Christ, he called this a libation. For a libation is said to be the pouring out of wine, which is done to expiate the divine honor.

4:7 *I have fought the good fight, I have finished the race, I have kept the faith.*

He says this not to congratulate himself, but he is speaking to exhort Timothy. That is, "during the time I had in this life I fulfilled everything that was soon to pertain to me." And what are the other rewards of his toils?

4:8a *For the rest there is laid up for me the crown of justice, which the Lord will give to me on that day, the just judge,*

He rightly called the crown given him in return for his toils *the crown of justice*. And he named *the just judge* to confirm [226] what will be his for his toil. And to show that it is not only he who may gain a profit of this kind, but also all those who are willing to toil carefully for it on behalf of the gospel—for this reason he says:

4:8b *and not only to me, but also to all those who love his coming.*

"And so there is held forth (he says) also for you the reward of a crown, if only you are now strong enough to exert yourself." And it is worthy of marvel that he did not say "to those who have toiled or suffered," but instead said *those who love his coming*. This is because there is not always a time for contests and sufferings, but there is always time for love. If now even in time of peace someone should be eager to preserve love as he ought, he would not be defrauded of his reward, although a time for contests were by no means his lot. Completing his advice with these words and concluding his exhortation by testifying to the teaching he is seen to have given Timothy, he writes further of things about which reason compelled him to write as to his own disciple and someone

pote ad suum discipulum et maxime sibi dilectum:

festina uenire ad me cito.

et causam explicans qua *cito* eum ad se uenire iusserat:

Demas (inquit) *me dereliquit, diligens praesens saeculum, et abiit*
5 *in Thessalonicam.*

hoc est: 'in deterius uersus est, totum se negotiis praesentis uitae implicans;' hoc enim dicit praesentis saeculi delectationem.

Crescens in Galatiam.

Galatiam dixit

10 †quas nunc nominamus Gallias;   τὰς νῦν καλουμένας Γαλλίας· οὕτως
sic enim antiqui omnes loca illa   γὰρ αὐτὰς πάντες ἐκάλουν οἱ πα-
nominabant,*   λαιοί.

sicut recognoscere quis poterit et ex multis aliis et ex historia Iu-
daica quam Iosephus descripsisse uidetur. nam et hi qui nunc di-
15 cuntur Galatae ita nuncupantur quos ex illis partibus ad ista loca
uenisse antiquorum insinuat narratio.

Titus in Dalmatiam.

hos non ad similitudinem Demae discessisse a se memoratus
est aut in deterius uersos, sed hac sola ratione qua non sint prae-
20 sentes.

Lucas est solus mecum. Marcum adsumens adduc tecum.

et quae sit ratio ut Marcus ueniat?

est mihi (inquit) *utilis in ministerium.*

'opportunus mihi est, eo quod cum summa sollicitudine uniuer-
25 sa adimplere deproperat.'

Tychicum misi Ephesum.

deinde praecepit ei etiam illa exequi quae oporteant eum facere
adseruientem:

paenulam quam reliqui Troade apud Carpum ueniens adfer; et co-
30 *dices, uel maxime membranas.*

†Latina lingua uolumina di-   μεμβράνας ῥωμαϊκώτερον τὰ εἰ-
xit *membranas.* secundum il-   λητὰ ἐκάλεσεν, ὡς ἀπὸ τῆς ἐν Ῥώ-

---

1 est (*aft* dilectum) *add C*   2 ad me u. *r*   3 quae (*for* qua) *C H*   5 The-
salonica *H*   9 dicit *H*   10 Galleas (*sic*) *C**   ‖   sq. Coisl. 204, f. 222 a [Cr.
vii. 79, Fr. 156] Θεόδωρος. τὰς νῦν, κ.τ.λ.   15 Gallatae *r*   17 Dalmaticam *C**
18 hoc (*for* hos) *H*   19 uersus est *H* uersus (*om* est) *r*   ‖   quod (*for* qua) *r*
21 mecum s. *r*   23 inquit m. *H*   26 Effesi (*sic*) *C r*   27 praecipiei (*sic*)
C* precepi ei *H* praecipit *r*   28 seruientem (*for* ads.) *r*   29 Troadae *r*   ‖
affert *H*   31 sq. Coisl. 28, f. 223 b Θεοδωρήτου. βεμβράνας [μεμβρ., Coisl. 30,
Reg. 222, 223], κ.τ.λ.

dearly beloved to him:

4:9 *Make haste to come to me quickly.*

And to explain the reason he had ordered Timothy to come to him *quickly*:

4:10a *Demas* (he says) *has deserted me, loving the present age, and has gone away to Thessalonica,*

That is, "he has turned to what is worse, entangling himself completely in the affairs of the present life." He means by this delight in the present age.

[227] 4:10b *Crescens to Galatia,*

By *Galatia* he meant

†the regions we now call Gallic, the regions now called Gallic, for this is how all the ancients for this is how all the ancients used to name those places,* used to call them

as anyone can discover both from many others and from the Jewish history that Josephus is seen to have written down.[30] Indeed, the story of the ancients conveys the fact that those who are now called Galatians are so named because they came from those regions to their present location.

4:10c *Titus to Dalmatia.*

He has not mentioned that they like Demas deserted him or turned to what is worse, but has mentioned them only because they were not with him.

4:11a *Only Luke is with me. Get Mark and bring him with you;*

[228] And what is the reason Mark should come?

4:11b *he is useful* (he says) *to me in ministry.*

"He is serviceable to me, because he is eager to accomplish everything with the greatest care."

4:12 *I have sent Tychicus to Ephesus.*

Then he instructed Timothy also to carry out the requests he ought to perform in serving Paul:

4:13 *The cloak that I left at Troas with Carpus, bring when you come, and the books, and especially the parchments.*

†He has spoken of the rolls He called the rolls in a Ro- in Latin as *parchments.* He used man way *parchments*, since he this word indifferently accor- was using the term indifferently ding to the way they speak in from the custom in Rome, from Rome, from which city he has where, of course, he also wrote

---

[30] Swete (2:227) cites Josephus, *A.J.* 1.6; 12.10; *B.J.* 2.16.

Iam consuetudinem qua Romae
loquebantur indiscrete abusus
est hoc sermone, ex qua urbe
etiam epistolam hanc scripsis-
5 se uisus est. in uoluminibus
antiquis temporibus habebant
consuetudinem diuinas scribere scripturas, sicuti et usque ad
praesens Iudaei multa in uolu-
10 minibus scripta habere uidentur. libros autem dixit secundum communem usum, eo quod
in alia specie erant libri. risui
uero dignum est de illis qui hoc
15 in loco paenulam apostolum non
indumentum significasse existimauerunt, sed speciem quandam libri. qui non intenderunt
illa quae subsequuntur; super-
20 fluum enim erat dicere et libros,
si tamen et illud libri species
erat, quod poterat etiam cum
ceteris significari.*

μὴ συνηθείας ἀδιαφόρως τῇ λέ-
ξει καταχρησάμενος· ἀφ' ἧς δὴ καὶ
ἔγραφεν τὴν ἐπιστολήν. ἐν εἰλητοῖς
γὰρ εἶχον τὸ παλαιὸν τὰ τῆς θείας
γραφῆς, ὥσπερ οὖν ἄχρι τῆς δεῦρο οἱ Ἰουδαῖοι τὰ πλεῖστα ἔχουσιν.
βιβλία δὲ εἶπεν κατὰ κοινοῦ, ὡς ἂν
καὶ ἐν ἑτέρῳ σχήματι τυχὸν ἔχων
βιβλία· γελάσαι δὲ ἄξιον τῶν ἐνταῦθα εἰρηκότων φαιλόνην τὸν ἀπόσ-
τολον οὐ τὸ ἔνδυμα καλεῖν, ἀλλά
τι εἶδος βιβλίου. οἳ οὐ προσέσχον
τῇ ἐπαγωγῇ· περιττὸν γὰρ ἦν εἰπεῖν
καὶ τὰ βιβλία, εἴπερ δὴ κἀκεῖνο βιβλίου εἶδος ἦν δυνάμενον τοῖς λοι-
ποῖς συσσημαίνεσθαι.

Alexander aerarius multa mala egit mihi; reddat illi Dominus se-
25 *cundum opera eius. quem et tu custodi; ualde enim restitit nostris ser-*
monibus.

hoc posuit ad custodiam et cautelam Timothei, non ad accusationem Alexandri; nihil enim pertinebat ei de hac. propter quod
posuit etiam illam poenam quae eum manebat a Deo pro quibus
30 talia faciebat. non maledicebat ei, sicut quidam existimauerunt,
sed ut hortaretur Timotheum multa ab eo sustinentem mala patienter sustinere. hac ergo de causa necessarie memoratus est uirum, praecipiens Timotheum ut pro uirium suarum possibilitate
declinare eius insidiis deproperet. non conuenit uero mirari si ab

9 δὲ om. Coisl. 28, Reg. 223   10   scriptum C* scriptura H   ‖   φαιλώνην
Coisl. 30 13 erat (for erant) H   14   καὶ τὰ βιβλ. εἰπεῖν Coisl. 30   21   specie H 24 egit om H   ‖   mihi ostendit r   ‖   reddet C (corr.) r   25   deuita (for
cust.) r   ‖   uerbis nostris r   27   ad eum r   28   de hoc H r   29   commanebat
H ei manebat r   33   Timotheo r   34   insidias C (corr.) r

plainly written this letter. In ancient times they used to have the custom of writing the divine scriptures in rolls, just as to the present day the Jews are seen to have many writings in rolls. [229] And he said *books* according to common usage, because there were books in another form. But it is worth laughing at those people who have supposed that in this place by *cloak* the apostle did not mean clothing but some kind of book.[31] They have not paid attention to what follows, for it would have been useless to say *and the books*, if indeed that were a kind of book that could have been meant along with the others.*

the letter. Of old they kept the writings of divine scripture in rolls, just as to the present day the Jews for the most part do.

And he said *books* according to common usage, since books happen to be in a different form. But it is worth laughing at those people who have said that here the apostle was calling a *cloak* not clothing but some kind of book. They have not paid attention to what follows, for it would have been useless to say *and the books*, if indeed that were a kind of book that could be meant together with the rest.

4:14–15 *Alexander the coppersmith has done many evils to me; may the Lord pay him back according to his works, whom also you guard against, for he has strongly opposed our words.*

He put this down to guard and caution Timothy, not to make an accusation against Alexander, for this was not his concern. [230] For this reason he also put down the punishment that was in store for him from God in return for such things as he was doing. He was not reviling him, as some have thought, but this was to encourage Timothy, who was enduring many evils from him, to endure them patiently. Therefore, it was for this reason that he necessarily mentioned the man, instructing Timothy to be quick to turn away from his plots with all the strength he

---

[31] *Paenulam,* φαιλόνην. See Swete's note (2:229): "The Greek lexicographers however admitted it as a possible meaning of the word ... placing side by side with it the alternative: ἡ γλωσσόκομον ["book case"]. ... It seems possible that the idea condemned by Th. originated in a misunderstanding or misreading of the Peshito."

aerario tanta tunc fiebant indisciplinate, quia et uulgares homines
insurgebant aduersus eos qui pietatem praedicabant; uulgus autem uel maxime omnes commouere uidebatur seditiones.

in primam meam defensionem nemo mihi adstetit, sed omnes me re-
5   *liquerunt; non illis imputetur.*

in prima defensione dicit quando inprimis Romae est uinctus ex
Iudaea, quando et adpellatione fuerat abusus. bene autem preca-
tus est *in illis non imputetur* peccatum hoc, eo quod perspexit alios
ob infirmitatem, alios ob imminentem sibi nccessitatem locum de-
10 disse.

Dominus autem adstetit mihi et confortauit me, ut per me praedica-
tio impleretur, et audiant omnes gentes. et liberatus sum ex ore leonis.

hoc 'leonem' in loco Neronem regem per aenigmata edicit. uult
enim dicere quoniam 'adsecutus sum Dei iudicium, a quo et con-
15 fortatus, de illis quae erga me fuerunt satisfaciens, dimitti iussus
sum, ita ut saeculum peragerem et multis pietatis insinuem dogmata, quod etiam et fecisse uideor.'

et liberabit me Dominus ab omni opere malo, et saluum me faciet in
regnum suum caeleste. cui gloria in saecula saeculorum. amen.

20 non ultra dixit: 'liberabit me ab eo;' praedixerat autem in superioribus quoniam non post multo tempore erat interficiendus.
quod et passus est, capitali a Nerone addictus sententiae eo tempore quo secunda uice Romae accesserat. sed dixit: *ab omni malo*
opere liberabit; hoc est, 'ab omni pressura praesentis uitae libera-
25 bit me, in suum me saluans regnum, quod et expecto.' post hoc
praecepit ei:

saluta (inquit) *Priscillam et Aquilam et Onesifori domum.*
indicat etiam ei et de aliis, ait enim:
Erastus mansit Corinthi.
30 designans quoniam Erastus Corinthi manserit.
Trophimum autem reliqui apud Miletum infirmum.

2-3   autem *om H*   4   in prima mea defensione *C* (*corr.*) *r*   4-5   dereliquerunt
H r   6   ductus Romam (*for* Romae) *r*   7   appellationem fecerat (*for* adp. fuerat
ab.) *r*   8   ut (*for* in) *r*   ‖   putetur (*for* imp.) *H**   9   loco cessisse *r*   13   leonem
hoc *r*   ‖   aenigma uocat *r*   14   iudicio *H*   16   cursum meum (*for* saeculum) *r*
‖   peragere *C*   ‖   insinuarem *C* (*corr.*)   18   liberauit *C* H r*   20   liberauit
H r   22   capituli *C**   23   Romam *r*   24   liberauit *C r*   ‖   me (*aft.* lib.) *add*
r   ‖   est *om C* H*   24-25   liberauit *r*   26   praecipit *C*   29   remansit *r*   ‖
Corinthe (*sic*) *C** Corinthii *H* (*bis*)   30   remanserit *r*

could muster. And we should not be astonished if such great evils were done disorderly by a coppersmith at that time, because the common people used to rise up against those who were preaching true religion, and it was the common crowd especially that plainly used to stir up all disturbances.

4:16 *At my first defense no one stood forward*[32] *to my support, but all deserted me; may it not be counted against them.*

By *at my first defense* he means when he first came to Rome as a prisoner from Judea and when he had used his appeal. And he rightly implored, may this sin *not be counted against them*, because he saw that they had given way, some because of weakness and others because of the constraint that hung over them.

4:17 *But the Lord stood by me and strengthened me, so that through me the preaching might be fulfilled and all the Gentiles might hear it. And I was freed from the lion's mouth.*

In this place by *lion* he enigmatically spoke of Nero the king. [231] For he wants to say: "I gained the judgment of God, by whom I was strengthened. Making my defense about the charges against me, I was ordered dismissed so that I could travel about the world and deliver the doctrines of true religion to many—something I also have plainly done."

4:18 *And the Lord will free me from every evil work and will save me for his heavenly kingdom, to whom be glory to the ages of ages. Amen.*

He no longer said, "he will free me from him." He had predicted above (4:6) that he would be killed not much later. And he suffered this, sentenced to capital punishment by Nero at the time when he had come to Rome a second time. So instead, he said *he will free me from every evil work*; that is, "he will free me from every harassment of the present life, saving me into his kingdom, which I also await." After this he instructs Timothy:

4:19 *Greet Priscilla and Aquila and the household of Onesiphorus.*
He also points out to him news about others, for he says:
4:20a *Erastus has remained at Corinth,*
Pointing out that Erastus remained at Corinth.

---

[32] *Adstetit.* The verse is cited in the commentary on Phil 1:12–14 (1:206), where the verb is *adfuit.*

Trophimum uero quod ipse infirmantem reliquerit Miletum insinuauit. quibus adicit:

festina ante hiemem uenire.

deinde significat scribens ei quoniam et fratres salutant eum, dicens:

salutant te Eubulus et Prudens et Linus et Claudia, et fratres omnes.

fratres (inquit) *omnes;* eos dicit qui utique eo tempore Romae erant. et illos quidem quos affectu iunctos sibi esse cernebat nominatim credidit memorandos; ceteros uero fratres in communi salutatione comprehendit. et primum quidem pro ipso Timotheo orans, dicens:

dominus Iesus Christus cum spiritu tuo.

post hoc uero consueto fine claudit epistolam:

gratia (ait) *nobiscum. amen.*

in fine consueta salutatione etiam seipsum illis censuit connumerandum.

1 relinquerit *r* 2 cecidit (*for* adicit) *H* 4 salutent *H* 6 et Linus *om H* || Cludia *C** 9 uinctos (*for* iunctos) *H* || cenabat (*sic*) *C** 12 dicit *C* (*corr.*) *r* 15 ait *om r* || uobiscum *r*

[232] 4:20b *and Trophimus I left ill at Miletus.*

And he conveyed the news that he left Trophimus ill at Miletus. To which he adds:

4:21a *Make haste to come before winter.*

Then, writing to him, he indicates that the brothers, as well, greet him, saying:

4:21b *Eubulus and Prudens and Linus and Claudia and all the brothers greet you.*

All the brothers (he says). He certainly means those who were at Rome at that time. And he believed that those whom he singled out as joined to him in affection should be mentioned by name, but he includes the rest of the brothers in a general greeting. And praying first of all for Timothy himself, saying:

4:22a *The Lord Jesus Christ*[33] *be with your spirit.*

After this he closes the letter with his customary ending:

4:22b *Grace* (he says) *be with us.*[34] *Amen.*

He decided that he himself should be included with them in his customary final greeting.

---

[33] The addition of "Jesus Christ" appears in the text used by Chrysostom and Theodoret, as well as Theodore, and also in the Latin versions.

[34] Another Antiochene reading: "us" instead of "you."

THEODORUS
MOPSUESTENUS
IN EPISTOLAM B. PAULI
AD TITUM

ARGUMENTUM

BEATUS apostolus Cretae accedens pietatis rationem illis qui illic habitabant tradidit. quia uero ad alias prouincias transire eum
ipsa pietatis ratio compellebat ut uniuersos per diuersa loca habi-
tantes pietatis instrueret rationem, beatum Titum Cretae reliquit,
5   sicuti et Timotheum Ephesi, praeponens eum illis ecclesiis quae
illic erant. scribit ergo ad eum, ut compendiose dicam, de ordinatione facienda, instruens eum quemadmodum conueniat ipsas
facere ordinationes; simul et de ceteris omnibus consilium ei tribuit, et docens qualiter de singulis agere oporteat eum. memora-
10   tur uero et eorum qui ex circumcisione erant, sicuti et in epistola memoratus est quam ad Timotheum inprimis scripserat; uehementer instruens eum ut ne quid pietati contrarium aut ipse doceret aut alios pateretur docentes. denique et multam similitudinem
haec epistola ad illam uidetur habere epistolam; nam et una cau-
15   sa erat pro qua et ad istum et ad illum scribebat. differri uero sibi
epistolae uidentur hac sola ratione qua Timotheo latius et cautius
de omnibus scripsit; in hac vero epistola quam ad Titum direxerat
compendiose de omnibus uisus est explicasse.

    epistolae equidem argumentum in his consistit. ego uero prae-
20   dicationem de singulis arripiens compendiose eam explicare ad-
nitebor; moris siquidem nostri est ut non absolute prolongemus
narrationem, quando sufficienter sensus ueritatis in paucis poterit

1   Cretam *C r*   2   ad aliis prouinciis *H*   8   ei *om r*   12-13   docere *H*   15
differre *C r*   17   dixerat *C* H*   19-20   precatione *H*   20-21   adnitar *r*   22
sensis *C* H*

THEODORE
OF MOPSUESTIA
ON BLESSED PAUL'S LETTER
TO TITUS

THE SETTING

[233] When the blessed apostle went to Crete, he handed over the pattern of true religion to those who were dwelling there. But because the pattern of true religion itself compelled him to go on to other provinces in order to instruct people dwelling in many different places about the pattern of true religion, he left blessed Titus in Crete, just as he left Timothy at Ephesus, putting him in charge of the churches there. Therefore, Paul writes to Titus, if I may speak succinctly, about ordination, instructing him how he ought to perform the ordinations themselves. At the same time he also furnished him with advice about everything else, teaching him also how he ought to act in the case of individuals. And he mentions those from the circumcision, just as he also mentioned them in the first letter he had written to Timothy, vigorously instructing him that he should not [234] teach anything contradictory of true religion himself or allow others so to teach. Finally, this letter appears to have a good deal of similarity with that one; indeed, it was for the same reason that he wrote to both Titus and Timothy. And the letters seem to differ from one another only because he wrote to Timothy at greater length and more carefully about everything. But in this letter directed to Titus, Paul seems to have given his account of everything succinctly.

The setting of the letter, then, consists in these points. And for my part, I shall strive to explain it succinctly by seizing upon particular statements, since it is our custom not to prolong discussion for no reason when the true meaning can be sufficiently

explicari.

Paulus seruus Dei, apostolus autem Christi Iesu secundum fidem electorum Dei et cognitionem ueritatis quae secundum pietatem est, in spe uitae aeternae quam promisit is qui non mentitur Deus ante tempo-
5 *ra aeterna, manifestauit uero temporibus suis uerbum suum in praedicatione; quod creditum est mihi secundum imperium saluatoris nostri Dei. Tito carissimo filio secundum communem fidem, gratia et pax a Deo patre et Christo Iesu saluatore nostro.*

longam fecit praescriptionem epistolae propter multitudinem
10 illam quam necessarie interiecisse uidetur. hoc etiam et alio in loco frequenter fecisse uidetur, sicuti et in illa fecit epistola quam ad Romanos dudum scripserat.

†praescriptionis igitur ratio in   τὰ μὲν τῆς προγραφῆς ἐν τούτοις·
his contineri uidetur: *Paulus se-*   παῦλος δοῦλος θεοῦ, ἀπόστολος
15 *ruus Dei, apostolus autem Christi*   δε Ἰησοῦ Χριστοῦ, Τίτῳ γνησίῳ
Iesu, Tito carissimo filio, et ce-   τέκνῳ, καὶ τὰ ἐξῆς· παρέθηκεν δὲ
tera quae subsequuntur; inter-   τὰ ἀπὸ τοῦ κατὰ πίστιν ἐκλεκτῶν
posuit uero ab illo loco quo di-   θεοῦ ἄχρι τοῦ Τίτῳ γνησίῳ τέκνῳ.
xerat: *sccundum fidem electorum*
20 *Dei* usque ad illum locum quo
dixit: *Tito carissimo filio.**

simile est autem illi principio epistolae quam secundo ad Timotheum uisus est scripsisse, ubi dixit: *Paulus apostolus Christi Iesu per uoluntatem Dei, secundum promissionem uitae quae est in Christo*
25 *Iesu.* hoc enim et in hoc loco dicit, quoniam 'apostolus constitutus sum ita ut per me credant omnes qui olim a Deo ob propositi sui bonitatem sunt ad hoc electi, qui et cognouerunt pietatis ueritatem ita ut perpetuam illam uitam quam expectamus adsequi possint; quam dudum Deus se praestare promiserat, in opere
30 uero nunc produxit per aduentum Christi, quando optime se rem habere existimauit; quem etiam et pro omnibus suscitauit. quod

---

3 cognationem *C* H* ‖ est iuxta p. spe, &c. *r* 4-5 saecula (*for* temp.) *r* 5 autem (*for* uero) *r* 6 quae credita est *r* 7 iuxta (*for* secundum) *r* 10 noscitur (*for* uidetur) *r* 13 praescriptiones *H* ‖ sq. Coisl. 204, f. 225 a [Cr. vii. 87, Fr. 157] θεοδώρου. τὰ μέν, κ.τ.λ. 14 continere *C H* 16 sq. et cetera … filio *om* (*per homoeotel.*) *H* 22 quae (*for* quam) *C* H* 26 a *om H* 27 bonitate *C* (*corr.*) 29 re praestare prom. *C*H* se repraesentari prom. *r* repraesentare praesumpserant *l* ‖ in opera *C* in opus *l* ‖ in opere … corrigas [*p.* 236, *l.* 12] *om r* 31 quam (*for* quem) *H*

explained in a few words.

1:1–4 *Paul, a servant of God and an apostle of Christ Jesus according to the faith of the elect of God and the knowledge of the truth that is according to true religion, in the hope of eternal life, which he who does not lie, God, has promised before eternal times and has manifested in his own times his word in the preaching, which has been entrusted to me according to the command of God our Savior: to Titus, dearly beloved son according to* [235] *the common faith, grace and peace from God the Father and Christ Jesus our Savior.*

He has composed a lengthy salutation for the letter because of the many words that he seems to have inserted necessarily. He is seen to have done this often, as well, in other places, for example, in the letter he had previously written to the Romans.

†Thus, the structure of the salutation seems to be confined to these words: *Paul, a servant of God and an apostle of Christ Jesus: to Titus, dearly beloved son* and the rest that follows. But he has inserted what begins at the place where he had said *according to the faith of the elect of God* and goes up to the place where he said *to Titus, dearly beloved son.**

The content of the salutation is in these words: *Paul, a servant of God and an apostle of Jesus Christ: to Titus, loyal child* and the rest. And he has inserted the words from *according to the faith of the elect of God* up to *to Titus, loyal child.*

And this resembles the beginning of the second letter to Timothy, where he said *Paul, an apostle of Christ Jesus by the will of God according to the promise of life that is in Christ Jesus.* He says this also in this place: "I have been appointed an apostle so that by me all may believe who of old were elected for this by God because of the kindness of his purpose, and who have known the truth of true religion so that they may be able to attain that perpetual life we await. Long ago God had promised that he would bestow this life, but now he has brought it forth in true deed by the coming of Christ, [236] at the time he thought best for the fact to come about, and he has raised Christ also on behalf

et cunctis cupiens manifestare, doctrinam mihi de hisce commisit,
ut cum sollicitudine et celeritate percurram diuersas prouincias et
impleam mihi promissam doctrinam.' hic enim est sensus inte-
riectionum. nam beatus Paulus ad exhortationem Titi causam sui
apostolatus necessarie uoluit insinuare; nam quod dixit: *Tito ca-*
rissimo filio secundum communem fidem, hoc est, 'qui secundum fidem meus es filius, secundum quod communis mihi factus es, per
meam doctrinam ad fidem accedens.' sicque consummans epistolam, incipit causam suarum explanare litterarum:

huius rei gratia reliqui te Cretae, ut ea quae desunt corrigas.
　　bene dixit *quae desunt;*

†nam pietatis ratio omnibus erat
tradita ab apostolo, restabat uero ut dispensatio erga credentes
impleretur, ita ut et ad consensum instituerentur per ordinationes ecclesiasticas.*

ὁ γὰρ τῆς εὐσεβείας λόγος παρα-
δέδοτο πᾶσιν παρ' αὐτοῦ· ἐλείπετο
δὲ οἰκονομῆσαι τὰ κατὰ τοὺς πεπιστευκότας καὶ εἰς ἁρμονίαν αὐτοὺς καταστῆσαι ταῖς ἐκκλησιαστι-
καῖς διατυπώσεσιν.

et quae sit correctio necessaria insinuat:
ut constituas per ciuitates presbyteros, sicut ego praecepi [*tibi*].
　　sicut autem errantibus pietatis cognitio est necessaria, sic et illis qui crediderunt necessaria esse uideretur commonitio pietatis;
quod non aliter fieri potest nisi omnes in unum conueniant, sintque ad hoc certi electi qui possint sua doctrina commonitionis implere officium. hoc uero implere poterant ex presbyteri ordinatione qui conuenientibus illis disputare et docere eos poterant de his
quae discere eos conueniebant; unde et in praesenti horum solummodo est memoratus, eo quod ob hanc ipsam causam plurimum
utilitatis in communi possint conferre. et quidem euidens est quoniam et ceteri erant necessarii, qui simul in ordinem clericorum

12 sq. Coisl. 204, *l. c.* Θεοδώρου. ὁ γὰρ τῆς, κ.τ.λ. 12-13 παρεδέδοτο Fr.;
txt., cod. Cr. 13 credita (*for* tradita) *l* 13-14 uero *om r* 19 sicut ego
praec. t. *om r* ‖ praecipio *H* ‖ tibi *om C H* 21 uidetur *C* (*corr.*) *r* 23
commonionis *C* communionis *r* 23-24 impleri (*for* implere [1º]) *C* H* 24
poterat *C H r* 24-25 ordinationi *H* 25 poterat *r* 27 hac (*for* hanc) *C* H*
29 ordine *C* (*corr.*) *r*

of all. Wishing to reveal this to everyone, he has entrusted me with the teaching of these things, so that with care and haste I may hurry through different provinces and may accomplish the teaching entrusted to me." This, then, is the meaning of the insertion. For blessed Paul necessarily wanted to introduce the reason for his apostleship in order to exhort Titus. Now when he said *to Titus, dearly beloved son according to common faith*, this means: "you are my son according to faith because of the fact that you have been brought into communion with me by coming to faith through my teaching." Finishing the salutation of the letter in this way, he begins to explain the reason for his letter:

1:5a *For the sake of this thing I left you in Crete, so that you might set right those things that are lacking,*

He rightly said *that are lacking,*

†for the pattern[1] of true religion had been handed over to all by the apostle, but it remained for the administration with respect to the believers to be fulfilled, so that people might be appointed in the interest of concord through ecclesiastical ordinations.*

For the pattern of true religion had been handed over to all by him, but there remained the administration of what concerned those who had believed and the establishment of them in concord by ecclesiastical regulations.

And he introduces what it is necessary to set right:

1:5b *that you may appoint throughout the cities presbyters, as I have instructed you.*

[237] And just as the knowledge of true religion is necessary for those who are in error, so, too, the reminder of true religion appears to be necessary for those who have believed. This can be done in no other way unless all come together as one, and unless for this purpose definite people have been selected who can fulfill the duty of reminding by their teaching. And ordained presbyters were able to fulfill this, since they could hold discussions with them when they assembled and teach them about what they ought to learn. That is why in the present letter Paul mentioned only the presbyters, because they could bring considerable benefit to the community for this very reason. It is, of course, clear that other people were also necessary, who would at the same time fulfill

---

[1] "Pattern" translates Latin *ratio* and Greek λόγος.

suum officium implerent, per quos explicari poterant illa quae ad communem pertinent utilitatem. deinde iterat illud quod dixerat: *sicut ego praecipio tibi*, docens quales debeant presbyteri ordinari:
    si quis autem sine crimine.

5   qui non ex crimine peccatorum, sed ex uitae suae cognoscitur integritate; ita ut ipsa uera ratione sine crimine esse cognoscatur, omnes calumniatorum insidias superans.
    unius uxoris uir.

dictum est enim nobis hoc idem latius in illa epistola quam
10 ad Timotheum inprimis dudum scripseramus quare dixerit *unius uxoris uirum*, et superfluum existimo ad praesens illa ipsa iterare. nec autem euidenter de illis quae haesitantur compendiose quis poterit explicare; et omnia illa quae ibi sunt scripta hoc in loco ponere non esse censeo necessarium, cum possit illam ipsam partem
15 epistolae quam ad Timotheum scripsimus decurrens uirtutem ipsius negotii ad plenum cognoscere.
    filios habens fideles, non in accusatione luxuriae aut insubiectos.

non reprobat patrum uirtutem ex filiorum prauitate, nam nec Samuelem indignum sacerdotii faciebat filiorum prauitas; sed ex
20 filiorum instituto patris studium probabile ostendere cupiens ista edicit. ideo dixit *aut insubiectos;* hoc est, 'si non filios suos ad idolorum culturam aut lasciuiam aut in deterius proruentes despexit, nec ullam uitae eorum uoluit facere correctionem; sed nec curam expendit ut subiceret eos sibi, aut prout conuenit uitam institue-
25 ret.' hoc etiam ad Timotheum scribens posuit, et hoc in loco similiter cupiens mores eius examinare qui aliorum proponendus est utilitati, si erga suos diligens fuit, erudiens eos de his quae discere eos conueniebant; eo quod si talis habeatur, manifestus est quod

4   est (*aft* crimine) *add* C (*corr.*) r   8-746.9 sq. unius ... mysterium *om* r
14   censio C* H   15   uirtute in (*for* uirtutem) H   17 habentes C H   18
prauiutem H 19 ex filiarum institutum C* H 20 iste dicit H 22 cultorum
H* 24 subiacerit C* subiaceret H 24-25 instituere C H 27 ergo C H
28 conneniebat C (*corr.*) || tales H

their duty in the clerical order and by whom what pertained to the common benefit could be accomplished. Then he uses again[2] what he had said, *as I have instructed you,* to teach what sort of people should be ordained presbyters:

1:6a *if someone also is without blame,*

Someone who is known, not because he is blamed for sins, but because of the integrity of his life, so that for true reason he may be known to be without blame, rising above all the plots of the slanderers.

1:6b *the husband of one wife,*

We have spoken of this same point at greater length in what we have previously written in commenting on Paul's first letter to Timothy, as to why he said (1 Tim 3:2) *the husband of one wife.* And I think it would be useless at present to repeat those comments. And clearly no one could explain concisely the points that are in question. In my judgment it is unnecessary to put down here all the points made there, since [238] anyone by tracking down our commentary on that very part of the letter to Timothy can fully understand the force of the matter itself.

1:6c *having believing children, not in an accusation of licentiousness or out of control.*

He does not condemn the virtue of the father because of the perversity of the children, for the perversity of his children did not make Samuel unworthy of the priesthood.[3] Rather, he declares this because he wants to show that a father's zeal is demonstrable from the condition of his children. For this reason he said *out of control,* that is, "if he has been indifferent to his children when they rush forward to the worship of idols or lasciviousness or into what is worse and has not been willing to set their life right in any way, but has expended no care in putting them under his control or ordering their life as is fitting." He also made this point in writing to Timothy (1 Tim 3:4), and in this place likewise he does so because he wants to test the character of the person who is to be put in charge of others for their benefit, to see whether he has been diligent in his attention to his own children, training them in what they ought to learn. This is because if he is held to be like this, it

---

[2] Theodore must mean that "as I have instructed you" belongs both with what precedes and with what follows.

[3] 1 Sam 8:3. See Theodore's comment on 1 Tim 3:5 (Swete 2:111).

diligentiam adhibebit etiam eorum qui ecclesiastico sunt iuncti
corpore qui erga suos diligens fuit; si uero suos despexit, nec istis
poterit diligentiam adhibere. et ostendens quoniam necessaria est
de hisce scrupulosa inquisitio, dicit:

5   *oportet autem episcopum inreprehensibilem esse, sicut Dei dispen-*
satorem.

'cui enim sollicitudo iniungitur ut illa quae Dei sunt dispen-
set, *sine crimine* esse eum conuenit ita ut aptus sit erga diuinum
mysterium.' duo hoc in loco ostendit quae a nobis iam dicta sunt
10 in prima epistola Timothei, quoniam illos qui nunc nominantur
presbyteri non presbyteros solum sed et episcopos tunc dicebant.
nam dum dicit: *ut constituas per ciuitatem presbyteros*, et de presbyteris disputans adiecit: *oportet enim episcopum inreprehensibilem*
esse sicut Dei dispensatorem. et quod dixerat per ciuitatem presby-
15 teros debere constitui, qui ecclesiarum possent implere dispensationem. prouincias etenim integras in idipsum committebant illis
quibus ordinandi potestatem praebebant, qui ciuitates peragrantes, sicut nunc episcopi regiones suas, eos qui in ministerio ecclesiae minus esse uidebantur ordinabant, et docebant quae eos
20 facere conueniebat; ordinantes, simulque et instituentes singulos
sicut expedire existimabant. tunc uero isti ipsi qui ordinationi
praeerant 'apostoli' dicebantur, contemplatione quidem reueren-
tiae; quo quidem nomine se uocari graue existimantes, praeelege-
runt ut secundum consuetudinem quae ad praesens habetur 'epi-
25 scoporum' sibi uocabula uindicarent, eo quod 'apostolorum' nomine se uocari sui meriti maius esse censebant. si autem non hoc
ita se haberet, non utique dixerit: *ut constituas per ciuitatem presby-*

7-8 dispensit *C**   11 dicebat *C* (*corr.*)   12-13 presbiteros (*for* presbyteris)
C* H   13 adicit *C r*   15 possint *C r*   17 praebeant *r*   18 nunc *om r*
|| ministerium *C r*   20 et *om C* (*corr.*)   21 expedire *om C H: txt r*   22
contemplationem *H r*   23 quo *om C* H r* || quidam *H: om r* || uocare
C H   26 maiorem *C H r*

is obvious that the man who has been diligent in his attention to his own children will be diligent also in his attention to those who are joined to the body of the church. But if he has been indifferent to his children, he would not be able to be diligent in his attention to those people. And to show that scrupulous inquiry about these matters is necessary, he says:

1:7a *And a bishop ought to be above reproach, as the administrator of God,*

"For the person to whom the task is enjoined of administering those things that belong to God [239] must be 'without blame,' so that he may be fit for the divine mystery."[4] In this place he demonstrates two things[5] that we have discussed in commenting on 1 Timothy. First, at that time they used to call those now named presbyters not only "presbyters" but also "bishops." For while Paul says (Titus 1:5) *that you may appoint presbyters in each city*[6] when he was discussing the presbyters, he added (Titus 1:7): *for a bishop ought to be above reproach, as the administrator of God.* What he meant was that presbyters should be appointed in each city so that they could fulfill the administration of the churches. As well, for the same purpose they used to entrust entire provinces to those on whom they used to bestow the authority to ordain. These people, traveling through the cities just as bishops now travel through their regions, used to ordain those who were seen to be of lesser rank in the ministry of the church, and they used to teach them what they ought to do, ordaining and at the same time appointing individuals as they thought expedient. And at that time those who were in charge of ordination were called "apostles" for the sake of respect. Then, because they thought it was too important to be called by this name, they preferred to claim for themselves the title of "bishops," according to the custom that prevails at the present time. This was because they decided that to be called by the name of "apostles" was more than they deserved. And if this had not been the case, Paul would certainly not have said *that you may appoint presbyters in each city.* Rather, he would

---

[4] See 1 Cor 4:1. The allusion, however, may be to the Eucharist.

[5] See Swete's note (2:239): "viz.: (1) that the second order of the κλῆρος in the Apostolic age bore the titles πρεσβύτεροι, ἐπίσκοποι, indifferently; and (2) that the members of the highest order were then entrusted with the oversight of entire provinces, the cities being left in the charge of presbyters."

[6] *Per civitatem* instead of, as in the text of verse 5, *per civitates.*

teros, sed dixerit: *ut constituas per ciuitatem* episcopum, qui ordinatus cuncta quae illo minus habebantur poterit adimplere. deinde ipsum episcopum designans qualis esse debeat dicit;

    non audacem.

5   hoc est, 'non ferocem aut elatum.'

    non iracundum.

    hoc est, 'reminiscentem iram et per longi temporis spatia te-
nentem.' nam qui alios regere constituitur, si hanc habuerit minorationem, magno praeditus malo, etiam illos poterit nocere quibus

10 praeesse uidetur.

    non uinolentum.

    euidens est ebrium dicit et qui nimietate potus delectatur.

    non percussorem.

    id est, 'non cito increpantem aut contumeliis afficientem ob

15 nullam utilitatem.'

    non turpilucrum.

    'non eum qui pecuniae lucris inhaeret.' deinde dicens qualis
non debeat esse, dicit et qualis debeat esse:

    sed hospitalem.

20   'eos peregrinos qui fide sibi sunt iuncti libenter recipientem.'

    benignum.

    ut erga bonitatem sit studiosus.

    pudicum.

    ut ab omni lasciuia sese superiorem contineat.

25   *iustum.*

    est, ut iustitiam studeat.

    sanctum.

    ut ab omni malo se superiorem reseruet.

    continentem.

30   quo non uoluptatibus delectetur.

    amplectentem id quod secundum doctrinam est fidele uerbum.

---

2 poterat *C* H r* 2-18 sq. deinde ... debeat esse *om r* 7 tempora *H* 8
constituetur *C** constituert (*sic*) *H* ‖ habuerint *H* 9 in illis (*for* illos) *C* 10
esse (*for* praeesse) *C** 12 ebriam *C** ebria *H* ‖ nimietatem *C* nimiaeta-
tem *H* ‖ delectat *C** 15 nulla utilitate *H* 17 inhiauerit (*for* inhaeret) *C*
(*corr.*) ‖ quales *H** 19 hospitalem inquit hoc est eos, &c. *r* 20 effidem
(*for* qui fide) *C* H*: *txt r* 24 ab omnia lasciua [=ab omnibus lasciuis?] *C* H*
26 id est *C* (*corr.*): *om r* 28 seruet *C* 30 quoniam *H* ‖ non *om C* H r*
‖ uoluntatibus *H r* 31 amplectens *C* ‖ est *om r* ‖ fideli *H*

have said "that you may appoint a bishop in each city," who, once he was ordained, would be able to fulfill all the tasks that were considered under his authority.[7] Then, to point out what sort of person the bishop ought to be, he says:

1:7b *not arrogant,*

[240] That is, "not fierce or lifted up."

1:7c *not prone to anger,*

That is, "not remembering anger and holding on to it for a long period of time." For the person appointed to rule others, if he had this failing, because he was endowed with great evil, would be able to harm also those over whom he would plainly be in charge.

1:7d *not given to wine,*

He obviously means a drunkard and someone who takes too much delight in drinking.

1:7e *not a striker,*

That is, "not quickly reproaching or given to insults for no benefit."

1:7f *not greedy for sordid gain;*

"Not the man who is attached to gaining money." Then, after speaking of what sort of person he should not be, he also speaks of what he should be like:

1:8a *but hospitable,*

"Freely welcoming the strangers joined to him in faith."

1:8b *beneficent,*

That he may be zealous for goodness.

1:8c *chaste,*

[241] That he may keep himself above all licentious behavior.

1:8d *just,*

That is, that he may be zealous for justice.

1:8e *holy,*

That he may preserve himself above all evil.

1:8f *continent,*

By not delighting in sensual pleasures.

---

[7] Literally, "less than he" (*illo minus*). Theodore's point seems to be that, since there are many presbyters/bishops in each city, the "bishop" cannot be a bishop in the later sense of a single bishop for each city.

hoc est, 'diligentem erga doctrinam pietatis.' et quia nihil proderit, si sit diligens erga doctrinam, si non etiam et possibilitatem
ipsius doctrinae fuerit praeditus:

ut potens sit [et exhortare] in doctrina sana et eos qui contradicunt
5 *arguere.*

oportet autem adesse ei uirtutem ut non solum docere possit
pietatem pios, sed ut et potens sit eos arguere qui resistunt, dogmatum fultus ueritate. et quoniam necessarium est ut et hoc illi
adsit, adiecit:

10 *sunt enim multi insubiecti uaniloqui et seductores, maxime hi qui ex*
circumcisione sunt; quos oportet arguere, qui totas domus subuertunt,
docentes quae non oportent turpis lucri gratia.

'multi (inquit) sunt qui obtemperare ueritatis doctrinae nolunt,
omnem uero uerborum subsequentes uanitatem seducunt multos.
15 tales et autem sunt hi qui ex circumcisione sunt, qui uolunt legis
doctrinam Christianorum subintroducere dogmati. unde et necesse est ut uehementius arguantur, utpote contra aequitatem docentes, ita ut ab eorum seductione simplices liberentur. nec autem
possibile est eos aliter a sua separari dementia, qui omne opus ex-
20 pendunt ut uerborum suorum uanitate uniuersas domus subuer-
tant, et in deterius deducant; quod maxime illa faciunt ratione,
ut cupiditatem pecuniae expleant, et tali ratione adquirere possint
pecunias.' haec dicens de illis qui ex circumcisione erant, qui subuertere et seducere multos adnitebantur, uertit sermonem suum
25 ad illos qui ex gentibus crediderunt; uehementer eos arguens quod
multi Cretensium seductoribus intendebant:

dixit quidam ex eis, quidam proprius eorum propheta: 'Cretes sem-
per mendaces, malae bestiae, uentres pigri.' testimonium hoc uerum
est.

30 quoniam autem hoc de illis dicit apostolus qui ex gentibus cre-

---

1   quae (*for* quia) *C* H* quod *C* (*corr.*)   1-2   prodesit *C* H* prodest *C* (*corr.*)
prosit *r*   2   possibilitate *r*   4   et exhortare *om C H*: consolari *r*   6   ei *om C**
‖ cupios sit pietatem pios est (*for* possit &c.) *C* H* copiosus sit piet. pios *C*
(*corr.*) copiose possit piet. pios *r*   7-8   dogmagtum (*sic*) *C*   8-12   et quoniam
... gratia *om r*   11   agere *C* H*   ‖   domos *H*   12   oportet *C* (*corr.*)   15   et
om r   16   doctrinae *H*   ‖   et *om r*   17-18   docens *C* H*   19   clementia *H*
20   domos *H*   22   cupiditatem pecunieam (*sic*) *C** cupiditate pecuniam *H r*
‖   tale *C**   ‖   possunt *C* H*   23-752.24   haec dicens ... dicebatur *om r*   27
qui (*for* quidam) *C* H*   ‖   primus (*for* proprius) *H*   ‖   Cretenses *C* (*corr.*)
28   uentris *C H*

1:9a *embracing the faithful word that is according to the teaching,*

That is, "diligent in the teaching of true religion." And because he would make no progress by his diligence in teaching if he were not also endowed with the capacity for teaching:

1:9b *so that he may be able both to exhort in sound teaching and to refute those who contradict.*

And he ought to have the power not only to be able to teach the godly true religion but also to be able to refute those who oppose it, supported by the truth of doctrines. And since it is necessary for this to belong to Titus, he added:

1:10–11 *For there are many people, disorderly, vain speakers, and those who lead astray, especially those who are from the circumcision, whom it is necessary to condemn, who subvert whole households, teaching what they ought not for the sake of sordid gain.*

"There are many (he says) who are unwilling to submit to the teaching of the truth, [242] and by pursuing every vanity of words they lead many astray. And such are those from the circumcision who want to introduce secretly the teaching of the law to the doctrine of Christians. For this reason it is necessary that they be rigorously condemned as people who teach against impartiality,[8] so that the simple may be freed from their attempts to lead them astray. Nor is it possible in any other way to be kept apart from their madness, since they expend every effort to subvert whole households by the vanity of their words, and they lead them to what is worse. They do this especially for this reason—to satisfy their lust for money and to be able to gain money for such a reason." After saying these things about those from the circumcision, who were striving to subvert many and lead them astray, he turns his discussion to the Gentile believers, vigorously condemning them because many of the Cretans were paying attention to those who were trying to lead them astray:

1:12–13a *One of them, one prophet of theirs, their own, has said: "Cretans are always liars, evil beasts, lazy stomachs." This testimony is true.*

That the apostle is saying this about Gentile believers is clear;

---

[8] *Aequitatem.* Presumably Theodore means that the Jewish Christians reject the equality in Christ of both Jews and Gentiles.

diderant, euidens est; 'proprium' autem 'eorum' poetam 'prophetam' dicit qui ista dixit; qui utique non fuerat ex Iudaeis, sed ex
gentibus. dictum est autem a poeta Cretensibus eo quod deroga-
re illis uoluit, ea ratione quam promittebant se Iouis posse sepul-
chrum in suis monstrare, non homine existente Ioue (ut poeta opinabatur), sed deo.

†illi uero qui contra Christia-num dogma contrascripserunt, hoc in loco dixerunt etiam bea-tum Paulum recepisse, eo quod iusta ratione haec poeta pro Ioue aduersus Cretenses dixerit; non intendentes neque modum apo-stolici dicti, neque illud quod dixerit: *testimonium hoc uerum est*. non enim poema neque poetae uocem recipit, sed quasi prouerbio quodam poetae uoce abusus, eo quod forte tunc hoc idem in prouerbio apud eos di-cebatur, sicut et multa alia apud antiquos dici solebant, quod usu ipso a posteris in prouerbium dicebatur.*	οἱ κατὰ τῶν χριστιανικῶν συντά-ξαντες δογμάτων ἐνταῦθα ἔφασαν καὶ τὸν μακάριον Παῦλον ἀποδέ-χεσθαι τὴν τοῦ ποιητοῦ φωνὴν καὶ ἐπιμαρτυρεῖν αὐτῷ, ὡς ἂν δικαίως ταῦτα ὑπὲρ τοῦ Διὸς περὶ Κρητῶν εἰρηκότι, οὐ προσεσχηκότες οὔτε τῷ τρόπῳ τῆς τοῦ ἀποστόλου χρή-σεως, οὔτε τῷ ἡ μαρτυρία αὕτη ἐσ-τὶν ἀληθής· οὐ γὰρ τὸ ποίημα οὐδὲ τὴν τοῦ ποιητοῦ ἀποδέχεται φωνήν, ἀλλ' ὡς παροιμίᾳ τῇ τοῦ ποιητοῦ φωνῇ χρησάμενος, τυχὸν καὶ τῶν τότε τῇ φωνῇ κεχρημένων, ὥσπερ οὖν καὶ ἕτερα πολλὰ τῶν παρὰ τοῖς ἀρχαίοις φερομένων ἐν παροιμίαις χρήσει τοῖς ὕστερον ἐγένετο.

hoc (inquit) *testimonium uerum est;* hoc est, uerum est illud; de
Cretensibus dictum est ab aliquo qui apud illos dudum magnus esse aestimabatur. 'hoc idem adsero (inquit) et ego de ipsis, eo quod
dogmate ueritatis nullam expendunt sollicitudinem, sed contrario
intendunt mendaciis eorum qui ex circumcisione sunt, qui nihil
uerum docere eos adnituntur.' quid ergo fieri debet illis qui tales
sunt?

1 eorum *om H* ‖ petam (*for* poetam) *C* H*   4 qua *C* (*corr.*)   5 ministrare *H* ‖ hominum existante Iouem *C* H* homine existante Ioue *C* (*corr.*)
7 sq. Coisl. 204, f. 227 a [Cr. vii. 91, Fr. 157] θεόδωρος. καὶ θεόδωρος δὲ ὁμοίως φησὶν [sc. σευηριανῷ (*v.* Cr. *l. c.*)]· οἱ κατά, κ.τ.λ.   8 scripserunt *C*   12
Cretensen *C** Cretensem *H*   13 modo in (*for* modum) *H*   15 ὅτι (for οὔτε)
cod.   17 χρῆσιν (for φωνήν) Fr. φ. om. Cr.; txt., cod.   18 uocem *C H r*   22
antiquis *C* H*   26 magnas *C*   28 dogmate *C H r* ‖ nullum *C** ‖ e
contr. *r*   30 adnititur *C* H* ‖ debet qui (*for* d. illis qui) *H* debeat quia *r*
31 illi (*aft.* sunt) add *H r*

he says that the poet who said those things is *their own prophet*. Certainly, he would not have been from the Jews [243] but from the Gentiles. The poet said this about the Cretans because he wanted to slander them on the grounds that they were claiming they could show the tomb of Jupiter in their land, since the poet believed that Jupiter was not a man but a god.[9]

†And those who have written against Christian doctrines have said that in this place blessed Paul has accepted the fact that with just reason the poet said this on behalf of Jupiter and against the Cretans. But they have paid no attention either to the manner of the apostle's words or to his statement, *this testimony is true*. For he does not accept the poem or the poet's voice but uses the poet's voice as some proverb, because by chance at that time [244] this was being said among them proverbially, just as many other things commonly said among the ancients were said by people later on as proverbs because of their constant use.*

Those who have written against Christian doctrines have said that here blessed Paul accepts the poet's voice and testifies to him that he rightly said these things on behalf of Zeus about the Cretans, paying no attention either to the manner of the apostle's usage or to his statement, *this testimony is true*. For he does not accept the poem or the poet's voice but uses the poet's voice as a proverb, since the people at that time used the voice just as many other sayings current among the ancients came to be used as proverbs by people later on.

This testimony (he says) *is true*; that is, what was said about the Cretans by someone who long ago was considered great among them is true. "For my part (he says) I, too, assert this same thing about them, because they expend no care on the doctrine of truth but, on the contrary, pay attention to the lies of those from the circumcision, who strive to teach them nothing true." Therefore, what should happen to those who are like this?

---

[9] See Swete's note (2:242): "Jerome informs us that the line cited by S. Paul is taken from the περὶ χρησμῶν of the Cretan poet Epimenides (comp. Socr. *H.E.* iii. 16), and that the first three words were either borrowed from Epimenides or cited as a proverb by Callimachus, when criticizing the claims of the Cretans to possess the tomb of Zeus. Th., like Thdt., seems to connect the quotation exclusively with the later poet."

ob quam causam argue eos uehementer, ut sani sint in fide, non in-
tendentes Iudaicis fabulis et mandatis hominum qui auersi sunt a ue-
ritate.

'uehementer (inquit) arguere eos ut in fide sana persistant, nec
5 ab illis seducantur qui fabulas quasdam et deliramenta referunt
composita, docentes eos legem seruare; quod mandatum hominum est eorum qui ueritati minime intendunt, et legem nolunt per
Dei cessare sententiam.' deinde et aduersus dicta illorum insur-
gens adiecit:

10 *omnia quidem munda mundis; coinquinatis uero et infidelibus nihil*
mundum, sed coinquinata est eorum et mens et conscientia.

†eo quod erga escarum in-   ἐπειδὴ περὶ τὰ βρώματα ἀκρι-
sumptionem scrupuloso agere   βολογεῖσθαι ἐδόκουν, ὡς ἂν κατὰ
uidebantur, pro quibus legis du-   νόμον τῶν μὲν δέον μεταλαμβάνειν,
15 dum latae tenore alia quidem   τῶν δὲ ἀπέχεσθαι· 'τῶν γεγονό-
debere insumi, alia uero repelli,   των (φησὶν) ἀκάθαρτον οὐδέν, εἰ δή
'illa (inquit) quae ad escam facta   τις αὐτῶν καθαρᾷ μεταλαμβάνοι τῇ
sunt nihil in se inmundum ha-   γνώμῃ· ἐπειδὰν δέ τις δι' ἀπιστίαν
bent, si tamen quis cum munda   ἔχοι τὴν συνείδησιν μεμολυμμένην,
20 conscientia uelit ea insumere; si καθαρὸν οὐδὲν τῷ τοιούτῳ, βλάπ-
quis uero per suam increduli-   τεται γὰρ ὑφ' ἁπάντων ὁμοίως.'
tatem habet conscientiam coin-
quinatam, nihil mundum esse
poterit illi qui talis est; nocetur
25 autem similiter ex omnibus*
illis sua perfidia.' et quoniam antiquam proponebant habere se cognitionem:

Deum (inquit) *confitentur se scire; operibus autem negant, cum*
sint execrabiles et diffidentes et ad omne opus bonum reprobi.

30 'negant (inquit) opere eius cognitionem, dum legibus eius nolunt obtemperare, neque aliquid de illis quae conueniunt agere.'
et dicens ista aduersus illos:

4 ueh. arg. eos praecepit (*for* ueh. inquit arg. eos) *r*   ‖   ne (*for* nec) *r*   5
liberamenta *C* H*: *txt r* 8-9 deinde … adiecit *om r* 9 adicit *C* 10 quidam
C*: *om r* 11 quod inquinata (*for* coinq.) *C* H* polluta *r* 12 sq. Coisl. 204,
f. 228 a [Cr. vii 93, Fr. 158] Θεόδωρος. ἄλλος φησίν· ἐπειδή, κ.τ.λ. 15 tenorem
C H r 16 sepe illi (*for* repelli) *H* 18-19 habet *C* (*corr.*) 19 μεμολυσμένην
edd. 22 habent *H* 24 nocitur *H* 26-29 sq. et quoniam … reprobi *om*
r 26-27 cognationem *H* 30 opera *H* 31 fagere [= facere?] (*for* agere) *H*
32 et dicens ista adu. illos *om r*

1:13b-14 *For which reason rebuke them vigorously so that they may be sound in faith, not paying attention to Jewish myths and the commandments of people who have turned away from the truth.*

"Vigorously (he says) rebuke them so that they may continue to stand fast in sound faith and not be led astray by those who retail certain myths and delusions they have composed, teaching them to observe the law. This commandment, one of human beings, is theirs, who by no means pay attention to the truth and are unwilling to put an end to the law by the verdict of God." Then, rising up against their words, he added:

1:15 *All things, indeed, are pure to the pure; but to the defiled and unbelieving nothing is pure, but defiled is both their mind and conscience.*

†Because they seemed to act scrupulously with respect to the consumption of foods, [245] since by the line taken by the law long ago delivered, some things ought to be consumed but others rejected, "what has been made for food (he says) has nothing impure in itself, if indeed someone is willing to consume it with a pure conscience. But if someone by his own disbelief has a defiled conscience, nothing can be pure to someone like that, and he is harmed alike by all*

Since they seemed to be scrupulous about foods, so that according to the law it was right to partake of some but to avoid others,

"none of the things that have come to be (he says) are impure, if indeed someone partakes of them with a pure judgment. But whenever someone by disbelief has a defiled conscience, nothing is pure to such a person, for he is harmed alike by all."

because of his own faithlessness." And since they were setting forth the claim that they had ancient knowledge:

1:16 *They confess* (he says) *that they know God, but by works they deny, since they are accursed and distrustful and unfit for every good work.*

"They deny (he says) by what they do that they know God, since they are unwilling to submit to his laws and to do any of the things they ought to do." And after saying those things against them:

tu autem loquere quae decent sanam doctrinam.

hoc [est:] 'illa quae ueritatis sunt doce.' deinde ad generalem exhortationem producit suum sermonem:

seniores sobrios esse, pudicos, castos, sanos in fide, in caritate, in
5 *patientia.*

deest 'doce;' uult enim dicere quoniam '*seniores* doce'—ut dicat, 'eos qui in ecclesia antiquiores sunt aetatis'—ita ut sobrii sint et erga illa sint solliciti quae fieri conueniunt pudicitiae simul et castitati.' *sanos in fide, in caritate;* secundum illam firmitatem quam
10 omnes habere oportet.

anus similiter in habitu decenti, non criminatrices, non uino multo deditas.

anus autem illas dicit quae aetate sunt prouectae, sicuti et de senioribus superius dixit;

15 †non sicut quidam errant, in ec- | οὐχ ὥς τινες ἐνόμισαν, ὅτι χειρο-
clesia ut mulieres quae prouec- | τονία τις ἦν τότε ἐν γυναιξὶν πρεσ-
tae sunt aetatis ad instar uiro- | βυτέρων. διδάσκει γὰρ ὁμοίως καὶ
rum presbyterii officium sorti- | τῶν γυναικῶν τὰς τὴν ἡλικίαν πα-
rentur. hoc enim instruit dum | λαιοτέρας τὸ σχῆμα ἔχειν ἱεροπρε-
20 dicit *similiter;* uult enim dicere | πές, ἵνα εἴπῃ 'θαυμαστὸν καὶ αἰδέ-
ut et mulieres quae aetate sunt | σιμον.'
prouectae habitu sint decenti
ornatae, id est, ut erga reuerentiam et uerecundiam sint per-
25 fectae,*

nec uino intendant multo aut ebrietati; sed nec istorum uerba ad illos nec illorum deferant ad istos.

bona docentes.

quae non modo diligentiam poterint adhibere bonitati, sed et
30 docere illa quae sunt optima. et qua de causa dicitur?

1 sq. tu autem ... sermonem *om r* ‖ docent *H* 2 est *om C H r* ‖ illi *C** ille *H* ‖ qui *C r* ‖ generali exhortationi *C (corr.)* 4 honestos pudicos (*for* pud. castos) *r* 7 antiquioris *C (corr.) r* 8 illi *H* 9 et (*for* in [2°]) *H r* 11 dicenti *C* H* sancto *r* ‖ incentrices (*for* crim.) *r* 12 seruientes (*for* deditas) *r* 13 secuti (*bis*) *C** 15 erat (*for* errant) *C* H* erant *r* ‖ sq. Coisl. 204, *l. c.* [Cr. vii. 94, Fr. 158] Θεόδωρος· οὐχ ὥς τινες κ.τ.λ. 16 melioris (*for* mulieres) *H* meliores *r* 17 aetate *r* 19 τό τε σχ. cod. edd. 22 sui (*for* sint) *r* ‖ dicenti ornatae idem *C* dicenti ornati id est *H*: *txt r* 24-25 prouectae (*for* perf.) *r* 26 intendunt *C** ‖ ebrietate *C* H* 30 et qua de causa d. *om r*

2:1 *But as for you, speak what becomes sound teaching.*

[246] That is, "teach what belongs to truth." Then he brings his discussion on to a general exhortation:

2:2 *the older men to be sober, chaste, pure, sound in faith, in love, in endurance.*

"Teach" is lacking. For he wants to say "teach *the older men*"— meaning those in the church older in years—so that they may be sober and may be careful about what ought to be done for chastity and purity." *Sound in faith, in love*—according to that steadfastness that all ought to have.

2:3a *the older women likewise in becoming behavior, not slanderers, not given to much wine,*

And by *older women* he means those advanced in age, just as he also said above about the older men—

†not, as some erroneously think, that in the church women advanced in age, like men, [247] were allotted the duty of a presbyter. For he gives this instruction while he says *likewise*, for he wants to say that women advanced in age should be adorned with a becoming demeanor, that is, that they should be perfected regarding respectability and modesty,*

Not, as some have supposed, that there was at that time any ordination of presbyters among the women. For he is teaching that *likewise* also those of the women who who were older in age should have a reverent demeanor, that is to say, "admirable and modest."

and not be intent on much wine or drunkenness; moreover, they should not carry the words of those to these or of these to those.

2:3b *teaching good things,*

Who may be able not only to apply diligence to goodness but also to teach what is best. And why is this said?

ut pudicas (inquit) *faciant adolescentulas, diligentes maritos suos et filios, sobrias esse, castas, domus suas bene regentes, benignas, subditas propriis maritis; ut ne uerbum Dei blasphemetur.*

illae etenim anus, si tales fuerint, poterint etiam adolescentu-
5 las docere ut et maritos suos diligant et sobriae sint et filios diligant suos sintque benignae et domus proprias optime regant et ab omni malitia se superiores custodiant, obtemperantes suis maritis; ut non ex earum uita mala et ferocitate Dei doctrina blasphemetur tales facere credentes sibi. et quia dixit de illis qui per ae-
10 tatem sunt antiquiores siue uiri sint siue mulieres, memoratus est et de mulieribus, simul instruens quales oporteat esse adolescentulas, quae etiam ab illis quae per aetatem sunt antiquiores instrui debent, adiecit:

iuuenes similiter obsecra sobrios esse.

15 sicut enim de illis dicens instruxit quales esse adolescentulae mulieres debeant, optime adiecit et de iuuenibus, dicens *similiter*; hoc est, 'et uiros iuuenes edoce ut sobrietati et pudicitiae studeant' et quoniam memoratus est omnium seniorum et iuuenum siue uirorum siue mulierum, consequenter adiecit:

20 *ad omnia teipsum praebens [formam bonorum] operum; in doctrina tene incorruptibilitatem, uerbum sanum inreprehensibile, ut is qui ex aduersis est erubescat, nihil habens de nobis dicere prauum.*

'in omnibus (inquit) bonis operibus de quibus alios doces, teipsum formam praebe, omnem castitatem ipsis ostendens operibus,
25 et omne quicquid bonum est et ab omni reprehensione est alienum enarra; ita ut uita nostra aduersarios erubescere facere, dum nihil de nobis possunt dicere prauum.'

seruos suis dominis subditos esse.

deest etiam hoc in loco 'doce.'

30 *in omnibus [placentas].*

1 adulestulas (*sic*) *H*   2 benignitas *C**   4 illi *H*   7-8 meritis *H*   10 est *om H*   11 oportet *H*   13 adicit *C*   14 inueni *H*   15 adulescentulas *C H*   16 debeant *om H*   17 sobrietate *H*   19 adicit *C r*   20 formam b. *om C** [*but with lacuna*] *H* exemplum b. *C* (*corr.*)   21 incorrectibilitatem *H*   ‖ inreprehensibilem *C* H*   ‖ ex aduerso *r*   25 aliena *H*   26 fac *C* (*corr.*)

2:4-5 *so that they may make* (he says) *the young women chaste, loving their husbands and children, to be sober, pure, rightly ruling their households, kind, submissive to their own husbands, so that the word of God may not be slandered.*

[248] Indeed, the older women, if they were like this, would be able to teach the young women to love their own husbands, to be sober, to love their children, to be kind, to rule their own households in the best way, and to keep themselves above all wickedness, submitting to their own husbands, so that the teaching of God would not be slandered because of their lives—if they were evil and savage—as though the teaching makes those who believe it wicked like them. And because he has spoken of those who are older in years, whether men or women, he mentioned the women so as to give instruction at the same time about how the young women ought to live and also that they should be instructed by the women older in years, he added:

2:6 *Likewise beseech the young men to be sober.*

For just as when he was speaking of the older women, he gave instruction as to what the young women should be like, so he quite effectively added instruction about the young men by saying *likewise.* That is, "teach the young men to be zealous for sobriety and chastity." And since he has mentioned all of them, old and young, whether men or women, in logical order he added:

2:7–8 *For all things furnish yourself as a model of good works; in teaching hold fast to incorruptibility,[10] a sound word irreproachable, so that he who is of the adversaries may be ashamed, having nothing to say of us perverse.*

[249] "In all good works (he says) about which you teach others, furnish yourself as a model, displaying to them all purity in the works themselves, and expound everything whatsoever that is good and foreign to all reproach, so as to make our adversaries ashamed because of our life, since they can say nothing perverse about us."

2:9a *slaves to be submissive to their masters*

"Teach" is lacking also in this place.

2:9b *pleasing in all things,*

---

[10] See Swete's note (2:248–49): "*Tene* has no authority in the Greek; ... of σεμνότητα our translation shews no trace, but it may be reflected by *castitatem* in the comm."

dicit: 'si hoc dominis libitum fuerit.' quod etiam in subsequentibus euidentius; *in omnibus* id dicit,' illis quae ad solum pertinent
obsequium.' nec autem ut ad impietatem uertantur publicauit, dicens:

5   *non contradicentes, non fraudantes.*

ita ut non spernant praecepta dominorum suorum, neque fraudem aliquam dominis suis inferant aut aliquid eorum furentur.

    sed fidem omni ostendentes bonam, ut doctrinam saluatoris nostri
Dei ornent in omnibus.

10   'doce (inquit) eos ut omnem fidem suis exhibeant dominis; sic
enim Dei doctrina mirabilis uidebitur, eo quod et seruos tales erga
dominos exhibeat suos.' et ostendens quoniam pietati studentibus
conueniens sit maxime uitam suam uirtutibus inlustrare, siue senes sint siue iuuenes, siue serui siue liberi, siue uiri siue mulieres:

15   *adparuit autem gratia Dei saluatoris omnibus hominibus, erudiens*
nos ut abnegantes impietatem et saecularia desideria sobrie et iuste et
pie uiuamus in hoc saeculo, expectantes beatam spem et aduentum glo-
riae magni Dei et saluatoris nostri Iesu Christi; qui dedit semetipsum
pro nobis, ut eripiat nos ab omni iniquitate et mundet sibi populum ac-
20   *ceptabilem, aemulatorem bonorum operum.*

    'talis (inquit) est nunc gratia quae per Christum adparuit, quae
omnibus est discenda, [ut abnegantes] impietatem et prauitatem
cum pietate et iustitia uitam praesentem transigamus, et pudicam
et castam uitam nostram per omnia demonstremus; ita ut statum
25 futurum quem expectamus prout potis est nunc informati imitare uideamur, quando expectamus Deum et communem nostrum
saluatorem Christum, qui adparebit in commune omnibus nobis
beneficia praestans; quia ob hanc ipsam causam pro nobis pati ma-
luit ut nos ab omni eriperet prauitate, et proprium sibi populum

---

2   qui (*for* illis quae) *r*   3   puplicauit *C*   5   fraudentes *C**   8   omnino (*for*
omni) *C* (*corr.*)   12   sq. et ostendens ... mulieres *om r*   ‖   pietate *C H*   13-14
seni *H*   18   seipsum *H*   22   discendae impietatem et prauitate cum pietate et
iustitia *C** discenda ut abnegantes impietatem et prauitate cum pietate et iustitia
C (*corr.*) discende impietatem et prauitatem cupiditatem et et [*sic*] iustitiam *H*
discenda ut impietatem et prauitatem cupiditatem et iniustitiam *r*   23   et (*bef.*
uitam) *add r*   25   potest (*for* p. e.) *r*   25-26   imitari *C* (*corr.*) *r*   28   ab hac
ipsa causa *C* H*

He means, "in all things that are just,[11] if this should be pleasing to the masters." Now this becomes clearer in what follows. By *in all things* he means "in those things that pertain to obedience alone." And he has not proclaimed that they should be turned to ungodliness when he says:

2:9c-10a *not talking back, not defrauding,*

So that they may not scorn the orders of their masters nor inflict any fraud on their masters or steal anything that belongs to them.

2:10b *but showing good faith in everything,[12] so that they may adorn the teaching of God our Savior in all things.*

"Teach them (he says) to exhibit all faith to their masters. For this way the teaching of God will appear marvelous because it exhibits slaves who are like this toward their masters." And to show that those who are zealous for true religion must illumine their life with virtues, whether they are old or young, whether they are slaves or free, whether they are men or women:

[250] 2:11–14 *And the grace of God the Savior has appeared to all people, training us so that denying ungodliness and worldly desires we may live soberly and justly and godly in this age, awaiting the blessed hope and the coming of the glory of the great God and our Savior Jesus Christ, who gave himself for us so that he might rescue us from every wickedness and might purify for himself a people acceptable, ambitious of good works.*

"Such (he says) is now the grace that has appeared through Christ. It must be learned by all, so that, denying ungodliness and perversity, we may pass through the present life with godliness and justice and display our life both chaste and pure in all respects. This is so that we may be seen formed to imitate as far as is now possible the future condition we await, when we expect God and our common Savior Christ, who will appear to bestow his benefits on all of us in common. This is because it was for this very reason that he preferred to suffer for us in order to rescue us from every perversity and to gain for himself his own people,[13] who may

---

[11] Following Swete's suggestion for supplying what seems to be missing. The sense appears to be that the obedience owed by slaves to their masters must be qualified by limiting it to just commands. This limitation, then, applies to 2:9c-10a.

[12] *Omni.* The Latin versions provide some warrant for this addition.

[13] Theodore's comment reflects the Greek: λαὸν περιούσιον. The NRSV has "a

adquireret qui bonis semper sit operibus praeditus.' et sic ostendens ex Christi aduentu et illis quae intentione facta sunt pietatis
eo quod apta sit illis maxime [erga] uirtutem industria, siquidem
et talia erga se futura expectant, optime adiecit:

5   *haec loquere et obsecra, et argue cum omni imperio.*

'quae ergo haec se habent ista dicito, ista doce, neque si opus
sit arguere grauiter dubites eos qui dictis his non suadentur.' et
quia diffidentibus dixit quos cum imperio arguere oportere dixit,
adiecit:

10   *nemo te contempnat.*

'contempnat uero te nemo (dicit), si et ualde sit aliquis ferox;
sed ut arguas eum peccantem, ita autem ut illum arguendo pudicos
ac sobrios et castos alios instituas.'

commone eos principibus et potestatibus subditos esse, dicto audien-
15   *tes.*

necessarie post ceterorum doctrinam adiecit quod oporteat eos
etiam illis qui secundum praesentem uitam in sublimitate quadam
sunt dignitatum subditos esse, obtemperantes de quibus imperant
pro communi statu et utilitate; eo quod multi bonum quid facere
20   se existimant si contempnant eos qui secundum praesentem uitam
praeesse ceteris uidentur, et maxime quando impietatem quandam
praediti esse uidentur. deinde dicit eos qui pietati studere cupiunt
de quibus oportet habere sollicitudinem, non tamen existimare
aliquid boni esse si iidem contra alteros litem exerceant aut con-
25   tendant:

ad omne opus bonum paratos esse, neminem blasphemare, non liti-
giosos esse sed modestos, omnem ostendentes mansuetudinem ad omnes
homines.

'nec enim uirtutis aut industriae est ut dicentes contra eos qui

1   sq. et sic … imperio *om r*   2   illorum *C H r* [*cf.* Rönsch, *Itala, p.* 442]
3   sit sit *H*   ‖   erga [1°] *om C H*   4   adicit *C*   5   eum (*bef.* cum) *add C**
H   6   quomodo (*for* quae) *r*   ‖   arguere oportet (*bef.* quae ergo) *add C*   ‖
habentur *C* (*corr.*)   ‖   dico tot (*for* dicito) *C** dico tu *r*   ‖   si opus *om H*   7
suaduntur *C* H* [*cf.* 1. p. 254, l. 20 (vv. ll.)]   ‖   etq: *H*   9   adicit *r*   11   ut
(*bef.* contempnat) *add r*   12   sed ut arguas sed ut arg. *H*   ‖   aut (*for* autem) *C**
H: *om C* (*corr.*)   13   alios *om H*   14   admone (*for* commone) *r*   14-15   obedire
(*for* audientes) *r*   16   necessario posteriorum (*for* necessarie poet cet.) *r*   18   et
(*bef.* obtemp.) *add r*   19   communis *H*   22   perditi (*for* praed.) *r*   24   idem
H r   26   opus *om r*   29   contradicentes contra eos esse (*for* dicentes … eos)
C (*corr.*)

always be endowed with good works." And so, after making his demonstration on the basis of Christ's coming and the deeds done by the purpose of true religion, because industrious application to virtue is especially suitable for them, if indeed they await such things to come for them, he quite effectively added:

[251] 2:15a *These things speak and beseech, and rebuke with all authority.*

"Therefore, speak of those things that are in fact the case. Teach them, and, if it is your task, do not hesitate to rebuke gravely those who are not persuaded by these words." And because he was speaking to people who lacked confidence, but who he said ought to rebuke with authority, he added:

2:15b *Let no one despise you.*

"And let no one despise you (he says), even if someone is quite savage. But rebuke him as a sinner, so that by rebuking him you may train others to be chaste and sober and pure."

3:1a *Admonish them to be subject to rulers and authorities, listening to what is said,*

After his other teachings he necessarily added that they ought to be subject to those who in the present life hold some high office, complying with their orders for the condition and benefit of all. This is because many people think they are doing what is good if they despise those in the present life seen to be in charge of the rest, and especially when they seem to be given over to some form of ungodliness. Then he tells those who by true religion wish to be zealous about what ought to have attentive care, that they should, nevertheless, not consider anything to belong to what is good if they stir up a quarrel against others or contend with them:

3:1b-2 *to be ready for every good work, to slander no one, not to be quarrelsome but gentle, showing all mildness to all people.*

"For it does not belong to virtue or purposeful activity to speak

---

people of his own," rather than the Latin, "a people acceptable."

dignitatibus sublimati sint; melius enim est ut cum omni studio
quae bona sunt agas, neminem blasphemiis pulsans. sed abstine
te ab omni contentione, uitam tuam cum omni instituens modestia
et mansuetudine, quam maxime et erga omnes homines ostendere
te conuenit, non solum erga illos qui principare aliis uidentur, sed
erga illos qui in plebeiorum sunt ordine.' et quia a principibus incipiens ad ceteros suum uertit sermonem, instruens quod conueniens sit ut erga omnes homines modestiam suam ostendant; obi-
ciebant uero ei illi quorundam impietatem, ob quam et usque ad
praesens multi fidelium bonum quid esse existimant, si aduersus
huiusmodi ipsi litem exerceant, bene adiecit:

eramus enim et nos aliquando sine intellectu, insuadibiles, errantes,
seruientes concupiscentiis et uoluptatibus uariis, in malitia et inuidia
degentes, odibiles, odientes in inuicem.

'si (inquit) propter impietatem eum odis, memor esto quoniam
antehac tales eramus omnes.' bene autem adiecit, dicens *odibiles;*
hoc est, 'digni eramus odiri, sed non utique uolebamus odiri.'

cum uero benignitas et humanitas adparuit saluatoris nostri Dei,
non ex operibus iustitiae quae nos fecimus sed secundum suam miseri-
cordiam saluauit nos, per lauacri regenerationem et renouationem per
Spiritum sanctum, quem effudit super nos ditissime per Iesum Chri-
stum saluatorem nostrum, ut iustificati illius gratia heredes efficiamur,
secundum spem uitae aeternae.

'quae ergo Dei misericordia adparuit per Christi aduentum et
ipsi adsecuti sumus, illa quae ab eo est salute non ex operibus nostris illam adsequentes—aderat autem nobis nihil boni—sed per
eius misericordiam qui per formam lauacri uirtute sancti Spiritus
renouauit nos et segregauit in ditissimam [quam] nobis bonorum
praestitit fruitionem, ut eius gratia iustitiam adsequi digni inueni-
remur, quam ex nostris operibus adsequi minime potuimus; quo-

---

2 abstinens *H r* 4 mansuedine *H* 6 plebe eorum *C* H r* 6-7 accipiens *r*
10 existimabant, exercerent *l* 11 ipsius *H r* 12 intellectum *H* 13 sq.
seruientes ... inuicem *om r* 15 propter *om H* 16 antea *C r* 17 odire *H*
18 bonitas (*for* benign.) *r* ‖ illuxit (*for* adpar.) *r* 19 non facimus (*for* nos
fec.) *C H* 20 lauacrum regenerationis *r* 21 Spiritus sancti *r* ‖ opulente
(*for* ditissime) *r* 22 efficiamus *H* 24 quia (*for* quae) *C* (*corr.*) 25 illa ...
salutem *C** illam ... salutem *C* (*corr.*) 26 nobis *om r* 27 pro forma (*for* per
formam) *H* ‖ Spiritu *H* 28 in *om r* ‖ quam *om C H r* 29 gratiam *r*
29-30 inueniremus *H*

against those [252] who are placed in high office, for it is better for
you to do what is good with all zeal, assailing no one with slanders.
Rather, keep yourself apart from all contention, ordering your
life with all gentleness and mildness, which you must especially
display toward all people, not only those who are seen to rule
over others, but also those in the rank of the common people."
After beginning from rulers he turns his discussion to the rest,
instructing them that they must display their gentleness to all
people. But they made an objection to him about the ungodliness
of some, on account of which even at the present time many of the
faithful consider it a good thing if they stir up a quarrel against
people of this kind. Because of this he rightly added:

3:3 *For we were also ourselves once without understanding,
disobedient, erring, serving various desires and pleasures, living in
wickedness and envy, hateful, hating one another.*

"If (he says) you hate him because of his ungodliness, remember
that we were all like this previously." And he rightly added the
word *hateful*; that is, "we were worthy of being hated, yet we
certainly did not want to be hated."

3:4–7 *But when the goodness and lovingkindness of God our
Savior appeared, not from the works of righteousness that we have
done, but according to his own mercy he has saved us, through the
rebirth of washing and* [253] *renewal through the Holy Spirit, which
he poured over us most richly through Jesus Christ our Savior, so that
justified by his grace we might be made heirs according to the hope of
eternal life.*

"Therefore, we have ourselves attained the mercy of God that
appeared through the coming of Christ, attaining it from him
for our salvation, not by our own works—and nothing good was
ours—but by his mercy, which has renewed us through the type
of the washing by the power of the Holy Spirit and has set aside
for us the richest enjoyment of good things, so that by his grace
we may be found worthy of attaining the righteousness that we
could by no means have attained from our works, since we attain

niam perpetuam illam uitam adsequimur, in qua constituti liberi erimus ab omni corruptela et omni peccato.' haec autem ideo memoratus est ut illos doceret quoniam ipsi misericordia sola tantorum bonorum digni sunt habiti. 'non ergo est iustum ut illos propter impietatem odiis prosequamur, et ipsi dudum [odibiles] fuisse uidebamur.'

fidele uerbum; et de his uolo te confirmari, ut solliciti sint bonis operibus praeesse hi qui crediderunt Deo; haec enim sunt bona, utilia hominibus.

'cum enim indubium sit et uerum quod ipsi misericordia Dei tanta sumus bona adsecuti—hoc enim dicit *fidele uerbum*, praecedentibus illud adnectens—necessarium utique est ut ipse cum multa fiducia de his doceas, et consilium des illis qui crediderunt Deo quatenus diligentiam conuenientium adhibeant, eo quod ista iuuare possunt homines. non ergo illa quae uirtutum sunt contentioni et liti deputari.' et quia aliorum impietatem quasi opportunam occasionem contentionis se habere existimauit, ideo omnia ista ad illud reddidit quod superius dixerat: *commone eos principatibus et potestatibus subditos esse.*

hoc quia in loco omnem sensum conclusit, deinde sermonem suum uertit, de illis dicens qui ex circumcisione erant:

stultas (inquit) *quaestiones et genealogias et contentiones et rixas legis deuita; sunt autem inutiles et uanae.*

eo quod illis in temporibus multa nociuitas ecclesiae ab illis inferebatur, ideo ipsa necessitate addictus et [in] principium epistolae et in finem memoratus est eorum; sic etiam fecisse uidetur et in illa epistola quam ad Timotheum scripserat. 'ne patiaris (inquit) conquirere et decertare de illis quae in lege praecepta sunt, neque genealogiis intendens opus tuum impedias, quae illi consulte praeferunt uerbositati studentes; ex his enim nullum iuuamen quispiam adsequi poterit, sed et multam sustinet nociuita-

1 adsequimus *H* 4 habitu *H* 5 persequamus *H* ǁ ipse *H** ǁ odibiles *om C H*: odiosi *r* 8 et (*aft* bona) *add r* 10 non dubium *r* 13 crediderint *r* 15-23 sq. non ergo ... et uanae *om r* 15-16 contentione *H* 16 quae (*for* quia) *C** *H* 17 occansionem contentiones *C** ǁ existimant *H* 18 commune *H l* 24 in *om C H* 27 ipsa (*for* illa) *H* 29 illi consuete praeerunt *H* illis consuete proderunt *r* 30-31 iubamen *C**

that perpetual life in which we shall be established free from all corruption and all sin."[14] Therefore, he mentioned these things to teach them that they are held worthy of such great good things only by mercy. "Therefore, it is not right that we should pursue them with hatreds because of their ungodliness, since we were seen to have been previously hateful."

3:8 *Faithful is the word. And about these things I want you to be confirmed, so that they may be careful* [254] *to be preeminent in good works, those who have believed in God, for these things are good and beneficial to people.*

"For since it is undoubted and true that we have attained such great good things by the mercy of God—for this is what he means by *faithful is the word*, connecting it to what precedes—it is certainly necessary for you yourself to teach about these things with much confidence and to give advice to those who have believed in God insofar as they display diligence for what is fitting, because those things can help people. Therefore, what belongs to the virtues is not to be defined by contention and quarreling." And because he thought that ungodliness presented itself as a favorable opportunity for contention, for this reason he referred all those statements to what he had said earlier (3:1): *admonish them to be subject to rulers and authorities.*

Because in this place he has concluded the entire meaning (3:1–8), he then turns his discussion to speak of those who were from the circumcision:

3:9 *Avoid* (he says) *foolish speculations and genealogies and contentions and quarrels of the law, for they are useless and vain.*

Because in those times much harm was inflicted on the church by these things, for this reason, bound by very necessity, he mentioned them at the beginning of the letter and at its end. So he is seen to have done [255] also in the letter he had written to Timothy.[15] "Do not allow (he says) questioning and controversy about what is commanded in the law, and do not hinder your work by paying attention to genealogies, which those who occupy themselves with verbosity deliberately bring forth, for from these things no help whatsoever can be attained, but they even support

---

[14]Swete comments (2:253): "The translation of this entire paragraph is more than usually careless."

[15]See Swete (2:254): "So 1Tim. begins (i. 4) and ends (vi. 3 sq.) with warnings against idle questionings."

tem.' deinde generaliter instruit, dicens:

haereticum hominem post primam correctionem et secundam deui-
ta, sciens quoniam peruersus est is qui eiusmodi est et peccat, cum suo
iudicio damnatus est.

5 'et ad plenum (inquit) illum deuita qui ea quae contraria sunt
pietatis praeelegit—hunc enim *haereticum* uocat—postquam enim
semel et bis eundem instruxeris et ostenderis ei illa quae conueniunt eius saluti, superfluum est diutius cum eiusmodi disputare, cum sit manifestus quoniam nullam percipit correctionem, ex
10 quibus semel et bis illa quae conueniebant sibi audiens cognoscere
noluit ueritatem. relinque ergo eum qui talis est ut iustam expectet a iudice poenam, eo quod [in sua pertinacia persistens] nullum
[ad correptionem suam] ex instructione [accipere uult consilium].
in his consummans plenarium consilium suum, scribit de cetero
15 utpote carissimo discipulo suo:

cum misero (inquit) *Arteman ad te aut Tychicum, festina uenire*
ad me Nicopolim; illic enim decreui exhiemare.

'atubi (inquit) misero Arteman aut Tychicum, festina uenire ad
me Nicopolim, ubi et persistere decreui tempore hiemali.'

20 *Zenam legisperitum et Apollo uelociter praemittas, ita at nihil illis*
desit.

deinde iubet ei [ut] Zenam legisperitum et Apollo uelociter
praemittat cum sumptu sufficienti, ita ut nulla parte indigeant.
euidens est autem quoniam et per hos scripsit, ad eum mittens eos
25 et alia uice ad auxilium eius et aliorum correctionem. et quia Titus
ex suis quod daret non habebat eo quod uirtutem studens [nihil]
possidebat, optime adicit:

discant autem et nostri bonis operibus praeesse ad necessarios usus,
ut non sint infructuosi.

30 'eos enim fideles qui diuitias mundi habent, conferant, ut copiosam mercedem pro tali opere adsequantur." post hoc uero dicit:

---

2 post unam *r* ‖ correptionem *C r* ‖ et secundam *om r* 3 quod su-
buersus est eiusmodi et deliquit qui est a semetipso. damnatus *r* 6 pietati *r*
9 manifestum *r*^{ep} ‖ correptionem *r*^{ep} 10 non (*bef.* conuen.) *add r*^{ep} 12
in sua pert. &c. *om C H r*: txt *r*^{ep}—*see note* 14-770.7 sq. scribit ... diligunt
nos *om r* 16 autithicum (*sic*) *C*** 18 adubi *C H* 19 Nicopolim ... legisperitum [2°] *om H* 22 ut *om C H* 24 per *om H* 26 uirtute *C** *H* ‖
nihil *om C** *H* 27 adicit (*for* opt. adicit) *H* 30 rogat ut (*bef.* conferant) *add*
C (*corr.*)

much harm." Then he gives general instruction, saying:

3:10–11 *A person who is a heretic, after a first correction and a second, avoid, knowing that he is perverse who is of this kind and sins; with his own judgment he is condemned.*

"And completely avoid (he says) the one who has chosen what contradicts true religion—for he calls this person *a heretic*—for after you have instructed him once and twice and demonstrated to him what is fitting for his salvation, it is useless to argue any longer with someone like this, since it would be obvious that he notices no correction, because even though he has heard once and twice what is fitting for him, he has been unwilling to recognize the truth. Therefore, leave the person like this to await just punishment from the judge, because by persisting in his stubbornness he is unwilling to accept any advice from instruction for his correction." After finishing in these words the full measure of his advice he writes further to his dearly beloved disciple:

[256] 3:12 *When I shall send* (he says) *Artemas to you or Tychicus, make haste to come to me at Nicopolis, for I have decided to spend the winter there.*

"When (he says) I shall send Artemas or Tychicus, make haste to come to me at Nicopolis, where I have decided to stay in the winter time."

3:13 *May you send on ahead quickly Zenas the lawyer and Apollo, so that nothing may be lacking them.*

Then he orders him to send on ahead quickly Zenas the lawyer and Apollo with enough provisions so that they may in no respect be in want. And it is clear that he also used these people to carry the letter, sending them to Titus also another time to help him and to set the others right. And because Titus had nothing to give them from his own resources, because he possessed nothing since he was occupying himself with virtue, quite effectively he added:

3:14 *And let our people also learn to take the lead in good works for necessary needs, so that they may not be unfruitful.*

"Let, then, the faithful who have the world's riches contribute to them, so that they may attain a plentiful reward for such work." And after this he says:

salutant te omnes qui mecum sunt. salutate eos qui nos diligant in
fide.

salutans eum ex omnibus qui secum erant, scripsit etiam omnes
salutare qui per fidei familiaritatem cum eo iunctas amicitias habere uidebantur. et sic consueto fine conclusit epistolam, dicens:

gratia cum omnibus uobis. amen.

hoc est: 'tibi quoque et omnibus qui diligunt nos.'

4 familiaritate *C H*

3:15a *All who are with me greet you. Greet those who love us in the faith.*

Sending him greetings from all who were with him, he also wrote [257] for him to greet all who were plainly joined to him in friendship by the close relationship of faith. And so he concluded the letter with his usual ending, saying:

3:15b *Grace be with all of you. Amen.*

That is, "with you and also all who love us."

THEODORUS MOPSUESTENUS IN EPISTOLAM B. PAULI AD PHILEMONEM

ARGUMENTUM

ARGUMENTUM epistolae quam ad Philemonem beatus scripsit apostolus Paulus in his habetur. Onesimus, seruus Philemonis cuiusdam fidelis et religiosi uiri, malum habens propositum
per fugam a suo discessit domino. hunc et praecedenti tempore
5 cognoscens beatus apostolus de domo et familia esse Philemonis,
cum esset in uinculis uidit; quem consiliis suis et exhortationibus
in tantum placauit ut pristinam malitiam sui arbitrii relinquens,
reuersus libero arbitrio suo obtemperaret domino, omne ei ut conuenit persoluens obsequium. quem placans atque instruens re-
10 misit ad Philemonem, non solum obsequiis eius idoneum eum exhibens, sed et pietatis eum habere docuit diligentiam. scribit ergo
in hac epistola Philemoni postulans ut ipsi Onesimo pro quibus
dudum deliquerat ueniam tribueret, reciperet uero eum in affectu
ob praesentem propositi eius correctionem.
15 sed argumentum quidem epistolae in his habetur. quid uero ex
ea lucri possit adquiri conuenit manifestius explicari, quia nec omnibus id existimo posse esse cognitum; quod maxime etiam ipse a
nobis disseri postulasti. primum equidem illud est perspiciendum

---

1 epistolas *H*   4   praecedente *C*   6   cumsiliis *H*   7   placuit *C* r*   12   in
hanc epistolam *H*   13   derelinquerat *H* reliquerat *r*   15-776.12   quid uero ...
similiter *om r*   16   lucri ex ea *H*   ‖   cumuenit *C**   ‖   explicare *C* explectari
(*sic*) *H*   17   eri iam (*for* etiam) *C** heri iam *C* (*corr.*)

THEODORE
OF MOPSUESTIA
ON BLESSED PAUL'S LETTER
TO PHILEMON

THE SETTING

[258] The setting of the letter that blessed Paul the apostle wrote to Philemon is as follows. Onesimus, a slave belonging to a certain faithful and religious man named Philemon, with a wicked intention, ran away from his master. The blessed apostle, who knew that he was from Philemon's household and family, saw him when he was himself a prisoner in chains. Paul conciliated him with his counsels and exhortations to such an extent that Onesimus, abandoning the earlier wickedness of his judgment, consented of his own free choice to return to his master, vowing to pay him all due obedience. Conciliating and instructing him, Paul sent him back to Philemon, not merely [259] presenting him as suitable for obeying orders, but he did so also because he taught him to have diligence for true religion. Therefore, in this letter Paul writes to Philemon, asking him to pardon Onesimus for the offenses he had previously committed and to take him back in affection because of the present correction of his purpose.

This is what the setting of the letter amounts to. But what profit could be acquired from it must be explained more clearly, because I do not suppose that everyone is able to recognize it. You have yourself asked us especially to discuss this problem.[1] The first

---

[1]Theodore's commentary is addressed to Cyrinus. See Swete's discussion (1:lxii-lxiii): "It is probable that the labour of composition was spread over several years. Whether from tradition or from the Syriac translation to which he had access, Ebedjesu gathered that the commentaries on the Pauline Epistles were written at the instance of six friends. The commentary on Romans was addressed to one Eusebius, the commentary on Corinthians to a namesake

quia quattuordecim numero sunt epistolae omnes Pauli. ex his uero aliae quidem sunt scriptae ad ecclesias integras, sicuti sunt epistolae quae ad Romanos et Corinthios et Hebraeos et Ephesios et
Galatas et Philippenses et Colossenses et Thessalonicenses scrip-
5 tae sunt. aliae uero sunt speciales ad aliquos scriptae, sicut sunt illae quae ad Timotheum et Titum sunt scriptae, quae pro communi
utilitate similiter scriptae sunt, licet speciales esse perspiciantur ea
ratione qua ipsae epistolae ad certas personas utpote speciales sunt
scriptae; tamen quia instruunt eos ipsae epistolae quid eos conue-
10 niat facere, ex quibus hoc commune esse uidetur plurima ex parte
ob insertam in hisdem uirtutem, illa quae in commune in ecclesia agi conueniant uel quali ordine agi debeant edocuit eos. euidens est autem quoniam omnis quicumque praeesse constituitur,
quaecumque doctus fuerit pro communi facere utilitate, haec ad
15 communia pertinent lucra, licet iuuari uideatur is qui id facit ut
cum conuenienti proposito suum impleat ministerium possitque
illa agere quae multos prodesse poterunt. haec uero quae ad Philemonem scripta est non solum specialis est quia ad certam personam scripta est, sed et ipsorum scriptorum tenore euidenter per-
20 spicitur. de seruo enim scriptum est qui pertinebat ad Philemonem, ut reciperet eum in affectum poenitentem pro illis quibus
dudum gesserat malis, ita ut de illis quae olim ab eo fuerant admis-
sa nullam rationem exigeret. ergo perfectum iuuamen in epistolis
quis intendens inueniat; maxime cum haec ecclesiis scripsisse ui-
25 detur, omnes erudimur ac discimus illa quae nos scire oporteant.
nam et dogmata scrupulositate ex illis instruimur, et conuersationis rectae institutum ex illis docemur. haec enim utraque in omnibus scripta epistolis quis repperiet aut pleniori prosecutione explicata aut infirmiori, sicuti et in interpretatione nostra cautissi-
30 me id designauimus. de illis uero quae speciales sunt multa ex illis
in commune uniuersi erudimur, eo quod de illis quae in commune

---

1 omnes ep. P. *H*   8   quae (*for* qua) *C** quia *C* (*corr.*)   ‖   ut (*for* utpote)
*C** (*but with lacuna following*) ut et *C* (*corr.*)   8-9   scr. sunt *H*   10   uidentur
C *H*   13   est *em H*   16   propositus *C** proposito *C* (*corr.*) propositum *H*
19   tenor euidenter *C* tenore uidentur *H*   21   in affectu *H*   ‖   pro i. pro
quibus *H*   24   inueniet *C* (*corr.*) *H*   25   discamus *H*   26   scrupulositatem
C *H* scrupulositatum *C* (*corr.*)   29-30   accutissime (*sic*) *H*   31   in communi *C*

point that must be noticed is that all the letters of Paul are fourteen in number. And of these some were written to entire churches, for example, the letters to the Romans, the Corinthians, the Hebrews, the Ephesians, the Galatians, the Philippians, the Colossians, and the Thessalonians. But other letters were written as particular ones to certain people, for example, those to Timothy and Titus. These were written likewise for the benefit of the community, even though they are seen to be particular on the grounds that they were written as particular letters to definite persons. Nevertheless, these letters instruct Timothy and Titus as to what they ought to do, including for the greater part what seems to be of general import because of the special character inserted in them. That is, Paul has taught them what ought to be done in the church generally and in what sort of order it should be done. And it is clear that everyone, whoever is appointed to preside, would be taught to do whatever would benefit the community [260] and that these matters pertain to what is generally profitable, even though the one who seems to be helped is the person who does this to fulfill his own ministry with a fitting purpose and so be enabled to do what will be capable of benefiting many. But this letter written to Philemon is not only particular because it was written to a definite person but is also clearly seen to be so because of the line taken in the letter itself. For it was written about a slave who belonged to Philemon, so that he would restore to his affection the slave, since he repented of the evils he had previously done, and so that Philemon would exact no reckoning for what the slave had once committed. Now then, whoever directs his attention to Paul's letters may find complete help. Especially when Paul is seen to have written these letters to churches, all of us are instructed, and we learn what we ought to know. Indeed, we are both provided with doctrines set forth in them with exactness and are taught by them the practice of a right way of life. For anyone will find both of these things written in all the letters more or less fully expounded, as we have indicated in our interpretation as carefully as possible. As well, all of us are instructed by the letters

---

Theodorus; Eustratius elicited the exposition of the Epistles to the Galatians, Ephesians, Philippians, and Colossians; whilst we owe the commentary on Thessalonians to a James, that on Timothy to a Peter, that on Titus and Philemon to a Cyrinus, who seems also to have drawn forth the commentary on the Epistle to the Hebrews." Cyrinus cannot be identified.

pertinent, sicut dixi, multa apostolus ad eos scripsisse uidetur. et specialiter iterum ad eos scripsit instruens qualiter debeant agere illi qui ecclesiae sollicitudinem habent iniunctam, eo quod tales erant et illi ad quos scribebat; qualia uero singuli adsequi possimus de quibus ad illos uisus est scripsisse. docuit enim nos quales debeant esse presbyteri, quales debeant diaconi, quales uiduae, quales serui, quales domini, quales uiri, quales mulieres. de his et autem scribens ad eos apostolus instruxit eos quales esse oporteat eos qui ecclesiae partem implere uidentur, edocens ut illa agant quae agi decent. et uiduae quidem instruuntur, quando illa quae de uiduis scripta sunt audiunt; diuites uero, quando illa quae de diuitibus scripta sunt, et ceteri omnes similiter.

quae est ergo utilitas etiam huius epistolae? ut omnes qui in ecclesiastica habentur functione, maxime illi qui praeesse ecclesiis uidentur, ut sciant quemadmodum oporteat agere cum illis qui nobis fide iuncti sunt, quando uel maxime de negotiis illis agitur quae ad illos proprie pertinere uidentur. quorum utilitatem tunc maxime quis poterit perspicere, si respexerit illa quae nostris temporibus a multis geruntur. nunc autem, sicut structores utilitatis aliorum constituti, commonere uolumus eos qui nobis fide iuncti sunt, de quibus conuenire oportet cum eo instituto cum quo Paulus uult summa cum obsecratione eos conuenire. sed quidam quasi domini eorum qui nobis fide iuncti sunt sic praecipere illis uolunt, etsi et de illis loquantur de quibus illos dominos esse res ipsa ostendit; multum autem interest ut consilium quis dans et de illis quae in diuina tenentur scriptura instruat eos cum modestia et non ex auctoritate praecipiat illis, et hoc de illis rebus de quibus legem nullam accepit ut ita faciat. audire uero Paulum de tali negotio non patiuntur: *non quia dominamur* (inquit) *fidei uestrae, sed cooperarii sumus gaudii uestri;* et hoc Corinthiis dicens, quibus

1 dixit *H* 5 usus (*for* uisus) *C*H* 7 et *om C* 13 haec (*for* quae) *C* (*corr.*) *r*
19 strictores *C** instructores *C* (*corr.*) *r* fructores *H* ‖ utilitates *H* 20
uolemus *r* 22-778.11 sed quidam ... peragit *om r* ‖ quidem (*for* quidam)
C H 24 ut etsi et illis *C H* (*corr.*) ut etsi etsi illis *H** 25 aut (*aft.* ut) *add H*
28 accipit *C* 29 dicentem (*aft.* neg.) *add H*

that are particular in many things of general import, because, as I have said, the apostle plainly wrote these people many things pertaining to the community. Moreover, he wrote to them in a particular way, instructing them as to how those who have the care of the church enjoined on them ought to act, because those to whom he was writing were such people. And each one of us can achieve the qualities about which he has plainly written to them. For he taught us what presbyters ought to be like, what deacons ought to be like, what widows, slaves, masters, men, and women ought to be like. Writing to them about these people, the apostle has instructed them as to [261] what those who fulfill a role in the church must be like, teaching them what becomes them to do. Indeed, widows are instructed when they hear what has been written about widows, rich people when they hear what is written about rich people, and all the rest in the same way.

And so, what is the benefit of this letter, as well? It is so that all who are kept in the service of the church, especially those seen to be in charge of the churches, may know how they must act with those joined to us in faith, especially when there is a question of matters that seem a personal concern of theirs.[2] Someone would then be able to see the benefit of this especially if he were to look at the behavior of many people in our own times. And now, as people appointed to build up the benefit of others, we want to admonish those joined to us in faith about what ought to agree with that mode of life with which Paul with his most earnest entreaty wants them to agree. But there are some, as though they were masters of those joined to us in faith, who want to give people orders this way, even if they are speaking of those whose masters the very fact demonstrates them to be.[3] [262] Indeed, it makes a great difference that someone in giving advice, even about what is contained in divine scripture, should instruct people with gentleness and should not order them authoritatively—and this concerning matters about which he has received no law that he should act this way. But they do not put up with hearing Paul about such a matter (2 Cor 1:24): *not that we are masters* (he says) *of your faith, but we are fellow workers of your joy.* And in saying

---

[2] "A personal concern of theirs" (*ad illos proprie pertinere*), as opposed to the public concern of presiding over the community.

[3] That is, even those in charge of the community ought not to give orders as though they were masters of slaves.

scribebat ut corrigerent se a peccato, cuius rei potestas nequaquam apud illos esse poterat, eo quod ad delinquendum nemo hominum dominus est. igitur cum posset cum multa auctoritate de his scribere, de quibus et uehementius uisus est increpasse quando tamen
5 sibi istius rei tempus adesse pro aliorum existimabat utilitate, ipsisque Corinthiis pro quibus delinquebant iusta ratione increpabat; tamen et hoc posuit, ostendens quoniam non tumore animi aut audacia quadam praeditus horum uerborum pondere abutitur, sed pro ceterorum utilitate illud exequitur quando res ipsa id fie-
10 ri exigit. sed Paulus quidem cum multa disciplina uniuersa peragit. plurimi uero nostris temporibus, nescientes quae qualiter et quando fieri debeant, existimant contemplatione pietatis oportere omnia praesentis uitae confundi et nullam esse discretionem inter seruos et dominos, diuites et pauperes, eos qui sub principatibus
15 sunt et qui principari aliis uidentur; sed haec solum sibi competere existimant ut cum multa auctoritate de his quae sibi uidentur imperent illis, nescio unde hanc potestatem sibi uindicantes. Paulus uero e contrario optimum esse existimabat ut singula in suo manerent ordine, saluo pietatis propositu; ualde autem erat pla-
20 catus, quoniam differentia haec inesse hominibus nequaquam poterat, si non Deus eam esse uoluisset; nec autem erat durum aut laboriosum Deo si omnes aequales facere uoluisset, si tamen hoc scisset hominibus expedire. sciens uero illud quod talis differentia nulla in parte pietatis laedat rationem, cum possent et diuites
25 et pauperes et serui et liberi si tamen uellent studere pietati; sicuti et e contrario possunt illud quod deterius est praeeligere, si

2 deliquendum C^* 4 uehementer H 6-7 increbat (*sic*) C^* 15 hoc H
18 sua H 19 proposito C r ‖ unde (*for* ualde) r ‖ erant $C^* H$ 21
ea (*for* eam) H ‖ nec autem ... uoluisset *om* r (*per homoeotel.*) 23 tali H
24 possit H possint r 25 uelint C r 26 pereligere H

this to the Corinthians, he was writing to them so that they might correct themselves from sin. He could by no means have had any control in this matter among them, because no one is the master of people for the treatment of transgression.[4] Therefore, although he could write with much authority about the things for which he is seen vigorously to have reproached them, at least when he thought he had the right time to do so for the benefit of others—and he reproached the Corinthians themselves for their transgressions with just reason—nevertheless, he put this down to show that he used these weighty words not because he was possessed by an angry swelling of the mind or by some kind of rashness but that he pursued this course for the benefit of others when the very fact required it to be done. Yet Paul, of course, carries everything out with much discipline.[5] But a great many people in our times, failing to know what, how, and when things ought to be done, think that for the sake of true religion everything in the present life ought to be confused and that there should be no distinction between slaves and masters, rich and poor, those titled rulers and those seen to be ruled by others. Yet they think they are the only ones competent to form these opinions, so that with much authority about their own views they give orders for those things, claiming this control for themselves from I know not where. But Paul, on the contrary, thought it best for individuals to remain in their own rank, provided the purpose of true religion was preserved, and he was quite reconciled to the fact that this diversity could by no means have belonged to people [263] had God not willed it.[6] Nor would it have been hard or toilsome to God if he had wanted to make everyone equal, if indeed he knew that this would be expedient for people. But Paul knew that such a diversity would in no respect damage the account of true religion, since rich and poor, slaves and free, if at least they were willing, could be zealous for true religion, just as, on the contrary, they could prefer what is worse, if that were what they

---

[4]That is, no one can compel vice or virtue.

[5]That is, if an authoritative approach represents one extreme, the opposite extreme is to pretend that social distinctions do not exist.

[6]See Swete's note (2:226): "The Ap. was satisfied to abide by the existing order of things, and that for two reasons. First, he felt that the inequalities of human society are permitted by the will of God; secondly, he knew that such accidents as poverty and servitude are no real obstacles to a religious life."

id quod uoluerint erit. quae cuncta in suo ordine manere uolebat; unde et diligentiam adhibere conuenientium omnes pariter
instruebat. ideo et principibus obtemperare iubet eos, inquiens
omnem potestatem a Deo esse dispositam; et ad plenum praeci-
5   pit ut unicuique debitum persoluamus siue tributum siue uectigal
siue timorem siue honorem; plenissime praecipiens ut quicquid in
debitum et contractum habetur persoluatur. sed neque de largitate quae fit in pauperes scribens praeceptiue id fieri iubet, sed melius esse existimauit concedere illis ut unusquisque propositi sui
10 agat arbitrio; adhuc et illud adiecit ut secundum uires suas praebeant; nec autem patitur ut alii quidem sint in requiem, ipsi uero
qui praebent penuria conterantur. seruos omne seruile obsequium
suis dominis praebere cum omni praecepit sollicitudine, siue impios habeant siue pios dominos. nam et in praesenti epistola, scri-
15 bens uiro fideli et suo discipulo magnus ille Paulus, et hoc de seruo
in meliori statu reuerso et promittente quod de cetero integro arbitrio cum omni deuotione seruiat domino, non iubet ut dimittat
seruum liberum per arbitrii mutabilitatem in melius, ueniam uero
dare ei precatur tantum de illis quae ante peccauerat; hoc fieri cum
20 multa postulat supplicatione. si uero aliquis de his qui nunc sunt
talem causam inuenisset, ueniam quidem seruo dari a domino nec
supplicaret nec peteret, sed cum multo scriberet imperio quoniam
'oportet seruum fide nobis iunctum et ad pietatem sponte curren-
tem liberari de seruitio.' tales enim multi sunt praesentis temporis,
25 qui cauti se uolunt uideri aliis onerosa imperando.

     hoc enim inprimis non modico ex ipsa epistola docemur, quod
a multis et ignoratur et neglegitur. aliud uero, quod in specialibus scriptis similis honor a Paulo et uiris et mulieribus praebea-
tur, licet in communi ecclesiae ordine pro ipsa honestate et ordine
30 decenti secundo in loco uelit eas esse et non debere usurpare illas agere functiones quas uiri agere uidentur. specialiter uero scri-

---

1   fieri (*aft.* uoluerint) *add* r   2   diligentia *r* ‖ conuenientiam *r*   3   obtem-
perari *r* ‖ in (*bef.* eos) *add* C (*corr.*)   5   et (*for* ut) *r* ‖ prosoluamus *C H*
7   contractu habet *H*   8   ad (*for* id) *H*   10   aures (*for* uires) *H*   11   requie
C (*corr.*)   16   stature uerso *C* H*   17   seruat *H*   19   cum *om H*   23   nobis
fide *r*   24   liberaliter seruitio *C** liberaliter seruio *H* liberari a seruitio *r*: *txt C*
(*corr.*)   25   cautos *r*   26-782.9   hoc enim ... praespicitur *om r*   29   licet in
c. eccl. [+ordine *H*] esse et non debere pro i. h. et o. d. sec. in l. uelit eas (*for*
licet ... debere) *C H*   31   agere uiri *H*

wanted. Paul wished all things to remain in their own rank, and that is why he instructed everyone equally to apply diligence to what is fitting. For this reason he orders them to be submissive to rulers, saying that all authority has been dispensed by God, and he gives complete instruction that we should render each one his due, whether tribute or taxes or fear or honor, giving the fullest instructions that whatever was bound by debt and contract should be rendered.[7] Moreover, when he writes about generous provision for the poor, he does not order this to be done by way of a command but has thought it better to defer to them, so that each individual may act by the judgment of his own purpose.[8] And he added besides that they should offer provisions according to their own resources, nor would he allow others to be relieved, while those who were offering provisions should be ground down by want. He instructed slaves to furnish entire obedience as slaves to their masters [264] with all carefulness, whether they had ungodly or godly masters. Indeed, even in the present letter that great man Paul, in writing to a faithful man and to his own disciple—and this about a slave who has turned back to a better condition and is promising that hereafter he will serve his master in integrity of judgment with all devotion—even here he does not order him to set his slave free because his judgment has changed for the better, but only prays him to pardon the slave for his previous sin and asks this to be done with much humble entreaty. But if someone nowadays found such a case, he would neither entreat nor seek that the slave should be pardoned by his master but would write with much authority that "a slave joined to us in faith and hastening to true religion of his own free will ought to be freed from slavery." For there are many people like this at the present time, who want themselves to be seen circumspect by imposing burdensome orders on others.

First of all, we are not in the least taught this on the basis of this letter, something many people ignore and neglect. Another consideration is that [265] in what he wrote about individuals Paul bestows equal honor on both men and women, even though in the common ordering of the church, for the sake of decency and seemly order, he wants women to be in second place and that

---

[7] See Rom 13; Titus 3:1.
[8] See 2 Cor 8:8–15; 9:7.

bens exaequat eas in honore suis uiris; quod et Corinthiis super
hoc scribens fecisse uidetur, ita ut non uideatur contemplatione
ordinis [eas exaequasse]; denique adiecit: *uerumtamen neque uir si-*
ne muliere neque mulier sine uiro in Domino. hoc uero in loco quis
5 melius haec ipsa cognoscere poterit, cum consideret beatum Paulum cum Philemone etiam eius uxorem in suis scriptis in praefatione posuisse.

licet uero uolentibus humilitatem apostoli praespicere ex hac
ipsa epistola, sicut non cito alibi praespicitur; nam in praesenti
10 epistola quis sic insuadibilis aut animum habens induratum qui
non demiretur, Paulum tam magnum et perspicuum per omnia
extantem et uirtutibus pietatis omnibus propemodum hominibus
praecellentem uidens discipulo suo cum tanta scribere supplicatione ob praebendam seruo ueniam? et hoc non apostolo existen-
15 te sed uiro fideli et moribus ornato, communem hanc exequente
uitam, sicut est id colligere ex illis quibus scribit ei, cum uxore
et filio—et quidem et hoc de seruo; namque qui eodem tempore
erant perfecti ab his omnibus erant alieni. itaque uidentur mihi
ad hoc uel maxime respexisse hi qui in primordio de legendis in
20 ecclesia epistolis statuebant iussisse ut ista epistola in ecclesia le-
geretur sicut et ceterae, eo quod plus quam ceterae epistolae haec
epistola humilitatem docere poterat auditores. nam non est simile
ut ad integram ecclesiam de tam magnis negotiis scribens humilia-
ret se; sed hoc est demirandum, quod ad unum scribens et hunc
25 discipulum et non adeo egregium, et de tam leui negotio. quod
cum tanta humilitate fecisse uidetur, de illis ei imperare [nolens]
quorum potestas penes illum esse uidebatur. de his et nunc superius dixi, quod non omnes similiter arbitror potuisse perspicere.
nam hinc disci potest quam magnum bonum est erga sanctos ex-
30 hibere sollicitudinem; quod manifestum tibi esse [potest], etiam
nobis non dicentibus. ualde laudat Philemonem hac ipsa de causa. incipiam uero interpretationem epistolae per partes facere, ut

2   uidetur *H*   3   exaequasse *om C H*   6   Philemonem *H*   10   sit (*aft.* insuad.)
add C (*corr.*) est *r*   13   tota (*for* tanta) *r*   15   exequentem *C H r*   17   nam *H*
18   uidetur *H*   19   quoniam (*for* qui in) *H*   ‖   primordiis *H*   ‖   diligendis
(*for* de leg.) *C H*   20   illa (*for* ista) *C*   20-21   legetur *H*   22   uerisimile *r*
23-24   humiliare *H*   24   est *om H**   ‖   demiraculum *r*   25   et *om r*   26
nolens *om C H*[?]: *conj. Pitra*   27-784.3   de his … poterimus *om r*   ‖   non
(*for* nunc) *C* H*   30   potest *om C H*   31   hanc *H*

they should not claim to exercise the services that men are seen to exercise. Yet when he writes of them as individuals, he makes them equal in honor with their husbands, something he is seen to have done when writing about this to the Corinthians in such a way that he might not seem to have made them equal from the perspective of order. For it was after he had said what was to be spoken from the perspective of order that he then added (1 Cor 11:11): *nevertheless, neither is the man without the woman, nor the woman without the man in the Lord.* And in this letter[9] someone could all the more recognize these very points, since he could take note of the fact that blessed Paul has also put Philemon's wife together with him in the salutation of the letter.

And those who are willing may especially discern the apostle's humility from this letter as it is not readily discerned elsewhere. For in the case of the present letter who is so difficult to persuade or so hard-hearted that he would not marvel when he sees Paul, standing out so great and illustrious in all respects and excelling almost all people in the virtues of true religion, writing to his own disciple with such great entreaty so that he would bestow pardon on a slave? And the letter was not to someone who was an apostle but to a faithful man and one adorned with virtuous habits, following an ordinary life with a wife and child, as can be gathered from what Paul wrote to him. Moreover, the letter concerned a slave, and, of course, those who were privileged[10] at that time were strangers to all this. [266] And so those who at the beginning appointed the letters to be read in the church seem to me to have ordered that this letter should be read in the church just as the rest, because they paid special heed to it, since more than the other letters this letter was able to teach those who heard it humility. For it is not the same thing for Paul to humble himself when he is writing to an entire church about such important matters, but it must be admired that he does so when he is writing to this disciple—not a distinguished one—and about so unimportant a matter. He is seen to have done this with such great humility, because he is unwilling to give Philemon orders about matters over which he plainly had authority and control. I have just now

---

[9] Literally, "place" (*in loco*).

[10] *Perfecti*. Swete suggests (2:265) that this means: "The educated, the upper classes, of S. Paul's day held themselves altogether aloof from their slaves, took no interest or concern in their welfare."

ex ipsis uerbis perspici possit beati Pauli sensus qui in hisce tenetur scriptis; nam particulatim interpretantes epistolam aliquid
amplius inuenire poterimus.

    Paulus uinctus Iesu Christi.

5   in praesenti negotio uel maxime est demirandum de apostolica
prudentia, quoniam scripsit quidem et ad alios plures cum esset in
uinculis, sicut ex ipsis epistolis id perspicere est possibile, et maxime in ea epistola quam [ad] Ephesios scripsisse uidetur; nullo
uero in loco 'uinctum' se in praefatione cum nomine suo posuit,
10   inquiens *Pautus uinctus.* hoc uero in loco neque 'seruum' neque
'apostolum' se dixit, sicut erat ei consuetudo scribendi; sed [quia]
de specialibus negotiis scribebat ad eum et de illis quae in potestate
ipsius Philemonis posita erant, hoc sibi magis dicere arbitrans, ut
non auctoritate apostolica abusus imperare ei ex tali praesumptio-
15   ne uideretur. sed illud magis proponendum esse censuit, quod et
ualde suadere poterat Philemonem, cogitantem quia non magnum
esset tam uilissimum praebere ei uiro qui pro aliorum salute habetur in uinculis cum et liceret ei si uoluisset ista minime pati; sicut
ipse quodam in loco dicit: *nam cum essem liber ex omnibus, omnibus*
20   *me feci seruum, ut plures lucrifaciam.*

    et Timotheus frater.

    et in hanc partem iusta ratione debet laudari Paulus, quod in
speciali epistola non dedignatur Timotheum sibi inscribendo as-
sociare.

25   *Philemoni carissimo cooperario nostro.*

    †'cooperarium' uocat ea ra-   'συνεργὸς' δὲ τῷ περὶ τὴν τῶν
tione qua erga sanctorum ob-   ἁγίων ἐσπουδακέναι θεραπείαν, οὐ
sequia sollicitudinem impende-   μικρὰ συμβαλλόμενον τοῖς τὸ εὐαγ-
bat, non minima conferens illis   γέλιον κηρύττειν ἐγκεχειρισμένοις.
30   quibus euangelii fuerat iniuncta
praedicatio.*

6   quo (*for* quoniam) *H r*   7   quod (*for* id) *C H r: see note*   7-8   *sq.* possibile ...
uidetur *om r*   8   ad *om C H*   11   quia *om C H r*   12   spiritualibus (*for* spec.) *l*
|| potestatibus *r*   13   arbitraris *C H*   15   quod ponendum (*for* propon.) *r*   16
Philemonem cogitantemque n. m. et *C H* Philemone cogitante n. m. esse *r*   17
uilissimam *C H* uilissima *r*   17-18   habebatur *l*   18   quod et licere *C** cum et
licere *C* (*corr.*) *H*   19   hominibus (*for* omnibus [2°]) *C* r*   20   seruum feci *H*
25   cooperatori *r*   26   *sq.* Coisl. 204, 232 a [Cr. vii. 104, Fr. 159] Θεόδωρος.
συνεργὸς δέ, κ.τ.λ.

spoken of this above, because my judgment is that not everyone has been able to see the question this way. Indeed, from this letter it can be learned how great a good it is to show care toward the saints; this could be obvious to you, even if we were not saying so. For this very reason let praise be strongly given to Philemon. And I shall begin to make a detailed interpretation of the letter, so that from his very words blessed Paul's meaning contained in this writing can be discerned. [267] For by giving a detailed interpretation of the letter we shall be able to find something more.

1a *Paul, bound a prisoner of Jesus Christ,*

In the present matter special admiration is due to the apostle's understanding, since he, of course, wrote also to a good many other people when he was bound in chains, as one can see from his letters and especially from the one he is seen to have written to the Ephesians. But nowhere has he put himself down in the salutation with "bound a prisoner" modifying his name, saying *Paul, bound a prisoner.* And in this place he has called himself neither "servant" nor "apostle," as was his custom in writing. But because he was writing about individual matters to Philemon and about what had been placed under the authority of Philemon himself, he decided to write this more on his own, so that he may not seem to be giving Philemon orders by using his apostolic authority from a presumption like this. Instead, he formed the opinion that what should rather be set forth was what could convincingly persuade Philemon to think that it would be no great thing to bestow such an extremely unimportant favor to him, as to a man held in chains for the salvation of others, since it would have been permitted to him, had he wanted it, by no means to suffer those things. For example, Paul himself [268] somewhere says (1 Cor 9:19): *for although I am free from all, I have made myself a servant to all, so that I might gain the more.*

1b *and Timothy, the brother:*

Even in this respect Paul should be praised for just reason, because in a letter to an individual he does not scorn to associate Timothy with himself in the address of the letter.

1c *to Philemon, our dearly beloved fellow worker,*

†He calls him *fellow worker* because he was devoting care to the service of the saints, not in the least comparing him to

And he is a *fellow worker* because he was zealous for the service of the saints, not in the least to be compared to those entru-

sic ad Philippenses scribens *dicit: benefacitis communicantes tribu-*
lationi meae; 'communicationem' uocans illa ratione qua in uinculis posito ea quae ad usus cotidianos necessaria esse ei uidebantur
idem miserint.

5 *et Affiae carissimae.*

Paulus equidem non solum marito in suis scriptis iungit uxorem, sed et aequum eis salutationis tribuit officium,

†'carissimam' eam uocans, si- καὶ ὥσπερ 'ἀγαπητὸν' ἐκεῖνον ἐκά-
cuti et illum 'carissimum'; eo λεσεν, οὕτως καὶ ταύτην, ἄτε δὴ
10 quod nulla in parte secundum μηδὲν διαφέρειν κατὰ τὴν εὐσέβειαν
rationem pietatis differentiam ἀνδρῶν τὰς γυναῖκας ἡγούμενος.
uult esse inter uiros interque
mulieres.*

nam istius temporis homines propemodum omnes in crimine uo-
15 candos esse existimant, modo si audierint nomen caritatis. apostolus uero non sic sentiebat; sed contrario, ut ego opinor,

†in illis hanc nuncupationem es- ἡγεῖτο δὲ ταύτην ἐπ' ἐκείνων ἁρ-
se aptissimam cognoscebat in μόττειν τὴν προσηγορίαν, ἐφ' ὧν
quibus turpitudo passionis ines- πάθους αἰσχρότης οὐκ ἐμεσίτευσεν.
20 se minime poterat,*

eo quod illi qui passionibus seruiunt non sunt in uera caritate; hos
uero scit iusta ratione esse in caritate, qui non passionis contemplatione exequuntur affectum.

 et Archippo commilitoni nostro.

25 †filium indicat Philemonis υἱῷ αὐτοῦ λέγει, τοῦ τε Φιλή-
quoque et Affiae,* μονος καὶ τῆς Ἀπφίας.

quem et 'commilitonem' uocauit ea ratione qua in fide erat ei communis. ostendunt uero scripta antepositum esse maritum uxori,
non secundo in loco uxores esse a maritis existimans, maxime si
30 erga pietatem plus fuerint mulieres sollicitae; sed ut naturae ordi-

---

1 si (*for* sic) *r* 3 necessarie *C H* necessario *r* ‖ ei esse *H* 4 id (*for* idem) *r*
5-788.16 et Affiae … existimauit *om r* 8 sq. Coisl. 204, *l. c.* [Cr. vii. 105,
Fr. 159] θεόδωρος. καὶ ὥσπερ, κ.τ.λ. 25 sq. Coisl. 204, *l. c.* θεόδωρος· ἄλλος
φησίν· υἱῷ, κ.τ.λ. 26 Ἀμφίας edd.

those upon whom the preaching sted with preaching the gospel.
of the gospel had been enjoi-
ned.*

So he says in writing to the Philippians (Phil 4:14): *you have done well by sharing in my affliction*, calling this "sharing" because when he was put in chains, they sent him what seemed to be necessary for his daily needs.

2a *and to Affia, dearly beloved*,[11]

[269] Paul, indeed, not only joins the wife to the husband in what he has written but also awards them equal respect in his greeting,

†calling her *dearly beloved*, just as he had called him *dearly beloved*, because in no respect does he want there to be a difference between men and women accor-ding to the principle of true re-ligion.*

And just as he called him *beloved*, so, too, he called her, since he considers that women differ in no way from men with with respect to true religion.

For men of this present time think that almost all people must be summoned for accusation if they merely hear the name of love. But the apostle did not have this opinion. On the contrary, as I believe,

†the recognized that this address was quite suitable for those si-tuations in which the shame-fulness of passion could by no means be present,*

And he considered this address to be suitable for those situa-tions in which the shamefulness of passion did not interfere.

because those who are slaves to the passions are not in true love. And he knows that those who are with just reason in love are those who pursue affection not for the sake of passion.

[270] 2b *and to Archippus, our fellow soldier,*

†He points out, as well, the son of Philemon and Affia,*

He is speaking of the son of Philemon and Apphia.

whom he also calls his *fellow soldier*, because he shared with him in faith. And what he has written shows the husband put before the wife, not because he thinks that wives take second place to their husbands, especially if they were, still more, women who cared for true religion, but so that he might keep the order of

---

[11] "Dearly beloved" instead of "sister."

nem custodierit. ex quibus memoratus est post mulierem etiam
Archippum, qui utique uir erat et non mulier, honorem et autem
aequum illis tribuit ob pietatis communionem, memoriam eorum
similiter faciens; ordinem uero naturae immobilem reliquit, pri-
5   mum memorans maritum, deinde uxorem, et tunc filium. et post
hoc adicit:

   et ei quae in domo tua est ecclesia.

   nec ceteros qui pertinebant ad eos fraudauit salutatione, sed in
ipsa praefatione etiam eos connumerandos esse censuit, eo quod et
10   illorum sit memoratus; custodiens uero et de illis suum ordinem,
non solum quia post illos memoriam fecit, sed quia nec nominatim
ceteros dixit. sed una uoce omnes pariter credidit significandos,
maxime cum euidens sit quia non a ratione qua serui sunt infirmiores dominis secundum rationem sunt pietatis; e contrario ue-
15   ro multis dominis serui meliores secundum propositum fidei sunt
reperti. sed nonnihil his curiose dicendum esse existimauit, custodiens uero et illis quam decebat sequentiam; sicut enim maritum ante uxorem dixit et parentes ante filium, sic post dominos
etiam ceterorum memoratus est qui in familia haberi qualibet ra-
20   tione existimabantur. et non dixit 'domui tuae,' sed *ecclesiae quae*
est in domo tua, ostendens quoniam ecclesiam esse existimat domum in qua omnes fideles haberi uidentur, et ita dignos eos existimabat suorum esse scriptorum quasi qui ecclesiae locum retine-
rent. nec enim multitudinem uirorum Paulus ecclesiam esse defi-
25   nit, sed propositum illorum qui pie in idipsum conueniunt. nam
et in circensibus et in theatris est multitudinem praespicere hominum confluentium, sed tamen non poterit dici illa multitude ecclesia Dei, propter arbitrii prauitatem eorum qui illo confluxerunt.
ecclesia uero Dei uocatur etiamsi duo uel tres tantum intuitu pie-
30   tatis in idipsum conuenerint, eo quod uerum est quod a Domino
dictum est: *ubi fuerint duo aut tres in nomine meo, illic sum in medio*
eorum. et quia ceteros in praefatione epistolae credidit illis adiun-
gendos, non modicum ei auxilium ad praesens confert argumentum; si enim fidei communio tantam fiduciam praebebat illis ut et

2-800.16   qui utique ... effectus *is wanting in H: see Swete note on l. 7 (2:270)*
‖   uir *om C** ‖   et *om C (corr.)*   7   eam (*for* ei) *C*   11   quae (*for* quia)
*C** quod *C (corr.)*   16-17   custodit uero apostolus ordinem (*for* custodiens ...
sequentiam) *r: cf. l.* 10 sq.   18   dominis *C*   19   eorum (*aft.* familia) *add r*
‖   habere *C*   22   habere *C r*   ‖   ista (*for* ita) *C**   23   ecclesiam *C*

nature. Because it was after the woman, that he mentioned, as well, Archippus, who was certainly a man and not a woman, he in fact awarded them equal honor on account of their sharing in true religion, mentioning them alike. But he left the order of nature unchanged, mentioning first the husband, then the wife, and finally the son. And after this he adds:

2c *and to the church that is in your household.*

Nor does he deprive the others who were connected with them of a greeting, but [271] he formed the opinion that they should also be numbered with them in the salutation, because he did mention them. But he keeps his own order about them, not only because he mentions them after Philemon and his immediate family, but because he did not speak of the rest by name. Yet he believed that all of them should be pointed out equally with a single voice, especially since it is clear that it is not by the reasoning that accounts slaves inferior to masters that they are accounted according to true religion. On the contrary, there are found slaves better than many masters according to the purpose of faith. Yet to some extent Paul thought it necessary to speak carefully of them, keeping even for them the order that was fitting. For just as he spoke of the husband before the wife and of the parents before the children, so, as well, he mentioned after the masters the others who were considered for whatever reason included in the family. And he did not say "to your household" but *to the church that is in your household*, showing that he thinks the church to be the household in which all the faithful are seen included, and he thought them in this way worthy of his writing, inasmuch as they held the place of the church. For Paul does not define the church to be a great number of men but the purpose of those who assemble in the same place in a godly fashion. Indeed, both in the circuses and in the theaters there can be seen a great number of men coming together, but, nevertheless, that great number could not be called the church of God, because of the perversity of purpose of those who come together there. But it is called the church of God even if only two or three [272] come together at the same place for the sake of true religion, because what the Lord said is true (see Matt 18:20): *where there may be two or three in my name, there am I in their midst.* And the fact that he believed the rest should be joined to those named in the salutation of the letter brings no small support to the present setting. For if communion in faith

coniungerentur suis dominis, iustum erat et Onesimum de cetero affectuose uidere, qui propositi sui communione hisdem se exe-
quendam sollicitudinem susceperat.

    gratia uobis et pax a Deo patre nostro et domino Iesu Christo.

5   haec quidem sunt quae et ex praescriptione discere possunt hi
qui cum sollicitudine scripta discutiunt. uideamus autem et illa
quae sequuntur. incipit autem in illam epistolam quam ad Philemonem scripserat hoc modo:

    gratias ago Deo meo.

10   a gratiarum actione incipit scribere, agens pro illis gratias Deo,
sicuti et in multis epistolis id fecisse uidetur. ut autem non uideretur nunc contemplatione litterarum gratias agere pro eo, optime
adicit:

    semper memoriam tui faciens in orationibus meis.

15   inquit: 'in orationibus meis memor sum tui et gratias pro te ago
Deo.' et causam ipsam indicans pro qua gratias agit Deo, ne uideretur absolute donans id dicere:

    audiens (inquit) *caritatem tuam et fidem quam habes ad dominum*
Iesum Christum.

20   et unde hoc cognouisti? incertum esse uidetur, si non donans
ei ista Dominus, eo quod caritas et fides quae in Dominum est in
propositu animae habetur.

    et in omnes sanctos.

     ex hoc ergo et illud cognoscitur; nam erga sanctos caritas in
25 operibus demonstrata affectum quem erga Deum habens comprobat. unde et optime adicit:

    ut communicatio fidei tuae perfecta fiat in cognitione omnis boni-
tatis quae in nobis est in Christo Iesu.

     nam quod dixit [*ut* non causam dixit], sed illud quod sequitur
30 consuete posuit, sicut est et illud quod dictum est: *ut iustificeris in*
sermonibus et uincas dum iudicaris. uult enim dicere quoniam 'fides tua—nam communionem fidei credulitatem dicit—quae in ip-

2   idem (*for* hisdem) *r*   2-3   exsequendum *C r*   5-8   *sq*. haec quidem … hoc
modo *om r*   10   illo (*for* illis) *r*   15   in or. m. inquit *r*   20   cognouistis *C**
cognouisset *r*   ‖   uideretur *r*   ‖   donans ei ista dicis *C* donata ei ista a domino
essent *r*   22   prepositu *C** propositum *r*   25   habet *C* (*corr*.): habes *r l*   26
adiecit *l*   29-792.6   *sq*. nam quod … frater *om r*   ‖   ut non c. d. *om C*   ‖
ut (*for* sed) *C* (*corr*.)   31   cum (*for* dum) *C* (*corr*.)   32   communicationem (*for*
communionem) *C* (*corr*.)

furnished them with such great confidence that they were joined together with their masters, it would have been right, further, to look with affection upon Onesimus, who had undertaken to follow careful obedience to his masters by sharing in their purpose.

3 *Grace to you and peace from God our Father and the Lord Jesus Christ.*

Of course, those who analyze with care what is written can learn about these words from the salutation. But let us look at what follows. He begins the letter he had written to Philemon this way:

4a *I give thanks to my God,*

He begins writing with a thanksgiving, giving God thanks for them, just as he is seen to have done in many letters. And so that he may not seem to give thanks merely because he was writing, he quite effectively adds:

4b *always making mention of you in my prayers,*

He says: "in my prayers I am mindful of you, and I give thanks [273] to God for you." And to point out the reason for which he is giving thanks, lest he should seem to say he was simply offering it:

5a *hearing* (he says) *of your love and faith that you have for the Lord Jesus Christ*

And how did you find this out? The answer seems unclear, unless the Lord gave him knowledge, because love and faith are held in the purpose of the soul.

5b *and to all the saints,*

Thus, it is from this that it is known. For love displayed toward the saints in works proves the affection someone has for God. That is why he quite effectively adds:

6 *so that the sharing of your faith may be made perfect in the knowledge of all the goodness that is in us in Christ Jesus.*

[274] Now when he said *so that*, he did not mean purpose, but he put down, as usual, what results, just as is also the case in what is said (Ps 50:6): *so that you may be justified in words and may conquer while you judge.* For he means that: "your faith— for he calls 'the sharing of faith' belief—is proved in the works

sis probatur operibus; ex quibus omne bonum erga sanctos facere
properatis contemplatione domini Christi.' et iterum illud resumit, quasi quia et magnum sit et dignum ut multae gratiae pro eo
agantur:

5   *gaudium habeo multum et consolationem super caritate tua, quo-*
niam uiscera sanctorum requiem inuenerunt per te, frater.

   'iuste (inquit) delector pro quibus cum multo affectu semper
obsequeris sanctos; ex quibus etiam sufficientem in meis tribulationibus consolationem inuenio, audiens intentionem studii tui.'
10 haec dicens in laudem et exhortationem Philemonis, solet autem
laus praeteriti temporis explicata alacriores eos facere in subsequentibus; unde adicit:

   quapropter multam in Christo habens fiduciam praecipiendi tibi
quod ad rem pertinet, prae caritate magis obsecro.

15   primum equidem non dixit: 'potestatem habeo praecipiendi,'
sed, *fiduciam.* deinde non dixit: 'propter apostolatum,' neque
'ob illam dignitatem qua praeditus esse uideor,' sed *prae caritate,*
quam erga omnes habebat; ut sit huiusmodi fiduciae uel causa ab
ipso Philemone tributa. unde et in laudem et exhortationem eius
20 adicit: *propter quod multam in Christo fiduciam habens,* et cetera; eo
quod idem Philemon tale habens institutum et propositum praecipere eum sibi cum fiducia adhortabatur, quia nec possit aliquando
postulationi eiusdem Pauli resultare. qui autem erga omnes sanctos sic liberalis est, numquam ob praesens negotium gratiam po-
25 stulatam dare pigebit. 'itaque tuum propositum et caritas quae erga omnes sufficiens est fiduciam mihi praebere ut et praecipiam de
quibus conuenit. ego uero hoc non facio, sed *obsecro magis.*' deinde et ad uerecundiam eum inuitans:

   talis cum sim qualis sicut Paulus senior.

30   tantam uim habebat sola Pauli nuncupatio. quid enim non expressit magnum et demiratione dignum in uoce hac qua dixit 'Paulum'? nam omne quodcumque summum bonum intellegi poterat,
hoc erat in Paulo. et quod adiecit 'seniorem,' non absolute eum ad
reuerentiam inuitauit, aetatis suae memorans longaeuitatem, sed
35 uoce 'Pauli' etiam illud ipsud faciens uenerabile; qui enim 'senio-

---

2-3   resumpnit *C**   12 *sq.* unde ... obsecro *om r*   14   prae caritatem *C** per
car. *C (corr.) r* propter car. *l*   21   Philemonem talem *C*   22   quae (*for* quia) *C*
23   resistere (*for* resultare) *r*   ‖ enim (*for* autem) *l*   26   praebet *r*   29   sis
(*for* sim) *r*   35   uoci *C**   ‖ ipsum *C (corr.) r*   ‖ uenerabilem *C*

themselves by which you are eager to do everything good toward the saints for the sake of the Lord Christ."[12] Then once more he takes up his thanksgiving, inasmuch as it is a great and worthy thing that much thanks should be given for Philemon:

7 *I have much joy and consolation over your love, since the innermost parts of the saints have found relief through you, brother.*

[275] "Justly (he says) I take delight in the fact that you always devote yourself to the saints with much affection. From this I also find a consolation sufficient for my afflictions, when I hear of the aim of your zeal." He says this to praise and exhort Philemon, and praise of time gone by, when expounded, usually makes people more enthusiastic in the times that follow. That is why he adds:

8–9a *For this reason having much confidence in Christ of ordering you what pertains to the matter, I rather entreat in view of love—*

He did not, indeed, first say, "I have authority to order," but *confidence*. Then he did not say "because of my apostleship" or "because of the high rank with which I am plainly endowed," but *in view of love*, which Philemon plainly had toward all, so that the reason for a confidence of this kind was granted by Philemon himself. This is why to praise and exhort him Paul adds: *because of this*,[13] *having much confidence in Christ*, and the rest. Because Philemon had such a way of life and purpose, Paul exhorted him with confidence that he could order him, since there could be no time when Philemon would turn back from his demand. And Philemon is so generous toward all the saints that he will never be displeased to grant the favor demanded on account of the present matter. "And so, your purpose and the love you have for all is enough to furnish me with confidence that I may give orders about what is fitting. [276] But I am not doing this; instead, *I rather entreat*." Then, also inducing him to shame:

9b *since I am such as this, Paul, an old man,*

The mere name of Paul had such great force. For what is there great and worthy of admiration that he has not expressed in the word he spoke, *Paul*? For everything whatsoever that could be understood as the highest good was in Paul. He did not induce Philemon to respect simply by having added *old man*, mentioning

---

[12] "Which" (*quae*) occurs in the text immediately before "is proved." I am following one of Swete's suggestions, that the word is an interpolation (2:274).

[13] *Propter quod* instead of, as in the citation of the verse, *quapropter*.

rem' audit, Paulum scire poterat eo quod longo tempore pietatis
studio inoleuerit, et multa fuerit hac de causa passus. inchoauit
enim praedicare euangelium cum adhuc esset adolescens; occur-
rit uero in senectutis aetatem semper Christo in passionibus per-
5 sistens. unde ne per aetatem eum absolute uideretur suadere, optime adiecit:

> nunc autem et uinctus Iesu Christi.

solum hoc non dicens: 'erubesce senectutem et canitiem in uinculis connutritam, et aetatem sic longam in passionibus illis quae
10 pro Christo sunt educatam.' et quia multis ex causis eundem ad
reuerentiam inuitauit, ad propositum recurrit:

> obsecro te pro meo filio.

sufficiens erat et hoc persuadere Philemonem, eo quod filium
suum esse dixerit illum pro quo fecit obsecrationem. et ut ne ui-
15 deretur absolute 'filium' nominasse, nulla existente causa, adicit:

> quem genui.

et ipsius generationis modum explicans:

> in uinculis meis.

'si enim eos qui cum dolore partus progeniti sunt amoris di-
20 gnos exhibet ratio naturalis, intellege uinculorum dolorem in quibus positus eundem pietate progenui.'

> Onesimum.

bene primum dixit propositi eius mutabilitatem, et sic posuit
nomen, eo quod sciret non bene habere de eo Philemonem prop-
25 ter pristinam propositi eius prauitatem. et cum memoratione eius
statim eius copulat mutabilitatem, inquiens:

> qui dudum tibi inutilis fuit.

nam adiectio dudum alterum esse hunc ostendit ab illo qui dudum fuerat. deinde et manifestius hoc idem dicit:

30 > nunc autem et tibi et mihi utilis.

demiratione dignum est quoniam inprimis dixerit
†tibi, deinde posuerit et mihi; ut   ἵνα μὴ δόξῃ τὸν ἀλλότριον οἰκέτην
non uideatur alienum seruum   σφετερίζεσθαι, διὰ τοῦτο Σοί, εἶτα
subtrahere ab eius domino. nam   ἐμοί· ʽσοὶ κατὰ τὴν ὑπηρεσίαν, ἐμοὶ

---

1 Paulus r   3   adesset (for adh. esset) C*   4   in (bef. Christo) add r   5   nec
(for ne) C*r   8   non om C (corr.)   10-800.1   sq. et quia ... faciens om r   25
mutabilitatem (for prau.) l   ‖   commemorationem C* post comm. C (corr.)
27   aliquando (for dudum) l   32   sq. Coisl. 204, f. 233 a [Cr. vii. 107, Fr. 159]
Θεόδωρος. ἵνα μή, κ.τ.λ.   34   μοί (for ἐμοί [1°.]) edd.

his own great age, but it was by the name *Paul* that he makes
even old age venerable. For whoever hears "old man" could have
known about Paul, because for a long time he grew old in his zeal
for true religion and had suffered many things for this reason. For
he began to preach the gospel when he was still a youth, and he
came to old age always remaining steadfast in sufferings for Christ.
Then, lest he should seem to be persuading Philemon simply by
his age, he quite effectively added:

9c *and now also bound prisoner for Jesus Christ.*

All but saying, "Respect my old age and my white hair, because
it has grown together with my chains, and respect my age that is
so long, because it has been brought up in sufferings on behalf of
Christ." And because he has induced Philemon to respect from
many considerations, he returns to his purpose:

10a *I entreat you for my son,*

[277] And this would have been enough to persuade Philemon,
because he said it was his son for whom he made entreaty. And
so that he might not seem to have named him "son" without
qualification, as though no reason existed, he adds:

10b *whom I begot*

And to explain the manner of this begetting:

10c *in my chains,*

"For if natural reason shows those born with the pain of
childbirth worthy of love, understand the pain of the chains,
placed in which I gave birth to him by true religion."

10d *Onesimus,*

He rightly spoke first of Onesimus's change of purpose and
then put down his name, because he knew that Philemon did not
have a good opinion about him because of the previous perversity
of his purpose. And at once he links his change with the mention
of his name, saying:

11a *who formerly was useless to you,*

Now the addition of *formerly* shows that he is different from
what he had formerly been. Then Paul says the same thing more
clearly:

11b *but now useful both to you and to me,*

It is worth admiring that he first said

†*to you* and then [278] put down *and to me*, so that he might not seem to be dragging the

So that he might not seem to make someone else's slave his own—that is why he said *to you*

quod dixit *tibi*, contemplatione   κατὰ τὴν βελτίωσιν τοῦ τρόπου.'
obsequii dixit; *mihi* quod au-
tem dixit, secundum correctionem propositi eius.*

5   et quidem quantum ad ordinem pertinet negotiorum hoc primum
fuerat effectum; nam Pauli exhortatio utilem eum [in] Philemonem et idoneum exhibuerat. sed et illud primum posuit, ostendens quoniam omne quod factum est ob illius lucrum factum est.
unde et factum? id faciens, adicit:

10   *quem remisi.*

uolens ostendere quoniam illi obsequiorum causa sit utilis, sibi uero causa fidei dixerit tantum. 'quid ergo est quod pro illo te
obsecro? non ut mihi concedas eum; misi eum ad te.' sed quid est
quod postulas?

15   *tu autem eum—hoc est uiscera mea—recipe.*

'hoc solum postulo, quod affectuose eum et recipias et uideas.'
uiscera autem sua nominans Onesimum sufficienter suasit Philemoni ut affectuose eum reciperet. oportet uero nec illum despicere. non dixit: '[ne] caede eum afficias, ne in uinculis mittas.' nec

20   enim existimabat Philemonem tale aliquid circa eum facere, quia
existimabat quod recipere minime pateretur ob morum et propositi eius prauitatem. et extendens, quoniam etsi maiora aliqua a
Philemone postularet non oportebat petitionem eius resistere, adicit:

25   *quem ego uolebam apud me retinere.*

'sic enim confido quod nihil ex illis quae ego gero te umquam
poterit tristem facere.' et quia audaciae esse uidebatur ut alienum
seruum absolute promitteret retinere, adicit:

    ut pro te mihi ministraret in uinculis euangelii.

30   *ut* posuit non causam dicere, sed ut illud consuete explicaret

3-4   correptionem (*for* correct.) *l*   6   in (*bef.* Philem.) *om C*   12   quod (*for* quid) *C**   13   concedes *C**   19   ne *om C*   ‖   cedi (*for* caede) *C**   23   petitioni *C* (*corr.*)   25, 26   ergo (*for* ego) *C*   29   unde (*for* ut) *C**   30   et (*aft.* expl.) *add C*

slave away as not belonging to his master. Indeed, when he said *to you*, he spoke in view of obedience, but when he said *to me*, it was according to the correction of his purpose.*

and then *to me*.

"To you according to service, to me according to the improvement of his manner of life."

And so, as much as belonged to the first order of business had been accomplished, for Paul's exhortation had shown that Onesimus is useful and suitable to Philemon. But he put that point down first to show that everything done was done for Philemon's profit. And so, what was done? To answer the question, he adds:

12a *whom I have sent back.*

He wishes to show that Onesimus is useful to Philemon because of obedient services, but he said he was useful to himself only because of faith. "Therefore, what is it that I entreat of you for him? Not that you may hand him over to me; I have sent him to you." But what is it you ask?

12b *But you, take him back, that is, my innermost parts,*

"I ask only this, that you both take him back and look upon him affectionately."[14] And by naming Onesimus his *innermost parts* he has sufficiently persuaded Philemon to take him back with affection. And he ought not despise him. He did not say "do not afflict him with slaughter, do not [279] put him in chains." For he did not think that Philemon would do anything like this to him, because he thought that he might by no means put up with taking Onesimus back because of the perversity of his character and purpose. And making the further argument that even if he were to ask something greater of Philemon, it would not be right to refuse his request, he adds:

13a *whom I wanted to keep with me,*

"For I am so confident that nothing I carry out could ever make you sorry." And because it seemed audacious simply to propose to keep someone else's slave, he adds:

13b *so that for you he might minister to me in the chains of the gospel.*

He put down *so that* not to mean purpose but, as usual, to

---

[14]See Swete's note (2:278): "Th. may have regarded σπλάγχνα as = τέχνον.... See however his exposition of Phil. i. 8 ... which suggests another sense—'the object of my tender affection.'"

quod sequi uidebatur; uult enim dicere: 'etiam etsi hoc fecissem, tuum erat lucrum ut is mihi ministraret; nam si tuus seruus ministraret mihi, mercedem utique pro tali facto tibi adquirebat, tibi lucra conferebat.' non autem dixit *pro te*, sed, 'pro tuo commodo,'
5 quasi quia pro huius ministerio competenter apostolo si ministrasset, lucra quae ex hoc adquirebantur illius utpote domini esse uidebantur. ideo adiecit: *in uinculis euangelii*, [ut] utrumque significaret quoniam uolens tenuerit eum, debebatur autem ei huiuscemodi ministerium qui pro uniuersorum patiebatur salute; et quo-
10 niam non minimas mercedes ex tali officio adquirebat Philemoni, in tali uel maxime negotio Paulo constituto, si praestitisset ei suum seruum in ministerium. hoc autem dixit non retinere seruum uera uolens ratione, sed ostendens quoniam si hoc fecisset non conueniebat Philemonem indignari. tantum ergo interest ut nulla in
15 suscipiendo Onesimo et praebenda ei uenia ambiguitas adnasceretur. tamen causam uolens dicere idoneam ob quam eum minime tenuerit, dicit:
sine consilio autem tuo nihil uolui facere, ut non quasi ex necessitate sit bonum tuum sed ex uoluntate.
20 'non uidebatur mihi esse iustum ut contra uoluntatem tuam eum retinerem qui ad te pertinebat. nam aequum esse existimo ut quodcumque bonum ex te fuerit factum pro tuo hoc impleatur arbitrio.' deinde quia tristem eum fuga serui ut moris est fecerat, sufficienter et pro hoc medere deproperat, dicens:
25 *forsitan enim ideo recessit ad tempus, ut aeternum eum habeas, iam non seruum sed super seruum.*
euidens est quoniam in fuga uersus est arbitrii sui prauitate; ex illis uero quae facta fuerant in praeteritum occasione accepta, dixisse uidetur hac de causa eum recessisse ut melior sui fieret.
30 praebebat enim firmitatem uerborum eius exitus ipsius negotii; unde nec definitiue, sed adiecit *forsan*, haesitatione dictum suum

---

1 uolens (*aft.* dicere) *add* C (*corr.*)   5   qui (*for* quia) C   ‖   petenter C*   ‖
ab (*bef.* apost.) *add* C   ‖   ei (*for* si) C   7   ut *om* C*

explain what was seen to result. For he wants to say, "even had I done this, it would have been your profit that he would minister to me. For if your slave were to minister to me, he would certainly have gained a reward for you by doing so and would have brought you profit." For he did not mean instead of you but on behalf of you, since if he had suitably ministered to the apostle on behalf of the ministry of Philemon, the profit acquired from this would surely have been seen as belonging to his master. For this reason he added *in the chains of the gospel* [280] to indicate two points— that he would willingly have kept him, and a ministry of this kind was owed to someone who was suffering for the salvation of all people; and that it would have gained Philemon no small rewards from such a duty, since Paul was appointed especially for such a matter,[15] if Philemon had handed over his slave to him for ministry. And Paul did not say with true reason that he wanted to keep the slave but to show that, had he done so, it would not have been right for Philemon to take offense. Therefore, the advantage is so great that no hesitation would arise in taking Onesimus back and pardoning him. Nevertheless, wishing to give a suitable reason why he by no means kept him, he says:

14 *And without your advice I have wanted to do nothing, so that your good deed may be not from necessity but from free will.*

"It did not seem to me just to keep him who belonged to you against your will. For I think it is fair that whatever good deed should be performed by you should be fulfilled by your own judgment." Then, because the flight of the slave had saddened him, as might be expected, Paul is eager sufficiently to remedy his sorrow for this, saying:

15–16a *For perhaps for this reason he has gone away for a time, so that you might have him back forever, no longer a slave but more than a slave,*

It is clear that Onesimus turned to flight by the perversity of his judgment, [281] but from what had happened in the immediate past by a welcome opportunity, Paul seems to have said that he went away for this reason, that he might become better than himself. For the outcome of the matter furnished a firm basis for his words. That is why he added *perhaps* not precisely but to make

---

[15] *In tali negotio.* Perhaps Theodore means Paul's suffering "for the salvation of all people."

non insuadibile faciens. intendendum uero est quoniam non dixit,
'ut habeas,' sed 'ut recipias;' non enim hoc dicit quoniam 'recessit
ut de cetero habeas eum pro seruo, maiorem erga eum affectum
ostendens'—nam ridiculum erat hoc de fugitiuo dicere seruo—sed
5   'ut recipias eum super seruum;'

†hoc est, 'recipias eum non so-   ἀντὶ τοῦ· 'ἵνα αὐτὸν κομίσῃ, οὐκέ-
lum seruile obsequium tibi per-   τι δουλικὴν εὔνοιαν μόνον ἐνδεικνύ-
soluentem, [sed etiam plus]   μενον περὶ σέ, ἀλλὰ καὶ μείζονα ἢ
quam serui solent suis domi-   κατὰ δοῦλον, διὰ τὴν τοῦ τρόπου
10   nis exhibere.' quod iure dicebat   μεταβολήν.'
propter morum et propositi eius
mutabilitatem.*

quid autem uult esse quod dixit *super seruum?*
    fratrem carissimum.
15   hoc est, 'fratrem ualde amantem te;' ut dicat quoniam 'etsi per
fugam recessit, sed tanto melior sui est effectus ut non solum debitum tibi obsequium ut seruus cum omni fide persoluat, sed et
sicut frater ualde amori tuo iunctus omnia pro te pati de cetero sit
paratus.' et quia incertum erat si haec ita se haberent, confirmans
20   dictum suum adicit:
    maxime mihi, quanto magis tibi et in carne et in Domino.
    est quidem obscurum quod dictum est ob nimium compen-
dium, eo quod apostolus saepe cupiens aliqua compendiose explicare obscuritate dicta sua inuoluit. 'testor autem Onesimo quo-
25   niam etiam tibi fuerit utilis'—post exhortationem et consilium
quod a se acceperat. uult enim dicere quoniam 'si erga me talis
extitit, mores suos demutans ita ut sponte uellet mihi omne obsequium seruile praebere; quemadmodum non erga te multo magis erit talis, cui et propter fidem utpote studioso pietatis carita-

6 sq. Coisl. 204, f. 233 b [Cr. vii. 109] ἄλλος φησίν· ἀντὶ τοῦ· ἵνα, κ.τ.λ.   8
sed etiam plus *om* C r: *cf. g*   15   te *om* r   16   sui melior r   ‖ affectus C*
23   se cupiens C   25   sibi (*for* tibi) C   26   acciperet C   29   studiose H r

what he said not without persuasion by its hesitation. And it must be pointed out that he did not say "so that you might have" but "that you might take back."[16] For he does not mean that "he went away so that you might have him afterwards for a slave, showing greater affection for him"—for it would have been ludicrous to say this about a fugitive slave—but "so that you might take him back as more than a slave."

†That is, "that you may take him back not only because he pays you servile obedience but also something more than slaves usually display to their masters." He rightly said this because of the change of his character and purpose.*

Instead of "so that you might receive him, no longer displaying only a servile goodwill to you, but also something more than what accords with a slave because of the change of his way of life."

So what does he mean by saying *more than a slave?*

16b *a dearly beloved brother,*

That is, "a brother who strongly loves you," meaning that: "although he went away by fleeing, yet he became so much better than himself that he may not only pay the obedience owed you with all faithfulness as a slave but has also been made ready from now on to suffer all things for you as a brother strongly joined to your love."[17] And because it was unclear whether this would be the case, to confirm what he has said, he adds:

[282] 16c *especially to me, and how much more to you both in the flesh and in the Lord.*

What has been said is indeed obscure on account of too much succinctness, because the apostle in his wish to expound some things succinctly often wrapped his words in obscurity. "And I bear witness to Onesimus that he will be useful to you"—after the exhortation and the advice Philemon had received from him. For he means that, "if Onesimus has come to be like this toward me, changing his habits so that of his own free will he is willing to furnish me all servile obedience, how will he not much more be like this toward you, to whom as someone zealous of true religion

---

[16]The Latin translation of verse 15 obscures Theodore's comment. The point is that the verse reads ἀπέχῃς rather than ἔχῃς.

[17]See Swete's comment (2:281): "A somewhat strange paraphrase of the passive verbal ἀγαπητός. Th. probably means, 'one who deserves thy love because he will return it.'"

tem persoluere debet, et sicut domino seruitium cum omni exhibere fidelitate.' haec enim dicit *in carne* quae 'secundum disposi-
tionem.' 'carnem' uero frequenter apostolica dicta interpretantes
significauimus, quia statum hunc temporalem qui in praesente ui-
5   ta habetur sic solet nuncupare.

    si ergo me habes socium, recipe illum sicut me.

    super omnibus dictis hoc uel maxime dicto persuadebat ei eo
quod ei decebat, ut ob communem fidem uniuersa quae sibi adsunt communia esse omnibus fidelibus reputaret. quod prae cete-
10   ris etiam sibi utpote praedicatori et doctori dogmatum pietatis Dei
ueri existimabat 'si (inquit) communicas mihi secundum fidem et
ad plenum existimas nobis omnia esse communia, recipe et hunc
propter me.' non hoc dicit ut in ordine eum recipiat apostoli; quomodo enim fieri poterat ut hoc suaderet? sed ut dicat, 'eo quod ego
15   eum recepi recipe et tu, si tamen communia nobis omnia esse existimas.' et iterum pro delictis et satisfaciens dicit:

    si autem quid nocuit te aut debitor est, hoc mihi imputa.

    hoc est, 'a me exige illa." et ostendens quoniam non absolute
ista scribens:

20   *ego Paulus scripsi manu mea, ego reddam.*

    promisit se redditurum, sciens quoniam dominis reposita est
apud Deum merces copiosa pro illa bonitate quam erga seruos
suos exercent, et maxime siquando delinquentibus illis ueniam tribuere uoluerint. et ostendens quoniam non debet haesitare de tri-
25   buenda huiusmodi gratia:

    ut non dicam tibi quoniam teipsum mihi debes.

    'et haec quidem promitto, sciens quoniam et ipse percipies per
Dei misericordiam copiosas mercedes pro ea bonitate quam erga
istum nunc exerceas; te autem conuenit cogitare quoniam et totum
30   te mihi debes, licet ego non dicam.' et iterum ad obsecrationem

2 est (*aft* quae) *add r*   3   erant (*aft* dispos.) *add C* (*corr.*)   ‖   freq. uero
carnem *r* 4   signifiuimus (*sic*) *H*   ‖   praesenti *r* praesentia (*om* uita) *l*   7   et
quod edecebat (*sic*) *C* et quod edicebat *H: txt conj. Pitra*   8   hoc (*for* ob) *C* H*
ad *r* 9   reputare *C* H* reputaretur *r*: *txt C* (*corr.*)   11   mihi *om r*   12   et *om*
H   15-16   existimans *H*   16   *sq.* et iterum … reddam *om r*   ‖   dilectis *H*
19   scribat *C* (*corr.*)   20   mea manu *H*   22   eum (*for* Deum) *C**   25   est (*aft*
gratia) *add C H*   26   mihi teipsum *r*   27   percipiens *H*   28   ergo non istum
exerceas *C** erga istum exerces *C* (*corr.*) erga non istum exerces *H* erga istum
nunc exercens *r*   30   *sq.* et iterum … in Domino *om r*

he should pay love because of his faith and to whom as his master he should display his service with all faithfulness." For this is what he meant by *in the flesh*, that is, "according to his station in life." And in interpreting the apostle's words we have often pointed out that he uses the word "flesh" to refer to this temporal condition kept in the present life.

17 *Therefore, if you have me as a companion, take him back as me.*

Above everything he has said, it is especially by this statement that he tried to persuade Philemon, because it would be right for him to consider that everything that was his belonged in common to all the faithful on account of the common faith. And Paul thought that this more than other things applied to himself as a preacher and a teacher of the doctrines of the true God's true religion. "If (he says) you are my companion in faith and think that everything should be completely common to us, take him back because of me." He does not say this so that he may receive Philemon into the rank [283] of an apostle, for how could it have happened that he would urge this? But he means, "because I have taken him back, take him back yourself, as well, if indeed you think that all things are common to us." And again to make amends for Onesimus's transgressions, he says:

18 *And if he has harmed you in anything, or is a debtor, charge it to me.*

That is, "exact those things from me." And to show that he is not writing those things lightly:

19a *I, Paul, have written with my own hand, I will repay,*

He has promised that he will repay, knowing that there is laid up with God a bountiful reward for masters in return for the kindness they exercise toward their slaves, and especially if at some time they are willing to bestow pardon on those who transgress. And to show that there ought to be no hesitation in bestowing a favor of this kind:

19b *so that I may not tell you that you owe yourself to me.*

"And I surely promise these things, knowing that through God's mercy you yourself will reap the bountiful rewards for that kindness you are now exercising toward Onesimus. And you ought to reflect that you owe me your entire self, granted I should not say

sese uertens adicit:

etiam, frater, ego tui fruar in Domino; requiescere facito [*uiscera mea in Domino*].

nam [quod] dixit: *ego te fruar in Domino*, pro adiuratione po-
suit. dicit autem quod det illi ueniam de praeteritis; 'suscipiens eum requiescere me facito.' *ego te fruar in Domino;* hoc est, 'sic uideam te in omnibus illis quae secundum Deum sunt profectum habentem spiritalem, quod meum esse existimo lucrum.' et quia larga supplicatione decebat rogare Paulum contemplatione humilitatis, uidebatur autem aliquam habere suspectionem ut forsitan Philemon non facile adnuerit eius petitionibus ideoque sit aposto-
lus coactus superabunde eum precari:

et confidens (inquit) *oboedientiae tuae scripsi tibi, sciens quoniam et super quam dico facies.*

'haec autem sic scribo, non dubitans quin uelociter gratiam tri-
buas; e contrario uero nec scripsissem si non nossem quoniam non solum hoc facies, sed et si aliquid plus postulassem.' in his postulationem suam terminans adicit:

*simul et para mihi hospitium, spero autem qnoniam orationibus ue-
stris donabor uobis.*

deinde salutat eum ab Epaphra:

salutat te Epaphras, concaptiuus meus in Christo Iesu.

'concaptiuum suum' dixit, eo quod communicauerat ei in illis maeroribus quos pro Christo ipse sustinebat.

Marcus, Aristarchus, Demas, Lucas, cooperarii mei.

necnon et a Marco et Aristarcho et Dema et Luca, quos etiam operarios suos dicit, eo quod conlaborent ei ob aliorum utilitatem. post hoc consuete adicit:

gratia domini nostri Iesu Christi cum spiritu uestro. amen.

in his consummauit epistolam suam.

2 me (*bef.* facito) *add C* (*corr.*)   2-3 uiscera … Domino *om C H*   4 quod
om C* H   5 do (*for* det) *C* r* do *H* [?]   6 mecum (*for* me) *r*   ‖ si (*for* sic)
C (*corr.*)   7 Deum *om H r*   ‖ prouectum *H*   8 aestimo (*for* exist.) *l*   9
contemplationem *H*   10 suspicionem *C r*   ‖ forsan *C r*   13 est (*for* et) *H*
14 id quod (*for* quam) *C r*   15 quam gr. uel. *C* cum uel. gr. *r: txt H*   16
sic (*for* nec) *r*   23 dicit *H r*   24 quae (*for* quos) *H r*   27 operios (*sic*) *H*
‖ collaborarent *C r*   30 *sq.* post hoc … ep. suam *om r*

so." And once more turning himself to entreaty, he adds:

[284] 20 *Also, brother, for my part let me have enjoyment of you in the Lord; make my innermost parts rest in the Lord.*

Now he put down his statement, *for my part let me enjoy you*[18] *in the Lord,* for an appeal. And he means let him grant pardon for what is past: "by receiving him make me rest." *For my part let me enjoy you in the Lord,* that is, "so may I see you having spiritual progress in all things that are in accord with God, which I think is my profit." And because it was becoming for Paul to make his request with copious supplication for the sake of humility, he seems also to have some suspicion that perhaps Philemon would not easily assent to his petitions, and for this reason the apostle has been compelled to implore him more fully than usual:

21 *And confident (he says) of your obedience I have written to you, knowing that you will do even above what I say.*

"And I am writing these things this way, not doubting that you will quickly bestow the favor. But, on the other hand, I should not have written if I had not known that you will not only do this but also anything else I should ask." Bringing his request to an end with these words, he adds:

[285] 22 *At the same time also prepare for me a guest room, and I hope that by your prayers I shall be given to you.*

Then he sends him greetings from Epaphras:

23 *Epaphras, my fellow captive in Christ Jesus, greets you,*

He said that he was his *fellow captive* because he had shared with him in those misfortunes that he endured himself for Christ.

24 *Marcus, Aristarchus, Demas, Luke, my fellow workers.*

To say nothing of Marcus, Aristarchus, Demas, and Luke, who he says were also his fellow workers, because they are toiling with him for the benefit of others. After this, as is his habit, he adds:

25 *The grace of our Lord Jesus Christ be with your spirit. Amen.* With these words he has finished his letter.

---

[18] *Te* instead of, as in the verse, *tui.*

Select Bibliography

PRIMARY SOURCES

Bruyne, Donatien de. "Le commentaire de Théodore de Mopsueste aux Épîtres de S. Paul." *RBén* 33 (1921): 53–54.

———. "Nouvelle liste de *membra disiecta*." *RBén* 47 (1935): 305.

Cramer, J. A. *Catenæ Græcorum Patrum in Novum Testamentum*. 8 vols. Oxford: E Typographeo Academico, 1838–44.

Dekkers, Eligius. "Un nouveau manuscrit du commentaire de Théodore de Mopsueste aux Épîtres de S. Paul." *SacEr* 6 (1954): 429–33.

Devreesse, Robert, ed. *Le commentaire de Théodore de Mopsueste sur les Psaumes (I-LXXX)*. ST 93. Vatican City: Biblioteca Apostolica Vaticana, 1939.

Fritzsche, Otto Fridolin. *Theodori episcopi Mopsuesteni In novum testamentum commentariorum quae reperiri potuerunt*. Turici: Meyer et Zeller, 1847.

Hill, Robert C., trans. *Theodore of Mopsuestia: Commentary on Psalms 1–81*. SBLWGRW 5. Atlanta: Society of Biblical Literature, 2006.

———, trans. *Theodore of Mopsuestia: Commentary on the Twelve Prophets*. FC 108. Washington, D.C.: Catholic University of America Press, 2004.

Lorimer, W. L. "Theodore of Mopsuestia: In *Ep. i ad Tim.*, ii, p. 123,11 Sw." *JTS* 44 (1943): 58–59.

Migne, J.-P., ed. *Patrologiae cursus completus: Series graeca*. Vol. 66. Paris: Migne, 1859.

Mingana, Alphonse, ed. and trans. *Commentary of Theodore of Mopsuestia on the Nicene Creed*. Woodbrooke Studies 5. Cambridge: Heffer & Sons, 1932.

———. ed. and trans. *Commentary of Theodore of Mopsuestia on the Lord's Prayer and on the Sacraments of Baptism and the Eucharist*. Woodbrooke Studies 6. Cambridge: Heffer & Sons, 1933.

Nau, François. "Controverse de Théodore de Mopsueste avec les Macédoniens." *PO* 9 (1913): 633–67.

Norris, Richard A., Jr., trans. "Fragments of the Doctrinal Works." Pages 113–22 in *The Christological Controversy*. Sources of Early Christian Thought. Philadelphia: Fortress, 1980.

Pitra, J. B., ed., *Spicilegium solesmense complectens sanctorum patrum scriptorumque ecclesiasticorum anecdota hactenus opera, selecta e graecis orientalibusque et latinis codicibus*. 4 vols. Paris: Didot, 1852–58.

Sprenger, Hans N., ed. *Theodori Mopsuesteni commentarius in XII Prophetas*. Göttinger Orientforschungen, Biblica et patristica 1. Wiesbaden: Harrassowitz, 1977.

Swete, Henry B., ed. "Fragments of the Dogmatic Works of Theodore. Pages 289–339 in vol. 2 of *Theodori episcopi Mopsuesteni In epistolas b. Pauli commentarii*. 2 vols. Cambridge: Cambridge University Press, 1880–82.

——. *Theodori episcopi Mopsuesteni In epistolas b. Pauli commentarii*. 2 vols. Cambridge: Cambridge University Press, 1880–82.

Tonneau, Raymond, ed. and trans. *Les homélies catéchétiques de Théodore de Mopsueste*. ST 145. Vatican City: Biblioteca Apostolica Vaticana, 1949.

Vosté, Jacques M., ed. and trans. *Theodori Mopsuesteni commentarius in Evangelium Johannis apostoli*. 2 vols. CSCO 115–16: Scriptores Syri 4.3. Leuven: Peeters, 1940.

Sachau, E. *Theodori Mopsuesteni fragmenta Syriaca*. Leipzig, 1869.

SECONDARY WORKS

Devreesse, Robert. *Essai sur Théodore de Mopsueste*. ST 141. Vatican City: Biblioteca Apostolica Vaticana, 1948.

Fitzgerald, John T. "Theodore of Mopsuestia on Paul's Letter to Philemon." Pages 333–63 in *Philemon in Perspective: Interpreting a Pauline Letter*. Edited by D. Francois Tolmie. BZNW 169. Berlin: de Gruyter, 2010.

Froehlich, Karlfried. *Biblical Interpretation in the Early Church*. Sources of Early Christian Thought. Philadelphia: Fortress, 1984.

Grant, Robert M., and David Tracy. *A Short History of the Interpretation of the Bible*. 2nd ed. Philadelphia: Fortress, 1984.

Greer, Rowan A. *Theodore of Mopsuestia: Exegete and Theologian*. London: Faith Press, 1961.

McLeod, Frederick G. *The Image of God in the Antiochene Tradition*. Washington, D.C.: Catholic University of America Press, 1999.

——. *The Roles of Christ's Humanity in Salvation: Insights from Theodore of Mopsuestia*. Washington, D.C.: Catholic University of America Press, 2005.

——. *Theodore of Mopsuestia*. The Early Church Fathers. London: Routledge, 2009.

Nassif, Bradley. "'Spiritual Exegesis' in the School of Antioch." Pages 342–77 in *New Perspectives in Historical Theology: Essays in Memory of John Meyendorff*. Edited by Bradley Nassif. Grand Rapids: Eerdmans, 1996.

Norris, Richard A. *Manhood and Christ: A Study in the Christology of Theodore of Mopsuestia*. Oxford: Clarendon, 1963.

Pirot, Louis. *L'œuvre exégétique de Théodore de Mopsueste, 350–428 après J.C.* Rome: Pontifical Biblical Institute, 1913.

Schäublin, Christoph. *Untersuchungen zu Methode und Herkunft der antiochenischen Exegese*. Theophaneia: Beiträge zur Religions- und Kirchengeschichte des Altertums 23. Köln: Hanstein, 1974.

Simonetti, Manlio. *Biblical Interpretation in the Early Church: An Historical Introduction to Patristic Exegesis*. Translated by John A. Hughes. Edinburgh: T&T Clark, 1994.

Staab, Karl, ed. Pages 113–212 in *Pauluskommentare aus der griechischen Kirche*. Münster: Aschendorff, 1933.

Sullivan, Francis A. *The Christology of Theodore of Mopsuestia*. Analecta Gregoriana 82. Rome: Gregorianum, 1956.

Trigg, Joseph W. *Biblical Interpretation*. Message of the Fathers of the Church 9. Wilmington, Del.: Glazier, 1988.

Wickert, Ulrich. *Studien zu den Pauluskommentaren Theodors von Mopsuestia*. BZNW 27. Berlin: Töpelmann, 1962.

Wiles, Maurice, and Mark Santer, trans. *Documents in Early Christian Thought*. Cambridge: Cambridge University Press, 1975.

Young, Frances. *Biblical Exegesis and the Formation of Christian Culture*. Cambridge: Cambridge University Press, 1997. Repr., Peabody, Mass.: Hendrikson, 2002.

———. "The Rhetorical Schools and Their Influence on Patristic Exegesis." Pages 182–99 in *The Making of Orthodoxy: Essays in Honour of Henry Chadwick*. Edited by Rowan Williams. Cambridge: Cambridge University Press, 1989.

———. *The Art of Performance: Towards a Theology of Holy Scripture*. London: Darton, Longman & Todd, 1990.

Swete-Greer Concordance

VOLUME I

Swete	Greer						
		33	51	66	101	99	151
1	3	34	53	67	103	100	153
2	3	35	55	68	105	101	153
3	5	36	55	69	105	102	155
4	7	37	57	70	107	103	157
5	9	38	59	71	109	104	159
6	9	39	59	72	111	105	161
7	11	40	61	73	113	106	161
8	13	41	63	74	113	107	163
9	15	42	65	75	115	108	165
10	15	43	65	76	117	109	167
11	17	44	67	77	117	110	167
12	19	45	69	78	119	111	169
13	21	46	71	79	121	112	171
14	21	47	73	80	123	113	171
15	23	48	73	81	123	114	173
16	25	49	75	82	123	115	175
17	27	50	75	83	125	116	175
18	27	51	77	84	127	117	177
19	29	52	79	85	129	118	179
20	31	53	81	86	131	119	181
21	33	54	83	87	133	120	181
22	35	55	85	88	133	121	183
23	35	56	85	89	135	122	185
24	37	57	87	90	137	123	187
25	39	58	89	91	139	124	187
26	39	59	91	92	141	125	189
27	41	60	93	93	141	126	191
28	43	61	93	94	143	127	193
29	45	62	97	95	145	128	195
30	47	63	97	96	147	129	195
31	47	64	99	97	147	130	197
32	49	65	101	98	149	131	197

132	199	172	255	212	311	252	361
133	201	173	255	213	311	253	363
134	201	174	257	214	313	254	363
135	203	175	259	215	313	255	365
136	205	176	261	216	315	256	365
137	207	177	261	217	315	257	367
138	207	178	263	218	317	258	369
139	209	179	265	219	317	259	369
140	209	180	265	220	319	260	371
141	211	181	267	221	319	261	371
142	213	182	269	222	321	262	373
143	213	183	269	223	323	263	373
144	215	184	271	224	323	264	375
145	217	185	273	225	325	265	375
146	219	186	275	226	327	266	377
147	219	187	275	227	329	267	379
148	221	188	277	228	329	268	379
149	223	189	279	229	331	269	381
150	225	190	281	230	333	270	383
151	225	191	281	231	333	271	383
152	227	192	283	232	335	272	385
153	229	193	285	233	337	273	387
154	231	194	285	234	234	274	387
155	231	195	287	235	339	275	389
156	233	196	289	236	339	276	391
157	235	197	291	237	341	277	391
158	235	198	291	238	341	278	393
159	237	199	293	239	343	279	395
160	237	200	293	240	345	280	397
161	239	201	295	241	345	281	397
162	241	202	295	242	347	282	399
163	241	203	297	243	349	283	401
164	243	204	299	244	351	284	401
165	245	205	301	245	351	285	403
166	247	206	301	246	353	286	405
167	247	207	303	247	353	287	405
168	249	208	305	248	355	288	407
169	251	209	307	249	357	289	407
170	251	210	307	250	357	290	409
171	253	211	309	251	359	291	411

292	413	298	419	304	427	310	435
293	413	299	421	305	429	311	435
294	415	300	421	306	429	312	437
295	415	301	423	307	431		
296	417	302	425	308	433		
297	417	303	425	309	433		

VOLUME 2

Swete	Greer	30	477	60	515	90	553
1	439	31	479	61	517	91	555
2	439	32	481	62	519	92	557
3	441	33	483	63	521	93	557
4	443	34	483	64	521	94	559
5	443	35	485	65	523	95	559
6	445	36	487	66	523	96	561
7	447	37	487	67	525	97	561
8	447	38	489	68	525	98	563
9	449	39	491	69	527	99	565
10	451	40	491	70	529	100	565
11	451	41	495	71	529	101	567
12	453	42	495	72	531	102	567
13	453	43	497	73	531	103	569
14	455	44	499	74	535	104	571
15	457	45	499	75	537	105	573
16	457	46	501	76	537	106	575
17	459	47	501	77	539	107	577
18	461	48	503	78	539	108	577
19	461	49	505	79	541	109	579
20	463	50	505	80	543	110	581
21	465	51	505	81	543	111	581
22	465	52	507	82	545	112	583
23	467	53	507	83	547	113	583
24	469	54	509	84	547	114	585
25	471	55	509	85	549	115	587
26	471	56	511	86	549	116	587
27	473	57	513	87	551	117	589
28	475	58	513	88	553	118	591
29	477	59	515	89	553	119	591

120	593	160	643	200	697	240	749
121	595	161	643	201	697	241	749
122	595	162	645	202	699	242	751
123	597	163	647	203	699	243	753
124	597	164	649	204	701	244	753
125	599	165	649	205	703	245	755
126	599	166	651	206	703	246	757
127	601	167	653	207	705	247	757
128	603	168	653	208	707	248	759
129	603	169	655	209	707	249	759
130	605	170	655	210	709	250	761
131	607	171	657	211	709	251	763
132	607	172	659	212	711	252	765
133	607	173	661	213	713	253	765
134	609	174	661	214	713	254	767
135	611	175	663	215	715	255	767
136	611	176	665	216	717	256	769
137	611	177	665	217	717	257	771
138	613	178	667	218	719	258	773
139	613	179	669	219	721	259	773
140	615	180	669	220	721	260	775
141	617	181	671	221	723	261	777
142	617	182	671	222	725	262	777
143	619	183	673	223	725	263	779
144	621	184	675	224	727	264	781
145	623	185	675	225	729	265	781
146	623	186	677	226	729	266	783
147	625	187	679	227	731	267	785
148	625	188	681	228	731	268	785
149	627	189	683	229	733	269	787
150	629	190	683	230	733	270	787
151	631	191	685	231	735	271	789
152	631	192	685	232	737	272	789
153	633	193	687	233	739	273	791
154	635	194	689	234	739	274	791
155	637	195	689	235	741	275	793
156	637	196	691	236	741	276	793
157	639	197	693	237	743	277	795
158	639	198	693	238	745	278	795
159	641	199	695	239	747	279	797

280	799	282	801	284	805
281	799	283	803	285	805

Commentary Index by Verse

1 Thessalonians

Index of Scriptural Citations
and Allusions

General Index

church; *see also* baptism, body of Christ, administration: as assembly of faithful, 209, 213, 273–75, 517, 607, 635, 645, 709, 717, 789; as support of truth, 609, 633; as household, 481, 717, 789; and Christ, 673–79, 791, 793; churches, 33, 455, 529, 595–97, 747, 773, 775; provision for clergy, 161, 519, 653, 703; provision for widows and poor, 471, 521, 637, 639–43, 647–53; public rebuke and penance, 351, 547, 561, 655–67

circumcision; *see also* Jewish Christians, law: 3, 7, 27–29, 45–47, 87, 119, 133–37, 141, 147, 163–67, 221–27, 291, 333, 335, 337, 349, 363, 425, 531, 663, 739

creation; *see also* Christ, heads up new creation: the first and second creations, 195, 219; harmony of first broken by death, 197; good of first, 617–19, 677,

deacons: 293, 607–9, 635, 649, 775; qualifications of, 599–603, 605; female deacons, 603, 635, 641; not mentioned in Titus, 743

demons; *see* invisible powers

devil; *see* invisible powers

dispensations of God; *see also* Christ, creation, grace, law: 3, 9, 21, 29–31, 75, 185, 193–95, 197, 235, 483, 509–11, 531, 695; permission of apostasy, 513, 531; will for the salvation of all, 551

disputes; *see also* Jewish Christians, heresy, working: 35–37, 147, 155–61, 171, 271, 291, 351, 451–53, 471, 521, 665, 713, 763–65, 767

elements: as luminaries defining times, 93, 99–101, 403; as earth, air, fire, and water, 195, 379, 415

Eve: 115, 275, 559–61

example: of God, 261; of Christ, 313–25, 443; of Paul, 311, 443, 513, 685; of Christians, 105, 445, 625, 759

faith; *see also* baptism, justification: in Christ, 29, 31, 37, 65, 75, 363, 553, 703; in God, 697, 709; in relation to preaching, 23–25, 51, 295–97, 305, 439, 553, 613, 741; and baptism, 3, 47, 71, 107, 199, 307, 407, 537, 577, 583, 587; in relation to age to come, 47, 55, 57, 61, 65, 75, 79, 149, 187, 199, 235, 363, 391, 399, 405–7, 443, 483, 501, 515, 531, 543, 553, 671, 697, 725; as gift of God or Spirit, 59, 63, 79–81, 515, 541; progress and remaining steadfast in, 139, 159, 237, 295, 311, 367, 391–93, 439–41, 445, 461–63, 465, 495, 497–99, 561, 607, 625, 679, 721, 753; expressed in deed, especially love of God and neighbor, 117, 135–37, 503, 539, 791; as opposed to law, 49–51, 57, 71, 79, 101, 141; as shield against devil, 285

firstfruits; *see* baptism, Holy Spirit, Christ